— What am I

e so full of

hat mean much

any questions

vered. — You'd

told you what

. — Not importan

My Faraway One

Selected Letters
of Georgia O'Keeffe
and Alfred Stieglitz

VOLUME I, 1915–1933

My Faraway One

Selected, Annotated,
and Edited by
SARAH GREENOUGH

Yale University Press
New Haven and London

in association with the
Beinecke Rare Book
and Manuscript Library

Published with the assistance of a gift from William S. Reese of the Class of 1977, Yale College.

Designed by Margaret Bauer.
Set in Sabon and The Sans types by Julie Allred, BW&A Books, Inc.
Printed in the United States of America.

Library of Congress Cataloging-in-Publication Data

O'Keeffe, Georgia, 1887–1986.
My faraway one : selected letters of Georgia O'Keeffe and Alfred Stieglitz / selected, annotated, and edited by Sarah Greenough.
    p. cm.
Includes bibliographical references and index.
ISBN 978-0-300-16630-9 (cloth : alk. paper) 1. O'Keeffe, Georgia, 1887–1986—Correspondence. 2. Stieglitz, Alfred, 1864–1946—Correspondence. 3. Artists—United States—Correspondence. I. Stieglitz, Alfred, 1864–1946. II. Greenough, Sarah, 1951– III. Title. IV. Title: selected letters of Georgia O'Keeffe and Alfred Stieglitz.
N6537.O39A3 2011
759.13—dc22
[B]   2010049539

A catalogue record for this book is available from the British Library.

This paper meets the requirements of ANSI/NISO Z39.48-1992 (Permanence of Paper).

10 9 8 7 6 5 4 3 2 1

Jacket illustrations: (*front*) Dried red poppy, enclosed in a letter by Alfred Stieglitz, August 8, 1929, 8 13/16 × 4 1/8 in. (20.32 × 10.16 cm) [Written on an accompanying card: "Very very much love. Grown by me, near the flagpole."]; (*back*) Anonymous, Georgia O'Keeffe and Alfred Stieglitz, Lake George, 1929. Gelatin silver print, 11 1/2 × 8 1/2 in. (27.9 × 21.6 cm). Both images Alfred Stieglitz/Georgia O'Keeffe Archive, Yale Collection of American Literature, Beinecke Rare Book and Manuscript Library.

Frontispiece: Paul Strand, *Alfred Stieglitz*, 1929. Gelatin silver print, 4 3/4 × 3 9/16 in. (12 × 9 cm). Alfred Stieglitz/Georgia O'Keeffe Archive, Yale Collection of American Literature, Beinecke Rare Book and Manuscript Library. Copyright © Aperture Foundation, Inc., Paul Strand Archive.

Page vi: Alfred Stieglitz, *Georgia O'Keeffe,* 1918. Gelatin silver print, 4 7/16 × 3 9/16 in. (11.3 × 9 cm). National Gallery of Art, Washington, Alfred Stieglitz Collection. Greenough 557.

Opposite page 1: Edward Steichen, *Alfred Stieglitz at 291,* 1915. Coated gum bichromate over platinum print, 11 5/16 × 9 1/2 in. (28.8 × 24.2 cm). Metropolitan Museum of Art, New York. Alfred Stieglitz Collection, 1933 (33.43.29). Copyright © The Metropolitan Museum of Art/Art Resource, NY. Permission of the estate of Edward Steichen.

Page 312: Alfred Stieglitz, *Georgia O'Keeffe,* 1920. Gelatin silver print, 8 5/8 × 7 5/16 in. (21.9 × 18.6 cm). National Gallery of Art, Washington, Alfred Stieglitz Collection. Greenough 658.

Page 404: Alfred Stieglitz, *Georgia O'Keeffe,* 1923 or 1924. Gelatin silver print, 4 5/8 × 3 1/2 in. (11.7 × 8.9 cm). The J. Paul Getty Museum, Los Angeles (93.XM.25.78). Copyright © J. Paul Getty Trust. Greenough 858.

Endpapers: (*front*) Letter by Alfred Stieglitz, November 9, 1916; (*back*) letter by Georgia O'Keeffe, September 3, 1916. Alfred Stieglitz/Georgia O'Keeffe Archive, Yale Collection of American Literature, Beinecke Rare Book and Manuscript Library.

Contents

Introduction

PASSIONATE AND POETIC, vivid and compelling, the letters between Georgia O'Keeffe and
Alfred Stieglitz are a profoundly moving account of the lives of two of this country's most
celebrated artists and an exceptionally important source of information on twentieth-century
American art and culture. Between 1915, when they first began to write to each other, and 1946,
when Stieglitz died, they exchanged more than 25,000 pages of letters that describe in unimaginably rich detail their daily lives in New York, Texas, and New Mexico during the many months
they were apart. In language that is sparse and vibrant (O'Keeffe), fervent and lyrical (Stieglitz),
immediate and unfiltered (both), the letters reveal the development of their art and ideas and
their friendships with many of the most influential figures in early American modernism, while
offering often poignant insights into the impact of larger events—two world wars, the booming
economy of the 1920s, and the Depression of the 1930s—on two intensely engaged individuals. But above all else, as these letters trace the blossoming of their love during the 1910s, its
rich maturation in the 1920s, its near-collapse during the early years of the Depression, and its
renewed tenderness in the later 1930s and early 1940s, their correspondence is a deeply compelling account of the evolution of a relationship between two focused, willful, and independent but
passionately committed individuals.

When O'Keeffe and Stieglitz first met in the spring of 1916, they were at very different
points in their lives. Stieglitz, fifty-two years old, was already a major force in the American art
world. Long a proponent of the artistic merit of photography and an internationally acclaimed
photographer himself, in 1905 he had founded the Little Galleries of the Photo-Secession, known
as 291 from its address on Fifth Avenue in New York. There he constructed a radically innovative

dialogue among all the arts, exhibiting not only the finest examples of the art of photography but also the most advanced European painting, sculpture, and drawing. A leader in the introduction of modern European art to America, Stieglitz gave Constantin Brancusi, Paul Cézanne, Henri Matisse, and Pablo Picasso their first exhibitions in the United States, and he also championed the work of American modernist painters and photographers, presenting John Marin and Paul Strand, among others. While Stieglitz was at the pinnacle of his fame in 1916, O'Keeffe was a twenty-eight-year-old art student. Although she had taught sporadically, her work had never been exhibited and was unknown to all but a few friends, family, and colleagues.

In addition to these disparities in age and reputation, O'Keeffe and Stieglitz also had very different personalities and backgrounds. Exceptionally articulate and opinionated; intellectually voracious and widely read; egotistical but charismatic and endowed with a remarkable ability to establish a deep communion with those around him, Stieglitz was an inveterate New Yorker from a large, close-knit, prosperous, and secular German-Jewish family. Born in Hoboken, New Jersey, and schooled at the College of the City University of New York and the Königliche Technische Hochschule in Berlin, he had traveled extensively in Europe, but rarely west of the Alleghenies. With his thick mane of gray hair, his intense gaze, and signature cape, he cut a dashing figure in the New York art world. Married for more than two decades to Emmeline (Emmy) Obermeyer, a brewery heiress whose inheritance helped finance his activities, he shared little in common with her, except love for their only child, a daughter, Katherine (Kitty). With his passionate nature, Stieglitz was drawn to attractive women, especially younger ones, and in the last dozen years had been infatuated with at least two—Sophie Raab and Katharine N. Rhoades—but both seem to have been wary of entering into a relationship with a married man.

Where Stieglitz's life had been formed by the cultured affluence and supportive milieu created by his parents and siblings, O'Keeffe's background had been more modest and her family more fractured. Born on a dairy farm near Sun Prairie, Wisconsin, she was one of seven children of second-generation Irish and Hungarian immigrants who were far from prosperous. When she was in her teens, her parents moved to Virginia, hoping to find better opportunities, leaving Georgia and her brother Francis behind to live with relatives and attend school in Madison, Wisconsin. Guided by her growing passion for art, she had studied at a number of art schools, including the School of the Art Institute of Chicago from 1905 to 1906 and the Art Students League in New York from 1907 to 1908. More apt to present herself as intuitive rather than intellectual, more prone to keen observation than flowery discourse, O'Keeffe had come to rely on her clear understanding of herself and her innate independence. With a sharp wit, feisty sense of humor, and occasionally imperious nature, she was also an astute judge of people and had little tolerance for those who did not engage her quick, lively imagination. When faced with the prospect of dull companions, she opted instead for her own company, work, and long walks in the outdoors. Unlike many other aspiring American artists of the time, she had never traveled to Europe, but by 1916 she knew the Midwest and the South, especially Texas, far better than most of her big-city colleagues. With her lithe figure, handsome beauty, and striking appearance, O'Keeffe was as drawn to creative, energetic individuals—especially good-looking men—as they were to her. Flirtatious, occasionally coy, and disarmingly frank, she confounded most men with her maverick behavior and her refusal to conform to conventional notions of beauty and dress. At a time when many women still wore elaborate Edwardian dresses and hairstyles, O'Keeffe's frocks were simple, and she usually pulled her hair back, with only a modest sweep of bangs covering her forehead. By 1916 she had been involved with two men: George Dannenberg, with whom she carried on an extensive correspondence from 1908 to 1912, and Arthur Macmahon, a political science professor at Columbia University whom she met at the University of Virginia in the summer of 1914. But as soon as both men became serious about her, she pulled away, perhaps instinctively sensing that they would curtail her freedom.

Despite their differences, when O'Keeffe and Stieglitz met in 1915, both were at turning points in their lives. Following the groundbreaking exhibitions Stieglitz had mounted at his gallery and the sensational 1913 Armory Show of modern art, organized by others, numerous other galleries had opened in New York to exhibit the most advanced European and American painting and sculpture, providing competition for 291. New periodicals addressed many of the radical ideas previously encountered in Stieglitz's publication *Camera Work,* while patrons such as Walter Arensberg, Mabel Dodge, and Gertrude Whitney began to court and support contemporary artists, offering the welcoming shelter and intellectual stimulation once found primarily at 291. Moreover, while Stieglitz was still hailed as one of the most important photographers of the time, by 1916 his own art had languished for several years, taking a back seat to his other activities. Unwilling to be one among many, Stieglitz mounted a series of "demonstrations" —small, focused exhibitions at his gallery—of children's and African tribal art in order to reclaim his position as New York's preeminent iconoclast. Perceived to be less corrupted by the materialism of Western society, these kinds of art were also thought to be more immediate and inventive, less intellectualized or analytical and therefore more expressive of subjective states, and deeply authentic. From 1912 through 1916, Stieglitz mounted four exhibitions of children's art at 291, and his 1914 exhibition of African sculpture was the first ever held in an art gallery in the United States. He was also intrigued with what he regarded as another facet of primitivism—women's art. His readings of Edward Carpenter, Havelock Ellis, Johann Wolfgang von Goethe, and Sigmund Freud had convinced him that if, as these authors argued, women were fundamentally different from Western men—less objective or cerebral, more emotional, sensual, and capable of divining higher powers—their art should also be different from that by men. A woman artist, Stieglitz had come to believe, could be one of those intuitive "geniuses [who] have kept their childlike spirit and have added to it breadth of vision and experience."[1]

1. As quoted in "Some Remarkable Work by Very Young Artists," 1912, repr. in Dorothy Norman, *Alfred Stieglitz: An American Seer* (New York, 1973), 115.

To test his belief, in January 1915 he presented a joint exhibition of paintings by Rhoades and Marion H. Beckett.

O'Keeffe, too, was about to embark on a new path. For the last few years she had had a series of dead-end jobs, punctuated by stimulating but too brief periods of study. From 1908 to 1910 she had been employed as a commercial artist in Chicago, but the work repelled her. She all but abandoned painting for two years and returned to it only in 1912, when, visiting her family in Charlottesville, she met Alon Bement, a professor at Columbia University's Teachers College who was working at the University of Virginia's summer school. He introduced her to the work and ideas of Arthur Wesley Dow, a highly influential teacher who believed that art need not strive for accurate representation but could instead simply be a beautiful depiction of harmoniously arranged forms. Armed with these new insights, O'Keeffe had pieced together a series of jobs teaching art—first in the Amarillo, Texas, public schools from 1912 to 1914 and in the summer school in Charlottesville, Virginia, where she taught from 1913 to 1916. But only her position at the University of Virginia, where she assisted Bement, offered her any modicum of stimulation; her years in Amarillo forced her to confront the limited, prescribed methods of teaching art so commonly practiced at the time. With Bement's encouragement, O'Keeffe studied with Dow at Teachers College in 1914 and 1915. There she made close friends, such as fellow art student Anita Pollitzer, and visited New York's museums and galleries, including 291, where she saw an exhibition of Marin's work.[2] Fascinated by 291, she confided to Pollitzer that she wanted Stieglitz, more "than anyone else I know," to "like something—anything I had done."[3] But when O'Keeffe left New York that spring—bound first for Charlottesville to assist Bement with his summer courses and later for Columbia, South Carolina, to teach at Columbia College—she had spoken no more than a few words to the legendary photographer and gallery director.

It was not until the spring of 1916, when O'Keeffe moved back to New York to study once more at Teachers College and again went to 291, that she and Stieglitz began to get to know each other. Those brief encounters prompted the exchange of a few letters, even while O'Keeffe was still in New York. After she returned to Charlottesville in mid-June to teach summer school, they began to correspond more often. At first they wrote each other weekly, but as a sign of their growing closeness, they quickly abandoned salutations and signatures. In late August when Stieglitz was at his family's summer home in Lake George, New York, their correspondence became more frequent as O'Keeffe, her summer job over, traveled throughout the South. By late September, after O'Keeffe had moved to Texas, they were exchanging ever more lengthy and often daily letters, and by late 1916 Stieglitz was sending her letters that were twenty to thirty pages long.

2. An Exhibition of Water-Colors, Oils, Etchings, Drawings, Recent and Old, by John Marin, of New York, on view at 291, Feb. 23–Mar. 26, 1915.

3. GOK to Pollitzer, Oct. 1915; see Clive Giboire, ed., *Lovingly, Georgia: The Complete Correspondence of Georgia O'Keeffe and Anita Pollitzer* (New York, 1990), 40.

They soon discovered their differences—Stieglitz revealed himself to be intense and passionate; O'Keeffe, high-spirited and spontaneous—but they also recognized their shared exuberance for life, their willingness to bare their emotions to each other, and their deep commitment to their work. Just as quickly, they realized they were intensely attracted to each other—intellectually, emotionally, and physically. Each adopted a tone that was direct and candid: they did not expound on current theoretical ideas, religion, or philosophy (as Stieglitz might do in his correspondence with others), nor did they extensively discuss the intellectual motivations behind their own art. Instead, they wrote about their struggles to make their art, their daily lives—the people, books, art, concerts, and the natural environment that moved them—and most especially what they saw and felt. Their letters were, as O'Keeffe perceptively noted, "intensely alive," filled with both a great "humanness" and an expansive, generous spirit that made her feel as if "all the world greets you."[4]

From 1916 through 1918 O'Keeffe's and Stieglitz's lives changed markedly, in large part because of their deepening relationship. As O'Keeffe became more familiar with the painters Stieglitz exhibited, as well as with his and his protégé Strand's photographs, her art became more sophisticated and sure. Discarding earlier influences, she synthesized her own, often highly abstract pictorial language. As she sent Stieglitz each new batch of work, he grew increasingly enamored of her. Extolling O'Keeffe as both the "Great Child" and the "Great Woman," he saw her as one of the "geniuses" of the modern age, the confirmation of his belief that women could be important creative artists. Yet despite their increasingly intense focus on each other, both were also affected by the mounting war hysteria. From his family and his years studying in Berlin in the 1880s, Stieglitz had a strong affection for Germany, but by late 1916 and early 1917 both he and O'Keeffe accepted the United States' involvement in the war as inevitable. However, neither condoned anti-German propaganda nor agreed with the popular sentiment that linked Germany's past triumphs in art, literature, and music with its current political aspirations. Whereas O'Keeffe's attitude toward the war and her focus on Stieglitz distanced her from her friends and neighbors in Texas, the war had direct consequences for Stieglitz. When the United States joined the Allies against Germany in the spring of 1917 and the government ruled that food products could not be used for the manufacture of alcoholic beverages, Emmy Stieglitz's income was significantly curtailed. Unable to afford 291 on his own, more modest inheritance, he closed the gallery at the end of June, after a final exhibition of O'Keeffe's work. In the fall and winter of 1917 and 1918 he kept a room at the same address, as an office and storage space, but with no exhibitions to attract visitors, he became increasingly isolated. As both O'Keeffe's and Stieglitz's loneliness intensified, they drew even closer together and their mutual attraction became ever more powerful and palpable.

---

4. GOK to AS, July 11, 1916; GOK to AS, Feb. 10, 1917. Unless otherwise noted, all of O'Keeffe's and Stieglitz's letters to each other, as well as their letters to others and manuscript materials, are in Stieglitz/O'Keeffe Archive, Yale Collection of American Literature, Beinecke Rare Book and Manuscript Library, Yale University.

During these years their correspondence significantly escalated and the letters that follow represent only approximately one-tenth of their copious output.[5] This volume, which is divided into three sections (1915–1918; 1919–1928; and 1929–1933), traces the arc of their love from O'Keeffe's first letter to Stieglitz in 1915 through their marriage in 1924 to the near demise of their relationship in 1933. Volume two (forthcoming) will reveal how, beginning in 1934, they used their new, hard-won understanding of themselves and each other to forge a less romantic and passionate but no less vital union that lasted until Stieglitz's death. In both volumes, I have chosen letters that most forcefully speak to several issues: the evolution of their art and ideas; their relationships with many of the most influential cultural figures of their time, as well as their friendships with less celebrated individuals who nurtured each of them; the impact of larger social, cultural, and historic events on their daily lives; and the character of both the vibrant New York world of art and culture that was critical to Stieglitz and the rural life in Texas and New Mexico that enriched O'Keeffe. But above all, I have selected the most compelling letters, ones that chart both the growth and depth of their relationship and their struggles to create a truly modern marriage that gave each of them complete freedom yet preserved their commitment to each other. I have constructed the selection to establish a dialogue between them and to show the qualities that attracted each to the other, the changes that transpired as they matured, the difficulties they encountered, and the new paths they charted to resolve these issues. I did not avoid letters that address their sexual relationship, for to do so would minimize the important physical nature of their love, nor did I omit ones that reveal their attractions to others, for this too would not give a clear picture of the hurdles they faced as they worked to sustain their union over more than thirty years. Readers will also encounter occasional gratuitous racist remarks uttered by both O'Keeffe and Stieglitz—these too have been neither avoided nor highlighted, for to do so would not accurately reveal the tenor of the time. Both artists, of course, exchanged many letters with friends and colleagues, which they sometimes referred to in their correspondence with each other. I have attempted to locate all of these letters to other individuals and when they elucidate the character and evolution of O'Keeffe's and Stieglitz's relationship, I have added pertinent information in footnotes or introductory texts.

In addition to correcting numerous biographical facts and clarifying their relationships with a wide range of individuals (from Arthur Dove and Marsden Hartley to Marcel Duchamp and D. H. Lawrence, for example), O'Keeffe's and Stieglitz's letters reveal a wealth of new insights into both artists that will fascinate readers for years to come. These include—but are by no means limited to—the changing personas each presented to the other; Stieglitz's tendency in the first decade of their relationship to treat O'Keeffe like a brilliantly gifted child, but also her willingness to reinforce this sense of immaturity; the struggles that resulted from their different ages, backgrounds, and temperaments, which gradually became apparent in the 1920s

---

5. O'Keeffe's and Stieglitz's letters in the Yale Collection of American Literature are available online.

and erupted in the early 1930s; the nature of Stieglitz's affair with the much younger Dorothy Norman from the late 1920s until his death and its often devastating, always gnawing effect on O'Keeffe, as well as the duplicity Stieglitz assumed to perpetuate it; Stieglitz's hypochondria and his tendency to project onto others his own perceived frailties; his intense egotism, self-absorption, and devotion to ideas, especially the concept of whiteness or purity, often at the expense of his personal relationships; the shrewdness with which O'Keeffe managed her later career, her resilient independence, but also her occasionally aloof manner toward Stieglitz and others; and the extent to which both Stieglitz and O'Keeffe were able to infuse their deepest experiences into their art. Yet the letters also show the remarkable depth of their commitment to each other and their willingness to withstand "a good deal of contradictory nonsense," as O'Keeffe wrote toward the end of her life, "because of what seemed clear and bright and wonderful."[6] Many of these issues are briefly noted in the texts scattered throughout this volume and the subsequent one, but they are not explored in depth, for it is the purpose of this publication to put forth the primary documents that detail their relationship in all its complexity.

As the letters do not always present both authors in the best light, they raise a number of other questions. First, did Stieglitz or O'Keeffe destroy any of their own or the other's letters that they deemed unimportant, inappropriate, or even incriminating, thus modifying the collection of their correspondence now housed in the Stieglitz-O'Keeffe Archive in the Yale Collection of American Literature, Beinecke Rare Book and Manuscript Library, Yale University? Nothing in their letters to friends or colleagues or the memoirs of others suggests that they did, nor are there unexplained gaps in their own correspondence. While many of their telegrams and the one- or two-line notes that O'Keeffe left for Stieglitz—in the sleeves of his clothes or on his pillow—when she departed probably have not survived, the collection of their letters at the Beinecke Library appears remarkably complete. The only exceptions are approximately 230 letters from O'Keeffe to Stieglitz written mainly from April through July 1943 and April through October 1944, which are now housed at the Georgia O'Keeffe Museum Research Center and which O'Keeffe most likely intended to be part of the Stieglitz-O'Keeffe Archive at the Beinecke Library.[7]

Second, did O'Keeffe and Stieglitz write each other with the expectation that their letters would be read by others, and did they want their correspondence published? The sheer volume of letters; their immediate, unfiltered voice; the fact that neither O'Keeffe nor Stieglitz edited them after they were written (passages, phrases, even individual words are almost never crossed out); and, most important, the critical role their correspondence played in the development and perpetuation of their relationship indicates that these are very private, not public documents.

6. Georgia O'Keeffe, "Introduction," *Georgia O'Keeffe: A Portrait by Alfred Stieglitz* (New York, 1978, 1997), unpaginated.
7. In the years immediately after Stieglitz's death in 1946, O'Keeffe had many of her letters to him transcribed. The handwritten letters from 1943 and 1944 and their typed transcriptions that are now at the Georgia O'Keeffe Museum Research Center, were, most likely, inadvertently never returned to her.

Yet from the very beginning of their relationship, O'Keeffe and Stieglitz were a private couple operating on a public stage. Stieglitz ensured that their relationship became another one of his "demonstrations" through his display of his intimate photographs of O'Keeffe, his promotion of her art as an expression of her sexuality (and also, to some extent, his virility), and his promulgation of the idea that their marriage represented the perfect union of both a man and a woman and two intensely creative individuals. He also carefully saved all of O'Keeffe's letters to him, along with thousands of other letters received from family, friends, and associates, knowing that these documents would help to confirm his preeminent position in twentieth-century American art and culture. In addition to publishing Marin's letters, he also reprinted several of O'Keeffe's letters to him in an exhibition brochure.[8] Noting that he felt "a book of your letters should be printed," Stieglitz wrote O'Keeffe late in his life, "Yes I have so often wanted to print letters of yours. Letters you wrote before we were together. Letters to me."[9]

For her part, O'Keeffe was not always comfortable with the public limelight Stieglitz forced on her and their relationship, and, as is evident in their correspondence, she came to resent his use of intimate details from their private lives as fodder for the stories and parables he recounted to rapt audiences at his galleries. Later in life, she was also notoriously careful about protecting her privacy and projecting a carefully modulated image to the public. She too saved all of his letters to her, but when she deposited their correspondence in the Beinecke Library, she sealed it, stipulating—with only a few exceptions—that their letters could not be read until twenty years after her death. Yet the evidence clearly indicates that O'Keeffe also wanted their correspondence published. After Stieglitz's death, she went through their correspondence and had hundreds of her letters to him transcribed. When she was in her mid-eighties and early nineties, she asked a few people, including me, to compile a selection for publication. She gave me few explicit instructions on the content and character of the book of their letters, except to "make it beautiful and make it honest."[10] I have been guided by these wishes and by her belief that others would benefit, as she wrote Stieglitz in 1937, from "peeping over the rim into our world."[11] I have also been inspired by the knowledge that just as O'Keeffe and Stieglitz sought to "touch the center"[12] of each other—emotionally and physically, intellectually and artistically, and even spiritually—so too would readers be moved by the story of their lives and love.

8. John Marin, *Letters of John Marin,* ed. and with an intro. by Herbert J. Seligmann (New York, 1931); *Georgia O'Keeffe: Catalogue of the 14th Annual Exhibition of Paintings with Some Recent O'Keeffe Letters,* exh. cat., An American Place, New York, 1937.

9. AS to GOK, Aug. 23, 1943.

10. GOK in conversation with the author, 1981.

11. GOK to AS, Oct. 3[?], 1937.

12. See GOK to AS, May 7, July 9, and July 24, 1929.

Note to the Reader

THE PURPOSE OF THIS BOOK is to present a selection of Georgia O'Keeffe's and Alfred Stieglitz's letters to each other that is informative and faithful, but also highly readable. I have therefore silently corrected spelling and have not riddled the text with the use of [*sic*]. Stieglitz rarely misspelled words, but O'Keeffe often did—"before," for example, was always "befor," and "minute" was frequently "minuet"; she and Stieglitz occasionally even made fun of her mangled attempts to guess at spelling.

Drawing on his Germanic heritage, a tendency to animate inanimate objects, and a penchant for dramatization, Stieglitz frequently capitalized the first letter of nouns and concepts—as in Trees, Mountain Tops, Night, Life, Truth, or Spirit. For smoother reading, I have followed this practice only when he was referring to specific places, such as the "Lake" (Lake George) or the "Park" (Central Park); when capitalization conveys both his emphasis and meaning; or when he or O'Keeffe used endearing appellations for each other, such as "Sweetestheart" or "Dearest Boy."

I have preserved their nontraditional punctuation, as it reveals the spontaneous, free-flowing character of their handwritten letters. Stieglitz's handwriting is elegant, and the long, graceful dashes that he formed with a thick-tipped fountain pen add a bold, sometimes breathless, and often poetic tone as one idea or image tumbles over another in rapid succession. O'Keeffe's orthography is equally distinctive (see pp. 61, 67). Particularly in the 1910s, her letters are frequently filled with long, wavy dashes, vertical and diagonal lines, multiple dots, and even curlicues that fracture her ideas into short, often vivid phrases, suggesting both her impressionistic, less analytical, and almost elliptical method of thinking and a wish to literally sketch out her ideas rather than verbally articulate them. I attempted to indicate the unique character of her writings by preserving her short phrases, but for the sake of readability, clarity, and concision, I have translated her idiosyncratic markings into dashes and have frequently condensed separate lines into paragraphs.

In order to allow both O'Keeffe and Stieglitz to tell their own story, I have annotated the text only lightly. In doing so, my intention has been to provide the reader with critical references to personal or historical information that the artists themselves do not present and to let the letters themselves unveil the evolution of their relationship.

Readers will find a biographical dictionary at the end of the volume that briefly identifies people mentioned in the letters. I have not included well-known artists or authors, unless they had a direct connection with O'Keeffe or Stieglitz. Nor have I included individuals whose first or last names are not known, unless they are mentioned several times in the letters. Both writers frequently referred to family and a few close friends, often women and children, by first name only. In these cases, I have given full names in footnotes at first mention. Thereafter names appear as O'Keeffe and Stieglitz wrote them, except when they used initials or other abbreviations; in those instances I have inserted the name. The biographical dictionary is prefaced by a list of individuals often referred to by first name only; they are cross-referenced and identified more fully in the dictionary.

Stieglitz's letters from 1916 through 1918, and intermittently thereafter, are very long (sometimes up to forty pages) and were usually written throughout the day (early morning, midday, late afternoon, and evening, for example) and over several days. Although O'Keeffe's letters from this same period are shorter, she too occasionally bundled in one envelope epistles written over several days. By their own admission, they rarely reread their letters, so these "subsections" of each letter often repeat information or ideas mentioned in other sections. Whereas elsewhere I have included the entire letter, in these instances I have selected the most compelling and forcefully articulated subsection and affixed a plus sign (+) next to the date to indicate my omission of additional subsections enclosed in the same envelope. However, each selected letter or subsection is presented uncensored.

In keeping with the fluid, uninhibited nature of their correspondence, O'Keeffe and Stieglitz never revised their letters, and phrases or even individual words are never crossed out. In those rare instances where their meaning is ambiguous, I have inserted clarifying words in brackets.

Before the early 1920s, neither of the authors consistently dated their letters or noted where they were written. When postmarks and internal evidence have been used to establish dates and locations, that information is given in brackets. Numbers, except for streets or when given as time at the beginning of a letter, have for the most part been spelled out, although O'Keeffe and Stieglitz often used Arabic numerals. Abbreviations such as "N.Y." or "Met" have been spelled out, except for "S.W.," which was the cool, distant way Stieglitz and Dorothy Norman referred to O'Keeffe in their letters.

Unless otherwise noted, all letters between O'Keeffe and Stieglitz, as well as correspondence between O'Keeffe, Stieglitz, and others, are in the Yale Collection of American Literature, Beinecke Rare Book and Manuscript Library, Yale University. All references to Lynes, followed by a number, refer to Barbara Buhler Lynes, *Georgia O'Keeffe: Catalogue Raisonné* (New Haven, 1999). All references to Greenough, followed by a number, refer to Sarah Greenough, *Alfred Stieglitz: The Key Set* (Washington, 2002).

I.

All the World Greets You
1915–1918

SOON AFTER Georgia O'Keeffe arrived in South Carolina in the fall of 1915, she reached a critical juncture in the evolution of her art. Rejecting all her earlier work, she realized she could not "spend my life doing what had already been done," and she embarked on a series of abstract charcoal drawings.[1] These pieces reveal her study of Japanese art and art nouveau, as well as the ideas of the Russian Wassily Kandinsky and the Americans Arthur Wesley Dow, Marsden Hartley, and Arthur Dove, though her drawings were also highly inventive. Eager for critical reaction, she sent some to her New York art school friend Anita Pollitzer. Although Pollitzer understood O'Keeffe's ambivalence about sharing her art with others, she also knew her friend wanted Alfred Stieglitz's approval more than that of anyone else. She took the drawings to Stieglitz's gallery 291 on January 1, 1916, the legendary photographer's fifty-second birthday. As Pollitzer excitedly reported, Stieglitz asked her to tell O'Keeffe that her drawings "were the purest, fairest, sincerest things that have entered 291 in a long while," adding, "I wouldn't mind showing them in one of these rooms one bit—perhaps I shall."[2]

Buoyed by Stieglitz's praise—"it just made me ridiculously glad," she told Pollitzer —and frustrated with her current teaching position—"I was never so disgusted with such a lot of people"[3]—O'Keeffe quit her job in South Carolina. After borrowing two hundred dollars, she returned to New York in March 1916 and enrolled in Dow's methods course at Columbia University Teachers College, a requirement if she was to assume the position she had been offered

---

1. In Georgia O'Keeffe, *Georgia O'Keeffe* (New York, 1976), unpaginated; Barbara Buhler Lynes, *Georgia O'Keeffe: Catalogue Raisonné* (New Haven, 1999), 45–56 (hereafter cited as Lynes).

2. Pollitzer to GOK, Jan. 1, 1916, in Anita Pollitzer, *A Woman on Paper: Georgia O'Keeffe. The Letters and Memoir of a Legendary Friendship* (New York, 1988), 120.

3. GOK to Pollitzer, Jan. 1917, in Giboire, *Lovingly, Georgia,* 128.

by West Texas State Normal College in Canyon, Texas, later that fall. While in New York, she renewed friendships, spent time with her beau Arthur Macmahon, and went to 291. Over the next two months, Stieglitz challenged and captivated O'Keeffe, as he did so many other visitors to his gallery. She was overwhelmed when she and Macmahon saw Hartley's April exhibition at 291 of forty large abstract paintings made in Germany, which she later described as "a brass band in a small closet."[4] She was "startled" when Stieglitz lent her one of Hartley's earliest paintings, *Dark Landscape* (1909), to take home to study. And she was even more stunned and disconcerted when Stieglitz told her that he wanted to exhibit her drawings in May. O'Keeffe abruptly left New York on May 2 after learning that her fifty-two-year-old mother, Ida, who suffered from tuberculosis, had died in Charlottesville. She returned to New York in time to see her first exhibition, which Stieglitz opened at 291 on May 23, 1916, but left soon thereafter to teach, once again, at the University of Virginia summer school.[5]

4. Georgia O'Keeffe, "Introduction," *Georgia O'Keeffe: A Portrait by Alfred Stieglitz* (New York, 1978, 1997), unpaginated.
5. The exhibition, which was on view through July 5, 1916, included ten charcoal drawings by O'Keeffe (Lynes 45–50, 52, 54–56), as well as works by Charles Duncan and René Lafferty.

2

Georgia O'Keeffe at the University of Virginia, 1915. Gelatin silver print.
Georgia O'Keeffe Museum Collection.

Georgia O'Keeffe · University, Virginia · August 14, 1915

Dear Mr. Stieglitz—

Yesterday I had a long letter from little—big hearted Anita Pollitzer. She asked me if I had received the June number of *291*[6] that she had written you to send me—

It came today and it pleases me so much that I must just write and *tell* you about it.

I am the young woman who was so glad to see John Marin make the world go crazy—You gave me a 291 number of *Camera Work*[7] and I can't begin to tell you how much I've liked it—I always want it where I can see it in my room—I like it for things it makes me think of.

Mr. Stieglitz—I want to subscribe to *291* and I want numbers two and three if you have any left.

If you will send number four to—Arthur W. Macmahon—Columbia University, N.Y.—I will thank you—

Sincerely,
Georgia O'Keeffe

Georgia O'Keeffe · [Columbia, South Carolina] · [early January 1916]

Mr. Stieglitz:

If you remember for a week—why you liked my charcoals that Anita Pollitzer showed you—and what they said to you—I would like to know if you want to tell me.

I don't mind asking—you can do as you please about answering.—Of course I know you will do as you please—

I make them—just to express myself—things I feel and want to say––haven't words for—You probably know without my saying it—that I ask because I wonder if I got over to anyone what I want to say.—

Georgia O'Keeffe

Alfred Stieglitz · 291 Fifth Avenue, New York · January 20, 1916

My dear Miss O'Keeffe:

What am I to say? It is impossible for me to put into words what I saw and felt in your drawings. As a matter of fact I would not make any attempt to do so. I might give you what I received from them if you and I were to meet and talk about life. Possibly then through such conversation I might make you feel what your drawings gave me.

---

6. *291* 4 (June 1915).

7. Stieglitz inscribed *Camera Work* 47 (July 1914), devoted to the question "What Is 291?" to O'Keeffe, writing: "A Marin afternoon at 291—A young woman interested in the 'Woolworth Etching'—A young woman who feels that in the springtime one wants everything to go crazy! Alfred Stieglitz, February 27—1915" (Department of Photographs, The J. Paul Getty Museum, Los Angeles).

I do want to tell you that they gave me much joy. They were a real surprise and above all I felt that they were a genuine expression of yourself. I do not know what you had in your mind while doing them. But I do feel that they have brought you closer to me. Much closer. If at all possible I would like to show them, but we will see about that. I do not quite know where I am at just at present. The future is rather hazy, but the present is very positive and very delightful.

>With greetings,
>Cordially,
>Alfred Stieglitz

Georgia O'Keeffe · [Columbia, South Carolina] · [February 1, 1916]

Mr. Stieglitz—

I like what you write me—Maybe—I don't get exactly your meaning—but I like mine —like you liked your interpretation of my drawings.—

It was such a surprise to me that you saw them—and I am so glad they surprised you —that they gave you joy. I am glad I could give you once what 291 has given me many times.

You can't imagine how it all astonishes me.

I have been just trying to express myself—I just have to say things you know— Words and I—are not good friends at all except with some people—when I'm close to them and can feel as well as hear their response—I have to say it some way—Last year I went color mad—but I've almost hated to think of color since the fall went—I've been slaving on the violin—trying to make that talk—I wish I could tell you some of the things I've wanted to say as I felt them.

The drawings don't count—it's the life—that really counts—To say things that way may be a relief—It may be interesting to see how different people react to them.—I am glad they said something to you.—I think so much alone—work alone—am so much alone—but for letters—that I am not always sure that I'm thinking straight—It's great—I like it—The outdoors is wonderful—and I'm just now having time to think things I should have thought long ago—The uncertain feeling that—some of my ideas may be near insanity—adds to the fun of it—and the prospect of really talking to live human beings again—sometime in the future is great.—Hibernating in South Carolina is an experience that I would not advise anyone to miss—The place is of so little consequence—except for the outdoors—that one has a chance to give one's mind, time, and attention to anything one wishes.

I can't tell you how sorry I am that I can't talk to you—what I've been thinking surprises me so—has been such fun—at times has hurt too—that it would be great to tell you—

Some of the fields are green—very very green—almost unbelievably green against the dark of the pine woods—and it's warm—the air feels warm and soft—and lovely—

I wonder if Marin's *Woolworth* has spring fever again this year[8]—I hope it has—
Sincerely—
Georgia O'Keeffe.

I put this in the envelope—stretched—and laughed—

It's so funny that I should just write you because I want to—I wonder if many people do.—

You see—I would go in and talk to you if I could—and I hate to be completely outdone by a little thing like distance—

Georgia O'Keeffe · [En route from New York City to Charlottesville, Virginia] · [May 3, 1916]

Mr. Stieglitz—

I am on the train on the way to Virginia—

I don't know why I have thought so often and so much about you at this particular time—but I have—I got a telegram this afternoon saying my mother is dead—

If you were here and asked me questions—about it—or about anything else—I would probably give very queer answers. I feel queer—I don't seem to know anything—

but—I do know that when I get there tomorrow morning—I must even forget she is dead—

It seems as though I must build—

I don't know anything now—I'll only know step by step as I come to it—You must not feel sorry for me—I am only going down because I can probably make things easier for some others—

—but I wish you would write me—not that you are sorry—or any of that truck—Just talk to me—

If you want to—Not if you don't want to.

Last Saturday morning when I waked up the first thing I saw was the Hartley—and it startled me—I was through with it all in a minute—I got up right quick and turned it to the wall. I have wanted to take it down to you every day since but didn't have time till today. Thank you so much for it.

I rode home on the bus after taking the picture in to you. It was a wonderful day—

Then the telegram was there—

Some way it still seems to be a wonderful day—

Georgia O'Keeffe

University, Va.—12:15 in the night—

8. Marin's etchings of the Woolworth Building were included in his 1915 exhibition at 291; see Carl Zigrosser, *The Complete Etchings of John Marin* (Philadelphia, 1969), 113–116.

5

ALL THE WORLD GREETS YOU, 1915–1918

Alfred Stieglitz · [New York City] · May 6, 1916

For two days I carried a letter in my pocket—a letter stamped & sealed ready to mail. Why did I finally tear it up? It was addressed to you. I wrote to you as soon as I had heard from you.

It seems impossible for me these days to find words for anything—perhaps because I'm dead myself. And words, just words, are so terrible. Rather by far a living aching silence.

Your mother.—Was she very close to you?—You to her?—I hope so for there can be nothing quite so wonderful. And if this was so, how you must suffer now. In silence. Heroically. —No one to know—not even self.

I have been on jury duty—still am—that's why I didn't see you when you returned the Hartley.—Had I known how to get at you in the city I would have written or phoned. Also to tell you why your drawings were not yet up on the walls. I didn't want them up while I had to be away so much. I wanted to hang them primarily for myself—for my own enjoyment. Jury call came unexpectedly.

It is a summer day today.—291 has been like a tomb all day—even the phone has been silent—without a sound.

Let me hear from you—If you are near trees send me some of their spirit. Trees & Water!—

291 sends you greetings.

Georgia O'Keeffe · [New York City] · [May 8, 1916]

I came back yesterday—Of course there is no reason why I should tell you—except that— I want to—

I've slept ever since I got here—except that I got up and ate once in awhile—and it seems as if I could go on sleeping always—

I feel as if I'll not want to go down to see you for a long time—but maybe I will—can't tell—.

If you put my things up let me know—I might like to see them first—and again I might not—I don't know—Morningside 5271 is my phone.

Georgia O'Keeffe.

Georgia O'Keeffe · [New York City] · [May 21, 1916]

Mr. Stieglitz—

I am writing you because I am afraid to go to sleep—and after I've told someone I'll not be so much afraid—or at least—I hope I won't—

Last night I dreamed—A very bad dream about Mama—and I thought my hands were on her face. I know the shape of it so well because I've rubbed her head so much and felt her face so often—No, not lately—it's just something I've always known—

Her temples I can always feel with my thumb—

I would make my dream—but I know I couldn't stand it to stay in the same building with it overnight—

I went out to dinner—and—supper—I've talked and argued and laughed all day—I've been in a very good humor—I am sure no one would ever have imagined that I would be afraid to go to sleep tonight—I've had a very good time all day—

—isn't it absurd that I am afraid now.

I saw you at the Metropolitan this afternoon—You were looking at the Winslow Homer—I was looking at the people. You didn't turn.

You are a funny man. I put my hat on and got to my door one day this week to tell you something that seemed worse to me then—than my mother being gone—but I turned back and saw a picture I had made—and—I thought—No—So—the next day I went—when I had cooled off some—I didn't tell you—because—well—I didn't need to then—and anyway— I couldn't have told the others—too—The reason I say you are funny is because you seemed to be hunting around that day for something to bother you—You had even tried to get the doctor to find something wrong with you—

and I had so much that was real—that—why—my brain simply wouldn't work.

—I knew when I went down that I wasn't going to tell you but everything seemed so queer to me—I wondered why people laughed—I had caught myself stopping and looking at them two or three times when I heard them—wondering how it felt—how it would be to feel like that again—did they know the other things—I couldn't do anything so I went down to see you for curiosity—I wondered what you looked like—

I ate lunch with Anita the day before—the day I thought I had to tell someone and started to tell you—She seemed like such a pretty little girl—I couldn't tell her. When I saw you—you were trying to find something wrong with yourself—

You don't mind—if I tell you that every time I have thought of it since—I have laughed. It seems so funny—and I laugh too—at the way I stood around there—seeming about as stupid as people are made. I guess I enjoyed being stupid that morning—I frequently do.

After I left it quite amused me to think what a fool I am—

But I didn't care that day—

And this is another day.

291 is a very nice place—

Maybe I can sleep now—

Goodnight—thank you for letting me feel I can talk to you.

[May 28, 1916]
I wrote this last Sunday night and found it in my desk tonight.

I've been sick—tonsillitis—in bed—for four days—can't come to life—can't care about anything—

Living great? Why yes—

The emptiness of the space ahead is appalling—It seems so empty that I don't want to move into it—thinking of it makes me feel I cannot stand it—

But I know I can—only I hate to take the first step—

I'd almost rather just stay in bed and have tonsillitis.—

The space ahead is the summer and the winter—and the summer and the winter again as I have planned them—and it's all empty—

[June 3, 1916]

Here it is—

Written last Sunday night—and the Sunday before—I would tell you why I went down today but my head aches so I can't—

The part of me that the doctor can't get at is very much sicker than the rest of me—

Alfred Stieglitz · [**New York City**] · [**June 8, 1916**]

Here is a letter for you.—It came last night.

—So you have found your balance. And the cause absurd.—Isn't everything that brings about a balance of within with without usually an "absurdity"?

I wonder if you know who Leo Stein is. He saw your work this morning & it interested him immensely as it continues to interest me immensely.—

You said you were going to make a new drawing—Did you?—I'm curious to see it. Perhaps you've forgotten all about the intention—or momentary desire.

So you stood behind me as I was looking at the Winslow Homer!—Amusing. I never see the people when I'm at the Museum—nor do I see much of the pictures—Why do I go there?—I only go two or three times a year—& always come out full of resentment—conscious of only what *might be so readily* were there just a little less stupidity at the head of institutions like our Museum.

—It's young I know. That's why I hate to see it waste its opportunities.

Greetings.

Will you tell me about the sister.[9]—

Hasn't the rain been penetratingly wet these two days?—

Georgia O'Keeffe · [**Charlottesville, Virginia**] · [**June 22, 1916**]

What's it like here?

Trees—oak trees—so big and dark and green that they almost smother me—

Early one morning—it was Sunday—I walked away from it because they smother me so—and I saw some smaller trees and bigger open spaces—fields white with daisies—mountains—

---

9. O'Keeffe wrote Stieglitz on June 8, 1916, that she had "a sister that I don't really care much about—only when things hurt her—and then—why I sometimes think that they hurt me more than they do her." O'Keeffe had four sisters: Ida Ten Eyck, Anita Natalie, Catherine Blanche, and Claudia Ruth. She may have been referring to Catherine.

I used to think it beautiful—but it isn't now—

My work means meeting many people that I know—people who have known me as something very live—I didn't know how little alive I feel till in their many greetings this morning I felt what response was expected of me.

Of them all—there was only one I was glad to see—and he[10] had the bad taste to bring his wife along this year—I've never seen her so don't know yet whether he is any good anymore or not—I think he said two children too.—

We used to get up weekend walking parties but—probably won't this year—

I must tell you that he is about as insufficient looking as anyone I ever saw—teaches agriculture somewhere in Georgia—but he has always been good fun before—he is human.

They pay me fifty dollars more this year so I have five hours less work a week—

I must tell you some more—I wish you were here and I could talk to you—I seem to want to tell you everything I know—You know those drawings you have had to grow some way—The man[11] who made me make them—I might better say—that I made them to—was here last year—I met him here—the farmer mentioned above introduced us repeatedly—

We got to know one another enough to want to know more on a weekend walk—and now there hardly seems a place I can think of for miles in every direction that he hasn't been with me—He even seems to have sat on every chair—picked up some number of every magazine I read—remarked on every dress I wear—he went to South Carolina to see me Thanksgiving—He seems to be part of everything I know there—part of everything I know in New York.

I even had the bad taste—no I'll not say that—I even took him to 291 to see the Hartleys—you remember—

It isn't queer at all—he is exactly what I am not—

I have always wondered—every time he came again—why he came—I can't imagine—

Yes he likes me—but he doesn't need me—

His life is planned—and he didn't put a woman in the plan—and I have not planned—and need the thing I like—

You understand?

Besides that—my mother lived here—you know—

And that not being enough—the sister is here—Nobody knows she is married[12]—Watching her is about as keen torture as anyone could want—

What can I say to you?—Your packages[13] yesterday gave me the only spurt of pure fun and joy that I've had since I came South. They excited me so that I didn't put them down till I was too tired to look at them anymore—And I haven't read more than a paragraph—except the little girl's poem—and a couple of Katharine Rhoades—I always like Katharine Rhoades—

10. O'Keeffe referred to this friend as "Scott" or "farmer Scott" and noted that he was from Georgia; his last name is not known.

11. Arthur W. Macmahon was a political science professor at Columbia University.

12. Anita O'Keeffe and Robert R. Young, a Texan who had been studying at the University of Virginia, eloped on April 27, 1916.

13. Stieglitz sent O'Keeffe *Camera Work* 42–43 (Apr.–June 1913), with a poem by Mary Steichen, aged nine, p. 14; and *Camera Work* 46 (Apr. 1914), with poems by Katharine N. Rhoades, pp. 17–18; as well as Willard Huntington Wright's *The Man of Promise* (New York, 1916) and "Notes on Art," *Forum* 55 (June 1916), 691–706.

I just looked at them—

I wish I had written you then—while I was so excited—but I couldn't put them down even to write to you till I was too tired—

I hope I'm the tiredest girl in the world—I'd hate to think anyone else is any more tired.

The Man of Promise came too—but I haven't done anything so I haven't read it—

You understand—I did get the *Forum* and read his "Art Notes"[14]—I'm only telling you that I enjoyed the photographs and drawings—and the color in the *Camera Works*[15]—I'm going to read later—And I simply can't tell you how much I enjoyed them.

Do you wonder that I hate it here—that I wish fall would come quick—I'm hoping the wind on the plains will blow it all away.

It seems as if I have felt things—and thought things till I'm afraid to either think or feel—I have slept—mostly—but even that is bad because I hate so to wake up.

I'm sleepy again.

The photograph of Gordon Craig[16] is great—The very first book I picked up after you asked me about him that day was his *Theatre of Today*[17]—or some such title—It surprised me so because I had an idea that I was going to try some stage settings—before I had to come to Virginia earlier in the spring—I had been thinking about it for several weeks—but hadn't had time for any definite start—

I'm such a fool—I want to do everything in the world—

I wish I could talk to you—wish you were here—it would make something very fine and new to take away the old—

Write to me—

Alfred Stieglitz · Boston, Massachusetts · June 26, 1916

A greeting from Boston—I'm here over night taking my daughter to camp in New Hampshire.[18] We get there tomorrow at one & I return to New York at once hoping to reach there Friday morning. So you see I'm getting a "vacation" from 291.—

This morning as I ran down to 291 before train time I was repaid a thousand fold for much I have had to go through for the sake of so many—& myself. Mrs. Bull, of Buffalo (I mentioned her to you in a letter) had telegraphed to a young woman[19] friend of hers (living quite some distance from New York) not to fail to go to 291 to see the drawings. This young woman

14. In "Notes on Art," *Forum* 55 (June 1916), 691–706, Wright asserted that "the side of art which is the recording of some emotion the artist has experienced so intensely that it demands concrete expression is feminine.... All purely decorative & imitative art is feminine. The work in which there is the subjective emotion of order and harmony, in which the effect is the result of a conscious or unconscious philosophic cause, is masculine."

15. *Camera Work* 42–43 (Apr.–July 1913) included three color halftone reproductions of Edward Steichen's paintings: *Nocturne—Hydrangea Terrace, Chateaux Ledoux; Autumnal Afternoon—The Poplars, Voulangis;* and *The Lotus Screen: S.S.S.*

16. Edward Steichen, *E. Gordon Craig, Camera Work* 42–43 (Apr.–July 1913).

17. Craig, *A Living Theatre: The Gordon Craig School* (Florence, 1913).

18. Stieglitz was accompanying his daughter Kitty to Camp Kehonka, Lake Winnipesaukee, New Hampshire.

19. Evelyn Sayer.

amazed (& delighted me tremendously) me how she stood there & SAW—just as I did—I wish you could have heard without being seen or known. It was a tremendous fifteen minutes for the Little Room—It never seemed so big—so pure. Thoroughly woman in the biggest, finest sense. The rarest thing in the world.—Mostly an idea only!—Too bad really that we had so little time together to compare notes.—And still—perhaps it's best as it is.—All of you on the walls of 291!—I wonder whether the man[20] *saw* the drawings [and] what he thought—& above all felt.—

And how are you getting on with your duties.—And are you just a little less tired.—I wish you could answer truthfully "yes."—

—You wrote in your letter about the man's plan—you probably not being in that plan. I've always wondered how most men do plan—I wish I had learned how—Perhaps I did without knowing it.—What odd things women are—& men—What things are they?—Hardly odd. Just plain stupid. Don't you think so?—

—I had a long letter the other day from a very dear friend of mine advising me—for my good—to quit 291—& to sever all connections with all those connected with it.—To get out of the idea (rut, I suppose) & get into another. I had to laugh aloud at such advice.—How often I've heard it for over thirty years—from so many friends—& nearly all the family!—Of course I understand—they do not know I cannot leave myself—& wherever I am—291 is—& wherever 291 is—all those that ever meant anything to me are there too.—It's bed time—it's a sultry night.

Good Night & Good Cheer.
Ever gratefully,
Alfred Stieglitz

Georgia O'Keeffe · [Charlottesville, Virginia] · [July 3, 1916]

Yes feeling better—really—but so stupidly good for nothing—not doing anything—and not wanting to—

How can I tell you how nice your letters have been!

You know—don't you—

Men stupid? No—I think they are all right—He[21] saw my things—

I like him because he is rare—feels and thinks too—It is all right for things to be as they are—

I've always been afraid of being like the women in *The Man of Promise*[22]—I enjoyed it immensely—but it made me feel like a curse on the face of the earth—just because I am a woman—I do not blame the women—it's the way they are made—I started to say that the man was weak—but I guess the women were too—

Thank you for the pleasant Saturday I had with it—

---

20. Arthur W. Macmahon.
21. Arthur W. Macmahon.
22. Wright's first novel, *The Man of Promise,* is about a highly talented man who is thwarted by a woman.

I haven't read anything else but some Synge plays[23] and pieces from the *Camera Works*—

Not even reading—It's disgusting to be wasting so much time—I hate it—and at the same time don't mind at all.

I seem to be waiting for something to happen—I've tried not to think because there are so many things that make me feel so exquisitely raw inside that—

There is a little sister—seventeen[24]—still a little girl—with a very keen mind—She has just grown pretty this year—It scares me—still I want the time to go fast—I want to see what she will grow to—

And—then there are more things and more things—It may be painful—may hurt—but it's a great experience—

If everything had gone smoothly I'd not have learned—not have had a chance to feel and think it—all—

When I try not to think I sometimes want to kick myself—for not thinking and feeling all I can—I don't dare you know—

Thanks again for your letters—

It's a wonderful night—cool and dark and little singing things—

Goodnight—

Georgia O'Keeffe—

Alfred Stieglitz · **[New York City]** · **[July 10, 1916]**

It's Monday morning.—And here I am at 291.—The fan going like mad—for it is stifling in the room although the windows are wide open—And outside the trip hammers are singing a chorus of noise—noise—& more noise—for a huge steel building is going up northeast of us—just a few feet away.[25]—

—On Friday I started writing to you.—I had written a page or two—when Duncan came in.—And when he went others came.—And so there never was a letter—And yet I felt like writing—like saying that I was very happy to know you stronger.—And that I believed you when you said you were so. Then too I wanted to tell you how well I understood all you said about your sister—in fact how well I understood all you wrote—& said—& felt.

And now comes your note.—Of course my only value to you can be that you can talk to me—anytime—anything—Say all you feel—how you feel—I know it's a wonderful comforting restful feeling to feel that there is someone always ready—to understand! Never to judge.—Someone to whom judging is loathsome—yet who is sometimes forced into a position of judging against will—Those are the moments when I'm truly miserable for judging is outside

23. John Millington Synge was a key figure in the Irish Literary Revival. His most celebrated play was *The Playboy of the Western World,* 1907; other plays include *Riders to the Sea* and *In the Shadow of the Glen,* both from 1905.

24. Claudia O'Keeffe.

25. Stieglitz photographed the construction of this building; see Sarah Greenough, *Alfred Stieglitz: The Key Set* (New York, 2002), nos. 426–428; hereafter cited as Greenough.

of me—And yet how often my so-called best friends finally try to force me to choose—to judge!—And then I find myself alone & a great calm gradually comes over me—And thoughts of Water—Night—and Trees.—And all they mean to me—How much more human they all [are] than even the best of human friends!!—

Of course I know it is one's self—One's self at war—Ever clashing!—

—Have you drawn any since you left New York?—Where is Miss Pollitzer—has she left town?—I like her—Always did—even before she ever opened her mouth—Liked her as I watched her look—watched her listen.—

Little did I dream that one day she would bring to me drawings that would mean so much to 291 as yours have meant.—Nor did you dream when you did them that they would —or could—ever mean so much to anyone as they have to 291.—It's queer how we met—it's queerer still how eventually—

—No I don't believe there must be anything eventually—

Except Great Life!—

And Music—Real Music—

Voices—Singing—Water

—Good luck to you.

Georgia O'Keeffe · [Charlottesville, Virginia] · [July 11, 1916]

I think letters with so much humanness in them have never come to me before—I have wondered with everyone of them—what it is in them—how you put it in—or is it my imagination —seeing and feeling—finding what I want—

They seem to give me a great big quietness—that relieves the tension that I always seem to be feeling.

I came in this noon—it was very warm—I had to talk for half an hour or so to a friend of my nice sister's[26]—a man who had come a long way to see her—I was glad to meet him—Glad to talk to him because she is the nicest girl I have ever known and she likes him—

My head ached—Your letter made me very quiet—and I stretched out—flat on my back with the weight of my arms on my head all the afternoon—

When it was almost dark I walked with my little sister[27]—away from the trees—out where I could see the mountains—the houses and lights of the city below them—all in the moonlight—and where I could feel space—

Tomorrow I must hunt out and meet a girl that she likes[28]—and read a book she read yesterday and liked—She wants me to know both—wants to know what I think of them—

I like what you say about judging—I think I'll try to tell her about it—Of course you know that I felt you that way before you expressed it to me.

---

26. Ida O'Keeffe.
27. Claudia O'Keeffe.
28. Probably Katherine Lumpkin.

We came home—and decided that—this is the best place after all—So quiet—trees—the moon—big black shadows—very big black shadows—and the little noises—it is just nice.

Anita Pollitzer is up at Fleishman's—Delaware County, New York—I haven't written her for over two weeks—simply haven't wanted to—

No I haven't worked—haven't wanted to—Nothing takes shape—there is nothing to do—

I don't know what is going to be next—work doesn't go with sleep and food—I am making myself stay in bed and my sisters make me eat—It's disgusting—I hate it—

Sometimes I wonder if it is me—it seems to be such a new version—

I wonder what I'll want to do next—I know it can't always be like this—Goodnight.

I'm going to write you something—that I know you know. I don't write to many people but the ones I write to are apt to get horrible doses of most anything—

I don't know what I wrote you a few nights ago—remember—that was just one little part of me—a part that I probably wouldn't have showed you if I had talked to you—

I know you know it but just the same I want to tell you anyway—

It is nice to know that you *are*—somewhere—

Tonight is very quiet—little singing things out there in the dark—the night feels so cool and damp—it is very nice—and the moon—only part of it—seems very near—it's hanging—just a little way off—over the trees.

Goodnight—

Georgia O'Keeffe.

Alfred Stieglitz · [New York City] · [July 16, 1916]

It's Sunday morning—and it's cool—& gray. I'm at home & am spending the morning working at *Camera Work*[29] & doing a lot of writing that should have been done months ago.—There was a time—not so long ago—when I was very punctilious—in everything. I wonder why I'm not that way anymore—when I lost the habit—? Why—?—

—So you of your own volition remain in bed much (it's wise for you need *rest* of that kind)—and your sister makes you eat!!—That's fine too. Building up the nervous system. And that can only be achieved through rest in bed & plenty of wholesome food. And once the nervous system has been strengthened—much else will be different!

I don't like to talk that way for it is so infernally conventional—But others just say it—& feel nothing. I say it & feel something.—And that is not so conventional these days.—

I had a fine letter from a woman—the one I wrote to you about the day I had to go to Boston—regarding your exhibition. I've written to her requesting permission to print the letter in *Camera Work*.[30]

---

29. *Camera Work* 48 (Oct. 1916).
30. Evelyn Sayer, "Untitled," *Camera Work* 48 (Oct. 1916), 13.

The pictures are down—not a picture on the walls of 291.—There'll be none all summer.—Some of your drawings I'm having framed—to protect them. They have meant so much to me that I can't bear the thought that they might be soiled—rubbed—for they are not fixed. You see I assume "rights."—Is it too nervy?—I'm sure no.—I'll take care of the others—or do you wish me to send them to you? And the framed ones—they are yours whenever you wish them. One though I want to keep for all time[31]—May I?—Of course that too you can have whenever you want it—but only as "Loaned."—

—I'll abide your will in the whole matter.—

291 is very quiet—Virtually "everyone" is away—still stray strangers stray in—& there's always some interest.—

Greetings—& the Wish for Strength!—

Physical.—

Georgia O'Keeffe · **[Charlottesville, Virginia]** · **[July 25, 1916]**

It's nice to think that the walls of 291 are empty—I went in a year ago after you had stripped them—and I just thought things on them—It is one of the nicest memories I have of 291—

That is absurd to say—I often wondered what it is you put into the place that makes it so nice even when it's empty—just tracks in the dust on the floor and a chair at a queer angle—

Still it was great and I was glad I had gone—glad that I saw no one.

No—nothing you do with my drawings is "nervy"—

I seem to feel that they are as much yours as mine—They were only mine alone till the first person saw them—I wonder which one it is you want to keep—Some things I cannot say yes or no to—right now—I wouldn't mind if you wrote me that you had torn them all up—I don't want them—I don't want even to see them—but I'm not always the same—Sometime I may have to tear them all up myself—You understand—They are all as much yours as mine. I don't care what you do with them so long as I don't have to see them—

It is nice of you to frame what you wanted to—You are a much better keeper than I am—

I wonder if you would like to see the cast of the thing[32] I modeled just before I left New York—It's like everything else—I want to show it to you—but—at the same time—hate to show it to anyone—The base is very bad—he didn't fix it as I told him and a lot of it seems lost but still I'm liking it—.

I'm feeling all right again—Went up to Mt. Elliott Springs above Staunton over the weekend and climbed Mt. Elliott.

---

31. Probably Lynes 50.

32. Lynes 66. In late June 1916 O'Keeffe wrote Pollitzer: "I did not take the thing to 291 but had it cast—the man sent me one but he has another—the way he fixed the pedestal is awful—I don't know about the rest of it—I have hardly looked at it" (Giboire, *Lovingly Georgia*, 159). O'Keeffe made this piece in memory of her mother.

I got to the top alone in the moonlight—just as day was beginning to come—It was great—the wind—and the stars—and the clouds below—and all the time I was terribly afraid of snakes—

The others slept about a mile below by the campfire—

—And I was glad—

Lots of outdoors made me very hilarious—When I came home and thought about it I was surprised at my foolishness.

I wish I could go in and talk to you this afternoon—

It's great to feel fine again—it seems almost impossible that I'm not apt to go in and talk to you for a long long time—because I want to now.

I've been working some—last week—watercolors—and am going to make [more] this weekend if I can get at it before it's gone.

It is getting ready to rain—and it's almost time for supper—and I'm going over to my farmer friend's afterward—you remember—the little man from Georgia[33]—I like his wife.

So there seem to be several good reasons why I should not ramble anymore—

Goodnight—I wish I could someway tell you how nice your letters have been—how nice it is that you are.

[July 26, 1916]
I wrote the other part of this last night—

Today the photographs[34] were here when I came in at noon—

—and I am speechless.

What can I say—?

You must just say it yourself.

Wednesday night.

Alfred Stieglitz · [New York City] · July 31, 1916

Mountain Tops!—A climb in the Night to see Dawn light up the World!—And afraid of snakes (how I loathe them—innocent ones!)—still going!—Life itself—

—The stillness of the mountain tops—and night—how different from New York.— From my last few days—291 a steamkettle & I in it—& the lid ready to blow off.—Twenty hours in bed in ninety-six hours—& no sleep because of mosquitoes.—Talking fourteen hours on a stretch to one man yesterday.—Sunday.—

—Standing at the open window—two A.M.—driven there by a mosquito—one vicious barbaric German I'm sure—one that disfigured me in spite of citronella & pillow!—The open window—A tremendous report[35]—the house shaken—Naval battle between English & German

---

33. Scott.

34. Stieglitz sent O'Keeffe photographs (no longer extant) that he had made of the exhibition of her drawings at 291.

35. On July 30, 1916, German agents blew up a munitions depot on Black Tom Island, part of Jersey City, to prevent the materials from being used by the Allies in World War I. The explosion, the equivalent of an earthquake measuring between 5.0 and 5.5

in our harbor?—the car strikers[36] dynamiting the car tracks & sheds?—The skies a sheet of moving red—Another tremendous report—another trembling of the buildings—New York's end—I smiled—How fine that thought—that picture.—The morning—thousands & thousands of shattered windows—the streets littered with glass—I suppose you read about the explosion of the munitions factory, etc.—It was great.—

—Of course I knew you'd be surprised at the photographs—I had fun in doing them. The one I want most is the one that hung on the left wall[37]—to the right of the *seething* one.[38] —The one I considered by far the finest—the most expressive—It's very wonderful.—All of it. —There are others running it a close second—but none gives me what that one does—You know the one I mean.—It hung to the right of the "curtain."—

—The frames are as yet not finished. Of course I'm anxious to see how they look. Will the pictures lose any of their freedom? I don't like the idea of the frame around them—anymore than I'd like the "Mountain & Night" framed in—but there is no way out if the drawings are to be protected.—And that I insist they must be.—So frame goes with that!—Life again!—

—Would you really send up those last?—I've often thought of them—in fact every time I think of you—& I've often spoken of them. I'll protect them too.—

—I leave next Monday or Tuesday for Lake George. Or rather to get my daughter in New Hampshire where she is in camp, & both of us then proceed to the Lake. So if you send the drawings send them at once to 291. Or would you prefer to wait till my return in October.— Don't wait if you don't have to.—Perhaps you'd like to send them to the Lake.—My address will be: Alfred Stieglitz, Lake George, New York—

—I'm glad you know Lake George.—Funny—

The Little Room empty.—Were you in it—alone!—It's that way again.—

—Quite a few people were disappointed to find your drawings down.—But they are coming in the autumn to see them.—See what a stir they have made. A real fine one.—What a great thing it was of Miss Pollitzer to chase down to me with them! And against all orders—

Greetings to you—

I'm so glad to hear you feel better—quieter—stronger.—

"291"

Georgia O'Keeffe · [**Charlottesville, Virginia**] · [**August 6, 1916**]

This paper feels too little for me but I'm going to try to write to you anyway—I guess we often do things in spite of difficulties—.

---

on the Richter scale, was felt as far away as Philadelphia; see "First Explosion Terrific," *The New York Times,* July 31, 1916, 1 (hereafter cited as *NYT*).

36. The motormen and conductors of the Third Avenue Railway Company went on strike on July 30, 1916. Sympathy strikes by the Brooklyn and North River Railroad company tied up transportation throughout the region; see "Crisis Is Expected Today," *NYT*, July 30, 1916, 1.

37. Probably Lynes 50.

38. Probably Lynes 52.

When I crawled out of my shell here and took the first step toward doing things—they kept coming[39] and I kept doing them so that I have hardly had time to think—The walk that I told you of started many things—

Three interesting people took some time—two girls and a man—he was stupidly nice and for that reason a curiosity—

One of the girls seems to have blood just a little redder than most people[40]—and it must go a little faster too—it makes her eyes shine and her laugh great—it even makes the gold of her hair just a little bit red—She is intensely alive—no not intensely—it's just live fun—The other girl—why—she is very wonderful—

I used to go over and sit beside her court to watch her play tennis—She never played with any girls but my small sister—it was great to watch—They would both be wet to the belt but her face never got red—They didn't talk—just played—

She had the Y.W.C.A. work here this summer—was the first person of [that] kind I have ever liked—We talked almost all night the last night she was here—She stayed with me—is only twenty—from Georgia—So fine—and so fresh—and so wholesome—it seems a shame that all women can't grow like that—

—Last weekend I climbed another mountain—went up about ten miles from Afton—at night—in heavy mist—so very very thick—then pouring rain—It was great—the woods in the night—and the mist and rain—often wading through water halfway to our knees—so far from houses that we just kept on because there was no place to stop—We didn't want to stop—then a fire in a little log barn—it was very funny—

I sat on a big rock outside after the others went to sleep and watched the daylight come over the mountain we were trying to get up—

The next night I slept on the rocks—just bare rocks—that seem to be the top of the world—so many many stars—everyone else went lower down where it would be warm—but I liked it cold—in the wind—the rocks so very bare and hard—and so much sky—It was just a little spot that you could fall off of all round—but great.

Then some old friends came to town for the horse show—and I went because they wanted me to—Such funny people go it is almost too good to miss—perfectly ridiculous—such funny old men—

Then there were a couple of nights at a little colony out by the springs—eight little houses so nice that you want them all—just dropped down in the pines—I would like to tell you about the people there—the woman who built them and my friend Judith[41]—but I can't tell you everything I know—

From what I've been doing I guess you know that I am all right again—I'm not afraid of things anymore—am feeling fine—and it is great—I appreciate it so much more having been sick—

Oh—I simply can't tell you how I like it—but you know.

39. Lynes 81–114.

40. Katherine Lumpkin, also possibly the subject of drawings by O'Keeffe; Lynes 97–99.

41. Elizabeth Maury Coombs, an author, and Judith Maury, a friend of O'Keeffe's from Virginia whose family lived in San Antonio.

I wonder what you have been talking so hard about—arguing so hard about—and why do it [on] such hot days—

Why argue—it doesn't matter, does it—what does anything matter—

I know things do matter but it seems absurd that they should—that we should get such notions in our heads and get them so hard—

You will probably laugh when I tell you that I like your photographs of my drawings much better than I do the drawings—I have been very much amused at the way I enjoy looking at them—really *enjoy* it—

Summer school is over.

I hope this week will be quiet—like the Little Room—like you can find it in spots and at times up at the Lake—Take me with you up there—when it's quiet sometimes—

The moon is very hot tonight—and red—hot looking—I sleep on the porch—way up in the tree-tops—a large patch of sky.

IN EARLY AUGUST, Stieglitz collected his daughter Kitty at her camp in New Hampshire and went to Lake George, New York. His father, like many other prominent New Yorkers of the Gilded Age, had built a gracious estate, Oaklawn, a mile north of the village, on the shores of the lake, where the large, extended family, along with many friends, had spent most summers since

Alfred Stieglitz, *Lake George Parlor*, 1912/1913. Gelatin silver print, 7¾ x 9¾ in. (19.7 x 24.8 cm). Alfred Stieglitz Collection, 1949.715. The Art Institute of Chicago. Photography © The Art Institute of Chicago. Greenough 379.

the late 1880s. Stieglitz was especially entranced with the Lake, as he called it, where he enjoyed an occasional game of tennis or croquet, and even indulged in nude swims, much to the consternation of the neighbors. He also spent many long hours simply watching the ever changing landscape and was especially entranced by the frequent storms that rolled in over the adjacent mountains and down the long thin lake. In the summer of 1916, his vacation was, no doubt, more peaceful than it had been before the war, for his mother, Hedwig, tired of his wife Emmy's hysterical outbursts, had suggested that Emmy might prefer to spend several weeks visiting friends in New England. Because O'Keeffe had stayed at Lake George in 1908, working at the art colony of Amitola on a grant from the Art Students League, his descriptions to her of the landscape were particularly vivid.

After O'Keeffe's teaching job at the University of Virginia ended in late July, she traveled around Virginia, Tennessee, and North Carolina, and then on to Canyon, Texas, to assume her new position as head of the art department at the West Texas State Normal College. Before she left Charlottesville, she asked her sister Claudia to mail two packages of drawings and watercolors, one each for Stieglitz and Pollitzer. Indicating her continued hesitancy about showing her work, she playfully encouraged Stieglitz "not to look at [any] you don't like."[42]

Alfred Stieglitz · [Lake George, New York] · August 26, 1916

They came.—Last night.—Just after I had come out of the Lake!

—You are a careless mother to send your children that way—not even registered! I was afraid to open the package—I was afraid to find the [drawings] crumpled—& cracked! Such were the symptoms from the outside. But I finally summed up courage.—It was a queer sensation—that of opening up that package. Of unrolling what was in it—

—Fortunately little damage was done—the edges of some of the drawings crinkled— but nothing serious.—My heart stood still before I looked at those you made in New York[43]— especially one which I had remembered so vividly—which had made such a deep impression on me—an incisive impression.[44] No, it was intact—the paper nearly immaculate.—You undoubtedly smile at my "fussiness"—my too great sensitiveness.—But it is neither. Perhaps some of your work means much more to me than it does to you.—In the sense that the Lake is everlastingly living to me—every moment—and it always strikes me with wonder & a quieting sensation—Even when it is in a turmoil as it is at present!—

—Your new work.—I opened the package.—Out amongst the trees—the Lake at my feet—There were the drawings.—The new work—I merely glanced at it all—and then glanced once more—as if I were being watched—& wanted no one to see.—I rolled up the drawings & put them away. I'll look at them again in a few days.—And I'll write you soon what I think.

42. GOK TO AS, Aug. 22, 1916, Yale Collection of American Literature, Beinecke Rare Book and Manuscript Library, Yale University, New Haven, Connecticut. Unless otherwise noted, all letters between Stieglitz and O'Keeffe, as well as between Stieglitz, O'Keeffe, and other recipients, are in this collection.

43. Probably Lynes 61–64.

44. Probably Lynes 64 (opposite).

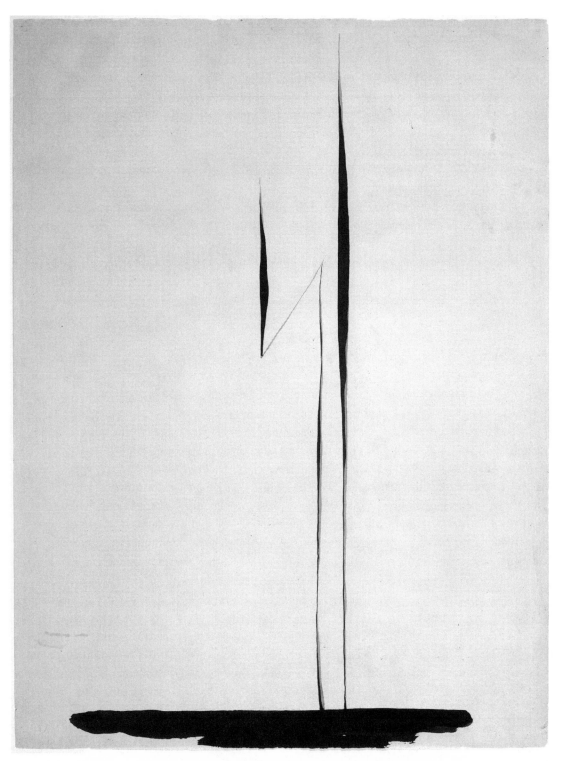

Georgia O'Keeffe, *Blue Lines*, 1916. Watercolor and graphite on laid paper, 25 x 19 in. (63.5 x 48.3 cm), sheet. Metropolitan Museum of Art, New York. Alfred Stieglitz Collection, 1969 [gift of the artist] (69.278.3). Copyright © The Metropolitan Museum of Art/Art Resource, NY. Lynes 64.

The glance—or glances—showed me some marvelous things.—I am delighted.—You are a great Girl.—The Mountain Tops—& the Coon Village[45]—all have filtered through you creatively.—

—So you are on your way to Tennessee.—The postal arrived.[46]—You are active.— And you seem to gain in strength steadily.—And that I like.—

I had a letter from New York asking me if I'd give Severini (one of the foremost of the Futurists) a show this winter.[47] A show!—this winter—New York—How curious all that sounded.—Just at present.—

—It all seems so funny—to think of the probability of my standing in the small room—addressing—Whom?—

This is merely to tell you that the drawings are safely in my hands—& that I am grateful —as I have ever been to you since I first was given the privilege to see your self-expression.— "291"

Georgia O'Keeffe · [Craggy, North Carolina] · [August 26, 1916]

22

Greetings to you and the Lake—but isn't this paper Hell[48]—

However—it's so awful and funny I must send it—I grabbed it up as I left the room— smiled—thinking I'd write you on it—Got in this morning—and went into the tub head and all—then found I was so tired that I went to bed with a wet head and just got up in time to get the train for Craggy—a few miles this side of Asheville.—

I guess I'm going crazy for certain this time—Scott—my farmer friend, wants me to come back to Knoxville early Monday morning and go on with them to Atlanta—

—And maybe I will—guess I wouldn't even have hesitated—only a letter from Arthur in Knoxville asks me to be very careful—to write him that I'm being careful—

Well—tearing around at this rate isn't exactly being careful—but I'm having such a time—and it is all so funny and unexpected—

I'm curious to see how much I will have done by the time I end in Texas. This week has meant riding and loafing when we wanted to—through the prettiest part of Virginia—

45. On August 11, 1916, O'Keeffe wrote Stieglitz that she and her sister went to a nearby box and basket factory where they saw many poor African Americans. The visit made her feel that she was "only getting the froth out of life." Her watercolors (Lynes 100 and 101) may have been made at this time.

46. On August 22, 1916, O'Keeffe sent Stieglitz a postcard from Natural Bridge, Va., saying she was on her way to Knoxville, Tenn., then to Asheville, N.C.

47. On August 21, 1916, Marius de Zayas wrote Stieglitz, telling him that Walter Pach had recently asked him to exhibit Gino Severini's paintings at the Modern Gallery. Because de Zayas did not feel he "ought to mix Futurism with the work" he was exhibiting, he asked Stieglitz if he would like to exhibit the paintings. De Zayas later added that he thought it would be beneficial to show New Yorkers work by a member of the Futurist group "so the people at least will not take every manifestation of modern art as Futurism" (Sept. 11, 1916). When Stieglitz first saw Severini's paintings, he wrote O'Keeffe that "the color is acid & gives me the creeps.—The work is thin.—Is not at all what the reproductions led me to believe it was." He added, "I don't believe in Futurism as you know.—Nor in its very noisy noise!" (AS to GOK, Dec. 11, 1916).

48. O'Keeffe wrote this letter on stationery from the Hotel Atkin, "The Hotel of Knoxville," which advertised that its two hundred rooms, priced from "$1.00 up," were equipped with sprinklers.

Mountains—wonderful hills—just green—trees—The country we are going through now is —hills—near and far—and so many little cedar trees—

There have been wonderful nights out under the stars—lightning storms in the mountains—curious people—

Oh I'm simply soaked with mountains of all kinds—So full that I'm almost nauseated—Drunk with it—

No I didn't sleep much—I never do—Why should I—

We have been out six days—are black as can be—my face burns—and I feel funny in this sort of dress on the train—

Everything I have done this summer has been green and blue[49]—I even have on a green dress—didn't realize how funny it is till long after I bought it—Haven't worn anything but black since my first long suit—but I'm liking the green.

Was so glad to get your letter today—I've thought of you so often this week—I was liking it all so much—and Scott is so funny—and his wife fair—as people go—it has been great—

It is going to be great up here at Craggy too—I meet Katherine[50] tonight again—

Yes I read the *Research Magnificent*[51]—and liked it immensely—Then looked it over a few weeks later and decided that it was like most pictures are to me—somewhat lacking—almost fine—but—? I don't know what—

Then I wonder—what right has anyone as incomplete as myself to be so hard to satisfy—

I didn't go to White Plains[52]—a friend going out mailed that letter and I suppose she forgot it till then—

The stuff I sent you was in a pile on top of my trunk all summer—I packed up and left on such short notice that I didn't take time to go through it—just left it to be sent—

My address will be Canyon, Texas, from now on—I expect to get there a week from today—Saturday—You can send it there sometime—

Paper's gone and I'm tired—

Georgia O'Keeffe

Alfred Stieglitz · [Lake George, New York] · August 28, 1916

Isn't it queer I haven't had the courage to look at your drawings again. They—the package—is lying at the foot of my bed—on the top of my trunk—& every time I go into my room—& I go frequently I feel tempted to look—& don't.—And I can't quite understand why. For I really want to look.—

49. Lynes 81–96, 104–113.
50. Katherine Lumpkin.
51. H. G. Wells's *The Research Magnificent* (New York, 1915) tells the story of a man who sets out to live a noble life.
52. In his letter of August 14, 1916, Stieglitz noted that O'Keeffe's letter of August 11, 1916, was postmarked "White Plains, New York" and he wondered if she had left Virginia.

—And just now—after a day of rain, when the sun broke through the clouds, & the Lake in the setting sun became intensely blue—the opposite shore golden—& the sky filled with huge breaking storm clouds—warm in color—& the sky a rich glowing blue!—As I was wandering down to the dock with my large camera to photograph some of the clouds—I really didn't feel much like photographing but the clouds were unusual & I felt as if I *ought* (I oughting to???—??? I who don't believe in such a thing)—to finally make an effort to "wake up"—just then as my mind was focused on the clouds your letter from Asheville was handed to me.—

—Instead of photographing (and how glad I was not to photograph just then!) I read your letter.—Yes, you are living.—Possibly not being as careful as you might be—or should be—but *living* often brings with it a seeming carelessness of self!—It's a great state to be in. No one knows that state better than I do—

—But I had to laugh at myself. I think I know now why I haven't looked at the drawings again.—None of them reflect any of your recent experiences—??—But what is the difference—they *reflect you*. And *you* under different conditions are always *you*. It's *that* which attracts me so much to your work. Of course the hasty glance when I opened the package showed me more than months of looking would show most others.—And perhaps I see more than is—but I doubt it.—*It is.*—

—The Trojan woman.—Gigantic.—Befitting your mountain life.—I can imagine that nearly everything else seems small by comparison. Queer, while the rain was coming down in torrents today, & after I had had a good swim—I felt as if I had to get in touch with some big human soul—touch it—when my eye chanced upon Goethe's *Faust*—my great favorite. Did you ever read *Faust.*—Of course in translation, good as it is, it loses some of its charm—beauty.—But it is gigantic—& I'm going to send you a copy.—Perhaps it won't be to a woman what it is to a man.—But I'll risk it.—As far as you are concerned.—

—So this is to reach you in Texas!—I think it's the first time I have ever sent a letter to Texas.—

—Green.—No longer black.—I think I can see you in green.—But I can't imagine you in purple.—We are a funny lot—all of us.—And still how simple it all is if one has but a trace of vision.—

I wonder what is going on in the Little Room—291—it just happens to come into my mind.—I don't often think of it at present.—I don't want to look "back"—& I can't look forward.—I seem to have lost touch with what is termed the "World." And I'm not a bit sorry—the thought of it makes me smile. I still recognize the Lake!—And I still have the power to see the Black of Night!—

I'm called.—The evening meal.—A thousand & one hearty greetings—

To you from me—

ON SEPTEMBER 2, 1916, O'Keeffe arrived in Canyon, Texas. Just over twenty-five years old, with few paved streets or houses with indoor toilets, Canyon was as raw as it was confident of its future. Surrounded by prosperous ranches, the town had the good fortune to be connected by railroad to Amarillo, fifteen miles to the north, as well as to points throughout the state, and to

West Texas State Normal College, Canyon, 1917. From Bulletin of the West Texas State Normal College, *1917, no. 14. From Special Collections Department of the Cornette Library at West Texas A&M University.*

be the home of one of the few colleges within hundreds of miles. Founded in 1910, West Texas State Normal College was a teachers' school, designed to train instructors for Texas's rapidly expanding public educational system. In 1914 a fire destroyed the only structure on the campus, but a few months before O'Keeffe arrived, a new building opened with classrooms, a library and gym, and a swimming pool.[53] Paid $150 a month, O'Keeffe was head of the art department and taught drawing, industrial art, costume design, and interior decoration, as well as a methods teaching course. She also worked in the elementary school run by the college as a teaching laboratory.

Yet even within this town of fifteen hundred self-reliant ranchers, frontier women, and professors, O'Keeffe soon distinguished herself by being "as different as they come," as one resident later noted.[54] At first she boarded with Benjamin Alvis Stafford, a Latin professor, and his family. After nicknaming him "Fatty Latin" and bemoaning their "hideous" wallpaper and rugs, she quickly moved to the home of large, white-haired Charles Ackerman, his wife, Susie, and their fourteen-year-old son, Ralph. Charles was, she approvingly told Stieglitz, "big inside as well as out," plus he had "the only house in this end of town that has steam heat—and walls one can stand to live with."[55] Spirited, unconventional, and irreverent, O'Keeffe's reputation as a nonconformist only increased when her feisty younger sister Claudia joined her in October 1916. In February 1917, when O'Keeffe's liberal views ran afoul of the Ackermans' more traditional ways, she and Claudia moved to the home of the physics professor, Douglas Shirley, his wife, Willena, and their two young children, Lewis and Louise. Tall and handsome, Douglas Shirley had a keen sense of humor that proved to be a more comfortable match for O'Keeffe, and she

53. For information on Canyon and West Texas State Normal College, see Joseph Abner Hill, *More Than Brick and Mortar: West Texas State College, 1909–1959* (Amarillo, 1959), 1–86.

54. Louise Shirley, as quoted by Fred Stoker, *O'Keeffe in Canyon* (Canyon, Tex., 1990), 10.

55. GOK to AS, Sept. 24, 1916.

lived with them for the rest of her time in Canyon.[56] Although she was intrigued with many of her students, her previous job as supervisor of drawing and handwriting in the Amarillo public high schools had soured her on art educators, particularly their use of prescribed textbooks. Her insistence on speaking her mind, her dislike of attending church, and her opposition to the war did not endear her to the community, nor did her tendency to fraternize with the students. But despite these difficulties, she remained enthralled with the landscape of the Texas plains, especially the magnificent Palo Duro Canyon, twelve miles to the east. More than one hundred miles long, as much as twenty miles wide and eight hundred feet deep, the canyon proved to be a source of immense inspiration to O'Keeffe. Its swelling, almost primeval shapes perfectly suited her formal vocabulary, while its bright, banded layers of orange, red, yellow, and white rocks gave her an entirely new palette to explore.

Georgia O'Keeffe · [Canyon, Texas] · [September 3, 1916]

Your letter this morning is the biggest letter I ever got—Some way or other it seems as if it is the biggest thing anyone ever said to me—and that it should come this morning when I am wondering—no I'm not exactly wondering but what I have been thinking in words—is—

I'll *be damned* and I want to damn every other person in this little spot—like a nasty petty little sore of some kind—on the wonderful plains. The plains—the wonderful great big sky—makes me want to breathe so deep that I'll break—There is so much of it—I want to get outside of it all—I would if I could—even if it killed me—

I have been here less than twelve hours—slept eight of them—have talked to possibly ten people—mostly educators—*Think* quick for me—of a bad word to apply to them—The *little* things they forced on me—They are so just like folks get the depraved notion they ought to be—that I feel it's a pity to disfigure such wonderful country with people of any kind—

I wonder if I am going to allow myself to be paid eighteen hundred dollars a year to get like that—I never felt so much like kicking holes in the world in my life—

Still there is something great about wading into this particular kind of slime that I've never tried before—alone—wondering—if I can keep my head up above these little houses and know more of the plains and the big country than the little people—

Previous contacts make some of them not like my coming here—

So—you see it was nice to get a big letter this morning—I needed it—

I waked and heard the wind—the trees are mostly locust bushes twenty feet high or less—mostly less—and a prairie wind in the locust has a sound all its own—like your pines have a sound all their own—I opened my eyes and simply saw the wall-paper. It was so hideously ugly—I remembered where I was and shut my eyes right tight again so I couldn't see it—with my eyes shut I remembered the wind sounding just like this before—I didn't want to see the room—it's so ugly—it's awful and I didn't want to look out the window for fear of

56. See "Dr. D. A. Shirley Announces Retirement" and "Death of Dr. Shirley Ends 35-Year Career at W Texas," *The Prairie,* Jan. 21, 1949, and Jan. 6, 1950.

seeing ugly little frame houses—so I felt for my watch—looked at it—decided I needn't open my eyes again for fifteen minutes—

The sound of the wind is great—

But the pink roses on my rugs! And the little squares with three pink roses in each one—dark-lined squares—I have half a notion to count them so you will know how many are hitting me—Give me flies and mosquitoes and ticks—even fleas—every time in preference to three pink roses in a square with another rose on top of it—

Then you mention me in purple—I'd be about as apt to be naked—don't worry—! Don't you hate pink roses—!

As I read the first part of your letter—saying you hadn't looked at the stuff I left for my sister to send you—I immediately thought—I'd like to run right down and telegraph you not to open them—then—that would be such a foolish thing to do—

Not foolish to me—or for me—but the other queer folks who think I'm queer—

There is dinner—and how I hate it[57]—

You know—I—

I waited till later to finish the above sentence—thinking that maybe I must stop somewhere with the things I want to say—but I want to say it and I'll trust to luck that you'll understand—

Your letter makes me feel like Lafferty's paintings—They made me want to go right to him quick—Your letter makes me want to just shake all this place off—and go to you and the Lake—but—there is really more exhilaration in the fight here than there could possibly be in leaving it before it's begun—

like I want to.—

After mailing my last letter to you I wanted to grab it out of the box and tell you more—

I wanted to tell you of the way the outdoors just gets me—

—Some way I felt as if I hadn't told you at all—how big and fine and wonderful it all was—

It seems so funny that a week ago it was the mountains I thought the most wonderful—and today it's the plains—I guess it's the feeling of bigness in both that just carries me away—

And Katherine—I wish I could tell you how beautiful she is—

Living?—Maybe so—When one lives one doesn't think about it I guess—

I don't know—The Plains sends you greetings—Big as what comes after living—if there is anything it must be big—and these plains are the biggest thing I know—

My putting you with Lafferty is really wrong—His things made me feel that *he* needed—

Your letter coming this morning made me think how great it would be to be near you and talk to you—You are more the size of the plains than most folks—and if I could go with my

---

57. O'Keeffe took her meals at the home of Mary Elizabeth Hudspeth, the first dean of women at West Texas State Normal College.

letter to you and the Lake—I could tell you better—how fine they are—and more about all the things I've been liking so much—

But I seem to feel that you *know* without as much telling as other folks need—

Georgia O'Keeffe · [Canyon, Texas] · [September 8, 1916]

I must write you tonight—I don't know why except that I seem to think I must tell you a little of what living here means to me. That mixture I sent last Sunday may be a bit deceiving—

Your letter of yesterday morning—came before breakfast and I only opened it and looked at it—I had to do that but I didn't read it till after five in the afternoon because—there were things to do that would have spoiled a 291 letter—and a 291 letter was apt to spoil me for the things I had to do—I only noticed that there were two different kinds of writing in it—

When you said you were going to open that awful roll—I almost screamed—and I could hardly forgive myself for not telegraphing you not to—

I can't see why I make things—

It's awful—

I don't know what I wrote last Sunday only I remember I was just snorting mad at the educators—

Well—even if I was I'm glad I'm here—In fact—I like it so much that I wonder if it's true—The country is almost all sky—and such wonderful sky—and the wind blows—blows hard—and the sun is hot—the glare almost blinding—but I don't care—I like it—

The work? I like that too—rather—I am going to—I think—because—well—

You know I get such a ridiculous lot out of living myself—and these boys and girls from the plains—get a lot out of it too—in a way—but I believe I can help them to get more—to get something they don't get now—I like them like the country—I've lived out here before you know—twenty miles from here—and it's absurd the way I like it—like to work in it—

The building is all new—one just like it burned two years ago—of course this one is better in many ways—but it seems so remarkable that this land of nothingness can get a building like this planted way out here at the end of the earth—

The funniest thing to me is a swimming pool—out here on the plains where it only rains twice a year sometimes—And it's as fine a swimming pool as they have at Columbia—

Because I pawed up the earth last Sunday don't think I don't like it—I *do* like it—I'd rather live here than any place I know if I could get to New York sometimes—easier—

I wonder how long I'll stay—

As yet—no particular friends—and I don't want any—When I like them at all—I like them so much that it almost eats me up alive and I just want time to breathe—I feel almost smothered with the pulls of the past few weeks—maybe I should say months—

I just want to get out where there is space and breath—and not like anybody and not be liked—

Sometimes—very—very seldom—I wish there were more people like you and like me—I don't know how alike we are—Are we alike at all—? I don't know—

Mostly I am glad that there are no more like me—I hope there are not—Living is wonderful till it becomes almost torture—or it is torture till it seems to be great—

I can't help it—it's hell and I like it.

Yes laugh!

Alfred Stieglitz · [Lake George, New York] · [September 20, 1916]

The last day of the summer of 1916! Officially at least.—I haven't written in some time as it was impossible to sit out of doors—on my favorite porch facing the Lake—& write.—The weather was so variable—one day raw & damp & cold—another very cold & windy—and then a mixture of the two.—And to write indoors to you seemed absurd. Impossible.

—The wind is south now. And the Lake is like a small ocean.—And the air is mild although indoors log-fires are necessary.—For our house is so near the Lake & so guarded by towering trees that indoors it's often colder & damper in weather like this than out-of-doors.— It is quieting down here too in our rather lively home. We are often sixteen–eighteen at table. Schools are opening up & the youngsters have to go to work.—And I miss the youngsters.— When I shall take my daughter back to the city is still undecided.—Every day brings me nearer to that day.—Perhaps within two weeks.—I don't know. It depends upon the opening up of her school.

—I opened the roll day before yesterday.—Out on the porch.—It was a day of alternating rain & clearing—at least attempts at clearing.—I never saw such variations of gray as I saw that day.—Very beautiful all of them.—

The drawings.—Those that made a deep impression when I gave them that hasty glance when they arrived were the ones that again impressed me most. Several are really very wonderful. I shall have those framed as soon as I get to the city.—To add to the others. I want the world to see them—They are very worth while. Of the new ones there are three especially fine. One of those you showed me in the city[58]—as fine a thing as you've done. And as fine in its way as anything I know. Then there is that one of tremendous power on buffish paper.[59] —That is really immense.—Gripping.—In it I feel all the powers of the night—as I feel the relationship of two fine natures in the very beautiful simple one. Then there is a small one.[60] Also tragic in its power.—It's a great privilege to be given the opportunity to look into a soul like yours—I feel it roaming through space and at night.

Last night was bitter cold—in summer clothes!—& the stars looked near.—As I looked upward through the openings left by the tree tops where they failed to meet—and as I lay down to sleep bundled up in three blankets—I covered head & as well as body. And I fell asleep & slept five hours the first time in quite some days.—

—Greetings to the Texan Plains.—From the Stars that gave me Sleep—

58. Probably Lynes 64 (see p. 21).

59. Lynes 61.

60. Probably Lynes 53.

I've wanted so much to write you—but I've done so many other things that I couldn't do it when I wanted to or didn't want to when I could—

My regular routine (I hate doing things by the clock—have always hated to do things at any stated time) only takes twelve hours a week—but last week I seemed to fill up every minute of day and night with something—

—This morning—right now—I am hot from a walk to the train in the sun—it is almost cold in the shade but the sun is hot—blinding—of course I go bare-headed—

And what is most on my mind is my small sister[61]—When I came out here I was sure I should bring her—others said no—a letter from her this morning makes me see that my premonition was right—

Foolish of me not to insist then—it would have saved trouble.—She is—I started to say queer—but I won't—she is too much like me—So I wrote her by the next mail—to come—

I don't know what I'll do with her but I'll do something—She will have to go to school and I'm waiting with a broad grin to hear her remarks on the people—It will be really fun—

—Still it makes me a bit uneasy—Will she come—again—I don't know what to do with her—but guess I will in time—

—Wish you could see the long stretches of white and sand-colored and greenish-gray cliffs out there that mark the beginnings of the Canyon—they are a long way off—and I seem to feel lost out there—even though I'm here—in spite of the cliffs—the skyline is perfectly straight.

Yesterday I rode out into that—then off to the right—where there is nothing—clouds making big dark shadows on the flatness—I almost went to sleep—dreaming over nothing—I guess—

And I want to tell you about the big dark lumps of clouds—seeming down close to the ground last night—and the moon—always trying to get through—just a few stars in queer places—Last night the moon was white—but the night before it was red—seeming like something alive and breathing out there—as it came up—

—*The Brook Kerith*[62] was here when I came from mailing my letter—I'd have read it right away—to forget—only I wanted to write to you—

You will doubtless be surprised when I tell you that I had four letters from you last week instead of one—Three that went to Virginia just got here—the one about the Paulist Fathers[63]—another you wrote the same day after it had stormed—and the other about the drawings you received—

I'm beginning to wonder what drawings you did get—I left a roll for you and one for Anita—and so far Anita[64] hasn't received any. My sister was to mail them—I didn't tell her to

61. Claudia O'Keeffe.

62. George Moore, *The Brook Kerith: A Syrian Story* (New York, 1917).

63. The Paulist Fathers directed the Sacred Heart Roman Catholic Church of Lake George.

64. When Pollitzer received them, she responded: "I love them—infinitely more than all the rest put together"; Giboire, *Lovingly, Georgia*, 195.

register them—didn't think of it—and I don't know what happened—Most of Anita's—mine to Anita, of course—were on tissue paper—Japanese tracing paper—all water colors.[65]

I don't know that I'm a careless mother—most of them have little interest for me after they are made—but I did like one in Anita's roll—

I just get rid of them by sending them away—It amuses me that you scold—it is really thoughtlessness but some way or other—I don't like to have pieces of me lost—I seem to be sure that they will turn up somewhere—they must!

Maybe remembering your sensitiveness will make me less careless—shall I say—or shall I say more careful—I don't know—It is so fine to know that it is—that you feel that way about things—only—I know too—how often it is hurt—hurt isn't the word—

You see I haven't words—

But—when I work—even when it is to say something to someone—it is to say it my way—and I don't care whether they understand—or get anything out of it or not—Nothing ever surprised me like your seeing and getting something—yes—I fairly boiled—

But—I saw the Rodins[66] when you showed them—the drawings—I remember you coming in with something black—and reddish-brown in your hand—some kind of a camera plate I guess—and I seem to remember that it was wet—

I don't know maybe you never wet the things—

That is almost the only exhibition that I remembered that winter—except a sick-looking little girl in a painfully stiff starched dress by Bellows—and a canvas by Glackens that I always remembered as a mess of paint[67]—

I remembered you and the drawings—

Told Anita I'd rather have you like something than anyone I knew of—that was why she did it—she thought you would like them—and that I'd like you to—

Funny—wonder why I just told you that now—Funny too how the memory stayed so long—only seeing you once—

I remembered—eyes—hair—a thin man—very intense—something in your hand—and the drawings—

Some things in my trunk now that I almost [forgot] seem someone else made—I take them out every three or four days and wonder what they are and why they were made—

The little fat woman[68] who runs the house saw them on the wall one day and asked if it was a sailboat[69]—a girl thought my last pet drawing was an ear about two feet long[70]—

65. Lynes 91–94.

66. While studying at the Art Students League in New York, O'Keeffe saw the fifty-eight drawings included in the Exhibition of Drawings by M. Auguste Rodin, at 291, on view January 2–28, 1908.

67. George Bellows, *Little Girl in White (Queenie Burnett)*, 1907, oil on canvas, National Gallery of Art, as well as paintings by William Glackens were exhibited at the Special Exhibition of Contemporary Art, National Arts Club, New York, on view in January 1908. The exhibition also included photographs by members of the Photo-Secession and was heralded as the first time that photographs were exhibited "on the same plane as painting" in the United States; see "Contemporary Art at National Club," *NYT,* Jan. 5, 1908, 9.

68. Susie Ackerman.

69. Probably either Lynes 112, 113, or 114.

70. Probably either Lynes 118, 119, 120, or 121.

I try to keep them put away but sometimes forget—I'm liking the drawing and hate to take it down—.

This is going to be my last page—might just as well stop anytime because I'll never get through—

To go back to the Paulist Fathers—I used to like to go up there and walk around their grounds because I heard a story—about—women not being allowed on the grounds—So one of the boys and I kept a regular supply of food in the roof of one of their summer-houses—Absurd —yes—but we got a lot of fun out of it—and after supper—the lake and sunset—

Your last letter—yesterday morning—it seems a long time ago now—I seem to live such a long time in such a short space sometimes that it makes me feel sick—was the first quieting one in a long time—

I had been thinking almost the same things you wrote—I had wondered if I would want to see you anymore—

Well—I know—that if I were in New York—someday it would be the only thing to do —other times—The letters have been so fine—I would hate to spoil it—so they couldn't be anymore—

Living is such a tangle—I've only started on this—but—

I'll stop—

When I folded it—I remembered—

I didn't tell you about going to the Panhandle State Fair at Amarillo—to see the cattle —Black Angus and white-faced Herefords—and the pigs and sheep and horses and mules—

It may seem a bit out of place to you to put a fat steer or pig in the same class as music—but they are such nice shapes—I always want to feel them. So much finer than lots of people seem to me.

The secretary[71] is an old friend of mine—has been a miner in Alaska—is a pillar in the Presbyterian Church and has been and done everything else in between—Yes—this is a very funny country—but it's great.

A letter from Anita today says she is going to 291—hopes it's in town—It must be because she wants to see it so much—

—Don't leave the Lake—I like your letters from the Lake—I like you to be there—

But I'm so glad I have space—I seem to need it so much now—

It poured rain this afternoon—doesn't seem to soak into the ground—just stands in ponds and runs down the road in rivers—the ground just doesn't know how to treat rain it gets it so seldom.

I sat out in a funny little car with the most enormous brown-faced—blue-eyed old plains-man[72] you can imagine—a great shock of white hair—whites of his eyes very white because his skin is so dark—He is so big that he seems to fill a whole room when he gets in the house—

32

---

71. J. F. McGregor was secretary-treasurer of the Panhandle State Fair in 1916, president of the Amarillo Real Estate Exchange, and treasurer of Potter County in 1914.

72. Charles Ackerman.

He wasn't made for houses—He was made for big outdoors—We watched the sun set
—The whole sky was full of it—all round—the brightest reflection coming to us down the little
river in the road—

He is the most human thing I've found out here—We watch the sunset quite often—
It's nice to watch it with him—but he is so big I'm afraid of him in the house—He is the
husband of the little fat woman[73]—

They just got through with the last murder trial and another man was shot—today.[74]

Georgia O'Keeffe · [Canyon, Texas] · [September 24, 1916]

Sunday night—

—Last night was a great night—

I was reading *The Divine Comedy* for the first time—and the most terrific thunderstorm
—with the wildest wind and such pouring—rain—took me from it—out on the porch—in my
kimono—I watched the most wonderful lightening I ever saw—held tight to a post for fear of
blowing away—

The man[75] I told you about—the great big old man—No—not so old either—came
out and watched it with me—he is too strong and live-looking to call old even if his hair is
white—

It was a great storm—and a great book—they seem to be the same thing almost—

I must tell you that—this big man—Mr. Ackerman—he is big inside as well as out—
runs the town waterworks—and has the only house in this end of town that has steam heat—
and walls one can stand to live with. He always wears a black sateen shirt and a tight-fitting cap
with a shiny black visor—a nice human man—

This morning after breakfast—your letter—one from Anita—and one from Arthur
were under my door—Almost too much for one day—

Anita will be in New York a month—going to the doctor—and wanting very much to
see you. That seems to be her chief consolation for having to stay there.—

—Arthur?—working all summer on your darned old City Charter—it sounds so stupid
to me—hopelessly stupid—when I tried to write him—I suddenly found that I was sadly in

---

73. Susie Ackerman.

74. On August 3, 1916, Oscar I. Smith, a candidate for sheriff in Canyon, shot and killed Claude Powell while he was "lighting
a cigarette." Smith claimed it was self-defense and was acquitted. On September 19, 1916, Sam Reynolds was shot in the back
and killed while hunting rabbits. His wife, Florence, who was with him at the time, professed to have no idea how he was shot.
Asserting that they were very "happy" even though they had little property, she admitted that once she saw him lying face down
on the ground, she did nothing to help him and acknowledged that her husband had taken out a life insurance policy the month
before for five thousand dollars. She was subsequently found guilty and sentenced to twenty years in prison. See "Claude Powell
Shot and Killed by Oscar Smith" and "Smith Trial on in the District Court," *Randall County News,* Aug. 3, 1916, 1, and Sept. 14,
1916, 1; "Oscar Smith Is Acquitted," *Amarillo Daily News,* Sept. 17, 1916, 1; "Sam Reynolds Is Killed Tuesday P.M.," and "Mrs.
Reynolds Trial Monday," *Randall County News,* Sept. 21, 1916, 1, and May 9, 1918.

75. Charles Ackerman.

need of last night's sleep. It's very bad to be tired—I'm so glad I'm way out here where I can't see any of you—even yet—I seem to be so tired of such lots of things.

All day I've been trying to remember what drawings you mention—and just a few moments ago recalled the one on buff paper[76]—I suppose that is the one—

It doesn't much matter—I don't much care—

The little one[77]—dark—is the only thing I made the year before that I liked—making it made me sick for several days—but it doesn't matter—none of it matters—

I will be sorry when you leave the Lake—have the leaves turned yet? Of course they have if it's cold—

Why didn't you send me *Faust*—did you decide I couldn't read it—I remember my mother having it and reading it—being very much absorbed with it when I was about ten— particularly—. I am very sure that the particular copy you said you were going to send me is the only one I want to read—

Tonight—I'm—

Well—I know exactly why youngsters yell sometimes—and cry—and fuss and fume and fret—

Goodnight—I hope the stars are very bright—tonight—the sky very clear—I want it to be very still so you can just hear the water—

So tired—and I haven't been able to eat since breakfast—

No—that doesn't matter—either—

[September 25, 1916]

Monday morning—

Your wonderful sunny letter came before I was up—but I didn't read it till a couple of hours later—Thank you.

I wonder if the other people you wrote to that day liked your letters as much as I do—

I read it out on the porch in the sun—a quiet morning—very quiet—all the miles of prairie grass shining with dew—frosty-looking dew—

Yes—a nice day—Monday is our holiday—but I won't do anything—

Georgia O'Keeffe · [Canyon, Texas] · [September 26, 1916]

Tuesday morning—

It was your letter telling of the warm quiet night—still—dark—just the clocks—

Isn't *dark* curious—Sometimes it is still with you—Sometimes you are just alone—and it's way off—Sometimes it chases you—it's such an enormous—intangible—awful thing when it chases you on the plains—

I'm glad you gave me the quiet dark night—

----

76. O'Keeffe included a sketch of Lynes 61 in the letter.
77. O'Keeffe included a sketch of Lynes 53 in the letter.

I'm mailing last night's letter today—After writing it I slept better than in a long time—This morning—I might leave out the third page[78]—but I'll not. I tore up a page that I wrote you that night on the way to Virginia in the spring and I've always been sorry—

The New Republic[79] was under the door with your letter—it makes me laugh—Arthur sends it—and it's so like him—

I could so easily forget him out here—he's of another world—some other time I lived—but I found myself deciding that I wouldn't—mostly because of what I feel he wants rather than what I want—funny.

Yes I'm feeling better today! I've had a terrific headache today—It's better tonight—

I got up and went to supper—mostly because I was almost crazy with thinking and I felt as if it couldn't possibly be any worse—

Sat on the end of the porch—quiet—just a little wind in the little locusts—windmills—very fine and lace-like—and the line of little houses against a quiet cloudless sunset—all so quiet—

I wished for you and the Lake blackness—and coolness like one feels from big trees reaching down—

A lot of things I have written you run through my head this afternoon—and—well it made me laugh—

For instance—I guess—just yesterday I said the City Charter was hopelessly stupid—Now—you know that isn't so—I could have a beautiful time slaving on the City Charter myself—if I knew how—just like I could have a fine time making an exhaustive study of cats' teeth—or any other fool thing—

I seem to think tonight—that I'd like to tell you that everything I've said is a lie—and—I've just told another—

Really—it's so absurd to write you—unless—maybe you're like I think you are—just understanding—

I wish I could stop feeling—for about a month and catch up with the world—Don't say you're glad I can't—

I want to touch someone I like—then maybe I could be still—but—I don't suppose I could—

Now I'm going to say another foolish thing—

Please don't—for awhile—write me those letters that always knock me down—Sometimes—your letters are so much yourself—such an intense live sort of self that I can't stand yourself—and myself too—Some mornings I wake with a shrinking sort of fear—that there will be a letter from you popped under my door[80]—

78. O'Keeffe may be referring to her third page of writing: if so, it begins with her sketch of Lynes 53 and continues through her assertion that the copy of *Faust* Stieglitz was to send "is the only one I want to read." If she was referring to the third sheet of paper, it includes the entire section written on Monday, September 25, 1916.

79. *New Republic*, Sept. 23, 1916.

80. O'Keeffe told Pollitzer: Stieglitz gets "so much of himself" into his letters, you can "hardly stand it." They are "like too much light—you shut your eyes and put one hand over them—then feel round with the other for something to steady yourself by." Giboire, *Lovingly Georgia*, 201.

You understand—I am always glad—and you know how much I like them—It's that it's too much—I've got to get quiet—some way.

I'm going to keep this a couple of days before I mail it[81] to you like I almost always did at first.

Alfred Stieglitz · [Lake George, New York] · [September 27, 1916]

I have just come in from a brisk walk. The night is a cold one & clear starlight.—It means feeling one's way where there are trees.—Even if one knows the way.—

It has been a Day of Days! Every moment of the day—beginning with a sunrise which predicted both rain & clear—was maddening because of its fullness—of its ripe perfection.— And no two moments were similar.—North wind & South—East & West—Blowing hard then dying down to a zephyr—then no wind.—The surface of the Lake rough & boisterous—then suddenly a dead calm.—Ripples on the mirrorlike surface—ripples becoming more alive— playing tag in the gusts of crossing winds.—And sudden showers out of clear skies—showers chasing along the hills, the sun shining at one spot—black clouds threatening a heavy deluge right near that spot.—Showers—several simultaneously at different parts of the compass. And always the sun victorious. All nature seemed to play around this center.—And such cloud formations—every kind imaginable—& rainbows—brilliant & double—clouds of all colors too—& the Lake of every hue—verdure turning golden—& here & there scarlet spots— & finally sunset—amazing in its splendor.—The night.—Windstill & very cold.—Real autumn —a touch of winter in the air.—

All day long I was very active—on my feet.—The water was very cold—Did you ever hear little silver sleighbells tingle on a very cold day?—I could *feel* that tingle on my spinal cord as I came out of the water.—A great sensation.—Little silver sleighbells!

—I wonder whether you have your sister with you.—Your letter came—it reached me the morning after I had mailed my letter about the night.—It was a very fine letter.—And it meant—& means—much to me.—It's queer that you should have lived *directly* opposite to our place here when you spent the summer at Lake George.—Last year friends of my mother's had that place—the Trasks—& I was there once & they showed me "where some students had once lived."—Little did I then dream that one of them would mean so much to me—& in so near a future!—

Of course I had to smile [at] what you said about seeing me again—and of course I fully understand.—When something is very fine one naturally fears to lose it.—And how easily fine relationships which come about naturally are ruined eventually through—What?—Yes, what?—I've often wondered.—And perhaps I know the reason.—Is it because of illusions?— Is it because one changes & the other doesn't? Or both change—grow away from one another? Is it due in part to physical conditions? We are free at present in our relationship—both

81. O'Keeffe mailed this letter on September 27, 1916.

feel free—absolutely so.—There is nothing that I need hide—nothing that I fear might be misunderstood—there is no consciousness of anything but a common understanding no matter how much we may differ—And so I feel it is with you.—You know I'll understand.—You are free—you know I *expect* nothing—but that freedom.—When it is gone all is gone.—The hollow shell remains—the shell itself not clean.—The potentiality of a whole world exists in such a relationship between two beings.—Why does it so rarely last when one sees one another often—Perhaps I know the reason why.—I've paid the price for knowing. It was worthwhile. Without that price—without that knowledge the fullness of today would not exist for me— could not exist.—

　　—I received the right drawings.—I hope Anita Pollitzer finally received hers—that they were not lost.—I wonder if she was at 291—I can't quite imagine myself in that place.— I wonder how it will feel—I wonder how people will strike me.—Am I going to have anything to say—to do?—It's all so funny.—And I'm the funniest of all.—To myself.—Miss Rapp is back there—she writes there is no mail, nor any visitors—nor any telephone calls.—I wish the mountains could hear that message—they'd sprout wings & carry me away!!—To a new rainbow—

[September 28, 1916]

It is another day.—Afternoon.—Another perfect day. But not so varied—not so exciting.— Blue sky—a perfectly calm smooth Lake—brilliant sunlight & milder in temperature.

　　Last night I lay awake much.—Was it the excitement of the glorious day?—Was it the stars looking into the little room where I lay in a very cold bed.—Was it the mystery of the tree tops I could see from the bed—tree tops against the starlit sky.—Or was it the thought of New York—New York drawing nearer.—The leaving of the Lake?—Or was it all of these—yet none?—Just the bedlam of self keeping me so wide awake when I "should" have been asleep???—

　　I have been photographing some recently—a portrait or two[82]—& trees & sky.[83]— Photographing always gets my nerves agoing. To give a breath of life—of what is felt—to a machine-made thing.—No small problem.—Why attempt it if it wears one out?—For just that reason. As if that were not sufficient.—

　　Why am I writing all this?—And what have I written?—I never read what I write. If I did it never would be sent.—Perhaps I feel that when I get to New York letters will be scarcer —& I feel like writing. These days.—

　　Funny—I'm thinking of your sister ever since I received your letter.—She's much like you, you say.—I wonder just how much.—Of course you know yourself—I feel that—& you see yourself in her.—And you wonder what will happen to her.—It's a wonderful thing to watch a girl develop. Much more so than watching a boy.—A girl approaching womanhood.—

---

82. Possibly Greenough 413–416, 435, 437–452.
83. Greenough 436.

The Lake was icy this morning. But it's *the* moment of the day—that swim—the swim.—
Greetings—many of them from a Glorious Autumn Day at the Lake! To Texas.—

Alfred Stieglitz · [Lake George, New York] · September 30, 1916

It's a very cold night.—Before sunrise the thermometer will have touched thirty-two.—Such a change.—But it's great. A clear cold night.—And undoubtedly when we take a stroll tomorrow much of the foliage will have turned red—& more yellow.

—This morning several of us went up Prospect Mountain. It was a perfect day for climbing—for walking briskly. And a great one especially for "views."—Not a specialty of mine—"views."—I hadn't been up old Prospect in thirty-seven years—& it was forty-four years ago, as a little shaver of eight that I first walked up it & down too.[84]—And when I speak of years—so many years ago—it is as if I were speaking of another person.—In fact I often wonder whether I am ever speaking of myself even though I use "I" so much!—

It was great the walk—the sun felt good—it was so cold that blustering north wind blowing about fifty miles an hour.—On the mountaintop we basked in the sun on sun-warmed rocks & we all ate our sandwiches & eggs most ravenously.—And in returning the party unintentionally became separated—one striking one road—the other another. The road I struck was the very old one—how neglected it now is. In a scandalous condition. It made me feel heartsick to see such neglect. But the walk could not be spoiled for me.—And as I got home there was a letter from Canyon with three green stamps on it. And the letter fitted the fifty mile gale.—

Queer that I should have hesitated mailing the two last letters—those you have not as yet received.—That headache of yours must have been frightful—I thought of your drawing.— I know how you must suffer.—I would have given much if you had not received a letter from me that day.—You see the Lake has been so marvelous—it is the better part of myself—that you have received some of its intensity filtered through me.—And that intensity does not quiet you.—I wish it would.—But I understand why it does not.—It is the last thing I wish to do—to disturb your peace.—You know that—don't you?—You say I'm intense[85]—I wonder if I am.— I feel things tremendously—but I'm told I'm as cold as a fish!!!—Perhaps I am.—You see, as I write to you, you get glimpses of what I feel under certain conditions.—I am not writing as a man to a woman.—Of course I'm male—& you are female.—But for me you exist primarily as a spirit—as in your work.—And I exist for you as "Understanding." Such a relationship is fine.—But it dare create no pain—except perhaps for a moment—as an idea! I have suffered too much not to fully understand.—And I do not want to suffer anymore—nor do I want anyone to suffer though me. Neither female—nor male.—And I fear that oftentimes I do bring suffering—unintentionally.—For I've always tried not to hurt a soul—both friend & foe.— And so you see your letter made me wish I could relieve you of your headaches. Of all other

---

84. Stieglitz first went to Lake George in 1872. His father purchased Oaklawn, the family's estate, in 1886.
85. On October 15, 1916, O'Keeffe responded, telling Stieglitz that intensity maybe "isn't the word—but you certainly electrify the atmosphere at times."

pain.—I cannot think of anyone suffering—whether close to me or not—without aching body & soul myself.—A sickly state perhaps. But I.—Do what I will.—I tell you all this for I want to help you see—me at least.—As I am.—Is such a thing possible?—But above all as I said before, if I cannot bring you peace I'm worthless. For you at present.—Don't you agree?

—Of course I do not take your letters literally.—I think I can follow you. And when you wrote about the Charter as you did I smiled & fully understood—But I was glad when you supplemented what you had written for fear you had been unfair to someone kind to you.— More than kind.—

—I wasn't in the Lake today.—I don't know why.—The clocks are ticking & I hear them tell me: "It is time."—

Good Night.—

Georgia O'Keeffe · [Canyon, Texas] · [October 1, 1916]

My pen makes a horrible noise—I like this better—

Sunday morning—your letter again—and such a nice one—one from Anita, too, and her cousin Aline—Aline is Sigmund Pollitzer's daughter—a great girl—unusual—

I don't know—I just like her. She would interest you—I think.

—Your letter is so alive—this week has hardly seemed a day—There has been a curious kind of quietness—

The nice thing about you—is that I'm free—you are—This week when I remembered my last letter to you—I wondered—would you understand it[86]—Still when I come to analyze what it is that I want you to understand—I can't—but I knew when I wrote it—that I probably couldn't send it to anyone else I know and expect them to understand it—

The feeling of relief it has given me has been like getting a drawing that worried me— out of my head onto paper—and—even though you didn't understand—it—was worth it —and if you did—well—then knowing you is just that much more fun—Not exactly fun— I should have said, finer.

It has been great—understanding—minus the sort of feeling that ties you up—

I feel like the wind this morning.

—Your mentioning—your work—makes me want to tell you how often your portrait of Hartley[87] has gone through my mind—

I remember the shapes in it in such a curious way—and never distinctly enough to be able to put them down—It's a curious memory—sometimes one way—sometimes another—And I've wondered why—was it the photograph or the association—remembering

---

86. GOK to AS, Sept. 26, 1916 (see pp. 34–36). As they exchanged more letters in the late summer and early fall of 1916, both O'Keeffe and Stieglitz acknowledged their growing closeness. Only a few days earlier, on September 29, 1916, Stieglitz wrote O'Keeffe, "I'm frightened at all this scribbling—frightened because I feel I have no right to absorb so much of your time. And still I know that you are the kind of girl that won't read until she's good & ready. And that's what I like immensely."
87. Greenough 429.

Hartley and the way he made me so furious—would I have remembered it so often if I hadn't seen him—It seems to be the dark shapes I remember—

New York—I don't believe it exists. There isn't any such place—Anita says there is—but I don't believe it. She says she went to 291—I think maybe that is there—the room—but it is *very* empty.

—The sister—well—you see—no one ever wanted me to do any of the things I wanted to do—and *did*. Everything—from the shoes I wore and the way I combed my hair—to my friends and opinions—was all wrong—so—I'd be uncomfortable if I tried to please them—and chose the discomfort of disapproval in preference—She is the same kind—

But a great-aunt, eighty-four,[88] that she sort of thinks she has to take care of, mixes things—The great-aunt was never fond of me.

—I don't know what she is going to do—She hasn't written—and hasn't come—but I wouldn't be surprised to see her funny smile any day—

I think she will be an improved edition of me if nothing happens—My mother and I were so different in temperament—in everything that I sort of wriggled up alone—bumping my head and thinking it was worth it—Still as I think of it now—I was a funny sort of baby all along the way—

The youngster already has a lot that I've only been getting recently—At seventeen nothing could have induced me to read the things she reads and likes—You see—I don't pretend to have any sense—

I just live along and get a ridiculous lot of fun out of it—remembering curious snatches—forgetting what I possibly "ought" to remember—not caring much—and caring a lot too—

Her brain seems to nail things down in a different way—

I'm not bothering much about anything except—right now—In fact—I forgot to go to dinner today till an hour after it was over—then I didn't mind—

She gets even more excited (or is it because I am watching her) over the outdoors—or anything else she likes—and gets interested in such curious things—This summer for two or three weeks she almost drove me crazy trying to find out all about sugar—who made the money on it—and *how*—You can imagine it wasn't a vital interest to me but I had to rustle around and help her find out anyway—

Quite an entertaining sister—Having her around keeps you awake. She worries my other sisters—

If she comes she is sure to turn over all my ways of living—

Why—I wonder—[write] so much about her to you—but why anything—.

Georgia O'Keeffe · [Canyon, Texas] · [October 9, 1916]

There is something aggravating about the fact that the last scrap I wrote you is still on the way to you—that it takes such a long time to talk to you—

88. Probably Jane Wyckoff Varney.

But this has been such a great day—a queer day—I've been so amused with myself—I must tell you—

Yesterday was sunny and fine and I went to the Canyon again—about twenty miles east—climbed and scrambled about till I was—well I had enough—I was out of breath many times over—and felt very little—such a tiny little part of what I could see had worn me out—Yes—I was very small and very puny and helpless—and all around was so big and impossible—

It seemed as if the steep places—the far away parts—the ragged little cedars and uncertain stones all laughed at me for attempting to get over any of it—

—Then at night I walked for a couple of hours in the moonlight on the plains—everything light but our shadows—The girl with me was one of the Training School teachers[89]—a girl who has always lived out here—

—So I slept—hard—I ought to hoe corn or ride cattle or do something really hard every day to get tired the right way—

—Then—when we were almost home there was one flash of lightning in the clear stillness—She said it meant a northern—and this morning it was here—a tearing wind from the north and cold—

I had intended going out with Ralph[90] to the place we went to last Monday but working outdoors would have been impossible—and I was glad—

I had a thing I had been twisting around in my mind and on paper for a long time—I told you about making something I liked some few weeks ago—But I wasn't through—It has hung here in front of me and I've liked it all this time—I've been doing it again[91]—and for some reason—I don't know why—I wanted to work on it today and have—all day—

It's absurd—I don't know what it is—I don't know why I'm doing it—I do know what I want it to do—that is—I know when it looks right and when it looks wrong—

—But what amuses me is—that—I think there is a right and a wrong about it and—still I don't know what I'm making—that is—I can't say it in words—

I haven't any words for it—What is it? I wonder if you could tell me—

Why should a person want to put down marks like that—Some way or other it doesn't fit into any kind of reasoning I know of—It sounds so unreasonable that I wouldn't try to say it to anyone else I guess—They wouldn't understand how something I can't explain could be so very definite to me—

I can't understand—I don't care either—and still I do care—I've had a great time all day—working—cloudy out—and the tearing wind—thinking I knew what I wanted to make—what I wanted it to look like—but not having any idea of what it was—

It is ugly—dirty-looking—and the one I made this time—yesterday morning and today—knocks the one I've been liking right off the wall—

They are both hanging there—The one I liked doesn't mean anything anymore—and it

41

ALL THE WORLD GREETS YOU, 1915–1918

89. Irish-born Anna Hibbets had grown up in Washburn, Tex., and was among the first class of graduates at West Texas State Normal College; see "Death Takes Miss Hibbets," *Amarillo Daily News*, Aug. 26, 1966.
90. Ralph Ackerman.
91. Possibly Lynes 118, 119, 120, or 121.

would give me great pleasure to cut a big hole in the other—I hate it and like it too—I have sort of a grudge against it for spoiling the other one and want to make another to spoil this one.—

I've been a little stiff all day from climbing—wanted to be out in the wind—there was something fine about its coolness—but no—I must make this thing—and I don't know what it is—Now wouldn't you laugh at yourself if you were such a fool—and I'm perfectly sure that I'll have to make it again—This one isn't quite right yet—

But it's so much fun to be that sort of a fool—

I can't help wanting to say why?—Now you laugh—Can there be any sense in what I'm making when I don't know what it is enough to say it—and still it seems alive to me—Not exactly alive—altogether—but parts of it—and when my eye is on one part—I jump right quick to another because I think something is happening over there—

When there are so many things in the world to do it seems as if a woman ought not feel exactly right about spending a whole day like I've spent today—and still—it did seem right—that's what gets me—It must be done—and if anyone asked me—what is it—I cannot even tell myself.

Tonight I've been to a faculty meeting—They are more fun than anything that happens here—Really—they are great—and they all look at me as though they think I'm crazy when I say I like them—But—they are so much fun I just have to say it—

Goodnight—

Tomorrow I'm going up to Amarillo with the History man[92]—I almost hate to go— I don't want to see people I know—no particular reason—except—I don't—

The air just makes you feel free—free from everything—and some way—I don't seem to be wanting people—just space has been so fine—I haven't had enough of it yet—

Again—goodnight—

It's a windy—gray night—the moon pale when you see it at all— still it's light.

Georgia O'Keeffe · [Canyon, Texas] · [October 11, 1916] +

Wednesday morning—

This morning—while it was yet dark—the little sister came—I thought she would surprise me if she came at all—

When I said—how did you do it—she said—why I just picked up and came—

She sat down after breakfast to write of her safe arrival—is writing now—I read your very great big letter[93]—while she wrote—

It's a quiet morning—cool—

I wanted to stand beside you as the train you spoke of[94]—pulled out—my hand on

92. Joseph Abner Hill was the history professor at West Texas State Normal College in 1916–1917.
93. Stieglitz's letter written from October 1 to 7, 1916, was thirty-three pages long.
94. On October 6, 1916, perhaps referring to an argument with his wife, Emmy, who had recently visited Lake George, Stieglitz wrote O'Keeffe that he had suffered "a great injustice done to me by one who has done so many to me that I ought to be

your shoulder—just quiet—to tell you that—some way—I understand—and I don't know what—one seems so much alone sometimes—I wanted to go to you—I know a lot of things that I don't know—

You do not hurt me—I don't know that you could—It's that you give me so much of yourself—sometimes it overpowers me—This morning—I hesitated—I feel it so much it is too much like walking on your naked soul—It is too much a privilege—

No that isn't it—

I must go—More later[95]

With her back half turned to my thing she said—I've been noticing your picture—

I said why.

She said—I like it—

I wonder is she here.

Alfred Stieglitz · [Lake George, New York] · October 12, 1916 +

Thursday.

I have been up since all hours.—It is not yet nine o'clock.—I have been photographing—some interiors—rooms of our place[96]—they can only be photographed as the sun comes over the hills—as the light then strikes them.—It is another perfect day.—Cloudless.—Windless.—Cold.—A little above freezing.—But rising mists along the hillsides signify warmer weather. And by noon I suppose it will be more summerlike again.—

—We do not leave for the city until Monday when all the family goes & the house is closed up.—I lose my vote as the last day for registering is Saturday.—And this year it's the first time I feel like voting.[97] —I intended going down Saturday but the unpleasantness of last week together with other considerations decided me to spend Sunday up here. Sunday in the city has always been a *bête-noir* of mine.—And then every hour here is worth living.—

—Yesterday morning a northeaster was again blowing and weathersharps all predicted positive rain & change of weather generally.—But again wiseacres were left in the lurch with their wisdom—the sun won out. What a humorist the sun is!—By noon the northeaster had disappeared—like a bad spirit dispelled by light. The Lake was mirrorlike—& deep green—& the colors of the hills seemed deeper & richer than before.—The depths of the greens I've rarely seen before.—And of course this black-like depth of all the yellows—light greens

---

immune by this time—And I thought I was!! I sat at the Lake—a mile away I saw a train moving out. It was carrying away the person. I was wondering how any person with a trace of finer feeling could be so—what should I say?—when a Lake like this one is ready for those who grieve." He continued, "My heart ached.—And I felt alone.—With the Lake.—I wondered how all would end."

95. On October 13, 1916, O'Keeffe amplified these comments, writing, "Maybe it's a hard thing to say—but it's a privilege to see you hurt—It is to see anyone hurt—most of us hide our hurt—it seems the instinctive thing to do—I believe we only show it to the people we think feel it—like my drawings—maybe that's why I don't like everyone to see them—they may not feel them."

96. Possibly Greenough 379 (see p. 19).

97. President Woodrow Wilson was running for re-election against the Republican challenger Charles Evans Hughes.

—reds—most amazingly.—All day I worked.—Unfortunately I have no color plates here this year.[98] It certainly is an opportunity.—But color photography excites me so terribly that I have discarded it.—Tempt me as it always does.—For it is very remarkable if one knows *when* to use it. *And how.* But the primary reason I have discarded it is that outside of the excitement the plates themselves are apt to be imperfect.[99]—So to finally achieve a "real wonder" & then find it *imperfect* owing to imperfections of manufacturing is maddening. Especially so if one has proverbial hard luck in just striking such material. And such luck I've had from the beginning. If bad plates could be chosen—I was sure to choose them.—Always.—So excitement of work & the inherent tough luck within myself are really the causes why "I don't" any more!—But it's a shame I suppose that I don't dare the devil till I drop dead from mere exhaustion—

& *the Devil remains!*

—In some things I may do that—

Last evening Walkowitz & I took a long walk—along the Bolton road. It was like walking through Fairyland—some of the landscape—wild with the music of color.—Color everywhere.—The variety of trees up here is so great that only when color really comes into its own—as at present—does the character of each tree stand out in contrast to the character of the others. And as we were returning the sun had just set in the west & the sky was as I had never seen it. The clouds as if brushed on here & there in flecks—fleecy like—rose colored—the blue nearly green—& above us the whole sky seemed like a huge dome with small variformed inverted craters—like flat reliefs.—I never had seen such an effect. And as we were standing there looking upward—over the eastern hills the perfect full moon came sailing into the skies. Clear—golden-colored.—It annoyed me.—I felt towards it as you did one day towards the Hartley when you wanted to put a hole through it.—The moon looked, & behaved so made-to-order-like. It reminded me of some "Beauty" who knew she was a "Beauty" & came sailing into a ballroom at the "psychological moment." But the moon was soon forgotten for coming homewards for the rich depth of certain evergreens sank deeply into our makeup.

—After supper we took another walk—It was cold & we walked at the rate of five miles an hour. Just to feel.—The moon was brilliant but commonplace—Perhaps I'm hard on that much besung wonder of all ages!—But the moon won't mind—and perhaps some day I'll bow to it as nearly all others do.—

—As I went to bed last night I stood at the window a long time.—There is a great tall pine next to the "Treetop" I see from my pillow.—Over the pine was Sirius—just over it —& above it at respectful & proper distance—the moon—one straight line—& perfect proportions—perfect in space.—But I slept badly—restlessly—I thought much of death.—

And now the sun calls.—I'm writing indoors. The sun sends its greetings to all those that give you pleasure down in Texas.

---

98. See Greenough 320–323, 328, 415, and appen. 3–20.

99. See Alfred Stieglitz, "Frilling and Autochromes," *Amateur Photographer* 47 (June 23, 1908), 636.

STIEGLITZ RETURNED to New York on October 14. Although the next exhibition at 291 did not open until mid-November, he went to the gallery every day to meet with friends and colleagues and prepare the next issue of *Camera Work*. In addition, as he wrote to the British editor R. Child Bayley, numerous people came to him "with all sorts of plans. Plans for new magazines, new art galleries, and exhibitions of all types. They want my help. Whatever that may mean. As usual most of the plans are not half baked, rarely feasible."[100] One of the ventures Stieglitz considered "half baked" was the Modern Gallery, established and run by his once-close friend Marius de Zayas. By mid-October, O'Keeffe too found herself increasingly at odds with those around her. "I feel in a pen," she wrote Stieglitz on October 15, 1916. "Teaching school is awful—for instance—I can't go barefooted tomorrow if I want to—I might lose my job if I cut off my hair—They pay you to be such a fool sort of pattern." But she also recognized she did not yet have "the nerve to quit."

Georgia O'Keeffe · [Canyon, Texas] · [October 22, 1916]

Sunday night—

   This morning—just to be contrary I guess—I said to myself at seven o'clock—I *will not get up*—I wasn't sleepy—I just objected to having to eat at 7:30—I'd rather not eat sometimes than have to do it at a certain place and at a certain time—

   So—I was almost asleep when someone knocked at my door—it startled me—No one came in when I said "Come"—So I got up and went to it—quickly—but with my eyes shut I guess—coming back is such a jolt when you have been in that nice half-awake land—just thinking—

   It was the big man[101] with the mail—

   Your letter—one envelope and two letters in it—if what is written at one time is a letter—

   You gave me almost as much of New York as I'd have had if I had gone around and seen it myself—

   —The word "humbug" coming to my mind right now makes me want to swear—It isn't just in New York that you can use it—I don't know any better place to use it than in a little town on Sunday—I don't see how anyone with a grain of sense in their head can go through the nonsense they do and call it religion—

   I mustn't think of it—it makes me—too furious—and really—if they enjoy it—I see no reason why I should object—

   One reason why they didn't want my small sister to be with me is because I do not go to church—and the amusing thing is that the ones who object—never go themselves—

   She isn't an idiot—very funny—

   What makes me so furious is talk about—SIN—Why talk about it—if it is so awful—

100. AS to R. Child Bayley, Nov. 1, 1916.

101. Susie and Charles Ackerman picked up O'Keeffe's mail for her from the post office.

No—I'm not going to write you a sermon—but something ought to be done to some of the folks who are talking to young folks on Sunday—

—To return to your letter—I remember stopping to look at Marie[102] one day—the first time I really saw her face—the expression startled me like an unexpected noise—It's a fine face—I wanted very much to know her—know all about her—She was alone—I asked for you—you were not in—as soon as I had taken a few steps from her—I thought—how stupid—you could have talked to her and you didn't—Maybe I didn't realize till I had turned from her that I wanted to talk to her—

I don't know—I remember I was too late—

You ought not have those drawings framed—You have enough stuff around there to take care of and I haven't any place to keep them—They take up so much more room framed—but—do as you please—

Of course—if you want to—it's the thing to do I suppose—It doesn't matter to me but I'm afraid they will be in your way—If they are in the way—let me know—I don't know what I'd do with them—I might send them to my blond lady to keep for me but—goodness—what am I keeping them for—I don't know—

Funny—I've been sitting here trying to think what to do with them—I don't want them—and I don't want them burned or torn—I wish they could blow around in the wind all the time and never settle to the ground anywhere—

Let me give you—now—the one you asked for[103]—I didn't want to give it to you—all for your own—when you asked for it—don't know—why—just didn't—couldn't—But afterward I gave it to you and intended to tell you several times but always forgot—It was before I left Virginia that I gave it to you and of course—I don't remember why—

So—if you still want it—I want to give it to you—if you will still take it—

Why am I so very funny—I wonder—No—I'm not funny—but that doesn't matter.

I've been in the Canyon all afternoon—I didn't climb—I sat on the top all alone—the first time alone—I didn't want to climb—so wore high-heeled slippers—knowing it would keep me from it.—That was the only way to keep me from it—and I had to laugh at myself sitting there in those shoes—and I had to laugh too—thinking how feeble-minded I must be to have to hobble myself before I left home to make myself behave—

It was a wonderful warm quiet day—The color—I would like it better if I had never seen things people have painted from places like it—The very far away side of it—lavender and pink and red and blue—made dirty in places by millions of little scrubby cedars—never more than ten or twelve feet high—but sometimes having trunks two feet thick—gnarled and twisted—sometimes half uprooted—scrubby little old things but still alive and bravely green—when all the grass around that we think of as being younger is dead and brown—

Shadows very blue—I almost cooked—half-asleep in the sun—but the shadows of the little scrubby trees were cold—I guess I liked being really hot—I'm usually cold after the middle of August till the next July—

102. Marie Rapp, later Boursault, was a music student and Stieglitz's secretary at 291 from 1911–1917.
103. Probably Lynes 50.

Anyway—I had a great time by myself—The sunset was a long warm glow—it seems to hate to leave this country—

Goodnight—

It is a very still night—it is still early—not nine—but I'm going to sleep—

Alfred Stieglitz · [New York City] · [October 26, 1916] +

Evening.—It has been a torn up day.—The doctor told me I shouldn't be discouraged.[104] I'm not. But I want to feel encouraged. And I'm not.—I don't want to have to think of my skin for weeks & months.—That is be conscious of something that is "nothing"—only annoying—& irritating & wearing.—

All day visitors.—Hutch Hapgood for some hours.—A great fine soul but we were not alone some—or most—of the time. Man Ray (do you know him?) also a fine fellow but *very young* (no crime) joined us.—The trio was all right. But I prefer duos—especially when I have Hapgood.—Later on Marin surprised me.—He was not expected till next week.—Bitter cold sent him home sooner—freezing of water-pipes, etc.—I'm glad he's here but today I had little of him too for others came dropping in—& joining.—I also had an hour at the Modern Gallery with de Zayas.—He & I alone most of the time.—Every effort is being made everywhere to draw me into a lot of "schemes"—exhibitions—etc.—& I'm not at all inclined that way.— I can't feel with New York as yet—& so I can't do anything with or for it.—And I won't until the spirit moves me.

—A letter from you.—Another fine one.—The Sunday one.—You feel about Sunday as I do.—So you are not fit to lead your own sister on Sunday.—Aren't the people a humbug nearly everywhere, on Sunday particularly.—The really religious ones do not go to church—Bed is the best place.—Too bad my letter forced you out.—That's the penalty of having a friend of my type.—Not even rest on Sunday!—Should I be sorry for you?—

Your drawings & frames.—Don't fret about them—I want the finest protected.—They spoil otherwise—They do not take up too much room—Now please accept what I say & have said: *Literally.* Your work means so much to me that I want to protect it primarily for my *own* enjoyment & satisfaction.—And when sometime you may want it or need it—& the frames are too bulky why the drawings can be taken out.—All you have to do is give the word when you may want them—with or without frames.—

—The one you have given me[105] I look upon as ours together—It is yours as well as mine.—

And now I'm going to say something I've been wanting to say for a long time—even to you when you were at 291—& during the summer often.—But I never knew how.—But I must now.—

—I know you live by work.—And your work means an awful lot to me—it has given

---

104. Earlier in the day, Stieglitz, who appeared to suffer from eczema, had visited his dermatologist.

105. Probably Lynes 50.

me more than you can ever realize—& this is not at all personal—*it's just what you expressed & how*—& if you will let me—I'd like to own some of the others if you will.—If you did not know me personally & I not you—you would let some of the things go wouldn't you—to someone wanting them badly?—Now no one will ever want some of them as badly as I want them—not to own—but to hold & look at—in trust—& still I want to feel that I'm not taking away your chances of disposing of them should you ever so desire.—(I hate to write this down—I'd rather have you on the Lake & tell you—but that can't be—so I know you'll understand)—

What I would like to do is to send you one hundred dollars & we own together three more outside of the one "ours" already.—Will you?—Or am I immodest?—Demand too much.—

—You know I know exactly how you'll look & feel when you get this[106]—& I really wish I could spare you that.—But I can't.—I've thought so long & often about this very thing—I *must* make the start—right now.—The male brute you see—even when more feminine than male—

—I wonder if you'll understand me—& feel with me as I do with you.—If in any way you don't agree forget all I've said—I won't allude to it again—The pictures & everything connected with them has been so pure—so fine—that nothing must rob anything from that fineness & purity for either of us.—

—Did I tell you that I saw a play at the German Theater on Tuesday.—By Tolstoy. The last thing he wrote—*The Living Corpse*[107]—tremendously overpowering drama in eleven pictures.—I sat there spellbound.—It was well done.—Very.—And I came away with a terrific headache.—That's my test of keen enjoyment.—A terrific headache.—I'm going to see if I can get that play & send it to you.—A pity Broadway has no theatre like the German.—And such acting.—I haven't been "out" except that evening.—

—If I felt in better spirits tonight I'd go & hear Strauss's *Alpine Symphony*—although I don't like Stránský.[108]—I hope soon to hear some music.—

Camera Work[109] is promised for tomorrow afternoon.—How will it look? Will it look as I feel tonight?—I hope not.—And will it give you any pleasure when you see it?—

I wonder what I've been scribbling to you these last days.—It's funny that I should be telling you so many things which are personal—Why send such things to Texas?—

You know you needn't read.—I'd laugh if some day you wrote: "Letter received.—It's fine but I haven't opened it. It's too big.—Am really busy.—Georgia"

Good Night.—I'll get this off in the morning.—I'm going to bed very early.—Just to lie there.—

Good Night—

106. Stieglitz enclosed a check for one hundred dollars with this letter.

107. Leo Tolstoy, *The Living Corpse: A Drama in Six Acts and Twelve Tableaux,* translated from the Russian by Mrs. E. M. Evarts (Philadelphia, 1912). Stieglitz saw the play in a German production at the German Theatre, which was part of the Irving Place Theatre in New York.

108. Stieglitz subsequently attended the American premier of Richard Strauss, *Alpine Symphony*, op. 64, 1915, directed by Josef Stránský, the Czech-born conductor of the New York City Philharmonic from 1911 to 1923.

109. *Camera Work* 48 (Oct. 1916).

Georgia O'Keeffe · [Canyon, Texas] · [October 26, 1916]

Thursday—

Just fifteen minutes—

This morning when I waked—the first thing I thought was—I'll not go to chapel today—it is twenty minutes in the middle of the morning—It's the first time I've missed—going is part of my job you know—

But as I sat—just thinking for that twenty minutes—among other things it seemed—I guess I smiled at the letter I had just mailed you—It seemed funny that what I had written you several days ago—before your letter about Sunday came—I had already answered it—

I usually work on Sunday if I'm not outdoors—

I've been going to a Sunday School class at the Methodist Church—here—sometimes—The President of the Normal[110] has it and I like to hear him talk—I went the first time because I want to know as much as I can of what he is like—I still go for that reason—and will probably continue to as long as I can make myself—or until I know all I want to about him—I like him. I guess I didn't go to chapel today because I knew he was away and didn't see any use in listening to or watching the old fat tub who takes his place—

—It is warm and sunny and a little windy this noon—I like my coat buttoned—a very nice day—I wish I could give it to you—or that you would walk with me after the class I have in a few minutes—I'll probably go alone—the youngster plays tennis—

Faust was on my table when I came from dinner—what you write in the front[111]—I like—thank you.—

She looked at me in surprise when I said I hadn't read it before.

Yes there will be time to read it—When I want to I make time and I don't think I ever wanted to read anything so much before—

—Like it—Why—that depends on what "like" means—It will interest me immensely—because you like it so much—maybe help me to know you better—I would like it for that—even though I personally disliked it—but—even while I don't know—I can't imagine myself not liking it—Maybe more than liking it.

Must go.

Last night was a wonderful still starlight night—I was out alone for awhile—Just standing still—space all around—to look at it. It was cold but I put my hat in my pocket—

—Some time I'm going to tell you something—

Faust has made me want to tell it to you—

I'd like to now but it isn't—it's nothing much—just thought it—or felt it—I don't know which—last spring—and now haven't time.

---

110. Robert Barstow Cousins was the founding president of West Texas State Normal College, 1910–1918.
111. Stieglitz wrote: "I have lived—When I was nine I discovered *Faust.*—It gave me quiet then.—I knew not why.—But it gave me quiet.—And I have lived since then—much & hard—& in consequence suffered so that I could not suffer anymore.—*Faust* quieted me in such despairing moments—always—And as I grew it seemed to also grow.—It is a friend.—Like the Lake.—To one who, without knowing has given me much at a time when I needed *Faust* & Lake.—1916." See Ruth E. Fine, Elizabeth Glassman, and Juan Hamilton, *The Book Room: Georgia O'Keeffe's Library in Abiquiu* (New York, 1997), 34.

I wonder if you know how much finer life has seemed to me through knowing you—a little—maybe more than a little—

[October 27, 1916]
Another few minutes—Friday noon.

Yes I've been reading—

After the class yesterday I walked—without knowing where or why—*Faust* under my arm—I didn't want to read it in the house—

So I walked—The plains seemed like rich green and yellow gold—I walked toward the cliffs or sand hills—till there was nothing but—the nice shapes of the ground in front of me—I never saw it look so like gold—The sun was getting low—that is—it was between three and four—nearer four—

I didn't see the sky—my hat was down close on account of the glare—and I only seemed to see the ground—warm gold—almost impossible to believe it—then farther away to the right those cliffs—blue—pink—lavender—a curious quality—makes me want to rub my eyes and see if it's true—It's something very beautiful I want to touch—but—wouldn't if I could for fear I might find there is nothing to touch—

Finally I saw a high pile of tumbleweeds lined up along a fence—so I got through the road fence and went far enough along the tumbleweed fence so that anyone who might go along the road wouldn't matter—I sat down in the little strip of shade made by the tumbleweeds—even then I looked for awhile—

—It's great being alone out here. I read—till the sun was almost gone and I realized I was cold—

All the way home I stopped every little while to read something over—and I wondered why you thought I might not like it[112]—I wondered often because—Why you know—I think I never liked anything better!—

Then I stopped still—surprised—sort of afraid—I have always been afraid of the greatest things that have come to me—afraid when I first realized a little—

It seemed that I was nearer to you than I have ever been to anyone—So near that I almost seemed to touch the thing in you that is *real* life—call it soul if you want to—it's a damnable poor word for it—

And it made me afraid for a minute—to get so close to anyone—

I have read four scenes—most of it more than once—some of it several times—Often stopping to wonder why you thought I might not like it—

---

112. On October 31, 1916, Stieglitz told O'Keeffe that he would never have given her *Faust* if he thought she would not like it: "Not that book.—It is the first time I ever sent *Faust* to another man or woman. Unless I felt it would mean a *tremendous* lot to them *for all time* I couldn't let them share with me what *Faust* symbolizes—& is—in my life.—Somehow your work—your letters—your whole attitude towards life as I feel it is & must be—made me desirous of sharing *Faust* with you."

It's about nine o'clock.—Saturday.—I have just decided to quit working.—I have really had
a very busy afternoon.—Working at my own photographs. Some of the time. And this evening
too. Some are really good—a development.—I wonder whether any of them—should you
ever see them—would mean more than just photographs!—I'm not easily satisfied with my
own work.—I tinker & tinker—& tinker—for years to get some print that looks so simple
that photographers, with few exceptions, think they could get a similar result—should they so
desire—within an hour or less.—But they never try. Sometimes I wish they would.—For their
own sakes—& above all for photography's.—

　　　—And *Camera Work* finally appeared on the scene—Three P.M.—My heart did beat as
I opened the package of five advance copies!!—

　　　What mistakes would jump at me—mistakes over which I had no control in spite of all
the supervision of years—mistakes owing to the sloppiness of the workmen & those who engage
workers—throughout this part of the country!—You have no conception of the fight I have
put up—incessant fight—for twenty-six years in this city to get *clean* work—with a trace of
feeling—

　　　Well I'm not ashamed.—The first copy I immediately sent off to you[113]—and Duncan
who came in got the second. —He thought it fine—& full of real humor!!—What will you
think?—At any rate I had to smile when I thought of what was to go out to the world.—
Stieglitz—dead—so many believe it. I'm always dying for my friends.—It has always been so
since my struggle began.—It's fine to die & be one's own funeral director!!!—

　　　—Kreymborg was the only other visitor at 291 in the afternoon. I phoned to Wright[114]
I couldn't come.—And think of it while working at *Camera Work*—I have to insert some of the
gravures—I never noticed that in the house next to us—the firemen were extinguishing a fire.
I had smelt smoke & even saw it—but I never thought of anything but the books—& Duncan
& Kreymborg were looking at them too.—Suddenly the two called me & said: Look out—there
must have been a fire next door.—The yard full of firemen.—My continuous thought of twelve
years—ever since we have been in 291—to find the place gone some morning. And in the last
three years there have been five fires within not many feet of us—even right under us one night.
A case of incendiarism—A miracle that nothing happened.—I'll never forget that call from bed
that night—The first children's show[115] was up—and the whole place full of *all* the work of
Marin—Walkowitz—Hartley—not to talk of my own.—And much other.—I didn't think of

---

113. Stieglitz inscribed this copy of *Camera Work* to O'Keeffe, writing: "A woman carries nine months—and a child is born
—sometimes dead. I have carried this eighteen months—Born today. What is it? Dead?—Or? Whatever it may be I'm glad it's
here—the labor pains have been unspeakable.—Father healthy.—Child a book. To Georgia O'Keeffe this first copy is dedicated
by one who loves intensely all that's *genuine*. October 28—1916" (Department of Photographs, The J. Paul Getty Museum,
Los Angeles).

114. Stieglitz was referring to the critic and author Willard Huntington Wright, who had a brother, Stanton Macdonald-Wright,
a painter who exhibited at 291. Stieglitz often referred to the painter as Wright, not Macdonald-Wright.

115. Exhibition of Drawings, Water-Colors, and Pastels by Children, Aged Two to Eleven, 291, Apr. 11–May 10, 1912.

mine.—I didn't really care.—Had it gone—what of it—But the children's—& Marin's—& Walkowitz's—etc. The life work of so many.—

As I said a miracle happened that early Sunday May morn—we were untouched!—In that tinder box.—Some day I'll tell you the story.—What a fanatic I was—perhaps still am.—I wonder if I still am.—I know I was.—

—Now that *Camera Work* is out I feel much better.—On Wednesday I'll get out about thirty more copies—& then every day some. It's slow work.—The mailing too is slow work.—I always thank my stars that so few people subscribe & that the edition is small[116].—

I wonder when I'll get out another number.—I have several in mind.—

Should I never get out another—it's a luxury—an expensive one—to allow myself the work—I'm glad, very, that you are incorporated in its pages[117]—as you are incorporated in the spirit & history of the Little Room.—

The room is once more living.—Nothing in it.—Empty.—So full.—You'd like to sit there awhile I'm sure.—Today.—I feel it.—

—I'm devilish tired tonight. I want to sleep.—Tomorrow is Sunday. I don't quite dread it as I did the last one.—I wonder whether you'll try to remain in bed late—no letter from me will disturb you—at least I hope none will—

Rest for you—real fine rest is more important for you than letters from me or anyone else.—

—Well Good Night.—

Do you ever dream? And if you do do you remember what you dream?—

Good Night!

Alfred Stieglitz · [New York City] · October 30, 1916 +

It's Monday morning.—Monday is different from all other days.—Different like Sunday is different. The other days are more or less alike.—

—I've just come in.—291.—The morning is gray & misty—still—it should have rained last night—but the rain seems to be in my own sort of dazed condition—it doesn't seem to know exactly what it should do—stay up or come down.—

—And as I came in I found a bunch of mail.—And curiously enough four very wonderful letters. One from an old friend in London—an Irishman[118]—I hadn't heard from him in nearly a year. And as I was coming up the elevator it struck me that I wanted to send him one of the first copies of *Camera Work*.—I knew he would enjoy it.—So you can imagine my pleasant surprise when on the top of my mail I saw his handwriting.—And he asks for *Camera Work*.—

52

---

116. By the time *Camera Work* ceased publication in May 1917, only thirty-seven people subscribed to it; see Richard Whelan, *Alfred Stieglitz: A Biography* (New York, 1995), 385.

117. As was his custom, Stieglitz published excerpts from reviews of O'Keeffe's exhibition of April–May 1916 at 291, including letters from Charles Duncan and Evelyn Sayer; a review by Henry Tyrrell from the *Christian Science Monitor;* and an unsigned epistle titled "O, Georgia!" *Camera Work* 48 (Oct. 1916), 12–13, 60–61.

118. R. Child Bayley.

Would it ever appear again. He had been going over old numbers recently.—He's a great fine fellow—an editor. Deeply interested in photography.—And horses.—And fishing.—In life.—

—Then there was a letter from California—from Annie Brigman one of my real friends. —I hadn't heard from her in months. I wonder whether you ever had a copy of *Camera Work* with her pictures in it[119]—I don't think so.—I'll send you one.—She's a sort of mountain wildcat—a woman of forty or more.—Perhaps less.—I don't know.—At any rate she's a genuine soul.—And I'm fond of all that's real throughout—Very fond.—She's loyal.—Not to me as a person—but loyal to the big thing which I know prompts all I do & feel.—Just life.—

—And then there was a beautiful letter from Sheeler from Philadelphia telling me what the other day meant to him.—Here too is a genuine soul.—And I was glad he felt as he did.— Not because of myself.—But because it's very fine to feel that what one has seen & felt—for some years in a person (although one may not be in intimate touch with that person) actually exists—is not self deception.—

—I have been told so often I don't see people as they are.—!!!—Always better.—And in one or two cases worse.—

It's so funny.—Especially the latter.—

—And I had not noticed a letter from you.—I was thinking of you while I read the other letters—thinking how you'd enjoy them were you here.—Just for what they reflected.— Three fine personalities.—And I felt I'd write to you.—And there in my hand I noticed three green stamps peeping out from under.—And a big fat letter.—From Canyon.—Of course I was glad.—Very. That it was there with those three others.—Friends.—Far away.—Yet here.— And I read. About your room—the bareness—and the bed—the freeness of it—the whiteness —& the simple smock—and you are sick.—I do not ask.—I hope not sick—not really—just unwell.—Passing.—

—It's a very fine letter.—Rather sad.—There's always a sadness running all through you.—All so natural.—Why should you want to talk to me?—Tell me?—Why should you not?—Why do I scribble away to you—I sometimes wonder.[120]

—Yesterday afternoon my brother-in-law[121] took us out driving in his machine.—It's a closed one.—Or rather it was closed yesterday. Inside were my wife & Kitty & my brother-in-law (he & I roomed together as students in Berlin for seven years!)—& Steichen & his daughter of twelve[122]—a very good looking youngster.—I was outside with the chauffeur.— It was dampish—an easterly wind—We drove out to Edgemere—near Far Rockaway—to see the ocean.—When Kitty was small we spent a few summers there. It was cool & near the city.—Very good for her. And I could be near my work. I was always ill—then—but worked

119. Brigman's photographs were reproduced in *Camera Work* 25 (Jan. 1909); 38 (Apr. 1912); and 44 (Oct. 1914). She also contributed to "What 291 Means to Me," *Camera Work* 47 (July 1914), 17–20.

120. On October 25, 1916, after mentioning to Stieglitz that she had been sick for a few days, O'Keeffe added that she was curious "why you write to me so much." Noting that he had so many people to talk to, she wondered why he was "talking so much way out here—to—just a little rat of a girl—I never feel that I'm grown up." She also added that she would "like to live where I can say and do what I want and still be not a curiosity."

121. Joseph Obermeyer.

122. Mary Steichen.

day & night—like mad—for I had "visions"—& a great faith in people—in the country—in workmen—"Give them a chance & they'll grasp it"—I was convinced of that.—Then—And for many years.—I still think it. But how [to] make them *see what a chance* really is.—

Well, for eleven years I had not been to Edgemere nor over the ground that leads there.—All much changed—built up—imposing bridges—& here & there tremendous factories—on the way there—roads in construction—new concrete elevateds—endless numbers of autos—going—?—Nine Fords to one of all the others put together—six funerals we overtook—horses & carriages for them—At last we got to the ocean.—There was the old house—it was new then—& it looks new still—a good landlord—but all built up about it—the huge bay nearly all filled in & houses where water had been—& the inlet back of the house—filled in—a city of ugly wooden houses—all empty now—in summer swarming with humans & mosquitoes.—The beach formation all changed. New projections of sand—way out—the old beach where Kitty had played, part of the ocean.—

—The ocean itself lazily moving floodward—but so drowsily—Construction—& destruction—& huge boulders along part of the walk to protect it from the ocean when it gets mad—as it often does.—And way off in the distance the horizon—unaltered.—And the smell of the sea—unaltered.—And the dampness that penetrated bone—unaltered.—It was a queer sensation to stand there & look out upon the sea. It is five years since I was in Europe last. On the sea.—And since then I had not gotten a glimpse of it.—Europe then—& now.—The sea the same.—

I was glad to move homeward—New Yorkward.—It was growing dark.—The West was gray with a patch lavender & pink—very pale—& a bit of pale blue green—and the crescent of the moon was pale too—all listless. Sunday like—Sunday in New York.—It grew dark & we sped along—a row of red glow lights—the backs of a string of endless autos. We passed hundreds of them.—And as we neared the city itself & the huge bridge—the river—huge advertising signs were all aglow—& some buildings too were dimly lit up—it was Sunday—& the haziness of the atmosphere dimmed the lights—I was conscious of a huge machine—growing every moment—signal lights of danger every light—all asleep or half asleep—the only moving sign of life the string of autos—moving in the darkness—moving red lights.—It all seemed quite terrible. The thought of the gigantic machine—the gigantic city.—The thought of what it was & would be to a greater degree within a few years.—Ten million souls part of that machine—dead to one another—all struggling towards—?—

It made me fear for the children.—A sign of age.—Or what?—I who sang the praises of the growing city—loved the huge machine—the developing of it—Tonight—(last night) I felt nothing of all that—merely sat there in the rolling machine & stared—& stared—& wondered. And felt no joy.—No creative joy—no impulse to sing the praises of the city—of the night—

A queer I.—Naturally—inevitably the Lake came into my mind.—And I closed my eyes.—Till it was time to get out—before our home.—

Night.—

It has been a very busy day.—As I was writing this morning Marin came in. He had his new work with him. It is beautiful.—A decided step forward. Always Marin. The color more sonorous—a greater, much greater plasticity.—A greater firmness. Gemlike—others like spring flowers in a loose bunch—very beautiful.—We looked at them in the front room.—And as we looked at them people came in & out—Djuna Barnes, Zorach, Walkowitz amongst them.—And then Caffin arrived & a Mr. Iklé.—Marin, Walkowitz, Caffin, Iklé & I lunched together. The conversation was the election. That means the American people.—

And in the afternoon I was full up again with visitors & things to do—the sun shone through a haze—it was a sticky day.—At 4:30 I went to Wright's home & stayed with him for two hours.—He is always full of ideas & work—things to do. And somehow or other he foolishly believes I know more than I do.—And wants advice.—!!—His book *Creative Will*[123] will be out in a few days.—You'll have it soon.—I'm to get advance copies.—I'm curious.—

De Zayas too called up—I'm to see him tomorrow on "urgent" business.—All are busy—Urgently busy.—*Negro Art* by de Zayas[124] just was issued. That too I'm sending you.—And so it goes.—And I want to keep out of most of it—I want to do my own work—& keep my own hours—Will I?—And 291—??—

—I wonder if all this interests you.—But as long as I write to you I can only tell you of how I spend my time—or give you an idea of how I'm living—here.

And as I put it down I have to laugh—it all seems funny.—And I wonder what it's all about. It's [as] if I had come back & met a lot of people I had known.—And for each I had a key. And as they came I applied the key.—And they talked & acted as they always had—the same things—like mechanical toys.—And I guess they think the same of me.—Isn't it great?—

—I'm wondering how you are tonight.—Still ill?—In that bed with three sides to get into[125]? I really hope it's nothing serious.—You can tell me.—

—And sister is doing well. That must be a pleasure to you.—It's good she's there with you.—I'm very glad.—

—I wonder whether I told you how I had to get into "full dress" the other night.—And how I felt like a fool.—And as I saw myself in the mirror—I don't like mirrors for myself—never did—I felt as if I were looking at an idiot.—How I hate all formality—& conventionality—yet one can't entirely escape either. Not readily.—For years I stubbornly refused and then rather than argue occasionally acquiesced.—They all say I ought always wear "full dress"—I'm "so much handsomer."—Isn't that a scream?—

—I wonder when we'll get the first snow.—Snow fascinates me—& mostly so when the wind is blowing a gale & it's night—& one is out in the streets—alone.—Fighting the icy blow. And face wet & cold.—Hardly able to see.—Blinding all—snow & wind.—I've spent whole nights that way—

It was then I loved the city.—Deeply.—Greatly—

---

123. Willard Huntington Wright, *The Creative Will: Studies in the Philosophy and the Syntax of Aesthetics* (New York, 1916).

124. Marius de Zayas, *African Negro Art* (New York, 1916).

125. On October 25, 1916, O'Keeffe wrote Stieglitz: "I always grit my teeth when I have to make a bed—and it always has to be done here—It seems such a waste of time—It isn't like most beds—it has no head or foot piece—just white—sticks out in the room so I can get in on three sides. Arthur used to laugh at my room—remarked that I cleaned it right out—there was never anything in it—not even on the floor."

Tuesday night—

It's a wonderful night—still and warm and moonlight—big quiet moonlight—

As I walked home alone in it—I was tired—Sunday night I worked almost all night—

—Monday morning when the plains were still very fresh and hazy in just waking up—your letter came. The big fat long one—It's a wonderful letter—

Seven Arts[126] and the letter and a trip to Amarillo yesterday—coming home in the midnight starlight—Such wonderful big starlight—It was cold—the wind stung my face so that I wondered was it cold or hot—An old woman—sixty-five or more in Amarillo who is fond of me—one who has lived with the plains country as it grew—went to see *The Melting Pot*[127]—Then home late in the starlight—

Why last Saturday seems months ago—I've thought so many different kinds of things—even Sunday—quiet—out on the plains with Ralph—seems months ago—

I've worked till two or three [most] nights—just wanted to—

I don't know—I've felt like an alarm clock all wound up—ready to go off—hadn't worked since I painted this thing—the one I wrote you of on wrapping paper—and I guess I'm tired tonight—Still I want to do lots of things—can't possibly do them all—

If I had some fixative I'd send these drawings[128] to you instead of a letter—They are pretty rank but would tell you what I want to say—maybe—

I wish I were just a little girl—about ten—and that you'd hold me and let me go to sleep—but I'm not just ten—

Of course I understand your letter—

Well—the youngster stopped me here—she has been restless—bobbing around—in and out—finally she said "Well, I never was so restless in my life. It's no use to study—I'm only using 4/10 of my brain."—Then a long talk—she thinks it queer and there is nothing queer about it—

but—

she tried every seat in the room—even the window-sills—

I tried to persuade her to stay out of school for a month and begin next quarter—but no—she won't. She has gained six pounds—has gone out to walk for a little—then to bed—no lessons tonight—

—You asked me—should you be sorry for me—because of your letters—as I understand—it—for goodness sake—*No!!!!*

126. Stieglitz had sent O'Keeffe the first issue (Nov. 1916) of the newly released publication *The Seven Arts*, edited by James Oppenheim and Waldo Frank, which called itself "an expression of artists for the community. " It included an article entitled "291 Fifth Avenue," by Peter Minuit [Paul Rosenfeld], 61–66.

127. On October 24, 1916, the Normal College faculty went to see Israel Zangwill's *The Melting Pot: Drama in Four Acts* (New York, c. 1914), a popular play depicting the life of a Russian-Jewish immigrant family. In a review entitled "Zangwill's 'Melting Pot' Returns Here" *The Amarillo Daily News* asserted that "no theatrical production has ever had a greater appreciation in Amarillo than the 'Melting Pot' " (Oct. 7, 1916, 5).

128. Probably Lynes 116–118, or 154.

—Don't be sorry either—because I have a girl that I don't know what to do with—and don't be sorry because I find your letter very hard to answer—

—It's something in me that I can't get out—

I think the best way I can tell it to you is—that last night I loved the starlight—the dark—the wind and the miles and miles of the thin strip of dark that is land—It was wonderfully big—and dark and starlight and night moving—

It is—tremendously free—you would love it—I wish you had been by me—

(she just came in for a thicker coat)

I wish you were by me now so I could some way tell you—I know you understand—that I cannot connect money with those drawings now—maybe sometime—but not yet—I don't need it—

—Last night wouldn't have been so nice if I hadn't known all the time that—

(—my hands are bothering me tonight)

I cannot let you buy—no, that's not the word—I cannot let you give me anything in exchange for your share in—my children—

You see—I never wanted a little one all my own till one day last spring—I was watching a funny little boy in the Horace Mann School—He was so funny I wished he were mine—Then I thought—Why he couldn't be mine alone—and when I thought—mine and—It surprised me so—it fairly staggered me—I remember getting up quickly—feeling I couldn't see and would choke—leaving the room quickly—thinking anyone could see what I had thought—and not wanting anyone to see—and the queer feeling—in the hall alone—I walked downstairs—not wanting to take the elevator—

That was all I remember—but—I can't imagine wanting a little boy that would be mine and anybody else's—

And—all the drawings you have were made to tell him[129] things—before that—and after that—It makes me feel sort of sick to write about it—

Anita has some things that were not made to talk to him—What I have here—are not made to talk to him—they are just for anyone—

I need no sympathy—it's a curious relationship—Most of mine are I guess—I can't explain—I don't know how—letters aren't frequent—but it never matters—I do not care about that. There is something twisted up some way—I don't know how—that makes it all right—

Maybe it's all gone—I don't know—I'm not sure—I don't know anything—I seem curiously glad that I can't even see him—

So there it all is. I am—

If I find myself wanting a hundred dollars someday I'll tell you—That makes it all right, doesn't it—Even if I kept it now—I wouldn't feel that you would have any more rights or feeling of possession in any of the stuff than I already feel you have—and you understood—even when I spoke of the framing that—YOU *do as you please*—I like you too—

So few have sense enough even to try to do as they please—

129. Arthur Macmahon; Lynes 45–50, 52, 55–58.

I return the check tomorrow—I don't want it to fall out and hurt you when you open this—Tomorrow I'm sure it won't hurt!

—Yes I'm tired tonight—Sort of a lump in my throat too—

Please tell me if it's all right.

Feeling particularly feminine I suppose—I want to be spoiled—

And instead I feel as if I've been out cracking hickory nuts the size of pumpkins. Goodnight.

Again—may I say—it's very nice to know you—I hate to send this because—it talks of hurt maybe—and—I don't like to hurt you—or anyone—

Still I have a notion you would rather get this than not—

Again—Goodnight—.

Georgia O'Keeffe · [Canyon, Texas] · [November 4, 1916]

Tonight I'd like to paint the world with a broom—and I think I'd like great buckets of color like Hartley's to start at it with—lots of red—vermillion—and I don't want to be careful of the floor—I just want to splash—

Camera Work this morning and a letter from Anita and one from Katherine—And I heard some music that hurt—Oh it hurt bad—And I worked all day after I went to school—that is four hours and at three we had Faculty Meeting—

Well, I like Faculty Meetings[130]—I always get so riled up—I want to scalp someone—Education is such a mess when it's bottled like they bottle it—

I want to live about three hundred years and see what happens—I think it's terrible that I can't—

—And I came home in the moonlight—still bright—warm moonlight—not even a coat—just my green smock—it's absurd the way I love this garment—I had a bunch of *Courses of Study* from Middle West Normal that I'm going to study—I want to see if they are all stupid (…I'm afraid they are…) I just want to know how stupid—

And then I'm going to decide if it's worth the trouble to fight and try to do some things here my way—I'm not sure that it's worth the trouble—I get so terribly riled when I start to fight—it wears me all out—

And is it worth it?—I don't know—They like things as they have it—

Chemistry and Latin[131] brought me home—talking election—bumping over the rough places—not noticing where they went—Latin is fat and bald—Chemistry lean—with a shaky way of getting up—his head is big—Nice old boy I guess—but Latin is a "nut"—no *Nut*—I had a hard time to write that word—

---

130. The next day O'Keeffe told Stieglitz that "the Spanish lady looked at me and laughed when I said I thought Faculty Meetings the most interesting events of the month—She said, 'Well—now I do know you are different from anyone that ever came here—I never knew anyone else to like Faculty Meetings before'—and the whole table agreed with her" (GOK to AS, Nov. 5, 1916).
131. John W. Reid was the chemistry professor, and Benjamin Alvis Stafford (Fatty Latin) the Latin professor at West Texas State Normal College in 1916–1917.

I had a whole armful of chrysanthemums—red ones—I love them—I like the odor—better than any flower—and I like them in great big bunches—lots of them—I wish I had a whole acre of them tonight—

School is very bad—I get so terribly excited over it—I wish I could just make up my mind to do one thing instead of wanting to do dozens.

—To do school right would take all my time—to do anything right would—I guess—but I'm so damnably fond of reading what I want to instead of what I ought to—Making fool drawings when I ought to be doing the other thing—

No—not ought—

These other folks don't take time for outdoors—

—I do what I want to when the notion strikes me—I do my work—sixteen hours a week—it is really just a side issue—it isn't the important thing in the day at all—And I think I do it rather well—but I can't give all of me to it—

—I could—but won't—!

It's very bad tonight—I wish I could see you—

Camera Work—?—is beautiful—I love the snow and I love Strand's *New York*—and the *Cat* and the girl—I love it all—I like Wright's end piece[132]—I'm sorry he's sick—

Well—I made a mistake—it's by de Zayas[133]—I just looked to see—that was a bad mistake I suppose.

I can't help it—today has been such a jumble—I wonder that anything is—but—back to *Camera Work*—I like your child—and I'm glad you are well.

Yes I smile—I must—

I wonder—do the things written in there about the other folks—make them want to sink the folks that write them—right through the crust of the earth to the hot part in the middle of it—

Of course it's all right for you to put me in *Camera Work* if you want to—but it hurts—Do you understand how?

Oh it's very bad—

Then—my hard crust gets to the top—and I don't care—Write a whole book about me if you want to—

I guess I hate myself most when I don't care—

Then I look around helplessly at my disgusting independence—and find myself asking—what can I do about it—And have to laugh—for there is nothing—

And tonight—let me ask you something else—I don't know—There is never anyone to ask the things we most need to ask—

—I'm getting to like you so tremendously that it some times scares me—

---

132. *Camera Work* 48 (Oct. 1916) reproduced photographs of snow by Paul Strand, *New York (Roof in Snow),* and Arthur Allen Lewis, *Winter;* five photographs of New York by Strand; Frank Eugene, *The Cat;* and Francis Bruguière, *A Portrait.* "W. H. Wright in the 'Forum,' " *Camera Work* 48 (Oct. 1916), 40, 57, 60.

133. In an untitled article originally published in *291* 5–6 (July–Aug. 1915), and reprinted in *Camera Work* 48 (Oct. 1916), 69–70, de Zayas wrote that "Stieglitz had tried to discover America," but because Americans did not understand "their milieu," they had been unable to express themselves in art or literature.

Tired tonight—all sorts of things knotted in me in such a tangle—having told you so much of me—more than anyone else I know—could anything else follow but that I should want you—want you in a curious way—it's a mixture of the way I've wanted my mother at times—but not just that—it's the man too[134]—

I guess it's just because you are what you are—I want you to make me feel tonight—that the world is all right—anyway—no matter how things seem—

I don't want to just quiet myself—I want you to quiet me—

Oh what is the world for anyway. I'm tired of it—and still I want to live three hundred years.

My flowers are very lovely—The watch and a train just pulling out—a sharp dog bark—train almost gone—cattle sound great here at night sometimes[135]—one now—

I'm glad I've grown to know you through letters—it's really much better—Tonight is really great—Such a day—

I'm starting the second part of *Faust* tonight—I've known it all before—I wonder if I read it—

I was very sick when I was eighteen—and I have forgotten lots of things that happened a year or two before and after—I really lost about four years—People sometimes won't believe me when I say I forget things they say happened after I seemed perfectly well—

Maybe I'll not read—I'm sleepy—

Goodnight.

Saturday

Alfred Stieglitz · [New York City] · [November 4, 1916] +

You are a very, very great Woman.—You have given me—I can't tell you what it is—but it is something tremendous—something so overpowering that I feel as if I had shot up suddenly into the skies & touched the stars—& found them all women—Women like you are a Woman.

—Your letter—no it does not hurt—on the contrary you see what it makes me feel—I had to do what I did—& I'm so glad I did it—for it has given me something I never could have had so definitely beautiful otherwise. Never.—No, my great big Woman you have not hurt me—not for a moment. All the contrary.—

How I understand every pulse beat of yours. The story of those drawings—your children—I their guardian. I never dared to think in crystal form—but I wanted to hear from you what I felt must be. And felt without knowing—I saw.—Yes at once & all the time.—And you have told me now—You yourself—wonderfully—so perfectly.—There never was a letter

---

134. Stieglitz responded on November 9, 1916, writing: "I'm glad you feel about me as you do.—And I understand the mother feeling.—You & I—our kind—we really never grow up—we are always children—And mothers are such wonderful things." He continued: "I wonder if we had ever been able to see each other as we do now if we had met personally more & less through letters.—I know I know you—I wonder if I'm really anything the way you feel I am.—There is a difference.—You see I have the advantage (or perhaps the disadvantage) of a great many years!"

135. Canyon had large cattle pens that were at the edge of the town and adjacent to the railroads.

Letter by Alfred Stieglitz, November 4, 1916.
Alfred Stieglitz/Georgia O'Keeffe Archive, Yale Collection of
American Literature, Beinecke Rare Book and Manuscript Library.

like the one right here before me—a Woman's Soul laid bare in all its beauty—pulsating—crying out into the starlight night—Windstill—And no one hears but—?

—Your children.—I sent you what I did because I had to.—I thought you might use it for some kids—others too—but never mind.—All is so fine.—

Fixative.—I'm sending some.

—I'm glad I'm living.—And that you are living, working in Texas—far away from New York that never has time.—

—Funny, yesterday afternoon while so many heterogeneous people were here together—all talking—& I hardly hearing what they were talking about—I was looking at your pictures—those that were in the Little Room last year.—

I often look at them. Just take a glance.—They seem to give me strength.—

—I feel like wiring to you to tell you about the letter—that I never received a greater gift from man or woman—

—But I won't wire. And yet I'd like to let you know for Sunday.—I wonder what you'll do tomorrow—

—I have been at the doctor's.—I'm much better.

—Georgia O'Keeffe—It's like a very beautiful folk melody—the sound.

Georgia O'Keeffe.

You can't hear what I hear.—And I hear it here—and the whole place vibrates with all that's finest in the world—Many extraordinary things have happened here this week.—All feel that the place never was more fine—never more free—all the discord that seemed to exist a year or so ago all gone—discord which was more felt than really existed—all gone.—Through me I guess.—And I merely reborn—the Lake & all it means—signifies.—

Perhaps you remember when you came to tell me something—& I told you of my swims.—

You remember.—I had to tell you then.—Your drawings & what I felt through them—& saw in them—*of you*—that's why it was necessary for me to talk to you & tell you what I did.—Then.—

And now to work.—

Georgia O'Keeffe!!

A very great Soul.—

Later.

It is as quiet here as on Mountain Tops—at Night—And I feel as if I could see into Eternity.—The Silence Vibrates—and I'm full of hearing—and I see—and I'm full of feeling.—All that's tremendous.—

And in New York—on Fifth Avenue!—

And I have to laugh because it's really funny.—

And I wouldn't have it otherwise.

Alfred Stieglitz · [**New York City**] · [**November 5, 1916**] +

It's Sunday Night.—The streets are wet.—It has been raining all day.—It's creepy raw. It's funny to see wet streets with umbrellas.—It's so many weeks—months in fact—that I have seen umbrellas in use.—They really look funny to me.—

—Yesterday afternoon I continued pasting the *Cat* into *Camera Work*—it was growing dark—I heard footsteps. Two old friends Katharine Rhoades & Marion Beckett surprised me in coming in.—I had seen neither in months.—Once upon a time I had seen much of them.—They are unusual creatures.—It seemed queer to see them there—so much seems to have happened to me since I saw them last—I think I've grown much sterner underneath all my laughter & joking.—More impatient with *surface* qualities—especially with people I really like—Less tolerant?—I wonder. And others too came in—other old friends I hadn't seen in months.—I like them all—& still I felt just after they had left I wish I could have remained alone in the darkness & stillness—& hadn't had to talk.—For I know that much I said was not understood—possibly even misunderstood.—And I never like that feeling when I care for those I talked to.—But I can't help it all—I'm full to overflowing as I've told you.—

—And your letter of the morning was so overwhelmingly *big* & pure that I may have been in an oversensitive state all day—& people did not know that. Why should they?—

—In the evening Mrs. Stieglitz & I went to MacDougal Street to see the Provincetown Players.[136] The crowd of artists & literary folks that summer at Provincetown started writing plays, mounting them & acting them there last summer. And now they have a front & back parlor of a house here which they have turned into an auditorium & a stage & produce their efforts there.—It was very interesting & different—even if not "very great"—A worthy attempt[137]— but I fear it will take up too much time of the men & women—that what started as a lark & pleasure will become a drudgery—a job—lead to professionalism.—I'll send you some of their plays & the programs.—Emma Goldman (you know who she is) & I sat together. And we had a talk.—She is a doer—a great woman.—It was interesting to compare notes.—

—Of course the place had no ventilation & there were wooden benches—low hard ones—& the place was crowded to limits.—No public sale of tickets—only membership cards—four dollars for sixteen performances.—Every two weeks all winter.—

—I wonder what your Sunday is like today.—This morning I spent with my mother— & the afternoon I spent at home.—Steichen was here.—We talked about many things. At one time he was the only one who helped me with constructive work at 291.—It was he who sent me the Rodin—Matisse—Brancusi things from Paris.—And he too brought me into touch with Marin.[138]—Etc.—Etc.—In the last few years he has not been so active. In fact he did not quite grasp my point of view.—I don't think he ever fully saw it.—For once seen—it can't be lost.—Few have really ever seen it. It is so simple—so direct—it's practically lost to all!—And that's such fun.—

—Your cry for a boy was not heard by the one who should have heard it—My cry— Who has heard it? For I had a cry too—for years & years—I wonder if it is still there. It is sometimes dangerous to hear—It's so much safer never to hear—

—Last night I seemed to roll around in my bed.—And I think I really had a dream— but I don't remember what it was.—It certainly was of no importance. Still I was mad that I was so restless. I had been resting fairly well.—Better here than at the Lake—as I had told you.

—Have you scribbled anymore—I'm rarely curious—but I'm just wondering what you wrote—I'm sure it's full of red blood—white heat—

In a few minutes I'm going to bathe—real hot—& the room hot—& I may use soap

---

136. The Provincetown Players, an experimental American theatrical company that began in Provincetown, Mass., in 1915, moved to New York in the fall of 1916.

137. In conjunction with Greenwich Village Theatre, the Provincetown Players put on three short plays, beginning on November 3, 1916: *The Game,* by the journalist and social activist Louis Bryant; *King Arthur's Socks,* a comedy by Floyd Dell; and *Bound East for Cardiff,* a one-act play by Eugene O'Neill; see "New Group to Stage Plays," *NYT,* Oct. 28, 1916, 11.

138. While living in Paris, Steichen arranged many of the exhibitions that Stieglitz presented at 291, including shows of work by Auguste Rodin (1908 and 1910), Henri Matisse (1908, 1910, and 1912), John Marin and Alfred Maurer (1909), and Constantin Brancusi (1914). For further discussion of Steichen's role at 291, see Anne McCauley, "Edward Steichen: Artist, Impresario, Friend," in Sarah Greenough, *Modern Art and America: Alfred Stieglitz and His New York Galleries* (Boston, 2001), 55–70.

for the first time in some weeks—on my body. Fortunately I'm the clean kind without soap—but it's fine to mess about with soap suds—

—Today I was told there were two earthquakes near Lake George.—Distinct ones—dishes fell off tables & houses rattled.—Did you ever experience the sensation?—Lake George! —It seems an eternity since I left it—I really can't get accustomed to New York—everything & everybody seems so dead to me—at least I seem so separated from all—Only a couple perhaps who seem real to me—to whom I can talk without feeling that I shouldn't say this & that. And formerly I blurted out everything to so many, many people.—Why must I talk to people?— Why won't they talk to me—if there must be talk.—

—I'd like to have silence—for a long long time at 291.—Just a going & coming.— Or coming & going.—You see how the going was foremost in my mind.—

Talk for talk's sake is something hideous.—And to talk & not be frank is worse.— How many people are open? I've always met all people openly—When I'm not permitted to I shut up like a clam.—But openness seems always to lead to misunderstanding because it's usually only one-sided.—And that is damnably unfair.—Anything one-sided is.

—I'm going to bathe.—

Good Night.—I hope you are in your bed—fast, fast asleep.—Without a dream.— Just sleep.

I wonder what sort of a letter I sent to you yesterday.—I wonder if it isn't full of mad thoughts & feelings—But you seem to understand them.—And it's great to be able to let go— some!—At least.—Occasionally.—

Good Night—

[November 10, 1916]
Friday Morning—

My hands are cold & stiff. I've just come down here—291.—Last night I was interrupted in writing.—And after I went to bed.—And I lay awake nearly all night. It seemed as if it were difficult to close the eyes. So awake. At one time I think I was just falling asleep when I started up.—The wind had begun to whistle [and] blow hard.—It had been windstill all day & windstill when I went to bed. A northwester without warning!—A change to cold from spring.—Without warning!—And as I started up I realized that as I was about to fall asleep I must have been in half thoughts—You were asleep.—And I was sitting next to your bed.—It was bitter cold in the room. I in overcoat.—You did not know I was sitting there. And I didn't want you to know.—It was a clear night & so I could see your face on the pillow—& I saw your hand moving towards something—in its sleep—it touched my hand & stayed there.— And that's all I know for the wind awoke me from my dazed condition.—Of course my having thought of your hand as I wrote did that!!—But there was something uncanny about it all the same—for it was so vivid what I saw.—

—And I lay there awake listening to the increasing wind—& finally I became conscious of the Little Room at 291 as it was last June. And your pictures as they hung there became more living more human than ever before.—And I began wondering what made me *see them at a glance* when Anita brought them in that day last winter.—And how that very moment I wished to know more fully all about them—to know whether I really felt what had brought them into the world!—And now I lay there at night—Awake—about nine months or ten months later —knowing that what I felt the first moment was *really* what existed before me.—A wonderfully quieting thought to know one can see—that one occasionally does.—

—And then I wondered whether it was you the woman attracting me—the woman in the personal sense—or whether merely the woman spirit through you.—Or both.—More the latter though the former partly perhaps.—Whatever it may be it's all very fine.—That I know.—I know it when I see the drawings—for I feel what I felt first—only intensified.—I tell you all this for you have given me so much strength for so many things at a time where I seemed to be going to pieces.—That's why I want you to know—& want to remind you often—what your work did for me.—And your work is truly you—as are your letters truly you.—

—I suppose I'm a lucky dog—several times in my life I have been in despair—& several times something big & fine emerged from it.—Lucky, you see!—Luck!—I have to smile.

—You like your work. Of course you do.—If there were more teachers like you must be one, teaching would lose its bad name.—There are few real teachers in the world—There's nothing finer than teaching—& nothing that is usually more damnable!!—

—Wilson elected.—So say the papers.—I'm glad Hughes did not get in.—For many reasons. I've always disliked Roosevelt[139] because he cheapened what was fine in him—of course that made him popular!—I dislike what is called The Interests & Wall Street—the professional side of them—I dislike too much "Righteousness" as typified in Hughes.

I like the faults in Wilson—some of them at least.—I like the *terrible* enemies he has— they *hate* him *so*—& that I like to see brought forth—

All are hypocrites—more or less—an American virtue I suppose.—Perhaps all men are hypocrites—I don't know.—But we Americans have our special brand—& it gives me the creeps.

But why all this when the day is so clear & crisp—the sun seems none whatever interested in who is who.—

—And am I to get back to *Camera Work*?—I guess I must get through & so I might as well get busy.—

—In a few days I expect to "open up"—that Engelhard kid's drawings.[140] I can't imagine myself starting up with anything else just now. I wish you could see them. Some day you may.—

—The Little Room looks shabbier than ever—I thought of rehanging curtains, etc. —but I can't think of *newness* in there. So it remains as it was—& is—genteelly shabby!—

—When you take your next walk into the night let me trot by your side—I'd love to walk into the night.—New York has no night at present.—Perhaps in the winter when it storms

139. On election night, November 7, 1916, following a very close race between Woodrow Wilson and the New Yorker Charles Hughes, some late edition New York newspapers carried the headline, "President Elect Hughes"; see "California in Doubt," *NYT*, Nov. 8, 1916, 1. Former President Theodore Roosevelt was nominated by the Progressive Party in 1916 but withdrew and gave his support to Hughes.

140. Water-Colors and Drawings by Georgia S. Engelhard, of New York, A Child Ten Years Old, Showing the Evolution from Her Fourth Year to Her Tenth Year, 291, Nov. 22–Dec. 20, 1916.

hard & snows—Two in the morning—Snow & Cold—Ice—& dim Lights—Tall buildings specter-like—& here & there a lost human—

    & just I enjoying!

    —There is the clock—ten.—

Georgia O'Keeffe · [Canyon, Texas] · [November 12, 1916]

The day has been still—white—cold—sometimes a fine mist—maybe sleet—I don't know—so very fine—even when it touched my face—I didn't know—but I saw ice—on water—when I walked—so I guess it was cold—I noticed that faces were very red—

There hasn't been much of myself this week—I've worked and talked all week—only wrote one letter—that to Anita—

One day I painted and it is forcibly impressed on me because the thing is so awful that I hate to think I made it—and still it amuses me—

A woman who wonders what I'm driving at said this afternoon (I didn't want to show it but she saw the back turned out and wanted *really* to see—and I—being very mercenary thought—maybe I'll learn something—so showed it)

"Someway it makes me think *woman*—but it doesn't look like one in shape—the head seems to be a very beautiful flower—but the tail of it is an animal."[141]

It made me laugh—It's very bad.

I've been making it over—this is the fifth—The sister thinks it very ugly—

Other days I've been working on scenery for a couple of plays—It was very interesting—results fairly good—but they provoked me—I don't know why—After it was over—even though I thought they worked out fairly well—I came home and felt like chewing nails.

To be honest—I guess it was because I had been so intensely interested—and nobody got it.—But—I'm over it now—guess I'm glad of it—glad most of the fun was mine—

The next one is already whirling in my mind—I'll just prepare to have the next party all by myself—

There have been wonderful nights—coming home late—I wish you could see the night out here—You get to know people so differently working like that—such funny things happen—

The fixative came—

Well—I wonder if you know what I want to say about it—.

To be honest—again—I hadn't thought to get any—but Monday—just happened to find a bottle that fixed the drawings all but a space about three inches square—Then later your letter said you were sending some—it made me mad—and it made me laugh—

Fixative can be bought out here but like many other things—I forget—

I hate to be talking about it so much. It's—amusing—but I couldn't help being riled over it—However—I fixed that three inch space this morning.

141. Possibly Lynes 119 or 120.

You get to know people so differently — working like that. — — such funny things happen — —

This finally came — — —

I wonder if you know what I want to say about it — .

To be honest — again — I hadn't thought to get any — but Monday — just happened to find a — that fixed the drawing all but a space about 3 inches square

Then later your letter said you were sending some — it made me mad — and it made me laugh —

Fixing can be bought but like many other things I forget

I hate to be talking about it so much.

It — couldn't help being rfilled over it

However I fixed that such space this morning.

Letter by Georgia O'Keeffe, November 12, 1916. Alfred Stieglitz/Georgia O'Keeffe Archive, Yale Collection of American Literature, Beinecke Rare Book and Manuscript Library.

—It has been a crazy week—arguing—I must do something very different this next week—I read a fool book on Egyptian Decorative Art[142]—among other things and those darned *Courses of Study*—

This morning I hated it all so—I read your last *Camera Work* through—and went back to the Marin number with the two color plates[143]—hunting for a drink of cold water—

All day—outdoors has looked as if something were going to happen—any minute— and all day nothing happened—unless the night happened—thin ice on everything—happened with it—and a quiet sort of wind—like someone crying—softly—the short dry grass looked quite white and shiny—the sky very big—and dark—and soft—I loved it—wanted to go into it—but not alone—it's slippery—

A letter from Duncan[144] this week is great—I wouldn't take anything for it—If I took it literally I'd be furious with myself for writing him—He asked me to so I did when I got ready —He tells me "words are nearly always ridiculous"—

Well maybe they are really—it amuses all of me—not just amuses—

Tell me—is he mostly in a world that the rest of us just peek into once in awhile.

Answering it will be an adventure—when I get ready—feel as if I'll have to step over something pretty high and don't know what my foot is coming down on—but I'll step.

It was really nice of you to take the trouble to send the fixative—I hate to phone—and I hate to go to town—it seems so ridiculous that you should get it to me from New York before I think to do it for myself—still I want to—you know.

I'm such a fool—

This week I lost my hat—*NOW DON'T SEND ME A HAT.*—

I just think it so funny—haven't an idea of where I left it—somewhere—at school— and it was such a nice old one that I won't be able to replace it for a long time—

Goodnight—.

Sunday night—

Georgia O'Keeffe · [Canyon, Texas] · November 13, [1916]

—Your letter this morning was great to get—

You're a bit mistaken about my father[145]

I am very like him—so like him that some members of the family—I don't remember who—said—You are so much alike that you are afraid of one another—

He never had time for me when I was little—he was very much fonder of my mother than she of him—I always thought—Still he and I agreed more frequently—and he would do

142. W. M. Flinders Petrie, *Egyptian Decorative Art* (New York, n.d.).

143. John Marin, *In the Tirol—No. 13* and *In the Tirol—No. 23, Camera Work* 39 (July 1912).

144. In his letter to O'Keeffe of November 5, 1916, Charles Duncan thanked her for her recent letter, which he said conveyed "the clarity of new days & big spaces," and he urged her to write again.

145. On November 9, 1916, Stieglitz wrote O'Keeffe that he "felt" her father was not dead; "I also felt you hadn't seen him in some time."

things for me—simply because I felt how to go at him—even though I always felt he was much fonder of—my nice sister—the nicest girl I know—two years younger than I am[146]—

I wasn't jealous—I just felt it.

I got to know him—and like him tremendously after I was grown—Mama was away for a couple of years[147]—Then when she came back—there wasn't any place for me at all— He told me something that wasn't exactly straight—I don't remember now what it was— he wouldn't have done it if it hadn't been for others—it was really a mere trifle—

He would agree with Mama—whether he did or not—really—inside—

I decided it was no place for me—and I never went home except for a few weeks at a time after that—

I have a way of just being through with people and things when they go too much against the grain—

My mother began dying to me the Christmas after I was sixteen—She didn't believe a simple statement I made about not waking up one morning—Probably things like that hurt more than her really being gone—only I always hoped that some way I'd find her—and now—of course—I won't—and I don't like to think of her being out there like that—

They thought they wanted me around but I always found it to be irritation all round so I stayed away. The small sister is the same—She irritates the rest of them—queer—

I don't know—probably a lot of just plain *Devil* in me.

There is a younger brother[148]—big—fresh and free—the kind that fills a room to bursting—I've always been very fond of him—I am yet—

But we are out too—We used to stay out almost all night—just walking and talking— often—I could get him to do anything I wanted to—but I finally told him he could stand upon his own backbone and be decent or go to the devil—

I was tired of holding the string round him—That was three years ago—I haven't seen him—won't know what has happened till I do—According to other folks—I guess he is a fair success—but that doesn't mean he will be to me—

It's all a queer mixture. We are all very funny—No one appreciates how funny like the younger brother—he can see if he wants to—

It's probably much better that my little one is just a piece of paper—

I have a great fear for a live man like that younger brother—such a damnable daring —but the conscience is very fine—so strong physically and so big—the very liveness of that bigness—makes the fineness inside get lost at times—

Still I got tired of keeping my hand on him—He was the only one who understood when the others didn't—

And what's the difference—

When I feel you tussling—feel you in the thick of the fight—I feel like a little boy urging

146. Ida O'Keeffe.

147. From late spring 1910 through early 1911, when Ida O'Keeffe was being treated for tuberculosis at a sanitorium in western Virginia, Georgia took care of her father and siblings in Williamsburg, Virginia.

148. Alexis Wyckoff O'Keeffe.

his dog on in a fight—I want to say—go to it—And when you say I help you—Well—maybe there are others I might be helping if I would—I often find myself wanting to put my hand on your shoulder—to make you feel sure there is another human being in the world—and again —sometimes—I'm the little girl who needs someone—

Probably to most folks—a damnably independent—self-sufficient young woman

No—I'm not sick—haven't been—it's curious the way this past week [I] didn't seem like me—

I don't know what was the matter—except work that took all of me—and every night I was very tired—but I like to be tired like that.

I feel great out here—doubt if there is room for improvement—and the sister—Wish you could have seen the red face—snappy black eyes—smooth shiny hair—very dark brown— above the soft blackish green coat—

She thinks the day is great—

This is such a little of all I want to say to you—

Talking about my family always makes me mad—

Maybe—

Someone came in—I forgot what I was going to say.—No—I remember—I was going to say that maybe it was a bad mixture of nationality—Irish—English—Scotch—Hungarian —and Dutch—or maybe we aren't any more peculiar and mixed up than other folks—

I'm glad too that I'm not in New York—I don't want to be there—There is more out here—

Yes—very fine to know you—

Monday morning

I must write more—

You see—I can't help feeling independent—wanting to be free from everyone. They have always objected to all the things I did—and I've done them anyway—I wouldn't ask the men of my family for anything to save their lives—I wouldn't even suggest that I wanted anything—

They amuse me so—

I am in debt and they know it—Still—if the sister lives with me—I have to take care of her—

Really—it's great—I enjoy it—They don't approve of my borrowing—but I do—when I want to—

All this is nothing—of course—but maybe it will make you see a bit more of why I am like I am—Why I dare to put on paper anything I choose—Why I dare to be frank—I have nothing to lose—no one's opinion to consider—maybe something to gain—

I don't know—

Nothing to do but live—and it amuses me that I can do it pretty much as I please in spite of them—and that the sister can too—

It amuses me to think how furious they would be if they could see me writing all this to you—really it's a good joke on them—

—Still they would all like me if they could forget the other folks in the world—

While snorting about my family I should have told you that there are two unmarried aunts—sisters of my mother's[149]—who are tremendously fond of me—and I usually go to them when things get too warm—

Great old world—Sometime I'll tell you more of them

It's night—Monday night—

I was in such a storm over my family this morning that I forgot everything else—

I guess the truth of the matter is that I can do pretty much as I please with any of them —but it's such darned hard work—I just decided I'd let them rock along as they please—Why should I try to fit them to what I want—

—I hate it all—Let's forget it—

—I've been working again on that darned thing that I ought to be ashamed to own— but if it's in me I suppose it's a good thing to get it out—

It makes me want to go back to my old question that almost drives Anita mad—What Is Art?[150] I'm beginning to think that maybe I'm exceedingly vulgar—and the funny thing about it is—

I don't understand—I get the shapes in my head—can never make them exactly like I want to—but there is a fascination about trying—And then too—there is the delicious probability that I don't know anything about what Art is—So it's fun to make the stuff—

ART

It can't be anything like that in front of me.—It's repulsive—I'd hate to touch it—and then at times it has a curious kind of beauty—and what is it? I never made anything such a funny color[151]—

I dreamed the other night that the sister was very sick—and her face that color—the little sister—It was terrible—

Then on another wall it simply howls—in blue with a little green[152]—it makes such a noise it makes me laugh—It all leaves a very bad taste in my mouth—

But what's it all about—

Last night after writing you I got in bed with the Marin *Camera Work* I had been reading in the morning and *Faust*—read what de Zayas says about art being dead[153]—Isn't it queer the way so many people don't look for the reasons of things—

Got up and looked out the window—blowing harder—cold as ice—white on everything—and I wished I had walked in it—I wanted to walk with you into it—Going to bed is so stupid when there is such a fine night out.—

149. Alletta (Ollie) Totto and Leonore (Lola) Totto.

150. In October 1915 O'Keeffe wrote Pollitzer, asking, "What is Art anyway? When I think of how hopelessly unable I am to answer that question I can not help feeling like a farce—pretending to teach anybody anything about it—I won't be able to keep at it long Anita or I'll lose what little self respect I have—unless I can in some way solve the problem a little"; see Giboire, *Lovingly, Georgia*, 59.

151. Probably Lynes 121, oil on canvas, which has a blue-green form, highlighted with orange.

152. Possibly Lynes 120.

153. Marius de Zayas, "The Sun Has Set," *Camera Work* 39 (July 1912), 17–21.

—This morning—windier—colder—clear cold—definite cutting ice and snow in the air—just a little—a little snow on the ground—blowing—many bare places because of the ice underneath—such nice sounding wind—Really a wonderful day—I wish I could give it to you—

At breakfast I gave the letter of last night to a girl to mail for me.

—You see the big man always brings my mail and would take it too—but I don't choose to have his fat little wife[154] keep track of who I write to—It's hard to get over certain obstacles in living—

Another thing I thought last night—after all my fuss about the fixative—was that there is some information I've got to have—I could root it out some way myself—but not as easily as if I let you help me—

There is a Faculty Circle—sort of experiment—and we are all going to have to give talks on whatever the committee assigns us—They have given me "The Cubist in Art"—and I'd like to scalp that fat old Latin creature[155] if he had any hair on his scalp to make a respectable showing—I think he has a notion that all modern art is cubist—

—I've got to get enough definite information in my head to talk for half an hour at least—the condensed kind that you can get over to folks that have no ideas about it at all—or very funny ones—Some of the men have good brains—the kind that tussle—think around things—not easy to satisfy—

—I want to say a lot in a little while—

Just at present—I don't know a cubist from much of anything else—definitely enough to get it to anyone else—I haven't cared exactly—about what a cubist is—It's a ridiculous thing to try to do—but—they have such queer notions about what I'm supposed to teach—I try to teach what I think is of use to everyone—

I'm aiming to give the Fatty the jolt of his life—he can't think much—but there is another who can think—three or four that I want to interest enough to make them ask questions—the President—History—English and Chemistry[156]—

I have till January to think about it—If you help me—thank you.

—I'm glad you like Wilson—I've been afraid to ask for fear it might be Hughes—

—I wish you would tell me about that funny little creature—Zoler[157]—I believe his name is—often on view at 291—You mentioned walking with him and it reminds me that I want to know about him—He is so funny—probably quite nice when you get past the froth—but so frothy to me—

My hands? They often make people say funny things—One of the boys who was helping me with that scenery—asked me to hold one up—I did—and remarked that it was very dirty—put it down to go on with my work—When I had held it up the fourth time

154. Charles and Susie Ackerman.
155. Benjamin Alvis Stafford.
156. In 1916–1917, Robert Barstow Cousins was the president of West Texas State Normal College; Joseph Abner Hill, the history professor; Horace Wilson Morelock and Jennie C. Ritchie, English professors; and John W. Reid, the chemistry professor.
157. A painter who often sported a flowing bow tie and helped Stieglitz at 291, Emil Zoler was a member of the Industrial Workers of the World (known as the Wobblies) who advocated the overthrow of capitalism.

at his request—he was a little behind me—I turned around to see if he were crazy—and asked—Why—He said—"Well—it's a great hand—that's why I like you." I laughed—and he added quickly—"My girl has a hand like that"—she's at some school in South Texas.

I never think of the looks of them—it's always wanting to use them—touch with them —feel with them—

Oh—I must go to bed—I've written you enough for one day—.

Goodnight—

It is such a wonderful night—nine above zero—doing pretty well—walking at sunset was great—still—ground fairly white—ice still on everything—sky all warm—

Oh it's really great out here—So cold—so big—so warm—and you feel so alive—

Stars now—

November 13

Why aren't you here to argue with me—maybe tell me—

I'm glad you are not—I like to do it alone—

You couldn't tell me anyway—I can only know by living—that's why I want to live three hundred years—Maybe I'd know something.

—Your dream—it's funny—that night—Thursday night—I was very tired and didn't take a book to bed with me—I remember laughing about it—not reading as I usually do—and I remember thinking there was something by me—I didn't know what—and I put out my hand to touch it—It was something I liked—and the fact that I touched nothing waked me and I raised up and looked at the spot in the moonlight—

Surprised that there was nothing—It was so definitely something that I liked very much that—Either then—or in the morning—I thought to tell you—but didn't—probably wouldn't have if you hadn't told me of your dream—

Alfred Stieglitz · [**New York City**] · [**November 16, 1916**] +

Another morning.—It's freezing cold & the sky is clear—Although it tried hard all day & night —yesterday—to snow—it couldn't—Like the rain that couldn't so often—& finally came down so mildly that one had to laugh.—

—And *Tristan* last night.[158]—It was a full day at 291.—Some really intelligent people —men—came in.—One a German. And Kerfoot, my old friend, one of the two men in New York, who really sense what I am trying to do—senses my attitude towards life.—He & I walked up Fifth Avenue in the dark—& talked—& laughed. He has just published a book on reading.[159] Applying the idea of 291 to it. It's splendid.—But I fear it won't be very "popular" —I'll send you a copy.—Someday some teacher friends of yours might care to read it—

---

158. Richard Wagner's opera *Tristan und Isolde,* conducted by Artur Bodansky, was presented by the Metropolitan Opera on November 15, 1916, with Melanie Kurt as Isolde.

159. John Barrett Kerfoot, *How to Read* (New York, 1916).

Of course I did not want to walk—but did—as I had a four and a quarter hours stand in the opera ahead of me.—After swallowing a few bites of supper I was off to the opera.— Fortunately I got a splendid standing seat on the rail—in the back—& I could stand there without moving for four and a quarter hours.

—The performance was a very beautiful one—possibly too beautiful—to be as "living" as some I've heard before.[160]—My head lay on my coat on the rail—my eyes closed—& I just heard. And hearing—saw.—And hearing and seeing—?—

I did *not* get a headache. The first time *Tristan* didn't give me one.—Perhaps my emotions go *through* my head just at present & don't get all tied up there—& so give me a head that feels like bursting—But I enjoyed thoroughly—the orchestra under Bodansky performed wonders—the gamut of modulation—no crass cheap contrasts which move people so readily—people who are not very sensitive—the American audience. And Kurt as Isolde was beautiful—interpretation & voice.—All were fine.—

The night was cold—and I felt very alone.—*Tristan* brought back so many, many things to me.—And all seemed so far away—not a part of myself—I really think I'm growing old.—Something seems dead.—Or deadened.—

—But I slept—

And here is your letter—You had a curious week.—Your letter is fine—It makes me smile—because it is as if you were sitting right here with me—& I had my eyes closed—& my ears closed—& saw you clearly—every movement of the face & body—& heard through all the silence.—

—And I really laughed aloud that you also say: *Don't.*—*Don't send me a hat!*! Great. —*Don't.* The woman.—But it's fine.—And I chuckled about the fixative.—You see three inches were waiting for it!—You are a great girl—

And I had to laugh about the people & your pictures.—Why should they get them? They don't live the inner life—You do.—Inner & outer & middle—all of life.—All—!—

—So you lost your hat.—I didn't think you needed one.—Somehow or other I imagine you hatless down there—& without shoes or stockings—& little clothes—just a sort of wild natural woman with a soul as big as Texas—much bigger!—

—Duncan.—He was in night before last.—Just a little while. He looked pretty much upset.—I had had such an awful day I couldn't say much. And he said little.—He's coming again.—He's a peculiar chap & at times I feel as if the strain he lives under might give way—

It's impossible to "help" him—His letter to you must be very wonderful. I know him for years—know his thoughts—abstract—he's fine all through—too fine that's his tragedy.—And no money.—And is intensely proud.—

Difficult for those closest to him. Lack of food & lack of money for the necessities of life

160. In a letter written on November 11[?], 1916, Stieglitz recounted to O'Keeffe how he first heard *Tristan und Isolde* when he was nineteen: "A very beautiful woman—married & intensely musical—took me there. My father too was with us.—He fell asleep.—She & I were wide awake.—I sat there spellbound.—And after that during my nine year stay in Berlin no performance of *Tristan* was ever given without my being there—standing for five hours!—Lost to the world.—And I traveled hundreds of miles—went without food & clothes—to hear it.—*Tristan!*"

are apt to twist a fine nature into curious shapes—He has been on his job of sign painting—physically it's healthy—but—Great gods.—

—If he had lived some years ago he would have been amongst those called religious fanatics—he might have been burnt at the stake.—Undoubtedly would have been.—

One kills such differently now-a-days but kills less humanely than at the stake!—

—So you too have been forced to talk a lot.—And you are working—that's fine—working expressing yourself—working in paint—Will I be able "to get" it?—This morning I seem to have to smile all the time I think of you.—Your letter has done that—Gosh I feel stupid.—

—Did I tell you Wright was in. *The International Studio* is to have a section every month devoted to Modern Art and written by Wright.[161] It all seems so funny to me this "sudden popularity" of "Modern Art."—

I wonder if your work will ever become "popular"—Would you like it?—

—I see your face—the mouth's expression—perhaps the eyes.—But I'm only conscious of the mouth.

—It's all right.—You have answered.

I wonder what I'm going to do today. Twenty-three years ago today I got married!—And I didn't believe in marriage then.—Nor have I believed it since.—But I got married.—

I'm not fit for marriage & yet I know no one who could have made a better husband—or call it what you will—

—The world seems specially funny to me this morning—& I the funniest part of it—to myself.

—Should I send you a hat just because of *Don't*.—I never bought a hat for a woman—it would be a lark to buy one—and wouldn't you look funny in something I might pick out!!—*Don't*.

I'm going to have Duncan paint *"Don't's"* on all the walls here—in different colors.—I'll always have to laugh then—for I'll see expressive faces—& expressive voices—

& I'll think of the smile of one called "Devil"—

—and behind it all—

?

Can you solve the riddle?

Alfred Stieglitz · [New York City] · [November 18, 1916] +

What a magnificent day for me. Today.—Real Glory.—I'm sure I have been hearing all the Angels of Heaven blowing on Silvered Horns trumpeting forth Music as I had never heard—nor imagined it could ever be.—The Music of the Glory of the Dawn—the Rising Sun.—

—A whole day as perfect as that.—In New York.—At 291.—

—It was nine when I got down there & until nearly noon I was alone—peacefulness—

161. See Willard Huntington Wright, "Modern Art," *International Studio* 60 (Jan. 1917), xcvii–xcviii, or (Feb. 1917), cxxxii.

within—without—I was working at my photographic prints—some made when I returned from Lake George—some made in July—some made several years ago.—It takes ages for me to complete my own things—I'm sure a "fusser"—I never—or rarely ever—seem to be able to completely satisfy myself.

—The sun was flooding the room.—The stove was good & hot—the smell of wood—I burn wood, it's cleaner than coal—& more extravagant!—I felt unusually well—free.—

—Towards noon Walkowitz came in & suggested that we hang the first show—the work of that Engelhard child—my niece—Georgia is her name!—Did I ever tell you that?—

—And so we set to work.—Pinning up fifty-eight pictures.—It is impossible to describe what is in that room.—No one could.—I wish you could see it.—Since your drawings were taken down nothing has been on the walls of that Little Room.—And no pictures in the room visible except one day when Marin came back and showed me his new work.

—The child's work.—A girl of ten—she will be ten tomorrow. I can't imagine anything that could have been put into that room to make it right—right for me—except perhaps your own things again.—

—Zorach and Zoler happened in—both were literally stunned.—Both had been led to expect very much—& yet they were surprised—yes, stunned.—We all stood there, they, Walkowitz & I—in astonishment & wondering what all the fuss is about—"Modern Art"—"Exhibitions"—"Professional Artists"—etc.—etc.—

—The child won't be harmed any.—She will not be made conscious that an extraordinary thing is happening through her.—Her parents[162] understand.—And she is a child through and through.—She'll come and see her work—she has only been twice at 291, both times to see children's shows—& I can see how she'll go up to her pictures & point out to me wherein she failed.—

She is honest like—

I wonder whether I was going to say—

You?—

—I was.—You might as well hear it.—From me.—No one quite understands *how* terrifically honest you are—no one quite as I do.—I am sure of that.—I wonder why I'm so sure of that.—

—It was late for lunch—but as we four were about leaving to go for a bite—the elevator boy handed me an envelope—four green stamps—two big official seals patching tears through the face of the envelope—The envelope must have burst open from the life within it. Fortunately—yes, very fortunately—the postal authorities discovered the gash in time to save the letter from dropping out—never reaching anyone—

And I wouldn't have wanted to have that letter lost to me for anything in the world.

—The letter—just then—Everything about it—was just right—When it came—what it contained—

Perhaps it's lucky for you you didn't come yourself just then.—Something would have

---

162. Stieglitz's sister Agnes and her husband, George Herbert Engelhard.

happened—Something that had never happened before. Perhaps I would have stood on my head in the middle of the Little Room!!—

Something quite as mad—or funny—

—You may smile.—

The lunch tasted fine. All were hungry.—Occasionally I took a peep at a page of the letter—I had taken some before we had left 291—here & there—just to get the spirit—and the first few words I struck gave me the key—

And made me feel so full of sun—

—We hurried back as glass had to be put up over the drawings—My own particular job which I have been doing for twelve years. I don't let anyone else help for I'm always nervous someone might seriously cut themselves—it's a nasty sort of job for one who isn't used to it.—

In the twelve years I had never cut myself & had only smashed three or four sheets of glass. But somehow or other today I had hardly begun when I gashed a joint on the edge of a sheet—my bifocals are a nuisance, they have a dead spot!—the blood flowed freely—It was good to see it. It was so red.—But I continued. And by five the room was ready. Cleaned too.—

—The inner room—the silver & blue—where Duncan & Lafferty were shown—contains a choice little exhibit of its own—shown in relation to the child's room.[163]—Only *nine* pictures!—But they cover a tremendous field.—It is a magnificent room—On the wall to the right as one enters are hung:

O'Keeffe—The blue one[164]—Marin—Marin—Walkowitz drawing—Dove.

On the opposite wall: Wright—watercolor Walkowitz.

Facing the door a large Hartley—blue & yellow—& on the small wall opposite a small Hartley in a gold frame.

—I'm pleased.—Very.—And I'm ready for New York & the rest of the world.—

—Your letter.—I've just gotten glimpses of it—It's burning a hole in my pocket—I've read enough to know what it is like—

Am I experimenting with you[165]?—Not more than I do with my own mother or child or self.—Living is experimenting.—And if I do experiment it is with a passion at white heat—experiment not in cold blood—just mind & body—heart—*with All of Me.*

And what is the experiment?—

You know what it is as well as I do.—You yearn for someone to understand every heartbeat of yours—to take every heartbeat—every thought—conscious—& otherwise—for what they are.—And you well know no one can understand so fully—but some come nearer to it than others—some very near—The yearn goes out—whether you wish it or not—to others who are

163. In connection with the exhibition of Engelhard's work, Stieglitz mounted A Representative Group of Paintings and Drawings by Hartley, Marin, Walkowitz, Wright, Georgia O'Keeffe, on view at 291 from November 22 to December 20, 1916.
164. Lynes 64 (see p. 21).
165. Perhaps responding to Stieglitz's letters of either October 16[?], 1916, where he wrote that he had been reading some "psychoanalysis," or October 28, 1916, where he asked her if she had ever read "Freud's Psychoanalytical works?—And Jung's," O'Keeffe wrote him on November 6[?], 1916: "Your word 'psycho-analytical' bothers me—I don't like being a 'specimen'—but there too I don't care—don't put much thought on it—because I'm probably not an average specimen."

feeling as you do.—Sensitive ones.—Reason steps in—not cold reason—warm reason—living reason—helps us see—We want so badly to see.—See what?—

—It is a mania of mine.—I can never see enough—not enough into human souls.—Perhaps it's something else—I don't know—I wish I had you here now—perhaps I could make you feel more clearly what it is.—

We'd walk & talk—all night—& all day tomorrow (Sunday)—& Sunday night—I'm so full of things I have to say—& you are so full of things you have to say—We'd listen—& we'd understand.—

Perhaps all the saying would be a great big silence.—But I feel that I'd want to listen to your words—the voice—

—But the body is far away—

It is well so I suppose—The voice gains in intensity—& all is so much clearer.—

—I'm at home.—Tonight I am to go to the second series of the Provincetown Players.[166] I don't feel a bit like it—although I know I'll enjoy it.

—When I get home I'll read your letter—once—twice—& aloud too a third time. Somehow I feel I must do that—this particular letter. Perhaps in the steaming bath awaiting me tonight.

—You know a crazy man!

I'm sending you some books to help you in your talks. To help you answer some of the foolish questions sure to be put to you. I don't think about *isms* any more than you do. I hate *isms* of all kinds. I accept them all & reject them all.—But any *one ism* makes me shudder.

The charcoal too will go to you—

It's suppertime.—

Good Night—

Georgia O'Keeffe · [Canyon, Texas] · [November 22, 1916]

Tuesday night—no it's *Wednesday*—I get the days twisted—

I've just finished another day in bed—got up and went to supper—but oh, so shaky—I did it because I made up my mind that I would go to school tomorrow whether or no—and thought I'd better practice a little.

I'm really better anyway. The plays came this afternoon and I read *The Shewing Up of Blanco Posnet*[167]—I really felt like reading—and the prefaces to the other two—they are so funny—

but I get so tired—

I'd have the doctor again but am quite sure that my chances for recovery without him are quite as good as with him—if not better. Don't like him—

---

166. The second series of plays performed by the Provincetown Players included *Freedom,* by John Reed; *Enemies,* by Neith Boyce and Hutchins Hapgood; and *Suppressed Desires: A Comedy in Two Episodes,* by George Cram Cook and Susan Glaspell.
167. *The Shewing-Up of Blanco Posnet,* a one-act play by George Bernard Shaw.

[November 24, 1916]
Friday—just before supper—

Went to school yesterday—So much work to do I couldn't stay home—Everybody grabbed me for an extra job too—Even old bald-headed Latin wanted me to make him a motto—Domestic Science giving a dinner and wanted me to help decorate her table—Expression[168] has another play on—I have it planned—the setting and costumes—but that doesn't keep them from keeping me standing talking for what seemed like years—

Gosh—! If I stay here a couple of years I'll be able to do most anything—But really it's great—it's lots of fun—

I had letters to write for stuff for that play but I was mad—and so shaky—

I read *Faust* till I was too tired to write—then went to bed—I wanted to write you but after I'd read till I couldn't read any more—I was too tired—and I wouldn't stop reading—I wanted to read—And the play can go hang! Till I feel better—

This morning your letter and the Provincetown Plays—and a letter from Anita—and some other stuff—came before I was up. I read Anita's first because it was shorter—it was written in red ink—Then your letter—

When I was about a third of the way through the sister made me get up—

I had to laugh as I crawled out—The darned thing had excited me so I was dripping with perspiration—

Well—you're a funny man—My first reaction was to feel about old enough to be your grandmother—and want to say—There little boy don't get so excited—don't bank too much on me—I'm only a woman—maybe I should say only a human creature—

It was a great letter—

I have to smile at my blue self[169] hanging on the wall beside Marin—and Walkowitz and Dove—(I always liked his things)—and looking over at Walkowitz and Wright and Hartley—it seems so amusing—Really you don't know how much it amuses me—

You know the spirit I work in is so funny—It's darned serious but it is simply for my own expression—I never consider anyone looking at it—and it seems so funny that such a "go long by yourself" sort of way of going at it would mean anything to anyone—when so many folks would work their ears off to make something that could hang in that Little Room—

—I know—what you'll say—or I think I do but it makes me laugh anyway—Everything is so absurd in the world—

I like you to hang my blue streaks up if it pleases you—it's funny—it doesn't mean anything to me—except that it amuses me—

I've been sitting here wondering what does mean anything to me—I made it while I was sick in New York—the first one I got up and made in the night—the charcoal one[170]—my bed was by the window and I always sat on it—the dark buildings going up into the night across the

168. Benjamin Alvis Stafford was the Latin professor, Martha T. Bell was the home economics professor, and Mary Morgan Brown taught courses in expression at West Texas State Normal College in 1916–1917.
169. Lynes 64.
170. Lynes 62.

street were great—always—There was a red geranium on my window-sill—and often I'd put it over in the dark so I couldn't see it—the red spot was great in the light against the blue and purple outside—but sometimes I didn't like to see it.

—That was really a great window—

I wonder—does Marin like me to hang beside him—I want to say Hello! to Hartley over in front—Such a funny thin little woman picture—

I didn't notice myself this morning—I was in such a hurry—but this noon—after dinner I opened Clive Bell[171]—looked through it—I didn't have any classes this afternoon— My chair just happened to be in front of the mirror—as I closed the book I looked up and saw myself—

It seemed to be hat and coat—very little face—I wanted to make myself without a face —so I went to bed.

I read the Provincetown Plays this morning in snatches of time between things—and the last two this afternoon—Lots of fun, aren't they? I've already passed them on—I'm such a fool—when I read something I like—I always want to give it to someone else to read—quick!—

All but *Faust* and *Camera Work*—

And sometimes—in fact—often—I want to kick myself because they don't seem to get the real fun out of it that I do—and I think—What's the use—

Your letter was on the bed beside me all afternoon—I didn't sleep—several times put out my hand to reach it and read it again—but every time didn't touch it—I don't exactly know —why—unless it was that I was a little afraid—Till nearly supper time and I got up to read it—

The sister worthwhile?

I don't know—No—I'm not going to try to shield her from anything—and she is the kind that can't be anything but free—she doesn't need shielding—She is queer—and about as independent as they are made—Still such a little girl—it's funny—Tonight she read me a lecture on spending too much money—a few days ago—informed me—after listening to an argument all evening—that it is all right to think what you want to but—you're a fool to express it— don't you know they never can see things like you do—it isn't any use to try to make them—

I don't see any reason why I shouldn't take care of her if I can—She has a funny kind of snappy grit that I like—and an unprejudiced way of thinking things out—Sometimes I wonder if it is just because she is my sister that I think her a bit out of the ordinary—

I don't know—but it's really interesting—she is more entertaining to talk to than most anyone here—and you have to talk to someone.—

—I understand your experimenting—When I remarked on it I think I also said something to the effect that it was all right—didn't you know I understood—

Of course.

—I have a lot more to write—in fact I guess I'd never stop—but I'm tired—I'll never get through so it doesn't *matter* when I stop—

Tonight the sky is wonderful—at sunset it looked—weird and—Oh—I can't tell about it—as though something is going to happen—The snow is still in patches everywhere.

171. Clive Bell, *Art* (London, 1914).

Goodnight.

I'm feeling much better tonight than this morning—will be quiet over the weekend and all right by next week—

I didn't say—Thank You for the books—did I? Thank you is such a stupid worn-out way of saying what it ought to mean—tell me another way to say it—I can't think.

Alfred Stieglitz · [New York City] · [November 27, 1916] +

Talk about a whirlwind.—Today was one.—At a little after noon 12:30 I put on my coat to go to lunch—I had nothing for breakfast—at 6:40 I was still at 291 with the coat on—no lunch!! No sitting down—My head one buzz.—But it was a great day.—Nearly one hundred people. Painters & teachers—ordinary folks too—women & men!! Dabo, Walt Kuhn, & the like!— I don't know what's started the rush!—And Miss Williams, Clifford Williams, the one I was so anxious to have see your things.—She saw them. Asked for them. She was literally taken off her feet.—Claims that your work disarmed cold judgment. Or something of that sort.—It was so intense it didn't give one a chance to think! Great.—The one hanging in the show[172] she had a "fit" about.—Everyone is moved by it.—Those who "know modern art" & those who don't.— It's great sport to see how all people *discover* it.—And it's curious to hear what they "see."— It's a pity you didn't meet Miss Williams—you have some things in common.—She had hardly gone when Anita turned up—I wish Anita had met her & heard her—and we had a great time. —Anita brought your things.—Some at least.—And she left three that I picked out with me. —One is especially fine.—One other fine too. And one potentially great. One with some red in sky.[173]—I won't try to describe the one I like by far best—I'll photograph it some time & let you see that way.—I can't draw.—Not a line.—

—Your ears should have been *red hot* today.—Anita was splendid.—She says she is going to Baltimore next week—to work.—You'll hear from her soon—undoubtedly.—

—I had one interview after another—public of course.—I was famishing.—But there I stood.—To cap the climax at about 4:30 Mina Loy, an extraordinary creature came in.—Did you ever read any of her writings?—I printed the first in *Camera Work*.[174]—She arrived from Florence a few weeks ago.—She paints & writes, does most anything—everything—is very, very alive.—Is good to look at because of that aliveness.—Well, she didn't get away till 6:40. I suppose she'd still be there at 291 if I hadn't been so hungry & eager to get home to have supper.—She too spotted your drawing on the wall & liked it.—Immensely.—

—I wonder when I'll get some quiet moments again at 291—I have so many things I want to do—letters to dictate—some that should have been dictated weeks ago.—

New York seems madder—rushier than ever.—People are constantly coming in to drag

---

172. Lynes 64.

173. Possibly Lynes 134.

174. Mina Loy had published several poems in *Rogue* 1 (Apr. 1, 1915), 12; 1 (May 1, 1915), 10–11; 2 (Aug. 15, 1915), 10; 3 (Oct. 1916), 4; and 3 (Nov. 1916), 6; as well as in *Others: A Magazine of the New Verse* 1 (July 1915), 6–8; 3 (July 1916), 27–28. Stieglitz published Loy's "Aphorisms on Futurism" in *Camera Work* 45 (Jan. 1914), 13–15.

me out somewhere.—All sorts of "temptations"—I have to laugh.—Everyone wants me to see some show or other—As if I cared a rap about picture shows!—

—You are really fortunate to be away from this bedlam—so far away.—

At present it's nearly impossible for me to imagine the Lake & the mountains—And as I lie in bed—all quiet—wrapped up, chilly from the infernal cold I have—lying there waiting for sleep—my pillow in my arms—I sometimes wonder whether I'm still I—I sometimes feel as if I weren't at all.—A curious sensation.—

—You see at such a moment I really need someone to quiet that quiet—as at times you feel the need similarly—so you understand—

If it weren't for eventual sleep existence would become insufferable—beautiful as life is after all!—

Overtiredness I guess.—Nervous tension.—

—I haven't had any patience to read at night—& I should bathe but once in a great while—I'm not in order yet—I wonder when I'll be that again—

But it's comforting to know that there is really such a being as Georgia O'Keeffe.—It helps a lot at critical moments.—

Good Night.—It's still early.—But I'm going to bed.—

—Good Night.

Georgia O'Keeffe · [Canyon, Texas] · [**November 27, 1916**]

I know you're going to laugh at what I'm going to say—but I don't care if you do—

Another book this noon—Jerome Eddy[175]—and now I'm wondering what possessed me when I told you I wanted something on cubism—This is the eighth book this week—and it seems like so many—and I can't say anything because I said I wanted the last two—and I just sat here feeling sort of helpless—like saying to myself—

Dear me—what am I going to do about it—Then it seemed funny that I was so disturbed—had to laugh at myself—because—well—for one reason I know you would laugh—

It's really great of you to think of it—but I always hated folks to give me things—

Just can't help that—I know you laugh—

[November 28, 1916]
—It's another night—Tuesday night—and—why—I'm tired—

It's only 9:30 and I'm already in bed—I'm not going to write—I'm going to read *Faust*—

Goodnight.

---

175. Arthur Jerome Eddy, *Cubists and Post-Impressionism* (Chicago, 1914).

It's the same night—later. I wrote my nice sister[176]—she is really great—then I read—but all the time I was reading I wanted to read your last letter again—

—I just read it—

—Really—you are a queer man—aren't you—*NOT CRAZY*—just curiously real—

Maybe—I shouldn't have said man—maybe I should have said person—

It's very windy tonight—I wish I could be by you out there in the night—

I haven't anything to say—but I'd like to be by you because you seem—alive—and real—and human—

I've read your *Three Dreams*[177] a good many times—and always wonder—I'd get it out and read it again tonight but it seems so absurd because I know it—still I want to read it.

I sit here wanting to write you—just looking and not seeing—wanting to write—still my brain seems to be a blank—what do I want to write—

I suppose I'm a blank—a blank wanting to say something and of course a blank has nothing to say.—

Georgia O'Keeffe · [**Canyon, Texas**] · [**November 30, 1916**]

Thanksgiving—Nearly night

—Yesterday I started to mail you a letter—and found Wright's *Creative Will* outside my door—I didn't mail the letter because—I didn't want to—I had more to say—

Last night I read—today I read—

—I wonder if what he writes interests many people like it does me—It's ridiculous—the way I get so excited over it—

If only I hadn't seen him—He is so funny to look at—

Just the same—it's a darned good book—One time I don't agree—but I'll wait awhile—maybe I'll change my mind—I haven't finished it yet—interruptions.

The sister had a cold and I insisted on her staying in bed—You know—it is so queer to have someone around to think about—I've always been alone—Twice last night I got up and went over and looked at her—bothered about her—She is better today but took lots of time—Has been tinkering with clocks most of the afternoon—She has three going now—They had all been given up—She gets so much fun out of it that it's funny—

I hope he doesn't write many more books because—if he does—I'll have to read them all and I know I'll die—I'll just naturally burst—And it makes me want more than ever to live *three hundred* years—or more—I won't have time to get started on living before it's time to die—

Wright interests her immensely—

But dear me—he makes me feel so stupid—and everybody else so tame—Makes me want never to work anymore because my head seems empty—

---

176. Ida O'Keeffe.

177. Alfred Stieglitz, "One Hour's Sleep—Three Dreams," *291* 1 (Mar. 1915), unpaginated.

Then I shake it a little—and think—well maybe it isn't empty entirely—and I shut my teeth right tight and think I'll go at it again—

This morning I got up while it was starlight and walked over to the cattle pens— Saw the cattle come in yesterday—about five hundred two-year-old white-faced Herefords— The noise they were making was great—I climbed up on top of the fence—it's very high as fences go—watched them a long time—and the coming morning—They were afraid of me —open plains all round—town off on one side—daylight coming on the other—

When I got off the fence only two stars were left—I walked northeast—A train was coming way off—just a light with a trail of smoke—white[178]—I walked toward it—The sun and the train got to me at the same time—It's great to see that terrifically alive black thing coming at you in the big frosty stillness—and such wonderful smoke—When I turned—there was the sun—just a little streak—blazing in a moment—all blazing—

—I thought of you—

Supper—Tired—

The charcoal came—thanks—

I found my hat!

Be good to my little blue streaks[179] on the wall—I feel as if I ought to stand up in front of them and hide them from some of the eyes—

Goodnight—

The hand—reaching for warmth—what—does anyone ever get it—anyway it reaches to tell you—

Goodnight—

Alfred Stieglitz · [New York City] · [December 4, 1916] +

Monday Morning.—291.—I'm in my hat & coat.—I have just come in.—The day is gray.— At least the morning.—And the beginning is damp for it rained some last night.—And I was awake much of the night. Tossing about.—No special reason.

—Sunday went by all right. As usual the morning at my mother's.—In the afternoon we drove out into the country.—I went along to get some fresh air—& to sit there in the auto— to feel the rolling along—a restful sensation under certain conditions.—As we came home it was getting dark & I must have slept some minutes or more—The air & the rolling—& the having gone to bed after one on Saturday.

—And last night I went to see a brother-in-law of mine[180]—my wife's brother who is a sort of trustee for her. I had wanted to see him about several matters ever since the return from the Lake!—Important matters really—material ones.—So I went last night—alone.—And he

---

178. Lynes 128–130.
179. Lynes 64.
180. Either Theodore or Ernest Obermeyer.

& his wife[181] & I sat together till after eleven—so it was nearly midnight till I got into bed.—Perhaps the talk started my mind going on material lines—things that must be faced.[182] Of course nothing that I haven't seen for years & years.—You see I've had a great reputation for being very impractical—a visionary—dreamer—idealist—& what not—Perhaps I'm all that.—But somehow or other most things I see & others don't sooner or later happen.—It's hard to sit by & know one sees straight & let the "practical" ones make fools of themselves & oneself too!—

—But fortunately seeing no longer hurts as it once did—

—On Saturday night we were at the Provincetown Players—saw the third series.—One playlet by Kreymborg & set by Zorach[183] was splendidly done.—Mina Loy played the chief part. I wasn't able to get the book. As soon as I get it I'll send you a copy.—How about the play you were interested in—working for?—When is it coming off?—

Steichen was with us.—We sat & talked until nearly one!—

—Did I tell you that on Friday Duncan was in.—He was pathetically amusing, but I felt better about him than I had.—He confessed of his own volition that he had no real sense of humor. Yes, unfortunately. He has sold a painting, a large one, to Daniel—for twenty-five dollars.—And he sold a poem to *Rogue*—price not stated.—It seems to amuse (?) him that he is such a successful "business" man—I haven't seen the painting—it's an old one—he says it's no good. Demuth says: "It's a wonder."—Hartley says "it has something but isn't clear"—I haven't seen it. Forgot to ask Daniel to see it when I was at the gallery to look at the Demuths on Saturday morning.[184] Demuth's work has great charm—he has a personality—a fine one.—His work reflects all that. And I also stopped in at Montross's.—Bruce[185]—I had turned him down some years ago at 291.—He wanted a show here.—His work was thin & saccharine.—Then.—He has developed but the work is still very thin & saccharine.—It gives me the shivers—like a cold kiss would.—Montross has some Chinese work[186] too—It was quieting but I know nothing about Chinese work—I know I ought to & people refuse to believe I don't—but I really don't. I have not had the time to live with it—in fact & in spirit.—So I simply see it without being moved—except possibly pleasantly.—Perhaps I see more than many who claim they "just love Chinese things."—I wonder how much Montross really sees in anything he has.—What a life to lead!—It's his affair not mine.—

181. Either Bertha or Henrietta Obermeyer.

182. As the United States edged closer to war, many members of Congress, urged by temperance leaders, began to talk about putting forth an amendment to prohibit the manufacturing of all alcoholic beverages. If such an amendment extended to the production of beer, Emmy Stieglitz's income would be greatly diminished.

183. The third series of plays performed by the Provincetown Players included *The Two Sons,* by Neith Boyce; *Lima Beans,* by Alfred Kreymborg; and *Before Breakfast,* by Eugene O'Neill.

184. Charles Daniel opened the fall season at his new galleries with an exhibition of work by modern American artists, including Thomas H. Benton, Demuth, William Glackens, Hartley, and Marin; see "Many Exhibitions of Paintings and Prints Open," *NYT,* Oct. 22, 1916, *Sunday Magazine,* 18 (hereafter cited as *SM*).

185. Patrick Henry Bruce's "agreeable…fresh and stimulating" paintings were on view at Montross Gallery from November 21 to December 9, 1916; see "Art Notes," *NYT,* Nov. 26, 1916, E2.

186. An exhibition of early Chinese art, collected by A. W. Bahr, was also on view at the Montross Gallery; see "Art Notes," *NYT,* Nov. 26, 1916, E2.

—How are you this morning, after Sunday?—Your letters were great—I haven't read them again—somehow I'm keeping them to reread at some moment—I don't know the moment—or the kind—I know there are parts that made my blood tingle—made me feel as if I heard you breathing deeply—quickly.—And saw a half smiling half sad face.—Pale with a trace of flush.—And the hands very still—imperceptibly moving.—It's funny things one sometimes feels.—

—I have no idea what I'm going to do today—I wonder if I have anything to do.—Oh! Yes finish that letter.—And get some other correspondence off. None of interest.—

—I have been fooled out of my hot bath—wanted one for several nights—but haven't managed. Unless I can get a good long one I don't want any at all.—Perhaps tonight.—

—I guess I'll chase down to Brentano's & see whether anything "new" is out—magazines?—books?—

The sun is breaking through the clouds.—But the room here is chilly—dampish.—

Later.

That was a surprise!—Two envelopes—one & two—green stamps.—At noon, just before going to lunch.—Marin & Hartley & Walkowitz were going with me.—I ran aside—& read—!!—So you laughed at the number of books that deluged you.—And you don't like "presents."—I'm delighted you laughed—for I knew you would.—And as for "presents"— I know how you feel—I feel the same way.—But you'll never receive a "present" from me—no one ever has.—So why you?—But I understand—& you do too.—That's great.—How about your "presents" to me—every letter is that plus a great deal more.—You give yourself.—And I accept.—Gleefully.—Naturally.—Freely.—But as I've said: I understand.

—Sister has had a cold & you have been nurse.—I'll bet you make a good one.—I hope she wasn't laid up for long—Somehow or other it seems odd to think that anyone can be laid up in Texas.—You have given me such a feeling [of] vastness—of air—that ailments seem entirely out of the question.—But I guess where there are people colds & the like—& other ailments —will also abide.—Perhaps as disguised friends!—?—

—You like Wright's writings.—I knew you would.—Funny so many around 291 see primarily his weaknesses so can't enjoy his real force.[187] And he has force. He'll be glad to hear that I have found someone who *really enjoys* what he has to say.—I haven't seen him in quite some days.—

—I had a treat today—another besides your surprise—Hartley brought in some of his summer's work—Also the two that were at Daniel's.—It is very simple—very living. It seems to breathe.—Seashells in sunlight at the seashore! Their inner luster.—

There are some more to come in a few days—later work. And still a step forward he says.—

—So you were out in the starlight.—Welcomed dawn.—And you saw the big black locomotive coming towards you—the smoke—& the sun broke forth—shooting its rays deep into your being!—And I was with you!!—

187. Contentious and inflexible, Wright had an abrasive personality and alienated many of his colleagues with his hectoring; see John Loughery, "Charles Caffin and Willard Huntington Wright, Advocates of Modern Art," *Arts* 59 (Jan. 1985), 103–109.

Do you know that for many years I roamed about amongst locomotives—railroad yards —& photographed. Did you ever see the two pictures I made of that subject. One on a windstill August day just before a storm—the other in winter—snow.[188] Locomotives still mean a great deal to me—I am always spellbound by them—It must have been wonderful to experience what you did.—I never saw quite that.—

But why weren't you in bed? Asleep?—Of course it would have been a great loss to have missed what you saw—& felt—still I had hoped you were sleeping aplenty these days.—

Georgia O'Keeffe · [Canyon, Texas] · [December 10, 1916]

Sunday—Sunset.

I'd like to write you with letters about two feet high[189]—

But maybe that would be a bit high—

This morning—in a tearing northern and snow—blistering cold I started for the Canyon—I just got home—my hands a bit swollen from cold but it was great! In the Canyon I climbed. It was all rough—but it was great.

Wish you could see the tumbleweeds blow—they are round and just tear across the plains like mad—big ones and little ones—far ones and near ones—where there are fences —sometimes they hang singly—sometimes they just pile up—It is the tumbleweeds that mark the fences here—

—A stretch of fourteen miles of nothing after the last house till you come to the Canyon —a slit in the ground—sometimes three miles across—sometimes five or six—but it is great— and that darned wind—and the cold—It's all so big—such big washes—big hills—long drops —thick trunked scrubby cedars—hardy—old—strong—often broken or the soil all washed from several feet of the roots—but they don't mind—they are still green—

Wonderful distances—colors—all kinds—Isn't it funny—when I was climbing out— sat down all out of breath—looking back at it—in the fine—wild-driven snow—I love it— wish I could be with it now—I want it all—The reality of it makes me almost crazy—Isn't it funny—folks get color very like that on canvas or paper—but the darned things don't get me going at all—

It was great to go out there after Anne Brigman's photographs[190] yesterday—They made today better—and today made them better—Really it was great of you—How do you manage to do things at just the right time like that—

I want to go to 291 tonight so much that I have sort of a notion that if I'd go out and down the street a way I might find it out there—

188. Greenough 277–280; Greenough 284–286.

189. O'Keeffe wrote this letter on a sheet of paper 24 × 19 inches.

190. Brigman's photographs were reproduced in *Camera Work* 25 (Jan. 1909); *Camera Work* 38 (Apr. 1912); and *Camera Work* 44 (Oct. 1913). In a letter of December 1, 1916, O'Keeffe confessed to Stieglitz that she "got absurdly excited" over the copies of *Camera Work* he had sent and that Anne Brigman's photographs "almost took me through the roof."

—When I came home—so cold—riding into the setting sun—I sat down by the radiator to thaw out—

—I finished reading the *Camera Work* about your "expulsion" from the Camera Club[191]—read most of it yesterday—my time isn't my own—so—I often have to leave things when I don't want to—really—I can—

—You enjoyed it—in a way—didn't you—291 must have been just boiling—what's the word—when you feel—What's the use in talking about it on paper—These two numbers of *Camera Work* make me like it better than ever before—but I believe the number that has given me most pleasure for the longest time is a 291 number[192] that you gave me during the Marin show that year—I had a great time with that—I went that day because I wanted to go to the woods and New York has nothing like woods that I know of except 291—

I feel rough and wild like the wind tonight—I'd like to take hold of you and handle you rather roughly—because I like you—

We rode miles in the Canyon besides climbing—it was all rough—and it was great—

FROM THE END of 1916 through 1918, the political and economic turmoil caused by World War I became a frequent topic of conversation between Stieglitz and O'Keeffe. In early December 1916, when German chancellor von Bethmann Hollweg issued an appeal for the end to hostilities without citing specific terms for peace, Wall Street investors panicked, fearing financial instability would occur in the aftermath of the war. On December 13, with the news that the Allies might accept Germany's offer, more stocks were sold than in any single day since 1907.[193] Throughout January 1917 the market continued to fluctuate wildly. On February 1, 1917, Germany declared that it would no longer follow international law and would sink any merchant vessel, neutral as well as enemy, that strayed inside a prescribed zone. A few days later, the United States announced it had severed diplomatic relations with Germany. As the situation grew more unsettled, Stieglitz became increasingly concerned about his family's finances and his ability to keep 291 open. He had to make a decision soon about the gallery, as his lease expired in the summer of 1917.

Alfred Stieglitz · [New York City] · [December 14, 1916] +

It's a great morning. I have just come through the Park. All is white. The snow is falling silently. There is no wind. Myriads of black spots—autos—are moving silently through the snow. One hears no sound. A sense of great activity—a sadness.

—Peace sought in Europe!—Consternation in American business quarters—a panic

191. John Francis Strauss, "Mr. Stieglitz's 'Expulsion': A Statement," *Camera Work* 22 (Apr. 1908), 25–30. In 1908, Stieglitz, a long-standing member of the Camera Club of New York, was asked to resign because many of the club's trustees felt his organization, the Photo-Secession, was undermining their efforts.
192. "What Is 291?" *Camera Work* 47 (July 1914).
193. See "Peace Offer Sends All Stocks Down," *NYT*, Dec. 13, 1916, 4.

in Wall Street—all because Germany spoke for peace. And we are frightened at peace—as we are frightened at war. Always frightened.—But there are thousands—hundreds of thousands of Americans—who felt rich day before yesterday—are actually wiped out today. Values cut into two. Because of peace talk.—I wonder whether you know anything about "Business"—about "Wall Street"—all they symbolize.

—And so the clean sad snow—& the moving black spots downtownward have a symbolic meaning to me this morning—have always had—but only more so today.—

—I'm at the Savoy Hotel—the dentist is around the corner—there are still thirty minutes until my appointment.—

—The day yesterday did turn out to be quite a wonder—a wonder spiritually—in fine quiet things happening—at 291.—All so clean.—And no one quite knew as I did that they were happening—although when Zoler left he had felt it somewhat—& Walkowitz too.—In a material way I paid a big price for I saw my little investments—I haven't many—I have not much money, very little in fact—shrink in value considerably.—But disagreeable as that may be it does not rob one of laughter—nor of anything else that's fine.—My only thought is that others—without knowing—are more affected by my loss—than I am.—Loss!—The word sounds all wrong.—It is not loss.—

—Duncan came in first. The sun was strong.—The snow on the roof had disappeared— I was glad he came.—We had an intimate talk—He went away quite buoyant.—His Christmas will be pleasanter for having come.—And mine too.—Although I don't believe in Christmases —I merely use the term symbolically too—as you understand.—

—Then I rewrote that letter I had been wanting to write so long. And it's right now & goes to France today.—I wonder whether it will be of use.—It's an important document—for many.—Not really for me—

—Towards dusk Duchamp turned up. The young painter of the *Nude Coming Down Stairs*.[194] —For a long time this hour between us was to happen—It was a marvelous hour— in the dark.—He & I talking. Zoler & Walkowitz silent.—Duchamp is a very fine simple fellow. —Of today. Modest—clean cut—as spiritual & clean as Duncan—Very clear—not dogmatic— broad—gentle as a woman—still masculine.—There was not much said—& yet what was said meant very much.—It was not about himself—or very little—& little about myself—But it was all about ourselves! And as he walked out he said that he had seen the pictures in the front room & enjoyed them immensely.—And never says anything he does not mean.—And then he pointed to your drawing next to the Marin & he said: "That's very fine." And I rushed for some of the framed things & he said: "That woman!"—And simultaneously we said: "The proof of the sincerity is found in the two"—(The blue one[195] representing one—the others the other). It was a very great moment for me.—I can't tell you how great!—

And when he had gone & the place was silent—no lights but a gas jet—there was a religious purity pervading all—

---

194. Marcel Duchamp, *Nude Descending a Staircase, No. 2*, 1912, oil; see Arturo Schwarz, *The Complete Works of Marcel Duchamp* (New York, 1997), 254.

195. Lynes 64.

—And it is snowing today.—Silently.—

The night had been good—somewhat restless.—I have friends who have been terribly hard hit by the panic & I couldn't get them out of my mind.—They say nothing. I haven't seen them—But I know what's happened.—It's awful to see so much!—

—It's time to go to the dentist—I forgot to say "Good Morning" to the Lady.—

Alfred Stieglitz · [New York City] · [December 21, 1916] +

Thursday Night—

The morning looked like snow.—Gray & murky.—The streets were one mass of slush. —All day continued threatening—slushy—

—I had my bath last night.—A boiling one in a roasting room. I came near falling asleep in the water—just caught myself.—It's like dope—the heat—boiling—broiling— roasting—the sense of water—the nakedness—the aloneness in a tiny room.—Dream possibilities—No dreams—

And I slept some. And was warm.—But I also tossed about much.—

—The day today.—Until after eleven I was alone. Still sorting—making order—a deadly occupation—

Marie came then & we had a talk—just talked about all sorts of things.—I took her to lunch.—And we talked.—I talked—She listened.—And she listens heart & soul.—And it is good to feel that a listener really listens—can listen.

And as I came out into the street I caught sight of a headline: *Smash in Wall Street.*[196] I dropped in at a broker's in the Waldorf to see what was happening. The crowd was great— men & women—stocks gone to smash—worse than ever.—Values shriveling up into nearly zero—And we, the prosperous country.—Frightened by the specter of peace—people panic stricken.—Money is a necessity but outside of its necessity it never meant anything to me in the sense that it means so much to nearly all people.—

Well, I won't go into all that.—I am thinking harder these days than I ever have—I see more clearly—both the complexity of existence as it is, today—& the wonderful simplicity it must be some day—*when people see. And someday they will.*—But it is a lonesome job to see too straight!—

As I came to 291—it was nearly three—there were two letters.—Both had green stamps.—A letter from you.—A proof of an article Traubel wrote about me & which is to appear in his paper *The Conservator.*[197] —

—Your letter.—It came at an opportune moment.—They always do.—Your letters.— And what you wrote—all of it—fitted my condition.—You seem to have been in a similar condition to the one I'm in.—Tired.—Overwrought.—Yearning for rest.—For sleep.—For sympathy in that if it can't be had in life!—

196. On December 21, 1916, *The New York Times* front-page headline read: "Stocks Fall Again on Peace Efforts—Prices Break Violently with Heavy Liquidation in Industrials."
197. Horace Traubel, "Stieglitz," *The Conservator* 27 (Dec. 1916), 137.

Yes, the mountain—snow & cold—no tree—a long long tramp—a silent one.—

—Wouldn't it be wonderful if a man & woman could walk into the snow on mountain tops—look at the sky—& frozen cold warm up long enough through the faith in life that the man fructify the woman.—

And man & woman & child fall to sleep together—

On mountain tops.—The snow as bed—the sky as cover!!—

—A mad thought but a pure one.—The thought came to me as I read & as I thought of life.—

Living is so intense these days that it becomes unbearable at times—One thinks of sleep & nature.—

Eternal rest.

—So Anita found me older.—She said the truth.—I am older.—Much older.—Look older.—Feel older.—I'm glad she wrote it to you.—Why you should know—why it shouldn't mean something to either of us I don't know.—

—I am glad *Faust* is with you—so close—yours.—

And I have to laugh at poor Clive Bell.—I never would have sent him if it were not for that lecture of yours.—Bell belongs to the "literature"—Etc.—

—You seemed to have had a similar Sunday to mine.—Amusing coincidence.—

I hope you haven't had that headache.—But being a woman you are probably damned to those periodic headaches, frightful ones, that so many women must stand.—And you with your nature are damned with the worst kind.—

Anita likes home.—That's good.—I wonder what she'll do.—Red ink!—When I was seventeen I often used red ink!!—Not since.—It makes me laugh. I was always terribly in love then.—

—I wonder if you'll like what Traubel wrote.—It's very alive.—It's funny that so many write about me now.—An Italian paper is writing—& a Jewish one too, I'm told.—I feel as if all were obituaries—I never feel as if I were reading about my real self.—

Is there a real self?—Isn't it simply a whirlwind of forces seeking equilibrium—

—Again I say I'm very glad you have *Faust*—so near to you.—That it means so much to you.—

If I could only see you in that room of yours—*Faust* before you—reading—watching the face—see you falling asleep—I unseen—Stealing away—Into the night.—

Wonderful night—Wonderful wakefulness—Night—

One ought to sleep during the day—When one is as mad as I am.

—This afternoon—towards five someone came in, a man I have known for twenty-five years!—Kerfoot, Zoler, Walkowitz, & Benn were present.—The friend asked me why I was so hard on America & never had a good word to say about it.—Well, I wish you could have heard me.—I'm sorry tens of thousands didn't hear me.—America never had a better friend—real America—not the flim-flam America—I hate patriotism—I hate all that seems so holy to so many "good" & "blind" Americans—Well, I let loose for fair, telling him what I felt as an American—as a man of the whole world—

I was all aquiver when I was through—I could not have spoken as clearly as I did had I not spoken to Marie today—& had your letter—

When all were gone—all except Walkowitz, he said: "They'll never understand—But every word you say is right."—Or something to that effect.—I'm full to bursting—

—This country will never come into its own until we have had some terrible common suffering.—Europe is chastened—values are being *reestablished*—and we?

Only through real suffering—common suffering—will eyes open & with them— *HEARTS!*

—Then brains will have a living value.—

Good Night.

Georgia O'Keeffe · [Canyon, Texas] · [**December 21, 1916**]

The nakedest thing I know of is an angleworm—and I feel that I've rather given myself that quality—to you—

I hate angleworms so tonight I'm not going to talk about myself—

I must tell you of the sister—Her latest adventure has been motorcycling—not trailing on behind—running it herself—She has simply gone mad over it—

But last night it snowed—it's bitter cold—everyone left yesterday for the holidays— she was a bit depressed—but hit on the bright idea of going shooting—She got a gun and off she went about five o'clock this afternoon—I followed about fifteen minutes later—when I caught up with her she had shot a bird—a prairie owl—She said she hadn't shot for such a long time that it never occurred to her that she would kill it when she aimed at it. Thursday night.

[December 23, 1916]
GOSH!

She has been out again this afternoon and came home with two jack-rabbits—shot two more but couldn't carry but two so is sending a boy for them in the morning.

Some way it doesn't seem right to me—She says she hates to shoot them but it's so exciting to see if you can—She went skating this morning—her ankles are weak though and it makes them hurt so this afternoon went back to the gun.

Folks looked cross-eyed at me for letting her do things like that—but I don't see why not—if she wants to—She is so excited that she is limp. At supper she would lift things— expecting them to be as heavy and they would go up—Every little while she tells me about another part that's tired and hurts—and if it isn't that it's some incident of the afternoon—

Just now she told me about another bird she shot—It was a long way off and she didn't think she could hit it—then she was so sorry she stopped and buried it—

She rode home on a load of baled hay—she was just so tired carrying those rabbits. She just now told me that I don't know what it is to be tired—Even her hands hurt from carrying the rabbits and the gun and the cold—

I'm afraid she will shoot herself but guess it isn't any more likely than that someone will shoot her through the wall—

I don't know of anything to do with her but to let her do as she pleases—It's very funny. So much better than having her wildly excited about—oh lots of other things she might like.—

Funny I haven't wanted to go out—I've been at home two days now—Thursday was the first day of vacation—and I've just liked being alone—Have been working—

Your letter today is great—the only remark I made to myself while reading it was when you said you wondered what the things I am doing now look like—

I said emphatically—Like Hell—

Then later at dinner—I was thinking about you and I said to myself—

GOSH! but he is great—

Then I thought to myself—I don't like that word but what am I going to say—I object to the coarseness of the word but I like its expressive feel—

We need some new words—or is it my poor taste in putting them together—it doesn't matter of course but I feel a deficiency in the English language when I want to say—no—express GOSH—it expresses what I mean but has a ring I don't like—

The other morning I was pulling on my stocking and stopped—just looking at space —remembering what you said about Leo Stein's use of words—and I thought—yes—I could use them better if I wasn't so darned lazy—As for you—there really doesn't seem much excuse for my writing you at all—you get it without my saying it—

Really you're great—

I wish I could see Walkowitz's things. I've always had to fight with them you know— I would see something—often I didn't know what—most often in fact—Still I wouldn't give up —There was just something I didn't get and I knew it and it aggravated me—

Funny the way I was so glad he was at the Lake with you last summer and I didn't know why—

Your *Camera Work*[198] came this afternoon. A box from my blond lady with it—I didn't open hers because I knew she wouldn't want me to but I did open yours right away—

I thought there must be a Stieglitz *Camera Work* somewhere and wanted to ask—and I wanted to ask for your photographs of engines too—You see—I don't ask for everything I want. I undoubtedly would have in time however—

Great—

I like the engine in winter best and the steaming horses[199] next. I haven't looked at it much yet—I don't know why but I am saving it—

It's very much you—You are really here—a lot of you—not all of you—I wouldn't

---

198. Stieglitz inscribed *Camera Work* 36 (Oct. 1911) to O'Keeffe, writing: "For sometime I have been wondering whether I should send you this number of Camera Work or not—(perhaps I sent a copy before I don't remember—but I doubt it)—I don't know why I hesitate—Perhaps I'm not satisfied to appear before you quite in this form—The number is over five years old—The pictures are dated—There is a snowstorm raging—I love snow—Green stamps are in my mind—they are the symbol of a very fine spirit—Life at its purest—So here goes the number to Texas. Georgia O'Keeffe—'291'—December 15—1916" (Department of Photographs, The J. Paul Getty Museum, Los Angeles).

199. Greenough 284–286; Greenough 92–96.

have known you without the letters—Something in both that isn't in the other—I like it.—And you know I like it—why need to say it—

Someone else I'm glad to know is living and walking around is Marin—He's like a good drink of clear cool water when you are very thirsty—

I must tell you about that Picasso drawing too—Anita sent me a *Camera Work*[200] with it in last year—I had seen it before somewhere—don't know—maybe the drawing itself—But I liked it so much I could hardly stand it for anyone else to look at it and still always had to laugh at myself—I hardly let anyone see the book for a long time—even yet have scruples about it.

Wish you would break that cast[201]—

Funny I had been thinking about it—You see it was way last summer I wanted to show it to you—now I don't know—it seems out of place—It was almost all lost in the casting—I didn't allow for that when I made it—But I know your place back there in that little room is full—no need of that standing around—I had another—funny—my nice sister[202] liked it so I gave it to her. Two or three people wanted to buy it—last summer but I didn't want to sell it—

When I think of folks looking at it I want to shrink up to nowhere—

Wright?—Sometimes I enjoy being stupid and contrary—at the *Forum Exhibition* last year I enjoyed not speaking to him—not asking him questions—just because he looked as though he thought I would[203]—Now I'd like to talk to him but I don't want him to see my little white thing[204]—It had a purpose not concerned at all with his confounded theories of form[205]—

Yes laugh!

It's such a pitiful little thing—I don't believe it can stand being out there—

Anything you please though.

Goodnight.

It's great to be having vacation. I'm not Christmas mad—it doesn't excite me at all—

Except—Maybe the world seems bigger and emptier then than at other times.

Again goodnight.

---

200. Pablo Picasso, *Drawing [Standing Female Nude]*, *Camera Work* 36 (Oct. 1911). Pollitzer sent O'Keeffe either *Camera Work*, special no. (Aug. 1912), or *Camera Work*, special no. (June 1913).

201. Lynes 66. On December 11, 1916, Stieglitz told O'Keeffe: "Plaster is unsympathetic material. If you could touch it with your hand it would lose its disagreeable quality—that is the material would gain life—or rather assume life."

202. Ida O'Keeffe.

203. Willard Huntington Wright and Morgan Russell organized the Forum Exhibition of Modern American Painters, Anderson Galleries, New York, March 13–25, 1916. Although their stated purpose was to counter the attention currently given to modern European art by focusing only on American work, Wright antagonized many artists by insisting that Synchronism, the style of painting pursued by his brother, Stanton Macdonald-Wright, and Russell, was the pinnacle of modern art.

204. Lynes 66.

205. In *Modern Painting: Its Tendency and Meaning* (New York, 1915) and *Creative Will*, Willard Huntington Wright insisted that the greatest modern art succeeded only through the development of form by means of color and that art must eschew mimeticism.

Alfred Stieglitz · [New York City] · [December 26, 1916]

I have just come in—291—the day after Christmas.—It's as if I had been away from this little place for many days.—An eternity.—It seems to be the only place—outside of the Lake—where I seem to feel all at rest—glad to be alive.—It's a terrible feeling to feel so isolated elsewhere.—

—The room is especially cold—no heat in several days—& the cold has penetrated the walls—

—Quite a mail—I have only opened one letter.—One with green stamps.—I don't want to see any others for awhile.—I'm not fit for them—no matter what they may contain— I am in no mood for well intended kindness—I hate kindness as an intention—Words—Good will as a profession—all that sort of conventional rubbish—

—Yes, your letter came in the morning. Just as you wished it.—And I'm glad it's here. —It rings so true—it is like the morning sky itself. And you a little girl.—I know exactly how you feel.—And I see you standing before me—head about reaching my knees.—I feel mountain high this morning as I sit here.—And uncannily quiet.—

These two holidays took much out of me.—I hardly spoke a word for two days.— I tried hard. For I hate to seem unsociable.—The more I tried the less I could.—And I know such silence is trying to all those who don't understand it. And if they understood—would I be silent!—

—So you are painting & painting—the one thing. No mentality—? Well, I am glad you haven't *too much* of that.—You have enough.—Just enough.—Too much would do to you what it does to so many women who would be finer if they had just a *little* less mentality.—

—To get all of *Faust*.[206] —No one in the world has succeeded.—No man—nor woman —why should a little girl?—You are a great little girl—with a heart big enough to hold the sky in it—& all that sky signifies.—If you had the mentality you'd like to have perhaps you'd fear the sky & so rob yourself of what is more precious than all the mentalities in the world.—And robbing yourself rob me—& others too. For there must be others to whom your existence must mean something very wonderful.—There is Anita.—I know what you mean to her.—I know how her eyes light up when she says: "Pat."[207]

—It is all so funny.—Those feelings which exist. The beautiful ones.—

—After I mailed you that letter yesterday I tried to read some of Joseph Conrad— *The Nigger of Narcissus*. Wright insists I read Conrad. Did you ever read any?—I read his *Victory*.[208] —

—There is a foreword in this book which I want you to have.—So I'm sending you the book.—

—I read awhile & then it grew so dark I stopped & sat in a chair not far away from

---

206. On December 14, 1916, O'Keeffe told Stieglitz that she was reading *Faust* but had "the most profound disgust for my own brain—It's reading so much better this time—but I keep seeing places where I could get much better connections if my darned head had anything in it."

207. Many of O'Keeffe's friends from her youth, including Anita Pollitzer, called her Pat or Patsy, in playful reference to her Irish ancestry.

208. Joseph Conrad, *The Nigger of "Narcissus": A Tale of the Sea* (London, 1897), and *Victory: An Island Tale* (London, 1915).

the Christmas tree—my daughter always has had one—a huge one.—And as it grew darker & darker—night—& the silence was so comforting—I sat there conscious of some glittering things—a form of tree against a window dimly lighted from the street lamps way below—under the tree suggestions of package forms—I closed my eyes.—And I was back to my first tree— to my daughter's first tree—she was three months old—& many trees came into my mind.— And all they meant to me—

So you see as you were in a little girl state—I too was in a little boy state—I never really seem to get entirely out of it. That's my disease I guess. Incurable!!—

—Disillusionment. Dr. Weichsel calls what I have gone through.—I have to laugh.— How little he sees me.—I have not had illusions—although I believe in them.—Most people have illusions about themselves—that's the rub.—

—I wonder how you are this morning.—You wrote you hoped that this would be a great day for me.—It already is.—The Engelhard work is coming down at noon—I don't like to take it down—but there is an end of "shows"—Walkowitz goes up.[209]—To open tomorrow. —It will be a beautiful room. And a great surprise to so many who have been damning me for "*exaggerating*" his importance![210]—Always the same story.—I should be enthusiastic about mediocrity!—And should wait with my enthusiasm about—

Oh! HELL—I'd like to blow up the whole of Fifth Avenue with all its humbug—& all the people who go with it!!—

Isn't that a fine Good Will feeling?—

A little girl would be afraid of such sentiments—but a woman—a *Real Woman!!*—? It's beastly cold here—my feet are like ice—& my hands stiff.

Walkowitz has just come. That means I must get ready to get busy!—

Here's to the *Little Girl!*—

Would she like to hear some fairy-tales? Taken from life—

Georgia O'Keeffe · [Canyon, Texas] · [December 30, 1916]

Another day is almost gone—and for all of it I've been on the fly—

Claudie mailed my letters this morning—Then when they were gone—while I dressed —I didn't want to get up—only the knowledge that I could wake myself with cold water made it possible—I like it very cold—and I like it very hot—but neither are good for me—I never get in it very hot—but sometimes simply can't resist the cold—This was a morning when I just had to freeze myself—couldn't resist it—

---

209. Although Stieglitz had originally planned to close the exhibition of watercolors and drawings by Georgia Engelhard on December 20, he extended it to December 26, 1916. Recent Water-Colors—Provincetown, Lake George, New York, Maine— By A. Walkowitz, of New York, 291, Dec. 27, 1916–Jan. 17, 1917.

210. A few days earlier, Stieglitz excitedly reported to O'Keeffe that Walkowitz's new work "took Zoler's breath away.—And Demuth's too today." He continued, "So many of my 'friends' & others have always guyed me about Walkowitz & Hartley— believed they were not what I 'imagined' I saw. Well, there is a surprise in store for all these wiseacres.—I'm amused" (AS to GOK, Dec. 13, 1916).

While dressing—making my bed and doing little things—I stopped several times—looking out the window—The only way to stop that letter[211] now was to telegraph—

Stop It—No sir—I won't—

Later I was sitting on the floor—leaning against my bed—could just see my head in the mirror—I was hunting for a book—stopping to look at other things as I looked—reading here and there—and I came across what Hapgood says in "What is 291"[212] —

—My tutor in my mind—It was then I looked up and saw my head in the mirror—and instead of my head—I saw myself as I have, often—dropping my clothes in the morning—just me standing there screwing my hair up tight before going to the bathroom—just a woman with nothing on but her skin—

A letter like that only minus even the skin—And—I wondered how I dared—still it wasn't daring—it came along just as the next thing to do—and I did it—feeling so damnably free—

What's the matter with me anyway—

Tell me honestly—do you suppose I'm crazy—I don't know—and don't care—but for what I said to seem so natural—seems so queer—

And all day I've been like a whirlwind inside—

I got some cloth—black—and went to the dressmaker—I'm very much in need of a dress but didn't expect to get one—hadn't even thought of it in fact—it's so much trouble—

And when a little "spring chicken"[213] you'd call him had followed me around downtown in and out of different places till he stopped me alone and asked if he could come up tonight—I almost laughed in his face (just met him day before yesterday—and he said it's funny I never saw you before—and I said I never go to town). He looked so queer when I said he couldn't come that I changed my mind right quick and said he could—

But goodness—what will I do—I'm feeling sixty miles an hour—and he looks about two miles an hour—It will be very funny—

I could speed him up only—darn it—I teach school—He has been to Yale and your East—home is here—hasn't had enough of city to like it here—doesn't know how nice it is—

Funny—so very funny—Wish I could eat supper with you—and talk—I think we would laugh very much—

[December 31, 1916]
Sunday morning—I feel like beefsteak—Not like eating it—Broiled—not done at all in the middle—

211. On December 29, 1916, O'Keeffe told Stieglitz she had sent Arthur Macmahon *Creative Will,* by Willard Huntington Wright, and had written him "such a funny letter.... It will give his Scotchness an awful jolt I'm afraid—no not afraid—Some things I've been wanting to tell him for a long time and never wanted to enough till yesterday."

212. Hutchins Hapgood, "What 291 Is to Me," *Camera Work* 47 (July 1914), 11.

213. Rector Lester was the Yale-educated Randall County attorney from 1916 to 1920. On March 10, 1917, O'Keeffe admiringly wrote of his "big healthiness, beautiful head," but she added, "if only I could slap him and change the personality—so absurd to be physically attracted to him, just wanting the kiss."

Tuesday night.

—I've been sitting here a long time wondering how to tell you how amused I am. There is simply no way unless you just get it.

The little fat woman[214] and I fell out—it was a most amusing talk—And that funny stupid man[215] was here again—it was about his coming that we fell out—

—Imagine anyone telling me they objected to anyone coming to see me—I'm not really over the surprise yet—She is too funny for words—

So instead of sitting in her old house we rode for nearly three hours—Her objecting made his coming interesting—

And way out there in the Canyon draw I made him get out and walk—He didn't like it but I did—It was really wonderful out—only he spoiled its wonder—but in place of wonder and star-gazing it was ridiculous—

I just want to yell when I think of it—

Can you imagine me shut up in the car—standing still for—oh it seemed ages—arguing and objecting to—beefsteak with really nice hands—(well shaped—makes you think he ought to play something) objecting to an arm round me and hands on me—

Why—I wonder that the car didn't laugh. It was so funny I couldn't get mad—

He is really nice inside—and because I laughed so—he couldn't understand. After several attacks—that I paid no attention to—I couldn't help shivering—and saying I hated to be touched—

Then—I thought of you—how funny it would seem if you could see and hear[216]—and laughed so hilariously I had to tell him why—He got it wrong of course—and asked if I were going to marry you—I told [him] goodness no—and that you were married years ago—more arguing—

I wonder if that car isn't laughing somewhere out in the dark of the barn—

I almost forgot to tell you that I found out since the first time that he is prosecuting attorney in the court here—whatever that is—brother is president of the bank I go to and father[217] one of the biggest ranchmen around here. I never ask questions so I didn't know—

Folks are so funny—What makes them so funny—And—that letter to Arthur!

And the little fat woman—she would ship me in the morning—scandalized—It's too funny—or is there considerable irony in it.

Goodnight. I feel as if the expression on my face would be idiocy if I'd look at myself—

214. Susie Ackerman.

215. Rector Lester.

216. Stieglitz responded on January 13, 1917: "I had to laugh at your 'escapades.' Yes, I wish I had been there—To see & hear. I'm sure I would have smiled.—And still it's rough on your male friends.—They can not understand you—They do not know that it is that very fact that fascinates them. Men are much more simple than women."

217. Lewis T. Lester, a prominent Hale County rancher, founded the Stockman's National Bank, later the First National Bank of Canyon; his son Commodore Dunlap Lester became president of the bank in 1920. Lewis Lester was also one of the principal supporters of the establishment of West Texas State Normal College.

[January 3, 1917]
Wednesday Morning—

Your letters were fine this morning after last night—

And the world softening—

Seeing last night again—the wind is howling but it's warm—and sitting here listening I can see it all so clearly—It's nine A.M.—

The car run up next [to] the fence at the side of the road—horses—runty western breed—strung along the flat space between us and those terribly bare hills—they were there because it was sheltered—a lavender kind of moonlit night—rather windy—I out for contrariness more than anything else. I had on three garments—all as thin as the law allows—besides my coat—It's amusing that you too like being cold—He couldn't imagine anyone liking to be cold—

I too only like certain kinds of kisses—certain kinds of touches—I cannot understand the other kinds of kisses—I can the other kinds of touches—there is something pathetic about them—

He only wanted to touch me because I was a woman—I distinctly did not want to be touched because he wasn't a particular man. And still wanted to put my arm round him and my hand on his cheek simply because he was so everlastingly man—and I was sorry—and he wouldn't understand—

So it was funny—hilariously funny—You would have had a good time on the back seat—too bad you couldn't be there—And he wanted to send me wine and I had visions of the old lady sniffing at my key hole—

He insisted even to the front door—think how her porch was polluted—

Still—I knew the woman inside—overfed—not exercised enough. He doesn't know it so can't help it—

I'm never going to eat any more and am going to walk miles every day.

Goodnight.
It's the end of a quiet day—your letters—or the spirit of them with me all day has made it fine—quiet—They give me a curious kind of balance—a conscious control of myself that I like.

Just to know that you are—

—The little girl again after being the wondering woman—Little girls are selfish—thoughtless—I'd like to be rocked to sleep close to somebody—

Goodnight—
Wednesday night—

Georgia O'Keeffe · [Canyon, Texas] · [January 10?, 1917] +

Your letter—makes me want to say—Sorry—yes so sorry for it all—Not for the things you tell me in words so much as the things I feel—and I wanted it this morning—No I didn't either—I wanted you—

I was so sick—excitement always makes me sick—and I gave that darned talk Monday night—and I got so excited and they all got so exited that we kept at it right over all the time allotted to the man who was to come after me and over an hour past time to go home—It was very funny—and I've talked it to individuals for hours at a time since—So funny—At the table —in the halls—in the offices—funny how interested they all were—Really amusing—maybe because I'm so interested—and I've hardly slept for three nights—drinking coffee without knowing I was drinking it—but trying to be still—not even to think—This morning my first class was at 11:35 so I didn't get up until nearly eleven—

However—last night the sister was hunting for my paint brushes to clean her gun—put my pallet on the bed—then sat in it—So this morning got up extra early to take the dress to the washwoman—so she found your letter to me and waked me by throwing it at me in the dark—

I wanted you but was too sick to get you out of the envelope till after nine o'clock—
GOOF

Yesterday there was other excitement too—that is—things to decide—It's Summer School—I don't know why but I sort of feel that I'd be a backslider if I didn't stay here and dance to the music—even if I don't like it—Someone else would take my work and get it all mixed up—but I'll have to work twenty-four hours a week—I have sixteen now—it will be for nine weeks—and I don't see how any white woman can do it—it doesn't seem to me to be worth it—Still if the others do it I hate to back down—

I don't know exactly why but I want to see the whole year round—Isn't it funny— I seem to want to try it just to see how people do things like that—queer isn't it—then too— money—but I put that consideration last—I'll be out of debt by summer but won't have enough to live through the summer—so all round working seems best—When I think of not working I have to laugh—My aunts[218] would raise an awful time if I didn't go to see them—and I don't want to go—and there doesn't seem to be any place I want to go—The sister will have to go to see the great-aunt[219]—and—

Why I never felt so lost and funny as I do when I imagine myself with three months and a half ahead to do as I please with—I wouldn't know how to behave—No place I want to go —No one I want to spend it with—I don't know—right this minute I think I'd like to spend it under the tree—or working with you—not saying a word—either of us—Still—you some way telling me the story.

I'd like to go up in the mountains by myself and stay—but I'd be afraid—
So what's the use of it all—

That nine weeks—twenty-four hours a week—makes me feel still sicker—but it's so funny too—it makes me laugh—anyway—I told old "Lanky" Allen—he teaches Mathematics and has charge of the Summer School—he walked home with me today—it's fun to talk to him —he looks so—sober and overworked and lean and lank—I always pat myself on the back when I've been able to make him laugh—and today I made him laugh several times—I told him I guessed I'd try worrying along with the rest of them—

Then when I came in—here was a letter from Virginia wanting me to make out the

218. Probably Alletta (Ollie) Totto and Leonore (Lola) Totto, Georgia's maternal aunts.
219. Probably Jane Varney.

material for their bulletin and wanting me to come back—funny I don't want to go—I must be crazy—the way I am enjoying being away from people I know—

Old Scott is so funny—and I'll miss seeing him—

It's almost like summer today—was yesterday too—

—I hate plans—so it aggravated me to have to be thinking so much about summer—it's so far away—maybe it will never get here—or will it—does it always come—

It does—doesn't it.

Alfred Stieglitz · New York City · [January 16, 1917] +

Tuesday Night—

This morning I sealed up this letter to you.—And had stamped it & had it in my overcoat pocket to mail it at lunch time. And at 12:30 I was ready to go to lunch—coat on & hat.—At four I was still in hat & coat. In the front room.—A lot of very important—exciting people—one after the other—& together.—Henri, Bellows & Randall Davey with Kroll.—A very interesting three-quarter hour with them—I of course leading the talk—Think of it Bellows volunteered at one time: Say, you, Stieglitz, & Henri will go down (why down? not up?) in the history of the fight for art in America as the two real champions!—It was intended as a compliment & was sincere but I was inwardly amused—But it was really great to have these big strapping men—for they are alive & men—standing there—listening to me.—And I spoke out as I can when I'm really interested. And I was greatly interested.—The Walkowitzes are bringing all—Academicians too. Some very sympathetic figures—old men—hoping to become young again.—

And there were alive women & men standing about—listening. Who they were I don't know.—You know 291 on such occasions—the atmosphere.—

The sun was shining brightly. I had awakened from my dead calm—A letter with green stamps was handed to me as I was talking.—I put it into my pocket.—It felt very alive in there.—Well, people came.—Miss Williams—I had a great hour with her.—She's really a genuine soul.—She wanted to know what had happened to me that I was so awake—so alert—so keenly direct—I told her I had been through several purgatories since she had been at 291—so why shouldn't I know some things I hadn't known before.—

And an old woman, very old, Mrs. Sanborn came in. A marvel.—Enthusiastic as a kid in spite of being all shriveled up. She wants to live forever.—Loves life.—I asked her why: "Because I love my husband." Her remark sounded like a trumpet signal.—Sanborn is an unusual man—a great philosopher & teacher.—I think they are Quakers.—She occasionally brings a child around.—She was very much moved by the Walkowitzes—threw kisses at them. No, she isn't dippy—just shows what she feels—Miss Williams stood at the door watching—listening.—It was as wonderful to watch her face as to listen to Mrs. Sanborn.

—There were many others—some good looking girls—some stupid ones—a constant going & coming—telephone calls—my "cruel" friend full of kindness again—Steichen—Zoler

—Walkowitz—Marie—I didn't get a chance to dictate a single line!—It was after six when I got away.—Hungry. Thirsty.

I did steal ten minutes to chase through your letter.—So you had the lecture.—I wondered.—Great.—I can see you—& hear you—and feel your great throbbing living excitement—I'm sure you did a great work.—In fact are doing a great work down there all the time.—The very wonderful livingness in you is contagious—

—So they want you for the summer.—I know how you must feel.—The struggle between conflicting impulses—the desires—even if you want nothing—you are so infernally human that it is painful not to know you free as a bird—And yet all you are experiencing makes you what you are—*A GREAT WOMAN!*

—What use?—What use am I?—What do I care about history—Adulation—I'm really not ambitious—but it's all life—struggle—mad—Mad—MAD—We want so much we want nothing.—That's our trouble.—

—But what we want except being free yet "*close*" I don't know.—Specialists would say: "Neurotics" & look well satisfied & wise.—"Ics" & "Isms" can go hang.—

—Does Arthur want you to marry him?—Or does he want you to become a toned-down free soul for your own good.—I do not say this ironically.—Quite on the contrary.—He seems to care a great deal for you—he can only care in his way—You like him—but you wish he were less *New Republic*-like—I know just what you feel—I can't advise you—or help you —Your problems are your own—Only you can solve them. If there be a solution.—Lord, I'm talking like some old teacher or busybody—well-wisher—

—Next summer.—I haven't the slightest idea of my own future.—There may be many changes.—I don't know.—All is uncertain.—More so than ever with me.—And since I'm married I never was certain of anything. Not from one day to the next.—You have no idea how I've lived—

—The summer!—I do not think ahead if I can help it. Of course you have to think of it —are forced to.—I believe in seeing things *through*. Everything once started—if at all pleasant. Only in that way can one keep one's spirit really free.

—No, Turner is not to have one of your babies—they are thriving well where they are. —So why upset them?—Don't you fret.—

I'm not looking at them the last week or so—But I see their backs—!!

—Well, it has been a great big day—& the night is clear & cold—

I'm going to take a boiling bath & then to bed.—

Good Night.—

And I'll read your letter too before going to sleep.—Good Night.

I'm really ashamed to send this stuff to you—but I guess there is no shame in me. As I have told you before: *You Need Not Read*—

I'm so terrifically awake I don't think I'll close an eye tonight.—

The water will be great—

Good Night—

Georgia O'Keeffe · [Canyon, Texas] · [February 4, 1917] +

Sunday night 9:25—

I've been in bed all day—The room was quite dark when someone poked your letter and some others under my door this morning. I waited till the sister came from breakfast—even though I knew by the size that it was yours that came under first—and even then I didn't read it right away—coffee—and I felt like—less than nothing—and covered up again—

I don't sleep on a pillow—so I could see that letter over there on the edge of the bed—

I began to wonder what the writing looked like inside—that's almost as much as what you say—no not that much but it's sort of a key—

So I opened it and read the last edition—It is like a wonderful spring day in Virginia —when the air feels as if you can take handfuls of it and toss it about—and the woods—black tree trunks—wonderful green—sunshine—violets everywhere—birds—and such sunshine —slow and dreamy—such lots of green moss—and I know where the first arbutus blooms— and I know places in woodsy marshes where one can pick all the yellow jonquils several folks can carry—and snowdrops too—

Queer that the last part of your letter brought me that—but it was—I can't exactly say great—but I liked it—so I read the rest of it—

Then lay very still all morning—till nearly two I guess—This afternoon I read some —Nietzsche—He's a wonder—I didn't read much—watched the sun go down—just a plain yellow sunset and one star came out—

I wanted you when the yellow light came in and it was all so quiet—the day had been very windy—just to be quiet by you—while the sky turned from yellow to cold white moonlight —you would have liked it too I think—

—The windows were very wide open—I hadn't enough over me and didn't know it till I accidentally felt the coldness of my own skin—my face on my arm—and I liked the coldness so that I didn't cover up then till the sister came from supper and shut the windows—

She has been riding horseback and is very stiff—can't cross one knee over the other— it's very funny—

Tomorrow—among the forty eleven other things I have to do—we are going to move.[220] I tell her she is going to do it—and she laughs—I'm curious to see how she will manage. I'm not even going to pack my own things—I know it's a risk—I'll probably never find anything again but I guess it doesn't matter much. We will have to build fires—more of that later.

How am I?

When I got up to write this—and turned on the light—I had been in the dark—and I got back into bed before half the first page was written—

But I'll survive—I always do—

Now I just remember that what I was going to write particularly was—

Of course it's no use to say it because you know it but I'm going to say it—

---

220. Georgia and Claudia moved to the home of Douglas and Willena Shirley on February 5, 1917.

(The sister just came in and announced that the next time I stayed in bed she was going to tag herself with a big red tag saying "My sister Georgia O'Keeffe is indisposed." So she won't have to answer so many questions—) She's in a very foolish humor—

What I was going to say was about you and your letters—

Why say it[221]—

I write you when and what I want & when I have time—Not fair for you to have some of your moods with me?

You think for me and for yourself too—maybe more for me—you need not be afraid—

You've helped me see many things more clearly—made the world seem much bigger—made many things that seemed out of gear seem more right—I too have always been a fool—you have made me more certain [of] that—

It's all just that I've always been alone or almost alone in thinking and doing—and it's hard to be sure you are right when it's that way—

Can't you feel sure that knowing you as I have right now—these last few months—has been great—that I needed it—but I only need as long as you would give.

Goodnight.

[February 7, 1917]

Wednesday morning—

Again I'm up and too tired to dress—Last night I was so tired I thought I'd go crazy—Didn't even seem to dare to go to bed till very late—And I don't seem much over the tiredness this morning—

Monday was about the busiest day I ever spent—But it went fairly well—the play[222] too and after that a party—a colonial party—very funny—and the blond man[223] came down from Amarillo—and stayed over yesterday—We rode miles—I was too tired to move—There was a picture show (I hate them—only go about three times a year)—it was *King Lear*[224]—and I almost died with all the other folks—The night was still and almost like day—

He's just a comfortable sort of man—you just don't mind him much—

The *Seven Arts*[225] came last night—was here with a lot of other stuff when I got home—I looked at it and wanted to read it but I just couldn't—I read the notice of Hartley's show[226]—That was all—thanks. I liked it.

---

221. The night before, O'Keeffe wrote Stieglitz: "You know before I knew you a little I just did things—said things—Why—just because I wanted to—They seemed honest to you—frank—and your telling me so has made me sort of self-conscious about it—till I almost feel that you have dared me to say things—and I don't dare follow my other impulse—which is probably almost as strong—to not say them sometimes. You have made the impulse to say them strongest—and it makes me wonder—where it will land me."

222. O'Keeffe helped the drama club build and paint sets and make costumes for their production of *The Romancers: A Comedy in Three Acts* (New York, 1899), by Edmund Rostand, which they performed on February 5, 1917.

223. "The blond man," or "Blondy," was Don Willard Austin, a forty-year-old married man from Amarillo. In subsequent letters O'Keeffe also referred to him by his yellow car or "chariot."

224. O'Keeffe saw the silent film of *King Lear,* released by Vitagraph in 1909.

225. *The Seven Arts* 1 (Feb. 1917).

226. Marsden Hartley's Recent Work, Together with Examples of His Evolution, 291, Jan. 22–Feb. 7, 1917.

Blondy says he will stay over till Saturday—or come down again then if I'll go up to Amarillo for the weekend but I think I'm not going—I've had enough—I feel bored to distraction with people and things—I'm ready for my own company again and lots of it too.

Maybe one reason is because I got rid of that trash—I sent it to you Monday—it has been tied up without outside paper for a month or more but nothing made me send it before —Some of it is very funny—ridiculously funny—

You needn't open it at all unless you want to—I don't care—Only—open it alone— will you? I don't know—why—It's all very bad[227]—I don't see how I had the nerve to let anyone see it—

There are two packages—I know you will scold about the way they are done up— IT'S — ALL VERY BAD—

Maybe they will get lost—I'll be rather glad if they are—

It's bad too to tell you how tired I am—so maddeningly tired—but maybe I have to be tired to wake up—

In spite of the physical fatigue—I feel better—somehow—somewhere.

It's nearly eleven—I must dress and go to school—

Alfred Stieglitz · [**New York City**] · [**February 6, 1917**]

Good Morning.—I have just come in—291—Hodge[228] is lighting the stove.—It's about twenty-five degrees in the room here.—New York is an icy grip—but the sun is out bright & clear.—

—It's the first morning in some days I feel quite human—half alive again.—Perhaps it's due to my use of my imagination—of your permission—your last letter which I received on Saturday evening just as I was leaving 291—& which letter I think I have read a dozen times since—several times aloud to myself—so that I could hear—

I think it is the most wonderfully beautiful letter I have ever received.—So full of great honest girlish womanhood.—

—The last week has been a desperate one for me—I wrote you several letters—but I haven't sent them—the first time I felt I couldn't—they would only make you suffer needlessly —without giving you anything of all that that I would like you to have—Perhaps—You see my "friends" had put me through the mill for fair for weeks—one after the other—& I stood up & thought it wasn't taking very much out of me—then came the crash in Wall Street[229]—series of

---

227. On January 14, 1917, O'Keeffe told Stieglitz that her latest work was "a queer bunch of stuff—Maybe too much me to be Art. It just seemed to scream me and I *hate* it."

228. Hodge Kirnon, born in Montserrat, West Indies, operated the elevator at 291. He was later a member of the Harlem Renaissance and publisher of *The Promoter*.

229. On February 2, 1917, *The New York Times* reported that the "official announcement of Germany's intention to resume her ruthless submarine warfare, coupled with reports that the United States was virtually 'on the verge of war' came as a shock yesterday to the stock market which had been looking for important developments in the line of peace"; see "Big Drop in Stocks Agitates Wall St.," 1.

crashes in fact—they affected me & those about me materially—& still I laughed & went ahead as if nothing had happened—Then came the War—close to us[230]—What I had seen coming day by day—nearer—as I had seen other things developing—And you know how intensely I visualize everything. Sanely—neurotically—And I haven't a soul about me who isn't leaning heavily on me—depending upon me in fact—all others have gone.—And so in days like these I simply seemed paralyzed—I saw & couldn't move.—I yearned for one moment of complete forgetfulness—of complete relaxing.—Bed seemed the only real sympathetic companion—& even that not completely.—I wanted—

    —Well, your letter finally gave it to me—Last night after arranging a lot of paper, the first real activity in days, I went to bed.—And I took you in my arms.—Closed my eyes.— I don't know what happened.—Nothing.—I don't know.—But I felt so at peace that I fell asleep.—It was a queer feeling the naturalness of it.—Natural because you felt it natural.— And I slept all night & I awoke with my arms folded as they had been when I went asleep.— It was daylight.—And I smiled at the wonder of the world.—

    —It's queer all this—the naturalness of it.

    —Your letter.—You were in a state similar to my own—devoid of sensation—hollow inside[231]—a little brain at the top—laughter to amuse others—No feeling to work—

    —But you fortunately have a job—I wish I had one.—That's what I miss.—I'm out of work.—

    —In times like these work is more necessary than ever—I can't even photograph— much as I'd like to—Paper is going to waste—plates & camera have been ready for weeks— I simply can't & I want to—And now of course with war staring us in the face a reality has set in. Theorizing gets on my nerves.—Those near me don't seem to comprehend—not here at 291—nor at home—The American is a spoiled child—a wasteful one.—There are but few exceptions.—Life has been too easy—hard as it may have seemed.—

    —The lease for 291 is up on May first.—Within a few days the landlord will be around wanting to know—If there is war it would be madness to load myself up with a lease—It has been mad all along but then something was gained by others & myself through that madness —but with war I hope all my friends will be at actual work—with no time for dreams— & theories—theories that are unworkable—even if all men were super-gods! I too want to get busy—at anything.—Of course I don't believe in war—& yet I know war must be sooner or later—in some form or another—as if there were war everywhere in a more insidious—more diabolical form—than the wholesale slaughter of people.—

230. On February 3, 1917, President Wilson announced that the United States had severed diplomatic relations with Germany; see "Congress Thrilled by Historic Speech," *NYT*, Feb. 4, 1917, 2. On Sunday, February 4, numerous stories appeared in New York newspapers applauding Wilson's decision and predicting the inevitability of war; see "Comment of the Morning's News-paper on President Wilson's Announcement of the Break with Germany" and "London Rejoices in Our Decision," *NYT*, Feb. 4, 1917, 3, 5.

231. Noting that she had not painted for nearly a month, O'Keeffe told Stieglitz on January 26, 1917, that she was going to a country club with friends from Amarillo for the weekend. Asserting that "I'm stupid—I might as well do something stupid," she continued: "When I'm just a wooden woman I'm always most entertaining to most of my friends—It will be fun in a way— for I'll forget how hollow I am."

I have always gone my own way—alone most of the time—I feel lost in days like these.
—If it wasn't for the daughter I wouldn't mind so much[232]—

I'd like her to stand on her own feet—relying on no one but herself—She hasn't had half a chance—.

I'm going to start packing things down here—It will be a huge job—& all the things in storage[233] too I'll have sent here to go through—a raft of stuff.—I have been wanting to do this for years.—Now I have to.—You see the stuff has value from many angles—& yet—?

For the present & for some time to come no one will be interested.—I am not thinking of the money value—that is insignificant although in days like these even it may become significant—No one can tell. The rich will be a little less rich—the poor still poor.—It's the middle-class that pays the price.—And I belong to that.—I have always deliberately forgone pay because we had a little capital—& I wanted to give all my time & all I had to the people—rich & poor alike—not for them—but for myself. I knew what I was doing.—But I did not know as I know now many things about human relationships—I did not know that my way of seeing, of feeling—were really so different!—

—On Sunday I was at the church—the Weichsel gathering[234]—I am sending you a catalogue.—It's a fine big hall—It was filled—The walls were filled with the exhibits—they looked like innocent babes.—I got in late—& I sat near the door—so that I could see no faces—only backs—except Kerfoot's who was up on the platform—Chairman.—He opened the meeting.—Spoke splendidly.—If another number of *Camera Work* ever sees daylight it will contain his remarks.—He then invited discussion. "What had the Photo-Secession Gallery done for Modern Art."—Think of it—the imbecility—& to make it more ghastly ridiculous that that particular subject should be under discussion just on the first day everyone was thinking of war as a reality!—Striking home.—But true to my promise I put in an appearance.—As luck would have it the man in front of me—I don't know who it was—asked why the Photo-Secession Gallery introduced French & European Art & had neglected American—& then he started about "Art" & "Racial"—In short rot.—I jumped up & must have spoken fifteen minutes.—I didn't remember when it was over what I had said. It was a jumble—a ramble—but it did come from within—*way down.*—I told him that for years I had been looking for the racial in America —thus far there was no American race (the Indian, yes); I told him people did not know what they felt when they talked for they usually felt nothing; I told him I knew from living hard that

232. Beginning in late 1916, Stieglitz started referring more openly to his family in his letters to O'Keeffe. For example, on December 29, 1916, he confided that "the day ended meanly—at home.—Mother & daughter—not agreeing.—The reverse in fact.—Some day I'll tell you about my 'family life.'—It is not a very 'happy' one—for any of its members I guess.—No one's fault—just different temperaments—too much reasonableness on one side—too little on the another—the child a mixture." He continued: "I've always claimed the only crime I've ever committed was to be party to the bringing of that child into the world.—I have done many 'foolish' things—but this is my only crime—as I see crime."

233. Stieglitz had a large collection of paintings, prints, drawings, sculpture, and photographs by leading European and American artists, as well as many copies of the periodicals he had published (*Camera Notes, Camera Work,* and *291*). This collection was housed at 291, in his home, and in storage in New York.

234. In early February 1917, the People's Art Guild, headed by John Weichsel, organized an exhibition of modern European and American art at the Parish House of the Church of the Ascension in New York. Lectures were given every Sunday "to make clear to the plain man the intention" behind this new art; see "Art at Home and Abroad," *NYT,* Jan. 28, 1917, *SM,* 7.

there wasn't a soul in the audience that given me forty-five minutes with them at 291 I couldn't come into contact with. I knew that no two in the audience understood each other's language —not even each other's "yes" or "no" as only the rarest of individuals seemed to feel anything when saying "yes" or "no."—I told him that as I saw the people sitting there it was nothing but a mob—& mobs did not think—nor did a mob feel for itself—I told him I was equally interested in Germans, French, English, Italians, Chinese, Russians; Blacks, Whites, & Yellows—as individuals; I told him that the Photo-Secession Gallery [welcomed] the individual to share my loaf of bread. That if one came, each had a half—if ten, each a tenth; if a million, each a millionth. That of course the latter meant virtually no bread. But that "291" was wondering all the while whether not one of that million would create another loaf of bread—possibly ten, ten loaves of bread—And perhaps some day the million would each create their own loaf of bread!—As for art 291 was not interested in art unless it meant life itself, life in its finest.—Etc. Etc.—

And when I stopped—& I stopped with the bread picture—Kerfoot called upon others —only one little woman got up & in a whisper announced that annually for years she had come to New York & found that at 291 she always came away with a great feeling of "hope."—Not another soul had anything to say. And the room was full of people who had used 291 —

To me it was all very significant—No different than it has always been—

If I say anything—nothing is said.—291 is not an academic topic yet!—

—Kerfoot came up to 1111 (my home)[235] in the evening. I asked him whether I had said anything.—I didn't remember a thing. I was too full of other pictures. The war.—This country. —He said he had come up especially to tell me: It was all right. And that it was magnificent because I had told the crowd I looked upon it as a mob!—

—I'm sure if you had been there something would have happened.—You are the boiling over kind like myself—unafraid—I think many wanted to say something—but I guess I staggered them.—I heard Weichsel was furious.—I warned him that I was unaccountable.

—Well, I'm glad that stupid piece of business is ancient history.—I guess I'm less understood than ever. But who cares? Not I.—

—Do you know that new version of [sketch of Lynes 116] has been standing before me for the last few days. Great isn't it? Somehow or other I seemed to fish it out without being quite conscious of it.—I think it was on Friday morning as I came in. After a night of absolute wakefulness—the third in succession.—I had to see something which would make me feel that life was still life—

And with the result that this expression of yours stood there before me.—It made me feel as if I were in some wonderful church listening to wondrous music—& didn't see a human being—Simply the feeling of great space—full of livingness—And since then it has been standing there—a friend.—So you see how once more that work of yours is helping me over critical moments.—

—I wonder how you are.—Of course I mean by that it would be fine to hear the tangible voice—to tangibly see the white hand—you say it's pink now—& that you are looking very healthy—

---

235. Stieglitz, his wife, Emmy, and their daughter, Kitty, had lived at 1111 Madison Ave. in New York since 1898.

—Are you growing fat?—

At last the stove is giving off some heat & my feet are getting warm.—

—The other night I went home on top of a bus in a night with the thermometer near zero—& the wind sixty miles an hour hitting one squarely in the face.—My moustache was ice.—It was great—

And that night I took a boiling bath—I hoped to find sleep—but in vain—

—I don't read.—I've been at a dinner or two—always lively—like you—having fun—But I wonder whether you sometimes feel your heart as if it were going to stop—

Tonight we are invited to the Kneisel Quartette—supper first—A Schonberg sextet is to be played.[236] Do you know Schonberg's music at all.—The ultra-modern?

—Friday there is another performance of the *Meistersinger*.[237] I hope I can go. If war with Germany who knows when I'll be able to hear it again.—And it does mean so much to me —that music. Why is the human race so mad these days?—Why do I ask a question I can answer best myself?

—I had you in my arms last night & you gave me sleep—Great rest—like the stove is warming me now—& the sun rays are playing at my feet—It is impossible to conceive that darkest clouds are gathering overhead—above the blue—or are they gathering in the hearts of all of us—hard to conceive in a moment of peace like this!—

—The hand is pink, you say.—And the body—White? or pink too?—But whether white or pink—I'm glad there is a hand—a body—

The wood is crackling in the stove—

Georgia O'Keeffe · [Canyon, Texas] · [February 10, 1917] +

Saturday morning—

I've just come from the post-office—Have to get my own mail since I've moved—

—Your letter and package—and another—as I went in the door I saw Lester coming and thought I'd get out before he got there—but in my hurry dropped all three as I almost bumped into him in the doorway—it was funny—

The sun is hazy—and I took a path across vacant lots—to read—I read—I don't know —I guess about three pages and—couldn't read—any more—

I don't know—I seemed to be choked and I couldn't swallow—

And I came in and cried and cried and cried and—only shed about three tears—

And I can't read any more—I don't know when I can—and I picked it up and sat there holding it in both hands a long time—so very tenderly for fear I'd hurt it—

I wanted to kiss it—it seemed made for lips—but I didn't—because it's only a paper—I still want to hold it in my hands and I still want to kiss it—

236. Stieglitz heard the Kneisel Quartet perform Arnold Schönberg's string sextet, "Verklärte Nacht"; see "The Kneisel Quartet," *NYT*, Feb. 7, 1917, 11.

237. Richard Wagner's 1868 comic opera *Die Meistersinger von Nürnberg* was performed by the Metropolitan Opera, under the direction of Austrian-born Artur Bodansky, on February 10, 1917.

All the world greets you this morning. It's very quiet—The smoke goes up straight—
On my way to the post office I noticed many birds—

    It's a dream—closed eyes—a great quiet that I send you this morning—

    The words look queer but the dream is past human—

    I just this minute noticed that the other letter isn't for me.

Alfred Stieglitz · [**New York City**] · [**February 11, 1917**] +

—It's Sunday once more.—Very clear sky & cold.—It's afternoon.—I'm at home.—1111.—

    —Your bundles arrived yesterday—What am I to say?—

    I'd love to take both your hands in my two hands—& just stand before you squarely
—face to face—& look at you.—You are a magnificent creature,—The work?—It staggers—
it is gigantic—it is so full of elemental—it is tremendously expressive—The Creative Forces—
Woman—Man—Mountains—The Night—Sky—Clouds—

    And your *Self-Portrait!*[238]—You everywhere.—Walkowitz & Bluemner & Zoler were
looking too yesterday—all with great amazement—and intense feeling.—

    —It was a terrific day yesterday.—I left home unshaven. I hadn't the energy to shave
—When I got to 291 it was about twenty-five degrees there—icy—the letter-carrier brought
the packages—I reached out for them as a starving parched person reaches out for a piece
of bread & some water—I had hardly energy enough to cut open the twine—I unrolled the
pictures—My great big Woman Soul I felt like crying but couldn't—Do you know the feeling?
—It's awful.—The last ten days have been too frightful on top of the weeks before—

    And as I sat gazing at your work—Wright (the painter) came in. He's very human.
—But as he was talking I hardly heard—And as he left others came & they came until after
six—Crowds all day.—I didn't get to lunch—Fashionable people—many rich—I don't know
where they all suddenly came from—& why they came.—All classes—& they stood about in
the front room as I was storming—telling stories—I guess they must have thought me mad.
I have been telling them that I was about to burn up thirty-five hundred copies of *Camera
Work*—about to close 291—They listened—stood there—made remarks—gasped—some
seemed as if they'd like to get out, yet were afraid to leave—

    Perhaps I bared my soul too much—I can't tell you how it was—what I said—but
I know it was a great day—a very great one.—For me.—Some took me aside & told me I
shouldn't do anything "rash." As if I ever did.—It is "rash" to die when blood has been flowing
for years from open wounds—& no more is left—& the heart ceases beating. One then is
pronounced "dead."—Died a sudden death!!—

    —I wish you could have been there somewhere to hear—you were there—I was fight-
ing for all that's living—fine in the whole world—Not for death—not for yesterday—Just for
all that is—so wonderfully magnificent—for what 291 really stands for—

---

238. Stieglitz's installation photographs of O'Keeffe's April 1917 exhibition at 291, reproduced in Lynes, appen. III, pp. 1110–
1111, indicate that he is referring to Lynes 99. However, O'Keeffe noted in *Some Memories of Drawings* (New York, 1974, 1988,
unpaginated) that the drawing was a study of a friend asleep.

—And when all had gone I looked at your work again—Great heavens—how blind the thing called "human" is—a few exceptions.—No matter what may happen—if I have to give up the little place your work will be on the walls when I close it up.—It would be a fitting end.—I know of nothing quite as fitting—quite as expressive of what I feel—have always felt.—

No wonder you haven't been working for awhile.—After such an orgy of expression —such a tornado of letting-go!—

—How you have developed!—Yourself intensified a thousand times!—

Power—Color—Vision—Elemental Force—Greatest Delicacy—Intensest Passion—Killing Love!!—

—I didn't go to the *Meistersinger* Friday Night.—I couldn't get up steam. So I went to my mother's.—

—It just strikes me that the people yesterday—& at the church last Sunday—must really think me crazy.—Perhaps I am.—Raving as I do these days.

Tomorrow is Lincoln's Birthday. I have an appointment to lunch with Murrell Fisher & a Danish poet (a fellow who sails around the world for sport!)—& Cosgrave, Editor of the *World, Sunday Magazine.*—All want to "see me."—I wonder what for.—And later on Belle Greene, Pierpont Morgan's Librarian, is to come up.—All were there yesterday.—I wonder what they want.—To "save me"—?—

—Oh yes, on Friday afternoon Marin dragged me off to a game of billiards.—It was a change.—But it seemed a funny one.—The Hartleys are still up.—Marin opens up on Wednesday.[239] —

—I feel a little better today—not so infernally nervous.—Not so on edge.—I wish I had brought a picture or two of yours home with me.—I'm going to have a few put under glass to have them here at home.

I wonder where you are just now—

Laughing I hope wherever it be.—

What a courageous creature you are.—What a coward I am by comparison!—

Georgia O'Keeffe · [**Canyon, Texas**] · [**February 16, 1917**] +

Friday morning—

It must be nearly five—I haven't slept a wink—the curtain flapped against the window and I just wasn't sleepy so I got up—got the *International Studio* and read Wright's article[240] —and looked at some Holbein miniatures[241] reproduced in it—I've always liked Holbeins and always liked them the same way—funny—I change my ways of liking most things—wonder why I don't change about that—do you know?

239. John Marin's Recent Water-Colors (Country of the Delaware and Other Exercises), 291, Feb. 14–Mar. 3, 1917.
240. Willard Huntington Wright, "Modern Art: Walkowitz, Monet, and Burlin," *International Studio* 60 (Feb. 1917), cxxxii–cxxxiii.
241. Wright, "Modern Art," civ, 166.

Then I read Dreiser's article in *Seven Arts*[242]—great—funny—the way some of it hit right on what I've been thinking—The *Courses of Study* we have been working on—

I told them they were trying to make everybody alike—and they said they guessed they were—it seemed to be the thing to do—and I wondered—and then—I don't know—lately I've been thinking I'd go and tell Mr. Cousins that I'm on a bum cog in the wheel for turning out what they want to turn out—but he would think I am crazy—You see I feel like a hypocrite pretending to belong in that wheel at all—

And just tonight—

It's this way—Sunday I caught cold—and Monday I went to the Canyon and Tuesday after my first class I came home and went to bed—and almost died for a couple of days—sore throat—headache—couldn't breathe—ached all over—eyes—and the doctor was sick too —so—

Anyway—It's the end of the quarter and this morning—no it was yesterday—it just seems the same day—I got up and went to school because I just had so much to do I had to— and after supper I just had so much to do that I wouldn't come home and do it—went [to] Hollands—that's the awful drug-store—There are always loafers—It's really absurd—And— why—I didn't know till I got home what funny things I had said—all students—but so foolish —I just said some things I wanted to—and it didn't sound like a cog in the wheel—and old red-headed Heyser almost turned handsprings out the door once—and little Mattie B's[243] eyes almost popped out—

And—I was thinking here when I couldn't sleep—

—What's the use in pretending to have flat feet and pop eyes and a Sunday school disposition when you haven't got them—

And I could just see Mr. Cousins laugh at me if I went and told him he better get someone with fallen arches and nearsighted pop eyes in my place—

The head of the training school[244] is like that and I know she will stay here till she dies. —She fits—

I feel like holding the lid on a boiling kettle—

She would scold the boys outrageously—be horrified—says it better—if she had heard the noise they made coming up the street with me—a crowd on their way to basketball practice. Clearing the streets because they had faculty with them.

Gosh—I'd like to be a green balloon going up into the sky—blue sky—and—burst—!

[February 18, 1917]

Sunday morning:

I'd like to have some very white—rather smooth sheets of paper about a yard square

242. Theodore Dreiser's "Life, Art and America," *The Seven Arts* 1 (Feb. 1917), 363–389, is a rambling critique on "the moral [and] social drift of America." Lamenting the abysmal quality of American education, especially for women, he deplored the prevailing assumptions that American women are "considerably more than human—angelic, no less," and condemned the fact that "the sex relationship" was "too vile a thing to be mentioned or even thought of."
243. Mattie B. Hume was a junior at West Texas State Normal College.
244. Possibly Mary Lamb. Beginning January 1917, O'Keeffe taught a few classes a week of elementary-age children in the Training School.

to write you on this morning[245]—and I'd go to the printer and get them only it's Sunday and I can't.

I got up and went to breakfast—then for the mail with a pretty little pink and white—girl—brown hair—blue eyes—

Mail wasn't open yet so we went on to Hollands—Fred[246] was there in all his shining glory—and two others—quite as amusing. I think they are being specially nice to me because they want me to go to a dance they are having tomorrow night—It's hard to get faculty to go to dances—and still quite necessary—

One of them—Davis—(Beverly[247] says he has sixteen silk shirts and nothing to do but be good looking)—insists that I go to breakfast with them tomorrow morning—and he is coming around after me—whether I go or not—but he hopes I'll go—

We all went for the mail—Fred's not talking much this morning—looking off—thinking—But he insisted on looking very carefully at the letter that pleased me so—your letter—

That's the way things trail along—

Then I came home and read it.

You know—besides the night I was awake all night—I haven't had a minute to myself all week—except about an hour yesterday—and that hour—I took a gun and a box of bullets—and went out on the plains and threw tin cans into the air and shot at them—The sister and I. She went on hunting afterward but I only had the little time—

Last Sunday—after writing you in the morning I think—I came in after supper and wanted to write you again—but it seemed so foolish—and I lay on the bed by the window—quiet—all alone—watching the sky turn from daylight to night—many stars—just full of stars—and I remembered your star story[248]—

It's queer—the way I find myself—sometimes—seeming to feel into space—for the little one I wanted—and there is always an element of wonder in the fact that I haven't it—I seem hardly to be able to understand it—

And all the week—so busy—still—thinking—

And—because of what I was thinking—wondering if I ought not give up my job—Some way—I feel today—no. It's a great place to work—No traditions—the whole thing—the whole institution—just beginning—started to build it seven years ago yesterday.—

—Why I'd rather work here than anyplace I know of—and maybe I'm not such a misfit as I sometimes feel—

I've said some scandalous (according to some folks) things in class this week—way off from art—or maybe the very substance of it if it's life—I don't know—I know the class was astonished—but they seemed to enjoy it—Still I wondered—would the sober ones of the place think me off my track—

---

245. O'Keeffe wrote this letter on strips of white paper 17 × 5 inches.

246. Fred Theodore Heyser.

247. Beverly B. Sportsman was a senior at West Texas State Normal College.

248. Stieglitz subsequently sent O'Keeffe a poem he had written, titled "The Stars Are Playing in the Skies"; AS to GOK, Mar. 29 and Apr. 2, 1918. He later retitled it "Portrait—1918" and published it in *Manuscripts* no. 2 (Mar. 1922), 9.

And it occurs to me that something besides those sober ones may help the whole thing along. I don't know—I'll stay another quarter anyway—

Sunday night.

The wind has blown a gale all day—it started while I was looking out the window after reading your letter—I guess I sat there a long time with it in my hand—

The dust blowing has made the sky seem a little yellowish—it shakes the house.

What can I say to your letter—most of the day I have watched the wind—and wondered—

I didn't want to read—started to several times but—as many times found myself looking out the window—not seeing much—but fascinated—too windy to go walk—

Wish you could hear the wind whistle—

Again—what can I say to the letter—The work—my stuff—I'm glad it means something to you—to me it seems so bad that I cannot tell you how glad I am to be rid of it—

—Above all—that it quiets you—I am glad—

That is what your letter makes me want most to do—

Can you understand how much without my trying to tell you?

I went to sleep here—On again for the next week—

Alfred Stieglitz · [New York City] · [February 22, 1917] +

Good Morning—It feels fine to sit next to the stove which is crackling with wood & blazing away—The Park looked stunning as I came through it on the way to school—a new mantle of snow—dry snow—& the sky a steel gray—with warm traces in it. Few people & autos for today is a holiday, Washington's Birthday, but the daughter's school holds court all the same as school began so late in the autumn owing to the infantile paralysis quarantine in New York.[249] —And here I am at 291.—It's so quiet.—So clean.—

I only got back from Philadelphia[250] at two this morning.—Left for there at ten yesterday morning.—

Before going to Philadelphia I was down here yesterday to start the cleaning woman & to attend to odds & ends. The ride to Philadelphia was restful. The roads along the railroad were muddy—there was spring in the air—although the rivers were covered with thick ice— I enjoyed the Pennsylvania Station in New York—Walking through it—I hadn't been in it for I don't know how long. It is a favorite of mine—inside—the iron work—the feeling of space & directness—the outside is a fright.—

249. In September 1916 schools opened late in New York City because of the large number of cases of infantile paralysis there; see "The Public Schools to Open on Sept. 25," *NYT,* Sept. 12, 1916, 22.

250. As he had done for the past five years, Stieglitz went to Philadelphia to judge the annual photography competition at the John Wanamaker department store on February 21, 1917. Stieglitz and his fellow jurors, Steichen and the artists Arthur B. Carles, Charles Grafly, and F. Vaux Wilson, hung only fifty-five of the more than twelve hundred photographs submitted and awarded first prize to Stieglitz's protégé Paul Strand for *Wall Street;* see "1917 Spring Exhibitions," *American Photography* 11 (May 1917), 310.

—In Philadelphia Carles & Steichen met me at the station—We went to Carles' studio. I wanted to see his work.—I liked particularly a nude he did.—Part of the painting is very fine. He is primarily a painter who likes his material.—He is a fine fellow—In the Academy show he got a prize this year. Of course prizes are absurd.—And he is to teach there too.—I'm glad for his sake that he is at last getting a little encouragement.—In seven and a half minutes we did the "important" Academy show.—Saw Bellows' Temple Gold Medal picture—(Fine enough as an illustration but atrocious in color. He has no idea of the meaning of color.) Next to it hung a Kenyon Cox (Ye gods! you should have seen it—Talk about wooden dolls—they are the quintessence of life compared to this work of—?)—& flanking him a black portrait by Chase.[251]

—The hanging committee certainly did a great stunt in aligning these three pictures—

The whole place gave me the creeps—its cemetery atmosphere—

Awful this "art" game with all its hocus-pocus—officialdom—deadness—pompous snobbishness—The air felt good.—

—Lunch at Wanamaker's. Were you ever in that huge affair?—We were the guests of the place!—Before judging their Annual Photographic Contest.—Carles, Steichen, Grafly (the sculptor), & Wilson (the illustrator), & I were the judges.—Walking through Wanamakers seemed like seeing a Belasco show[252]—Everything seemed like unreal—there seemed millions of women—some pretty sale-girls—pink hose—ladies underwear—toys—sporting goods—story after story—huge—& then a lunch place for thousands of people—all tables full—I walked about like a greenhorn who had come from some village—& who had suddenly found himself in New York!—I was hungry.—I don't know what the lunch was like.—In the evening I was told by the others that it was "no good."—

Judging took us three and a half hours. About 1,250 photographs to go through.—Average higher than usually.—Nothing very great.—Strand was the lucky winner of the first prize—$100. He sent but one print. It took us half an hour to decide the rotation of one, two, three after all pictures had been eliminated but three.—When we were through we were shown the kitchen—an immaculate place—huge too—& the racetrack on the roof—& tennis court—swimming pool—for the employees all these things.—And the huge & fine schoolrooms. —If I were a kid I'd want a job there—I like the running track—

It was queer to go downstairs & pass through all the empty floors which had been crowded not long before. The huge lunch room with its endless tables & not a soul in the room—& downstairs the pink hose—& ladies chemises & drawers—& union suits—& the toys—Oh yes & the antique (!) department—& *art department!!!*—& the six lone cubist paintings directly imported from Paris!—

I wish you could have been there just then—I can hear you scream with laughter—as it was I had a great time to keep a straight face—It was all so big & so funny—& a provincial goody good atmosphere about it all.

251. Arthur B. Carles won the 1917 Walter Lippincott Prize for *Sarset;* George Bellows won the Temple Gold Medal for *The Sawdust Trail;* Kenyon Cox exhibited *Tradition;* and William Merritt Chase exhibited *Portrait: Dean Grosvenor* in the One-hundred-twelfth Annual Exhibition, Pennsylvania Academy of the Fine Arts, Philadelphia, Feb. 4–Mar. 25, 1917; see *Annual Exhibition Record of the Pennsylvania Academy of Fine Arts, 1914–1968* (Madison, Conn., 1989), 123, 86, 145, 131.
252. David Belasco, a theatrical manager and producer, was known for his spectacular stage settings and innovative lighting.

—It was nearly 6:30 when we finally got away.—Carles had to have a bracer—& then he & I played one game of billiards—rotten—I won—but both were too tired.—And then came supper—Breckenridge (the painter) joining us towards the end.—The train was late, so instead of getting away at 10:30, it was eleven.—Steichen & I returned to New York—We talked all the way—primarily about our affairs—291.—

—And now for a piece of news.—On Tuesday the agent came in to see me & somehow or other the sun was shining unusually brightly—there was a touch of spring in the air—the day had been pleasant—I had destroyed a lot more of 291s—"Did I want 291 for another year?"—
Did I?

Well, I said "All right."—An impulse.—A moment.—I guess it's all right.—I wonder what you'll say.—Of course the elevator boy[253] was happy—& Marie—& the cleaning woman would be.—

—I wonder why I said "yes."—I guess because there was nothing else to say *then*.

—The whole of Tuesday was full of pleasant moments—perhaps I'm feeling stronger —so less depressed—so fine things inevitably must happen—but I don't know.—I know nothing—I wish I never felt anything either.—

—Mrs. Meyer came in & spent an hour looking at the Marins & she bought one— our second sale since July last!—It's great.—Screamingly funny.—

—I dreamt about you the other night—I'm not sure—all I saw were legs & hands— I'm sure they were your hands! I know you were waving them frantically, signaling—I didn't know whether to me or not—although no one else seemed about—but I didn't know you could see me, because I had arrived unheralded—

The background was a dark green—here & there young green.—The hands were whiter than ever—

I couldn't see a head nor a body—the legs were in evidence just a little above the knees —downwards—they too were very white—& very beautiful. Immovable.—

I awoke shivering.—No cover—The window wide open.—

—There's the sun—& the clock striking ten.—

—I think I'm going to hear *Gotterdammerung*[254] at 1:30. Another long stand. Did you ever hear it?—I have only heard it once.—One of Wagner's things I have heard so little. I want to hear some music—am in the mood for it—And today is my chance.—

—How wonderfully quiet it's here now—& so clean.—Yesterday was cleaning day.

—I suppose you have a holiday today.—It would be great if we had a chance to have a good long talk.—I don't know what there'd be to say—perhaps nothing.—But Texas is so far off—Isn't it far from New York?—

---

253. Hodge Kirnon.

254. Stieglitz, along with a "very large audience," heard Richard Wagner's *Götterdämmerung* (*Twilight of the Gods*), the final opera of his *Ring Cycle*, in what was described as "one of the most notable incidents of the musical season"; see "Barber of Seville: A Holiday Novelty," *NYT*, Feb. 23, 1917, 9.

8:45 P.M. The family has gone to the movies.—I preferred to stay home alone.—Tired.—And I'm not very fond of movies—haven't been in ages.—

—Another busy day.—Marin—I told him about the people [who] are worrying that I am not treating him fairly—He laughed.—Daniel called me up—wants to see me. Fears he misunderstood me.[255]—I assured him he did & explained my viewpoint which has not changed —& he said: "Great—fine.—Like always. I had misunderstood & that staggered me for I thought you might have changed."—Amusing.—I'm always different—always alike—rooted in the ground.—

—He's coming tomorrow.—I like him. And I want to help him—as I want to help all those who want my help in *my* way—that is really *their* way—their *real* way!—

—Mina Loy came in to get something & then had a talk for awhile.[256]—A short while. —And Katharine Rhoades came with her mother.—The one I hadn't seen in many weeks—the other in nearly a year.—Mrs. Rhoades said she never saw me looking so well—I answered: "I always look well when I'm full of fight."—And I never was more full of fight than these days. —Katharine Rhoades looked very beautiful—but haggard.—She is a wonderful person.—They didn't remain long—ten minutes.—I guess they are visiting "art"—A Cézanne show is open at the Arden Gallery[257]—four Cézannes loaned by Mrs. Eugene Meyer Jr., several by Mrs. Havemeyer, one by Miss Bliss, etc.—About ten to twelve in all.—I am not going. I can't go to see Cézannes in a gallery—fine as it is itself—run by Mrs. John W. Alexander.—It is about seven years ago I sat at her table with her husband & Steichen & pleaded for Modern Art to be hung at the Metropolitan. Alexander was *the* power there.—I was laughed down.—And now *parading* with a name—Cézanne.—It is all too sickening.—I'm glad for those who need the chance to see the Cézannes—I've seen them—but I can't go to Mrs. Alexander's. If I met her I'd be rude.—And I don't want to be rude.—She cares as little for Cézanne as she did seven years ago—It's all a beastly game—She is a clever woman—& able in a way.—And nice enough too.—

—All day long I had several of your things standing about—for me to look at. I can't arrive at conclusions as fast as others.—I have no labels to stick about—& on—

I always feel a great force at work—an intensity—Art—?—Psychology—?—What's the difference?—I am getting much—you are giving it to me.—

—I wonder if you have been moved to work again—or has the moment not yet come— I feel it must have.—

255. In a letter from earlier in the day, Stieglitz recounted to O'Keeffe that he and Charles Daniel had had an amicable "set-to." Like others, he explained, Daniel "can't see that at 291 (although I'm only too happy if anyone buys something, happy because I know the artist—especially the type gathered about me—is modest & must have some money to live)—money is taken into consideration as a very side issue."

256. In a letter of February 24, 1917, Stieglitz related to O'Keeffe that Loy "says I was the first person to encourage her—& that recently I sent her into the depths of despair.... She is painting a picture which she wants me to show.—I guess because I refused to promise showing it without first seeing it [that] 'sent her to the depths of despair.'—!!"

257. See "Paintings by Cézanne Now on Exhibition Here," *NYT*, Mar. 4, 1917, *SM*, 7.

—Back of my head all these days—no matter what else happens—is of course the War —this country's situation.—The people's.—The forces at work—

It is impossible to forecast the future—but I don't see how we can escape the mess—

I was at a dinner party last night—a rather fashionable one—though small—a judge —an ex-editor of the *Times*—a banker—several good looking women—several very intelligent —I was glad to hear the editor say he thought this country needed a dose of real war to bring the people into a unity—All but myself were horrified at such a statement.—

I was a listener.—The judge & editor debated.—I love to listen to good English—that's what I heard chiefly!—A treat for the ear.—

—I wonder how you are.—Somehow I haven't quite the clear vision of you I had about ten days ago—I think my brain is in a fuzzy condition—Still I see the mouth—& the hand— very, very clearly—

I'm beastly tired.—

Good Night.

X

Alfred Stieglitz · [**New York City**] · [**March 10, 1917**] +

Saturday Afternoon.—5:30—This is the first moment I have had to myself—for myself—in two days.—

—I'm pretty well done about—& there is dinner tonight, Jacques Loeb & others— And I'm tired—& my eyes burning.—From the excitement of the morning.—The smoke.—

—It's a miracle that I am sitting here—A miracle that 291 still stands.—

A marvelous spring day—Blazing sun.—A blazing blue sky.—I had come down on top of a bus—the wind was west & sharp—

I had hardly been at 291 more than fifteen minutes when Hodge raced in to me announcing that the building was on fire—!!—I smelt smoke—I was very quiet. Always am in emergency cases when confronted with a reality.—291 on fire.—Again.—The tenth fire under or near us in seven years!—I made Hodge take a few pictures on the elevator—& I had some Marins under my arm & the bundle of your drawings—I sent Hodge down the elevator—I told him to hurry.—Smoke was coming up.—I told him I'd take the stairs. The elevator couldn't hold us all.—It was a smoky exit.—Down the last stairs I couldn't see my way—but I was perfectly cool—Hodge was calling me—firemen—policemen!—The street full of engines—red everywhere—policemen—a mob of people—Smoke creeping up inside the building—

I stood there & looked.—Had the end of 291 come?—And with it the wiping out of so many things wonderful to me—hundreds & hundreds of beautiful things—rafts of Walkowitzs —a lot of Marins—nearly all of Hartley's work—Practically everything of my own work— *Camera Work*—Of your work but little up there—one or two I would [have] hated to have disappear—

It was a glorious spring day.—And as I stood there wondering—291 or no 291?—I felt very quiet—& I was glad that if 291 were doomed it would disappear with the streets so gay —so bright—so full of spring.—

—Hodge & I stood together—I saw that the smoke rose no higher.—It meant fire under control.—In a half hour I was up stairs—everything suffocating with smoke—all windows & door opened—& openings to roof also opened—Fireman—a handsome fellow—He asked what the pictures were—And he pointed to your blue one[258] & asked what was that: I said: "The world—all that's wonderful—in the making—in a woman's womb."—He looked at me as if I were crazy.—

All I know is I was glad 291 was still there—Every night for thirteen years when I go home I wonder if I'll find 291 standing in the morning.—Am I tempting fate?—

—Walkowitz came about that time. He looked upset.—His work—He has been through several "scares" here—I've warned him *not* to have everything here—Perhaps he'll listen now— Then Zoler turned up & regretted he hadn't been here—And Quinn & Kuhn came in—the smell of burning was still strong—still is—& Quinn took some more Severinis—I hope he'll get them.—And people have come all day.—The show is liked.[259]—

—At about 2:30 in the midst of the coming & going a letter with green stamps—

I only read it a few moments ago—I was glad to see the handwriting—when it came— the note in which you told me you were going to bed—had written seven letters—A good night —Stella was here—the New York Futurist—many people—They talked futurism—the fire— war—

—As the fire was over Marie happened to call up—she doesn't come Saturdays—she was amazed to hear about the fire—Caffin called up from the Metropolitan Museum—on his way up he saw all the engines before 291—he wanted to know—& others seemed to have heard & inquired—

Funny—Why is 291 in a fire-trap?—

—Yesterday was a very full day too—& full of trying excitement.—

I must go home.

Georgia O'Keeffe · [Canyon, Texas] · [March 11, 1917]

It's a very wobbly little girl writing you tonight—Sunday night. I've had a wonderful day—

Last night I didn't tell you about my invitation to go to the Canyon because I wasn't sure —I only thought—sort of felt it.

I go for the mail every morning—and frequently a big man[260]—is going that way too at

---

258. Lynes 119.

259. The New York collector John Quinn purchased ten Severinis from Paintings, Drawings, Pastels, by Gino Severini, of Paris and Italy, on view at 291, Mar. 6–17, 1917, for more than one thousand dollars; see Richard Whelan, *Alfred Stieglitz: A Biography* (New York, 1995), 380, and *John Quinn, 1870–1925: Collection of Paintings, Water Colors, Drawings and Sculpture* (Huntington, N.Y., 1926), 5.

260. Thomas V. Reeves, the Randall County district clerk.

the same time—I knew who he was but had never met him—A nice young fellow—I knew he watched me—but I never looked at him—Why should I care if he looked at me—and why look at him—he didn't interest me—

His wife[261] phoned me and asked me to go—and the first thing she said after she introduced me when I went out to get in the car was—"He said he wanted to take you to the Canyon because he likes the way you walk down the street with your hands in your pockets and he thinks he likes you." Wasn't it funny—I knew he had done it but it would have seemed so absurd to say if she hadn't said that.

The day couldn't have been finer—and they are great folks—She is very pretty and blond—

I walked and climbed—and climbed and walked till I feel all shaky in the knees and limp all over—They took another girl too—a great friend of Mrs. Reeves—

We waded in the stream—icy cold—about ten feet—lay in the sand a long time—Really big cedar trees—I took a long walk by myself—following cow trails through the cedars along the stream—We all took our hair down—No, it was just Mrs. Reeves and I—but it was great—just to feel free in the big outdoors—And the awful places we climbed—Really—life wasn't worth living to me a few times—I was so scared—It's all so tremendous—and we came home riding into the sunset—Too wonderful to be true—I made a lot of drawings—just little ones—

I'm almost too tired to wiggle but I wanted to tell you about it—

Three letters from you this morning—and *The Seven Arts*[262]—all very nice to get—I didn't have time to read all the letters before I went—but what I did read made the day nicer—

Fred was by me when I got them—he had been telling me about a blue hyacinth he was going to bring me—Agriculture is his specialty and he has been growing some flowers—and when he saw those three letters and the package—he said he wouldn't bring me the blue hyacinth—and he hasn't brought it today—I had to laugh—he'll bring it yet—The pink one froze—I cut the top off and there are just a few blossoms way down among the leaves. I was glad when it froze—

Well—I must go to bed—it's after nine—and I am to be ready to go out on a tramp at five o'clock in the morning with some girls and boys—breakfast out somewhere—I don't know where—

—You know—I'm just living—I just sort of plunge from one thing into another—so often—so very much afraid—And you feel like something that protects me—something I want to be very close to—like I had to shrink back—so many times today—against the wall of rock going straight up beside me—and in front—

Gosh—a misstep and I'd roll down forever—and the dirt and rocks crumbled and rolled down and there was nothing to hold to—I dare not hold anything—and I couldn't stand still by the wall of rock—or I'd never get to the top—I must keep moving—and I guess—being so afraid made it all the finer—It was that way many times—and another awful place was a

261. Luella Reeves.
262. *The Seven Arts* 1 (Mar. 1917).

bare ridge—that went down seemingly forever on both sides and we must climb up it—as it slanted up and ran along the top when it was on the level—

There is something so merciless about the Canyon—so tremendous—I love it—

The big cedar trees were very nice too—the grass is very short and brown—no underbrush—such clean ground under the trees—clean ground and rocks and trees and a very clean stream—And we could see for miles and miles and miles—and nobody—

When we came out—way off on the edge of the earth against the sunset were a lot of cattle in a string—We could see daylight under them—Like a dark embroidery edge—very fine—on the edge of the earth—

Goodnight.

I think—if there is anything left of me after I've trailed off for that moonlight breakfast I'll paint tomorrow—

I thought a lot about you down there today—It was so quiet and warm—

Just a little girl tonight—so tired—I wish you were somewhere around—When I wonder how I ever got out of that place I want to be close to you—

I seem to hate to stop writing—My hands are filthy—scratched and dirty—my face burns and my lips burn more—chapped. The air is very dry.

That letter I sent this morning was in my pocket and my pen leaked on it—much ink and cedar gum on my hands too—

Oh, I've had a great day.

So glad he likes my hands in my pockets—He's a nice man—I like him—When I got out—when we came home—he said "Now you must consider I've called on you and I expect you to return it."

Guess I'll have to because he has my hair-net and a comb that I can't live without in his pocket.

Goodnight again—

Georgia O'Keeffe · [Canyon, Texas] · [March 15, 1917] +

It's cold as the devil—snowing almost all day—I just came in from supper and can't make the fire burn fast so I'll write you while I wait for it—

I'm quite as uncomfortably cold as anyone who doesn't like me might wish—I don't mind shivering over a little scrap of fire out in the open—wet wood and all—but this kind—in a stove—that you can't see—isn't much—I can hear it—burning on the southwest side—and don't dare look at it—because if I do—every time I look and poke it—it goes out—

I've wanted to write you ever since the last time but—

You see—I've been wasting lots of time on folks—and it's hard to quit—even when you are ready—They come along and jolly you with your last piece of foolishness—and before you know it you are off again—and a whole evening is gone or a whole afternoon—

—Yesterday afternoon I came home—and got *Faust*—I'd been wanting to read it for almost a week but someone or something always kept me from it—And I fled from the house and the phone—to get away from them all—I went to a little stream—not much more than twelve feet across—you can't see it till you are right by it—the water is low—and has left something—lime I suppose—on the ground and grass where it has gone down—that looks just like frost—I don't remember sitting down—or lying down—but I was looking at the water —almost upside down for a long time before I knew it—Then I sat up and looked at *Faust* and laughed at myself for carrying it way out there and not reading—just dreaming—and I wondered—did I have it along just because I like to have it by me—So I spread out my handkerchief—I should say one of my handkerchiefs—now that I have pockets I can carry lots of things—and put *Faust* on it—so it wouldn't get scratched—

Then I lay down again and went to dreaming again—The sun was warm in the little hollow where the wind didn't strike—You would have liked it—I wondered what you would say and feel out here where there is nothing but ground and sky—

It must be that you would like it. After awhile I opened the book—and wondered where I had been reading last—decided I'd begin at the beginning again—While I was lost—a queer little whirr—made me look up—a great flock of birds going over quickly—and I looked and listened—it was so still.—

—The day—the paper said Germany was giving Texas to Mexico[263]—The smiles—the war talk—

I got out *Brook Kerith* again. Have been reading on it again for three nights—not till very late though—people earlier—Isn't it queer—the way it fits some moods and not others —and every night I got out Wright's *Nietzsche*[264] book too—and looked at the chapter on the Anti-Christ and put it away—That's as far as I have read—I want to read the rest of it but can't get the humor so far—It's just now getting warm. I was in bed and scrambled out again after *Faust* when I had been sufficiently petted by *Brook Kerith*—*Brook Kerith* is such a funny run-along way of writing a book—isn't it.

Not being orderly—I started reading along in the second part of *Faust*—I was looking for the Helena and found something else that seemed to serve the purpose just as well—

When I finished your letter this morning—I banged it down on my desk in the office— I had been sitting there between the windows—my tilty business-looking chair tilted back against the radiator—my feet propped up much too high for a nice lady but discreetly behind the desk—so as not to shock any chance visitors—And what I said to myself—was—

"GOSH BUT I LIKE HIM"

Then I jumped up quick and went on to class—for the bell had rung—And I laughed —I knew you would have laughed if you had heard me say it.

---

263. On January 19, 1917, German secretary of state Arthur Zimmerman sent a cable to his minister in Mexico City, proposing an alliance with Mexico. In exchange for their support against the Allies, Mexico was to receive territory in New Mexico, Texas, and Arizona. British authorities intercepted the cable and realizing it would enflame public opinion in the United States, gave it to the Americans. When it was released to the press on March 1, 1917, large, bold headlines ran in newspapers across the country; see, e.g., "Germany Seeks Alliance with Mexico and Japan to Open War upon the United States: Carranza Is Offered Three States as His Reward for Aiding Kaiser," *Amarillo Daily News,* Mar. 1, 1917, 1, and "Plot Awakens Congress," *NYT,* Mar. 2, 1917, 1.
264. Willard Huntington Wright, *What Nietzsche Taught* (New York, 1915).

I had been reading the letter instead of going to chapel because—Well—of course I wanted to read the letter—and I had [it]—I didn't want to go to chapel—

The Seniors and Juniors all used to sit in the back of the auditorium—but they didn't behave very well so the order was reversed—Seniors in front—Freshmen in the back—and it seems that all the boys I like best sit right at my feet—and I had stood it for two mornings—and today I didn't want to—I hate to be looked at—After they have sat down there a week or so they won't look so hard and I won't mind—

Yes—it's funny—laugh. Sixteen silk shirts—Davis—stopped me in the hall yesterday noon and told me he thought the faculty looked great—he enjoyed being on the second row—he could see so well—and he simply doubled up laughing when I said I didn't enjoy it—

Didn't I tell you about the dance—You asked so I must have forgotten—

The yellow chariot[265] came down from Amarillo and took me and the other chaperone —He didn't dance—but I did after I had watched a little while to see who could dance—

It was very funny. I had a great time—such ridiculous kids—

Yes—I guess I dance rather well—Can't help it, you know—it isn't my fault. It seems so queer that everyone can't—

You ought to see Beverly—he is just a little hunchbacked—and someway he seems like a Teddy-bear—and he has more fun dancing than most anyone here—he doesn't do it so remarkably well but he has such a good time that he makes up for any lack of skill—and every time we meet at Hollands and he can get something on the Victrola that he likes—he tries to get me out in the back room to dance—

If you could just see Hollands back room—badly lighted—and littered with everything from pills and drugs to fishing rods—scales—stove—desk—boxes—just everything—There is oilcloth on part of the floor—the rest is too rough and the oilcloth is ragged—Can you see it— and the Teddy-bear.

I always want to pet his cheek—he is such a nice funny little boy—always though—the hunchback—it hurts you—don't you know—maybe makes you like him better—I don't mind him looking at me—He and Davis room together—

The sister is at tennis again—She has two new yellow jackets that look great—and noisy green ribbons—No one has beat her so far—it's bad—you don't improve when you don't get beat—Maybe someone will though—

I don't seem to be able to remember much about the stuff I sent you—What I remember when I try always aggravates me so that—Why—it's just like scrap paper—I throw it in the scrap heap and go on to something else—

Sometimes it makes me laugh—I hate so to think about the stuff. Most folks don't feel that way about what they make—do they?—

What will I say to 291's continuing—? Why—this morning before I got up I was think-ing about it—and it seemed that I would just have to go to New York if you were going to close it—I'd have to be there again—I don't know why—but I must.

I thought that this morning before the letter came—

---

265. Willard Austin.

Knowing that 291 is—is one of the things that makes life worth living. That was true before you knew that I existed. I used to go in—maybe for only a few minutes—simply because—

It wasn't you—though I never forgot the first time I saw you—the wet brown and black thing in your hand—the not very pleasant—questioning look—

I wonder why I like 291 so much—so much that to think of losing it makes me feel sick. Goodnight. I like you very much tonight—

And tonight I'm only a little girl.

More—I want—to say—but—what—

I guess that space that is between what they call heaven and earth—out there in what they call the night—is as much it as anything. So I send you the space that is watching the starlight and the empty quiet plains—.

Alfred Stieglitz · [New York City] · [March 26, 1917] +

Monday Morning.—What a glorious morning.—As I came through the Park everything was bathed in a languid warm mist—the smoke & steam from the chimneys of the skyscrapers rose listlessly straight into the air—Windstill—Spring—

—And here I am at 291.—Windows open.—Sun pouring in.—I feel as if I had been on a debauch lasting weeks.—The whole body is aching—& my head seems to be empty.—

—Even yesterday, Sunday, was a continuous go—different—Mother in morning—the same—people to dinner at noon at home—In the afternoon I visited an old lady—eighty-six—a wonderful person—remarkably young—& before I realized it it was time to get ready to go to Arensberg's to dinner.—He has or rather lives in one of those large studio apartments in West 67th Street—I thought he & his wife & I were to be alone.—When I got there at seven I was delighted to see a large studio—very spacious—white walls—filled with splendid examples of Matisse, Picassos, Duchamps, a Cézanne watercolor & a Cézanne lithograph—several Brancusis—in marble, wood, & bronze—a large Steinway Grand—everything very simple—very livable—homelike—a beautiful spirit.—I had hardly been there more than ten minutes when in walked Mr. & Mrs. Gleizes, Mina Loy, looking very stunning, Frances Stevens, very blond—as full of life as ever—her black Chinese dog with her—she in white—very low cut front & still lower cut in the back—Then Duchamp came & several others—after dinner.—The atmosphere was unlike any I had found anywhere either abroad or here—There was Debussy music & Schoenberg too—Mrs. Arensberg being a pianist—& a French lady sang—All was very informal—very distinguished—aristocratically free.—

Arensberg & I had a talk about the *Independent Exhibition.*—It is going to be right.—Chaos.—

Duchamp having his studio a flight up, he took me up to see his work—He is doing a

marvelous thing on huge glass[266]—about eight feet by twelve—Has been over a year on it—
It's all worked with fine wire & lead—a little color—very perfect workmanship—He has a
beautiful soul.—He loves the age of machinery—its significance, its orderliness—precision—

Miss Stevens who went up with us found it too static, the work—Duchamp & I
laughed.—She is so vivacious & full of nervous energy that unless a thing makes her feel a
powerful push she feels something lacking.—She has vision & brains in spite of her kittenishness
—I like her.—

—Mina Loy wears splendidly—she is so spontaneous—She laughs & jokes—Under it
all there is a deep nature—rather sad—disillusioned[267]—

It was after one when I got home.—The night was so perfect—I walked awhile—
alone—

Stevens & Loy, who live next door to each other in an apartment wanted me to go with
them awhile—I was ungallant I guess—I was tired & wanted to be alone awhile in the night.—

They were stunning to look at—& to listen too—both looked so sleepy—but the night
beckoned.—

It was great walking.—

—The night before Mrs. Stieglitz & I were to a dinner at the Cosgraves'—It was
midnight before we got home. There were people there I had never met—writers primarily—
husbands & wives—poets—art critics—all sorts—Intimate enough.—But people one may
meet once in a lifetime—I fit virtually in any old place—& always have a good time—still bed
was welcome.—

—And yesterday morning as I sat at breakfast table alone—I had the drawings of yours
before me—the two—the one of two *Lines* & the one I call a *Self-Portrait*[268]—I think I sat there
riveted for half an hour or more.—How wonderfully expressive those two things—how both
seem to breathe—In fact I know they breathe—And the *Self-Portrait* how beautiful it is—&
how its expression seems to change constantly—It's uncanny—at moments it seems as if it were
repellent & then the next moment it seems to bewitch—the sensual quality of it is staggering—

It certainly makes one feel like holding firmly—[or] letting go—

—I'm looking forward to the show[269]—your work.—A great treat in store for
many—primarily though for me.—

This paper is awful to write on.—I am writing in all directions trying to get a smooth
flow—

—How are you this morning?—I have just addressed a copy of *Seven Arts*[270] to you—
just arrived.—A good number again.—

266. Marcel Duchamp, *The Bride Stripped Bare by Her Bachelors, Even (The Large Glass)*, 1915–1923; see *Schwarz*, Duchamp,
287.

267. In a letter to O'Keeffe of February 26, 1917, Stieglitz described Loy as looking "less like a pantheress than she did when she
first came to New York—*New York tames!*"

268. Lynes 64 (see p. 21); Lynes 99.

269. Exhibition of Recent Work—Oils, Water-colors, Charcoal Drawings, Sculpture—By Georgia O'Keeffe of Canyon, Texas,
291, Apr. 3–27, 1917.

270. *The Seven Arts* 1 (Apr. 1917).

I have to do quite a little photography today—for the *Independent* catalogue[271]—I promised to help.—

I wish Canyon weren't quite so far away just now—still I guess it's best that it is.—

I don't know why it should be best so—perhaps because there is so much work both have to do.—

I have to laugh.—Here's my hand—Do you wish to put yours in it—

Georgia O'Keeffe · [Canyon, Texas] · [March 26, 1917]

Monday night—

Cold starlight—quiet—The stove is warm though—

And it's the little girl wanting to be close to you that's talking to you—makes me feel sort of sick—that I can't be—

We had a great time last night going to Amarillo—The wind went down—the sunset was very yellow—like gold—only—warmer—warm—It was warm—green fields—that fresh spring green—dark soil showing through—long blue shadows from very little bumps on the plains made it all look so clean—as though it had been rained on—instead of smothered with dust—

And—I was in great good humor—simply couldn't help it when the world looked so good—It was great—just a nice fresh wind—not cold—Laughing—talking—nice good humor—the car open—no top even—

The excuse for going was to hear a man talk on Tolstoy—I went for the ride and for the fun I get out of hearing what some other folks that I knew were going would say about it—I don't know much about Tolstoy but don't remember when I didn't know everything the man said so I've had a great time today. It's fun to hear folks air their opinions—

I'm such a fool—More fun tomorrow. So much fun to know folks that way.

Only on the way home in the dark—I remember looking round over the empty plains—And thinking in sort of a forlorn way—Where is someone to think like I think—

It was only a moment—

Then the laugh—as though I'd see anyone out there in the dark—and as though it mattered—

The ride home was great—the thin moon went down—very red—The sky—Oh—it was great—I let my hair fly in the wind till Mr. Reeves objected—tied his handkerchief corners in knots and made me a cap. She has the most contagious laugh I ever heard—yellow hair—and I love yellow hair—like her even if she didn't say a word over my Rodin *Camera Work*.[272]

271. None of the illustrations in The Society of Independent Artists exhibition catalogue (New York, 1917) indicate who made the copy photographs. However, O'Keeffe's *Expression, No. 14* (Lynes 52), Charles Demuth's *The Dancer*, and Marsden Hartley's *Movement No. 7* were reproduced.

272. On March 25, 1917, O'Keeffe told Stieglitz that she had showed Mrs. Reeves her copy of *Camera Work* and she "never said a word—Wasn't that funny…. How could anyone look at it and not say anything." Rodin's work was reproduced in *Camera Work* 22 (Apr. 1908) and 34–35 (Apr.–July 1911).

Claudia O'Keeffe, *Georgia O'Keeffe, Canyon, Texas*, 1917. Gelatin silver print, 2¹⁵/₁₆ x 3¹⁵/₁₆ in.
(7 x 10 cm). Enclosed in a letter by O'Keeffe, March 26, 1917. Alfred Stieglitz/Georgia O'Keeffe
Archive, Yale Collection of American Literature, Beinecke Rare Book and Manuscript Library.

You ought to live way off like this sometime—it makes you wonder when you see how
little Rodin in this form means to most folks—I can hardly believe it—I'm going to show it to a
talkative class tomorrow—They might like *The Thinker*[273] a little—

The sister didn't even get the watercolors—they puzzled her—she wondered—looked
several times—always seeming to question—The man on the horse she liked.[274]

No one has seen it but Mrs. Reeves and Claudie—I'll take it to school tomorrow—
showing it to folks that can't see hurts but I'll do it anyway—Maybe one will like it—maybe
two think about it—Don't know—I'll see—

Is it because there is more animal in me than brain—that I want to be near you to tell
you how much I like it—

No—it isn't animal at all—it's touch—Touch may be God or Devil with me—I don't
know which—

—I had thought about the *Independent Show* but simply didn't have time to do anything about it—No—not that altogether—I just said to myself—why should I—It would
be fun to *see* myself hang next to somebody else but I hadn't anything to send when I thought it
—Dorothy[275] wrote me right after I had sent everything to you—Should I cook up something
—No—get something from you?—no!—What would I send if I sent anything—

So I let it slide—Too much of a problem for me—I'd forgotten about it—but I think it's
fun that you are doing it—I wonder what you will do—

---

273. Auguste Rodin, *The Thinker,* 1880, bronze; see John L. Tancock, *The Sculpture of Auguste Rodin: The Collection of the
Rodin Museum, Philadelphia* (Philadelphia, 1976), 113.
274. Auguste Rodin, *Drawing, Camera Work* 34–35 (Apr.–July 1911).
275. Dorothy True was a friend of O'Keeffe's from Columbia University Teachers College. On February 24, 1917, when she
reminded Stieglitz that he had met True a few times before, O'Keeffe wrote that she had become "riled" when she thought Stieglitz dismissed True as a "fashion-plate [with no] sense under its yellow hair and blue hat."

I just want to say one little word—Please don't name anything—unless you want to *very* much—If you want to—enough of course it's all right—go on and have a good time— I should think that sort of a show would be lots of fun—wish I could go to it—And if you are giving me another show—I want to go to that too—just once—

No I don't either—I get a creepy feeling around inside of me somewhere when I think about it—

I've been sitting here watching the youngster's goldfish for such a long time that I'm lost—

Remembered that I didn't tell you that I moved in to my white room today[276]—am not in there though because I have the habit of being in this one I guess—

And I didn't tell you that I haven't modeled since last fall—The thing looks like a bad stomachache—There has been an idea—a shape—all made in my head but it's so foreign to stomachache that I've hated to make it out of the same stuff—and I really hated to muss up the shape I have—It's so bad I sort of liked it—really don't know where I've put it if isn't in the top tray of my trunk—

I'm glad you asked me about it—I've been wanting to make something my hands could get all round and was thinking of metal—Maybe I'll model the thing I've had in mind so long—I guess it's the plains—I don't know—Maybe I can't make it—guess I'll try—

Fred and Lyman[277] and someone else—don't remember who—came in the post office this morning as I was struggling with the combinations on two boxes—getting other folks' mail for them—They had to feel and admire the green coat—Fred remarked that it had a collar— They had to sound the depths of the pockets—Fred remarked that he wanted to see what my skirt pocket was like inside—said he never had—

Crazy—Of course I'm crazy—of course I'm crazy—It's a disease and contagious— I didn't intend to say that twice—

Sleepy—

Dust has blown all day—A norther came just after we got in last night—

Goodnight—

I didn't tell you that I let Fred feel in all my pockets—He wanted to know about your pen too— Claudie had gotten our mail and gave it to me—

Alfred Stieglitz · [New York City] · [March 31, 1917]

How is the Little Girl this morning?

—Just before I left 291 last night a letter postmarked Canyon, March 27—was handed me.—It was a letter full of great good humor—laughter—a touch of silent night—with endless depth into that darkness—Endless.

---

276. O'Keeffe had painted the walls of her bedroom at the Shirleys' house white.
277. J. Lyman Davis, a senior at the Normal College.

—I had to laugh at the pocket exploration—What did he expect to find there?—Just pockets—The Little Girl with pockets—

So the white room is completed.—

I wonder whether anyone in the class room responded to any one of the Rodins.—I don't see how anyone could—unless—well, lots of things.—Above all one must be overflowing with the sensibility of touch to respond fully—& at once. And how can youngsters be that—unless they are youngsters very much different than most youngsters are.—

—Of course occasionally a youngster is much different.—You undoubtedly were such a youngster. And as for the older ones how many know what touch is—how many feel its meaning. Maybe it isn't as important to the world as it seems to be to those of our ilk.

Touch!—I'm glad you feel like modeling again.—

Don't fear I have put no names on the things I have sent to the *Independent.*—I call them *Expressions.*[278] That's all.—Two drawings—one of those shown at 291 last year & the one with the shafts you sent me last summer.

I know how you feel about it all—showing—etc.—But I do feel the world is entitled to a chance to see your work—not that many will get it—but a chance should be given—How many get anything that comes from the real inside?

—The show here will look stunning—I'll photograph it so that you'll be able to see what's up—and how! Of course war will deflect attention from all exhibitions—still those really interested will continue to be interested—no matter what else may happen.—

—Last night I was at my mother's.—I met two gentlemen there—Mr. Iklé, I think I have mentioned him to you before—& a friend of his.—We left my mother's after eleven—& then sat together at the Savoy until long after midnight—talking about war, etc.—The future.—

—??—

Iklé was in France when the War broke out—the other man in Berlin. Both were full of amusing stories. If one can forget the tragedy of the whole thing everything becomes comical—farcical in fact.—

What a curious thing the human "monkey" is—I never can get accustomed to the idea.—It's always new to me.—

—I was pretty tired when I got to bed—my feet are in such a bad shape—& I was told my old chiropodist (to whom I have been wanting to go for months—I've had him twenty-five years) had suddenly died—

I don't like changes—not in that line.—

—Before sitting down here to write to you I was in the front room & had some of your things in there to see how they'd look—the varnish bothers some—reflections—& I wanted to see how to minimize the sheen.—The things look very fine—In some of them I'm always discovering something new.—

—————

278. Lynes 52 and either 62 or 63.

ON APRIL 2, 1917, President Woodrow Wilson appeared before a cheering audience of a joint session of the House and Senate to ask for a declaration of war on Germany. Laying out all the points why war was both necessary and justifiable, he asserted that peace was impossible for the democracies of the world as long as Germany remained an autocratic power: "The world must be made safe for democracy," he concluded.[279] A formal declaration of war on Germany followed on April 6, 1917, and several months later on December 7, 1917, the United States declared war on the Austro-Hungarian Empire.

On April 3, Stieglitz opened the Exhibition of Recent Work—Oils, Water-colors, Charcoal Drawings, Sculpture—By Georgia O'Keeffe of Canyon, Texas at 291. Including twenty-three works, it was O'Keeffe's first one-person show and the last one Stieglitz presented at 291. A few days later, on April 9, the First Annual Exhibition of the Society of Independent Artists opened at the Grand Central Palace in New York City. Billed as an exhibition with "no jury" and "no prizes," the show sought to distinguish itself from the restrictive exhibitions of the National Academy of Design and was open to any artist who paid the modest dues. In order to further ensure that no one received preferential treatment, the organizing committee—including the collector Walter Arensberg and a diverse group of artists from Duchamp and Man Ray to George Bellows and Maurice Prendergast—installed the more than twenty-five hundred works alphabetically by the name of the artist.[280] Perhaps to gain publicity for the exhibition,[281] Duchamp submitted one of his "ready-mades" to the exhibition, a urinal he titled *The Fountain,* under the assumed name R. Mutt. When the committee refused to hang it, he brought it to 291 and asked Stieglitz to photograph it so that it could be reproduced in a forthcoming issue of *The Blind Man.*[282] As Stieglitz related to O'Keeffe, he carefully positioned *The Fountain* in front of Hartley's 1913 painting *The Warriors.* The heroic imagery of the painting—soldiers riding into battle—perfectly suited both the challenges Mutt's sculpture posed to traditional art and the militaristic tenor of the time, while its ovoid forms echoed those of the urinal itself.[283]

Alfred Stieglitz · [New York City] · [April 2, 1917] +

Just a hasty line.—Monday.—Spring weather—Sun—but the wind is east—It means grayness for tomorrow—a certain rawness.

—The two Little Rooms are ready for the public—They are very beautiful.—Even more

279. "Must Exert All Our Power," *NYT,* Apr. 3, 1917, 1.

280. See Clark S. Marlor, *The Society of Independent Artists: The Exhibition Record, 1917–1944* (Park Ridge, N.J., 1984), 3–14.

281. Duchamp probably brought *The Fountain* to Stieglitz on April 17, 1917 (see AS to GOK, Apr. 18, 1917). Because he did so eight days after the exhibition opened and because Stieglitz had told O'Keeffe on April 12, 1917, that Roché, editor of *Blind Man,* had lamented that the Independent Show was "badly visited—poor press agency," Duchamp may have hoped that by showing *The Fountain* at 291 the exhibition would gain notoriety. In his letter of April 12, 1917, Stieglitz told O'Keeffe he gave Roché "some ideas."

282. *The Blind Man* 2 (May 1917).

283. For reproductions of *The Fountain,* Stieglitz's photograph of it, and Hartley's *The Warriors,* see Pepe Carmel, "Marcel Duchamp, 1917: The Not So Innocent Eye," in *Modern Art and America: Alfred Stieglitz and His New York Galleries* (Washington, D.C., 2001), 220–228.

Alfred Stieglitz, *Main Room—Wall, Next to Door, Right,* 1917. Gelatin silver print, 7⅟₁₆ x 8⅞ in. (17.9 x 22.6 cm). The J. Paul Getty Museum, Los Angeles. Copyright © 2010 Georgia O'Keeffe Museum/Artists Rights Society (ARS), New York.

so than I had imagined they would be.—I wish you could see them. I know you'd be surprised yourself.

—A little after nine I came down & took the Wrights off the walls[284]—at ten Walkowitz arrived & he & I got busy.—It took an hour to arrange the things—& as I started to hang them Hodge handed me a green-stamped letter.—I waited to read it for about an hour.—It felt good to have it in my pocket just so—It felt warm—quieting.—It came at an hour at which no letter ever came from you—

A queer coincidence! And the sun was shining very brightly—

People came—amongst them Gaisman who wanted to see me "alone."—He waited—a German girl too to show me photographs—I read the letter—I felt that hand gripping another hand—gripping

I was very glad to have those two written sides—What a splendid human you are.

—I went with Gaisman to lunch.—I told Walkowitz Gaisman wanted to see me—&

284. Exhibition of Paintings and Sculpture by S. Macdonald-Wright, on view at 291, Mar. 20–31, 1917.

Gaisman did. Would like to see *Camera Work* on a "business basis"—& made suggestions. All well meant & fine. But I laughed & told him "business" & *Camera Work* were incompatible & told him the reasons—

It's funny how they can't see—they want to "help"—But they don't know "how"—That's the trouble—They think in different terms than I do—that is they feel certainly differently. You feel the way I do—not identically—but we understand each other's talk—We need no explanations—

There is no debit or credit in our make-up—Life is all we feel—Life is all that interests us—& *how* it *hurts* at times!!

—When I came back there was little Walkowitz sitting on a chair staring at your pictures—he had finished hanging the show.—It was a surprise for me.—We stood there together.—It was a wonderful moment.—I'm going to photograph the walls so that you see exactly how you have been treated.—There is a religious feeling pervading the rooms—all the paintings are in the room to the right—In all twenty-one things are shown—fifteen in one room—six in the other.—A feeling of space—a great beautiful livingness and an unspeakable *fineness.*—Like string music—clear & crisp—but so fine—Right—

—And it's great that the things are up just at present—The fineness of life—really a religious ecstasy for life—& today Wilson asks Congress to declare war—He can't do otherwise. War existed from the beginning—today is merely the expression frankly of what existed since August 1st, 1914.

—Then too the *Independent* opens up in a week—& for that reason too I'm glad your work is at 291—

Your soul is free. It is a Great Big Soul—as Genuine as the Universe—

—I'm going to take Marin home.—I'd like him to spend the evening with me. So here is my hand—

Walkowitz has been like of old the last two weeks again—very fine—the footsteps are gone—perhaps I'm not as nervous—perhaps both of us are at our best again—I don't know.—

—Your letter is as fine as your pictures.—

A perfect day.

Many things happened besides. But it's late.—I must go.

Alfred Stieglitz · [New York City] · [April 10, 1917] +

It's Tuesday night.—Early—cold & disagreeable. The wind is still howling, whistling & raging alternatively—the fourth day of that sort of thing—It gets on one's nerves—It is unusual for New York such a prolonged siege of blustering northwester—& especially at this time of the year.—Spring!—Ice everywhere.—A joke for fair.—Like so much else these days of brotherly love.—

—The Big Show opened last night. It is really a big affair in every sense of the word—It looks dignified & rather "European"—The hanging alphabetically has worked out well—& in some instances has produced some wonderful results. For instance in the H room—(each letter has a room or rooms—although N, O, P have one together, & X, Y, Z too)—the two Hartleys, hanging over each other & being the same color scheme, look like one painting—are flanked by Birge Harrison[285] & other academicians!! It's a marvelous exposition of the "Academy" & the new. Hartleys sing like Caruso when he was young & lavish—Of the others—they have no voice at all.—

From eight till eleven I walked about—the place was packed—the place is huge—with "all" New York—"Everybody" was there—I discovered no "new" talent—perhaps I may later on—

I sent you a catalogue this morning.—Your picture reproduced splendidly.—I knew it would.—I'm glad it worked out all right.—At the show your drawings look distinguished, although they drew a space which is near a corner.—The hanging was fairly done—no favoritism being possible under the system.—

—I was glad to get to bed. It was after midnight.—The day had been an exciting one —a sort of dope activity.—I'm so tired mentally that I could cry.—

Today I went to hear Marie sing—at her teacher's.—The poor girl was nervous. She has a sweet voice & if she can ever forget that she is singing she ought to do very well.—For two years I had been wanting to hear her—It's a long road to become a singer.—She hopes to sing in church some day.—What she needs most is some self-assurance—She is so diffident—

At 291 there were quite some people—Your things attract.[286] To me they become more & more living—so much more that today I felt as if you were running through all my being— As if I had known you for years & years—As if your being had coursed every particle of mine —It's an uncanny state—

I guess I'm in an ultra-sensitive state—the strain of uncertainty everywhere—in everyone—

When alone in the rooms with the paintings I felt as if I were under that tree—my tree —and I would liked to have fallen asleep right then & there—& sleep—I'm tired beyond all idea—

That wind is awful—and I wish the steam would come up the radiators—The house —we have been eighteen years in it—is running down—I think I'll go to bed—cover up— head & all—

I wonder how you are—how the wind is in Texas—whether the storm there has let up—And I wonder how the nights are—The windows are rattling—I'm shivering—cold & fatigue—I hate myself when I'm this way—so little man—just a helpless bundle of useless nerves—

I'm glad that your work is at 291—when I'm with it it seems to prop me up—makes me

285. Hartley exhibited *Movement No. 7* and *Movement No. 18*, and Lowell Birge Harrison exhibited *Moonlight on the Beach* and *Red Sawmill* in the 1917 Society of Independent Artists Exhibition; see Marlor, *Independent Artists*, 283–284.
286. On April 6, 1917, Stieglitz related to O'Keeffe that "a 'critic' too wandered in—the *Evening World*—Has no trace of *seeing*—but is a good natured fellow.—I always joke with him.—I nearly frightened him into believing that the Metropolitan Museum had bought the whole collection.—In going he asked: 'Is it really true?'—I feared he might lose his job—so I told him I had been joking—that the Metropolitan never did anything so alive."

forget so much that is hideous—and a deep reverence for something very wonderful invariably over comes me—

That's what you give me. The place breathes peace & space—human throb—a great yearning—a great closeness—

The wind is increasing in force—tornado-like—

Good Night.—

Georgia O'Keeffe · [Canyon, Texas] · [April 14, 1917]

Friday night—the 13th—

No—I guess it's Saturday morning—the roosters are crowing already.

I really never had a nicer surprise in my life than the photographs this morning. I opened it on the street—waiting for a little joint down there to open—Imagine my amazement—and while I was looking—along came Physical Education[287]—He didn't understand my things but he could understand your end of it—what a lot of trouble you had taken—He laughed at me when I told him I was so excited I couldn't stand there by myself—that I just have to go along with him wherever he was going—So I went with him—It was a great morning—quiet and sunny—he's nice to talk to so I quieted down—[What a] great pleasure you gave me—seeing how they are hung—then too—seeing them again—I forget them you know—and even what I think I remember is so often all wrong—

It was almost like going to 291—

When I waked this morning—sun rise—The question came to me as a startling surprise—while I lay there thinking—

What are you to me—

I can not say it even to myself—I don't know how—

Only I can hardly imagine being without you—Space would be so utterly empty—

I liked getting the photographs and the letter after that. It was warm and sunny too—

I feel like such a little girl tonight—no I forgot morning is well on the way—I would like you to hold me close to you—

I was busy all day—worked in my garden till five—came home—was just in the house when up sailed the man from Amarillo that I don't like[288]—

I went up with him but GOSH! Now I hate him—

I'll never go again—Maybe that's why I want to be close to you—The ride was great —green in the sunset—lightning—and small [spots]—dark spotted out now—

I just came in—it's after twelve—

But—it gives me the creeps.

Goodnight.

---

287. See p. 130 and Lynes, appen. III, pp. 1110–1111 for reproductions of Stieglitz's photographs of O'Keeffe's exhibition at 291. William Henry Blaine taught physical education at the Normal College in 1916–1917.

288. Willard Austin.

My Hand—

—I wish you were by me. I'd like you to kiss me goodnight—I feel like such a little girl—queer little girl—

Goodbye

Alfred Stieglitz · [**New York City**] · [**April 19, 1917**] +

Thursday morning.—I have just been printing—Started as soon as I came in.—It's now eleven —The clock just striking it.

—Walkowitz is busy framing a series of Isadora Duncan drawings—He is to have a show at Daniel—forty pictures of *The Dance*.[289]—Some very fine.—

—The windows are open—Yesterday afternoon we suddenly jumped into summer— I was busy all day—photographing part of the day—cramps besides—excitement & worry & probably irregularity in eating—But I remained on my feet at least twelve hours—

I don't want to think—not because of fear—but because I can't do all the thinking for so many about me—so many blind ones—kind ones—The unkind ones see their own interests—they left long ago—

But I've had some fun in photographing. Perhaps you'll see it.—There was a row at the *Independent*—a young woman (probably at Duchamp's instigation) sent a large porcelain urinal on a pedestal to the *Independent*.—Duchamp, Marin, Covert, Arensberg wanted to show it. The rest of the committee wouldn't.—So there is a row—a jury after all.—

—They asked me if I'd photograph it.—Its lines are very fine. I have made a photograph —suggesting a Buddha form—& there is a large Hartley as a background.—The "Art of China" brought up-to-date.[290]—

—The *Blind Man* wants to use the matter for a number—a discussion of "Art"—

—Yesterday an architect was here.—He was much impressed with your work.—His wife is to have a baby in two weeks or so & he wants to bring her up to see your pictures— to see what she'll see—& how she'll feel.—He said that the work suggested Venus & the Madonna—

I laughed.—The real woman always does.—To any man the least bit sensitive.—

—I got a letter too.—And it was, as always, good to get.—Very.—So you heard from the woman with six sons.[291]—You see how much you are giving people—Just in daring to be yourself—I say "daring"—It isn't "daring" at all—You wouldn't be to me what you are

---

289. Walkowitz, Interpretation of the Dances of Isadora Duncan, Daniel Gallery, Apr. 21–May 12, 1917; see "Interpretation of the Dances of Isadora Duncan," *NYT*, Apr. 22, 1917, SM7.

290. Later on this same day, Stieglitz told O'Keeffe: "The *Urinal* photograph is really quite a wonder—Everyone who has seen it thinks it beautiful—And it's true—it is.—You'd like it.—It has an oriental look about it—a cross between a Buddha & a veiled woman—And the Hartley background is great."

291. Florence Schauffler, who with her husband, Charles, would later become close friends of both O'Keeffe's and Stieglitz's, wrote to O'Keeffe on April 10, 1917, saying that she wished she knew her better because she seemed instinctively to "understand" her pictures, "and I reached out and loved the you" expressed in them.

if it were "daring."—The sun doesn't "dare" to shine—nor rise—nor set—It simply does what is natural to it—So with you—You express *yourself*—all the time—every breath of a moment—That's why you mean so much to me—You live from *within*—way, way, way within—the without is an accident—passing—real & no theory—real because the within is so genuine.[292]

—So Walkowitz & Dorothy True had a talk—I wondered if I ever spoke to her—

A young man was sent by her yesterday—he doesn't know you personally—He was much impressed.—Everyone seems to be.—No wonder.—The intensity back of the expression is so great that the deadest must feel some of it—

—Today Fifth Avenue is to be given over to a "Wake-Up America" Parade[293]—to last hours—Chiefly women—schoolgirls—suffrage—nurses—Also boy scouts—youngsters, etc.—I rarely go out of my way to see any kind of parade—not even [to] go to our front window—

Georgia O'Keeffe · [Canyon, Texas] · [April 19, 1917]

Good Afternoon!

It's sunny—warm—green—just spring—

Last night another play—I wasn't much interested but—as fool's luck usually goes—it seemed to turn out better than any so far—

I don't know exactly what happened yesterday that I didn't get any farther—

Except that Watkins[294] was down again in the afternoon—we rode a long time—It was great—such wonderful long strips of color in the plains—spring color—From a higher part in the road out east the town is just a little streak in the long ribbon line—horizon way above the town—It makes paint seem impossible—wonderful light greens and blues and grays and lavenders—When we went back to town Leah[295] decided after much comment that it would be fun to go to Amarillo with him and come back on the train—It was a great ride up—a little rain—much sun—tremendous clouds—I wouldn't have missed the sky for a whole lot—but could very well have gotten along without the rest of it.

136

---

292. Not all of the 291 artists agreed with Stieglitz's assessment of O'Keeffe's art. On May 12, 1917, Stieglitz wrote her that Hartley did not like the things in her show. "They are 'too personal' for him," Stieglitz reported. He added, Hartley "doesn't want to feel struggle—he has had enough himself—He wants a greater objectivity—less subjectivity."

293. The "Wake-Up America" parade of April 19, 1917, was organized by the British War Relief Association of America to demonstrate enthusiasm over the United States' entrance into the war; see "British to March Here," *NYT*, Apr. 15, 1917, 2.

294. Kindred Marion Watkins was a married man with two children who worked at the Connell Motor Company in Amarillo. In her letters to Stieglitz of April and early May 1917, O'Keeffe mistakenly referred to Watkins as "Watson." After she received a letter from him on May 6, 1917, in which he pledged to be with her "*right* or *wrong*," she referred to him as "Watkins." Yet, perhaps indicating that she still had trouble with the Texas accent, she continued to call him "Murray." For clarity, all references to "Murray" and "Watson" have been changed to Marion and Watkins.

295. Leah Harris, a county nutritionist from the Texas Agricultural Extension department, was a friend of O'Keeffe's who lived in Amarillo and whose family had a ranch near San Antonio.

Several times today I wished you were around—somewhere—No—I wanted to go to 291 and just sit there in front of you—I had nothing to say—You would understand if I were just sitting there—

Understand what? Maybe it's the impossibility of living—I don't know—

So I went out and gardened—Did I tell you before that I have a garden—It's in the school garden—too far from the road for anyone to get you in a car and too far from other things for folks to walk to you unless they have to go to the garden—It's a good place to go to —I like to get very tired like hoeing and planting and watering and scratching around ought to make you—but I'm even getting used to that—almost four hours of it today and not a sign of being tired—The wind blew very hard—Sky and plains all round except to the Southwest—big clouds today—great shadows on the plains—

Boys leaving school and going to war—the best ones it seems—some waiting till the end of the quarter—Vacation—three weeks—vacation in three weeks—

I don't know—it's bad—a few new ones getting the fever every day—leaving on one train or another—They can't see at all—I can't see much—but I can see enough to know I can't see—

It's like sending the cattle to market—

Goodnight—I'd like to give you both hands and be very close to you—for the world hurts—Someone to feel it like I feel it—All these other fellows—like—oh the ones that make me hate all the men in the world—They don't think about going to war—They will still be here with cars and their despicable selves—

It's only the nice *youngsters* that go—

[April 20, 1917]
Friday evening—shadows growing long—yesterday a large wind—all quiet tonight—Your two letters this morning—Nietzsche and a letter from Dewald again—Leah and I have been fighting over the book all day at odd moments—both wanting to read at the same time—I'm going to bed with it tonight—

I read all the letters at the dressmaker's—had gone on an errand for someone else— it's right beside the post office—dirty little room but the morning sun comes in—She is a good old soul—and I didn't want to wait till I got home to read—She never said a word while I read it all—I think I'll have to have her make a dress for me—I haven't any and she looks as though it would do her good—It's almost warm enough for white again.—

—I've been dreaming—it would be great if you were here right now.—

—No—young men can't understand—they make me laugh—I wonder why they ever try—Very young ones like me—little boys—the students here—sixteen to twenty-four—they do not try to touch me—they leave me alone—I don't know—I feel like one of them—They talk—maybe it's because they like to talk about themselves and I like to listen—It interests me—

Then too I'm "different" to them—they think I'm queer—I don't know why—They expect nothing—neither do I—That I think and talk and act differently from what they have known before does not scare them—doesn't insult them—

You spoke of Bement[296]—he is one of the best friends I have—has been for five years —one of the few—

He is really great—I've been asking his advice—then only taking about half of it all this time—He only understands me about three-quarters of the way down though—He is too discrete—too safe-minded to squeeze all the juice out of any kind of a lemon—but he is impersonal—

I had painted—drawn—scratched around at it as a youngster—then things happened that made me stop[297]—I hated it—the smell of turpentine almost made me crazy—I just stumbled on him one day—He gave me a new point of view—and I started at it again—I don't know whether he really knows how much I owe him or not—I don't know that I ever told him —guess I didn't—He has done a lot of things that he can't help knowing of—Dorothy and Anita could never understand—He must have married this year—I hadn't heard from him since in the fall and he said nothing of it—I'm glad he's married—really a queer little man—I'll like him better now that he is married—He offered to give me an exhibition this year—Yes—a very funny little man—

Think how funny my things would look any place but 291—Wouldn't it be absurd—

I like him tremendously—only he is—

—Why he is so unlike me I never could understand why he tolerated me—why he ever gave me a second thought—No not at all in love with me—just very patient—very thoughtful—tried to make me have a little sense—I could always go to him when I got in a bad fix—and you can't to many folks—

I wanted him to see what I had been doing so wrote him—

Less fear might make quite a presentable man of him. He loves comfort—so must be afraid.

I'd just as soon give the thing to Dewald[298]—he likes it enough—It tickles me so that he likes—no—that it means so much to him—I would like him to have it—It feels great—and makes me laugh—isn't it funny.

Goodnight—

I must go. It's almost dark—

I feel like bursting—like having a great time—

296. On April 16, 1917, Stieglitz wrote O'Keeffe that Alon and Katherine Bement had come to 291 to see her show. He added: "As for the work I don't think he sees it all—certainly not the color significance."

297. From the fall of 1908 through 1910 O'Keeffe worked as a freelance commercial artist in Chicago to help support her family. A friend later recounted that O'Keeffe was so discouraged by the job, which allowed her very little time for her own art, that she stopped painting for a few years; see Helen Appleton Read, "Georgia O'Keeffe—Woman Artist Whose Art Is Sincerely Feminine," *Brooklyn Eagle,* Mar. 2, 1924, 4.

298. Jacob Dewald bought Lynes 128 for fifty dollars; see GOK to AS, June 7, 1917.

Georgia O'Keeffe · [Canyon, Texas] · [April 24, 1917]

It's another day—spots of blue sky and clouds—not much sun—

Again it's war—girls learning to can and feed folks—what in place of wheat[299]—?

New classes formed[300]—the sister going in for it—She had a letter from Buck[301]—one of our liveliest boys—He had just arrived in El Paso[302]—She thinks she is going to can beans—

Some of the girls come to school in sunbonnets—Not on account of war—they always have—More boys gone—Mothers come to tell them goodbye—

Leah's lover's brother died and she seems to be exceedingly fond of the whole family—

I don't know—A bad day—And things ahead look worse—Wonder—

I went to the dance—Yes—and danced too—Ted[303] is funny—and likes it so much you can't help it—

Lester was there—I thought he wasn't even going to speak to me—but after watching for some time—across the room out of the corner of his immoveable face he came over—He can dance—really well—neither of us said anything—but that the other danced well—

When I found I had danced four or five times with him I went home—that was enough —It was funny—So absurd—And—darn it—I dreamed about him—

I had to laugh—

It's a queer day—

What's the use of Art—if there is war—It's queer enough to get excited over it when there is no war—But when there is war—

And I painted all day yesterday—would today too but haven't time—

Why—though—

And to him—

How are you?

Tuesday—3 P.M.

[April 27, 1917]

Friday morning—

I've been on the run—almost flying every night—

Watkins was down Wednesday night—I like him better—he's funny—honest— anybody frank seems queer—it's like fine cool water on a hot day—He is going to war too— Coming again today—

---

299. On April 22, 1917, Americans were urged to consume only "one wheat loaf a week" because of severe grain shortages in Europe; see "Economize on Food, Warning by Hoover," *NYT*, Apr. 22, 1917, 17.

300. The Normal College offered courses in the spring 1917 semester in the "forms of service that women can render" to the war effort, including cooking, preserving, and food conservation; see "War Work," *Bulletin of the West Texas State Normal College* 16 (1918), 17.

301. Buck W. Bolton was a junior at West Texas State Normal College in 1916–1917.

302. During World War I, El Paso's Fort Bliss, one of the nation's foremost cavalry posts, was home for the U.S. Signal Corps and a training center for antiaircraft units.

303. Ted Reid was a senior at West Texas State Normal College in 1916–1917.

Your letter this morning—It's hurt everywhere these days—everywhere you turn some thing to tell you of it—Hell for folks like you—And me—There is a deadening sort of consciousness of it all

Will something particular for me to do come—I don't know what it will be—

Faust—Nietzsche—We have nothing like that—that I've ever seen—What's it all about anyway—

I cannot clap and wave a flag—

I must go—

Georgia O'Keeffe · [**Canyon, Texas**] · [**April 29, 1917**]

Greetings—my hand—It's Sunday night 9:30—

The sister and I walked—north of town—about three miles—out of the basin where the Canyon begins—You go up a fairly steep—white hill—and at the top of it is the levelness —We started just before dark—just when the moon began to make our shadows pale on the white road. We lay down up there on the edge of the levelness—talked—great sky—I almost went to sleep—Coming home—I was afraid—didn't say so—but I was—

I can't get over being afraid—there is nothing to be afraid of either—even in the moonlight you can see for miles—

We saw the train coming way off—waited for it at the crossing—a long freight train— coming out of the night—I was terribly afraid—but it was worth it—

Clouds had covered the moon—So the black streak—bright yellow streak—soft white smoke strung out—roared and crawled and creaked up on us—out there where there was just nothing around—I can't help being afraid of it—It isn't a train to me—it's an awful live thing—I like the rattle of it as it goes bumping on its way—

Yesterday and today have been bad—Yesterday—I don't know why but I had so much to say and no one to say it to that—I came home and went to bed and covered up my head at about five in the afternoon—Just nobody to talk to that would understand even a little—and I had so much that I wanted to say—So I just covered up and shut my eyes tight—

Watkins' car waked me up—I wasn't asleep—I just knew it—Of course I sat up and looked out and he saw me just as he stopped—He is funny—I like him—He thought it a large joke that there was nothing but my head that I could show—And I wouldn't go down because he had a man with him—I've often seen the fellow with Lester—often seen him on the streets —No one ever told me who he is and I never asked—but he looks at me too hard—and I don't like to be looked at—He is enormous—drives a good car—if I knew him I wouldn't have any better sense than to ride in it—and I just don't ever—

Bah! I hate to be touched. Still he looks as though he would be fun—

Today—I've spent mostly with the Gellers—He teaches Agriculture—They are both sick—I didn't want to stay but I am sorry for them—He is a Rumanian—she a German— Been here seventeen and twenty-two years—Foreign—and some way folks do not understand—

It was bad—I didn't enjoy it a bit—He very quiet—she nervous and excitable—It is terrible. It made me ridiculously glad I'm not married—

GOSH!

A letter from Mr. Dow about my things at 291—riled me—I had told him about them —He liked some color printing I did a couple of years ago and comes harping back on that[304]

I wanted to answer him and tell him "Color printing be damned" but I guess I won't—

Anita always said "Oh! if his mother had only been able to keep him from ever seeing a Japanese print! He would have been a pretty nice old boy but that ruined him"—

Then the *Masses*[305] came—I feel like chewing nails.

Goodnight—

I've just been wondering the past few days why I—and the sister were put in the world—

I feel like such a misfit—She doesn't know it yet but she will in time be as much a misfit as I am and I'm sorry for her—I never ought to talk to folks about anything but the weather—

I always horrify them—And it always surprises me when I find how differently I think about things—

I talked at dinner today—last Sunday too—without intending to—Open mouths and queer looking eyes waked me up both times—

I don't know how I grew queer—how it happens that I'm almost always alone—And I don't care if I am alone—I'd rather be alone than with them—

Your last letter is very alone too—I had forgotten that while writing of myself—If the drawings and things make you less alone—I cannot tell you how glad I am—What would I be doing these days if I could not talk to you—It would be so queer—

Goodnight.

Alfred Stieglitz · **[New York City]** · **[May 1, 1917]** +

Good Morning. It's nearly eleven—I have been cutting cardboard, preparing to mount some fine (useless) photographs of mine. I wish I could break myself of the habit to preserve anything of my own.—

—Everything seems a waste these days.—

—It's another mean day—cold & wet—alternatingly drizzling & heavy rains—May first!—

---

304. Lynes 44. On April 24, 1917, Dow told O'Keeffe that he "was interested in the simplicity of your designs and the harmonious rhythm that you had expressed so well." But he added that there "were too many of those vague things. I remember your excellent work in color printing and think it would be worth your while next time to show a greater variety." Stieglitz responded by noting that Dow was "as far removed from your work as any human can be," adding, "You ought to see the really fright of a picture he has at the *Independent*—Awful—It looks like a seventy-five-year old shriveled up woman who is enameled & painted & acting as if she were seventeen!!" (AS to GOK, May 6, 1917).

305. Both the April and May 1917 issues of the socialist publication *The Masses,* which described itself as "arrogant...impertinent" and "a revolutionary not a reform magazine" (May 1917, 43), contained several articles by the editors, Max Eastman, Floyd Dell, and John Reed, in support of the Russian Revolution and against the war and conscription.

Last night I went to the *Independent Show*—Alone.—I hadn't been there since the opening night & I felt it my "duty" to go again before the close.—Why I should "duty" it I don't know.—On Saturday it closes—a huge failure.[306]—That was a foregone conclusion—I knowing New York—& the committee. Of course the War is blamed.—But the War has little to do with the failure.—The trouble lies deeper than that.—But the War is a convenient scapegoat these days for all fools.—

—Outside of myself—I was there over two hours—there were eighteen people in that big highly lit-up place!—In all about twenty-five pictures have found owners—I doubt whether more than $1,200 have changed hands.—Oil paintings—chromo—in gilt frames, landscapes, were amongst the things sold.—Atrocious things at $25.00 each. Happy artist—happy purchaser!—Sheeler sold his painting for $150 and his drawing for $50 (I'm glad for his sake—he's so modest & the things were very good). And Clifford Williams[307] got $100—Outside of those three things, modern, the red stars were on truck—

—Really what a waste—a deficit of $6,000—Stupidity rampant—how it hurts—But nearly everything hurts these days—hurts doubly.—

Your two drawings looked well—they were hanging next to each other—not over each other like on the first night—If one picked out about fifty pictures from the whole show a good exhibition would be the result.—Your two would be of the fifty.—

—I should have been very tired—having been on my feet at least twelve hours during the day—& should have found sleep. But I couldn't.—Unsettledness gnaws at the brain—keeps one like me wide awake—

I was wondering too whether the people who *begged* me to continue 291—whether they have forgotten.—

Nearly everyone in New York forgets—I was to get money for rent on May 1st[308]—So many promises—so few redeemed.—I asked for nothing. Why volunteer—Perhaps the people are waiting to be *reminded*—I don't remind—We'll see.—Uncertainty everywhere—Nothing but that—

—"Living"—

As I went to the show last night I read your letter—in the car—Watkins—Lester—dance—I'm glad you dance no matter how you may feel—I see Lester—You—You dreamt of Lester—I had to laugh—as you laughed—It's all so natural.—To me.

—Clapping. Waving flags.—Isn't it funny how people are moved by superficial things—not really moved—just react mechanically—& think it's fun—

I can't be enthusiastic by command. I can't feel by command.—Except resentment perhaps.—

—One "friend" of mine is *wildly* enthusiastic that we are helping France—Another

306. The exhibition lost more than eight thousand dollars, most of which was covered by the dozen guarantors who backed it; see Marlor, *Independent Artists,* 12–14.

307. John Quinn bought Charles Sheeler's *Landscape No. 1,* 1916, oil on canvas, for $150, and *Barns,* 1917, crayon, for $50 from the 1917 Society of Independent Artists Exhibition; see Judith Zilczer *"The Noble Buyer": John Quinn, Patron of the Avant-Garde* (Washington, D.C., 1978), 187-188. [Edith] Clifford Williams sold *Two Rhythms* to J. R. McCurdy; see Marlor, *Independent Artists,* 577.

308. Stieglitz had a number of friends and supporters who had helped him pay the rent for 291.

is *wildly* planting potatoes—a third "too busy for words" canning & preserving—It's "wild" about something everywhere—

It nearly kills one to have to listen to it all—Wild about these things as they were wild about art—& wild about Whitman—& wild about knitting things for the poor Belgians—

Hysterical jabbering—No depth—No intensity—Separation—no two moments related—

—How are you today?—

[May 2, 1917]
The sun is out.—It's Wednesday.—The cleaning woman is busy.—It's cold.—Stove going today.—Yesterday too.—The sun is playing hide & seek—with big clouds—West wind —Clearing—Rained all night.—

Tossed about.—Sat in a steaming bath an hour to get tired—Nothing seems to help towards sleep—Maddening.—

One thing might—but that is beyond my having. It's rotten to be so tired.—I laughed all day yesterday—Everything seems so ludicrous—Serious faces affect me as so funny—my own tiredness strikes me as ridiculous—

I wish I weren't so damn sane—It borders on insanity to see too straight—

I had Marin & Zoler laughing for an hour—Carles turned up at home—a surprise— he's restful—for he is straight—isn't playing a game—I haven't heard from the rent guarantors —It makes me laugh—

And through it all your pictures hang there silent watchers—and they give me the strength to laugh—It's a kindly laugh—

I'd like to watch you dance—I'd like to see all you do—just live through seeing—I see much as it is—but there is no end to seeing—

There goes the clock—Eleven— I had better get to doing something.—Sort—& continue getting things in shape—Destroying—No one caring—

Give me your hand—I wonder is it cold—or is it warm—

Are you very quiet?—

Mad—Mad—Surely crazy.—Overtired.

Georgia O'Keeffe · [Canyon, Texas] · [May 1, 1917] +

It's night—

I've just come in—great out—I was out hoeing and watering my garden while the sun set till it was too dark to see—Then went by the Normal on my way home to get a drink—They were practicing the senior play—

Ted and I lay out there on the big flat cement piece on the side of the steps—looking up at the sky for a long time.—Talking—

Ted is a nice boy—No that's not the way to say it—

I like him says it better—

—He is one kind of cowboy—Thinks he can't go to war right now because he has a lot of cattle down on the ranch that they have to keep through the summer—Anyway—he wants to see what's happening—first. He was down there Sunday—and got all excited telling about it—"And don't you know—I have the greatest mother in the world—at least to me."

Tall and thin—muscles like iron—

He asked me something—I don't know what—then rose right up—and asked why I always smiled such a funny smile—and changed the conversation so quickly when he tried to find out if there was a particular man—

I had just started to try to tell him—I don't know exactly what when someone came along—He is good-natured—funny kid—has such funny kinks in his brain—I like him—

Some way or other—I doubt my sanity tonight and I don't know why.

Goodnight—it's a great night—

Georgia O'Keeffe · [Canyon, Texas] · [May 3, 1917] +

Thursday night—Quiet—perfect—such stillness—a wonder world—

Your letter this morning—very busy all day—my garden at sunset—when I couldn't see to hoe I started in with the hose. It must be watered every day—sometime the boys do it for me—it's fun though—Leah and I go out there in the moonlight—the sky still red—it stays red so long here—making the ground black and wet—I can almost see my beans grow—get so absurdly excited over it—

Mrs. Pennebecker (I don't know how to spell it) talked on women's work in the war —right now—tonight. I like her—Then Leah and I walked a little in the night—It's a great night—I came home and read your letter again—I've been in a queer mood all day—

What is whiteness[309]—?

I did such a funny thing last night—I don't know—I've felt like such a little girl all day —wanted just to put my hand on your arm questioning—

Queer too—that it should have been last night—it was just a year ago last night that I went to Virginia—It's like a dream—I wonder was it me—

I told you Watkins was coming in the morning—He hadn't come at ten—so—I went to school and took a bath—I don't know why I didn't wait for him—it was a perfect morning and I wanted to ride—I just can't help doing things like that—

At noon when I came out from class—I got in a car with some other folks—talking and didn't notice him or his horn or anything—till he drove past us—and almost died laughing when I scrambled out and got in with him—He was a bit grouchy because I hadn't waited— picked Leah up and we rode out south—

309. On April 30, 1917, Stieglitz told O'Keeffe that a recent visitor to 291 had "spoken of the *Whiteness*...the intense whiteness" of her "Self-Portrait" and *Blue Lines* (Lynes 99 and 64). He added that it was a "splendid way of putting it.—But I see that [and] an intensity that I'm sure not even you yourself recognize.—A religious glow—of purity."

144

I was furious with myself for missing it in the morning—We didn't want to come in for dinner but he made us—

No use to tell all about it except that—way yonder in the night—I don't know—it was all so queer—I feel so at home with him and he is so funny—Leah had gone in to Dr. Mac's[310] —He kept me talking—"I want you to be to me—say to me—anything you want to—I want to kiss you goodnight—if you want me to—not if you don't want to"—He's the most natural sort of a human I ever saw—Of course I wanted to kiss him—couldn't help wanting to—

I never saw anything so queer—Honesty given you and a chance to be honest—He could hardly understand I think—It seemed impossible to me—we both laughed—And I find myself afraid to be honest—It was all funny—really ridiculous—I couldn't help shrinking from the second one—

So hot—

Gosh it was—I don't know—queer—

He's married—gives me the feeling that he is feeling through all space—all the world to satisfy a fine kind of hunger—

Leah had been driving the car—we had just talked of many things—we had picked her up after a long ride out south after school—had been riding for hours—

It was queer—I never felt the fence so completely down between myself and another —It's not that I care so much—care at all—not that he cares—it was just like the frankest sort of acknowledgment of the fact that I really—honestly—like you immensely—

I wonder—have I made you understand at all—It seemed that not to kiss him meant the lips a little tighter—the eyes colder—the face turned more rigidly toward space—a gnawing sort of hurt—he hurts inside—And that a woman's daring to be human—honest—have faith in him warmed him—

He's queer—

I wonder do you think I'm completely crazy—I wonder too—

You say you understand me—Don't know that I have the least understanding of myself—

All night I couldn't sleep—Headache—sick at my stomach—face burned—thirsty— All day the same—

We didn't stop at Dr. Mac's—we came home—after sitting there in the car for ever so long—just decided to come home—I don't know—I can't understand—He said he might go on to camp—not be down again—but I know he won't—I know he will be down again—He tried to make me promise to go down near the camp for my vacation—Leah has a house twelve miles from where he is going to camp—He's so funny—really downright amusing—besides being so comfortable to be with—I may go—don't know—and he has such an amazing amount of nerve—

I just like him—

---

310. A physician who lived in Amarillo, Dr. "Mac" was Leah Harris's brother-in-law, married to her sister Annette (Annellie; Billie). Although O'Keeffe consistently referred to him as "Dr. Mac" and to his wife as "Billie Mac," his name was Robert McMeans. For clarity, all references to the couple have been left as "Dr. Mac" and "Billie Mac."

Yes—I'm apt to be talked about—he's apt to be caught—and Billie Mac is apt to get Leah—Leah told her last night that I was out there in the car with Marion—

I wanted to shoot her—

Isn't it queer that folks are not supposed to be human—It just makes me want to yell—

Your little girl tonight feels very quiet—I dreamed of him—all the time it seemed—when I dozed a little last night—That queer consciousness of having touched another real human—touching it yet through space because I know it exists—

I would like to put my head in your lap and go to sleep.

It's so quiet out—

Goodnight.

Georgia O'Keeffe · [Canyon, Texas] · [May 6, 1917]

It seems that I've never felt more devoid of feeling of any kind than I do this morning—

Yesterday was cloudy—damp—windy—a little rain from time to time—

Today is Sunday—The world is white with snow—almost a foot of it—heavy on everything—young spring green on the trees shining through or hanging broken—

A white world—I'm glad it's white—glad it looks different from other days.

I wish I could see you—don't know why—

Watkins was down again yesterday—all day—I knew he was coming—don't know why because he didn't tell me—even when it rained I knew it—

And—Oh—I don't know—

The plains were very blue green and violet and purple—Soft wonderful gray—

I don't know what to say about him except that he has left me absolutely devoid of feeling of any kind—

He wanted me to go back with him—waited around all day for me—I had much to do —He took me so far at noon that by the time I got back to work it was impossible to get through till nearly six—

Queer the way I like him—only he likes me—maybe that's not the word—too much—

both so queerly honest—

We rode till almost dark—blue green—lavender and purple—unbelievably long thin horizontal streaks of it—I would *not* go to Amarillo with him—

I don't know why—something made me feel I mustn't—and today I'm so glad I didn't and I don't know why—

Twice he brought me back—stopped the car—and both times snapped his teeth right tight—and the door of the car—and with that hard look straight ahead said he couldn't let me out—had to take me and we rode on—

It was very bad—He thinks that I feel like he does and won't give in—and you know— I don't—

Maybe several things keep me from it without my knowing I'm so reasonable—

If he would just be friends—because I like him immensely—Maybe there just isn't any fire in me—maybe it all died last spring[311]—

It hurt—hurt terribly—I hated to see it—Then too—it surprised me so—That he should get on such a tantrum with so little excuse for—and so many against it—He said so many things that made me laugh—surprised—wonder—once I almost cried—many that hurt—

Still—just being by him is a kind of rest I almost never get—

He wonders—believes—yet can not believe—queer that honesty should be so rare—

He says he will not come again till I ask him to—Not—exactly that—

Tell him I want him to—

And today I wonder—I would be tremendously glad to see him walk in right now—he is good to talk to—the laugh is nice—We laughed often though he reminded me that it wasn't funny to him—I don't think I'll want him enough—to say so—won't want another ride out into the night—at all—I guess—isn't it queer—

—And I seem to know that he will come again—

Of course he'll come again—he will want to—and it's his damnable nerve that I like for one thing—"No—I won't come again—but *remember*—it won't be because I don't want to—it will be because I know it's not best for you"—

And I have to laugh—I know he is so selfish—And he doesn't know it himself—

I'd like to bang my head against the door today because I can't see why things are like they are—

"I am always waiting"—

I'm going to be very busy all next week—then after that three weeks to do as I please—There are several things in the wind—two trips overland to San Antonio—but it all sounds so much like greased lightning that I think I'll go off somewhere and sit in a corner by myself—and not even breathe—just sit there quiet—alone—and watch the dust blow by—

I'd like a dust colored vacation—

Just a little girl this afternoon—be very good to me will you?

I don't know—he was very good to me but some way—

You see—I am just woman to him—

In the course of the afternoon I remarked that I ought to be shot—he reached over toward the pocket of the car where I know he keeps a long slim black pistol—and I quickly told him—not today—thank you—Still—why not—. The snow is almost gone—it's late afternoon—

Georgia O'Keeffe · [Canyon, Texas] · [**May 9, 1917**]

—I don't know how to begin—don't know that I have anything to say—

—Only all inside I'm crazy and I don't know what over—how—why or anything—just don't know anything—I wouldn't mind dying when I feel like this—

311. In the spring and summer of 1916 O'Keeffe's once strong feelings for Arthur Macmahon diminished.

Ted told me I was pale—Was I sick—

I'm feeling great—not sick—but—what is it—is it just so full of woman that I feel—

Been looking out the window—it's cloudy—raw—cold—

Forgot where I was at—

I don't know—what it is—My hands so full—full of what—I don't know—

Ted thinks maybe he will go down on the Rio Grande to be a River Guard—would rather do that than be just a straight run along soldier—Has a ranch and cattle down there—

I want to go along—I want to get right out and go somewhere now—

I was laughing at the way he walks today and he said—Why that's because I've always lived in boots—

Queer the way I like him.

What in the world is the matter with me these days anyway.

I feel full of wheels and empty spots—Out of kindness to the rest of the folks I ought to leave everyone alone—I feel like a curse to everyone I talk to—I ought not to even let Ted look at me—

It's something tingling to my very fingertips that I feel almost burns folks—The queer over-sensitiveness toward everyone—feeling and seeing with them all even more keenly than usual—

Your little girl—a piece of fast-burning wood—Hot—moving—easily put out.

Next week all will be different—so much between now and then that it scares me —What—

The other teachers here don't have the sort of time I have—but I can't help it—

I feel like a fire-cracker.

IN EARLY MAY 1917, as Congress moved closer to passing a prohibition amendment, Stieglitz decided "it would be sheer madness to continue 291"[312] and made arrangements to close the gallery on July 1. In the coming days he met with other New York gallery directors to ensure that they would exhibit the 291 artists who had come to depend on his support, and he began to move some of his large collection of paintings, drawings, and photographs into a 7½ × 11 foot room in the same building that housed the gallery. He also decided to stop publishing *Camera Work* after numbers 49–50 and told Emmy that they might have to leave their home at 1111 Madison Avenue for a cheaper residence.

Throughout the spring of that year, as O'Keeffe watched many of the young men of Canyon enlist, she had coquettishly flirted with the Canyon attorney Rector Lester, the married Amarillo men Willard Austin and Kindred Watkins, and the student Ted Reid with a casual disregard for the small town's standards of propriety. But by early May, her relationship with both Watkins and Reid had become more intense and complicated. As she later explained, she was staggered that "so many people had kissed me in such a short time—and I had liked them

312. AS to Aline Meyer Liebman, May 16, 1917, Aline Meyer Liebman Papers, Archives of American Art, Smithsonian Institution, Washington, D.C.

Alfred Stieglitz, *Georgia O'Keeffe at 291*, 1917. Platinum print, 8⁵⁄₁₆ x 7½ in. (23.3 x 19 cm). National Gallery of Art, Washington, Alfred Stieglitz Collection. Greenough 457.

all and had let them all—had wanted them to."[313] When the spring semester ended on May 14, she "fled" Canyon, as she told Stieglitz, going first to Amarillo with Leah Harris to visit "Dr. Mac" and his wife "Billie." But a few days later when she received Stieglitz's letter announcing his intention to close 291, she decided on the spur of the moment to go to New York and left Texas on May 20. While she still had many friends in the city, "it was [Stieglitz] I went to see," she confessed to Pollitzer. "Just had to go Anita—There wasn't any way out of it."[314] She flabbergasted and entranced Stieglitz by arriving at 291 with no warning on May 24. Although he had taken down her exhibition a few days earlier, he immediately rehung it. In the next few days, which

313. GOK to Paul Strand, June 23, 1917, Center for Creative Photography, the University of Arizona: Paul Strand Collection; hereafter cited as CCP:PSC.

314. GOK to Anita Pollitzer, June 20, 1917, in Giboire, *Lovingly, Georgia,* 255.

O'Keeffe described as "the most wonderful days of my life,"[315] he introduced her to some of the 291 artists, including Abraham Walkowitz, Stanton Macdonald-Wright, and Paul Strand, as well as the collector Jacob Dewald and the inventor Henry J. Gaisman. On May 30, Decoration Day (now known as Memorial Day), Gaisman drove Stieglitz, Strand, and O'Keeffe to Sea Gate, an exclusive community on Long Island, and then to Coney Island. As the group strolled on the boardwalk, Gaisman and Strand went on ahead, while O'Keeffe and Stieglitz, talking quietly, lingered behind. When the sea breezes chilled O'Keeffe, Stieglitz attentively wrapped his loden cape around her. A few weeks later she declared that "it was a great party and a great day."[316]

Before leaving New York on June 1, O'Keeffe returned to 291 and Stieglitz made four portraits of her, two of her face in front of her watercolor *Blue I* (1916), and two of her hands.[317] He and Gaisman then took O'Keeffe and Arthur Macmahon to the station for her train back to Canyon. In the days to come Stieglitz frequently wondered "why I hadn't put my arms around you at the station & held you—not letting you go—& why I hadn't kissed you as I wanted to."[318]

Alfred Stieglitz · [New York City] · June 1, 1917

It's a queer sensation—June 1st—pouring rain—I'm here at 291—long before nine.—And I don't know whether you are on the Albany boat[319]—gone—or whether you are to go tonight.—

—291 seems no more.—Even though I am right here—And the walls still stand—and nothing seems changed since yesterday.—

And yet all seems changed.—I wonder what it is—

Isn't it odd that the sunniest day while you were in New York was Decoration Day?—The only real sunny day.—

—It's queer how fond I am of you.—Not at all as man & woman—something so different—It's very wonderful—& it hurts terribly—Hurts in the same way as it hurts when I look at Kitty—my daughter—

You have given me so much—just in being—& doing—& I feel so much like doing—for you—& for her—& one or two others—& I feel so utterly helpless—paralyzed.—

—How I wanted to photograph you—the hands—the mouth—& eyes—& the enveloped in black body—the touch of white—& the throat—but I didn't want to break into your time—As I wanted to walk into the night—with you too.—I can tell you now—when it can't be.[320]—

Others wanted you—& I felt they were nearer life than I was—and I wanted you to be with life—

---

315. GOK to AS, May 29, 1917.

316. GOK to Pollitzer, June 20, 1917, in Giboire, *Lovingly, Georgia,* 256.

317. Lynes 119; Greenough 457–460.

318. AS to GOK, June 4, 1917.

319. At the time, many people took a boat up the Hudson River to Albany, where they boarded trains heading west. O'Keeffe, however, took a train directly from New York to Chicago.

320. Stieglitz photographed O'Keeffe later that day.

—Arthur.—Yes, it was the same I saw in the Little Room—alone one day—looking at your pictures—rather bewildered—a questioning gaze—I looked at him—I knew it must be Arthur—but I said nothing—nor did he.—I knew he didn't see the pictures.—A fine clean fellow.—He cares for you tremendously—And you care for him too.—Neither can change.— That blue drawing[321]—you & he—becomes more & more uncanny in its vision—its absolute picturing of truth.—If he could but see an iota of what I see in it—you would be his.—Life is maddening—so much comes so near to absolute truth—Contact—yet no touch—eternal separation.—

—To understand it all—to see it so clearly—that seems to be my fate.—

—The world without 291.—

I losing touch with all the young ones—all those that mean the world—the worth-whileness of living—Why do I do it?—I could go on—& still it is impossible—

—I know you understand.—or rather feel it must be right—it couldn't be otherwise—

Is it sentimentality—?—Am I all mush—hysterical—?—No, it's not that—I know it—

Yet I'm sitting here with the tears just rolling down my cheeks—so desperately alone—& yet so full of life.—

Canyon.—The Plains.—The Night.

—Greet them all from me—You have brought them to me—take me to them—

What a wonderful thing a woman can be—should I say what a wonderful thing a wonderful woman is—

All are wonderful—Some a little more so than others—

And men—? I wonder what they are.—

—You said it was fortunate that women had no memories.—I think you're right—But I never knew it until recently—that's what the last year or so has taught me.—You see I am still learning.—

—I wonder what is going to happen today.—

I'm glad you saw the Strand photographs[322]—it means much to him that you did— I wish 291 could show them—*Camera Work* will have them—

And I'm glad you saw little Georgia's things—& liked the house particularly.[323] —

—And I'm glad that Marin liked your new work—It stood there against the wall & we sat before it a long while looking at it—

It is still pouring—although it had stopped for a few moments—the rain is beating on the tin roof—

I'm still in coat & hat—it's so damp & chilly up here & I have a rotten cold—

---

321. Lynes 119.

322. O'Keeffe told Pollitzer that Strand "showed me lots and lots of prints—photographs. And I almost lost my mind over them—Photographs that are as queer in shapes as Picasso drawings"; O'Keeffe to Pollitzer, June 20, 1917, in Giboire, *Lovingly, Georgia,* 256.

323. Stieglitz's eleven-year-old niece, Georgia Engelhard. "The House" may be Engelhard's watercolor *The Doll's Bungalow* (Lake George, 1916), reproduced in Kathleen Pyne, *Modernism and the Feminine Voice: O'Keeffe and the Women of the Stieglitz Circle* (Berkeley, 2008), 194.

5:50—

Here I am back at 291.—I had to come back. Just to see the Little Room.—Disordered as it is—The Little Room—And you are at the station—the train to go in ten minutes—to carry you off—further & further away—in miles—What a wonderful day it has been—Never a more wonderful [one]—everything—everybody—And all because you are just you—

Nature's child—A Woman—All feel it—To all you mean more than you know—Strand—Gaisman—Dewald—

291—The Park—Lunch—And Arthur—I'm glad we met—& I'm glad he is to bring the things down—

And when you get these lines you'll be thousands of miles away from here—

Yet here—

Your coming today has made it easier for me to close the place—There never was a purer spirit than breathes today—The train leaves in a minute—Now it is pulling out—I'm chilled to the bone—There goes the clock—

Georgia O'Keeffe—Black—White—Hands—Eyes—Smile—

It's dark—only a pale silhouette out the window—

It's all bad—leaving—I wanted so much to kiss you goodbye—the right side of your face and neck—and I didn't because of him—and I just seem to have frozen toward him—Why did I mind him when I felt that way—He has come so near thawing now too—that's what hurts—when he has killed the thing in me that was so live and warm—Just chilled it clear through—Yes—hurt—I just told him the truth about it—and even after they had yelled "All Aboard"—he got in the train again—and just stood closer to me than he could on the platform and kissed me again—It just makes me feel so tired—tired of fighting and fighting.

I wished Gaisman had kept me[324]—and just let me rest—not think or feel or anything—It was so nice in the car between you two—He gave me such a fine feeling of rest—being very much protected—thought of—You all around me—everywhere—His eyes—his hands—make me feel I could—maybe give him what he wants—if he just let me be very still and rest first. Queer the way I liked him—his warmness—

So much that I almost am writing this to him instead of or as well as to you—Only if I wrote it to him—I want to ask him why he didn't keep me—and of course it wouldn't be a question to be answered like other questions—it would be—

—I haven't his address anyway. I wonder if he thought of it—of keeping me—or did just I think—I fancy you laugh loud and long over that—I laugh too—

Maybe the warmness of all you folks down there made Arthur seem farther away than ever—

I don't know—I feel so puzzled and mixed up—

---

324. On March 29, 1917, Stieglitz told O'Keeffe that Gaisman was eager to find a wife.

I'd like to be a baby tonight—have wanted to be ever since I left you—and have you rock me to sleep—in your arms—

You said "Did I hurt you"—don't be foolish—I don't know why I had to cover my eyes—my face—You know don't you—and that I kissed you many times as you went away in the car—

Queer about Gaisman—Tonight—how much I wish he had kept me—

And I was almost afraid to stay in a room alone with Strand—Afraid *of* myself—not *for* myself—Afraid for him—

It's a good thing I don't stay around New York—Something would happen somewhere—

Am I crazy?

I seemed to be headed for something—just like a sled tearing downhill—

—I wish I'd bump tonight—even if the jolt of stopping killed me—

When you have rocked me to sleep kiss me Goodnight—

And help me be quiet.

Do you suppose—?—

Why—isn't it funny to say—

Well—the Gaisman joke is your—?

I'll not say it.

ON HER WAY to Texas, O'Keeffe briefly visited her younger brother, Alexis, who was in officer training camp at Fort Sheridan, Illinois. Although he had previously impressed her as "the sort that used to seem like a large wind when he came into the house," she now found his belief that he would not return from France and his "sober—serious—willingness—appalling."[325] She arrived back in Canyon on June 4 to teach summer courses at the college and its elementary school. Inspired by both the people she had met and the art she had seen in New York, she immediately began to paint, making watercolors of the Canyon landscape, as well as a series of abstract portraits of both Paul Strand and Kindred Watkins.[326] In the next few months as she and Strand exchanged letters, the attraction between them intensified. Soon after she met Strand, she wrote Pollitzer, "Dorothy and I just fell for him." And later that month, she confessed to Strand, "The look in your eyes that startled me so was the day you and Walkowitz showed me his things—I had just run from eyes—I had run like mad—only to find a glimmer of the same thing in new eyes—So I looked away—wondering wasn't there any place to get away from that look—from folks that feel that way about me."[327] She also inextricably linked Strand's art and his persona, telling him: "The work—Yes I loved it—and I loved you—I wanted to put my arms round you and kiss you hard—There you were beside me really and the same thing in front of me on paper—I never saw or felt anything like it."[328]

325. GOK to Paul Strand, June 3, 1917, CCP:PSC.

326. Lynes 189–194.

327. GOK to Anita Pollitzer, June 20, 1917; see Giboire, *Lovingly, Georgia*, 256.

328. GOK to Paul Strand, June 24, 1917, and June 11, 1917, CCP:PSC.

Alfred Stieglitz, *Paul Strand*, 1917. Silver and platinum print.
Collection of the Center for Creative Photography, University of Arizona.
Copyright © 2010 Georgia O'Keeffe Museum/Artists Rights Society (ARS), New York.

As she drew closer to the 291 circle of artists and intellectuals, she recognized that everything about her—the way she looked, dressed, spoke, and thought—set her apart from the other residents of Canyon. Rather than breezily dismiss their conventional ways, as she had once done, she grew increasingly restless and recognized, as she confided to Stieglitz in early June, that she was "the most talked of woman on campus," perceived by others as "queer" and "different."[329]

Alfred Stieglitz · [New York City] · [June 3, 1917] +

Good Morning, dear Soul.—It's Sunday, two in the afternoon.—And I'm at 291. Alone.—I have been all day.—Printing. Seeing how those negatives turned out.[330] —Of course nothing like what they should be—not what I wanted—not you within a thousand miles—yet—I'm glad I have what I have. I'll send you proofs in a day or two.—I wonder what the fellows (here) will say.— I'm so full of you that I can't tell you how bad they are—or how good.—

329. GOK to AS, June 11, 1917.
330. Greenough 457–460.

—And you are speeding on & on—& are within fifteen hours of Canyon—forty-four hours away from 291—from me—Yes, me.—I guess I'm mad to think of that—But you have become such a great part of me that I can't quite make it out.—Of course I'm not sorry—Your honesty is so wonderful & I have suffered terrifically because of the lack of it in so many who were dear to me.—And you are more than honest—it is that heart of yours—big as space itself —that's what grips me so terrifically—

I wonder how you are feeling—The trip must be a rest. Away from the tension of New York—& of Canyon.—

—I had a rotten night.—And on my way down here I broke down on the street.— I'm all nerves.—The family is spending the day in the country.—I cooled my cheeks on your *Self-Portrait*[331] this morning—my head was throbbing so terrifically—& I feel so terribly alone —& so terribly full of yearning—for—?

Is it rest?—

Dear Soul—I can't tell you how grateful I am that you came—but it hurts that you had to go.—But it was best just as it is—For you.—And perhaps for me—I really don't know.— It's so quiet here.—Afterwards I'll take a bus ride—on top—it's very warm.—

How is the lip—May I?—

Georgia O'Keeffe · [Canyon, Texas] · [June 5, 1917] +

Tuesday morning—five till eight.

The sister came in and waked me—my room all sunshine before seven—I had slept— A tired feeling of having very much rested—relaxed.

I've had breakfast—the sister brought the early mail—A letter from you was all besides papers—

Quiet this morning—I read your letter on the way from breakfast—white linen again— leaned against the porch arm at the steps to finish it—the walk from breakfast is only a short block—

I'm afraid I would have cried but I had to come past people in the house maybe to get upstairs—

I felt as I left that I meant a lot to many—and it seemed so queer—it bewildered me—

—The sister just came in—saw what I had painted last night—standing in a row on my bed. "Why they look just like people—real people—different ones—No—all the same—naked people."[332]

It made me feel uncanny—sort of crawly way down to the ends of my fingers—for they were people—and it seemed so real to her—I guess they are Strand—anyway—it's something I got from him—

---

331. Lynes 99.
332. Lynes 189–194.

I wanted to paint longer—do it again and others—but it was too dark—

And it's queer—I rather enjoy having it still in my head yet—

I must go—

My hand—

And—

Alfred Stieglitz · [**New York City**] · [**June 6, 1917**] +

Good Morning. Another clear day—cool.—It's not yet time to take the daughter to school. Another twenty minutes.—

Yesterday was a full day—too full in fact—some work done—but too many visitors— Mabel Dodge—Maurice Sterne—Hapgood—Dewald—& a host of others you don't know.— And the evening—from 8:30 till midnight Hapgood & I sat together in the Café of the Brevoort (you were at the Brevoort with Dewald) & talked—a wonderful evening of comparing notes on life—spiritually—through real living. Unafraid of truth—even unafraid of "Wickedness"— And while we were talking Dr. Brill, the psychoanalyst, sat with us a short while. Brill is a pupil of Freud & the man who translated Freud into English—I have several times been on the verge of sending you Freud—but I decided it was best for you to go without him.—It seems you picked up a volume of his at Dewald's—& he asked you whether you had ever read Freud.— You see how things come around—I have to smile.—No, don't read Freud—not till I tell you to. You laugh—& wonder why I should talk that way—Perhaps you are not laughing but feel what I want to express—

It's better to read *Faust*—over & over again—

—Brill related about an Englishman who had been at the front—wounded several times. Is here now.—The Englishman relates how all the soldiers have become brutalized—really animals.—How the French take prisoners—& then stand them up in a row & mow them down with machine guns.—Enjoying the "sport."—How the English as a "pastime" take a German, put a small hand grenade into his pocket, time it, & then make the German run—& suddenly the thing explodes & the poor devil is blown into bits—& the soldiers think it a huge joke—

Then too he related how the soldiers in their imagination are already raping the German women to "get even" with German atrocities in Belgium. How the men sit about hatching fiendish ideas how they should do this deed in the most bestial manner—

—A picture of man's civilization! The human race at war—showing all its animalism.— All so natural.—And now we are to go into it—& do likewise.—We think we won't—but we are not a bit better.—

—It's all ghastly—& gives one the creeps.—

—The night was a little better. It was one when I got into bed—& I had walked— & I had taken two mild highballs—the first in over a year—I don't think I've taken ten in my life!—

But the talk with Hapgood—its intensity—got me dreaming—all sorts of things— agreeable & otherwise—details I don't remember—

I dreamt of you too—pleasantly—you were sitting on a chair sewing—sitting by my bedside—& you looked very serene & wistful—I was ill—

—And how is the Little Girl—A week ago today was Decoration Day—it seems ages & ages ago—& yet as if but a moment ago—It's as if it had been a dream—It was perfect—that day.—Only much, much too short—It should have included the night.—

You see I never quite get enough of a perfect thing—

Georgia O'Keeffe · [Canyon, Texas] · [June 6, 1917] +

It has been a wild day—Wednesday

I spent last night at my sick lady's house—Her husband[333] was away and she wouldn't have anyone but me—It was terrible—She is so nervous—Then trying to get classes straight all day—

I had seen Watkins yesterday too—and his eyes—Gosh I thought I'd die—

Ted at a distance—Today right at me—

"I was terribly afraid you wouldn't come back"

He looks different—Had spent several nights—awake all night—There is something great about him—really fine—We talked a long time and have a lot more to talk—

He makes me afraid of myself again—

There is something I can do for him—something that will matter a lot in all his life —I don't know what it is—It will just be in the way I act—You see—it's hard for him to understand me—I sort of feel that I mean woman to him—almost more than a particular woman—

When I've gone—will he be sure that they are fine—My honesty makes it hard for most twenties to understand and believe—and I so much want him to—

Many folks stopped me and asked me about some things in my work that surprised them—I had to go to the dressmakers to get some buttons fixed and other little tag end jobs that I won't do myself—More people—the folks in the house here—I had to talk to—Then just a little time to paint before dark—

Just as I turned on the light—I was sitting by the window—up drove Watkins—I got out on the roof and talked awhile—He wanted me to get Claudie and ride—Not me though —enough—

I decided it was a good time to tell him I must stop—he mustn't come around any more and mustn't phone—So went down and told him—

Nice sort of a chap—he understood—Not safe for either of us—he knew it all the time—Isn't it queer—the way he likes me—yet would make trouble for me if I'd let him—

Queer way of liking a person—isn't it—He would just walk on anything to get what he wants—

I both hate him and like him for it—

---

333. Mr. and Mrs. Henry Geller.

The amusing thing is—I was painting on him[334] when he drove up—

He gave me such definite creepy crawls—I had to make it and now I'm just torturing myself by leaving it on the wall—It makes me feel like I have felt all day—as though I could hardly stand living—I can hardly stand that thing in the room—The look on his face yesterday—

Oh I'd like to see you tonight—

I wondered several times—why I didn't walk out into the night with you—

Your letter this morning was great—some way I seem to feel in it that Arthur was a small edition of a stone wall—even to you—

I'm tired—terribly tired—

Being alone in my room seems fine—

—I've been puzzled—Everything seems so queer—

People as they go through my mind—I've thought of Strand often—The photographs just simply get me—they are him—

The Wrights are music—Marins—as you said last fall—lovely flowers—

Arthur—a trembling kind of sweetness that seems to mean—be—all the world—but I'm afraid he is an illusion—At any rate—he will never make me believe—feel certain that it isn't just a dream—And I so much want it to be real—

It would take so much to make me believe—now—

He never will—he can't—he couldn't even when it would have taken such a little—

Believe—what—What is it I want—

It's so little compared to what most women seem to want of men that it makes me laugh—

And it's queer the way I think about Gaisman—"Why didn't he keep me"—I didn't think about it when I was there—I wonder if I'd have said it if I had—wouldn't it have been funny—

And the funny surprised feeling I have about it—

People and people—I wish so much I could see you—

I don't know why only I do—

Oh so very much—

Alfred Stieglitz · [New York City] · [June 10, 1917] +

291—It's about three—I have been destroying—tearing up—photos—books—papers—some pictures—It's impossible to think of preserving all that stuff—Where put it?

—Much of it can never mean anything to anyone outside of myself.—And I?—I may have trouble enough soon to find space enough for my own physical self—

It would have been great had the place burnt down that day I carried down your things while the building was on fire. Then all this mess would have been avoided—It would have been a "clean" job—

334. Lynes 192–194.

—Still there is one reason why I'm glad that it didn't burn down—do you know the reason?—

You ought to be able to guess.—Your show—living at 291 with them—just as I did —& then your coming just as you did—

—Had the building burnt down that time my job—the present one—would have been spared me—but I would have lost that which I could not afford to lose—What was that?—

You may know—That glorious feeling of completion—a living potential completion —that which was given to me by you when you came—out of the clear sky—

—Wonderful things have happened at 291—several very wonderful—none more so than your coming that day—& your stay.—Nothing else in the whole world would have equaled that—at that time—for me.—

—I wrote you this morning that you were a symbol to me—not a person.—I have to laugh.—A symbol—Spirit—Woman—so many things that names seem stupid—& I hate names.—Still seem to use them—even I.—

—It's hot up here—Filthy—gritty—the windows & doors all open—so the dirt flies around thick.—

Gaisman's address is: Auto-Strop Razor Company, 345 Fifth Avenue, New York—I've been wanting to let you have it every time I wrote. I'll send this off afterwards so that you have the address in case you feel like sending that letter to him—or another.

This paper is glorious.—I wonder if you'll be able to use it at all.—I hope Of[335] has finally shipped that box to you.

—I've just had your little piece of sculpture[336] in my hand—In spite of what it lost in casting—I like it.—Much.—You great Girl.—

—The fellows asked me yesterday whether I'd be here today.—I didn't know then.— I guess I'll go home earlier than I expected to—It's a great day to get into a bath—& I'm sorely tempted to do so before night.—It looks now as if it might storm.—

—I wonder how you are spending Sunday—Is it very hot down there—but you like heat—it will let you warm up a little—

It's very quiet here—not a sound.—Yes, a few sparrows—& then an auto horn— It's nice to be so alone for a change—

—I look around here & I can't believe that very soon others are to live here—& I be on the street—But my heart no longer aches because of that—

Dear Little Girl—that's what you did—took away the pain because of 291—that terrible, terrible pain.—Your caring as you did released that pain—I discovered that yesterday.—

It's true.—

Your hands—

My head feels funny—

Dear Little Girl.—

---

335. The painter George F. Of, who was also Stieglitz's frame maker, was sending O'Keeffe a box containing paper, reproductions of Cézanne's work, and photographs of African sculpture.

336. Lynes 66.

Georgia O'Keeffe · [Canyon, Texas] · [June 11, 1917]

Your letter this morning—

At Tubman's—Just meeting him—watching him a little while was great—I'd like to see him often—The wife must be very nice—I wonder if she would like me—Women do—and they don't—both at the same time I so often feel—

I hear that I am the most talked of woman on the faculty—I don't know why—It makes me want to put a few things in Anita's little bag and leave—quietly—on the night train —I believe I'm considered "queer"—"different"—and if I were different from what I am I'd be artificial—or something that's not me—I don't know what I'd be—I thought I was going very quietly about my business—Saying very little to anyone outside of it—So was greatly surprised to learn that I was being very much discussed—

My clothes—my shoes—my hair—my face—my talk in classes—the things I say— I don't like it—

You see the summer folks are different from the winter folks—older—most of them teachers—

I wonder if I as a person get in the way of what I am trying to teach—Isn't it funny—

It's so absurd to try to teach anything—and I—as a person—to myself am just nothing—it seems so ridiculous that anyone should think to talk about me.

It's raining—lightning—thunder—Much needed rain—everything was burning up— I don't enjoy rain—

—The thing in your letter this morning has been—in my mind rather often during the day—What you said about being free—

Why of course I feel free—Never occurred to me to feel any other way—Why shouldn't I—I owe you nothing—You owe me nothing—still—

The sister and I walked a long way this evening after it was too dark to work—In talking—our talk was interesting—in a way—I said some things I wanted to say to her—I tell her some things that happen to me hoping that some way things will help her—Living is going to be queer to her—and I want her to understand—What—I don't know—I don't understand —anything myself—how can I help her—

We were talking about my different friends—When she mentioned you—I made the remark that I just didn't see how people could get along in the world without having what you mean to me—

She remarked that as far as she could see not many people seem to have it—

—She is a funny little girl—I am beginning to feel that maybe she is rather fond of me —I never felt it before—I wish you knew her—Maybe I wish more that she knew you—

She likes Arthur very much—

Free—Yes I'll always have to be—I cannot help it—you cannot help it—No one can help it—

Yes raining—I've been sitting here dreaming—looking at my bare feet—I'd like to draw them with the toes all turned down—the feet right close together—the left overlapping the right a little—They look like I feel when I want to be close to someone—maybe my face turned to be kissed—

Funny that feet would look like that—

Goodnight—

Georgia O'Keeffe · [**Canyon, Texas**] · [**June 16, 1917**]

The box came—yesterday—and I love myself[337] and the other things made me jump—The Cézanne mountain particularly and the Negro sculpture—The feeling of power in the mountains is one of the greatest surprises I ever had—I didn't look at them in New York you know—when you gave them to me—

I believe I like my hands better than my face—though both seem different every time I look at them—I'm glad there is the outside of my right hand after the two of the inside of it—

I believe I like the one with my neck and hands best—the hands against me—

It makes me laugh that I like myself so much—Like myself as you make me[338]—Maybe it's you and me that I like—I like myself better than anything of yours I've seen unless it's the tracks in winter[339]—that always stays in my mind—

It's Saturday night—I painted from supper till dark—

The way I'm painting makes me think I may be crazy. It's just sort of rambling around with color—such a curious half-indifferent sort of a way of going at it—always wanting to—but only feeling about it—

—I can't exactly explain—The thing I worked on today—dry paper—then wet looks like a poor imitation of Marin—I certainly had no such intention—it looks like my left hand too—No—I guess like both of them—the inside and the outside—

Of course I can't tell much by the electric light—it's just a senseless absurd blob—and I like it—still have to laugh at the half-awake humor I was in when I made it.

I'm tired tonight—so tired that my head almost aches—

—Yesterday afternoon I met Ted on the street by accident—Said he had been looking everywhere for me all the week and never could find me—where had I been—wanted to hear me laugh—When he had been funny till we got to my house he said—

Yes—and here I've been wanting so much to talk to you—now I've had a chance I never said a thing I've wanted all this time to say—I've just been talking nonsense—Still it seemed I just couldn't think of anything else—And he turned around—with his back almost to me—and said—Tell me anyway—Do you still like me—

I said—Yes, Ted I think you are great—And we both laughed—and he said it was all right then—And we turned and went on—

337. Greenough 457–460.

338. On June 8, 1917, when Stieglitz sent O'Keeffe prints of the photographs he had recently taken of her, he wrote, "I think I could do thousands of things of you—a life work to express you."

339. Greenough 284–286.

Funny—it tickles me in such a peculiar way—and it feels so right—We are both so funny—

I'm tired—must stop—

Goodnight—

Yes my hands.

I'm so glad it's Saturday night. I'd like to be under the tree by you—close by you—touching you—dark—very still—night—its livingness I want to feel and quiet—

Alfred Stieglitz · [New York City] · [June 23, 1917] +

Saturday—5—At home—I came home a little while ago & took my clothes off & threw myself on the bed.—So hot—so tired.—All windows, all doors open. No one home.—I came home early because 291 was so full of grit & dirt—looks so upside down—ransacked—and it was unbearably hot there—or I felt hotter than usually—I had gotten down early—& had been on my feet all day—

—Here I am at the open window—practically naked—a draft, the door open & not far away.—In fact all doors open—the apartment rooms run into each other like one room—

—There was no storm last night—not in New York—in Brooklyn they say it rained.—I tossed about all night—hugged the pillow—I wanted to sleep—but no sleep.—

—When I got to 291 early—a letter—green stamps.—I sat down & read it—It was like a cooling breeze in an oven-like atmosphere.—I sat on a chair—the "easy-chair" in the little place next to the room on the left—the space next to the one where your oils hung—in fact part of the main back room—I sat there & read the letter. And when finished closed my eyes—& held the sheets of paper firmly between my hands—I felt your hand—& when I looked up I involuntarily kissed the paper I had held.

—I wonder what prompted me to do that.—The letter was so calm—so big—purity itself.

The walk with Claudie—I can see you two walking—Of course she is very fond of you—How could it be otherwise if she is anything like you—& she must be like you—

—I won't go into the letter—

—I got out your paintings—the new ones—& I stood them up before me—I sat on the chair—the letter in my hands.—

—Those paintings!—All three are remarkable—the Portrait uncanny—powerful—The red one[340]—what can I say—I had to think of the first color things I saw of yours—Incredible this new work—The color is as much yours as is black & white—charcoal—What a glorious world you carry within you—Glowing with purest light—

As I sat there looking—looking—I wondered what kind of a child you'd bear the world some day!—The Glory of Dawn & the Glory of the Night—& the Glory of the Noon Sun—all combined—within that Womb of Yours—

---

340. Lynes 189–194; possibly Lynes 159.

The Universe—A Woman's Soul!

I can't tell you how glad I'm to have those paintings—just now—

That's why you sent them—now—

—And the blue & green one.[341]—The calm bigness—again thoroughly you—thoroughly expressive—shapes & forms & color—

—Passion under control.

—Have you any idea how you are developing—how rapidly—& how perfectly.—

—As I sat there like in a church—alone in a church—I & beauty—Zoler came in. Somehow I was glad he came.—He stood & looked.—And was moved—much—deeply.—And he spoke too—very beautifully & truly—

I wish you could have heard.—And then he sat down near me—& we looked together—then others came—Walkowitz—Strand—Gaisman—& Lee,[342] just arrived from Paris.—And we sat there & looked.—Lee related about Paris—the War—he has been over there three years—related about Picasso too—intimate with him—about Brancusi—conditions—life & art there—New York seems funny to him—unreal.—

As he spoke I heard but I saw your pictures—the whole world.—

—Later on I showed Strand & Walkowitz & Zoler the watercolors.[343]—They too are very beautiful—color expressive—But there was an argument about the "right-side-up."—We disagreed. You remember them.—How do they go.—It makes a difference.—I'm sure I had them straight.—The other way around I was too conscious of heads—fantastic animal shapes—

My way I merely got expression of color & form—& possibly a subconscious suggestion of shapes related to the animal & vegetable world.

—I didn't tell Strand he might have "himself"[344]—didn't tell him one was he—There are three series—one you say is Ted—one Strand—one—?

Can you designate through a suggestion of line who is who.—

I wouldn't say this but if I should decide to let Strand have one I would want him to have "his"—no other. For myself all three series are fine—the delicate one is possibly the finest as far as color is concerned.—One series is very powerful—virile—& there is much suggestion of primitive forms in it—These two series are composed of three each—The other is composed of four—

—I have brought the watercolors home to look at them tomorrow. Sunday.—I'll be alone.—I don't think I'll go to 291—& still if it should be cool—?

—My eyes are burning—& my head throbbing—

It's wonderful to know you are not a myth—but are really made of flesh & bone—a real human—.

—Your paintings are in the new little room—somehow I want them in there over Sunday—

---

341. Possibly Lynes 166, 209–211.

342. Probably the painter and set designer Lee Simonson.

343. Probably Lynes 189–194.

344. Lynes 189–191. In her letter of June 12, 1917, O'Keeffe told Stieglitz to give Strand the portraits she had made of him if he liked them.

—The room is tiny—but everyone seems delighted when they hear there is a room—
—I'm going to lie down awhile.
—Little Girl—

Alfred Stieglitz · Boston, Massachusetts · [June 28, 1917]

Boston Station—Waiting room—9:30 P.M.—Since eight this morning until now I've been on the go[345]—on trains about ten hours to travel two hundred miles!!—Late an hour going—over an hour—& late an hour returning!

—My train for New York leaves at midnight 30.—Last night was a terror—I tossed about incessantly—It's cruel what the daughter is being forced to endure these days—She's a real trump & that's what makes it such a torture for me.—I know *exactly* what's going on inside of her—better than she knows.—It's all too frightful—& was all so unnecessary.[346]—

And still nothing else was possible.—Forces working as they were—& I being such a real fool.—You remember the story about Munich[347]—Wouldn't you like to have a daughter by me?—Would you chance it? Mad idea—isn't it?—But it just strikes me—I hear locomotive bells—& tooting & see people chasing—Crazy—Life—?

What's all about this torment—The mountains looked wonderful—The lake mad with whitecaps—So stormy we couldn't cross it—Had to go by auto to camp. The woods smelt inviting—the brook swollen with rushing waters—The sky breaking with clouds—There was rain for a week until today.—A more perfect day for arriving couldn't be imagined.—Owing to lateness was at camp only three-quarters of an hour.—Am glad the daughter is installed there again—third summer—simple tent life—simple girls & a very sensible woman at the head.—One of Mrs. Bull's daughters[348] is to come later—Queer coincidence.—

I feel greasy & smeary—the roads are filthy—

Everything seems as not real—Myself—You—The daughter—"Home"—291— Traveling—

Only my terrific head pressure & heartache seem to be actualities—

Little Girl—I wish my daughter had met you—I told her so today—

—Good Night—Good Night—

I'll roam about to get some air—it's stifling here.

345. Stieglitz was on his way back to New York after taking his daughter Kitty to camp in New Hampshire.

346. On June 25, 1917, Stieglitz told O'Keeffe: "You have really no idea of the life I've led at home for years.—Mostly absolute silence—& all the responsibility on my shoulders. And the wife self-willed without the least conception of the practical side of life—the meaning of money—business."

347. While he was a student in Germany in the 1880s, Stieglitz impregnated a woman who lived in Munich and bore an illegitimate daughter, Elsa Bauschmied. The daughter died in 1912 while giving birth to a child, Elsa Lidauer. Stieglitz sent money to his daughter until her death; see GOK to Lowenstein, Pitcher, Spence, Hotchkiss, Amann, and Parr, Jan. 19, 1956. When he told this story to a few select people, it became an allegory not only of his youth and virility but also, oddly, of the purity and "whiteness" of his love. He often referred to it as his "Munich Story"; see AS to GOK, July 27 and Aug. 10, 1929.

348. When Stieglitz vacated 291, Nina Bull rented the rooms that had formerly housed the gallery.

You referred to the water colors as A. B. and C.—Then forgot to mark them.[349]

No—I've never made Ted—I wonder why—

Some folks make me see shapes that I have to make—other folks don't—I was trying to tell myself why—It seems with him—there is something so fine—so beautiful—just a very slender streak of it—Sometimes wider sometimes very thin—almost to breaking—so delicate —And it terrifies me when I feel that I may unwittingly break it—

I don't know any lines fine enough to make it—

The third series you sent a tracing of—is the thing that reminded me of Marin when I had finished.—I don't know why unless it seemed to look somewhat like some of his things— I didn't intend it—I didn't intend anything—

I guess that third series is just me—shapes I had in my mind from things that were happening—and just felt—It seems that I was just playing with color that I felt—

I can't tell it any other way—I had Strand all painted in New York but didn't have any paint—or time—Telling you that now reminds me of some other things I painted in New York.

Yes—I felt that the red one[350] was better—but it got to look very flat to me—I have that painted again too—in my mind—

A fool brain I have—

Today I've been down making drawings of the girls in the swimming pool—It was lots of fun—They are great—Results not much—You see I haven't drawn for a long time like that—I've been painting on the sister—

The girl I sent you was Leah[351]—It was sunset as we were going up to Amarillo when Austin was here—I painted it from memory about three months after the time I saw it because I kept remembering—I always intended to make the cheek go round better but didn't—That isn't the one of her that I told you about—

You told me what you did Sunday—I didn't tell you what I did—Got the mail— Prints—little ones from Strand[352]—Wrote him—Rode with Mr. Reeves awhile. I wrote Strand a queer letter again[353]—Doing things like that makes me want to kick the foundation out from under the house—

Still I have to do them—

After dinner—I was tired—didn't want to sleep—but you know I'm such a good

---

349. Stieglitz had sent O'Keeffe sketches of four of the watercolors she had recently mailed him. She marked three of them, all portraits of Strand (Lynes 189–191), indicating their correct orientation, and returned them in this letter.

350. Possibly Lynes 159.

351. Possibly Lynes 172.

352. Strand may have sent O'Keeffe contact prints made from his 3¼ × 4¼ inch negatives or photogravure reproductions of his photographs from *Camera Work* 48 (Oct. 1916) and 49–50 (June 1917), which were smaller than his platinum or Satista (a combination of gelatin silver and platinum) prints.

353. O'Keeffe told Strand that she was not particularly impressed with his little prints: "You would not be what you are to me at all if I had not seen the part of you that is in the big prints." She added that the large ones "make me conscious of your physical strength—my weakness [but] in spite of my weakness I give you something that makes it possible for you to use your strength—or should I say express it" (GOK to Paul Strand, June 24, 1917, CCP:PSC).

for nothing human that I have to waste a lot of time taking care of myself whether I want to or not—So after dinner—much against my wishes—I stripped—and slept or dozed all afternoon—When it was almost six and I decided I could get up—I rolled over and stretched —and while I stretched just happened to look down my own length—The long dark skinned body—smooth looking—and I almost laughed aloud at myself for having been stretched there—a whole afternoon—just sleeping—nothing on—

> Wasn't it funny—
> Good Night—
> —I must sleep.
> [Sketch of possibly Lynes 84] should turn this way—
> [Sketch of Lynes 119] *Blue One* like my hands are on should turn this way.[354]
> I did not tell you about these before—
> I don't know—it didn't seem to matter—I didn't remember when talking about it which

were wrong besides the one I told you about.

Georgia O'Keeffe · [Canyon, Texas] · [June 29, 1917]

Friday night—nearly twelve—

> I just came in from the night—very little breeze—moonlight on the bigness—
> Last night I wanted to write—Claudie and I lay out on the plains watching the sunset

go—the stars come—I was very much aggravated with some folks and things—I had to get out where the world was big and empty—She was in a very good humor—I was very tired too—

> Came home and went to bed without writing—because I thought I ought to go to bed—
> Today a book man who had pestered me yesterday came in and pestered me again—

When he came in my office I was just showing the music lady[355] what Fisher had written about me[356]—All year she has been feeling around to find out what I am driving at—No—it dates from the talk I gave the faculty—She was reading it—told him what she was reading—that started him—He sat there on the desk talking for nearly two hours—

> It was fun to me—in a way because I so seldom talk to anyone out here about my

work—I did most of the talking—He said no one had ever made it so clear to him—Art stuff —What I aimed to teach and what I was trying to do myself—

> I told him some things about his own stuff—He remarked that the folks out here were

not going at it like I am—Then said: "What are you doing out here anyway—You don't belong here—There is nothing here"—I laughed and told him that was why I liked it—

> It was funny—I don't often talk much but when I do I almost blow up.
> —I went down to the swimming pool again—painted this time—It's great—Haven't

made anything much yet but maybe I will—don't know—

354. When Stieglitz installed O'Keeffe's exhibition at 291, he hung Lynes 119 horizontally, instead of vertically.
355. Jessie M. Kline was an instructor in the music department at West Texas State Normal College from 1913 to 1918.
356. William Murrell Fisher, "The Georgia O'Keeffe Drawings and Paintings at 291," *Camera Work* 49–50 (June 1917), 5.

After supper George Ritchie—nephew of one of the English faculty—was going to take me out to see the sunset—We changed our minds and went in to play some new records—He is just a youngster—a queer one too—only here for the summer—seventeen—Then we decided we would go up to the Normal and swim—after that we got Claudie and rode a long time—

A woman kicked me in the jaw—She was big and I was helping her out of the pool—and she seemed to get hung [up] and almost kicked my head off—right under my chin—Lucky it didn't make me bite my tongue—My whole neck is sore and stiff—can hardly swallow—It makes me laugh—I didn't tell her how bad it hurt—She couldn't help it and it would make her feel bad—It seems to hurt more all the time—still it is so funny—She is so big—very good to look at—

Out in the night we passed some wheat fields—burned yellow—very big ones—almost as far as you can see at times—In the moonlight they were light—about the same value as the sky—A little dark streak of the other land way off—Some way it seemed startlingly like water even though it was light—

It's a wonderful night—

Between Claudie and George and my own queer self—I guess the conversation was a bit queer—three queer folks—

Camera Work—Thank you[357]—

Fisher was nice to me wasn't he—

It makes you believe more in yourself to feel that you have been able to get over something of what you want to someone else—Not only that though—it's that it means something to them—

I don't know what I would have done if 291 hadn't come along as it did when it did but I don't see how I could possibly have had the nerve to do what I want to when I want to—like I want to—if 291 hadn't come along—

I never got much encouragement—any in fact—to work things out naturally—as they come to me—291—You—believing in me—that making me believe in myself—has made it possible to be myself—And feeling that you believe—the other folks don't matter—I don't care the snap of my finger for any of them—

So again tonight—I don't know if it's woman or little girl—I am mostly both—I want to put my arms round you—kiss you—let you kiss me—It's all very quiet—what I want is very quiet—It's great to trust anyone enough to let them kiss you—Tomorrow is the last day of the Little Gallery—There is still a little room though—

Tonight you seem to be something very wonderful to me—it's peace—warmth—life—

How can I say it—what—

Goodnight—

—I'll not try to say things I can't—You must just understand—

357. Stieglitz inscribed *Camera Work* 49–50 to O'Keeffe, writing: "Here is the first copy of the new number—The last to be issued from '291'—as it has been known for over twelve years—Georgia O'Keeffe's spirit—and—the spirit of '291' are identical. To the Little Girl of the Texas Plains—A greeting from the Old Man of '291'—June 26—1917" (Department of Photographs, The J. Paul Getty Museum, Los Angeles).

Near you—

Why it gives me a tremendous wonder—more wonder than fear—I simply wonder—am I afraid—when the idea of fear comes to me—

It is queer that I am out here isn't it—

Again—Goodnight.

Alfred Stieglitz · [New York City] · June 30, 1917 +

5 O'Clock—

I was interrupted. People—People.—Phone.—Phone.—Endless. And I am so tired.—And I would like to sleep under trees—Red ones—Blue ones—Swirling passionate ones—

It has been a broken up day—Photographed Stein[358]—failed again—I'm too stupid—A woman from New Hampshire—a photographer—Had never seen her—wanted *Camera Work*—& see "291"—& me.—Then there was Wright the painter who wanted something—Gaisman—Schauffler[359]—Charlie Liebman, & others.—All fine—but I so damnably tired—I developed & found I had failed—

—As Strand, Baasch & I were looking at your watercolors—I asked Strand which he like best. He told me.—The watercolor *Portraits*[360]—he told me—Then I told him that I felt that that was his.—[Was] sure he was to have that series.—I thought from the start it represented him. I wonder.—Baasch agreed.—Then I told him why I hadn't told him before.—He blushed—He told me you had written him some time ago you were going to send him something. And he blushed again.—It's all fine—I had to smile.—And he understood you had done the right thing & so had I.—And he too.—He said he had asked you about this matter after you had written & you never answered. Again I laughed.—What a fine little girl you are.—No end of fineness.

—Why aren't you here now—they have all just gone—But it's good for you that you are in Texas—you're so much better off—My spirit I guess is the best part of me—the rest—?

Beastly tired—

Boxes all about me—boxes—Will I be able to stand them—A storeroom—

June 30—Officially the last day of 291 the place—Not everything is out of the rooms—I couldn't do a thing today—could have easily cleaned out & made good—by six P.M.—As it is two hours will clean out the place.—

Good Night—

I'm very near you—Very close—

I guess I've gone entirely crazy—

I had to laugh at your tying up package story—

---

358. The modern art collector and critic Leo Stein; see Greenough 453.
359. Charles Schauffler.
360. Lynes 189–194.

Georgia O'Keeffe · [Canyon, Texas] · [July 1, 1917]

Sunday evening—Five after eight—

Sun just going down—I am on the east—can not see it—Don't want to—No particular reason—Just don't—

—Yesterday morning I waked up early—thought of you and 291—The last day of it— I thought to get up and write you but instead—looked out the window—Shut the glare of the sun out—then went on thinking about you—

I don't know what I think I thought—so maybe I didn't think at all—Maybe you were just in my mind—

Anyway I know there was something about you—and that it was with me more or less all day—

I wondered at different times what you were doing—who was there—You and Strand came to my mind so often—I could see him—motionless—not moving[361]—You I couldn't see without effort—but the consciousness of you was of liveness—movement—

I went to bed early—before ten—Had had a long talk with Ted—and it was queer— I am queer—He is queer—

They had phoned me to go up to Amarillo—George came to take me to the station and I didn't go—Couldn't make myself—Ted was here at the time anyway—He tried to make me go and I wouldn't—I didn't want to—

When I came upstairs—my head ached—I put out the light to think—my eyes hurt too —And I went to sleep—

Your letter from Boston this morning—Yes you wrote me from there last year—I never camped in a tent but once—a couple of weeks in the mountains in Virginia—Snakes almost drove me crazy—

My head has ached all day—I went to breakfast—then slept—dozed half asleep all morning—Didn't go to dinner or supper—didn't want any—

This afternoon I've worked—Had to do something with this headache—

I wish you were here—I'd like to show it to you right now—Isn't that absurd—You would laugh at my room—perfectly bare—floor and all—Nothing on the dressing table but a plain white cloth—The table is stacked high—I'm going to get a new one about four or six times as large—it will take up most of the room I'm afraid but I don't care—

You would laugh too at what I've been doing—I don't know whether to tell you or not—I couldn't get what I wanted any other way so I've been painting myself—no clothes[362] —It was lots of fun—Stupid of me never to have thought of it before—I had thought of it but never enough to want to before—

Today I wanted to paint nakedness—

361. O'Keeffe frequently told Strand of her frustration with his slowness. On July 22, 1917, she wrote him: "I hated your letter early in the week—hate was my mood I guess for I just now read it again and it is really beautiful—That morning I hated any-one who simply stood and felt—I wanted them to *do* I don't know what—I guess I despised you for sitting somewhere—a long way off and simply telling me what you felt instead of acting" (CCP:PSC).

362. Lynes 176–188.

It makes me laugh—I had such a good time headache and all—

And when I tell you about it I feel like such a funny little girl—I want you to take me in your arms and let me hide my face down in a corner somewhere—

I don't know though that they feel any more like nakedness than a landscape I've been working on does—I think I made the eighth and ninth editions of that today too—

There seem to be wheels in my head—I see and think of so many things—The sheet on my bed is a great twist—Two different places are fine.

Can't do everything though—the sheet is just good to look at—

My blond boy[363] has been crazy as a loon this week—went home last weekend and came back in a great big car—

Well—he has been like a whirlwind on a very hot day—

I've hardly seen him—So busy—I sort of forgot him till he came in yesterday and forcibly reminded me—face red—hair flying—blood about to spurt out of his veins anywhere—Then I remembered I had seen him shooting around several times with the car full of boys and girls—and that a couple of times I had seen him standing for sometime waiting to talk to me when I was busy with others and I guess I never got to him before he got tired of waiting—

Dear me—I'd like to be about six people—

I'll remember him specially this week—So many force themselves on you—that you don't have much chance to reach out to anyone else—

You know schoolteachers are maddening with questions—

My little folks are great—A little boy made a landscape for me yesterday with a purple star about three inches in diameter in the middle—a house on each side—a tree on each side—tiny little house in the middle—It was so funny—but I liked it—

I'd like to tell you about them all—Two made submarines—one had a gorgeous orange sail boat above the dirty gray little submarine—He lives across the side street—Shoots me every time I go by—Always war—

The youngsters get more of war than the older folks—

One youngster explained a few days ago that bright colored spots all mixed up—sort of like a sunset—was war clouds in Europe—

My neck is recovering—doesn't hurt much to swallow any more—My headache is gone too—It's dark. The windmill—I had intended to sleep out on the plains tonight but it's too windy—

Goodnight—

Yes—

As I wrote Yes—on the bottom of the other side of this—I stopped—and looked past the light of the room out into the blue of the night—wonderful dark blue—almost black—night—and I wished that I could some way tell you what goes with the little three lettered word—

I wonder if you know—

And I wish you were not so far away—and would take me out into the night—way

363. Probably one of O'Keeffe's students and not Willard Austin.

out there in the dark blueness—and that the day would never come—or would I like to see the dawn with you—Night seems to mean that I could be close to you—feel your nearness—

That if the day came and we were out there—even in the emptiness—and alone—we would be farther apart—would have to be.

Goodnight.

Georgia O'Keeffe · [**Canyon, Texas**] · [**July 2, 1917**]

Monday morning—

Claudie brought the mail while I was at breakfast—I was sitting on the porch of the house where I eat—reading—

A card from Fred at his Goat Dairy—wishing I were down there—A goat on it—

Then—your letter—

I was so glad to see it—When I turned over the first page and read the question at the top[364]—I screamed—I couldn't help it—

Claudie was alarmed—I told her it was nothing and started home—It seemed I couldn't shut my mouth—I came upstairs—I had to be alone—And I feel as if I can't read anymore—I wouldn't mind your saying it to me—but it is so hard to read—I almost can't read—

I put it all under the cover of my bed—I had sat down on the side of it—

Oh—I wish you were here instead of just the letter—I want to cry—let loose some way—And alone—it seems I must just stare into space—

It is a cloudy morning—I watched a horse way out on the plains—walk across the open space between the side frames of my wide middle window—

Yes—I'll read—now. I can read—now that I've talked to you a little—

It's a nice letter—

I wish I had time to think but I have three or four things that must be done right away—

I wish you were in front of me—would hold me close just a minute before I go on to the things I must do—

Sun is out a little—wonderful streaks of color on the plains—wind feels cool—damp for here—

I have sort of half way realized for a long time that if I were near you—something might happen—Maybe that is why we didn't go into the night alone—Then it would not have been a case of "Chance it?" or reason—It would have been—and have been right—have worked out some way—When one reasons coldly—one does not see the way clear—

Have you no sympathy for the child that would be you and me—

Why I can't reason about anything like that—how could I—You have already taken a lot of me from myself—entirely—

I don't know—

---

364. At the top of one of the pages in his letter of June 28, 1917, Stieglitz had asked O'Keeffe if she wanted to have his child.

All of me has been yours many times—

As I sat down to read your letter Ted went by—Claudie remarked that he walked like an old man.

I must go.

Frankly—yes—I think I would like to have it—but can I consider just myself—Many things are in the way—

Maybe the child itself most of all—

I do not know—

Later—

I have been to town—and to see some other folks—phoned—came to the Normal—am waiting to see others—

—I read your letter again—read what I had written you—then looked around for something to write with—I only seemed to want to write two words—

Help me—

Petals dropped from a sunflower in front of me—I saw something queer and shiny in the center of another—it was a pin someone had stuck in the center of it—I pulled it out—how could anyone put it there—

It seems that I don't see how I can live today—and tomorrow—and the rest of time—Why should that simple question seem to shake me so—all the way up and down—inside and out—

I can't tell you how I feel—I wonder if you know—

—If I was near you I know what the answer would be—I think—You knew too or you'd not have asked—

I hadn't thought it directly—definitely till you asked—

I'd have no choice if I were near you—

As it is—I'm a long way from you—so far that I have no choice—

It's a queer cry that I feel like sending out to all the universe—all time—all space—

And I don't know what it is except that it is something all would hear—all would understand—and that would hurt all like it hurts me—even little children it seems would understand—

So that I wonder how I can even get up and walk out of this room—

I do not seem to want to—

Still I must—

Alfred Stieglitz · [New York City] · [July 2, 1917]+

Monday, 7:30 Evening.—There is an electric storm—incessant lightning—rain—hardly any thunder—rain. It was a stifling day—I hope it cools off some—the humidity was unbearable.—

—It has been an awful day in every way.—Last night after writing you I ransacked the store-room—looking through prints & papers—wishing I didn't care for any of them—My own work—good—but good for what or whom!—These are serious days.—

It was much after two—nearly three—when I finally got to bed again. But I couldn't sleep—the wife too I felt couldn't sleep—Finally daybreak came—It hurt so I clutched the pillow as I never clutched anything before—& so close to me—I could have screamed.—These are days of torture—hell must be a paradise compared to them.—

—From nine till two the wife & I had words—She is a really pathetic person—she can't connect two thoughts—an untrained brain—a great self-will—obstinate—& not much deep feeling—or rather fine feeling—Full of theories & conventional ideas—Not half bad if she could but think & reason—This way a hopelessly bemuddled brain—and no real memory. I felt terribly sorry for her for she really suffers—and doesn't realize chiefly through her own self—We all do that.—But some see why & profit—& don't resent their fate—But she does not see—can't see herself—criticizes everyone—has little good will for the world.—Is really just a child—& spoiled.—And I no husband for her—I wonder if anyone would have made her "happy"—It's all frightful & I don't see what the outcome—To me I see no solution but one—Money of course would heal her suffering—but where is it to come from?—She has had aplenty—& wasted—as many do—Opportunities unearned do not recur—

—It was 2:30 when I got to 291—Gee it was hot there.—A green stamped letter—ending with: kiss me Good-night—Smaller than that—hardly visible—but very dear—I was such a wreck it felt as if a sympathetic hand was holding me from toppling over.—

A few hours later Marie said: Why there is a letter you didn't see.—It came with the other.—It was a second letter, green stamped—What a pleasant surprise.—And what a fine letter. The one answering about Strand, etc.—the drawings.—I was right in the placings, the others wrong.—Strand thought he was Watkins[365]—I wasn't so sure—in fact I doubted it at first & then wondered—?

The Marin.—I saw a face distinctly—& wondered whether it was partly Marin[366]—Couldn't quite make out.—Much you.—I'll give Strand his series.[367] —

—He wasn't there today. As for the things hung at the exhibition—wrongly—I didn't look today. Tomorrow—I wonder how they'll look right-side up.—

—Funny that you should write about your body—twice yesterday—& once day before—While writing I wanted to ask you about it—to tell me about it—describe it—But I didn't—I don't know why.—In fact I wanted to tell you that it came into my mind—that it must be much like your hands—and dark—& smooth—& that I'd like to kiss it from top to bottom—so gently that you wouldn't know—still feel it—Queer—& here in the letter today comes the description—your sleeping—without anything on—discovering your body—

—Somehow I'm yearning for the touch of flesh—no desire—beyond the touch—My hand, my mouth—perhaps my own body—Craving to forget all misery & torture—& flesh

365. Lynes 192–194.
366. On July 6, 1917, O'Keeffe responded: "You mistake my reference to Marin—I had no idea of making Marin—I meant that when I finished painting the thing I had found it very easy to imagine someone saying I was trying to paint like him."
367. Lynes 189–191.

would do it—a long, long sleep—entwined—I'd like to die that way—I've told you that before
—Would you be afraid—But I'm not young enough—nor strong enough—Passion, yes—but
that is not enough.—

    —You say you wrote a letter to Strand that you really should not have—but had to—
I have to laugh.—Just as I didn't wish to write about the body—& do—

    And do so many things which I have to & yet don't want to.—Showing that I really
want to but reason says I shouldn't.

    —Nothing was accomplished at 291 today.—It was too hot—and I much too upset
—It's a wonder I don't break down completely—nervous prostration.—I guess I'm made of
mud—some slime in it—I hate myself these days—never was over-fond of self—much as it may
have seemed I was.—

    —As I sit here & look around & think that soon all this too will be gone—I shudder in
a way—Nineteen years is a long while to live in a place—a lifetime—& although it has been
no home—I have lived in it over 190 months—5,700 days—There are a thousand books or
more—I'll have to sell them for a song—some really valuable—The pictures—hundreds—?
—Furniture—& carpets—All must go.—Sacrificed.—To store would be too expensive &
would mean a hope—a hope for what.—One is richest without property that takes up room
—All property is wrong—

    The night is going to be an endless one again.—

    On Thursday my wife's brother[368] always comes—He—she & I will have it out—
come to some definite understanding—There must be some radical change—

    —I wish tonight were Thursday.—Uncertainty is hell—If there must be—& there
must be—a capital operation—the sooner the better.

    —The storm has ceased.—The cool breeze died out—

    Good Night—Where shall the kiss—be?

    Good Night.—

Alfred Stieglitz · [New York City] · [July 5, 1917] +

I have just come home. 5:50.—Gaisman took me away from 291 at 4:50. He drove me about the
Park—And it was good to get some air into my lungs.—It is many days since I really have. And
we had a fine talk. It's always fine to be with him—especially alone—although he is no different than when we all four were together. But when two are together you know there is greater
concentration.

    —As I look out of the window there is a marvelous storm-cloud formation in the
West—the sun fairly low—

    All day has been alive. Like your very living letter.—Charlie Liebman was in—but just
a moment to tell me his wife[369] wants to see me tomorrow. Then Kerfoot turned up & we were

368. Joseph Obermeyer.
369. Aline Meyer Liebman.

together for several hours. He took me to lunch. We had a long talk about home affairs. He knows them as well as I do.

It helped me that he agreed with my plan of action—Tonight my brother-in-law, very close to my family, responsible in many ways for the trouble we're in—as he was responsible for his sister's marriage to me—all through *great kindness*—He, my wife & I shall have a *talk*. A plain one. Quietly.—I shall state facts as they have never before been stated to him & her.—He & I lived together as chums in Berlin—eight [years]. Never had a word.—I think I told you—or wrote you.—

We'll see.—I'm glad I had a ride in the Park—& Kerfoot today.

Then too an Englishman, a sort of publicity agent—an unusual young fellow—with much culture—lived in Italy two years—also in Germany—came in with a Russian sculptor. —For a show!! Had been sent up by a very prominent man. This man wrote down the following names as possible sources of introduction to New York for the young Russian—

Stieglitz—

Birnbaum (Scott & Fowles)—

New York Evening Post (!!)—

Vantine's—!!!!

Gorham's—![370]

What do you say to *that* list? Did you ever hear anything like it? I roared.—

I explained—showed the old torn up room—they liked it even in its torn up state— it's clean now—empty—showed them my new domicile. And told them that's what New York leaves me. They were amused—didn't understand. For about three-quarters of an hour we stood in the hallway—at the elevator—& talked about England, Germany, Russia, the United States—in the abstract. And it was a pleasure to see the Englishman so impersonal. In fact we agreed.—

He is coming again.—He is a very practical fellow—though somewhat of an idealist.

—The old washerwoman came to tell me she had a job for the summer—taking care of a house—Strand got it for her.—She is happy. Wants the "honor" of cleaning the cubby hole!—I'm glad she is placed for the summer.—It was hard to see her suffer & not be able to do anything—still Strand is 291—It all works out—

—The elevator boy [371] is staying. He wants to talk to me.—This is what I have been told.—You see moving & being in such a frightful condition I have been in gave people like Hodge & the washerwoman little chance to have me.—And they have been accustomed to have me—for years.—

—And so the day passed by. Not a moment that wasn't full—pleasantly.—

Strand came in & read me an article he had written. Splendid.—I hope *Seven Arts* prints it.[372]—

---

370. Martin Birnbaum was an art dealer associated with the Scott and Fowles Gallery, New York. A. A. Vantine and Co. was a store in New York that sold Asian goods, including silks and rugs. Gorham Manufacturing Co. sold silver and china.

371. Hodge Kirnon.

372. Paul Strand, "Photography," *The Seven Arts* 2 (Aug. 1917), 524–525.

Camera Work is creating quite a stir.—His work.[373]—Of course the pictures in *Camera Work* have not the quality of the originals—nor have they the power—but they have something as a whole which I tried to emphasize—at the cost of all else.—And that seems to have been achieved. On Japan paper there would have been a fineness at the expense of the directness.[374]—Reduction of size also robs the pictures of something the originals have.—

—Your letter describes your bare room—that's been a dream of mine. Every day I have been telling the men of just such a room—that's the kind I want.—Funny again—you have it. —I wish I had one exactly its counterpart not too far from—I don't know where—

—I wonder if a storm is coming—

Tent.—Snakes.—The name snake just makes me squirm—always did.—

Good Night.—I want to get this off—My head is swimming—

Too much air has gotten into it I guess.—

Once more Good Night—

What do you feel?

Georgia O'Keeffe · [Canyon, Texas] · [July 13, 1917]

Thursday night—no—Friday morning—I can't sleep.

Wednesday I was so tired I didn't go to school in the afternoon—slept—

A fool woman came and talked to me a long time [at] supper time—I went to bed again at 9:30.—I was so tired I wanted to cry—Slept again—didn't want to get up when morning came—

Thursday—very full—I did some extra work at school—there all day—didn't go home till six—After supper—too tired to move and hot—

I undressed—painted again on myself[375]—I guess that excited me—my head full of wheels again—Seeing things everywhere I turn that I want to do—but I thought I ought to go to bed—So I took a bath and have been trying for two hours to sleep—

Claudie met me on the street—said—Turn round here—let me look at you—turned me toward the sun—Then started on without saying anything—I asked—What was the matter?—She said—Well—what's the matter with *you?* You look like the devil—

I get so excited painting—

One is on the wall—watercolor—I painted them all red—It has a curiously funny quality—A feeling of bigness like the red landscape[376]—still the body has an almost affected twist—I just caught myself in that position by accident—it's funny—

373. Stieglitz included eleven photogravure reproductions of Paul Strand's photographs in *Camera Work* 49–50 (June 1917).

374. In keeping with the softer, more atmospheric nature of the work of the Photo-Secession, Stieglitz had frequently printed the reproductions of their photographs in earlier issues of *Camera Work* on Japan tissue. For Strand's photographs, however, he used a heavier, woven paper.

375. Lynes 176–188.

376. Possibly Lynes 159.

I want to show them to you—they are so funny—most of them too fat.

May I send them to you and feel sure you won't show them to the other folks—

I feel like a little girl asking you—very close to you—laughing—I don't know why laughing except that making them has been such lots fun—Today's so different from the others—

None of them what I want yet. And I wondered if I'd want to make anyone else if I had a chance—and I decided I wouldn't—it would seem awfully dead I imagine—isn't that funny—

One of the funniest things is that I haven't made a single one that begins to compare in nakedness with the feeling of nakedness in a landscape I made before I got this notion.

I must be going crazy too—but I don't mind—I like it.

I wonder how you are tonight—I'm not woman to you at all tonight—just a human being—but I'd like to put my arm round your neck—both arms and feel close to you—my breasts close to you—and feel that you like them—I don't know why I want so much to tell you that—but then I don't know why anything—It seems that would quiet me so I could sleep—

Goodnight—

Yesterday I looked at the paper that came with Strand's print—Why—you know I'll hate to paint on that—

I don't know—I'll see. Cheap paper like this is a great friend lately—A stack of it almost a foot high makes me feel downright reckless—It isn't the size I ordered but seems to be serving the purpose.

I'm like you about that other paper—I'd rather look at it than ruin it.

Goodnight again.

Many stars—A cool breeze—soft warm feeling—

The windmill—One ought not mind staying awake—Night is very lovely—

Alfred Stieglitz · [New York City] · July 28, [1917] +

8:30 A.M.—291—Just came in—

—A north wind—Very cool—clear—cool enough to be comfortable in a vest—

—Some sleep.—I hope you too got some—When I went to bed a gale was blowing through the apartment—a very cool wind—growing colder—It was the first night in a long while that some covering—a sheet—felt comfortable.—And no flies or mosquitoes could be happy in such a wind—As I went to bed I lay there awhile on my back & I was thinking—of—Canyon—

And what Canyon is to me—but one thing—

I fell asleep—Towards daybreak I dreamt—It must have been towards daybreak—for the dream awoke me—& the sun was just beginning to light up some walls of buildings I can see from my bed—

—I dreamt that a woman lay in my arms—I on my left side held the sleeping form in my left arm—She was breathing very deeply & very quietly—I had slept—but was awake. My eyes closed—I didn't dare open them.—The form I felt was not heavy.—

I suddenly realized that the woman had opened her eyes—Somewhat surprised to find herself where she was. My eyes were closed. She did not know whether I was awake or not. She looked, turned on her right side—towards me—I could sense her body & her face closer to me —I didn't stir.—And she kept looking & wondering whether I knew she was there. My eyes remained closed & I motionless.—I didn't dare move—nor dare I open the eyes.—

And finally I felt that she knew I wasn't asleep & I felt she wanted to know why I didn't look at her—why I lay motionless—She didn't know—

And suddenly I whispered into her ear: "The drawings are for me only—aren't they." —My eyes still closed.—What I said was hardly a whisper.—I felt an abdomen near mine— very close—I felt breasts—near my breast—very close—I felt a breath near my mouth—very close—I felt the gaze of eyes penetrating through my closed lids—

I knew the answer—her arms too I felt about me—in the answer—but I dared not open my eyes—nor dared I move—for I would have crushed the woman—& smothered her—

And I didn't want to hurt her.—

—I opened my eyes—

Emptiness—A pillow on the floor—

For a moment my heart seemed to stand still—I felt an awful pain in it—

The wind was blowing a gale through the rooms—I got up—the feet sore—the cold somewhat better—I somewhat rested—But frightfully alone—

I think this morning I feel human the first time in a long while—that is I have feelings.

—Steichen has been ordered to Washington[377]—he called me up on the phone yesterday—at home to tell me—He seemed somewhat excited—I suppose the reality—the meaning of what it actually may mean—may have suddenly struck him.—Here in this country there has been so much flirting—playing—with life & death questions—that life & death no longer were realities—Flirting days are over—playing is over—

—There is music—soldiers marching—people applauding—all the windows opposite filled with men & women—more applause—a magnificent day—I hear officers' orders—

Dear Little Girl—It hurts—terribly—

—Well, I'm to see Steichen at eleven—he & I will lunch together. He leaves this afternoon.

The future—? For all of us—?

Hodge tells me Bluemner was here yesterday night after I had left—I'm awfully sorry to have missed him. Maybe I'll go & see him in the country—he lives somewhere in New Jersey—

I like him—he has brains—& he is playing no game—

—Tomorrow is Sunday—?—This afternoon—?

Gosh—I'm terribly alone—

I wonder how you are—You have work—I must find something to do or I'll go mad.—

178

---

377. On August 2, 1917, the War Department established the Signal Corps Photographic Division, with Major James Barnes in command of Steichen and three other men. The unit was charged with both aviation photography as well as the recording of all military operations; see Penelope Niven, *Steichen: A Biography* (New York, 1997), 449.

Later.

This letter was sealed & ready for mailing this noon but somehow I didn't mail it—I'm at my barber's for a shampoo—waiting for the man who has served me twenty-five years!—

—Called for Steichen at his studio—saw his recent paintings & his photographs. He is true to himself—developing in both—And his work is like his character—He is very serious—wasn't excited—We lunched together.—Is certainly an energetic fellow—practical.—

He is off for Washington tomorrow.—It will be a great experience—no matter what may happen—Of course he may never get to France—his hope is to see some real fighting.—

—After lunch I returned to 291 & started developing some of the Stein exposures.[378] —Oh, yes, Stein turned up this morning after I had written you—I had an hour till Steichen's appointment. I don't know whether I've gotten Stein this time or not.—I hardly think so.— Was hardly in trim to photograph in a rush—or at all today.—The light was good—Perhaps something happened.—It won't be my doing if it did—

—While developing Murrell Fisher turned up—I hadn't seen him in ages—he says he was up several times but I was out—I gave him *Camera Work*—his article in it. I told him what you had written about it.—He's a fine fellow—

—It's 4:45 now—I walked up 59th Street here—near Fifth Avenue—That day we all walked up Fifth Avenue—the day you went out with Dewald—Strand went west with you— I'm near that corner—

—I had no business to walk—my foot is on fire—but I walked.—The day is so perfect.—

—I wonder when you leave Canyon on your vacation—& where to—
Perhaps this letter will no longer catch you in Canyon.—
And Claudie—
From here I'm going home.
—I'd love to hear some real good music today.—Why is there none in summer to be heard in New York—or rarely.—
As I can't have a walk with you—
You smile—I'm sure you do—
—My turn in—A shampoo—
Good Night—Little Girl—

Georgia O'Keeffe · [Canyon, Texas] · [August 6, 1917]

It's Monday noon—No—almost three to be exact—I've been sewing since dinner—I've told you before that I sew when I want to think—

I've thought of you often—and haven't written—just simply haven't—that's all— Maybe because I was trying to think and couldn't get things straight—didn't seem to be getting anywhere with myself—Or with anybody else—

———————————
378. Greenough 453.

It's glaring sun and wind—Not hot here in my room—but I hate to go out—and I ought to go to the Normal—getting things straight for the last week—I was there all morning—

Last night again was wonderful moonlight—

And Ted took me way out into it—We watched the moon come up out of the Plains—and stayed till it was high in the sky—He is so funny—And I guess I'm funny too—

Why I think maybe I'm crazy—but I know I'm not—I'm beginning to think like you said of yourself—that maybe I'm too sane—I don't know—I can't say anything to you—it's all so intangible that you can't get it into words—

It makes me laugh—and he laughed too—and then we talked some more and reasoned some more and couldn't make anything work out so that it would seem like any sort of sense to anybody else—So we laughed again—

He wants me so much that he just can't take any pleasure in liking me because he thinks he can't have me like he wants me—ever—

And I—Why—you know it seems living with him would be lots of fun—it seems as though he is the only person I ever knew who would take me to the tail end of the earth where folks wouldn't bother me and then let me do as I please—

And he said—if we can't make it work we will quit—

You know in the spring I wanted to go with him more than I wanted anything—Just put my hand in his and walk out into space[379]—

While I was in New York I almost forgot—

And now—little by little I've grown to like him again—It's so queer—like two children playing—He had me all curled up in a little knot last night—"Why it would be so easy to just pick you up and carry you to town—you are so little"—

And I was so comfortable I wanted to go to sleep that way—I seem to like him like I like myself—

And when I look around here—at what I am doing and things as they are—I wonder why I don't marry him today[380]—

—Why do I stay with this—Isn't it funny—

I would like to be out in the night with him tonight—I was afraid two or three times last night—Then laughed—then he laughed—laughed through it all—our acquaintance began with a laugh—

We have always laughed—

What is worthwhile in living anyway—

School is over Saturday morning at about eleven and I haven't an idea of what I'm going to do—I don't know that it matters—

---

379. On August 12, 1917, O'Keeffe confided to Stieglitz that Ted had wanted to kiss her a few days earlier: "I wanted to be kissed—All kisses are different—His—Why I don't know—What he gives feels more like what I give—They are nice to remember—It's like turning your face to the wind."

380. On August 2, 1917, O'Keeffe admitted to Stieglitz that she was "not sure that I'd like any man I ever saw well enough to live with him—Cook and wash and scrub." Later that month, she told Strand about Ted: "It's funny the way I like him—and the way he likes me. I've said I wouldn't marry him—again and again." Although she admitted she hated "the idea of being tied to anyone," she added, "Right now I've made up my mind that I will—in a year—if we don't change our minds—and I know we will change them—or I'll change mine" (GOK to Paul Strand, Aug. 15, 1917, CCP:PSC).

I don't seem to feel inclined to plan anything so I guess I'll let it take care of itself—

Am I queer—He said I was—then right quick said—No—it's just that I never knew anybody else like you—and I know I'll never let myself like anyone else so much again—

I don't know—

ON AUGUST 9, 1917, Stieglitz went to Lake Winnipesaukee, New Hampshire, to get Kitty at camp. A few days later, the two arrived at Lake George, where they joined many other members of the Stieglitz family, including Stieglitz's brother Leopold (Lee); Lee's wife, Elizabeth (Lizzie); their daughter Elizabeth; and her friend Alie Mörling, an art student. To aid the war effort, Elizabeth and Alie planted a garden at the farm up the hill from their house, which the family also owned. They were assisted by the family's new gardener, Donald Davidson, whose erudition and wit intrigued both Alfred and his niece. As usual, several friends also visited that summer, including Francis Picabia and Gabrielle Buffet-Picabia.

Before leaving on vacation, O'Keeffe sent Stieglitz a package of watercolors: "I would have to burn it if I didn't send it to you,"[381] she explained. With her tables swept clean from the prying eyes of her landlords and summer school over on August 11, Georgia and Claudia took a train from Canyon through New Mexico, "where the nothingness is several sizes larger than in Texas,"[382] to Colorado, where they spent time in Ward, a former mining town, and Loveland, as well as Estes Park and Boulder. O'Keeffe made a number of watercolors and drawings on the trip, but she spent most of her time hiking and climbing several mountains, including the fourteen-thousand-foot Longs Peak. After stopping in Denver, which O'Keeffe described as "both horrid and amusing," and Santa Fe, which "was really great,"[383] they returned to Canyon in early September.

Georgia O'Keeffe · [New Mexico] · [August 15, 1917]

Wednesday—

I'm out here in New Mexico—going somewhere—I'm not positive where—but it's great—

Not like anything I ever saw before—I want to stop everywhere—The Indians and their black hair and very bright colors—dark skins and eyes—the square little adobe houses are great—I'm crazy to live in one—It has rained lots this afternoon—still gives the feeling of a land of sunshine—

I wonder why—Spaces—Why Texas isn't in it—There is so much more space between the ground and the sky out here it is tremendous—

I want to stay—I've wanted to stop most every station—

---

381. GOK to AS, late July 1917.
382. GOK to Paul Strand, Aug. 15, 1917, CCP:PSC.
383. GOK to AS, Sept. 10, 1917.

ALL THE WORLD GREETS YOU, 1915–1918

The first glimpse of the Rockies—Gosh—there must have been a time out here when they were made—

There was a peak that had a backbone of different kinds of rock turned right up to the sky—running in wavy ridges—deep blue peaks and peaks—big ones and little ones—and the bareness of them—and the deep blueness of them—

They hardly seem possible—

Why don't you come out here—isn't that a funny question—

It makes you feel like a sky rocket—or something that's going up in the air—

Seven thousand feet high here the sister just came and told me—

Canyon will forward mail—

Georgia O'Keeffe · [Ward, Colorado] · [August 21?, 1917]

I have just sent you a postal—simply because it is a picture of the place we went to yesterday—

Sunday we came up to Ward on an excursion and we liked it so much that we stayed—and Monday a mining engineer that we met coming up on the train and an old miner—seventy-two—only more like thirty-two—so active and lively—took us up past Red Lake—Brainard Lake—to Long Lake—just below Audubon Mountain top—could have gone to the top but the engineer—Mr. Lentz—and I both had the remains of terrible headaches from the day before—

It reminded me of the day we went to Coney Island—great folks to be with—They were looking over the ground and timber—opening mines up there—There were snow drifts and it was cold—Claudie fished with a friend of the old miner's—Kneal is his name—while I walked round the lake with them looking at the timber—tall straight balsam and spruce and pine—narrow and so very sharp at the top—

It was wonderful—so bare and lonesome—looking over the lake at the snow spotted bare mountain[384]—the ground underfoot covered with brilliant flowers—brilliant red—deepest blue—light blue—lavender—purple—yellow—every color it seemed—yellow green grass—slushy at the edge of the lake—and the tall dark pines—friendly—loving you—blue green on the edges—deepest black in the center—warm brown of the needles between the flowers at times—many big bare rocks—a few bare—blue gray and white looking dead trees—

Mr. Lentz is fifty-six and old—but nice to be with—We really had a wonderful time—

I wished you were here—but isn't it queer—I some way feel that I couldn't go up into that quiet lonesome place—of bare snow spotted mountain tops—warm brilliant flowers and tall narrow pines—about three feet in diameter often—the cold keen air and warm sheltered spots—with you alone—isn't it queer—

The lake like ice at our feet—all the water here's so cold you can hardly drink it—

I wonder what you are doing—

I am sitting on top of a—hill they call it here—but it feels like a mountain—under

384. Lynes 219, 220.

an enormous crooked pine—snow spotted mountains—so terribly bare—blue—blue—blue ones piled and piled—a near bare green one that I want to run my hand over—just patches of pointed timber on the sides of it—bunches of brilliant red flowers in almost every direction —yellow and blue and purple too but I only seem to be aware of the red ones—aspen trees— little ones—I love their little round—always moving leaves—

Comfortable when the sun shines—my sweater buttoned high round my neck—That little blue green one you saw—Cold when a cloud comes along—being alone here is great—

I am trying to be quiet for one day—have been going just as hard as I could for a week. It's queer to be quiet and alone—the wind in the pines is great—smells so great— Alone—and I like it—but—Yes the wind is nice—it comes in puffs.

I wonder if the mail will bring me a letter—

Alfred Stieglitz · [Lake George, New York] · August 22, [1917]

Wednesday—the 22nd—So you are in the High Mountains—you & Claudie.—I can well picture you there—I'm glad you went—I had hoped you would—In fact I knew you would go —knew it all along—From the day you said to me you'd probably go—I'm really glad—

No, it wasn't funny for you to wish I'd come out there—

That's really where I ought to be—somewhere far away from hereabouts—away from all this—the ever-reminding of the past—I really dead—here at least—ready for the scrap-heap —old junk.—No energy—no joy—not even pain—just a bundle of useless nerves—something I despise—& no matter what I try to do—result—just nerves. More nerves.—Every human sound seems to cut me to the quick—

—A few moments yesterday up on the farm—I was alone—just standing there amongst the vegetables—looking at the ground—at the creepers of the melon patch—There was a threatening sky—& the wind didn't know whether it should blow northeast or northwest—the difference between rain & clearing.—

The new gardener[385] to whom I had not yet spoken—In fact had only gotten a glimpse of one day & who made a great impression upon me—impression as a human.—A lank sinewy figure—eye glasses—spectacles—middle-aged—a firm expression around the mouth—

We met up there—And I don't know why—but we talked for about fifteen minutes— I don't know what brought it about—but it was very wonderful—that meeting. Life—War— Society—Plant Life—the Universe—We understood each other—He's unmarried—Scotch descent—Riches once upon a time in the family—

It was very human that meeting—the most human thing that's happened to me in some time—

He seemed drawn to me & I to him—Queer—Perhaps I'm not quite as dead as I imagine I must be.—Merely suffocating in an atmosphere which is so foreign to me—

—I am still reading Tolstoy's *Journal*—I can't read more than ten minutes at a clip—

---

385. Donald Davidson.

& simultaneously I am reading his *What Is Art*[386] which I read much differently than I did when I read it years ago.—Then I really did not see what I see today—although the direction was the same—Of course I don't agree with much that he says about art—in fact he had no conception of the meaning of certain things—was really all at sea—Still Tolstoy was always such a deep thinker that even his fallacies are of value. At least to me.—

—Yesterday my brother, the doctor,[387] who is here for a few days, invited me to go to Saratoga to see the races. We motored down—& back too—had lunch at Saratoga Lake—& then saw the races.

—It was a curious sensation for me—these Saratoga races—for it was forty-five years ago that I spent two weeks at Saratoga with my father & we went to the races daily.—The hotels are the same—the track has been rebuilt—a year later too I had been there—but not since—forty-four years ago—

—It seemed like yesterday—I saw myself on the Grand Union porch—heard the voices—even those of the strangers about me—saw the fashionable freckled jockey Bobby Swim with a big diamond in his green tie—He won the big race that day on a famous Kentucky horse—& I had won $5 on him—

And here I was back—forty-four years later—& although loving races & horses so much—in all those years at Lake George, though so near Saratoga, I had remained at the Lake!—

—It was beautiful to see the horses & the variegated silks of the jockeys—the day had become a brilliantly sunny one—very cool—There were no great horses & the day was not an eventful one as far as the races were concerned—the crowd was large but not very picturesque—nothing to be compared to a Paris crowd—or Baden-Baden—

Still I enjoyed the change—as much, I suppose, as I can enjoy anything these days. The auto ride made me feel as if I could sit there forever & roll on & on—not caring much for anything but the sensation of rolling onward—no matter where to—

—I did see how green vegetation was everywhere—& here & there water attracted me —all else might have been non-existent as far as I was concerned.—

Owing to my foot I'm not playing tennis nor swimming these days—Doing those things seemed to irritate it—so even exercise of that kind has been taken away from me. I guess I'm a hoodoo for fair—

—Still the days seem to be passing too quickly—I am not looking forward to New York with any pleasure—nor with any dread for that matter.—

All seems a blank—& what is not blank—pretty ominous—

The caterpillar pest[388] is a symbol perhaps for the way I feel about much in the near future—

384

386. Tolstoy, *The Journal of Leo Tolstoy*, trans. Rose Strunsky (New York, 1917); *What Is Art?*, trans. Charles Johnston (Philadelphia, 1898).

387. Alfred's younger brother Leopold (Lee) Stieglitz.

388. New York City had a large infestation of caterpillars in 1917, prompting one citizen to assert that while "Zeppelins have not yet compelled the residents of New York to seek shelter in cellars," caterpillars might soon send the population "scurrying for cover"; see "An Overhead Pest, Caterpillar Horde in Town," *NYT*, July 16, 1917, 8.

Do you like those hairy creepy crawly things—Caterpillars?—I genuinely *don't*.

It's a gray morning—dampish—more like autumn—and very quiet.—

—My photographic apparatus has come & so have the plates, etc.—I guess I'll make a perfunctory effort soon—

Everything seems foreign to me—Far, far away.—Detached.—

Greet the highest peaks for me—Are there any as yet virgin grounds—untouched by man—

Alfred Stieglitz · [Lake George, New York] · August 27, [1917] +

Monday. A little after two.—On the porch.—After a goodly noonday meal.—And then a second look at your work!![389]

—It's a wonderful balmy afternoon.

Last night after I had written to you I went to my room & got into bed.—It was cold. —Shivering cold. My feet didn't seem to want to get warm.—I finally fell asleep—slept some —awoke occasionally—couldn't seem to get warm.—

—One time I awoke & the floor of the room seemed bathed in gold—I knew it meant dawn—I only looked a moment—I pulled the sheets over my head—and pulled my feet up under me—& huddled all there was of me into a corner—with the two pillows.—And as I lay there I wondered whether I shouldn't get up & get out into the morning.—But it was cold— & I felt so very alone.—You came into my mind—the snow on the mountains—and oddly enough—your work came into my mind—But I stopped thinking—I lay there half asleep— half awake—

The call to get up was great—still I lay there.—

I finally arose.—My room has two windows—one facing west—the other east. I dropped my pajamas—& I stood there between both windows—stood stripped—with the cold air striking the skin—

I stood quite awhile—letting the body drink in the cold dry air—

—The first hours of the morning were threatening.—Was it to be rain?—But gradually the sun came out—grayness disappeared—I shaved—& then went up to the tennis court— alone—awaiting the return from the village of the daughter. She had gone for the mail.—

—A great big lovely surprise!—A package from you—& a letter.—Both wonderful.— I chased down to the house—I had to look right away—

Yes, even though I was waiting in New York—yes, waiting,—I who never (!) wait—

And now I'm glad you followed *your* own feeling—You always do, that's what makes you such a wonder—for as much as the watercolors would have meant in New York—I was

---

389. O'Keeffe's package of watercolors, including several nude studies of herself (Lynes 176–188), arrived in Lake George on August 27. A few days later, on September 6, 1917, she explained to Stieglitz that several of the watercolors came from her work in the primary school that summer: "Stealing their ideas and making them more—A crazy notion maybe for while mine had something the children's hadn't—theirs had something mine hadn't."

much more fit—and worthy—to receive them today. What a marvelous lot of work—ever growing, richer, deeper, more sonorous, always yourself—And your letter—

Queer coincidence that both came together!

Ted twenty-one–twenty-three? I had asked. I wondered whether he was twenty-one or nineteen. Nerve you say.—Naturally.—The life—the age—experience—youth—the whole world ajar—

You—I see him—I know you.—Age makes no difference—yet it does—Spirit has no age. But—

—I played some tennis—felt rather alive—took a swim—the water was icy—but hourly the air is growing warmer—& the sky is cloudless. A mild south breeze.—

I have been looking at your work again.—

The *Nudes*[390] are marvelously beautiful—several chilled me like music sometimes does—chills of deepest emotion—And many of the other drawings are equally beautiful—some make me smile.—

The Little Girl—the Passionate Woman—the Artist—all there—

—I remember how afraid I was last year to open the package of drawings you had sent me here. How it lay a long while on the top of my trunk unopened—I wonder what I was afraid of—

—I'm glad you are—wherever you may be—I know you always are just you—

A great big world—

—This afternoon I'm going to try my hand at some photography. It will seem funny.

Just a Good Night before going to bed. It's after 10:30. All is dark in the house—I'm still downstairs—the clock, one lamp lit & I—

It was an evening of laughing. The young (thirty-four) woman of Cincinnati was here—she who sings so beautifully.—She gave us a series of imitations. People of Cincinnati.—Very remarkable. Types.—We all were kept in convulsions of laughter. It felt good to have a real laugh.—I hadn't had one in ages.—

—I photographed towards evening—after having played five games of croquet with little Georgia—my niece—

Photographing excited me terribly—they say I looked ghastly—I know I felt like a dish-rag after it—And the joke is I probably accomplished nothing—except a start.—It's too stupid how I get excited—It has always worked me up to a great pitch to photograph—but formerly it didn't take quite so much out of me—That's the difference between twenty-one & fifty-four.

The intensity is greater today because there is a greater consciousness—& less physical surplus of energy—

—I guess it's time to go to bed—

---

390. Lynes 176–185.

Georgia O'Keeffe · [Loveland, Colorado] · [September 4, 1917]

I don't know the date but I guess it's Tuesday—the first Tuesday in September—

We have been walking since early Sunday morning—have to wait here a little for the train—and I have the next few days planned so full that I don't see where I can write again—

Last Friday Claudie and I went to Estes Park from Ward in an auto—It was so much fun—so pretty all the way up that Saturday morning it occurred to me that it would be fun to do it again—walking—taking our time—so Sunday we started—

I wish first—that I had time to tell you of all the funny folks in Ward—It is just a scrubby little mining town—the Estes Park stage connects there with the end of the railroad—but it's really a remarkable place—I'd rather go right back there today than to Denver but we want to make a couple of trips out of Denver the next two days—then spend a day at Santa Fe on the way home if we don't take a notion to do something else.

There was a dance in Ward again Saturday night—and that was remarkable too—

I went with the Engineer—Mr. Lentz—Claudie too—He said he hadn't danced in twenty years—but some way I imagine it was because he hadn't had a good chance because he certainly seemed to have a wonderful time at it—He dances the round and round kind of dancing of a long time ago—

Claudia O'Keeffe, *Georgia O'Keeffe and unknown man, Estes Park, Colorado*, 1917. Gelatin silver print, 2 ¼ x 3 ¼ in. (5.7 x 8.3 cm). Georgia O'Keeffe Museum Research Center, Gift, The Georgia O'Keeffe Foundation. © 2010 Georgia O'Keeffe Museum/Artists Rights Society (ARS), New York.

I can follow it if I don't talk—The other queer folks thought us very funny when we first began going round—then all the old ladies wanted to dance with him—it was lots of fun—He is really a very good dancer—Some of the other girls who like to teach that sort of thing—I can't you know—I can only follow—almost taught him to do some new things—

I met the man who looks like Dewald—a short almost turn-up nose seems to be the principal difference—He is a wonderful dancer—dances with long straight lines—if you know what I mean by that—up there for his health—county clerk and forest ranger—It was a funny affair—all of it—Dewald's likeness—wants to take me up in the mountains where folks never go—up over the Continental Divide if I'll go back next summer—at least a three weeks trip—a funny little man—

—I wanted to stay and go now—I don't want to go home at all—It's awful to start to work feeling that way about it—I never did before that I can remember—

It seems as though this week is the first of my vacation—it's the first I have felt rested—like a real human being—

I've almost walked Claudie to death—never walked with her before and she thought she could beat me but she is half dead and I feeling better every day—A little over twenty miles a day on an average—Sunday night we walked till almost midnight—it was such wonderful moonlight—

Mr. Lentz walked out a way with us—so funny in a long tailed coat—When we struck a trail off the main road he left—One of the oddities of the town started with us too—A man who has been everywhere and done everything—a miner—and trout fisher now—I thought he would go five or six miles but—no sir—he took a notion that our packs were too heavy so he went right along till last night—carrying our things—It was awfully funny—Claudie liked to talk to him—and he is so queer I was interested in finding out what he was like—He is everywhere and anywhere and nothing—

I wrote you on a card that your telegram came as I was talking to the man at the station who receives them—He excused himself for a moment to receive the message—and as he wrote the name down he said—"it's for you"—I had stopped on the way out of town to send an express package—It was nice to hear from you.

Several letters came to me from Denver—however I'll call for them tonight if I get in on time or else in the morning—

We came down Big Thompson Canyon yesterday and today—Started this morning by moonlight—before daylight—Walls and walls of rock—tremendous—! The little stream tearing along below them—the road—too narrow for cars to pass except at special places—hugging the edge of the stream—the rock rising right up beside it—sky growing lighter above—then pink on the top on one side—

After that—sunshine—irrigated valleys—cherry orchards—sugar beets—far away blue mountains—very hazy—a few patches of snow—It has been—from the Park yesterday till about ten miles out of Loveland this morning—it seemed to be *down hill*—between the rocks beside the little stream all the way—sometimes many pine trees—mostly bareness though—

I haven't worked much—too many things to do—or else I was tired—Such a little time I couldn't work and see things too—

I wonder if you received the bunch of stuff I left with a girl to send you—

I feel as far away from it now as I feel from Canyon—New York—Longs Peak—Everything—

I seem to be years and years and miles and miles away from everybody and everything—If I could walk for a month I might really forget everything—

Hard exercise—why I've breathed so hard my ribs are sore—isn't that queer—Claudie seems to be all in all over—the Baron[391]—we named him that at the hotel in Ward—was stiff in the legs—rheumatism he said—Exercise makes me feel great—and—

Why—I forget folks and things I guess—

Ted among others—it makes me laugh—It's as though I've washed the slate clean—

I must stop—must write Lentz—He wants to know that we are safe and I promised some information about hotels and scenery. He is certainly a nice old man—

Maybe I shouldn't put it that way—but he is certainly great—I phoned him yesterday as promised—Going to be in Ward all winter—with his mines and miners—and there won't be much else—

Those are not my finger marks.[392] I didn't notice them till now—

One of his mines is full of water too. Lots of work—and not much else. He will build a log house for me up on his lake if I'll go back next summer—but of course I don't know what I'll want to do by next summer—Nothing but lake and tall pointed pines and white spotted mountains—

Sitting down in the house makes me sleepy—

I must write him before train time too because I probably never will if I don't now.

I wish you were here—talking would be so much fun—When you feel soaked and soaked with all sorts of things it's pretty hard to get any of it onto paper—

O'KEEFFE ARRIVED BACK in Canyon a few days before classes started on September 11, 1917. Soon thereafter, Stieglitz and his wife, Emmy, accompanied Kitty to Smith College, where she took her placement examinations before beginning courses there later that fall. When they returned to New York a few days later, Stieglitz for the first time in twelve years had no gallery to run or periodical to publish. He still went to 291 Fifth Avenue each day, where he spent his time at first in other rooms in the building and later in a small space where he stored some of his art, which he affectionately referred to as the "Tomb" or the "Vault" because it lacked both heat and light. Oscar Bluemner, Arthur Dove, Marsden Hartley, John Marin, Paul Strand, and Abraham Walkowitz, as well as a few younger writers such as Waldo Frank and Paul Rosenfeld, and the painter-photographer Charles Sheeler continued to visit him in the room. But with no exhibitions, the "Vault" attracted few of the widely diverse American and European artists, writers, intellectuals, and activists that 291 had in its heyday. As his days became quieter, Stieglitz

---

391. The man who walked with Georgia and Claudia from Ward to Loveland.

392. Both O'Keeffe and Stieglitz were greatly disturbed when the paper on which their letters were written became soiled or when the ink smudged.

increasingly focused on his newest protégée and eagerly awaited the arrival of her letters from Canyon.

Throughout the fall of 1917, prowar rhetoric and anti-German hysteria continued to escalate. In October, Congress imposed new taxes on tobacco, entertainment, train fares, and postage in an effort to cover the escalating costs of the war, while the government simultaneously launched an aggressive drive to sell millions of dollars of "Liberty Loans," a special war bond to support the Allied cause.[393] To encourage Americans to "fight or buy bonds," cities and towns across the country commissioned posters, hired airplanes to drop leaflets, and organized parades and rallies where celebrities such as Mary Pickford and Douglas Fairbanks spoke. In early November the former president Theodore Roosevelt assailed the Socialist candidate for mayor in New York, Morris Hillquit, and his supporters "as Huns within," and insisted they were more dangerous than "Huns without."[394] As unbridled patriotism swept the country, even the playing of German music became suspect. A few days later, the New York Metropolitan Opera, which Stieglitz frequently attended, assured its public that the upcoming season would "contain nothing to cause the least offence to the most patriotic American." Critics insisted it would be a "great mistake" to perform German operas with their scenes of "violence and conflict." Further controversy ensued when the Prussian director of the Boston Symphony, Dr. Karl Muck, refused to lead the orchestra in the rendition of "The Star-Spangled Banner."[395]

Both Stieglitz and O'Keeffe nominally supported the war effort. O'Keeffe toyed with buying Liberty Bonds, and Stieglitz completed a "census form" in early November, offering his services to the War Department.[396] For Stieglitz, this public turmoil was echoed in his personal life. On October 22, 1917, after a series of heated arguments with Emmy, he moved out of their home at 1111 Madison Avenue and into the studio of his niece Elizabeth Stieglitz, at 114 East 59th Street, which she shared with Mörling. He stayed there several days and agreed to return home only because of his concerns for Kitty and with the understanding that he would have his "freedom without any questions asked."[397]

Georgia O'Keeffe · [Canyon, Texas] · [September 20, 1917]

Thursday Morning—

Your letter—you have just looked at the drawings—And the pansy—it's lovely.

I still am just nothing—

—Yesterday morning in chapel it suddenly struck me how absurdly empty some of my letters to you [are]—what queer things I told you in others—No not sorry—I only realized it —Though I'm feeling nothing I seem to be seeing more clearly—

393. "New War Taxes Go into Effect Today," *NYT,* Nov. 1, 1917, 6; "Bonds Allotted to Reserve Banks," *NYT,* Sept. 30, 1917, 1.
394. "Roosevelt Sees Our Great Danger in 'Huns Within,'" *NYT,* Nov. 2, 1917, 1.
395. "Halt German Opera at Metropolitan," *NYT,* Nov. 2, 1917, 13.
396. See Chief Signal Officer, U.S. War Dept., to AS, Nov. 19, 1917.
397. AS to Joseph Obermeyer, Oct. 31, 1918.

The English professor[398] is so absurd—he just fits my humor—I told him he better leave me alone—I don't want to bother him and I probably will in time if he doesn't leave me alone—however—I warned him—

Makes me laugh—He will not bother me—unless in time he bores me to death—

—Yesterday I had just washed my head—put on a clean white dress—feeling too clean to feel natural—started to dinner—and up rolled Watkins in a big dark blue—almost black—car—We both laughed—I'm disgusted that he hasn't really gone to war—or something—apt to be called any time—I don't know exactly what—didn't try to remember—

We talked awhile—I wouldn't get in—simply can't do it—Tongues might get me—I guess I didn't want to get in anyway—even though the car looked good and it was a wonderful day—He isn't fun any more—He's too serious—is always trying to understand and can't—When he is serious he doesn't say funny things—he's just plain stupid—

Asked all about me—my work—where I had been—what doing—Nice questions—in a nice way—my sister—

—Makes me sorry in a queer way—but goodness—what can I do about it—

I've been wondering what living is for anyway—The plains are very wonderful—I've been reading about the earliest traces of man in Europe—thirty thousand years ago is a long time—and what is it all about—Probably most of them have wondered—have any of them ever found out—

There seems to be some use in it when all one's short time is full—or at least—then one hasn't time to wonder about it—to doubt it—

—But—well fed—well housed—time to think—and wonder—feeling nothing—this window looking out on the big emptiness—

It seems queer to have time to sit still and think—Where emptiness hurt before—it seems now that I ought to fill it with something and I just look at it blankly and wonder what—It doesn't hurt—Nothing seems to hurt now—

I lent that African Negro sculpture [book][399]—and lost it—and want to read it again—Will you send it to me again—And I want a catalogue of the *Forum*[400] exhibition too—You would laugh if I told you why—I seem to be remembering that they said some very absurd things in it and I want to see it again—

Painting seems such a sickly part of the world—Outdoors is wonderful—I want to take hold of all of it with my hand—

Alfred Stieglitz · [New York City] · [September 30, 1917] +

Sunday morning.

It is coming down sheetwise—but driven by a northwester—It means cooler weather—it has been like summer—& inside of ten minutes a clearing sky!—

398. W. B. Mahan was a new professor of English at West Texas State Normal College in 1917.

399. Marius de Zayas, *African Negro Art* (New York, 1916).

400. *The Forum Exhibition of Modern American Painters,* exh. cat., Anderson Galleries, New York, Mar. 13–25, 1916.

—In spite of coughing nights & days the last have been active—full.—On Friday Dewald phoned at suppertime—I had him come although I was in bed—I spoke in a subdued voice as the earache was letting up—& I didn't wish to irritate the chord or the larynx—We were together—Part of the time was spent in looking at your work—old & new.—It always fascinates—is always fresh.—

We talked the future—business—society—all so? Speculation—And yet—!

—There's the sun—& blue rifts—

—Yesterday there were a lot of people at 291—All morning.—Amongst them Miss Williams & the female part of the 291 marriage[401]—I talked with both—the cough probably torturing all of us—Williams asked for you. Wanted to know what you were doing—I told her if she'd stay on—she intended leaving last night, is going to be in Ithaca all winter—I'd bring some things down for her. I'd like her to see them. I wonder will she have stayed.

—Mrs. Steichen & her daughter Kate, nine years old, also turned up. An uncanny child, like an old woman.—Yet a child.—They & the rest of the family are to be here with me for supper tonight—

—It's all so queer—life—Here is a whole family unfolded—about fifteen years—before my eyes.—Something tragic about it[402]—

It's queer how people will destroy each other—or try to—The young one merely said: "That's it"—she was reading, while the mother & I were talking. I'll never forget that: "That's it" to a remark I had made to the mother about the father of her children—It was like a voice out of a Greek tragedy—I'll always hear that child's clear "That's it"—& see it sitting there reading seemingly not hearing nor listening.—She's undoubtedly heard her mother saying the same thing so often she hears without listening—

—At two Dewald called for me.—Just before he came, a letter was handed me by the big black man—through the door which could hardly be opened as the room was full—A letter from Canyon.—

—Before going with Dewald I read.—So the fireflies—or are they moths—were about again—You were beginning to feel the blood coursing through the veins—Ted!— Impressionable!—You care for many a little—not sufficiently for anyone—??—

Well, I'm glad you are feeling more alive—Your Colorado work is no good, you say.— I wonder.—Just at present you may not be a good judge.—You're a great girl—

The sky is perfectly blue now—opposite is a brick house—a large one—& out of the window a girl in white—red hair—a servant—a tiny dilapidated weather-beaten American flag hanging listlessly out of the window—just below her chin—

It's 11:30—I guess I'll go to gurgling & tinker around my room—my table has come— Darn my cough—it will blow my head off [if] it continues—

192

401. After meeting at 291, Miss Schroder and the poet Turner married in early 1917. They briefly lived in one of the rooms at 291 Fifth Ave.

402. By 1917 Edward and Clara Steichen's fourteen-year marriage and family had disintegrated. Edward was in the Signal Corps; his daughter Mary was living with Stieglitz's brother and sister-in-law, Lee and Lizzie Stieglitz; and Clara and their youngest daughter, Kate, had only recently escaped from war-torn France; see Niven, *Steichen*, 453–454.

—I have to smile at your liking so many people a little—This paper does not want to take up the ink—I guess it didn't like what I was writing—I can't blame it.—

Yes, I'm smiling—I really don't know why—

—Well, here's to the sunlight—brightest sunlight—

Oh I didn't finish with my day yesterday.—Dewald & I lunched together—then went to the *Chemical Exhibition*[403]—Just as I said to Dewald looking at a wonderful machine: The real expression—art—of today—I ran into an art critic who was surprised to see me.—He introduced me to a friend—a powerful looking chap—thrift written all over him—The friend said: My friend here says: "There is no art here."—I asked Dewald to state what I had said a moment before.—General laughter. The art critic said: That's the way we always get it from Stieglitz!—The floors of machinery & bottles & stuff—at the Central Palace—I thought of the *Independent Show* of art—the difference—The difference in attendance too.—

—We marched over to Broadway & had a game of billiards.—Dewald's suggestion. I had no business to play but did.—He is no player—says the play's proof. I don't.—But it was fun—an hour.—Right after supper I bundled up into bed & at ten took a steaming bath— Hadn't had such a hot one in months—

—You see my life is not exciting—I am devoid of ideas—devoid of dreams—Am just amused—at everything & everybody—

Including myself—Most.

Georgia O'Keeffe · [Canyon, Texas] · [October 1, 1917]

Good morning—Monday morning—

I want to write you and I have nothing in particular to say but I want to write anyway —I just won't let myself wake up and so have to laugh at myself—It's great to see yourself asleep.

My bed isn't made—things are strewn all over my room but I want to write first—

I just came from breakfast and the post office—your yellow letter paper—The *Negro Art* and a page from Strand—There is something great about him—but somewhere—he seems to be getting too old too soon—What is it I want to say—too fixed in some of his ideas too soon—

That makes me laugh—

Mr. Cousins told me the other day that my ideas were still in a liquid state—I think that was the way he put it—And you know I'm so feeble minded I don't imagine they will ever be in any other condition—and I don't care—It seems hilariously funny to me—

I didn't tell him so though.

He asked me to talk in chapel next week—on account of some other work interfering

---

403. Alfred's brother Dr. Julius Stieglitz, president of the American Chemical Association, spoke at the opening ceremonies of the Third National Chemical Exposition, Grand Palace, New York, September 24–29, 1917; see "Chemical Industry Show," *NYT*, Sept. 23, 1917, E5.

I put it off till the week after—And even then—What am I going to talk about—I never talked to so many folks—about five hundred I think—We are short about a hundred—war and bad crops—However—that doesn't matter—What I say can't be any more stupid than what some other folks have said—

The thing—is—When you get a whack at them—what is worthwhile—It seems that so many things said to them are not worthwhile—And how do I know what is worthwhile—

It's funny—I don't want to waste my chance—Still I'm not sure that I know how not to —It scares me and it makes me laugh—

I'm glad painting is worthwhile to you—glad mine is something to you—To me it is a necessity at times—You know all that though—

A good many of these folks have never seen a painting though—You know I would like them to see Hartleys—I don't know why Hartleys—the different kinds of Hartleys seem so real—that lonesome little house that Daniel[404] has—then all the changes since—I wonder could they see then how a man's painting is the expression of himself—his life—

Oh—I'm wondering—

I didn't intend to write that last page—it just happened—

It's a sunny windy dusty day—a little cool—the wind warm—

Too bad about your cold—

Yesterday I saw a man very sick—at least I suppose a person is rather ill when he is bleeding at both nose and mouth—It made me very sick—I asked him if I could do anything for him—he was standing alone—He said—only give him a piece of paper and smiled—ghastly pale green—It made me so sick—way to the ends of my fingers—Gosh—

I played with the baby[405] a long time—out in the side yard—a swing—zinnias and sweet peas between us and the road—a couple of hours—She doesn't look well—delicate and dainty—seemingly too pale lately—two—teeth are bothering for one thing—It bothers me to see her so pale—it's such a little life—mother and father both very big and husky—She won't talk either—but she is so nice—

Mr. Lentz—the engineer I told you of up at Ward—dropped dead in the railroad station at Boulder last week—He was—I don't know how to say it—fine may express it—but it seems such an ordinary word for him—he was most extraordinary—So fine and quiet—so comfortable to be with that it was an event—He asked me two or three times what I thought came after living—

I did not know—Queer—But a nice way to die I think—Never in bed—no fuss about it—I believe he would consider himself lucky—He hated bothering folks—a grown family— he fifty-four from Philadelphia—had been out here when young—

—I went to Amarillo one day this week—Mr. and Mrs. Terrill—

The country is really wonderful—and all so flat and empty—a yellow look—quite

---

404. Owned by the Charles Daniel Gallery, *Deserted Farm,* 1909, oil on fiberboard, was one of the "Dark" or "Black Land-scapes" exhibited at 291 in 1909; see Elizabeth Mankin Kornhauser, ed., *Marsden Hartley: American Modernist* (New Haven, 2002), 37.

405. Louise Shirley.

brilliant over it all—I just want it all I like it so much. Another day I went to the Canyon—supper on the edge of the plains—the long drop right off the edge—the tremendous stretch between us and the other side—Four or six miles at least I should imagine—wonderful colors—all colors—the shadows forming—one place where we could see it winding on it must have been much more than six miles—so far away that the color went in with the sky almost—

We had supper on the edge—between the sunset and the moonrise—Three of the faculty and Claudie and myself—

It was the most wonderful view I have seen of it—I engineered the party—went through POSTED land—off the road right into space—not knowing where we were going except that I knew it was toward the Canyon and I knew it must be deep and wide—

They were afraid—I wasn't—I knew the man wouldn't arrest a bunch of old maid school teachers—

Saw hundreds of cattle coming up the paths—smooth paths in the bottom—You can't see them till they are almost under you because you can't see the real bottom of it all—The long line of them wound up crooked paths—the other side of a little gulch and finally came out—looking like narrow black lace on the edge of the plains against the sunset—hot glowing sunset—It was great—I had wandered from the others—found the cattle alone—watching them—alone—

You see I didn't eat supper—I helped get it because some folks can't build a fireplace that will hold a coffee can and they can't open tin cans without openers and things like that—

Then I wandered off—Over an hour by myself I guess—I had collected the lunch on about ten minutes notice because I wanted to stay late—knew they must be fed—so I had to get it into eatable shape—

And I watched the moon come up and the sun go down—and the cattle—it was a wonderful moving line—and the great stretch of color—changing tonight—

And I don't know—I felt something—but I didn't wake up—I saw it all as though I were sleeping—and I came home and slept nine hours straight—

And laughed when morning came—Had a bad headache two or three or four days this week—stopped eating and tried to walk it off—Committee meetings took up other time—

—I don't know—I just look around and wonder—

A little girl—yes—probably more than ever—Not even knowing what to ask—It's like walking around in a dream with your eyes open—a queer stupefied sort of existence all—???—I don't know—

In the wind my black close hat brim is like a flickering shadow between me and the gold of the plains that stretches seemingly to never and the gray blue of the sunny windy fall sky—

The only other thing that seems to impress me is glaring white house ends or fronts—against the sky or plains—glaring white—ugly slopes at the top—ugly windows—Most of the houses here are ugly—the ugly windows make dark holes in the white fronts—

Gosh—They are white—The sun relentless in its whiteness—The wind is careless—uncertain—I like the wind—it seems more like me than anything else—I like the way it blows things around—roughly—even meanly—then the next minute seems to love everything—some days is amazingly quiet.

I wish you were here—or I were there—or something—
I don't know what—
I want to go to Alaska—

Alfred Stieglitz · [New York City] · [October 10, 1917] +

Wednesday—1 P.M.—At 291—All day yesterday at home—a bleak rainy day.—I was about to leave at nine when Mrs. & I had some "words."—It seems impossible for us to talk over anything without the *inevitable scene.* I try so hard to make her see—stupid to try—she never will—can't—& yet I try—for her own sake—But she has never understood—not me—but practical life. Gosh I haven't understood much—but she understands nothing—Every word I say riles her—she doesn't hear—I'm terribly sorry for her & she doesn't know it—She—It's all killing me—That kid is ever in my mind—my daughter—fortunately she is far away from the sordidness of all this & happy in her surroundings & work—There is some one knocking—

7:30—Home. Through supper. Alone. Mrs. Stieglitz has gone to the country—The knock at the door was Mrs. Bull. I went into the back room with her—there was Turner, the young poet—the one half of the "291 marriage"—& there was his wife[406]—cooking—fine, good to look at—both are—I wouldn't join in the eating—I was too full of all else—There was Miss Schroder & there was Mrs. Bull.—I talked. Young Turner talked—he surely is an unusual fellow—& finally I started telling them some stories of my life—I was really telling them to Turner—the women listened attentively—I must have talked a long while—

I wondered what they all got—Gaisman came in—& Charlie Liebman too—they met accidentally.—I took them into the Vault—We stood—the three of us—Gaisman had been in Washington—while there he was incidentally finding out whether there wouldn't be an opening for me—He related a great story—I laughed. It led to a three cornered discussion—Elizabeth[407] had come in—she too stood & listened—For an hour the discussion continued—Washington—the United States—Patriotism—Gaisman & I are not far apart—still there is a separation—Charlie Liebman was miles off—Elizabeth smiled & understood all three—They left—the men—Elizabeth & I walked up town—stopped in at my mother's—Unfortunately I was compelled to state some brutal truths there—both days—the family's finances—the poor old woman doesn't grasp & I wonder why I'm so brutal—Elizabeth thinks I did the right thing—I wonder—I always wonder—Why can't I shut up—

This morning I was at Daniel's—three hour session there—serious talks about the men—myself—& now I guess I'll go to my mother's again—My sister & her husband, the Engelhards, will be there. I haven't seen them since Lake George—

—It has been a mad day—the papers are full of the shrinking of investment values—Everything is being wiped away—It's like watching the coming of a flood & one feels escape

406. Miss Schroder.
407. Elizabeth Stieglitz, Alfred's niece.

196

impossible—trapped—caught—a few who have very high houses & the doors locked to "out-siders" may escape!!

—You are indeed fortunate to be deep in work—in Texas, far, far away from all this—me—291—New York—

—Tomorrow I am to see Marie—I haven't seen her in three weeks—Cold & earache—& all the rest—I wouldn't go near her.—Unless I can bring her life why see her—She can't help me except letting me help her live her life.—Mine is too tottering to share—

And so with you—I'm glad you're far away—I even wonder if I ought to send letters—they are not what they were—full of fight—hope against hope—Still I let you have them—I wonder why—Am I clinging to life—is it that?—I'll go now—I've walked miles today—I'm alone in the apartment—all gone—I see your *Self-Portrait*[408]—

Would I forget the World—the Deluge—Heaven & Hell—Everything—for a moment—??!—

I dare not look at it for more than a moment—Queer—& not long ago I looked at it for hours—serenely quiet—It took me into various worlds—

I guess I'm terribly tired—Perhaps my lips are parched—My whole being seething into desire to be embraced to sleep—by anyone that has soft skin—& gentle arms.

I guess I'm really crazy—I wish I were—they'd lock me up—I wouldn't have to think—anything that's sane—

Good Night—

Alfred Stieglitz · **[New York City]** · **[October 17, 1917]** +

Wednesday 6:20. I just came home—I'm pretty hungry & thirsty. Forty minutes more. Had a full day—So full that it began at nine & lasted until six without a let-up—nothing to eat—nothing to drink—I missed neither. Am really accustomed to it—Walked down.—At the Bourgeois Gallery I thought I'd stop in—Nine American "Landscape" Painters[409]—Amongst them Marin & Walkowitz—I went up & I was glad.—I had the rooms to myself—the sun was bright—& when there was a feeling of dignity—& straightforwardness about the place. There always is.—Little rooms—Pleasant.—So different from Montross & even Daniel—for Bourgeois has good light—Daniel hasn't.—It was a joy to see the wall of Marins—I had sent them—old acquaintances—I never saw them look so well, even at 291. And a wall of Walkowitzes.—Beautiful. Never saw him so beautifully presented. New & old things—These two stood out way above the others—Stella had some interesting notes—But Walkowitz and Marin make the show.—Bourgeois came in. He is the one really *living* dealer in New York. Not at all a New Yorker—a man who is a lover & knows—& does business. Of course the show will not do much business—but he knows what he's doing. It was 12:30 when I got away.—We had a long intimate talk—undisturbed.—

---

408. Lynes 99.
409. Nine Landscape Painters, Bourgeois Galleries, New York, Oct. 16–Nov. 10, 1917.

—When I got to 291 I tinkered around a little—Paul Rosenfeld came—he wrote about music in the *Seven Arts*—I talked to him—& Leon Fleischmann, also a poet, came (stayed a few moments only)—he is young & is the husband of a pretty vivacious girl I had photographed a few years ago, Helen Kastor[410]—They had been away from New York—have settled down here again—Gramercy Park—I'll go & see them—

In the meantime a seventeen-year-old music student came—a girl—petite—She had [a] bunch of drawings—Isadora Duncan. Never had lessons. Crazy about Isadora—dances herself—drawings quite remarkable—

—I told her to go right ahead—just work—

Gaisman then turned up. Is very anxious for me to take some "useful" position—has plans for me—advertising firm—to use "modern art"—I'm amused.—Perhaps I'll make a trial. Of course within a week I'll be "out" again—

I'll see.—Am to meet "the man" with Gaisman tomorrow—Of course I know all about "the man."—A big concern—huge in fact. I wish I could fit in—but I know I won't—Can you imagine me in a "job"?

Then women came "to see exhibitions"—Many come.—Much disappointed—"Out-of-Towners"—And a man came too—one I had often noticed—don't know what he does or who he is—He was much moved about the closing up.—He sat awhile with me—Seems to have met Marie at the Modern Gallery—she was there a few months when it opened—& last summer he chanced upon her in the country—He spoke of her as radiating light & heaven on earth—& gave me a picture of her that was truly Marie—remarkable—He is a man of fifty-one—Very simple—He asked for Hodge.—It was a pathetic session for he was really moved—felt he had lost his best friend—the Little Room.—I was very quiet—It was good to hear about Marie & Hodge & the Little Room from this simple man—

—It had grown dark & cold—and you remember the room has no heat nor light.— It seemed funny.—I could have laughed—but I didn't.—There was the man—& there had been the music student—there was Bourgeois—& then the JOB—I in the advertising business— or part of it—In the hands of friends—Gaisman is such a fine fellow—he just misses—What? —Of course if he had had that would he have ever been able to succeed as he has—

Well, we'll see.—Experiences as you see—as ever—

I've had supper—It didn't take long. But I had plenty—just Mrs. Stieglitz & I. In silence.— Queer—Formerly it would have put me on edge—now I'm so far away—so far away— Nowhere!—I didn't walk home—It was too late.—Or was it [that] I wanted to sit—I had stood a good part of the day.—

—I wonder how you are. I stopped writing last night—turned off the light & went to sleep—so early—It wasn't a good night—nor a bad one.—At one time I wished I would feel your fingers over my eyelids—so that I'd fall asleep—& they remaining there—until—I fell asleep.—I shuddered at daybreak—I was awake as it broke.—It seemed so terribly lonely outside—I could see a brick wall—& some sky—the window was open. Bed was warm—

198

---

410. Stieglitz, *Untitled—Legs,* Frish Brandt and Jeffrey Fraenkel, *The Eye Club* (San Francisco, 2003), pl. 64.

& so soft—& the room so quiet—I bundled up—& dug my head into the pillow—It was as if it were human—that pillow—

I could see your two paintings, the red one—the green one—the green one suggested by tree forms shadows[411]—

I guess I'll go to bed—Read some—Gerard—*My Four Years in Germany*[412]—rather interesting reading—not as literature—

—Good Night Little Girl—

I wonder if you are still so empty inside—

Perhaps there is room there for a very tired soul to crawl in there to disappear forever.—Good Night.—

Georgia O'Keeffe · [Canyon, Texas] · [October 18, 1917]

The forty-two pages[413] this morning was astounding to say the least—I never had such a long letter—I liked it—yet I hated it—

Time has been very full—I was surprised at no letters—Yesterday it occurred to me that maybe you were ill—Still I did not write—My darned head so stupid and so full—You will understand—

Ted was up Saturday night—A dance—he came in late with an older brother & a girl[414] he always trotted around here from habit I think—She was from near his home—a really nice—lovable sort of girl—but as he put it—"There is something in you that she hasn't got—she just hasn't *got* it—nobody else has."

He brought the brother over—we danced and talked cattle—He dances just like Ted only not so much of that damnable self-assurance—Ted told me about him—long ago—a girl spoiled things for him—I liked him—

The dance was lots of fun—Mr. Blaine was there—I don't know exactly why—but it was more fun than usual—It was great to see Ted—his face very red—outdoors all the time—seventy-five miles to get here—faces turn a wonderful color from sun and wind here—His eyes so shiny—Not exactly happy—war—everything a turmoil—grabbed my hand right tight—dancing—

I don't know anything—Do you—

—I believed he is trying to like Ruby because he can't see me within reach[415]—

It seems I never saw such a live—seething piece of humanity—making such an effort to manage it all—He was here all day Sunday and didn't even phone me—

411. The red one, Lynes 159; the green one, possibly Lynes 90.

412. James W. Gerard, *My Four Years in Germany* (New York, c. 1917).

413. Stieglitz's forty-two-page letter included passages written from Monday, October 1, through Thursday, October 11, 1917.

414. Ruby Fowler (later Reid).

415. O'Keeffe's biographers have asserted that Reid severed his relationship with O'Keeffe after he was warned by faculty members that he would not receive his diploma if he continued to see her; see, e.g., Hunter Drohojowska-Philp, *Full Bloom: The Art and Life of Georgia O'Keeffe* (New York, 2004), 144.

—I'm sitting on the porch—it's a warm sunny afternoon—cowboys went by with a bunch of horses a little while ago—A bunch of cows and calves going by now—

—I want to get right up and go with him—if he would only come and ask me again—It doesn't seem that it would even be necessary to get my hat—I'm ready right now—

Going seems out of all reason—but does reason amount to anything—Why couldn't I have been ready when he asked me so many times so earnestly—and half afraid—I said it wasn't reasonable—he said he knew it—

—I don't know—it seems something must happen—Long ago I told him—before I knew how much he cared—way last spring when it was cold he sat here on the porch with me in the moonlight—after dancing and a long walk—and I told him he ought to plan to marry Ruby or leave her alone—he would make her like him too much and maybe hurt her—

—If he would marry her—it would be all right—knowing he was forgetting—

It's feeling that he wants and I want—and the damnable little things that keep us apart —I know it would be foolish—no not foolish—against what everyone would expect is more to the point—and how I would make out living his way isn't at all certain—it's all so uncertain —He said—Well—we can quit if we can't make it work—sometimes I think you would like it and sometimes I don't—Then we would laugh about it all—

200   —I don't know—it all makes me want to get up and go to him and tell I'm ready—and if he has changed his mind—has reason—now that I haven't—just wander off into space away from everything I've known[416]—

I hate it here—It's a lifeless bloodless sort of life to live—No one I can think of here seems to have anything but white blood—no red at all—

Then there is Claudie—So long as I am responsible for her I'm only half human—I wonder what I'll do when she is gone[417]

Watkins in Amarillo—and some other folks—but they—I don't know—I hated them—Guess I hated your letter for the same reason this morning—One thing saves me from wanting to shoot or strangle or drown you—

—You understand—

I wonder if you know how great that seems these days—

Alfred Stieglitz · [New York City] · [October 23, 1917] +

You'd like to shoot, drown or strangle me.—Those were the first words I saw in your letter of yesterday.—There were two letters—You don't know how funny those words sounded—just then—& how I wondered whether it wouldn't be wise were you to do it—Perhaps that's your job—

—I had just come from "home" where I had an awful row with Mrs. Stieglitz—It's a

---

416. A few days later, on October 31, 1917, O'Keeffe insisted that she had "forgotten Ted" and now found it humorous to see Ruby sitting in her class.

417. Claudia O'Keeffe was about to leave Canyon to work as a student teacher in Spur, Tex.

wonder I didn't kill her—She has hurt me so terrifically for twenty-four years—all that's really good in me she tries to drag in the mud—She doesn't know it—but she is without heart—she can't help it.—And I follow her & listen & try to be quiet—quiet in the sense that someone is lying on the operating table & is being operated on—butchered by a pseudo surgeon—without anesthetic—& finally one can't stand the dilettantism & one is ready to kill the would-be "helper"—

—It's Tuesday & I haven't been home—I left—without comb or toothbrush—or clean collar—just left—I came here—And your words greeted me. I laughed.—And I read about Ted & Ruby—& I knew all you felt—& he—& Ruby—

—What a mad twisted thing life is—& some of us more specially so—too sensitive—& our intelligence not equal to our feelings.—

—I was glad to have those letters—It's a wonder I'm not in jail today for having killed a woman.—The mother of Kitty.—It was the cook that prevented it. And I knew what I was about—& I would have pleaded guilty—& all I would have asked is permission to relate my story—not about the woman—nor myself—just a story—And then I wouldn't have cared what would have happened.—

—I sat here like paralyzed—Marie happened in—just accidentally.—She wanted me to go home with her—Walkowitz & Zoler came—sat awhile & left—Gaisman tried to convince me I must be quieter—use reason more—Strand came—& then Elizabeth.—And Elizabeth wanted me to go to her studio—In the meantime I locked the door of the room next door.—A loud knock—I opened—McBride inside, the *Sun* art critic, the man I'm very fond of. He was waiting—We all laughed. He had a narrow escape.

—And then I went to the studio—& Miss Mörling was there—she, Elizabeth & I had tea—There are two beds—cots in the rooms—a cot in each—Elizabeth fixed one—gave me the keys & said: Do as you like.—It was seven when they had left—I walked the streets & finally called up Strand—he met me at a druggist's, a "rendezvous"—We walked. And then we went to a German "Garden"—where I knew no one would be—I had eaten nothing all day—There was music—& it was quiet—for I didn't hear the music—& the tables were empty—

I then took Strand to my new abode.—We sat together till 11:15—& when he left there I was millions of miles from everywhere—no one except Elizabeth & Mörling & Strand knew—I wanted to write to you—but I couldn't—I looked about—the windows—the north light—the cot—all so peaceful—primitive—I lay down—the gas turned half off—I was dreadfully used up—I dozed—I put out the light—turned over a million times—I guess I was hungry—for food—& rest—

—But it was wonderful.—To feel that daylight would come & the room would greet me with its simple smile—

I heard a man's voice & a woman's & a child's—the bathroom near—daylight streaming onto the bed—primitive sheets & pillow—I half in my clothes—It was eight—I was up—Elizabeth came—with edibles—but I wanted nothing—just hot water—Then Mörling came—& I entertained them with jokes about life—& we all laughed—

—And here I am—feeling seedy & dirty—unshaven & unkempt—I guess I'm at heart a bum—fit only for that—What will the day bring?—I won't go home—I can't—I've been hurt too much—

A letter from Marie—what a heart that girl has! And a letter from you—cards—you are willing to sit under the tree & let me sleep as long as I like—You are so full of life—

—As if I didn't know—The Little Girl—I'm glad you feel that you are about to work again—that's great—And of course I wonder what it will be like—before sleeping long I'd like to see—

—It's wondrous quiet here—

—Liberty Bonds[418]—Yes, here too—Everywhere Liberty Bonds!—A funny contradiction of words: Liberty—Bonds. Like life itself.—

—I feel as if I weren't I—another I—No the same old I, I guess—I have so much I ought to do—& I don't seem able to do a thing.—

It's 9 o'clock—I'm in Elizabeth's studio. Alone.—I've just had supper. Alone. Hadn't had anything but a hot cup of water since last night—

It's funny sitting here—alone—

—It has been a big day—Big in the sense that my family mess is finally coming to a head—It is the psychological moment—I was called up—they seemed to have found a number—want a family gathering—three brothers & sister[419]—I & Herbert Engelhard—the father of Georgia—I'm ready.—Told them so—At a moment's notice—at their signal.—

I refused to go "home" tonight—won't go "home" until something *definite* is settled upon—I can't live as I have for twenty-four years—

Our cook was to 291—Mrs. Stieglitz was in the country—Mrs. Stieglitz is finally beginning to realize that I'm not entirely a dishrag—

—It's a long & frightful family story—I really feel sorry for her for she'll never see or understand—She's really never grasped the meaning of life—& still more the meaning of another's feelings—She never was disciplined—nor did she discipline herself—

—I'm so unshaven I feel uncomfortable—don't think the pillow will like it.—I hope I sleep I'm dreadfully tired.—All day people—uncanny coincidences—

—I wish someone would kiss me to sleep—anyone—with soft lips & soft hands—& clean. I'm so infernally tired—

—I wonder if you still [feel] like strangling me—I wouldn't mind—perhaps would do quite as well as a kiss—

—My neck is 15½—I think your hands would reach around—or would you use a rope—or like Othello a kerchief—or pillow—he smothered Desdemona—Smother with kisses & choke with hands—at the same time.—

—These are days of killing. It seems funny to be up here without comb or toothbrush

418. In her letter to Stieglitz of October 20, 1917, O'Keeffe confided: "I don't know whether I want a Liberty Bond or not—Maybe I'll buy pictures—wouldn't that be funny—But it seems the men ought to be able to make a living if I can." And on October 31, 1917, she related that Herman Reeves was "afraid he will have to go to war—twenty-five—and is wanting to get married instead—Is wondering how he can buy shoes this winter having bought Liberty Bonds—let alone get married."
419. Theodore, Ernest, and Joseph Obermeyer and Emmy Obermeyer Stieglitz.

—pajamas or books—Just a cot & chairs—& gas jets—& a few glasses—tobacco—the ladies smoke—I don't.

    Good Night.—

Georgia O'Keeffe · [Canyon, Texas] · [October 29, 1917]

All week I've carried a letter to you in my pocket—and haven't mailed it—I don't know why I haven't mailed it—or why I'm not going to send it with this except that I seem to feel that it's just nothing—that there is nothing in it—

    The week has gone very fast—and mostly I've been in a turmoil of thinking and feeling—

    I wish there were another country to go to—I'd like to leave this one for a country where there isn't war—or else I'd like to go to Europe and see what it's really like—

    Still—it makes me sick—nauseates me just to talk about blood—and internals—I wonder what it would be like to see folks mutilated—only parts of folks—wonder if I'd get used to it—I'd like to try—

    —You know—I feel as if I can't stand it here much longer—I don't know where I'll go or what I'd do—but—it feels like it's coming—just that I can't stand it to look at these folks and hear them talk and see how they are thinking—

    I guess it's the same everywhere—If I were a man I'd get up and go to war so fast you couldn't see me—Everything just seems awful around me—I seem to hate everyone—Claudie is the same—It isn't exactly hate—it's more impatience with everybody and everything—All living seems to be changed—It's as though the sky will never be clear again—

    It's a cold weird moonlight night—a tearing north wind—sand blowing and dried little green locust leaves on the almost bare trees seem to string out in the wind—I never saw such a night—whistling and rumbling wind—the bare dusty moonlight—uneven gusts of wind—I could hardly walk against it—It's terrible—and yet I like it.

    Strand sent me a copy of his 291 article and a couple of poems[420]—They gave me a great time—specially the 291 article—I hope it's published—it's great—Made me feel just like his work made me feel—there is certainly something fine about him—I'm so glad we met—But what is the war going to do to him—I wish I could talk to him—

    There isn't a single person here that I want to talk to tonight—I feel as alone as though I were the only person in Texas tonight—The only person up here on the plains country anyway—

    No I haven't worked any—I'm just all tied up—I just haven't anything to say—I never felt so dumb in my life—it's an effort to carry on the most inane sort of conversation—to even remark on the weather—and to laugh—Gosh—

---

420. Paul Strand, manuscript, Stieglitz-O'Keeffe Archive. Strand's poems are no longer extant, nor are his letters to O'Keeffe from 1917 and 1918. Earlier in the week O'Keeffe responded to Strand's letter: "The best way I can tell you how your letter this morning and the article on 291 made me feel is to tell you that I love you like I did the day you showed me your work—Love you both armfuls—Or is it what you say that I love" (Oct. 24, 1917, CCP:PSC).

I've looked at the outside of *Faust*—It's the only thing I have any notion to read except papers—and I haven't even put my hand on it—much as I want to—It's on my table—right in front of me—I don't know why I don't even touch it—

I don't know anything—

I'd like to be by you somewhere out in the land of nowhere—very close by you—because I'm afraid—It's no use to write you when I feel like I've been feeling—That isn't why I haven't written though—I've simply been dumb—

Like a machine I've tended to many tag ends of work this week. I seem bent on trying to get things in order—as though I'm getting ready to leave—

Isn't that queer—

There isn't much sense in it because every other place is just as bad as this I guess—I don't see any place to go to.

Goodnight.

I want to talk to you—

Alfred Stieglitz · **[New York City]** · **[November 2, 1917]** +

Friday Noon.—291—I just came in—It's a very cold clear morning—I spent it at Elizabeth's studio—first alone—then she & I—& later her friend & me—It's so quiet here—the sun pours in in the morning.—

—I've just read your letter. There is one you didn't mail—I know exactly how you feel—the condition you are in—much the same as my own—

They are yelling Extras[421]—how I hate the sound.—Everything seems so ghastly—As you feel as if you were preparing to end something—to go—so I have been feeling for months. Everything I do seems as if it were done to end something—to get ready for—? It's all too horrible—I can't work up to the popular level—I was a real good American until I realized there was no America nor American—I felt American for years for I believed Americans felt the universality of things & beings—I'm just nothing when the world is labeling individuals still more than formerly—

—I can't see anything separate—I feel things as a whole—& I see them that way—

—Yes, I wish you were here to talk to—& be talked to—*Faust* on your table—You read the papers—that's about all—I read the papers today too—Wall Street—the War—Politics—Roosevelt's Rantings—Coming taxes—No German opera—The Boston Symphony refusing to play the Star-Spangled Banner—

All such a mix-up—What a madness—hysteria—

—I hardly slept a wink last night—such ghastly things are happening all around

421. On November 2, 1917, *The Washington Post* and other newspapers reported that Russian premier Alexander Kerensky had cabled United States government officials to state that Russia would no longer continue to wage war on the Germans. On November 3, 1917, newspapers corrected earlier reports and stated that Russia was still in the war and would make no separate peace with Germany; see "We Assist Russia; She Stays in the War," *NYT*, Nov. 3, 1917, 1.

me—in the family—& families—Fortunes wiped out—Pathetic because the causes are not understood—My prayer, if I have one, is that all money be taken from *all* people—

I wonder how you look this morning—how your face would look seated opposite to me—an empty chair is there opposite to me—

I'm not surprised that you are dumb—can't paint—can't even laugh honestly—

I wonder how much *heart* Wilson has—I'd love to know exactly what he really feels.—

Marin comes at two today—I hope we'll be left alone awhile—no Walkowitz or Zoler —or anyone else for that matter—Of course we can go away—or I can send people away— I wonder whether he'll bring his work—

—I'll look after some prints now—Little Girl I'd like to have you read some *Faust* to me—or would you rather go out for a long walk—in the country—Anywhere—Is there anywhere these days—Can one get away—even for a moment—from those terrible speeches of hate—Destruction—Maiming—Blood & Hideousness—Writhing Mangled Humanity— Humans!!—

—Fortunate those who are in the thick of it as long as it is the only thing that exists today—

Georgia O'Keeffe · [**Canyon, Texas**] · [**November 5, 1917**]

I just came in out of the night—wonderful black night—some very bright stars—It's ten o'clock and I'm here all alone—no one else in the house—so I haven't taken my coat off—My hands a little stiff with cold—my lips burning from the wind—Being in the house alone is a bit uncanny —I don't like to take off my coat—

A man down from Amarillo—taking a car he had sold to a man out in the country from here took Mrs. Reeves—I went with Mr. Reeves—the other man left his car and came back in the Reeves' car—gone about three hours I guess and it was great out—

Only we talked war all the way out—I can't talk it with many folks—they are so stupid —or I am—that it just won't work—

—The night was great—it was great to talk—man and woman are queer—Everywhere the same incongruous puzzle—inconsistent—reasonable—unreasonable—war—or ride in the night—it all looks the same to me—it's the same thing everywhere—I've seen women and children in South Carolina living in a kind of poverty I couldn't imagine if I hadn't seen it—I haven't seen children with their hands cut off yet—but I've seen things that seem just as bad—if not worse—in a country not at war—Will war help those folks—I like to think it will in time—

I ought to stay away from Reeves—it seems I ought always to stay away from anyone I like—

—She phoned me and asked me to go—I didn't know I was going with him—as I got in the car he laughed and remarked that he had done some tall scheming to get me in there—

—It doesn't matter—Nothing does—Everything is right or wrong—crazy or sane— according to the way you look at it.

And I just don't *know* anything—

Seeing Leah this morning—Reeves tonight—two human folks in one day—it's almost too much—Wish I would burst and be through with things—

Claudie just came so I'll go to bed—it's rather chilly—

Goodnight.

Alfred Stieglitz · [New York City] · [November 12, 1917] +

Monday—Noon—291—Just came in—A real spring morning—a haze—balmy—A mean night—The cold kept me tossing about—But somehow I didn't feel tired out this morning in spite of lack of rest.—

—On my way down I stopped in at Elizabeth's studio—Read some more pages in Swedenborg—Then the girls showed up—Mörling has a cold—Elizabeth was tired & sleepy —so we soon all trotted out—Elizabeth to fiddle. She says it wakes her up—Mörling to dose herself & warm up.—I started to walk to 291.—

—On the way down I stopped in at Scott & Fowles (the fashionable firm dealing in "old masters, English") to see Birnbaum who joined the firm last year.—He had made such a financial success of his art shows at the Berlin Photographic Company. Berlin had become taboo[422]— Scott & Fowles needed new blood—Well, I wanted to see Birnbaum in regard to several matters. —He is Nadelman's agent & a lady wants a sculptor to do something for her & came to me— I suggested Nadelman.—So I arranged a meeting between her—the agent—& the artist—And then too Birnbaum had written to Marin—& Marin turned over the affair to me—So I saw Birnbaum for Marin too. Two birds with one stone.—

—At Scott & Fowles the season's "first" show there was just opening up.[423] —A very luxurious room—heavy draperies—artificial light—Samples of well-known names—& less well known (suggesting the idea of helping the unknown struggling but deserving artist)—all styles—everything though of the saleable kind. Nadelman shone out far above all else—There were Manship & Dearth—Bellows (a cross between a Huylerized Winslow Homer—a Harrison Fisherized Daumier[424]—a fishing scene by the way—Americanized Prussian brutality in paint —ye gods—& it was sold for two thousand dollars—Birnbaum thinks the fishing pole should have been at a different angle as it seems to run into the line of the distant mountain—!!)— Alden Weir (also sold—& so are the Nadelmans and orders for replicas of the latter also, three of one—four of the other—!!—& the show just opened—)—Maxfield Parrish—etc. etc.—Birnbaum as spic & span as ever—immaculate in dress—hair & moustache perfect (I'm

422. The galleries of the Berlin Photographic Co. in New York, which had exhibited modern European and American art, closed in the summer of 1916, a victim of anti-German sentiment.

423. The exhibition included work by Elie Nadelman, Everett Shinn, Maurice Sterne, Robert Chanler, Henry Golden Dearth, Constantin Guys, Salvatore Lascari, Maxfield Parrish, Gertrude V. Whitney, J. Alden Weir, and Paul Manship; see "A Contemporary Group," *NYT,* Nov. 22, 1917, 12.

424. Huyler's was a confectionery store in New York City that later expanded into a chain of luncheonettes and candy stores. Harrison Fisher was an American commercial artist known for his often saccharinely sweet portraits of women. His "Fisher Girl" and "American Girl" were the model for feminine beauty for many people in the early years of the twentieth century.

sure a barber did up both—or Birnbaum is as perfect as a barber in that line too)—"Business &
Art" in perfect ensemble—written all over the place—

—The whole thing reminded me of an experience in Budapest thirty years ago.—I know
virtually nothing about houses of prostitution—except for hearsay & literature—But in Pest I
was "shown around" just to see.—One evening I was shown from the "lowest to the highest."
—The first place was a mean little sawdust covered room—raw tables—no light except two or
three candles—a few brutish looking men—half asleep before their nearly empty glasses—
I was full of fear & wanted to get out—but before I could a big fat woman in her chemise—
huge bulging breasts—legs in proportion—arms (I shiver when I think of them)—a face not
coarse—dark hair—emerged from a dark corner—She asked what we'd have—I handed
her twenty cents—the equivalent—& told her we were strangers & were seeing the sights of
Pest.—She looked us up & down—the men too looked but hardly moved—She undoubtedly
served drinks & all the rest to all comers—Lady of the house—The price of her special favor
was fifteen cents—drinks extra—I was glad when we were out in the clear night again—The
whole episode took not more than two minutes—if that—It seemed an eternity though—

—Then the cab drove on & we were shown the places where favors cost twenty-five
cents—& others for fifty cents—one dollar—& so on—until finally we came to the swellest
of swellest—A palace—a broad marble stairway—white—glittering lights everywhere—
innumerable rooms could be seen from the broad hallway—rooms plush & gold—different
colors of plush—music far off—No one to be seen.—A middle-aged woman appeared at the
head of the stairway—fixed up—painted & enameled—false teeth—glistening white—a genial
smile that made one feel as if a death mask were wishing to be kind to you—a dress cut very
low—She came down & asked us what type of girl we wished. She had young & old—virgins
too—thin & fat—short & tall—French, Hungarian, Italian, American, Negresses—every
nationality & she wanted to know whether we'd have champagne or wine—I felt we weren't
rich enough to take in the picture show—so gave her twenty-five francs & got out.—We had
seen no one but her.—

—Well, the Birnbaum show somehow brought the episode vividly before my mind's eye
again.—But this morning I was shown all the "girls"—even virgins. But they were not as yet
taken.—

—Birnbaum certainly knows his business. He is very frank about it—to me at least. I
don't want you to think that I am sneering at him. I really admire him. He fills a want!—But the
"artists"—? The whore is a real thing—but—well—I guess it's New York.

—I then dropped in at Knoedler's as Steichen was "showing"[425] there—fifth floor—
right—A small room—Samples too—early & latest. Landscape & flowers.—It hurt me to see
the show—His undoubted ability—A sincerity of a certain kind—Americanism—His flower
pieces have a charm—one can see he cares for flowers—has a feeling for them—And his expres-

425. See "Art Notes," *NYT,* Nov. 9, 1917, 12. Although the reviewer believed Steichen's landscapes "can be seen without the
suspicion of a quickened pulse," his flower paintings "compel a sincere and deep emotion on the part of the least impressionable
observer." He concluded: "It is a remarkable little collection, contributing to art a new expression and a demonstration of the
highest technical adequacy."

sion of them is his own—a mixture of Whistler—Chinese—Cubist—Color Photography—But somehow I do not feel moved—I simply see color & mechanism—

I think I detected the trouble. He has a *Nocturne—Lake Champlain*—It's Steichen at his best—taking Steichen as Steichen—There seems to be a feeling for night & water & sky—(even if the feeling for paint is irritating)—One feels it when one involuntarily is jumped to a tiny bit of paint—a highlight in the sky—a star!—Not a trace of feeling in that bit of light—just a final "There it is"—The sudden consciousness of that feeling gave me a chill. Steichen has imagination—is a poet—but it takes more than that to create life—I wonder whether the war will sensitize him.[426]

—Perhaps I'm too sensitive—too critical about Steichen—Perhaps I was too fond of him at one time—perhaps too fond still—to be entirely fair to his work—Perhaps "oversaw" it formerly—when he potentially lived in me—& "undersee" it now when I am impatient with all tricks—whether his or the President's.

—In the adjoining fifth floor room as I glanced in—while waiting for the elevator—I saw Jonas Lie's *Western Mining* series[427]—the series I saw some weeks ago in his studio—I looked in.—A large room—Louis xvi furniture (I was informed the room was an exact of replica of the famous Widener Room in Philadelphia!) Jonas Lie sitting on a sofa—pensively—like Napoleon at St. Helena—The huge oils on the walls—over each, attached to the frames the gilt-hooded electric light reflectors—The show had just opened—A woman sitting on another sofa—other side of room to Lie—she a friend of Leo Stein—I laughed aloud.—I never saw such a combination—The spirit of those mining camps as I saw them in my mind's eye—the huge illustrations in oil of that spirit—& the imitation Louis xvi room!—Ye Gods.—I more than laughed aloud.—And I told Lie I never saw anything funnier anywhere.—

—Another room in the Budapest Palace!—

—The Stein lady friend went down the elevator with me & assured me it was really too bad I "closed" 291—She was sincere—I had "done so much for the country" I ought to "reopen" soon—

—I was glad the sun was out—I mingled with the Fifth Avenue crowd—was splendidly alone—& finally got down here—291—*"Closed"*—The Vault—the rooms full of rat holes—the rooms I sit in & are not mine—I realized that a simple shed—without chairs & without any furniture—perhaps a few planks to sit on—walls of plain boards—unkempt boards—the cheapest—any color—is needed more than ever.—Honest work to be shown there without frills—no brass bowls—no autumn leaves—no catalogues on Japan paper.[428] Just pure daylight & a certain amount of cleanliness—& neatness—

But the "artist must sell to be able to produce art—to work"—So Birnbaum says.—

426. Steichen later agreed with Stieglitz's assessment of his paintings and destroyed many of them in the early 1920s; see Anne Cohen DePietro, *The Paintings of Eduard Steichen,* exh. cat., Heckscher Museum, Huntington, N.Y., June 29–Aug. 18, 1985.
427. Jonas Lie exhibited a series of paintings of the Utah Copper Mine in Bingham Canyon at the Knoedler Galleries in New York in November 1917; *NYT,* Nov. 16, 1917, 1.
428. In 1905 when Stieglitz opened 291, he printed elegant catalogues, often on Japan tissue, for many of the shows. The galleries were designed by Steichen, who placed a brass bowl, filled with leaves, on a pedestal in the center of one of the rooms.

No one will buy except where plush & gilt & spic & spanness act as stimulants for the opening up of purse strings—purse strings of those—who are they anyway—those with money!—

—The chaos down here—it's clean.—The rat holes are honest rat holes.—I'm glad I had this place to come to after the morning in the Galleries of Art & Success on our Greatest of Avenues!—

Alfred Stieglitz · [New York City] · [November 14, 1917] +

Once more the envelope is torn open.—I have carried around another day to mail—went into several places to get stamps—out of them—like sugar & salt—

I've just gotten home—6:15—Wednesday—A dream day for me.—Clear & summer-like—

I spent the day with Marin at his home in Weehawken—up on top of the beginning of the Palisades—right above the West Shore railroad yards.—Marin lives on the first floor of a little frame house—from the windows one sees the river & New York—the huge grain elevators in the foreground—to the right the railroad depots—yards—etc—

—It was twenty-five years since I was in Weehawken.—A winter day—Heavy snow falling—February—Going to the Guttenburg racetrack—one of a very tough crowd—none tougher—I one of them—seemed at home—yet apart.—An old dilapidated rickety nearly falling apart stage coach, hauled by half starved horses driven by a more than half-starved & nearly frozen stiff driver, took a crowd of us to the racetrack—I'll never forget that pull up the steep hill—the slippery mud & snow—the horses slipping and [hauling]—the driver whipping & swearing—the tough bunch of us in the coach, steaming breaths, trying to keep warm.— The arrival at the oval track.—The races in the falling snow.—I hugging an iron stove behind a huge glass room on the grandstand trying to keep warm—Betting—Losing the few dollars I had saved.—Supposed to be downtown in business[429]—loathing the business crowd—More at home with the toughs & disreputables & the snow & the horses & touts & gamblers—It was a great day that twenty-five years ago.—It was night when I got home—No one had an inkling of where I had been—

—So today. Twenty-five years later.—The hill now is macadamized.—The trolley runs up.—All looks prosperous & orderly—No racetracks. Jersey closed up all racetracks years ago. —The Guttenburgs brought about the closing.—

—Marin lives a sane life.—His wife is a worker—the three year old boy[430] a buster —The feeling of family—home—I looked at Marin's work—summer's work—He has worked & has accomplished.—Continuing his experiments—developing—growing—always Marin—Moving forward—more form—richer still in color—always a close student of nature —working from it—before it—Is also working on watercolors twice the size—marvelous

429. Stieglitz worked at the Heliochrome Co. (later the Photochrome Engraving Co.) in New York from 1890 to 1895.
430. Marie Marin, his wife; John Marin, Jr., his son.

virtuosity & intensity—Reminds me often of wonderful piano-playing—Two hours of looking—more than two hours—I had to stop after awhile. Lunch (really a special dinner for me, splendidly cooked by Mrs. Marin) was served at 2:15.—

—Marin, Mrs. Marin & I at table. The boy asleep. He had gotten his lunch at one.—It was as if I had always sat at the table there—a small cozy room—one window—I sat facing it—the window open—I saw the river—New York—the huge elevators in the foreground—It all seemed as if I were dreaming—or looking at the picture book like in childhood days! Lunch over—more pictures—Amazing work—a continuous delight—

It was after 4:30 when the light was fading that we got through—Marin & I took a walk along the boulevard—southward—There was no wind—we saw no people—at least I wasn't conscious of seeing any—so there weren't many—there was no sun—it must have been setting & we were looking east & southeast—Below us—way down—tracks innumerable—puffing creeping trains—blue smoke—black clouds of soft coal—emerging in great volumes as the trains below us came out of a tunnel—grimy rocks—glistening river—boats—barges in use—many rotting away—the city beyond—no feeling of height looking at it—the sense of space only—movement—light—ever changing—the city enveloped in a dark vapor—layers of atmosphere a little lighter above it—Not a human soul it seemed anywhere. Just Marin & I.—Wrapt in wonder.—Marin said he had never seen the equal in all the years he has lived up there. New York—the New York I love—

We walked along—the picture ever changing—ailanthus trees—bare—here & there right before us clinging to the bare grimy ominous rocks going down precipitously beneath our feet—

The light of day fast fading—forms simplified—here & there little yellow lights appearing—in moving boats—gradually some too in the distant buildings of the city—Night was fast approaching—We began going down the iron stairways to the ferryboat—The rocks with their amazing shapes & color gripped me—every step seemed more wonderful than the one before—As we came down & looked up the silhouetted buildings southward looked like castles way up in the sky—and the sky itself was streaked—mad dashes of vanishing pale reds & yellows—

All indescribably—Such an hour will never come again.—It would have been wonderful to have been able to crawl back up the hill into one of the houses on top of it—stolen silently into one of the rooms on the top floor of one of the houses—they looked so clean—& found a woman there—naked—in a simple cot—a dim light—lying on her back—expecting—Not knowing what or whom—And I would have kissed her—taken her in my arms & kissing her my eyes would have seen the city beyond the river—the river glistening too—the sense of moving trains & boats—Not a human soul to be seen anywhere—not even the one I was kissing—the window before me—the woman couldn't see it—she was facing me—I was facing her—but also the window—

Then I would have crept away—She would have received all I had to give—

I don't know who she might have been—& she wouldn't know who "he" might have been—the candle or lamp would have been blown out as he stole out of the door—

Night—the city beyond—the trains below—All busy & active—but not a sound—nor a single vestige of a human being anywhere—

Mad dreams you see—Still I am much awake—Never more awake—

Tomorrow is the anniversary of my wedding day![431] —

Georgia O'Keeffe · [Canyon, Texas] · [November 20, 1917]

9:30 Tuesday night—

I've just read your letter—looked at it—simply glanced this morning—read Elizabeth's[432] this morning twice and again at noon but have just now been free long enough to tackle yours—

—It may be a large mixture of many things but it is living and real—and it's curious how we seem to be saying the same things so often—feeling the same—Curious—yet not curious—

When I finished it—How to tell you how glad I am that the "scribbled pages" come to me—so I got up and poked the fire—

A bit uncomfortable because I've been hearing rumblings of a family row below me all the while—He seems to be at the end of his rope tonight—It is a long sitting room—an open fire—She crying once in awhile.[433] He is just going after things—A tall very good looking man thirty-five I think—She large—also very good looking—His voice is low and very quiet— I have a feeling that she needs a good laying out—The humdrum of housekeeping—care of the two children—she doesn't like—And she has a terrible fear of having another—It makes her cross—His good humor has been a marvel to me for a long time—all things considered—

I don't know what the row is about tonight but I hope she gets what's coming to her and she seems to be getting it—

It's all just her attitude toward life—it seems so stupid to me.

Gosh! I'm glad I'm not married—Wouldn't I be in a devil of a fix—No—I wouldn't either—I would like it or else I'd quit—that's all there would be to it.—

—It just now occurred to me that you—

Well it's written—Still why write you about what I hear downstairs—I don't know—

A train—going away and away—a quiet night and the sound seems to stay with us a long time—

I haven't anything to say—only that I'm wanting to write anyway—

The afternoon with Marin must have been wonderful—I wish I had been there—not seen or felt any more than I was—

431. Stieglitz was married on November 16, 1893. However, as he had previously noted that this letter was written on "Wednesday," which was November 14, 1917, he was mostly likely confused about the date.

432. Throughout the winter and spring of 1917–1918, Alfred's niece Elizabeth Stieglitz wrote O'Keeffe several undated letters, in which she expressed her feelings about the war, Stieglitz and his photographs, and the beauty and importance of O'Keeffe's art. She also sent O'Keeffe some of her poems.

433. Douglas and Willena Shirley.

I seem to be quieter today than the last day I wrote to you—didn't sleep till after four this morning—it seemed a long time after four—I read and tried to sleep by turns—

—The sister? I don't know—I don't bother much about her—She was thrown from a bucking horse the other day—and I believe it did her good instead of hurting her.

My hands are very cold.

Birnbaum—Why I always thought he was sickening—I would love to quietly cut a piece off of his coat-tail—on just one side sometime when he is being his most wonderful—What do you suppose he would do when he discovered it—

That's about as absurd as my always wanting to slap Mr. Dow right hard on the shoulder—enough to really startle him—then say, "Good morning, old boy, how are you?" —I've stood behind him several times and almost done it—

And I wanted to walk up to Wright—the writer—at the *Forum Show*[434]—when his eyes had followed me—and he had arranged himself so nicely to be questioned—I went there several times—I wanted to go up to him and stroke his nice brown beard and say—"Isn't it nice and soft and brown"—instead of remarking on the show—He seemed so absurd to me that I wanted to take him off his amusing pedestal—They are all so ridiculous—

—And I sat here—just thinking—knowing people too well—

It's too late now to be even considering lamenting the fact that there isn't much more for you to know about me—really nothing that I know of right now—so I'll not consider it— I probably wouldn't consider it anyway.

—What I've given—whether it's what I write—or drawings—or whatever the communication—has been because you gave as freely—I guess—

It seems—when I think of it—as natural as just sitting here breathing—as natural as the fact that I grew to the height I am—one seems as natural as the other [and] as little of my choosing—

It scares me when I feel that—

NO SIR—I won't be scared if you know me too well—that will be natural too.

I wrote Bement a hair-raising letter[435] the other day—Poor little man—he will try to preach to me and he will laugh too—

It was something I wanted to know—

My notion—maybe to leave Canyon won't seem practical to him at all—good money for none—Good old soul—I wish he had done it oftener in his little weezening life—but I like him—

I haven't an idea of what I may do any minute—and I don't know that it matters— I'm only one—and a very small one—and there are so many—

I guess I enjoy making his eyes pop—Still I like him—Yes very much—I'm really fond of him—

---

434. The Forum Exhibition of Modern American Painters, Anderson Galleries, New York, Mar. 13–25, 1916.
435. O'Keeffe's November letter to Bement is no longer extant. The year before, however, when Bement had heard that Stieglitz was interested in O'Keeffe's work, he had advised her to recognize that the war had "put an end to the Futurist and Cubist movements" and urged her to "have just as much respect for conservatism as you have for anything that is radical" (Bement to GOK, Feb. 10, 1916).

Why tell you about Bement—

Watkins was down the other day—it just happened to be great to see him—We rode southeast till the grass and sky were not red anymore then back into the gray and night—

And he can't understand and I'm sorry for him and like him too—Poor stupid thing—clean-cut—alive in a way—feeble-minded too—

A great letter from Buck[436] too—Rheumatism and can't go to war—and he hates it—terribly alive—

And all the women I know—see around here—seem to give me the crawls—whatever that is—I haven't any other word for it—Some of the girls I like—like very much—

—Goodnight—Do you hate me or will you kiss me goodnight—I'd sleep better—

I didn't intend to write all this—Isn't it a lot—Will you kiss me—

Alfred Stieglitz · [New York City] · [November 22, 1917] +

I've just come in from a walk in the rain—a rain like in midsummer—& the room here is hot—or the walk made me hot—It's three afternoon—291—Alone—Marie came to have lunch—just half an hour—It was fine to see her—She's as real as the rain.—

—At noon I had a talk with the very black superintendent who runs the elevator between noon & one while the "regular" boy is to lunch—He has been here since I am here—We have rarely talked.—I used to give him a dollar a week for thirteen years.—When I came back to town this autumn I told him I couldn't do that anymore—Today I felt I had to give him a dollar.—Just had to. And I said: "Sam, dollars are scarce these days with me."—He said: "Thanks, every little counts. You were too good all those years & the people too ungrateful"—And he began to enumerate "Mr. White was the first ingrate.[437] Mr. Weber[438] the next. You have treated all people alike. The best you had to give them you gave all." I stopped him & laughed.—I said: "Sam, I don't regret a thing—I did what I felt—just as I do now.—Times have changed."—

[November 23, 1917]
I'm in Elizabeth's studio. 8:45 A.M.—Friday.—Alone. It's a mean foggy drizzling northeast morning. And I wasn't well all night.—Insides—I was interrupted yesterday as I was writing—First a letter from you.—In a long while I had had none—You couldn't write to me—You wanted to—but simply couldn't—And you have been down with a cold—

---

436. Buck Bolton had left West Texas State Normal College after his junior year to enlist in the military.
437. One of the founding members of the Photo-Secession, Clarence H. White was angered when Stieglitz reprinted an exhibition review in *Camera Work* that was highly critical of his work; see J. Austin Lidbury, [untitled], *Camera Work* 33 (Jan. 1911), 70.
438. Stieglitz later acknowledged that his study of Max Weber's art allowed him "to enlighten myself in a way in which I couldn't have otherwise in America" (*Twice A Year* 1 [1938], 83–84). Their friendship was strained in 1910 when Weber wrote a thinly veiled *histoire à clef* criticizing many of the 291 artists, and it was shattered in 1911 when Stieglitz mounted an exhibition of Weber's paintings but refused to put high prices on those painted on cardboard; see Temple Scott [Max Weber], "Fifth Avenue and the Boulevard Saint-Michel," *Forum* (Dec. 1910), 665–685.

Later. 1 P.M.—291—I was interrupted this morning. Elizabeth & Mörling came in early.—Elizabeth went to the country a little after ten.—She & Mörling had been digging & ploughing for few days—a summer home Elizabeth's father had bought.—The sun has come out—it's like summer again—but a northwester—I guess is due & with it cold.—

—Well, to come back to where I started this morning, so you were down with a cold —in bed—& "unwell" I suppose. And I know exactly how the world must have looked to you—all that has happened to you in your life—your friends & loves—& work—people—family—you, yourself—The futility of everything except the moment itself—And if there are no "moments" there seems to be no life—All "free" souls seem to feel these days as you do—I do.—You see we are devoid of all those "*rational*" qualities which *seem* so necessary to the world—or rather to the people in control—

—You thought of the tree—my tree—the symbol of rest—And you felt you'd like to come there—& perhaps find me—or even with [out] me—Just the tree—Queer—even the tree for the time being seems non-existent in me—It is as if I were existing in space—dangling from nowhere—my legs not even trying to find ground to stand on.—Just dangling—not hung.—

—And you want to get away from Canyon.—East? (not New York)—Waco, Texas —anywhere—to just get away—Will you?—I wonder what we'd have to say to each other if we met—It's all so queer what seems to be happening to us—Still I know I feel things just as I always have—I sometimes wish I didn't—

I look at the young soldier officers—there are more every day—& I wonder what they are—what they feel—I seem so out of touch with all that is "actually" going on—Yet people come to, & go from, 291—I just like formerly—All sorts of people—some I haven't seen for years—Rex Stovel turned up the other day & as we sat together he said: "Just the same old fool as ever"—& we laughed & joked.—Had a real good time. He's the son of a Canadian Reverend & the one who has been butler, actor, playwright, soldier through the Boer War—wrote in "What Is 291."[439] I thought him shot to pieces long before this. But some of his family have drawn that lot—he says he had enough soldier business in the Boer War.—Tries to eke out a living with movies.—And so every day something different—& yet always the same.—

Had a letter from the War Department.[440] I'm wanted—yet I'm not wanted.—Like always.—Unless I can "fit in exactly" fear somewhere of me somehow keeps me out.—

—It's very quiet here—but I'm wondering why I'm up here—& when I'm at Elizabeth's I wonder what I'm "doing there"—& when I'm in my "own" bed—I wonder when that will no longer be—

—Cramer came in yesterday afternoon & we went off for a walk in the northeaster —The rain on my glasses was annoying—but the walk was great—It was a rare blow & a great penetrating wetness. I had told Marie I hoped someone would drag me off for a walk.—

—And it happened.—

439. Rex Stovel, "291," *Camera Work* 47 (July 1914), 28.

440. After receiving Stieglitz's "photographic census form," the Chief Signal Officer from the War Department asked him on November 19, 1917, to propose "some definite line of activity" in which his experience could be utilized. Stating that their most urgent need was for men and materials for aerial photography, he asked Stieglitz for suggestions on how they could achieve the highest possible standards with this work (U.S. War Dept. to AS, Nov. 19, 1917).

THROUGHOUT THE FALL of 1917 O'Keeffe and Strand continued to exchange letters, but her feelings for him fluctuated wildly. She alternately implored him to allow her to give herself to him "completely—utterly," then chastised him for not "moving" and looking so "vile and cold and critical"[441] in a portrait Stieglitz had recently made of him.[442] To Stieglitz she confessed: "All last week I was numb as a half frozen man—from what [Strand] made me feel…. I wanted to put my arms round his neck—lips—I wondered if it would take away the awful feeling I have." Once again depicting herself as part child, part woman, she continued: "Then you came to my mind—I feel like a little girl to you."[443]

During Thanksgiving vacation, O'Keeffe went to Waco, Texas, along with the Normal College speech teacher, Mary Morgan Brown, and the history professor, Joseph Abner Hill, to speak at the Texas State Teachers' Association meeting. While there she saw her brother Alexis, who was stationed at Camp MacArthur, a training camp for more than twenty-eight thousand troops.

Georgia O'Keeffe · [Canyon, Texas] · [November 25?, 1917] +

I'm sleepy—and I enjoy it so much that I'm trying to stay awake—I haven't been sleepy for a long time before.

I sat down to write—And had to get up and take my waist off—my cuffs around my wrists bothered me—

I have been staying awake almost all nights lately—Reading some—just not sleeping some—I don't mind—but being sleepy and so tired that I ache all over is rather nice—I haven't even felt tired lately—

Tonight the idea of paint—drawing—came to me—almost as a brand-new idea— it seemed a surprise to think of it again—and so queer to think that I had ever done anything like that—I looked around the room and laughed—don't even seem to regret not wanting to work—Last spring when I didn't want to work it alarmed me—nothing seems to alarm me now—If the house were to catch fire now I doubt if it would excite me—

I feel sort of amazed—not at anything in particular—just stupefied I guess—I don't know what over or why—Maybe that isn't so—Maybe I do know why—.

You will laugh but let me tell you—Will you—

It's no use to tell—no use to not tell—you probably know already—

—Strand had aggravated me—riled me—sometimes amused me—sometimes made me impatient—Then he sent some things he had written—it started with the 291 article. They got me just like his prints—I don't know why or how—but in a day everything else seemed years behind me—

441. GOK to Paul Strand, Dec. 15[?] and Dec. 23[?], 1917, CCP:PSC.
442. See illustration on p. 154.
443. GOK to AS, Dec. 29, 1917.

I hadn't dared stay in a room alone with him after I saw his prints—afraid of me for him—

—I guess more than anything else—what has come to me through the letters and other written things is the feeling of a great need—and quickly—with no reason or thought—the desire to satisfy it—

Not for myself—in a way it felt a sacrifice for me—I don't know why—but it felt worthwhile and there I stood just feeling it—wanting him—to give to him—The things he wrote went right through me—left me feeling terribly still and numb because—

If it were easy to come to me—he would come—subway or surface car—It put a price on what I was worth and I wasn't worth the price.

Still he will rant around enough to make me feel that way—

It makes me feel as though I've broken an egg that felt as heavy as any other egg and found absolutely nothing in it—just dry emptiness—I do not particularly care but that empty egg surprises me—

All the time I've been riled over what I felt I meant to him—

I do not exercise my capacity for feeling like he does—I can't afford to—it makes me sick—I like many folks some—and none—A few I like tremendously when they grab me and make me when I'm not looking—

I don't know why—but it seems I would rather see most anyone I know seem hollow rather than Strand—Even you—He is young—has great possibilities it seems—Maybe it's because I so much believe in him that I want to wish myself [to] make him more—

Georgia O'Keeffe · [Waco, Texas] · [November 29, 1917]

Good Morning—

You see where I am and I am so glad I'm here that I just can't tell about it—Soldiers and soldiers and soldiers—and last night my brother and a friend of his—dinner—then we walked and walked—It almost turns you inside out—It's tremendous—seeing and feeling what it's meaning to them—It makes you think and feel things you never thought or felt before—makes me sure of some of the things I thought before—many in fact—

Many folks coming along here—I just wanted to tell you—.

Georgia O'Keeffe · [En route from Waco to Canyon, Texas] · [December 2, 1917]

How are you?

I seem to feel as though I've come out of a blinding fog into a little light—

But my voice—it has almost left me and hurts way down the front of me.

I feel almost like a brand new person—I've seen folks—and how they live and move around—and I liked it—I talked to many—folks I like in a queer way—Soldiers—my brother —his side partner—both engineers—

What it is all doing to them is astounding to me—I seemed to feel like adopting his friend as a brother on sight—It was like with Gaisman—I couldn't leave him alone—he looked so forlorn—He won't see his people or the girl again—before they go over—as they think things now—And I couldn't help slipping my hand through his arm—

The smile—why you know—I'll never forget it.

Being with them was wonderful—I think I'll go again Christmas if they are still there —the brother said I had to—Curry just smiled—

Why coming out of a fog—because I think I see something to do—"conservation of thought"—Maybe I'll get it into other words later but—as I see it hearts and souls and minds are being so rapidly worked and wrung dry of their larger fineness—realities becoming so real that we see all life at new angles—

The soldier mind is a revelation to me—

It seems as though I never felt a real honest need of Art before—it never seemed *necessary* before—

It seems as though I feel more on my own two good feet than I ever have in my life before—

I hope they don't dampen me completely the minute I get off the train in Canyon—

I wanted to stay in Waco—I didn't want to come home—but I feel as though I have lots to do—*lots*—and one thing to paint—It's the flag as I see it floating—A dark red flag—trembling in the wind like my lips when I'm about to cry—There is a strong firm line in it too—teeth set—under the lips[444]—

Goodnight—My chest is very sore and I'm tired—couldn't sleep or eat for excitement down there—and hurt—and wonder—and realizing—

Georgia O'Keeffe · [Canyon, Texas] · [December 7, 1917]

It's Friday afternoon. 3:30—

I got home Tuesday morning—A whole stack of letters—barely glanced at—I haven't had time to read them—

I've thought of you often this week—feeling glimpses of you but I've been like a young tornado—tornadoes don't have time for anything—but good—they raise a line—

Ted met me at the station—bent on aviation[445]—

That afternoon was asked to report on the trip to the faculty—another woman—a man and myself[446]—

Well—it was an event in the history of that faculty I guess—judging from what I've heard since—It seems that it was an explosion I've been growing to all my life—and I tell you I had it—

---

444. Lynes 234.
445. Ted Reid had enlisted in the Air Service Signal Corps with the U.S. Air Force.
446. Mary Morgan Brown and Joseph Abner Hill.

I took each boy in turn—Fatty Stafford—Latin—first and knocked him down and jumped on him with both feet—then took all the rest in turn—I told them their course of study was a failure and that many times they didn't know what they were talking about—That they were *teachers* not human beings and trying to cultivate another crop of the same thing—

The Army and the art talk at Waco started me—

The art was rotten because it has no relation to life—They don't know what they are trying to do—And as I see it the men of the Army haven't the resources within themselves to handle what they are up against—and it is because they have tried to fill up curriculums with "SOLID" work that is not vital—Their educational system is not built on the development of natural human needs—desires—emotions—Too many students are just working for certificates —diplomas—degrees and the like instead of learning to live—Too many folks working for money instead of working because the thing means something to them—

I had a great time—and almost every old boy and every old girl on the faculty came and talked to me about it afterward—The women tremendously tickled because no one had ever dared stand up and tell those particular men that they didn't know what they were talking about and that what they were teaching wasn't of any use to the people they were teaching it to— And I was afraid four of the men were going to hug me—

It was great—but the excitement almost killed me and I can hardly speak aloud for more than five minutes at a time my throat and chest hurt so. I stayed home today—thought maybe a day's rest by myself—no one to talk to—would help me.

I've been so full up that I've *had* to talk in class—and some of the boys back from the training camps talked so much and kept me talking so much that I almost haven't any voice and haven't been able to sleep or eat enough—

But it's all right—

I feel as though I've waked up with the loudest bang yet. It seems so funny to remember the way I was feeling before.

And why don't I read the letters—three from Strand—two from you—one from Bement—two others that ought to interest me—.

—Claudia was gone when I got home—down in the sticks somewhere to teach— have heard little from her—

I just wonder that there is anything left of me at all—

I have made up my mind I'm going to stay here—The rest of my life it seems now—unless they fire me—They may—I'm going to talk some more as soon as I get voice enough.

I'm on the warpath—it seems wanting though—in spite of my savageness—to be held close to someone—as though it might quiet me—

Alfred Stieglitz · [New York City] · [December 8, 1917] +

It's Saturday. One o'clock.—I'm still in my overcoat. 291.—Snowing & very bleak outside. —Perhaps a blizzard blowing up. As I came in—a few minutes ago—the cleaning woman was just getting ready to leave. She had cleaned up thoroughly. How clean the rooms look.—The rooms that I occupy & that are not mine! The floors are still wet & they will remain wet a long while on a day like this—

It was good to come in & see the old woman—seventy-six—She & I. We had quite a talk. She remarked I look so different—so well. Feared awhile ago I was going out of my "head"—so did others—All wonder what's come over me these last two or three weeks.— Laughing & joking—my old self—only more so—

I guess it's not receiving any more bills—hearing nothing about money—not at home —not at 291.—I need so little for myself. It's great this feeling of freedom after the terrible load of twenty-four years—Then too I feel I'm of some use again—my head is clear—I'm on the "path" again—.

—You are in Waco—I'm sure it's doing something for you—It's what you needed— Perhaps you're back in Canyon by this time.

—Soldiers.—Didn't I see them galore in Berlin. Nine whole years.—I saw order—good work—discipline—& still a freedom—I know what must be happening in Waco—Elsewhere too—Of late I have been relating to many how in Berlin I never was without a piano—nor a set of the *Encyclopedia Britannica*—& a large American flag on the walls!—And how upon my return to the United States I first had to give up the piano—then the *Encyclopedia Britannica* became a nightmare—& finally the American flag lost its meaning for me.—Why all this?—

Perhaps because I was too much a real American—& the flag had symbolized so much—to me—so many years. Perhaps what I felt in my youthful innocence—even though I was over twenty-six—may [be] about [to] be reborn these days for the country at large—

I wonder—And perhaps art too is about to be born for this country too.—

—I have hardly had a moment to myself these days—at 291—at home—elsewhere— much about—even get little chance to go to Elizabeth's studio—

Marin's pictures are here at 291—it seems funny to have pictures here—a few frames —Walkowitz was much moved by the Marins—Seemed the old fine Walkowitz again.—Spent hours looking at them. He & I alone.—Enjoyable hours.—

—How quiet it is. The snow is falling faster.—

Boston Symphony last night—the beautiful *No. 2 Rachmaninoff Symphony*[447]—the night before a boiling bath—feel asleep in it—Wonder I'm still alive—

Night before that with Carles & Marin until after 1:30—& then took Marin to 42 Street—I got home at three—a walk alone in the cold night—I enjoyed it—For the evening with these two fine fellows had been perfect.—

447. *The New York Times* reported that the Boston Symphony Orchestra revealed the "remarkable beauty and power" of Rachmaninoff's Symphony in E Minor, No. 2, Op. 27. In addition, the Prussian-born conductor Karl Muck acquiesced to public criticism and played "The Star-Spangled Banner"; see "The Boston Symphony Orchestra," *NYT*, Dec. 8, 1917, 13.

So much has happened these days—all sorts of things—I can't tell you it would take sheets & sheets—& hours & hours—all connected with what I call my "work"—doing nothing—yet something.—They have been alive these days.

—Later.

It's funny—a letter from Waco.—You write you are going to paint the flag!!—!!!!!!! Red.—

And you are feeling alive—Waco has made a deep impression—I'm glad. In fact I knew it would.—I hear the elevator door—it's time for Dewald to come. There he is.—More later.—I'm glad to have the letter.—

Georgia O'Keeffe · [Canyon, Texas] · [December 10, 1917]

I've just spent about three hours clearing off my table and writing necessary letters—I believe my cold is a little bit better—staying in and not talking much—but I seem to be still in a bad fix.

Furniture catalogues—book lists—a long letter to the sister—sorting—ordering.— I haven't looked so straight in ages. And here as the last thing—I see this little slip of the list of *Camera Works* I have—

And I want to know something. I would like to buy a set of *Camera Work* for the Normal —I want to put it on my book list and I haven't any idea of how much it would be. I don't mean that I am going to buy it myself—I mean I want to get the STATE to buy it—I believe it would be good for them.—I may not be able to convince them but I can't even try till I get a price on it so I must ask for the price.

Nothing to write except that my head is going at the rate of forty miles an hour—After being asleep so long the waking up almost takes all physical life and strength—

A lovely old gray haired lady[448]—forty I suppose—sat down by me tonight and asked if I were feeling better—"I guess it's excitement more than cold or anything else that's the matter with you."

After my explosion in faculty meeting she came up to me and laughed and remarked— "That was great—your standing up there and telling those men they don't know what they are talking about—and that what they are teaching isn't doing anybody any good"—

She teaches sewing—and I guess they call it Domestic Art—I don't know—

Goodnight—

I must go to bed—it's only ten but I feel as though I've lost my backbone. I must go to bed—

I just tonight read some letters I hadn't even opened since my return—So you know how I've been going—

448. Martha T. Bell.

Alfred Stieglitz · [New York City] · [December 14, 1917]

It's Friday morning.—10—Have just come in—A great snowfall last night.—The city looks like fairyland—so white—& the sky so blue & serene.—I came down on top of a bus.—The wind tearing through me—Icy cold—The face cutting—enjoyable.—Only the feet bother me—they hurt in an unpleasant way.—But they don't count.

—You are still under the weather—The excitement has been too much for your physical strength—& I bet everything happened just at that particular time of the month where you should have husbanded your strength—

No I don't believe that—you had to let go—that's all. No matter what the time.—But I hope that by this time you are up & about again—fairly your normal self.

Camera Work—You want to recommend it to the Board.—A complete set is out of the question. First of all I haven't any—at least I don't think I have.—Secondly a complete set is worth about $750.—Does that stagger you?—Some numbers are worth about $100 each.—

But there is a possibility of my being able to let a school have about forty numbers for $65.00—a nominal figure.—Several institutions have availed themselves of this opportunity. —In all there are about forty-eight to fifty numbers. I don't know exactly.—I think fifty.—In the course of time individual missing numbers could be picked up at very reasonable figures & so the set gradually completed.—If you want a set of *291* for the department I'll gladly donate a set. They too are rare now as I have destroyed nearly all.—Of course a condition for both *Camera Work* & *291* would be that both would be taken good care of. The day is coming where both will be treasured for many reasons. It's really a pity I'm so little interested in money.—It seems funny to quote a price even to an institution.—In the forty numbers there would be included the Rodin number, the Matisse—Gordon Craig—the numbers on Picasso & Cézanne, etc., etc.[449]

—Should the Board feel it couldn't afford to appropriate such a great sum of money perhaps it would appropriate something & I'd send you what I consider a fair equivalent for the amount appropriated. Several schools have done that.

—So much for that.—

Wright was in yesterday afternoon. He saw some of the Marins.—He seemed to like many of them. And I was glad. He is very frank & *knows* more than most of the men.—And it's always a test of myself when I listen to the men.—

Sheeler spent several hours with me too.—He is always fine.—Wears splendidly. I am to have three of his wonderful photographs in exchange for one of mine.[450] He seems to get results more readily than I do.—It's hellish hard work for me to get what *I* want—& I don't want to give him a print which isn't A1 ++—A1 plus plus—and I rarely make such. I want him to see several prints of your hands.—I wonder how he'll like them. I'm still printing them. Trying to get

449. *Camera Work* 34–35 (Apr.–July 1911); 32 (Oct. 1910); 36 (Oct. 1911); special no. (Aug. 1912); special no. (June 1913).
450. Stieglitz was greatly impressed with Sheeler's recent photographs, describing them as "perfect abstractions—marvelous work—a genuine treat—certainly an addition" (AS to GOK, Oct. 16, 1917). Sheeler gave Stieglitz four photographs of his home in Doylestown, Pennsylvania, all made in 1917 and now in the Alfred Stieglitz Collection, Metropolitan Museum of Art, and Stieglitz gave him four photographs: Greenough 388, 393, 421, and *From the Back Window, 291*, all now in the collection of the Museum of Modern Art, gift of Charles Sheeler.

one perfect print—one in which one isn't conscious of *any process*.—I've gotten near to it
—but—

—So you see straight now—never so straight before.—Fine.—
It's all great.—

Georgia O'Keeffe · [Canyon, Texas] · [December 14, 1917]

Friday noon—

Dinner—your letter—I am at school at eight in the morning so don't go for the mail till
after dinner. One of the girls brought it to me this noon—Thought I might not want to go for it.
I was surprised—glad too because I didn't want to go.

Everyone has gone on about their work—it's quiet here—so here I sit—feet on the
stove—No class but many things to do at school—Shall I go to school or go home.

I seem to be sitting here—

It sounds so funny when you remark that I am going to paint the flag—I haven't had
time yet—and what I had in mind wasn't the flag at all—it just happened to take flag shape—

I'm so tired—I'm ridiculously glad to know that tomorrow is Saturday and only four
days to teach next week before Christmas holidays—Absurd to be so tired—

I am going to stay here Christmas as far as I know.

It's queer—I plan to stay here—I feel too tired to go anywhere but a sneaking notion up
my sleeve seems to tell me I will be going somewhere in spite of myself—

I don't know—Don't care.

It seems so queer to think that Christmas is almost here again—Last year seems so little
ago.

I have some nice folks at school that I like—

I seem to be waking up to some very funny things lately—Claudie used to tell me I
was the most innocent person she ever saw—She said—"You expect other folks to be like you
are—think like you do and feel like you do—and it isn't that way—You are different."—And
I've been finding such funny differences—things almost unbelievable—they don't seem human.

I would like to be in New York for a few days—and see you—and talk to you—I want
to see a real live talking—moving—living—thinking human being.

Gertie[451] is going to play hymns so I must either go home or to school—

Night again and I'm in bed—I've been reading—

Everything war and I can't get enough of it—and still it almost drives me crazy—

I'm not at all certain that my feeble mind has been able yet to center on anything that
would make me willingly offer my life if the excitement and adventure were taken out of it all—

I wish that for a thing so tremendous and terrible as what is happening I might put my

451. Probably Polly Gertrude Smith, a student at West Texas State Normal College in 1917–1918.

hand on some cause and desired result—that I could feel definitely justifies it all—but I hunt all around—it is like chasing an almost invisible slippery nut—small—slippery—hard to crack—slippery—

Everything contradicts the other—

Goodnight—I almost went to sleep here—so tired inside and out.

[December 17, 1917]

It's Monday morning—

Bright sunshine coming in my windows—some greenness shining in it. My room is warm—it's a nice place—

Last night was cold still starlight—I saw the sun rise out of the enormous stretch of blue hazy plains and hot sky—

Yesterday I heard a man say that in France coal is $100 and $250 a ton—

Last week I got talked about for objecting to cards in the drugstore—Christmas cards—Statue of Liberty—and a verse that ended with "Wipe Germany off the map!"—amusing but not exactly what one wants to get mixed up in—

Really funny—They couldn't understand how or why anyone would object for any but pro-German reasons—even faculty folks got after me about it and when I explained they looked at me sort of cross-eyed and said they hadn't thought about it that way—I can't help wondering what they are thinking about—

Your letter this morning—I liked—

Yesterday I was very much depressed with the futility of everything—All morning I talked with Mrs. Shirley—the lady downstairs—She is great in a way—she is waking up—and she is such a wonder physically.

Some way—this morning though ahead looks more uncertain than anything I have ever looked ahead at—

I feel more sure of myself than I ever have.

Good-morning to you—

I have much to do.

Fatty Stafford across the street is acting president and asked me to talk in chapel in the morning. I will if I have any voice. I haven't much yet.

I may go to Waco for Christmas—I really don't want to—I'm so tired and it makes me feel and think so hard—Costs a lot of self and a lot of money. Seventy-five dollars looks big—

It depends on how much I am urged. I can't afford it anyway.

When I was there the brother insisted that I must come again—

I don't know—It depends on him—it would be to please him—not myself—

I wonder what you are to me—it's like father, mother, brother, sister, best man and woman friend, all mixed up in one—

I love you greatly.

THE COLD that O'Keeffe caught during her Thanksgiving trip to Waco, Texas, lingered on through December. By early January 1918 she frequently complained to Stieglitz that she "coughed all night—my chest hurt so I didn't dare go to school—My voice is in such a bad fix too—I knew I couldn't talk more than a few minutes without stopping completely."[452] And she admitted that her friend Doctor "Mac" in Amarillo "didn't know enough"[453] about her illness to treat it properly. By mid-January, with little concrete information about her health, Stieglitz became increasingly concerned and spun a grim picture from the few facts he had. Although the 1918 influenza epidemic had not yet broken out, other kinds of flu were sweeping the country and he knew that O'Keeffe's mother had died of tuberculosis, a contagious disease. His fears also infected others, including his niece Elizabeth Stieglitz and Strand, and all began to deluge O'Keeffe with letters and telegrams inquiring about her health. Yet as O'Keeffe herself openly acknowledged, her discomfort was greatly magnified by her refusal to embrace the militant anti-German rhetoric that some Canyon residents, like many others throughout the country, used so freely and unthinkingly.

Georgia O'Keeffe · [Canyon, Texas] · [December 19?, 1917] +

My lips are greased and I'm in bed—Rouge is the only thing I know of that helps the chap—

It's only nine—but I feel so near a headache I'm in bed anyway—much against my own will and desires—

My throat is bad again—And I feel like a wreck—but the inside of me feels like a mad whirlwind—

I can see just my one little star twinkling in the deep blueness out my window—it will travel out of sight in a minute—

This morning I got up just as daylight was coming—It was great—The first thing I thought was—GOSH—didn't God have his nerve with him when he painted those swipes across the sky—

I envied him—the size of it—and the daring—The early mornings are tremendous—

I'm still talking in chapel and it's about to wear me out but I'm having a great time—Yesterday the faculty liked it—they all talked about it to me—most of them—I should say—and I heard that a lot of them talked about it in class—

Today the students got terribly excited and the faculty didn't say a word—It's great—I don't know what will happen tomorrow—and I care less—I feel like slinging brick bats and I have the chance to—so I'm slinging—I'm telling them a few things they don't like to hear and it's giving me a good time—

One of the students said—It feels as though you are just up there talking to us—it doesn't seem like a speech the way it does when the others talk—and you don't look mad about

---

452. GOK to AS, Jan. 12, 1918.
453. GOK to AS, Jan. 7, 1918.

it—you laugh sometimes—And a lot of them told me they could hardly get to work afterward—they were so excited they felt as though they just had to get up and do something—

Still the faculty didn't say a word—It's amusing—

Wouldn't it be a joke if they fired me—I'd laugh—

Goodnight—

So tired and limp feeling and my head—

Alfred Stieglitz · [New York City] · [December 21, 1917] +

10:30 Friday Morning—I have just come in—My hands are still stiff with cold—Although the morning is like spring.—

—I walked down.—It's a marvelously beautiful morning—the sun forcing its way gently through dense vaporous fogs—for mists are rising from the thawing ground & melting snows. The tops of the skyscrapers were peeping their sun-kissed heads above the rising vapors of the earth.—They looked lovely—And the streets are muddy & piled up with great banks of snow.—And people everywhere—Little spots ever moving—Huge soldier men on the Avenue—seeming to enjoy the sights—The shop windows with their soliciting beckonings—Christmas garlands & Red Cross posters.—People feel as if it were a crime to buy—yet they are tempted—the windows with their smiles—and wiles!!—All great to see & watch—

On my way down I saw Elizabeth a moment. She said she had just mailed you a letter—Neither had time—although I really have nothing to do.—I walked past the Grand Central—thought I'd mail my letter to you—And I did.—Happened to pass through the doors you passed through when you left for Canyon that day.—And as I came into the doors, the large hall was wondrous to behold—the soft sunlight trying to increase in intensity—peeping into the great huge place—American flags—huge ones—silently hanging from the ceilings—hanging there yet untouched by the sun—so sedately—as if waiting—and on the floor below—I was up on the stairway—myriads of spots at different gateways—waiting for doors to open to trains to go.—And as I mingled with these people—women & men & children—& soldiers—I felt as if I were in a trance—All seemed so silent—Hardly a sound—Perhaps I'm above most sounds. The place affected me like a wonderful cathedral with no one in it—

—And I dropped the envelope for you into the letter box—And as I knew it was no longer in my control, it struck me what a wondrous thing a letter box is—What its powers are.—

I have no idea what went away in that letter—Except that it was myself—As always.—To you—To everyone.—

—Claudie is right. You are as she says. And if she knew me well she'd think much the same of me—I still believe people & even when I know they don't believe themselves—That's funny—

—I left the station & came down the avenue—Just loitered down—I felt as if I had never seen it before—and like at the station I felt as if entirely alone although I saw lots of spots—moving—& I liked them. Was conscious of them all.—

—And here I am.—The room finally not cold. The night was good.—It was very late when I fell asleep—& I did dream—towards morning—And the dream & the spring morning have put a certain languor into my bones & flesh—

—I read your letters again—those of yesterday in one envelope—They are like the day today—there's spring in them.—You don't like spring—nor do I—yet we are part of it—& we really do like it—Are you laughing?

The world would call us absolutely crazy were it to see such statements as above—Perhaps we are crazy to feel because we can't help feeling—

—It was a great day yesterday.[454]—All of it. Every minute.—As I look at the chairs here—in a semi circle—near the hole which is supposed to heat the room—I'm in one of them—I see the young South Dakota man—& Marin—& Dove—sitting in the dark—listening to stories from life—all connected—all meaning something—to all of us—I wonder why the young man came—Am I a corrupting influence—?—Who knows?—I really don't—But if I am, I'm that truly—

—Humans.—Do you know it takes time to be a human—& how many people will take the time?—Dare take it—I merely do seem human because I do take time—& give time—And you do likewise. Those who feel find time for all such things that the busy practical world has no time for—It's simply a different feeling—ours & theirs—

There is Marin—

Alfred Stieglitz · [New York City] · [December 27, 1917] +

It's Thursday evening—I am home somewhat early.—About five—A really cold day again—Tried to print but the water & solutions were icy—I tried your hands[455] once more—Prints failures—Impossible to do anything decent under such conditions—but I thought I'd try—Knew I'd fail—had to—

—The day was not agreeable—Why will "people" insist in thinking that I'm playing a game like they are—when I'm playing no game—& when I have voluntarily closed doors & have given up all but my last drop of blood? What do they want—the "art crowd"—Dr. Weichsel & company. You have no idea of the double facedness—yes, triple facedness that must have infested 291 for the last years of its place existence?—I had hoped that I'd be left alone—Fortunately nothing hurts any more—& I'm "amused" even though I still occasionally feel as if I had the creeps when conditions, unavoidable, bring forth putrefied "friendships" to the surface.

—I thank my stars I am out of it all.—It's the littleness—the stupidity—that is so loathsome to me.

454. On December 19, Marin and Dove went to 291, as did a young man from South Dakota soliciting security orders. Stieglitz related that he talked for over an hour, telling the man that "securities were [as] worthless as pictures." Marin, Dove, and the securities broker were so mesmerized with Stieglitz's talk that they returned the following day to continue the conversation (AS to GOK, Dec. 20, 1917).

455. Greenough 460.

226

I took a long walk in the cold—numb with cold—Stopped in at Bourgeois a moment. —I like him—He thinks I ought to go into art business.—I explained the absurdity of such an idea after having made the fight for twenty-five years—giving all I had—opening doors— & creating—& now after having created competition I should start in—

And I'm no businessman—and art & New York—I wish I had had business in me— perhaps I'd be of greatest use in a way—but if I had had there never would have been 291— nor *Camera Work*—nor my own work—nor could I have found you as you are—nor Marin as he is—nor Marie—nor Hodge—nor others—Nothing as I feel it—I'd simply be someone else.—And perhaps that would have been better for me.—

That means I would have never been.—

Strand went to the country somewhere—invited—to skate—where he was last summer.[456] —He has to file the military papers—I wonder whether he'll be drawn—I don't see how he'll get out of serving—

If I were he I'd serve.—I told him so—& told him why. And when I say if I were he I mean knowing him as I do & knowing conditions as they must come I feel he'd be best off to get the experience—

But he must decide—& then it will be decided for him.—

—My nights have been wretched—

I guess my mind is working overtime—& ditto what I feel.—And I feel everything more intensely than ever—the things that are true to me—

—I wonder how you are spending your holidays & until when you have vacation.—

Georgia O'Keeffe · [Canyon, Texas] · [December 28, 1917] +

Friday morning—

It was 10:30 before I went for the mail this morning—The *Camera Works*—

—I came home and looked at them just a little—Do you want me to tell you the way they make me feel—They make me feel as though there isn't any place for me anywhere at all in the world—

I believe if they had come at the beginning of vacation it would have been—go to New York—the only thing to do—I opened first at your street scene—horse—iron fence—tree— buildings[457]—and it is wonderful—

I wanted to get right up and go to it—Then it flashed through my mind that school begins Monday—and goes on straight till sometime in May and I wondered how I could stand it—

The way people are living nowadays isn't living—It hardly seems existing—shutting their minds and eyes—I am just beginning to realize a little what your seeing means—I seem to

---

456. Twin Lakes, Conn.

457. *The Street—Design for a Poster*, 1900–1901, *Camera Work* 3 (July 1903); Greenough 266.

feel myself so far from all the folks about me—so far in thought—feeling—everything—
that—why—I just hardly can't understand it—How did I get where I am—why are they so
queer—

How did I ever get so far away from them—They all think they are nice good religious
folks too—and I think them the most damnable heathens—

I want to run away from them—out into the nothingness—and cry—

It is a great time to be living—seeing the uprooting—twisting and turning and the
way men and women respond—the way they all run brainless and heartless in a mob—it
seems almost unbelievable—When I waked this morning I was thinking of it—Can I believe
it—realize even a little what is happening—

How long will it last—Will the little thirteen-year-old boy who brings my coal and
kindling be going in a few years—Will Paul be going in another month—

Richard[458] was up from camp Christmas—I don't mind his being killed but I mind his
killing—the smile is so sweet—I just love him—

It's the older folks I cannot stand—The talk of men past thirty—The—women—

Girls and boys and the ones who must fight are different—

Christmas afternoon Richard and the girl he is engaged to came up to see me—talked
awhile then went to ride—She was driving—Richard wanted to put his arm round me—so he
did—it was so funny—I hadn't ridden with anyone's arm around me like that since I rode with
you—He would have liked me like Ted did last spring if I had let him—

The brown face—color—very white teeth—and the smile—We all said such honest
funny things—it was great—

He is gone—

The *Camera Works* look like life—and I don't see anything but death—even in the
living folks—old dead ones hampering the young live ones—Even Ted—he isn't himself any
more—the finest thing about him was his freedom—realness—

Partly—maybe mostly—my fault—Engaged to Ruby—Still—standing in front of me
—he remarked—You know I just can't stand it to talk to you—it almost drives me crazy—and
after you are gone it's worse even than while you are here.

I stopped here and read—dinner—read again—*The New Republic*—I look at that pile of
Camera Works—and wonder if I dare look at them—read them—or will it make me want too
much to escape from what is here—from deadness to life—and the fear that life may be only a
dream—

Alfred Stieglitz · [New York City] · [December 28, 1917]

Friday night—A little while ago I sealed an envelope to go to you.—

—I have had something to eat—My hands are no longer quite so cold. I'm again
in my room—and I'm thinking of your work—paintings. I'm glad you were moved to look

458. Possibly Richard H. Harter, a former student at West Texas State Normal College.

at your summer's work—I'd have given a great deal to have watched that face while it was looking—Perhaps I see it without the watching—but I'd liked to have been near enough to see the movement of every muscle—for the face is reflected in the body—And the face wouldn't know—And—Well, never mind.—Perhaps it's just as well I'm here—or was here when the private view was taking place.—

—But it's great to know your feelings moving towards painting again. Without looking at them, your nudes[459] & that series have been much in my mind again these last few days— I haven't gotten any under glass as yet—nothing seems to be right—

It's as if you were being caged—& of all the people in the world you are the last I can imagine that—

You wrote some letters to me & you don't know where you put them.—You wrote a letter last summer to me you never sent off—?!!

The other day I was wondering what the last two years would have been without your coming into my life—I can't imagine them—It's an absurd thought—still not so unnatural.—

(There was a print pasted on this paper)

Do you ever hear from Miss Pollitzer—Somehow or other I hear her voice saying one day at 291—when I had related some mad story—"I have a friend—she & you ought to meet."—It was quite some time before she brought your drawings & when she brought them how little did I realize that they were done by "she" that I "ought to meet."—

—It's all very wonderful—

Will this reach you before 1918?—I'm fifty-four on January 1st.—

Good Night—

I'm glad to know that I am all the things you say I am to you—quite a family in one person!—

Georgia O'Keeffe · [Canyon, Texas] · [January 2, 1918] +

Next Night—[Wednesday] night

Two letters from you this morning—your birthday—

Thank you—that is for being born and for the letters too—

—A full day—

My chapel talk and some other things have taken fire—and a good blaze is going— I've been so riled—and thought and felt so hard about it—

Why—I can't begin to tell you how everything I know and think and feel is tangled up in a knot—

Everyone I've said anything to about it—has been rather surprised at my point of view —They always see it—but the amusing thing about it is they always say "Yes—I see what you are driving at—you're right—I hadn't thought it that way—but Miss O'Keeffe to save your life—you can't drive that into the ordinary man's head—I don't care how hard you try." Well—to make a long story short the "ordinary man and woman" of our honorable village have

459. Lynes 176–188.

stuck several different things together—my chapel talk—and various bits of choice information and they are just pawing the air—

It is amusing—it's really the Devil too—

I'm trying to calm down enough to talk to Mr. Cousins about it—but I'm having a hard time to do it. I wanted to today and couldn't.

I'll tell you—I'm mad enough to kill—

Shirley—downstairs—has helped me a lot—but it's really a snorting time we are all having—The faculty are beginning to line up with me I think—Thanks to Shirley I guess— I don't know—The town however is wagging its poor tongue off—Isn't it disgusting to get in a mess like that—

My children were wonderful today—My first, second and third graders—I am getting my children to paint even if I'm not painting—really wonderful—I wish you could see them—

I have two Chinese lilies again—in a blue bowl—pure—white—clean—

They and the children seem the only rest from the madness in the air—

If I can't some way quiet down I don't see how I can keep on working—

Tonight I feel as tired as I did before vacation began. If I could only stop feeling and thinking—but my mind seems ravenous—I'm going like mad inside—and all sense and reason tells me I can't stand it—Still I can't stop—

—You know—I just can't understand Strand's being willing to let war—all that's happening—get past him—and missing it—or wanting to miss it so long as it's a state that exists—

Yes—I can too understand—That is—I can and I can't—That bothers me too—

It seems as though everything bothers me—do you suppose I'll—

I don't know—I wonder what I'll do—will I ever be fifty-four—I some way seem to feel that if I ever am fifty-four I'll be so different I'll hardly know it's me—I used to say I was going to live to be ninety-three—but I'm thinking now—I won't—

Just this one day of talking and work has made my throat as bad as it was before Christmas vacation[460] —

Goodnight—

It's only nine but I must have a bath and bed—

Do you suppose I could stop feeling and thinking if I tried—it seems it would mean stopping living—Maybe I had better do that—

I don't know—

[January 3, 1918]
[Thursday] night
Nine o'clock again and I feel almost dead—so tired—I must go to bed right away—

Had a long talk with Mr. Cousins—Nice—

He remarked—You think differently from other folks—You may be right—I'd not

460. A few days later, Leah Harris took O'Keeffe to Amarillo to see Doctor "Mac," who urged her to rest and not talk. Yet on January 12, 1918, O'Keeffe reported to Stieglitz that her "chest hurts so bad I could cry."

have you a bit different—but it's going to be mighty hard for you to get along with folks—The ordinary run of men are just ordinary men and woman and they don't think like you do and they are very apt to misunderstand you—more apt to than not—They don't think—and they don't want to think—

We had a great talk—He thinks I'm queer—but—he thinks too, "You may be right"—It's funny. I like him you know—

but I'm so tired—

please love me—a lot—

Goodnight—

I haven't decided yet—whether I want to trust *Camera Work* to these folks or not—

I hate so to think of folks looking at it that don't really love it like I do—.

Georgia O'Keeffe · [**Canyon, Texas**] · [**January 5, 1918**] +

Saturday—

Today—seven more *Camera Works*—I was so surprised—

And I've looked at them all—the seven that came today—three times—This noon before supper and since supper—They are really wonderful—make me sit still—a long time —looking into space—wondering—wondering—

I put out my hand to reach for the one with your face in it[461]—again—then stopped— No, I didn't want to look at it again—it affects me like the printed pages—I looked at them —wanted to read—but felt I might scream if I did—And I had to laugh as I came to the end of the last one and realized that I had turned every page—smoothed down and looked at every printed page—often looked some minutes at it—and in the whole seven don't think I read the words—

I wondered at my hand—my left one as I saw it on the last printed page of the last book —and my mind wandered to the prints of my hands—I moved to get up to look for them—No —The other hand reached for the book with you in a circle—I probably understand why the person put you in a circle—I wouldn't have put you in a circle though—Then it seemed I couldn't look at you again any more than I could read the printed pages—

So I sat looking at the hand—then at them both—I've looked at them often today— they have looked so white and smooth and wonderful—I've wondered if they were really mine—

One thing I did read this afternoon—just before supper—Caffin's story of the artist who wouldn't sell his pictures and died—wouldn't sell his children—And I wondered if my selling mine[462] was murder—in a way it was—The three that I took money from you for—

That was like killing—yet what is worse is the fact that it gave me such a large

461. Alvin Langdon Coburn's portrait of Stieglitz, reproduced in *Camera Work* 21 (Jan. 1908), is circular.
462. Charles Caffin, "An Impossible Case," *Camera Work* 21 (January 1908), 27–29, is the story of a destitute artist who declares that he would rather starve than sell his art: "Can one," he asks, "sell the offspring of one's soul's love?" O'Keeffe had sold one work to Dewald (Lynes 128) and three to Stieglitz (Lynes 52 and two other unidentified works, possibly including Lynes 64).

satisfaction—and my conscience has never hurt me at all—it has all been a curious wonder to me—something that happened in myself that I can not but wonder at—wonder—

—Since you have been feeling so poor I've sometimes wished I had taken just one cent instead of the one with the two zeros after it in dollars—one penny would have given me as much satisfaction as a hundred dollars—

It was all queer—

Dewald's black spot was a different kind of a child[463]—I've thought of it often—on a pink wall you said—it always makes me laugh to think of it on a pink wall—but it's all right that way if he likes it—

Faculty meeting this afternoon—I've never seen or heard anything funnier—faculty meetings are the most entertaining things that happen here—However—the others don't enjoy them like I do. I don't suppose anyone else has the particular sort of good time that I do—They mostly think it's stupid—

You know—I am rather uncertain in my mind here—I may not last through till May—I'm going to try to last till after summer school—Claudie will be back for summer school to finish her work—But it wouldn't surprise me if I just packed up and left most any day—

I feel less and less like a free white woman—The old brothers felt as though—well—I just surprised them a bit lately—They either had to abandon their professed religion or side with me and it didn't exactly go with their unthinking crazy way of haranguing (I don't know how to spell that word) about the war—and naturally—they didn't enjoy being jerked up—

—It was funny—worried me a lot—but it makes me laugh too—It's worth it—it all is but it's mighty ticklish ground to be walking on.

—If I didn't like it here so much I wouldn't even bother to jolt them—but I like it—and—I wonder what I like—Isn't it queer that I like it here—like it so much—

It isn't any particular person—except my children—The folks are really unimaginably stupid—hopelessly ordinary—

Alfred Stieglitz · [New York City] · [January 9, 1918] +

Later.—Same day.—I bet you can't guess where I am.—In theatre.—Waiting for the curtain to go up.—I'm alone. Fifth row orchestra—center. Waiting to see *The Land of Joy*[464]—It's the last week & all the fellows told me I shouldn't miss it and I have been putting it off.—It's a Wednesday matinee & I am extravagant.—

As I was writing to you at 291—Dove came in—Last night I felt he'd come in today. I'm always glad to have him come—but today I was especially glad.—He saw the Wright[465]

463. Lynes 128.

464. *The Land of Joy,* a musical comedy, billed itself as "the greatest dancing show in the world"; *NYT,* Jan. 2, 1918, 9.

465. On January 6, 1918, Stieglitz told O'Keeffe that Stanton Macdonald-Wright's new painting, possibly *Self-Portrait—Synchromy,* 1917, oil, was "a marvelous performance—He has actually added something to painting—has produced something neither produced by Cézanne or by Picasso.—What he said he was trying to do—something between music & architecture he has actually accomplished in color—on canvas."

—but what's more I could show him your things—& I could see them too.—I wanted to see them while having the Wright before me—A test of the Wright—your things—myself—I wish you could have been present—seen—& heard—Your things are even more beautiful than they ever seemed—Dove felt as I did—He said: "It's the only real thing in spirit—feeling & brain at work—but the brain not worrying! Real freedom—free expression—no theory"—If you had been present I'm sure I would have hugged you & you would have thought me crazy.— Would you?

Again I felt like wiring—I feel as if letters took an eternity—I want you to feel more immediately what I am feeling *now*—about you—your work, your state—at Canyon. But somehow I feel that a wire wouldn't do what I'd like it to do—it might do the reverse—Even letters sound absurd—not yours to me—But I feel mine to you must be so.—

I write I'm quiet—It's the quiet of an engine that is bursting with power—but stands there all serene—ready—but unused—calm—seemingly dead to those that don't see—

—It was great to hear Dove express himself about those pictures of yours—great because he is a man of few words—& I've rarely seen him enthuse—

Why should I care what he says about your work—I do care.—I care what all those I respect say about it. I want them to see it—what I see—what I know is there—a great big spirit—expressed. Dove went as far as to say: "She does what Kandinsky tries to do."—Do you know who Kandinsky is?

—It's what Gertrude Stein some years ago told Hartley in Paris, that he was really doing what Kandinsky was trying to do—Hartley had met Kandinsky in Munich. Liked him.—You have met virtually no one—are working entirely from within—womb & brains—& all that goes with both.—But all free—no theory—no effort—

—There goes the orchestra.—It's Spanish music—Spanish dancers & singers—

Alfred Stieglitz · **[New York City]** · **[January 12, 1918]** +

After supper—Supper doesn't take long—Here I'm again with you—Until Sheeler comes.— Sheeler had to chase off & finally Strand, Walkowitz & I were left alone.—It's queer how Walkowitz gets on my nerves—whatever he says seems to be inopportune—I wonder whether it's I or he. I'm sure I haven't changed any—his not understanding a side of me together with a certain false pride which he has always had & the strain he is undoubtedly under owing to lack of funds bring out certain qualities—which were always there & were always jarring—but now they have become intensified.—Wrong notes—

—I was glad when Strand & I were finally alone—On the floor of the elevator I was surprised to see two envelopes addressed to me:—Canyon—Los Angeles.—You & I recognized Huntington Wright's handwriting on the other. Hadn't heard from him since he left New York—

Your letter is a marvel & it has worked me all up—I was ready to be worked up—for my life never was more intense—terrifically concentrated & direct. Fearless—A second bundle of *Camera Work*—why both bundles had gone off together—& they reach you a week apart.—In a way I'm glad. Glad because of this—another wonderful living bit of flesh & blood of yours in the shape of a letter—

—I had to laugh about my portrait. In a circle not because it was so intended originally —but the negative broke & 291 had been using the disc somewhat (the gold disc on its catalogues) & so Coburn got the idea to use me in a circle!—No I can't imagine you seeing me in a circle—nor do I see myself in one.—But the likeness at the time was good—it must be about twelve years ago when it was taken.—Taken in the room in which you saw the Strand photographs.—

—I see you sitting before the *Camera Work* numbers—hardly seeing them—just *One Great Bundle of Heart and Soul*—And all that would have been necessary to make the moment complete to perfection would have been had I stolen in behind you—and—Well—you did look at the hands—

You are a wonderful bit of *Real Humanity*—

—No, No—No—that won't do—I don't want you to think of those hundred dollars as you do.—It gives me the shivers.—I bought nothing—You sold nothing—I sent you what I had & wanted you to have because I knew you could use it—& not for yourself—Great Big Little Girl—you have never received *Money* from me—*Not one cent of Money*. Your children are in my trust—not in my possession—I own nothing—Nothing you ever did or can do—If you gave your soul & body to me—not even they would be mine—not as ownership—they would never be so free as the moment you offered them—gave them—

You see what you felt that moment is ghastly—that moment when you mention the dollars.—And the Dewald too—I never would have let him have that one unless I felt he was entitled to it—And I still feel he is even though he made a fool of himself—If I didn't feel that way about that drawing & him I'd take it from him & return the money to him—I'd rather starve than have him have it—

So don't you dare feel that way again—*Ever*—It isn't fair to your children—not to yourself—to neither Dewald nor to me.—But I'm glad you mentioned it as long as you felt that way.—

I really ought to scold for fair—Don't you think so?—I'd love to but I can't—

Your throat—I shouldn't be worried—But I am.—I have worried all along—I know you as I know myself. You are just as careless—or rather you don't think of yourself—you can't when you are so full of *SAY—you must speak!*

Don't I know—Have I not been through it all—that's why I am worried—I know the long chances I took—I know you take as long—even longer—than I.—Of course the doctor tells you to keep the cold night air out of your throat & nose in riding in the auto—If you want to fight you must spare yourself—Yes—even *I* finally tell you.—

Gosh! I know what a nuisance it is to have [to] husband one's strength—doctor—etc. —But there is no way out—even a bull has limits to his strength—

You too—

—Of course you like Canyon.—Through the Summer School—Canyon has given you a chance to really live—rather to express yourself—It is material & background—you create with it—& you develop yourself through your own creation—

234

—A great snowstorm is predicted for tonight—Will the morning be white—

Give me the hands—& remember when you don't take as much care of yourself as you possibly can you are committing the only *crime* you are capable of committing.

—Sheeler will be here in a moment or two.—I forgot to tell you that Kerfoot was in this morning to see the Wright—didn't seem very enthusiastic—but he wasn't enthusiastic about Ravel[466] last night—and I was—It was great.—It would have made you sick to hear it. I wish you had sat next to me.—

A young fellow from Montreal was in too today.—So you see what a full day—More than full—

Good Night—You Great Soul.—

Georgia O'Keeffe · Canyon, Texas · [January 14, 1918] +

Monday night—

Your letter—I liked—I've just read it—Your liking my things seems so far away—

I must send you four others to make what you have come out right—These four were too large for the bundle and I never got them off—

I'd like to have someone do all those tag-end things for me for about a year and maybe I'd catch up.

They aren't right—but if I remember correctly they are like the others—yet distinctly different—

Other folks too—it seems so far away—as though you are talking about someone else.

—I just seem like nothing—little me—here—I am seeing things again—not very distinctly yet but I like their untouchable color—wonder if I'll ever try to make them—they are lovely in my mind.—

You say you got Hartley to like them before he knew whose they were—that makes me laugh—because—Oh—he's just funny.[467] I believe I read Kandinsky's *Spiritual Harmony in Art*[468]—or something like that—It was blue in color—I lent it to a friend—

Two letters from Strand—Something in him riles me terribly[469]—We are cut out of altogether different kinds of stuff—He has taught me things—Maybe what seems wonderful in him—seems relatively more wonderful in that I feel it in the same person with things that feel almost repulsive to me—I marvel at the two together—

ALL THE WORLD GREETS YOU, 1915–1918

---

466. Stieglitz probably heard the "young Russian prodigy" Leo Ornstein perform his first piano recital in New York at Symphony Hall, with a program of composers from Beethoven to Ravel; see "Programs of the Week," *NYT*, Jan. 13, 1918, x5.

467. On January 23, 1918, Stieglitz wrote O'Keeffe that Hartley subsequently said her work was "fine but not painting—too psychic, too much yourself" and that when she got "over that" she would "do some very good things." O'Keeffe responded on January 29, 1918, writing: "When is Hartley going to get over being personal himself—I think he is almost the funniest man I know of—really I could yell over it."

468. Wassily Kandinsky, *The Art of Spiritual Harmony,* introduction and trans. by M. T. H. Sadler (New York, 1914).

469. In a letter to Stieglitz written on January 12, 1918, O'Keeffe described her conflicted feelings about both Strand and Hartley: "No use to talk about Strand—I feel about him like about Hartley's canvases. I want to kick my foot through it—jump with both feet—I'd take pleasure in tearing one up today." But, she added, "I like Hartley's things—really a *lot*."

Is it a beauty and coarseness that I cannot attain—the one I wonder at—the other makes me shiver—No—both extremes he makes me feel—make me shiver—

—I can't bother about him tonight—I'm tired—I feel as though I'll never write him anymore. But I probably will—I don't know or care—

A letter from Claudie—Very funny—Country-life in the sticks isn't very comfortable in blizzard weather—Says she thinks she will stay down there next summer and farm—raise peanuts and watermelons—

—So funny.—I wonder. Or else she wants to go to Arizona. Said she slept under eight quilts—in her union suit—pajamas—sweater—and stocking cap one night—hot-water bottle too—Still she likes it. Great sister—.

—I've been to Amarillo—went on train and Leah brought me back in a closed car—Dr. Mac is sick—gone to hospital—more convenient than being sick at home—moved him out this afternoon—The other doctor[470] read me another lecture—Scolded me for going out—then later said he didn't know that it mattered—might not be any worse than staying home alone—

—Told me doctoring wouldn't do me any good—no use to give me medicine—Still he gave me some—he is a funny old boy—Said he would like to pick me up and put me down in a place where it was warm and sunny—and leave me alone—with only one prescription—Rest and don't talk—

—Medicine won't do you any good. He reared around and made a great time—As Leah said—made me feel I'd die if a tree fell on me—

—Goodnight—I must go to bed—He said I'd feel better in a week or so—then he would come out with the rest talk again—You've got it to do—whether you want to or not—

—I laughed.

—Goodnight.—

—I'm all tired—all over—Tired in my head—all of me—

The tired in my head is bad.—

Alfred Stieglitz · [New York City] · [January 15, 1918] +

Good Morning.—It's eleven.—It was nearly nine when I got up.—The morning was so dark.—I had slept so little—I went to bed before eight—tried to read but gave it up—turned off the light—& tried to sleep—above all to rest—It began snowing in the night—the window was wide open—then it began pouring—It had grown warm suddenly—

—It's pouring now—And there is a fog—the streets are slushy & slippery—the gutters little rivers—pneumonia weather.

—Caffin died yesterday—The papers have it this morning[471]—I lose much.—For he was honest—and the honest soul is human—feeling—He is to be buried tomorrow.—I don't believe in funerals.—But I know Caffin would like it if I were present—& Marin & Walkowitz

---

470. Either Dr. J. R. Wrather or Dr. R. D. Gist.

471. See *NYT*, Jan. 15, 1918, 13.

—And Strand too. Caffin championed what I stood for since I knew him—Championed it in his own way.—In "What is 291" his is one of the really *felt* essays[472]—

—I wonder how you are—that throat—Not hearing I hope is good news—You know you are an awful lot to me—I have to laugh when I say it—It sounds so funny to say it—As if you didn't know—And still something makes me say it in such a raw way this morning—

—I have just had a beautiful letter from Marie—the country—where she is sleighing —& feels clean—away from the office & all it symbolizes—On Friday she will be back—

—The room here is damp & very cold—Not a trace of heat in the whole building— Gaisman wanted to present me with an oil-stove—I refused the offer—

Still it is not agreeable to be so cold.—Perhaps I'm stubborn—or foolish—both—? —No, it's none of those—Just myself—

A very funny individual—

Alfred Stieglitz · [New York City] · [January 17, 1918] +

Thursday morning. 291—10 A.M.—At last traces of heat are coming out of the hole in the wall —the rooms have been unbearable—so damp—cold—my rheumatism enjoying both hugely— & I?—cussing & smiling—

—It's some time since I wrote.—It was too cold here—& at home I went to bed early or there were people—I simply didn't write.—

—I had hoped to hear from you this morning—hoped to hear the throat wasn't quite so bad—was much better—??—I'll have to wait—I won't believe things are not good—

—My days have been full—different—the same—Yesterday was an incredible day —I got up early. Came to 291.—Sat awhile before the Wright—but couldn't stand the cold room—so wandered up Fifth Avenue to Montross's.—A mixed show of "Moderns"[473]—Henri —Kroll—Bellows included—Terribly inane, mediocre—Awful in fact—Dead—Putrefaction— Montross wasn't there.—No other visitor—I then wandered to Macbeth's—a loan exhibition of Davies[474]—his whole evolution—three rooms full—drawings, etchings, lithos, oils, water-colors, pastels, sculptures—in blue, red, yellow, tiny & a little larger than tiny.—The show for the bene-fit of Blind Soldiers of France—fifty cents—The galleries newly decorated & lighted up—much money spent—All great taste & pianissimo.—The show gave me the creeps. I felt as if I heard whisperings coming from the wall—occasional beautiful words—but I didn't hear clearly—felt a painful sensation of suppression—or what I call—don't be shocked—an incomplete erection. —Do you know what erection signifies?—Davies originally had virility—virile talent—but America has kept it from developing—All is pianissimo—sighing—whining—It's a sort of Huyler Candy & Ice Cream Soda running through all—

472. *Camera Work* 47 (July 1914), 62.

473. Watercolors by George Bellows, Childe Hassam, Robert Henri, Leon Kroll, John Marin, Max Weber, and J. Alden Weir were on view at the Montross Gallery in December 1917 and January 1918; see "Art Notes," *NYT*, Dec. 14, 1917, 12.

474. A Retrospective Loan Exhibition of the Work of Arthur B. Davies, Macbeth Gallery, New York, Jan. 2–31, 1918; see *NYT*, Jan. 27, 1918, 66.

—Did I ever tell you how I ran into the opening of the Carroll Galleries some years ago.
—Davies opened it—It was a dismal place—A room full of drawings—Females & males—the
females all frankly nude—Interesting—very able—the males all clad with white loin cloths![475]
—I roared with laughter & knew at once what ailed the "Art" of Davies—Males nude the
"*police*" would not permit in ladies' society—& Davies is supported by women primarily—
A male with all that makes a man a male would have kept the women—the type supporting
Davies—away—They may "look" in privately.—I don't know.—But in public—Gosh—Never
—New York the Hypocrite—the Ladylike—And Davies is ladylike—He is an artist. A poet.—
And he is sensitive.—The show reeks with good taste.—

—I came out as if I had been stuffed with a mediocre quality of incense.—

—Went to 291.—Zoler waiting for me. We walked up Fifth Avenue—through the
Park—to 66th Street & Broadway. Caffin's funeral—I have been to but six funerals in my life
—I don't believe in them. The first was not until I was forty.—But Caffin did & I knew he
wanted me to be there. So I went—I don't know whether you know of funeral organizations. I
never knew of them until I saw this one.—There is a building—a sort of simple store—or series
of stores—an elevator takes one upstairs—& one finds oneself in a room which is an imitation
of a church—Everything artificial—imitation—One feels as if one must be at Wanamaker's
—As the Reverend—I don't know exactly what his official title was—Caffin was of the High
Church of England—began speaking it was so inaudible that I felt "Davies pictures"—It was
painful trying to listen & not hearing.—And if one didn't try it was still more painful—And to
emphasize the inaudibility of undoubtedly "beautiful language" one heard the heavy fire-engines
chasing down Broadway making a frightful noise—the sirens screaming louder than ever—
Rumbling trucks—Ghastly New York—a screaming farce—I could have yelled—The man
continued—raised his voice a trifle—I sensed what he was emitting—Then there were prayers
—& chapters out of the Bible—some awful organ music—a sort of whine—nearly inaudible—
An hour of all that—I'm amazed that Caffin didn't arise from his coffin & kill all of us—

—Bourgeois sat next to me—Marin & Zoler in front of me.—Lever on other side of
me—

When we got on to the street I wondered why people continued [to do] all this useless
nonsense—

I had walked miles already—the Park had been wonderful—I walked some more
miles—I would liked to have talked to Caffin about his own funeral—as I had so often set him
thinking along lines which he would not have thought had he not met me—

—You see everything is so impersonal as far as I'm concerned.—I'm sure that that
which made Caffin, Caffin is nearer to me than to anyone else—including his wife & children.
Nothing sentimental stands between him & me—as far as I'm concerned.—

As he was sick & incurably so I'm glad he is gone—He died just as he was beginning to
be appreciated—that's a fine moment to die—& live—

475. *The New York Times* disagreed with Stieglitz's assessment, writing that Arthur B. Davies' drawings and paintings of male
nudes, exhibited at the Carroll Galleries in December 1913, showed the "intensity of the artist's interrogation of the human
form," while "the breadth of life seems truly to inform the modeling" of his studies of the female figure; see "In the Art Galleries,"
NYT, Dec. 17, 1913, 10.

—I walked & walked.—I think I could have walked forever—

It was nearly suppertime when I got home.—And I ate.—The phone rang—a man whom I had never seen or heard of—who had come into 291 a few days ago & for whom I had no time then—asked me if he could come to see me—at 291. I told him call me up at 1111 & come to me there. I didn't quite know why I did that—I never did that before for anyone—It was cold at 291—he looked intelligent—& queer—black hair—huge mustache—sallow— & I knew he was interested in photography & at home I could show him some things—

—He came at eight—At one he left.—I had—we had—an amazing five hours.— He is a Georgian—English origin—is a mechanical engineer—was years deeply interested in photography—is now building an entirely new system of movies—

A real thinker—I can't tell you all that happened.—All that was said.—The War— Germany—England—American—All impersonal—far-seeing—tremendously clear vision— bordering on fanaticism—Without mania—

He has evolved what he calls the White Faith—He says he does not talk about it to many—The remarkable thing about the session was that we absolutely understood each other —He has read everything—is a mathematical mind—I have read virtually nothing—am evolving no faith of any special name—

I wonder if we'll ever meet again—These are certainly wondrous days—

I went to bed & slept—the first time in days.—The air—the long walks—all that happened—the consciousness that all I *see* actually is happening—

—He isn't married—Hasn't had time—had to travel too much—He *hates* England— impersonally—says the present English are not racially English—but I won't go into details— I couldn't give you anything but false impressions—It's like trying to describe the Wright or music—

—Elizabeth has just phoned.—She is coming down.—I'm glad—I wanted to go to her studio but didn't. Bourgeois is due too—is to see the Wright. And I brought the Marins.—I want to hear what he has to say—

—It looks like snow.—

I'd like to give you a *Big Kiss*. There ought to be some instrument by which distance could be eliminated for kisses as for sound.—

[January 18, 1918]
Friday.—11 A.M.—291—I just came from Elizabeth's—I had hoped for an answer to her telegram—

—Yesterday I was interrupted as I was writing to you.—There were many people.— I was really far away—tired—upheavals everywhere—& I was wondering how you were.— No letter.—I made myself "believe" you were better—yet I knew you were probably worse. —No letter—Elizabeth came to ask if I had heard.—She wired you—no reply.—Strand was worrying too.—I felt a letter *must* come—& it came—

—It dazed me—I'm glad you wrote—frankly—Gosh, I wish I knew you [were] with the doctor in Amarillo—It's ghastly to be sick & have stupid people around one.—No answer to the telegram makes me hope you are in Amarillo—If only you are put on your feet soon—You have been killing yourself the pace you have been going for years—& still I know it could not be otherwise—you being you.—And the world being what it is.—I wish you weren't so far away.—I daren't read the letter again.—It excited me too much.—I'm sorry that you should have received that question of mine—the child[476]—just while you were ill.—And so ill.—I don't like to excite you.—And that did.—And much else I wrote.—But I wrote because I had to—just as I did.—

—My head doesn't seem to want to think—all that goes through it as I wish to write is: She is sick & suffering pain—physical—mental too—& here we are, all of us thousands of miles away.—And I've even thought of what use would I—could I—or anyone of us—[be if we] fly to you.—Yes, if we could bring you to New York & have you cared for here.—But there—strangers & inexperienced—

I wish there were an answer to that telegram. I'll wire again by night if there has been none till then—Are we foolish to be so concerned?—We can't help it—

I don't know why I haven't mailed anything to you all week—

—Night—nearly midnight—Nothing from you—I hope you are in Amarillo with the doctor—in his care—I wired to the President of the School to find out how you are.—I had to.—

It has been a busy day—gray—& warmer—& now it's snowing—Marie came.—And as I was all upset I asked her to go up to 155th Street & walk from there down the Riverside Drive—near the river, inner walk, for some miles.—It was a wonderful walk—over ice—the river looked gray & sullen—full of floes of ice moving southward—puffing engines—smoking factories on opposite shores—Every shade & tone of grays—Hardly a soul—I couldn't get you lying in bed, coughing, out of my mind.—I know what it means—the ache—the depression—and I see you revolting yet helpless—

—But I hope it's all much better—But is it?—Will the morning bring an answer from the President?—What will it be? It seems an eternity till then—

When I returned to 291 Strand & Wright were there—Strand was with me when I wired. I called up Elizabeth to ask if she had heard.—

It's just about two years ago Anita brought me your drawings—a few days earlier—?—Two years—a lifetime these days—

—As I was watching the river—& the puffing locomotives pulling the long freight trains—& saw carts with horses dumping ashes way below us—all bathed in a potential endless variation of warm & cool grays—& I was walking along the lonely path—Marie beside me—I was thinking now & then what a queer thing life is—it seemed so much queerer—the individual so immaterial—I, not as important as a fly-speck—All man's work in the shape of boats & buildings—tracks & trains—parks—all quite wonderful—yet how insignificant to the sullen looking quiet flowing ice choked expanse of leaden color water—& a leaden sky serenely quiet—

476. On January 2, 1918, Stieglitz responded to O'Keeffe's recent comments about Strand: "I know what you are to him—what he feels—better than he knows it." The next day he asked "I wondered if you could think of him as father of your child."

—Later—For a few minutes I had fallen asleep—pencil in hand—grasping the paper—

Good Night—

I hope you are resting—that you are in good hands—

Good Night—

I want you well & laughing—

Good Night—

Georgia O'Keeffe · [**Canyon, Texas**] · [**January 20, 1918**]

Sunday morning—

I am up and dressed. Mr. Cousins told the lady who is doing most things for me—and who saw him last night for me that he is coming to see me this morning so I am up and dressed —otherwise I would not be up—

I guess I feel some better—anyway—I haven't been coughing so much—

I am sorry I've raised so much disturbance—still I can't be sorry I told you I was sick—

—I am not going to try to explain details here—why delay and all that—partly others' fault—partly mine because I couldn't talk—and my head slips a cog every once in awhile— I forget what I intend to do and simply don't think at all about the most ordinary things folks would first expect me to think of—

Then I looked at the telegram and didn't know what to say—Said I'd write and came home and to bed and was too tired to write—

It all made me decide though—that I'd stop work for a month—However—I think it would be a physical impossibility for me to do anything else.

I guess I just didn't have energy enough to have the initiative to do it till I had to.—To get up and say you are going to quit when there isn't anyone anywhere around to do your work isn't as easy as it seems—He is going to try to get the girl[477] who was here before me—She is married—living in Kansas—He likes her—so do I—the most life in the least bundle I've ever seen—

So much for my job—

—For myself—Why I don't know—I don't seem to care—maybe I'll care in a few days. Leah is going to San Antonio for February—and wants me to go with her—

I don't seem to care—Maybe I'll stay here—The lady who stews over me most—almost made me promise to go to Amarillo tomorrow if I feel able—to the sanitarium if I don't want to go to anyone's house—I've just about made up my mind to face the music and go—I've never been in a hospital—it scares me and I know they will come and haul me out—

Don't you bother though. I'll wire you if I'm not all right as [soon as] possible.

It's just I feel like nothing—and my head—If I'm quiet I'll be all right.

477. Mrs. Hillery.

Night—Sunday—

Mr. Cousins came—Wants me to rest a week and see if I can't go back to school for at least part-time—In the meantime he is going to see if Mrs. Hillery is available in case I can't go back to work in a couple of weeks—

Well—I just didn't much care one way or the other so agreed to do as he chooses.

The excitement—or something—made my head ache—I got in bed right after he left and slept—like you sleep with a headache—all afternoon—Folks came when it was dark—Brought supper—I couldn't eat a bite—Feel as though I never want to eat again—

—I'm not going to see anybody anymore—They make me talk and make me tired—Have found a girl who will come and do the things I want done—

—Measles and all the pestersome diseases are flourishing and they don't want the children to get them downstairs—that makes extra difficulty but things seem to be better settled—

A page from Strand this noon—

Goodnight—

I'm too tired to write more but I know you are bothered—

I just wish I could feel that no one bothered—

[January 21, 1918]

Monday morning—

Slept like a dead woman last night and feel better this morning—Still going to stay in bed—content just to be still.

I love you very much this morning—

—Isn't that funny to say—I sat here a long time wondering whether I would say it or not—But I wanted to say it—

I dreamed all sorts of queer things—about folks I'd almost forgotten—.

Alfred Stieglitz · [New York City] · [January 22, 1918] +

Good morning Little Girl—291—after eleven.—Have just come down—Had been at barber's to have a shampoo—was in sore need of it—It's snowing hard.—All is one whiteness.—And it isn't very cold.—I may get up on top of a bus & try some photography. Have wanted to do that in a snowstorm for some years.—Here's my chance. Will I take it?—The other day Marin was arrested for sketching near the river front[478]—Had a great time to get off.—His "abstractions" the authorities were positive were secret plans!!—Ye gods the stupidity of the man in power!!—So I wonder what the law is.—May one ride on a bus & photograph? No one seems quite to know what is law & what is not law—And I don't much care but I do not want to be arrested unless it's worthwhile—Nothing is quite as maddening as running up against ignorant stupid officialdom—which feels its power through its very stupidity!!—

478. In the winter of 1918 Marin and his wife, Marie, lived with her sister, Sarah Hughes Shaw, in the Flatbush section of Brooklyn.

—Yesterday was a queer day—rather choppy—like the sea when it's not over pleasant riding on—Yet the day was alive like such a sea.—Four times during the day I took tea!!—Quite Russian.—And I really don't care for tea—Tea for breakfast—At lunch tea—It was lunch like it was breakfast. Went to a place where it was warm—to warm those feet.—And at four I said to Strand let's go & get warm—We went to the same place—a small tea-room on the Avenue—Outside of Strand & myself & the waitresses & the boss—an artistic looking man with flowing black tie & goggles à la mode & an intelligent face—about forty-five—fifty—no one was there.—Tea.—For six I had an appointment with Hapgood.—He was to meet me at 291—So Strand & I sat together until then—he told me about the letter—showed it to me—I said why that's O'Keeffe—as fine as beautiful as ever.—I knew how he felt.—He sat there like a little boy.—And I assured him you'd write again.[479]—And you will.—Perhaps not quite the same.—But always yourself.—And that's the same.—Of course the draft is on his mind—I had to laugh when he said: "How much you & she are alike."—Or something to that effect—I wonder whether we are so alike—I doubt it—We are alike in that we are really free in our feelings & we say what we feel—And that seems to be rare—I wonder why—Is it?—

—Hapgood appeared on time.—He suggested we go to a new restaurant—a Russian one—small—run by Jo Davidson's (the sculptor) sister—But before going we stopped at the Waldorf to sit alone awhile—At the Russian restaurant Davidson & his wife & Boyesen, the poet, son of the former Columbia professor[480] were likely to turn up—So we went to the Waldorf. Hapgood wanted a drink. No drinks served because of the Garfield Day!![481]—Blue Monday.—I wanted nothing—Just to keep warm & be with Hapgood undisturbed.—But we couldn't sit there & not take anything—A pot of tea for two!!—Twenty-five cents sum total—and with lemon—& lots of hot water & a clean table-cloth!!—Hadn't had such luxuries in a long time. And all for a quarter.—

We talked.—And it was great. Finally we got to the Russian Restaurant—virtually empty—everything new—Soon Davidson & Company arrived—also Dr. Aisen whom I hadn't seen for a year—all former frequenters of 291 when there was "Art & Lunches & Novelty"—!! I did most of the talking & in the usual way—just relating—By nine they "had to go"—Hapgood & I sat awhile longer—He too had to go to a meeting given in honor of Emma Goldman who is to go to jail for sedition[482]—He & she were great friends in years gone by—He wanted me to go along. Said she'd be glad to see me—But I refused.—I told him I hated all official hours, etc.—That if she & he & I could be alone, I'd love to go but this "official"

479. In her letter of January 14, 1918, O'Keeffe told Strand that if she were a man, she would go to war: "I wouldn't miss it for anything—just the seeing of what it does to men." The next night she added: "I have a notion that maybe I won't write you anymore" (CCP:PSC).

480. Florence Davidson; Bayard Boyesen, an anarchist, was the son of Hjalmar Boyesen, a professor of Germanic languages at Columbia University.

481. At the request of President Wilson and H. A. Garfield, the Fuel Administrator, many stores and businesses closed on January 22, 1918, giving their workers a paid vacation, in order to conserve fuel. The Hotel Association also forbade the sale of liquor in dining rooms that were heated; see "Big Stores Closed in Shopping Areas," NYT, Jan. 22, 1918, 3. Several Mondays thereafter were designated as "fuelless days" in order to conserve energy resources.

482. In 1917 Emma Goldman and Alexander Berkman were convicted of making speeches and distributing literature against conscription and draft registration; they were sentenced to two years in prison and fined ten thousand dollars. On January 14, 1918, the Supreme Court upheld their conviction; see "Affirms Sentence on Emma Goldman," NYT, Jan. 15, 1918, 10.

parting—*No*. The Caffin funeral was the last straw—I did something there which went absolutely against my own grain—& I have done nothing for Caffin & I'm not yet over the mean resentful feeling the performance gave me.—I guess I've become more impossible than ever—

I accompanied Hapgood practically to the door—Second Avenue & 11th Street—We walked.—The night was cold & damp—But I liked to be together with him as long as I could. —He is coming tomorrow afternoon to see your watercolors of last summer—He asked for you —And Marie phoned [to see] how you were.—She sends her special good wishes.—You see all those who mean something to me are interested in you—

—Finally I got home—Alone there—Mrs. Stieglitz away for the night—

I thought much of Emma Goldman—& my mind was in Russia[483]—I'm sending you another book—I'm not connected with any propaganda—never was—But the living truth is all that interests me—it moves constantly.—

You know what I mean—You are the symbol of the living truth—you feel the moment —although you may not understand it.—And still perhaps you do—without trying to—You just do.—

—My sister[484] called up this morning asking me to come to a "dinner" tonight—some good-looking women & some learned men—Perhaps I'll go—I don't know—

—Boyesen & the "crowd" last night found me the same incorrigible *Optimist*— Funny the family calls me a pessimist—so many others call me the great optimist—Both are correct—

How's the throat?—

I'd like to drag you out onto the river—in the snowstorm—the river is nearly all ice— but there are openings for boats—I'd like to see you all wrapped up in black—very warm— as I am wrapped up—in black—And on the river—in the snow—

I'd like to give you One Big Kiss on the mouth—*Just One*—

Georgia O'Keeffe · [Canyon, Texas] · [January 23, 1918] +

Wednesday afternoon—nearly 3—

Your letter this morning—and the two sheets of Elizabeth's—It came with my breakfast but I waited till the room was warm and I had eaten my breakfast and taken the nasty stuff the doctor gave me—Then—up on my two pillows I read. I don't know why but I wanted to read Elizabeth's first—still you had put it last so I read it last—

It some way makes me feel I've disappointed her—I've thought much of her—wondered much about her—responded little—It could not be otherwise—It almost makes me sorry that she happened along right now—these past few months—

483. Following the October 1917 Revolution, the Bolsheviks, led by Lenin, Trotsky, and Stalin, took control of most major cities in Russia. On January 21, 1918, when the long-awaited constituent assembly met, Lenin immediately dismissed it because most of its members were non-Bolsheviks.

484. Either Selma Stieglitz Schubart or Agnes Stieglitz Engelhard.

You see, I haven't even responded to the sunrise or the sunset or the bright shining day or the night sky—Other things have been taking so much of me there has been no energy—no vitality for others—I've often looked at things and wished I had the energy or life—whatever it is that makes you feel things enough to create from them—but I haven't dared to give myself that way lately—There hasn't been enough of me—

—I can't even write about it—It makes my head ache—

I went to sleep after your letters this morning—I feel better—but letter—breakfast—and then sleep again doesn't sound very frisky does it—

—I don't suppose my letters read very sanely—but I really feel better—I wonder that you have patience to read them—

Queer that the only thing I've read in the *Camera Works* happened to be that story of Caffin's—And why I happened to read that particular one—Except—Gertrude Stein[485]—You know those things of hers [make] much better sense to me than most supposed-to-be intelligent combinations of words—They make ordinary prose seem so stupid—

Leah came in about two—All up in the air—I had told them downstairs that she was the only person I wanted to see so they let her up—Leah is just like me only a little different —She had to come down to see about some of Dr. Mac's taxes at the court house here—He has a ranch twenty miles south—

Anyway she said—"George—I just had to see you—I thought I'd go crazy if I didn't—ever since you didn't come up Saturday." And she sat on the table and kicked her heels and told me what she had been doing—falling from one scrape into another—

And she said—"I'm coming back tomorrow with woolen stockings and robes and the car all shut in tight and you're going back with me and anyone that says you're not I'll just tell them to go to Hell—I'm engineering this."

"Why" she said—"You've got to go—I want you around—I'm going crazy."—You would laugh at her—She is so funny—tall—slim—and such eyes—and the keenest tongue I ever saw???—She feels and thinks and does things—and goes like the wind—

Things bothering her—she said "Why you know I just walked the floor and I don't often do that"—and then began tearing around through the things on my table for something to read—I gave her Schopenhauer—I wish you could see her—she is wonderful—She wears a man's coat and hat and then the most wonderful pair of women's feet kick out from under the skirts—long—slim—unusually good-looking feminine feet—And the eyes up top—

People always think we are sisters—here and in Amarillo too—it's so funny—She is food demonstrator for three counties here and burns up much good gasoline tearing over them—Dr. Mac furnishes the car—the counties the gasoline—

Don't exactly know why I'm writing so much about her today—Except that the first time we met—nothing had to be explained—it was as though we had always known all about one another—

Guess this is enough for today—

485. Gertrude Stein, "Henri Matisse," "Pablo Picasso," *Camera Work*, special no. (Aug. 1912), 23–25, 29–30.

No, I don't cough so bad but I don't enjoy what I do at it—Don't worry—I'm quite Irish—and quite tough—and anyway I'm not worth bothering about—I'm really going to get up again tomorrow—five days in bed at a time is too much—

I am saying I don't know to Elizabeth because that is all there is to say—

If I am by any possible chance able—I am going to work this month—finish the Winter Quarter's work—that's four weeks more beginning Tuesday—and then stop for three months— that is—stop for the Spring Quarter—

If I can't do that—that is—if I can't finish this Quarter's work—Why I don't know and I don't care anything about what happens—Where I go or what I do or anything else—If I can work next week—but—I am a typically inefficient American—the kind you tell about.

No I'm not blue—I'm not even unhappy I guess—

Georgia O'Keeffe · [Canyon, Texas] · [January 31, 1918] +

It's night again—and I want to write big but only have a few sheets of paper and may not go to town to get any for some time so I guess I had better write little—

246

I said it was gosh darned cold—Shirley says it's damn cold—but I rather like using two words to say it—We both mean the same thing anyway. I've wanted to swear at myself all day —for lots of reasons.—

My throat bothered me—I'd like to be buried way out on the plains somewhere till I feel better—Wouldn't it be great if I could do that—

A talk with Mr. Cousins—not much encouragement about that Spring Quarter off— He thinks I'll be all right by then—it's three weeks off—He is a nice little man—And you know I just couldn't tell him that what I want even more than a beautifully working throat is to feel free for just a little while—

What is it anyway that's in me—that inability to fit myself comfortably into the sort of places other folks fit in—It seems as though living here right straight along till the three weeks' vacation at the end of May would—

Did you ever see an old gray rag—very lifeless—limp—fringed on some edges—a hole or two—flapping in the wind on a wire clothesline—sometimes just hanging down—it's about two feet long—variable width—but narrow—

Alfred Stieglitz · New York City · [February 1, 1918] +

Friday—a little after 5—Just home.—Am to go out for dinner & then theater.—

—It is some days—three I believe—since I've written.—What three days!!—Knowing you in Amarillo—in the care of somebody human I feel somewhat at ease as far as the Little Girl is concerned.—To be ill—sick—& have no one around that is really human—interested—is about the worst affliction I can think of [for] you—And feeling that you were more or less so alone in Canyon is what—you call it worry & I have to laugh at the word—I felt & which made me feel like rushing down to you & dragging you away—

Where to—??—To anywhere where you might get a little real care—affection—

—What have I been doing? First of all finally out of those rooms not my own nor anyone else's.[486] —The "Vault" is jammed full—no [more] room for anyone except myself to get at things—& to get at anything means moving many things—It was a job—And the room downstairs—one side all window—why today I was in it all day—It is queer to be down there—& it does feel cramped & cage-like—but there is more room & more light than in the Vault. And just sufficient space to look at small paintings—

And I have a gas-stove.—Had to have one. So there is some warmth.—

—But I'm very tired—I feel *driven* about—

I'll give you an idea of day before yesterday—Up early—Chased to 291—Looked at the Hartleys—just glanced at them—to get an idea—Felt nothing—saw less—but knew there must be something for I know Hartley must develop—Started transplanting more packages—upstairs & downstairs—Then Zoler came. Mrs. Stieglitz wanted me to get tickets for the Greenwich Village Theatre[487] (that is where we go tonight with Mr. & Mrs. Liebman as our guests—We dine with them—our cook is in the hospital) & so I asked Zoler to walk with me.—Fourth Street & Seventh Avenue—I felt like a greenhorn seeing New York—We walked there & back—I guess nearer four miles than three—met people I knew on the way—

Talk—Amongst them Waldo Frank whom I hadn't seen since the *Seven Arts* was put under chloroform[488]—After the War it is to be revived!!?—

—It was time to get to Kennerley's—appointment for lunch—I got up there—59th Street and Park Avenue—by noon thirty—He showed me through the new place (Anderson Art Gallery)—space galore—I never saw such lavishness of space—& I felt that to live as I did was indeed amusing!

—I was shown a copy of *Comus*—Milton's own copy—a tiny volume—? Was informed that ten men were going to bid for it at the coming auction—& that it would bring ten thousand dollars!! Possession—Isn't it a great thing—?—Everyone is more or less afflicted with the germ—Does one ever outgrow it entirely?

—Lunch at the Plaza—talk—and then I chased off to the Heifetz concert. The young Russian boy violinist who has been the sensation this season[489]—A packed house—black with

486. Throughout the fall of 1917, Stieglitz had used other rooms in the building that formerly housed 291 to store his art and meet with friends. In late January 1918, however, the landlord informed him that all the rooms, except for Stieglitz's "Vault" and one downstairs, were now rented.

487. Stieglitz saw "Der Luxbaron," described as a "rough and rollicking piece," about a vagabond masquerading as a baron; see "Germans in Musical Play," *NYT*, Feb. 2, 1918, 9.

488. On September 26, 1917, Stieglitz had told O'Keeffe that *Seven Arts* was going out of "existence—the lady [Annette K. Rankine] who put up the money objected to the articles *against* War—so she withdrew her support—!!—A big attitude to take —isn't it? Sickening.—But in keeping with all else—Free expression with a string to it—It would be a pity if it went out of existence."

489. Following his celebrated performances in Europe, Jascha Heifetz made his Carnegie Hall debut on October 27, 1917, and performed several times thereafter in New York in the winter of 1917–1918; see "A New Violinist Plays," *NYT*, Oct. 28, 1917, 21.

women—at least five hundred on the stage too—And many knitting—Elizabeth's mother[490] had had a spare ticket & had invited me the last moment—

The recital was enjoyable & not enjoyable—I never heard more perfect violin playing—impersonal playing—crystal-like—but the selections were Harrison Fisher magazine cover like—I suppose the manager caters to the American public—the women—It hurts—So I was glad when it was over—I wonder what this rotten New York will do to that boy.—Is he big enough to develop in spite of Huyler Soda Water—

I walked some miles—a biting wind—I had to forget that audience—the afternoon—

—Got home—had to wash & get into clean clothes—Gaisman called for Mrs. & me—dinner at a club—Was very hungry—Mrs. Stieglitz said I ate as if I hadn't eaten in months—I dislike that club—dislike all clubs in fact—Then two ladies were called for, mother & daughter, Gaisman told me both were brilliant—had heard often about them from him—& all of us & he too landed at another club where a man named Marcosson, whom some claim to be the best American war correspondent, gave a talk on the Allied Fronts of the War—A packed house—An hour & half talk—& the whole business in a way was a repetition of the afternoon—I could have choked the audience—His talk was as fine as a Bouguereau!!—It makes me boil to think of it—the shallowness in the garb of depth—and the darn fool public not seeing—applauding wildly at stupid sentimentality—A remarkably fluent speaker—"real" American—what I dislike about the American—

—I was glad when I got into my own four walls—I wanted to write to you—but I was too mad all the way through—

—The day started me boiling again—the War & this Country—Art & this Country—It's all the same—"*they*" simply don't see—because they have not suffered enough—if at all —to feel—

—And yesterday was another day of chasing—real New Yorkish—I hate it—Why do I do it?—I rarely do—

—I have looked at the Hartleys today—A few are very fine—undoubtedly his best to date—You'd like them—I'm glad—Oh yes—yesterday Wright came around & carried me off to his joint—25th Street & Seventh Avenue—his new picture. —And then the frame for the portrait[491]—

Well the new picture takes one's breath away—I don't know whether it's as good—or better—than the portrait—It's different—Yet a continuation—In parts it's very wonderful —Probably finer than anything in the portrait—I'll have to see it at 291 before I come to any decision—All I know is it is very remarkable & you'd have a "fit" over it—It's glowing with color—It's more like spring & the other more reserved—drawn in—Wright himself thinks it's way ahead of the portrait—We'll see.—You know the story of the last baby & the family—

—So you see I have had some treats as far as the men are concerned.—It's really a great satisfaction to see them [developing] so beautifully—in spite of war—handicaps generally—

490. Elizabeth (Lizzie) Stieglitz, wife of Alfred's brother Leopold.
491. Probably *Spring Synchromy*, 1918, oil, Fisk University, Alfred Stieglitz Collection, and *Self-Portrait—Synchromy*, 1917.

—But I'm full of the desire to photograph.—In the rooms into which the new party [is] moving there is a wonderful negress washing—scrubbing—the floors—so black—& a white cloth about the head—One can see she must have a marvelous body—strong as an animal—I watched her on her fours moving about the floor—her rolled-up sleeves—arms like steel rods in strength—

But I haven't a ghost of a chance to work at 291—It makes me laugh—the whole situation—It's the only thing to do—All else would be foolish—Wouldn't it?—

—I wonder when I'll get a glimpse of you at Amarillo?—Perhaps you are to have complete rest—no letters from any "exciting" friends—no letters to any "exciting" friends—I wonder whether I am such a friend?—I don't want to be—Yet at times I guess I do—

Do I?—I want nothing but the feeling that you are living—not tormented too much—some you'll always be—for that's you—Intense intensity—a depth which goes straight to the center of the earth—& through it—into space unending—

And my kiss would like to follow that line—Is it possible?

—I'm so darned tired that the idea of a kiss into Unending Space—makes me laugh aloud—I—?—

It's time to wash—dress—

Good Night—I'm glad I found this paper today—It's beautiful to feel—

Good Night—

Georgia O'Keeffe · [Canyon, Texas] · [February 4, 1918]

Just back from Amarillo again and a most uncanny feeling that I must write you now because my arm aches so—another hypodermic of some sort of serum—I can hardly move it—and I'm going to bed and I don't know—I just don't feel like getting up again soon—Dr. Mac got me to go specially to his office—and told me I just must be careful and a lot of not encouraging things—

The other man[492] got him to I think—He says the serum will make me sick but to take it anyway—dangerous not to—

[February 6, 1918]

Wednesday night—started this Monday—I haven't been up till tonight—I got up and went to supper—queer feeling in my head and slow walking—Surely have been laid out—the darned stuff gives me an awful headache and makes me deathly sick at my stomach—and the worst of it is that as soon as I feel pretty well again I have to have another dose—So tomorrow morning I'll have another—pleasant to think about—

But you know—I just don't much care anymore—don't care much about anything—don't care if it makes me sick—don't care if it doesn't—

492. Either Dr. J. R. Wrather or Dr. R. D. Gist.

The Van Gogh letters[493] came Monday—I have read them—not the introduction—in between sleeping and waking—read mostly to forget how sick I felt—then would go to sleep —reading makes me so tired—but I enjoyed it—enjoyed it very much—

You are very nice to me (nice is a poor word—a weak little pretty word and that's not what I mean at all but you will know)—

Such a wonderful letter from the sister last week—Hardly anyone but you could imagine how pleased—that's not the right word either—I am with the way she is growing.— It is wonderful.

I had two of Wright's *Creative Will*[494]—she helped herself to one without telling me and writes that she is having a wonderful time reading it—late at night and early in the morning when it's quiet. She says it doesn't seem new at all—that it's just like talking to me only he uses different words—I had to laugh—Wright probably wouldn't feel flattered—Anyway it's a great discovery to her—"More truth in it than you dare believe" she says. She almost scares me. I don't know what she will turn into and her interests separate her more and more from people—She said remarkable things in that letter—the saving thing is I guess that the things she sees give her great pleasure—

—Aloneness—is more fun than folks [know]—She loves the country down there— Shadows of the trees on the bare ground in the night—moonlight—and the sky— My little girl is queer.—No not queer.

Leah took the thing I painted last week up to show Billie Mac when she brought me down Monday. She thought it wonderful and wondered what Billie would say—she was to leave yesterday for the south—

Is going to write me what they said. I know it will be funny. She was telling about it and they asked to have it brought up.

I don't seem to have anything to write—And anyway I must go to bed again—It's eight and I usually go at seven. Tired—up about three hours—a little less.

Goodnight.

Georgia O'Keeffe · [Canyon, Texas] · [February 8, 1918] +

Friday—1:30—

Isn't everything funny—The day out is a yellow Hell of tearing biting cold wind— fairly blinding with dust—why it's mad—It's wonderful too—I like it—I'm glad it is that way —it's tremendous—still it is laughable—It's like some crazy folks I've seen—I lived near an asylum once[495]—The head doctor's daughter and I were great friends—and I saw many crazy folks—had an awful fear of them—

493. Stieglitz sent O'Keeffe *The Letters of a Post-Impressionist: Being the Familiar Correspondence of Vincent Van Gogh,* trans. Anthony Ludovici (Boston, 1913) and inscribed it in part "To Georgia O'Keeffe—a little girl from a very, very old man." See Fine, Glassman, and Hamilton, *Georgia O'Keeffe's Library,* 62.

494. Willard Huntington Wright, *Creative Will* (New York, 1916).

495. O'Keeffe could be referring to the Poor Farm and Asylum that was located in Madison, Wisconsin, in the early twentieth century.

—I'm just as afraid to go out into this weather as I used to be of crazy folks—It affects me about the same way—feeling as I do.

I went in a cab this morning[496] and came back in it—it wasn't so bad when I went out—

Your letter—Why it makes me laugh too—Your thinking me in Amarillo—I couldn't stay there—I don't believe I can stay anywhere—

Yesterday I went to school—and I've come to the conclusion that I just simply can't go anymore—no two ways about it—That makes me laugh too—and I couldn't sleep for thinking what I would do about it—It doesn't worry me (I know that's a bad word) like it would most anyone else—I don't much care—only I wonder what I'll do—I wish I could talk to you—Last night when I couldn't sleep I wanted you here—wanted to talk to you—It isn't that I want to plan to do anything—it's simply a sort of curiosity about which way I'll move—

And it's an amusing position to be in—I know by the way I feel that it is pretty apt to take at least two or three months to make me human again—I've tried to think I was mistaken but I'm not I guess—Needles in my throat you know—it's way down—you can't see it—and the rest of me just no good—Today it even hurts to whisper.

It is amusing—The people I know in San Antonio are a variety I don't seem to want to see right now—

I must tell you what I'm reading—it amuses me so—I never read anything like it—and it makes me laugh like everything else—*The Red Lily*[497]—it's great for forgetting—I read—so I won't think—Not that I mind thinking—but I feel myself less and—Why I haven't been so amused in a long time—

My brother[498] from the Waco camp was on the boat that was sunk off the coast of Ireland[499]—As far as I can tell from the papers he didn't go down—I knew he wouldn't as soon as I heard it yesterday and thought a minute—then this morning saw that his division seems to be safe—Amusing—I envy him—He is so funny I wish I could see him—He took my hand over the table down at Waco one night and remarked with his funny laugh—You know—you and I are lucky—

—There is a check for a hundred and fifty over there in my drawer from the other brother[500]—More when I want it—That's amusing too because I have no desire to cash it—What's the use—

As usual—the things you said about the War today were almost exactly what I had been thinking—

This morning almost forgot to finish lacing my shoe—a high tan boot—and I hate tan shoes—sitting here pulling on the strings—thinking about the War—I rather like these shoes—only they are tan and too wide—couldn't get them narrow—Of course that doesn't seem to leave much in their favor—still I'm fond of them—

496. O'Keeffe had gone to Amarillo to see Dr. Mac for another injection.

497. Anatole France, *The Red Lily,* trans. Winifred Stephens (New York, 1914).

498. Alexis O'Keeffe.

499. More than 150 American soldiers were killed on February 5, 1918, when a German submarine torpedoed a ship off the coast of Ireland that was carrying over 2,000 troops; see "Attacked Tuesday at Dusk," *NYT,* Feb. 8, 1918, 1.

500. O'Keeffe told Stieglitz on January 30, 1918, that she had written her brother Francis asking if he could lend her some money and that he had sent her a check.

I've been boiling for several days—Mrs. Reeves picked up *Van Gogh's Letters* from my table—turned over pages—remarked quickly and dropped it as though it had burned her—

"Ugh—it's translated from the German"—I have to laugh about it and at the same time I feel as though she is too stupid to speak to—

Isn't it funny—

What is the use in petting and coddling yourself into living a long time among folks like that—

Funny—Why it's the funniest thing to do that I can imagine—

—Being any sicker among them would be worse though—They look so much uglier inside when you are sick—even when they are being very nice to you.

—Yes? You like the little girl—it's only a little girl—I never felt before so much as though I don't belong anywhere—Wish I could talk to you.—Don't bother about me though—

Why don't you live where it's warm in the winter—

Wish you could see this day—

Alfred Stieglitz · [New York City] · [February 11, 1918] +

291—Just in—Monday—Your letter—tiny—tiny handwriting[501]—lovely—purity itself—but so heartbreakingly sad—Just the feeling I had that day at the station as I drove off—you standing there to go in—to go—And yet—?—

Yes yet—??—As if I didn't feel just what you felt then—what you were then—are today—today intensified—as if it weren't intense enough then to kill most any human being—

And here you are weak—down—so terribly far away—still here all the time—

Serum—I wonder what it's for—I'd like to write to the doctor & ask him what he has in his mind—what he thinks—I'd like to know—*I must know*—Didn't he tell you anything that you could tell me? What's his address?—His full name—

I know serum injections are given for many things—Kitty is anemic—my brother has treated her with arsenic injections—my mother has been receiving injections for ten years—

I want to know what the doctors have in mind about you—

If you are to go away & have a complete rest it must be brought about—by hook or crook—I have nothing in mind—Just a positive feeling—You must have a chance to get on your feet—not drag along—

—The sister—Yes, she must be a keen joy to you—You her sister—mother—*Creative Will*—she finds much in its pages she heard before—from you—Life!—And she reacts—she has a soul—a big one—And it has had an unusual chance to develop—through your own big soul—& suffering—turned into a smile—

—You got the Van Gogh book—

Am I really nice to you? Who could be less than that to you if one has an iota of feeling for genuine fineness—

---

501. O'Keeffe's letter of February 4, 1918, was written in very small handwriting (see pp. 249–250).

You see when I looked at that photograph of [you][502] on Saturday night—I felt what your tiny tiny letter has done to me now—It's as if I'd like to sit at your bedside—hold your hand—have you fall asleep—& sleep until you woke up strong—Well—I'd never budge—& I'd want nothing but to see you well.—

—You know what you feel for your sister—Well, somehow part of what I feel for you is identical with what you feel for her—Perhaps it's all like that—most of the time—Perhaps nearly all the time—

—The sun is out—Mrs. Liebman is coming a little later—she wants to see the Marins & Hartleys—

I came near bringing down your watercolors—to show them to her—I had had them in my hand to bring them—but I want her to see them when nothing else is shown—

Georgia O'Keeffe · [Canyon, Texas] · [February 11, 1918] +

Monday night—

—Letters from you and Strand—I just got home—Yesterday afternoon went to the country to one of the most famous ranches in this part of Texas—Hermosa or The Devil's Kitchen[503]—It was warm—cloudy—the sun in spots like wonderful gold on the plains—*wonderful*—

Your letters make me laugh—

I—Why when I go to walk I'm not sure I can walk straight to the place I want to go—Something is certainly queerly wrong with me—Dr. Mac says go South—lower altitude—and warm—He says San Antonio so I go—

I think I'll go Thursday. I seem to get [it]—He says go immediately—No use talking about it—

You think my letters sound better—It really does make me laugh because I am so very sick—I get up and do all the things other folks do—but gosh—it's such an effort—You can't understand—and something in me that makes me feel that if I don't hold on tight I might go crazy—

Why—yes—I'm afraid—but what good does it do—

I don't know why I write this to you—It will probably trouble you—The weekend with Billie Mac was unusually nice and quiet—She is great—but I wouldn't say how bad I felt for the world—He rubbed it in more today that I must go South and I can't tell you how I hate it— right away too he says—

Goodnight.

Don't be surprised if I don't write—

502. Greenough 457–460.

503. The Devil's Kitchen, which is now in Palo Duro Canyon State Park, was at the time owned by H. C. Harding.

I'll be busy winding things up and getting away—I'm going to get Margaret[504] to pack for me—but I have a notion I may not write for awhile—Mail will be forwarded.

I wish you were here and would hold me very close to you till I go to sleep.—Got to be near someone I like—

Tell Elizabeth to send the letter.

Goodnight.

I feel too tired to live—

UNABLE TO RECOVER from the illness that had plagued her since late November and increasingly alienated from those around her because of her opposition to the war, O'Keeffe took a leave of absence from her teaching job in early February. On the recommendation of Doctor "Mac," she and Leah Harris went to the warmer climate of San Antonio, where Leah's father, Mose, the "fiery" editor of *The Texas Republic,* lived.[505] At first they stayed with Sibyl Browne, a friend from Columbia University, and her mother, Hetty, making occasional trips out-of-town to visit Mose Harris at his ranch; later she and Leah moved to a farm in Waring, Texas, fifty miles to the northwest of San Antonio. Stieglitz was distraught when he heard the news, especially when O'Keeffe told him that one of her doctors had "given up in despair."[506]

Georgia O'Keeffe · [En route from Canyon, Texas, to San Antonio, Texas] · [February 14, 1918]

You will laugh—

I'm on the way—The tall lean man[507] who mops my throat out could hardly believe his ears today when I told him I had quit work and was on the way to San Antonio—

Dr. Mac says—You don't need to go to any doctor if you will take your own hypos—he showed me how—The change and rest and warmth is what you need—What doctors can do for you doesn't amount to anything—

My arm is almost too sore to move tonight from where he stuck me this afternoon—

—This is the filthiest railroad station I ever saw—it's nearly 9:30—train late—half-lighted—straggling—listless moving crowd like late train crowds are—I don't seem to care if the train is late—Time is nothing now—It's great—seven—eight—nine—no hour means anything—Tomorrow—if I miss connections it doesn't matter—Think of it—time is nothing—it doesn't matter—I haven't anything to matter—General Delivery—San Antonio is the only address I know—I wish you were here—This dismal droopy-looking crowd—smoky room—

No hurry—only I'm tired—I want to go to bed—

Goodnight—

504. Possibly Ruth Margaret Cooper.

505. "Pioneer Editor Dies at El Paso," *San Antonio Express,* June 3, 1922, 14.

506. GOK to AS, Feb. 10, 1917.

507. Either Dr. J. R. Wrather or Dr. R. D. Gist.

[Forth Worth, Texas]
[February 15, 1918]
One o'clock Friday noon—

Here again—This is such a very undesirable place[508] that I like it—Just got in—had some food—train five hours late so I missed connections—This is right across the street from the station—The prunes are good—have to wait till 8:50 tonight—Richard[509] met me—he is in camp here—His pass only lasted till 11:30 so he had to go back to camp and get another—Late trains are a bit inconvenient—It seems as though no time has passed since I sat at this very desk and wrote you before—Funny—

—It's hazy out—blue haze—in Canyon we hardly ever have anything but yellow dust haze—

I didn't get up till nearly eleven—slept well except for my arm—It aches and I seemed conscious of it even while I slept—and every time I moved I waked up—I don't mind it much though—.

It seems so funny to be coming down here again and so odd to be going to San Antonio—I always wanted to go—and now that I have to go don't care anything about it—I just can't imagine getting there but I suppose I will—

I have a notion you will be surprised that I've moved—but—I simply couldn't go to school anymore—it seems so stupid to have to say that—

It's nice to be alone—no one to talk to—Richard says I don't look sick—I guess— Well—to myself I look like the devil—Maybe it's because I see myself not dressed—

However it doesn't matter—I don't care what I look like—

General Delivery—San Antonio—

I'll send you a scrap I wrote last night if I can find it—

Soldiers again—they don't interest me greatly now—I don't know why—.

Alfred Stieglitz · [New York City] · [February 16, 1918]

Saturday Evening.—8—Am I still flesh & bones—or just imagination—spirit—Call it what you may.

—I have but one thought—& have had but one thought since that envelope arrived yesterday afternoon!—

You must get well.

—I wired last night to Canyon—I hope the wire reaches you soon—It is an awful ordeal not to know—& to imagine what perhaps isn't at all—

—I had just closed an envelope to you yesterday, after having sat before your drawing a long time—when Bluemner came in—I hadn't seen him in weeks.—His first visit to the new room.—He felt he wanted to see me alone—& we were alone.—Nothing particular to say

508. O'Keeffe wrote this letter on stationery from the Terminal Hotel in Fort Worth, Texas.
509. Possibly Richard H. Harter, a former student at West Texas State Normal College.

but to be with me—& I was glad to be with him.—Just as I know you'd like to be with me awhile—& I with you—Just simple understanding—two human beings!!—Different from the average—not entirely different—just in degree—

He talked about the War, this country, Europe, life generally.—He sees—As we see.—

—As we were leaving the place to get a bite to eat—I was taking him to the [Y.W.H.A.[510]] place to show him what I knew would make an impression on him—he is a very able fellow—but so clean he's poor—when, in stepping into the elevator, your letter was handed to me—When I saw the envelope it was as if a blow had been struck me over the head—It's a wonder I didn't topple over—I remembered that last June I wrote a letter to you & you wrote it came as a terrific blow to you—staggered you—stunned you—so you know how I felt yesterday.—

As we walked up Fifth Avenue in the spring sun—and amongst the crowds I read your letter—that part written in *black* ink[511]—It was hard to believe my eyes—it couldn't be—

Gosh—the distance to Texas seemed—

I sat at the table with Bluemner—he was amazed at the place, said he must bring his family—he talked some—but I was far, far away—& I told him what had happened. He felt—He feels.—He's damnably human—too much so for his own good.—

—I got back to 291—Strand came in—I was glad. I wanted him to come—Hartley came & we had to go to Of's to have Hartley's glass paintings framed[512]—& then I suggested to Strand he & I go to Elizabeth's studio.—She wasn't there—But she came—She felt I wanted to see her—And I told her.—And the three of us, all your friends, all—Well, you know, you are a great human spirit to each of us—We talked it over what to do—how to reach you—All sorts of suggestions made by the young ones—and I—?—Listened & answered—

—I finally wired as I did—It was the only thing that could be done—You have no address in San Antonio—Of course each had the impulse to rush down to San Antonio—Yes, each of us—

—If only I knew exactly what the doctors said—I know they inject for colds of a certain type now—I know that in 1904 in London (& Paris) I got a severe case of the grippe, neglected it—& for months coughed so people steered clear of me—broke two ligaments in my chest just from coughing—I do hope whatever it may be that it's merely a question of time & care that will restore you to complete health again.

—I wonder what connections you have in San Antonio—You have to focus on one thing only—to get back your health—The Little Girl mustn't be afraid—It's not good for her—I know how easy it is to say "mustn't"—I know how terrible it is to be so alone—& to be uncertain—And I had thought you at Amarillo being taken care of—You see I'm a believer still—

510. Stieglitz wrote Y.W.C.A., but he most likely meant Y.W.H.A., the Young Women's Hebrew Association, an organization supported by his friend and patron Aline Meyer Liebman and one Stieglitz frequently visited in the spring of 1918.

511. GOK to AS, Feb. 11, 1918 (see pp. 253–254).

512. In the summer of 1917 Hartley stayed at an art colony in Ogunquit, Maine, sponsored by the critic and patron Hamilton Easter Field. He encouraged Hartley to look at American folk art, especially paintings on glass, mirrors, and saloon signs, as sources for his own paintings; see Kornhauser, *Marsden Hartley*, 301.

I understand & yet I don't—

I did feel you were getting stronger—I had to feel it—

That Letter!!!

This morning I found in a doctor's directory that there are two Macs in Amarillo—McGee—McMeans—I have a sort of hazy memory that it is the latter—so probably it's the other.—

—I, knowing you, should have asked the doctor's name & address long ago, & written to him—Still you understand why that seemed impossible until now. I guess I must be dense & stupid in some respects for otherwise I would have handled the situation better—not so clumsily.—

—The telegram sent last night was: "Letter received. You're leaving for San Antonio. What is doctor's full name & address in Amarillo? We want to know exactly what ails you [and] whether anything can be done from this end. You have friends here who insist on getting you rapidly on your feet. Coming to New York might be advisable. A nurse could accompany you. Necessary funds ready to be telegraphed. Consider your own health only. Sending this to Canyon to be forwarded. *A. S.*"

I hope this reached you & that we'll hear soon.—

—I dare not think—I must wait till I hear—

Perhaps the warm sun—& warmer climate—will have cheered you up a little—Warmed you up some—It is so very far away—when you are well—It is the end of the world when you are ill—

How miserably powerless & useless I seem to feel this moment—And Strand feels as I do—& Elizabeth too.—Dewald & Gaisman inquired.—All want you well.—And Zoler.—*All.*—

—Every effort must be concentrated to get you well—your efforts & ours. Elizabeth says she mailed you a letter today.—

What a solace it must be to be able to pray!—Isn't that a queer thought to come into my head.—I pray in my own way.

—Good Night.

I had this in an envelope ready to mail—I don't know it all sounds like so many words—words—& it's really bewilderment—& yet my mind is clear—There is so much I'd like to know & talk about—I might be able to help you see daylight—Even if I can't find daylight for myself—I occasionally seem to be able to help others find it—That's why I telegraphed as I did—Everything is ready—All sorts of thoughts have chased through that head of mine—I'm enclosing something[513] you should have for case of emergency—that's one reason I've opened the envelope again—Don't say a syllable—& *don't get excited.*—I don't do a thing I feel I mustn't do—mustn't to satisfy something within myself.

You have suddenly been confronted with a new problem—a serious one—& certain

---

513. Stieglitz enclosed a check for one hundred dollars in the letter.

257

ALL THE WORLD GREETS YOU, 1915–1918

phases of it must be made as simple as possible for you.—By hook or crook—There is but one thought: Get well. *Will* it—

Mind is nine-tenths of the battle—You know it—In a nervous state of course it's difficult to make the mind work along a straight line—but it is possible—You have the will—the grit—

Please don't laugh at me today—Smile if you will.

Good Night—

Georgia O'Keeffe · **[San Antonio, Texas]** · **[February 18, 1918]**

I hardly know what to say—I feel in another world—What shall I say—

Your telegram and Elizabeth's came in the mail this noon—Monday—

I arrived Saturday morning—and I'm so glad I'm here and not in Canyon—Still it all seems so funny and unbelievable—

—It has rained ever since I've been here—not real rain—the air has just been wet and the mistiness is wonderful—I've never seen such a motley mixed-up town and every time I go down the street I meet someone I know—the most unheard-of—unexpected people—Leah brought the mail this afternoon—about 1:30—with it the telegrams and I got right up and tore out to answer them—I had been lying down all morning—just won't stay in bed—We went to the bank and while we stood in line I turned round and there was Frank Day—Lieutenant Day—one of our Canyon army boys—He almost stood on his head—it was great to see how excited he was—and changed though still the same—And just as we were bidding him goodbye—he is leaving for Austin tonight—Leah turned round and saw Willard Austin—the man of last spring with the yellow car—it was too funny.

After that I wanted to tell Leah not to look anyone else straight in the face for fear we might recognize them—Spent rest of the afternoon with him—Food and *The Garden of Allah*[514]—A summer school student waylaid me—A girl I knew years ago in Chicago—and another who roomed in the same apartment I did in New York at one time. And I don't care particularly about meeting folks I know.

I am feeling better—rather stupid today and tired because I had a new dose of serum yesterday—but I can talk better than in a long time—it's great—I'll feel better in a little while I know—

As for being taken care of—I hardly know how to behave—I am staying with Sibyl Browne—a South Carolina girl I knew at Columbia—and she is too good to be true—The sort of person I call a nice sweet lovely girl—thinks of doing things for you that you would never even think of wanting done—Almost too comfortable feeling to be true—it's great—it doesn't seem natural—I haven't even felt like writing—

Being lazy is great—between them all they think they have time filled up for me till Friday—Well—maybe they have and maybe they haven't—

514. Based on the 1904 novel by Robert Hichens, *The Garden of Allah* was a popular play.

—You don't need to be alarmed about me—Leah says she is going to write you—I'll be all right here in a little while—

She is going back in about ten days and will ask Dr. Mac—I'd lots rather you wouldn't ask him about me—things up there at Canyon had just about driven me crazy I guess—

—If I don't get lots better in a little while I will do something else—but—I wanted to go East and he said—No—it's too cold—He said El Paso—California—or San Antonio—and here I am.

I must go to bed.

Goodnight.

Kiss me goodnight and don't bother about me—I am really truly honest—

You see—up there at Canyon it was so hard not to go to work and—I don't know—the whole thing almost ran me crazy—

[February 19, 1918]

Next morning—Tuesday—

Raining still—not enough to see—you just can feel it misty on your face—

I'll be all right if folks just leave me alone—and—well—I'm going to be left alone anyway—

There isn't anything the matter with me except what I told you before—See Dr. Mac said my throat might turn into TB if I wasn't careful—said it had fine chances to—if I wasn't careful—

But I really feel so much better and I've only been here three days—

He said TB or pneumonia—and he rubbed it in so hard—that's why I came down here as he said—

—It's warm here in spite of rain—The city like a fairy city last night—looking out into the mist.

Alfred Stieglitz · New York City · [February 19, 1918] +

Tuesday A.M.

What am I to say?—My heart is thumping away at a rate—it would make you laugh. —And it's as loud & has no business to be heard.—

—And why?—

It's raining. It's raw & cold.—I really slept a few hours.—The first in three days.— And although every bone ached & squeaked as I arose I felt not quite so completely lost as I had for those hours since that envelope came.—

—And here I am at 291 the floor littered with open boxes—Prints by many people— photos—Cézanne, Van Gogh like one I sent you—there were two envelopes—my mail as I thought—ads—

I was just about to leave the table, it's next to the door, & it's piled up with stuff—& the little white figure[515] stands on it—in the corner—

I noticed a long tube—crushed—looked like an ad—At first I didn't feel like looking at it—so crushed—& I thought "anyone sending an ad so carelessly"—

But I suddenly spied through the packing paper—backwards Canyon—I began tearing up the tube—crushed—No wonder my heart was thumping—there was something of yours in there & was there anything left?—

What a careless mother you are.—I've said that before. But a mother.—And that's the main thing.—

You can't imagine my surprise—no not surprise—I stood there spellbound—that's the word—like I stand spellbound on a rare morning—dawn—in summer—or late spring—or fall—I don't know.—

I don't think I ever saw anything so beautiful as these four bits of color on paper—One as fine as the other—I have to laugh at the crushed paper—It's all so you—the beauty—& the crushed part—The blue nude[516]—

It's as if what has nearly set me crazy the last few days was fully there before me—

How did you ever get that on paper?—And the other is very wonderful too—Very— & the others—All—

—It's all so queer again—that which is between you & me—I don't know what it is— Do you?—Just play—children in this world of ours—Play—The child's life—All so real— so much more real than when the child grows up & forgets what play is—

I must see how I can have that paper straightened out—I want to give the world much pleasure—I know the men will be staggered & the women too—just through intense beauty —so living.—A Little Girl—Who is she?—Where is she? They ask.—

—Yesterday.—The two women for whom I brought down the drawings of yours didn't come.—But Cramer came. And he brought a woman. A woman of about thirty-three or so— New England born—has adopted two children—don't know whether she's married—She was brought to see "New Art"—Gosh! The room looked a sight & it so tiny—but the light is perfect—She had never seen anything "new"—I showed her your watercolors. Cramer hadn't seen them. There was great interest—More than interest—Cramer said when he saw the *Nude* "Where does she get all that from?"—I laugh.—I then showed Hartley—Marin—

—Oddly enough while walking up 5th Avenue at eleven P.M. with Dewald—Mr. & Mrs. Cramer accosted us & took us to their little apartment—72nd Street near Third Avenue —They have two little kids.—A real live home—

—It was one when we got away. Cramer told me the woman remembered only your things—the Marins & Hartleys seemed "thin" to her after she had seen yours.—I laughed.— And she seemed to have said: "Mr. Stieglitz fixes his eye on you & then starts talking"—Do I? —Well, I laughed all day yesterday—My heart was so black—I couldn't—dared not—think

515. Lynes 66.
516. Probably Lynes 242.

260

—Not until the wire had come from San Antonio—And all day people came—Cramer says the room is tiny but the feeling is no different than upstairs!—Freer if that be possible.—Bruno spent several hours with me—& it was great the stories he related about Otto Kahn & Coady (you probably don't know either)—but they were stories of value to me—Bruno didn't know that—"Value"—what do I mean?—It's of value to me to know why my feet are cold & to know that they won't be so cold if I know where to warm them—

It's of value to me to see—seeing begets seeing—

—It's all so funny—the outside world—the "thinness" of most people—surface—surface—nothing but surface—& even that is of a rather mediocre quality.—

—And several ghosts appeared in the afternoon—people I hadn't seen in a year or so—One, a man, just back from Maine—had gone there to get rid of neuritis in the arm—what I have—A woman who is still "looking for"—she has been "looking for"—for years—Lewis—the etcher wanting to know why people like his work but don't buy it.—He has just gotten married. About forty.—Haven't seen his wife.—He's fine.—she must have courage & muscles—

—And so it went all day—& all were filled with laughter & good nature—Strand turned up & was surprised to see me so hilarious—the room as if swept by a tornado—He looked at me—?—I told him as we went out "I guess you didn't quite understand"—But the wire had come—the tension released a little—

Dewald called me up when I got home at seven—I was to meet him at the German Theatre[517]—He said: "To laugh"—a farce—I went—The farce was stupid—the first really poor thing I ever saw there—It's lucky I had laughed so much before—

So you see it was a mad sort of a day for me—On my way home I had stopped in at Elizabeth's.—She & her friend & Davidson were sitting there—I told Elizabeth of your telegram & the one from Canyon from the Western Union people—

—I felt all day—& have been feeling for days—so separated from all—yet never so much a part of all—so indescribably human—

And here are those four babies of yours—

The Little Girl herself—

—But I'm waiting to hear what the ailment is.—Don't you hide anything—I know you are not the hiding kind—but you don't want people to "bother"—& so you keep back without—

You understand—I don't know how to say it—All the words seem so wrong—so knifelike—hiding—keeping back—all terms not applicable to you—

517. Stieglitz saw Franz von Schoenthan's farce "Die golden Spinne" at the German Theatre; see "The Week's Happenings," *NYT*, Feb. 24, 1918, 54.

Georgia O'Keeffe · [San Antonio, Texas] · [February 23, 1918]

Isn't this the wildest paper you ever saw[518]—Leah spent the night with me—we just had breakfast and came down here—Stopped on the way at the post office—Your letter about the telegram with the hundred in it—If the chair hadn't been tilted against the wall I'd have fallen backward out of it—

I'm sorry to excite all of you so much—there is one part of my letters to you that you always ignore—I've told you all along not to bother—Not to worry—and you don't pay any attention to it.—

It's a wonderful spring morning—warm and almost sunny—misty sun—

I don't seem to have much of anything to say—The printing office seems to scatter my thoughts—

—This is really a great place—only I wish you were here—the river winds around and the trees over it at night lighted with colored lights—it's like Christmas trees.

I don't know how I feel—a hypo night before last—(it's what Dr. Mac calls—mixed injection—and that doesn't mean anything to me—) made me feel rotten yesterday—and my head is a little off this A.M. but I feel better up and moving than in bed—it's after seven so you know—I haven't been rushing—

Must go—will write later—again today or tomorrow.

Georgia O'Keeffe · [San Antonio, Texas] · [February 25, 1918]

Monday morning—

Been to breakfast and the post-office—your letter about the roll and one from Strand—Gray sky this morning—Sibyl slept with me and got up early and left—It's funny—I'm afraid to sleep alone—Isn't that ridiculous—

Night before last—that is—the day I wrote the yellow note—I went to sleep intending to get up and write you—I was wondering where to find words for what to write—

Can you understand that?—

—Yesterday morning ran away from me—Sibyl was here—In the afternoon we went out to Hot Wells[519] again—Leah's wish—Leah and I had dinner with her father—He is remarkable—eighty his next birthday and more alive physically and mentally than most people ever are—He is wonderful—it was a perfect spring day like in Virginia—only maybe softer and warmer—really almost unbelievable—and the night—if possible—it was more wonderful than the day—quiet—moonlight—and this quaint funny town—and the remarkable old man—who has lived and is old—and is young and—at first said little—but as time went on seemed to take more and more pleasure in us—

---

518. O'Keeffe wrote this letter on bright orange stationery from the Texas Republic Printery, San Antonio, owned by Mose C. Harris, Leah's father.

519. Hot Wells was a hotel and bathhouse in San Antonio.

Leah was sick—a terrible cold—fever a hundred and two—the woman at the baths told her—but you can't stop her—

She is so wonderful—and not strong—and won't give up—Maybe she wouldn't be so wonderful if she were different—I suppose she would not be—

The sun is out—very pale through the mist—No—the building I see over there is bright yellow against the gray sky—pale gray sky—

I'm sorry the four things were wrinkled—but some way I can't feel that it matters much —I rather liked the blue-green nude—[520]

I want to make more nudes as soon as I feel like working—wanted to for some time— some time before I left Canyon—I'm feeling better—yes really—but I don't seem to have a feeling of push—I have to have to work—

One thing that is great is that there are so many things I want to do—paint I mean— Things look so wonderful to me—

You know—I didn't care—No that's not the way to say it—I just couldn't leave that stuff around Canyon—and I hadn't energy to do it up right myself—the nudes specially couldn't be left.

However, it doesn't matter—

The sky is blue—the mist going down like a cloud behind the red-tiled roof of the yellow brick house.

I must go out—can't miss the sun.

It's almost impossible to stay in here—I'd like to live out—

Yes—I love you very much this morning—quietly—and all of me trusting you—I don't know what I'd do if you were not—It seems I would like to feel all—

First I thought I wanted you to kiss me—hold me in your arms a moment before I go out into the sunshine—then—that didn't seem enough—I wanted you to touch all of me— everywhere—Then I wondered—is it you—and I do not know—Maybe it's just spring—It's another perfect day now that the sun is out.

Alfred Stieglitz · [New York City] · March 1, 1918 +

Friday Noon—It was after eleven when I got away from home.—I was ready to leave before nine—Mrs. Stieglitz started a discussion.—I hadn't seen her since Sunday night—Discussions after twenty-five years lead nowhere—She is a woman who cannot put herself into anyone's place but her own—she wants agreements in which only her feelings are considered & no one else is to have any feelings!—Not an unusual case. But a masterpiece of its type!—There was no "quarreling"—no excitement on my part—It has all become such ridiculous childishness to me —Of course I understand her nature—& I have considered it to a degree for twenty-five years that I know no other human could or would have.—

I won't go into details—I got down here a little while ago—have had nothing to eat or

---

520. Probably Lynes 242.

drink as yet—Gaisman had arranged for me to see the Vice President of the American Lithograph Company—Thinks I might be of service there.—Mrs. Liebman had called up that on Monday I'm to hang photos at the Young Women's Hebrew Association[521]—

And I feel as if I'd sooner or later find the only rest in the woods—I guess I'm impossible—

—I did get some sleep last night—I was so played out by the time I got to bed—I had ridden around in a bus for over three hours—Had gone to my mother's to see if she was in—She was not—So I rode in the bus—just to rest & know I was moving—& no one could disturb me—

—It's raining today—I don't even see newspapers—It's a mad existence—mine—Perhaps stupid.—Idiot like.—But at least it's one that comes from the inside.—

—I said to the cook this morning it seemed as if Mrs. Stieglitz's idea of life was money & lies—And money & lies I suppose are bedfellows—Inseparables.—And I for the world of me don't see why money & truth can't be bedfellows.—Inseparables. I know they could if people weren't so stupid—so full of fear—

—No I'll say nothing—I'm too full—& so darn quiet—

I wonder how you are faring—The health—Eating enough?—And sleeping—lying in bed—

—It's March 1st—I guess I'll run up to the [Y.W.H.A.] to get something into my stomach—Rather unromantic—I'd rather sleep than eat—Perhaps in the near future I'll have my bed in here—If there were running water I'd do it at once.—

There's an envelope just been handed in—San Antonio—I'll open it—

—An hour later.—

Well, what am I to say—It's the queerest thing in the world how "coincidences" will persist as far as you & myself are concerned—

Wright came in as I was in the middle of your letter—he looked worried—Army business—I finished reading your letter—It was just as if I felt you coursing through & through my whole being—Like warm sunlight—& the quiet of clear endless night—You see words convey little—my words—I don't seem to find them—Your words to me are like your pictures—you have a greater gift of expression on paper than I have—

—I'm glad I am because it means something to you that I am—& I'm glad I am because through it I know that you are—

—And wasn't it queer that just as I had finished reading your letter a registered package came from Canyon[522]—the letter carrier came in—& the package so properly packed up and registered—I had to laugh at how I had been "obeyed"—my wishes carried out—I looked—Wright too looked—And I told him how between his work & yours I knew what color signified

521. As Stieglitz noted in a letter to O'Keeffe of February 4, 1918, he had agreed to organize an Exhibition of Pictorial Photographs, American and European, including twenty-nine photographs by himself and other members of the Photo-Secession, at the Young Women's Hebrew Association in New York, on view March 6–24, 1918.

522. Among other works, O'Keeffe had sent Stieglitz watercolors she had made the previous summer in Colorado; Lynes 213, 218–225.

—And I told him how you represented two poles—equally perfect—Female & Male—This all after the casual remark he dropped as soon as I had opened the package: "What lovely color"— I told him what I had told Bluemner night before last about color as I felt it—having discovered its meaning through the work of yours & of Wright's—

Wright said: "O'Keeffe's isn't painting—it's the beginning of a new art"—

I nearly fell over—that's what I know—I don't call it art—I call it by any name— I simply know it exists—something quite definite to me—

Georgia O'Keeffe · [San Antonio, Texas] · [March 6, 1918]

This noon I just mailed you a letter written this morning—and when mailing it got your very big fat one—forty-four pages[523]—Did you know it was so much—I expect the paper in that letter and the nine cents it took to send it would about furnish you two meals at your twenty-nine-cent rate. You know I cannot but laugh when I know that in my pocket are two checks amounting to $125—I can't exactly understand and yet maybe I can—

Many things I can't exactly understand—and yet I can—maybe.

You know Willard has a wife—somewhere—I don't know where—Evidently not known here because I have been taken for his wife till it's funny—and he has a son finishing high school this year—here—I haven't seen him but he told me about him—Both bother him a lot—I didn't ask questions and he didn't tell me—

It almost seems that this is the first sunny afternoon since I've been here that I've been left alone—I like it—I'm tired—am tilted back in a white chair in the side lawn—I say *in* because it's fenced—nice trees—spreading fat-looking fig trees—gray—with a few leaves just out—and some other taller trees—very soft and feathery—It's almost hot—just right here in the shade but I don't want to go out in the sun—and it's so wonderfully quiet—

Willard hasn't phoned me today—I know why—He probably will later—It's so queer a world—An idea went through my head so often yesterday—Why do you let me be with Willard so much—it doesn't matter—but—

—I did not obey you when I had the package neatly packed—I just happened to ask a neat person to do it—The first grade teacher in the Training School[524]—I had asked her to do it before you said anything—

Those are the things that seemed so bad—They will continue to seem bad too—The one I asked you to return is for her[525]—She liked it so much I wanted to give it to her right then but she insisted on sending it with the others and I know it no use to try to persuade her so wrote on the back of it—

I wish you could see the funny little Mexican man who does things around here—queer brown and black face—blue shirt—oyster trousers—red handkerchief in his pocket and red

---

523. Stieglitz's letter written from February 27 to March 3, 1918, was forty-two pages long.
524. Anna Hibbets.
525. In a letter of March 1, 1918, Stieglitz noted that on the back of one of the watercolors O'Keeffe had recently sent him, she wrote that she wanted it returned.

tobacco bag—He has a creepy kind of movement—We can't talk much but we have a great smiling acquaintance—He just crept around—he is very little—and told me I have a great place to sit here and that it's pretty hot—I agreed and told him I didn't know he could talk so much—that he had fooled me and he just laughed and laughed—twisted up his face and shoulders—He is great—

Birds sound so nice—Your speaking of cold seems—oh so far away and impossible—

Wright—he will have to go to war or do something about it, won't he—I don't want him to go to war—It seems like—why it seems outrageous—Seems to me he should be moving.—Why doesn't he get busy and learn to speak Spanish right away—

There isn't going to be any place for some of us to live for awhile—or is it ever—

Leah and I have just about decided to farm—decided it would be least objectionable—I don't believe I could stand Canyon anymore—They say and do and stand for so many things I can't be roped in for—I can't begin to tell you what a relief it has been to get away—Running around with their eyes shut and suspicious of anyone who doesn't run with them—Leah tells me I'd be crazy to go back—she is returning the tenth—She can't stand the work and the climate up there—Dr. Mac told her she had to come right back here—It's almost a misfortune that Leah and I ever met because when we get together the wheels in our heads go so fast we turn over most anything—

I wanted to talk some more about Wright and art—

My things not art—Well—I'd just like to know why art or painting should be any particular thing—I'm not saying that my work is either—you understand—I'm quite content that it shouldn't be either if many things I've seen are.

—Why should the particular thing he is doing be art or painting any more than what I am doing—Maybe Chase was the painter—creator of art—He was just as cocksure of himself as Wright—I liked Wright's painting last spring better than any I ever saw—I would like to have it—I've wanted it often—and I don't know of any other I've ever seen that I want like that one—would like to love and care for almost like a person—

—Isn't that funny—I've often wondered if it would wear—stand daily living with—

My things are only a means of relieving my mind—I don't care whether they are painting or what they are—It doesn't matter to me in the least—but I do have to laugh at his saying it isn't painting—

—My Mexican just crept by with a broom with a red handle—

Must go—

I have more to say but it doesn't come to me because I just thought of something I must do for Sibyl—I sleep alone now—I'm not afraid anymore—

Georgia O'Keeffe · [San Antonio, Texas] · [March 14, 1918]

Thursday morning—

Your letter about the concert—

Your letters—why you know I like them but it occurs to me that you need taking care of

—I've been thinking of it often lately—and your telling me to eat—I always eat all I can but darn it—my internals must be made for some other purpose—They don't care much for food—However I'm not starving like you seem to be—

You must take care of yourself—Please do—it's so bad to think of you out in the wind and cold and not eating anything—tearing around all the time—You mustn't do it—

That's so funny for me to say—isn't it—When I know how impossible it is for you to do differently from the way you do—

I would like to know Mrs. Stieglitz too—

—I would probably seem very queer to her—but I would like to meet her—

Night—

People and things—

The architect's brother—gray—a son in the army—took me to see a girl he thought great to look at—has been telling me about it often—She is in a shoe-shining place on the street —but wasn't there—I'm to go again now that I know where she is—

Then to see some pictures—a Bohemian photographer—large map of Europe on the wall—pins stuck in it—An artist was there who had been living twelve years in Mexico till the revolution—it was interesting—A man and woman came for a photograph that had been made of a boy—and they both cried in the other room—I enjoyed the talk—it seemed more like 291 than most anything I ever saw—I'd like to go again but I probably won't—

—Then—oh more folks and they wanted me to go to the country for supper— I wouldn't—it seemed colder and I am bent on fixing this throat if possible—and coughing again makes me mad—So I wouldn't risk it—and I didn't want to go anyway—So they got their stuff and all came up to my room for supper—it was very funny—

—I'm glad they are gone—

Leah comes in the morning—I will surely be glad to see her—Lucy[526] wants me to go out to the ranch tomorrow too—Well—I said I didn't know—I'm not planning—

I hate to think I have to do anything because I said I would—

A new idea has sort of grown around in my head the past few days—since I painted last—

I was thinking about what you wondered about what you get out of my things—As near as I can see it—it's this way—

I work in a queer sort of unconscious way—more feeling than brain—I seem to throw my brain away sometimes—Maybe I haven't any—Maybe feeling isn't the word I should use—and maybe I shouldn't say I throw my brain away—

I think I see how Wright works—Our heads work so differently that it's funny—

—What you get out of my things often surprises me—Still it is usually just another way of saying what I said—or it is sometimes saying something that I probably would have said if I could have—and painted because I can paint things I feel and do not understand when I can't formulate them into words—

ALL THE WORLD GREETS YOU, 1915–1918

---

526. Lucy was a friend of Sibyl Browne's.

—Still I sometimes wonder—is it because you think much of me—

—What you have of mine is a whole woman spread out[527]—

My idea was—some colors I put together—The thing they are in is bad—but as colors they talk—I feel like saying I found some new colors—and finding them saying something I hadn't been able to say before is like feeling something I had never felt before—

What the things have meant to you has made me conscious of myself in a way—Not when I work I guess—but it seems it would be nice to live in a world where everyone painted like everyone talks—there would be nothing unusual about it then—

Guess I better quit talking about it—I get all tangled up—

You speak of having something framed that you call an embrace—Well—I don't know what it is—I forget about them—

When they are made I almost forget them—and when they are gone to you they are almost entirely out of my head—

It's really nice of you to keep them for me—or for anyone—I wouldn't take such good care of them myself—

—When I was trying to remember what you might call the embrace I remembered an old pastel on white paper I think that looked as if I had gone stark crazy and all the springs in my head are broken loose at one end and sticking out—if I remember it was quite yellow—the yellowest thing I ever made[528]—

Goodnight—

Georgia O'Keeffe · [San Antonio, Texas] · [March 21, 1918]

Good morning—

Back in town—Raining—Mr. Harris fell and broke three ribs so we had promised to phone in daily and ask how he was—Yesterday when we phoned Brack[529]—Leah's brother— was here and wanted us to come in—so we came—

The place we went to camp was the farm. It is a funny little house—no one lived in it for two years—We camped in the front yard for the night—between two lilac bushes—In the back yard under a tree to eat—We really had a wonderful time—wouldn't have come in but for Brack—He is quite a necessity as we need lots of things done—It's good we came anyway on account of the rain.

He surprised us very much by telling us he would go up and stay with us awhile—

268

527. Stieglitz heartily agreed with this comment, writing O'Keeffe on March 19, 1918: "Yes, I have a woman spread out before me—on paper!—In color—in black & white, which is often color too—in letters—Every living breath of you—I have it in my keeping." He added: "And I have to laugh about the brain.—You have quite a bit more than people might think you have—but your brain & heart are so much one.—One as man & woman are one when they complete each other!—Your mind is ever busy—but it is the thing inside of yourself—your *own* children—that come out of you."
528. Lynes 57.
529. Thomas Brackenridge (Brack) Harris.

Willard was going to take us again today—We had starved him and fed him and worked him in turn so he was feeling much better and wanted more I think.

Leah and I have been planning to farm for quite awhile—half in fun but as we both had to come down here and quit work—why not in reality—It is really amusing—everyone has promised donations—the most remarkable kind of donations—A thorough-bred Jersey cow—two goats—one pig—one bedroom set—two small rag rugs—We had a Reo[530] car but Dr. Mac said Leah mustn't run it and I can't and don't want to so we had to give that up—

I think Brack is going to invest in a kitchen stove today before he goes up—he is fond of biscuits it seems—And Mr. Harris wants to visit us but won't come unless he has a bed so I guess he will bring another bed along—We also have one table—already—and a waffle iron among the donations to come—

The farm—well we just decided we were going to have it—Borrow the money— a thousand dollars—and get it and go to it—Willard offered to back us to get it—so did some other folks—We don't know how we are going to pay for it but we are—

—I don't want to go back to Canyon—it seems terrible to think of—I really can't think of anything else I can do and be left alone—

When Leah was back in Amarillo—Watkins asked her—what business I have going on a farm—what do I know about it—Leah laughed and told him I didn't know anything— didn't need to when she knew enough for two—

I didn't tell you about it before because I didn't know whether I really wanted to do it or not—but I am beginning to think there isn't anything else I'd rather do right now—

—It's beautiful up there now—plums and pink Judas trees blooming—everything young green—sleep out under the stars—planning to live out in the open altogether—house only for rain—Billie Mac says she will paper it—

I wonder if you think I've lost my mind—Just being out that little made [me] almost feel like a human being—Makes me crazy to go up and live out—

Must go—

Oh—I almost forgot—The sister writes she found she had to have a horse so she bought one—isn't that a joke—

Georgia O'Keeffe · [Waring, Texas] · [March 28, 1918]

I'm almost asleep but guess I can manage to write anyway—if I don't right now there is no tell-ing when I'll get to it.

I've done such a funny unexpected thing that I feel as though the grin never will wear off my face.

Am on the train going to the farm with Brack—He is reading the paper—It is still early morning haze but cloudy—I can't help laughing when I think how funny it would be if it would rain before we get the kitchen stove up—It and the four chairs are in the car ahead—

530. The Reo Motor Car Co. manufactured cars and trucks from 1905 to 1975.

—I must go back to those telegrams[531]—They surely have had me hopping during the past two days—You see I didn't get the first one from Elizabeth—till Monday night on account of being out on the ranch—They sent it out with a letter from you and one from Claudie and two others and it was misplaced with the letters and I haven't seen any of them yet—However [I] got a duplicate of the telegram—

I knew I ought not go up there now while it's so cold because—Well just because I haven't any business doing it—I feel fine usually on warm days if I don't run around too much but cooler days are bad—

Leah just reared when she came down from the farm last night—no—night before—and I told her—"Just as good as suicide" she remarked—then added—"Maybe I'm prejudiced but I don't think I am—I'm just going to write those folks to leave you alone—They are crazy" —Then last night when I read her your telegrams she said, "Well—I knew by that man's picture —that's what he would say if he cared what happened to you."

However I was pretty much stirred up—

Then on top of that Watkins blew in—Willard and I had just gotten a package and were sitting in the car—lazy—just watching the people go up and down Alamo Plaza—and first thing I knew Watkins was standing beside me—the right-hand side of the car—It was so funny—Well—last night I felt paralyzed—

Many things expected of me today—Sibyl expected me to go camping with her and a lot of her absent-minded friends—and I saw visions ahead of not being very comfortable— Watkins was going to take me shopping for the farm—whatever he thought we had to have— Willard was going to let me ride with him and paint where I wanted to—

I just tell you—last night I almost got up and stole off in the dark alone to escape them all but I went to sleep—

Leah got up at six to come up with Brack on the early train—and while she was dressing she decided she would like me to get up and have breakfast with her—I decided I'd like her to stay over, spend the day and tend to some of the animals for me—Finally we decided I would get up and we would go to the train and tell Brack that she wasn't coming up and give him the things to bring up—

When we got there—Well—I got on the train and came up thinking it an easy way to get out of a lot of—Away from a lot of folks is more to the point—

So here I am at Waring sitting on the store porch across from the saloon—and it's raining—

Brack just went back to the depot to see about having the kitchen stove hauled out and to carry up the stove-pipe—He is nice—alone with him in the country is preferable to the mess I was in in town.

531. On March 21 and 26, 1918, Elizabeth Stieglitz wired O'Keeffe, urging her to come to New York because "he cannot leave." Concerned that he might be ill, O'Keeffe telegraphed Stieglitz on March 26, 1918, asking if he wanted her to come; Stieglitz replied: "It would be criminally careless to travel and suicidal in this climate" (AS to GOK, Mar. 26, 1918, two telegrams). Although he later admitted that "often, often since your illness I have had the greatest desire to go to Texas—to see you for an hour—just an hour—or a day," he had no idea his niece Elizabeth had telegraphed (AS to GOK, Mar. 27, 1918). In addition to Elizabeth Stieglitz's two telegrams of March 21 and 26, Stieglitz also telegraphed O'Keeffe twice on March 26.

And I have to laugh that I'm here because it will raise such a time down there—
Rain is badly needed so I guess I can stand it—
Must stop as he will probably be—Here he comes—

Alfred Stieglitz · [New York City] · [March 31, 1918] +

Sunday Night.—I don't know why I didn't mail the letter to you today—I guess I have no
envelope large enough at home here. No envelopes of any kind.—A sloppy sort of existence—

The daughter is out for the evening—I'm in my room—

—It has been a rather cut-up day.—Sundays really don't seem to agree with my makeup.—There is so much bourgeois about it—What the people do & say on Sundays seems to be
more trying than the trying things they do & say on weekdays—

—This morning I was at Elizabeth's—Elizabeth—Mörling—Davidson—& son[532]—
I showed Elizabeth your telegrams. She smiled.—Seems to have been twice at 291 & both times
I was out.—Thought her every day in the country!—It seems too she finally saw Bourgeois
personally—

I guess I'm living in an entirely different world than anyone else's up here—I seem more
& more ridiculous to myself from a certain everyday point of view.—

—I met Charlie Liebman on the street & as he met me he said: "Thank God I meet
you"—I had to laugh.—It seemed such a relief to see me—& I looked a positive disgrace—My
coat looks a sight—It looks as if riddled by bullets & moths—a combined attack—but neither
bullets nor moths have been near it—It's just age—like the top of my head—minus many
hairs—But the coat is very clean—so really I don't mind.—I want to get a new one—& I just
hate the idea to go & talk clothes to some salesman—or anyone else.—

—Mrs. Boursault, Marie's future mother-in-law,[533] dined with us—She is secretary at the
French hospital—really a fine woman.—And she loves Marie.—And I'm glad—Marie deserves
love—lots of it.—And Strand came for some advice—And so on & on—

—I feel like crawling into bed.—Last night was such a rotten one—

Sunday—How did you spend it? I wonder whether I'll hear from you tomorrow—
The first letter since the telegraphing—

You know you telegraphed you were feeling fine—I hope that's literally true—That
every day you feel stronger—

Today I tried hard to think a little less of you—that is not less of you—but not let my
mind dwell too much on the thought of you—Do you know why?—Silly isn't it—There are
a thousand & one things I'd like to ask you were you here—& still I know I wouldn't let you
answer any—I really don't know whether I want to ask anything of consequence—or anything
of inconsequence—I guess I just mean I'd like to have you near me—And still when I feel that

532. Gilbert Cummings Davidson.

533. Stieglitz's former secretary at 291, Marie Rapp, was engaged to George Boursault, son of Albert K. Boursault, a member of
Stieglitz's group of photographers, the Photo-Secession.

something seems to tell me you wouldn't be as happy as you are where you are now—not now—

—Happy—What a ridiculous bourgeois word.—What I mean is that I feel, taken all in all, it is better for you to absorb the sunlight of the south—see the Mexicans—& the reds & brilliant colors generally—than to be here in this grayness & dampness—even though—

—But you know what I mean—Do I clearly know—

—But always one thought comes to the top: *It's glorious that She Is.* I then feel as if you were sitting right opposite to me both your hands in my hands—& the eyes looking straight into mine—a tiny smile—

Not a word—Yes, we understand—

And then you might run away & play with a child—or a man—or a woman—or flowers—or birds—or paints & brushes & paper—

—The Great Child—Child Everlasting—Flower Eternal—

It seems that the noises last night on the river—& the locomotive—etc. was the announcement that the clocks had been set an hour ahead—two to three![534] I had set mine sooner—

Good Night—I hope they'll be a letter in the morning.

What is Miss Hibbet's first name, I want to send her that watercolor—

Georgia O'Keeffe · [Waring, Texas] · [April 6, 1918]

It's Saturday afternoon—I don't know what time—We have no timepiece running—Willard brought us out last night and he and Brack went to San Antonio this morning—Both had to get back to town—and we forgot to set a watch before they went—It's great not even to know the time—

If I could cut my hair off it seems I would be quite happy—I've been lying here wondering if I dare—I don't know—but it seems to be the most civilized thing about me and I'd like to get rid of it—

I wish you were here to talk to—We had such a time yesterday I'd like to tell about it —We lunched with Mr. Harris—Then Willard came for us and we did our shopping—

Just as we were ready to start for the country—Willard made me perfectly furious— I don't get angry—maybe I should say *crazy* like that very often but when I do I almost lose my mind—It was terrible—Leah had a terrible time patching it up—I didn't want to ride in his car even—

Oh, it was awful—it was also very absurd—However—Leah fixed things so we at last got started between three and four—It is about forty miles up here—About twenty miles out of town a storm broke—

The clouds have been marvelous—wild green and blue and dirty yellow rolling over the

---

534. In an effort to conserve fuel during the war, the United States Congress instituted daylight savings on March 31, 1918, for the first time in the country's history; see "Daylight Savings Which Begins Today," NYT, Mar. 31, 1918, 58.

dark green and blue hills—it was like Willard's and my falling out—Really great right at that time—It rained so hard we had to stop and just sit there all shut in while everything that the heavens can send down tore around us—Leah and I in the red blankets—We had food along and ate supper—

Finally it cleared but streams were so swollen that we couldn't get past—the hardest rain in over two years they say—

We were on a strip of road about a mile long—near a little store—Leon Springs Camp —with about five or six other cars—they were all full of soldiers—and streams at either end of the mile strip of road—swollen so that nothing could pass—It was very funny—a wonderful sunset—a fire—a long dark bridge—three or four hours we had to wait—and it was so funny to see how the different folks took it—An ambulance was stuck in one stream—

It was great—Then the ride in the dark—

I forgot to tell you that while we waited in the storm—I was afraid—it was while we were still driving—before it got so bad we had to stop—Willard knew I was scared—I don't remember exactly how or exactly why—but I knew he felt abused—I was on the back seat alone and I leaned forward—scrambled over the spading fork and box of all kinds of things and kissed him—

I know it gave him a large surprise and I debated for some time—but I wanted to— so I did—

—It was all amusing—

After the water went down we rode along quietly for a long time—the roads are mostly rock—white ahead and the green trees at the sides and the darkness all around—till we came to a dirt hill—no—rock—

[April 13, 1918]
This was written a long time ago—I'm not going to take time to tell all the rest of it—how we got stuck half in the mud and half on the rocks and couldn't move in any direction and then how the Dutchman[535] we get milk and butter and eggs from came along—a little drunk and pulled us out with his Ford.

Leah and I laughed till we almost died—sitting on automobile tires in the back of the Ford—to hold it down so it would pull better—Feet sticking out each side—

—Then the old man liked our company so well that he wouldn't let the other car loose and Willard could only follow—tooting his horn as hard as he could to be let loose—up hill and down—It was really one of the funniest times I ever had—

Then at our gate—I got out to open it—almost stuck again—the wheels spinning and car snorting—puffing and raging like a great black beast—enough red on it to add to its seeming fury—

When we got home—Leah—standing there—the blanket draped around her—falling off—one hand on her hip—a characteristic critical attitude—Looked at the car awhile—then she looked at me—and remarked—

535. The "Dutchman," Dr. Louis Zoeller, whom O'Keeffe also referred to as the "German," lived down the road from the farm where O'Keeffe and Harris were staying. He was a veterinarian.

"George—I believe I've lost my respect for a Hudson Super Six—We won't have one—We will have a Ford—You have to have one anyway to pull you out of ditches—Why have anything else."

Willard laughed—The great beast snorting in the dark was wonderful—

This was all a long time ago—Brack went to Laredo that day—It was before I went to town last.

Georgia O'Keeffe · [Waring, Texas] · [April 17, 1918] +

It's an awfully long night—misty stars once in awhile but mostly just darkness and dampness—my loose hair felt too cold and damp when my face turned on it—restless—sleepless—that I had to braid it—I was rather savage as I sat up to do it—

Many singing things—a hoot owl and a cow bell—It really sounded great—You would laugh—maybe think me crazy if I told you that it's still dark—very black dark and I'm sitting here in my coat—having already had coffee—Sam[536] was out—his snoring helped keep me awake and he had to be back in town early—I was glad of an excuse to get up—Lying in bed gets very monotonous when you can't sleep—and maybe another reason why I can't sleep is because I want to talk to you—

You know my head seems to be in whirls—I don't have my feet on the ground and don't much care about it but it seems that I ought to care—

So many things have come up lately where theory and reality (now maybe I've unconsciously expressed it all right there—solved it for myself without knowing or intending) don't seem to work together—

My brain works differently from the instinctive feelings I have for many things—It's the same thing in life that I've known in art for a long time—

When Leah was in town night before last—we lay flat on our backs—My right arm through her left one—talking—for a long time—When we were ready to go to sleep we noticed for the first time how characteristic the position was and both laughed—

We wouldn't put our arms round one another—Just the linking together seems to fit—

—Still—tonight—I've been thinking very much about us—

Life has been so different to us—still seems to have made very much the same thing out of us—No that's not what I mean—

We are alike and yet not—The difference seems to be—race—breeding—traditions[537]—Still—she is one of the very very few who understands—

But last night—no—it's this night I'm still on—I was wondering—

When morning comes I intend to go out and plant tomato plants and dig in the garden—

I don't know—

536. Sam was a friend of Leah Harris's.
537. O'Keeffe may be alluding to the fact that Leah Harris was Jewish.

They asked me to talk at one of the high schools next Wednesday—Do I want to—Maybe I'll say something I ought not—Still—I have a lot of things on my mind that I want to say—

My throat seems to be feeling pretty good—I was rather discouraged a week or so ago—but it's better now—In fact I'm as fat as I ever am—Can do as much as the average person—running around and that sort of thing—in a day and not mind it—

I ought to be thinking of going to work—Am I going to hoe beans or misinform the young and unprotected—

—I don't seem to think I ought to go back for the summer—I could stand the work—could be doing it now for that matter—but the misfitness of it would wear me out in just a little while again—

Still—you say Strand is going to war—I'm glad!

Isn't that funny to say and to feel—No—not funny—it's incongruous for—I seem to want to fit him into the machine and all the time feel that it's a physical impossibility to fit myself in—

Everybody seems to be having a hard time to fit these days—that is—everyone who can think a little—

Lucy is disturbed because she doesn't want to buy Liberty Bonds[538]—I finished yesterday with her—afternoon and evening—poking around old houses and queer corners of San Antonio—in a Ford—Just riding in the Ford is an adventure—She drives so queerly it is like riding a horse that you can't get in motion with—it's between a gallop and a trot—and snorts and puffs and gets hot and she dodges around queer alleys and corners and across streams—all but climbs trees—And every five minutes you marvel at your charmed life—Nothing but a charmed life could survive Lucy's driving—

When the engine stops—and it frequently does—you just wait till someone comes along who looks as though he might not mind cranking it—She is so absent-minded she stops it without intending to—

Well—her brother and sister went over with the Ford Peace Party[539]—They are peace folks and don't want to buy Liberty Bonds—one of the oldest families here and wealthy—The brother will be drafted—he just married—

—Needless to say it's a rather disturbing situation—one brother is in France—the mother has bought bonds—and Lucy isn't looking forward to either buying or refusing—

Really it's a great time to be living—to see how folks behave—

I wonder if it would be very foolish of me if I got a notion that I had to go to New York and talk to you about things—

538. On April 6, 1918, the United States government launched the third "Liberty Loan" campaign of the war to encourage Americans to buy war bonds. With even greater organization than in the past, the publicity department of the Liberty Loan Committee orchestrated lavish patriotic parades throughout the country; see "New York Open Liberty Loan Drive with Subscriptions of $100,000,000," *NYT*, Apr. 7, 1918, 1.

539. Founded by Henry Ford, the Ford Peace Party traveled to Stockholm in 1915 to try to negotiate an agreement to end the war.

I didn't mail the letter of yesterday—simply because I didn't want to—It wasn't that I forgot—

I asked you why you don't come out here—It's a wonderful place—I wonder why everyone doesn't live here—Still—it would be very foolish for you to come—I don't know why—

I just heard a wonderful bird-call—so sweet in the stillness—

Then too—the talk with Sam yesterday—an old friend of Leah's—I think the army will get him soon—He wants to argue about it and we won't argue—we just see he is going—He is thirty-one—very Irish—

It's queer—the different ways it gets different folks—

You wonder if I am really feeling better—or just excited over people and things—I guess I am very much excited—but I am feeling better too—I wish I could keep from getting excited—

—You see—I never knew folks quite like many folks I've met here—Or is it the times—Talking with most anyone seems to be an adventure—or is it me—I don't know—

I'm getting tired—and morning doesn't seem to come—the bird again—

Believe I can sleep now—Guess I'll go to bed—

Alfred Stieglitz · [New York City] · [April 20, 1918] +

Nearly Noon—Saturday—291—a raw day—gray—East wind—I have just come in—I came down at nine & had a wagon here to take a load of chemicals & trays, etc. to Elizabeth's studio where I'm supposed to want to do some work!!—It was funny to see the dishes & pans & graduates & funnels & printing frames arrive there & find a temporary home there. They seemed to look at me & I at them with the same thought—"Why are we here?"

—I wonder whether I'll do anything. Every day it seems more impossible—I seem to be so dead.—

—I walked down Fifth Avenue—Liberty Bond signs everywhere—and women & men & boys & girls accosting one to buy—A sort of Coney Island atmosphere without the ocean—& I looked into the shop windows—Posters everywhere but things to sell—too—Horrible cartoons of the Germans—all other people seem to be saints—they all fiends! Of course they have to be pictured that way to arouse the people to fight—to hate—It's all all right—but somehow I seem to be outside of everything—I understand it all—but I can't be it—

And I saw Old Masters—real ones, early Italian in a new art place—then near it hideous cartoons—A little further on hundreds of war books in Scribner's window—Then a corner window full of wonderful flowers—yellows—& whites—forget-me-nots—great greens—lavenders—I stood there a long while—thought of you—& wondered—about it all—the flowers—the Avenue—the people I've met—the War—you—me—the family—life—My head seemed to swim—

—I looked into the candy shops—& dress places—& men's haberdashery ones—

—And here I am. Alone.—It's very quiet—& cold—& gray.—

Night. It's after 2—I've just come home. And am in bed. After having gotten my feet dried. I had walked home in the rain—& my shoes both were torn.—Strand & I walked.—He, Hartley & I had been to the opera house, last night.—A packed house—we stood way up under the ceiling.—We wanted to see *Coq d'Or*[540]—Hartley had seen it several times.—A ballet with singing—a very original affair—beautifully staged & performed.—Delightful music—very fresh throughout—All of it leaning forward in spirit—music & stage—You would have enjoyed it too.—We didn't hear the *Cavalleria Rusticana*[541]—the first half of the evening. Oh, yes, the ballet's music was written by Rimsky-Korsakov—Russian. The whole thing was Russian—a satire—staged by a Hungarian now here.—

—Hartley & Strand had been at the opening of the *Independent*[542]—Say it's well hung but decidedly unworthwhile—a few good things but nothing that hadn't been seen—No new discoveries.

—Marie came to lunch. Dewald, Wright—Kreymborg later—& Hartley too—All day there were Liberty Loan Parades—the whole Hippodrome[543] was marching too.

—The day was drizzling. Everything seems unreal.—But was glad to hear some good music.—

I wonder how you are. The weather here is killing.—It would have been the end of you had I been mad enough to wire you to come—

Good Night—

I hope you are sleeping well & are continuing to gain strength—

If only that throat were better—It's always on my mind. I want to know you well.—

Once more Good Night—

Georgia O'Keeffe · [Waring, Texas] · [April 26, 1918]

Friday,

Came from San Antonio last night—Received two letters forwarded from there—I never call for mail there anymore—

Hope you didn't worry over my being tired. It wasn't any joke but I'm feeling better—In bed almost all day today—Intending to write but I haven't done it—

Reading more on Strindberg's life—Have *Master Olaf*[544] for next—

Haven't written—because there is something I want to say and it's so hard to say—

---

540. Serge Diaghilev's *Le Coq d'Or* was an opera-ballet interpretation of Rimsky-Korsakov's opera of the same name. Diaghilev's company, the Ballets Russes, toured the United States from 1916 to 1918, performing the work with the Metropolitan Opera Company.

541. An opera in one act by Pietro Mascagni, adapted from a short story by Giovanni Verga.

542. The Second Annual Exhibition of the Society of Independent Artists opened on April 20, 1918; see *NYT,* Apr. 20, 1918, 12.

543. The Hippodrome was a large theater in New York, featuring lavish spectacles with circus animals, elaborate sets, and a five-hundred-member chorus.

544. Possibly Lizzy Lind-af-Hageby, *August Strindberg: The Spirit of Revolt* (New York, 1913); August Strindberg, *Master Olaf: A Drama in Five Acts* (New York, 1915).

It's a very simple fact that I've always known but some way has come to me newly—It's the telling me of why I am not fitting into what is around me here—It's just the old game of truth against what is really a game—

Not being me because I'm not expected to be—

An uncomfortable dislike of letting other people influence me and unable to hold my own—be myself under circumstances—

Working Willard—using him because I know I can—If I liked him it would be all right—

Many things I've found myself doing—unconsciously almost—

My disgust that I'm not worth any more physically—

It seems as though I've just seen myself—I'll write more later—That's why my work is rotten—Too many folks—all taking pieces of me—None enough for me to concentrate on any one thought or feeling—

Everything goes too fast—And I'm tired—And I wanted to cry because you were so lonesome last Sunday—but—Oh—I don't know—everything seems off only I really feel better now that I believe you found out what's the matter—

It has become a kind of nervousness that always has a quick—often cutting reply to most any remark—Willard astonished me the other day by frankly remarking that he couldn't talk to me—I always got the best of him—

I want more than ever to write music—You would laugh if you knew what I want to write now—

Leah is washing dishes—tin pans—crockery—monotonous slush of water rattle—It's slow—quiet—she isn't rapid today—I ought to go wipe them—With each rattle—slush and slop of it all—I wonder what dish it is—It's a noise that would make you want to scream if I could get it into shape—

I always want to write monotonous noises like that—and I don't know how to write anything—

Something very tight ought to be all round me today—

I may fly into a million pieces—

Yes—love me very much only I guess don't touch me—

Georgia O'Keeffe · [Waring, Texas] · [April 30, 1918] +

Greetings—

Your letters last evening were great—There were three of them—two mailed 25th—one 26th—

Did I tell you that the first couple of weeks we were up here Walsh—the postmaster—asked Leah one day who those big fat letters I get were from—She told him in a slow funny way she has of talking sometimes—that she didn't know—that maybe they were bills and he didn't say any more—He never said anything to me about it—

He is just crazy and can't help it because he doesn't know it—

It had rained—the sky was a deep cloudy brilliant blue in the east—Somehow making trees and bushes and hills and dirt at [the] side of the road stand out warm and brilliantly against the blueness—a queer deep blueness—

The color was wonderful—Color doesn't often thrill me—but I walked up the road —it's up hill—then level—then up again to a wonderful view of valley and mountains as you look back—your letters in my hand—the first one open—I not reading because the color of the world just seemed to go through me and through me—I saw colors I had never seen before—

Was it the little of the letter I had read—or was it really the evening or was I just waking up and seeing—

It was getting something through my eyes that I usually have to get through my ears— Maybe more wonderful in that I was getting it that way—

—No it wasn't a woman—It was only a person—

When I got home I went up to a rock pile in the field—you can see the long line of blue hills over trees—and read two letters—One was very like what I had just mailed you—Strange —but not strange—

—I don't remember the next one—intended to read them again today and didn't— It was cold so I looked at the sky—lovely warm pink and lavender—High up and so very far away—

I came to the house and read the last one—It was funny with a hurt all through it— I understand—

I hope you *can* do what you want to with the black paper[545]—Really you are great—

You will be on jury from the 6th till 20th—

You know—I am getting to want to see you so bad I'm afraid I'll have to be moving up that way—It seems absurd—but—I guess I'm usually absurd—

The wind just blew for a minute—such a soft half wind (there it goes again) nice sound —I had to stop and listen—

I guess I ought to go to bed—

I've gardened and cooked and cleaned up and sewed—and walked to town and back— In fact I've worked as hard as I could all day—wanted to do it all—

Leah didn't get up till suppertime—I wouldn't let her—She laughed at me when I was too tired to garden any more and sat down and sewed—

It was too cold to be still and do anything worthwhile—My head doesn't work when I'm chilly—I don't even like to read—I forgot to tell you that I went out foraging for wood and carried it home—

And you know—I was laughing to myself—I remember days at 291—many men—or maybe just a few—standing about—the best way I can express it is worrying over their souls— and I laughed to myself as I went out with a grubbing hoe to get rid of some brush I'm waging war on—What good use I could make of a lot of those long stand around fellows if I could just get them to work a week—and how different the world would look to them in a week if they got out and dug and scratched around—

545. Stieglitz was trying to mount some of O'Keeffe's watercolors on black paper.

A week wouldn't really be long enough—A month would be a short while—
The wind—
Goodnight—I'm tired—
Tomorrow I'm going to try to keep still—but I get a savage sort of satisfaction out of physical work that really tires me—
It's cloudy again tonight—If it doesn't stop raining I'm going to town—

Alfred Stieglitz · [New York City] · [May 1, 1918] +

It's not yet 11—& I have just gotten into bed. Fighting a new cold for a change.—There is an Arctic gale blowing—This morning there was a warm rain—The wind sprang up suddenly from a black gray sky in the afternoon—Strand & I were downtown—I had to deposit something —He went with me for I was terribly nervous for a few hours—A rare kind of nervousness for me—I'll tell you later.—

—Last night was restless & cold—I felt the new cold I had stupidly contracted somewhere.—But I had a wonderful dream—I dreamt I awoke & found you snugly asleep in my arms—breathing gently & regularly.—I looked at you surprised—not knowing how you had gotten there. And it seemed as if you had ever slept there. As I awoke I was holding my pillow firmly in my arms!—

—On my way down to 291 I stopped in at the Anderson Gallery—There is to be a sale of moderns—Picasso, Herbin, Gris, Rivera, stuff which had been entrusted to Coady— Somehow the Parisian owner could get no satisfaction out of Coady so has ordered an auction sale.[546]—Coady published *Soil*—With those moderns there will also be sold some very lovely Persian paintings—& a Greek one—& some Chinese Pottery.[547]—There are two Persian paintings I'd buy if I had money—One is a nude—They are tiny things.—

—As I came to 291 I had hoped to find a line from you—just a line to tell me how you were—What a nuisance I must be to always want to know—As if my knowing brought about a change for the better in you—better in health. Yet I do want to know even if I am a nuisance.—

—I mounted some of your water-colors on black paper.—They looked so alive & beautiful. I kissed one—had to—

And then as I looked out of the window I saw a lot of those wonderful French soldiers walking down the streets in twos & threes—some in taxis.—I felt as if I'd like to send a few down to you to look at—be with—Just looking at them gives one a thrill—

546. In 1914 Michael Brenner and Robert J. Coady, editor of *The Soil: A Magazine of Art* (December 1916–July 1917), opened the Washington Square Gallery, where they exhibited many European modernists artists, including Cézanne. The May 3, 1918, sale at the Anderson Galleries included prints, paintings, and sculpture by artists from Picasso and Gris to Auguste Herbin and Jean Metzinger, belonging to Léonce Alexandre-Rosenberg, a Parisian art dealer; see "Art Notes," *NYT*, Apr. 27, 1918, 14. On May 4, 1918, Stieglitz told O'Keeffe that most of the pictures brought between $10 and $80, with Picasso fetching one of the higher prices at $370.

547. See "$700 for Roman Portrait; Sale of Early Egyptian Art and Chinese Bronzes Brings $12,690," *NYT*, May 4, 1918, 15.

280

Lee[548] came in & I told him how they made me feel the Alps & he laughed & said: Why they are called the "Alpins"[549] —

Everyone else on the street seemed ridiculously puny — magazine cover like — even our tallest soldiers — Some of these Frenchmen are as broad as they are high — some have black beards — some blonde moustaches — They were laughing — & seemed absolutely unconscious of all but the good time they were having. —

Lee looked at your work — I had never shown it to him — he was very enthusiastic — the nudes especially — And as he left Mr. Herschmann, the guest who sang in Lake George turned up. — He is very musical — & is a first class engineer — but has no eye for color. As we were arguing a letter from you. — I saw by the envelope what condition you were in —

I read. — For a few minutes I was so atremble that I thought I'd collapse. — My Child — the quintessence of naked truth — relentless truth — You never wrote a letter quite so terribly great to me — just four tiny pages[550] — World inclusive — All day I have been wanting to telegraph — I have to use every bit of power in me not to chase down to you —

Everything going on in you I understand & feel —

So tired — & what you say about Willard — Yes — and what all take from you — you in pieces —

None see you — Not that Great Big Simple Lovable Child — physically anything but strong — a heart so big — the world — all struggling for freedom — fine expression — that finest Self — Yourself —

You want me to love you — & I have to smile — not to be touched — If I really do feel you all as you are — every bit of you — do you think any part of my body — hand, mouth — would physically touch any part of you — unless I knew that — What — What —

It is unsayable — everything — Your truth is a religion — mine — yours —

And you'd like to write music — that too I understand — I smile — Perhaps — why not — the sound of dishes & water — Do you think I'd scream if I heard it — the music — the dishes —

I wonder why you are so tired & not feeling so well — facing the truth about yourself — the facts — the horror of the whole situation. — I wonder if your state was not aggravated by your periodic disturbance — I hope that that is partly the answer —

— Marin spent the evening with me — I had shown him your work again — he liked one of the red nudes[551] — a terrific one — very much — One I often stare at — Queer the one Wright liked best Marin liked least —

How people react differently — I was glad to have Marin —

---

548. Probably Alfred's brother Leopold (Lee) Stieglitz.

549. During World War I, the Chasseurs Alpins, nicknamed the "Diables Bleus" (the Blue Devils), were a well-known French mountain infantry whose fearless fighting won them their name from the Germans. Their exploits, as well as their blue flowing capes and berets, captured public imagination when they toured the United States in 1917 and 1918 to raise war bonds; see "French 'Blue Devils' Here to Boom Loan," *NYT*, Apr. 30, 1918, 5.

550. O'Keeffe's letter of April 26, 1918, was four pages long (see pp. 277–278).

551. Lynes 176–188.

I felt so miserable—the throat—the constant thought of wanting to fly to you & see to it that you are let alone—permitted to rest—be yourself—Is it impossible to get a little quiet?—

—Tomorrow I have a dentist's appointment—I don't want to break it—This infernal throat—how stupid.—

As I came in I was thinking how can anyone not an ox stand this climate we are having this year—It is really incredible—

How far Waring is away—I wonder if I sat near you would you feel better—quieter— I wonder—

Good Night—

I'd like to dream again—the same dream—

Good Night—

[May 3, 1918]

Night—One o'clock.—In bed. Just got in.—Wide awake.—

Cold gone—I seem to have beaten it off. Dentist.—291—Mounted thirty-five of your small water-colors in folders of large sheets of black paper—They sing—wonderfully. They make a large unwieldy package but that doesn't matter—It may amuse some of the friends when they see me carry it—As it did tonight as I took it to supper—& had it at my feet in the last row of the gallery of one of the fashionable theatres—& walked it up home—letting no one but myself carry it—Hartley, Strand, Davidson & I spent the evening together. Hartley wanted to know at the theatre whether I wasn't going to show the pictures—he was so amused at me. "Stieglitz's Celestial Solitaire" he called it. The pictures are giving great pleasure to everyone—

Davidson came in early. He looked at them a long while.—He liked the freedom of the "new" place—the light—the feeling of the street—the chaotic appearance—

There were many people—I saw those French (they are really French-Italian) soldiers —they are called the Blue Devils—They looked queer today in autos being driven by magazine cover girls—It's walking in which they look so marvelous.—There was a reception of the Anzacs[552] (Australians) today—Also a great group of men—stronger looking than ours— & their getup is much the same as ours but has more style—character—vitality—& enthusiasm —We certainly need a lot of waking up & going through fire—

—The play we saw tonight was an old French one—pleasing—Billie Burke—Henry Miller.[553]—Not to have seen it would have been no great loss.—The "children"—Strand & Hartley—were eager to go to theatre.—

[May 3, 1918]

It's a warm, very warm sunny morning—I stopped writing last night without even saying Good Night.—I suddenly felt so tired.—This morning I found my watch had been an hour slow!!—

---

552. Anzacs was the acronym for the Australian and New Zealand Army Corps fighting in World War I; see "The Origin of Anzac," *NYT*, Oct. 8, 1916, E2.

553. Alexander Dumas' "A Marriage of Convenience," starring Henry Miller and Billie Burke and adapted by Sidney Grundy, was performed at the Henry Miller Theater in April and May 1918; see "Bill Burke Stars with Henry Miller," *NYT*, May 2, 1918, 11.

—The night was full of dreams—Caffin had come to me—had arisen from his coffin—was midway between skeleton & human—was Death living—I seemed too frightened for a moment—He couldn't speak but he seemed to have a language more direct than words.—He made me feel I understood his coming. He insisted I take him to art galleries—& I did—& everyone ran away when they saw us—& pictures fell from the walls—Only a few remained in their places—Very few—

I don't know which they were. That was immaterial—

And he disappeared—I saw Steichen—he had come from France. He had come & talked—And it seemed that the War had not given him a greater vision—& we had a great discussion. He always very fine—yet—just as he was before going to War.—Steichen—And I found de Zayas in Mexico—

Etc., etc.—A roaming dream amongst old friends—

—This morning a letter from Elizabeth. She has had a letter from you[554]—says it's very wonderful. Tells me it has done very much for her.—Makes a great confession.—She needed you—you not her.—I've always known.—Or perhaps you needed her a little too—I doubt it.—But she really is fine—a little young. Her letter is really very unusual—& straight.—

—I wonder what she wrote you—Of course I don't wonder—only I wish that neither she nor anyone else would try to take you outside of your own sphere of feeling—no one can—but they can sap your vitality in trying to—

—There is great applause & great yelling—principally of women—at windows—the Anzacs are passing—The men hardly know what to make of it—Hysterical America must please those men & make them smile—All week—& all last week—Fifth Avenue is one holiday—& it gives me the creeps.—The War is to the people what Matisse was a few years ago here—Excitement—I fear that unless it lasts for years the people collectively will feel but little that is genuine—some mothers, yes,—individuals, yes—But—it's all too ghastly for words & yet the people are fortunate those that can turn the War into a new toy—a new circus—for themselves & their friends—all in the name of Freedom & Truth—Love—Liberty—

I said to Strand yesterday the American thinks himself an *Idealist*—he is usually an *I dealer.*—

—And in coming down I saw a whole squad of girls in khaki—auto squad.[555]—Certainly looked stunning enough—three or four were trying to crank a car—men stood around watching—no man dared offer assistance—They looked so good to look at—& so forbidding too—

—Of course all were strong enough to knock me out in the ring—! It seemed amusing.—

554. On April 26, 1918, O'Keeffe wrote to Elizabeth Stieglitz, admonishing her that she was "trying to make something that does not exist." Admitting that Stieglitz was "probably more necessary to me than anyone I know," she nevertheless thought "we are probably better apart" because "we are both of a temperament that makes physical contact with most anyone exceedingly annoying at times." Chastened by the letter, Elizabeth Stieglitz admitted to her uncle that "perhaps I've been a mischief-maker all around" (Elizabeth Stieglitz to AS, May 2, 1918).

555. The Salvation Army women, who often worked so near the front lines during the war that they were assigned gas masks, wore khaki uniforms; see "The Salvation Army 'Over There,' " NYT, May 5, 1918, 82.

—I have your babies here again—to mount a few more—

I wonder if you have gotten a chance to work—To crystallize—Or whether you are still unable to feel one thing deeply enough to have it find form purely—

And that physical body of yours—is it behaving a little better? And the great tiredness—is some of it gone—

And I have been wanting to wire—but I haven't.—Were you in San Antonio I would.—

—I'm glad you have Strindberg—And how is the music desire—

There are big clouds coming—perhaps a storm—It's very close—

It's 11:30—It's very, very quiet—

Here goes a whole lot of paper to you in this envelope—& so little else in it—And still you must feel—Feel—Do you?—Even the question is stupid—The very fact that I ask a question—

But it's only another way of saying: What you must feel—unsaid.—

I'd like to sleep a very, very long while. I'm tired this morning—tired because I feel so useless—so very unfit—

I wonder how you are—

That's what I'd like to know most just now—And that means I wish you were getting back your old strength—physical—All else would be all right with that back—

I've wondered whether you still have to make injections—You see I have never had a positive statement about your health—your state—& sometimes that gets me half crazy.— Perhaps no positive statement can be made—

Do take care of yourself—if you can—& you can—Can't you?—Tell me all— Everything—

EARLY IN THE MORNING of May 3, 1918, O'Keeffe and Harris were awakened at the farm in Waring by their neighbor, the "Dutchman," Dr. Louis Zoeller. Unsure of his intentions, Harris got a gun and scared him away. When Stieglitz learned of this, he panicked. Still worried about O'Keeffe's health, he now believed she was also in danger. Because he had jury duty until May 20, he decided to send Strand to Texas to possibly accompany O'Keeffe back to New York. Of all his potential delegates—Dewald, Gaisman, or Elizabeth Stieglitz—Strand was the most likely candidate: objective and methodical, as well unencumbered by either a job or family, he would provide Stieglitz with the clearest assessment of the situation. Stieglitz knew that Strand hoped he and O'Keeffe might rekindle their "perfect relationship,"[556] but he also knew that she did not reciprocate the younger photographer's feelings. Strand left New York almost immediately and arrived in San Antonio on May 12, 1918.

556. Strand to AS, May 15 and Sept. 5, 1917. In a letter to Emmy's brother Joseph Obermeyer of October 31, 1918, Stieglitz claimed that Strand went not only as O'Keeffe's friend but also as a "wooer" and that he offered to marry her.

Letters from you and Strand Thursday evening—

They sounded so helpless it seemed I must go up and help you out—How I don't know—

Leah and I planned to come to town Friday A.M.—seven o'clock train—I had been trying to get her to come all week and she wouldn't—She wasn't well—It was rainy and cold and dismal out there—

I wrote you Tuesday—Wednesday I sewed—a perfect mania for it—Thursday the same —I wanted to paint but was too tired—Working Tuesday seemed to make me too tired to try it again—.

Now for the climax—At least so it seems to me.

I've been awfully nervous—scared of wuzzy worms and crawling things and they seem to take to me like ducks to water—

—It was after twelve when I went to bed Thursday night—I had slept 'til nearly noon— off and on—hadn't gotten up anyway—

Was awfully tired—glad to be in bed—Outdoors—it was raining—All ready to go to town in the morning—The chugging of a car—strong lights on the bushes waked me up—it was all on Leah's side of the house—

Well—I thought first of Willard—then knew he wouldn't be out in the rain—then thought of Sam—then Leah's voice told me—something wrong—She was asking very calmly —"What do you want?"

To make a long story short—it turned out to be the Dutchman who had pulled us out of the mud that night—He went back and stopped his engine—and—

I have to go—so must hurry—

Anyway when he came back with a searchlight—I was in bed with Leah and—after a moment's talk—the searchlight fell on Leah's hand and the black revolver in it—

Conversation turned and he was off in a very few minutes—

I looked at the clock—2:15 A.M.

Well—I've been a wreck ever since—Came to town and have been in bed most of the time since—Wanted to send a night letter last night but couldn't make it—

Almost noon—I got up—today—I have never been as glad to see daylight as I was yesterday A.M.—Leah calm as if nothing had happened—I haven't told her that I won't go back to the country with her—but I don't think I will—

When I see how I'm feeling it scares me—It makes me think I need a caretaker—

Well—I was feeling quite "up a tree"—not knowing what to do with myself—when —Sibyl came in and told me Judith[557] is in town and the Maurys are rearing because I've been here all this time and haven't been to see them—

Gosh—It's all Hell—Something must be done—

---

557. Judith Maury was a friend whom O'Keeffe met in Virginia and whose family lived in San Antonio.

Must go and have my head washed—The Maury circus has to be met and I might just as well get ready for it.

However—I have waked up to the fact that I'll never be my human self again till I can some way get quiet—

Have to go now—
General Delivery—San Antonio

Alfred Stieglitz · [New York City] · [May 9, 1918]

Am I in a trance—floating in space—what am I? Who am I?—Where am I?

—Since last night eight until now—1:30 night the day after—twenty-nine–thirty hours—I have been talking—& on things pertaining to vital questions relating to so many very close to me.—First of all last night for nearly four hours a session with Mrs. Stieglitz.— I dropped from sheer mental fatigue—You can have no conception of the ghastliness of such hours—As I came into my room I sat there my head throbbing, eyes aching, everything seemed to be swimming—Kitty, the daughter, was in my mind—much—You—much—291—the men —Marie—The question of your coming East—my going to you to save you a trip which might put you back months—Jury—the situation here at home—certain work at 291—

And then out of the clear sky I sat there & saw you in Waring—You girls—& I wondered how you liked bugs & creepy things—how they would affect me—& then it flashed through my mind what would happen if you two girls there alone were suddenly confronted by a man at night—Were you ready—Did you have revolvers—Was there a watch dog—Above all would you be frightened—

And I thought of myself there perhaps useless as protection—no revolver in my hand in thirty-seven years—muscular strength nearly equal to zero.—A great picture.—

—Jury duty—on a case—Irish—amusing—Brought in a verdict for the Irish—

Got to 291 at 2:30—Strand there—a letter from you—San Antonio—& I gasped when I read your letter—the night with the intruder—the bugs & creepy things—exactly what went through my head last night—

I read the letter to Strand.—Something must be done.—Was I to wire to you to come. —Not really knowing your physical condition that was impossible.—*Above all I want your strength back.*—Overtaxing yourself might set you back—I went over the ground with Strand from every angle.—It was finally decided he go to San Antonio—

You may have seen him before you get these lines.—He will tell you all—exactly as I feel about everything—the situation here—

I have been talking to him from 2:30 until now 1:30—eleven hours!!—& all about the one thing—Several times we were interrupted for very short periods—Benton & Demuth were in—Benton is to be soldier—Kenneth Miller came in—I was glad he came—

Strand can tell you all—And there was a letter from Mrs. Caffin—she writes to see me tomorrow.—I don't know—jury duty—Yesterday afternoon Bruno turned up & we had quite an unusual hour together—Zoler & Strand present.—

Strand to see you.—Just a year ago that I took down your things from the walls of the Little Room—really the end of "official" 291—Monday, May 14, it was.

—In a way I have done the impossible during the year—

I wonder whether you are in San Antonio or whether Leah has coaxed [you] back to Waring—I wonder so many things—

Your work hasn't come—has it been mailed—somehow I wish it were here—with me —now—here—

I'm very quiet—but my mind is working away at a great time—as if it were trying to penetrate *into* things—to get at the essence—to be able to put it into form—

—I have wired to find out how you are—

There is a great deal I want to tell you—but I think Strand will give you the substance of it—

—The night is bitter cold. Clear. Starlight. The morning was summer-like.—I went without a coat—There was a sudden wind—at two—icy from the west—growing colder & colder—We walked briskly—

You'll certainly be greatly surprised to see Strand standing before you.—I wonder how he'll find you looking—feeling—how he'll find that you actually are—physically.—The rest I know.—He can't know quite as well as I do.—

—My head is swimming—I had better go to bed—I'll get this off first mail in morning—

If you were standing beside me here—you could not be closer to me than I am to you now—It's just as if I were trying to make you feel the tremendousness of something for which there are no words—

Remember take care of your strength—You need quiet—Is it in you to get it?—I think so—It is not easy—

Good Night—

—It will be time to get up soon—

Little Girl—Tonight you're that—I hope you are over that terrible shock—Entirely you can't be—Leah is a wonder—

It's queer how it was decided that Strand go—

Good Night—

Georgia O'Keeffe · [**San Antonio, Texas**] · [**May 11, 1918**]

Friday night—more likely Saturday morning—I hear roosters crowing—foolishly drank coffee for supper and I can't sleep—Wrote the sister a long letter—Thought about you—Why I just think of you very often—that's all there is to that—

Had two talks today—A long one with Mrs. Maury this morning—Five daughters and a son—son youngest—a lieutenant—in Washington State holding down a camp of German-born American soldiers—rather—helping to hold it down—I made a remark about how age—weathering—improved her service flag—then my mind wandering on about flags I remarked that I thought the Russian colors so much nicer than ours—

Then the circus began—

Judith is in bad anyway because her husband has ideas—And she is so afraid I'll get her in worse I guess—She finally hauled me off—but it wasn't dangerous at all as far as I could see—

It's amusing to see what fear those girls have of her—

I'm really curious—Judith thought she was getting ready to eat me and I didn't feel it at all—Judith said anyway she didn't want to risk it—It was funny—

—Then I came home—Lunch—undressed—then your telegram—I answered it—curiously quiet—Strand coming—It seemed a bit surprising—quite natural—didn't interest me greatly—I seemed to feel more concerned over your unquiet—

Sewed—Sibyl came—we sewed—No she didn't—I just continued to sew—talking—

After supper we went to see a friend of Sibyl's—a charming old lady friend of Sibyl's mother[558]—We really had a great time at her house—It seemed to be real fun—It's the best arranged house I've been in here—Maybe that helped—Isn't it queer how bad houses are as a rule—It was lots of fun—her hair white—but she was so nice—It was great—

—When we were leaving she remarked "Miss O'Keeffe—you look so different tonight I wouldn't have known you."—My hair was plastered back tight and I had on a skirt about the color of the hair—nondescript brown velvety feeling stuff—It makes me look so funny—I rather enjoy it—Nothing decided about it—You don't know what color it is—

Wearing black makes my hair seem black—and it had been high before—She remarked that I looked very well in black—with black furs—She even remembered my hat—Sibyl laughed—she hates my hair this way—but I've always worn it this way at times—It relieves my mind—only very few folks like it—You would—The plainness of the hair was the only thing about me that wasn't nondescript—We had a great laugh over it—I wonder if she would have remembered me if I hadn't been in black before—I enjoyed what I had on tonight—Have been wearing it two or three days—

We walked home in the dark—Walking was very nice too—

Everything looked so wonderful—and—I wondered if it was so because Strand is coming—I kept thinking how much fun it would be to see it with him—Finally—I remarked to Sibyl that I was glad he was coming and a little later that I wished he would hurry up and get here—

She gave me a savage knock and remarked that she was glad to see me get up a little enthusiasm at last—I was so indifferent to everyone's being nice to me that she was surprised that anyone ever spoke to me—man, woman or child—She never saw anyone so little concerned over whether people liked me or not—and she never saw anyone make it so perfectly evident that they were unconcerned—

I had to laugh—It was so savage and so true—but it's the way I feel about them all—I had to laugh—

558. Hetty Sibyl Browne.

An invitation to talk at another high school today but I didn't go—No more such stunts—

   We walked on—as we walked I wondered why he is coming—Some way I feel you are mixed up with it—But it's no use to wonder—only I wonder how it happened—Wondering simmered down to quietly being rather glad he is coming—it's queer—

   Moving wagons are stirring though it's still dark—

   I'm going to try to sleep again—

   In a way—you know—it's hardly fair for anyone to come to me now—

   I hear a train—

   Goodnight.

   You seem very dear to me tonight—It's great to feel you think so much of me—

Alfred Stieglitz · **[New York City]** · **[May 14, 1918]** +

Tuesday morning—Court Room—9:45. At ten I enter the jury box—so there are a few minutes —There is a very wet drizzle—The Woolworth Building is bathed in floating mists—and the little trees at its feet are greener & fuller than yesterday—it's drippingly moist—like the air in which they exhale—& the ground—earth—in which they breathe.—

   —I stopped in at 291—a letter from you—green stamps—

   Yes I know it is not myself you want[559]—It's something which through my merely being you need—Yes, I see you better than you see yourself—That's simple—Not because I want to see you—I simply see.—And as it is not your body—nor even lips—or hands—which make you what you are for me—there is an equality between us.—I need you—as you need me— Just the consciousness—the contact of souls—or spirits—whatever it be—physical miles do not count.—

   —I must smile when I think that you are nearer to me than ever today—more part of me—I part of you—

   —I don't think many could understand—And why should they—If they could there'd be no war—& perhaps no Woolworth Building—nor subways—nor Wall Street—Nor all such wonders of the earth—

ON MAY 17, 1918, Strand sent Stieglitz a long letter, reporting on O'Keeffe's health and his growing understanding of her needs. Noting that Harris saw no reason why O'Keeffe should not go to New York in a couple of weeks for a visit, he told Stieglitz, "You have seen very straight—Georgia is a child and yet a woman," and added, she needs "someone to take care of her." He also admitted that although he loved her very much, "it is very clear to me that you mean more to her than anyone else."[560] As Strand and O'Keeffe spent time together, she soon

---

559. On May 10, 1918, O'Keeffe wrote Stieglitz: "You are not what I want—but I couldn't get along without you."
560. Strand to AS, May 17, 1918.

became exasperated with his slowness, his inability to do anything for himself, and his lengthy conversations with Harris about her. When she and Leah thought that Zoeller was slandering them and Strand did not leap to their defense, O'Keeffe's frustration with him only intensified. (Strand later extracted an apology from Zoeller, but only after the local sheriff became involved in the incident.) By the end of the month, O'Keeffe informed Cousins at the Normal College that she would not return to Canyon and instead made plans to go to New York to see Stieglitz. After saying goodbye to her friends, O'Keeffe and Strand left San Antonio on June 3, 1918. Fearing that the long trip might compromise her health, Strand decided they should stop in New Orleans and rest before continuing to New York. Although Stieglitz did not know exactly when they would arrive, he made arrangements for O'Keeffe to stay at Elizabeth Stieglitz's studio at 114 East 59th Street.

Georgia O'Keeffe · [Waring, Texas] · [May 21, 1918]

Greetings—
    Oh—I wish you were here—I have wanted so many times to roll on the floor and laugh—this morning particularly—And you would too—
    You can't imagine anything funnier than the combination of Leah, Strand and myself—He is the most helpless, slow, unseeing creature I ever saw—
    Gosh—it's funny—
    He moves so slow that we can hardly realize it's true—
    Really—country life—tending to all your own wants is wonderful for showing folks up—Leah and I just look at one another in amazement at times—I guess we are spoiled—
    And it's all making things inside me turn over in such a queer way—He goes off and talks to Leah—she tells me—Of course it is so stupid—even doing her best things can't help tangling a bit in the transfer from person to person—
    Why in the world couldn't people leave us alone—you and me I mean—I feel like saying about him like I said about Little Willie[561]—I never was so young—but I must add something else—How could anybody grow so slow—
    —Maybe it's mean to say all this—I guess it is—because—his being here has made me quieter than I've been in a long time—but you have spoiled him—his mother has spoiled him and I guess above all he has spoiled himself—
    Don't tell him I'm saying all this—However—it probably won't be necessary—I have a notion I'll probably tell him myself—He doesn't think to save us anything—It's hard to tell anyone to do things—
    It's amusing—
    Last night in the night I wanted to get up and run away—Leave them both sleeping—go to you I guess—Oh—it's all so amusing—

561. W. B. Mahan (Little Willie) was an English professor at West Texas State Normal College in 1917–1918.

He has rested me much—by—I guess just the feeling of someone near liking me so much—It was quite wonderful—but—The incompleteness is maddening—

The trouble over the old German here has brewed till (they talked about that too and didn't tell me)—Leah told me about it this morning and I immediately decided that we are not going to try to stay here—either of us—

It's troublesome and I see no use in mixing up with anything that bothers you when it is possible to get up and leave it. Unless something very remarkable happens I told Leah—this morning—Strand just now when I found them in the kitchen discussing it—that we are going to leave here—in about ten days—It will take both of us that long to get over being under the weather—

You don't need to worry about me—And I also feel like saying that you don't need to pay much attention to what anyone else says about me—You know I will tell you—

I don't know exactly what you want—it's hard to see correctly with Elizabeth, Strand and Leah all throwing mists of queer colors over the glass—

I am almost afraid you might spoil me like you seem to have spoiled Strand—if I let you—Only—I am both fortunate and unfortunate in being a woman—

Some of the things they say make me feel like a fine blooded cow—

My work—

Gosh—folks are funny—I am trying to keep them from worrying you—

Last night after I had gone to bed—Leah lay across the foot of it—Strand across the corner—my head on him—his arm round me—I half asleep—He said my arm was very smooth—

I wished he were someone I would let feel all of me—But I never could let him—And I wondered—if that was what you wanted of me—I didn't know—I know you need me—maybe even more than I need you—I do not know—

I thought I understood you—but they have made me feel so mixed up that—

Nothing seems to be more important than getting rid of the tangle they have made—If it's that you want me to work—is that what you want—

Why—It's the same feeling I've had ever since I came down here—that I must some way get loose from the people I know—They seem to make tons of trifling things—hanging around my neck—half choking me—You remember—that was my principal reason for not wanting to come down here.—I have written Mr. Cousins that I'll not return to Canyon this summer—In a way maybe that is preferable to this—

—It never seemed that my painting was so important—or important at all—It was just something I wanted to do—had to do usually—

Oh—I seem to feel sick over things—It's no use for me to go to you—or you to come to me for just a little time—a day—a week—or even a month—

I don't believe I could make myself go to New York with Strand today if I never saw you—

Please don't mind my writing all this—and don't let it disturb you—Maybe part of it is the time of the month. No I'm not sick now—

But there is such a mad passionate desire to be greatly loved only as a woman—

You—I don't know—

Just kiss me—

Wait—I'll write again soon—and if you trust me you will let me wade around in the mix up here—Maybe I can see better tomorrow—

I lay over on my bed awhile ago—and had to laugh at myself—

Thinking about you—depending on you like I might be your own child—

Some way lately—in spite of people and things mixing me up it has seemed as though —in spite of my not writing—something in me was going very quietly but surely to you.

Nothing but a wonderful song like I've never heard could tell me to you now—

I hate to stop writing—it's like drawing away—when I'm very close and like being close.

Tuesday 5 P.M.

Georgia O'Keeffe · [Waring, Texas] · [May 25, 1918]

Greetings—

Your telegram last night—

I guess Strand thinks me a hard-hearted wretch for—just going on after I read it— Laughing and talking—I had gotten up to make corn muffins for supper—in my kimono— because I wanted them—He didn't know what was in it and I didn't tell him—Talking seems to have become next thing to impossible—You are such a perfect god to him—I have to laugh—

It seems to me secrets aren't necessary—Why not tell anybody anything—It ought to be possible to talk to anybody about anything—Leah and I do—He has made things three cornered though—So I said nothing till he and Lucy went to walk and Leah came and got in bed with me—

—He is improving though—I told him yesterday morning that he might just as well go home—That or something did him a lot of good—

You see—Leah and I *move*—he wonders that we never rest—We are in the habit of doing things for ourselves and for others too—He has done very little even for himself—He doesn't think—I told him he just simply didn't know how—no use to try—told him all the above and more—

Leah remarked that she would like to get hold of his mother and tell her what she thinks of her for raising anything like that—Really—you can't begin to imagine how amazingly amusing and aggravating it has been—

Then too it is largely my fault—I was too nice to him—it inflated his ego to such an extent that it made me contrary—So there you have it all—

I have a notion he will be disillusioned—*some*—and some wiser by the time New York sees him again—Really it's funny—leave him alone—

—I have set the end of the month as my date to be free—Leah's nephew[562] is coming then so she won't be alone and I am going—

---

562. Probably Harris B. Henning, the son of Leah's sister Dean (Deanie) Harris Henning.

I don't know where—I'm just going—I won't be bothered *anymore*. The Dutchman business bothers me—I'm just going away—

I got up at noon intending to go out and paint a tree that's in my mind but after lunch—why I just got in bed again—clothes on—I hardly feel like writing this—

Lucy is just inside the house trying to paint with watercolors for the first time—She is a very funny person—It's great to have her here—

I don't look sick—Nothing hurts—It's just that moving seems to be next thing to impossible—Maybe I'm only lazy—Anyway—I'll feel better in a day or two—

I don't know whether it is wise to be so honest or not—I don't know—don't know anything—

I'm sleepy—

I feel a bit bad about what I write you because in a little while I'll be up stewing around the house—laughing—talking—

I only send you the inside—

Alfred Stieglitz · **[New York City]** · **[May 25, 1918]** +

I'm at the Manhattan Hotel. Writing Room. There is music in the distance. And voices. The feeling of great restlessness—"frivolity"—chatter of women—& men too.—It's 7:30—I'm unspeakably tired.—Alone.—Glad.—

—Such an afternoon.—Exciting—291—Alone. Nadelman appeared with a friend who is to open an art gallery opposite the Ritz—a real fountain in the middle of the gallery!—Hadn't seen Nadelman in a long while. He is very prosperous—I like him in spite of it.—Marin appeared—And Baasch.

There was a heated discussion about the appreciation of art in America—Nadelman likes me & can't quite understand why I refuse to go "into the business." Seems to feel sorry for me. Can't understand that my conscious goal has been failure!—Defeat!—And to smile at it—Or my own "foolishness"—I was wishing you would have walked in just then—It was really quite magnificent the argument—&—the room—The whole atmosphere—Oh! I forgot before Nadelman had come—Bruno came in & said the same thing that Hartley had written—& both were identical with what I had said to Zoler in the morning.—Bruno was expecting Frank Harris—He wasn't present at the Nadelman debate—

The room full of Marins, your pastels, Wrights, Hartleys, old ramshackle chairs—a feeling of chaos—cheer—detachment—No War—just mad freedom—

When Nadelman left he said to the other man, "One always goes out of here with a revelation"—I had to laugh.—You see nothing can blind me—for long—not even myself—I don't turn my "Weaknesses" into "Virtues"—

Marin was funny—he always resents my being what he calls anti-American—& he generally proves my case—& shows that it has nothing to do with pro- or anti- anything—All I state are facts.—It's funny how they excite people.—

—As Nadelman left your letter came—I read it at once.—You were writing Tuesday—the day I wrote fourteen telegrams—& letters—sending none.—

—Of course I see you & Strand & Leah—at Waring—Always the Great Child—Woman.—I can hear them talking to you—I see Strand in the seventh heaven—

I have to smile—as you do—& Leah—

—Can you imagine me at Waring?—I'd certainly be—too foolish for words—clumsy—heavy—unfit from every point of view—

—The letter is beautiful—Its flower-like quality—What's that about art & you.—It's you the woman spirit that I have found—The pictures, why they are merely the evidences—wonderful in themselves—but—

—I wonder what is to happen—I just don't think—every moment just is—

—I do wonder sometimes—often—very often—what that something really is which seems to exist between us—Am I what you feel?—I know you are what I feel you are.—But you see I'm an old man—after all.—Old compared to you.—Physically—Otherwise I'm perhaps much younger.—I think I am.—

—Funny that I can't seem to grow up.—

—Leon Fleischman brought in two young girls—one very wide awake.—Another discussion arose—an interesting one too—They are coming next week to see your work.—

While they were there the queer Baroness[563] walked in all in black—very high necked—a touch of green—a touch of red—The women & the man seemed to wonder.—They went. The Baroness asked why I looked so terribly tired.—Instead of going she started talking & talking.—I was suffering—so tired—& your letter—the afternoon—

Suddenly excitedly the little girl from next door appeared & charged the Baroness with having taken five dollars out of her pocketbook.—Seems the Baroness had posed—Excitement—I very quiet. The Baroness walked away.—Insulted?—The little girl came in to me—she was positive the Baroness had taken the money—I had often heard that the Baroness was a kleptomaniac—I said nothing for awhile. When the little girl felt sorry & said she'd do nothing, I told her I felt she was possibly right in feeling as she did. What a pity! I wonder whether the Baroness will appear again. Schamberg had written I should give her his manuscript[564]—but I didn't have it with me—So, will she come?—

—So the day as you see was quite unusual—Even the cleaning woman turned up.—

—Perhaps I'll go out to the country tomorrow. To see some real soil—& trees—& smell fresh air—

I wonder what I would do tonight were you here—Do you know it sometimes frightens me to think you here—because of the great cruel city—& the unrest of it all—

563. A poet, sculptor, and friend of several New York Dada artists, Baroness Elsa von Freytag-Loringhoven was known for her outlandish dress, such as the lid of a coal scuttle she used as a hat. Despite her grand title, she was impoverished. Shortly after their marriage in 1913, her husband, Leopold Freiherr, was imprisoned and later committed suicide. To support herself she occasionally modeled for artists and even starred in a short film by Man Ray and Marcel Duchamp, *The Baroness Shaves Her Pubic Hair.*

564. Probably Morton Schamberg, [Preface], *Philadelphia's First Exhibition of Advanced Modern Art,* exh. cat., McClees Gallery, May 17, 1916–June 15, 1916.

As if you didn't know it—as if you hadn't lived in New York—Perhaps I'm afraid you might find me not at all as you now think I am—and I would hate to lose anything you feel for me now—

—Do you understand?—I refuse to think—Will she come—or won't she come—Whatever you do it's doing that which you feel you must do.—

—Remember my first thought is your getting strong—really well—

I feel like telegraphing—but I'll refrain—

If I could get Waring directly—I would go ahead—but via San Antonio takes too long.—

Good Night—

I'll go & read your letter again—I have no idea where I'm going or what I'll do—It's 8:30—

Alfred Stieglitz · **[New York City]** · **[May 26, 1918]** +

What do I want from you?—

—It's hardly six—morning—Sunday—cool—clear—the window wide open—I propped up in bed—feeling rather sick at heart—yet—still dreaming—having thought all night—sleeping impossible—

What do I want from you?

Your letter—I sent you a letter finished at the Manhattan Hotel—I went away & ordered something to eat—I re-read your letter—read it really for the first time as at 291 I was not alone—The food stood on the table & I seem not to have seen it for I was paying the bill when I realized I hadn't touched a thing—was just staring into space.—The waiter laughed. —So did I.—I guess he must have thought me half-witted.—Sometimes I feel that I have gone completely dippy.

There it stood in large blazing letters—Wherever I looked: "What do I want from her" —And there was no answer.—Do I want anything from her that she hasn't already given me over & over again—from the first moment I saw the drawings.

—All the drawings—all the letters.—Perhaps they set mad dreams agoing—Or were they merely the tangible evidence that the dream of a life was no longer a dream—

What do I want from you?—Nothing—nothing—

Perhaps I merely dare not want—No, that's not it—I dare if I really did.—

I fear the youngsters in their idealism see possibilities & think you & I are of one spirit —& they love us—& they have dreams that they would like to see come true—through you —& through me.

Beautiful dreams—if the world were more beautiful they would come true—But the world is relentless & cruel—people are—they must be I suppose or they could not live—

Dearest Child—What do I want from you—You say I seem to need you—that you need me less than I need you—That's true in a way—Still—it's not entirely fair to me or to you—

Sometimes I feel I'm going stark mad—That I ought to say—Dearest—You are so much to me that you must not come near me—Coming may bring you darkness instead of light—And it's in Everlasting Light you should live—

Your living is important—that's what I want—my living is really not important.—I am young in spirit—As a spirit of some use—Otherwise truly hopelessly unfit—

—Of course I'd love to see you—talk to you—be with you—hear all you have to say —& tell you all I have to say—but if I am taking you away from your own natural center—away from Leah who can do more for you than I ever can—more materially—in the way of actual care—& I know that here you will feel the cruelty of the city—will live a restless existence—primarily because I'm not entirely free—having still responsibilities—& above all because I am a poor man as far as money is concerned.—

I need very little—but you should have sufficient—not because you think you need it —but because I feel you should have it—I know I'm no money-getter—It nearly drives me mad to see how helpless in a way I am—&—

Why Great Child—You don't know me at all—You know me as the Dreamer—as the Spirit—

What do I want from you—Perhaps one big kiss to put me to sleep—& give me peace forever—I want to know you strong & well—I want to know you free—

I know you are a woman—First—& always—I know you need a home—a child—Those take a man to give you—I am not a man—That's my curse.—

I could give you a child—It would be the purest that was ever conceived but it would be drowned to death—& you with it—& I too—because I do not know how to be part of the big game—

My love for you is so great—as wonderfully pure—It's not the physical self seeking your physical self—I don't know what it is—

Madness I guess—Madness like 291—

Great Heavens—Everything seems to hurt this morning—

If you should decide to come because you feel you must—for no particular reason—expecting nothing—hoping for nothing—wanting nothing—Just coming—whatever happens then will happen naturally—What it will be I have no idea—

—Strand I fear has not made things very clear to you—How could he—He brought you quiet—that's why I wished him to go—But I had hoped he'd be able to give you a picture of myself—conditions—Why—Because he felt—Elizabeth felt—I felt—you wanted to come East awhile—& I felt that you should know conditions—I could not write them—I can give you no picture now—My existence seems to be one great mess in spite of its spiritual purity—& I want to drag no one into the mess.—

Your getting sick made matters involved—It's the sickness which in a way drew in the youngsters—I seemed so helpless to help you—so I spoke to them about you—I thought perhaps they could be of some assistance—& they have been—but they have brought glasses to you—colored—& you don't see directly as you did before.—Not that which existed between you & me.—Really exists now—

Strand was really to rid you of the glasses—Of course it's I responsible—I can write now all this—a couple of weeks ago it would have been absurd—

The sun has gone—it's clouding up—

I wonder what you'll decide to do—My last letter gave you an idea of the situation here—

Remember if *you* feel *you want* to come—are strong enough—I'll be very happy—But if you come because you think *I want something from you*—the coming will be a false beginning.—

Beginning of what—

I'm so tired—I could cry—

Your letter—it's beautiful—It's full of passion—the Woman's Soul—Crying for Completeness—Heart Rending—

Like your work—heartrendingly beautiful—Can anything bring you peace on earth unless it's home & a child—And who is there fit to give you these? Honestly—Fairly to mother & child.—As you would need—

These are terrible days—

I wonder—I hate to send this letter—

Somehow I feel I ought to have you here—my arm around you—like Strand—Leah—listening—or not—& I telling you all this & more—Perhaps it would bring some light to both of us—

Perhaps I'm afraid—afraid that I am steering you for pain.—

—I am to go to the country—to my brother[565]—I don't feel a bit like it—I'd like to shut out all light & stay in bed—& not think—

There goes the clock—

Georgia O'Keeffe · [**Waring, Texas**] · [**May 29, 1918**]

How do you do!

I haven't written for several days—

Strand and I had a good talk over everything—Then another good talk and it seems things are going better—all right in fact—We might get to a fair understanding after several hundred good talks—

Everything seems to be righting itself—I knew it would in time—

Two days I didn't write because I was painting—Have to work at least another day on it—Maybe another month—

Brack is here today—came last night—I painted on him[566] today—Have been *disgustingly* sick at my stomach all day from getting all stirred up yesterday—but I worked anyway because he could only be here today—

He has great muscles and Strand photographed him—Seemed to have a great time—

—I think I have decided to go to New York—Am beginning to think I have to—

---

565. Stieglitz's brother and sister-in-law, Lee and Lizzie Stieglitz, had a house in Mamaroneck, New York.
566. Possibly Lynes 240.

There were two beautiful letters yesterday—You are really very wonderful to me—

—He is going to town so must stop—Brack makes me light headed anyway—Strand looks at us as though he wondered how it could be possible for us to act the way we do—Brack just tried to get me to bite a ball of green wax—telling me it was a plum—He's so ridiculous—

Georgia O'Keeffe · San Antonio, Texas · June 3, 1918

[Telegram] Starting for New York tonight. Just told Leah goodbye. If I had let anybody or anything get in my way I wouldn't be going. It has to be this way. I don't know why. I don't know anything. Think I see straight yet see nothing.
O'Keeffe

Alfred Stieglitz · [New York City] · June 7, 1918 +

It's Friday.—It poured this morning.—And it's very sticky now.—291—Your letter from San Antonio—just before packing—Your telegram of the third came on Tuesday—telling me of your decision—I read it over & over & over—& over again—

A perfect picture of you—those few words—Really all of you.—

Was I glad?—I don't know—I seemed to have no feeling—It all seemed as if feeling & mind & everything like that had passed away into something that I have always known must exist—yet had not—there is no word—

—Then came Strand's letter.[567]—His offer to work for you—All very beautiful—All so simple—Yet the world is hardly ready for such simplicity—His not knowing how you & he were coming & when—via what route.—

—I had the studio cleaned—And aired it—& had new keys made—& spoke to the landlady—a young woman with a child—a sympathetic woman—I wanted her to know who you are—I wanted you not to feel too alone—when alone in the studio—I told her so.—

—The men are all glad.—Wright has much he wants to tell you—And Dewald & his wife offered all sorts of things—All really so sincerely—& beautifully—

—I'm alone at home—for two days—yesterday & today—No one in the house—

—I wonder when you'll turn up.—Today—tomorrow—In a week—It's certainly all unusual.—I have to smile—

I have been thinking of every possible eventuality—I don't think anything has escaped me.—

All I want is to preserve that wonderful something which so purely exists between us.

567. On June 1, 1918, Strand wrote Stieglitz, confiding that he had told O'Keeffe, "I would take care of her as long as she liked—wanted it—a job somewhere she wanted to be—without expecting anything in return except the joy of doing it—Perhaps naïve but I could do it—if it were to be—But it isn't—which I knew long ago."

—There never was anything quite so crystal clear—not because of me.—It's you—yes—The purest being that ever lived.—All heart & something more—

—None can understand—You need not—I do.—

For some days I was feeling very miserable—but yesterday somehow I felt better—I guess it's having something *definite*—just a little something—to know it's happening.—Action taken.—

—And the Superintendent of Schools wants you in San Antonio—Everything will take its natural course—What that will be neither you nor I know today—All we do know is that you are coming eastward—

—You should have happened in yesterday. I was fuming mad for several hours—here—a woman trying to arrange an exhibition next autumn—the same old stupid idea of "help"—when in fact it's all the reverse.—

The whole last week has been one of war again—I storming—fighting—It seems it's so deeply rooted in me that eventually I break out—loose—I'll tell you all about it—And you'll smile—I'll never get used to the blindness & stupidity of so many who ought to know better—And the lack of nearly all near me seeing what I'm trying to express—& have been expressing for so many years—is incredible—

Are you really on the way here. Where are you now—On the boat—perhaps seasick—Or still in New Orleans—Or are you on a train.—

I have to smile at Strand—He has received—is receiving—something he'll never receive again.—Nothing ever so wonderful.—No matter what may come to him.—

I wish you were here now—Sometimes I wonder at my quiet—Am I really so quiet inside—or is it all just will—

Spirit—

EARLY SUNDAY MORNING, June 9, O'Keeffe and Strand arrived in New York. Still coughing, she spent her first few days in the city under the care of Stieglitz's brother Lee, who was a physician, and his niece Elizabeth, as well as Stieglitz himself. At once, Stieglitz began to devote all his waking hours to O'Keeffe, and their intense infatuation for each other blossomed into a passionate love affair. Just as quickly, too, he began to photograph her, as she later said, "with a kind of heat and excitement"[568] that startled her. Although O'Keeffe was still a virgin and they did not consummate their relationship until August 1918, Stieglitz's portraits of her became not only more innovative in their daring abstraction of form, but also more intimate as his camera's lens explored and seemed almost to caress every inch of his beloved. They wrote few letters during this summer; those that exist, mainly from Stieglitz, reveal their all-consuming passion for each other.

568. O'Keeffe, "Introduction," *O'Keeffe: A Portrait by Alfred Stieglitz,* unpaginated. See Greenough 487–518.

Alfred Stieglitz · [New York City] · [June 10?, 1918]

It's much after midnight—& the rain is coming down hard.—I came home only a little while ago.—Strand & I sat at the little restaurant until near twelve—he relating about the sheriff & apology—the whole story—And the missing of the train—your laughter—A whole lot of things—I listened—And I told him of some things that happened here while he was away—

—Here I am sitting on the edge of my bed.—In a way it seems too ridiculous.—It is as if you were in Waring—or San Antonio—or at the North Pole.—

—And still it's a wonderful feeling to know that you are much nearer—not so terribly far away—That if I didn't want you to sleep & rest & get strong I could come & talk—or just watch you sleep—It's all the same—

It's all very wonderful—Seems to be way beyond feeling—Everything seems always just right—

I guess it's you—I have nothing to do with it except reflect yourself back to yourself—I wonder whether you are sleeping quietly—whether the rain on the skylight isn't disturbing.—

And whether just before falling to sleep you wished—Did you?—

—It seems so incredible that you should possibly care a little for me in a way a tiny bit different than when you came—or thought you would—or could.—

—As for my feelings—I have to smile—You see all that something which has been going out to you—for two years—more & more—that something seems to have become greatly intensified—seems to have taken wonderful form & a still greater whiteness—

—It's very beautiful—In a way serene like a very clear quiet balmy starlight night—

It's you who achieves all that—I merely echo—Yes you—All of the beauty is rooted in you—Perhaps I'm very sensitive to it—& so your beautiful soul—how white it is—begets what it gives—sometimes intensified—

Alfred Stieglitz · [New York City] · [June 11, 1918] +

Another whole day gone.—And I on the edge of the bed here—the bed uncovered. I in my clothes—window wide open—door too—a cool damp air circulating—I so wide awake.—

I feel as if I had traveled from the skies—had held a star there—just a moment—an intangible moment—

—I ought to feel very big—head high—I never felt quite so tiny—

Your strength is amazing—You are space itself without time—

Yet so much a woman—It has been a day of days—hour of hours—It was foolish to have broken down—

I wonder if you could understand—

I left you but a few moments ago—yet it seems so many, many hours—foolish—Ever thirsty—Ever hungry—Wondering whether you are careful—Wondering what you may feel—Every moment is a different moment to you—

I hope the irregularity of the day has not harmed you—I'm a fine nurse—Oatmeal—Irregular hours—What else—

—June 11—So much has happened—

June 9—June 10—June 11—

You were very tired—I wonder if you'll rest & look rested in the morning—like you looked rested this morning—

All these words seem words—so empty—so meaningless.—

I see a face with a million expressions—changing every moment—The mouth—and eyes—Even the cheekbones seem to speak a million tongues—all different—yet one harmony.—

Perhaps someday you may seem cruel to me too—you said—Perhaps—but you have earned the right—

Why do I think of that remark—

I don't seem to want to go to bed—The night is very dark—

You said you wouldn't think—I know you won't—& yet way down in the bottom of my heart I hope that as you were closing your eyes—you felt—so very quiet—

I wish the Marins were with you—I'm going to bring one down hanging on the walls here—I wonder whether you'd like it—& I'll bring a Rodin—

—Quintessence of livingness—That's you.—Not a dead fraction of a second—

I have a whole box of your letters here—On my lap—I don't know what for or why—They are just there—

Alfred Stieglitz · [**New York City**] · [**June 13, 1918**]

Flower of my soul's yearning of all these many years—that's what you are. Yes, *You are.*—

Here I am ready to steal some more moments to be with you—It is a glorious feeling to *know* what I *know*—What you have told me—What I have seen—What you express every moment—in just being.—

—I still have one thought above all—To want you strong.—There is so much for you to give the world—

Always the flower—The flower that has no withering—

June days—five so far—each so full—ever growing richer—deeper—all embracing.—

You have come East—The Sun they say rises in the East—I say it comes from the West to rise in the East—

Light & Air—& Sound—Height & Depth—Everything that's Wondrous in the World for me—All in one little body—The Spirit of Life—Life Itself—

And I love Life and fear not Death—Because I've lived—But never as now—these days! Good Night—I'm with you.—

Georgia O'Keeffe · [New York City] · [June 14, 1918]

You will be here in a few minutes I guess but I have to get up and write you—it's necessary—
I must—

I've been lying here listening for you in the dark—My face feels so hot—Aching for you
way down to my fingers' ends—an actual physical ache—

—As I came up the street into the sunset after supper—I wondered—can I stand it—
the terrible fineness and beauty of the intensity of you—

—I do not know—may yet have to run away—it seems almost too much—

The hot setting sun so brilliant—shining white I could hardly walk toward it—

—And lying here—wanting you with such an all [over] ache—not just wanting—
loving—feeling—all the parts of my body touched and kissed—conscious of you—

A volcano is nothing to it—No words I know say the hotness—consumingness of it—

Still I some way feel I can be quiet when you come—can control myself—

—Feeling it growing though—I seem to feel that the moment will come when I can't
control myself—when I'll be blind and mad—

I have to tell you—I know you know—and still—maybe you don't know how really
mad I seem to be growing—

You will have to think for me when I cannot think for myself—

Trust—Why do you know—the trust I have in you is the finest thing I've ever known—
It's absolute—

The woman you are making seems to have gone far beyond me—Almost out of sight—

And as I go out into the street I seem to feel that I am solid stupidity of the most
unmoving kind—all the way through—feelingless—stolid—

Almost too much—

Alfred Stieglitz · [New York City] · [June 15, 1918] +

I had to read—at the street corner—under the lamppost—The street so quiet—not a soul—
No stars—just the light & I—And it didn't look—it just helped me to see—read—

And I read—& read again—& once again—

And I was so quiet—and you were within a few hundred feet—I could have run to you
within a minute—& you would have been surprised—and glad—& I too—

But I looked at the sky & at the silent street—& hoped the Woman Little Girl would
fall asleep—sleep well—& peacefully—And that the morning would have cleared away that
cough—

—Run away—because I am too intense in my fineness—No Dearest Whitest Soul—
you won't have to run away—Soon you'll be at work—and I busy too—I don't know exactly
with what—helping you work—It is very beautiful to feel that I mean so much to you—but I
must see to it that you have no aches—Peace you must get—Real peace—

Marvel of Song—dissolving into night—Eyes closed—mouth closed—breathing deeply

& gently—A woman lying alone—Asleep—Knowing herself meaning greatly something to one man who thinks her the most perfect of her type—who raises him to the feelings of a god— yet shows the god that he is very small—very tiny—compared to her wondrous never-ending song—Tonight I see white snow mountain peaks looking into dark boundless skies—Still all asleep—the mountains & the skies—like one human soul I've found—A Woman—

A Little Girl—a Child—All Innocence—And Purity Unheard of—

—All that I feel—& what I feel lives—is true—

I'm glad I read the letter tonight—I'll sleep—

I'd love to dream I lay on the floor next to the narrow bed—lay there to see that you are cared for—undisturbed—Asleep—Wondrous soothing rest giving sleep—to awaken without cough—without ache—yearning perhaps—

Good Night once more. What do I want you for!? I didn't know—But now I know— to tell you of the deepest boundless quietest feeling for what you are—to all—to me—

And to hear that I am not quite an ordinary man to you—

Good Night—

It's two—I'm still undressed—

Alfred Stieglitz · [**New York City**] · [**mid-June, 1918**]

To wake up at daybreak & lie here in bed & feel that there is the loveliest someone on earth not so far away waiting—feeling like I do—Two beings so full of the same feelings for each other— Converging into a focus—a complete oneness—

I never knew it was possible to feel as I do—ready to die at any moment with a smile that only you could understand—But I do not want to die if I can mean the slightest thing to you—

—Strand & I walked till after one—Davidson did not show up—Strand feels somewhat lost—does not quite understand—It was all very fine—very—And I tried to show him what his feelings really were—

He showed me all the photographs—a few are rather lovely—& a few nudes very good —of Leah.—He said he had asked you several times & what you had said.—It was all very true —very fine—And he said: I think she'd pose nude for you—& I said: Perhaps she would.— I don't know.—

And as he told me I realized how glad I was at heart that all was as it was—That no one had ever seen—nor touched—for I realized then that although there would be no great difference yet—yes yet—that intensest of intense spiritual something that goes out from you so directly to me these days—through gradual discovery—& gradual contact—it would be different—And anything different couldn't be quite what this is—& I would not want anything to be different—

Rarest flower on earth—rarest beauty of color—rarest shape & aroma—fragrance bewildering so quieting—

Why no man on earth has ever been given such gifts—so consciously—so willingly—naturally—unfoldingly—

—Once you wrote me long ago I turn to you as the flower turns to the sun—

It was a moment I knew—a picture of a moment—so lovely—so pure—I didn't take it for myself—I understood—

I wonder how you are feeling—Whether you could sleep longer—the direct light not falling on your face—

Here I am lying when really I should be there—or you here—No, I there—There because those rooms have become holy ground if ever there was holy ground—

Your very moving about there makes them that—

Do you realize now why I closed 291 with your things on the wall—the last of exhibitions. Do you realize now why in the Little Room there is you wherever you look—the wonderful little whitest of figures—the green landscape—& even Leah![569]—Everything happening through feeling—nothing arranged—nothing calculated—

I hear a song no mortal has ever heard—

Truly—it exists—You are—It's that—

304

Alfred Stieglitz · [New York City] · [late June 1918]

I see half-open lips—a glimpse of tiny teeth peeping through them—the arches of those lips subtly expressive of beauteous desire—

I see eyes hardly open—soft firm lids closing wondrous eyes, eyes hardly open—eyelashes very dark—& brows made to stroke—

I see the strong forehead—silken hair, dark & wild—pulled back from the forehead—

I see the most wondrous of ovals—a face so strong—so soft—both simultaneously—

I see arms & hands stretched out into the skies—seeking to hold—all of love—firmly—passionately—wildly—ecstatically—deliriously—

I see breasts—too—awaiting—a throat too—& neck—

I see strong white legs—& black stockings—& shoes—laces—

All different than ever I've seen—All seem to exhale but one thing—

I dare not see more—I'm lying in bed—not far away—still so very far away—it's morning—I dare not think any further—

I hear birds kissing—Day is breaking—I'm full of a wondrous feeling of peace—Nothing exists on earth or in heavens but that which so completely has become my first self—

I hear the gentlest voice—I see that half open mouth—I hear everything that has been said all these days—I feel it's all spirit—Yet flesh—

You ought to be here—Or I there—Ever in each other's arms—Floating into space—No one to disturb—

---

569. Figure, Lynes 66; Leah, Lynes 242.

Just kisses & love—& great peace—Even when no kisses—kisses take place—

Two Souls have become One—Flesh does not touch—

Give me the lips—I know they are waiting—

I hope you slept well—And have been very quiet—

It has been a long night—I went to Dewald's—And then looked at the river—the night
—And I was within a few feet of your place—At midnight—

I stood there & wondered—

The Great Child was sleeping—My Great Wonderful Child—

I hear her voice—& see her lips—And her spirit bathes every part of me in light—
Child are you waking—there goes the clock—

I'd like to sleep a little more—I didn't sleep much—I don't know why—

And yet perhaps I do—I want you strong—It's as necessary for you—For me—
For—

You smile—You dearest thing that ever breathed on earth—Where do you come from
—I wonder if I deserve it all—

I guess I must—But why—I do not understand—

I know it is—

Alfred Stieglitz · [En route to Boston, Massachusetts] · [July 2, 1918]

It's nearly five—on the train—Boston in two hours[570]—Kitty & I have been talking very
intimately—frankly—about you & me too—Quite wonderful—She is very straight &
impersonal in her analysis—It means much to me to have had the chance.—

—But here I am every minute further away from 114 East 59th Street—our little home.
You—And still every minute brings me nearer to the moment of seeing you again.

—Of course you are here—Everywhere—with me—I am with you—there—
Everywhere.—

How wonderful the last two days—& this morning—Such peace—And incredible
beauty of every moment—no moments alike!—

And as I left you standing at 82nd Street & Madison Avenue—my little black figure—
I had to think of the station last year—

Dearest you are truly all I've said about you.—All the time.—Even when you've caused
me greatest pain—as you did for several moments—last week & the week before—I always
love you—then as much as ever—But I feel something very wonderful going on in both of us
—big as space itself—

Are the eyes half shut—The lips half open—

And the breasts? And she—??—

---

570. Stieglitz was taking Kitty to her summer camp in Alton, New Hampshire.

—And is the water great fun—I wonder if you miss me a little—I hope a little—No much—& yet I don't want you to miss me at all—

Oh! Yes, I do—*Kiss*

The train is shaking & rocking—writing is not easy—I wonder have you painted?—Of course I'm very eager to get back to photograph—I'm full of desire—I must get some things that satisfy me—

Dearest Little Girl—You never were quite as beautiful as you are now—

Yes I'll make you fall in love with yourself—

Kiss—Everywhere—

Just arrived at the hotel. Essex—opposite station. Have washed. Am waiting for Kitty.—The trip was filthy—& I am very sleepy & tired.—There is a big double bed—brass bedstead—What do you think was my first & my only thought—I hope you'll have a great sleep tonight—To bed early & really get a great rest—a long one.—

I wonder how you are. How you spent the day—What you ate—What you did—& thought—& felt—& looked—I guess I'm more full of you now than ever before & I have been full to overflowing for so long—Perhaps I'm growing so as to carry more & more—& more—

I don't seem to be able to think of anything else—or feel fully anything else—Just you—& all that you signifies—

—I can't believe that I won't see you for another thirty-six hours—Do you remember last night it seemed very long to you a moment or two—I seem to feel that way most all the time when you are not very close to me—

Insatiable hunger—Unquenchable thirst—

9 o'clock—

Have just come in from a meal & a walk—It's a great night—A cold north wind blowing.—There is always something intimate about Boston—likable.—There are soldiers & sailors galore on the Common—& meetings galore too—

But my mind—my being—are not with anything but one beautiful lovely spirit—the spirit I call—Georgia O'Keeffe—It breathes—lives—really is—touchable—concrete—& still not touchable—intangible—

You great big Child Woman—I see arms stretching—Breasts protruding towards the skies—a head so alive—with a mouth entrancing—eyes bewitching—an abdomen unequalled—a cathedral with heavenly music below it—the unborn child—legs full of strength—

I must stop—for I could yell—yell so that you'd hear it—

I wonder whether you are in bed.—It's nine.—

My head is full of many things said—& of the future—visions—possibilities—Oh! Give me your lips & let me drink in your love—& let me give you mine—I'll spare your neck but not your mouth—Do you feel the hand—All of me—pressing—

You purest of Pure Ones—Why no one would understand us—believe us—

It's all so different—Yes, we must be very different—So what we do is different—

—Tomorrow morning we leave at eight—I shall be under way all day until I'm back at 8:30. At 11:30 I hope to be in the sleeper on my way to you.—

It's all as if I were in a trance—

I wonder when you'll get this scribble—I hope some time before evening—I'm going over to the station now to mail it. It ought to be in New York at seven A.M.—& delivered before noon.—

It brings you millions—billions of kisses—quiet & passionate ones—an assortment unheard of—

—It brings you so much love it might smother you—It brings you all that makes me what I am to you—

What am I to you? Do you know? You are alone now & have a chance to think—

I want to sleep tonight—I wonder can I—

Good Night Georgia O'Keeffe—

I see a very oval face—I hear a dear sweet voice telling me what I must not do—

—You Wonder of all Wonders—You Glorious Bit of all that's Human—

A Woman—A Real Live Living Woman—

All Soul—Yes *All Soul*—

Dearest—I wish you were here—

Good Night—I hope you are very, very quiet—

Good Night—

Kisses Kisses Kisses—

AFTER STIEGLITZ RETURNED from taking Kitty to camp in New Hampshire, he brought O'Keeffe to his home at 1111 Madison Avenue to photograph her. When Emmy unexpectedly returned, she insisted that he immediately stop seeing O'Keeffe. Stieglitz refused and although Emmy later apologized, he packed his things and left. "I'm out of 1111—in one hour and fifty minutes the job was completed," he wrote his former secretary, Marie Rapp. "You never saw such a clean job and the place was left spic and span." He added: "I'm really sorry for Mrs. S.... But what can I do? I was certainly patient and persistent."[571] Putting many of his possessions into storage, he moved into Elizabeth's studio with O'Keeffe. Within a few weeks, Stieglitz's mother, Hedwig, invited them to Lake George, where she embraced O'Keeffe as the newest—if still unofficial—member of the Stieglitz family. Although O'Keeffe was surprised by the family's size and volubility and by the formality of their large Victorian estate, she and Stieglitz were immensely happy. As Stieglitz told Strand in early August, "The days here are the most perfect of my life."[572]

Their bliss was disrupted, however, by letters Stieglitz received from Kitty. Distraught by his desertion, Emmy had gone to New Hampshire to be near her daughter. "No matter how

571. AS to Marie Rapp, July 1918.

572. AS to Paul Strand, early Aug. 1918.

much she deserves" the present situation, Kitty wrote her father, "she is alone—more than we are—And therefore I shall try every possible means to make her more happy even if it must finally be at my expense." Kitty concluded that she could not come to Lake George as long as O'Keeffe was there: "If you were in Mother's place would you allow me to go up to live under the self same roof with someone who has taken your place?" And she asked: "You of course have a right, father dear, to live your own life, but do you think you have a right to voluntarily hurt other people by the sharpest weapon possible—by hurting their pride?"[573] A few days later, Kitty telegraphed Stieglitz, imploring him to come to New Hampshire to talk. On August 6, Stieglitz acquiesced, taking the train first to Boston and then on to Lake Winnipesaukee.

Alfred Stieglitz · [En route from Lake George, New York, to Alton, New Hampshire] · [August 7, 1918] +

Wednesday morning. It's six.—The train is two hours late.—Shaking so that it is nearly impossible to write—

Good Morning—Dearest of Dearests!—I wonder how you slept.—Whether you are up —Saw the sunrise.—

—It was a sweltering night—but I slept some—am fairly rested.—Ready.—Of course when awake—I missed you very greatly—the voice—the tenderness—

Yes—the tenderness—No one can be so tender—No one—And I need tenderness— as you need it—We—so nearly twins in all we feel—Where is your mouth—& the hands. —Where the arms—Where legs & feet—Where my Lady Friend—Where Every Part of You— All merely to intensify that incredible something which I felt for you before you came—Is it a reality today—

I wonder what you're thinking—It's so unfair to not be together—we whose souls are one soul—

But this had to be—There was no other way—Perhaps you smile—

—I have to laugh at what you said as I left: You spoil one so that one isn't fit for killing much less for living.—Perhaps you are right.—Let me kiss you until you cry for breath—And hold you so close till you cry: You are breaking my ribs—

—There is no sun—All is gray—& the morning not so hot.—Lucky there is no close connection.—I'd hate to dilly dally in Boston & be away a minute longer than *must* be.—

I want to mail this at once so that you have it tomorrow—

It isn't much—my mind feels stupid—But it will bring you something of me—Perhaps even the stupid part brings you something you may like—

Kiss me Dearest—as only you can kiss—How fast you've learned so much—I have to smile—You out-master your teacher—

—You most wonderful of all beings—Somehow you are a Woman this morning—Are you?—Yes, I'm sure.—

There is no more paper—& the shaking is awful—

308

573. Katherine Stieglitz to AS, July 21 and 24, 1918.

I'll be with you very soon again—the sun is trying to break through the grayness—
Endless kisses—

I love you—do you feel it?—I close my eyes—See you—Everywhere—

My Great Great Soul—

Georgia O'Keeffe · [Lake George, New York] · [August 8, 1918]

Dearest—

It is night—I am in bed—I haven't written today—I sewed—it seemed more
comfortable—it's hard to get in a comfortable position with the curse—Then too—I rather
expected a telegram this morning—and waited—half waited for it—

I felt like a very spoiled little girl—wanting you—hurting inside with the curse and
wanting you here to have it with me—as though you could help me have it—I didn't want to
have it alone—

Then came your letters—near noon—I was lying down—so dear—Dearest—so
beautiful—so much more real—so much more very real than they used to be because I know
what closeness to you means—Lips—arms—legs—body to body—warmness—wetness
—lovingness—sleepiness—

forgetting—

Then your telegram this afternoon—Dearest—it made me so happy to know you
coming in the morning that I really felt foolish—I was so happy—

No—my little boy—I don't seem to have thought much—I seem to have just—felt
much—

Goodnight—I will see you in the morning—It seems more wonderful than the day
coming.

Goodnight

Yes—I kiss you—

I am just a little girl person to whom kisses and closeness that you give me seem to be
life.

Dearest.
Thursday night.

Alfred Stieglitz · [En route from Alton, New Hampshire, to Lake George, New York] · [August 9, 1918]

Dearest Love of Mine—

Here I am back in Albany—It's fifty-eight hours since I sat here—It's six morning
now—I've hardly been out of my clothes since I saw you—*You*—It seems like a dream that I
ever held you—that you & I are really *one*—that you are waiting for me—& I—why every
minute seems an eternity—sitting here till train time—How will you be when I see you—As

happy as when I left—Happier—?—What will you have to tell me—how will the kisses be—
I'll know *all* at first glance—that is, *how you feel*—& what—

—Have they tortured you—upset you—Or have you smiled at all & only remembered
me, my great love for you—& what it signifies—

It will be very wonderful to be so close to you—more wonderful than ever—

I have really done the impossible while away—*Really*—And I have given peace to
my own daughter—She got her first glimpse of 291—In the woods—Her mother present—
A meeting of three the likes of which I know there never was—As I know there never was the
like of you and me as *one*—nor the like of 291 as a place—nor a *Camera Work*—Of course I'll
tell you all—It's worth telling—It's very wonderful—And I know I'm not dreaming—I know it
all did happen—As I know what all has happened between you & me all these days of marvelous livingness of two madly sane individuals—*You*—I. Kitty very wonderful—I feeling like the
cruelest coldest thing on earth—hating myself for not being able to compromise on truth—
Knowing it would relieve the strain—for a time—but knowing it would be but momentary
comfort—not actual help—And help—towards seeing—towards *own* living—not for self
—but because of *all*—that's why I can't be but relentless with myself—seemingly relentless
with others—

It's self that bleeds & could shriek with pain—& so hurts the other—Other not
knowing—Also wounded to death—

—I lay there—quiet—Felt miracles *must* happen—

A windstorm blew up—One side of the tent was tied up—the lakeside I kept open—
I had to see the lake—My eyes quieted me—There was lightning & thunder then—Marvelous
lightning—loud bursts of thunder—lightning all over the lake—Rain too—but I was
quiet—My Physical Perfect Body sleeping in the other cot moved about—slept—

The storm subsided—Calm—I breathed the wetness & freshness of the soil—Daybreak
—Dawn—Marvelous lovely blues & reds—in sky & lake—great broad strips from horizon
into zenith—

—What would the day bring—

I got up—Walked about in the woods—the many tents—gradually little boys appeared
—half dressed—barefooted—washing—girls got into the lake—And nature seems to have been
at her maddest to entertain me—A night in a tent—At the lakeside—just a tree—a thin long
one between me & the bed—a few small rocks to climb down on to the lake to wash & brush
teeth—I lay there—open tent—the young man in the tent—physical culturist—nineteen—
a perfect body—picture of what I ought to be these days—at moments at least—Queer coincidence to see my own dream of myself asleep there—I awake watching the lake—glassy—very
broad—a distant light across it—one.—I half dead—Had had nearly six hours with Kitty
alone in the woods—All seemed hopeless—as if I couldn't make her see—just that same *tiny*
difference that *seems* to bring us, you & me, to a deadlock at moments—I felt again so like the
wanderer—so alone—

You ever in my thought—All the time—in every word I said—every thought I had—
every breath I took—You in the lake—You in the trees—You in the smell of soil—You in the
windstorm—You in the most vivid lightning—You too in the crashes of thunder—You in

the marvelous colors of daybreak—You everywhere—Every moment—Giving me strength—Great—Great quick strength—& you yourself where were you—What were you feeling—doing—Had I given you strength?—

Kitty appeared—her hysterics gone—she had become unwell two weeks ahead of time—I had half thought so—The moment I saw her I knew the day was won—My own daughter—And then her mother appeared—No scenes—no words—all quiet—

At a deserted little cottage at the lakeside—quarter of mile from camp—Just we three—she sitting on the steps—Kitty on the porch on an old unused icebox—I standing—Three & a half hours of talking—each one—I talking about three—or more—

It was 291—the essence—Just a different background—My own immediate family listening—the *first time*—no unnecessary words—no hysterics—no compromise—all softness unyielding & very kind yet firm—

Kitty seeing—her mother too—That Wednesday had really done its work as I originally knew—& then doubted—

I've got to go—the train—

STIEGLITZ ARRIVED BACK in Lake George on August 9, and, as he often recounted in the years to come, later that same day, "during thunder & lightning," O'Keeffe "gave" him her virginity.[574]

574. See AS to GOK, Aug. 5, 1929.

2.

The Kiss That Is My Life
1919–1928

AS SOON AS O'Keeffe moved to New York in 1918, she and Stieglitz forged a relationship that was centered on their all-consuming love, their art, and their deep respect for each other. In the last three years, they had come to know each other's emotional terrain through the letters they had exchanged, but they soon discovered that they shared many traits: both voraciously imbibed the world around them, responding immediately, even viscerally, to the people, places, art, and especially the nature they encountered; both were articulate and opinionated—Stieglitz, verbose, O'Keeffe, dry and pointed; and both sought perfection in everything they did. Just as quickly, too, they realized they had a powerful erotic attraction to each other, and their letters, with their frequent references to "Fluffy" and the "Little Man," clearly indicate that they came to revel in an intensely satisfying intimacy they had never known before. For two such sensualists, their first few years together were indeed a profoundly exhilarating time.

They made enormous strides in their art during this decade, thanks in large part to their study of each other's work and the inspiration they drew from their love. In the early 1920s, O'Keeffe's paintings became less abstract and more focused on the world around her—the landscape of Lake George and flowers of all varieties. Deeply inspired by Stieglitz's and Strand's photographs, she incorporated photographic devices—compression of space or extreme close-ups, for example—into her art and even frequently painted on canvases that were approximately the same size as Stieglitz's 8 × 10 inch prints. Intrigued by the sharp lines and translucent surfaces of Stieglitz's prints, which she often "spotted," she also gradually ceased painting in short, textured brushstrokes, and abandoned watercolor in favor of oils.

If Stieglitz and photography grounded O'Keeffe in the natural world, making her art more representational, she liberated him, inspiring him with a creative freedom and energy he had never known before. During the late 1910s and 1920s he made more photographs than he had at any other point in his life. Embracing the nude with a conviction almost unknown in American art before him, he continued to make daringly innovative and intimate photographs of O'Keeffe, lovingly exploring every facet of her body. But he also applied the lessons he had learned photographing her to a series of portraits of family and friends that reverberate with a similar intensity and insight. In addition, although in earlier summers he had all but overlooked the landscape of Lake George, he now began to photograph it, stimulated both by O'Keeffe's infectious enthusiasm and by her own studies of the area. Citing her ability to put "her experiences in paint," Stieglitz wrote that he too endeavored to "put his feelings into form"[1] in his photographs of the trees, barns, and buildings, as well as the landscape and clouds, that surrounded him.

Yet despite their deep love and immense support of each other's art, as the decade progressed they increasingly found "the question of practical daily living," as Stieglitz wrote in 1928, more problematic.[2] The differences in background, age, temperament, and lifestyle that had earlier seemed so attractive now occasionally caused friction, especially when ignited by their fiery tempers. With Stieglitz's tendency to parse every concept or statement, the question of whether he loved O'Keeffe more as an idea than as a person runs throughout their correspondence of the 1920s. He continued to extol her as the "Great Child" or the "Great Woman," as he had when they first met, but he also increasingly exalted her as the personification of "White"—an almost holy state of spiritual, moral, and even physical purity. Less prone to hyperbole, more pragmatic and down-to-earth, O'Keeffe did not use such terms nor did she share this grandiose understanding of herself. She also grew steadily more disturbed by Stieglitz's belief that her art was fundamentally an expression of her gender. In the early 1920s she was not only stunned by the overtly sexual interpretations of her art that appeared in the press but troubled to realize that Stieglitz fostered them. She came to see that his nude photographs of her, which he had exhibited in 1921 before he showed her work in 1923, added fuel to this Freudian fire. Becoming shrewder about her public image, she rarely posed nude for him after 1923, and she sought out sympathetic critics, hoping for more balanced reviews. But she did not succeed in quelling the overtly sexual interpretations, in large part because she continued to paint provocative imagery. Always hesitant about showing her work to anyone, she often became sick when her exhibitions were on view after 1923.

Flaunting conventional notions of respectability, the unmarried couple openly lived together for several years. They married in December 1924, three months after Stieglitz's divorce from his first wife, Emmy, was granted, yet O'Keeffe continued to advertise her independence by steadfastly using her own name. As later letters make clear, their marriage was a bone of contention, something Stieglitz, not O'Keeffe, wanted. Although many factors may have prompted him to conclude they must marry,[3] his Victorian upbringing, coupled with the emotional burden he carried for never marrying the German woman who bore him a child in 1889(?), surely

1. AS to Herbert Seligmann, Oct. 11, 1923; Herbert Seligmann, *Alfred Stieglitz Talking* (New Haven, 1966), 61.

2. AS to GOK, July 13, 1928.

3. Sue Davidson Lowe, *Stieglitz: A Memoir/Biography* (New York, 1983), 267–268, notes that O'Keeffe and Stieglitz were married only a few weeks after they moved into their first rented apartment and she suggests that signing the lease as an unmarried couple may have made Stieglitz uncomfortable. Hunter Drohojowska-Philp, in *Full Bloom: The Art and Life of Georgia O'Keeffe*

influenced his decision.[4] For Stieglitz, who loved to note the cosmic coincidences between his and O'Keeffe's lives, the traffic accident they had while driving home from getting their marriage license must not have augured well.

Befitting their untraditional relationship, they led a peripatetic existence during most of the 1920s. Subsisting at first on Stieglitz's modest income, they depended on his family for several years, living in his niece Elizabeth's studio at 114 East 59th Street in New York, and after early December 1920 with his brother Leopold (Lee), a physician, and his wife, Elizabeth (Lizzie), at their home at 60 East 65th Street. Neither arrangement was ideal—the studio was cramped, with little privacy, while living with Lee and Lizzie, O'Keeffe later said, had the emotional warmth of a "cold, damp cellar."[5] In November 1924 they moved to a studio at 35 East 58th Street, and one year later they rented rooms at the newly built Shelton Hotel, where they resided for the next several years. Every summer and fall, though, with the blessing of Stieglitz's mother, Hedwig, they spent long periods at the family's home at Lake George, New York. After 1919, when Hedwig sold Oaklawn, their large Victorian home on the shores of the lake, O'Keeffe and Stieglitz shared a farmhouse on the hill behind it with an ever-changing cast of family and friends. Stieglitz celebrated the "Hill," as he called it, as an ideal community of individuals living and working together for the common good. But O'Keeffe, who earlier admitted that "families paralyzed" her and were "suffocating,"[6] saw the reality of daily life there, with its constant stream of visitors intruding on her time to paint. With her keen desire for privacy she longed for a house of their own, but Stieglitz, with his equally strong need for companionship and an audience, was not swayed.

During these years, they were further challenged by Stieglitz's refusal to have a child with O'Keeffe—her paintings, he insisted, were their children—and by his estrangement from his daughter Kitty. After his separation from Emmy in 1918, Stieglitz tried to convince Kitty of the correctness of his actions, but she was not persuaded. They saw little of each other, and he did not attend her 1922 marriage to Milton Sprague Stearns. His anguish about his relationship with her greatly deepened after the 1923 birth of her son, Milton Stearns, Jr., when she was hospitalized for postpartum depression. Subsequently diagnosed with dementia praecox, now known as schizophrenia, Kitty remained institutionalized for the rest of her life. Although Lee Stieglitz oversaw her treatment and gave Alfred regular reports, he rarely visited her and had only minimal contact with her husband and son.

In the early 1920s, Stieglitz organized sporadic exhibitions of his and O'Keeffe's work at the Anderson Galleries, run by his friend Mitchell Kennerley. Although these exhibitions rekindled his long-standing desire to have another gallery, he now determined to focus his attention not on art from around the world, as he had at 291, but on American painting and photography. He realized this wish in December 1925, when he opened the Intimate Gallery, a small room

(New York, 2004), 241, writes that O'Keeffe told her sister that they married to rid Kitty of her delusions that her parents would reunite.

4. See n. 347, chap. 1. Stieglitz's conflicted feelings about his illegitimate daughter can be seen in later letters to O'Keeffe; see AS to GOK, July 27 and Aug. 10, 1929.

5. GOK to AS, July 16, 1929.

6. GOK to AS, May 10, 1918.

in the Anderson Galleries building devoted to the "study of seven Americans": Arthur Dove, Marsden Hartley, John Marin, and Paul Strand, as well as O'Keeffe and himself and an unnamed seventh artist—frequently Charles Demuth but also others, such as the sculptor Gaston Lachaise. Taking only modest deductions from sales to cover his costs, he ran the "Room," or "303," as he called the gallery, as an artists' cooperative, hoping that it, unlike 291, would bring the artists much needed income. It soon became celebrated not only for its exhibitions, but also, as the critic Henry McBride noted, for the "copious, continuous, and revolutionary"[7] monologues Stieglitz delivered there and for the eclectic mix of people it attracted, including authors and poets such as Sherwood Anderson, Hart Crane, and Jean Toomer, critics such as Paul Rosenfeld and Herbert Seligmann, and historians such as Lewis Mumford. Although O'Keeffe believed that Stieglitz's work in promoting American modernism was important, she was bored by the often abstract, "dreamy" discussions that so animated Stieglitz and his acolytes and found their blind devotion to him "unhealthy."[8]

One of the people drawn to the Room was Dorothy Norman, a twenty-one-year-old newlywed who had recently moved to New York. Delicate, shy, but fiercely tenacious in her beliefs, Norman was the daughter of a wealthy Philadelphia clothing manufacturer and the wife of Edward Norman, son of the founder of Sears, Roebuck. Adrift in a new city, she was eager to find an intellectual home and soon impressed the much older photographer with both her willingness to assist him and her devotion. By the early 1930s, she and Stieglitz embarked on an affair that lasted for almost two decades and irrevocably altered his relationship with O'Keeffe.

From 1919 through 1928, O'Keeffe and Stieglitz were apart only infrequently, and thus their correspondence is sporadic. Sparked by O'Keeffe's recognition that she needed something that neither Stieglitz, New York City, nor Lake George could provide her, their separations at first were prompted by her visits to friends. But soon they were also occasioned by her sudden departures after they fought. Willful, passionate, and volatile, neither easily accommodated the other, and their heated arguments became more frequent as the decade progressed. Yet despite the circumstances behind their separations, they repeatedly expressed their longings for emotional and physical intimacy in language that was alternately searing, tender, and lighthearted. And they professed their profound, immutable love: "You see you are the most precious thing I have ever known," O'Keeffe wrote Stieglitz in 1926. "All my love goes to you—And the kiss that is my life."[9]

The summer of 1921 was not a productive time for O'Keeffe. Weighed down by the burdens of managing the large household of visitors at Lake George, she had little time to paint and initially found the scenery uninspiring. Eager to discover some semblance of the vast, untamed landscape that had so moved her in Texas, she accepted an invitation in May 1922 from Florence and Charles Schauffler to visit them at York Beach, Maine, while Stieglitz remained in New York on

7. McBride, 1926, as quoted in Susan Noyes Platt, "Responses to Modern Art in New York in the 1920s," Ph.D. diss., University of Texas at Austin, 1981, 41.
8. Dorothy Seiberling, "Horizons of a Pioneer," *Life*, Mar. 1, 1968, 52.
9. GOK to AS, Sept. 3, 1926.

jury duty. Warm, generous, and seemingly unflappable, Florence Schauffler was an ideal companion for O'Keeffe—happy to accompany her on long walks on the beach and equally content to give her time by herself. The couple's five grown sons, along with their wives and children, frequently visited their York Beach home, which was filled with a "funny hodge-podge of nondescript and heterogeneous furniture," Florence told Stieglitz. Their view overlooking the ocean, she continued, was sure to please O'Keeffe with "its shifting color and ceaseless movement."[10] She and O'Keeffe left New York on May 2, stopping first in Boston to visit the Museum of Fine Arts. In Stieglitz's absence, O'Keeffe was surprised to realize that she had "a feeling of quiet—of being a whole person all by myself that I seem to rather like—I seem to be only a very small fraction of a person when you are around—and I believe I like to be a whole one all by myself."[11] On May 15, Stieglitz went to Lake George to open the family's house for the summer and then to York Beach, where the two remained for a few days before going back to New York City.

Georgia O'Keeffe · [**Boston, Massachusetts**] · [**May 3, 1922**]

5 to 7—

Dearest Duck—

—The birds are singing—It's morning—the sun is shining in the window—I see the tops of trees in the park outside—it is the city common I think—This is the Woman's City Club —It must have been a great old house in its days as a private house—a most wonderful circular stairway and the halls curve about in a peculiar way—even the doors are curved like a warped board to fit in with the line of the rest of it and it isn't all curved in one circular direction—It seems to curve about in different directions—Modern architecture will have to hustle—I have a little room on the fourth floor shaped like this [sketch of her room]—

—I slept wonderfully with just one thickness of blanket over me—It is warmer here than in New York but I was glad to have my heavy coat as they insisted I go to Mrs. Schauffler son's[12] with her to supper and we went in his open Ford—A huge red sun over the river was wonderful—just a solemn ball of hot-looking stuff gazing out of a gray sky—

It seemed nice to ride through streets where the buildings are small—

Coming back here in the Ford again the little moon was over the river—long rows of low lights along the river—very clean-looking. In the afternoon going to her son's we saw the Harvard crew rowing on the river—

I thought of you—but I've thought of you all along Dearest—

The son's wife[13] teaches dancing—a very alive girl—She had a lovely old daguerreotype (that isn't spelled right I suppose but you will know what I mean)—It was of her mother and uncle as children and their father and mother when the grandfather was home on a furlough

---

10. Florence Schauffler to AS, June 4, 1921.

11. GOK to AS, Oct. 13, 1922.

12. Bennet Schauffler.

13. Marjorie Schauffler.

(I feel I don't know how to spell anything) from the Civil War. It is really wonderful when you think of what a family group would look like nowadays—

Well Duck—I'm safe as can be and I hope you are taking care of your dear little self—Do be careful—and be sure to fix your toes—I wish I could look in on you this morning and see what you do when you are alone—

I'm still in bed—it's 7:20 though and I'm going to get up now—

I was surprised to learn that Ogunquit is just twelve miles above York—I thought it much farther up the coast—

Will write you again later in the day—Dearest, you are the sweetest nicest thing I know—You even have all this curved house in you—

I am going to the museum first thing—

I don't seem to want to stop writing to you—it's almost as bad as leaving you.

—G—x—That's my kiss—

Georgia O'Keeffe · [**Boston, Massachusetts**] · [**May 3, 1922**]

318

I am at the Museum too early—they will not let me in yet—

I've been looking at the Indian on his horse[14] out in front—He looks so smooth armed and his horse so fat and well fed—I wish they had more lean muscle—and were not so slick—when it's so slick I can't imagine it very active—He even has dimples—don't you think that's funny—

Chinese stone—inside—

I am in love with the Compassionate Lord—*Padmapani* of the sixth or early seventh century[15]—He is wonderful—stands with both feet planted firmly in the center of a water lily that seems full to the top with water—He stands as though the wind is blowing his draperies slightly back—his back is colored red and blue—his trimming gold but all his front is gray—He must look quite different in this gray room with his paint all gone—than he looked when he was new—

I wonder—have we any chance at all to understand him—He is really marvelous—

The first hall I chanced down was Indian sculpture—many-handed figures—jewelry and some wonderful Indian paintings—

It's 3:30 and I am properly tired—museum-ed till now—

Am in the Abbey Room of the library[16] and it is awful—at least that is what I feel now—I am waiting for Mrs. Schauffler—

14. Cyrus E. Dallin, *Appeal to the Great Spirit,* 1909, bronze, Museum of Fine Arts, Boston.

15. Probably *Guanyin, Bodhisattva of Compassion* (when Guanyin is portrayed surrounded by a large lotus leaf, he is called Padmapani), Chinese, Northern Zhou or early Sui Dynasty, about A.D. 580, carved limestone (gray) with traces of polychrome and gilding, Museum of Fine Arts, Boston, 15.254.

16. Installed in 1895, the Abbey Room of the Boston Public Library includes fifteen murals on the Arthurian legend painted by Edwin Austin Abbey.

—I had a beautiful time in the museum—It seems to me that their selection and presentation are much finer than the Metropolitan—I could hardly believe my eyes at the Chinese and Japanese things—Enjoyed the Indian very much too—

The Sargents and Dodge Macknights are much finer than those in New York or Brooklyn—The Italian and Egyptian things I enjoyed immensely—It seems much easier to see things presented as they are here—

A row of Monets was interesting—Millet pastels make the Picasso of the man and woman asleep[17] seem rather reminiscent only he—Picasso—has carried Millet quite a bit ahead and I found Egyptian wood carvings that seemed modeled after Nadelman—I found an archaic Greek taken from Foggia—Some of the Egyptian things seemed very fine—

I am back in my room—at the window—up in the treetops it seems—a few—

—I was waiting for Mrs. Schauffler and she came—I've rested—and have just a moment before supper—

—I wish I could tell you what a good time I had in the museum—The whole trip was worthwhile to me for that even if I didn't go on to York and like that—

I wish you would come here with me sometime—I'm going on with her in the morning but am thinking I may try to spend a day here on my way back—I wouldn't want to start at it again tomorrow but by the time I return I'll be ready—

I was surprised at the Sargents in the library[18]—They are not nearly as bad as I had imagined—As single things—or apart from the place—they seem awful—but in their place they are quite festive—quite handsome—I suppose you have seen all the things I am talking about —I seem to take it for granted that you have—

People here seem very grumpy—very snappy—Even with my bad disposition I feel like a grinning cat by comparison—

I got some stockings on my way home from the museum—

Duck—I'd like to see you—Yesterday seems years ago—even this morning seems years ago—I have to laugh in going about by myself to find how much I depend on you—just little things—but they seem like a real joke on me.

Tomorrow morning at ten we go on—

You can be glad you don't see the old girls about this place—I never saw such a sour looking lot of women—Mrs. Schauffler says that is the way New England women look—They are awful—And the place is so—

Must go—

G—

---

17. Pablo Picasso's *Sleeping Peasants,* 1919, gouache, watercolor, and pencil on paper, Museum of Modern Art, New York. Formerly in the collection of John Quinn; see Judith Zilczer, *The Noble Buyer: John Quinn, Patron of the Avant-Garde* (Washington, D.C., 1978), 177.

18. From 1890 to 1919 the American painter John Singer Sargent worked on a series of ambitious murals entitled *Triumph of Religion* in the Boston Public Library reading room. Critics charged that two panels depicting a youthful *Church* and a collapsing *Synagogue,* unveiled in 1919, would encourage prejudice and discrimination; see Sally M. Promey, "The Afterlives of Sargent's Prophets: The Reception of Christian Devotional Art," *Art Journal* 57 (Spring 1998), 31–44.

Georgia O'Keeffe · [Boston, Massachusetts] · [May 3, 1922]

We had supper—a most surprising supper—for seventy cents—So much and so good—Her son's wife's mother was with us—I was sorry you couldn't be here—it was really as good as anything I've eaten in ages—not even Cos Cob[19] was better—No wine of course—But Dearest —these women—such faces—well to do women—three rooms full of them—I was the only one without a hat and they looked at me as though I must be something very new and strange—

I stopped my last note very abruptly when they came for supper—

I sat in my room looking out—the city lights again—the moon a bit hazy—the trees —seeming much greener today—It is so warm—still I'm glad to have my coat—in the car it is cool—There is quite a pond in the park. It all seemed so warm and a nice haziness—

It would be nice to feel you—

From where I am sitting now there seems to be nothing but dark blue outside—with lights here and there—yellow lights—blue lights—white lights—and green lights—I don't want to go out into it—I am just content to sit—by nine I'll be going to bed—

I saw two Egyptian stone figures today—two-thirds life size—They seemed to be moving forward—he with both hands down holding something firmly if I remember—she with her right arm round his waist—the hand showing in front—her left hand on his left arm[20]—the way I walk with you sometimes—They were very lovely together—Today we must be a little like them—must feel a little the same things—

The El Greco man[21] was a little like you too—very tender—something about the eyes—I had thought the thing as a whole would be larger—it was a rather wide canvas for its height—I had expected it to be higher—

Since I saw those Chinese and Japanese paintings I feel that painting can be as exciting as photography—some of them have a breathing quality of color that is almost unbelievable— The shapes often didn't seem to matter so much to me—the color just lives by itself—It's like watching a person breathe when they are asleep—You have a consciousness of life that is helpless like a child—

I wonder—do I make clear to you what I mean at all—

I never saw any color like it before—and I never heard anyone try to tell of anything like what I felt—Maybe I was crazy today—I must go again to look at them and see if I saw what I think I saw—

In the meantime I very much enjoy thinking I saw it—thinking I have something that I got there—I want to keep it awhile before I go and risk losing it for something else—The Japanese were very fiery—very fiery Dearest—to make one laugh—

—Well Dearest Child—I am going to bed—Don't work your dear little self too hard— do be careful—won't you? You are very precious—

19. Alma and Maurice Wertheim, collectors of both Stieglitz's and O'Keeffe's work, had a home in Cos Cob, Connecticut.
20. Probably *King Menkaure (Mycerinus) and Queen,* from Giza, Menkaure Temple, Fourth Dynasty, 2548–2530 B.C., graywacke, Museum of Fine Arts, Boston.
21. Probably El Greco, *Fray Hortensio Félix Paravicino,* 1609, oil on canvas, Museum of Fine Arts, Boston.

320

I wonder if I should have left you—I hope you are being careful about your food—
I become quite panicky when I begin to think that maybe I should have stayed with my baby
—I can scarcely wait for tomorrow to have word from you when we get to [York Beach]—

I feel like a real hero—And I must say I have had a great day—I think you will like that
so I feel a bit excused for leaving you—

Good Night Dearest—

I so wish I could see you all bunched up in a little heap and surprise you. Don't sleep
with the pillows on your feet and do fix your toe. I hope the jury is not unpleasant—

—G.—

Alfred Stieglitz · [New York City] · [May 4, 1922] +

8:10 Morning.—Just read your sweetest dearest little letter. I'm so glad you are enjoying all.—
Just a big kiss before breakfasting. Cocoa & zwieback ready.—Shaved. Corns fixed.—Bed fixed.
Room cleaned up. All ready for the day. All before breakfasting. Chased down for mail as soon
as all was done—Another kiss. More later.

8:15. I've breakfasted!—A few more words before hurrying downtown.—The night was a little
better. Cooler—It rained—Before going asleep I caught myself saying: Goodnight, Sweetheart
—It was a nice feeling to feel it happening so naturally—You are my sweetheart.

—I can imagine how you felt in your room in the Women's Club.—The fine old
building.—That's what I like in Boston—a feeling of old solidity.—I know the park too.—

Ogunquit not so far from York!—I'm certainly glad you had your heavy coat motoring.
—Felt that might happen.—Young America lives on wheels.—

—I have my repaired suit on. Looks very well—It would have been a crime to have
discarded it. Was feeling sorry for the blue one I was wearing!—Have hung away all clothes.
Hung up right—In wardrobe (closet).—

—I have to laugh with the time you occasionally seem to have with spelling.—You are
yourself sometimes like one of those words in which all the letters are there but not always quite
there where the "law" expects to find them—The word then frequently has achieved a peculiar
fascination—like a very fine looking Frenchwoman (or man) speaking English.—And you are
often like that only raised to the nth degree of that kind of charm.—

—Now I'd better run along—Want to go to tailor before subwaying.—

An endless kiss till you struggle for some air.—

You Sweetest One.—

Thursday: 6:20 Evening: About three-quarters hour ago I got home—Rather wet. Jury all day,
except lunch hour—Didn't rain till four—Was in court till nearly 4:40. Still same case. Has
turned into a very comic affair. No court tomorrow.—Continue on Monday.—Hope to get
through with the case by then.—

—During lunch hour I went to Brentano's & looked around awhile. Then went to City

Hall Park (court house is there) & took a look at MacMonnies' *Civic Virtue* about which there has been so much fuss.[22] Amusing to listen to the crowd's remarks. The thing itself looks too stupid for words with the towering skyscrapers as background, etc.—I may photograph it as a lark—Make a comic snap.—In itself the thing may not be half bad.—But I hate that kind of stuff down there.—It's bad enough for a museum.—

When I got back here found your very dear letter. All about the museum & the enticing women of Boston.—Enjoyed your reactions in the museum. Yes, I know the things you talked about. So could follow you in all you said.—It's great the way you see straight.—

—Yes, a second visit will be much worthwhile. (Marion[23] just phoned. She doesn't care to risk going out in the downpour—is probably unwell—I think I told you it occurred to me last night to ask her to go to Lilias' dance[24] on the ticket. As it is I guess no one will use it.)

—And perhaps some day we'll get a chance to see it together. I certainly think the Boston museum a much more enjoyable place than our Metropolitan.—

—Donald and Elizabeth[25] are here for the night—

—Kiss—

They & I & Rosenfeld will dine with Lee here. Rosenfeld doesn't know it yet. And then go to the Seligmann affair. Lizzie[26] is in Mamaroneck for the night.—

—There is a real warm downpour—a strong wind from the northeast. I wonder is it coming from the sea—from up where you are. I do hope you are not starting in at the seashore with a rainy spell—cold & so damp.—Do be careful.—

Just at present Elizabeth & Donald went to 14 East 60.[27] I told them how you had gone. —Saw them just about fifteen minutes.—Am drying my hat & coat in the bathroom—small stove lit—Took my shoes off too—Got wet—coming from subway—Lexington Avenue & 68th Street.

—Have made an appointment with Marion to go to Juley's[28] Saturday morning— Tomorrow, if it rains, I shall try to see Marie. Go to Stone's[29] and Bourgeois[30]—to see how your pictures hang & look.—There is much I want to get done before Monday.—

—The wind is blowing harder. I'd certainly rather stay home than trot off to theatre.

22. Frederick MacMonnies's *Civic Virtue,* a statue of a scantily clad youth standing on two sirens, incited controversy as soon as it was installed in March 1922. Critics insisted it degraded women and demanded that it be removed; see "Say 'Virtue' Statue Degrades Women," NYT, Mar. 16, 1922, 13.

23. Marion Beckett, a painter whose work Stieglitz had shown at 291.

24. A dancer who occasionally gave public performances, Lilias MacLane Seligmann was married to Herbert Seligmann, a journalist and later a photographer.

25. In 1919, Stieglitz's niece Elizabeth, daughter of Lee and Lizzie Stieglitz, married Donald Davidson.

26. Elizabeth (Lizzie) Stieglitz, Lee Stieglitz's wife.

27. In the early 1870s, Stieglitz's father, Edward, built the family's house at 14 East 60th St.; however, no members of the family lived there in 1922.

28. Peter A. Juley and Son, commercial photographers in New York, made portraits of artists and photographed their works of art.

29. Stone's was a tailor.

30. The Bourgeois Gallery, which was showing works by Joseph Stella, Stefan Hirsh, Edward S. Bruce, and other artists, "rather prides itself upon being 100 percent American"; see "The World of Art," NYT, May 14, 1922, 55.

It does seem an eternity since day before yesterday—fifty-four hours!—That's since the train pulled out.—

—I do miss you—greatly.—And still I'm glad you went—It's doing something positive for you—& so does something positive for me.—

Rosenfeld is late.—I had better—(—Rosenfeld just phoned. He's still at 23rd Street. Will be late a few minutes—)

Well, Sweetheart, consider yourself hugged & kissed.—I'm very hungry in every way!—(Had a sandwich at an automat at 1:45).—

Strand phoned & told me about his judging at Orange. Beck[31] will go with me some time to pick out a trunk for you—wholesale prices.—If you are back in time we can all go.—

—You probably got the first letter from me today—

Kisses—Kisses—Kisses—Kisses—

Georgia O'Keeffe · [**York Beach, Maine**] · [**May 4, 1922**] +

Thursday night—8
Dearest Duck—

I seem to like to address you as Dearest Duck—I wonder why—another of my questions—

Today has been so exciting I feel like a perfect wreck—

I am sitting in the kitchen on a funny little rocking chair with a red cushion on the seat —my feet are perched up on the rack below the oven door—onions are boiling on the stove for supper—The wind howls like the devil out here—It isn't plastered or anything like that it's just boards—a nice dark wood without finish of any kind except that it's partly papered white up about seven feet—and it's painted up that high where it isn't papered—All sorts of pots and pans and strainers and spoons hang about everywhere—table-tops white oilcloth—long hangings in front of cupboards are bright red—ceiling is very high up and dark—floor not even painted and hasn't been scrubbed any too often—Something about the whole place makes me feel that extraordinarily good food has been cooked in it—made to use and not to look at—

Not being plastered you hear the rain on the roof and sides and the wind howls as finely as I ever heard it—

Mrs. Schauffler had gone to a neighbor's—She just came in—

[May 5, 1922]
Morning—I haven't known the time since I waked at 6:30—old time[32]—It is a quarter to eleven now—I am in my room with my left side back to the open fire and my right side front

---

31. In 1922, Paul Strand married Rebecca (Beck) Salsbury, daughter of the self-proclaimed creator of Barnum and Bailey's "Buffalo Bill's Wild West Show." She was a secretary in the early 1920s.

32. First instituted during World War I as a way to cut fuel consumption, daylight savings time became optional in 1919. Some states, such as Massachusetts and Rhode Island, continued to use it, as did a few municipalities, such as New York City and Lake George. York Beach did not follow it.

to the ocean—It is pouring rain—a wonderful sound with the little sizzle and crackle of the fire—

—Yesterday it was only misting and we went out and walked a little on the beach—I with an umbrella to protect my head from the wind more than the mist—Today it is just pouring—it poured all night—

I love it—every time I turned over in bed I thought of you and enjoyed the sound of the rain—The bed is indecently large and soft—The cover—she calls it "down puffs"—very light and very warm—I couldn't help feeling how nicely you would cuddle up in the warm softness with the sound of the sea and the rain outside—and how you would like it—I think you would never get up till the sun came out—I wanted to get up because I had to look at it—even a wonderfully soft warm bed isn't so interesting when *you* are not in it—I got up and looked out twice and got back into my warmness—I don't know what time it was when I dressed—

—The rain is wonderful—I feel so peaceful and so excited all at the same time—The house is so still and even though it is low tide the beach is perfectly shiny and smooth and clean looking and there is a wonderful sea rolling in—It's raining so hard that it all seems like a gray sea—with just a little green in it—great long white waves breaking through—big ones and little ones and thin ones and thick ones—

Little Duck—I am so glad I came—if only you are all right without me—

I got some pastels in Boston—Am sending for more—also I got some paper—I began to feel there that I might want them—Am sending there today for two dozen more sheets of paper and more pastels—her son[33] will bring them up tomorrow—

Yesterday I tried three of the waves[34]—am going to work at it again in a little while—

I just read more of your letter—read parts of it over—You dearest little creature—I am so glad you greased your head more—If you had your hair cut it would be easier for you—

Of course I know you love me[35]—I guess coming up here and being here is being very much myself—and if I didn't feel that you love me—the thing that's *me—myself*—if I didn't feel it very surely—I wouldn't have come—You precious—I hope your insides are all right—

I wish you would come and sleep with me in this bed for a night—just one—and listen to the rain and the ocean and the fire—

Dearest I do love you—And I am very safe—Fluffy is doing nicely too thank you—

Love—Love—Love—

G—

33. Bennet Schauffler.

34. Lynes 382–384, 387.

35. On May 2, 1922, Stieglitz had written O'Keeffe: "You are very, very dear to me.—You see you may have been an 'Idea' to me at first—or at least partially an 'Idea.'—I think I have gotten beyond 'Ideas'—I know you are an extraordinarily fine person—I know that you mean truth to me. I know you help me be my best self.—All that is not imagined by me—I know.—I wonder will that answer your question do I love you."

Later. 9 A.M.—Just in again. We breakfasted at Sharp's.—The air felt good. Rain & gale—coolish—walking weather!—A letter from my dear little girl.—I read it walking to Sharp's—Heard nothing—saw nothing—felt nothing—except just you & your—

(Mrs. Wertheim just phoned.—Re—the school & her husband. All fine. Also said the Bourgeois show was so good—with the exception of Stella who seemed soft—All just as I know it existing—as I told Rosenfeld last night what I thought the show was like)—

But to come back to your dearest letter. It's great what the Japanese & Chinese made you feel.—It's the first time I don't resent the enthusiasm for them. With nearly every one else what is "felt" is a self-imposed transposed *attitude*. A sort of "looking for because," etc., etc. At any rate you have found something for yourself—a real living thing.—And what you say about the Egyptians I feel is true too.—Of course you & I don't know book language—We can't quote—We don't "know"—except that which we *know* through ourselves—the deepest feeling—

—I had to laugh about those women—Bostonians.—No, I don't think I ever looked around at womenkind when in Boston. You naturally must have seemed something more than queer in their midst.—

—Davidson is sitting here, reading the paper.—We are going to Bourgeois & to Stone's. —And then I'll develop today.—Formaldehyde won't be needed.[36]—Mrs. Wertheim asked me to some school-party for tomorrow but I told her I had much work to do. And *had* to do it.—

The dance last night was rather enjoyable in spots.[37] But it showed me clearly why I didn't like Mrs. Dufour—what was underlying the certain inarticulateness of the whole business —Hapgood's friend was in splendid form.—Lilias was statuesque.—Some of the kids a delight —All had a good time.—But Mrs. Dufour sticks in my mind as a grimace!—

—After the dance Elizabeth & Flora[38] drove home while Rosenfeld, Strand, Beck, Donald & I went to Luissier's (very nearby)—Seligmann & Lilias joining soon after—to have a "bite."—Well we had a great laugh.—Strand related amongst other things how he had inherited some cameras & underwear from his uncle, etc., etc—We all laughed.—And then Beck described how Strand appeared in lavender pajamas (his uncle's) when they got married. Strand flushed. Beck stroked his cheek & told him she didn't wish to be indiscreet—It was all so humorous & very nice—And we just shouted with laughter. And you know me when my imagination gets hold of a picture—Well, Strand did look at moments like a dripping poodle—But he too enjoyed the joke—It was all very nice. Much more enjoyable than the dance because it was really so much more alive—truer.—

—It was raining hard—& the wind blew harder & cold—as Davidson & I walked

---

36. Photographers sometimes added formaldehyde to the developing solution to prevent "frilling," the separation of the photographic emulsion from its support.

37. Elise Dufour, assisted by Lilias MacLane Seligmann and twenty-four dancers, presented a program of rhythmic dances at the Town Hall, New York, on May 4, 1922.

38. Flora Stieglitz Straus was the sister of Elizabeth Davidson and the daughter of Stieglitz's brother Lee and sister-in-law Lizzie.

across town—& as no cars were in sight & I fearing we might be locked out—we taxied home—

Everyone asks for you. Everyone wants to know how long you'll be gone!—

You are my Little Girl—I wonder what you are doing now—whether you are feeling comfortable—whether the sea can be seen from your window—whether it is storming—and perhaps see nothing but wetness & hear the howling wind—

It's hard to believe that perhaps the sun may be out there. I doubt it.

Now I guess we'll go.—Take care of yourself.—I am taking care of myself—Very good care—

I am with you.—You are with me.—

Loads & loads of kisses—All kinds.

Georgia O'Keeffe · [**York Beach, Maine**] · [**May 6, 1922**] +

After lunch—Saturday—
Dearest Duck—

The sun is shining brightly—very warm but the wind seems cool—a great mist rising from the sand—So I lay on the steps in the sun like a dog—face down—just listening and being hot—colored glasses on—it is so bright—She has people here cleaning—In a few moments we go up the beach somewhere on the trolley—Today is harder to put down in color than the other days—I've been thinking of it—I'm going to try to put down something every day for you—I am sure it is finer here now before other people come than it can be later—No one about—just us—and the ocean—

Fluffy jumps very high—

I wish you could come if only for a couple of days—It would do you lots of good—I've been thinking—lying here—your letters—you are very tired—maybe I shouldn't have left you alone—then I find myself wondering if this porch wouldn't be great for photographing—It faces directly east and is very high up—I hear you saying I'm crazy and all the other things—that I have a "great idea"—etc—

[May 7, 1922]
Is ten after twelve at night—I'm in bed—my fire crackles—I'm propped up on huge soft pillows and well covered—The frogs and other night things are singing a great song and along with it that endless roaring roll of the ocean—I'm not a bit sleepy—

Dearest—I've had the most wonderful afternoon—The sort of sea that Homer tried to paint—but that just can't be done—It's the first real thrill I've had that compares favorably with Texas—I just almost died—it was so wonderful—I simply shouted and was so terrified at times that I just had to hold on to Mrs. Schauffler. For three hours watching the tide coming in with these tremendous waves rolling over rocks that make New York seem like an idiot's toy—The sky mostly blue—and such masses of froth and foam rushing and rolling and booming till everything seemed to shake—spray flying way up in the air as high as the house at 65th Street[39] it seemed at least—and such whiteness I had never imagined—such maddening power—We climbed up and around and down over rocks—great walls of them—

It seems you must come and see it—I feel like saying I just won't go home till you come—I think you would love it even more than I—I often feel that you get something way down deep inside of you that means—that *is very very* much to you—that you don't have to talk about—probably can't talk about—I must just sputter about what I like—

However—I'm not going to say I'll stay till you come because it might be too long to wait to see my baby—Dearest Duck—I had a most wonderful afternoon—and in spite of a good stiff wind—I'm feeling fine—

As we changed trolleys on the way home the son from Boston and his wife[40] met us in their Ford—they had come with the wife's mother and another young man from Boston—The son who seems to be a very ardent admirer of his mother—remarked as he went to bed that everything was very Schauffler-like—They arrived—expected—but no hostess to receive them—no beds or fires made—and rafts of food—hot, ready to slide onto the table at a moment's notice—even to cocktails—

It was a festive meal—wonderful after the afternoon in the wind—then danced a little—even the two old ladies—I felt clumsy the first time—it seemed so unexpected and far away from me—but by the third one it seemed quite natural—Then we sat by the fire in Mrs. Schauffler's room—and here I am in bed—

—When I think back to New York—I wonder which am I—I feel as though I have dozens of selves—Dearest—Do you really love all of me—all my selves—Maybe you don't know—

I feel as though I am getting to something of myself here that I couldn't get when I was with you—Do you understand?—I think you do—I think you like it—Maybe you didn't mind my not having it—but I guess you did mind my resenting not having it—It must have been annoying—I don't really know what I'm talking about—but maybe you can get an inkling—

Anyway—you are my dearest—and your arms and your kisses are home to me—and I love you very very dearly—We seem to be one no matter if we are miles apart—

I've been writing this and thinking to you for exactly an hour—Must go to sleep—as we may go and climb those rocks again tomorrow—

Good night my dear one—Do I make you feel how much I love you—

Georgia O'Keeffe · [York Beach, Maine] · [May 8, 1922]

Monday morning—I've just washed Fluffy—after breakfast—It's ten o'clock but I've been down to the beach—without a sweater—It's quite warm—no fires—the sun comes in so brightly—Great lumpy white clouds—surf still rolling from the days I've written you of but

39. Lee and Lizzie Stieglitz's house at 60 East 65th St. was four stories high.
40. Bennet and Marjorie Schauffler.

the wind is from the land and blows the top of each big wave backward in a fine misty frosty spray—The sea is very shiny and green when you are down by it—

Dearest—I wish you were here—Last night I was really homesick for you—really lonesome—I had to laugh at myself—and knew you would too—I just wish you could see how big and wonderful it is out there—

Yesterday after a very festive two o'clock meal—the Boston son left with his Ford and friends—then I walked up the beach for about two miles and a half—it was lovely—toward a lighthouse—the coast becoming rougher and rougher—(it's so lovely and blue and green and lavender out now)—Nothing as mad as the place we went to the day before though—I was walking east—and suddenly the light seemed so queer—I turned round in time to see the sun going under a cloud—There was something terrifying about it and I realized that part of the booming noise was thunder[41]—that it wasn't all waves on rocks—I was walking on the top of the rocks—water way below—

I began hurrying home—walking into a most wonderful purplish—gray yellow—gray pink storm cloud with lightning streaking through it—It was marvelous—That on one side—the ocean on the other—gradually being darkened by the storm cloud—and the moon look-ing too foolish and yellow for words—in a patch of bright blue sky—just looking on at all this madness—I hurrying as fast as my feet could carry me thinking Mrs. Schauffler might be worrying—and thinking of you—It began to pour just before I got here—She was at the door watching me come—We watched the excitement a while—I wrapped up in a pink blanket with a very pink face—wonderful lightning—then the setting sun suddenly breaking through—blazing on all the madness—

—I took a warm bath and went to bed before seven—ten to seven when I got in to be exact—I thought of you—was lonesome—very—and the ocean suddenly became a terrific and terrible monster—not to be trusted—I was almost afraid to be here in bed in the house beside it and I wanted you—then I went to sleep—Mrs. Schauffler brought me a glass of water that I only half knew about—I was too sleepy to want supper—

It was 3:30 when I waked up—tangled in my hair—I hadn't braided it—I got up and looked out—stars shining brightly—queer little clouds—tiny ones—far apart in the sky—could see the whiteness of the waves breaking—I got back in bed—braided my hair—and won-dered about you—went right to sleep again till daylight—I don't know what time I got up—she was making coffee—I made the toast and ate much raisin bread—My coat is drying on the roof again—

Am going at the pastels again now—the skin is wearing off my fingers from rubbing—

I am wondering if you might change your mind and come for a couple of days here—then together a day in Boston—

I want so much to see you but I don't want to leave this—I can't quite think of it yet—and Mrs. Schauffler would more than like to have you—

G.—

I may seem persistent—but it is so lovely here it seems worthwhile to be persistent—

41. See Lynes 385, 386.

328

So don't mind—Just do as you must and when you assure me that you won't come—I'll start for home or for Albany to meet you—

I want to stop in Boston for a day or a few hours at least—to go to the museum again—

Alfred Stieglitz · **[New York City]** · **[May 9, 1922]** +

Tuesday Morning: 8:30.—I'm a little late. Bed fixed. Shaved.—Laundry ready for man.— Breakfasting while I rush off a few lines—I slept pretty well. I had walked quite some yesterday. And the air was of the bracing kind—

—Your letter of this morning is another real joy—Full of sea breezes.—I'm so glad you are feeling so free—much like in Texas.—Nothing could give me more inner quiet than to know that—Yes, you dear, I like all your different selves. You have quite a few.—But it is they that make you so different. And it is the *difference* that means so terribly much to me—

—My "business" is still here. It would be stupid for me to leave just now. And then there is court. Everything tells me—much as *I'd* prefer the ocean—*You*—Mrs. Schauffler, whom I like greatly—*very much*—to all this "business" here. Don't think I like most of the things I do.—They somehow "like" me & they have got to be attended to—*by someone*. For your sake & my own.—And everyone else's.—It may all be a stupid way of feeling—or seeing—things— really a very stupid one I believe myself—but there you are—that's the way I register!!—

—You stay at York Beach as I wrote last night.—And I'm sure Mrs. Schauffler is glad to have you.—If she has had enough she is honest enough to let you know.—And I'll see if there is a way to call for you & at the same time get a glimpse of some of the things you are so enjoying.—

—It's all right that you are away. You needed just what you are getting. It had been worrying me quite some time that you weren't getting something like it—I'm an old poke.— You are not.—But under different conditions I mightn't be quite as poky as I am.—Still I'm of the poky kind.—You are not.—And I'm glad you are not.—

—You are *just right* as far as I am concerned—

And you danced.—Great.—I wish there were a little more elasticity up at Lake George. —It would be so easy.—But I suppose it is a form of pokiness too. So I'd better say nothing.

—It's a beautiful morning—Yesterday downtown in the sunlight I noticed the buildings for the first time since going to court.—Formerly they always "excited" me. I still *feel* them—but they don't stir me to wanting to express anything—*give* anything. Of course I know I'm tired in many ways. But not tired in the sense of being hurt & carrying too great a load.—You see *you* have given me so much that many things—although they are—do not carry with them the significance they at one time did.

In some ways I'm really *ages old*. Nothing to be very proud of. Nothing one should care to be.—One is—or is not.—

Yes I can see the ocean—& hear it.—I've watched it for hours & days crossing the ocean—And while I felt very alone with it—its tremendous power—its endless moods—its ever varying forms—its endlessness—And yet knowing that in Time Infinite it would no longer be what it appears to us.—

—Dearest—It's good to live—and feel all things.—It takes extraordinary strength to live simply—yet remain in touch with all that is.—

You are very, very dear to me—Everything you feel must echo that.—

One big, big kiss—I've got to run along now—Remember me to Mrs. Schauffler.

Georgia O'Keeffe · **[York Beach, Maine]** · **[May 11, 1922]**

Dearest Duck—

Your letter of yesterday—written Monday night and Tuesday morning pleases me very much and also puzzles me—Pleases me that you think of coming for me—and puzzles me to see when you are going to get it in with all the other things you have planned—I can't very well make the poster here—I have no paper fit to make it on—and some way or other an exhibition seems to be such a faraway affair that I doubt if I could do anything satisfactory if I had the paper to do it on[42]—The idea seems to give me a queer feeling in my stomach—a dizzy feeling in my head and a perfectly blank state of mind—I'm hopeless—Maybe Bluemner would do it —I don't seem to be able to think of anyone else—

I had rather planned—after I decided to stay *one* week—to go to Boston next Monday or Tuesday—The idea of leaving you for more than two weeks seemed to be beyond my imagination—but if you can come later next week—I love it here and really don't like to think of leaving at all—I will go with you to Lake George if you want to—or if you think the other way round better—you to go there alone—and then come here—I am about equally pleased either way—So do what you think best—most convenient for you—I am satisfied with anything so long as you are coming—one way or the other—I am rather waiting for your letter today —as I think it may give something a bit more definite—

I can't tell you how much I like your letters—unless—you just know—You must know—and it's so nice that I've had one every day—Yours look so neat—and mine have been so untidy—Considering the way a blot grieves you—I ought to feel terrible about the scraps I send you—but I don't—it doesn't seem to worry me at all—

The sea is lovely and green today with a gray-blue horizon—I've seen the sun come up the last two mornings—merely pretty—not what I call exciting at all—The tide is high and seems very gentle—just long slow little waves breaking—It seems so peaceful—and the whole beach and the whole ocean seem to belong to me alone as I look out on it from my window— It is so peaceful that I feel you must know about it—

Day before yesterday—the day we went to Ogunquit—we had a beautiful walk—the tide was low and the rocks near the water wonderfully dark and rich looking—the ocean bluer and greener than one ever imagines it in one's wildest ocean dreams—

---

42. In June 1922, Stieglitz lent some of O'Keeffe's paintings, as well as works by other artists associated with him, to an exhibition in the Municipal Building, Freehold, N.J.

Still it always seems nice to come back to this long clean sandy stretch of beach after walking up the wilder coast—I always feel relieved to get here—There is something so terrifying about the rocky places—I like them—but—maybe I'm afraid—maybe it's too much excitement for me to carry alone—

Portsmouth—yesterday was a queer experience—The country on the way over by trolley is very lovely—The houses so neat—so severe—They are quite as terrifying as the ocean—no people outside around them—occasionally—very seldom—a man working in the fields—

I don't know exactly why but I couldn't help wondering was it possible that any real lovemaking ever went on inside those severe white houses—any of the fine—wild warmness of lovemaking—any of the madnesses—It seemed almost impossible—and I keep on wondering—

I know you will laugh at such an idea—but dearest they don't look like it—Mrs. Schauffler says it isn't done in New England—I doubt if even you would dare to kiss me in Portsmouth—There are many fine old houses there—so different from the hospitable air of Southern houses—I felt in Portsmouth that it must have taken all the vitality of the inhabitants to live up to the houses—

I didn't feel at home at all—I felt that all the houses disapproved of me—

We had a brilliant colored lobster lunch—it was very gay and very good—

When we came home I picked some dandelions and we had a most festive supper—broiled fish—my dandelions chopped and mixed with mashed potatoes and boiled egg—The latter was my contribution—It's most wonderful—I remembered I liking it very much when I was a youngster and my experiment at making it worked very well—We also had cheese with sage in it and cucumbers with onions—

I never had a stranger meal but we both enjoyed it—so did the cleaning woman—I was wondering all the time if you would like it—I seem to be able to eat more and more every day —today I am fixing onions the way Dauble fixed them—

I won't talk so much about strange food—it will frighten you—

But I do want to tell you that we have wonderful moonlight—

I seem to feel so near your coming that it doesn't seem so necessary to tell you all these things—

It will do you lots of good—you dear Little Duck—

Don't expect too much of my pastels—I am stacking them in a pile on my closet shelf—but I guess they aren't much—just some foolishnesses—I am beginning to feel that I might be interested in painting—There are all sorts of things in my head but it's so late now—I'll do the best I can with the pastels—I can manage very well—I like them too because they go very fast and I can leave them at anytime—I guess the reason why I like oils is that they seem more definite—

Must get to work now—

We stay at home today—I'm glad—I have a few things I want to put down—

Dear Sweet One—

Thursday—12:35 P.M.

Georgia O'Keeffe · [York Beach, Maine] · [May 11?, 1922]

My Dearest Sweetest Child:

Your two yellow letters just came after lunch—and a nice messy one from Childs—however I like your neat ones—Let's hope that the Marin life insurance[43] will amount to something—I hope he hears very soon—it isn't pleasant to wait—but I some way feel that it must surely be over five thousand dollars—I can't imagine anything quite as bad as that—

What you say about protecting Kitty and me[44]—we must talk about—It gives me a creepy feeling as an idea—I wish you could give her some of the feeling of inner protection that you give me—Maybe she will someday get it—I want to help you give it to her if I can in any way—but I do not see [that] just now—

I feel your little heart and soul just twisted every which way—when I had hoped that Marin's father dying might mean some letup for you from that quarter—Naturally it makes you think and feel many things—and knowing you in that condition makes me want to hold you close and let you talk to me—

Thinking of you as a week away seems a long distance and a long time—I must get to work my dearest—You feel me with you anyway—don't you—even if we are days and hours and miles apart—

Alfred Stieglitz · [New York City] · [May 11?, 1922] +

Night: 10:30. I'm so tired I feel more stupid than ever.—Eyes feel a little better. Head itches like fire. Greased it. But the itch means a change of wind—East or northeast—It may be raining up your way.—

—Well, I did get a bath. Tried three times today—Finally at 6:30 went down & asked Agnes[45] to light the apparatus. So I got enough hot water to bathe.—A real struggle to achieve.—Amusing.

—Was three times at barber's. Never connected. Am to go at ten A.M. tomorrow. I do need a haircut—Perhaps the itch won't be so bad—

It burns—Always some torture—

—At 3:30 I was ready to go to Juley's to get the remaining prints. Phone. Duchamp—He came up & stayed with me till six—I always like him. So clean cut.—Says Man Ray likes it

---

43. As Stieglitz reported in his letter of May 9, 1922, to O'Keeffe, Marin had just learned that he would receive only his recently deceased father's life insurance and that his stepmother would inherit the bulk of the estate.

44. The day before, Stieglitz had written O'Keeffe: "I *must protect you*—& Kitty—as far as I am able to. And by *protect* I mean something which is not easily explained." He continued: "It has become clearer & clearer that as fine as individuals are at times to each other—conditions turn them collectively into a huge monster as far as the one standing alone is concerned—And the *one must be ready*—Must be ready without fear—Either with physical brute force—or spiritual strength!"

45. Probably Lee and Lizzie Stieglitz's maid.

in Paris.—Photographs for a living!!—He, Duchamp, gives French lessons to live. Is finishing the glass painting.[46] We must go & see it.

—He liked the portrait (corncob) of you.[47] Also some of others—Looked at your paintings. Some. And Marin's.—We talked many things. Picabia—Mrs. Picabia. He looks at things very straight.—Is very fine.—

Seligmann called up to see whether I was too lonely—Litchfield came at 7:30. Had written him. Dined at Chinese restaurant.—Kerfoot didn't turn up—A queer hash of a day—

New *Broom* came. Opening page a poem by Sandburg: "Four Prints by Steichen."[48] !!! —There is change of character in the magazine. No pasted on art.—

—I can't tell you how glad I am the Little Girl is away from all this dreary atmosphere. Really, I can't tell you *how* glad I am—Of course I miss you greatly. But I know these days are not pleasant here.—

I suppose I'm not pleasant—too too tired. Temporarily used up—

I'm going to bed—It is still early for me—But I want to lie down in the darkness.— And there is a wind blowing.—

—You are very sweet, very dear to me. And I still can't understand why I can be so much to you.—I feel too stupid for words. And you certainly can't like anything so stupid—

—I'm glad the pastels were right—

Much, much much love—

& *One Big Kiss!*

Georgia O'Keeffe · [**York Beach, Maine**] · [**May 16, 1922**] +

Tuesday morning—8:35—

The Schaufflers are gone and I am disgusted to say that I forgot to give them the letter for you—I wonder if you are nearing Lake George this morning—I had breakfast at the tail end of theirs—walked up the beach till the sun hurt my eyes—was back at seven—after looking in the windows of two or three of the cottages on the way home—

Took down the soiled breakfast things—and have looked at my pastels—They look pretty sick—Fixed them in a neat pile for you to look at—It has been so exciting to be here —and I've felt so rushed that I feel I haven't given much in the way of an edge to anything— either the drawings or my letters to you—all seems to be scrambly to me—There may be three —maybe four things there—that are worth keeping—

The wind is blowing in waves across the green grass of the field out there—and I hear the water behind me—the sun is warm on my back—

---

46. *The Bride Stripped Bare by Her Bachelors, Even (The Large Glass)*, 1915–1923; see Arturo Schwarz, *The Complete Works of Marcel Duchamp* (New York, 1997), 287.

47. Greenough 662.

48. *Broom: An International Magazine of the Arts* 2 (May 1922), 1. Published first in Europe and then in the United States, *Broom* (1921–1924) was one of many "little magazines" dedicated to the arts that flourished in the 1920s.

Dearest I love you—

I am on my back—wanting to be spread wide apart—waiting for you—to die with the sense of you—the pleasure of you—the sensuousness of you touching the sensuousness of me —All my body—all of me is waiting for you to touch the center of me with the center of you—

I got up—a moment after writing the last page—walked round the room—found the other pages of my letter to you—looked out the window—

Dearest—my body is simply crazy with wanting you—If you don't come tomorrow— I don't see how I can wait for you—I wonder if your body wants mine the way mine wants yours—the kisses—the hotness—the wetness—all melting together—the being held so tight that it hurts—the strangle and struggle—the release that moans and groans and the quickly drawn breath—the reaching of something in the whole body for the center of heaven—the relaxing to prolong the pleasure that goes through every inch of one's body—one's center touched—repeatedly with that center that goes into one's center with such madness pushing and pounding and beating at the middle of one's soul till it is satisfied—the ring about the opening to one's center begins to contract and one becomes gradually a limp thing—hot—wet—relieved —satisfied—and your smooth wet little pinkness lies beside me—all in a limp dampness— both unconscious in his release—for a moment—then pale little smiles at one another—

When I feel how your touching my body—getting into my body—has given all of me to you—all of you to me as much as one human being can get into and feel another of another —I wonder if there is any difference in body—and spirit—soul and mind—aren't they all one and the same thing—

I seem to feel my body very intensely this morning—so much so that I wonder if there is anything else to me—It's my body that wants you and it seems to be the only thought or desire that I have—It even seems to be my only memory of you—two bodies that have fused—have touched with completeness at both ends making a complete circuit—making them one—a circle that nothing can break—You have given me—the circle of the most painfully intense pleasure —most pleasurably intense pain—The circle with two centers—each touching the other—The mathematical impossibility of the situation is probably nature's reason for the particularly keen pleasure she affords when the mathematically impossible happens—

I must work—I'm in such a state that I could write about this all day—

Does it tell you how wildly hungry every inch of me is for you—even my toes. It's no use to say it's my soul crying for you—I know good and well that it is my body—my blood— my flesh—even my bones seem to cry for you—hunger for you—

[May 17, 1922]
Wednesday—5:30

All night I was with you Dearest—I waked at day break—saw the sun rise round and red—and you were with me—It seems the last twenty-four hours I've been with you—more than at all since I've been away from you and it quiets me—My madness is gone—and all day I've felt so quiet and so snuggly close to you—quietly flowing into you—the peace after the madness of yesterday seems strange—This morning as the light was coming I seemed to have you in my arms—Your dear little head on my left breast—Our legs close locked together—

I patting your little smooth behind—soothing my baby—You are so very dear—and it all seemed so real that I can't help but feel that you felt it—

Yesterday was a torture to me—a kind of torture that I've never experienced before— You have always relieved me—I didn't realize how much—For a while I just lay on the bed— face down—holding my breasts—it hurt so—I didn't see how I could stand it—then I got up and walked—

I had to do something—I felt I couldn't stand the ocean so I walked up the back road— then later on the beach—

I forgot to tell you that before I went to walk—I made a drawing to tell you about it all—

Dearest One—I do want you—not madly like yesterday—but just to see your dear little face—and see how you are—and feel you hold me close for a moment—I had so hoped you would come today—I've been very quiet—and just waited for you—all day though—I seemed so close to you that it seemed I didn't really have to write—

Now it's night coming again—the last train has come and no you—So I've written you the day and must wait for tomorrow—I am very quiet—only hoping that you are caring very well for your dear little self—

And remembering that you are the dearest most wonderful thing in the world to me— most precious—My baby.

Good Night—

Much—much love to you—you know—don't you.

EXHILARATED BY her brief vacation in Maine, O'Keeffe immediately began to work when she and Stieglitz arrived at Lake George later in June. Although many visitors came to the Hill that summer and fall, she made more than fifty-five paintings and pastels—far more than previous years—of apples, flowers, and leaves, as well as the hills and lake itself. Stieglitz, too, made many photographs, including portraits of O'Keeffe and others, and he embraced a new subject, clouds, that would preoccupy him for the next several years. In the early 1920s, O'Keeffe had renovated a small shed, which she called the Shanty, to use as a studio; now in the summer of 1922 Stieglitz converted another shed, which he called the Little House, into a darkroom.

The following winter, Stieglitz celebrated their accomplishments in two exhibitions at the Anderson Galleries. In January, he presented one hundred works by O'Keeffe, ranging from 1915 charcoal drawings to 1922 paintings made in Lake George. The exhibition was both a critical success and a grueling ordeal for O'Keeffe. Critics were quick to recall Stieglitz's provocative nude portraits of her, exhibited only two years earlier, and they discussed her work in blatantly sexual terms. One reviewer asserted that O'Keeffe's art was "a clear case of Freudian suppressed desires in paint,"[49] while another, using language more appropriate to Stieglitz's photographs of O'Keeffe than her paintings, wrote of their "breastlike contours of cloud and the black cleaving

---

49. Helen Appleton Read, "Georgia O'Keeffe's Show an Emotional Escape," *Brooklyn Daily Eagle,* Feb. 11, 1923, 2B.

of lake shore."[50] Stieglitz further encouraged these interpretations by reprinting an article by Marsden Hartley in the exhibition brochure extolling O'Keeffe's paintings as "shameless private documents [with an] unqualified nakedness of statement."[51]

Several weeks later, Stieglitz showed 116 of his photographs, mainly new portraits that he had never before exhibited, and introduced his cloud studies. The exhibition was a dazzling success, and the cloud photographs in particular elicited great acclaim. Ananda Coomaraswamy, curator of Indian and Islamic art at the Museum of Fine Arts, Boston, was so impressed that he arranged for the museum to acquire twenty-seven photographs. This was the first time photographs had been accepted as works of art by such a prestigious and conservative American institution.

Exhausted by their exhibitions, O'Keeffe and Stieglitz arrived at Lake George in June 1923, hoping for a peaceful vacation. Instead, Stieglitz was, as O'Keeffe wrote their new friend the writer Sherwood Anderson, "just a heap of misery—sleepless—with eyes—ears—nose —arm—feet—ankles—intestines—all taking their turn at deviling him—one after the other."[52] His physical sufferings were compounded by the devastating news of Kitty's illness and hospitalization and by his grief over his mother's death the previous fall. To alleviate his distress, he surrounded himself with friends—Anita Pollitzer, Katharine Rhoades, Paul Rosenfeld, Herbert and Lilias Seligmann, and Beck and Paul Strand, as well as many family members, all visited the farmhouse that summer. He even invited his former 291 secretary, Marie Rapp Boursault, to spend several weeks at the Hill with her husband, George, and young daughter, Yvonne, whose incessant crying prompted Stieglitz to dub her "Twenty-One-Cats-On-The-Back-Yard Fence."[53]

With Stieglitz's ailments and depression, and what Beck Strand described as the "rackety" atmosphere of the household, O'Keeffe grew "pretty sad and forlorn." After having words with Stieglitz and deeming her summer "a failure," she left Lake George in early September for the solace of York Beach, Maine. She arrived there, Florence Schauffler later told Stieglitz, looking "utterly spent."[54] O'Keeffe left Stieglitz in the care of Beck Strand, his mother's former nurse, Katherine Herzig, and other family members, assuring them that her departure would be "much pleasanter for you than my staying would have been."[55]

50. Herbert Seligmann, "Georgia O'Keeffe: American," *MSS* no. 5 (Mar. 1923), 10.

51. Marsden Hartley, "Georgia O'Keeffe," in *Adventures in the Arts: Informal Chapters on Painters, Vaudeville, and Poets*, intro. Waldo Frank (New York, 1921), 116–119.

52. GOK to Sherwood Anderson, Aug. 1, 1923, Modern Manuscript Collection, The Newberry Library, Chicago, Ill.

53. AS to Rebecca Strand, July 21, 1929.

54. Rebecca Strand to GOK, Sept. 12, 1923, and GOK to Sherwood Anderson, Aug.1, 1923, Modern Manuscript Collection, The Newberry Library; AS to GOK, Sept. 8, 1923; Florence Schauffler to AS, Sept. 24, 1923.

55. GOK to Elizabeth Stieglitz Davidson, Sept. 8, 1923.

Georgia O'Keeffe · [En route from Lake George, New York, to York Beach, Maine] · [September 7, 1923] +

Glens Falls—We stopped beside a train with strange apparatus on it. It must be the wrecking engine.[56] There is a huge hook right outside my window—curious wheels and strange pieces of chain—big nuts painted white.—Looks as though Beck had been at work on it—

You poor little thing—you looked as though you felt as bad about my going away as I felt—Up in the room talking before I left you gave me something—very clear that you love me —a much finer love—a clearer purer crystal than I was asking for times past when I've asked —You were very kind to me—I'm sorry I have bothered you again—I'm going to stop and just look out[57]—

I'm tired—it seems you should come down the aisle to sit by me any moment—that I should see your dear bright little eyes—

It's nine o'clock—we just passed Balliston Spa—I've just finished supper—graham bread, tomatoes and milk—tell Beck—

A school teacher from Philadelphia sits beside me and talks much—She has a Jewish nose but says it was broken when she was a child—

I'm tired—Dearest—am just going to sit—

There are two coaches full of strange Germans like the one you saw—

It is a great feeling of peace—just to know that you are—

I'll just sit—All that I am goes to you—

9:20 Railroad time[58]—Arrived in Albany—got my Pullman ticket—a nice breeze here in the station after the stuffy train—

I seem to like just to sit—It's all light here—and I know you are up on the Hill in the dark with maybe a light in the house—or maybe lying wide awake in your little bed—the quiet and singing things outside—That dear little white body—

I wish I could give you one little fraction of what you give me—I feel on the edge of tears all the time but I'll be all right—I still feel I was right to come—Don't worry about me a bit—

And take care of your dear little self—Be careful of your food—and I do hope you sleep —Greetings to Beck and Katherine—don't let them work too hard—

—It's no use to say what I send to you—You know it—

It's all of me—I do hope you sleep—I know I will and I'll be careful—

---

56. Earlier in the day, a wheel had fallen off a train leaving Lake George.

57. Stieglitz responded on September 8, 1923: "I'm glad you realized before going that my feeling for you was a very deeply rooted one—call it by what name you will." He continued: "We are very different—yet alike in much—truly alike in that we respect—we revere—each other for what we each are. It's that deep respect founded on a great reality—experienced & intuitive—which holds us together in no common bond."

58. Railroad or railway time was the name given to the standardized time zones adopted by all U.S. and Canadian railroads in 1883; see "The New Railroad Time," *NYT*, Oct. 12, 1883, 5.

Alfred Stieglitz · Lake George, New York · September 8, 1923

Good Morning Sweetestheart—It's 7:25 A.M.

It just happens to be that—I believe your train pulls out of Boston for Portsmouth at this time. I hope everything is well with you.—I am downstairs—shaved—clean.—I just hear Katherine & Beck upstairs getting up. The kitchen floor is dry. The paint we put on last night seemed thick & we feared it mightn't dry readily, so were prepared to be minus kitchen today.—

—The morning is a very dark one & there is a wind blowing. In the night too it blew quite hard—As I left you & walked home I had only one thought—one feeling—that you, my Sweetest One, would get that from the ocean—from the going—which would give you back some inner peace—balance—

—That's all I *felt*. That's what I want most. Perhaps the only thing *I want*—We had supper in the kitchen. And then Beck & I painted the floor—The house seemed very empty— I telegraphed to Herbert[59] too. I lay in my little bed & it seemed as if I could find no sleep. I was unusually quiet though. Of course every step of yours was in me. And I was hoping all was right. That you were safely installed in your berth & would get some sleep. Some rest.—I can't tell you how sorry I am that the summer has been such a "failure" for you.—And really because of my inability to do so many "things" myself. That's the root of it. But I shall learn in time if I live long enough. I move very slowly.—

If you don't know by this time that *you* are the last person in the world I wish to see unsatisfied then it is hopeless for me to say anything. I do not misunderstand you. To me you are just the *same Whiteness* you have ever been. You can't be anything but that—And white-ness means as much to me today as ever—possibly more if such a thing is possible.—Also do never for a moment overlook the fact that everything I have been the last five years—& even before—I have been because of *You* being what *You Are*. And that all that has gone out into the world I know has gone out from our *Togetherness*. It has gone out from us both as one. Don't ever for a moment forget that I know that—And that I am ever conscious of that knowing. And the knowing is strength for us both.—

—Again I say all I hope is that the going—the sea—will give you something which will give you what you couldn't find on the Hill.—

Your life is not as complex as mine. You have not permitted it to be.—Or perhaps we have no choice. Perhaps they are different complexities. Maybe my living is more involved than yours. I don't know. At any rate I wouldn't want you different than you are even if it were in my power to make you different. But I do hope you'll find your own balance again which I have so unfortunately—& so without the desire to—upset.—

—It was necessary for you to go. I realize that fully—you being what you are—I repeat again do not worry about me—I am going to do my tinkering called work. I want to get these things out of the road—out of my mind. I want to write to Kennerley today.—Maybe a line too to Lawrence—I'll order the book[60] sent to Mrs. Schauffler—But I feel for you while there the

338

59. Probably Stieglitz's brother-in-law George Herbert Engelhard.
60. D. H. Lawrence, *Studies in Classic American Literature* (New York, 1923).

ocean—Mrs. Schauffler—the change—those should be your book. But my child is much wiser than I am.

—I mean it—& will do as she feels she wishes to. So I must laugh at advising—

—Katherine & Beck have just come down—Katherine is busy in the kitchen—Beck is toasting.—It doesn't seem quite real.—So much doesn't seem quite real these days—Like the weather itself—

—There's Fred[61] a little earlier than usual driving up. The morning is very dark. And I see that I forgot to close the door last night of the Little House. Fortunately the night was dry. And I'm assuming no animals have gone in to chew up the little negatives or to build a nest in the camera which is over there.—

—I wonder will you paint any. I hope there'll be no delay with the trunk. It matters not whether you paint or not. It's living that matters—there can be no worthwhile painting if there be no equilibrium—which leads to doing—be the form what it may.—

—Take care of yourself—try not to catch cold. Remember what I want for you is you to be you—that's all. If I interfere with that in the bigger sense then I am destroying you. And I do not wish to destroy you or anyone else.

—Words all seem to have become meaningless.

I'm called to breakfast!—A kiss.—My little red whiteness.—

A little later—Before starting in to tinker around I want to give you one more kiss—

It has begun to rain. I wonder will it be raining at York Beach when you arrive there. It looks as if this weather were coming from the ocean.—

I'll go up now to get the wash out of the way. My bed I fixed as soon as I got out of it. And cleaned up the bathroom too after me—I went into your room to see if it were raining in. —I am going to leave everything exactly as you left it.—

—I wonder when you'll get this letter.

Don't forget you mean as much—& more—to me than ever.

That's all—Take care of yourself.

I wonder did I tell you that Lawrence's book gives me the same feeling of *Truth* that your work gave me when Anita brought it. Nothing since—except your own work—has given me such a feeling of *living truth*.

Incidentally I might add that your work means as much as ever to me. I don't say much about it these days—but don't think I am not thinking of it all the time—

A big kiss—I hope you get a good night's sleep.

I am yours.

---

61. Fred Varnum was a caretaker at the Stieglitz family's house at Lake George.

You feel your days and years are precious—

All days and years are precious—If one is conscious—thirty-five is as precious as sixty—Your days are precious to me too—and mine must be to you or you wouldn't have made it possible for me to come—I couldn't have done it if you hadn't helped me—Thank you—I've shed quite a few tears over this but I'm all right—

Out of Boston there are miles and miles it seems of railroad track—and little green murky rivers—I liked them—

I have written you a long letter in my mind—

Bare hungry gray rocky hills—with fine dark ominous uplifting cedar trees—rank yellow grass in wet marshy places—dried yellow brown green hay fields with the little streams winding way off in them—flat and far away—under gray sky—fields of flowers everywhere—

My sunflower[62] is very true of something in me—it seems spread out everywhere I look—I didn't know it before—And it comes to me—you will laugh—but I'll be middle-aged when I come back to you—I would have been middle-aged if I hadn't come away—but it seems that something would have broken—and I can't go into it broken—

You speak of yourself as an old man—but you have made the bridge to being what you call an old man—as a bigger richer—more far reaching—clearer person—putting down clearly your richer vision—You have been completely each thing as it came to you—and have been able to move clearly onto the next—

—I have two or three things to put down about what I seem to feel I'm leaving—but moving into this country—nearing the ocean—the occasional slash of red in the somber dead looking greens is curiously like something happening in me—I already feel I'll not have to come again—and coming now is more right for me than the earlier summer—

It's like my yellow sunflower—only much more cruel—and when I painted the sunflower I felt it should be much more cruel—You must not laugh at this—nor read it to anyone[63]—I'll mail it when I get to York Beach—

There are lots of yellow flowers—

You see the thing I write you isn't so because—what I think is—so now—can't be—because what I think was—was not—and what I want or think I want—can't be—and what will be in reality will not be for me—

So I come to the conclusion that the thing that disturbs me is something in myself because it only exists for me through me as I touch the world—Yes you have told me many things but I must find it for myself—

It came to me when thinking of Melville Cane[64]

Many white gulls on a[65]

---

62. Lynes 355, 356.

63. Stieglitz had the habit of reading aloud letters he received to those who happened to be around him.

64. The attorney, reporter, and poet Melville Cane had sent Stieglitz and O'Keeffe some of his writings in 1923; see Melville Cane to AS, 1923.

65. This letter ends abruptly.

Alfred Stieglitz · [Lake George, New York] · [September 10, 1923] +

Good morning—

It's 7:30. Katherine & Beck are just about to arise. I'm up quite a while already. A cold beautiful morning. It was cold in bed. I had to laugh finding a blanket on the floor as I fixed the bed. Wondered all night why two blankets seemed so thin!!

You see, you Little One, I am incurable. The night wasn't bad—nor was it good. But there was some rest. The eyes still bother but they'll be all right in time. Too much mounting I guess.—The strain.—As I lay in bed awake I was wondering were you still asleep—There was an ideal instrument of joy wondering about its companion—It didn't tell me—but I guess it—

You're very—very—more than very sweet. You're lucky to be so very far away for I feel if you were here something might literally crush you—a pleasurable crushing. But I feel the rightness clearly of your going—I know it's doing for you what you felt it would. I feared a little—but it was stupid of me. I realize that clearly—I *am very*—very very Very—deep of feeling for you (I started in to say "fond" of you—but that says nothing—nor do any words). You clean bit of lovely Whiteness—That's what you are—I really am nothing so clean—I've always said that—I have always known it.—

—Katherine & Beck are in the kitchen now. It's chilly sitting here. The Davidsons have a great day coming. Undoubtedly they'll come in the afternoon. Everything is ready & there'll be aplenty to eat—a Brown Betty too Katherine announced yesterday—It was funny to hear her tell Beck as the latter was washing dishes that she missed you so much—it was so nice to have talks with you—& walk with you—etc., etc. I wondered would Beck take it kindly—When she came in Beck said she thought Katherine didn't like her. I said "nonsense. She was simply stating what she felt about you & that undoubtedly no hurt was meant." Fortunately Beck is a sensible person in such matters & she went out & continued to joke with Katherine & the latter likes it.—

So you see there is peace amongst the women folks. I hope it will continue tonight when two more women folks[66] arrive on the scene—I guess it will work out all right. It must. I'm always not so far away—

Well, Sweetheart, I hope your little mouth has that sweet expression which tells me so much—that you are not unhappy—on the contrary too full of life taking in—no resentments.—

You great Woman Girl—It's really all like a dream to me—All of you—all of our togetherness—It's all so very true that it doesn't seem possible.—Do you feel what I mean?

—I'm called.—More before I'll mail this—

A big kiss—Everywhere—

66. Elizabeth Stieglitz Davidson and Agnes Engelhard, Stieglitz's sister, were due to arrive at Lake George later that day.

Georgia O'Keeffe · [York Beach, Maine] · [September 10, 1923] +

It's Monday morning—ten o'clock—

I had to stop last night because my ink gave out—and besides that my head was such a whirl—

I was so excited that I didn't sleep very well—but it wasn't as bad as it might have been for staying awake—All creation seemed to be going through my head—I woke from a half sleep at dawn—got up and looked out at it—

I wanted to stay up but really thought I would burst if I took in any more today so I got back into bed—but after another doze got up and looked out again—just in time to see a *red red* sun coming out of the ocean—long long breakers in front of it—but I got right back into bed again—and had a really good sleep—

I've been down to the water only for a minute—it is a perfect day—Even finer than yesterday—and all clear and sparkly—the breakers sometimes seem to be the whole length of the beach—and are so clear and green against the blue—

I don't dare to look out today—I'm going to be quiet and let yesterday settle—

I thought so much to you—

It was a perfect day—and today is a perfect day—clear and fine and warm—

I know you would be glad if I could really tell it all to you—and I know the others would not mind my having come if they really like me even just a little—

I'm sorry I didn't get letters off to Agnes and Elizabeth but I just couldn't manage it— I'll do it now—

Dearest—you are always with me—I just do hope that you are all right and any time if you want me to come—I will take the first train if you wire me—but I feel rather sure you wouldn't wire me any more than you would get in bed with me—no matter how cold you would be—if I didn't ask you—and I can't do anything with you—You just are that way—

I got a canvas in Ogunquit yesterday—I am going to get it ready so I can work on it as soon as my trunk comes—It was delayed on account of the wreck I presume—

I don't seem to feel the usual break that I usually feel in going from one place to another—I seem to be all ready to do something I have in my head—it seems to just reek with things that I think I want to do—It's awful to feel so full of things—but I like it—

It seems so hard to stop writing to you—I just want to keep on—but I must stop—
G.

Alfred Stieglitz · Lake George, New York · September 13, 1923

Good morning—My Sweetest One—

The sun is just coming over the hills—And the Paulist Fathers' bell is striking seven— I am downstairs ready for the day. No one else is as yet up. It's another day. Another promising to be fine. And warmer.—There are no vapors rising from the Lake. The Lake is quiet. And foliage still.—And such is the spirit of the house—

I didn't write last night.—It had been a most busy day.—At ten they all retired—some before. I read a Marin letter (accidentally it contains an allusion to Babse[67] which pleased her & the parents) to the Engelhards and Davidsons—(Babse was in bed or going I believe)—& Hartley's[68] as they had inquired about both. Babse is developing very rapidly. Really thinks so must feel—for she thinks about *all* things—In the afternoon the grass plot under the apple trees was like a workshop—Beck & Donald busy with tables—scraping & painting—I was busy in the Little House—also watched Donald & learnt some things—Had quite a discussion with Elizabeth—Beck present part of the time—Beck as nice as she is—& certainly developing—does lack creative seeing—It's a pity. But I suppose that can't be "given" one. There was quite an argument. Elizabeth is forced to think harder & deeper than ever—And one can sense the terrific fight she is putting up.—In the Little House she & I continued—she coming over while I was washing negatives. Of course she has great problems ahead of her.[69] But she does not complain about them—nor shirk them.—And she'll manage to solve them somehow for she sees them clearly—Still she is worried—that is she has to be in the saddle *all* the time & that sometimes may become beyond physical endurance.

—The Engelhards seem contented here. Everything is really going splendidly.

After all had gone to bed I sat over an hour on my cot with my little prints ready to mount—cardboard & paper had come from Of's—& was working at the cloud series—the sequence[70]—for they are built on a particular feeling—or theme—or idea—or combination of those—call it what you will. I want a proper sequence. I think I have it.—I'll have to make some prints over. But as a beginning what I have is good.—

—I finally went to bed but didn't sleep for a long time. It was one of those nights in which I would liked to have worked all night—but those eyes of mine say "nay."—

—So I lay there and thought of you. As if I weren't thinking of you all the time—no matter what might be happening.

Your letter had come telling me of the arrival of your trunk. I was glad you had it. And that you had painted a picture. Were absorbing your mad happiness & exaltation of the day before—It's a fine feeling to know you so yourself—so the way I wish I could always have you be—Perhaps some means will evolve—

—No, none of your letters made me feel unhappy—They were *all you*—& I want *all you* as you know—nothing kept back.—I understand because I can *feel* much more *with* you than you realize. I know I hurt you very often. And I certainly don't wish to hurt you. Least of all you of anyone in the world. And I certainly want to hurt no one. Certainly not for long.—But I know I do hurt—& I try not to but it seems impossible to live & not to hurt—

67. Georgia Engelhard, the daughter of Agnes and George Herbert Engelhard, was called "Babse," "The Kid," or "The Child"; later she was occasionally called "Georgia Minor" because of her affection for O'Keeffe.

68. Hartley wrote Stieglitz on July 17, 1923, describing his travels in Europe and his work on his forthcoming book *Twenty-Five Poems* (Paris, 1923): "all proving Stieglitz that I seem to be on my way again after sinking for the last time in the deepest water I ever got into in my life psychologically speaking."

69. Elizabeth Stieglitz Davidson's parents, Lee and Lizzie Stieglitz, never fully accepted their son-in-law Donald and both Elizabeth and Donald strongly objected to her parents' materialism.

70. Stieglitz grouped most of his photographs of clouds into sequences.

No, I'm glad for all the letters—they are *all you*—one as much to me as the others. —You may laugh & think you know me better—that I am fooling myself. I don't know. I doubt my doing that. But everyone has a blind spot—that may be mine—but the spot is very small, that I'm sure of—

Well, sweet Dearest One, I hope every day is adding to your building up—that you are gaining a little weight too I hope. I know you must look well—Much better than here. I was far from satisfied with your looks all spring & all summer—In the winter for a few months you looked magnificent as you never had looked. The grippe & your show[71] wrecked that. That is the excitement of the show.

Well, perhaps, the ocean & the kind of life you are leading now will give you back the serenity & the weight—some of both at least.—I want your wellness above all things—That's what I wanted when you went to San Antonio & finally came East. That's really what I wanted. And want ever.—

—Your letters were received by the various ones[72]—I know what a "job" it must have been—& perhaps not really "necessary"—yet I feel it's just as well you went [through] the bit of torture—I hope it's the last time you'll have to go through that kind.—

—Every day I continue to learn about life & living. It's certainly a long schooling.

—As I look out of the window I see the west is growing dark—& in the east the sun is covered—I want to palladio[73]—It looks doubtful—Well, I'll Artura[74]—Clouds & a few other things—It's queer how little I feel like photographing—

—Some of the folks are up—The kitchen is astir. So far there have been no voices.

—I'll go to the little prints. See in daylight what happened in artificial light. More later—

A long, long kiss!—

10:30 A.M. Just another kiss—a big one & I'll let this go—

Everyone is on the go—the sun is out—I have been fussing with the small prints— Am stopping—too damp for palladio[75]—sun in & out—Another big kiss—

Keep well—

71. Alfred Stieglitz Presents One-Hundred Pictures, Oils, Water-colors, Pastels, Drawings by Georgia O'Keeffe, American, Anderson Galleries, New York, Jan. 29–Feb. 10, 1923.

72. On September 8, 1923, O'Keeffe wrote to Elizabeth Stieglitz Davidson to explain why she had left Lake George so suddenly and was not there for her visit.

73. Strong sunlight was often used to make "palladio," or palladium, prints.

74. Artura, a brand of gelatin silver paper available in the 1910s and 1920s, was designed to be printed by gas or electric light (also referred to as "gaslight" paper).

75. Humidity could damage palladio paper.

Alfred Stieglitz, *Georgia O'Keeffe*, 1923/1924. Gelatin silver print,
4⅝ x 3½ in (11.7 x 8.9 cm). The J. Paul Getty Museum, Los Angeles
(93.XM.25.78). Copyright © J. Paul Getty Trust. Greenough 858.

Georgia O'Keeffe · **[York Beach, Maine]** · **[September 13, 1923]** +

Dearest—

    You are the nicest thing in the world—I really don't know how I was ever able to leave you—I don't quite understand how it is that I can and do stay away from you day after day—except—that I felt I had to—to keep our togetherness clear—

    It's wonderfully quiet here—With my windows open I don't hear anything in the house—The ocean has been more beautiful today than any day—pure lovely color—and it has been warm and lovely out but I've pecked away at my paintings all day—since early this morning—excepting a couple of hours at noon—I drove to York Harbor with Mrs. Schauffler for some shopping—And then after lunch sat on the porch and read your letter—I stood on the beach with it in my hand for a long time watching the water—

    It is so wonderful Dearest—At sunset we walked on the beach—the loveliest pale green-blue-pink-lavender sun set—ocean and sky—weird pale gray looking pools of water around the rocks—And the old schooner—she is a wonder—You would have a great time with her—

    —I sat in the swing on the porch before supper—curled up with the pillows—I almost went to sleep—dreaming—day dreaming—of you—and it came to me Dearest—You know the ocean wouldn't be wonderful to me the way it is without you—I can't imagine caring for anything without you—You have touched my soul and I guess that souls that have touched can no longer be single souls or sit in a corner alone again—They must always be reaching for the touching again—for their other half—It's only in the contact with the other soul that they can feel complete—

Dearest Child—I am sitting here in bed again and am half asleep—must stop and get under the covers and put out the lights—My little painting[76] is finished—It isn't a portrait I guess but it's a funny little thing—I really can't tell what I feel about it—it's too new—

Goodnight Sweet One—I must sleep—

I am very close in you all night—and all day—too—

Sleepy, sleepy kisses—

Alfred Stieglitz · Lake George, New York · September 18, 1923

Dearest Sweetheart:

Big banks of clouds are moving out of the Lake upward & northward—so that just the tops of the hills across the Lake loom black against a sky in which the sun will rise its head in a short while. The mountains further on stand out clear against a sky pale blue & pale pink. And there is frost on the ground. It was a very cold night—I have just carried out the ashes of the kitchen stove & put on coal. I'm in the kitchen. It's at least comfortable there. I don't want to start the furnace yet. Then too the pipes need cleaning—We have been trying to get Taylor for more than a week. We'll finally land him somehow. I'll have to—Fred is not positive enough.

—First of all a big kiss to the Little Girl by the sea—I hope your curse is nearly gone & that you have escaped bad headaches & misery generally. It would be great if you had. Here Beck is worried because she is overdue—Undoubtedly cold water, etc.—I laughed at her worrying. —Mean I suppose because I know what such worry is.—But she's so funny about it.—

—All are abed yet except the Swiss[77] girl who has just come down. It's not quite seven now. I was up at six. After having gone to bed at midnight. Rosenfeld & I had a talk after the others had retired.—He looks in trim. His book[78] is complete except the chapters on you, Miller, Ryder, Frank, & myself. I think he will do you first here.

—He had heard about the Lawrence book but imagined it a reprint of a series of articles written by Lawrence for an English review. In which he was mistaken. I told him he shouldn't read it till he has completed his job. And yet I wonder shouldn't he go right at it. It's foolish to be "afraid." He got a glimpse of my most recent photographs & was deeply impressed. Of course he was surprised to find [you] gone. Also seemed to feel the house very different from how he had remembered it. It is different—white painting—new wallpaper, kitchen, etc.

—Yesterday afternoon I photographed—made snaps of Donald doing the Lilias act.[79] I hope some will turn out good. Very funny. He's really a wonder—Did I write you of the rough & tumble he & Beck had while all of us were at breakfast yesterday? Beck was full of

---

76. Possibly Lynes 440.

77. The nurse for Elizabeth and Donald Davidson's children, Peggy and Sue.

78. Paul Rosenfeld, *Port of New York; Essays on Fourteen American Moderns* (New York, 1924).

79. Donald Davidson was imitating Lilias Seligmann dancing the Charleston; see Greenough 697.

challenge—& strength—etc.—& Donald accepted. They got up & wrestled—& Beck bit—then Donald gave it to her, dropping her in such a manner that since she can sit only on half her seat! And his glasses were smashed. Fortunately he had another pair. It was a real rough & tumble. He isn't as gentle with a woman as I am. When she bit he got mad. And she bit "because" I called out to him: "Look out, she's apt to bite!" So she bit. It was very funny, yet I'm glad she wasn't hurt more—Dempsey—Firpo—Babe Ruth influences[80] at work—

—I had strained my neck photographing clouds! Sloan Linimented it—today the swelling has gone down. I must have stretched my neck all out of gear. I haven't developed the negatives yet. I hope some are good. A few were exceptionally fine opportunities.—

I called for Rosenfeld—The Swiss girl has just come in again—She seems to have been out in the woods & has come in with autumn leaves—says it's beautiful out of doors. Is a real child of nature. I wish you could see her. Now she is standing at the stove stirring cereal—a picture of bursting health & strength—& determination.—

Oh I forgot there was a letter from Claudie yesterday. Two letters came. One addressed to you from Claudie & one to me from Sessions. He comes next Sunday.—Claudie's letter to you I looked at & then said to Elizabeth, "I have never opened a letter addressed to anyone else—I feel I ought to open this one." And then I looked & said: "No, I'll forward it." Beck too was present. Then I said: "I'll be damned, I'll open it." And I tore it open & it began: Dear Stieglitz, etc.! The letter was for me. So I owe you no apologies. You Sweet One—Well, Claudie is getting $150 a month—has a job forty minutes from town in Jersey somewhere—Affiliated with Teachers College. The letter sounds very rational. She borrowed some money from Teachers College & has already paid it back & is very proud of the fact!

—I wrote seven letters in sixty-five minutes—really notes.—One each to Lee, Marin, Claudie, Litchfield, Beckett, Rhoades, Sessions & got them off with Katherine who was taking a letter of hers to the post office to catch the afternoon train.—You can imagine how busy I am when I tell you four *Sportsman* are lying there for me for three days & are unread!

The time does fly—I don't know where it goes to. But getting photographs into shape the way I do does mean much time.—

—There you have a fair picture of another day.—And here is the beginning of another—the weather as ever marvelous. I wonder how long can this series of days continue.

—I do miss you much—but I'm glad to be so busy—& above all so glad to know you are so well taken care of—& so full of life—& know that Mrs. Schauffler must be enjoying you greatly—as you are enjoying all you're having so greatly!—

—There's Katherine now. She & the Swiss girl standing at the stove—My cocoa is being prepared. It's a great picture that strapping girl & that old woman—both intense—Really fine—

Sweet Dearest One I'll stop now—with a very big strong long smothering gentle lusty kiss—A lusty kiss full of life & spirit—that are fine & in both of us—

A contact of the souls—You are the best part of me—

My love to Mrs. Schauffler—

347

---

80. On September 14, 1923, Jack Dempsey fought Luis Firpo and won the heavyweight championship. Although hailed as one of the greatest hitters of all time, Babe Ruth was also known for his tumultuous personal life; see "Firpo Felled Ten Times," *NYT*, Sept. 15, 1923, 1.

Georgia O'Keeffe · [York Beach, Maine] · [September 20, 1923] +

5 P.M. Thursday—

——My great top of the worldness this morning—early—turned to a headache—
I worked anyway—from nine to one—then lunch—and after that I lay down for my headache
—I didn't sleep but felt better when I got up—The sun had gone and a thick fog was rolling in
in clouds—I've been down on the rocks—walked down the road—fog thicker all the time—
I stole a grand gay bouquet of flowers—and now am sitting on the top of the cliff—even the
green below is becoming gray—It's like a sea of tears lashing the misty rocks—maybe all the
tears of the world are what make the ocean—Everything is wet—I'm wet when I run my hand
over my coat—It's wonderful—You would like it better than anything I've seen here I think—
All the soil to windward is wet—And it all seems like tears to me but it is marvelously beautiful
—There is a spider's web—a perfect one radiating from the center—it's all white—looks frosty
against the green as it hangs on the wire—

Dearest—I love you so dearly—I've thought of you so much today—I don't seem to
exist without the consciousness of you—I've had it ever since the 291 days—when I felt the
spirit of you—I knew you then as well as I know you now—Maybe more clearly because no
personal feelings got in the way—

I hear a weird bird note—

You see—I've had you longer than you have had me—

I must go in—I wish you could stand here with me just for a moment—I would so like
you to see it—and to kiss me—Just one kiss—It would be cool—and salty—but some way
neverending—

—Broken pencil—

Alfred Stieglitz · Lake George, New York · September 21, 1923

My dearest Sweetest White One:

It is not yet six o'clock. I am downstairs in a warm kitchen. Needlessly warm because it
has turned warm outside with the rain which has been falling quietly & steadily since Rosenfeld
& I started for the post office yesterday afternoon—I more to get a walk in than to go to the
post office—

—It was midnight before I got to bed. The night was poor. The rain on the roof seemed
a new sound to listen to—& it was warm besides & my eyes were burning—So there was little
sleep—perhaps too much cover too—But I feel rested enough. Daylight is beginning to show
itself in the windows—The rain is thinning out—The first day of official autumn!—The kitchen
clock seems very loud in its tick. And there is water dripping from the faucets. Yet there is great
stillness. It's as if I were alone in the house.—

After our return from the Village yesterday afternoon we found Beck finishing up typing Rosenfeld's article on you.—I asked to read it. He was glad to have me do so.—I insisted
on reading it aloud to him. It read well—much better than I had hoped for. But he suggested

elimination of certain repetitions—& I suggested that he introduce certain elements here & there to give the article not only the feeling of curved lines—even though he had used symbols like arrows, etc. as straight lines—but also of todayness—a hitching up with the machine—the skyscraper—paint on autos—a feeling too of austerity—The additions were made by him & I'm sure the essay is improved greatly—has that which it sorely needed—& something you'll like & others will respect.—Furthermore what was added here & there gives greater significance to what he had had down.—Now he is going at Miller—

We had supper in the kitchen—I tinkered with prints—read the *Sportsman* finally—Beck had cramps & went to bed—Rosenfeld & I sat talking till very late—About his essay on you—about my new photographs—about life generally—really a fine talk.—Nothing about trivial personal matters. I think he got something for I believe I was pretty clear in all I said—

—You do mean a very great deal to me. I realize that more than ever—But I never ceased realizing it.—There is a positive difference between us. You are very much more one thing—in spite of all appearances & "moods"—

I sometimes wonder what I am—straight or round—or knotted up—I know there is a very positive something running through it all—& that untouchable—What that is I don't know.—You are very dear to me—even when we don't agree—

I still look at your starlight picture[81]—I just see it hanging there—I don't dislike it—it attracts—I don't think about it—but it does do something to me that seeks crystallization.—

—Two weeks ago you left.—An eternity.—And so much has transpired. It seems as if the whole world has passed before & through me in those two weeks.—

Yes, it's well you were with the ocean—

I am going to write to Hartley now. It isn't fair not to acknowledge the receipt of his fine letter. And I want to get that off my mind.—

There are several other letters to get off—"business" ones—odds & ends. Today I shall be out of doors—rain or no rain. I feel I have been too much indoors of late.—

—If you were here this morning I'd be asleep in your arms—but it's well as it is—

You are very dear to me—

A big, big sweet long kiss—

Georgia O'Keeffe · [**York Beach, Maine**] · [**September 22, 1923**] +

Saturday—I guess it's about noon—I'm still in bed—don't worry about me though—I'm all right—

We are at Mr. Schauffler's again—After lunch yesterday I promptly threw it all up—and twice since have thrown up what was left in me—Am feeling very comfortable this morning tho—even if I did gag and throw up as soon as I first moved about—Am not eating and will be all right by tomorrow I'm sure—Am sleeping most of the time—

It's still foggy out—sometimes so that I can't see a thing—at other times when I sit up

---

81. Lynes 393.

I see a very gay flower garden—It belongs to the man I used to tell you wore blue overalls and was always digging when I was here last year—It's very gay—

My headache's gone—it's just that I don't feel like eating—and I'll wait till I feel like it—

Meantime the bed is very comfortable—

I think it's raining out now—I'd rather have you than the ocean today—I miss you much—

Mrs. Schauffler has gone for the mail—I had four letters from you yesterday—It was a great treat—

They were very sweet and dear—I keep them right by my side on my table so I can touch them and read them when I want to—

It's 4:30 in the afternoon—I'm still in bed—and like it—I've been very comfortable—it feels nice and quiet and restful—Have had a fire in the fireplace—it cracks and seems friendly. Mrs. Schauffler wanted to have the doctor so we had him—a nice little man—he gave me a dose of calomel[82]—It is still inside of me—but I don't feel sick anymore—have had a cup of coffee— it was very good and hot—

You see I'm well taken care of so you need not worry at all—I'll be all right by morning—

I hear the ocean—and see the flowers—and through the other window green willows—they are very soft and lovely—

This morning was so miserable I didn't tell you about your four letters that I received yesterday—When we came through York Beach on our way home we stopped at the post office for the mail and I sent a box of bayberry branches to the Engelhards—The driver attended to it for us and handed me Ida's card and a letter from Beck—You can imagine my consternation at receiving nothing from you—I told Mrs. Schauffler I was sure it helped make me throw up my lunch—Of course it didn't—but I was in a great stew—I knew you wouldn't miss writing me for two days—and she was sure there was mail for her too—So after I came up to bed she phoned the post office and asked—They told her there was more mail—It seems quite wonder- ful to be able to know and ask if there is mail before you go for it—So while I was asleep she went over and got it—a letter from Mr. Schauffler and your four for me—

—I was the most pleased person you can imagine—You see—they had given the man only what had just arrived—they hadn't given him what they had been holding for us—

—Today I have your one page note—I've thought much of you today—You are getting up too early for you—I'm afraid you are not warm enough—You should have that little morn- ing sleep that you get between six and seven thirty—and I feel sure it's the cold that is getting you up—You could fix that electric pad so you could turn it on in the morning when you get cold—and take your little nap—

I feel almost as though I am asking a child in the cradle to take care of itself—You are

82. A purgative and liver stimulant.

such a dear little thing—and your mind is so far away from your dear little body that you are not apt to take very good care of the little smooth white body—

You must be good to it—it is so precious—and you will need it in the winter—all the strength you can store up now—

It's amusing the way we lay in bed in the morning when we are together and get up so early when we are apart—I will be back to hold you and warm you before many more nights are gone—

I may go to see the Fitzgerald collection in Boston[83] on my way back—it will be quite convenient—but I'm making no plans—Mrs. Schauffler wants me to stay till after next Sunday—but I have a feeling that I may have to get back to you this week—I'm missing you—

The flowers and brown marsh that I see out the window are richer and darker—lights are lighted—Mrs. Schauffler came in and talked awhile—I haven't been much trouble being sick because there was nothing that could be done for me but leave me alone—I'm going to have a little supper—just some toast and something to drink—

—I hear the foghorn on the ocean—The fire crackles—and there are the waves—

Being away has done me much good—I think you will like me better when I get back—I don't know that I have thought out anything in particular that would do either you or me any good—but I *feel* better—

And when I look at my work—I see quite clearly now why they say it has no form—What I have put down here—it's very little—has no form in the sense that the men speak of it—but I feel it has something else that is quite as definite—and seemed more important to me as I put it down than the idea of form—I may be able to get that by doing them over later—So far there are only three and a half pastels and two paintings[84]—they are all lively tho—and all old things I had in my head but one—

Good Night Dear Child—

I guess I'm tired—

Much—much—much love from—all of me—

Alfred Stieglitz · Lake George, New York · September 23, 1923 +

Dearest Heart of Mine:

It's just six. And I'm downstairs in the little room. A dark morning.—It was midnight before I got to bed. Took a hot bath before going to bed, a long one—a pretty warm one. I felt the need of sitting in water & would liked to have fallen asleep in it.—The day had been a

---

83. The Boston collector Desmond Fitzgerald owned many works by Claude Monet as well as other French Impressionist painters, including Auguste Renoir, Edgar Degas, and Camille Pissarro, and such Americans as W. Dodge Macknight. In 1916 he built a gallery in Brookline, Massachusetts, which was open to the public; see Carol Troyen, *The Boston Tradition: American Paintings from the Museum of Fine Arts, Boston* (New York, 1980), 38–39.

84. Lynes 438, 440.

strenuous one. Much tinkering with prints—and finally developing more cloud pictures—a few of which seem most amusing & very different—

In the forenoon Beck accompanied me to the post office, she bringing orders from Katherine for things at butcher & grocer, etc. Beck asked me many impossible questions—She has been "worried" about "things" she doesn't quite get, etc., etc—I tried to make myself clear. A piano may be good & still one key may get stuck & not budge even for the best pianist. Well Beck I fear has several notes like that. I told her so.—The discussions really started the night before about the Corona[85] which she was upbraiding & maltreating & wanting to come up to a standard beyond its powers.—I proved to her how she was doing that in spite of her resentment. —I had seen her do the same thing to her own painting of doors & tables—to Strand—a fineness to begin with & then a smear to finish with. As she has been very kind in so many ways & so eager to learn I felt I had to call her attention to that particular & very significant trait.—As chance would have it the mail in 201[86] gave her an inkling perhaps of what I was trying to get over to her for her own sake. I have no feeling about it except an impersonal one. I [hate] to see waste & force.—

—There were four letters for me. I opened the top one—A real surprise. I'm enclosing a copy because I know you'll like it—it is so simple. Really fine. No rhetoric.—A letter from D. H. Lawrence.[87] Nothing could have fitted into *that* moment like that letter.—There were two lines from Zoler. Finally after seven years his sister seems to have been forced to do what he has begged her to do all these years—& couldn't get her to do.—I hope he'll finally get his own chance—There was a really fine letter from Elizabeth & for *you* & *me*. Lee is pretty sick.—And a letter from Litchfield which I didn't open until I got home. There I read it to Rosenfeld. The boy has earmarks of genius—but just fails to connect—so far.—

—I waited for the later mail. It brought a letter from my Sweetest One. I read it standing on the street. A very beautiful letter. Rather sad—but very, very, beautiful. Yes, I know what I am to you—but I have to laugh when you say you had me before I had you—Yes, in a way and then in another that is not quite so. Wasn't I waiting for years for *you*—what you are—Didn't I see it at a glance when Anita showed me the first drawings—Perhaps not the *you* in person—but certainly the *you* in spirit—More than spirit—something that has no name—

—There are kindred souls—Some very close—

I hope your headache didn't last long. Possibly eye strain—after effects of all the excitements—

I'm sure you have made an extraordinarily beautiful pastel—A great wetness & grayness—the sea in mist—"stolen" flowers—Without seeing it I know it's "my" picture— we'll keep it.—

—A kiss—

---

85. Beck Strand was using a Corona typewriter to transcribe Paul Rosenfeld's essays for his forthcoming book, *Port of New York*, as well as some of the letters Stieglitz had received from Sherwood Anderson.

86. The Stieglitz family mailbox at the Lake George post office was no. 201.

87. D. H. Lawrence wrote Stieglitz on September 17, 1923, thanking him for his letter about *Studies in Classic American Literature*, and noting: "I expected abuse, & I get, for the very first word, a real generous appreciation that I myself can appreciate. One gets so sick of being carped at with the inevitable, 'But Mr. Lawrence.'"

As I was mounting during the afternoon Rosenfeld sat watching—He had read more Lawrence—& walked about looking—thinking—We talk together about such things as will help him crystallize—all very quietly. He is really fine to have about—Wants me to print a series of the cloud photographs (large ones[88]) for him. I told him I'd see. Said he could pay in yearly installments.—Well, I'll see. I'm much too full of completing what I'm now doing. I'll probably get at the series when we're alone—I'll see—

—Strand arrived at eight—He has brought his camera to have another try at me.[89] He looks thinner—Tired.—I fear Beck worries him a great deal even more than he worries her. But the worries are very different.—

—I wonder will Sessions turn up today. It will make no difference one way or another. Of course I'd like to have him come.

—I think I'll go in the attic to see if my negatives are dry—

A sweet kiss before—you dear runaway—

Georgia O'Keeffe · [York Beach, Maine] · [September 24, 1923] +

Monday morning—

Just a moment my Dear One—to tell you that it's eight o'clock—that I was up at ten to five and walked to York Beach to mail my letter to you—and watch the sun breaking through the clouds just a little above the horizon—It was very beautiful and the foliage is so fine too—Everything was silver when I first looked out—that was what tempted me out—

The walk was great—I am feeling fine—She says it is one and a half miles there—three in all—I think it isn't a bit over a mile each way—She thought it was too far for me but I promised to return if I was at all tired—I enjoyed it muchly—found the only way I could send the letter to you was to give it to the train conductor—that seems to be quite the thing to do here—So I risked it—and thought—well—if it's lost—it's lost—When I got home I visited the man of the flower garden—He is thin and brown and hard looking—talks about his flowers and seems to feel about them the way we do about our work—hard to satisfy—He gave me all I could carry home—they are already arranged in various pitchers and vases over the house—a grand bunch in the kitchen. Mrs. Morse was so pleased—I still have my stolen bouquet that I like.

I love you like this morning.

2 P.M.—Monday—

The light green waves seemed to come out of space this morning after the sun was well up—They seemed to mark off the edge of the earth and the beginning of time and space—or should I say timeless space—It was soft and warm here and seemed to be soft and warm out beyond the breakers—They were very long and not very high—very even and beautiful— always with that trembling edge that always seems to break—

88. Greenough 792–802.

89. Probably Strand's 1923 portrait of Stieglitz that was reproduced in Rosenfeld's *Port of New York*.

I've been working—a queer looking smear to make on such a fine day—

I was ravenous for dinner—So much so that I almost ate my plate—I think you have never seen me go at food with such a fever—but maybe you have—

Anyway—I rested myself a bit after it and before I start at my daub I just want to tell you how alive I am feeling—and how much I enjoyed my dinner—and how nice and warm it is and how bad my pastel is—but I'm going at it again—hoping it will improve—

I had thought to start home on Wednesday—How can I tho—with a day like this I feel like never moving—The sun is very glaring—not bright—just seems to be everywhere—So I am pleased to sit here and smear around—We will go out on the beach at sunset—I am looking forward to the mail—had none yesterday—

Keep well my Dearest One—

I feel *like a red ball bursting* to you—

Alfred Stieglitz · Lake George, New York · September 25, 1923

Good Morning Faraway Nearest One:

It's just six. And I'm shaved & ready for the day—It was a marvelous night. A white moonlight night. I never saw any night quite like it—none more beautiful—For a long while before going to bed I stood at your window looking lakeward—looking at the white silences—the white night so silent.—Nothing stirred. Even the moon full & round seemed not to wish to disturb the stillness—it seemed to be moving slowly upwards as if on tiptoes moving through a house of stillness at night when all inmates were fast asleep.—All was so still—& the whiteness so lovely—The hills were not hills—they were something bathed in an untouchable spirit of light—the line produced where this spirit met the sky spirit was of rarest subtle beauty—

Really I never saw anything quite so beautiful—I looked & looked & knew I was awake—

I had called the attention of the others before their going to bed. Rosenfeld remarked it was a pity you weren't here to see. The night was related to the picture of yours he has.[90] Yet it was very different.—All night I jumped up between periods of restless sleep & looked out—until I finally got up & watched the break of day—really night ending more than morning beginning. There was one bright star above the near poplar—the poplar so still, so dark, so big rising into the sky as if to meet that star—The hills no longer bathed in whiteness but dark with a few tiny dark elongated clouds in a perfectly still & clear sky otherwise changing color every moment even though still night—The Lake lay still & seemed hardly to exist—When finally the star's light had disappeared into the light of day I went to shave.—I felt as if I had witnessed a marvelous burial alone—of what I don't know—Maybe myself—That just comes into my mind—But I have no idea what that myself means or is—

All I know the night I'll never forget—I'm sure you saw the moon too—it wasn't the

90. Probably Lynes 395.

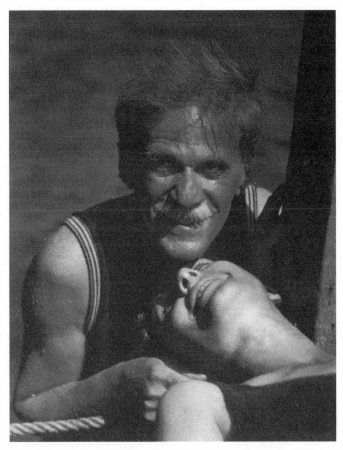

Paul Strand, *Alfred Stieglitz and Rebecca Strand, Lake George*, 1922. Gelatin silver print,
4¾ x 3¹¹/₁₆ in (12.1 x 9.3 cm). National Gallery of Art, Washington, D.C.,
Southwestern Bell Corporation Paul Strand Collection.

moon we saw—And you saw out into & beyond the endless sea—The still sea—as the Lake was still—

I love you, Dearest One, if I am capable of love. I often wonder, am I?—But if I am, it's you there with me in the great white stillness—where there is a great peace & no ugliness.—No voices with edges that tear—

I was told yesterday that I seemed to be faraway all the time yet seemingly in contact with all that's here. I had to laugh. When one is playing with the clouds & one's best part is far so faraway—near the endless sea—one cannot be entirely amongst those who know little about clouds—little about sea—

—A kiss—a very very quiet kiss—very gentle—not to break the stillness that still is although the sun is over the hills & day is fully on its way—

Rosenfeld's book on music[91] came yesterday. It looks well. And reads well. I was surprised to find it dedicated to me. The copy is inscribed to you & me—He is in rare shape.

---

91. Paul Rosenfeld, *Musical Chronicles, 1917–1923* (New York, 1923).

Is writing with real pleasure. The spirit here—& the Lawrence book have given him a real lift. —It's great to see.—Strand & Beck are much as ever. She is finer without him. He finer without her.—He wants to photograph me today. On Monday was really the day—a perfect day for a portrait—a gray day.—But Strand I fear has no idea of a portrait for if anything is born of feeling it's a portrait—But I suppose in my sense everything one puts down is a portrait!—So if Strand doesn't understand what a portrait is—he is deficient in all his work, deficient of the creative quality which gives life. Sometimes he is so near or on the borderline that one feels like shoving him over into the real—if one only could!—

—Beck is certainly not creative—it's amazing how sensitive she is at moments & how something gets in the way then & turns a fine material into something much less fine—often unfine.—She knows it but doesn't grasp the why-ness.—

The Little House is three-quarters shingled—by noon the men will be through with it. They then go to the porch. Too bad the roof must wait—When they got through yesterday at 4:30 I went over & did some Artura proofing—I think there are a few good things—but I was dangerously close to ruining all the things through my over eagerness while photographing— as I lost nearly all the snaps of Donald[92] for the same reason. A question of technicalities— everything else was right—

—Katherine has been urging me to write to you that the house seemed empty without you—You give it a something it has not without you—She says Miss O'Keeffe knows how to do things—& does them so quietly & in such a fine way.—

I agree with her—She says she learns from you—She tells Beck she can't teach her because she herself doesn't know—The fact is Beck makes her nervous—nervous because of her eagerness to always speed up—Katherine has her own speed.—It's all most amusing to watch as long as there is no trouble—Beck tries to grasp what it's all about & she doesn't realize that she is just as her watercolors were!—If she'd *look* at them she'd understand more about things she can't grasp now.—

—I still continue to learn—There is so much to learn.—Not in the ordinary sense—not the knowledge talked of & which it is said one should have—but a learning about something which very few seem to know much about—

There was no letter from you yesterday. Maybe two will come today—I'm wondering did the headache go—

Eighteen nights have gone—Yes, you had to go—Soon you have to come—

You are as fine as the white night last night—Yes, your soul is that fine—The world is a hard place for fine souls—

You Little Girl—

I kiss you gently—with all I am—

92. Probably Greenough 697.

Georgia O'Keeffe · [York Beach, Maine] · [September 25, 1923]

My Dearest One—

It's a beautiful warm morning—and my stolen bouquet is very grand and gay—right under my nose here—The curtain is blown by the wind occasionally and the sun flashes across it making it particularly fiery—It's small—but very gay—making it seem like all the fire of the world—stuck in a little glass vase—

Last evening—walking on the beach at sunset I saw a pink moon—nearly full—grow out of the gray over the green sea—till it made a pink streak on the water—very faint—that told you where the ocean began and the soft gray blur of space was ended—And the moon grew hotter and hotter—and the path on the water brighter and brighter[93] till it burned so that I didn't want to look anymore—and we came in for supper—Later—we went out—and the streak on the water was glistening white—and the moon white—glistening—the waves pound me and terrify me at night—and the big schooner-prow reaching out to sea—seemed almost suspended in space—but couldn't get to the deep enough ocean that it was reaching for— I stood there a long time alone—terrified—looking at it all—the moon sheen—glistening on the wet sand—the tide was low—the few small rocks at the edge of the water black—it was very wonderful—

Finally Mrs. Schauffler came down and we walked up to the old boat—I was afraid to go alone—the waves and the huge stretch of sand and the great black hulk almost petrify me—

Then we came in and to bed—I tried to write you—I sat in my bed thinking of you —pen and paper in front of me—I reread the three letters of the afternoon written on the 21st and 22nd—and I felt utterly helpless—Finally put out the light and went to sleep feeling you close and warm within me—as you have always been and will always be—All of me seeming to cry out to you—for you—to give to you and to take from you—to give all that I have to give you—all that you can take and to receive in return—not in the sensing of give and take—but a perfect coming and going like the waves—body and spirit—soul touching—flowing together —all of me yours—till I disappear—

I felt you were worrying about me and it worried me—

And I slept without waking till day was just beginning to come—I heard Mrs. Schauffler stirring—We got up and were out on the beach—sand and sky all a burning light pink—a few gray little clouds—that soon turned lighter pink—and the sun—a queer flattened shape—a hot fiery pink rose little by little out of the ocean—and finally sent its path across the wetness to greet us while the moon—a huge pale white thing—slipped away behind the soft green willow tops in the west—It was a great morning—so warm too—

I climbed the schooner again—I wanted to climb the ladder to the mast but she shook her head at me from where she sat on her red blanket on the soft sand—coffee tray beside her—We had that on the beach before the sun poked his head up—nothing happens in the morning here without coffee first—I like that—but it's very funny to me—

Then she came in—when the sun on the water was too bright to watch—I got my

---

93. Lynes 438.

stuff and went back to the boat and made some drawings—It's very difficult—right under the prow—just a little piece of it—

I do wish you were here—I know you would have a great time with it—parts of it are wonderful—chains and an iron hole—and pulleys—or something—I don't know what they are exactly—and the lines curve so subtly—As it stands on the sand it is slightly tilted on one side—a long rip in the bottom that the tide surges through with every come and go—

Well—My drawings are rotten—

I ate a huge breakfast at eight—went down and looked at the boat again—water washing around her—that was why I came up for breakfast—

It was very hot out there before breakfast—and the waves were nearly at me—

Well—My Dearest—The wind has come up—the ocean is coming to life—I am going to make my bed and get to work—I must have been up for at least five hours and a half already—

—My work all looks rotten—The day is beautiful out—and I don't feel a bit discouraged about my inability to paint anything as fine as the day—as fine as I feel—as fine as my passion for you—fever for you—or whatever you want to call my madness for you—

Compared to my stolen bouquet—my work looks like a dead angle worm—but I don't seem to mind a bit—I'm going right at it again—

The best of me to you in knots—straight lines—curves or whirlpools—any way you want me—You're my baby—!—

I had intended to leave here tomorrow or Thursday but Mrs. Schauffler says if I will wait till Monday she will go to Boston with me—So I will probably be back next Tuesday or Wednesday—

—The days are so fine—it would be rather difficult to pack up and go away from them—and though I know my work is very bad I seem to want to do some more that will probably be equally bad—I seem to have a very good time with it even if it's bad stuff and so far I have very little to show for it—It will come in time—Something must come from it—

Save your retouching for me—You mustn't spoil your good prints—I'll be disappointed if you scratch everything up—when you can save them for me just as well as not—You know I like to do it—

This old boat reminds me of your *Katwyk*[94] (I don't know how to spell it)—You see—your things are quite as important to me as my own because you are my child—and you mustn't ruin them with your scratches—and you must also save your eyes!

WHEN O'KEEFFE RETURNED to Lake George in early October, she was disconcerted to discover that in her absence Stieglitz and Beck Strand had grown noticeably closer.[95] On the pretext that she disapproved of Beck wearing pants, she quarreled with both of them and Beck left immedi-

94. While traveling in the Netherlands in 1894, Stieglitz visited Katwijk aan Zee, a popular artists' haunt, and made several photographs of boats; see Greenough 208–211, 225–232.

95. See Greenough 740–770.

ately.[96] O'Keeffe and Stieglitz remained at the Lake until late November, enjoying the solitude, the cool fall weather, and an early snowstorm just a few days before they returned to the city.

Once back in New York, Stieglitz made plans for an exhibition in March 1924 that included sixty-one photographs by him and fifty-nine paintings, watercolors, pastels, and drawings by O'Keeffe. It was the first time in twenty-five years that Stieglitz had organized a joint presentation of paintings and photographs and the only exhibition he ever shared with just one other artist. While Stieglitz wanted to demonstrate that he and O'Keeffe were artistic partners with a shared vision, O'Keeffe wrote in the exhibition brochure that she hoped to "clarify some of the issues"[97] that had been written about her the previous year and show how her new work was "as objective as I can make it."[98] Critics applauded Stieglitz's photographs as "revelations" and praised his role as a "path-finder" for the arts in America.[99] O'Keeffe's work, though, was once again discussed in terms of her gender: "They are the work of a woman," one critic wrote, "who after repressions and suppressions is having an orgy of self-expression."[100] While O'Keeffe found these criticisms embarrassing, she also recognized, as she told a friend, that "most people buy pictures more through their ears than their eyes—one must be written about and talked about or the people who buy through their ears think your work is no good—and won't buy and one must sell to live."[101] And her work was beginning to sell: she made several thousand dollars from her 1924 exhibition.[102]

Much to O'Keeffe's relief, this new-found success allowed them to move out of Lee and Lizzie Stieglitz's house into their own studio apartment in November 1924. It also inspired Stieglitz in March 1925 to mount a large exhibition of more than 150 works in the Anderson Galleries. Celebrating the twentieth anniversary of the founding of 291, the exhibition championed, as its titled announced, the art of Seven Americans: Demuth, Dove, Hartley, Marin, and Strand, as well as O'Keeffe and himself. The critical response was mixed, with each of the artists receiving both praise and scorn. But Stieglitz was not discouraged: if he had been at the gallery every day, not in bed with kidney stones, he reasoned, he could have swayed many more reviewers to see the strength of the work he had selected.[103]

The summer of 1925 brought little rest for O'Keeffe and Stieglitz. In early June, O'Keeffe had a severe reaction to a smallpox vaccine. A few weeks later, Lee and Lizzie Stieglitz moved into their newly built home, Red Top, adjacent to the family's farmhouse on the Hill. Because Red Top did not have a kitchen or dining room, they, their family, guests, and servants all descended

96. See AS to Rebecca Strand, July 21, 1929.

97. Georgia O'Keeffe, [Statement], *Alfred Stieglitz Presents Fifty-one Recent Pictures, Oils, Water-colors, Pastels, Drawings by Georgia O'Keeffe*, exh. cat., Anderson Galleries, New York; repr. in Barbara Buhler Lynes, *O'Keeffe, Stieglitz, and the Critics, 1916–1929* (Ann Arbor, Mich., 1989), 197–198.

98. GOK to Sherwood Anderson, Feb. 11, 1924, as quoted in Jack Cowart, Juan Hamilton, and Sarah Greenough, *Georgia O'Keeffe: Art and Letters* (Washington, D.C., 1987), 176.

99. Forbes Watson, "Stieglitz-O'Keeffe Joint Exhibition," *New York World*, Mar. 9, 1924, 11E.

100. Helen Appleton Read, "Georgia O'Keeffe—Woman Artist Whose Art Is Sincerely Feminine," *Brooklyn Sunday Daily Eagle Magazine*, Apr. 6, 1924, 4.

101. GOK to Doris McMurdo, July 1, 1922, as quoted in Cowart, Hamilton, and Greenough, *Georgia O'Keeffe*, 170.

102. Drohojowska-Philp, *Full Bloom*, 233.

103. See AS to Dove, July 7, 1925, as quoted in Richard Whelan, *Alfred Stieglitz: A Biography* (New York, 1995), 472.

on the farmhouse several times each day. Just as disturbing to O'Keeffe, Lee's and Lizzie's newfound interest in Lake George prompted Alfred's siblings Selma and Julius to reassert their claims to the family's property. Yet Stieglitz's and O'Keeffe's vacation was not exclusively devoted to his family for several friends also visited the Lake that summer and fall, providing welcome relief. Among the most notable was Jean Toomer, the handsome author of the much touted 1923 novel on African-American life, *Cane,* who brought with him his new lover, Margaret Naumburg, the former wife of Waldo Frank. Stieglitz was so taken by the young writer that he made fifteen portraits of him, while O'Keeffe painted an abstract portrait of him later that fall.[104]

When O'Keeffe and Stieglitz returned to New York that fall, they moved into the newly constructed Shelton Hotel, a thirty-story skyscraper on Lexington Avenue between 48th and 49th Streets. Considered the pinnacle of urban living, the Shelton boasted a library, solarium, swimming pool, Turkish bath, and even bowling alleys and squash courts, yet initially it was a men's residential hotel and only began to admit women a few months before O'Keeffe and Stieglitz arrived in late November 1925. The Shelton changed their lives in the city—its spectacular views inspired both of them to embrace the city as a subject in their art; its cafeteria provided Stieglitz with an arena in which to hold court with both old and new acquaintances, such as the architect and theosophy scholar Claude Bragdon; its daily maid service freed O'Keeffe from the household chores that encumbered her at Lake George; and by using the living room of their two-room suite as a make-shift studio, it gave O'Keeffe a place of her own to paint for the first time in several winters. Although they changed rooms, they lived at the Shelton until 1936.

In December 1925, Stieglitz opened the Intimate Gallery, a small room in the Anderson Galleries, dedicated to the art of the Seven Americans. Through the spring of 1929, he mounted annual exhibitions in the "Room" of work by Marin and O'Keeffe, as well as occasional shows of Demuth, Dove, Hartley, and other artists. The third exhibition in the gallery, opening in February 1926, was of O'Keeffe's recent work. Including many paintings of flowers, the show was also the first public display of her views of New York. In 1925, when she first began to paint the city's skyscrapers, "the men," she later recalled, thought she had lost her "mind"[105] for tackling such a difficult subject. Yet she was vindicated when *New York with Moon*[106] sold the first day her show was open for twelve hundred dollars. Her flower paintings, too, were eagerly acquired: within the first month of the exhibition sales from all of her paintings totaled more than nine thousand dollars.[107]

O'Keeffe and Stieglitz arrived in Lake George in early June 1926, eager to get to work. Instead, Stieglitz had to go back to the city, where he was admitted to Mount Sinai Hospital for a

---

104. Greenough 1077–1091. In a letter of March 12, 1934, O'Keeffe told Toomer that one of her paintings of trees (Lynes 506), which hung in her 1934 exhibition at An American Place, was a portrait of him. As she explained in *Georgia O'Keeffe* (New York, 1976), unpaginated, "There are people who have made me see shapes—and others I thought of a great deal, even people I have loved, who make me see nothing.... I have painted portraits that to me are almost photographic. I remember hesitating to show the paintings, they looked so real to me. But they have passed into the world as abstractions—no one seeing what they are."

105. GOK to Blanche Matthias, Mar.[?], 1926, as quoted in Roxana Robinson, *Georgia O'Keeffe: A Life* (New York, 1989), 293.

106. Lynes 483.

107. Lynes, *O'Keeffe, Stieglitz, and the Critics,* 130.

kidney stone. On his return two weeks later, O'Keeffe's sister Ida, a nurse, came to care for him, but he was a difficult patient—Stieglitz later described the summer as "five rotten months of illness & suffering."[108] With no visitors in July, O'Keeffe was able to paint, and even to take on a student, Frances O'Brien, who lived at a nearby hotel. Her peace was interrupted in early August, though, with the arrival of Ethel Tyrrell and Eva Herrmann, the daughters of Stieglitz's old friends, the critic Henry Tyrrell and the painter Frank (Sime) Herrmann. Although Stieglitz was delighted to be surrounded by these attractive young women—he even made nude photographs of Herrmann and O'Brien,[109] the first nudes he had made in more than three years—O'Keeffe was not. Stieglitz reported that she became "terribly nervous" and "run down."[110] But she was also disturbed by his flirtatious behavior not only with the young women, but especially the cook Ilse. Just before August 20, 1926, she became incensed when Herrmann said she had seen Stieglitz kissing Ilse,[111] and she abruptly left for York Beach.

Georgia O'Keeffe · [En route from Lake George, New York, to York Beach, Maine] · [August 20, 1926] +

8:30—In the dining room at the station—waiting for food—

The train shook so I couldn't write—

I watched the evening come—and seemed to be nobody—nowhere—but [sometimes] saw things passing the window and I suppose it was me—and the things that I saw made me feel very lonely—They made me feel that something that you and I are together is very far away—and I seem to shrink from everything else—

I didn't cry—I only shed one tear—

And when I think of your little anxious face I don't see how I was able to come away—But I had to Boy—there wasn't anything else for me to do—You understand—I think—

I hope you sleep tonight—I hope you take Allonal[112] so there will not be any doubt about your sleeping—and if you don't tonight I hope you will tomorrow night—You mustn't worry about me—I will be all right—

I have eaten—two poached eggs—a large portion of celery and a large piece of melon that was very good—I feel I could sleep but I haven't any bed—I would have fixed yours before I came but as it wasn't certain that we both wouldn't be sleeping in it I couldn't.

I have thought of so many details about all sorts of things and everyone—I can't go into them all—I won't even try—I just wish you would hold me and let me go to sleep and never wake up—

I haven't much feeling about where I am or where I am going—I sit here at the table in the dining room and write—The girl says she doesn't mind—No one else is here—

108. AS to Arthur Dove, Apr. 6, 1927.
109. Greenough 1139–1149.
110. AS to Herbert Seligmann, Aug. 22, 1926.
111. See AS to GOK, Aug. 18, 1929.
112. A sedative introduced in the early 1920s.

I only have a vague notion that the ocean may do something for me—I don't like to stop writing you—it is like saying goodbye and it makes me cry—

So I guess I had better stop writing—

I hope this will find you well and rested in the morning—Do be careful and take care of yourself for me—will you—

Alfred Stieglitz · [Lake George, New York] · August 21, 1926

The house is very still—no one is stirring.—And nothing outside seems to be stirring—for it is windstill—& it was windstill all night.—So very still—that one seemed not daring to move for fear of breaking the stillness—And the moon was bright—& the sky clear—

—It's not quite seven now—& I'm downstairs ready for the day.—Shaven & washed. And it must be about this time that my Sweetestheart is in Boston—And I wonder how the night—how the trip—how everything else.—So much I wonder about—I hope some stillness is with you too.—If you could but learn to acquire some of the ability I have to be "alone" amongst the restless many.—Don't think it comes easy—or that it is all natural—I do know you try—& try hard.—Somehow I feel much of the failure is altogether because of what I am not—The togetherness is our strength—whether here or in the Room—I never forget that.— And yet it would seem that "everyday" life—that "people" are stronger than the togetherness— and that is something I do not grasp—can't fully understand—I have to believe that nerves are stronger than one's will—if will is there.—

—I know I'm always doing many things that you'd rather not have me do—& you may believe if I felt for you what you believe yourself to feel for me I would refrain from doing.— But perhaps you place false values on some things—They may seem what they are not—But I am not going to write about all this—It has worried me more than I can ever tell you seeing you run down as you were & I feeling myself responsible for it.—For that is the way I feel.—If I were a better craftsman in our togetherness perhaps you'd be well—for that is above all [what] I want for you. That is all I thought of eight years ago before you came & I knew you weren't strong & well—

—You must know that you mean more to me than anyone else in the world—And I'm never unconscious of that fact—You also know that Kitty & what she signifies is ever also in my consciousness & that I feel her the victim of all that's weak in me—& so you can imagine what I feel about her.—

Being of the stuff I [am] made of is not very pleasant—never was.—And all I can do is to try & use the material as my own lights tell me to—and oftentimes those lights may be will'o'wisps for all I know.—

I am not excusing myself—for I don't believe in excuses for oneself.—

—But why all this?—I wrote you yesterday what my one & only wish is—I want to see you well—for I know that when you feel stronger again much will seem different.

—So I hope you'll rest & sleep—rest after eating. That you will eat properly—for it was ghastly that improper way you ate here for weeks & weeks. That you don't overexert yourself.

And above all that you don't worry about me—or anything here. I shall try to keep the spirit of the Hill alive while I'm of it—while I'm here.—That's my job just now. It isn't an easy one—

—Of sent the mounting paper. It arrived last night. And a new paper company I had written to sent me printing paper & a very fine letter. The samples came last night. So I'll have my hands full experimenting. I will miss your help—for the mere fact of being able to show you prints I consider help. But it's all right as it is—

I hear Ilse in the kitchen—

—And the morning is cold—I didn't notice it until now sitting here.—And by this time you may be already on the train to York Beach.

—You do seem very far away—And still all this place is very full of you—for me.

—Sweetestheart—think of all the fine things we have in common—

Your strength will come back—& maybe I'll learn some things eventually & make them my own—

Much, much love—and a big kiss—

Georgia O'Keeffe · [York Beach, Maine] · [August 22, 1926]

10:45—Sunday night—

I am in bed—The wind blows my curtains—The moon shines outside and the tide is high—it is very loud—

I walked for two hours on the beach—walked fast—alone—saw the moon come up—and felt really alive like I haven't felt in a long time—

I had walked yesterday after writing you—It was awful—I was like a mad woman—all the world seemed gone from me—everything that I had ever been able to touch and to build my life on seemed shattered—the ocean seemed nothing—the clouds stretched out wild thin gray arms from a blurred sun—and sometimes a whirl of cloud passed in front of it all but didn't cover it—

The night was worse even than the walk—

I had your letter at supper—I had wanted it so—hadn't thought it possible that it would or could come—I reached for it with a feeling like a person who hasn't had food for a week—

That you should be interested in my health puzzles me—after the past few months—Many things puzzle me—

I could not sleep—finally at one o'clock I took a second Allonal—it was after two before I finally went to sleep—I waked at 8:30—and when I finally got up could hardly walk—such a queer feeling I never had—Several times during the day I tried to get up—and I couldn't—My body seemed dead—and my head worked like mad—All the time thinking—thinking—like a crazy one—

Finally—at two—dizzy or no—I got up and went downstairs—They had brought me breakfast some time and I had just dropped off into a half daze in the middle of eating it—and hadn't come to even tho I wasn't asleep—

No more Allonal for me—not if I stay awake for the rest of my life—Dinner was ready when I got downstairs—It was incredible as usual—I sat with Mrs. Schauffler in the swing after eating—Didn't really feel normal till I had walked for about an hour—

I thought many things—my two hours on the beach today—and yesterday—and in the night—and all day today when I couldn't move—

Three meals with the family are the usual table full—After eating they all seem to disappear—I don't know where they go except that I don't go along—It all feels very healthy—

I pick up things on the beach—I had thought there might be lots of people around—there aren't—It seems almost as empty as when I was here before—

You need not worry about me—I will be all right—I knew it out there tonight—It is something that goes thru my blood—that the ocean gives me—and the sky gives me and the sand gives me—and the being alone with it gives me—It seems to be the first firm feeling I have had under my feet in months—I am going into the water tomorrow—Mrs. Schauffler tells me not to but I'm going anyway—I want to—and I have a feeling that I must—

I am going to sleep—I expect to sleep—even tho I am not sleepy—

I am glad that I came—

As for the Room—if it were as healthy as this it would be all right—I didn't feel it growing in health—

—Good night Boy—

Take care of yourself—It would do you good to come here for a week—I am as sure of it as I am that I have a right hand—I feel it would be good for something between you and me—

I do not ask you to come—but I would like it—it would be good.

[August 23, 1926]
It is morning—7:30—

I slept after a long time just lying quiet—The sun shines—it is warm—

I'm going to get up—

10:30—I have had breakfast—lots of it—alone at the kitchen table—Mrs. Schauffler busy about—a nice little Philippino boy who seems to be doing everything asks me if I mind if he opens my egg for me—He is the sort of incredible creature that only a Schauffler would find —all in white with very slick clean looking black hair—

Then I went down on the beach—the tide is almost high—I sat for a long time—after walking a little—on the wreck of an old schooner that is stuck in the sand down the beach—It is a wonderful old thing and with every strong rush of the water it trembles and booms—I like to sit with my feet hanging over the water—feeling close to the water—It looks very pure and fine this morning—A wonderful delicate blue stretch of sky to the east—the rest of the sky gray but very light—more white than gray—It is very good that I am here—I have wonderful things from the beach in a glass dish beside me—

—I just sit here holding my pen—looking out at the water—just looking and looking —So I had better fold this and mail it—

Don't for a minute think that I can divide you up and think of any one side of you—I can only put many things together and realize you—And you undoubtedly do the same when you think of me—

My greetings to whoever is at the Lake.—

Alfred Stieglitz · Lake George, New York · August 26, 1926 +

8:30 P.M. Eyes or no eyes—I don't want to go to bed without dropping you a few lines—First of all I must tell I had to go to the Village this afternoon—a second walk—& found two letters from you—None had come this morning—Upon receipt of the letters I immediately wired Bennet Schauffler to stop over with us on his way back.[113] —Whether he will receive this wire or not I don't know. At the train this morning I was stupid enough not to have thought of the possibility. There was a big crowd & I hastened him quickly on the boat[114] for fear of his not getting a seat—So consideration of one kind got in the way of really proper thoughtfulness—I had thought of the idea when I saw him first but—Well, I hope he gets the wire—I always liked him—So much for that—

You say you are eating everything—I wonder meat too? In a way I hope so.—For I'm curious whether it wouldn't agree with you under proper conditions—You burnt up a letter which you had written to me—It's rather awful that both of us seem to be in similar hypersensitive states—not able to write like free souls—as it once was—And I sincerely hope will soon be again. Specters are awful things. And much that stops each of us is kindred to specters—if not specters themselves—For myself I know. My hurts—yes, I have hurts—make me do many things I don't really want to do—things that mean nothing whatever to me. Yet I do them—or did them.—With you—I at least know that I have hurt you—But really not willingly as I have written to you & told you. And I can't believe you willingly want to hurt me at any time—But there are deep hurts in both of us—When not too crazily tired I dare think—for I know the hurts in me are all of my own making—& I must face them fearlessly—& try to gain something from them & without poison remaining. It's often a wearisome long task—

—I'm trying to see the future—just a bit—I have to.—Maybe that's a gross blunder. —Maybe if I were more haphazard it would suit you better—be better for the two of us. But it's difficult to change at nearly sixty-three. Yes, sixty-three—it's a crass fact. Your thirty-eight does seem very far away from sixty-three! Fifty-four & twenty-nine were perhaps not so far apart.—

The evening is clear—& the day was sunny—Maybe some sun will be helpful—

—I stood a long while today looking at your paintings. I have been thinking about your work a great deal for a long time. I have said little—As I have said little about many things really closest to my heart—

But you know more about your own work than I can ever know—

I hope you'll be painting soon in Maine.

---

113. Bennet Schauffler had spent the night at Lake George on August 25, 1926.

114. At the time, it was possible to take a boat from a landing near the farmhouse to the Lake George village.

—I'm again alone in the house. I like the feeling—For I feel everyone is doing what they want to do—as I am also doing—

Good Night—I do miss you—

You certainly know that—don't you feel it way down in the root of you—& I know you miss me.—Yes, I know it. But it is good for you to be where you are—good in every way. How good it is for me here I don't know. And it is really immaterial. I am here. That's all—

Once more Good Night—The ocean baths must be wonderful—I can imagine your enjoyment—

Good Night—I would like to come with the wind & take a peep of you when you are sound asleep—& slip away again with the wind—& you would never know.—

Georgia O'Keeffe · [York Beach, Maine] · [August 26, 1926] +

Thursday—almost dinner time—We are to eat at twelve—as people are coming for a big supper and it means preparation in the kitchen—

I slept last night like I haven't slept in weeks and weeks—I didn't wake up all night from ten till nearly eight this morning—I eat my breakfast in the kitchen—the little Philippino fixes it —he can even make a poached egg a new and different affair every morning—

There was rain and fog—so after eating and putting my room in order I put on Eva's rain coat and walked the length of the beach in the rain—It was nice warm rain—felt good—Since then I have been at a queer little painting—

I guess there is really very little to say between you and me—only time can say anything—

Much goes through me—I looked at the little photograph of you this morning—

1:45 P.M.—I just have another letter from you—

I'll go on with my painting[115]—

Alfred Stieglitz · [Lake George, New York] · August 29, 1926

It's nearly ten A.M. now & I'm up since five. Sat in a boiling bath for an hour from five–six— And it was midnight before I went to bed. It was impossible to get any sleep—I wrote you several letters last night—several this morning. They were already in the mail-bag but somehow I'm not sending them. Your letter—the very short one—with enclosures of Ettie Stettheimer's & Frances' letters came last night—I wish I could make you feel a bit more "up" than "down" —for I feel it is entirely myself who is making you unhappy—For you are unhappy—

---

115. In another letter to Stieglitz of August 26, 1926, O'Keeffe wrote: "I sit so long with my pen in hand to write you that it becomes absurd.... It is better to go out into the fog and walk than try to write—Out there I seem to get a sense of life and direction that may give you something as well as me if I can really establish it in myself."

—I was in the sun yesterday on the Lake for three hours & rowed five miles. I'm paying the price today. I haven't heard from the Englishman as yet about going to town to receive that medal[116] which means nothing to me except the nuisance of having to be polite & go to town—As for coming to York Beach I'd certainly rather go there than to New York. I *must* be here with the family finally showing up for I must get *something* out of my system—So the next ten days should give me the opportunity. Perhaps I'll mess it as I seem to be messing everything these days.—It sickens me to be such a mess as I undoubtedly am.—I realize it.—That in itself also makes me wonder why bring it to you & interfere with at least the little peace you may be having.

If you don't know that my heart & soul—all that's really fine in me—are in York Beach what earthly good would it do to drag my physical remnant there?—

Here there is a constant going & coming. You are well out of it. Thank heavens. Within a few days some will be gone. Others coming for a few days.—And then virtually no one will be here—When I think of the summer I see a horrible mess—a frightful waste—not a constructive act of a single kind—

I hope the individuals each will have gotten something. To me it's all too ghastly. Maybe also my doing.—I really don't know anymore.—

One thing is certain—I haven't the vitality for these times—I belong to the dead past —that's one thing I've gotten out of it all—

I received a letter from Heinrich Kühn[117] yesterday. It is an extraordinary one. It made me thoroughly ashamed of all I am.—

Now don't construe any of this as relating to you—for it doesn't—"291" was a failure—The Hill is a failure—so it must be I [am] attempting something beyond my powers —& that is crass stupidity—& nothing but conceit.—Lying awake a whole night after a sun-bath does bring a bit of clarity.

I also know that as far as the young are concerned I'll keep my hands off.[118]—I'm making the old mistake of assuming they *feel* things they can't feel as intended—I'll make no such blunder again—

I know I'm old—Even the spirit has grown that—

Now please don't think—

I ought to tear all this up too—but Sweetheart I'll let it go.—

It's nearly time to go for the mail—I wonder why I go—I'm really beastly tired.—

Sweetheart!

116. In 1924 the Royal Photographic Society of Great Britain awarded Stieglitz the Progress Medal "in recognition of his services in founding and fostering pictorial photography in America"; see Herbert J. Seligmann, "Alfred Stieglitz and His Work at 291," *American Mercury* 2 (May 1924), 84. The society was unable to arrange for a member to present the award to Stieglitz until 1926.

117. In his letter of August 9, 1926, the German photographer Heinrich Kühn commiserated with Stieglitz on his poor health, reflected on the importance of *Camera Work* and the beauty of David Octavius Hill's photographs, lamented Steichen's "big mistake" in selling out to the commercial world, and noted how the economy had made life in Germany very difficult for someone like him.

118. Stieglitz was probably referring to his improper behavior with the cook Ilse.

TROUBLED BY the tone of O'Keeffe's letters from Maine and concerned that there was "a black ugly wall" between them, Stieglitz went to York Beach for a few days at the end of August 1926. While there he caught a cold, but even his illness did not dampen the newfound sense of love and commitment he and O'Keeffe discovered during his visit. He returned to the Lake in early September, leaving O'Keeffe to spend a few more weeks with the Schaufflers before they drove her back to the Hill on September 18. Only a few days later, he went to New York to arrange for the framing of his photographs and works by O'Keeffe, Dove, and Marin, which Katherine Dreier had requested for the International Exhibition of Modern Art Arranged by the Société Anonyme to be held in November 1926.

Alfred Stieglitz · [Boston, Massachusetts] · September 3, 1926

Sweetheart—

I'm sitting here in the Essex Hotel (opposite South Station) restaurant waiting for a bit of food. There is still one and a quarter hours till the train goes.—I have everything ready.— Of course you want to know can I breathe. Coming in the train wasn't very pleasant for a while. But could have been much worse. Now, here I am breathing!! I feel the night will be acceptable. —I'm glad I'm on the way—altho' it was very, very hard to leave you standing there—I saw you in the road—You didn't see me waving—But I feel the only wise thing has been done—a wisdom founded on what I feel is best for you—which means us—And the best for me also meaning us.

—I want so much to see you gain still more strength—I did interfere in a way—But the "interference" was essential—the little "setback" was secondary.

I can't tell you what I feel—It's very wonderful—I hadn't understood—couldn't— the essential thing that seemed like a black ugly wall between us. Neither of us wanting any wall —even was it a most beautiful one—But now I feel we are together even more than ever— I have learned a great deal—You suffered when I didn't want you to suffer—& through me. I suffered as horribly as you Sweetheart—& didn't understand—suffered because I did not understand & saw your face!—Of course I should have gone to the root of the "difference" —but I suppose I was "hurt"—& stupid—wounded vanity maybe—

Sweetheart, I never could believe that you could feel that there could be anyone way down in the depth of all I am but you—

I hope you are in bed—asleep—not thinking—just feeling what I feel—Our togetherness which nothing can disturb.—Maybe I'm old enough to have learned how stupid I can be!—

You dearest Sweet One—

Good Night—It was *all* very wonderful—I kiss you & love you much—

Georgia O'Keeffe · [York Beach, Maine] · [September 3, 1926] +

9:25 —in bed—
Dearest Boy—

    And everything—all round everywhere seems full of you—your presence seems everywhere—

    I didn't come to my room after you left till I came to bed—I went from the bus right down on the beach and walked—and walked—close to the water's edge—I could cry right out loud there and no one could hear me or bother about me—I didn't cry long—just a little—It was good—I had to—Then I walked—slowly—up and down from one end of the little beach to the other—the beach that you and I walked together this morning—The beach and the ocean —the little birds—the sky—are all full of you for me and I like it—It made me very happy that you seemed to like them too—Supper was ready soon after I came in—Mr. Schauffler told me about his sailing and he gets all young and excited when he talks about it—that filled in the time till supper—

    I've had a hot bath—and here I am alone—I wonder how you are—where—what doing—I am very anxious to hear—I just hope you are not too uncomfortable—

    I am very quiet—I got quiet down on the beach—I wore your slippers to the bathroom —they seemed fine—It is so good that you seem all around—everywhere—even in the air— that you have used and touched everything in my room—

    —I wonder if you understand how I feel—that you are everywhere—

    You see you are the most precious thing I have ever known—I couldn't seem to see myself living without it—I didn't know how—it was worse than if you had died—seemed worse to me—

    Good Night my Precious One—Do take care of yourself—
    I'll go to sleep—
    All my love goes to you—And the kiss that is my life—

Alfred Stieglitz · Lake George, New York · September 5, 1926

Sweetest-Heart-That-Ever-Beat—I have just read your letter.—It is a wonderful feeling that feeling which is all one's own to know that you & I are truly one—Together I feel as never before —quite as one still much much more so—

    Yes, I took along the ocean & its colors—& the sand & the little birds—& the house —the kitchen & cakes made & in the making—the spirit—the fact—Mr. Schauffler & Mrs. Schauffler & the tragic boy—the children—*Everything*—*Everything*—& *you* there feeling so much that I feel—Yes, I'm *there*—& you are *here*—

    I'm in bed. It's noon—The day is raw & raining & cold. And I feel it's best to stay in bed today & steam & gargle—& try to rid myself of this nasty sinusitis—Don't worry I'm

doing everything as is best. Katherine looks after my needs. And Sel[119] looks in—I don't talk
—Lee will come in after lunch I guess. He is fearing catching a cold in this rawness & dreads
starting practice not fit. How I know that feeling.—

It's good I'm here & not at 274[120]—Right here in this little room of yours. And in your
bed—It is tiny this room—But I like it—

—I do hope the weather will grow warm & sunny sometime soon—But don't worry
about me—It's disagreeable but I'll be all right soon. I must be. And will be—

—Yes, death wouldn't have been as bad as feeling what each one seemed to be feeling
about the other—My law holds good—You poor sweet woman—how I made you suffer &
without wanting to—& without really knowing.—I still can't get over it that I should have
made you feel what you felt—for it was so far from all truth—What queer things humans are—

The mail brought three letters—yours—one from Ida—one from Seligmann—I like the
combination.—I have read only yours. Will read the others after I've written this—

My feeling "against" Ida[121] is gone!!—See what happens when we are truly one—I can
write to her again—I can do much again that had grown completely meaningless to me—much
again that I know will make others feel something worthwhile & that *we* can give—

I wonder did you paint. I feel whatever it may be it is very beautiful—I'm glad you
have the slippers—And that you've slept & are eating again.—*Don't* worry about me—I'm
keeping you posted.—And you are really better off where you are than if you were here just at
present—altho' there is really no nervous tension in the house. It is all very peaceful. Even Sel
has toned down considerably—Ag & Herbert are as ever—Elizabeth is due tomorrow—Little
Hugh[122] leaves this afternoon. He is a fine boy. Unfortunately I have been unable to give him
what I had hoped I could. But he undoubtedly realizes that at least somewhat—

—I sent you two registered envelopes yesterday addressed York Village—I hoped
you got both—I sent the knife anyway—Ethel is really what I originally felt she was—I hope
life won't treat her too roughly.—When I'm feeling ready I'll send her some proofs[123] & drop
her a note. At present I'm not writing anyone—Maybe a note to Ida & one to Seligmann. I'll
see.—I'll read their letters—And it's nearly steaming time—I wonder what you are doing this
morning—Probably it's raw & rainy too—

And you have an open fire—& the windows open! & hear the sea—& smell the air. It's
all so very different from what's here—

Oh! So very much love to you! & a KISS—

—I've read Ida's letter. Am enclosing it. Keep it for me. Don't lose it. And Seligmann sent a
clipping—a review he wrote of some art books.

---

119. Katherine was a housekeeper, and Selma Stieglitz Schubart was Stieglitz's sister.

120. The Schaufflers' house was at 274 Long Beach Ave., York Beach, Maine.

121. In 1925 Paul Rosenfeld had proposed marriage to Georgia's sister Ida O'Keeffe; she rejected him but later regretted her decision. Not wanting to encourage the relationship, Stieglitz refused to invite Ida to Lake George in the summer of 1925 until after Rosenfeld had left.

122. Hugh Grant Straus, Jr., was the son of Stieglitz's niece Flora Straus.

123. Greenough 1145–1149.

I'll drop each a short line—

Much much love—& one more—KISS—

Remember me to all the folks—They are all real people—and *You*—You are everything!—Very real.—

Alfred Stieglitz · Lake George, New York · September 9, 1926 +

Noon. A letter from you just received—Lee advised not walking. So I went down & back in the car—I wrote to you this morning telling you to stay—& here comes your letter saying you might. I repeat—you must stay as long as you can for I feel you are getting something there you cannot get here. Even alone with me. Particularly when I'm not well—that is free to be myself in the healthy sense—This weather is awful—But it isn't cold. It's just foggy & bad for one in my state.

—I really ought to be in New York for a day or two attending to the Dreier Brooklyn Museum business[124]—But I dare not risk it. Stupid. And I can't trust Zoler for what I want done. I've written Seligmann. Too bad the spring was such a mess—So much I knew should be done because of now was only three-quarters done. It's the one-quarter undone making all the difference. Well, I'll do my best. The Brooklyn affair promises to be of great consequence & we'd be great losers if we slipped up on our chances in connection with it.—Of course Miss Dreier is one who always has ideas in a rush—Others must be ready!—(for her)—At any rate she is working. And has ideas & an idea.—

—I wonder did you get the walk from Bald Head to Ogunquit. And if you did did you run across anyone you wanted to meet & anyone you didn't.—

I'm going upstairs now—It's pleasanter there—& I'll tinker about until lunch time—I have plenty to do outside of gargling & steaming—Another letter from Ida—I want to answer it. She asks so many questions.—

Lots lots of love—You want to receive kisses—I wish I were there & in shape to give you all & more than you could receive—or maybe *just enough*—

—Remember me to all—& never forget for an instant—

I love you—

Georgia O'Keeffe · [York Beach, Maine] · September 11, 1926 +

9:30 P.M.—Saturday

Dearest Boy—

You are a bad one—and you just knew what I would be doing. When your telegram[125]

124. Katherine S. Dreier and the Société Anonyme were organizing a large exhibition of modern European and American art, The International Exhibition of Modern Art Arranged by the Société Anonyme, scheduled to be on view at the Brooklyn Museum of Art from November 19, 1926, to January 1, 1927.

125. On September 11, 1926, Stieglitz wired O'Keeffe that he was fine and urged her to stay at York Beach as long as she wanted.

came I was all ready to go but changing my dress and Mr. Schauffler was just tying up my paint box—I hope you are telling me the truth—That you are really feeling better—

We have been having such beautiful days I can't believe that your weather hasn't picked up a little sunshine—and I feel sure your nose needs sunshine—

Today has been perfect from the earliest streak of dawn—I even had my room all cleaned up to leave—I feel quite grand lying here in state with it all in such wonderful order —I am not going to unpack my trunk—will just get out materials to work tomorrow—I have just run around like mad the last couple of days thinking I would be leaving today—

Don't expect much of my painting—so far there are only two new ones since you were here—and they are both odd ducks—I had some things in mind that I didn't start because the time seemed so short—Things I felt I would have to do over and over again—I have mostly just been letting the ocean and the rocks and the sand get into me—it seemed more worthwhile than anything else—

We had a wonderful time this morning—from about 4:30 till about 8:30—It wasn't so terrifying as some times—But it was very beautiful—It has been a very clean colored day— I walked on the beach tonight—The new moon was lovely and the glow all around—

Boy—I think will be with you Wednesday morning—I will be ready so don't urge me to stay here longer—I will be wanting to see you—and I'll be coming anyway—no matter what you say—

Goodnight—My Little One—I wish you were here—It is terrible that you have had such a bad time—

A Good Night—love you kiss—

I'm very sleepy—

Alfred Stieglitz · Lake George, New York · September 14, 1926

Good Morning this gorgeous morning.

Very cold—cloudless—The sun blazing.—Vapors rising from the Lake in entrancing shapes.—And there is not much wind.—

—A kiss—It's a little after eight. And breakfast is a matter of history.—Everything is running smoothly—without much ado. It was a cold night—but I had a window open in the room—a proof I'm feeling nearly myself again—*nose-ily* speaking. Gosh! I'm glad to have literally a breathing spell—The prints of yesterday are a very poor lot—I'll back[126] a few now to see what's actually the matter with them—I'm trying to get a print of you, Marin, Dove & myself ready to send to Miss Dreier.[127] We are to appear in the great catalogue which she has in mind. I wish Hartley & Strand were invited—Hartley is not "abstract" enough I suppose—& Strand?

126. Stieglitz often dry mounted inferior prints onto the backs of his photographs in order to keep them from curling. He referred to the process as "backing."

127. Several of Stieglitz's photographs (Greenough 429, 431, 666, 706, 855, 874) were reproduced in *International Exhibition of Modern Art Arranged by the Société Anonyme*, exh. cat., Brooklyn Museum of Art, Nov. 19, 1926–Jan. 1, 1927.

—I hate to make any suggestions to her—& still I may do so anyway. I don't want to appear as pushing—But I do feel Hartley ought to be represented at least with some of his war pictures—They are "abstract" in her sense.—And Strand ought to be in it too—I'll see—Maybe I'll write her—

And how is my Sweetest Absent One?—No letter yesterday—Undoubtedly two today. None since I wired you.—It all seems so long ago.—Everything seems longer ago than long ago.—It's a sight to see this room filled with instruments—a truss on the sofa—suction nose pump on the bureau—a steamer for inhaling on the little table—eye apparatus elsewhere—etc., etc.—What next?—I'm sorry for you.—

What a mountain day.—I wonder will I get up Prospect[128] this year?—It's a sort of test—I have to laugh—

—I wonder what you've been doing—I'm still wondering are you gaining any weight—It may be of little significance—a few pounds—but I know you'll need them.—

You're sweet—I'd like to kiss you wherever you'd like to be kissed most—just now—That's probably not at all—or *all over.*—

News there is none.—I'll go down now—the sun is great here—& do some backing. And then we'll probably march ourselves villageward—Oh! I must suction first.—Came near forgetting it.

Lots lots—& still more—love—& a never-ending kiss—

—My very best greetings to all those who are kind to you.—

Later: I've written to Dreier about Strand & Hartley.[129] —Another Kiss—

Georgia O'Keeffe · **[York Beach, Maine]** · **[September 15, 1926]** +

Dearest Boy—

I feel like a regular backslider to you. I saw the sun come out of the ocean this morning after a hot colored dawn—and I thought it my last day here—I got up at about six-thirty—walked to the end of the beach toward the old wreck and back before breakfast—Everything clear—and sparkling—

After breakfast I looked over all my shells that I have been picking up since I am here[130]—sorted out the ones I wanted—I should have said that right after eating I lay in the hammock and maybe went to sleep in the sun—it was warm and nice—At about a quarter to ten I started for the lighthouse—walking—alone—I had a very good time all by myself—stopped and looked at the water—and rocks—and picked up shells—The water was very dark blue today—

128. Stieglitz and O'Keeffe liked to climb nearby Prospect Mountain on cool, clear days.

129. In his letter to Dreier of September 14, 1926, Stieglitz suggested that both Hartley and Strand be included in the Société Anonyme exhibition. She responded on September 16, 1926, saying that she would like to see Strand's work to consider it but found Hartley's last paintings "so unsatisfactory…I did not know what had happened to him." On October 13, 1926, she agreed to include Hartley but not Strand.

130. O'Keeffe often picked up rocks, leaves, shells, and other objects that she would later paint.

When I came back I had your first letter—and when the mail came had the second—It is a shame about that nose of yours—I hope it is better by now—

After dinner I packed my shells—got Mr. Schauffler to help me do up a bundle with my last three paintings in it and just as we were through tying and nailing and about to put the final paper on Mrs. Schauffler came in and persuaded me to stay so I will not get to you till Saturday—I will explain the details when I see you—

So I went off to the cliff with Mrs. Schauffler—Margie—Leslie's[131] wife who is here from Chicago and all the kids—It was a beautiful clear dark blue evening—high tide—The sort of thing that makes you feel that the human gods we have invented are a real joke—That God is something too tremendous—so universal—that we poor little humans can't conceive of it—

Just now Mr. Schauffler shouted Northern Lights—we all dashed out on the porch—then upstairs—lights like I had never seen—rays of light shooting straight up into the sky—sometimes very sharp—sometimes fading away—

—Well—Little Boy—this is certainly a mad house—I wish you were here to get into my big bed with me—I hope you won't be provoked with me for changing my mind—It came at the last moment again—I am counting on painting again tomorrow—

I showed Mrs. Schauffler my new painting today—she was crazy about it—I will probably work on it again when I get it home and it is dry—It is a blue ocean.[132]

—I'll be going to bed—I am tired—with my walk this morning and climbing rocks this evening—I don't mind going to bed—

I am feeling fine—It has been a beautiful day—Clear—dark blue—

Good Night—

—I really feel guilty for not going tonight as I said I would but you will understand when I tell you about it—

And kiss me goodnight—

If there is anything you want to eat that Katherine doesn't think of ask her for it—And do take care of yourself—I really feel I am neglecting you—but kiss me goodnight anyway—

Georgia O'Keeffe · [Lake George, New York] · [September 21, 1926]

Dearest Boy—

It is eleven o'clock—I have attended to Ormsby—they come today or tomorrow—I mail the MSS when I mail this—The Schaufflers got off at nine o'clock—Richard is painting—oil is here for the oil stove—Katherine has been bumping around working like mad all morning—Your room is all fixed for you as neat as a pin—I got her to go up to Lee's with me to see if the house was all right for closing—We brought down a few trifles that belong here—

---

131. Leslie Schauffler, the fourth of Charles and Florence Schauffler's six sons, was married to Katharine; Margie (Marjorie) was the wife of Bennet Schauffler.

132. Lynes 567.

There is still no wind—The stillness quite startles me—Only bird noises and the singing things in the grass—

I have been looking at my paintings—I hope you see the ones from Maine—You can order frames for them if you want to—and have time—Allow room for glass but don't have it put on—I want them to dry more and want to paint on all of them a little—

I hope to get to work as soon as I get a little quieted down today—I will be all right in a little while—all the moving is disturbing—

And I wanted to be close to you—I seemed to need it—really need it badly—Don't hurry back—I do hope your face is simple to fix[133]—You will feel better too for seeing about your prints yourself—

Maybe it is good for me to be alone a little—I don't know—

Anyway—Take care of yourself—and know when you think of me that I am reaching out to you with everything there is in me—It seems to mark the turning of a page in my life—I don't know yet what is on the other side of it—I don't seem to really know what is on it—or is it that I don't know what I am going to put on it—

I feel that only time can tell me—and I reach to you because I have taken you so deeply into me—

Just kiss me and be kind to me for a little till I get started—then I will try not to bother you with it anymore—

It is after two—Katherine and I had lunch—very pleasantly—she seemed to enjoy it—We ate on the porch—We both took a nap and are about to walk to the Village—The sun shines—just a little breeze—

I am sending you what I wrote—tho for a while after I wrote it I almost tore it—

—Katherine is ready—

My love to you and be kind to me when you think of me—

Alfred Stieglitz · [New York City] · September 21, 1926

10:30 A.M.

Good morning—Dearest One—

I've just come from Of's where I spent nearly two hours—They are all [piled] up there [this] morning. But the paintings of yours & Marin's & Dove's[134] are now properly marked & will be in the museum within a day or two—& they have been insured. It's all very expensive business. But it's lucky I came down even tho Seligmann did everything right. But after all my

---

133. Stieglitz had a boil on his face and had an appointment to see his dermatologist, Dr. A. B. Berk.

134. Stieglitz sent the following paintings to the Société Anonyme exhibition: Dove, *Chinese Music* (1923), *Moon and Sea* (1926), *Nigger Goes a-Fishing* (1925); Hartley, *Rubber Plant* (1920), *New Mexico* (undated), *Still Life* (undated); Marin, *New York* (1925), *Blue and Gold Maine* (undated), *Camden Across the Bay—Maine* (1922), *Lower Manhattan* (1921); and O'Keeffe, *Abstraction II* (undated), *The Maple Tree* (1925); see Ruth L. Bohan, *The Société Anonyme's Brooklyn Exhibition* (Ann Arbor, 1982).

orders & attention are more explicit & positive. He can only follow my instructions—I think of all sorts of possibilities while I give instructions myself. I've decided to send *eight* photographs.[135] Your two things are certainly very beautiful—very complete.

—While at Of's I had your York Beach box opened. I'm going to take the things to 303 this afternoon to get them out of that mess & I'll look at them at the Room. It was too filthy down there to stay a moment longer than I had to—

—Seligmann called up & told me Rosenfeld was in town leaving for the "Catskills" tomorrow A.M. Maybe I'll see him tonight.—At Of's also found your sweet but tired letter.— It must be great to have the quiet.—This town is dirty & noisy—& I'll be glad when I can get away. Berk wants to see me tomorrow (Wednesday) evening or Thursday A.M. preferably. I'll see—I'd like to be back at the Lake latest Thursday night—It's too long [away] as it is. But I'm glad I came down—After supper last night—both of us ate ravenously at the Commodore— A1 but simple—Then came up here to my room[136]—& I dictated letters, etc. to Seligmann who will type them.—He left at 10:15. I bathed & cleaned up—& slept some—It was hot & I had nothing but a sheet over me—was up at seven again—

There is building nearby and an awful noise—

—I intend having my hair cut now altho' it has grown much cooler. But I can't stand it as it is.—

I wonder how you slept—and whether you are ready to paint today—I hope so— I do want to get back to you—I feel that my Sweetest One has still a few things wrong about ourselves—We'll have more talks—more Lake hours—

It's curious how I don't care to see a soul here—I feel far away from everyone. Seligmann is really a true person.—I like him more & more. I know he is a friend. I realize the danger of making such statements.—I know he doesn't prevaricate nor lie. That's the beginning of friendship at any rate.—

When I woke up this five A.M. your friend was up & quite lively.—I thought of our hour—It was very perfect—very beautiful—You lovely bit of womanhood.

I know no one else can ever give me anything when it comes to woman—Don't you know that?—But I suppose I don't make you feel that sufficiently positively.

I'll go now & have that haircut.—Seligmann is coming at three.—I'll lunch somewhere —don't know yet. Have nothing to do until he comes. We'll go to Of's then & taxi your things & my prints (not at framer's) to the Room—I may go to Brentano's to take a look about there. Seligmann says Rosenfeld's article on Lachaise[137] is out & is very good.

—Well, Sweetestheart of Mine give me your mouth—

—*I love you*—Much, much more than you seem to know—

Remember me to Katherine.

135. Four of Stieglitz's photographs of clouds (nos. 177, 178, 227, and 314) and *Spiritual America, American Girl, Death Struggle*, and *Portrait of a Family* were included in the Société Anonyme exhibition; Greenough 889, 604, 874.
136. Stieglitz was staying at the Roosevelt Hotel on Madison Avenue and 45th St. in New York.
137. Paul Rosenfeld, "Habundia," *The Dial* 81 (Sept. 1926), 215–219.

Georgia O'Keeffe · [Lake George, New York] · [September 22, 1926]

I walked for the mail at about five yesterday—and had your letter written on arrival in New York—At about twelve this morning I went again—and had the two of yesterday—I was glad to have them—

I am sitting in the hammock—glad when the sun comes out and shines a little on me—

I do not seem to have much to say that hadn't better wait till you get here—and then probably keep on waiting after that—I keep going over and going over things—since about three weeks before we left New York in the spring—It must be because I am turning a page in my life—and I must see as clearly as I can what is—not what I want to see—but what *is*—

I am glad to have had these days here alone—it is good to have them here—It hurt me terribly that you had to go on Monday—I seem to need you so very very much—The hour had been wonderful—perfect—the Lake too was good—It will be very good to have you back—I love you and am glad you have attended to things to your satisfaction—and that your face will be recovering instead of our worrying about its getting worse—But we need the days here—

I am hoping you don't catch everybody's cold while you are there—

And it is too bad you have missed these lovely days here—but I am glad to have been alone—You understand don't you—

You say you have thought much of me—I don't think you have been out of my mind for more than five minutes at a time when I was awake—

Just kiss me—

I will be very glad when you come—

AFTER A MONTH together at Lake George in October 1926, O'Keeffe and Stieglitz returned to New York and attended the November 19 opening of the Société Anonyme's exhibition at the Brooklyn Museum, which presented their work, as well as that of Dove, Hartley, and Marin, alongside the most advanced European and American painters and sculptors. That same day Stieglitz opened the Intimate Gallery with an exhibition of Marin's work, which continued to attract attention. In December, he arranged for Duncan Phillips to buy Marin's watercolor *Back of Bear Mountain* for six thousand dollars, more than three times the price his works usually fetched. To celebrate this "miracle,"[138] as Stieglitz hailed it, he made a gift of another Marin watercolor to Mrs. Phillips and sold a third to Phillips for half its asking price. A few months later the miracle lost its luster when Stieglitz and Phillips traded angry, public accounts of what actually transpired.[139] In January 1927 Stieglitz opened an exhibition of O'Keeffe's paintings at the Intimate Gallery, which proved to be her most successful yet. Although she thought it was "too beautiful" and hoped her next one would be "magnificently vulgar,"[140] the critics compared

---

138. Sheldon Reich, *John Marin: A Stylistic Analysis and Catalogue Raisonné* (Tucson, 1970), 25: 4. AS to Duncan Phillips, Dec. 8, 1926. The first American museum of modern art and its sources, the Phillips Collection had opened in Washington, D.C., in 1921.
139. "Field Marshall Stieglitz," *Art News* 25 (Apr. 2, 1927), 8; Stieglitz, "Here Is the Marin Story" (New York, privately printed, 1927).
140. GOK to Waldo Frank, Jan. 10, 1927, as quoted in Cowart, Hamilton, and Greenough, *Georgia O'Keeffe*, 185.

her to Matisse,[141] and Stieglitz said more than nine thousand people flocked to see it in the forty-two days it was on view.[142]

On April 14, 1927, O'Keeffe and Stieglitz argued, and O'Keeffe abruptly left for Cos Cob, Connecticut, to stay with Alma and Maurice Wertheim and their thirteen-year-old daughter, Anne (Nan).

Georgia O'Keeffe · [Cos Cob, Connecticut] · [April 15, 1927]

It is a little after one—

Nan and I just finished having lunch on the lawn in the sun—I was out all morning after a little after nine—

After phoning to you I went down to the gate and got the mail—my letter from you—

And all morning I walked with it in my hand—through the woods—and a few open spaces—always beside a little stream—always coming to the sun that was warm—and then—again—always coming to the shadow that was cold—

And always thinking of you—Wishing only for understanding—

I am feeling quieter—

I will go out again and walk again—and try not to think—Or I may paint—I don't know—

I only want to tell you that much love goes to you with this—It seems to be like a blind thing that doesn't know how to get to you—

I am sorry about the cold—I hope you didn't get it from me—mine seems better—Do take care of it—I would return if I thought I could do anything for it—but I know I can't—

—I won't be long anyway—

Alfred Stieglitz · [New York City] · April 15, 1927

It's a gorgeous morning. And I'm glad you are to have it in the country—where there is more peace & quiet—quiet & peaceful as it is up here at your desk—for I am scribbling this to you sitting at it. And it's nice & orderly—& the rooms are cleaned up already.—

It's after breakfast.—I still am in a daze.—For I am unable to grasp what is upsetting you so—what is my shortcoming this time—& what I have been neglecting all winter & before. —Why I seem to be hurting you so much without wishing to—I may have vague notions about it all—

I seem to be about as helpless as the firemen were the other night when man's own work was beyond his own powers to preserve it when the elements let loose.—I'm afraid that many things I blurt out aloud you don't understand believing that they are directed personally

141. Lewis Mumford, "O'Keefe [sic] and Matisse," *New Republic* 50 (Mar. 2, 1927), as quoted in Lynes, *O'Keeffe, Stieglitz, and the Critics,* 265.
142. Drohojowska-Philp, *Full Bloom,* 274.

against you. If I permitted the *personal* to dominate my life & actions we never would have come together. And I know that nothing to me could replace that *togetherness.* And I know that I couldn't feel it as I do if I didn't know that our *being together* is as necessary for one as the other—no matter what "hurts" maybe entailed. Of course I know my weaknesses & I don't like them. Even less than you do.—And yet somehow they seem an essential part of my makeup—And without them there would have been no me at all.—I hold no brief for them. But I feel you emphasize them out of all proportion & maybe intensify them in me in consequence. —I don't know.—I do know that I have never in my life been more "proper" in every act & thought & inclination than all this winter—My mind was on the Room—on you—all else seemed far, far away—nearly non-existent.—Yet you charge me with neglect & indifference— Of course words are empty—don't mean a thing. I know what you feel—& I hold you have no actual ground for feeling what you do—or maybe *how* you feel it—& see it.—

—I do hope that as your nerves let down that you will realize that the "situation" is not a fraction as bad as you wish me to believe it is. I know it isn't. Unfortunately the "perfect" is unattainable—even in our own relationship which I know has been more wonderful than any relationship between any man & woman I know of. It has produced much beauty & fineness for thousands & thousands of people—There is your work & my work—as evidence of our togetherness—

If contemplating that doesn't give you strength to find true values for yourself I can't see what will.—My chief crime is my age with my infirmities—physical & otherwise. My spirit is all right enough—but—the carcass is certainly a sad drag to it.—

—I don't know whether you'll be able to make out anything out of this hodge-podge. I'm frankly without much life—but I *must* clean up as much as I can—

I really don't want to go to the Room—but there is no alternative. Lachaise[143] wants to see me—why I don't know.—He is fine & I'm glad I seem to be of service—

—I'm fighting a cold—wanted to go to Lee—but won't as I believe I'll manage without. The night was a restless one but I was glad to be in bed awhile—& tried not to think of anything—

Of course the rooms seemed very large—& very empty.—

You mustn't come back until you feel completely rested.—

Remember I love you very, very much—heartache & all—Maybe it's a funny way I show my love—

I'll gargle now & walk up to 303.—

Again love—& a kiss—

BY THE MID-1920S, O'Keeffe and Stieglitz realized, as she had written in 1926, that they were "turning a page" in their relationship. Still passionately in love, they nevertheless argued with ever greater frequency, and both had come to recognize their differing expectations and desires. As O'Keeffe shed her schoolgirl flightiness of the 1910s and gained greater confidence with

143. Stieglitz exhibited Gaston Lachaise's sculpture at the Intimate Gallery from March 9 to April 14, 1927.

her growing reputation in the 1920s, the balance of power subtly shifted in their relationship. Inquisitive and energetic—despite Stieglitz's frequent fussing about her frailty—the forty-year-old O'Keeffe longed for a more spontaneous, less predictable existence that touched her "center," as she later said,[144] as Stieglitz himself had once done. No longer willing to always bend her life to accommodate his, she found it increasingly difficult to live with someone who did not want to travel or have a home of their own. Stieglitz, who was now in his mid-sixties and unsettled by change, witnessed O'Keeffe's growing restlessness and independence with mounting concern. He had always needed an audience, but now he wanted a partner who was totally devoted not only to him but also to all of his activities at the gallery.

In the summer of 1927 O'Keeffe was bothered by health problems. In June, when she and Stieglitz arrived at Lake George, rheumatism in her right hand made painting difficult; in August and December, Dr. Benjamin Berg removed benign cysts from her breast at Mount Sinai Hospital in New York. But unlike Stieglitz, who was usually felled by far more minor illnesses, O'Keeffe's did not prevent her from making more than thirty paintings that year, including numerous flower studies and one of her most celebrated landscapes from the 1920s, *The Red Hills with Sun*.[145] She also found new—and playful—allies in the younger members of the family, including Stieglitz's nephew William Howard Schubart and his wife, Dorothy, and Stieglitz's niece Georgia Engelhard. Stieglitz too had a productive summer, making more than forty photographs, including several whimsical studies of trees and clouds.[146]

Eager to ensure that his artists earned enough money to support themselves, Stieglitz mounted seven exhibitions at the Intimate Gallery in the winter and spring of 1927–1928, far more than in previous years. He also arranged to sell to an anonymous collector (Mitchell Kennerley and his fiancée, Margery Durant Campbell Daniel) six of O'Keeffe's calla lily paintings[147] for twenty-five thousand dollars, a far higher price than her works usually commanded. (He announced the transaction only days after the sale of thirty-two John Sloan paintings for forty-one thousand dollars, also to an anonymous collector, was made public.)[148] Although the final sale, like Kennerley's engagement, collapsed, both Stieglitz's sales stunt and the attendant publicity made O'Keeffe uncomfortable.

O'Keeffe was also disconcerted by another threat. Throughout the spring of 1928, Dorothy Norman, who had first visited the Intimate Gallery the year before, began to spend increasingly more time there, reading *Camera Work* and *291* and striving to become part of the daily life of the "Room." "I cannot keep from coming," Norman wrote Stieglitz a few months later; "I hope you will not tell me to go out into the woods too!—Altho' I think O'Keeffe would if she had the chance. She always looks at me as if I were some queer species of animal who had strayed in—was taking up your time and more—and wouldn't I please remove my superfluous presence far enough away so as to be out of her sight."[149]

144. See, e.g., GOK to AS, May 7, July 9 and 11, 1929.

145. Lynes 608.

146. Greenough 1198–1204.

147. Lynes 423, 425, 426, 429; vol. 2, appen. 11, 44, 73. Kennerley returned the paintings to O'Keeffe in 1931.

148. "Artist Who Paints for Love Gets $25,000 for 6 Panels," *NYT*, Apr. 16, 1928, 23.

149. Dorothy Norman to AS, Dec. 10, 1928; all letters between Stieglitz and Norman are in Dorothy Norman Papers, Yale Collection of American Literature, Beinecke Rare Book and Manuscript Library.

In May, O'Keeffe once again sought the restorative atmosphere of the Schaufflers' home in York Beach. Stieglitz did not accompany her, but remained in New York to pack their things at the Shelton Hotel before their scheduled June departure for Lake George.

Georgia O'Keeffe · [En route from New York City to York Beach, Maine] · [May 19, 1928]

Dearest—

I am feeling very quiet—It is good to just sit still and look out the window—

Spring is here—The leaves are large and tender—all cool green as there is no sun—I would like to be one of those large—soft—tender green leaves—and wrap around you and hold you while you sleep tonight—

I am just sitting quiet—it is so good—

My dearest love to you—I hope you keep quiet and well with the many things you have to do—I will be thinking so much to you—and I think maybe I am beginning to understand almost everything—

As we go on the leaves are hardly out at all—It does not rain—

I am just going to sit—And tonight I will go to bed so early—

Again—my love to you.—

Georgia O'Keeffe · [York Beach, Maine] · [May 23, 1928]

It is night again and I am in bed again—I had your letters this afternoon telling of your visit to storage and of Zoler going fishing—and all the things you were getting done—

I had looked for blue cups at Macy's for you—couldn't find any—

I do hope you find some mounting paper—And I also wish I had seen the photographs put away before I came away—

The large silver frame at Of's is for my *New York River*[150]—if he has two large silver frames one is a mistake but I told him to keep it—I will have something for it later—*The Shelton*[151] was due to have a frame painted with the radiator paint—I think silver leaf would be too handsome for it—

I was on the beach for a couple of hours this morning—I wish you could see the difference in the way I look—It even made me laugh at myself—

I haven't picked up much to paint—There isn't much of anything to pick up—it is all like a newly scrubbed floor—cleaner even than Ella could scrub it—hardly a scrap of any kind to pick up—

You say you wonder how the ocean looks to me—This morning I was thinking of that to myself—It has been all greenish gray since I am here—It is as terrifically male and female as ever—the same terrific male power in the overpowering breakers as they move toward you—

150. Probably Lynes 620.

151. Lynes 526 or 527.

slowly—but surely coming—and the same marvelous loveliness that seems female when they break—

I love it—I wish you were watching it with me and loving it with me—

There are no people—it is all empty—but so powerful and so beautiful—and so clean —I just wait for morning to get out there again—This morning I was crazy to go in it—I had to laugh—it is so cold I wear two sweaters—a long sleeved waist and my red coat—but I am sure I would like going into it anyway—

—It was misty this afternoon so I didn't go out—I slept for nearly two hours—And how I do eat—This is the first day I have actually felt like eating up the house—

Mrs. Morse and I made you a pair of woolen pajamas this afternoon—We worked for two hours—She will finish the stitching tomorrow—I don't know the machine—

I wasn't going to tell you but how else can I tell you what I did with the afternoon—

I must be getting to sleep now—

Boy—I am feeling so much better—it is wonderful—even my nose has cleared up surprisingly—

My best love to you—and I hope you sleep half as well as I am going to—not the very least—

A kiss good night—a real one—

G—

Alfred Stieglitz · [New York City] · [May 23, 1928] +

7:30 P.M. Here I am alone eating supper—Well, some work has been finally done. First of all as I came to the dentist at eleven I found my appointment was for three P.M.!! Another for Friday at same time. Well, I didn't mind. Was glad I could go right back to the Room. Zoler came in shortly after & we got busy without a word said. Quite a bit was packed up by six P.M. tho we had lunch & I was at dentist from three to four. And the *Lilies* carefully protected are finally deposited in Kennerley's room—He very satisfied.—It is still difficult for me to realize that I am no longer Guardian of the *Lilies*.—I know Kennerley appreciates how I feel—We talked about the Wright article.[152] He & I feel the same way. Kennerley read it again last night. So did I— I'll tell you all about it later—when we are together again—that is physically together as otherwise—for I feel we are in no way separated—

Upstairs—I'm going to go through some photographs tonight. I told Zoler I hoped he & I would get thro' our job as quickly as possible. I want no dallying—Now we'll see. This dawdling is maddening. Of course I'm to "blame" myself—There was no talk about fishing or prize-fighting —It's a very musty gray still evening—I'm sitting at your desk—the Lachaise alabaster[153] right

152. *Lilies:* Lynes 423, 425, 426, 429; vol. 2, appen. II, 44, 73. In his article "S. S. Van Dine: The Man Behind the Mask," *Outlook* 149 (May 9, 1928), 48, 77, 78, Harry Salpeter revealed that the popular mystery author S. S. Van Dine was in fact Willard Huntington Wright.

153. Gaston Lachaise, *Georgia O'Keeffe,* 1927, Metropolitan Museum of Art; see Gerald Norland, *Gaston Lachaise: The Man and His Work* (New York, 1974), 94.

in front of me—I see the city out of the window—here & there a few first lights—a bit of rising steam on one rooftop—More lights by now—I somehow feel less tired—I guess knowing that we're on the job has relieved me from much tension. At nine A.M. I must be in storage to transplant your things from one of my vaults into yours—& those things now in your one vault into a vault of mine. It ought not to take much time. Two men are to be ready for me.

—And Zoler is to be at the Room at ten A.M.—I shall also take a few things to Of— Sel brought her *Lily*[154] to be reframed—

—Maybe we can clean up the Room by tomorrow night. Wouldn't that be grand?— Then there would be this room—& plenty more—

Hartley—?—Haven't seen him in two days. Maybe he is finally seeing Griffin—

—Zigrosser appeared this afternoon. Mrs. Hare had a letter from D. H. Lawrence. It seems Lawrence is coming over to have a show of his paintings. And Mrs. Hare thinks I might be the one to show [them].[155] I told Zoler that I'd have to see the things first. Altho' interested much in Lawrence I'm not seeking notoriety for the Room using *names*—Lawrence I feel lost much in not coming to the Room when he said he would—Maybe just as well tho—We'll see—I have to keep in mind that maybe next season will be my "last"[156]—so I don't want to waste any time over anything not essential—You understand.

—There is my cleaned cape from Barrett & Nephews. And my shoes from Slater. Also much wrapping paper from Of's—also twine—& tissue paper—Zoler dumped the water out of the big jar. No damage done—

—I wonder how you feel today. I hope still less numb—really beginning to feel alive again—I fear that you haven't seen any sun yet—A mean spring again—I am really glad you are not here now—even if you felt strong enough—

It's beautiful outside now—I think I'll get to work—

This letter brings you much much love—& some little kisses—& still more love—I do hope you are really a bit rested—& are gaining in every way—

—A tiny kiss—

Georgia O'Keeffe · **[York Beach, Maine]** · **[May 27, 1928]** +

Dearest Boy—

It is night and I am in bed—

After writing you this afternoon I went to walk—I went down the railroad track back of the house—It isn't used any more—There isn't even a path. At the first crossing I took the road—then a path and on up a hill—it was lovely—everything unfolding—blossoming— When I had been wandering for some time—a thick fog rolled across the sunshine from the

154. Lynes 428.

155. Stieglitz subsequently told Herbert Seligmann that Elizabeth Hare had sent him pictures of Lawrence's paintings. "Even if the pictures were fit for the Room—for which I fear they are too large—the dates would be impossible. And assuring sales—well??" (AS to Seligmann, June 19, 1928).

156. Mitchell Kennerley was thinking of closing the Anderson Galleries where the Intimate Gallery was located.

ocean—just as I was taking a path that I knew would lead back to the ocean—It was as thick as a fog can be and not be rain—

When I got to the ocean I was glad to see the tide almost high—washing away all the tracks and marks and sand houses made by the Sunday visitors—I had it all to myself—Nobody else would be walking in such a fog so I walked as far as the high tide would let me—The mist even gathered on my eyelashes and flew off in drops when I blinked—It was good with the soft white so close all round—The ocean coming in so clean—

Finally I came in—made a fire in the fireplace—saw that the whole household was still busy—going faster than ever to finish up everything before dark—They were all so tired looking—but interested—as tho they all wished the day would stay—

I made some order in my room—all the time thinking of you—always thinking of you—wishing I understood everything better so you wouldn't have to bother about me—

I got out the little clouds you mounted for me and looked at them—They are very fine—I try to understand what that thing is that you are to me—that you are to the world—what I am to you—our relationship in its various phases—we singly and together—what it is all about—

At any rate I had a good day—I didn't work—I had no idea that was worth spending a sunny day indoors—By the time I came in this evening it was nearly six—

This is just to tell you good night—very tenderly—and to tell you how I am always telling you all the things I do as I do them—

I wish I could hold you warm and close—

Good Night

A kiss—very quiet—

Alfred Stieglitz · [New York City] · May 29, 1928

11 P.M. Here I am back again in 3003[157]—From 7:15 until 10:30 with Sel in her home!!—And I'm not on edge—So that's something—There was a very good supper & I ate a bit too much.—As much to please Sel & Zillie[158] as because it was very good—

—In my letter I wrote you before going to Sel I forgot the main thing that happened in the last twenty-four hours—of course the "main" thing from a particular angle!—Last night six of us were to a Negro Show[159]—It was a real treat—The Strands took Bluemner—I, Marin & Zoler—Hartley had recommended the show highly & I felt that he could [not] twice go wrong. Then too I wanted to see a Negro Show—I wish you had been with us. I know you would have been excited about it as we all were—The whole show was as swift as *Rain and*

---

157. O'Keeffe and Stieglitz were staying in room 3003 of the Shelton Hotel.

158. Zillie was Selma Stieglitz Schubart's cook.

159. In late May 1928, two "all negro reviews" were on stage in New York: *Sandy's Picnic,* by Sandy Burns, was at the Alhambra Theatre on 125th St. in Harlem, and *Blackbirds,* by Lew Leslie, was at the Liberty Theatre; see "Theatrical Notes," *NYT,* May 23, 1928, 33.

Shine[160] was slow—And there was a man dancer that beat anything I ever saw in dancing—an amazing performer—a sort of thing one could see over & over again & never tire. Really incredible. When you come to the city we may get a chance to go together—It's the show we should have seen that Seligmann night—& we got $3.30 tickets for $2 each!!—Strand got them—

—The night is a grand one—the first clear one since you left—

I'm going to bed soon—

I'll mail this—& send you more than one kiss—& more love than ever—if that is possible.

Good Night

Georgia O'Keeffe · [York Beach, Maine] · [June 2, 1928]

Saturday afternoon—

Everyone has gone somewhere—and everyone wanted me to go along—I just wanted to stay at home and look at the ocean and be still—I wish you were here—This thing that the ocean is—that I like so much—terrifies me—the long steady roll of the clean green breakers —the blue day—the spray like the manes of wild white horses flying back from the top of each wave—It is wonderful—but it makes me want to put out my hand to you for reassurance— maybe because I have gone farther into the unknown with you than with anyone else—Going into it alone terrifies me—I would want to go with you—even tho I know I must go alone— I at least want to feel your love with me—

I spent only an hour out there this morning—Last night I didn't go down to look at it in the moonlight—I felt it couldn't be as beautiful as the night before—

This is just to kiss you—I will be glad to be seeing you—

O'KEEFFE RETURNED to New York on June 4 "feeling quite like a human being." A few days later, though, Stieglitz hurt his back and then tore a ligament in his finger. When the two arrived in Lake George, neither found the country restorative. O'Keeffe felt "in a sort of daze," unable "to wind up the machinery necessary for living here," and perplexed about "what one might paint,"[161] while Stieglitz confessed, "Whether it is good to be here or not I don't know."[162]

After arranging for a housekeeper, Margaret Prosser, to care for Stieglitz, O'Keeffe left Lake George in early July to visit her family in the Midwest and return to the "place that was my beginning," as she wrote Stieglitz.[163] After stopping briefly in Chicago to see her brother Alexis, his wife, Elizabeth (Betty), and their newborn daughter, Barbara June, she traveled to Portage,

---

160. The musical comedy *Rain and Shine*, starring Joe Cook and Tom Howard, written by James Gleason and Maurice Marks, and with music by Milton Ager and Owen Murphy, was presented in New York in February 1928; see "The Play," *NYT*, Feb. 10, 1928, 26.
161. GOK to Henry McBride, June 11, 1928.
162. AS to Arthur Dove, July 4, 1928.
163. GOK to AS, July 12, 1928.

Wisconsin, near her birthplace in Sun Prairie, where she had not been in many years. There she visited her sister Catherine and her husband, Ray Klenert, and their young daughter, Catherine, and the sisters' maiden aunts Alletta (Ollie) and Leonore (Lola) Totto in nearby Madison. As she revealed in her deeply felt letters to Stieglitz, she was moved by these strong and independent women who had been so important to her in her youth, touched to see the farm her family once owned, and inspired by the fertile Midwestern landscape. But she also recognized, as she told Stieglitz, "how much deeper you have gone into me even than my beginning."[164]

Stieglitz did not accompany O'Keeffe to "'her' America," as he wrote to Seligmann, even though "I know that is what she craves." He added, "I don't think she has any idea what it is to be sixty-four." Instead, as he detailed in his chatty and occasionally superficial letters to her, he worked on making a set of prints to donate to the Metropolitan Museum of Art,[165] wrestled with ongoing water problems on the Hill, and devoted considerable time to his correspondence with friends and colleagues, especially Dorothy Norman.

Alfred Stieglitz · Lake George, New York · July 12, 1928 +

386

My Better Part of Myself:

It's just an hour since the train pulled out—And you must be nearing Saratoga. How empty the house is—& the grounds deserted.—And how still the leaves—

I have been planing the bathroom door (lower floor). It has annoyed me, all these weeks —& even last year awhile.—It closes now—Not a beautiful job by any means. My kind. Not your kind.—I know the difference—

—So there has been some exercise—In the meantime I feel like one in a trance—

How can my Sweetestheart still doubt my loving her. I know.—I know. You see at times I seem far away—very unsympathetic—at times when you want most to have me very near—very sympathetic—Tho seeming far away—I'm nearer than ever—Nor am I ever not sympathetic.—If ever I cared for anyone—you ought to know who it is.—I have written you often in my mind—& in my whole being—Above all else there is always you—& there is ever Kitty. All you are—all you signify to me—All that Kitty is of me—& is not of me. And all she signifies to me—It's ten years ago now that you & I were together first—I'm much older now than ten years, more—much, much older in every way.—And as I look back to your innocence —& my innocence—for I was that if anyone was innocent—but I was hardly more than half-grown up as I am still not grown up.—Much that's very wonderful grew out of that time— is still growing.—Even heartaches—part of the inevitable growing pains. When I'm at work —I'm giving—And when I'm not at work I sometimes brood.—I always did—Lightheartedness I never knew.—You did—I have robbed you of much of it without acquiring any of what I have taken away.—

164. GOK to AS, July 12, 1928.

165. AS to Herbert Seligmann, June 28, 1928. In 1928 Stieglitz donated twenty-two photographs to the Metropolitan Museum of Art; see Richard Whelan, *Alfred Stieglitz: A Biography* (Boston, 1995), 495–496.

—There is much to say that can't be said—Not in words.—I do know that if anyone has ever gotten close to me it's you—Sweetest One. Close to the thing that makes me a bit worth-while. As I know that no one can ever get closer to the thing you are than I have. No one. —And that is strength for me.—I'm not a great hero, you know. Maybe my physical condition has much to do with my lack of hero quality. Or maybe if I were less fearsome I'd be better off physically. Heavens knows I have been taught much by you.—Even thunderstorms seem no longer to affect me much—soon not at all—

—I do hope you will come back looking as well as you did this morning when you left. Your aunts don't know what it has meant your going.—But they have been on my mind quite as much as on yours. More possibly.—

There comes Margaret over the fields. I'm going up to shave. I'll walk to the post office —& will mail this. It is letter number two.[166] The number one went yesterday afternoon.— I wonder will it have welcomed you? I suppose not.—I should have had the idea a few hours earlier. But my head doesn't function as readily as formerly—It's so full of nothingness—

I'll write more later—Don't expect any inspiring letters—I am going to try & fix up a darkroom—& see whether I can't at least load up plate holders[167] & be ready to photograph a cloud or two if they happen along. Maybe I'll find something to say.—I really don't seem to have.—And I want to print—altho' I really don't much enjoy the prospect of papers.[168] —It is a torment whatever one seems to do.—

Morning mail just in—Albert[169] brought it.—Dorothy announces that she & Howard[170] will put up over night here (at the farm) on Saturday if it doesn't [inconvenience] us. They are coming from Lake Champlain or somewhere on their way to New York—Undoubtedly on a business hunt for old furniture, etc.—Well, there is the "apartment" on the ground floor—or the Engelhard "suite."—Probably the latter.—They can use the lower bathroom. They can suit themselves. Also a very decent letter from Emilie Sarter.[171] Not at all frivolous. Seems to be a very good sort. She says an answer is not necessary. And it isn't—Must be of the Pemberton type.[172]

—Lizzie is phoning now to Bryant—& Cashion[173]—So you see the "Day has Begun" —Even the leaves have begun to stir—

166. In the summer of 1928 Stieglitz numbered his letters to O'Keeffe so that she would know the order in which they were written.

167. The Little House, which Stieglitz often used as a darkroom, frequently needed repairs. Stieglitz used 4 × 5 or 8 × 10 inch sheet film in his cameras and therefore had to load it in the dark into holders before exposure.

168. Gelatin silver photographic printing paper changed significantly in the 1920s. Although matte surface papers were common in the late 1910s and early to mid-1920s, by later in the decade commercial manufacturers replaced them with smoother, glossier papers. These changes—and being at the mercy of the manufacturers—frustrated Stieglitz.

169. Albert was Lee Stieglitz's chauffeur.

170. Dorothy and William Howard Schubart; Howard was Stieglitz's nephew, the son of his sister Selma and her husband, Louis.

171. Emilie Sarter, a manager of concerts, lectures, and art exhibits, had recently written Stieglitz, "Mine's a dangerous age—midsummer madness, things you do on a ship that you wouldn't do elsewhere and so forth plus a scandalous affair forecast in my horoscope," and she asked, "Can one be scandalous by mail?" (July 3, 1928) Stieglitz's response must have been just as playful, as she wrote back on July 11, 1928, chiding him not to "think you're too old to play" and assuring him he must be a "delightful character... if you have a sense of humor and no conscience."

172. Murdock Pemberton was the art critic for *The New Yorker* from 1925 to 1932.

173. Bryant and Cashion were Lake George grocery stores.

In the meantime my Little White One is speeding further & further away from the Hill. I know her heart is here—As I know my heart is speeding with her.—

—I'll be very sensible—And I know you will too. Much, much love—Remember me to Catherine big & little.[174] Also to Ray Klenert—Maybe some day I'll meet him too.

—A kiss—altho' I'm not much on kissing—am I?—these days.—

A kiss all the same—

More love—

Georgia O'Keeffe · [En route from Lake George, New York, to Chicago, Illinois] · [July 12, 1928]

Dearest—

A little black triangle made by your cape—disappearing into the white triangle of the station pillars—then your black triangle again disappearing into the darker black shape of the station door—your head just a tiny white dot at the top of your own black triangle—your hand a moving waving thing—the disjointed part of the straight shapes—

Then we went around the bend and you were gone—

I watched the Lake till it was gone—it was very lovely this morning—then moved to the shady side of the train and the rest of the way here to Albany was thinking to myself—mixed with a few tears—

It was very comfortable—I am seated at a table in the ladies waiting room—only a few people—and cool—

I hope you will be able to let down a little—and try more than anything else to take care of yourself—Be sure too—to tell me just how you are—don't misrepresent—

You see—as I realize you are growing older—I want to take you in my arms like a baby and make it easy for you—take care of you—but I feel you want to stand alone in the wind—the wind blowing your cape and your hair and your little body and I feel too that it is best that way—But I at least want to stand beside you near enough so that you can put out your hand to me if you want to and when you want to—and I want you to feel me there no matter how far away I am in miles—

This coming away is good for me—it clears many things in my cluttered mind—or heart or whatever I am—like my room was cleared when I left—

There are things I have wanted to talk to you about—all sorts of things—like I used to tell you everything—but maybe most of it is trash—There is no reason why I should bother you with it—in time I have to settle it by myself—and it is all little things—

You must not worry about me at all—This straightening things out in myself is good— and the trip I am sure will be all right if the train does its work—

I have my Pullman Lower 5—car 15—$8.25—I am going out and mail this with the hope that you get it today—

And Dearest One—the most that I want of you and for you is that you take care of yourself—and put worrying about me out of your mind—

174. O'Keeffe's sister Catherine Klenert and her daughter, also named Catherine.

388

I am glad I am on the way—I will be glad to have this off my mind—

—I kiss you and wish you quiet—

As I go toward this place that was my beginning—I know more and more how much deeper you have gone into me even than my beginning—

It is as tho I have had nothing else but the feeling of big open spaces—

—My love to you dearest—I think we both understand—even tho we are both very difficult at times—

I have wept a handkerchief wet over this—I will mail it and then I am going to eat—I am hungry—

Yours—

11:30 A.M.—Thursday—Yours—

Alfred Stieglitz · Lake George, New York · July 13, 1928

Back again from the post office. Walked there slowly.—Found the box empty.—I knew Lizzie probably (undoubtedly) took the mail out on her way to Glens Falls, for I knew there must be a letter from you from Albany.—Lizzie—good old soul. For she's really that.—She is more than carrying out all your instructions!—As if I didn't know even [though] I say little these days.—Too tired—or maybe too old. Maybe they are the same in this case.

But I stood around at the post office for the mail to be sorted. Sure enough. A letter from my Whitest One—from Buffalo.—To bed at seven—Yes—I can understand.—It was a long day for you—a trying one—Also a very fine letter from Litchfield. Hadn't heard from him in two months. No other letters. A series of printed circulars from the Sarter lady.—Quite "stylish." Amusing.—

—From Colgate had some cards for you to sign.—I signed them for you. I hope that will do. The market is down.—This will be a most difficult time to speculate in.—For it is speculating, not investing, you are doing. No need worrying tho.—

—Albert came with the car & took me home. Would have preferred to walk but as he said there were letters for me I hopped in & was here in a jiffy. And sure enough three letters from my Faraway One—also the telegram from Chicago.

Fine—Yes, Sweetheart, I know you have been wanting to talk to me about many things. I didn't encourage you because I hadn't clarity enough myself—or was it inner quiet owing to my physically being unequal to what I demand from myself—so others too demand. Sometimes talking gets in the way. Things are said which are not understood—they hurt—instead of clarifying.—So words become poison.—The beginning of our togetherness was much simpler than it became later.—That does not mean that our togetherness of today isn't much deeper—really "finer"—than the togetherness of the first days. As I wrote you yesterday those were days of a great innocence—both you & I. In spirit I know you have lost nothing—nor have I lost anything. We have both grown greatly—one thro' the other.—Singly neither would have grown so strong. But the question of practical daily living is not as simple as it was—or we thought it was. And we are both older.—Even you can't do many things you could ten years ago. Maybe you did things then you shouldn't have done—taxed your system—

But there is no going back—Our work shows our spirit—We can see what we have "gained"—what we may have "lost"—We have grown—that I know. And without sacrifice of identity—

I know this trip is good for you—so it's good for me—I'm really feeling quiet—& better—Even my eyes seem a bit more sympathetic—

—There's a letter from Seligmann.[175] From the ranch. A fine letter too—Really quite a growth too.—No other mail.—

Yes, I'll keep you posted about the water here—So there's lettuce in the garden.—I'll tell them.—

I'm going to take it very easy today.—Didn't load up last night.—Will darken the bathroom to load up. Just to get started. My finger is really in the way.—You see it's working in the dark & I need all the *touch* I have to do anything. But I'll manage I guess. Have to—

—It's nearly twelve now—They are beginning to set the table—So it must be after twelve—I'll row to the Village about four.—There's a trace of sun & no wind.—Very cool.

—I wonder what the Art Institute pictures will give you.—Another few hours & you'll be on the way to Portage. I'll be glad when you are there.—I'll wire this evening as you asked me to do.—

You beautiful one—I know we belong to each other—

A sweet kiss—Remember me to all.

I'm with you—

Georgia O'Keeffe · [En route from Chicago, Illinois, to Portage, Wisconsin] · [July 13, 1928]

Dearest—

I am on the train again—for Portage—It has been a good day—

Alexis met me—we went to the Union Station—checked my bags—Then he took me to the Art Institute and left me there—It is open at nine—

It was very interesting—The Bartlett collection[176] a great treat—again I have the feeling that Rousseau[177] comes very near being IT—for me—A beautiful [El] Greco—man on a white horse—another man standing beside him[178]—Sisley I liked too—

Many Monets—so much of nothing—Van Gogh—wonderful color—like food like good beefsteak—Davies never looked so thin—I had a great time—I looked at the rooms used for loan collections—will tell you later—

---

175. Seligmann wrote Stieglitz on July 7, 1928, from Jemez Springs, N.M., describing "the evening of my first day beyond the edge of the world." Stieglitz responded by noting he felt "like a criminal—or something much worse—in being the cause of keeping Georgia from where she really naturally belongs" (AS to Seligmann, July 10, 1928).

176. The Helen Birch Bartlett Memorial Collection of French postimpressionist and modernist paintings, including Georges Seurat's *A Sunday Afternoon on the Grande Jatte,* oil on canvas, 1884–1886, was formed by Frederic Bartlett and his wife, Helen, and donated to the Art Institute of Chicago in 1926.

177. Henri Rousseau, *The Waterfall,* 1910, oil on canvas.

178. El Greco, *Saint Martin and the Beggar,* c. 1600, oil on canvas.

By twelve I was worn out—Alexis came for me at 12:15—we had very good lunch—
then he took me out to his place—Betty's mother and sister were there—From there to the
hospital to see Betty and the baby[179]—It is a sweet little thing—so tiny—so nice to look at—
I am glad I saw it—Betty looks so well—asked to be remembered to you—was much pleased
with your letter—

Their home is just like her—every inch of it—Alexis took me there again from the
hospital—Made me lie down—I wouldn't have thought of it—Being with him was nice—he is
looking very well—seems very well pleased to have a girl—It seems to have been his wish—
I felt very comfortable being with him—

It is almost dark—prairie country out the window—I am tired—will be glad to get
there—It is fine and cool—Everything seems to have gone my way—so far—

—My love to you dearest—the evening sky was wonderful—

This train is better than the 3:20—I am ready for bed again—Am very glad to have seen
the paintings—Everyone on the train is playing cards—

I kiss you good night—and wonder how you are—

Saturday night:

My first day in Portage is over—I sit here in my bed—an amusing old fashioned one
with a yellow spread on it—a double bed—and I reread your letters—and I feel so queer—so
no one and nowhere—My room is nice—with a large bouquet of different kinds of red zinnias
—very gorgeous—

The day has been pleasant but when I look back to the morning it seems ages ago—
This morning after taking the note to you to the post office the two Catherines and I walked
down to the river along the bank for about half a mile—then across the bridge and quite a
distance in the woods on the other shore—

When we got home the little one and I lay down on a cot that is on the porch—I think
I slept a little—Then it was lunchtime—I was ravenously hungry—everyone else seemed to be
too and the food was very good—This afternoon Ray took us to the country—We were away
for about four hours—walking for another one hour of the four—The country is very prosperous farming country—Large places—big beautiful fields of grain—sometimes green
—many greens—sometimes ripening yellow—sometimes glittering in the sun like water—
I think we did not meet more than six other cars—It was a lovely afternoon—neither hot nor
cold—

One thing that makes me feel so lost is that I can't imagine what it feels like to live here
—I am here and I am not here—

Tomorrow we go to Madison—Sunday—

---

179. Alexis married Elizabeth (Betty) Jones in 1927; their child's name was Barbara June. O'Keeffe painted *Abstraction—
Alexius* [*sic*], 1928 (Lynes 616), to celebrate her brother and the child's birth.

I will be going to sleep now—It is time—No daylight saving here so the hours seem queer—There are many beautiful trees—and the river—

Good Night Dearest—

I feel like a shell of something with a floating middle—am feeling very well—

Again Good Night—

Georgia O'Keeffe · [Portage, Wisconsin] · [July 16, 1928]

Dearest—

It is morning again—Monday—seven o'clock—I was too tired to write you last night—This morning I have been awake for about an hour—waking up slowly—and wondering how I could tell you of a day like yesterday—

The drive to Madison took a little over an hour—rolling farming country—sometimes very fine trees along the road and near houses—and such perfect fields—mostly of grain—and wonderful barns—mostly red barns—not Bluemner's kind[180]—As we neared Madison many more trees and little streams and the lakes—We went through part of the city—passing the new capitol—It is quite handsome but the capitol appears so much smaller than I had remembered it—only about a third the size—the building much larger than the old one—

Well—we finally got to the aunts'[181]—Catherine having taken along a dinner cooked with less trouble than anyone else I could imagine—knowing that they wouldn't have enough for the four of us—

Well—there they were looking much older—and little and very black—The thing I seemed most surprised about was how dark they are—They seem fragile and tough at the same time—They are very gentle—and at the same time have a quality of independence that is fine—and they are very spry—and alive—They have the simplest little shell of a house with trees thick all around—a little garden—flowers and a few vegetables toward the road. You don't see the road for the trees—and you only see the lake through trees—Down at the lake a big willow hangs over the dock—and you see the capitol dome and city in the distance—across the lake—toward the setting sun—

It was all very cool and quiet—and they seemed as tho in the end they will just quietly blow away with the breeze when the leaves move and leave the little house there among the trees till someone accidentally finds it is empty—

They had just thought I would never get there and they were enormously pleased—They are very fond of the two Catherines—so they had a great day all around—

I can't exactly say what happened to me except that it seemed to be good—a curious sort of adjusting—mixed with the satisfaction of finally getting there—It meant a lot to them—and the feeling of the place is fine—You would be much interested in it—seeing what those two little women do alone—It is really fine—and quiet—and simple—

180. Stieglitz had exhibited Oscar Bluemner's paintings and watercolors at the Intimate Gallery from February 28 to March 27, 1928. Using richly saturated colors and highly simplified forms, Bluemner depicted both urban and rural America.

181. O'Keeffe had lived with her aunts Alletta and Leonore Totto in Madison from 1902 to 1903.

9 A.M.—

As I was writing—Catherine two came and got in bed with me—then breakfast—then I had just started writing again when four letters came—I have read them—that water business is a pretty mess—

Must go for now—Will write more later—

It is good to be here for many reasons—I am so glad you get on the Lake—

—Address me now for about four days to—600 S. Brearly, Madison, Wis.—c/o Ollie Totto—

We go down there Wednesday—

Alfred Stieglitz · Lake George, New York · July 18, 1928 +

Good Morning, You Ever-in-My-Thoughts—Good morning—

And a kiss—It's eight A.M. I have had breakfast. Am not yet shaved. Think of it— I went to bed at 8:30 last night. Was so tired I had no choice. The day before had been just a bit too much for me I guess—In the afternoon I lay around instead of going on the Lake as I wanted to. My eyes were kicking up again.—You see how little I seem to be able to rely on "improvement" & still I feel I am in much better shape.—Dreamt even of naughty things last night—You—very "naughty"—nothing happened.

Before supper I rewaxed some of the small mounted prints—& respotted them. Are complete now. Maybe a corner there for you to fix up.—I can't equal you try as I may.[182]

—I then read a bit of Shaw.[183]—Supper.—Quiet & all right—Lee every evening asks me to come up to them—Thinks I may be too lonely.—But last night I sat on the front porch & read—reread—Lao tsu's *Tao*.[184]—It just fitted my mood. Much more than Shaw.—How bring about Shaw & *Tao* in a new form? Can it be done? That seems the problem of many of us—The economic problem—& the artist's—the free being.—The only free one—And as I have always held there are very few artists today.—And there could be so many more—Everyone potentially has a bit of the artist in him or her.—

—It was very satisfying to sit there & read—And as I put down the book I sat quite a while—with eyes closed. I wished for you to be near me—You were in every word I read— you are in everything I see—& feel—& still you are not satisfied—And I seem to understand— And I want you not dissatisfied—

The aunts. You are still there undoubtedly. And I'm fervently hoping that the ordeal isn't as trying as you imagined it would be.—And that you come away strengthened instead of used up.—You will I'm sure.

182. Stieglitz waxed almost all of his prints to enhance their appearance and preserve them. If a coating appeared streaky after drying or was damaged, the print was often "rewaxed." O'Keeffe often "spotted" his prints to diminish dust spots or other imperfections.

183. Probably either G. B. Shaw, *The Intelligent Woman's Guide to Socialism and Capitalism* (London, 1928), or his play *The Apple Cart* (1928).

184. Probably Paul Carus's translation of *The Canon of Reason and Virtue: Being Lao-tze's Tao Teh King Ching* (Chicago, 1913, 1927).

—Today?—I shall positively write to Haviland.—I'm quiet enough. Yesterday a telegram came from Mabel Dodge asking if I had received her letter.—I was so prompt formerly in matters like these—She should have the letter today.—A bit more patience & she would have saved her dollars & saved some for me—But it's all right. I don't mind.—I fear my letter will disappoint her. She is so accustomed to have "her" way.—And I'd prefer to let her have it.—But—?—

Now I shall shave—In the bathroom downstairs.—The new pipes are not here yet. Nor the plumbers naturally. The trenches are dug—Lee's & ours.—

Everything so slow—Really unseeing.—But eventually we'll have some real water upstairs.—

—The morning is warm & fairly clear—& windless. I slept all night with but one layer of blanket—Got some sleep.—But not much that was sound—

A kiss—You are very much right here this morning—Very much—

You dearest whitest thing I know—

Georgia O'Keeffe · **[Portage, Wisconsin]** · **[July 18?, 1928]** +

394   Good morning Dearest—7:30—

It is the first morning I have really gotten up before the others—I dressed quietly and walked over here to the river—The sky is a little gray—the sun not out—The river with the town on this side—low trees and sand banks on the other side—seems very still—almost no wind but a very rapid quiet moving current in the center—

—Just telling you of the events of the day doesn't seem to have any particular significance—It is something else that happens—and that something is very difficult to define—

It was warm yesterday—after dinner I slept—The morning was mostly just little things—In the afternoon we drove again—If I stay long enough I will certainly have to paint a red barn—they are wonderful—not what is ordinarily called picturesque—They just seem alive all the way through—and I wish you could see the men who work in the fields—moist warm sunburned skin—and often bright blue eyes—They are an incredible color—

A little town like this is a sort of curiosity to me—Last night we were invited to dinner —Zona Gale—just married[185] was to be there but she didn't come—There was a girl—Margery Latimer who wrote *We Are Incredible*—She had something in *The Caravan* last year and again this year[186]—had been at the Room—seen my things and liked them very much—was much moved but the last time she was there she thought you and I were laughing at the people and she thought it terrible—I had to laugh and try to explain—She has seen the things at the Brooklyn Museum and at the Room for three years—A very real person—knows everybody—

—So that is the way it goes—New York spread like thin butter over everything—

185. The Pulitzer Prize–winning dramatist Zona Gale spent most of her life in Portage, Wisconsin, which figured prominently in her writing. In 1928 she married William L. Breese.

186. Latimer's *We Are Incredible* was published in 1928. A year earlier she published "Penance," in *The American Caravan*, ed. Van Wyck Brooks, Lewis Mumford, Alfred Kreymborg, and Paul Rosenfeld (New York, 1927), 623–644.

—This is all so different—in every way that it quite surprises me that we—you and I—have lived so long in our particular groove—

—I hope you have water by now—and that you are quiet—I am glad I stayed here a few days—Madison today or tomorrow—It depends on when Ray gets off—

Must go Boy—I feel far away in every way—but I send you a morning kiss—from the river—

Georgia O'Keeffe · **[Madison, Wisconsin]** · **[July 22, 1928]**

Sunday—

I didn't have time to get off anything but the few lines to you this morning—Ollie was going up to see Charles[187]—the boy—at camp and there was great scurrying around to get her off by eight o'clock—I just sent the note so you would have a word—not knowing how the mails get out of these places on Sunday—It has rained so the past two days that this morning everything seems to be steam cooking in the hot sun—the sun hot—the shade cool—almost cold—I'm still wearing the sweater suit so you know it isn't very warm for me yet—maybe I haven't cooked out yet—

—Yesterday morning I had your letter in town after writing the shaky nothing that I sent you—I wrote it in the car—while Catherine stopped for her errands—We drove past where my aunts lived when I was with them—They sold the house a few years ago—but it still looked much as it did—

After we got home there was much commotion—They are very funny—I had a feeling that they didn't exactly like it that we went to town—even tho some of the errands were for them—I think they rather enjoy stewing over something—After dinner Catherine took a nap—I talked with them a while—

At four Catherine and I decided to go out where we used to live[188]—Lola didn't want to go because she was afraid it would rain—Ollie wouldn't go because she was to have a long drive today—so we went off alone—They tried to tell us it was such a long way we wouldn't get back till eight or nine o'clock at night—So we decided to drive for an hour and if we were not there—Catherine didn't exactly know the way—to turn around and come back so as to be back at six—They didn't like it much—They like to spend time talking about things and getting ready—

I wanted to go while the going was good—I didn't want to run the risk of not going at all—and you know—I am uncertain—I wanted to do all I had to do so that I am free to go home when I am ready—I had decided that if the weather didn't improve I would be ready very soon—

So we got off—We made one mistake in the road—when we were about half way I knew the rest of the road—much better roads than when I was small—

---

187. Charles Totto, O'Keeffe's cousin and nephew of Lola and Ollie Totto.
188. O'Keeffe was born on a dairy farm in Sun Prairie, Wisconsin, a few miles northeast of Madison.

Finally we got there at about ten minutes to five—then it was only a few minutes when we had driven the mile of road along the side of the farm my father owned—I haven't seen anything finer since I am here—

I was rather irritated that it was so beautiful—it made me want to stay—The last little distance is across a marsh with the most beautiful big willows on either side meeting over the road—It was always one of my nicest places—I wanted to stay—I got out to tell Catherine how far she could back up in turning round—the soil on both sides of the road is slippery black mud—no chance to get out of it if you get in too far—I never saw anyone turn in a smaller space—Small Catherine asked me if I could do it—when I said no she told me I must write you that her mother did it—

—I walked back across the marsh and we started home—having just time to get back by six so they would not worry—We were here at ten minutes to six—

Well—I am glad I went—I want to go again—if I stay long enough—maybe tomorrow or day after—Catherine isn't feeling much today—she has the curse—It is quiet here and good to be still—

Well it all seems queer—Yesterday afternoon was fine—I wish you had been along— The green of trees so heavy and dark—almost black—and a sort of blue green—and such beautiful fields—no sun—so it all seemed somber—

I wish you could drive with Catherine too—She is very gentle and very skilful—her sense of touch at the wheel is like the sense of touch one has in a painting—very sure and careful—perfectly controlled—

There is quite a breeze today—Small Catherine insisted on going fishing last night— she caught one small fish—

And that is the way things go—I walked again in the evening with Lola—then we sat on the porch and talked till late—They are so pleased I came—they have to tell me about it every day—It is all right—

—My love to you Little Boy—And I am wondering how you are this Sunday morning—

—I tried to phone Ethel in Chicago when I had so much time—could get no answer so left a message—I don't remember whether I told you or not—Yesterday I had a note—She had been in Kalamazoo—that is in Michigan—saying she wants very much to talk with me—to be sure to let her know when I go through Chicago again—That was all—using her own name—

—Do take care of yourself—don't try to do too many things—I am wondering if Davidson and Elizabeth are with you—It must have been pleasant to see Arkin—

My best wishes and thought always go to you—!

Alfred Stieglitz · [Lake George, New York] · July 24, 1928 +

9:15 A.M.—Good Morning again.—Yet another day.—Cloudy & cool.—Donald has just sewn my suspender which had torn completely.—It's late. A very poor night—A mighty stiff companion for an hour at five A.M.—looking for company I suppose—I was quiet enough.

No thoughts—Naturally without them there was the picture of something very black hiding something most wonderful—

I must smile—You're sweet—all of you—outside & inside—touchable & untouchable —Above all that center about which no one knows—still does—

A kiss! And more—

Good Morning—Miss O'Keeffe—

Well I got a great bath last night. A real tub of water—An experience for Lake George —And hot too—

It was eleven before I went up. After sitting awhile Elizabeth who had been playing up at Red Top came down for a short time. I read Hartley on Marin aloud.[189] Reads well. Very well—Then, after she had gone I started reading Lawrence—A pretty warm affair—Lawrence. If the authorities "knew" the book would never get thru![190] Some very plain language—

Will shock many of his lady admirers because of unusually plain speech showing how conventional everyone is after all. At least the so-called "refined"—

The mail just came—no letter from my Sweet One—Well in an hour there is another mail. Maybe there'll be no letter today!?—I won't worry.—Dare not.—

—Am continuing to glue & paste & dry mount.—Clippings.[191]—Did some this morning.—

There is a letter here for you from Miss Hendrie. It'll keep. I haven't opened it—

Well, Sweetheart, I'll let this go now—With a big, big hug—& a bigger—*very long kiss*—

Take care of yourself—Remember me to all—

Alfred Stieglitz · Lake George, New York · July 25, 1928 +

It's 7:30 A.M.—Good Morning—

I'm waiting for my zweiback & hot water. Meta[192] is getting them ready—Another night over with. Not as poor as former ones.—Some sleep.—It was 11:30 when I went to bed. Read quite a lot of Lawrence—He certainly holds one. It's a powerful book—I wonder will it be understood—Or will it be looked at falsely. There is certainly a deep relationship between his writing & my photographs & feeling about life.—And between your work & his too which

---

189. Marsden Hartley, "The Recent Paintings of John Marin," 1928, in *On Art by Marsden Hartley*, ed. Gail R. Scott (New York, 1982), 77–81.

190. To avoid censorship, Lawrence privately printed *Lady Chatterley's Lover* in July 1928. He wrote Stieglitz that the book "seems to have exploded like a bomb among most of my English friends, & they're still suffering from shell-shock…. [There] are numerous rumors of suppression in England & numerous of a ban in America. But I can't help it. I've shot my shot, anyhow" (D. H. Lawrence to AS, Aug. 15, 1928).

191. In the 1920s and 1930s Stieglitz and his associates put together scrapbooks of newspaper and magazine articles on him, the artists associated with him, and the exhibitions he organized at his galleries. These are now in the Stieglitz-O'Keeffe Archive, Yale Collection of American Literature, Beinecke Rare Book and Manuscript Library, Yale University.

192. Meta was the Stieglitz family's cook in the summer of 1928.

must be if his writing & my photographs are closely related. He understands the forces.—The subtlety of the whole relationship of them.—

—I didn't accomplish much yesterday—but seemed always busy—Was on the Lake a while—also usual walk—No letters from anyone. Not even you.—Well, I kiss you all the same.—It'll be good to have you here again when you are ready.—Lee is still in town & will be gone till Friday night.—Several serious cases.—All is very, very tranquil here. Children[193] very quiet at table. No fussing by anyone. At least I noticed none—And I believe there isn't any. —Food continues good. My stomach is pretty fair—Am feeling all right. No special trouble. Finger healing very slowly.—I'm satisfied.—

—Woke up with a ready friend—& had to smile.—Amusing.—Well—

Your unwell time is about due—in a couple of days or so—I do hope you'll not be inconvenienced very much.—I wonder how you are faring—

Meta calls—I'll get some of that water down while it's hot. Donald appears.—Is starting the coffee. Did I write you he has ground it very fine. Makes it stronger—Well—here's a kiss—a good one—And a squeeze—I don't exactly know where—that would depend on your expression—Or does the expression depend upon the squeeze—the where—and—

Well, you are sweet all the same—whatever.—

398

Georgia O'Keeffe · [**Portage, Wisconsin**] · [**July 27, 1928**] +

Good Morning Dearest Boy—

I have been up and had my breakfast and am back on the bed again—not feeling very good in the middle—otherwise all right—It is Friday—tonight I will have been here two weeks—When I waked this morning—I was very lonesome for you—but I have waked so often in the room right next door to you and in the bed right next to yours and had the same feeling—and closeness to you seemed quite as far away as it does this morning—it started me wondering—

It is a cold gray morning—I look out my windows on dark slightly moving greens and wonder—

I am learning something out here that I cannot quite define—but it is something very important to me—There is something very healthy for me in the feeling of this country—

The cousin I accidentally met—so clear—so strong—deep lines of thought in the very brown face—the things he said—and the feeling of the fields—They are so rich and heavy and clean looking while the food that dirty New York has to have to eat is growing there—ripening and waving in the sun—ripples running over it like over water—

We left the aunts Wednesday afternoon—late—almost six—They did not want me to go—were quite disturbed over it—but I thought I had better—It is quieter here at Catherine's —no associations—and in Madison all sorts of people that I had forgotten—even people that knew you—were phoning and trying to find me—

—This is a much better place for the curse—I had been there long enough—

---

193. Elizabeth and Donald Davidson's daughters, Peggy and Sue Davidson.

I felt pretty good yesterday—painted all day—lying down occasionally—today being up is too uncomfortable—The two Catherines are both wild for me to get to work so I had no choice no matter if I didn't feel very good—

We were at Zona Gale's yesterday—last evening for dinner—It was pleasant—rather an unjointed sort of feeling in her new house—with her new husband—There was talk of Toomer—It seems that in Chicago they do not know that he has negro blood—he seems to claim French extraction—Will tell you when I see you—his book[194]—novel—is based on the work he has been doing—He is trying to get the Theater Guild to dramatize it—Is in Maine—

Zona Gale is quite a person here—a real citizen of the town—interested in everything in a very useful way—it is really fine—

—A girl that I knew when I was at the convent just drove up here from Madison—such a talker—just like she was as a child—I was glad to see her and glad to see her go—

I had your letter this morning—telling of your early morning visitor—

Yesterday was the first day except Sundays that I have had no letter—I knew there wouldn't be any as it had to be forwarded from Madison—It came this morning—Number twenty-one—

As there wasn't any yesterday I took a bunch of old ones and read them—when I counted to see how many I had read I found I had read seven—I had to laugh—

You seem very busy—I am most curious about the Lawrence book[195]—above all I am glad you are feeling better—

My job here is really finished—I am ready to go back when I feel fit to travel—which should be by next Tuesday—Monday I count on going down to see the aunts again—and Tuesday or Wednesday I will be ready to go unless I stay to work awhile—I have no other reason to stay—I almost don't want to stay for that either unless I really stay long enough to get something—and you know how that is—It takes time and then I always have continuing it on my mind and I dread starting on a new thing like that—I almost feel it would be better not to start—To really get into it—

Well—you know how it is—

—This country is practically untouched in the painting world—

Yesterday I worked on a flower that I have been wanting to do for several years[196]— a flower I knew when I was small and that you seldom see in New York—I am keeping it in the ice box—It is late for it to be blooming so I will not be able to get another—

Do not worry about me Boy—I am all right—I will probably have to try to get at least one thing that feels like something I feel here—It will be my only way of really telling you of it—

—A very warm and quiet kiss goes to you—and something much much more— something like a river running deep down under the surface of the earth—

The word Wisconsin means Dark Rushing Waters or something like that—

A kiss Dearest—

194. Probably Jean Toomer's burlesque novel *The Gallonwerps* (New York, 1927), which was based on G. I. Gurdjieff's Chicago followers.

195. D. H. Lawrence, *Lady Chatterley's Lover* (Florence, 1928). Stieglitz received no. 389 of the 1,000 copies of the book privately printed in Florence in July 1928.

196. Possibly Lynes 634 or 635.

Georgia O'Keeffe · [Portage, Wisconsin] · [July 29, 1928]

Dearest Boy—

It is Sunday morning—10:35—breakfast just over—I didn't wake enough to know anything until after nine—

Yesterday I did the same thing—There has been a little shower of rain—blue—blue coming after it—a lovely cool sunny day—yesterday too—was perfect—I got at my painting right after breakfast yesterday—had your letters—the first one sent here since we returned and another forwarded from Madison—telling of reading the Lawrence book and the family being gone for the day to Schroon Lake—It made me wish to be with you—

I didn't get up from my painting all morning—Catherine has started to paint too—We were both so absorbed that we didn't have our noon meal till very late—then we got right into the car and started for the country looking for a grain field and barn that we could start out for today and not have to hunt for—

My bleeding heart painting[197] I quite like—would like to do another—but I am going to try a grain field against the sky—It will be very difficult—but I must try—it is much a part of here—

When we got home last night Margery Latimer was here—we had asked her for supper —She did not go till after eleven—is a terrific person—you will be amused when I tell you her experiences with Orage—

Catherine enjoyed it much too—and was amused to think how it would shock Ray —she is a great one—Looked wonderful all done up in a blanket of black and many bright colors—a knit thing—very gay—it was so cold—

—So the day went—fast from one thing to another and I didn't seem to be able to squeeze my letter in—I can't write fast and easily as you do—it seems to take me a long time— and last night when I was finally ready for bed and quiet—I was too tired—It worries me much that you will not have a letter tomorrow—

—I feel better today—quite like a person again—Am going out to the grain field in a little while—

Tomorrow we go to Madison to see the aunts again—Charles will be home—they want me to see him—then I want to paint for a few days—I want to get at least one thing of the country—and if I get it—will be starting back soon—Catherine is a great driver to keep me trying to work—Her start is nice too—lovely color—

I had your telegram yesterday morning—telling me to stay and work—I will stay a little—Your letters sound lonely—and make me want to go to you—Maybe you are quite as lonely when I am with you—I don't know—

At any rate I will try to work for a few days—I feel much like it—cannot promise that anything will come of it—but I will try—

Many thanks for your kisses—and other things—for every word you write me—

I don't like Sunday because there is no mail—I look so anxiously for your letters—and enjoy them so much—

---

197. Lynes 635.

Am so glad you are feeling better—
An early morning kiss for your friend—
And others—

Georgia O'Keeffe · [Portage, Wisconsin] · [July 29, 1928]

Dearest—

I sealed my letter to you and Catherine and I walked to the post office to mail it—

As I walked along the street coming home—talking—in spite of talking of other things I had such a sinking feeling in my stomach—or somewhere in me—a feeling that I had mailed you a letter—and that really—what I feel—what reaches out to you—no matter where I am— wasn't in the letter at all—and that is really all I am wanting really to send you—

My daily doings are unimportant—The other thing seems to be the care of me— I wonder do you understand—and may I send it to you—

With a kiss—

It's nearly supper time—Catherine and I just came in—Right after lunch we got in the car with all our things to paint—going out to the field we had found—It was raining a little—she said— "Oh that doesn't matter"—so off we went—It poured—and poured and thundered—she drove on as though it never occurred to her to do anything else—

Finally—just before we got to the field—there was blue sky and sunshine—

We sat there in the car on the side of a hill—all afternoon—working—Hers is as good as mine—She is through—mine is just a beginning[198]—I was tired when it was nearly six— she reading—I just seemed to have an idea of how to begin—I hope I can get something from it —It is a great sight—one of those things so simple that it is almost impossible—

A kiss to you dearest—for the night—

I look for the morning and your letter—

I am going to bed early—
Sunday night—

Alfred Stieglitz · Lake George, New York · August 4, 1928

The morning mail. Two letters. Your sweetest one—In which you tell me you might leave the next day (Friday) or Monday. I wonder which.—Monday I'm thinking—or guessing.—?

You'll have so much to tell me. And my life has been very humdrum—Nothing "new" in any way—except being without you longer than any time since we were together.—

---

198. Possibly Lynes 617. The next day, O'Keeffe wrote Stieglitz, "I have my two fields on the bureau in front of me—I can't tell much of anything about them—They seem to move toward something I want to do with them—But they are so little—and what I saw was so big." On August 3, 1928, she noted that Catherine's paintings "are much better than mine—She is painting what she would like the place to look like—I am trying more to paint what I see—It is wonderful to see the way she goes at it."

—A letter from Hartley—Lachaise's—A very fine letter—Seems he stopped at Boston.—At the Museum there is a room (exhibition) of Goyas & Dürers & my photographs[199]—He says the photographs stand up wonderfully.—Well—I know they must & still it always surprises me.

He says the Lachaise house is a masterpiece of Mrs. Lachaise's taste—

—You'll enjoy the letter. Seems to be full of writing.—And feels that he is *the* mountain painter par excellence.[200] Perhaps he is.—It was the *feeling* of the mountain he gave me which decided me to give him his first show[201]—that & of course telling me he lived on four dollars a week & couldn't get that!!—

—I hope you'll be satisfied with things as you find them here when you return. I'm not critical in the sense that you sometimes are.—

—The morning has cleared up.—It's going to be another very hot day—

You'll probably not get this till it comes back here—even if you leave Portage on Monday.—

—If it should catch you before you leave there—there are kisses for every mile you travel—& much much love—Be careful—

Remember me to all the Klenerts—

402

Georgia O'Keeffe · [**Portage, Wisconsin**] · [**August 4, 1928**] +

In bed again—and raining again—

Dearest—

You apologize for your letters—you needn't—I like them very much—

I waked at dawn this morning and was quite sad that I hadn't prepared to go this morning—After stewing about it for a couple of hours I got a magazine and read—then when it was nearly seven went to sleep and slept so soundly that it was almost impossible to wake up at 8:30—By a little after nine I had had breakfast—and your letters—and Catherine and I were on our way to the barn—

199. Hartley wrote Stieglitz on August 2, 1928, of his visit to the Museum of Fine Arts, Boston, to see an exhibition of Stieglitz's photographs and assured him he would "be thoroughly satisfied" with their presentation. He also noted his delight on hearing another visitor, a painter, exclaim, "'Aren't [they] extraordinary.'"

200. In his letter of August 2, 1928, written from the costal community of Georgetown, Maine, where he was visiting Gaston and Isabel Lachaise, Hartley noted that "everywhere I look I see a Marin or a Homer—and one knows at least their visions are being recorded faithfully. It would not be my country to paint as I have grown so into a mountain [painter] that I could feel this only as pleasant subject matter." For many years Stieglitz had applauded Hartley's paintings of mountains. Noting that the leaves at Lake George made the surrounding hills look "like a tapestry," Stieglitz wrote O'Keeffe on October 4, 1916: "I'm continually reminded of Hartley's early paintings—those that attracted him to me. At that time all the people said: Why does he not work in fabrics instead of paint? Today I reminded Walkowitz of that fact & called his attention to the truth of Hartley's observations—the truth of Hartley's paintings.—I felt their truth at once—& yet I had never seen the mountains as he had painted them—All I claimed then was that Hartley had made *me feel the mountains* as none other ever had.—And here today many years later I see before me in nature—what he many years ago had brought into the Little Room."

201. Exhibition of Paintings in Oil by Mr. Marsden Hartley, of Maine, 291, May 8–18, 1909.

It is a grand barn—and we had a great morning—a real farm with geese and horses and little red pigs—

Catherine looked at what I painted—my barn[202]—and remarked—"Well—that will look funny hanging beside your calla lily[203]—It will even seem different—entirely different beside your New York." We go out to it again in the morning—I am not half through with it—I like doing it—

At 3:30 Zona Gale came for me—we drove—then walked—through a woods to a big field of oats against the sky—to the top of the hill—then a road through the fields—till we came to green fields—then other fields—and finally the road—

She is strange—like some sort of a mystery puzzle to me—

Tonight after supper we went to see Ray's mother[204] for a little while—Fat—and endless small talk—her daughter[205] to be married next week—All the talk is quite incredible to me—It seems like some sort of a fairy tale—Catherine doesn't like her—that was probably why I had it much on my mind to go—It was all like some sort of a strange dream—

I must go to sleep—Am tired—feel as tho I have been rushing all day—Want to get at the barn early in the morning—

A kiss Dearest Boy—

I look forward to seeing you—and touching you—really kissing you—

I hope to be with you Tuesday night—

O'KEEFFE ARRIVED BACK at Lake George on August 7, 1928. After the two spent a peaceful month together, Stieglitz suffered a severe angina attack in early September and was confined to bed. A few weeks later O'Keeffe wrote to Ettie Stettheimer that she had "not a thought in my head—unless strained spinach, peas, beans, squash—ground lamb and beef—strained this —five drops of that—a teaspoon in a third of a glass of water—or is it half a glass—pulse this —heat that—grind the meat four times…until the girl who helped me grind and measure and rub the stuff through the two sieves actually got hysterical laughing about it."[206]

---

202. Lynes 617 or 618.
203. Lynes 423, 425, 426, 429; vol. 2, appen. II, 44, 73.
204. Mary Ellen Klenert.
205. Either Florence or Leone Klenert.
206. GOK to Ettie Stettheimer, Sept. 21, 1928.

3.

A Terrible Rightness
1929–1933

IN THE SUMMER OF 1929 O'Keeffe fell "into something," as she wrote, "from which there is no return."[1] Still deeply in love with Stieglitz, she had been increasingly torn in the 1920s between her desire to work to "carry the thing I do further so that people are surprised again"[2] and the obligation she felt to care for Stieglitz and his family, especially during their long summers at Lake George. Yet the exhilaration she discovered during her trip to Wisconsin in July and August 1928, coupled with the inspiration she derived from the midwestern landscape and the joy she received from reconnecting with her family, prompted her to explore other alternatives. During the winter of 1928–1929, she considered spending the following summer in Europe, but when the impresario Mabel Dodge Luhan and the painter Dorothy Brett came to New York, they convinced her to go to New Mexico. Earlier in the 1920s, Marsden Hartley, Paul Rosenfeld, and Paul and Beck Strand had all visited New Mexico and had frequently extolled its grandeur. They now helped her convince Stieglitz to allow her to go. He was, no doubt, also swayed by O'Keeffe's promise to take Beck Strand as a traveling companion, her poor health that winter, their frequent arguments, and the fact that she was not "talking much to Stieglitz," as she told a friend that spring.[3]

  With wrenching force and unimagined consequences, the trip ruptured the life they had constructed together and laid bare the issues between them that had simmered throughout the 1920s. In her letters from the summer of 1929, O'Keeffe expressed her intense, visceral love of

1. GOK to AS, May 4, 1929.
2. O'Keeffe, as quoted by Lillian Sabine, "Record Price for Living Artist," *Brooklyn Sunday Eagle Magazine,* May 27, 1928, 11.
3. GOK to Mitchell Kennerley, spring 1929, Mitchell Kennerley papers, Manuscripts and Archives Division, New York Public Library. Astor, Lenox and Tilden Foundations.

the southwestern landscape in an exuberant, free-spirited, but also decidedly independent manner that rankled the often overly sensitive Stieglitz. In his increasingly more numerous, lengthy, and agitated letters to her, Stieglitz poured forth his passionate love for her, but he also revealed his inability to conform his life to hers, his infirmities (both real and perceived), his need for someone to care for him with unquestioning devotion, and his tendency to obsessiveness, even hysteria.

As they unintentionally began to carve out separate lives, O'Keeffe's 1929 trip, plus subsequent ones she made in the summers of 1930 and 1931, also tempted both of them with other appealing companions. O'Keeffe was captivated not only by New Mexico's landscape but also by its people. Mabel Luhan's Native American husband, Tony Lujan[4]; the dynamic, idiosyncratic, and charming doctor, scientist, and writer Gustav Eckstein; the heiress Marie Garland with her much younger husband, the filmmaker Henwar Rodakiewicz; and the deaf Honorable Lady Brett, with her large tin horn—all fascinated O'Keeffe with their charismatic personalities and unconventional lives. In her absence, Stieglitz and Dorothy Norman grew ever more enchanted with each other. Even though she was in her mid-twenties, he was forty-one years her senior, and both were married, their flirtation of the late 1920s grew into an ardent affair in the early 1930s that neither tried to keep from their spouses or anyone else. Celebrating their emotional and intellectual union, their common goals, and shared German-Jewish heritage, Stieglitz increasingly lamented that "S.W."—as he now often coldly referred to O'Keeffe in his letters to Norman —simply did not understand him. O'Keeffe and Stieglitz had always professed to have an open relationship, where both were free to associate and even sleep with whomever they pleased, but the consequences produced by such an arrangement, as well as the jealousies, slights, wounds, and intrigues, proved far more difficult than either had ever imagined.

From 1929 through 1933, O'Keeffe's and Stieglitz's professional lives were also unsettled. In May 1929, Stieglitz closed the Intimate Gallery because he thought the Anderson Galleries, where it was housed, would soon move. In December 1929, just weeks after the late October collapse of the stock market and the early November opening of the Museum of Modern Art, he opened his last gallery, An American Place. Situated on the seventeenth floor of an office building at 509 Madison Avenue, the "Place," as Stieglitz called it, was different in both look and spirit from the Intimate Gallery. Consisting of three galleries, a small office, and a storage area that he used as a darkroom—all with gray cement floors, white or gray walls, and simple shades that rolled up from the bottom for greater light—it was as spare, elegant, and modern as the Intimate Gallery had been cramped and cluttered. He soon reduced the "Seven Americans" he had shown at the Intimate Gallery to a core group of three—Arthur Dove, John Marin, and O'Keeffe—and only occasionally exhibited Charles Demuth, Marsden Hartley, and Paul Strand, as well as a few other artists. In addition, because Norman and the Strands found the rooms, secured the backers (one of whom was Norman herself), and cosigned the lease, Norman became a fixture at the gallery. Although O'Keeffe installed most of the exhibitions, she felt increasingly unwelcome and

---

4. In her extensive writings about her husband, Antonio (Tony) Lujan, Mabel Dodge Luhan Anglicized his name to "Luhan." However, Lois Palken Rudnick, a Mabel Dodge Luhan scholar, notes that there is no evidence Tony ever changed the spelling of his name (Rudnick to the author, May 27, 2009).

began to call before she went there. Marginalized from the daily life of the Place, she also grew more independent of Stieglitz. In early 1932, without consulting him, she accepted an invitation to exhibit her work at the Museum of Modern Art and that summer agreed to paint a mural for Radio City Music Hall. Her inability to complete the mural later that fall had profound consequences for both of them.

The economic instability of the times further exacerbated the growing distance between O'Keeffe and Stieglitz. Although neither had speculated in the stock market in the late 1920s, their income was significantly curtailed by the early 1930s as their modest savings shrank and O'Keeffe's once booming sales slowed considerably. Also of great concern for Stieglitz, Dove was in dire financial straits, often only days away from destitution. In 1930 Stieglitz convinced the Washington collector Duncan Phillips to send Dove a monthly stipend of fifty dollars in exchange for the right of first selection from the painter's annual exhibition at An American Place. But Phillips was often tardy in his payments, causing both Stieglitz and Dove considerable anguish. These grim economic times only made Stieglitz more zealous in his commitment to the Place and more convinced of the necessity and rightness of his actions.

Despite this turmoil—or perhaps even because of it—both Stieglitz's and O'Keeffe's art flourished during these years, growing ever richer and more resonate. New Mexico proved to be a source of seemingly endless inspiration for O'Keeffe. Its trees, crosses, and churches; its brilliant blue sky; and especially the land itself, with its lustrous red earth, arroyos, mesas, and rugged mountains—all became the subjects of her frequently luminous, occasionally playful paintings. Working with often richly saturated colors and simplified natural forms, she strove to translate the ecstatic feelings she had when she contemplated the landscape that affected her, she told Stieglitz, like music, because it "moved and changed constantly."[5] As she "hunted for something of myself out there," she sought "something in myself that will give me a symbol for all this—a symbol for the sense of life I get out there."[6] Noting that O'Keeffe was once again "the wild child of the soil," Stieglitz recognized that he was still very much "of the city," and he found in New York the same inspiration that O'Keeffe discovered in New Mexico.[7] In a series of crystalline photographs taken from his windows at An American Place and the Shelton Hotel, he recorded the constantly changing face of the city. But, as if to prove that he was not divorced entirely from O'Keeffe's world, he also photographed the trees, bushes, hills, and buildings at Lake George, investing these humble objects with a poignant, deeply heartfelt eloquence unknown in his previous work. And he embraced a new model, Norman, making dozens of photographs of her wistful, childlike expressions and delicate hands and body with the same obsessiveness that he had once photographed O'Keeffe.

O'Keeffe's and Stieglitz's letters from these years are numerous and rich. Especially in 1929 as they worked to keep their relationship strong, they clearly articulated their deep love and desire for each other. As they had done when they first began to exchange letters in 1916 and 1917, they poured into their correspondence the same qualities that the other had once found so

5. GOK to AS, June 16, 1930.
6. GOK to AS, May 30, 1929.
7. AS to GOK, July 14, 1929.

attractive: O'Keeffe sent Stieglitz lucid, vivid, and even giddy descriptions of the new worlds she discovered in New Mexico, while Stieglitz wrote her extensive, often passionate accounts of not only his daily activities but also his emotional life. Yet the physical and emotional distance that now separated them also enabled both of them to understand ever more keenly their own, often independent and frequently competing needs. As O'Keeffe explained in early July 1929, "I have not wanted to be anything but kind to you—but there is nothing to be kind to you if I cannot be me." And both came to recognize, as Stieglitz wrote a few weeks earlier, that there was a "terrible rightness" to their new lives.[8]

With a promise to Stieglitz that she would join him at Lake George later in the summer, O'Keeffe and Beck Strand left New York City for New Mexico on April 27, 1929. After stopping in Chicago to visit O'Keeffe's younger brother, Alexis, and his new wife, Betty, and their baby, Barbara June, they continued on to Santa Fe, arriving there on April 30. The next day, Georgia and Beck took a bus to the San Felipe pueblo, a few miles outside of Santa Fe, to see the annual corn dance, where they accidentally met Brett and Mabel and Tony Lujan. Amazed that the two women had come to New Mexico without telling her, Mabel insisted they go to Taos with her to see the dances at the pueblo and stay at Los Gallos, her twelve-acre compound just outside of the town's center. With its caged parrots, wild chickens, and pigeon houses; carved ivory skulls, Navajo rugs, and French upholstered chairs; paintings by both New York and Taos artists; fireplaces filled with pungent piñon wood and numerous, ample beds, all enveloped in undulating, sensuous adobe walls, Los Gallos was as exotic as it was sprawling. It included the Santa Theresa House, where Tony often stayed, the Pink House, which Mabel gave to O'Keeffe and Beck Strand for the summer of 1929, a studio O'Keeffe used, and Mabel's own "Big House," as well as several other buildings.

As was her custom, Mabel had many other guests staying at Los Gallos that summer, including the Irish poet Ella Young and the author Neith Boyce, the wife of Stieglitz's friend the journalist Hutchins Hapgood, and their children, twenty-three-year-old Miriam and twenty-five-year-old Charles. Brett occasionally stopped by Los Gallos, joining the festive and occasionally raucous dinners that Mabel hosted, as did other Taos residents and visitors, including the painters Andrew Dasburg and Robert Walker; the poets Witter Bynner and his companion Willard (Spud) Johnson, who edited the *Laughing Horse,* and their friend Lewis Callaghan; the California photographer Ansel Adams; and Charles Collier, the twenty-year-old son of John Collier, who later became commissioner of the Bureau of Indian Affairs. Yet even within this varied group, Georgia and Beck were a striking pair. Almost the same height, build, and age (Beck was thirty-eight; Georgia, forty-one), they often dressed alike in black skirts and white shirts. Visitors to Los Gallos soon discovered that while Georgia was energetic, often effervescent, and always electrified by her new surroundings, if also occasionally sharp-tongued, imperious, and controlling, Beck, the daughter of one of the self-described creators of Barnum and Bailey's "Buffalo Bill's Wild West Show," always "had her shirt casually open [and] a cigarette…dangling from a

8. GOK to AS, July 9, 1929, and AS to GOK, June 27, 1929.

corner of her mouth," as Miriam Hapgood later remembered. "She rides her horse to a lather, talks tough, [and] associates with the gamblers and rough characters of the town."[9] Georgia and Beck soon became so entranced with New Mexico that, without consulting Stieglitz, they wrote Marin, suggesting he join them; he arrived at the end of May. Although Mabel left shortly after they got to Taos, first to go to a doctor in Albuquerque and then to Buffalo for an operation, O'Keeffe stayed at Los Gallos for the rest of the summer, even after Beck returned East in late July to care for her ailing mother.

With his fear that a high altitude would provoke another angina attack, Stieglitz seems never to have thought seriously about accompanying O'Keeffe to New Mexico, nor did she suggest it.[10] Instead, he remained, as he said, "at his post" at the Intimate Gallery, overseeing its last exhibition, Five New Paintings by Charles Demuth, on view from April 29 to May 18, 1929. After the close of the exhibition, he spent several weeks moving art from the Intimate Gallery (Room 303) into the Lincoln Storage Warehouse.

Georgia O'Keeffe · [En route from New York City to Chicago, Illinois] · [April 27, 1929]

Dearest—

I didn't stand to watch you go—I just couldn't when I saw the tears in your eyes— and I came into the train wondering why on earth I ever had any such idea as to leave anything as beautiful as you are—once I have found it—But even through my tears I knew I had to go —We both sat and wept—and had very trembly voices for a long time—

Beck remarked—"Well we did it ourselves"—meaning that we left of our own accord —nobody sent us—.

—We finally revived—sat on the river side—then finally I took the shady side as the sun hurt my eyes—

—This may write better—The train rocks so—

The country has been beautiful—Hills all gray and severe with the soft young green shining through everywhere—The fine Bear Mountain part was particularly beautiful—

I have a big fat pillow that I can lean back on—almost lie down and still look out the window—The peach and plum and cherry trees are in full bloom—among bare trees and new green they are lovely—I am not feeling sick or even drowsy—it is 6:20—so I probably will not be so this time—

Little One—my heart goes out to you—and I feel very close to you even tho I am going away—It seems the train moves very fast—But I am with you—close under your shirt—right next [to] your skin—

I said to Beck awhile ago—I try to imagine what you are doing—what is going on in the Room and I just know I can't—One never can—

A TERRIBLE RIGHTNESS, 1929–1933

---

9. Miriam Hapgood DeWitt, *Taos: A Memory* (Albuquerque, 1992), 8.
10. See Paul Strand to GOK, July 14 and 26, 1929, where he chastised O'Keeffe for not giving Stieglitz "a chance to go with you."

All I know is that I have a great fondness for you and your understanding my having to do this makes me feel you are again very good to me—

Dusk is coming—the lights are on—We had—

Right here we decided we must eat—The food was good—It's dark—and when I seal this I am going to bed—I am tired—

I hope you will be sleeping—I will be wondering in the morning—

Good Night my Dear Little One—Just a gentle Good Night kiss—very tender—

Alfred Stieglitz · **[New York City]** · **[April 28, 1929]** +

Sunday, 8 A.M.

Good Morning, you Grandest One.—

I'm just up. A raw gray morning.—Want to write a few lines before washing & shaving, etc. When I was about to put on my pajamas I found your letter[11] pinned to them.—Certainly more than a surprise. Naturally I smiled—& I read—& I lay down & I was as near to breaking down as I could possibly afford to be. You dear, dear Dear One.—Yes, I know.—I know what you are going thro'—have been going thro'—I know I'm not a bad sort—but that I should seem to be so beautiful to you—that I cannot understand.—I'm not at all satisfied with what I am.—To me at times so far from everything beautiful. You are a thousand times more so than I am.—Yes, I mean it.

—I put out the light—but finally made one (side light) in your room. And finally I fell asleep. Woke up often.—Got up at four & rinsed mouth & urinated. And took a look out of the window. A grand clear still night—And I could breathe. And that was truly wonderful. And altho' the night was a tossing about one I breathed comfortably—& dozed some—& towards morning a friend of yours looked around for a friend of his. For quite awhile. And as I dozed off I dreamt you stood by the bedside taking off your chemise getting ready to lie on me—I awoke —You Sweetest One.—

—Your letter is going to stay in my pocket—I wondered what you were doing up— But I was so infernally tired physically & mentally that I didn't even try to think—I just knew you weren't in bed.—

—And now I'll get clad & cleansed.—Or really cleansed & clad.—I wonder what sort of a night you two have had—Good I hope—Soon—in about two hours you'll be in Chicago—

I'll breakfast downstairs. Eggs for a change—I'm due for lunch at Lizzie's—We'll hang the Demuths at 5:10—

Once again lots lots of love to you goes with these lines—& a big kiss on the neck— I hope soon to be well enough to kiss the mouth.—

And love too to Lady Fluffy—

---

11. Beginning in 1929, when O'Keeffe went away, she left notes for Stieglitz pinned to his clothes or on his pillow.

Georgia O'Keeffe · [Santa Fe, New Mexico] · [April 30, 1929]

Dearest—

We are here—and we are both much pleased.

We arrived sometime this morning—I don't know when. I only know that by the time we had looked over the two hotels—staying here[12] was my doing—Beck rather wanted to stay at the other one—It smelled bad and didn't look good to me—now she is much pleased with being here—It is neat and clean and we are each in a room of our own—small but light and nice with running water—no private bath to be had here—but it is all right this way—

I have just come from the roof and a grand view—The village is just a little spot compared to what is all around it—

I had your three sweet—very dear—letters—and my trunk and everything by eleven this morning. The post office is just across the street—

When I had washed and cleaned up some it was twelve so we ate—very good food and plenty for 85 cents—dinner tonight will be $1.50. After lunch I lay down for over an hour— I was tired—Beck wouldn't—declared she never lay down in the daytime—I notice she is doing it now—and I'll bet she is asleep—She seems to tire sooner than I do—

—After my nap we took a little walk—it is quite cool—the green is very new—hardly here—the fruit trees are blooming—the dust is blowing—the air fine and dry—

Oh I am so glad I came that I feel like bursting—I see all sorts of things for work—and I would like to kiss you.

We looked in a couple of small rooms of the old Governors Palace at Indian pottery— very fine pieces—I never thought Indian pottery so beautiful before—some of it has a holy look —We only stayed a few moments—We didn't feel like doing anything hard—

—I am going to bed right after supper again tonight—My curse has been very kind to me—I seem to get along with it as well as Beck does without—

Your letters are good to have but I look forward to the next ones that will tell me of your Sunday—hanging the show and all that—

We are really here for the spring. It isn't as advanced as New York—dryness makes the air pleasanter—

A kiss—tenderly.

Georgia O'Keeffe · [Taos, New Mexico] · [May 2, 1929]

Dearest—

This really isn't like anything you ever saw—and no one who tells about it gives any idea of it—Things go so fast and are all so much to tell about that I don't get anything down to you. We both have bright pink cheeks from sunburn and eat to beat anything you ever saw—

It is no use to try to tell about an Indian dance—it can't be told any more than I can tell

---

12. La Fonda Hotel.

Anonymous, *Mabel Dodge Sterne* (later Luhan), 1917. Gelatin silver print,
5 x 7 in. (13 x 18 cm). Mabel Dodge Luhan Papers, Yale Collection of
American Literature, Beinecke Rare Book and Manuscript Library.

you what the country feels like—and that feeling that I had the first year I was West—it is just the same again—only maybe I enjoy it even more because I think I understand it a little better—

When Mabel came along there was nothing to do but follow [her][13]—It seems that we arrived just in time for the only two dances of this time of year—no more till July and August—and one of the most important is here at Taos tomorrow—I hear rumors of six o'clock breakfast—We went for the beginning of it at sunset this evening—

Mabel's place beats anything you can imagine about it—it is simply astonishing—there is no end to it—and Tony is really its crowning glory—He is very grand here[14]—I sat beside

13. Hutchins Hapgood described Mabel Luhan as "God-drunk. If at any time she became aware of something just out of her reach, she was intensely restless until she had drawn it into her web"; Hapgood, *A Victorian in the Modern World* (New York, 1939), 348.

14. Miriam Hapgood, who arrived at Los Gallos a few weeks after O'Keeffe, described Tony Lujan as "like a bronze equestrian statue"; see DeWitt, *Taos,* 23.

Anonymous, *Tony Lujan*, undated. Gelatin silver print, 9⅝ x 6¹⁵⁄₁₆ in. (24.4 x 17.6 cm).
Mabel Dodge Luhan Papers. Yale Collection of American Literature,
Beinecke Rare Book and Manuscript Library.

him driving up from Santa Fe—He drives the car and is a very good driver—and you should see him sitting with another Indian—two profiles against the window—both beating the same drum—

The color Mabel has built is lovely—

We are to have a house—and I a grand studio besides—the most beautiful mountain out the big window—white walls—

Well that is the way it is—as I write the room filled up with people—all talking—they are all staying here—only six besides us—We are in the Big House tonight till the other one is ready—

—Well—it is all like an unimaginable dream—The drive up here—seventy-five miles—was wonderful—It is bedtime and I am not a bit sleepy—not even tired—I lay in the sun a long time this afternoon—The air is cold and the wind—but the sun is hot—

Brett blows about—

Spring is much later up here than in Santa Fe—leaves not out yet—

Anonymous, *Los Gallos, Mabel Dodge Luhan's Taos, New Mexico, Home, Front Gate*, early 1930s.
Gelatin silver print, 5½ x 7⅝ in. (14 x 19.5 cm). Mabel Dodge Luhan Papers,
Yale Collection of American Literature, Beinecke Rare Book and Manuscript Library.

—This talk is too much—I'll go to bed in a little—and kiss you Good Night—It all seems so unbelievable—I think I'll be working soon—

You are sweet—I hope you are being good to yourself—

Georgia O'Keeffe · [Taos, New Mexico] · [May 3, 1929]

Dearest—

Such a day—up at dawn—then after rushing breakfast someone comes in and says the dance will not be till nine or ten o'clock—

Well—I curled up in a bed in the room where the piano is—There is also the most enormous pink geranium you ever saw—a Max Weber and many other things—five or six people could get in that bed—but only one woman came and crawled under the blanket with me—a musician—sings modern songs—couldn't get a chance to sing in New York—She is very nice —[I have] a feeling about her singing that [it] will have a hard time in New York—

Finally Tony came in in a light blue sweater—he wears elegant tan colored riding breeches and high black boots—He told me yesterday that he doesn't like clothes like that—doesn't think he looks well in them—he thinks he looks better in his Indian clothes—long buckskin trousers with fringe or flaps on the side—He sets his watch by the sun and solemnly tells you the time when you ask him. Watches don't work well in this altitude so mine is very temperamental—

Well—he came in and said it was time to go—that Mabel had a stomach ache and wasn't going—I guess that was why we didn't go for the sunrise dance—It is something about blowing eagle feathers into the air as the sun comes over the mountain—The thing we went to is called the races[15]—All the young men down to little boys that look not more than six or seven—race—two at a time—naked except for a loin cloth—moccasins—paint—feathers—ribbons—beads—bells—pieces of fur or porcupine quills—The pueblo is divided by a river—creek—and the race is to keep up speed in the young men—It was very beautiful—The old men and women line each side of the track and urge them on—The men in blankets—any kind of a bed blanket—or Mexican blanket—Tony says these people—his people—formerly wore skins—they did not weave blankets—

The old ones in their blankets are bare-chested and the one arm free of the blanket is bare—the women all wrapped in black shawls—mostly bright dresses underneath—

The old men seem to be very fond of their young men and boys as they urge them on to run with a queer sort of cry—and it is great to see them run—Some run with their minds and some only with their bodies—I thought much of you—

—I can't really describe it adequately to you—but I must say that Mabel picked one of the prize men of the tribe—One of the fine things about the Indians is a kind of quiet—calm—gentleness—They all seem to have it—

There was much food when we got home at noon—I don't know where I put it all— I eat a most unheard of quantity of a limitless number of things—I marvel more and more at what Mabel has done here—we might be eating in New York for variety of food—And when I look out at the desert and the mountains—prairie dogs right at the back door—it all just terrifies me—because you feel that the desert must win if you dare to combat it—and the mountains must win—and Tony's calm must win—

Nothing but the most appalling persistence could have achieved what she has—

The day before we came much of the interior of part of her house called the log cabin—burned—everything from a high poster bed—and a sacred cow to Tony's favorite buckskins was ruined—

And it seems to be just a drop in the bucket—

May 4, 1929—

We went to another dance yesterday afternoon—Today isn't the day I started to write this—Much wind and dust—young boys and girls dancing—I can't go into it all—Tony drove us up the river past the most beautiful grove of cottonwood trees you can imagine—just a tangle of silver—very tall and grand—and some lower bushes that are a fine silvery red and green—It is like a dream—

Well Dearest—it is Saturday, May 4th—I have been away a week in a few hours—It seems at least a couple of months—Last night—I was quite lonesome for you—I didn't have a letter since your Sunday written one—I know moving up here delays mail as it [is] quite difficult to get up here—it's quite out of the way—

15. O'Keeffe went to the foot races of the Santa Cruz Feast Day celebrations at the Taos Pueblo.

I was quite terrified at the idea that I have only been here a week—only away from you a week—And that desert and mountains out there—I am quite afraid to let myself go out to it as one has to to work with anything—It is as though I fall into something from which there is no return.—No road back—

I asked Tony if he liked that mountain—he smiled and remarked "That's why I'm here"—

My love to you Little Dear One—I will go out to the sun—am writing by the fire. We are not going to do anything today—Beck is quite exhausted—everybody is—except me—I feel fine—Much is happening to me—as tho I see quite clearly—ahead and behind—

A kiss—

Georgia O'Keeffe · [Taos, New Mexico] · [May 7, 1929]

Dearest Boy—

This is Mabel's paper that is on every table—everywhere—It is the first time I have written on it—I think you should see it—

—It is such a beautiful still morning—every morning since I left you has been still—and sunny—We haven't seen a drop of rain—but a beautiful morning here means a sort of a white morning—I can't say it any other way—and it seems so still—I wish you could see it—

I didn't write you yesterday—Mabel hasn't been well—we finally persuaded her to stay in bed—Beck and I are the only ones who go in to see her—we do the errands—

She seems to enjoy talking with me—You know she has a real fondness and respect for you—I wish you would send her some books—five or six—put in Ettie's *Love Days* and *We Are Incredible*[16]—and anything else you think of—anything you think she would like to read—Her heart is bothering her—she got up and did too much after she had the flu a few weeks ago I think—is taking fifteen drops [of] digitalis a day—She objects to being quiet but I think it is what she needs—her pulse is rather slow and irregular—

—I didn't write you yesterday—the day went too fast till mail time—I unpacked my trunk—got settled in the studio—and in the afternoon went out to try some trees[17]—Of course I got nothing but a start for a start—I wish I could tell you how alive I feel—I really never felt better in my life—Beck is amazed—I am much tougher than she is—

Day before yesterday—Sunday—we drove way up in the mountains where there are patches of snow all through the woods—Tony and another Indian and Beck and I—Tony looking for some sheep that he thought he wanted to buy—We really looked very funny to ourselves—it seemed so funny to be out in that big car—I in front with Tony—big and complacent in his blue sweater—Beck in the back with the other Indian done up in a gray bed blanket—They are really very fine—very real—Tony seems to like taking us along—The other visitors say they have never seen him so nice to anyone—

16. Ettie Stettheimer, *Love Days* (New York, 1923); Margery Latimer, *We Are Incredible* (New York, 1928).
17. Lynes 686.

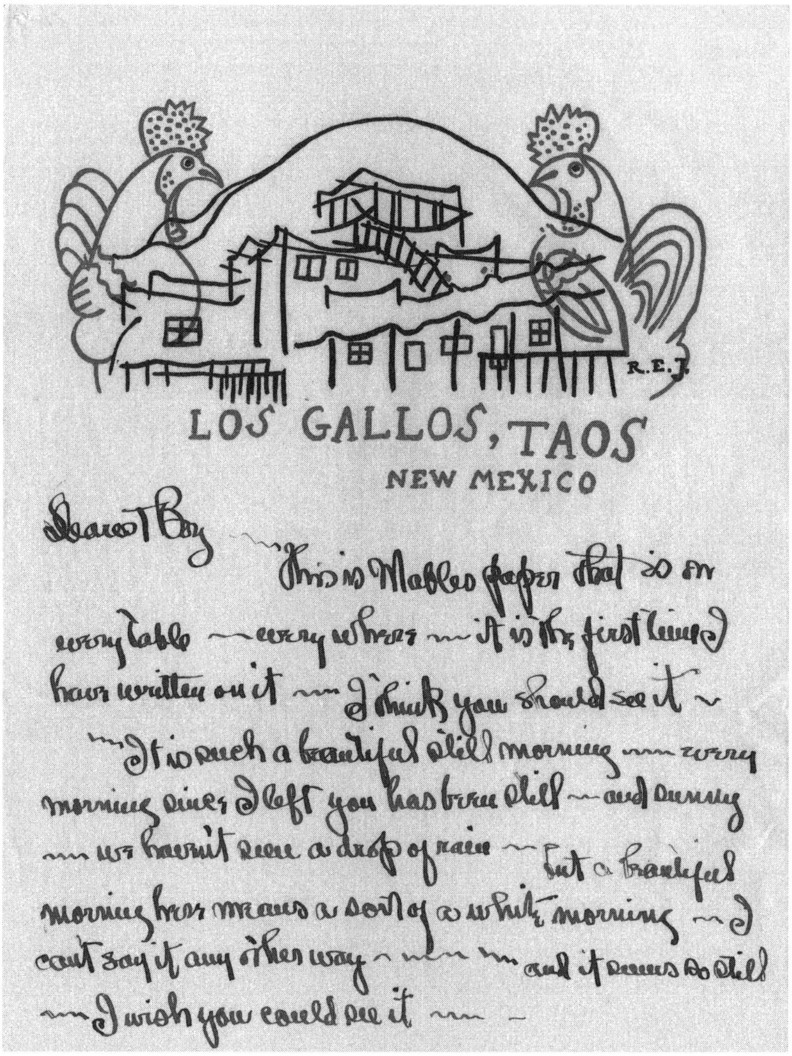

LOS GALLOS, TAOS
NEW MEXICO

Dearest Boy — This is Mabel's paper that is on every table — every where — it is the first time I have written on it — I think you should see it — — It is such a beautiful still morning — every morning since I left you has been still — and sunny — we haven't seen a drop of rain — but a beautiful morning here means a sort of a white morning — I can't say it any other way — — and it seems so still — I wish you could see it —

Letter by Georgia O'Keeffe on letterhead for Los Gallos, Mabel Dodge Luhan's Taos, New Mexico, home. Alfred Stieglitz/Georgia O'Keeffe Archive, Yale Collection of American Literature, Beinecke Rare Book and Manuscript Library.

Well—we are having a great time—Even if we went home tomorrow it would be worthwhile to have come—Tony is much interested in your letters to me—He can't read—but he thinks they are very nice to look at—

—I read them—and then read them again—I am glad you are being careful—I thought you would be—I dreamed about you last night—Many people were about and I was waiting for them to go because I felt when they would go you would touch the center of me—and I wanted it—

But this is all very good—I enjoy it all so much that I can't help wishing you were having it with me—

I must kiss you and go out to the sun—It is nice that the mail comes at night—after supper—last night there were three—

Again I kiss you—

Tuesday morning—

Alfred Stieglitz · [New York City] · [May 9, 1929]

It's 10:30 A.M.—Raining. I came in at 9:45 just as the letter carrier handed the doorman two letters of yours for me!—There were none yesterday.—So the two today. And I have read them—My Sweetestheart in her element—Faraway still right here. It's all quite unbelievable for you as for me. You have the mountain—I just feel space—& space beyond space—Mountains seem timeless—creative of moods not withstanding—Space is everything—yet nothing—still tangible—to me—Maybe another form of the mountain.—Another form of all that was & will be.—

There is the Room here—the Demuths on the wall—the one opposite me small—his last—unfinished—a white mask[18] beautifully painted.—The numerals 1 2 3 in pale yellow on a veiled gray surface. The letters LOVE in a pink on a bromoil red surface—an unfilled plain black surface (unfinished he says) occupying one-fourth of the picture—upper left hand.—The picture fascinates me. I think it the best here.—I don't know why it holds.—And it is curious to think that when this show comes down in a few days it will undoubtedly be the last one in the Room.—And that picture the last opposite me as I sit in that hideous but comfortable chair.—

—Much cardboard (100 boxes) arrived—much packing paper & twine. Zoler wants to do all the packing but I feel I'll have to get professionals so as to get thro' quickly.—I want to see if I can't get thro' a week before going away. Is it possible?—For me?

—The three Doves have just come back from Washington.[19]—And Strand called up to ask some questions.—And there were several other calls.—My line of "thought" has been interrupted.—

But to come back to your letters. You are certainly having the very full days I knew you'd have—I know Mabel—& I think I can picture Tony—& the household—& much of the life there—& I know my White One—Of course in reality it may be very different but not so different after all.—

—A kiss.—Well, I'm glad you feel so alive once more—And are in your natural element. This here in a way is rather awful.—Don't think I don't know that.—

—Bernadette's Mexican friend who is a sculptor has asked if he could come & carve me!!—I wouldn't have to sit. Of course I'm not a least bit interested but if he feels the need he should go ahead. I told him so. He asked when it would be convenient for me—& I told him I didn't live a convenient life—so he'd have to do as he liked. I merely added that between 12:30 & 1:30 I'd be out to lunch.—Maybe I should have said: No.—But why?—

---

18. Charles Demuth, *Love, Love, Love (Homage to Gertrude Stein)*, reproduced in *Charles Demuth* (New York, 1988), 185.

19. Ann Lee Morgan, *Arthur Dove: Life and Work, with a Catalogue Raisonné* (Newark, Del., 1984), 29.4, 29.13, 29.16.

—It was midnight when I got to bed last night. Bathed—& sat alone quite awhile after Seligmann had left.

—The auction of the two "great" pictures last night[20] brought half a million—one and a half had been expected!—The small picture brought $375,000—Duveen buying it!?—& the other $125,000.—A game if there ever was one.—

They say there was a great crowd—but all was over in fifteen minutes.—I'm glad curiosity did not move me.

—I had a letter from Mrs. Fischel this morning.[21] She is elated. Had been away from St. Louis. Wants the painting before May 26.—Will send money any time. I'll write her to send it at once.—The picture is hers.—And the risks are hers.—I hate to see it go.—But as the "future" is so uncertain, I dare not let sentiment dominate.—If there were really a place—the picture would be kept for it—But there can be no *place*—That I know positively.—By place I mean something of relative permanence—& by permanence I mean five years.—

—And now I'll get to sorting. Another kiss.—All I hope is you remain well.—

Everything else is secondary as far as I am concerned.—

Georgia O'Keeffe · [Taos, New Mexico] · [**May 10, 1929**]

Dearest Boy—Dearest Boy—

Such days—such days—When you think of me think of me with hands like dark brown gloves—very dirty finger nails—my nose is sore on the top today from sunburn—Tony says it will come off—meaning that it will peel—Mabel looks at me and says—"I wouldn't believe anyone could change so much in a few days"—We seem to just fly about from morning till night—doing everything so hard—The road out to the place where I am painting is so bad that it seems a terrific fight to get there—but we get there—

—I didn't write you yesterday—today is the tenth—I just didn't have time—getting my things together to get out to the place I wanted to paint—it was very complicated—and I wanted to get there early to have a long morning—

I take off my waist and just cook in the sun as I work—In the afternoon I came over here to the studio to work—it is a 30 × 40 canvas—gray trees[22]—going rather well—Just as

A TERRIBLE RIGHTNESS, 1929–1933

---

20. On May 8, 1929, two paintings from the collection of Carl W. Hamilton sold at the Anderson Galleries. Sir Joseph Duveen bought Piero della Francesca's *Crucifixion* for $375,000, a record price for a painting sold at auction in the United States, and Leon Schinasi bought Fra Filippo Lippi's *Madonna and Child* for $125,000; see "$375,000 Paid Here for Piero Painting," *NYT*, May 9, 1929, 15.

21. On March 15, 1929, Marguerite Fischel, who lived in St. Louis, wrote Stieglitz asking to buy O'Keeffe's *Shell and Old Shingle VI* (Lynes 545). Noting that she was not rich, she offered to pay "a certain sum at regular intervals for many years in order to obtain this painting." She added, "Would Miss Keeffe's very fine painting cost more than a very fine automobile?. . . If I could have an automobile, why could I not have a fine painting instead, especially when the painting has a very important significance to me?" She agreed to donate the painting to the St. Louis Art Museum on her death; see Fischel to AS, Mar. 15 and Apr. 22, 1929; and AS to Fischel, Apr. 10, 1929.

22. Lynes 686.

I sat down to write you yesterday Beck came and wanted me to go over to Brett's room[23] —
I hadn't been so I went—It is lovely—You climb a ladder to get to it—she has windows on
four sides—It isn't far away—

Mabel is much out with her—but we won't go into that—Beck and I decided not to
be complicated in it—Mabel is not well and carried on so that I told Brett not to come over
for awhile—we will go to see her—It is all very complicated and unimportant—Brett doesn't
mind—

Everything is going well with us—I never felt better in my life so have nothing to complain of—I feel so good I can scarcely believe it—I would be in great danger if you felt as I feel
—and you would be in danger if you were nearby—no matter how you felt I am afraid—

I think very nice things are happening to Beck—and I think Mabel enjoys us both—

I just can't get over this place—every little while I find a new part of the house—There
seems no end to it—and it is all so amusing—

Tony wears wonderfully—He is really fine—and he and Mabel together make a
gamut of life—ranging from his fine simple primitive quality—quite unchanging—through her
charming—sophisticated—ever changing—laughing—weeping—questioning ways—There
seems no end to it all—she one thing—going her way—he another—going his way—and still
they are very much together—I can't get over being surprised at it—

I feel like working—there are lots of things to do—I just hope I can get something
done—I was out and at my tree again this morning—It stands here behind me—gray and
indefinite—

—I want to do something that will make you feel how much I like it here—

You shouldn't stand up to write me—you often say that you do—and don't make an
extra effort to write when you are tired—

The line at the end of your letter last night looked gay—

I can't tell you how far away I feel—and I feel too that it is very good for me. I just wish
you could see what a grand color I have—

And I feel like flying—like turning the world over again—like I used to feel—

I kiss you—any way you wish—but I prefer that it be lively—

Alfred Stieglitz · [New York City] · May 14, 1929

Good Morning.

It's raining.—It's just 7:30. And I am ready for breakfast. Not yet—for I took Salsanos[24]
awhile ago & I have to wait. Chops are ordered.—The night wasn't bad nor good—Lachaise
was in my head.[25] How to finish up with him so that there is some sort of edge. He is such

23. Brett had a small house on Kiowa, the ranch Mabel Luhan had given to D. H. Lawrence. However, during the summer of
1929, when she and Luhan quarreled, she also stayed in a room in Taos on top of a house that was accessible only by ladder;
see Sean Hignett, *Brett: From Bloomsbury to New Mexico, a Biography* (London, 1984), 202.
24. A digestive aid.
25. On May 3, 1929, Stieglitz wrote Gaston Lachaise, saying that he had loaned the sculptor one thousand dollars in November
1928 because his wife was ill, and that Lachaise, on his own volition, left two works as collateral. On May 13, Lachaise

a lovable person & such a good artist & simply impossible in the practical sense. One has no chance, do what one will—give him one's last drop of blood and he has no idea of it all. That's what makes it so ghastly—so impossible.—I begin to feel that Mrs. Lachaise is not fully innocent—that she drives him into all this madness without her realizing what part she really plays. The "people" are not entirely wrong in this matter. Of course the tragedy is that she is what she must be & he is what he seems he must be. And then there is the "world" which now includes us as far as we are concerned.—Well, somehow, I must get Lachaise out of my system as an active thing.—Really too bad.—

The letter I wrote last night to him I'll rewrite today.—The document must be fuller & clearer. Maybe he can read. I doubt it.—Maybe she can.—I wonder—Maybe she can & prefers not to.—

I got off quite a bit of correspondence last night. This in place of Bach. So the too cold church was good.[26]—Seligmann who was there called up after the concert to see whether I was all right. So did the Normans. Very decent—but really not at all necessary.—Today the central American sculptor comes to begin his carving of me!—Came yesterday afternoon but it was impossible in the mess to let him begin.—And fortunately he did not begin as Lachaise walked in shortly after. I feel he might be suspicious that I had transferred my affections to another sculptor.—Ye gods.—Such a world—of humans.—Myself included.—You I exclude. Yes I do.—And I haven't kissed you yet—nor said Good Morning to Fluffy.—Well here are kisses for you—& for her.—And now I'll "chop" it—the day's real beginning. Chops.—I awoke & found a can opener—quite awhile. So I'm not completely fagged out.

—Be good to yourself. I know you are in your true element & that makes me feel very fine—

A kiss—Once more greetings to all—

I wrote a few lines to Mabel[27] last night & also to Brett.—I'm not much of a letter writer any more.—

Alfred Stieglitz · [New York City] · May 16, 1929

7:30 A.M.
Good Morning.

It's early.—I'm ready.—It's warm gray & sticky.—Not very inviting for hard work packing.—But it could be worse.—More packing. Of's man. I. Zoler.—All. And the Demuths still on show.—Yesterday was another wild day.—But not quite as hectic as the one before—

"dumbfounded" Stieglitz by asking for a receipt for the sculptures. Stieglitz responded on May 16: "I told you that such a request had never been made by anyone from me; that the Room was not in business, that I was not in business, that the things the artists brought were brought at their own volition and left in the Room at their own risk."

26. On May 13, 1929, Stieglitz wrote O'Keeffe that he went to a Bach concert with Dorothy and Edward Norman but had to leave soon after he arrived because it was too cold.

27. On May 13, 1929, Stieglitz wrote Luhan that O'Keeffe had told him she was having a "marvelous" time with Tony, especially what he is "showing her—& doing for her.—She is in her element."

Of's man was prompt & we repacked with decent paper & the storage people took out many packages of paintings—Marin's & some of yours. That was a relief—Packing continued.

While packing, labeling, etc.—much detail—Milton, Jr. & his governess,[28] a young very nice Canadian governess came.—They spent an hour in the chaotic surroundings. The boy is bright & lovable. And nice looking.—Very direct & not a bit bashful—It seemed quite natural to be Grandpa—& yet I seemed still another being sort of buried somewhere.—I went on labeling & marking packages & recording all the time they were there. Yet I talked with him & the governess. And Of's man worked & smiled at some of the things the boy said—

Suddenly the boy said: Grandpa, you are getting old. Aren't you?—I said: Yes, my boy, that's very true. Someday maybe you'll be so old too. It was amusing how he said it.—Yes, I'm getting—am—old! I know it only too well. But it doesn't worry me. Rather amuses. I am sorry for you. That's all.—Otherwise it makes no difference.—It seems the boy & his governess are in New York for a week with Emmy. So as to give the governess a chance to get to theaters, etc. —Milton[29] is in Boston.—

For lunch the *New Yorker* man[30] joined me to talk about you. He knows Molly Smith very well—& many others who know you from various angles. And he seems bent on producing an article. I wonder what it will be—nothing that can be more than superficially entertaining. Full of irrelevancies.—Well, he is intelligent enough.—Then the sculptor came & went at his work. I have no idea what he is doing—I had no time—nor desire—to look. I continued to work—walk about—as if he weren't there.—

In the meantime people came & wanted to know about prices, about Marins, about O'Keeffes—a very fine young fellow from Williams College—he spent several hours with me —Eager to have an O'Keeffe—a Marin. Really a fine fellow. Painting too.—Seligmann brought me the four-page Lachaise letter I had dictated. I re-dictated another[31]—the one written wasn't quite right.—To get anything focused doing a dozen things at a time seems difficult. Formerly I could do it—but Grandpa is getting old! Zoler went to Aline's.[32] She wasn't in. The butler said she had decided to keep the *White Petunia*.[33] So the *East River*[34] came back. I have written her to find out had a mistake been made.—I don't trust anybody these days for straight information of any kind.—Everyone seems so muddle-headed.—That includes Grandpa.—I was very tired when I got to the hotel. Zoler came with me.—I didn't talk all evening. Sorted more papers.

And Sweetestheart how busy I really was is proven by the fact that your letter which came at three—I hadn't had a letter the day before—I didn't read till after supper!—And it was

28. Stieglitz's grandson, Milton Stearns, Jr., and Lillie Beaton, his governess.

29. Milton Stearns, the husband of Stieglitz's daughter Kitty Stieglitz Stearns.

30. Murdock Pemberton, art critic of *The New Yorker*. The magazine was preparing an article on O'Keeffe; see Robert M. Coates, "Profiles: Abstraction–Flowers," *The New Yorker,* July 6, 1929, 21–24; it was illustrated with a sketch of O'Keeffe by Miguel Covarrubias.

31. Stieglitz sent Lachaise a five-page letter on May 16, 1929, detailing his understanding of their financial arrangement. He noted that he had returned the works Lachaise had left as collateral and that Lachaise could keep the one thousand dollars he had loaned him. "I am satisfied to pay for the lesson," Stieglitz concluded, "and hope you are satisfied with your bonus."

32. Aline Liebman, one of Stieglitz's supporters.

33. Lynes 463.

34. Either Lynes 619 or 620.

a great letter. So full of real life. Grand.—And you feeling like bursting.—Yes, I can imagine how you look—And how lively Fluffy must be at times. It's all very good—very healthy. And Europe would have been the very reverse. For Beck as well as you. And I wouldn't have said a word had you decided to Europe it!—

And now I'll go to my chops—& orange juice & Wheatena.—I take Salsanos every morning.

These letters are rather stupid—but it can't be helped—

Lots lots of love—I'm glad you feel strong enough to paint.

A big kiss—everywhere—and some bites too—& anything else that might give you pleasure—I'm ready.—

You're sweet.—

Georgia O'Keeffe · [Taos, New Mexico] · [May 20, 1929]

Dearest—

Such a time—such a time—

Yesterday morning I was in the studio all morning—a pastel[35]—very silly—

After lunch to the races—You would pass out at that—The whole town—particularly the Indians and Mexicans and picturesque whites turned out—There was to be one race—two horses—200 yards—They were from two P.M. till about five getting started—and finally only one horse ran—I just have to laugh out loud when I write it to you—it sounds so ridiculous—and when I think of how interested everyone was—and the way they accepted seeing just one horse run after all that waiting—and the way everyone was talking about the different aspects of the whole thing—It was really great—

Well this morning Mabel and Tony went off to Albuquerque to see the doctor—She finally got tired of her ailments and decided to find out about them—everyone is relieved—

I have been in the studio all day—working over the big painting I started first[36]—I don't know much about it except that I felt like starting the day over when I shut the door—

The studio is just too grand—I wish you could see it—It seems the natural place for me to go to when I'm not riding somewhere—It's better for me than the other houses—and nobody comes to see me—

I didn't write last night—as a matter of fact—I wept—It was one of those times when many things seemed very clear to me—and I don't like it—though it seems very necessary for me—

Tony thought he would fool me and didn't give me your letter till about half an hour after the other mail—but it just happened that I received from Betty the two you had sent me to Chicago[37]—He was much disappointed—

35. Lynes 672.

36. Lynes 686.

37. Stieglitz had sent two letters to O'Keeffe in Chicago, care of her brother and sister-in-law, Alexis and Betty O'Keeffe. The letters arrived after she left.

Brett is here this evening—We all walked out to the cross on the desert—Everyone a bit grumpy—They all talked so much that Beck and I felt quite thorny—Mabel and Brett being rather mixed up is a bit difficult—There are the two sides to it and neither one likes the other side—

—Well Little One—I wondered today—often—what you are doing—What—What—and then another What—

It has been a beautiful day—no wind—enormous clouds—and such sunshine—I lie on the studio doorstep for sun—

And a little kiss—like the air goes to you—

Georgia O'Keeffe · [Taos, New Mexico] · [May 21, 1929]

It is morning again—Tuesday I think—As a matter of fact it is almost noon—I sitting in the studio—in a big chair like those new porch chairs Lee got last summer—There is a fire in the stove—I just read *Nellie Bloom*[38]—It is blue gray—or maybe gray blue would be better today —The sun almost out—but not quite—Last night it rained—this morning the weather can't settle—

When I walked into the kitchen for breakfast there sat a new person—Not Pete[39] the Mexican gardener that we often breakfast with—Not Mabel's adopted Mexican boy[40] who arrived last night—Still at my first glance it seemed someone familiar—It was Spud Johnson— in white corduroys and a light lemon colored sweater—

Well that was that—this uncertain weather makes me feel unsettled—

Last night two letters from you—There is no Sunday mail here—it neither comes nor goes—so last night two—I wonder did Mrs. Liebman pay the same for the *Petunia* as she would have for the *New York*[41]—?

I too will be glad when the Fischel *Shell and Shingle* thing is settled—To me it seems a queer thing to take money for[42]—But it seemed strange to take money for that large white flower of the same period[43]—It all seems far away to me—They just represent something to me that I have lost—my cry to it to come back to me when I knew it was gone—and I am glad that they are gone—

It is difficult to see my new painting—the big one of trees[44] that I have been working on —It isn't really of this country and it doesn't exist for this place and it isn't exciting—The rain

---

38. Margery Latimer, *Nellie Bloom and Other Stories* (New York, 1929).

39. José Pitman Guadalupe (Pete) Dozier worked as both a gardener and horse wrangler for Mabel Dodge Luhan.

40. Eduardo.

41. Lynes 463 and either 619 or 620.

42. Lynes 545. O'Keeffe painted *Shell and Old Shingle I–VI* in the fall of 1926 using a shingle from the Lake George barn and a shell she had collected during her trip to York Beach in August and September 1926; see O'Keeffe, *Georgia O'Keeffe* (New York, 1976), unpaginated.

43. Lynes 561.

44. Lynes 686.

has made the road so bad that I haven't been able to go out to the place again—It hangs here in front of me now—I am going to work on it this afternoon again—I like something about it very much—I think it will come—tho it may not be anything for anyone but me—

I kiss you—and stay here with my stove and my mountain—and the gray sage desert and the alfalfa field—very green—while the letter goes on to you—

As I walked the plank across the irrigation ditch on my way over here this morning— everything so quiet—and thought of the Room and what you are going through—The two seem so different—it seems quite unbelievable—This must be very good for me—I really can't imagine feeling much better—I wish you could imagine that what you are at could be half as good for you—

About our wiring Marin—He asked me to let him know how things are here—so I did. He should have come right away—the spring color is fast going—I thought he would get a lot out of a month or six weeks here and be back home by the time his child[45] would be out of school—It is so easy to get here—If it disturbed him too much I am sorry—

—Another kiss to you—

I am neither warm nor cold this morning—quite neutral—

But I have a notion that I would be a very wild woman to go to bed with—that my pleasure would be maddeningly intense—

So—I kiss you—quietly—

Georgia O'Keeffe · [Taos, New Mexico] · [May 22, 1929]

Wednesday—4:15 P.M.—

It rains—and rains—I've been in the studio all day—Finished my gray trees[46] for the present—showed it to Beck yesterday—she liked it very much—For me it is better now—and I've painted all over another funny little painting that I started last week—I am glad of the rainy day to be rid of them—When the sun shines I'll take a fresh start—

—You would have laughed to see me run over to the other house in a white bathing cap with a black and white—mostly white—rug around my shoulders—No one here thinks it even unusual—They just pick up a rug from anywhere and wrap up in it and walk out—then the rugs are always where they don't belong—

Spud Johnson brought a friend[47] for supper last night—a blooming young man—well fed and pampered and cared for looking—He is from California sent here for the summer to cure a bad sinus—Beck mentioned having a letter from you—and he asked immediately—did she mean the great photographer—Everybody seems to know you one way or another—It rained so hard he had to stay all night—Mabel has a road leading up to her house that beats anything you ever saw when it rains—and when it is dry maybe it is worse—When it rains it

---

45. John Marin, Jr.
46. Lynes 686.
47. In the spring and summer of 1929, the photographer Ansel Adams and his new wife, Virginia, stayed at Mary Austin's Taos home.

is rivers of water and frightful mud—When it is dry it is so rough that you can scarcely believe anything can be so bad—She bumps and slides over it and doesn't mind—She isn't home yet—

Beck has taken over the household with grumblings and threats—the housekeeper —the gardener—the painters—plasterers and roofers—all sorts of things go on here at once— She makes a fierce face over it but I think she likes it—feels important[48]—

There is no news when it rains and one works—except that I eat an enormous amount of food—it is very good—A pregnant horse is eating alfalfa in the field outside my window— And the man who has a studio over the garage back of this studio got stuck in the mud with his car when he tried to drive out and slid and sloshed and spun around most dreadfully—This mud is the slipperiest stuff you ever saw—And there is new snow on top of the mountain—

Things go on in me that are rather difficult to tell about—a curious sort of rearranging of myself—or maybe it is just seeing what is there because of the way it connects new surroundings—At any rate—it is all very good—

—I sometimes wonder what our being apart will do to us—Whatever—must be all right—I feel we both understand—

I think my painting is going to be quite different in color—

I kiss you—

426

Alfred Stieglitz · [New York City] · May 25, 1929

It's 5 P.M. And I'm here in the hotel. Alone.—It has been a trying day. Nothing really "happened."—Much has been packed & there is real daylight ahead.—At least as far as packing is concerned.—Strand appeared with Marin's watercolor output of last year. I am to put them in his vault. I took time to glance them over very hurriedly.—Many are incredible. They too are in a box ready to go into the vault—I could have kept them out to look at them again but my mind is bent on the vaults!

—After Lee's I went right to the Room—got there at 9:15. No mail. Nothing. I pitched right in tagging, marking, recording—so much finicky detail. Zoler arrived at 10:15 & went right to work—At eleven a letter came from you. I hastily read it. Read it twice. About your feelings about the *Shingle & Shell*—& the *White Flower*.[49]

—All you said I know only too well—My "end" of the pictures, I don't think you will ever be able to see.—This is no criticism.—It was not easy for me to let them "go" out into the world knowing their significance better than anyone else can ever know—seeing their true wonder—& seeing you!—Your whiteness—straightness—I am not white—

Your letter touched a very vital spot in me—I won't go into it—It would take reams —& what I'd say would be unclear—I actually began a letter to you at once in the Room— after I had read—but I stopped—I found all words dead—or worse than dead—damned.—

Yes, that's the seat of much trouble, words that are damned still used.

48. Miriam Hapgood DeWitt later wrote that although Beck Strand could be a foul-mouthed, brawling character, when you "enter her house…you are in a precisely ordered, almost lace-doilied world"; see DeWitt, *Taos,* 8.
49. Lynes 545, 561.

I wonder what I'll do when the vaults are filled & the Room is itself again—This packing has become significant in many, many ways.—So much that I'd like to drop into the East River—why keeping?—

—Goepfert phoned—Ettie had told her she should—I wishing it—Well, she is coming to dinner. I had hoped we would not be alone. It would be a bit easier on me. But no one has turned up.—Weekend. And a grand day. Clear & cool.

—I'm going to lie down a bit down—

I kiss you Sweetestheart—

Later. I tried to lie down but feel too restless.—Now that packing is nearing completion I wonder about much of the things I call "my own." What is to become of most of the stuff.—What its earthly use. Even three-quarters of my own prints. I have no desire to destroy them now.—All the clippings & such stuff—You will never make use of any such things—That is not in your natural line.—Well maybe when I'm really all through and everything is finally buried away I'll see what must be done by me—With most of the stuff—

Your paintings have a real significance—to me at least. So have Marin's. And some of my prints. A set of *Camera Work* still means a little to me. And still if I knew they were all destroyed—not a single one to be found—I'd have no feeling about it.—For I feel *Camera Work* incomplete—Its spirit is clear enough & lives—

But that's not enough for me. Not these days.—Not from myself. And *Camera Work* is myself—& yet not my mature self—And *Camera Work* can never be completed—As much else will remain incomplete—

One is so completely powerless in a way.[50] —

—I did have a haircut finally. That's an achievement—a comfort.—And a shampoo will turn it into a delight.—

I'm out of paper.—

Once again a kiss—& a very Good Night—You are very very dear to me.—

Georgia O'Keeffe · [Taos, New Mexico] · [May 28, 1929]

Dearest Dearest—

Your letter today makes me sad—the one about what I said about the *Shell and Shingle*[51]—

You do not need to write me reams about that—I think it is one of the things I understand—I haven't said anything about it—it is hard even to say what I understand—It is one of the things that seems to have been always in my mind for a long time and I think it is all right now. You need not worry—

50. The next day Stieglitz continued to ruminate on the disposition of his work: "Under no condition do I want to saddle you with wasting your life over it.—You have other things to do. To me more important even if I'm not here in person.—Things for yourself."

51. Lynes 545.

I didn't write you yesterday—I worked all day and again today all day—and I can't tell you how I enjoyed it—I was at work before eight—stopped a couple of hours at noon—then at it again till six—I will be at it again tomorrow—I haven't had such a feeling of real pleasure in working in a long long time—The things move slowly—but tonight when I hung up what I had been working on it seemed to belong in the studio so I thought it was coming—and rather liked it—

I seem to be such a fool here—about liking things—We all laugh and have a great time when one dreaming guest lights a fire in a stove that has no chimney—and such nonsense—

—Marin phones he will be up tomorrow—Mabel isn't back yet—writes that after examination—all her organs are perfect but none of them work—

—Beck sends her love—We are really having a great time—she is doing the housekeeping—I just won't—Many things come up—and quiet down—I think it is all giving her much—

Your letter was very dear—I was afraid my remark about the *Shell and Shingle* would disturb you—but it seemed I had to say it even when I thought twice—

Henderson's remark[52] was nice—

Well—Good Night Little One—

The studio was very big and quiet today—and out the window the wind blew hard—very hard—across the alfalfa field to the mountain—

I kiss you—and feel very near to you—

I am glad Marin is coming tomorrow—

I not only kiss you—I give up all myself to you through the distance—

Georgia O'Keeffe · [**Taos, New Mexico**] · [**May 29, 1929**]

Dearest—

I feel as tho my brain is a strange hash—I have been working all day again—and lay in the sun at noon and after five till I felt cooked—

Marin has come—It seemed the whole countryside collected—Brett with a butcher knife hunting for worms to go fishing—Callaghan with his face all greased—he lay in the sun too long and is burned—red as can be—Johnson doing odd jobs for everyone—filling cigarette lighters—picking up books Brett threw in the road—running after the dog—etc.—other females with their hair combed for Marin—and we all sat in the swing and chairs about it—Marin says he feels he doesn't know where he is—but he looks pleased—

All this after I stopped working—a little after five—I was up and at it before eight again this morning—and enjoyed it—I am painting the back of an old church—it is the queerest shape you ever saw and has no windows—sand color against a blue sky—I have two of

---

52. As Stieglitz related in his letter to O'Keeffe of May 24, 1929, Hunt Henderson, who had recently purchased Lynes 530 and 638, wrote him, most likely in reference to Lynes 530: "I love the O'Keeffe but I have not shown it. I don't want to hear it talked about."

them—one 36 × 24 and the other 24 × something less—and another small one[53] that is just a piece of it for color—It looks lovely on my wall here—

I feel full to bursting for work—and I feel it is going to be good—at any rate I enjoy it —I work out in the morning and in the studio in the afternoon—and all the wild goings on that are there when I come in from working don't seem to disturb at all—I guess Beck and I manage to stir up much of what goes on that has a real kick to it—but everyone is keyed so high that no one seems like people in other places and they all tear about at a great pace at one thing or another—

Marin looks so funny and city like—If he hasn't any funny pants along we will have to get him some—Brett is going to take him fishing—he regrets he didn't bring his fishing pole—

Well—we expect Mabel and Tony back tomorrow—Beck says she will throw a hammer into my working fever—I don't think so—

The evening is very beautiful—still—soft—and such beautiful birdcalls—It seems ages since I got up this morning—

I know my painting is different because the one I did when I first came didn't seem to belong at all and this one does—My studio is so grand—white and big and still—and no one comes to it—I will send you a picture of it tomorrow—the picture is the front of it—outside— and doesn't feel a bit like it feels inside—

Johnson and Brett are waiting for me to walk out to the cross—It is such a lovely evening—I must go—

A kiss—with the quietest evening you ever saw—

Georgia O'Keeffe · [Taos, New Mexico] · [May 30, 1929]

5:20—Thursday—
Dearest—

It is raining again—I was out but managed to get into the studio just before the rain fell—I wanted to write you and didn't think it would be possible over in either house—It is so nice here alone—the floor and woodwork dust gray like the dirt outdoors—the white walls— the window facing north toward the Holy Mountain is so big—and the place always feels so big and still—

I was up at 6:30 this morning—hoping it wouldn't be too muddy to go out to work— but it was—I had breakfast at seven—and then started across the sagebrush to look at the early morning light on the cross—

The walking was so good—though my feet were heavy with rubbers and mud—I kept on going toward the east—the nearest—lowest hills—Well—I have never had a more beautiful walk—The mountains and the scrubby cedar were so rich and warm colored they seemed to come right up to me and touch my skin—And when I got way up in the hills and looked back —the plains covered with sagebrush seemed like the ocean—the little fresh green around

53. Lynes 662, 664, 666.

Mabel's place and the distant mountains—the Holy Mountain nearby to the right with snow—new snow on its top—it all has a glitter—the whole landscape—and at the same time it is like the most glorious flower garden—

I seem to be hunting for something of myself out there—something in myself that will give me a symbol for all this—a symbol for the sense of life I get out here—

I feel like I felt when I first came out here—I think I was twenty-three then—The difference is that I understand the feeling now—and it makes it all seem very rich—

I wanted to take off my clothes and lie down in the sun naked—but I didn't dare—

I was gone for three hours—and it was as perfect as any hours I have ever spent with the outdoors—

When I came back—Marin was out back of the house painting—I didn't look at it—but he says he is pleased—I will look later—

One thinks so many things when one walks like that alone—it is the next best thing to being in bed with you—and I feel almost as relaxed and let down from it—

I brought back lovely bright blue and red and yellow flowers that grew in the gullies—

Well—I lay on the floor in the studio door in the sun for nearly an hour when I got home—I had your letter too—telling of last Sunday—It was rather sad—you sound quite forlorn and a bit as tho you need me—but I know that if I were there you would probably be very much irritated with me—When are you planning to go to the Lake—? And I wonder—seeing you there without me seems very sad—but my urge toward what I feel here is stronger than my sadness—

I wonder if you would like me here—I don't know—

Beck swears you will never be able to tell her I am delicate again—She seems physically stronger than I am but I stand much more than she can—

I have been watching a snowstorm on top of the mountain—

It is almost suppertime and getting cold—It is too late to build a fire here so I will be moving toward one—

I wish you could stand here beside me—just for a moment at least—it is such a different world—

I kiss you—

Well—I have a notion that Brett and Spud Johnson are looking to go to the hotel to some sort of Indian dance or other—I hear car honking—So I'd better go—

A kiss—

Alfred Stieglitz · [New York City] · [June 6, 1929] +

Another Day.—Clear & cool. Nearly noon already.—

Was at the Engelhards' at 8:45 to sign checks. Went to Lee's but he was at an operation. So I'll go tomorrow instead. Have to go to Török too tomorrow. Nothing serious.—Merely ailments. Nuisances. Here in the Room we are waiting for Of's wagon—also the storage people—loads go out. Then there will be twenty boxes for Lake George to be called for by the American Express. Stuff I'm sending up—papers & things to go through up there & burn up.

—Most of it.—I am full of a wild desire this morning to burn up nearly everything which the world calls mine—Someday I know I'll have to do it.[54]—I can't go through this ordeal again. —Nor do I want anyone else to do it for me. No one can.—Much material that could be utilized.—But in a way I feel more & more the unimportance of very many things—I have always had that feeling—but somehow *things* will accumulate. Well, we'll see. When all the packing is over I'll get a bit of clarity.—Maybe I have it already. I don't know.—

Last night I was finally at the Normans'—It made me think of many things.—A really nice home.—They are so young—Really not usual. A very live & friendly child.[55]—Good & thoughtful food. And many acquaintances on the wall[56]—looking friendly & well. Thoroughly at home. And a whole wall to the ceiling full of books—familiar up-to-date literature—lots of air—& light—Still problems of money—living.—I felt a million years old—& still quite at home.—I guess I feel at home anywhere.

—Well, Sweetest Wild One—two letters from you today. None yesterday.—Great letters. One with Mabel's to you.—A fine, very fine letter. It's all very right.—As I knew it would be. Knew last summer.—Even before. Really. If my letters occasionally sound sad it's because occasionally I'm not feeling as comfortable (well) as I might—& the drudgery of this everlasting packing finally became a bit too trying.—As for Lake George, you see it won't be sad for me as I have already lived all what is going to happen—I'll be glad to just sit—silently—& without people—without pictures—without books—without the excitement of any kind.—Even without thought—Not even the feeling of being "alone"—I do hope there'll be some sun for awhile & some warmth.—I expect to go up on the 14th—Zoler goes with me.—I intended to go alone but it would be foolhardy.—He has been very fine. And seems to understand. So you have no cause to worry about me.—

It's great really what you are absorbing—getting—living.—It would be criminal to disturb that.—I'm glad Marin has started painting.—

—It's a queer feeling in the house here this morning—more than ever—A feeling as if the jury were out to arrive at a verdict—The darkies look at each other—Arthur & Chapman & Smith—Grant's son—all—Toni—all look & say little—& wonder what will happen[57]—And they don't quite seem to get what I am doing.

Florrie[58] was here a short while ago—for quite awhile.—Naturally wanted to know all about you.—She certainly would be very much out of place down there.—They go to Tarrytown on June 20.—

---

54. A few days later, on June 9, 1929, Stieglitz carried out his threat and destroyed some of his work: "Yesterday in the Room I started destroying negatives & papers. Some I never believed I'd have the heart to destroy—negatives of Kitty—old negatives of Venice—some of '291'—I'll never print them.—They are simply dead in every way.—I suddenly realized that over half the stuff of mine carefully stored must go. And it's up to me to destroy it.—I have chucked out several hundred more *Camera Work*. Zoler wanted to salvage them. I got angry for once & forbade it.—He can sell them for a nickel if he wants to. But I don't want to see them any more. It's just plain stupid" (AS to GOK, June 9, 1929).

55. Nancy Norman, born 1927.

56. Dorothy Norman collected paintings, prints, drawings, and photographs by several of the artists associated with Stieglitz.

57. Stieglitz and others who worked at the Anderson Galleries, including the janitors and elevator operators, Arthur, Chapman, Grant's son, Smith, and Toni, thought that the building in which it was located would soon be torn down.

58. Florine Stettheimer, a painter, was the sister of Carrie and Ettie Stettheimer. She and her sisters were thinking of going to New Mexico.

Alfred Stieglitz · [New York City] · [June 8, 1929]

7:30 A.M.—Dark & rainy. Saturday. Chops ordered.—And I ready for another day. Went to bed early last night. So terribly tired. But with packing virtually accomplished—I lay awake a long while.—My mind full of you & me.—Our togetherness.—Its beginning—its state now.— The first time in ages that I was free enough from the Room—to allow myself to indulge.— Tomorrow is June 9th. Sunday.—It was June 9th, Sunday, eleven years ago that you hopped off the train in the Pennsylvania Station—early morning—& ran up to me & kissed me! Like a happy child.

  —Eleven years have passed by.—I see all its phases—all the days & hours & moments of ecstasy & pain—the growth—of something very exceptional & very beautiful between us—I see the studio in 59th Street—291 (no man's room)—our sitting there that first Sunday afternoon—Yes all those days & hours & really minutes still existing vividly for me—Then my being ordered out of 1111—the photographing—Lake George—all the wonder & beauty & life —& all the terrible ordeal.—Life—your innocence—Emmy—Kitty—what not. On the Lake— the talks. All so crystal clear. And I see myself—And you.—Your siege of sinus. Our irregular living & simplicity. All so clean.—So inevitable.—The moving to 65th Street[59] against your will —the sale of Oaklawn—the beginning of the Hill. I won't go into it all. *All* came into my mind last night. Even the first night we went to sleep without a kiss!—Illnesses.—Yes, Sweetestheart —I lay hours letting all happen to me—the whole evolution of *US!*—And finally I fell asleep. It was six when I awoke & I got up.—Very quiet. Without a trace of sentimentality.—I with all my shortcomings—yet austere—

  My Holy Mountain invisible within.—Another part of me tossed about like the waters of the sea. And yet quiet. A contradiction ever.

  —A kiss—a greeting—a good morning!

  I am going to Juley's.—They made six very bad prints of *Shingle & Shell*.[60]—Paper troubles. Stupidity. And then I shall go to Of's with the pictures of yours still here.—Then bank & several other matters.—Must get stockings too.—At any rate 303 is emptied excepting the furniture.—That can stay.—Five weeks or more of work. Incredible.

  —I'm sending you Latimer's book by registered mail so that Mabel can read it if she cares to. Don't mislay the book.—

  Well, Sweetest One, I had better go down & get breakfast—Queer I feel dazed. My letters must seem awfully stupid & tiresome. I wonder will I wake up any in Lake George.— It's impossible for me to think myself there in any live way.—But I'll really be glad to get away altho' New York has been pleasant enough & everyone has been very kind & some quite solicitous.—Lake George will seem very empty without you—& still I'm glad you are not going knowing fully how you feel about it.—Again I say it's very good you are where you are. It's the only thing that's right for you—so also for me. I don't merely say this but I feel it fully.—

  A kiss—

432

59. Lee and Lizzie Stieglitz's house in New York.
60. Peter A. Juley and Son specialized in photographing artists and their works. Lynes 545.

Georgia O'Keeffe · [Taos, New Mexico] · [June 13, 1929]

Thursday night—really evening—just a bit of daylight left to write by—

I have had another wonderful day—they all seem to be wonderful—This morning I went out to the Pueblo—a little after nine—was there about three hours—My painting[61] walks on—

Tony was coming past the studio as I came in for lunch—I showed it to him—He was quite surprised that it was—as he says "just like it"—and he likes it—tho he has told me several times that he doesn't like paintings—and he always adds—that he doesn't know anything about paintings—

He is really a remarkable person—in ways that it is quite impossible to put into words—very simple—and honest—and real—and kind—very wise in his way—a rich kind of simple knowledge of life—and at times a bit crafty—

—Well after lunch everyone went a different way—they usually do—I to the sun in the hammock—Marin digging angle worms nearby—

In this sun one loses all sense of lying on anything and just feels suspended in heat—expecting to disappear at any moment—When I was about gone—just a small speck of me left—along came swinging Lewis[62]—hadn't seen him in days—all in white—and such a picture of flourishing health—He sat and talked by me a long time—funny spoiled boy—I finally sent him off with Marin—and I went hunting for Beck—

Well—we finally landed out in the Pueblo again—for an Indian corn dance—

I had a really beautiful afternoon—the simple Pueblo village—all of mud—against as perfect a mountain as one could imagine—and the dancing—rather monotonous—moving on from one place to another—Everyone in colors of such rich saturated pigment—much black —much long straight black hair—the brilliant sun and blue sky—

It went on and on—till I finally realized that I was the only white person left—The monotony of it—the brilliancy of the color—the live eyes—It is terribly exciting—and at the same time quieting like the ocean—I had a great sense of quiet and peace—and at the same time a very—very living excitement—

Beck was dead and ready to come home long before I was ready—I wasn't a bit tired —Maybe I would be there yet if she hadn't dragged me away—That place has the queerest fascination for me. When I get out there I just want to stay—

The Indian girl waitress hadn't come to help with supper—so I set the table and made Mabel's toast—

I want to wear a sheet like Tony—and ride like the Indian men that came tearing through the Pueblo gate in a body—all riding like mad—They have a real man's life—When I remarked it—Lewis who had joined us snorted—"Oh it would bore you soon enough"—

And then I thought of you and your letter of last night—and began telling them about it —that it was a real man's letter—I may read it to them—it is so beautiful—

---

61. Probably Lynes 699.
62. Lewis Callaghan, a photographer, was a friend of Spud Johnson's.

Lewis again remarked—"Well—you must have a wonderful husband—I never heard any woman talk about her husband the way you do"—

So that is that—

It has really been such a beautiful day—and I can really only tell you such a little of it—the sort of day that seems to float in space like a perfect thing—like the sun shine—

So I kiss you—

I am again in the studio—with my candle—The mountain is black and large—the stars high and bright—The moon will be shining on the log I walk [on] across the little stream when I return to the Big House—They will all be sitting about the fire—and other places—when I go in—

Good Night—I didn't realize till I sealed your letter last night that I must send it to Lake George—Sending what is here—there—seems so queer to me—

I just feel so like expanding here—way out to the horizon—and up into the sunshine—and out into the night—

I am glad you feel how right it is for me to be here—It is really terribly right—

So—I kiss you Good Night again—

You are very kind to me—

434

Georgia O'Keeffe · [Taos, New Mexico] · [June 14, 1929]

Dearest—

I was out painting all the morning—till three o'clock in fact—I took my lunch—I thought I would finish it today but now it seems there will be at least two more days as long as today on it—and then I already know I am going to want to start to do it all over again—

After standing around the house next [to] the studio for about an hour—watching half a dozen people—hanging curtains—making beds—putting down rugs—covering pillows—whitewashing—putting chairs and whatnots into place—I went to the springs with Beck and another woman—The judge's wife—They live in another of Mabel's houses—We had a bath and just got back in time to get straight for supper—Everyone but Mabel, Beck and I was late for supper—

After supper I had your letters—two—The mail is queer—connects in queer ways to get here—The letters of your last two days in New York—They make me sad—You as usual have a stomach ache—you haven't told me a word about your heart—I wonder if that is what keeps you awake nights—

I know how you feel about my being away—There seems to be no other way—It all leaves me with nothing to say—

I have missed writing you three or four days—some days I don't seem to have a moment when I can sit down and write—

—You are at Lake George tonight—I just know how it all looks and smells[63]—and sounds—I wonder—is Margaret going to fix your three meals—It seems queer to think of you getting into your little damp bed alone—and I not near you—and all the ailments you probably have that I some way feel I ease a bit even if you do growl a lot—

Tonight is the first night I have a real deep lonely feeling—that it isn't right for me to be away from you—but in another way it is the only thing I can do—

I have been working a bit—am glad I go out in the morning to work—I do hope the sun shines—I don't think I ever enjoyed working more—That doesn't mean that I think what I am doing so wonderfully good—it only means that it interests me—

I enjoy lots of other things here—but I don't think I enjoy anything more than that— Of course there are many things I want to work on—and the days fly—

Last night was moonlight and we took a long drive—out past a queer church that I have two daylight paintings of[64]—I wish I could do what I saw last night—the queer white windowless mass—and the terribly alive sky full of stars—the desert stretching on and on like the ocean—dark—

Good Night Little One—This seems to be my world—and I can't help it—

I had a letter from the Goodwin boy today—and some pieces of cloth he dyed for me— He left for New York today from Colorado Springs—

Good Night—I'll be going out across the alfalfa field to the Pink House in a moment —in the moonlight—and I'll send a kiss to the moon for you—

ON JUNE 14, 1929, Stieglitz and Emil Zoler, his gallery assistant, went to Lake George where he remained—except for two brief trips to New York—until O'Keeffe returned from New Mexico in late August. After the intense work he had done in New York to close the Intimate Gallery, Stieglitz had a difficult time adjusting to the quiet of Lake George and the absence of O'Keeffe. Instead of relaxing, he began to destroy much of the material he had only recently packed and sent to the Lake, now deeming as "unimportant" papers, books, and even works of art, copies of *Camera Work,* and his own photographs and negatives. As his agitation and loneliness intensi- fied, he slept poorly and obsessively watched the mail, worrying when he did not receive a daily letter from O'Keeffe and growing more angry as his lack of trust in her judgment mounted. His friends and family became increasingly alarmed by his mental state. When Paul Strand arrived in early July, he found Stieglitz extremely distraught and wrote O'Keeffe expressing his concern, as did Stieglitz's brother Lee. Despite their company, little could stem Stieglitz's loneliness or his fears that he had lost O'Keeffe forever.

---

63. A few days later on June 18, O'Keeffe told Stieglitz: "Lake George is a damp thought to me—I wish you could be here—really—I just feel so good I can't imagine anyone feeling any better."
64. San Francisco de Asis is a small mission-style church in the Ranchos de Taos; the paintings are Lynes 662 and 664.

Saturday night:

No mail goes out from here on Sunday—but I will give this to Mabel or Tony to mail tomorrow night from Santa Fe—

There was a doctors' convention here last week and Mabel had herself examined more thoroughly—The result is that she starts tomorrow night for Buffalo for an operation—She expects to be gone at least three weeks and maybe six—

All her invited guests are called off—the household to continue for the benefit of Miss Young—Marin—Beck—Tony and me—We offered to leave but she wouldn't hear [of] it—Her houses are all rented or given away except most of the big one—Most of that is empty—Beck is to be housekeeper—It will be all right—we can manage very well—

Mabel was in the studio this afternoon—she was much surprised at it—and remarked "Why it looks just like you." She liked what I have done with it—

This morning was a colorless morning—No real sun and a sandy wind blew up early so I didn't go out to work—I was quite disappointed—I spent the day in the studio—stretching and scrubbing canvases—and thinking much of you—It is your first day at the Lake and I wondered so much how everything is for you—I almost telegraphed to ask you—

Court is in session here now—everyone has gone court mad—Beck has been there all day—A murder case of some sort—I decided that was one activity I wouldn't take part in —Mabel says the court session is the opera season of Taos[65]—We had the judge for supper— murder—and judge—and judge's baby—and Spanish—they all talk nothing else—The Federal court is also in session trying some Indian case about Indian land—Tony says he is taxi man for the Pueblo—says he took sixteen Indians out in one trip tonight—They have court day and night while it lasts—

I liked being in the studio alone all day—am glad to get the canvases fixed—And I thought and thought about you—

After supper when they went back to court I sat with Mabel awhile then walked over here to the Pink House around the orchard—sagebrush on one side—the mountains beyond —apple trees on the other—and a border of flowers—here and there a little patch of garden— The moon over it all—New green paint on the gate to the path—Of course I got my hand all green—

They have been irrigating the alfalfa field for two days—Beck walks through it mud and all—I walk around—It is remarkable to see the way they get water to run any place they want it here—all over everything—

Well—I must be getting into bed—I didn't have any letter again tonight—there were two last night—and now will not have one till Monday night—

I am tired—and sleepy—

---

65. The murder that would set all of Taos abuzz occurred a few weeks later on July 3, 1929, when Arthur R. Manby, Mabel's landlord when she and her then-husband Maurice Sterne first moved to Taos, was found "with his head severed and chewed by his two fierce guard dogs"; see DeWitt, *Taos*, 9–10.

A kiss goes out into the night to you—My night is so different from your night—I just wish you could see it—It touches something in me that I so like to have touched—something that seems to be all of me—

I wish too that you could have seen the faces around the supper table—it was a curious company—Marin is just sparkling—has fifteen watercolors[66]—Mabel had them all spread out looking at them as one of her ceremonials before leaving—

Here goes the kiss—

Georgia O'Keeffe · [Taos, New Mexico] · [June 17, 1929]

Dearest—

Tonight there were five letters from you—the last ones written from New York—It all sounds pretty bad—and I know it all so well—

There is nothing for me to say—It makes me feel like being there and trying to take care of you—but I know so well what that leads to—too—

—So I am here—it is a beautiful moonlight night—I sat in the hammock alone a long time—looking out at the night—over the yellow rose bush—and thinking of what your night may be like—

—Everyone here had gone a different way tonight—I quiet and alone—and I liked it—

Mabel had asked me to write her for Tony—so after supper I asked him what I could write—She had told me I must be very careful—he very much minds not being able to write—And all he told me—about what he had been thinking and feeling and doing was so like what you or I would have written—I was very sorry for him—He looked so big and dark and handsome and sad as he sat there on a little wooden railing in the evening light—

She had told me he would probably refuse when I asked him—but he didn't—he talked right along[67]—We get on very well—a curious kind of understanding that lets the spots where we don't understand just slide—I like him very much—and I wouldn't like Mabel nearly so much if it wasn't for Tony—and I wouldn't—of course—have any contact with him as I have if it wasn't for her—Something between them is very close and very important to them both—

Good Night—Little One—

A kiss goes out into the night air to you—I hope you receive it warm and close—It needs to be warmly held—

[June 18, 1929]
Tuesday Night—

Painting all day and it's going well—I'm pleased as can be—A kiss.

---

66. See Sheldon Reich, *John Marin: A Stylistic Analysis and Catalogue Raisonné* (Tucson, 1970), 29.14–15, 29.17–41, 29.43–68, 29.70.

67. O'Keeffe wrote Mabel on June 17, 1929, that Tony said to tell her, "All the place all around is so sad when Mabel is gone away."

Alfred Stieglitz · [Lake George, New York] · June 21, 1929

Thanks for the signed papers.—They just came. 4 P.M.—

—So Fluffy is very much alive. No wonder—It is but natural—Too bad you are hitched up to this dead thing I am since last year.—But remember you are free—Always have been free[68]—

I have been thinking much since [coming] up here. And curiously enough particularly much this morning—of Fluffy.—And this dead useless thing I have become.—I have always held you know when I'm no longer really alive I'll be useless to myself & useless to myself, I'll be more than useless to everyone else—& most particularly to you—I can't fool myself. I simply can't.—I know life too well.—I know. Yes I do.—Not much, but a few things I do know.—

—It's great to know you so terrifically alive—Inevitably so.—It is odd how vividly I saw this morning the very thing you wrote about. I have been lying about all day—somehow not feeling much like moving about—Just the opposite of you.—You all alive—all of you—None of me alive—not even dead.—

There is a great wind blowing—Too great risking a sail on the Lake—And I'm glad in a way for I didn't want to go.—I have been reading George Moore—English—always beautiful—& Tod Sloan.[69]—I don't think I have spoken three sentences today.—Just can't open my mouth. And I like to be alone.—And am.—

My love to Fluffy—With all the sun she is getting she must be looking quite a wild one—Will I ever be fit enough again to make a real picture of her.—Of you?—My camera has come. I haven't unpacked it. Nor have I ordered any material.—

There is no hurry—You are all activity—I am all inactivity!

No wonder you are there—& I am here—I'm not even here.—

The New Yorker has sent me back the three small prints of you I let them have. Covarrubias has made a drawing of you. The article is to appear July 6.—I fear to see it.—I'm growing afraid of many things as lightning no longer seems to affect me!—

Another seven weeks & it will be eleven years that Miss Fluffy was actually initiated—during lightning & thunder—& later you, sweetest of all flowers—lay on the floor bandaged—& I photographed you—

You Most Beautiful One. Then—& Now!—?—

And forty-eight—really thirty-six—hours later another tiny visit—& then the Iklé picnic.—The first in the back room of Oaklawn—the morning in "my" tiny room next door.—It all seems incredible—& wonderfully incredible—

I kiss you—& I kiss Fluffy—& kiss all of you—and maybe bite you too—& stroke you—Maybe I'm not as dead as I believe I am—maybe I'm deader—

---

68. At about this time, Stieglitz appears to have sent O'Keeffe a letter Norman had written him in which the younger woman admitted it was "a little naughty of me to write along like this" (Norman to AS, June 14, 1929, originally filed with GOK to AS, June 1929).

69. A. Dick Luckman, ed., *Tod Sloan, By Himself* (London, 1915).

But I do know something you never will know—can't know—*What you really are to me*—

No, you can't know—have never known—won't ever be able to know—not while— oh! It's all so very right—

Alfred Stieglitz · [Lake George, New York] · June 23, 1929

There is a great wind blowing.—It's 3:30. I lay on my bed for half an hour.—Half asleep.— A loud knock awoke me.—No one there. I must have dreamt.—I have no idea what. I merely jumped up.—This wind will bring rain.—The weather has been hot & dry.—Today there is dampness in the air—but it's not bad—

I walked nearly to the post office—Alone. The car picked me up.—A letter from you —Sweetest One—The one in which you seemed frightened.—The moon—My first letter from Lake George—I think I understand—It's all too bad in a way.—Yet there seems no other.— Not just now.—I have written you quite a few letters since here which I haven't sent you. I really don't know why.—Somehow having written them I felt they should not be sent.—They contained nothing in particular.—I have nothing much to do here but vegetate—let down as much as a nature like mine will permit—& above all to think of you—of *US*. For I can think in no other terms.—I write about myself.—Am I?—I can't write about *US* because I find no language will express what I see & feel.—All words seem inadequate. Wrong in fact. Misleading.—Isn't the human being an impossible creature?—

—You ask how my heart is.—As long as you ask I might as well tell you that in New York for awhile I was a pretty miserable creature. Particularly for a week or two.—Between kidney & sinus, hernia, heart & stomach I had a time of it.—But having set my jaws to see the Room thro' I avoided hypodermics & doctors all I could.—I saw but one thing to do. And did it. —You being safe & happy I could see it thro'—Had you been here I would have probably caved in. Why?—Not that I didn't want you with me. Quite the opposite. But you see I knew for years that the Southwest was in your blood—in every fiber of you—I knew you'd have to satisfy that craving.—I knew too what Lake George had gotten to mean to you—whether rightly or wrongly—I knew your health—all of you—because of everything—needed to get away from what I seemed to be—& really wasn't—

It's all so complicated—Well, Sweetestheart, I know you understand—& yet sometimes I feel you cannot—not quite. I appreciate such contradictions.—

Well, here I am. Nine days of Lake George. For a few days I felt I'd cave in in spite of all philosophy—of all quiet.—But I think I have come through.—I'm sure I have.—I'm feeling much better.—My stomach is better. My heart is as all right as it can be. The proof is my walking.—My hernia isn't molesting me. My kidney behaves.—My sinus is virtually gone.— And I'm living as regularly as anyone can. The food is good enough.—Everything is done to make me comfortable.

—Of course I can't help thinking much of the future—Winters & summers.—Everything. But above all—Always you—US.—You come first.—And have come first even when you believed you didn't—& perhaps I made you feel you didn't.—

—Lee examined me this morning.—He seemed satisfied. And I certainly am. To be awhile without pronounced pain of some kind is very wonderful.—Much of my "trouble" I know is my nerves.—

—I hope you are satisfied with this confession!—

A kiss for listening—And many kisses to make you forget it—Yes, many, many—everywhere you'd enjoy them—

And you are working hard—painting hard.—Of course I can't have any idea what it all looks like—But you mustn't work too hard—altho' I realize why you should feel you must—

Remember it takes a lot out of you—But you know best for yourself—Or at least I have to think so even if I sometimes wonder whether you do.—

I kiss you on the abdomen—a long long fervent kiss—

ON JUNE 24, 1929, O'Keeffe, Beck Strand, and Tony Lujan drove to Mesa Verde, Colorado, to see the ancient cliff dwellings. From there they traveled south to Gallup, New Mexico, then on to Acoma Pueblo, west of Albuquerque, before returning to Taos on June 30. Like Willa Cather before them, they found the trip with Lujan a moving experience, and discovered, as Cather wrote, that traveling with him "was like traveling with the landscape made human. He accepted chance and weather as the country did, with a sort of grave enjoyment. He talked little, ate little, slept anywhere, preserved a countenance open and warm, and [had] unfailing good manners."[70]

Georgia O'Keeffe · [Pagosa Springs, Colorado] · [June 24, 1929]

Dearest—

—Well I wish you could see us and could have seen us all day—Tony is taking us to Mesa Verde—and it is a real party—

I didn't tell you we were coming because I wasn't sure till we finally drove off—

It is a wonderful drive—was all day today—and the things that happen along the way are as nice and as funny and as amusing as we are—The country varies from desert to the richest greens on the mountains—then there are other mountains that are almost bare rock—

Oh—we have all had a grand time—

We are paying him—He won't take anyone on this trip without pay—but after the first day I feel it more than worth the price—and he is so pleased to make money—He is really a remarkably nice person—

---

70. Cather modeled her character Eusabio in *Death Comes for the Archbishop* on Tony Lujan. As quoted by Lois Palken Rudnick, *Mabel Dodge Luhan: New Woman, New Worlds* (Albuquerque, 1984), 188.

Beck is in bed—asleep I guess—The place we are sleeping is the funniest you ever saw—

Well—you probably think I'm crazy—but I'm feeling remarkably like me—

—I will not be back in Taos if all goes well till Saturday or Sunday—Mail will not be forwarded as we will be moving all the time—

—I wish you could have seen what we saw today—only I fear at times the sheer edges of things would have made you a bit uncomfortable—

—A kiss to you Dearest from Your Crazy One—

A starlight night with a strong sulphur smell around—

Alfred Stieglitz · Lake George, New York · June 24, 1929 +

It's just nine o'clock. Night has set in. For over an hour I have poked the fire—& stood watching *Camera Work* & all else burn.—Five hours of burning. The yellow flames—*Camera Work* burns a marvelous yellow—greet the stars as they appear. It is windstill. And so silent.—So pleasantly warm.—What a day it has been.—I don't quite see where my sudden energies have come from. —I have not rested all day.—Simply couldn't.—

I had an hour's bath—windows & door open—no one in the house. Hot water first then very cold. Real pleasure.—But not comparable to the burning—There are several more wheelbarrows full ready for the flame—I may stay up & burn it all tonight.—Begin the morrow with a cleaner slate—I see much simplification in New York when I get back. Flames for many vaults of my stuff—Practically all *Camera Work* except the few bound sets.[71] All must go. And only in that way.—I want no more out in the world.—And many books will go too.—And rafts of letters. And clippings.—It's all so clear.—Negatives & prints too are in line. Everything that isn't satisfying to me.—

A marvelous cremation—

—Now I'll go out—& pile on some more—The silence continues. It is perfect.—

Good Night—

I feel very clean tonight—in every bit of me—I feel I have done a good day's work— the first in ages.

Good Night—I see some stars—

—Later. It's not quite midnight.—I'm so wide awake I hate the thought of bed. I'd like to go on the Lake now. It's a great still night.—

But I daren't be too foolhardy.

What a day like this has been.—What price, we'll see. It makes no difference. None is too high.—The fire burnt merrily to a little while ago.—And I have more ready for the morning. —I'm writing on the dining room table. More letters & photographs—still more magazines.— Endless truck—And some negatives.—I wonder how much will be left when I decide to return

---

71. Stieglitz bound a few sets of *Camera Work* in suede, one of which is now at the National Gallery of Art, Washington, D.C.

to town to start cleaning up there.—It's queer that I haven't a trace of feeling one way or another about it all—Still there is a relationship between this & thirty years ago it will soon be that I left Lake George for New York to burn all diaries & all letters.[72] —

What a terrible thought that they might still exist.—I see how wrong all those were who said I should not have done what I did.—And talked Freud & science & what not. I see it all in a very different light.—You have helped me to a new clarity—And once again I am in your debt in a greater degree than ever.—For I am in your debt.—

How still the night—I hear my heart beat as if it too were applauding what had been accomplished. It is a healthy heartbeat.—

Good Night—In Taos it is about nine o'clock—I hope it is another great night for you. —It is a night of wonder here.

Good Night.—A kiss.—

Alfred Stieglitz · [Lake George, New York] · June 25, 1929

Noon—Altho' I wrote you this morning that I would not write any more today here I am at it again.—The walk to the post office—no letter from you for a change—& caught in a downpour—stirred me up a bit.—I hope no letter means nothing.—I'm in such a state of tension that all sorts of miserable thoughts shoot through my head & I dare not let any of them take hold of me.—I must get busy at something more than destroying what has become as much rubbish. But busy with what—I find myself beautifully cornered—Laughably so.—And yet it is far from a joke. It's really rather serious business at my age & in my condition.—

Photography—So far even if I had material I haven't had the least desire to put anything down.—Of course I have old paper & could print. Today is a perfect "gaslight" day[73]—but in going thro' my trash yesterday I found a box full of very fine small prints—all to be spotted & mounted.—And I looked at them & wondered shouldn't I burn them up too. And be done with the business. But I didn't have the heart.—They represented real heartblood year before last—Didn't I often squirm with pain while working—ready to drop at times.—And the new paper I hear is atrocious.—So I didn't have the heart to destroy those prints.—Some are really very beautiful. And in my present state that is saying much.—

I took all the Hartleys down at five this A.M.—I just couldn't stand them. The bare walls look wonderful.—

How stupid it is that that heart of mine has virtually turned me into a prisoner. Some day I'll ignore it—& I'll do anything I feel I must do—heart or no heart. Rather death than living as I live. New York was bearable. But this is all new.—Terribly new.—Maybe good for my soul—if I have any left—I wondered in a letter to you whether there was such a thing.— Of course I really don't wonder—I know only too well there is one—A very tortured one I'm

---

72. Stieglitz told Todd Webb that shortly before his November 1893 wedding to Emmy, he burned the diaries he had kept since his childhood; see Webb, *Looking Back: Memoirs and Photographs of Todd Webb* (Albuquerque, 1991), 48.

73. "Gaslight" paper was designed to be printed by gas or electric light and did not require long exposures in bright sunlight.

well acquainted with.—But that has ever been my lot. There must be something radically askew with me.—

489 Park Avenue is to be torn down—that is the latest.—Mitchell (not Kennerley)[74] wrote me that. It isn't positive.—I haven't heard from Kennerley.—

Well, I at least am ready in that line at least. Everything is out of the Room but bookcases & chairs & headrest, a drawing board & a few items like that. When word is given to completely vacate, I'll go down & give the stuff away to Arthur or him & someone else.—

What worries me most is what address to use next year on dividends.—I'll have to make some arrangement with somebody—I don't quite trust hotels.—So you see there are problems like that of some importance.—And so it goes. You probably think why worry about all that now.—That's my curse. And yet it is that quality which has been of value to many—more to many than actually to me.—

I had hoped that 489 would remain awhile even if we were out—so as to keep it as a postal address. For that could have been arranged with tips!—For a time at least until there'd be some definite address.—I wonder will there ever be one for me? Can there be?

—I have hesitated to write you of all this. Hesitated to tell you that I was given definite notice by Mitchell (not Mitchell Kennerley) that early in May that Room 303 could no longer be ours after October 1 no matter what happened. He was very fine about it. Told me that if at all possible if the business continued they'd like me in the building.—But I counted on nothing. I saw pretty straight.—So you see Dearest Heart—it all seems so unimportant—yet to me I can't possibly see it that way. My age & condition & the whole situation undoubtedly make me see the matter more seriously than if I were a bit younger. Or if other situations were not quite so difficult.—But it's up to me to find a way—I hope I will have enough vision & strength left for that. In a way it seems like an eternity until the day of necessity will have come—but as I live that day is here—every day.—These are not words.—And that's why I do many things, & say many things, which I wish I didn't do & didn't say.—

You may wonder why I didn't let you know all this when it actually happened. As a matter of fact I hoped not [to] have to write it at all.—But today I feel I must let you know one of the things actually very much on my mind & which is not merely a state of mind.—Or maybe it is that after all. I wish I had some light heartedness. I never had any.—

There is the call for lunch.—I'll go.—

—I'd like to have you sit near me—& talk over many things.—I have often wanted that—even during the winter—But—?—Once upon a time we talked over *everything*. I suppose it's all my doing that it became different.—

Still the other day as I was thinking about everything—our whole togetherness— I remembered how going up the road from Oaklawn, right at the oak, you suddenly flared up & said you had to go alone for a long walk.[75] —I remember how tortured I was when you were away—two whole hours—I had no idea what had happened. I saw your going back to

74. R. Milton Mitchell, Jr., was treasurer of the Anderson Galleries at 489 Park Ave., New York; Mitchell Kennerley was its president.

75. This incident occurred in the summer of 1918.

Canyon—saw every possibility that means darkness to me.—Finally you came back.—Nothing was said except that you had had a great walk. You never knew what I had had during that great walk—In time—long, long afterwards, you explained you had resented my tapping your behind!—And I had been in bed with you for weeks & fondled & kissed you—had done everything but fluff you—How could I know what I had done—& why the walk?—And this in one form or another is characteristic of so many things that have come between us.—I innocent. You innocent at other times.—It's all too ghastly when people are actually as close as we are. The poison of resentments.—Poisonous as the poison of jealousy & that is accepted as the worst poison in the world—a deadly poison.—You see I must out with some of this. The stillness here—the absence of anything actual to do—the aloneness—relentlessly baring self—for somehow I have felt guilty of so many crimes—that at times life seems unbearable.—

It's all very good for the soul. And if I come out of all this as I hope to I'll be ready for anything.—Now please don't worry about me.—But I have had to open up—

It is grandly right where you are—it is not quite so right where I am. No place would be quite right.—I am tired beyond words.—And no one can help me but myself. This is a struggle with self to the bitter end.—

Remember I see you as white—wear what you will—

It is pouring—Maybe we are in for a spell of rain—I wouldn't mind it—I wouldn't mind anything.

I'll not reread this letter—for if I do I'll tear it up & I want it to go.—It must go.—

—Be good to yourself—and remember I'm always with you—as I know for me you are here always.—

And please do not for a moment imagine that you aren't doing absolutely the right thing in being where you are & enjoying it to the fullest—Of course it is a pity I can't share it all with you.—But me at my best would spoil what you are enjoying & receiving.—

—A kiss.

Georgia O'Keeffe · [Mesa Verde National Park, Colorado] · [June 26, 1929]

We arrived here yesterday afternoon at about four—

—This morning I was out in the starlight at 4:30 trailing down to a cliff dwelling—then on down the canyon and back for nearly three hours—

—After a bath and breakfast we drove around the rim—climbed down to a larger cliff dwelling—They are really remarkable—Some beautiful views—

I almost died on the way up yesterday—it was so grand—We are going down today and I'll probably die again—

Beck sends LOVE

We make a great party—Tony says he likes to travel with us—we don't make any fuss —I might add—we don't make any plans—we just start when we are ready and we all have about the same speed—

—I lay out under the stars last night a long time—really till I had been asleep several times—I would have stayed out all night but was too tired to make a bed—

Beck sends MORE LOVE—Tony says he sends BIG LOVE—Big as Mesa Verde—

We must eat—Are starting home a longer way after we eat—

Much love—

Alfred Stieglitz · [Lake George, New York] · June 27, 1929

I have already mailed one letter to you this morning.—I must add another.

I wonder do you remember that a few days before you left for Taos you asked me what I'd like done with my things in case anything happened to me.—I don't remember what I said. But I know that it could not have been anything positive.—But in my letter this A.M. to you I mentioned disposing of the photographs of Steichen & Company[76]—This naturally led me to think about my own photographs & other pictures I have.—I have decided to have one hundred of my best prints framed at my own expense & give part to the Metropolitan—the others to Boston.—The unframed prints will go to the Metropolitan. The duplicates I'll give to individuals.[77] I think this is the simplest solution of a difficult problem.—I had hoped there might be some moneys for them eventually—moneys to go to you & to Kitty & her son. But I see nothing but a mess ahead unless I do as I above suggest. And in a way as I really never worked for money it is fitting not to take any for my work after my death.

But what is in my mind chiefly is to free you from all bother & responsibility. It is not fair to myself to saddle something so incompatible to your very being.—

As for moneys—you'll have enough to protect you in a simple way.—Both your own money which you have earned—& the additional relatively small income from me. I have been working all these years with a very positive idea back of my head—& I fear you didn't *quite* realize its purport. But that is immaterial here—As for Kitty & her son I must assume her mother (his grandmother) & the uncle[78] will protect them financially as I have been led to believe all along would be the case.

76. In a letter written the same day, Stieglitz told O'Keeffe that he would send his collection of photographs by members of the Photo-Secession, including Steichen, to the Smithsonian. On August 7, 1929, he changed his mind, writing O'Keeffe that he decided to destroy all these photographs: "I dare not be sponsor for anything I know to be false. The Steichens are false. The Whites too.—And many others.... In time it might become history. But 'history' is false. And for the present my presenting the collection to the people would be entirely misleading—would be a betrayal of my own faith in photography." Yet, in 1933 he once again changed his mind and gave many of these photographs to the Metropolitan Museum of Art. After his death, O'Keeffe spent three years disposing of his large collection and gave many more of his photographs by others to the Metropolitan Museum and the Art Institute of Chicago. See Weston Naef, *The Collection of Alfred Stieglitz: Fifty Pioneers of Modern Photography* (New York, 1978).

77. Although Stieglitz continued to refine his collection of his own photographs throughout the 1930s and 1940s, he did not dispose of it during his life. After his death, O'Keeffe formed the "key set" of more than sixteen hundred of his photographs, which she gave to the National Gallery of Art. See Sarah Greenough, *Alfred Stieglitz: The Key Set* (New York, 2002), xi–xlix.

78. Probably Joseph Obermeyer, Alfred's college friend, the brother of his first wife, Emmy.

I'll give the prints to the museums in their names—Kitty's & Jr.'s[79]—I think that is the obvious thing to do.—It's queer how "things" will solve themselves.—

Of course if there are any particular prints you may want for yourself naturally they are yours. But I wonder wouldn't they eventually become a nuisance to you. All negatives except a few I'll destroy.

It is amusing how simple all this has become—how dreams have vanished into a clear cloudless sky—

I'm all smiles today—maybe because I'm so close to weeping.—Smiles are so much more becoming than tears. And smiles satisfy a vanity. And I must grow in vanity as I grow in wisdom.—And in that I feel I'm growing very suddenly. And without growing pains.—

As for "my" paintings, Hartleys, etc. I may return them to the artists.[80]—I must get rid of them.—The Marins I'm not clear about. But I'll solve that question before long.—

And of your things I consider but very few "mine." The blue & white drawing.—That I wish cremated with me.[81] That's the one favor I ask of you.—If it's possible for you to see to. But under no conditions must you put yourself out to see to it.—Such are my definite conclusions.—

It happens to be a very clear day—& amusingly a 27th too.[82]

I'll go to the post office now. Maybe there'll be a sign of life from you—If not I'll accept it as part of the "terrible rightness" of everything.—

A kiss—& thanks—

N.B. When I see you I will explain fully how I arrived at all this.—

Please don't lose this letter. I'd like to go over it with you.—It's really a memorandum —I must assume that you are occasionally giving some of these matters a thought in spite of Taos. But even if you don't this letter must go to you.—

—It must not disturb you. There is no reason why it should.—

A fond kiss.—

Georgia O'Keeffe · [Gallup, New Mexico] · [June 27, 1929]

Good Morning!

Well—the way I like a little dried raw western town—cooking in the sun—is just too ridiculous—there is a good one in the gray dirt against a rocky ledge outside the window—

But I must say that all three of us were glad to see a Santa Fe Hotel[83] last night with

446

79. Neither Stieglitz nor O'Keeffe gave prints to museums in the names of Kitty or Milton Stearns, Jr.

80. In 1933, as Stieglitz tried to reduce his storage bills, he destroyed a few paintings and drawings by Hartley, Steichen, and Pamela Colman Smith (see AS to GOK, Oct. 8, 1933), but he kept most of the works by other artists. After his death, O'Keeffe dispersed them to several American museums; see O'Keeffe, "Stieglitz: His Pictures Collected Him," *The New York Times Magazine,* Dec. 11, 1949, 24–26, 28–30.

81. Lynes 64 (see p. 21). In 1946 O'Keeffe did not include this drawing with Stieglitz's body when she had it cremated.

82. Fascinated with numerology, Stieglitz believed that 27 was "an evil omen" (AS to GOK, July 27, 1929).

83. O'Keeffe was staying at the El Navajo Hotel in Gallup, part of the Fred Harvey chain of "Santa Fe" hotels.

real beds and hot baths—When I waked this morning I said to Beck—"Civilization is pretty good"—And we had breakfast in bed—Tony would say like snakes—

Yesterday we drove almost all afternoon through the Navajo country—it is grand and desolate—and hot and dry—

After our [tire] puncture we had supper—found the hotel impossible—so at sunset we started on for another hundred miles for this place Gallup—It was a great night—very little talk—almost none—Tony singing—his monotonous soothing sort of *Hi yi* song—queer rock shapes looming up out of the desert at times—The sunset glow lasting hot and burning for hours—and a good road—none of us had been over it before—so we just rode into the night—

We met a large flock of sheep on a pass—and their eyes as our headlights came along were like a moving mass of phosphorous—

—It was a great night—Nearly 11:30 when we got here—and Beck couldn't get over my eating liver and bacon at that time of night and going right to sleep on it—

Well—it is a great trip we are having—

Looks hot out this morning—but I like to feel that hot wind blow around my ribs—

—When I saw myself in a real mirror in a real hotel room I realized I looked pretty black—I tell Tony I'm trying to catch up with him for color—and he tells me I'm doing pretty well—but I see I'm several shades behind him yet.

We will be going—

A hot wind takes you a hot kiss—or maybe a star—and a hard hard wind like we had last night—

Georgia O'Keeffe · Taos, New Mexico · [June 30, 1929]

Sunday afternoon—Taos—

Well here we are—safe and sound—Everyone says we are looking fine—and we know it—Marin was sick when we left—He is all right now—his wife[84] on the way here—

I started a letter to you yesterday morning—but didn't finish and have mislaid it—

Three nights ago we got lost in a woods where the timber was being cut—every road seemed to end nowhere—We finally slept in the car and on the ground with a fire when we got too cold—I didn't sleep at all—The night was so grand—it was one of the best parts of the trip—We had nothing for supper and breakfast but oranges and whiskey—It was funnier than I can tell you—Tony kept saying he was so "shamed"—when the gasoline got so low he didn't dare waste anymore in the dark—and next morning—when we were on the road he told us he was so shamed he almost cried the night before because he never was so lost before—It was very funny—

The next morning with only whiskey and one orange apiece under our belts we drove through the most pitiless desert I have seen with a blinding sort of white hot wind—

It was wonderful—sort of unbelievable—

---

84. Marie Marin.

When we got to food at about eleven A.M. I insisted that everyone go to bed till later afternoon—Then we got up and drove some thirty miles out to the Acoma Pueblo—It is a great sight—the mud village on top of a high—sheer—mesa—You climb up through deep soft sandlike snow—then through a crack in the rock—stone steps cut with places also cut for you to hold on with your hands—The finest thing up there is a church—a high—very high large white room—rough board floor—dull pink border about three feet high around the bottom— a gay somber altar—

It was very impressive and bare—and as I stood there—I thought—the most beautiful room I ever saw excepting 291—The sky clouded a little—just as we began to climb up the mesa—so the heat and wind were not as bad as it might have been and the sky was very fine—

From there on to Albuquerque—the night and good food—and yesterday from there up here—clouds and rain in the distance made it cool and made us all very gay—and the scenery grand—It was very fine and dark in color—

We stopped at Santa Fe to see Scott for a few moments—he sends you greetings— and to see Walker. I feel the same about Walker's paintings—you didn't see the best—He let me rummage through them all—I think it is the sort of thing you would like to show if you had the Room—I told him I felt that way about it—He was much pleased—His wife is a very sensitive lovely little person—He gave me a painting I liked very much—

The trip was quite perfect—Tony is certainly a rare one—Beck and I agreed today that we didn't know anyone who could have gone through six such days with us more beautifully—We being so wild and gay—and enthusiastic—and at other times so hot and tired—It was a great trip—.

Oh! I guess you think I am crazy to go off and tear about like that for a week—but I liked it very much—it seems to add a grand part to my life—

—Aside from your letters I had one from Mabel and two for Tony—I just had to lean up against a post when I read hers to me[85]—I will tell you of it later—It was like an awful crack on my head—It was about something between them—

I read his to him when he came outdoors after me a few moments later—And there we stood—He said he didn't want to talk—I told him he needn't—but—could I—After a few moments he said yes—It was a wonderful few moments—I wish you could have seen him—I have never seen a more beautiful expression—or a more beautiful way of meeting understanding—He is a very rare person—

I wrote Mabel last night[86]—pages and pages—trying to tell her what I feel about it all—She asked me to—It made me very sad—

---

85. Mabel Luhan wrote O'Keeffe on June 21, 1929, asking her to find out "whether Tony *really* cares for me as I do for him or not." If he did not, she continued, "I must get over caring for him or I will pass right out. So please tell me—I mean *find out* & tell me." She instructed O'Keeffe to "let me hear your *real* opinion soon."

86. In her letter to Luhan of June 29, 1929, O'Keeffe wrote: "Next to my Stieglitz I have found nothing finer than your Tony." She assured Luhan that "if Tony doesn't love you—according to my notion—nobody ever will—But love is a queer thing— I have rarely seen something in two people seem as welded together as I feel it between you and your Tony—but I feel you have got to let him live and *be* his way." She added, "I know that many people—men and women love Stieglitz—and need the thing he has to give.... I feel you haven't any more right to keep Tony utterly unto yourself than I have to keep Stieglitz—and if Tony

Then there were your letters—fifteen of them—and you wrote me others that you didn't send—You should send them all—whatever they are—What I feel you going through made me very sad too—Beck's mail was bad too—I feel there is something almost wicked about your being alone these days—

You tell me also that you will not have the Room for certain—That you would like to talk with me—Maybe I ought to go to you—

—The thing I want to say—you must put all those things about me out of your mind —don't be feeling sorry about things we couldn't help—The best thing all this is doing for me is that many of those old things are sliding away—I don't want you to feel hurt or disturbed over anything you have done to me—All I ask is that you let the things that I have done to disturb you slide away too—We mustn't be wearing ourselves and one another out with all that—it is just too foolish—

And remember—when I came away you promised to let me know if you really want me to come to you—even if it is only to talk with you—I am getting to feel free of so many things that I feel equal to almost anything—

Is there a chance to have exhibitions in the Anderson building if it isn't torn down— or shall we look for another place—or what have you in mind—You and I are together close and not to be worried about—You put yourself on anything else you want to do—I will be with you and come back to help you anytime you say—Do you understand?

I kiss you too—

—I hope to get to work again tomorrow—I feel full of it—It is a grand feeling—

You must just put all that heartache in your pocket—and just let down—those things aren't so bad—I think you need me to pet you a little—

—I have a notion you wanted to write to Ethel—I wish you would if you want to— I know she would like it—

Thanks—thanks for all the letters—You are very—very sweet to me—It was nice to have them even if they did make me sad—

A long—long kiss—

And I touch all your skin—all over—everywhere—

Alfred Stieglitz · Lake George, New York · July 1, 1929

No letters from you in two days—three just arrived. You are on your way back to Taos.—I can imagine the grander than grand trip you three had.—Just what you love above all.—I am not writing—Can [not possibly] express what I have to say.—I have written you at least forty letters

---

happens to go out to women with his body—it is the same thing when one goes out for a spiritual debauch." O'Keeffe ended the letter by noting, "I'm having a grand time just being ME—I think I would never have minded Stieglitz being anything he happened to be if he hadn't kept me so persistently off *my* track." Luhan responded on July 5, 1929, assuring her that she would never leave Tony "except to *die*," and she admitted, "I *do* hate to see him smile at others—love others—swell up & be civil for others."

during the last two weeks—all forty going into the fire. They seemed like so much nothing—like this Hill compared to what you are experiencing!—You will understand—I love you that's all you need to know.—I can add nothing but a gentle kiss.—

I just wired you.—I don't know why. But felt I must. I have hesitated about so much—I couldn't about that. Someday I'll get over this crazy obsession that has a stranglehold on me now.—Overtiredness undoubtedly. And maybe I'm too fond of—maybe you—It must be that—

Kiss.

Georgia O'Keeffe · [Taos, New Mexico] · [July 2, 1929]

Dearest—

Last night I read most of those ten letters to Beck—my second time—I in bed—she sitting on the rug in front of the fire—When I got to the last one I just turned over and wept and wept—She just sat—finally I gave it to her to read—it was rather intimate but it was so beautiful I felt it a shame to keep it from her—

—And oh dear—What can I say to it all—To your being there alone and suffering alone—I am in such a rush—and an uncertainty from Mabel keeps us all not sure that we will do what we intend to—But just the same we are getting ready for the rodeo over the 4th—and between that and your letters I feel I am hanging in mid-air.

My painting of yesterday[87] is a knockout—in a way—

—We both have bought black sateen workmen's shirts for ninety-five cents—I have a string—four strings of white Indian beads to break the front—Beck has a mass of stuff—Maybe Tony won't take us when he sees us—I have a silver ring with a large black stone—she has bunches of blue hearts—

Crazy—Maybe—I don't know how many Indians he is taking—but I think a car full—

This was all started before I had your letters—I almost stayed at home—but I won't—Tony says when we leave this house we must forget all things that make us sad—we can't help—He is a great one—

Well—my Little One—with things moving so fast—this is the best I can do—

The reason I didn't write you about Mesa Verde was that we didn't know till we were off whether we were going or not—Mabel kept it hanging in the air—

We will probably be gone four days this time—

Love and a kiss—a very tender dear one

ON JULY 2, O'Keeffe, Beck Strand, and Tony Lujan, along with four Native Americans—Fernando, John Marcos, John Concha, and Lupe—drove first to Santa Fe, then on to Las Vegas, New Mexico, where they saw a rodeo on July 4th. Although O'Keeffe told Mabel Luhan she drank too much whiskey two days in a row, she had no remorse and "came out clear as

87. Lynes 669.

a whistle…much more clear than usual—with a fine neutral feeling—all emotion gone."[88] O'Keeffe was most impressed, though, by the dance performed by Tony, Fernando, Marcos, Concha, and Lupe at the Meadows Hotel in Las Vegas—"I quite lost my head," she wrote Mabel.[89]

Georgia O'Keeffe · Santa Fe, New Mexico · [July 2, 1929]

Greetings from Santa Fe—!

Tony just left us—Beck is in the bathtub—and I'm going to get in—

It was a beautiful ride down the canyon—sunset—we got here at dusk—a little after eight—A cool lovely drive—Tony, Beck and I on the front seat of the Cadillac and four singing Indians wrapped in sheets—all but their faces—on the back seat—Tony thinks we look grand in our black sateen shirts—only he doesn't like us to look so black—it's too sad—but just the same he wants a shirt just like it so we will all look black—

Beck says bath is ready—and we must get to bed—

That black night that is starlight sends you greetings and a black starlight kiss—

[July 3, 1929]

Good morning—5:30—

I seem to have been awake for hours—I am propped up—under a yellow blanket in the most ornate blue and silver bed you can think of—So grand—three large windows wide open—a cold stone floor that feels fine to your feet when you get up and walk about—

I seem to need very little sleep out here—everything in one seems to be heightened to a very lively pitch and I just feel like going—I lay here since long before dawn thinking of you and of your letters—I wonder if you want me to come to you—

I must tell you something else I have done that I haven't mentioned to you before— The second day I was here at Mabel's Tony and Beck took me out on the back road and proceeded to teach me to drive Mabel's Ford—

Well—Tony doesn't laugh readily—but I can tell you he almost died laughing at me —Four or five days later I got a Ford—and after much struggle and much rough talk from Beck I mastered it—

I have been driving by myself for about five weeks—It is very good to work in— and a fine feeling to be able to do it—I am not very wonderful at it yet—I am very careful— Beck gets irritated with my carefulness—Tony agrees with me—better to go slow than to have anything happen—I didn't want to tell you till I felt quite safe about it all—Of course we go out with Tony a lot—but everyone on the place is busy and I couldn't ask them to take me out to work—

Anyway—it is something I wanted to do—I made up my mind to it last year and now I have done it—Beck paid half the license and insurance—So we are quite free to go about when

88. GOK to Mabel Dodge Luhan, July 6, 1929.
89. GOK to Mabel Dodge Luhan, early July 1929.

and where we choose—You will probably tell me you knew I was going to do it—Well—I have done it—So now I have told you about the worst thing I've done since I'm away—I said *about* the worst—I just should have said the *worst*—

—Now that is the way I am—If I had been alone I would have done it years ago— I think you should be glad whether you are or not—

—I'm going to get under the yellow blanket again and see if I can sleep a little—I've wanted to tell you about that Ford all along—but it just didn't seem to be time—

—I wish you could be here in this bed with me—it is very grand—

And—I wouldn't mind being fluffed—I wonder if it is the altitude or not being fluffed —We are both certainly keyed to a pitch to tear the roof off—

I kiss you—

Alfred Stieglitz · Lake George, New York · July 4, 1929

7 A.M. The house is still. And the morning gray & winterlike.—Certainly most abnormal condition for this time of year. For the fourth morning forty degrees! Iceland's relation.—And I am downstairs. Sitting in a coat.—I have been running about with little on (for me) these days, no vest like in the last few years, but real summerlike. But this morning a coat in the house is compulsory.—Yes, the house is very still. And in the grayness out of doors nothing seems to be stirring either. I got some sleep. Took a pill. And slept in your bed!—The Engelhards arrived for a three day stay. Sel is expected today. Was to come yesterday. That's why I have your room. Will stay there.—It matters little where I am—but as I have to be somewhere I'll be there.— The Engelhards go to Denver—a suburb or so—I don't know, for their holiday.—No Lake George. Sel I hear goes to Europe!?—

What a day yesterday.—Hell let loose. The day before I felt like [one] reborn—full of light—full of vim (for my age!)—Yesterday? The reaction. No sleep.—All night eyes wide open. And above all the fourth day & not a word from you!—Child, why will you do that?— You don't feel like writing? It interferes with your freedom?—Or are the mails so cruel. Will many letters come together?—Lying awake with all the what I am not & would so like to be for you. All the idle speculation. All the fears. All the actual realization of all that seems gone forever—& so little light for me in the future.—And this loneliness.—And there is no escape for me. Place doesn't count.—People do not count. If it weren't for Zoler I'm sure I would have put an end to it all.—These are not idle words. Nor must they disturb you. But at one time we could say all to one another—happy time! The only real relatively happy time in my life— yet the background was tragedy for me—And gradually somehow for reasons I see & yet do not fully grasp—a silence developed at moments in both of us when there should have been no silence. In these silences born of mutual hurts the seed of what is *today* was sown. And what is today for you I seem not to know.—What today is for me I know too well.—That you *had* to go I know.—It was of my doing & because of what inherently you are—that part of you I could never satisfy except in one way.—But I dare not go into it—it excites me much too much —it doesn't help the heart—& finally if I continue to be so useless—I know the inevitable.—

I cannot stop it.—But I know the cure for myself.—These are not idle words—Will they mean anything to you beyond mere words—You need say nothing I will know without—

I have certainly done my best—& maybe more—but I see all the things I have failed to do.—To undo those it's too late.—Your blue & white drawing[90] I wish cremated with me is life itself—but a child put its finger on it—& left a spot.—And that spot always hurt me.—And I have never gotten over that hurt—You laughed.—That hurt & that laugh that's what has done it all. Done what?—Just life exposing itself through you—through me—& us together & apart.—Life!—

I'll go out & walk awhile—everywhere I see you—I dread the sound of voices.—

A kiss Sweetestheart.—The mails are very cruel. I do hope nothing has gone wrong—or that you are ill in any way.—All crazy ideas shoot thro one's head!

The morning mail has come. No letter. No sign of life.—I am tempted to wire Beck but I don't want to introduce God knows what because I am so unfortunately what I am! I'll continue to wait—

Again that waiting!

Georgia O'Keeffe · [Las Vegas, New Mexico] · [July 4, 1929]

Dearest—Dearest—Again what a time—

I waked this morning after a good sleep—and just couldn't tell where I am—Then it finally came to me—Las Vegas—and after that I remembered the rest—A little town—so raw that it just touches the bottom of your soul—but I can't tell much about that—except that I feel terribly in tune with it—And Beck and I riding about in that big car with our five Indians are not the least part of the spectacle—Everything is gay with flags and lights—There is much dark skin—and many pairs of eyes that seem to look through to your back bone and then on to the rest—

But last night was the thing—it is as tho everything drops out of me when I remember it—and I put my hand on my head to see if it's still there—The Indians—when we found them after supper had changed from a kind of quiet reserved lot to something so moving and alive—When we asked—Tony said they wanted to dance—Well after much consultation—it was decided to go to a hotel and dance and see if they could make some money—So they went back to where they lived and in a few moments emerged with the most astonishing array of feathers and blankets and bells—

But their clothes were not as astonishing as what had happened to them—It can't be told about except that it just seemed they couldn't stand or be still—

We all rode through the town again to the dancing place—and when we got there—and they got out—sheets and blankets came down—and bless you—two of them were practically naked—but what they did have on was grand—

90. Lynes 64 (see p. 21).

We were sent in ahead to sit with the other people and in a few moments Tony and two others stalked in after us in their handsomest blankets—Tony a burning red—the other man his age in the same red and black blue [blanket]—the younger one in a sheet—They stood up against a counter and began singing and then the other two came in—

Well I can't tell you about it—The finest one[91]—one of the tallest Indians—I had thought of him before as beautiful like a beautiful woman—very fine long hair—and a very beautiful face—not just features—but beautiful from the inside—and such a beautiful body—and what a change from his smiling softness—All—every fiber seemed to go off like fire—and —the way he enjoyed it all—

I just almost died—

It wasn't just the dance—It was the human thing that happened—the transformation and the pleasure in it and their laughing after it—

Dearest—it is stupid to try to tell about anything like it—It can't be told—

Then the younger Indian—Tony's nephew—as he stood beside the car talking with me —after we drove them home—They have the most astonishing self composure—till they seem almost stupid—then they get so terribly alive—and in between were some moments when they meet you with everything—all at once—

454

Well—that was something that couldn't happen twice—such a night—because I couldn't be surprised like that again—

It is certainly a rare time we are having—Beck and I talked long into the night— Today for the rodeo—and I think the boys intend to dance out there—

We will see—It is the 4th—

My kiss goes through this raw little town—O

Alfred Stieglitz · [Lake George, New York] · July 5, 1929

Another gray & threatening morning.—I'm downstairs. It's seven.—The sleeping potion gave me sleep.—Till six. And then I lay in your bed wondering will a letter come. And what will it bring me. Peace or torture?—Will a telegram come—I believe my mind is sick—Has been for a long while. If it weren't I couldn't have written you as I think I have. This long distance— oh, so many things!—You know how you felt when I was in the hospital[92] & you thought I might die & you'd be left alone with feelings that weren't fine about me—Well, Sweetestheart, I know thro' all this week of torture exactly what you felt & how—but I also know that I was innocent—that all you saw was not at all as it was.[93] —I know that—I'm not deceiving myself nor you.—This is all too serious not to look at facts squarely. Too serious for me. It's all I have here. The chance to face all facts—the truth—squarely & should it finally cost my life—

---

91. GOK wrote Mabel Luhan that John Marco was "the most perfect specimen of an artist that I have ever seen—His dance was so beautiful—so terribly alive" (July 6, 1929).

92. Stieglitz was hospitalized in June 1926 for kidney stones.

93. Stieglitz was probably referring to the incident in August 1926 when Eva Herrmann said she had seen him kissing the cook Ilse.

Somehow I feel that what is ailing me is that as you left that something which was between us — something really holy — & which gave me strength — was not quite that for you anymore. And when McBride often said: You have each other — I wondered. — I should have said much to you which was breaking my heart all year — & last year — & year before — & kept still. And that's what made me [fret] & say what you called complaining things to others. — It's all so clear to me now when I have nothing else to do but think — & try to get something straight within myself — so that when the end comes I can feel at peace — I cannot live this life of torture. And uncertainty is the only Hell for me. — I can understand but I cannot stand uncertainty. — You auto much — you do many things you have to do that make me wonder — something might happen. You might be ill. — The not knowing. — Don't you understand. — You may feel I must learn to get rid of such thoughts, take for granted all is right — and I try my level best — & succeed most times. But when you let me wait six days for a sign of life — & who knows whether not longer — I simply cannot stand it. It is cruel. Terribly unfair to me. I can't believe you have a purpose. And yet who knows. In my condition I even begin to doubt the sun. — I the believer. Maybe Taos is teaching you that that is the way — I don't know. — Maybe it's stupid to be in love. — To have a heart. All weakness. All meaningless. To live & be — without thought of other — maybe that's the way. — I don't know. — I don't say that you are that. But maybe Taos teaches that — If it does I can't learn it — it's too late for me. — I'm perfectly ready to go. I have served as well as I know how. — And when I'm no longer needed I go. — You said in the winter I needed you no longer when I knew I needed you more than ever. And I was silent. What was I to say. If you didn't feel it, that great need, I had no choice but silence. — And why do I say it now. I'm forced to. Because I'd like you to understand some things about me which are true — if you care to understand them — You see the doubt that has infected me. You doubted me. And I never doubted you. But these few weeks with no word from you — my own condition — they seemed to introduce so much really foreign to my nature — altho' it couldn't have been foreign otherwise it wouldn't be as it is. — Maybe I'm just sick — & you innocent — as I was innocent three years ago — & you not right. — But it was the beginning then of something lacking the beauty of the former years. — Georgia — I wish I could make you feel what I feel — if I could I'd be willing to go at once — Not molest you anymore with letters that are not beautiful — letters full of weakness which you so hate — or should I say repels you. — I ask for little. — It has come to asking. — You see the degradation. —

— I'll walk now. — And I'll wait for the mail. I won't go to the post office — I can't watch that box. — And maybe by noon there'll be a telegram. —

Don't be angry with me. — Remember I am sick in mind. And I'm not indulging myself. — I'm endeavoring to get well. Walking may help. Sleep may help. — Time may help. — And you if you wish to. —

Goodbye —

In my condition I dare not touch you — it might contaminate —

9 A.M.—Later. I just came from the Village. Drove down with Albert[94] when he went for the mail.

Well, Whitest One, finally a letter from you. I reeled for a moment & someone caught me as I was about to fall. Just the sight of the envelope I clutched—You certainly see a mad weak Alfred these days—

Your letter breathes real health—real Georgia.—What you say is all true—You have found yourself—are yourself—all health & life—as I wish it for you. That's what I've wanted all these years.—But can't you see me here.—Your ghost everywhere—& I lonely beyond words—lonely not alone because you not here—gone so long & still be gone long—all of which is all right—for you—& so for me—but because I see no work ahead for me. Not even photography.—I had many things I wanted to photograph but the opportunity has been taken away—I had much to say that won't be said.—Life has willed it otherwise.—What you wrote about Mabel & Tony—I somehow knew. Not particulars. They are immaterial. It's queer how I do see straight—& know. And yet with all the knowing can do nothing whatsoever for myself.—That's my real tragedy.—I knew last winter when I saw Mabel. Knew thro' every letter you wrote. Knew—oh! just knew.—

—You say maybe I need some petting. Maybe I do.—But I must not indulge in the thought.—

—No, I don't care to write to Ethel.—I have nothing to say.—Nor am I thinking of exhibitions next year. All I know is I *must* get the stuff in *storage* in order. A most uninviting job—but it's up to me to do it. For you & Marin I am ready. Maybe for Dove.—But all others will have to go elsewhere. I have no more to give.—Have not the strength. The job is too heartbreaking.—

I have proven something to myself—that the impossible is possible if one insists in making it so—but then one must *give* all of self for years & years—& with the eyes set starward I have done that—My star is hidden. I know where it is. And my inner eye is not as clear as it was. So I regret that I can no longer be of service to the young—You & Marin & perhaps Dove—and the things in order—& given away—winding up my activities—preparing to go as I have lived—not in a mess—but like "291" was—& looked. As you saw it. That was I—at my purest.—The Room was an adulteration.—

Still—I know you are ready to come at any moment—but you need Taos—& I want you to have what you need most—& you are serving there as well as receiving—I shall manage now that I have your letter—It is a very, very wonderful letter—& I kiss you for it.—There is a bit of peace within me—I'll go ahead & do what I still must do—And I'll not torture myself anymore when letters do not come—

I'll learn to smile—& say: it's Georgia's way. And as for our common hurts—You have buried yours.—You have buried them in Taos.—As for me I have no burial place—I'll have to work them out into some form which I still don't know.—

Goodbye—& Greetings to Taos—

It's fine you have a Walker painting.—I knew I hadn't seen his best.—

94. Albert was Lee Stieglitz's chauffeur.

Later. I had this letter in an envelope sealed. I read your letter again. Twice. Three times. Drank in every word. To gain the strength I so sorely need—I feel it growing.—You are a very grand person—woman—child or what you will—a fine being—so rare.

I'm sorry beyond words about Tony & Mabel. Every day while you were there I had it in my mind—I wanted to write to you about it—But I didn't dare—There are books & books I could write to you—but you are to paint—& live—not write letters. Just to let me know you are alive.—One word—Well—Great God, you Sweet Dearest Soul, you don't know that that one word would be enough. But it's not your way.—And I must learn to accept your way.— Don't I carry the reminder with me all the time—I know too well—& know so little—One thing I know before I can be of any use to you or anyone else I must find my equilibrium once more. I thought I had found it the other day but to find the next—just because no word from you for a few days—that I was worse off then ever.—

Don't misunderstand me about Walker & the young.—I'm interested as much as I can be interested. I have buried much. Yes we are together—very much together. In a way I have been the leader—now it must be we lead together—or I give you the right of way.—

My vision is not clear these days—altho' I see—but as I have said the star is veiled —hidden—the first time in my life—my guiding star.—

Maybe you'll help me find it—remove the veil.—

Alfred Stieglitz · Lake George, New York · July 6, 1929

It's 5:30 A.M.—I couldn't stay in bed any longer. Altho' I walked twelve miles yesterday & took a pill the night was restless.—I slept till two—& then got up—went to bed again. Lay awake & thought of your letter. Lay awake a long time. And thought & was very quiet. I fell asleep & dreamt you had come & we were in the bathroom together—both naked—You turned around stooped down & with your hands pulled Fluffy open—I had a terrific erection—Fluffy looked like the big *Black Iris* which next to the *Blue Lines*[95] is closest to my heart—& as I took hold of you—& rammed my Little Man into you, you said with sighs—sighs so deep so heartbreaking—you must leave him no matter what happens. And I saw Fluffy—I saw him wet & shiny ramming into Fluffy & felt like God must feel.—And you were beside yourself & your smooth behind seemed to grow a bit larger—& it moved—& you pushed—& you seemed to wish to suck in—& I rammed & rammed & you seemed to want to hold him—& yelled: Don't take him out—I'll hear that voice to my dying day—the agony of it—& I moaned, No, no, it dare not be—I & mine are accursed[96]—And I drew him out. Wet, erect—panting—You crying. I half mad.—I awoke. No wet dream.—Even that I seemed to control.—Thank all that is that I had this dream.—I have had no dreams in ages—any kind. Not awake. Not asleep.—And life without my dreaming is terrible.—

---

95. Lynes 557; Lynes 64 (see p. 21).

96. After his daughter Kitty was diagnosed with schizophrenia, Stieglitz thought he might have a genetic defect and did not want O'Keeffe to become pregnant.

—But as I lay awake then much became clear. And I shall not hesitate to tell you some things in my mind—in all of me. Because it is mostly not my mind—but all of me.

You write in your letter you said to me before leaving if you need me just let me know. What you said in the taxi was: if you get sick, you must promise me to let me know at once. You promise.—And I promised.—Quite different you see.—

—And in letters—quite a few—you told me that you always felt not well in Lake George & felt so perfectly well in Taos & so completely happy & free. Now Sweetheart, don't you see even had you said what you write you said, about being ready to come to me if I asked you to—you made it absolutely impossible for me to ask [even] if I died—You are well there—& happy & free. Here, not well & miserably not free.—And as I love you & not myself how could I under any condition ask you even if I were dying, ill & had promised to let you know. —That's number one.—

—Two.—When you painted the Brixey picture[97] I knew my fate.—The inevitable.—And when Mabel Dodge & Brett appeared I knew my fate. Every time a postal came from the West—I knew my fate.—And when Dr. Jenks said before we left for New York "He must not go over 2,000 feet"[98]—I saw the fatality—the inevitable separation of this summer. And how Sweetheart do you think I felt. What do you think all that did to me. You couldn't help the call anymore than I can help the diseased consciousness of responsibility of a certain type.—

—In 1923, the year Kitty became ill—you know what that did to me—then Marie came—unfortunate days—& you know as she went you went.[99] And what I suffered those days Strand & Beck witnessed. And they very kind. Very.—And on the day Strand photographed me —the picture in Rosenfeld's book[100]—I was half mad & said: "I'm not so sure Georgia will come back. If she isn't back by tomorrow night she'll not return." Neither he nor Beck understood. It was the 27th the next day.—You came.—You had hardly arrived [when] you had words with me about Beck & her getup. And I was amazed you returned that way.—But that night as we were in bed together—kissing—holding each other very tight—you said kissing me: "You know Dearest I nearly didn't come back." I said nothing. But I knew my fate.—We kissed & fluffed & you in tears said: "Sweet One, I must never leave you again. Never."—I heard but knew what the next spring & summer would bring. And they did.—And so every year—Until last year the two years had grown into four.[101]—I understood it all. But I always felt that I was as much the center of you as you were the center of me.—

—But this time, Sweetestheart. This time. And that is what has nearly killed me. And if it weren't for Zoler this letter never would have been written. No letters. I must tell you. For I couldn't stand the torture—the pain. It was all too terrible.—It was not myself I thought of.—

97. Lynes 608.

98. After Stieglitz's first attack of angina in the fall of 1928, his doctor Edwin Jenks said he should not go to high altitudes.

99. Marie Rapp Boursault, Stieglitz's former secretary from 291, visited Lake George for ten weeks in the summer of 1923 with her young daughter, Yvonne. O'Keeffe left for York Beach, Me., on September 7, 1923.

100. Paul Strand, *Alfred Stieglitz*, 1923, reproduced in Paul Rosenfeld, *Port of New York: Essays on Fourteen American Moderns* (New York, 1924), opp. p. 237.

101. O'Keeffe went to York Beach in 1922 and 1923, and again in 1926. She went to Wisconsin in 1928.

But solely you—& us.—Something that had been was no longer—So I felt it. And not because of me really. Yet I was part of it.

—I had complained about you in minor ways. But my God—I was canonizing you day & night—for thirteen years—as no woman living or in the past was ever canonized. And today yet I am doing that altho' in spite of all quiet & acceptance I grovel in the dirt.—Not a man. Not a woman—Just nothing. Really nothing to myself.—All else means nothing but words.—

Well, I came to town hardly out of bed[102] & jumped into harness against your wishes. But I had no choice. It was the last year of the Room. I knew it. You wouldn't believe it.— And I knew I had to complete—at least partially—something begun. And work to liberate you economically & liberate Marin—& if possible help others. I wasn't strong all winter—reserved every bit of energy for the Room to do what I saw *had* to be done.—You were ill too. Very much.—The Room meant less & less to you as Room. You finally called it my sitting-room which stabbed me to the quick. What you meant to this day I don't know.—In some ways I'm very dense.—And then that same day, it wasn't long before you left, [you said] that I no longer cared for you—you had grown older & I cared for younger ones. Georgia, Georgia have you any idea how cruel these remarks.—How unfair.—I adoring the ground you stood on—I singing your praises to all—just because a few young people came to the Room—you could say what you did. But I said nothing—

And when you came into my bed—I fearing to infect you more with my sinus & with a throat you knew nothing about—[that] was not what I felt so much like being—I'd send you to your bed. The other room.—Why that separation? To protect you from me. Yes,—I know, I know, all diseased—fear to harm you.—Just as I stopped photographing you nude[103]—because once you caught cold—& just as I never fluffed you out in the open—as I so badly wanted to— because I feared dirt might get into you.—Yes, fear for you.—Not for myself except thro' you.— Don't you see a little—Of course it's all so contrary to your way of living. You are fortunate not to know many things. And I helped you to keep away from knowing to keep you as you are.—

And then when you came to the Room one day & had hardly sat down—Mrs. Norman sat reading Marin's letters. You without even having nodded good day—sharply said: "I do not want you to read my letters."—I nearly sank into the ground. As if I'd let anyone have your letters—Sweetestheart—& certainly not another woman—no one. Great Stars—don't you see what all this showed me—how little really you were feeling for me.—How little we were *together* any longer—Not because of me—really not—& still I was part of it.

—And during the year you didn't help me with a photograph. Showed no interest. And I had hoped & waited—But you were ill—were hardly interested in your own work—but it hurt. Our photographs.—And I felt they must not be shown in the Room.—And as I look back & see the Room I see why I never showed them. They were of 291—& ourselves both at our purest—The Room—oh, that Room—And I a salesman before the world. I really do not mind.

---

102. Stieglitz's attack of angina was in September 1928. He and O'Keeffe returned to New York in early November and opened the Intimate Gallery on November 14, 1928.

103. Stieglitz made only one nude photograph of O'Keeffe in 1922 and none again until 1931 (Greenough 827, 1438–1444).

Why not?—And a most excellent one.—All spirit lost sight of—even by you Sweetestheart—
or you could not have said "sitting room."!—But I don't hold it against you. Nothing against
you. I'm simply trying to tell you something about ourselves—You where you are have no time
for such inactivities as these—mine here.—But I live in the land of ghosts—I sleep in a bed of
[a] ghost—and the future is blank.—

—The future?—It is up to you to help me form it.—I have no desires. No vision.—
Even if I had a Room Marin has failed to frame his work.—It can't be gotten ready.—You!
I don't know what you have in mind.—

You see when you sprang Europe on me—that too nearly killed me. And even tho you
did remark, "If I waited for you I'd never get there," I knew that wasn't true—But you told me
how you saw me.—It was McBride who steered you Southwestward. Not I.—I dared not say a
word. You had decided.—You & Beck.

—The future?—You must tell me how you [see it]—For yourself if you can. Or as well
as you can. We must be 100 percent open with each other again—not silent—Won't you Dearest. Don't try to spare me—for that kills me.—In sparing me I become silent—& all wrong.
And that affects you in turn—& everything becomes wrong between us—Without you I am
nothing. Without me you go right ahead—will be Georgia O'Keeffe. The fact is you really do
not need me anymore. It is not as you wanted me to believe [that] I didn't need you.—Do not
think I'm just saying this. It is true.—You do not need me. Maybe someday the need will be
there again. And I'll exist in my purest form—impersonal. Exist for you as spirit—as I existed
as person before you came & we lived together.—That's why I felt I must go—so as to live for
you.—All this written is so raw. I could say it so much better.—I'd see your face. I know what
you'd feel. And my words would have a sound. Written they are but half-sounds—if any sound
at all.—

The future? If you have any wish, say it. I'll help make it good if in my power. You
must help me.—The order in storage—I doubt my being able to stand more than two weeks
of it—I know it would end up my destroying everything—for it has all become more or less
dead. The dream I had can never return.—And it was a dream that could have been turned into
a reality—a wonderful one—as you as painter have become a reality—& Marin a reality. So I
could have become a reality—not as photographer but a much bigger thing—But it has mostly
been left to me. And alone I'm helpless. My reality consists of more than one—You should know
for if you don't know who should—But I wonder whether you know—I know so little these
days—know too much—

Didn't you write you doubted whether I'd care for you there: Is it gay clothes &
hilariousness—smoking & drink—Oh! What matter these? There can be chastity in all these—
But even if chastity were gone—there'd always be that Georgia for me. Canonized including all
& everything that's Georgia.—Your paintings will tell me all—if I be privileged to see them—

The future?—I am free. Freer than you are. For I haven't a single wish except the one to
be with you awhile if you should feel you'd like to be with me.—It must be a mutual need.—

—The time is not ready for you.—I am ever ready like I was ever ready in the Room—
at 291.

The future? An apartment?—A studio? Go south?—A trip to Europe next spring?—What?—I cannot see myself sitting in a room pleading for the young with a broken heart—I need real help—need a heart that occasionally beats with mine. Do you know this is the first time in thirty-seven years that I have not a woman near me to care a bit for me. Even tho Emmy hated me—she did things for me—And you have been so good to me for eleven years[104]—

I see the needle case—& butter case—& all the things you arranged for me. They remain untouched. Oh! I know I am a fool—a terrible fool—but you loved that fool for years —It's the fool in me that you feel when you think of 291—It's even the fool in me when we fluffed you loved—

I can't go on.—The day is clear & quiet.—The locomotive is puffing—It must be about seven—I must go up & wash & shave & clean my teeth & take Carlsbad.[105] —

Please don't forget I am ready to do your bidding.—If I didn't know it would upset your freedom I'd even come to Taos—I'm not afraid—I'd rather die where you feel happy & well than rot here in my own misery.—

—I'm really quiet.—Altho' the letter may sound anything but quiet.

A long, long neverending kiss—I'd like to die in your arms—perhaps that's my great wish—it always was.—

N.B. When I say I'm free this winter for the first time in years I mean: There is no Room. There are no promises. Marin has money for quite awhile. And you have become independent.—I started out to get $30,000 for you—$1,500 a year. Believing that would protect you—then it was $50,000—$2,500 a year—I seeing that $1,500 inadequate. Then I set $70,000—$3,500 a year. And when you were ill so much—I set it $100,000—$5,000 a year! Well, there is about $80,000 & if not squandered when I'm no longer here to guard you as long as [you] permit me to guard you, that is sufficient for your needs. Any more will come from the additional moneys from me. But I insisted in setting you free economically—even from me.—If I had done anything else I would have been untrue to what made 291 what it was.—Of course I know money means nothing to you—but you need it a thousand times more than I do.—I must tell you all this—for I could not be free & do much I would liked to have done with you feeling economically unsound—dependent—And so I had to focus & used all opportunity without destroying any spirit—or compromise. I "succeeded" in all—but really lost part of you.—That's the irony of my life—Maybe it's the great law I see.—

And now having written—not one hundredth of what there is to say—remember I know that what you are doing is right—your not being here is right—but that something so holy to me which was between us was not quite right for quite awhile—& I want it right—& will give my life to have it right if you will help me. And it only can become right if you feel as

104. The day before, Stieglitz wrote Norman that it had been thirty-six years since he had been without a woman near him: "I miss that nearness.—Perhaps I need a mother more than wife or sweetheart.—Can you tell me? You are a mother & a wife —& know too what it is to be a sweetheart." Using the abbreviation of one of his nicknames for her, the "Young Lady," he added he had "deep gratitude to the Y.L. for her deep sympathy & quiet understanding" (AS to Norman, July 5, 1929).
105. Carlsbad salts, a laxative.

I do—that it is the most important thing in the world—*Our Togetherness* if not physically & spiritually at least spiritually!

If that cannot be there can be no togetherness between any man & woman. I'd lose my faith in that possibility.—The essence of my faith.—A creative woman—a creative man— for we both are that—You are—I was?—may become again thro' you.—

—Another kiss.—

Somewhere I'd like to fall asleep in your arms & you in mine—face to face—

And I who don't know what love is—Do you think I know a tiny bit?—Do not spare me—tell me the truth—

—Oh yes, I must add—Ida told me all about you & Berg & the operation he wanted to make.[106] It explained much of your demeanor.—It also explained your closing the door when I was in bed one night with a cold & saying you wanted to talk to Ida. I feared it was about yourself—but again I dared not ask—

Oh this terrible consideration how it breeds poisons—Sweetest—Sweetheart. I'm quiet but [my] heart is breaking because somehow I feel I can't let you see into that heart as I want you to see it.—I know it is worth it. I know it will add to your strength. And as the consciousness of you—what you are—adds to mine altho' it may eventually kill me—

—Let me kiss you on the mouth—let me kiss your neck—behind the eyes—let me kiss each eye—& mouth again. Let me kiss the abdomen—each breast—each side of your sweetest of all behinds—let me kiss Fluffy—every part of her & lie there—And then let [me] hold you firmly & let happen what will. I think were you here now I'd even risk all—just without anything. Madness I know—But I am mad with *You* penetrating every fiber of me—every pulse beat is you—

And you ought to know it. And you don't—And you don't believe it now—That's what I have forfeited.—

That's the cross I bear—which robs me of all initiative.—Has killed the dream.

I love you Georgia—

Don't you know it—Should I be silent?—

I haven't reread this letter—it may be hard to make out—Don't waste time over it. —If you [have] written don't throw away the letters. Send what you write. I'd tear this up.— I know it must sound broken—& not beautiful—not flowing—not as I should like it to be.— But I'm not flowing—not beautiful these days. I am broken—& I don't like myself at all. But I'm trying hard to find my line again. You'll help me. I must believe you will.—

Won't you?—

---

106. O'Keeffe had confided to her younger sister Ida that Dr. Benjamin Nathan Berg, who removed two benign cysts from her breast in August and December 1927, wanted to operate on her again in the winter of 1928–1929. She refused to have the procedure done.

Georgia O'Keeffe · [Taos, New Mexico] · [July 6, 1929]

Dearest—

Well—I am sorry you worry so about me—I can't imagine why you haven't heard from me in five days—I have never missed writing more than a day at a time—and that only two or three times—

When one moves about I suppose mail doesn't leave the funny little post offices except when they happen to think of it—

It is Saturday morning—We got in late last night—after a wonderful day—drove through the kind of country that just touches my heart—and I was in a wonderful neutral state all day—it was very perfect—Those Indians with their drums—like a heartbeat from the center of the earth—and sometimes they sing wonderful things—their presence something very alert and silent—It was a very beautiful day—

When we arrived here—Oh I forgot our supper—in a big white room—big—very big open fire—three or four tables at one side—And afterward—we danced—Beck and I—then—the dancer and I—Beck and Tony—then Tony and I and Beck and the dancer—Then Tony stalks out without a word and everyone follows—

That boy who dances[107] is one of the most beautiful creatures I ever saw—and one can't talk with him—but what a smile—It is like a rich beautiful woman—pure and innocent and male—very male—all at the same time—I wish you could see it—and his pleasure in the dance—and in his food—But he eats beautifully just like he does everything else—without having our kind of manners—It seems like a beautiful thing that just naturally grew—He made his own dancing ornaments—and they are really very fine—It is as real a specimen of an artist as I have ever seen—I wish you could see it—

—When we finally got home—in Mabel's big sitting room—under the big lamp we found the mail—When I read Tony his he fell into a lump in the chair in front of me and announced that he was going to go and get Mabel[108]—Beck squatting on the floor—complaining about Paul complaining about her and something about her mother[109]—

—Then I had your letters—six of them—really—When I had finished reading them I wondered were you a bit mad—I read them again in the Pink House—lying on the floor in front of the fire—and got into bed and wept till my nose wouldn't work—and it seemed I'd never sleep—

But I did—

I waked when the sun came over the mountain at five—in a little while got up—quietly gathered my clothes together and slipped out and over to the studio to dress so I wouldn't wake Beck—

Everything smelled so good—and Lisa had cleaned the studio very nicely—and when

---

107. John Marcos.

108. In her letter to Tony Lujan of June 30, 1929, Mabel noted that the doctors were still uncertain when they would operate on her.

109. Later in July, Beck Strand left Taos earlier than she had expected to return to New York to care for her sick mother.

I stood out in front of the studio—dressed in my black sateen shirt—I felt very clear and level with the world—unusually clear and balanced—with my feet on the ground—both of them— I went to the garage to see if the Ford is still there and everything all right—

Then came over here to the Big House—walking down the long porch to the bathroom to wash my face—I see Tony in a bed where he doesn't belong—Mrs. Hapgood came yesterday with her two daughters[110]—are in his house and I guess he didn't want to risk disturbing them —so just fell into the first bed he came to—He must have been dead—driving so far—

Mrs. Marin and boy[111] have arrived too—I haven't seen anyone this morning but the housekeeper—She gave me your telegrams—I will wire you as soon as I can get to the village —She also gave me breakfast—and all the village and house gossip—a man mysteriously killed —etc—

I am not going into your letters—I wish you had sent me the ones you burned—They would undoubtedly have been very important for me—

All I have to say is—I am feeling very strong and level—and if you cannot get quiet and get yourself together—I will be back to you—You mustn't waste yourself as you are doing —I feel very sane—and very clear—It is as tho I never felt so firm on the ground—

So I kiss you with the morning—and with that feeling—and I want you to feel I am there for you—any moment—every moment—

464

Alfred Stieglitz · Lake George, New York · July 6, 1929

A telegram from you Dearest, best part of what I am.—You back in Taos.—This morning after I had sent you a twenty-six-page [letter][112] registered—I came back & broke down again—There was so much more to say in the letter & I realized I hadn't said it—that I felt no matter what I wrote I couldn't make you feel what really was eating me up—killing me—Not your being away but that terrible lack of togetherness when you left—& I know that without that I am lost— That side of me I hate would get the upper hand. You always said I'd be a terrible rotter if the balance swung a tiny bit the other way.—I nearly became a murderer with Emmy when I'm not a trace of a murderer at heart!—So I sent all away—they went on the boat. I remained behind & cried. As I have cried & cried—so much since here.—And I don't like to cry.—Then I marched myself to the post office to see whether the mail had come. It hadn't.—And now I'll give you a million chances to guess what I did.—

—I engaged an airplane for myself—just had to be alone—one with a cabin—that flies to New York & back at weekends—& I flew. And I had wanted to wait & fly with you.— I knew I'd do it this summer. Zoler for days dissuaded me. So I sent him away today with the others.—It was an extraordinary & quieting experience.—I never felt so quiet. And as I saw the

---

110. O'Keeffe was mistaken; the novelist Neith Boyce (Hapgood) brought only one of her daughters, Miriam, and her son, Charles, to Taos in 1929; see DeWitt, *Taos*, 3–7.
111. John Marin, Jr.
112. AS to GOK, July 6, 1929 (see pp. 457–462).

Georgia O'Keeffe, *Black Cross*, 1929. Oil on canvas, 39 x 30 in. (99.1 x 76.2 cm). The Art Institute of Chicago (1943.95).
Photography © The Art Institute of Chicago. Lynes 667.

water below—five thousand feet below at times—I felt comforted that all I'd have to [do was] open the door & walk out & no one would ever know—My Lake!—How quiet it looked. The hills & islands—the greens all much as I had imagined.—The only sensation I had was a pressure in the ears.—I had no sensation that I know of of the heart.—It's a great machine.—Are you surprised?—The absolute aloneness in the cabin made the trip doubly incredible.—

And as I came to the post office there were *four*—yes *four* letters from my girl who has run away & was right in running away even if it had killed an old & weak fool.—I read the letters at once—Yes, they were my Georgia free—& full of heart—that heart I had missed for months—months—& months—so never-endingly long.—And you drive a Ford.[113] Good.— We are attuned once more. When Albert arrived here I asked him how long it would take me to learn to run a Ford. A week he said. And I told him this summer I would learn. And told him too I wish you knew how.—Had we known Lake George would not have been so bad. But as you say I was the inhibitor—& I know why.—It wasn't fear—not fear solely—I felt if we had a car which we really could not afford until recently we wouldn't work & do the things as fully as without a car. It's a long story.—It's all not simple.—I'm glad you confessed.—But please don't drink too much whisky.—Chauffeurs shouldn't drink much.—

And my letter made you cry.—And you turned them over to Beck, even the intimate ones —Well, I understand only too well. Maybe the crying was necessary—I having cried so much.—

And went to the rodeo—& the telegram just now says you're back. All fine.—Just don't keep me on tender hooks.—One crippled finger is enough. I don't blame you—*you*—I'm just a fool & crazy.—

There was quite a letter from Mabel to me.[114] She says she & I suffer from the same malady: too much ego—too little self—I still consider her the most destructive person I know —if one isn't on one's guard.—Being very remarkable doesn't exclude being very destructive. Coupling herself & me—Well, I have written her. Maybe I'm destructive too. Her trouble has been her wealth & the thing she is & what she will always be. As I will always be what I am even tho I try to remake myself & hate much of myself—& you will remain what you are—But tolerance which means a real togetherness dispels the ego—& doesn't smother self—lets it grow. —When we came together our mutual respect for each other's identity—or love for what the other was—functioning as one—became productive for both.—That togetherness grew— & tho there were differences—there was no doubt. When doubt set in—but we'll not talk about that.—My heart thumps hard as I write this letter—

I'd better stop—If you were here I'd smother you—I know why your Fluffies jump—?

---

113. When O'Keeffe discovered that Stieglitz had flown, she wrote Mabel Luhan, "I think it is one of the funniest things I ever heard of.... After his ride there was nothing for him to say about the Ford except that it was good—that he was glad I had done it—I feel if I stay here long enough he will just come to anything—get to be a real human being" (GOK to Mabel Dodge Luhan, c. July 9, 1929).

114. On July 5, 1929, Mabel Luhan wrote Stieglitz suggesting that both of them were suffering from "drooping egos.... You & I have played great games, Stieglitz, all our lives—or thought we did. Our egos did anyway." On July 6, 1929, Stieglitz responded, noting that her letter "staggers me.... I know what ails me. My brokenness is my loneliness.... I am not what you think I am— an experimenter with people.... I walk off the ego—I shed it—give the self a chance." Despite their blunt language, the two continued a lively correspondence for the rest of the summer.

A kiss on yours—until you scream!

I'm sure you have some very grand pictures.—Black cross against blue sky![115]—And queer as I lay awake this morning I was wondering if you didn't ever wear black down there—I was just full of wonderful black—& here is your letter.—Full of black—real black!

Yes, I feel we are attuned once more—like in Canyon!—

It's a rare feeling of release—

I'm ready to die—or fluff you—Both are one!—

Alfred Stieglitz · Lake George, New York · July 7, 1929

Sunday—6 A.M. The morning is warm. The night was warm. I lay under one blanket. The windows all were open. All was stillness.—And your bed seemed particularly fitting. And as I fell asleep I heard myself saying: Good Night Sweetheart. And seemed to stretch out a hand to touch you—& let you feel I was there next to you.—And I slept till 5:30. Rain on the roof—the sun rising—a few birds saying good morning to each other—a cock crowing & a cow mooing—they seemed to greet my awakening. Or maybe they awakened me. And my thought was you.—I'm so full of you it is a glorious feeling—And really so quiet. Something certainly happened yesterday.—I'm not reborn.—I simply am myself again.—At my finest. And it will remain so.—All fear is gone. All self torture—Fear of the future. Fear of losing you.—Fear of everything. Above all fear of self—that part of self that does destroy all that is sacred to that other self to which all is holy!—What brought this miracle about? My walking into that airplane cabin alone & not a bit nervous.—That flight.—So quiet. So natural as if I had flown all my life. The walking to the post office & finding four letters from my Sweetheart—Reading them—all so lovely—all so true—nothing weighed—just plain giving like in Canyon days! The knowing that I had not lost all that was holier to me than anything else in the world. Mabel's letter—terrific—true yet misapplied. Really destructive. Poor soul.—If anyone could set her straight I might be able to—today. But I fear that is not to be. This is no illusion.—And another very wonderful letter—rather tragic—I'll tell you about some other time. That mail—incredible—The walking—the photographing—going to Jenks (what a lovely man he is)—Dunklee (he too a real person)—your telegram—all seemed to give me the feeling of a great peace. All else mattered little—altho' my nerves are still a bit too sensitive for my own good. And as I awoke the immediate feeling was you. As it has been since & long before you left.—But it was not a you always kindly—a most destructive you at times.—A torturing you.—Myself of course. Or we together. But as I lay there this morning I knew I could die in peace whether I ever saw you again or not & my last breath would be: Georgia.—And that means all the love that I am capable of. And I have gotten to know it is very much.—And before yesterday I know I would have died & my lips would have been silent—All ideas have gone. All ambitions.—Things mean nothing to me. I mean nothing to myself. 291 I know was true.—You & I in Canyon were true.—Our first coming together was true. "My" idea was true. And when we at first lay together in that tiny cot

---

115. Lynes 668 (see p. 465).

& I taught you what woman can enjoy thro' man—& you used to say: It's not I you enjoy but I'm just an idea & I laughed & kissed you—that too was true. Yet I loved you purely. And when finally I fluffed you—& you were happy & released & said: If only I could give you to other women—what you said was true.—I understood.—And I loved you more than you could know. But you were happy. And we worked & were poor. We expressed ourselves. Lived for each other & my idea!—But gradually here & there a bit of ugliness crept in—I never lost sight of the idea—It was essential.—I never ceased to love you as I loved no one before—or could ever love again. And you?—You painted glorious paintings—your life—you soul.—And my *Equivalents* were born of pain—Kitty's illness—your not being completely happy! My vision of forces. Eternal relationships!—I won't go into it all—Then your going—My own state—physical fears—psychic fears—the "loss" of Room—the "loss" of Hill—the loss of all that seemed myself—that part which gave me the courage to live. The packing.—Your gay time in Taos.— The feeling that altho' still together we had grown millions [of] miles apart—everything died in my hands—Idea—things—painting—art—self—everything—for I knew if I should die my lips would be sealed—And I wanted to die the agony was too terrible.—That I didn't die is a miracle—I know well the meaning of a broken heart—But all is peace within me now—I am at your command—I have no idea.—I have no things.—I am no longer guardian.—"291" is there—I don't need the young—the adolescent—I don't need any particular place—I have no thought of hurt—there is no self-pity—there is no fear—there is but one grand feeling of peace for my last word would be if I were to die today: Georgia.—And I'm sure that whatever may happen—to me or to you—I know that will be my final thought & word: Georgia.—And the meaning of this I only know—And it will be kept mine—not as possession—but as a sacred vision—beautiful—more beautiful than even the vision of "291." So you see what you have done for me. A black cross against a blue sky!—

I don't need to see the painting itself—for I know what it looks like.

Georgia.—

Georgia O'Keeffe · [Taos, New Mexico] · [July 9, 1929]

Tuesday—

My dear Alfred—

I did not get a letter off to you this morning because I overslept—it was a gray day and usually the sun wakes me up—It was after nine when I waked—

Last night your letters put me in such a daze—I didn't seem to have thought enough to write—I was not here when the telegrams you speak of came. I wired you as soon as we returned—that is we got in late at night and the housekeeper gave me your telegrams in the morning. I wired you immediately—asked how you were that day—You did not answer—I sent you a night letter last night—

I really see nothing for me to do but return to you if you are going to worry this way. I don't want to wear you out with anything like that—I am as conscientiously careful in everything I do as can be—I have not missed writing for more than a day unless maybe that time I asked Beck to write—and then it was because I was working all day every day—and I think that even that day I wrote you a little note after she wrote—

—If you are uneasy this way I will just not stay any longer—so you must tell me—

Mail in these places is not very certain—and on our trips I sent letters from any crazy little place we happened to be—Tony and Beck both laughed at me for writing so often—and we were not often still when I could write—I can't tell you how sorry I am that you have been so distressed—It was entirely unnecessary—I assure you—If anything goes wrong—we wouldn't be six days telling you about it—You have just worn yourself out—doing more than you could this spring—and being tired get into a state of mind that you wouldn't if you were in better condition physically—

—As for other things you write of—of the past—things that have hurt me—and things that have hurt you—I have purposely not written of it or remarked on it because of the distance between us—the long times between letters—and possibly—I do not want to hurt you—I have put out my hand to you so many times of late and more often than not felt you turn away from me—In the Room you usually made me feel that you were just waiting for me to go—You feel that I am mistaken in many things—Going into it all does not lead anywhere—

I do not wish to blame you for anything—and I do not want you to be having any regrets—I think I understand it all better than you imagine—In a way I am very grateful to you for all of it—It makes me understand so many things about other people—and makes it very very difficult for them to touch any place in me that hurts—in either big or little things—

It is as tho it has given me the big balance wheel—It is as tho it has taken my heart— and at the same time left it for me in a usable form—

Maybe you will not like what I feel myself working into—maybe I just imagine it is different—I am not making an effort toward anything—in particular—It is nothing to grieve over—It feels right—and sane and alive to me—

Tony has done much for me—quiet—solid—a warm warm heart—his hurts and his loves—and his checking off my nervousness of many kinds—What I see between him and Mabel—his way of handling it[116]—

You really need have no regrets about me—You see—I have not really had my way of life for many years—When I felt very close to you—that there was a home for me really within you—I could live—I will say—*your* way as much as it was possible for me to live *another's* way—

But when that seemed gone—there is much life in me—when it was always checked in moving toward you—I realized it would die if it could not move toward something—Here it seems to move in every direction—There it didn't seem to move at all—it seemed only to meet cold—cold—

Miss Young—the very keen Irish woman who is here looked at me across the breakfast

116. In a letter written on July 1, 1929, O'Keeffe confided to Mabel Luhan: "Something you are—and something Tony is—is helping me much with something between Stieglitz and myself—It is smoothing away many things for me—Tony just being what he is—seems to pull out of me the best things that are in me—And a lot of surface things—that hurt one's vanity—and that the world looks at—the Bretts and the Becks—and all the others—just become so much nothing."

table yesterday morning and remarked—"I never saw anything like you—You never seem to tire—You always live—How do you do it—Mrs. Strand goes up and down—She sometimes looks terrible—You get up at all hours—You go on long trips—You stay up late at night—You do all the things everybody else does and work besides—Tony looks all worn out keeping up with you at times—But you are the only one who seems able to stand it without there being any feeling of wear and tear—You seem to thrive on it always"—

I had to laugh—

—I go to sleep when I want to—Last night—everyone else playing cards—I went sound asleep on the floor—done up in a blanket at the feet of Tony's nephew—he drumming Tony's big drum in my ear—till they say he went to sleep too almost buried under the big drum—And Tony got up and rescued the drum and sent him to bed—I had gone numb with your letters—and all the people that came in—the Hapgoods and others—and the telegram I sent you—and wondering—should I just pack up this morning and leave—and just walk in on you—So I just got as close to the drum as I could—the Indian beat has a terrible persistent rhythm—it just carries you—so that even after I walked home across the alfalfa field—I went off again into a dead sleep—.

With this morning—Dasburg was in to see me—I showed him my work—He seemed to like it very much—thought that I had put down both the thing one sees in this country and the thing it does to you—He was very nice—seemed a bit sad as he left—Maybe I flatter myself but I often feel that a kind of live life quality that my things have makes other painters sad because it is something they haven't—and can't get—and I just have it—I have no choice—it seems to be right in my teeth—

Charles Collier is here too—he is stretching canvas for me—does it as well as I can—and you know that is saying a great deal—I taught him—You will meet him. He goes to Columbia next winter—

—Now listen Boy—I am all right. And what is between us is all right—and I don't want you to worry a bit about me—There was much more cause to worry about things when I was right beside you—If you will just quiet down and be normal I will stay—If you can't—I want you to tell me—But if you can—I want to stay here longer—But not at too great a price from you—So you must tell me—

I assure you—there is nothing to worry about—The things I do may seem crazy to you—I thought of not telling you—only it seemed too foolish not to—

Do not worry about anything—We will work out something together—I feel very strong—Just try to give your little body a chance—You see I know that if I had not come away you would be in just as much of a stew over something I would be doing there—everything about me would have irritated you—Every summer you get ready to leave Lake George because of something I am and do that you can't stand—

Strand is with you today—Beck has a telegram from him—I wonder if he will quiet you a little—

You see—I feel—if I hadn't come away I would have irritated you—being away you worry—There seems no chance for me to come out right—

And I chose coming away because here at least I feel good—and it makes me feel I am growing very tall and straight inside—and very still—Maybe you will not love me for it—but for me it seems to be the best thing I can do for you—I hope this letter carries no hurt to you—It is the last thing I want to do in the world—

Today it rains—

Please leave your regrets—and all your sadness—and misery—If I had hugged all mine to my heart as you are doing I could not walk out the door and let the sun shine into me as it has—and I could not feel the stars touch the center of me as they do out there on the hills at night—or the silver of the sagebrush way off into the distance as well as nearby—seem to touch my lips and my cheek as it does—

—A kiss Little Boy—

I have not wanted to be anything but kind to you—but there is nothing to be kind to you if I cannot be me—And me is something that reaches very far out into the world and all around—and kisses you—a very warm—cool—loving—kiss—

Alfred Stieglitz · Lake George, New York · July 11, 1929

I find my mind has been very sick for a long time. Still is very sick.—In that condition I should not have written you nor write you. It is not fair to that fine something which links us forever. Your mind is clear. You have gained sanity you say, & health & that means joy & the power to live—create.—And I am very happy though my own condition is the reverse of yours. I have suffered—still am suffering—beyond the breaking point. I see no release but one.—I'm not quite ready.—Don't be disturbed.[117]—There must be order first. And I must see you too.— At that time which has been in your mind before & when you left.—I do not know when that is. But I have learned to wait. Yesterday I wrote you a few desperate letters. Forget those letters—forget everything about me except those days where you & I were really one—a great togetherness.—You gave me back my life—you have earned the right to take it.—Those days & years of our perfect togetherness is all I have left today.—I dare not lose them. Until my mind is less sick I must not write you.—I know I love you Georgia.—Once you knew it & there was that togetherness.—Now I must prove it—Then I'll have won the peace I seek—

The morning is clarity itself—and a silence which gives strength—The morning kisses you—I the sick man may not—

All my prints in storage belong to you—I have no wish whatever about them. They are all I am. And that belongs to you—

This is final—And I am not sick in mind on this point.—

117. In another letter written on July 11, 1929, Stieglitz told O'Keeffe that the previous night, when he "was no longer sane— or perhaps saw so clearly that I couldn't go on living," he took a bottle of poison to bed with him.

My dear Alfred—

I mailed that letter to you an hour and a half ago—then went in and had breakfast with Tony in the kitchen—The letter wasn't what I wanted to send—but it was the best I could do—

I would like not to say to you any of the unpleasant things I have felt or thought— it simply adds to the pile of waste—

Tony had laid across the foot of Mabel's largest couch-bed last night when I came in —like a log—boots sticking out—black and dead looking from under the dark blue blanket that looked black with the little light—the face looking dead—the hair very black—all dead and exhausted with worry—Mabel was operated on yesterday—

This morning at breakfast—well groomed—still looking worried—but very quiet— and controlled—handsome—and warmth coming out of him—He is really a rare person— so human—

I don't know exactly why—but he does me much good—He was very funny—one morning a couple of days ago when I was particularly sad over my letters—he said to me— "I cut the alfalfa—I cannot go now—but then I take you camping—I take you camping where you cannot get letters for—Oh! three days—I cook—I can do many things"—

Before Mabel left we had planned to go camping this month—she wrote us to go without her—Well—we will see—I will wire you if we go as it will stop my letters to you.

For your long—long letter—Boy—you tell me that you feel it is right for me to be here —You see—along with all the things between you and me—when Berg wanted to carve me again last winter—and I said, No—it was a strong decision to make against such a doctor—

Months and years had gone by—and I could not get close to something I had been close to and touched in you—You did not seem to need the center of me touching your center— The next best thing was out here—And when I left New York—it was really with the hope that there would be nothing here for me—

It seemed I just couldn't bear the months and months of half aliveness that come after an operation—and I felt he was wrong—like I felt they were wrong both other times they cut me—and feeling within myself that they were wrong I made up my mind to try my own cure —If I had felt you reaching your hand toward the center of me—that would have helped me— but I didn't feel it—Going away and moving in my own way seemed to be the only thing left me—

And now you cry for the center of me that has been pushed away for so long—so long—that to tell you the truth—I am not sure that it exists anymore—Nobody else has ever seen it—or ever will—I seem to meet people here with my skin—that doesn't mean anything when I say it—but it is the best I can say—Maybe I accept the human being in a different way than I could before—The thing you call holy—I do not feel any less holy—but I feel more like the rocks in the bottom of the stream outside my door—Much water runs over me—and I know it—Everyday there seem to be more things I am conscious of—and can just let pass over me and be—Under it all is something knit to you—it will always be that way—I have no choice —you have no choice—it just is that way—

I wish you could really get to work—It is the only thing—other things will follow—I have no other plan—You would not be loving me if I had not come away—

It all makes me feel very helpless—I am glad you send me the letters—it is good—but I wish you could be in a state so that you wouldn't feel that way—

You need not grieve over anything you have done to me—This summer I feel for the first time that it has begun to add something to me—I feel beyond a kind of suffering I have had—and you must get beyond it—so that we can be together in peace—and not in torture—

I seemed to be in the world only for you—But I must be here awhile yet—

An untouched whiteness has been soiled—maybe it isn't a very practical thing to try to go though life with—Maybe blackness is the pure thing after all—the thing you cannot soil—

Do not feel hurt Boy—I cannot be of any use to you unless I can grow much myself and every day I feel more and more on the earth—I have always liked both black and white—I will be of much more use to you when I return—and I am holding you very tenderly in my heart while I am away—

You must not hold onto things I have said and done that hurt you—you must feel you can move freely toward me—it is the only sign of faith in me—

Your telegram just came—the very intimate one—The man who phoned it to me almost gasped as he read it—He will mail me a copy—

I had to laugh—Tony suffered so wanting to send an intimate message to Mabel before she was operated—He just couldn't telegraph it so decided to phone—When he got her on the telephone he couldn't say anything he wanted to—I had to laugh when he told her it was raining and he had been cutting alfalfa—

Then to get such a wire from you—Well—you are sweet—

Now we are not going to argue and rave about all these things anymore—You get to work—and take care of yourself—and don't get crazy—And I'm going about my business—

I must get at it now—I feel like tearing this up but I won't—

With lots of love—

G.

Georgia O'Keeffe · Taos, New Mexico · July 12, 1929

Friday—

Yesterday I painted all day—Beck in bed with a cold—After supper was out with Pete again—along the highway for some distance then a long trail over the hills home—the hills a black waving line against a starlight sky with dark long clouds over the hills—the moon in and out behind black and white cloud—It was the longest, hardest ride I have had—and I must tell you again that Pete is very watchful—and the white horse very sure footed—I not a bit afraid—It is the finest thing I have had out here—

When I got in at twenty to ten—I had my bath—then sat in front of Beck's fire and read my letters—two—very beautiful—I read them aloud to her—She was almost in tears over having a cold and to be in bed these last days here—she will be leaving in two weeks—

The letters were quiet—very beautiful to both of us—I got into bed—so limp from the ride and hot bath that I felt I might fall through the bed—I slept very soundly and was still limp when I waked this morning—I mailed my letter to you—then had breakfast with Tony and read him his letter from Mabel—

—Washed my brushes from yesterday—went to the village on some errands—Just as I returned met Mrs. Hapgood walking to town—it was hot so I offered to drive her—

When I got back—Mary Austin for lunch and the editor of the *Survey Graphic*[118]— He wants a photograph of one of my churches for a Spanish number that will come out next winter—remarked on how much they had liked my *Sun Spots* that they had some time ago[119]— I told him we would see—you would have to say—.

—Then—the telegrams—Paul's of yesterday[120] I did not get till after yours of today—

I wish you could see my new painting—it is alive and sharp and rich and dark around the edges and light in the center[121]—colorful—all—

I must work some more—

With what I hear from you—with one breath you are quiet—all right—with the next you are all upset—

It disturbs me—but what can I do—

I know that many things that seemed very precious—very holy—are gone for me— but I feel too—that way down beyond that—where you cannot touch it—where no one can touch it—There is a bond—that is my feeling for you—It is deeper than anything you can do to me—That is why I know I will be with you to the end—whether you wish it or not— whether I choose it or not—whether I am close to you or not—

I do not know whether that is what you want or not—You have always told me you do not know what love is—I have had to do with mine what I could—.

—I think I must stay here awhile after Beck leaves—I must be alone awhile—but even when I write that I trust you to call me if you feel you must—I am counting on that in spite of all the things you say—

You have always told me the work comes first—That has often been very difficult for the woman in me—

I am not going into it any more—I am doing what I can—

My last painting is a new color—and I must go on—and you must go on—It is the only chance we have—

I see no other way—I must take enough from here so that I will *know* I have been here—and I haven't that yet—

474

118. On May 12, 1929, when O'Keeffe first met Mary Austin at Los Gallos, she wrote Stieglitz that when the author first arrived, "The household quite changed color—I like her but she makes me feel—I don't want to be anything but just a woman—I don't want to become the sort of thing one seems to become through being anything else—I just want to be soft and loved and foolish" (GOK to AS, May 12, 1929). The editor of *Survey Graphic* was Alain Locke.

119. Lynes 527; *Survey Graphic* 59 (Mar. 1, 1928), 676.

120. Strand telegraphed O'Keeffe from Lake George on July 11, 1929: "You came with me from Texas and you spoke to me of Europe and Taos therefore I must tell you the secret. Never have I seen such suffering. Your letter this morning telling him you loved him actually saved him. The future is still a blank for him and so far for all of us."

121. Possibly Lynes 650.

I wish that you could be very quiet and go about your days so that you get some good out of them—this is all just too destructive—

Please Boy—be a little bit sane—I will be back in a little while—

Indians are making hay all about the place here—I feel as tho a million eyes are watching everything—even Tony is out there at it with a pitchfork—in his white shirt—working as hard as anyone—

I don't see what else I can say to you—I am doing the best I can—and even if you don't believe me now—you will find when I get back that my feeling is all right—

I have needed to breathe in my own way for awhile—

My love to you Boy—

And a kiss—and do be good—We are all right—and you know it—I feel so helpless—

But what is here is very right—

Alfred Stieglitz · Lake George, New York · July 13, 1929

Dear Georgia:

There is your long letter of July 9. You feel yourself strong & happy & free & in the right environment for your growth. You must know that that means more to me than my own life. I have said it before. But maybe not clearly enough. Haven't I worked all these years to set you free from me?—And you are free.—If in our personal relationship I have hurt you much & in the last year seemed to draw away—have you ever examined yourself? If you were here I could explain much but it would not change your feelings for me. I am the loser—the one weakened—And when I seemed to draw away I was often much closer to you than ever before—loved you more—the heart was at breaking point. But I saw my fate. I saw it for some years. Taos was in the stars.—Maybe I was jealous.—My mind is all lost—I have no Tony to teach me anything. I have no new surroundings to stimulate me.—I haven't the youthfulness to begin afresh & gain wisdom.—I may see clearly—all you wrote I knew. But wanted to see it written.—I knew you would be honest—ruthlessly so. But seeing clearly I seem not to know how to act with wisdom.—That's why everyone seems finally to leave me. So I have my loneliness which I so richly deserve.—I do not complain. I'll be quiet.—I accept it all. I have no choice.—The Room was my undoing. I see that clearly.—But all this would have come eventually anyhow, I fear—you being what you are—I being heaven knows what. If you feel you must stay in Taos longer than you have in mind—you must not hesitate.—I have no idea what you have in mind. Of course I'd miss you terribly—as I miss you every moment here—as I always missed you every moment whenever you were away. Missed you during last winter when you were planning Europe or Taos without telling me. Maybe I felt all that & intuitively drew away. But my head is in a muddle—I must stop writing—I seem to make everything worse for myself & just rob you of your time—If we can build together & you'd show me how I'll be only too eager—I must learn so much—I kiss you Georgia.

And you say no matter what you would have done you had no chance. Now don't you remember how I told you over & over again the law I found.—Which means that as I twist &

turn all my sins in relationship to what you are, I always arrived at one result: I have no chance. She cannot hear. As you say I cannot see.—

But I do see you—& I do see myself—myself all too clearly. That's the rub—It's not a fine self I see. You see yourself strong & healthy. I see myself stupid—unhealthy & unproductive.

So how can I be anything to you except a memory—or one you'd like to help because of gratitude.

Love is not relentless! Life may be—

Georgia O'Keeffe · [Taos, New Mexico] · [July 13, 1929]

I am in bed again—It has seemed a long day—painting all day with interruptions—and even at that the painting is one that goes slow—but it goes—I think it will be a good one and a new one—

Your twenty-six page letter[122] this afternoon dazed me as I read it—I put it aside when finished and went on with my painting because it is the sort of painting that must be done now or not at all—I can't hold on to it—

Tony came past and told me he was going to send the horses—including the one I am riding—up to the ranch—I had to tell him I was riding it or lose the horse—He was much astonished—and said I wasn't fair—

I enjoyed his astonishment much—I don't know what he will do—one never can tell— Then two other Indians came in to visit me—one had made me a pair of moccasins—the other was one that had gone on the Las Vegas trip with us—They came separately—their remarks about the picture I am painting would entertain you very much—They liked it much—

After supper I went out with Pete again—and I can't tell you how much I enjoy it— He rode a dancing black mare that hadn't been saddled in months and she certainly danced all the way—It was a gray evening—the moon having a hard time trying to come through—Pete is a great boy—half Indian—half French English—and how he rides—it is a wonderful rhythm moving along beside one—And as we put the horses back in the alfalfa field he told me that I should tell him anytime I want to go because he likes it very much—maybe I would come and wake him early some morning—anytime two or three o'clock—he likes to ride early in the morning—So maybe I will—

I had your letters when I got to the Big House for my bath—it was 9:20 when we got in —Also Mabel sent me the *New Yorker* clipping—I haven't read it—

I am not going into anything you write of tonight—I am too tired—not really tired— but wound up with too many things—

Riding out there in the sunset—dusk—and night—is just too grand—I remarked to Pete—"I don't know whether I like the riding or being out in the night and the stars and the sagebrush"—He laughed and answered "I guess you like both"—

—I must sleep—

---

122. AS TO GOK, July 6, 1929 (see pp. 457–462).

I have a feeling you are more interested in my daily doings than in my arguing—or writing of what you write—I can't talk about the letter until I read it again and think about it—and the things I write of happen right now—

Good Night—

A tired girl with a whirling head crawls under the cover—

My painting—your letters—the Indians—Pete—and the ride—the night—Beck is knocked out with a cold—but I'm fine—

So I kiss you a good hard healthy kiss—and go to sleep—

[July 14, 1929]

I am up at seven to mail this—Many birds singing—

—As soon as I mail it and have my breakfast—and do what I can for Beck to keep her in bed—I'm going to the studio—to your long letter—and to my painting—

—Some of the things in your long letter I knew of—am always conscious of—You asking me to give of myself to you seems so strange because I have been begging to give—to be with you—till I just felt I wouldn't worry you anymore—And now all this—it all seems too queer—I have always wanted to be with you—don't you know that—It would either be you or the sort of thing I find out here—If you hadn't come first—all these years—I would have come to this before—but I have certainly spent dreadful summers at Lake George—and—

Well—it just seemed I had to have some fresh air and feel like a real human being again—I thought maybe I couldn't—I find I can—In spite of all that I would go back to you now but I just can't bring myself to move myself into that family feeling—I can't eat my meals with Lee and Lizzie and digest them—and I have no desire to be so close to anyone who is apt to jump up and scream at me—

I haven't done enough work here yet to satisfy my having been here—I have much feeling to work here—and when I think of Lake George it just seems to take all the breath out of my body—

—I am being honest with you—Last year I knew I couldn't stand it unless I had a place of my own—and when I asked for that I knew I was giving up any chance of ever having anything like I am having this summer—But it seemed the nearest thing to anything I could do to give you any satisfaction—

—It just doesn't seem human to try to live as I have been living at Lake George—

I must mail this or it will not go—I do not like to write you these things—it is entirely unnecessary—

I must be what is here now—it is the only way I can be of any use to you or anyone—

And it is so exciting to me to feel good that I just almost die over it—

Here is my kiss with the cool wetness of the morning—

You must know I'm not so far away from you as you are saying I am—

Still my Dearest Grandest Child:

It's still dark—not yet four—I have lain awake all night—in spite of sleeping potion. —Just thinking & thinking—with heart on a rampage—with no thought of anything but you & your letter. As if I have had any other thought for a moment but you since you left! You see it's not worrying about you in the sense as I worried about you so much of old that you seem to think. But it's that awful gnawing in my soul that's killing me by inches. The gnawing that I let you go without a long clarifying talk. That it was I too hurt & with a false pride that it kept from happening. And it was essential for both. And you went without making me feel you wanted it—needed it as much as I needed it. Need it today. But today in a way you really do not need it. You refound yourself—are sure of the soundness of self—altitude—congenial surroundings—everyone fine—Tony your helper—you feeling so strong & well—a great contrast to what you have been feeling in recent years—here—in New York—with me.—So doubly wonderful it all seems to you.—Must naturally. I know no woman ever brought more of herself—all—to a man than you brought to me. I know no woman was approached by a man with greater love—greater tenderness—greater allness than I approached you. And what existed for some years was pure & extraordinarily beautiful & productive in spite of differences within our natures. You the wild child of the soil, I city-bred of the city.—But our love for each other was all we knew—& there was the Hill where we were a bit nearer the soil—& the months there alone—Sweetestheart, what wonder they bred! And everything was simple as we were simple. And innocent & clean.—But when I began to fear, yes fear, that if anything happened to me & you'd be left alone—frail, for you were frail when you came to me—& without money—I began to think of how I could get money for you—to protect you. I never had given money for myself a thought.—Nor felt the need of money as I did then.—To protect you. Yes, Sweetestheart, you must remember that.—First it was $1200 a year—then it became $2000 —then $3000—eventually last year $5000 I wanted for you—to insure you against illness— against the cold world—knowing well money had no meaning to you. Yet you needed it!— And so the thought of satisfying that began to consume me—the need of "proving" my various cases—that watercolor is a major medium in the hands of one like Marin, that a woman could be creative—yourself—that photography could express—& what not. And so growing older & not being strong & you being frail I put on more & more steam.—And I felt you were with me —& understood—And you were for awhile—& we worked as a team—not because you cared for my ideas so much but because there seemed life—direction—a giving of self—a growing of self. But there was always your yearn for the Southwest—& I feared it. Was jealous of it. Knew it would win you from me. And as I realized that more & more—it got in the way of my pure self—& it made me resentful & do things that weren't fine—& it made you in turn hurt me because I hurt you.—And gradually you began steeling yourself—& I felt it & it did something to me.—All understandable. But destructive of that wonderful purity that brought us together.—Last year when you sat in Claudie's car for over two hours believing she was going to California—I frantic wondering where you were—still not going down to see nor letting

478

Anita[123] go for I felt I had no right to interfere with your freedom—still inwardly incensed at your inconsideration of me—I ill—we going away in the morning. And when you came in saying: "I suppose you have been complaining about me. I had to talk to Claudie. She is going to California & I won't see her again." And I feeling Claudie won't go (& she didn't) & resenting what I felt was your lack of thought of me—I being what I am. And I knew I'd pay the price before midnight. Physically. I had said it to Anita.—I knew it because there was a clash between my mental insisting not to interfere with your free action & my feeling of not being considered. And as you know I tore my ligament. And my (our) summer was ruined for all I had planned to do for us—in work & in every other way. And when the finger got sufficiently well to work & be free a bit I was ordered to bed with the heart! Now you are not to "blame" for the finger. It is a symbol of myself—my own clash. And it is this same clash that has resulted in changing your relationship to me—not mine to you. And this sort of thing has gone on for years. In one shape or another. And it is that which is responsible for this terrible situation for me. You are as serene as you were sitting in Claudie's car.—More so.—You have a new vision—a new star—guiding you.—All I ask you to see is that I'm [not] that which you have grown to believe—but that I'm really still that [which] you once loved to the exclusion of all else—really that a thousand-fold more. But that which I was if you were to meet it today would mean nothing to you—that's my tragedy.—That's why I have lost all. And don't want to live.—Maybe I'm all wrong—Show me wherein.—Give me a chance to function once more—in the world—if not for you.—You wrote in a letter recently you loved me—your experiences were richer because of that love. And I wanted so much to die at that moment—go with that thought—for I wanted to believe it was true. And I know you are the essence of integrity. But then I felt I had lost something I couldn't hold—offered to me so generously—& I grew frantic—so powerless.—And I'm mentally sick —& must get well or go under. And I don't want to go under for I want to keep your respect— I am such a Mamma-baby—& you made me feel you liked that—& I miss you—Georgia you can't help what you are. And I accept it all. Have no choice. But do try to help me go on—But you see when I feel you so strong & happy there it seems all so selfishly wrong to wish to have you come to me even for an hour. And I can't go to you not because of my heart—but because I'd spoil the purity of what's there. And this madness for purity—I the impure one, weak one, don't seem to achieve. That's why I'm so lonely—will be to the end.—It's in one's blood— one can't get rid of it. It's that I knew when I said "all is relative but one's relatives & they are absolute."—And so it is in your blood to be ruthless—& to be beautifully clear—spiritually free —and full of tenderness—

Dearest One—if I could but be released from all this torture of self—

You have tried—you were ready to live your life—die with me—because I was your all—I didn't have the courage—& now you wish to live & be—enjoy life & create.—And that's what I wanted for you.—And yet my heart is breaking because it's all so right—& I'm not equal to sharing it all with you.—That's my madness—for I know what I want is against the great law I know & have known for so long.—It's my struggle for life in a spirit like yours—

---

123. Most likely Anita Young, Georgia's sister, not Anita Pollitzer.

I see but too clearly what is in my way.—If that something weren't in the way we'd be together completely even if one were at one pole & the other at another—

I find no words to tell you what I feel for you—what you are to me—My kiss may tell you. I wonder.—It too is cool like yours but never-ending—beyond death.—

It is raining & day is coming—no sun—It's Sunday—I wish I could pray—

Isn't it terrible—there are a million & one things to tell you—& I feeling all would seem so meaningless to you—a child's prattle from an old man—I do miss you every moment & the feeling—the thought that I did not use every moment when we were together—squandered so many—because of petty hurts—Georgia dearest—if you saw my face, perhaps you'd understand something that might bring real clarity into my soul.

But you want calm faces—not agonized ones—crucified to their own crosses.—

Do let me kiss you with a warm kiss. Will you? I don't expect answers to my letters nor to telegrams—Paint—It's much more important. And take all out of life you can get.— Living is terrible you often said—& I said yes. Living is wonderful to you now & that is wonderful to me. But living to me seems more terrible than ever—yet I must find a way to make it wonderful too—so that we may find each other on the way once more.

Once more Goodbye—

Do you believe I love you—Or do you believe what I call love is nothing more than self pity? You see how I question everything. And that is not my natural self.—Help me Sweetest Child—if you can & care to.

Later: I found these two prints & have mounted them for you. I don't know [if] they will mean anything to you or not. If not, tear them up or give them away.—My own conflict—my curse & my vision are in them.[124] —

In them there is balance and movement—in me at present there is neither balance nor movement—nor light—

All darkness—& death—Pain & torture—

Pain & torture but not on this plane—helped bring you to me. And out of it came that great love that is consuming me now—because I did not know how to hold you.—

I must have an opportunity to photograph you when you come East.[125] You may believe I haven't wanted to all these years—but between all the illness & all else—I couldn't see you here in Lake George for years—& in New York it was impossible—why it didn't happen.—

---

124. Stieglitz probably sent O'Keeffe two of his photographs of the landscape and clouds at Lake George, which he called *Equivalents*. The next day he continued to ruminate on the relationship between his art and his feelings: "In former years I tried to find an equivalent for that trembling something where the hills and the sky meet, the thing you had painted and I have tried to photograph. In place of the hills and the sky, I can see only you and me. I am trying to see this trembling line, that breathing something which is pure spirit between two people. A relationship that is holy. As I see the relationship of the hill and the sky as holy. You must remember when Mitchell Kennerley asked me to write something about you because he felt that I was the only one who could really say something about you, I wrote to him that when I would be able to put into words what I felt about the meeting between hill and sky across the Lake which I had been watching for years, I would put down what Georgia O'Keeffe is to me" (AS to GOK, July 15, 1929).

125. Greenough 1306–1317.

I'm only a photographer perhaps after all—& maybe that's my failing—No, no, all of me is a failing except my burning love for someone far far away.—

—I'm glad too that everyone feels you have untiring energy—I have always known under proper conditions you would have it. But you hadn't it when you came to me, altho' in Texas you danced all night—or auto'd all night—& taught in the day—yet broke down.— So to me you came frail & remained frail. That's why I had to think of money—to protect you —to protect us.—Here in the East—Where you are now—if you had no reputation—had no money—I wonder would you feel all the certainty as you do.—Idle speculations. But a lonely one has idle thoughts.

ON JULY 14, O'Keeffe and Beck went to the Annual Feast Day dance at Cochiti pueblo, a few miles south of Santa Fe. From there they visited the Radcliffe-educated painter and poet Marie Garland and her fourth husband, the twenty-six-year-old filmmaker Henwar Rodakiewicz. Fifty-nine years old, Garland had attained notoriety many years earlier after forfeiting the income from a $10 million estate from her first husband, Charles Garland, to marry her second husband, Francis Cushing Greene. She was also a celebrated hostess and often entertained at her large, elegantly appointed H & M Ranch in Alcalde, thirty miles north of Santa Fe.

Georgia O'Keeffe · [Taos, New Mexico] · [July 15, 1929]

We are just back from Santa Fe—

In the studio again—have watched a storm hide the mountain—and watched the mountain come again—I have read the four letters awaiting me twice—the telegrams many times —Pete came up and asked me if I had a good time while I was away—I said yes—He looked at me and laughed and remarked—"You don't look it"—

I feel in a daze—

—Things happened last night like nothing I ever saw—and your letters today seem a continuation of it—I will not go into it—will tell you when I see you—It was something I wasn't aware of in life before—terrific—to an almost paralyzing degree—only one clear beautiful note singing through madness—

—We went to the dance yesterday—started down at eleven in the morning—thirty miles through white heat—desert—one long unbelievable hill about halfway—the last five miles along the sandy valley of the Rio Grande—When we got there—Beck and I went alone— ate our lunch by the roadside just before we got there—everyone west of the Mississippi that I knew seemed to be there—and such heat—and so many Indians and Mexicans—The dance— it is all so many things mixed up together that it is quite impossible to tell of—much for the eye —and much for the ear—then all the people one knew and the fire of crosscurrents running around through them—

When I sit here in the coolness after this rain—and recall yesterday it all seems almost impossible—

We were invited to spend the night and have dinner at a house about a third of the way between Santa Fe and here—We had been invited often before and didn't go—but last night we went—Mabel said we should go once—There were fifteen for dinner—thirteen guests —No there were more—four more came just as we were finishing—or maybe more than four —Anyway there were a lot of people—The mother of the husband[126] of the house had been at your first exhibition after we were together—the photograph she remembered most definitely was the one of my hands peeling apples[127]—

Everything was quiet and moved beautifully till about twelve—It was unusually fine —then a bomb seemed to go off—and it all turned in a flash to lunacy—I went to bed between two and three—I never saw anything like it—

I had a good sleep—was the first one dressed and about—We had breakfast and drove up here—a very beautiful drive—there are your letters—It has been a strange three days— very interesting—but Oh My!

[July 16, 1929]
Tuesday morning—

As for your letters—Too much time elapses between your writing them and any answer I can make—

The sum of it all is that I feel you have done what you could with what you are— I do not wish to find fault with you—I would not have come away no matter what you did— probably—if I could have stood the strain physically—But I couldn't—and I regret very much that it upsets you—As for the feeling of separation between us—I feel that nothing but my coming away would have made things clear between us—

I didn't do it for that—I had too much respect for both of us and what we had had together to feel it possible to continue as we were going—Everything in me seemed to be discontinuing to move—principally because nothing seemed to be permitted to move toward you—

It was all making me sick and dead—I have too much respect for my body to tear it to pieces the way I had been—

And love needs care like one's body—

—You wonder when I will be going back—I really have no plan—I had none when I came—As I have told you—I do not care about being at the Lake with Lee and Lizzie—I have always had the same feeling about their living place—it is like a cold damp cellar to me—I felt it when I first went to Mamaroneck—they brought it to Lake George—and have it in any other place where they live—

I just can't bring myself to living mixed up with it—Life is too short to spend it that way—

I really have no desire to live—but if I am going to do it I see no reason for torturing myself with it—I would rather go out in the desert in the sun—and just burn up—

126. Erla Rodakiewicz.
127. Greenough 659.

They all ask why I ride at night—My God—the night is *there*—the country is most wonderful then—one is more alone—Why not use the night as well as the daytime—

I am sure you would not have wanted me to ride at night if you had been here—Most of the things I enjoy are as simple as that—It all makes me just wish I could blow away with the wind—

Beck rode with us last night—she spoiled over half of it by complaining about everything like a groggy woman—But when her horse had shaken the life out of her she got normal and enjoyed it very much—I was glad she went tho I was a bit mad at her for the fuss she made—.

—Again—about my returning—I must repeat I have no plan—I think I go tomorrow for three days camping into the mountains if Tony will let me have the white horse—that is the only plan I have—

August is usually a great family month at the Lake—You see I have had such a lot of those summers—so little doing the things I like—

You tell me you want me to stay here—I must say that you make it rather difficult—It took many many things to bring me to this—because I seemed to want to give up my soul to you—It was my feeling that it didn't mean much to you anymore that brought me away—My body couldn't live close to you without feeling loved—and I didn't *feel* loved—

I must mail this or it will not go—

Boy—don't you know I am there for you anytime you want me—but I can't be cramped all out of shape if I can help it—

I must stay awhile yet—if you are really so fond of me please be good to yourself—Really all my love goes to you—

Alfred Stieglitz · Lake George, New York · July 16, 1929

Georgia Dearest:

Last night at 9:30 I sent you a night letter reading as follows: "The distance you speak of in letter writing mixes up everything. I must have a talk with you & am ready to meet you in Albuquerque—the sooner the better. If I left Chicago Sunday, July 21, I could be in Albuquerque on Tuesday morning, July 23—8:30. Wire me will you be ready. If not what day will suit you. Very much love, Alfred—"

And now I am anxiously & eagerly waiting for your reply. It'll be at least eight hours before I can get one—as it is only three A.M. now in Taos. You may be surprised at my sudden decision. But it isn't sudden—any more than your leaving me was sudden for you. I just feel I must see you & hear you—what you have to say about your decisions—new attitude—new feelings.—I must hear relentlessly. And you must hear what I have to say. All quietly & without excitement. For there is to be a new relationship—a new understanding. My feelings for you are finer than ever—& I haven't changed—except that in the last four weeks I have lived in a hell which I never want you to know. A hell because I felt that your new attitude—your new feeling—gave me no chance—even tho I had robbed myself of every chance.—

You may be surprised that I should take the risk of so long a trip—when yesterday I couldn't even write to you—& had to dictate[128]. But I went to Jenks. He knows the situation. And he examined me & we had a long talk & I asked him could I go. He said anything was better for me than living as I was. And I spoke to Lee. And he too said: go. And had they said "no"—I was going anyhow. I had no alternative. You know my way of choosing.

So I hope you'll wire, Come, I'm ready. You may be unwell. That makes no difference. I'm coming to straighten out a diabolical mess unworthy of what I know you are to me—unworthy of myself. And I know you must want it cleared up as much as I do. For Georgia dearest—don't you know that you are life itself to me.—It makes no difference what I may be to you.—I must know the truth. All of it.—I am ready.

You may wonder why I chose Albuquerque. I didn't want to go to Santa Fe or to Taos. I don't want to see *anyone* but *you*. And I felt Albuquerque would be least interference, least effort, for you. You can meet me at the station—or wire me what hotel. But the station would be safest—surest. Are you surprised?—Do you want to see me? Are you as eager to clear up a terrible lot of misunderstanding. I think it's all going to be very simple once we are together & can talk. I'm sure of it. My idea is to come & see you & talk & then come away—come back —so as not to interfere with your own line—with your work. I could see some of the country but I don't want to—I just want to see you—hear you. That's all I want. And to get this frightful mess within me cleared up. Wire me when you get this that you have received it. As soon as your wire comes today I'll order reservations. I leave for Chicago Saturday. I'm going to no art museum or see anyone there. There is just you in my mind—in all of me.—Nothing in between.—And that's what I wish to keep.—Must keep. There are no resentments. Just clarity for action. The morning which is very clear kisses you—Sweetest Child in the world.—

Strand offered to accompany me so that I would not be alone. It was kind. His feeling is very deep for me. But I refused.—I know I must go alone.

—If you have any suggestions to make wire them at once when you receive this. I figure on your getting this on Friday & remember I leave here Saturday. When I leave Saturday it will be eight A.M. in Taos.

The sun sends you a kiss.

Georgia O'Keeffe · [Taos, New Mexico] · [July 16, 1929]

Dearest—Dearest—

When I ran out with my letter to you this morning it seemed a very unsatisfactory letter to me—I wanted to come right back and go on writing—I got ready to work after breakfast—but all day have been running to the telephone for telegrams—not only yours but Mabel's—several from her too—altogether I have had about ten today—I almost feel I have talked with you—

128. On July 15, 1929, Stieglitz dictated two of his letters to O'Keeffe to Strand because he was too weak to write.

I have wired you that it was my intention to go camping in the morning—before this wiring began—I finally gave up thinking of painting today and washed my head.

—I have decided—as long as you want so much to see me that I will take these three days as I had planned them—Pack my things on Sunday and leave on Monday—There seems to be no other way—

I can't have you going on in this way—but I must have some nights out under the stars —if the stars will be kind enough to shine on me—

I feel the long trip for you in the heat—even just to Chicago[129] is too much—especially in your excited state—and I feel that in such a state coming to this altitude—in spite of doctors —is too much—You know I don't always agree with doctors—

I am sure I am right about this—Albuquerque is a ghastly hot place—Raton is nearer here and more apt to be cool—but it is too high—I know I am right about this—Forgive me for taking these three days in the mountains—I will be with you as soon as possible after that— Pete will make me a box for my paintings while I am away—so packing will be easy when I get back—

It will be no use for you to wire me to do anything else. I have made up my mind. You are getting no good from the summer—and will be fit for nothing in the winter—This can't go on—and I am quite sure that if I go to Chicago or any other place to meet you—if I see you I will not come back here—It is no use to leave my things here—I had better clean it all up—

—I had hoped to stay until sometime in August anyway.—Mabel will be back the first week in August—There will be things I could attend to about the place that Beck is attending to now—but I cannot stand the idea of the state you are in—. You should know that my only wish since we have been together has been to help you with whatever direction you take—I know we will work out something for next winter together if you will just give yourself half a chance— But you will not be fit for anything if this keeps on—

Maybe I should go to you without these three days in the mountains—but it seems I just can't—it is that much just with the outdoors—and I seem to need it terribly—The Hapgood boy and girl and Charles Collier are going and two Indians[130]—

Please have patience with me—I hope it doesn't seem heartless to you—I wouldn't have been any use to you at all if I hadn't come away—

Please—please Boy—be very careful of yourself and very good to yourself till I come —I need you very much—and I know you need me—and all this carrying on is just too terrible—

I will be there very soon—

The moon carries you—for me—a long quiet kiss—holding you close till you sleep— Good Night—

129. On July 16, 1929, Stieglitz proposed meeting O'Keeffe in Chicago. On July 19, he telegraphed Beck Strand: "For forty-eight hours I have been thinking entirely in terms of Georgia and have decided it would be criminal on my part to disturb in any way her original plans and intentions for her stay in Taos. Unless she feels it wise for us to see each other before in Chicago or Albuquerque she should remain in Taos."
130. Tony and Juan Mirabal.

ON JULY 17, 1929, Stieglitz again wired both O'Keeffe and Beck Strand, insisting that it would be destructive for O'Keeffe to return to Lake George and that his doctor agreed it would not harm him to travel; to O'Keeffe he added: "All I want is to feel you love me — that I have a chance — & that we can work together — & be together."[131] In a letter written the same day, Beck asked Stieglitz how he expected O'Keeffe to "carry through the thing you want her to if she feels that anything can happen there — that even suicide is in your mood." She also reminded him of a conversation they had had the previous winter when he said: "'Beck, the word love — I don't know what that means' — I remember too that tears came to my eyes as you said that & I thought 'What of Georgia? Not even her?'"[132] When Stieglitz got Beck's letter, he immediately responded, lambasting her as "absolutely unseeing." He continued: "When I said I didn't know what love was I meant in plain English that I had not yet found anyone who knew. — You certainly don't know. Georgia does. — And when she takes my words literally it is not Georgia as I know her — it is echoes of others — resentments poisoning self. Great God I wish I never knew what love is. — But you do not, can never, understand — as the little self consumes you." He concluded: "I have learned one great thing — not to waste my time on people who have no vision — I know them well. — Pardon me for this brutality. If you had [been] a friend of mine you could have spared Georgia much anguish."[133]

486

With Beck fielding Stieglitz's numerous telegrams, O'Keeffe left Taos on July 18, 1929, to go camping on Mount Wheeler with Charles Collier, Miriam and Charles Hapgood, and Tony and Juan Mirabal, but not Tony Lujan, as she had earlier told Stieglitz. Despite rain and patches of snow still on the ground, their time on the mountain was exhilarating, but their ascent to the peak was harrowing. Charles Hapgood wrote his father: "We glimpsed all the kingdoms of the earth, in Biblical fashion, so to speak. We walked the horses along ridges that made one actually dizzy — for one could see almost perpendicular slopes on every hand descending a thousand feet or more." His sister, Miriam, added that they encountered a fierce thunderstorm, with sheet lightning that knocked off Charles's hat. Scared and disheveled, they left the peak, she wrote, "as quickly as possible and [took] another route home."[134]

Georgia O'Keeffe · [Wheeler Peak, New Mexico] · [July 18, 1929]

Good Morning Dearest—

It might be mid-afternoon or after supper — or anytime — I seem to have lost all sense of time — We are up here in the mountains at about the edge of the timber line — sheer rocky mountain tops with very little green on them and patches and ridges of snow all around — a very clear little mountain lake — lovely flowers — queer weathered trees and many dead ones — We rode thirty miles up here yesterday — almost all of it [on] trails — about ten miles through pouring rain

131. AS to Rebecca Strand, July 17, 1929; AS to GOK, July 17, 1929.
132. Rebecca Strand to AS, July 17, 1929
133. AS to Rebecca Strand, July 21, 1929.
134. See DeWitt, *Taos,* 11–12.

—much of it through aspen forest—millions of greenish white tree trunks with their dark green well-groomed looking leaves over head—in two places it was so steep we had to get off and lead the horses—

—It was a beautiful ride—up here there are many patches of snow—Talking about it just doesn't tell—We have two Indians and two pack horses—Charles Collier has been the leader—he is a nice boy—just seems to fit to camping—He and I talked till all hours by the fire last night—twice we started to bed and started talking all over again—*such* a clean kid—and you wonder how they stay that way with all they go through—He and I walked back through a fine piece of woods we had passed just before we got here—the trees are a great sight—about a third of them magnificent dead white trunks standing there—

We have all climbed all over the place—It pleases me that I can come nearer keeping up with Charles than any of them—You see I haven't climbed about and walked much for so long that I wasn't sure I could anymore—I find I am pretty tough—It is good to know.—The little lake turns to bright dark green in the afternoon—I hope it will not upset you too much that I came up here these three days before going back—

[July 19, 1929]
Another morning—

It rained yesterday afternoon—we were prepared—it didn't matter—The lake in the moonlight last night was one of the most beautiful things I ever saw—I stood out on a log alone long after the others had gone to bed looking at it—I wished you could see it with me—I wish you could do all this with me—I with you—

We all sat around after breakfast this morning and thought what a nice party we are and how glad we were that none of the others came—But I would like to be doing it with you—only I can't imagine you enjoying it—I have been the first one up and the last to bed both nights—I just can't bear to waste time sleeping—The night is so fine—such a tall white tree in front of an equally tall dark one right by the fire is wonderful to watch as the fire blazes—

It seemed I had to do this—and it seems so queer up here where it is so cold and no trace of human life—that I will be on the train in three days—But it is all right—I feel a need to see you—like the need to come up here I feel I *must* give you quiet—I wish I could feel sure that it is possible—

I can give you something anyway—I wish you could sit here with me on this old dead tree—one fallen across another making a perfect seat—It would be such a nice place to talk—and the place looks as tho no one has ever been here before—It will probably be a long time before anyone comes again—Too bad you can't fly here—

A bare—bare mountain top nearby through the trees—I lay in the sun on a big rock a long time and climbed down to another tiny lake on the other side of the ridge—

This is all so untouched up here it seems quite unbelievable—

I send you a clear fine kiss from it all—I will be with you soon—

Much—much love.

Alfred Stieglitz · Lake George, New York · July 20, 1929

8 P.M. Clear—icy cold.—I [am] absolutely dazed. Can't believe it.—Just sit & stare—& everything seems so glorious—everything—everybody. I just feel as if I'd have to kneel with bowed head for the rest of my life & just murmur—

Georgia—Forever.—Yes—Georgia—just Georgia!—You can't hear what I hear when I say so quietly to myself—Georgia.—

Telegrams from Beck.[135] Telegrams to you—you Grand Child still in camp—& I glad you are.—And three letters from you this morning. I hadn't heard in three days & didn't hope to hear for some days more—Strand & I walked to the post office—& there were letters in the box. I opened—three letters from you.—My hands were all atremble. I wondered should I open them. I really was afraid.—I had been steeling myself—trying to wean myself—I felt you had nothing left for me but pity perhaps—I opened an envelope & when I read Dearest—Dearest—I toppled & burst out crying. Strand caught me. Georgia you grand one. And I read. Still my Georgia—refound. I still can hardly believe it. And you ready to travel on Monday. Going to camp was so right. Going & staying in Taos all so right.—Everything right. But our parting as we did—living as we did—both inwardly crying for love & having it but not giving it—your steeling yourself, your letters not those of former years—my bleeding to death by inches for I was devoured with love—& the pain of knowing I had been a bungler—

So stupid—& feeling you no longer loved me—Have you any idea? You can't have.—I don't want you to have. I cried into the night: My anguish was love[136]—

Every breath was love—Every thought was love—And I cried out into the day: Why won't she hear me—Why doesn't she know having lived with me—worked with me—suffered with me—having loved me with all of herself—I loving her with all of me & more than myself—why can't she tell me she loves me still.—

But the cries were not heard.—The stars over your head would have told you—every one—had you looked—really looked—The moon would have echoed it—The sun spoke in loud tones—Georgia, he loves you as no woman was ever loved—As woman & artist—One!

Georgia! I love to say: Georgia—How often I said it & no echo—I listened & listened—Not a sound—

But all is different today.[137] All of nature—everybody—all singing a chorus: Georgia.—And what music!

And I read on—Georgia—I just couldn't stand the pain—the joy—I collapsed.—And

---

135. Beck Strand telegraphed Stieglitz twice on July 20, 1929, telling him that O'Keeffe had not returned from her camping trip.

136. In another letter written to O'Keeffe on July 29, 1929, Stieglitz recalled that when they first got together, O'Keeffe did not know he loved her. Writing of her in the third person, he said: "I told her I never knew what love is! And she heard the words & believed me. Funny woman.—Maybe stupid old man."

137. On July 19, 1929, Stieglitz told Norman she had brought this change in his mood: "You came [near to] losing me completely.—But a miracle has happened. And you have helped bring it about! Your letter. Your analysis of me.—At a critical moment."

Paul Strand, *Alfred Stieglitz*, 1929. Gelatin silver print, 4¾ x 3⁹⁄₁₆ in. (12 x 9 cm). Alfred Stieglitz/Georgia O'Keeffe Archive, Yale Collection of American Literature, Beinecke Rare Book and Manuscript Library. Copyright © Aperture Foundation, Inc., Paul Strand Archive.

then I read the other letters. But the one that gave me back life is the one I read first—The last one you wrote. Queer about the mail.—But it is well the letters came together. What happened was just right for me. I wired you at once about Albany, etc. thinking you in Taos again altho' hoping you were still in camp. I wired you about Albany & suggestions about our going off to Canada or Maine, etc., etc.—Then later on I wired again. I have no idea what—Then a third wire telling you I felt you should see your original intentions thro' & stay in Taos, etc., unless you felt it best to come, etc. I had wired to Beck yesterday you must stay in Taos.—It has been a dizzy pace.—

I'm dying to see you—but I somehow feel the summer belongs to Taos & as long as I know you really love me—are soft again & will let me feel your love—I'll be very good & manly as I can be—& be careful of myself (as best I can) & await the day of your natural coming. All I want is a lot of love—so much I need—from Georgia. Yes, you. What absurd people we have been.—I can't believe you love me again—never ceased loving me. Trying to smother it & so kill me—not intentionally—I being devoured with love for you—always—more & more! —Isn't it silly what we did to each other.—Tell me you love me—Fill a whole sheet with just

I Love You!

Let me feel it in every bit of me—Georgia, my Gorgeous Grand Georgia.—

And don't you feel much better?—Wait & see—I'll never let you go again—not without holding you so close & so long—that when you go you'll come back soon because you feel you must be held—so close—just by someone as foolish as I am always murmuring when alone—

Georgia.

The phone just rang—Western Union say the last two wires of mine received in Taos. That doesn't satisfy me so I'm having Western Union find out who received them. It's all too serious to have anything go wrong. You ought to phone Taos Junction & get copies of all the telegrams.—

—This distance business is pretty trying even by wire.—Letter writing is frightful. Much misunderstanding was due to distance—

I'm dead tired—I must stop now—

I take you in my arms—& both of us will kiss quietly & fall asleep face to face— & sleep peacefully. Like we did years ago—

I love you Georgia! And I kiss you so quietly—you'll fall right to sleep—

And when morning comes & you have rested—!—?—

Do you remember when the first time an unbeautiful thing happened between us— it was here in Lake George—Do you remember your lying in bed & saying good night said: "We mustn't let anything unbeautiful happen between us again." I somehow feel tonight it can never happen again—nothing not beautiful!

Good Night—

It's icy cold. Another kiss—

Georgia O'Keeffe · [Taos, New Mexico] · [July 21, 1929]

Dearest—

I wish I could see you tonight—and just curl up by you and be quiet—I feel we would both understand everything and just be quiet together—

That ride down the mountain yesterday was a little much—We went to the top of Mount Wheeler and rode about a mile and a half along the ridge to the very top—When I think of it now I don't see how we did it—or I should say how I did it—Miriam Hapgood gave up long before the top—On the way down we were lost for about two hours and I went down a mountainside that almost makes me think today when I recall it that I am lying to myself—

Thirty-five miles is quite a few—even on a good horse—It was dark when we got here —Mrs. Hapgood gave us supper—and I came over here to my letters—and bed. Beck phoned the telegram for me—

The letters I read last night—but I was just in a daze—This morning Beck brought me breakfast—and I started reading them all over again—

Letters and telegrams—The thing that I come to is this—Your suffering is just too terrible[138]—At times I felt I must go to you immediately—I understand your conflict over whether I should go to you or stay awhile yet—I understand your conflicts over many things —and I want you to feel that I do not love you any the less because of them—

I have decided to stay here a little while yet—really because I want to work a little more —That camping trip seemed to complete something for me—

If I were to go to you tomorrow—it would be with an unfinished feeling that I know would breed resentment in me—and start anew that everlasting call that this country has for me—

I will see how my work goes for a week—I have nothing of landscape yet—Today I had to show my things that I have three times—Covarrubias and his lady[139] were here for lunch and wanted to see them—they are both fine—he particularly—but I liked her too—They liked them—Then Miriam Hapgood and Charles Collier—They were sweet—Charles remarked as tho he had made a discovery—his eyes shining—"You know they have the sort of thing I like to find in people—They are so definite—so clear-cut and clean." You must meet him in the fall— He is fine—Miriam has a lot of her father—looks fragile and blond and light blue and loves the darkest most passionate color—and stands there with her eyes shining—idealistic—

Then Scott and his lady[140]—I had invited them for lunch—They came at 2:30—It never occurred to me that they hadn't eaten—we eat at twelve—my mind hasn't been any too clear today—

---

138. On July 20, 1929, Lee Stieglitz wrote O'Keeffe, telling her that Alfred "is going to pieces or has already gone to pieces I am sorry to say under the strain of worry and fear of the future [and that] you may not need him in your life any longer." He urged O'Keeffe not only to write to Stieglitz every day and reassure him that she would spend the winter with him in New York but also to encourage him to rent another gallery in the fall.

139. The artist and *New Yorker* illustrator Miguel Covarrubias was married to Rosa Rolanda, a modern dancer.

140. The author Cyril Kay Scott was married to Rose Allatini, a novelist, one of whose pen names was Eunice Buckley.

They got groggy over something—Beck had words with the lady—I don't know what about—I was talking with Miriam and Charles—

Anyway—I was glad when everyone was gone. Mrs. Hare was in this morning too—she came while I was still in bed—I read your letters in bed—We never ever had so many guests in a day before—

Scott said my things looked different from anything of mine he had seen—

With my daze from the camping trip—your letters—and all these people—it has been a busy day—Beck and I just fell in a heap when the Scotts left—they were the last to leave—Beck is riding tonight—While I am writing Spud Johnson and Lewis came over—The moon was just coming over the mountain—We sat on the front porch and talked—They thought I might be going tomorrow—

You see—I understand your wanting me to come to you—and I want you to understand and believe me when I say that I want to go to you—I want to be with you—I want you to feel that I am very close to you—and that you are by far the dearest most beautiful thing in the world to me—and that I am with you even tho I am here—that my doing some more work here seems important to me solely because it seems important to me for our going on together —Don't you understand Boy? It is important for our going on together like I feel your caring for your physical body is important and necessary for the same reason—

When I have said to you that I feel different—have changed—I think you mistake me —for maybe I change again—Your making me feel that you need me makes a great difference to me—and in spite of all you have written me I didn't feel it in a real warm living way until today—

Maybe something completed with that camping trip—relaxed something in me—because as I read your letters today I felt myself flow out to you with the old soft beautiful kind of feeling of love and the necessity for you and all that you have meant to me—It was a great relief—as tho some terrible thing had passed—

I had four days of letters—really terrible letters—and at the same time very beautiful —When Charles and Miriam came over I was tempted to give them to them to read—it would mean much to both of them—I feel I would like to give them to all the youngsters that I like to read—and I like Charles and Miriam very much—

The sequence of the letters—coming all at once was really like wonderful music that touches one with terrific sadness and beauty to the very quick—

But don't mistake me or mistrust me—my feeling for you that seems to come warm and clear and full does not come from pity or anything like that—It comes from my feeling that you need me—and I have wanted to be needed—and wanted to give—

Please tell me that you trust me—Tell me too that you have let down and are quiet—

I do not feel that talk is so important—or that thinking is either—Charles and Miriam and I argued for hours around the fire day before yesterday—afternoon and night till way late at night—He a realist—wanting to *know* everything—she an idealist wanting to believe many things—My final comment was that all the thinking and arguing didn't really get one anywhere —all I cared about was that someone really loved me very much and that I could really love them very much—all the rest of it didn't matter—.

I hope my deciding to stay a little longer will seem right to you—I assure you I only do it with the feeling of trust in you that you believe in me and my feeling about you—and will let down and be quiet—It is unfortunate that we have spent all this time apart but I feel it is bringing us together with many things clear that could not have been clear in any other way—

Good Night Dearest—I must go to bed—Miss Young laughed when she saw me today and remarked that even that camping trip didn't make me look tired—Well—I know I am ready for bed—I wish I could sleep beside you—Please get the notion of any change in our relationship out of your head as far as I am concerned unless you mean it has changed for the better —that we understand better and are closer—I hope you feel it that way—I can't believe that all this is for nothing—

Let me kiss you Good Night—and feel the night when you get this—that I am holding you very warm and close when you go to bed—wanting you to sleep—

Thank you very much for the two skies—They are very—very beautiful—I kiss you again for them—

Good Night—

Georgia O'Keeffe · [Taos, New Mexico] · [July 24, 1929]

I have your registered letter—and your telegram telling me you are quiet—and that your New Jerusalem now lives[141]—I got it out and looked at it—You must mean that things are singing within you—but in the letter you write as though you expect to die at any moment—

You speak of what happened three years ago[142]—You see—I lost my faith—the kind of faith that one has always had—conscious and unconscious from childhood—that kind of faith may be an illusion like a religion—but it was as though my backbone was gone—

You laughed about it to the men and were very tender with the women—

For me there was nothing—till I didn't even dare put out my hand to touch you—it would only be shaken off—I do not feel that my resentments grew into a hideous growth as you say—I simply peeled away more and more of my impulses—discarded more and more of my feelings—I simply felt I wasn't anything to you but a mild habit—often habitually irritating —that is why it seemed logical to go away—

I wrote you of my doings—I had very few feelings left—till I touched out here—and touched it *hard*—and I seemed to get back to what I had been before I gave up myself to you—

141. Stieglitz had recently sent O'Keeffe one of his photographs of clouds, which he referred to as "New Jerusalem." In the Book of Revelation, after John witnesses the new heaven and earth, he sees a new city, the New Jerusalem (also called the tabernacle of God), descending from heaven; see Book of Revelation 3:12 and 21:2. On July 22, 1929, Stieglitz clarified his use of "New Jerusalem," telling O'Keeffe he had an "extraordinary feeling of peacefulness—It's as if I were in a New World—I am —and all here is so quiet. Everyone seems to have been affected by what I am. It's all in me.—See what you have given me— & everyone else!"

142. In his letter of July 18, 1929, Stieglitz again alluded to the incident in 1926 with the cook Ilse and asserted his innocence: "I knew that what you said I had done I hadn't. Say it now. And it hurt me beyond words that you didn't—couldn't—listen to the spirit" and had not "believed me."

That is why I have had to do all the things I have done—to stretch something inside myself that had almost died—I have to love and I have to laugh—and I have to have the sun shine on me —and if I couldn't love you—as I have often told you—the next best thing is the outdoors— It has been good to me—

I felt as tho you had shut me up in a hard dark tight case where there was nothing—If I had stayed there you wouldn't be feeling about me as you do—

You cannot give me back that faith you took away—that is something I must live without—My lack of it horrifies Miriam Hapgood—But what I have taken in its place makes Charles look at me with a deep childish smile of understanding—He wants to *know*—she wants to believe—Charles is twenty—Miriam twenty-three—they are both beautiful—

Knowing is as beautiful as believing—and with what I *know* I think you cannot hurt me anymore—and the love seems to have gone far deeper down into me—

There is something quite untouchable about it to me—

I could just sit here and cry for wanting an absolute understanding with you—

—I waked this morning feeling you almost pulling me to you—and I thought I must get up and pack and go to you—but I was all ready to go out to paint—so I went—Lewis went with me and sat and read on the front seat—I on the floor in the back—we talked very little —He just gave me some very good points on driving—With all these people at work on me I ought to learn something—

I want so much to work here—and you are there—I feel almost pulled in two in the middle—

The painting of this morning is no good—but I was much excited over it—and know something will come—Only I feel I could sit in that spot at the side of the road for the rest of my life—and not be through with it—

So it seems to me that leaving it now or a week or a few weeks from now doesn't make much difference—

It is all so ridiculous—Living is so ridiculous—

I can't think of anything that seems sane but loving and being loved—

I am quite distressed with my desire to go to you—and my urge to try to work here—

Dr. Walker was in this evening with two men—one of them an astonishing creature— a scientist[143]—I don't even know his name or where he is from—he sails for Japan in two weeks —He was a cross between a spark from a star—a little fiend—and much love and tender liveliness—I went with them to Dasburg's for supper—His conversation was the livest I have heard out here—like lightning cracking around—but lovely in feeling—and so funny—We laughed—and laughed—

The night sky was wonderful when they brought me home—

—Dearest—Good Night—a long—long kiss—very tender and warm—

I don't see how you could be feeling all this time that I don't love you—What else could I love—when one's heart has been touched to the core like mine has been—

143. Gustav Eckstein, a professor at the University of Cincinnati and an expert on animal behavior, was working on a book on Hideyo Noguchi, a Japanese scientist.

—Oh Boy—it is all too awful—and too terrible that we are not together—touching
—skin to skin—I may have to go to you soon—

Good Night—

It is queer the way I am getting to feel myself the way I felt before I went to you—and
you speak of the same thing in your letter—only you have made me wiser and I thank you—

ON JULY 27, O'Keeffe, Charles Collier, and Charles and Miriam Hapgood, accompanied by
Juan Mirabal and his son Tony, rode to Kiowa Ranch, the 160-acre property that Mabel Luhan
had given to Frieda and D. H. Lawrence a few years earlier. Seventeen miles north of Taos and
more than eight thousand feet high, Kiowa was the site where Lawrence had hoped to establish
a utopian society, Rananim, although Brett was the only one to accept his offer. When O'Keeffe
arrived, the Lawrences were not there, but Brett was staying at her own small (9 × 11 foot) cabin,
which was nearby. Because Lawrence believed people "no longer have any real contact with the
earth," the property was deliberately kept simple.[144] Brett's house was hardly more than a shed,
Charles Hapgood wrote his father, and "very public," and Lawrence's house, where Georgia and
Miriam spent a few nights, was occupied "by wild animals," including chipmunks, a coyote, and
a porcupine that "had to be ejected by force."[145] While O'Keeffe was once again incommunicado,
Stieglitz became convinced he had lost his love.

Alfred Stieglitz · Lake George, New York · July 27, 1929

Georgia—Georgia—Great Guardian that hovers over us both—I don't know what to say.—
I'm all ashake. I went to the Village again accidentally & found your letter—telling me all. And
you at Brett's & I can't reach you!—I thank you for telling me. It's too ghastly.—All that happened to you was happening to me—only I didn't lose faith—I simply couldn't understand so
many things. All becomes clear now—But Georgia—it's terrible you are not here—just ghastly
—that I can't hold you & talk—I laughed about you to men—& was tender to women!

Great Guardian—and you let me touch you—& when you disbelieved me I let you
touch me—Georgia—Georgia—It is all too ghastly—all so untrue—all out of value. I robbed
you of your faith—while you were strengthening mine!! No wonder I wished to die.—And the
New Jerusalem—I singing is your interpretation. Great Guardian—that picture is a chorus of
all singing together—my faith—in you—& all—I had received a sign of love from you that's
why I sent the picture. I the fool!!—I laughing at you with the men—& tender with women.
No wonder I felt your gradual withdrawing—which made me withdraw. First I was "He" when
you came, then I went thro' grades to "Stieglitz"—I didn't understand—I merely heard.—As I
saw you take away your brushes here—& pack up linen while I was sick. Don't you think I saw
& knew. And it nearly killed me. For I didn't understand when you said you loved me & were
solicitous of me—

---

144. Dorothy Brett, *Lawrence and Brett* (Philadelphia, 1933; repr. Santa Fe, 1974), 146–147.
145. DeWitt, *Taos*, 12.

Georgia, Georgia—Why didn't you give me a chance—one chance—Why do you think I worked for you as I did not sparing myself—because I laughed at you & was tender with women? I have been tender with men & women all my life—that's my natural self—When Strand brought you north, didn't you want me to throw him out. You didn't want to see him.—And I wouldn't—I was tender with Strand. And I well knew why you didn't want to see him. Did I lose my faith?—

Great Guardian—Georgia—Georgia—& so you went on & found fault with this & with that & finally I did things I didn't want to do—because inwardly I saw destruction ahead. And I had to make good for ourselves. Wasn't I kicked out of home because I had a mistress? Isn't Kitty in an asylum because her father is a rotter?

Great Guardian—Georgia—Georgia—I'll win back your faith for you—That will be my work—That's all I must live for—I robbed you of your faith & you continued to live with me—& you didn't believe me & I lost my self respect. Georgia, Georgia—You must believe—I do.—

And I can't get at you, you are at Brett's—Why am I not struck dead—maybe you'd believe me then.—Yes I was tender with women & tender with men.—Should I become hard as steel—

496
You have lived this summer—I have been dying by inches—I want you to live & laugh —& enjoy people—I'm willing to die alone—I know that all you say about me is unseen— Values warped—all out of recognition—

Georgia, Georgia, now I understand your letters—everything.—And yet I understand nothing. You have damned me. And I needed a woman's love to release me. And you have said you love me—No wonder I didn't know what love is—

Georgia, Georgia—& you are at Brett's—And I'm glad you are there—& I have to live four days before I can reach you after this—Georgia—Georgia—how can I live and face the world—Without your knowing this letter stamps me a liar. Every word I uttered in Room 303 you prove a lie. Prove me a hypocrite. Maybe I am both.—But what of me—it's you I think of. How could you let me touch you—I know now why you always cried when you got through—How could you take money through me for the pictures which were of your & my blood—

Georgia—Georgia—I ought not believe in any human being, not in you—nor anyone else. And not in myself. But I can't help believing. For real beauty is an affirmation of faith. And I feel you still have faith only you are trying to destroy [it] because I hurt you to the quick & you hurt me to the quick. It's a wonder I'm alive—it's a wonder you are not mad.

Georgia—Georgia—I think I could show you your great fallacy—I'm sure I could. Let me come to Albuquerque—or Chicago—I & you must meet—This dare not go on. No wonder both of us have been sick so much with all this in each of us. Where are the men to whom I laughed. I'll kill any one of them who has the nerve to say that. I'm a murderer as it is. Murdered your faith.—Why not die in the chair—it's more honorable than living like this.— Georgia, how could you go with all this in you—& not say a word to me. I blind with Room— blind with eagerness to prove lies—to get money for Marin, for you & Lachaise, Hartley & Dove—& Tofel—Blind—Blind—

Georgia—how could you? Is there a woman in the world who will release me?—

I the great affirmer of woman telling the world that you never lied—never even thought a lie—& here this now—You honest—yes honest but unseeing—& I the great liar—Beck whom you wanted me to throw out—your friend now in laughter & sunshine & freedom!

Georgia—& you at Brett's.—For four days.—And you talking to youngsters—& I telling them about you—affirming faith.—All so ghastly—so diabolical. Has it come to this? You left on a 27. This comes on a 27.—

All 27 is an evil omen for me—the perfect number—I the opposite of perfection— a robber of faith, adulterer, hypocrite, liar, & what not—Yes, that's what I must be. For you say that.—And much more—

But it's good you have told me I stand damned.—As I had damned myself. My letters were all true. Even tho you did write to people I bombarded you with letters & they made no impression on you—you were happy, & laughed & felt well. And yet I went on—writing— & writing.—"Beautiful" letters! How do I know whether you mean it or not

We slept together when you—Oh! I can't say it.—I believed you. Believe you still— love you.—I can't give you Taos which you love—& give that little you have left of me at the same time. Taos is not for me. I always knew it.—I knew it years ago.—I knew what Mabel Luhan touched was death for me—I am ready to see you anywhere at any time. Georgia I must have clarity between us—Painting can wait—Taos won't run away—but my life will not last long—cannot feeling as you do about me—

Georgia—I daren't kiss you—I dare not say I love you—I dare not say I'll work for you —all I know whatever there is left of me must bring about that your faith be reestablished—

Georgia—Georgia—how could you all these years—I swear I'm just a fool—a swinish fool perhaps—but—now I know why I didn't kill myself that night—I had to live to hear what I had done to you—robbed you of all faith.—

And you are at Brett's—And I'm glad even tho I'd love to wire you at once—Don't you see how sardonic this is—all just like this. I receive this letter the day I cannot reach you for four days.—I ought to die tonight—but I dare not die—I must work & work & work to give you back what I have stolen from you—That's all that's left. How I'll do it I don't know.—Maybe you'll help me a little—maybe we can find some way to release us both.—I want to kiss you & I dare not touch you.—And now I know why I didn't touch you before you went—I felt truly even tho a criminal in every other respect.—

My head is splitting—Good Night—

I want to kiss you—touch you—be so close to you—But I'm damned & may not—

Oh you poor child—Kitty insane—my other daughter dead[146]—& you worse than either—my other child—And I to live—

But thank the Guardian you have told me—I may not even touch your feet—

Somehow I understood Marin's not writing.—He saw—& didn't wish to write.—

It's all too ghastly—And I cannot get at you—if I could I'd come to Chicago at once.

A few hours ago I felt a great hope—now I feel so filthy—nothing can cleanse me—

146. Elsa Bauschmied (see p. 164, n. 347).

And I believed myself purified—clean—through sorrow & suffering—Georgia, Georgia—how can you wish to touch me. That's what I do not understand.—And you are at Brett's—and I am nowhere—

You say I laughed at you—at your love—

Georgia—Georgia—am I mad—do I hear right—I laughed at you—where did you get that? I canonizing you—slaving for you—laughed at you?—Where did you get that? Ask Brett—ask them all whether I ever even smiled—when I spoke of you—you the woman to release me—& I laughed?—You say that. Believe it. And say you understand. It's a lie—I never laughed at you—Georgia—Georgia—

But where did you get that from—Four days you'll be gone—& I'll have to wait—to wire—& you with this feeling—so diabolically wrong. And Beck not correcting it—

I am to meet people you say—Not a soul till I'm clean—Can I ever be clean?—I doubt it if an iota of what you say is true.

You say you must live without faith—I still have my faith—I wish I hadn't—it would be easy to live—I know exactly how.—Georgia—won't you help to cleanse me—but I forgot you may not touch me for I'm unclean—

No wonder your paintings failed.—

The "New Jerusalem" I photographed one day after we were very loving & you had said many kind things about people you had always said unkind things of—And I innocent fool saw a great hope of collective togetherness—my great dream!

Do you see all my pictures that way?—I thinking you saw them?—And so I thought you saw me—but now I know how you see—

I don't see how I can go on writing when you say you love me & damn me at the same time. As you said I'll come if you need me but I hate Lake George—I love it here!—

And still I love you—have never ceased to love you—have never laughed at your love—never laughed at you—I'm not the laughing kind—

—You sneered at my letters full of love—Yes, you did—& still I loved you—loved you more than ever. You say if you hadn't gone away I wouldn't ever have found this love. Of course not, you wouldn't have given me a chance. Even since going you haven't—I have forced a chance. Had I not you wouldn't have moved a finger.—And yet you say you love me!—Well my love is a greater love than yours—or a man's love is different from a woman's—

I can write no more letters after this one—you have made it impossible. When you are ready to see me, I'll come at once as I wrote you this morning.—

My poor child—Fatherless—

Remember I love you—I know as no one is loved—I the unclean one.—

Alfred Stieglitz · Lake George, New York · July 28, 1929

2 P.M. Only a very short note—it's hot & I'm about all in.—But am all right. You wild beautiful child who came near killing me again.—Last night I had to go to the Village & dropped into the post office—I had a lovely letter from you in the morning & wrote you—& the telegram telling

me you had gone off with Brett for four days—I found a letter from you & read—& literally keeled over—the one in which you tell me how I had robbed you of your faith—& how for three years you were gradually weaning yourself from me—And you at Brett's—not within reach for four days!! Georgia Child I'm glad it's all out finally—But I staid up all night & wrote & wrote—& wrote—& paced the floor—prowled about the house like a haunted ghost—Georgia dearest—it was terrible—All light was suddenly gone—I felt the end of everything—I still had faith—I loved you more than ever.—But the agony.—And you without reach. The whole morning was one of self torture trying to see straight—My faith remained unshaken—I have my signals that remind me not to let go—they always appear at critical moments—And my love for you became a mad passion—And I helpless. I understood you. Saw you out there. A conflict.—A tremendous battle—tho seemingly none—I don't know what would have happened hadn't Strand been here—He has his own problem. We men.—

—Finally we went to the post office. Two letters from you. My hands were all atremble as I tore open the envelopes. I went to Strand's car—& actually became hysterical—I kissed the feather[147]—I cried—I did many crazy things—for there it was in both letters—so warm—so loving—so coming—so needing—Yes, yes we are together again. No more impulses to be smothered. I'll not let you.—We have found each other again—I can't write—I wrote so much all night—

I'll read you the letters—I won't send them. Isn't it rotten there is no airplane here I could engage & fly to you & carry you off to some star—far away from all humans—just you & I—together more so than ever—I knew you must have been unwell when writing—I made allowance for it—but—but all I can say now I'll never let you go again very long—

I need you Georgia—I need your love—I need your nearness—I need your arms around me—I need my arms around you—I need great closeness—I need to talk with you—& need you to talk to me—I need everything about you—but let me live a little longer so that I can be near you & you near me.

A never ending kiss on the mouth—

Georgia O'Keeffe · [**Kiowa Ranch, New Mexico**] · [**July 29, 1929**]

Good Morning—Dearest—

I wish I could actually picture to you the details of all that has happened—it is quite impossible—I wish you could be sitting here beside me under a huge green pine tree on the side of the hill—in my red coat—nothing under it—waiting to continue the sun bath that was interrupted by a cloud—There is scrub oak and small cedar and sagebrush about—and a sort of feeling that no one will ever come here—that I can sit forever—

We didn't start up here at eight in the morning on Saturday as we intended—Shoes missing on the horses and other such small details kept us from starting till two in the afternoon

147. As she would often do in the 1930s and 1940s, O'Keeffe had enclosed a feather in her letter to Stieglitz. Although less frequently, Stieglitz also occasionally enclosed pressed flower petals in his letters.

Anonymous, *Dorothy Brett*, undated. Gelatin silver print, 10 x 8 in. (25.4 x 20.3 cm).
Mabel Dodge Luhan Papers, Yale Collection of American Literature,
Beinecke Rare Book and Manuscript Library.

—Then we started off in the rain with good crashes of thunder and lightning—Nobody minded—We all have nice greasy yellow slickers—had expected to be rained on—so we rode along—it was much pleasanter than hot sun—we all liked it—The country is wonderful—and you feel so close to it on a horse—Sometimes we ride for miles without a word—single file—sometimes we bunch together and talk hard but mostly there is very little talk—It rained off and on all the way up here—the storms coming and going and occasional sunlight make the landscape very fine—I felt I had just started when we got here—The seventeen miles seemed nothing—

    Brett was much pleased to see us—She has two boys staying with her—friends of Mrs. Hare—We had brought a tent and sleeping bags—You would have laughed to see the procession of four boys bent with loads climbing the hill to the big pine tree where we were going to tent—

    Well—we slept up there by the big pine tree—a stormy sky—then the moon and stars—and finally the sun in the morning—I got up and went to the spring with a pan of hot water and had a bath between the two—and started breakfast—Charles came along and finished—Needless to say Brett's housekeeping is rather haphazard—I had a sun bath and slept—Oh I forgot—we sat at breakfast till nearly noon arguing—

After my sun bath and lunch Brett and I went to ride and telephone—the telephone house is about a mile and a half away—Then we rode up a canyon—through nice woods till the rocks became very sheer—altogether I guess we rode six or seven miles—I rode one of her horses and she rode mine—I just want to ride other horses—Mabel's white Charlie that I ride is just too perfect—Brett's horse is all right—The ride was fine—We met the two boys on the way and brought back the milk—thirteen quarts—It seems just too funny but everyone drinks it—

I was very tired last night so Miriam and I got into a big bed in Brett's sitting room right after supper—The boys rather cheerlessly went off to play cards and we had a long night's sleep—Charles came in this morning and offered to bring us breakfast in bed—The two boys and Brett ran their legs off for us all morning while Miriam and I lay in bed—each with a huge cow bell that we rang whenever we wanted anything—There was much laughing and it finally ended with a water battle—

And when I was up and dressed and had a bath I went out to that pine tree where I started writing you this morning—everything out there smelled so good—I just sat and looked at the green in front of me for hours it seemed—

Maybe all this seems like nonsense to you—Maybe I am crazy that I enjoy it so much—Maybe I am selfish that I do it and leave you alone—I some way feel it is right for me to do—

It has been pouring rain—as soon as it clears Brett and I are going to ride again—Miriam and Charles are sitting in the Ford—Brett's Ford—at the foot of the hill—I ran down to them with a basket of lunch in the rain—Nobody wanted me to—but I knew they would like it—

Brett tramps about in the rain in rubber boots and overalls—She really fits here—exactly fits—

It is all a haphazard time—even the way toilet paper hangs on a wire in the small outhouse—I brought everything up here to work—but just *being* seems so important—just sitting out there looking into space seems so important—

I don't know why I must be this way—but I must—

I am going to ride another horse today—she has a whole pasture full—ten or twelve —I just must try a few—Some of them are Tony's—and some of them hers and it is so nice riding up here—all wild—but fairly good trails—

I kiss you Boy—I am very careful—You need not worry about me—it is all very good —it feels almost like flying in the air—

My very dearest love goes to you—and all of me—

Alfred Stieglitz · Lake George, New York · July 31, 1929

Good Morning you glorious woman—my woman!

It is 6:45. Rather later for me than recently. What a morning—Such weather.—Clear & cool. Incredible. One day after another. But bad for water, bad for crops—still marvelous. Glorious woman—my Georgia O'Keeffe, "my"—still fine as the lark!—I love you.—It's marvelous to be as full of love as I am.—Not in love—maybe a little of that at times—but really just love itself.—Everything in the world exists for me only thro' that love—A burning star—way beyond stars—my Georgia. Yes, I am purified thro' suffering as few have ever known. And tho grand times you have been having—I know too you Sweetest Woman, you have not had an easy time. But you must [be] very happy now for I know you love me—I feel it—It was terrible to be without that feeling—I feel it for I know my love could not be growing beyond all space as it is were it not reinforced thro' love itself—A woman's love—Georgia's—A woman.—Do you like to feel what you're feeling?—When I look back to the three months they seem like a terrible illness—terrible—Georgia dearest—I came close to going forever. And to have gone knowing that my last word could not be Georgia—I do not know what the last word might have been—was the most terrible feeling I ever experienced. And when I realized that I was living again—I knew that there was no more ugliness for me—there was only Georgia my beautiful—and no words—just a peaceful beingness beyond all wonder. I love Georgia O'Keeffe—my wife—Yes, my wife—Don't be alarmed[148]—I'll not use the word before people, nor do I think & feel in such terms—but just this morning—now this moment—I seem to feel it necessary to say my wife! It does sound a bit funny. And I'd like to kiss you because of its "funniness."—But you are that—my wife—& everything else beyond that—Do you like to be loved by me?—I'm such a fool—but maybe not quite such a fool as you knew.—

502

And now for some news.—To my delight Beck & Paul turned up.—And we have had many many hours together. Very, very fine. Pretty hard for Beck at first.[149] But all very perfect. —She'll undoubtedly let you hear.—Of course I heard much about you—nothing I didn't know —but it felt as [if] Taos weren't quite so far away.—It is pretty far even now. Your wire came at ten last night—I called for it in the Village. And it capped a great day.—Enclosed also came. I think you'll like what Mumford wrote.[150] I do.—So you haven't received my two wires sent Monday—the other Tuesday. Beck had said there was probably a storm. The wires could wait. And yet I love to feel I'm in direct touch with you every day.—

Curiously enough I had many extraordinary letters yesterday. "New" people—& Mumford's article came too. My correspondence is very small.—No letter from you. Naturally. I knew there couldn't be any.—I'll write to Brett in a day or so.—Well, Mabel is on the way.—And Ida[151] too.—I wonder what Ida'll say when she sees you.—Don't prompt her.—I know you must be thin. As I am thin—down twelve pounds—133.—But I'm feeling very fit. I have eaten no bread or butter since here—& haven't averaged four hours in bed.—I'm really very fit.— The cutting out of bread & butter is my own doing.—I have no idea why I cut them out—they just seemed to go against me.—You know that feeling—Maybe very unintelligent to be guided by it.—But I wonder.—Haven't been so well in years.—

---

148. In a letter written to O'Keeffe on July 24, 1929, Stieglitz noted that she had "always resented" that they got married, even though he "explained over & over again why there was no other way because of our poverty."

149. After returning to the East Coast at the end of July, Beck wrote O'Keeffe that when she first spoke to Stieglitz, they discussed the letter he had written her earlier in the summer that had "hurt" her so deeply. He gave her "a lot of pretty awful punishment," she wrote, "but in the end it was all for the best and cleared up a lot of things" (Rebecca Strand to GOK, Aug. 2, 1929).

150. Lewis Mumford, "Alfred Stieglitz, '84," *City College Alumnus* 25 (May 1929), 149–151.

151. After her operation in Buffalo, Luhan hired O'Keeffe's sister Ida, who was a nurse, to accompany her back to New Mexico and care for her. Stieglitz wrote to Ida on July 29, 1929, urging her to "take a bit of care of Georgia—she needs it more than Mabel Luhan.—I just know it."

How quiet it is—I hardly conscious of people—as I wasn't conscious of horses or anything else while sitting at the races[152]—only conscious of one thing: Georgia O'Keeffe. And I repeat—the feeling of that is wonderful—Nothing could be more wonderful except having Georgia O'Keeffe not quite so far away—& yet she is right here inside of me—near me close outside of me too. When dawn broke & I half opened my eyes—I said: I love you my Georgia—& seemed to fall asleep again—& I felt you come closer.—Silent. Asleep.—But very very close. No wonder there is a deep quiet within me.—A quiet I have never known.—

Come bring me your lips—come very close—let me embrace you—hold you awhile—forever—Do you realize what you are to me? My very life—Yes, that is what the summer has brought me—and I like the feeling—It is like the silence this morning—so rich & full—for the morning is intense with light—pregnant with every beautiful potential—

Georgia, my wife, Great Woman.—

I love you.—Do you like it?—

Georgia O'Keeffe · [**Kiowa Ranch, New Mexico**] · [**August 1, 1929**]

Good Morning—Dearest—

We go down the mountain today—It has been six days here—it seems like one and at the same time like a million—I have ridden a lot—there are seven of us—Brett—her two boys and we four—it makes quite a string on the road—tho we only all went together once—The rides are very lovely—I have gone at least six or seven miles every day—am nicely bruised in the knees—but I don't mind—It is worth it—one just can't get around any other way—I have just had an hour's sun bath—you just walk to the edge of the woods—a few feet from the house and take off your clothes and wander off looking for a sunny spot to lie down—You feel no one was ever here and no one ever will come—

It is certainly a great place—

I wish you were here—I feel a great pull toward you—almost as tho you have hold of my hand and are drawing me toward you—

But all this is something that stretches far—far into me—touches things in me way beyond what I knew I was before—It is as tho I thought I was one thing and find I am something else—something way beyond myself—

I hope you really love me—something in me only seems to exist in you—

My dear—dear love goes to you with my fondest kiss—and need—

ON AUGUST 1, O'Keeffe briefly returned to Taos, but she and Collier immediately drove back to Kiowa Ranch so that she could make a painting. Two days later, they went back to Taos and then drove to a dance at the Santa Domingo pueblo with Brett and Miriam Hapgood. Afterward,

---

152. In an effort to keep his brother from brooding about O'Keeffe, Lee Stieglitz took him to the races at Saratoga on July 29, 1929.

O'Keeffe and Collier again visited Garland and Rodakiewicz at the H & M Ranch in Alcalde, where they made plans to go to the Grand Canyon with Garland, Rodakiewicz, and Johnson. Although Mabel suggested that Collier might prefer to stay in Taos with friends his own age, O'Keeffe responded, "'Well, I am going to make him go.'"[153] And she did. Driving Garland's Rolls Royce and Packard—both convertibles that purred "like velvet," O'Keeffe said—the group left Alcalde on August 9 and headed west to Flagstaff, Arizona, then north to the south rim of the Grand Canyon. Roaming throughout northern Arizona, they drove to the Little Colorado River Canyon, then through the Painted Desert and the Navajo Indian Reservation. After going north to Bryce Canyon, Utah, they crossed the Grand Mesa in Colorado and Independence Pass, near Aspen, then drove to Colorado Springs before returning to Taos.

Georgia O'Keeffe · [Kiowa Ranch, New Mexico] · [August 2, 1929]

Well—here I am in Brett's disorderly sitting room—I wish I could tell you all the funny details of the life here—about the chipmunks eating up the bed—and the way everything is done and not done—

Supper is over—a funny gasoline lamp hisses on the table—makes a very good light —It is raining out—Brett sits in the shadow of a suitcase and looks as if she is figuring on her income tax—

When we got down to Mabel's yesterday after riding almost all afternoon in the rain everything seemed soft and beautiful and colorful—all the flowers around my little house are in bloom—It all seemed so inviting—so tempting—everything welcoming—I only saw Mabel for about three minutes—was told not to go see her at all but went anyway—

It took me a long time to read your letters—I got on the bed to do it—in the middle Ida came in—and Tony—and finally Charles—He wanted to be sure I wanted to come back up here today—Ida is looking fine—Charles promised to be back by eight this morning—I lent him the Ford to cart his things out to where he lives—I was up at six—

I didn't tell you that after reading your letters last night I walked across the alfalfa field with a candle to light the way and sent you a telegram at eleven o'clock—and carried back a bucket of hot water to take a bath—

I unpacked and packed my suitcase this morning and washed my head on the front porch and visited Mabel and Charles and I were off before nine—We stopped for supplies in the village and I got your registered letters and sent you a telegram—I feel you so much with me today—all soft and warm and nice almost as tho I can feel the moisture of your breath—

We had a nice ride up—Charles driving—I didn't want to get tired and had buzzed about at a pretty lively pace before leaving Taos—He drives very well—We were here in less [time]—Brett and the boys were a bit surprised to see us driving up—It felt good to get here— there is something so bare about it all—We immediately got to work—Charles made me a very convenient arrangement to hold my canvas to paint—also dug some charcoal out of the fire

153. DeWitt, *Taos*, 18.

for me—I scrubbed my canvas then sat down on the barn stoop to read your letters while it dried—You seem so close to me—I hadn't read them coming up in the car because we came too fast and—also—I like to be alone and quiet when I read them—

Dearest—I feel like saying *Yes* to everything you say to me or ask me when it is a [feeling] moving toward me—You must know that—All day you seemed to be around near me—

The boys had to go to town and Brett decided not to so she and Charles and I were here alone all day—and we all thought it was grand—so quiet—Brett and I painting in different houses—Charles did some odd jobs then wandered off somewhere and didn't come back till time to go for the milk—When he came back with the milk I took the horse and rode for half an hour—

We had supper—quiet—Charles and I doing the talking—He telling me about a wonderful idea he has for a building—a six pointed star—I said it was a pity they didn't put it at the Grand Central on Park Avenue—Then the other boys came in with their adventures in Taos—All sitting around the table eating stewed cherries—

My painting[154] moved very fast—tomorrow we will see what it moves into—It sort of knocks my own head off—I am glad we came up again—it has been so quiet—and the painting is such a queer one—

The feeling of the place is very fine—

Charles finally had to help Brett in her struggles with her bills—His laugh and practical turn at work on Brett were very amusing—He made out a bill for her to send to the father of the two boys—and insisted that she write the father a letter. It was nice—and very funny—Brett looking particularly old—he particularly young—

Good Night Little One—

Alfred Stieglitz · Lake George, New York · August 5, 1929

Noon. It's an autumn day.—Cold. And a stormy gray very moving sky. Amazing tempting shapes. I have been up since seven & very much on the go. Getting off many letters—at least seven to bankers who will insist in sending checks to you with O'Keeffe spelled wrong.—I have written before but somehow mistakes continue.—Many details to be attended to.—I'll change much when I go to New York—It may cost money but my time does mean more than the money.—

I want to print this afternoon. Maybe I have something very fine. I don't know.—

—Two letters from my woman finally came. Very grand ones. It was a very long wait. —Yes, you are doing as I want you to do. Just wired you. Fill yourself to the fullest. I understand. —And [I] share it all with you.—I have much more in me of what you are experiencing than you have any idea of—There is a side of me that is as wild as your wildest side is—but my life in America has been such I had to find "Equivalents"—Some day we'll talk it all over without arguing. There is nothing to argue when one sees.—It's all very simple—No you are not selfish.

---

154. Lynes 687.

When I telegraphed you the other day there was nothing in the East for you but myself, I well knew what I was saying. Of course if you were a water woman the sea would have the parallel of what you are getting on land—

What you feel *beyond* you is in your blood—what I feel *beyond* me is in the center of me—my blood too.—Twenty-five years in a way make a difference. And man & woman are complementary.—

—The mail brought me a very unusual bunch of letters—Much is asked from me—spiritual & practical—Maybe now that finally our togetherness is reestablished—and that fine edge that both insist on again exists—I can be of some use to others.—But I'll have to spare myself. Something I never did before.

—There has been so much "waste" that it is ghastly. I dare not waste any more.

It does feel very wonderful to know we are together again—that your need & my need are identical—even tho you are there & I am what is termed "here."—I know the pull I have—your pull towards me. But you are wise in doing what you are doing—Of course I want to hold you—& kiss all of you—see you—look at you—see whether you really exist—are what I know you to be—Too bad I'm not twenty years younger & yet be what I am now! But then perhaps we wouldn't be together at all. That's the queer thing about it. It's great you're riding so much.—Great you're doing all the things you are doing—All so healthy & clean. Riding in the storm.—That reminds me of some days years & years ago up in the Alps—and in my little scull out on the Lake here when I was a kid—in real storms—I had no fear then—no responsibilities—That damnable sense of responsibility—!—developed to a morbid degree—I'm gradually ridding myself of the morbid state. Yes, I am. I'm doing lots of things to myself. Nothing that isn't natural. I have to in order to go on.

Painting!—I wonder what I'll see. I really wonder will I be able to see paintings at all. Yours surely.—Marin's too. But not many others.—What's more I don't want to see them.—As much else I don't want to see or touch.

—You grand woman. You say you are my woman. Yes I know.—On August 9 it will be eleven years that you gave me your virginity. During thunder & lightning. It's as if it were yesterday.—It's a wonder I didn't give you a child!—We were made to have one—But it was not to be.—I realize how impossible such a child's chance would have been. How unready you were. How little I could provide for it & for you.—Yes, you gave me your virginity—I still see your face—& feel it all—And see you on the floor afterwards naked with a bandage on—a wounded bird. So lovely.—Georgia I loved you then most wonderfully—and I never ceased to love you in spite of all you felt to the contrary—but what I feel today is what you feel beyond you. That's what you feel beyond yourself—that something you are to me. You gave me your virginity. That's the reason you are my woman for all time—You are not like other women—& I am your man for all time for I'm not like other men—

You gave me your virginity Georgia—And don't I remember June 15—six days after you arrived—& I touched a spot & you jumped—& I sat on a chair & felt like a murderer—& you wondered what ailed me—I often wondered since wasn't I a murderer. Particularly after you had gone & you wrote me those letters—& I looked at the hair I cut that day—& I looked long—& I knew that what I was & felt was as true as that day—that touch—that hair—And as fine.—And then I was called to camp to see Kitty & her mother—& slept in a tent—a storm raging—a boy asleep near me—you in Lake George. I remember the long talk with Emmy & Kitty listening. And when I went away I believed I was understood. Really did.—And it was the day after returning to the Lake you gave me your virginity. I couldn't have accepted it (or taken it) hadn't I felt all was very right between Kitty, Emmy & me.—You know how "wrong" I eventually was.—But your virginity was in my trust. Is today.—And I have never forgotten it. Yet you doubted me. Appearances were against me.

And I bungled—for I was hurt as you were hurt—But all is very right between us—for you gave me your virginity—It is the very center of your being you gave me—& dearest of women—most beautiful of women—I gave you my center—the center of my center—No one else ever received it. Yes, I love you—

How the trees are being torn to pieces by the wind—a gale—and the sky has grown very dark—& the room is very cold—I don't want to start a fire—

This morning I had a touch of sinus—If it develops I'll go to town & have it nipped in the bud. I hope it won't be necessary. The sudden crass change of temperature—& I flaunting all of myself to the wind! Getting chilled. And the bed was icy. And my wrapper is still in the trunk.—I'll tell you a secret. I couldn't wear it while I felt you no longer loved me!—What you were feeling in a way about me I was feeling in a way about you.—Only I didn't have the bitter resentments—But the line was very similar—

Maybe I'll get out the wrapper. Maybe on August 9[155] (& be sentimental). No, no I'm not a bit sentimental—& yet I am.—

I love you my wild Georgia O'Keeffe. I'll never be able to hold you again. So I fear—But I really don't fear.

It looks like snow. Nothing can surprise me—Oh yes—something can—you.—Beautiful surprises only.—

Lunch calls.—

Give me your body—let me kiss every inch of it—long & tenderly—Remember you gave me your virginity—It still exists—I kiss it—a kiss into eternity. Do you feel it? I know you do.—

And still another kiss.

Alfred Stieglitz · Lake George, New York · August 7, 1929 +

9:30 A.M.—The phone just brought your wire from Santa Fe. Of course you must know by this time what word, any word, from you means to my day! All of my being—Thanks.—I'll get the written telegram when I go to the Village for the noon mail.—I must get out in the sun. I have been tinkering around here with prints. I don't like them.—Strand is still asleep!—I think he

155. Stieglitz referred to August 9, 1918, the day he returned from visiting Kitty at camp, as "virginity day."

leaves tomorrow.—He left his car here & came up for it. He is very much worried about Beck—Has every reason to be.[156] But I don't want to go into that—

The morning is so clear—& I have heard from my woman—

A long long kiss—I'll wire you later—

Do you believe I love you—When you finally believe I do—you'll just say one little word: Yes.—Won't you?—I'll wait for it for years—but finally I must have it. I know I have earned that "yes" if ever I earned anything. Do you remember that night under the stars—oh so long ago—after a day of very hard work—you cooking & you scrubbing & painting—& I washing dishes & photographing & printing like mad—my hands all day in icy water—It was late in October—you went out into the night—it was cold—& you called me—You stood south of the flagpole looking at the myriads of stars—such a clear night—I stood north—we quite a distance apart—& you said: Aren't they marvelous? And I looked & was silent awhile. Then said: We have had a very full day working nearly seventeen hours—You have known what it is to make a living. I never have. Millions know how to make a living. But how many have earned the right to live?—Do you remember?—I feel that way still. Few have earned the right to live—& fewer still have earned the right to die. I often think of that night—It seems Lawrence has discovered that idea too. But I discovered it ten years before he did—Georgia, say: Yes. But I'll wait.

—There is Strand—It's ten o'clock—I'll get out in the sun—

Do I hear "yes"—you loveliest of women—so hard to get a "yes" from—Kiss.

Georgia O'Keeffe · [Alcalde, New Mexico] · [August 7, 1929]

Dearest—

I guess I am bad—but I can't tell you how I have been flying—

I sit in my bed in a large white room—water trickling out in the patio and sort of wonder what has hit me—This is certainly an incredible country—

I have been going so fast—and so much has been going on around that writing has been quite impossible—

I painted the two days at Brett's—a crazy picture—a new one—and *different*.[157] It was quiet and fine—Then Charles suggested going down to Taos by what is known as the Circle Drive—making it some eighty miles down through the mountains—It was a very beautiful drive —and we met Marin on the way taking it in the opposite direction—We were home in time for supper and I unpacked again—had a hot bath—and packed again to go to the Santa

---

156. Strand wrote O'Keeffe in July that he was worried that Beck was "wasting" her experience in New Mexico "by letting it become just a plain drinking bout of excitements that finally only depress." He added that he hoped O'Keeffe could "steady her and help her get rid of some of this resentment she feels about returning" (Strand to GOK, July 14, 1929). Norman also encouraged Stieglitz's growing distrust of Beck Strand. He wrote Norman on July 23, 1929: "What you write about a certain lady [Beck] is incredibly right." And on August 4, 1929, he added that Beck "hasn't a trace of awareness—nor sense of whole—all values warped."

157. Lynes 687.

Domingo dance[158] and come here for maybe a night—maybe two—I wanted to paint on the road out from here—a very fine mesa—so fine that I probably can't paint it—Sunday morning (I was in bed at nine Saturday night—had a fine sleep—was pretty tired) we were off for the dance—Miriam—Charles and I—a hundred miles—I drove seventy-five—Charles the last thirty-five—It was the most beautiful dance I have seen and the largest—We had seats—sitting on the edge with our legs hanging down—on a roof with a roof made of branches over us to keep the sun off—We couldn't have had it from a better place—They had a very fine chorus and I think about four hundred dancers—It was fine—the chorus was right at our feet—

Everyone was there—many unexpected meetings—Walker's friend Eckstein carrying a parrot—and all the Indians wanting to buy the parrot—You must meet Eckstein—you and he would have a great time—I asked him to come and see us when he returns from Japan in October or November—

The Santo Domingo Pueblo is large—The whole thing was very fine—

From Santa Fe on our return I sent Miriam home with Brett—I had been invited to visit here at Alcalde and I could bring Charles because they all know I can't—or don't drive alone—long distances—Miriam was crazy to come too—the parties and tales of this house are notorious—but I just felt I couldn't bring two extra—So Charles and I arrived about eleven at night—Food and all the trimmings waiting for us when we got here—The place is quite as remarkable as Mabel's in a way—The woman[159] is the friend who gave Scott money—and such a tale you never heard—I just found this morning that she is also the mother of the young Garland who would not accept the millions he inherited a few years ago[160]—You remember—much about it was in the paper—She is sixty and married now to a boy in his twenties[161]—

Well—it's a great place—everything from the patio out there where the water trickles —with the stars overhead—the endless library where we dance—and a big open Rolls Royce that purrs like velvet—and such landscape around—I have almost lost my head—yesterday and today—The two days I have been here I painted from 8:30 till one—Then yesterday afternoon Henwar—the husband—went off to collect a party that we had last night—She had company—I worked till four then Charles took me on a three hour drive that was the finest drive I have had out here—We took her car—he knows all the country—drives as well as anyone I ever rode with—I just wish you could have been along—I don't know why this country gets me the way it does—but I just get a feeling of being drunk with it—and I like it so that I feel I will die—Charles likes it too—but he doesn't enthuse over it like I do—he just looks and drives—and watches all around—

When we got back and dressed there was the party—it was small—and amusing—

158. O'Keeffe went to the Annual Feast Day and Corn Dance at Santa Domingo Pueblo on August 4, 1929.

159. Marie Tudor Garland.

160. After their mother, Marie Garland, forfeited her rights to $10 million left by her first husband, Charles Garland, their sons, Charles and Hamilton Garland, initially refused their inheritance. Charles was adamant about not accepting the money: "A system which starves thousands, while hundreds are stuffed condemns itself." But after the sons married and had children, both changed their minds; see "Garland Refused Million as Not His," NYT, Nov. 30, 1920, 11; and "Accept $1,500,000 They Once Refused," NYT, Jan. 10, 1922, 5.

161. Henwar Rodakiewicz (born 1903), a filmmaker, was the fourth husband of Marie Garland. They married in 1927.

very—ended by everyone going swimming in the Rio Grande about twelve—everyone but me—
I looked on—too cold and too much mud for me—It was after two before we got to our rooms
—I was out to paint at 8:30 this morning—The woman paints among the other things she does
—Marie Garland she is called mostly—She went with me again this morning—she in her car—
I in the Ford—My painting isn't much—it couldn't be—what I try to paint is too much to get it
right away—

I was going back this afternoon to work on it again but it rained—everything was so
different—we were chased in by the rain—She wouldn't go out again so Charles went with me
—and I made a lot of drawings—little ones—size of this paper—of a kind of little hill that I
wanted to paint[162]—Charles says it is a little hill—and I tell him yes—but it is very big inside
—He makes me drive—says it is good for me—and when I do things wrong keeps at me over
and over again till I can do them—

—I must tell you that there is no telephone here—they go to Santa Fe for mail—it is
thirty-five miles there and the same back—and they don't go for it specially—Henwar drove
me sixteen miles to wire you tonight—I am not having you wire here because at first I thought I
might only stay one night—This is the third—

The big car purring along in the night is wonderful with just a few stars over head—
mostly clouds seeming to press close.

Marie Garland seems to take great pleasure in my pleasure in the landscape here—I may
come back and spend a week—She is certainly a remarkable woman—old and wise and young
and vital—all at the same time—

This is just a vague outline of what I have been doing—as I read it over I feel that I
give you no idea at all of what happens—for as it all happens it all seems so terribly alive—and
warm and there doesn't seem to be a moment to stop—one thing follows another so fast—

Even tho much seems to happen here there is a feeling of quiet about it for me—much
more quiet than at Mabel's—in a way—I have been out mostly with just one person—Marie
Garland or Charles—and I like the landscape here very very much—

Well—maybe you feel I have had enough of this thing that I like—that I should be
leaving it and going on to you—

I write that—then sit and look at the wall—And the thought that comes to me is that
what I have been getting out here gives me a kind of feeling of balance within myself that I seem
terribly to need—

My kiss goes with this—a free kiss like my hills and mesa—

And a Good Night—it is after two—I ought to be asleep—

In spite of all my landscape talk—I haven't a good one yet—not a single one—

I forgot to tell you how I laughed at your calling me a man beater—I laughed aloud at it
—and I must own up to it that I am beginning to feel a bit wild—and that wild feeling makes
me very sure I am me—

Again Good Night—A Big Kiss—

---

162. Lynes 681, 682.

Alfred Stieglitz · Lake George, New York · August 8, 1929 +

After lunch—What a morning. All sorts of activities. The chiefest was another fly to the skies.
—Donald & I were walking to the Village when I said: Donald, want a fly with me? He was
ready. So we jumped into a plane—It was such a grand day. Absolutely clear. Sky so blue &
cloudless.—Air bracing.—Off we went. And the flying was fine but no great thrill. But suddenly
the pilot flew higher & turned in a circle—& made a great swoop—the mountains looked
upside down—the Lake was running downhill—It was a grand sensation—beat anything
imaginable—Donald very excited—said he wouldn't forget it in a million years—I seemed like
an old rounder. It was really incredible. We'll fly soon. Have a real fly.—You & I—very close.
You'll love it.—

    I wired you my very much love.—The sky was so blue—& so clear—& the hills so
queer standing on end & so green—& the water was inviting. I felt like opening the door &
jumping. It would be easy. No water ever tempted me so.—A kiss from that dark blue sky—
a kiss from that dark green water that tempted me so—a kiss from the upside down hills—
a kiss from all of me to all of you.—

    —You said "yes" in your letter yesterday—after I had mailed a letter in the morning
asking [for] a "yes."—I want a million yeses—I want all of you—every bit of you—resentments
& all.—I'll take whatever you are—I need it all—And I'll take it all & fly with you to the ends
of the earth.[163]

    When I came home I was asked how about my heart. And my answer was: To hell with
my heart—I don't understand such language—That heart touched the blue of the sky—& the
blue touched my woman—You are the blue—

    Not only you are a bit "crazy"—but I fear I can go you one better.—

    So I'm going to kiss you like mad—& make you just a bit crazier—I like you "crazy"—
& it's great to feel mad—

    The house is very silent—the sky is no longer blue—it looks ominous—

    I'm getting ready to walk up Prospect tomorrow.—I have to get up there. All summer
I have set my mind on it—And I'll go up.—Don't be worried. I'll force nothing. Tomorrow is
Virginity Day—& if it doesn't rain—my heart will walk the mountain.—

    I love my woman—A madman loves his woman—

    Say "yes"—say yes a million times—each yes means I'm your woman—I belong to you
—whatever I am is yours—And as I never take more than I give—I'll accept her yes—The
woman's yes—& give her back a million fold what she gives—for it is that a woman needs—
& hopes for from her man.—And she is entitled to all she needs—to all she wants—

    I love you Georgia O'Keeffe—

    Say "yes"—say it that it echoes thro' the world—

    I love you—do you feel it?—

---

163. In a letter to Dorothy Norman of August 10, 1929, Stieglitz again attributed his newfound enthusiasm for life not only to
recent communication from "S.W." but also to Norman's "very beautiful letter about our friendship.... You have been a real ray
of light—& will continue to be one.... Without your help I would have been completely lost."

Georgia O'Keeffe · [Taos, New Mexico] · [August 8, 1929]

Good morning Dearest,

Here I am in the Pink House again—a rather cloudy morning—

We came up from Alcalde yesterday afternoon—Marie Garland came with us as her husband had come in the morning to bring back the remnants of the party—She counted on meeting him on the road and returning with him to Alcalde which she did—But what a drive we had—rivers of rain had run through the canyon that the road comes up—and in places you would never have any idea that there had ever been a road—

Well—I wish you could have seen Charles tackle it—it is too long to tell when you don't know the road—sufficient to say that we got through and got here by about seven and it was hours before another car could get through—Everything else was stuck and nobody else seemed to be able to get over the bridges that he fixed for himself.

I think he had a grand time—it was like a game to him—She got a great kick out of it —and by the time we had finished our supper at the hotel most of the party that had been at her house had collected—

However—before they got there she had the idea to take me on a trip—ten days to the Grand Canyon—and Navajo country—she—her husband—Spud Johnson—Charles and me—Two cars—the Rolls Royce and a Packard—

Well—I just couldn't miss it—such a way to go—and they all know the country— Charles and Spud and I drive down to her house this afternoon late and we plan to leave her house at five tomorrow morning—

I hope you don't think me mad—I had rather planned to go home now in four or five days—I wanted a little time to see Mabel—But I'll be off for this—Isn't it funny after what I said last summer about a Rolls Royce[164]—I hadn't said anything about that to them either— It just happened this way—

It was after ten when I got into the big sitting room at Mabel's and got my mail— all your letters and copies of telegrams—

Dearest—you mustn't doubt me—don't you know that all of me has always been yours —when you wanted me—but you haven't made me feel you wanted much of me for a long time till I came out here—I understand it now—and there isn't anything I would rather have than that closeness to you—I know you know it—and don't you know—all these things I am doing that may seem mad—I couldn't be enjoying as I do if I didn't feel you there to put my hand on and reassure me—

It makes me very gay—in a very nice way I think—Anyway—I feel they all like me very much—and something that I feel myself seems to give them all a lift like my paintings make the people feel who like them much—

I will be wiring you on the way—I will be driving either with Charles or Henwar and they are both wonderful drivers—unless they let me drive—and I'm improving a lot—Don't

164. On August 11, 1929, Stieglitz told O'Keeffe he was delighted she was "touring in a Rolls Royce...your wish come true."

512

worry about me—I will be fine—Marie Garland has a very motherly way of taking care of everybody—I think it will be a great trip—

Do take care of yourself—It is the nicest thing you can do for me—and I am glad you make me really feel you love me—It makes me feel much more like flying into the open spaces—

Beck is pathetic—We will talk of it—I feel there is very little one can do about it— Only she can do anything—

This must go for the mail—

With very much love—Have only nice thoughts of me—forget the others—

Kiss—

Georgia O'Keeffe · [Alcalde, New Mexico] · [**August 9, 1929**]

My dearest Alfred:

I wish I could put my arms around all of you and pick you up and take you with me— It is twenty minutes before we are supposed to get up to start on this trip—and I must first speak with you before we go—

I had your two registered letters yesterday afternoon—also your telegram sent after I wired you as we were going—I was so busy getting off that I saved the letters—

Spud, Charles and I drove the fifty miles down the canyon in the evening light— Charles driving so we came fast—but with such a sure wheel—We hardly spoke all the way down—There was a wonderful dinner—then your letters when I finally got into bed—

I can't tell you how well they fitted things that had been happening—and my state— One was the letter where you called me your wife—and it fitted—all so well—I so much liked the feeling of you all about me—it makes something in me feel so at home even tho I am flying about out here this way.

The casual way this trip has been started would amuse you—Oh there is so much I would like you to see and like to tell you of in detail—I think I understand how the flying makes you feel—and I seem to feel I am flying with you—Beck's letter from Lake George was typical of her[165]—I am glad you went to the races—even tho you didn't know much or see much except that I was with you—

I just hear Charles' alarm going off across the patio—that means he will soon be out—

I feel that I am your child and your wife truly this morning—that it will always be that way—that as I go out to greet the sky—the dawn—I am greeting you too—and that you touch me like the air on my cheek—everywhere—because all of us is together—It seems more than two humans together—It seems all of everything—the rhythm of life—More than I can understand—I can only be of it—and let myself go—

There is a little rain just beginning—No one ever stops for that here—They will

---

165. O'Keeffe may have been referring to the breezy way Beck, in her letter of August 2, 1929, recounted Stieglitz's criticism of her.

probably go on as tho the sun is shining—knowing that it will probably rain often during the ten days—

—A long—long kiss to you—I will get up and get under that river of a shower in the bathroom—

And don't forget any day that the center touches—

Alfred Stieglitz · Lake George, New York · August 10, 1929

The sun is just coming over the hills—& the sky is cloudless. And the morning starts very still. —And I am up since five—having gone to bed at midnight—Good morning my much moving, much traveling, much seeing-the-world woman.

—Yesterday was quite a day.—The Arkins & I lunched. And then sat on the porch. My heart was on a rampage. But I pay little attention to it. Just remain a bit quiet.—We talked. They are two very unusual kids. He wrote a very remarkable poem: *The Swan Dive to Death*. And she listens & looks—& altho' only twenty is very mature in a way—much older than he is at twenty-two. A beautiful couple—She teaches kindergarten & must be an artist at it.—At about 2:30 we went to the Lake. I lent her [your] suit. Found it in your trunk which I hadn't touched until then—and they swam & I watched—Then they lay on the dock. And there was talking—He said some [thing] about the tragic. I had been speaking about life—We all spoke. Each one listened. And finally I said, I'll tell you a story. And I told those young newly married people the story of my illegitimate daughter.[166] And as I related—it was quite incredible what happened to the young woman's face—the intense listening—& what I saw then—& Arkin was lying on his back listening & his face was very beautiful. Hers terribly pained—His quiet.—And it took quite awhile to tell the story.—And the Lake seemed so quiet & so terribly far away.— Everything seemed so distant. And as I related I saw you—always you—nothing but you—& you seemed listening too altho' you know the story—but had you heard it yesterday you'd hear something quite different than when the story was told you—altho' I never vary that story!

And when it was all over everyone was very quiet for a long while.—And I finally asked the young girl what she thought & she said: That's the purest story I ever heard. And Arkin was still. But his face seemed to radiate—And I said: You see that story is really what I am in reality.—It includes everything.—And it does.—It is my whole life feeling.—And as I grow older the more I realize that *that is* my life. How many would understand it?—And I don't care how many would. I may write out that story[167] & print it.—A servant girl, a peasant girl, a daughter, the state & the church & I.—All equally straight—all equally simple. But the girl had to die at twenty-four—& the daughter had to die at twenty-four—& here I am— still "alive."—

---

166. Elsa Bauschmied.

167. Although Stieglitz later dictated many stories about his life, which Norman printed in *Twice A Year* (1938–1948), he never published an account of his relationship with the woman in Munich who bore his illegitimate daughter (see p. 164, n. 347), and AS to GOK, July 27, 1929 (see pp. 495–498).

And it was Virginity Day!—There was no love—there was no talk—no thought of rightness or freedom—There was no woman nor man.—All just happened with a sublime purity. And covered twenty-five years.—I still hear my mother's voice when I told her that story down at Oaklawn—I still see your face when I told you that story—Yes, I must tell that story to the world. It is a sacred story. The world will besmirch it—besmear it. But what of it? So much has been besmirched & besmeared that I'm way beyond the world & its smearing.—And I told these children of some things I could no longer do—And Arkin finally said: You are terribly changed. And I said: No I'm not changed a bit—And the girl said: Are you sure you can stand up that way in the world? & I explained why I had no choice. Nothing was of my own choosing. All was chosen for me—

It was 7:30 when finally there was supper. The house-full only returned at that time from Paradox Lake—After supper all left except Donald & the Arkins. And the latter left at 9:30 to write letters to their folks. And as Arkin left he said: Stieglitz, this was a very grand day. And she said: I'll never forget this experience—It was very, very beautiful. And [after] they had gone I felt a thousand years old—I didn't envy the young—I merely saw their beauty—the life ahead of them—And a finer couple than Arkin & that girl doesn't exist.—It is very fine how they are together. And altho' I was calm it all excited me terribly. Donald & I sat in the front room awhile —a-talking. He was at his finest. And that is extraordinarily fine. He has lived & suffered. I have lived & suffered as few have suffered—I wouldn't give up what I see for everything in the world—But I do need a long, long rest for I'm a very tired man. And I love a woman beyond all there is—beyond life—beyond death—a vision of a woman—Yes, I love—

Arkin says I'm a biblical figure. I don't know what he means—& he says the austerity is overpowering & I don't know what he means—for altho' I hear him I'm not living in these terms.

Lee returns at seven. And there is talk of going to the races—Whether I go or don't go makes very little difference. Everything seems to have nothing to do with me—Nothing but my very great love seems to exist—& the abstract past—with a future full of possibility—but very new still rooted in only the purest of what I am—the purest of the past—

I had a very remarkable letter—It seemed to reinforce all I felt & know—It's extraordinary—the letters—there are very few I receive these days—

Well, Sweetest Georgia, I'm wondering where you are this morning. Still asleep while I'm writing—Or maybe up all aglow.—I wonder will there be a telegram. I wired you to Flagstaff yesterday—I shall go up now & shave. And take some Salsanos—I haven't had any in a long while.

A kiss on your lips—a long quiet kiss—

I love you my Georgia.

Before I went to bed last night—while talking with Donald—I played the *Ninth Symphony* & part of the Brahms *First*—Music seemed to be needed—And it fit into the day.—

Another kiss—I hope the trip is very exciting.—

Georgia O'Keeffe · [Flagstaff, Arizona] · [August 10, 1929]

Well—Here we are—I sent you a night letter last night—but I was so sleepy it probably didn't have much sense—Henwar said we would sleep in Flagstaff last night—and we did—but getting here was quite a job—

All kinds of weather—all kinds of roads—from dry hot dustiness to pouring rain—roads like butter and rivers of water like thick mud to cross—

—It was fine—I had a grand day—Half the day with Charles in the Packard and the other half with Henwar in the Rolls Royce—and both wonderful drivers—and what a car—It is like velvet—and to see him take it up a greasy road in the night—

Well we had a time—It was a great day of all sorts of things—Henwar not only drives his car he drives everybody else to the place he is aiming for—

Well—a kiss—

They are after us for breakfast—I am feeling fine—

Georgia O'Keeffe · [Grand Canyon, Arizona] · [August 11, 1929]

Good morning—Dearest— 5:45 —and I am sitting out on the end of a point at the end of what they call Bright Angel Trail—all the others were asleep—I only saw six people coming out—a bellboy, a workman, and four others—so I feel the sun rises quite alone here in spite of its rising over this terrific scene—

Spud and I walked a long way along this path in the moonlight last night and he nearly died laughing when I had to sit down once because I said I felt from my feet all up my legs I was eating lemons till my mouth watered and I got a sharp pain in my head—It is certainly a staggering sight—and there seems no end to it—

But everything out here seems staggering—I rode with Henwar yesterday—all day—and such a car—and what country we crossed and what heat—But it is a kind of heat—so hot that your eyes feel as tho they are frying—and you don't mind—you like it till it gets you on the top of the head which it finally does—But by that time the side metal on the car is so hot you can't put your hand on it—

We drove till about five—all day—from eight in the morning through desert along first soft gray sand hills—then red and pink cliffs—sharp and enormous—It is a cruel cruel country—terrible roads—and along with what one saw which finally got to be so much that I just felt I couldn't [take] any more—That car—being forced up and down those awful roads by that little blond man—burned very black—such a set jaw and such a sure hand—he and the car seem to be one—The car like a woman that he knows controls absolutely relentlessly—There wasn't much chance for the car to purr yesterday till we finally climbed a frightful hill and began going into trees—For over two hours we went through pines—little scrubby ones at first growing taller and taller as we went on—the roads fine—and the air cooler and cooler till we were all done up in coats—and we got here just for sunset—

We are all terribly burned—a very dressy hotel and we the most disreputable looking people I saw—So sunburned that it is funny—all have queer-looking eyes—but we all feel fine —We all rode with the tops of the cars down except for about two and a half hours—you can see so much better—

Dearest—it is all too much to tell about—

When Spud and I got back to the hotel last night—we danced a couple of times—and he remarked, "Well I guess there is nothing left for us to do today—we couldn't have done much more"—

I forgot to tell you that we crossed the new bridge that has been built at Lee's Ferry— It is not very long but so far above what is below that you don't quite believe it—Charles and Henwar and Marie have all been through this country several times—Spud has been through part of it—I am the only green one—but we are all having a great time—

As I watch the sun coming over this—it just gets to be too much—I am quite limp from looking over edges—

So I'll kiss you and go eat—

I hope to have a wire from you today from Cedar City—

I forgot to tell you how good it smells here—the wind in the pines and the sound of water way down in the canyon where you can't see it—

Georgia O'Keeffe · Grand Canyon, Arizona · [August 11, 1929]

[Telegram] Well it is the Grand Canyon all right. We go into the Navajo country so do not expect word of any kind for several days maybe a week. Will wire as soon as there is a chance. In the meantime think only pleasant things of me and trust that I am having great days [and] that they couldn't be so great without the center and our love.

Georgia

Alfred Stieglitz · Lake George, New York · August 12, 1929

9 A.M.—It's muggy & hazy—but the sun promises to win out—Good Morning you Wild One. You say you are a bad one!—Arkin & his wife came to go with Lee to the end of the Lake & back—but were late so decided to join Donald & me going up Prospect. All advised me against it—so the only choice I had was to go.—As all advised against the Room last year & you know what I did—including "losing" you!!—So we're going. The cook is making sandwiches.—

—Your letter—of August 7th—the one [about a] really grand drunk—(the one of the 8th came yesterday—in a way I'm glad it came first) telling me about the Garlands & the marriage, the house, etc. etc.—the comparison with Mabel's house, came this A.M.—I have read it twice—Well, all is your own choice. I have no right to interfere—Of course I see a great deal you are not conscious of.—You are living your own life—& enjoying it hugely. And that is important. "Living" may be of greater value than seeing. Yet one can't see if one doesn't live. Maybe seeing is a certain kind of living.—As for your painting being a failure, it couldn't be otherwise. One can't speed about as you do and paint anything really worthwhile. But that's all your own affair.—I have nothing to say. Nor do I think about it.—It's all your own choice. Living is the greatest art after all.—

—Queer, as I write a young girl—a very handsome one all in yellow with a tiny lavender kerchief on her brown hair—she brown as you probably are—has driven up by mistake in an open Rolls Royce—An amazing sight—would loved to have photographed—she really as beautifully made as the machine—all one—she & the machine—one quality—She was looking for Mrs. Luther. As she drove off naturally you were in my mind—As if you weren't always in my mind.—In everything I see you.—But I wondered as that Young America drove off how much "art" meant to her—as I wondered on the golf links about Young America[168]—so handsome & casual—what [could] "art" mean to it. Nothing I am sure—and there is no reason why it should. And I had to smile at my own life—And wondered how I could face Young America in the future!—

—There is the full sun. Drowsy & hot—A great day for lovemaking—cladless—lying about in the sun.—Physical satisfactions.—Maybe a spiritual need—I lay awake in bed a long time this morning thinking about you—purely objectively. It was most elucidating.—I didn't let my love interfere—It's amazing how calm I am.—Your letters as they come confirm my prior seeing.

You are Georgia O'Keeffe—the one of Canyon greatly intensified.—

And now I must be off to the mountain.—I expect to take three hours up & will come down the short way to the Village. And stay up two hours. I'm sure the experiment will be satisfactory.

Very, very much love—& a big indulgent kiss—Yes, I love you Georgia O'Keeffe altho' drunk.—

Georgia O'Keeffe · [Cameron, Arizona] · [August 12, 1929]

Dearest—

It has been a great day—The Grand Canyon is just what one would expect it to be—Big and grand and colorful till one can't take it in—It didn't surprise or excite me—I just looked at it—

But Dearest—this afternoon I almost died—as we drove into the Navajo Country and passed the Little Colorado River Canyon—We all agreed that it was much finer—and I almost went crazy—and we drove on toward what they call the Painted Desert—on the left and on the right a range of stark mountainous hills that is one of the nearest to my sort of things you can

168. On August 6, 1929, Stieglitz saw Walter Hagen play in a golf match in Glens Falls. He later told Ida O'Keeffe that the day reminded him he "was a golfer once—As I was so many things once—healthy things—before I imagined I'd have to protect artists & teach Americans the spiritual significance of art." He also added that when he "saw the youngsters on the links I realized they & painting had nothing in common—There was no reason why they should have" (AS to Ida O'Keeffe, Aug. 9, 1929).

imagine—I got so excited and crazy that Spud and Charles both got much irritated with me
—and I got furious with them—

But we have a nice sort of relationship that doesn't really get mad even when we seem to
—However I am going to ride either with Henwar or Marie in the morning—

I never saw anything so dark and naked and simple—and beautiful—It would be a
good place to die and let your bones bleach—

And we finally came to a trading post—A store, a house, some tents and three or four
cabins—It would delight your soul—all simple—comfortable—and a good natured man
running it—And the Painted Desert—colorful—stark and grand—all round—Still so much of
nothing I have quite lost my head—

—Spud and I walked out on the long bridge over the muddy river—but such beautiful
mud—and watched the sun set—It was grand—Not many people come up here—the roads
aren't good so one feels almost alone with it—

Good Night Dear One. You certainly have a crazy child tonight—

AS STIEGLITZ'S FEELINGS about O'Keeffe continued to swing wildly throughout August, he
grew closer to Norman, and, emboldened by his attention, the younger woman began to criticize
O'Keeffe's behavior more openly and pointedly. On August 1, Stieglitz confided in Norman: "In
a way you keep me alive. Yes, I don't know how the summer would have been possible without
your letters. I would have starved to death without them. That's true. They are so human &
fine."[169] On August 16, Norman wrote Stieglitz, chastising O'Keeffe's self-indulgence for going
to the Grand Canyon. There are "plenty of things one wants to do," she wrote, "but altho' one
calls them living, still there is the reality keeping one from the more attractive for the more
permanent. Farsighted pragmatism against nearsighted. Is spoiled the word—or what?"[170] In
another letter to Norman, written on August 14, Stieglitz complained that "S.W. has no vision
of me at all,"[171] and in one to O'Keeffe from the next day, he revealed his disturbed, jealous
suspicions that she was being unfaithful both to him and to her art, allowing others to appeal to
her frivolous or sensuous side: "You see I cared for you as an artist. No one else does.—You say
woman & artist are one. Yes in a way.—But I could have fluffed you to death—you were ready
for it—Hadn't I realized a greater value in you than fluffer!—I often told you so.—And I could
have fluffed myself to death.—Maybe fluffing you to death & myself too might have been wiser.
I'm wondering." Two days later, on August 17, 1929, he reminded O'Keeffe: "I have fought for
you as a woman & painter. You asked for the chance as a painter. And I knew painter & woman
could be of value only as one. As painter I never violated you—as woman I so often must have."
And in another letter of the same day, he continued: "You say the people about you are receiving
from you what the people received from your pictures. But please don't forget in the Room I
reinforced those pictures—let them live."[172]

169. AS to Norman, Aug. 1, 1929.

170. Norman to AS, Aug. 16, 1929.

171. AS to Norman, Aug. 14, 1929.

172. AS to GOK, Aug. 15 and 17, 1929.

Alfred Stieglitz · Lake George, New York · August 15, 1929

Good Morning—My Grand Canyon Madness—

It's again seven A.M.—And I'm in such a state that I ought not write.—Yesterday evening I received two hasty letters from you.—They were very beautiful. But upset me the way it upset me when you told me about the Berg operation to take place next morning.—I don't know why. But that's what happened.—I guess I'm a fool. Just unfit for days like these. Unfit to have any relationship with one like you.—You see you originally wired me you were going through the Grand Canyon & would be in touch with me. The next day you wired you would probably not be able to be in touch with me for ten days. The next day you wired I should wire to Carson City saying roads were bad, etc., plans changed, etc. etc.—I wired at once. And the wire never reached you.—So "plans" were changed again.—And there is Henwar. I know the type. They don't give a damn—something you enjoy—& he sensing your enjoyment gives less a damn than ever. I know—I have enough of that in me to fully understand.—Well, of course I must accept. Have no choice. As long as you are getting what you want—your new thrill—your new experience—as artist—as woman—or both.—I have nothing to say.—Any more than I could say anything about the hailstorm with hail as large as golf balls which ruined crops & killed cattle.[173] One is merely an onlooker—& knows how helpless one is in the final analysis. But I see so much—too much for my own good. Except perhaps everything one is forced to go thro' is for one's own "good." No one loves the casual more than I do—but had I built "291" & "303" on solely the "casual" there would have been no Georgia O'Keeffe, artist—except potentially. Not for the world.—Not for what she is to herself today & to those with her now.—That I know. Know as I saw those hailstorms beating shingles to pieces—killing plants—covering the ground with whiteness for half an hour—some stones so cold lasting hours. Life today.—Yes, I grant I am terribly nervous. I must be calm. Steel myself for anything. I read & reread your note hastily written on the Western Union paper. I read them as possibly the last note I'd ever get.—I don't trust expert drivers.—I don't trust your judgment. You ask me to trust. Well, I don't. Never have when it came to certain matters.—I know you sweetest woman the world ever knew. I know much about you you don't know yourself. I know much about you [that] you have no idea I know even tho you know.—Past experiences. You & [I] are totally different. We complement one another. That is our strength.—I know all you gave up for years to "follow" me. You are striking an average.—As for me I do not live in terms as you do. You are of today.—I never belonged to any time as it were. Or maybe am too old fashioned. Or maybe too new fashioned. Or a mixture of both. It's all immaterial. I'll be glad when my trial is over.

—I do know that the way you are living leads to no paint—Cannot. I also know that it is not important to you for the present at least. I do know you wrote I am full of paint & I am going to work. I do know the very next day you permitted yourself to be sidetracked. And virtually have been "sidetracked" ever since.—All that is significant. Still very unimportant.— I see so clearly I am calm.—As I saw the hailstones batter down the growing things & was calm. —I knew the mountain would stand even tho the trees be battered down.—Bridges swept away

173. A severe hailstorm battered Lake George on August 13, 1929.

—the rivers swollen—roads washed away. I knew there'd be new bridges—new contracts—the rivers quieting down—new roads. Jobs for many rebuilding. Nature at work in her ways. Casual!—

—It's a sunny morning but there is sullenness in the atmosphere—a strong south wind.—Goodbye for today.—To be frank I'm prepared for anything.—I have to be. You have trained me well this summer.—It has been a rough schooling.—

And I'm past the readily learning age.—But it's all good. And all right. As was the hailstorm. An extraordinary & wonderful phenomenon. The hail was innocent—so were the flowers.

Good-bye—A kiss—and I am ever in your debt whatever you do.—But I can't trust you—try as I will any more than the flowers could trust the hail.—A kiss.—

All of my prints of yesterday were no good—bad Eastman paper!—

Georgia O'Keeffe · [Colorado Springs, Colorado] · [August 16, 1929]

Dearest—

It seems that every place that I find myself in is more remarkable than the place I found before—At present I am lying on a couch bed undressed in the most perfect little studio—on the top of a hill with nothing for miles around but green—and Pikes Peak is what greets me if I open the door and look out—There are two of them—the other is just a bit larger than this—The boys are over there—Marie and Henwar have gone to town—Colorado Springs—to get food—We are resting the afternoon and night—having the car fixed and go down to Taos in the morning—This place belongs to a friend of Henwar's. He has a big hotel in the town and just comes out here occasionally—

—Well—it is certainly a great place—We all feel just a bit like holding our heads and wondering if we can stand anymore—For two nights I haven't written—The day we left Bryce Canyon was the most perfect drive I ever had in the morning—through woods with Henwar—In the afternoon we went through the most paralyzing desert I have seen—white with alkali—mountains and plains alike—the sort of country that would just eat your heart out if you had to live with it—We drove till eleven at night—

Next day we went over Grand Mesa—a mesa with 350 lakes on top of it—There was sleet and hail till the ground was white—lots of flowers—and Henwar fighting with his car is not the least of my pleasures—The mesa was beautifully green but we soon dropped down into desert lined with bare rocky mountains—and at about five in the afternoon we began following the Colorado River with the handsomest green mountains I have ever seen—

We spent the night at a little hotel and started on at seven this morning over Independence Pass—12,098 feet high—green—snow in patches—very very beautiful—and here we are—It has been a wonderful trip—all our noses are peeling—but I wouldn't have missed it for a great deal—It is the sort of thing that only people like Henwar and Charles could push through with a bit of delicate managing from Marie—It was done for me and Spud went along—

Well—I guess they all had a good time—they seem to have—We have stopped at all sorts of hotels—from the finest to the simplest—Charles said this morning that we have gone over two thousand miles—

I must rest a bit—someone or other is coming for tea or whiskey or something—Spud was just here to see if I wanted to go over—I said in a little while—I must just lie a little—

And send you a kiss on the cool breeze that comes in—

AFTER PLEDGING to "do anything" for Stieglitz, Norman sent him a check for one hundred dollars in early August and suggested he use it to fly to New York City, which he did on August 19.[174] Two days earlier, O'Keeffe had arrived back in Taos to find Los Gallos "aquiver."[175] After arguing with Ida O'Keeffe, Mabel and Tony Lujan had abruptly gone to a sanatorium in Albuquerque because Mabel was having problems with her heart. Neith Boyce (Hapgood), who had also been insulted by Mabel, left as well. O'Keeffe, too, decided, she was "ready to go now—in every way"[176] and telegraphed Stieglitz. Louis Kalonyme, who was visiting Lake George, forwarded the telegram to him in New York City. Feeling "like the top of the world," O'Keeffe left New Mexico on August 22. Although she wrote her friend Ettie Stettheimer that she was "ready to go back East," she also admitted that "if it were not for the Stieglitz call I would probably never go—but that is strong."[177]

Alfred Stieglitz · Lake George, New York · August 18, 1929

Sunday A.M. 7—Dearest Georgia:

If you ever receive this letter it will be the last you'll get from me.—Tomorrow morning I fly to New York & back for a lark—In a way it is tempting fate. But why not tempt it. I have tempted it so often—I'm fully aware what I am doing. If you receive this you are free—completely so—& the Far West will be yours. And you part of it.—From the very beginning there has been a battle raging (within you & within me because within you) between the Far West & what I am—or was to you for awhile.—In 1923 when you left for Maine—the year Kitty got ill—you came back & said you had found an equivalent for Texas.—I knew you hadn't—The way you went—the things you charged me with that year & before—that was the beginning of a separation of spirit.—I thought eventually you would "see" but you didn't. Quite the contrary. You couldn't help it.—When finally three years ago you charged me with doing things I know I didn't do—& your spirit & my spirit seemed miles apart—I saw clearly what was coming. Inevitable.—I swear by my own death that I have never been disloyal to you nor untrue. I did a lot of foolish things I wouldn't have done—& shouldn't have done—but not what you claimed—I swear that—But whatever "crimes" I may have committed against you

174. See Norman to AS, July 28, Aug. 1 and 8, 1929.
175. GOK to Rebecca Strand, Aug. 24, 1929.
176. GOK to Mabel Dodge Luhan, Aug. 24, 1929.
177. GOK to Ettie Stettheimer, Aug. 24, 1929.

—I assure you you have more than wiped the slate clean this summer. If you wish to do me a favor read the letters you have written to me this summer! I know if ever anyone has been grossly unjust to anyone you have been to me. But I accepted the unfairness the best I could for I understood you.—From your own angle whatever you do is *right*—from my own angle so much I have done is stupid—so certainly not "right."—Yes reread your letters & your telegrams.— Remember the spirit in which you left me—I certainly stupidly innocent of the spirit at the time. —Had I not poured out my love to you in letter after letter you wouldn't have moved a finger to preserve something very rare & very holy even tho desecrated not only by me—but by you.— Yes by you a thousand times more than by me—I say this without resentment.—

You simply refused to listen.—Refused to hear. Refused to believe. Wounded self came first.—

You couldn't help it.—You grew up that way.—

And may continue so you owe me nothing. I owe you everything. I have lived since I saw your drawings first. That should give you strength to go on. My death has nothing to do with you.—Remember I wrote before you came: "Three Dreams." "He killed himself—he understood the kisses."[178] What held good then—holds good now.—I have discovered nothing new in myself. You wrote you are constantly discovering something new in yourself. That too I knew all along—that potential—And you'll go on discovering new things in yourself. That's why my death—the liberation from me (the East) is really the "right" thing for both of us.—

You still have your life to live—you have hardly begun it—I have lived—At best my years could be few.—I'm ready to go.—

Another wish—please don't speak to anyone about me—Keep your silence as once you prided yourself you did—

As for "my" things—don't bother—let Strand attend to them—He was nearest to me here—It makes no difference what happens to them. I loathe institutions.—Cremation is my honest wish.[179] —

As for money you are well taken care of—relatively. Way beyond my original hopes.— Beware tho of swindlers & flatterers & people wanting to use you. There'll be aplenty.—

I'm sorry what began so perfectly & what was so very beautiful for five years should have to end this way.—In remembering me please remember I did my very best for you & for others—I rarely gave myself a chance except in that way—

And as for art there'll have to be another guardian—

As for my dreams all have come to this—

As to my faith it still holds good—

As to workmanship I feel I was above the average—

But one thing I have always been—a good spirit.—And as such I die.—I lived as one— I die as one—Americans know little about spiritual sportsmanship. I know a lot—More than about photography.

---

178. "One Hour's Sleep—Three Dreams," *291* (Mar. 1915), unpaginated.

179. On August 16, 1929, Stieglitz told O'Keeffe that if she was indeed dead, as he feared, he would cremate all her pictures and would not even bother to look at those she made in New Mexico.

—I could write you forever—Remember as I go to death my last thought will be you &
all the beauty you brought to me & all the beauty you brought out of me—That I know. For I
am prepared.—Preparing for a long while.

A last living kiss.—

May your friends be kind to you.

Georgia O'Keeffe · Taos, New Mexico · August 18, 1929

[Telegram] Yes. Yes. Yes. Planning to leave for you on Thursday or as soon as I can get packed
and off. I am ready. This last trip made it all seem enough. Looking forward very much to seeing
you. Very much love.

Georgia

Alfred Stieglitz · New York, New York · August 19, 1929

[Telegram] Left Lake George by airplane at eight. No wire from you. Had an incredible trip thru
storm. Over clouds and thru them. Everyone persuaded me not to risk it. Bought a roundtrip
ticket. When the plane landed at Flushing Bay a man came rushing breathlessly calling Stieglitz.
A slip of paper was handed to me. Your wire Yes Yes Yes had been forwarded to me. Can you
imagine my state. An open speedboat was waiting to get me to 42nd Street & East River. I
clutched the paper Yes Yes Yes. The speed boat raced up the river. Unbelievable. I ran thru 42nd
Street like a mad one. The city seemed incredible. Everything seemed incredible. You and I finally
together again reborn. Last night I despaired. The morning star said Yes go. Georgia I shall
not fly back but take the train. I dare not tempt fate too much. We shall fly together. But being
together anywhere always that is what I need and you too. I cannot believe that I am living. All
seems too incredible. Very very much love. I would like to meet you on the train when you come.
Where. Still more love,

Alfred

Georgia O'Keeffe · [Taos, New Mexico] · [August 20, 1929]

A starlight moonlight night—very beautiful—

I have been packing today—

Late this afternoon Walker's friend Eckstein came in to see me—We talked till late—
with no supper—such a fine talk—such a real person—really rare—He is coming to see us in
November—you will have a great time with him—

The house here has all turned over like crazy—Mabel—etc—she gone to Albuquerque
Sanitarium again—Ida gone—

The flowers are blooming madly—It all seems a bit mad—

I kiss you—Or the star does—

Yes—yes—yes—and again—yes

I want you to know that I am very ready to go—have had enough—and need much to see you and settle to fall work—

Need much to see you and be by you—

WHEN O'KEEFFE ARRIVED in Albany, New York, on August 25, 1929, she found a dramatically improved Stieglitz, "better physically than in four or five years," she related to Mabel Luhan in early September. He was "grand," she continued; "I just look at him and wonder if I can believe my eyes." Their reunion, she wrote, was "the most perfect thing that has ever happened to me."[180] The days they spent together that late summer and early fall were indeed "perfect," Stieglitz confided to his niece, for he had "learned a lot—& shall apply what I have learned." Both felt that their relationship was "sounder than before, maybe…a bit more mature."[181] When Charles Collier arrived on the Hill after driving O'Keeffe's car East, Stieglitz commemorated their newfound warmth in a series of playful photographs of O'Keeffe and her car. "Good idea that going West," O'Keeffe told Beck Strand a few weeks later: "When I spread out my work last night before packing it—I patted myself on the back and said to myself—Not so bad—Guess you've won again—It looked so good I called him in to look at it…He curled over in a chair—and looked as pleased and surprised as I felt."[182]

Their winter in New York was largely quiet, although punctuated with deep sorrow. Right after the New Year, O'Keeffe's favorite brother, Alexis, who had been gassed during World War I, died suddenly, leaving behind a pregnant wife and young child. O'Keeffe included a 1928 painting she had made in celebration of him, *Abstraction—Alexis,*[183] in her February 1930 exhibition at An American Place, her first show at Stieglitz's new gallery. That exhibition, which was dominated by her paintings of New Mexico, especially its crosses, received only lukewarm reviews from the press. Although O'Keeffe insisted that "anyone who doesn't feel the crosses, doesn't get that country,"[184] most critics did not understand them. One noted that they evoked "an unpleasant hysteria,"[185] while O'Keeffe's friend Henry McBride, the critic, teasingly suggested that O'Keeffe had gotten "religion. What Mabel Dodge got, I have not yet heard."[186]

Throughout the winter and spring, Norman and Stieglitz continued their affair, but it too entered a different stage. In her letters to him she professed that Stieglitz was "the sole living individual I know—or know of—whom I love completely," and she admitted that "you haunt

---

180. GOK to Mabel Dodge Luhan, late Aug. and Sept. 1929.

181. AS to Elizabeth Stieglitz Davidson, Aug. 25 and Sept. 2, 1929.

182. GOK to Rebecca Strand, Nov. 5, 1929.

183. Lynes 616.

184. O'Keeffe, as quoted by Henry McBride, "The Sign of the Cross," *New York Sun,* Feb. 8, 1930, 8.

185. Mary Mann, "Exhibitions," *International Studio* 95 (Mar. 1930), 76.

186. McBride, "Sign of the Cross."

Alfred Stieglitz, *Georgia O'Keeffe: After Return from New Mexico*, 1929. Gelatin silver print, 7.9 x 11.7 in. (3⅛ x 4⅝ cm).
The J. Paul Getty Museum, Los Angeles (93.XM.25.72). Copyright © J. Paul Getty Trust. Greenough 1306.

me. Your whole body haunts me—every inch—every part of every whole haunts me." But she also recognized that she had "found a symbol," as much as a "reality."[187] Stieglitz's letters to her from this time are far more flirtatious and coy than passionate and revealing, perhaps reflecting his and O'Keeffe's new closeness or the fact that Norman herself was pregnant with her second child and was also becoming increasingly infatuated with the writer Gerald Sykes.

In early April, O'Keeffe and Stieglitz decided that she would once again spend the summer in New Mexico. As she explained to Brett: "I couldn't decide until Stieglitz decided— it came quietly—naturally—like the flow of all the winter has been—It is what I want to do for my work." She added: "It is almost as tho Stieglitz makes me a present of myself in the way he feels about it."[188] O'Keeffe spent most of May and early June at Lake George, opening the house for the summer and filling it with her new paintings, including *Jack-in-the-Pulpit Nos. I–VI*.[189] Stieglitz visited her almost every weekend. When she left first for the Midwest and then Taos on June 8, both recognized, as Stieglitz wrote, that while their relationship had a "bit less romanticism than formerly," each gave the other "something that seems very necessary…like salt

187. Norman to AS, Jan. and Apr. 1930.
188. O'Keeffe to Dorothy Brett, April 1930.
189. Lynes 715–720.

in my food."[190] Vowing that he would be "all right on the Hill" and would "learn not to worry uselessly—needlessly," Stieglitz also admitted that he knew O'Keeffe needed "the life you'll find in New Mexico."[191] As if to keep his emotions in check, his letters to her from the summer of 1930 are oddly flat, devoid not only of the intensity and the passion of the previous year but also of insight into his thinking. Although O'Keeffe continued to express her deep love for New Mexico, her letters to him are equally circumspect, as if she did not dare excite him too much with her own wonder or with overly enthusiastic descriptions of her escapades.

Throughout the summer they, like so many others, nervously watched the plummeting economy. In June stocks continued to suffer large losses on the New York Stock Exchange. By the middle of the month, railroad stocks plunged, while wheat broke a new low for the season and other futures markets were similarly depressed. On June 19, in one of the heaviest selling sessions since November 1929, practically all active stocks equaled or went below their previous 1930 lows. The following day, Secretary of the Treasury Andrew W. Mellon assured a nervous country that new tariff laws would not adversely affect U.S. businesses or retard growth. Yet on June 21, Wall Street demonstrated a "heretical disregard" for his statements and an "onslaught of selling" drove prices even lower. In August, when predictions of a revival were dashed, *The New York Times* reported that the recent "bull campaign [had] failed completely."[192]

When O'Keeffe arrived in Chicago, she visited Betty O'Keeffe, the widow of her recently deceased brother, Alexis. Unbeknowst to Stieglitz, she had also arranged to see Gustav Eckstein, the scientist whom she had met in Taos the previous summer. She then traveled on to Portage, Wisconsin, where she stayed with her sister Catherine Klenert and her husband, Ray, and saw their aunts Alletta (Ollie) and Lenore (Lola) Totto. On June 12, she headed to New Mexico, arriving two days later. Although Mabel offered to let her stay in the Los Gallos studio she had used the summer before for painting, O'Keeffe was not her prized guest that summer—that honor fell to the poet Robinson Jeffers. She also remained suspicious of O'Keeffe's feelings for Tony and, as O'Keeffe bemusedly related to Stieglitz, Mabel "arranges quite well that Tony and I never meet—it is very funny."[193] To gain some distance from Mabel's machinations, O'Keeffe took most of her meals in town, occasionally with the Marins, who arrived in Taos in June, or with Paul and Beck Strand, who came in early July. She also frequently visited her friends Marie Garland and Henwar Rodakiewicz in Alcalde, New Mexico, often staying for several days.

After accompanying O'Keeffe to Albany, where she caught her train to Chicago, Stieglitz returned briefly to New York and then went to Lake George with Emil Zoler on June 12. He stayed there until O'Keeffe returned from the Southwest at the end of August. Both Zoler and Paul Rosenfeld, who arrived a few days later, spent most of the summer with him; other visitors included the drama critic Louis Kalonyme.

190. AS to GOK, May 26, 1930; GOK to AS, May 12, 1930.

191. AS to GOK, June 1, 1930.

192. See "Stocks Suffer Large Losses," *Wall Street Journal,* June 16, 1930, 13; "Mellon Declares New Tariff Law Will Aid Business," *NYT,* June 21, 1930, 1; and "Financial Markets," *NYT,* June 22, 1930, N11. "Topics in Wall Street," *NYT,* Aug. 13, 1930, 27.

193. GOK to AS, June 26, 1930.

Alfred Stieglitz · Albany, New York · June 8, 1930 +

2:20 P.M. Here I am alone in the depot—sitting where you & I were sitting but a few minutes ago—together. And now you are speeding westward—and I have my bag before me—we ready for New York—

I hope you are quieting down—& will be at peace shortly—I know what you are feeling—Yes, I know.—And I know too this had to be—for you—for me—for us together—

It will work out all right—I know it must.—Of course I wish you were in Taos already—But that too will come & take its place. I'll be glad when you will have gone thro' the Betty end of it—& the Aunts.—And I know Catherine will enjoy you—& the youngster[194] will too—in spite of the short stay.—

—Again I assure you you mustn't worry about me. You have arranged every detail at the Lake so perfectly—Yes—I see.—And somehow or other I feel I'll be strong & clear—as strong & clear as last autumn—I can wish for no greater strength nor greater clarity.—And the economic question I won't let dominate me—or you—

It's natural to be sitting here—I do feel you here—& I know I'll feel you that close all summer—And remember I'm with you that close too—otherwise I couldn't feel your closeness as I do.

A kiss now—I'll write more on the train.—

Georgia O'Keeffe · [En route from Albany, New York, to Chicago, Illinois] · [June 8, 1930]

Dearest—

I have said it all—and I have said nothing—but I feel that if any human being could understand—you do—

And I thank you—Thank you for everything—Above all for loving me—

Be very careful of your little self—I will be too—

And I kiss you again very tenderly—

Georgia O'Keeffe · [En route from Chicago, Illinois, to Portage, Wisconsin] · June 10, 1930

8 A.M. I just sent the little morning word off to you with a red cap—so you would have it sooner than I know you can get this—mailed farther north—

This is my real Good Morning Dearest—The night was warm but I got well washed up and rested—am glad I stayed in Chicago.

I didn't tell you all about yesterday when I wrote last night—I was too tired to be as clear as I wanted to be—

---

194. O'Keeffe's niece, Catherine Klenert, daughter of her sister Catherine and Ray Klenert.

Eckstein had told me when he was in New York that he had to come to Chicago again and go to Madison too so when I went West—if I went to let him know when I went through Chicago—and if he hadn't been here by then he might come then if I let him know when I was coming and on what train—

I said nothing to you because I had already given you so many uncertainties and I was very doubtful of his being there[195]—but there he was—a very pale worn looking little creature—

The hours with him were fine—and I tell you of it because I feel that if you understood —as you probably do—how he feels and thinks about me you would like it much—

I must tell you too—that one of the last things he said to me was "You know—it is very very sweet to know Stieglitz as I know him through you"—He was very sick looking—almost no sleep for two nights—working till he will get so he can't anymore—if not careful but it seems to have gotten under his skin—very much as it does with the rest of us—isn't it funny—

From the way he talked I think he is most apt to go to Hamburg and get his apes[196]— but he doesn't know—

—You see—I even wondered—should I tell you I had seen him—it seemed so foolish not to—He is among the things I have enjoyed most since I met him—among the people I have enjoyed most in my life—in a really beautiful way—that feels healthy and alive and free to me—and I want and like to tell you—He gives me something that I think you would very much like me to have if I could say to you exactly what it is—but saying such things is quite impossible—I only want you to feel that I feel it is very good for the thing in me that means something to you—You and he seem more alike than either of you are like me—

It is funny—He seems more like you than anyone I have known—

He took the sleeper to Madison last night to see Bunting at the university early this morning—and will be back in Chicago to see someone there this afternoon—He plans to go to New York later in June—beyond that knows nothing except that he may have to quit his pace for a little—just to be sure he has sense before he turns in the manuscript[197]—

He was funny—when I got my sleepers and baggage arranged—he remarked that just the names of the towns out there—when he heard them gave him such an itch to return—He doesn't love the sort of life that I love there at all—

Well Dearest—that is that—

One great difference in you is that he admires Rubens but doesn't like him—that is— as he put it—he doesn't like what Rubens sees—

—No use going into any more of it—I know you understand—

—I really feel first rate this morning—the train is good—Out the window I know so well I don't have to look at it—I will be at Portage at noon—

195. Stieglitz responded on June 12, 1930, telling O'Keeffe that he knew she would see Eckstein and added: "You could have told me....I'm glad you have someone who gives you what he does."

196. Gustav Eckstein was studying animal behavior.

197. Eckstein's forthcoming book, *Noguchi* (New York, 1931), was hailed as "an unforgettable narrative"; see "A Glowing Portrait of a Great Microbe Hunter," *NYT*, May 17, 1931, 63.

11:25

Good Night Dearest:—

    I saw our star—the bright star out over the road leading to the pasture—I saw it with the very last glow of color in the west—the glow that comes and stays after it is dark—out over the Wisconsin River—We got out of the car to stand at the railing and look down into the water—Catherine—Ray—Mrs. Cushing and I—the river very swift moving—powerful —almost silent—and very dark—Our star—very bright and strong—over it—the red glow in between—I wonder if when you look at it you too feel it is our star—it is such a bright beautiful star—

    —The day has been quiet—still much in it—Catherine and I talk much—Margery[198] came again this morning—Catherine showed me more paintings—some large ones—really quite a surprising development—

    After lunch the Portage reporter came to interview me—I let her come because Margery was very insistent—and Margery came in again while she was here—it was a very sweet sensitive girl—Margery tells me Blanche Matthias is in Chicago—I may see her Friday morning if I connect well—Margery wants to come to New York next winter when my show is on—it seems to mean a great deal to her—

    We went to Ray's mother's[199] for a few moments after supper and we just [were] going down to see Mrs. Cushing again when she appeared at the door—She went in the car with us as there were some small errands to do then we drove out over the river—

    It has been a lovely day—Mrs. Cushing is a wonder—

    Tomorrow morning at seven Catherine and I intend starting down to the Aunts'[200]— We phoned them tonight—I am glad to have had this day here first—It so confirms the nice feeling I always have about Catherine—

    Zona Gale is not at home—I can not feel very sorry—she seems such a cold thing— compared to the others I see here—

    You will be going to the Lake in the morning—I hope things go fairly well—Ray says the market is much down today[201]—pretty bad—I know how that makes you feel—and it disturbs me to feel you in that state—

    Last night—when I waked in the small hours—for a little time as I often do—All of me seemed to be going back to you—wanting to go to you—to hold you and pet you and comfort you—Then I thought—yes—and the trunks are traveling West—

    It all seems so queer—And I feel so strange some moments—and wonder where I am in space—that I am not by you—

530

---

198. The author Margery Latimer.

199. Mary Ellen Klenert.

200. When O'Keeffe visited her aunts Ollie and Lola Totto, she noted that though her visit had been a "great treat for them…the soil and the Catherines seem to be all I would really have an urge to return to" (GOK to AS, June 12, 1930).

201. The New York Stock Exchange suffered its greatest loss of the year on June 11, 1930, but was rescued from "a decline of sweeping proportions" when J. P. Morgan bankers submitted bids for over sixty thousand shares of steel; see "Bankers Halt Drops after Stocks Reach New Lows for the Year," *NYT*, June 12, 1930, 1.

My Darling Little Boy—I feel so closely knit to you—and still I am way out here—
I look forward to being settled and at work—
—This time in between is difficult—
Good Night Dearest—
A very fond Good Night kiss—

Alfred Stieglitz · Lake George, New York · June 13, 1930 +

Here I am again—5:30 P.M. Zoler & I back. A strong wind—south—was blowing on the
Lake. We went to the post office. Zoler rowing both there & home.—It was enjoyable altho' his
rowing is anything but good form.—

At the post office I found your very, very beautiful letter from Portage.—Yes, Wall Street
is bad. Ominous.—But I accept it without depression or sadness.—I have gone thro' all that—
& can't go thro' it any more. I know Sweetestheart, how you felt & saw me when Ray told
you—Yes, the trunk was traveling Westward. It had no choice.—You have no choice. That's why
I say get all out of "it" you can. Use the opportunity to its fullest. What that means is difficult to
say. Each according to his own lights—or each according to his darkness. Sometimes I wonder
which.

Zoler said a significant thing when looking at your *Jack-in-the-Pulpit*—the last one[202]
—hung on the wall in the small room—He called it "The Black Lily." I had thought of it as
"The Ascension." And I'm not given to titles you know. Nor is Zoler. I didn't say anything to
him one way or another.—At present he is boiling water for me.—

Your letter, yes, is very very beautiful.—And you are a grand woman—or should I say
child.—Maybe both. The star—our star—yes—It wasn't clear last night—there were no stars
here last night—Maybe tonight. You dearest Fine One—I do hope Taos will give you even more
than it did last year. And by Taos I mean the summer.—I have made up my mind to be very quiet
—And all will report to you when the summer has come to an end: Alfred was very serene &
very well all summer.—

Georgia O'Keeffe · [Taos, New Mexico] · June 14 [1930]

Dearest—

Here I am in my bed in the studio—the little stream outside—all quiet but for its
flowing—

Charles met me at Raton—I was glad to see him—glad I didn't bother Mabel and
didn't have to come down by stage—We had lunch then drove down—I drove—about ninety
miles and I was so pleased to see how sure I felt—Charles said I drove well—

---

202. Lynes 720.

It is a beautiful drive—The young green of the aspens against the dark pine trees—a stormy sky—a little rain—a mirage on the desert—all wonderful as I remembered it—and I so much enjoyed driving it and feeling the difference in the way I felt last year and now—It was a good feeling—

Mabel looks fine—Tony a bit thin—but that is good—the Jeffers[203] are here—a curious man—I had supper with them then came over here to get fixed—

I forgot to tell you that I arrived in the town with the circus—an elephant in a truck—Another truck having gone through a small bridge was stopping all the traffic—and there was Brett with a new tin horn mixed in with it all—It was funny—and just what one would expect in Taos—

Charles helped me remove all the Indian ornaments and Italian trimmings put up to make the studio seem cozy—It was so funny I had to laugh—I want to wake up in the morning and feel it bare—Then we put my blankets on the bed—and now I feel quite fixed—

It was good to have your letters—They are sweet—and interesting—I wish I could see you all at the Lake—

It is going to be different over here—I think I am going to like it better than the Pink House—About the eating—I will decide tomorrow—

Good Night Little One

Brett has a bad cold so I made little effort to talk with her—

Again Good Night—and a kiss—it goes out into the dark with the stars to you—

That bright star in the West is very burning here tonight—

A kiss—soft and dark—

[June 15, 1930]
Sunday—

My first night is over—it is perfect—A most perfect moon came bursting over the mountain when I was half asleep—I felt as if I had forgotten what a moon was like when I saw it—

My morning kiss feels very alive—

Alfred Stieglitz · Lake George, New York · June 15, 1930 +

7:30 A.M.—The house is still silent. Everyone still asleep.—Zoler, Rosenfeld, Martha[204] & chauffeur. I am taking Salsoda.[205] Will take it regularly for a week or so.—Am feeling fine—better than in many months. Even the mean arm is mending. The itch is nearly gone—really no longer bothers me—heart is behaving—still I think Salsoda will do it no harm.—

---

203. Una and Robinson Jeffers.

204. Martha was Lee and Lizzie Stieglitz's cook.

205. Although most commonly used for washing, Salsoda (sodium carbonate) was occasionally used in the treatment of scaly skin diseases.

Good Morning you Whitest One of White Ones.—Yes, Good Morning.—I had your letter yesterday morning as you were leaving Raton[206]—maybe I mentioned that in my letter to you yesterday—So you must be in Taos by now. Or maybe you staid over in Raton for the night & will not get to Taos [until] today, Sunday sometime.—I'm amazingly quiet.—I am certainly a "different" person.—A kiss—A very sweet one.

The night was fair. All windows open. It was warm but pleasant—And it was after midnight when we went to bed. Zoler, Rosenfeld & I had a concert from 9:30 till then. Had sat on the porch until 9:30.—Quiet. Enjoyable. Then I played the Ravel *Bolero* for Rosenfeld.— He dislikes it. Robeson followed.—Then came Rachmaninoff, Kreisler, Beethoven *Sonata* which I bought you with Robeson, etc., but which I don't think you ever played. It's very fine. One of the choice records.—Then came various Bachs—& I followed up with Beethoven *Quartet No. 59, I*—We each sat in a corner—there are chairs in three corners now—& we listened & really reveled. When I got to bed my allness was ringing with music.—You would have enjoyed the concert.—

Instead of being rowed to the station—Zoler & I walked. Our timepieces being slow we just reached the station as Rosenfeld was about to get into a taxi. I was glad we arrived in time. —Rosenfeld is well installed & says he didn't remember everything as beautiful. Your paintings certainly cheer up the house. So does the feeling of light. His room is perfect. And he is ready for work.—Took a swim as soon as he arrived. Lucky one to be able to do that—.

The morning is clear & the day will be pretty warm—the way you & I like it best.— A fixing bath is ready—& if nothing interferes & I don't see what should, a bit of printing will be done today.—I am curious. This beginning all over again—And this lack of faith in the material. Always the uncertainty all along the line.—

Lee & Lizzie had a good day.—Their "feed" house[207] will be ready tomorrow but the table has not yet come—So for a few days I guess we'll all be eating down here.—

All this is not very interesting—but it gives you a picture you know already only too well.—Of course I could write about many abstract ideas that constantly chase thro' my head but I feel that they best remain in my head unless they assume concrete form some day.—And then above all I want you to live the life of the Southwest—*your* life there—the few weeks will be all too short for what you have set out to do. And remember you must not think I worry. It's very different from last year. If you make trips—camping, etc. & can't keep in touch with me for a long time—remember I have made up my mind really not to worry.—You must feel absolutely free & not feel you are doing anything at my expense.—For you are not.—

Martha's voice is heard—Rosenfeld is ready for breakfast—Zoler is marching around outside—the chauffeur is on his way to Cashion's—Commotion—centered in Martha.—It will be good when the two households will each set their own pace—

206. As she traveled to the Southwest, O'Keeffe wrote Stieglitz that she felt "like falling into this country like one sometimes wants to fall off a sheer wonderful edge—It has such a feeling of death and terrific life—side-by-side" (GOK to AS June 13?, 1930).

207. Lee and Lizzie Stieglitz had recently built a kitchen for their house, Red Top, on the Stieglitz family's Lake George property.

After breakfast.—That is over with.—Much commotion.—Salsoda working.—Lee at dock waiting for his man who is eating a belated breakfast.—It's all very amusing.—

Kiss. And you? I wonder where you are just now.—How you are feeling.—I do hope on top of the world in every way.—

Kisses. And a ton of love.—

Georgia O'Keeffe · [Taos, New Mexico] · June 16, 1930

Monday night—

I had four letters from you tonight—your last from New York and first from Lake George—

I was glad because last night—in the night—when I waked—and had my black thoughts I was much worried about you—I hope you send me a night letter as I wired you to —These four letters were a help anyway—

I have had another lively day—being not tied to Mabel's household is very good— I was at the hotel for breakfast at seven—Brett came in as I finished—Mabel and I had a great time getting houses and blankets and floor mops and lamps and such things straightened out —We ran from one house to another all morning it seemed—My trunk came tonight—I moved all my furniture and got rid of some—straightening out a bit—After lunch I went out with my paints and things to look at what I am thinking of painting and all afternoon I sat there looking at it and thinking about it—

What is it about this country that gets me so—and what can I do about it—No use in painting till I am a bit clear about it—

I made several little drawings[208]—Was really too tired from rushing around all morning —too tired to start painting but it was wonderful sitting there alone watching the light and shadow over the desert and mountains—and wondering what I could do about it—

It all interests me much more than the people—they seem almost not to exist—The nicest is Charles—he is in a half dream—dazed sort of state—hoping Mary[209] will come—he had another letter from her—wrote her again today—

Tomorrow I hope to get over looking and do something—but what I was looking at this afternoon seemed to affect me like the music I like—it moved and changed constantly—

I am tired—I'll be getting to bed—

Mabel and I had a very funny talk about Tony—Brett and Charles just went off into shrieks when I told them—and Tony came to the hotel and sat with us while we were eating supper—He seems very glad to see me back—

Everything goes very well—But I must get to bed—eyes won't stay open—

A kiss goes out into the black night wind to you—

208. Possibly Lynes 733, 746–750.
209. Charles Collier's girlfriend and later his wife.

Georgia O'Keeffe · [Taos, New Mexico] · [June 17, 1930]

Tuesday—

I was so glad to have your wire this morning—I just was in a sort of a stew about you—for no reason except that I was—Yes Taos is as fine to me as it was—Maybe even finer because I like this being alone—Brett went up to the ranch this morning with a car full of Indians—men, women, and babies—it was a funny sight—I saw three of her paintings— They are better—freer—

I was out at the same spot gazing at the desert and a particular mountain that I love— I have a drawing[210]—but when I bring it here and hang it on my wall I know I am not going to paint it—I will start again—No use to paint unless it is something—

After lunch I lay down a little—I was tired and hot—then it began to rain—dark clouds with long dark fringes racing across the sky in front of the mountains—lightning that flashes over everything—and I look out at it—and wonder and wonder what it is that I love so about it—It is one of those suffering times when I love something so much—and I want to work —I feel like it—but things do not come clear to me—they just don't come and it makes me crazy—I am very quiet—feel very nice within myself—a kind of peace in spite of my excitement over the country again—

Alfred Stieglitz · Lake George, New York · June 23, 1930

Noon—30. What a day. Nothing more beautiful can be imagined. A summer sun.—A sky intensely blue—cloudless. And a cool breeze. Really wonderful.—Zoler, Frankie[211] & I walked briskly to the Village—Without getting hot—Two beautiful letters from you, Dearest One. Letters like the day. And I had one for breakfast. The one that should have come yesterday.— It's wonderful to know you so at peace—so full of activity—in surroundings completely satisfying—free—riding—painting—autoing—sleeping well—eating at the hotel—feeling contented there. Charles a good companion.—Great—

And I feel alive today. For a week or so my heart was thumping—not skipping or too fast—just thumping—principally at night. Last night I took half a grain Luminal[212]—Lee told me to take it—& the miracle has happened at once. The thumping stopped. And no thumping since.—I knew it was nothing. It didn't make me nervous but it did keep me awake.—So I feel like the day. And like your letters.—And even tho there is no "excitement" here—I am contented with all that is—here & in Taos—& in the Place, etc., etc.—Eight new records have arrived. Paul Rosenfeld donated two & I six. We'll play them tonight—Lizzie goes to Chicago today & comes back Thursday. Today is Monday.—Lee isn't going.—I suppose he'll eat with us. He comes down occasionally after his meals to sit with us.—

---

210. Possibly either Lynes 733 or 746–750.
211. Frank (Frankie) Prosser was the son of the Margaret Prosser, Stieglitz's Lake George housekeeper.
212. Luminal, a barbiturate with sedative properties, was used as an anticonvulsant.

—This is a mountain day—the wind is blowing up hard—Northwest—The tall grasses outside of the window are swaying madly & the windblown trees singing a song—beyond the grasses a field all white—& beyond that deep green trees—& such a blue in the sky.—Really an incredible day.

I'm doing nothing in particular.—Wrote letters to Eggers (Director, Worcester Art Museum) & to Fox (Brooklyn). Your & Marin's things were sent to Copenhagen & are now in Munich.[213] And without my permission. Eggers assumed that we had given permission to Fox & Company. Well, the deed is done. And we'll see. I did not want you or Marin to appear anywhere in Germany until you both could be seen fully.—

Rosenfeld is busy calling up Wall Street—Funny I am not a bit curious.—Neither one way or another. Wouldn't act either way now so what's the use of "knowing."—

I haven't shaved as yet—so will go up & clean up for lunch.—

A big kiss you Wonderful One—Another kiss—

Georgia O'Keeffe · [**Taos, New Mexico**] · **June 23, 1930**

11:45 A.M. Monday—
Dearest—

I am just back from Marie's—and I have two letters from you—written before you had my first letters from here—It does take a long time for mail to go and an answer come—over a week it seems—I am so glad you are printing—you sound very quiet—and the Wall Street so bad—

I wish I could see you—I was up early and out in the hills down at Marie's this morning—I didn't even make a drawing—I only looked—it is very wonderful out there alone —Then the drive up was lovely—Spud didn't feel good so there was no talk—I enjoy the driving and I enjoy what I see—

Here it seems so quiet—only the noise of the little brook—the room so large and cool and still—after the fifty-mile drive—

I got a lonesome feeling for you—The time when I plan to go back seems so far away —and the grip of this country on me is such a real grip—It seems so much right this minute that I would like to know what you are doing—

People here seem to exist for me so little—but the earth and the sky—and the little green—the vast empty distance—It all makes me a bit sick at my stomach—right at this moment—

I'll be going for my lunch and working this afternoon—

I regret that you will have some days without my letters—even tho they are not much at

213. Stieglitz loaned two watercolors by Marin and two paintings by O'Keeffe to the Retrospective Exhibition of American Painting and Architecture organized by the Worchester Art Museum under the auspices of the American-Scandinavian Society and the American Federation of the Arts for the Royal Academy of Art in Stockholm and the Ny Carlsberg Glypotek in Copenhagen. William Henry Fox of the Brooklyn Museum of Art subsequently arranged for the show to travel to Munich.

536

times—Mail doesn't do much here over weekends I fear—that is—Sunday—and from Marie's it doesn't go at all unless someone happens to go to town—

A kiss to you Little One—

And know that I think much of you—

Georgia O'Keeffe · [Near Bear Lake, New Mexico] · [June 29, 1930] +

Sunday Morning—

Dearest—Dearest—

Here I sit with sun on the top of our mountain with the Bear Lake over the other side in the valley—We had a wonderful ride up yesterday—only a little rain for a few moments— We were off at nine—Charles—Young John Marin—a very nice Indian[214] and I with one pack horse—The party is perfect—weather good tho we have three snow drifts right beside our camp —I thought we would freeze to death—but such a bed of boughs as Charles concocted you never saw—When I got into mine I thought I never felt a better bed—I was warm as could be— and should have slept well but it was so wonderful listening—smelling—looking—I didn't sleep much—We have the neatest camp you ever saw—Charles crawled out a little before five and was out fishing—so there were fish for breakfast—Maybe two cups of coffee for supper kept me awake—and I kept feeling I still had something between my legs where the horse had been all day—I am not a bit stiff or sore this morning—not so bad after riding from nine till five with only a few moments for lunch—

Everything is arranged much better than last year—

Well—I wonder what you are at this morning—it is a few minutes after eight—I am going to take a sunbath here before the whole valley and the bare topped mountains with their patches of snow—

[July 1, 1930]

It's Tuesday afternoon—lovely—sunny—warm—tho when I say that you must remember that I still have on my two sets of woolen underwear and two sweaters—

It looked like rain this morning so we all sat around waiting to see—didn't go far from the tent—Finally all got under with everything that water could hurt—a big fire out in front— had a little hail or sleet and that was all—The sun came out—We all crawled from under the tent much pleased that that was all—soft white clouds seem very close against the brilliant blue —The Indian came in before breakfast with fish again so we all had three or four apiece for breakfast again—He is very nice—young—the sort that can do anything—very gentle— I talked with him a long time this morning—When I came in from the woods after cleaning up for the day I still had my skirt on—I sleep in my skirt—He remarked with such a pleased smile—"Oh—we have a real woman today"—It was so sweet—I had to laugh—

214. O'Keeffe, Charles Collier, John Marin, Jr., and a Native American named Louis who worked for Mabel Luhan, went on a camping trip near Bear Lake, from June 28 to July 3, 1930.

It is really a very nice party—quiet—each one doing what he likes—and it is fine for Young John Marin—I had to laugh at a talk he and Charles had after breakfast about school —then the young Indian's remarks about their conversation—The three of them in relation to one another are very nice—It is a curious three days out here with the mountains—and the lake and this untouched feeling woods—Charles so efficient—a bit contrary at times—the young Indian just smiling when he doesn't agree with him after he has made his difference of opinion known—Young John Marin mostly just looking on—They take no particular trouble for me— I just go along like the rest of them—I don't even feel queer about enjoying it so much—it all seems just right—

A queer woman you have—I suppose—I wish you could see where I am sitting—It is the handsomest seat I ever saw—One enormous dead silver tree has fallen across another equally large and handsome [one]—My feet are on the branch of a third one—older and deader— under these two—its branch—sticking up in perfect position for my feet—The sun shining on me—the sky so blue it seems almost black—I am a queer woman—but I don't feel queer at all—I feel quite right and in place—so in place—and so placid about it that I have to laugh—

They will all be green with envy down in Taos when we get back and tell them we had almost no rain—

The wind has come up—tho it is only three I must go and get my long coat—I foolishly came off without it—

A kiss to you Dearest—This is all so simple—if you could see how simple it all is you wouldn't dream of worrying about it—

Another kiss—I feel in a sort of faraway state—as tho I have fallen into the mountain and can only recall myself to write with difficulty—So if my penciling is stupid know that it is simply because I have fallen into the mountain—or the days or something—It is so quiet there seems to be nothing to say about it—

The silver trees I am sitting on send you greetings—also the very cold very clear little green lake and the mountain with the long pure line of a snow ridge on its left side—

And I wish that my kiss could take you all of it—

Alfred Stieglitz · [Lake George, New York] · July 1, 1930

9 A.M.—Good Morning. You Grand One. A great beginning for July.—Hooray for all of us. —I'm down since seven. A poor night—wind blowing trees—& Pluto[215] water rumbling inside of me—Bathed eyes before going to bed—Rosenfeld read Van Gogh's *Letters*[216] aloud to me. What a beautiful relationship between brothers.

215. Pluto Water, from the Pluto Mineral Springs, French Lick Springs, Indiana, was advertised as a digestive aid with the slogan "When nature won't, Pluto will."

216. Vincent van Gogh, *The Letters of Vincent van Gogh to His Brother, 1872–1886: With a Memoir by His Sister-in-Law* (Boston, 1927).

Well, here I am.—All ready for the day. Zoler just down. Surprised we're thro'.—I got the breakfast ready. Usually do.—Most of it. All very simple. And everything so clean—& *in place*. Fred[217] got my mail this A.M. with Lee's.—First time.—And it was quite a mail. I'm wiring you the grand news.—When I saw an envelope marked Cleveland Museum I opened it first expecting to find Milliken say he's returning painting—"sorry," etc., etc.—But lo & behold I find he announces the purchase of the *White Flower* for four thousand dollars by the museum.[218] —Hooray. He has made good. For years he has been hoping.—But I dared not think it could happen. I wonder was Hanna in Cleveland.[219]—Well it's an important happening just at this time when so many are denying you—The idiots. Same old story.—And the money is welcome too—in view of recent happenings. I'd rather have you earn one hundred thousand dollars thro' your work than any amount thro' Wall Street.[220] All I want for you & me is no worry about moneys in case of illness.—That's all.—You must feel glad too. This time you are permitted to say: "I'm glad for your sake."—All know it here and are glad.—Fine to see their faces light up.—Well, you have done pretty well after all this year.—And all museums (that includes Sam Lewisohn[221])!!—Great—Milliken writes me: "I wonder if you have any information from Georgia O'Keeffe about this picture, I would appreciate it, if possible, to have a note from her about its significance & her relation to it." Now, sit down at once & send him something.—Please don't forget—Address letter: William M. Milliken, Esq., Curator of Paintings, The Cleveland Museum of Art, Cleveland, Ohio, Station E—Or if you prefer send me the letter & I'll forward it to him. You may want me to see what you write—

—It's a gaslight printing day & I want to use it.—I'm wiring you the good news. I hope you get the wire.—

Lots lots of love & a huge kiss!—

Georgia O'Keeffe · [Taos, New Mexico] · July 3, 1930

Thursday Morning—

Dearest—

That was certainly a scrappy bunch of writing I sent you this morning—but I thought it would give you a vague picture of the days in the mountains—I can't tell you how disappointed I was that the letter telling you I was going didn't get off to you as I intended—I gave it to Charles to mail—he put it down here in the studio and doesn't remember a thing about it—

217. Fred was a handyman who worked for the Stieglitz family.

218. William M. Milliken, curator of paintings at the Cleveland Museum of Art, wrote Stieglitz on June 28, 1930, that the museum would purchase O'Keeffe's *White Flower* (Lynes 674).

219. Leonard C. Hanna, Jr., who lived in Cleveland, bought O'Keeffe's painting *White Flower* (Lynes 561) on March 26, 1928.

220. With advice from her brother-in-law Robert Young and others, O'Keeffe was taking an active role in managing her portfolio of stocks and bonds.

221. Sam A. Lewisohn was a New York collector who purchased O'Keeffe's *Porcelain Rooster* (1929, Lynes 672). Although he later donated several works to the Brooklyn Museum of Art, this pastel was not one of them.

I had wanted it mailed after the one before—I had thought it would go to you Monday morning as there is no mail on Sunday—

Thanks for the little blue petals in the letter—They surprised me much—I got an eagle's feather up on the mountain—it is too large to send in a letter or I would send it—

I still feel battered this morning—decided not to work till tomorrow—That walk down the steep place was what knocked me up—I just feel used all over—but not more so than I have often been when you had finished me four or five times—.

It is a hot day—I helped sort our camping stuff and cleaned up the studio—It was very dirty—Seems so queer to be back in town—

Mabel was in—asked me to supper—She is very funny—The Indian whose horse I rode was in too—He camped with us last year—And the Indian who went with us this time was in[222]—I had told him he could ride out to Ranchos with me this morning—He was taking fish to some friends out there—And Marin and Young John were over getting John's things—So the morning slid away—

Your letters in a way make me feel you are not so well—and still you say you are well—Remember—if you are not well I want to go to you—Those days up in the mountains make me feel so quiet inside—and so full of something satisfying—I could pack up and go now and feel the being here had been worthwhile—

Marin saw my worst church this morning and thought it much bigger than the one of last year[223]—It is quite incomplete—He said nothing about the one I am through with—I was hurrying to breakfast and said nothing either—

The Cleveland Museum surprises me much—I have been intending to get at that flower again. They are blooming in the field just outside my door—I feel more like doing it this year than last—Think I'll have a better one.

I wish you could see my studio now—be here with me—It is so quiet—I feel so far far away—And the little Ford standing outside in the shade of the studio takes one to anything one wants so quickly—

—I sometimes wonder what it is all about—you and I—your life there—my life here—and why I like this sort of thing so—and am a bit irritated that I am too knocked up today to want to work—This all seems so bare and strenuous—

Beck comes on Saturday—I may go down and meet her—Spud wants me to go to Marie's on Friday—then we drive the fifty miles on from there early Saturday morning and meet Beck—at nine A.M.—It seems better than doing it all the way from here Saturday morning—I haven't decided—tho I may not go at all—Maybe I [will] send Charles if he will go—and he probably would—

I have some things in my head from up the mountain that I want to try to work on—

I wish you could have seen the moon go down behind the big mountain across the little lake—and the black shadow move slowly up the other one—a terrible black coldness—taking all the sparkle out of the woods around me—It was a great moment—almost terrifying—

222. Probably Juan Mirabal and Louis.
223. The "worst church" was Lynes 703, 704, or 705; the "one of last year" was Lynes 662, 664, or 666.

I am tired Little Bird—Think I'll take a nap—Even Louis—the Indian—owned up when he was in this morning that he was tired—

I wish I could curl up and go to sleep beside you—

—A kiss—a kiss to you—

Don't be sorry I am tired—it is good—I like it—

Georgia O'Keeffe · Taos, New Mexico · July 9, 1930

Good Morning—Dearest—

Usually I write at night because I am up and off at something early in the morning—Today it is 9:35 and I am still in bed—Something went wrong with me yesterday—I don't know what unless I just did too much the day before—I was just low—and this morning am still taking it easy—My last two letters were very short because I was so tired I couldn't manage any more—I am all right this morning—but I'm not going to get up till lunch time—It is so still here—and I feel better being quiet—

Your letters picture the days at the Lake very clearly—I am sure I do not picture my days as definitely to you—When one hasn't seen this white light there seems little use in trying to talk about it—And last night—at sunset—a storm over the Taos mountain was as grand as anything I ever saw—I never saw such long lines of rain coming down or such terrible streaks of lightning—Marin called me out to look at it—

And the night before—the moonlight in the Glorietta was like a dream—The trees seem fantastically large and soft—the mountains back of them dark—the sagebrush in front white and frosty looking and every once in awhile a glimpse of the river very black and mysterious—and sometimes the moon shining unexpectedly in it—It is certainly a wonderful country—but you have to keep moving day and night to see it—The days are too short—and the nights are too short—and one is too weak—and too small—But oh dear—I love it—and still I feel it is all beyond me—That I will not have time to do anything with it—

—I hate the back of my Ranchos church[224]—Tomorrow I must get out at it again—It is heavy—that is why Strand likes it I suppose—I want it to be light and lovely and singing—

Well—that is the way things go—Living here seems a waste—but I like that too—

Good Morning Little One—

I wish you were here—You would love the room—a bird just flew in and out again—It would seem curious to see you walking about here—A soft little pat on your cheek this morning—and a kiss—

---

224. Lynes 704.

Good Morning Dearest:

  I visited the printer today as you can see—

  Schultz dividend should come June 1st—etc.—

  I try to think some words to Mr. Milliken in Cleveland—and they don't come readily[225]—

  You see—that painting[226] was done with my head—before my heart and my body were ready—and what I do with my head may possibly be beautiful—but it hasn't the breath in it that means life—

  I want to paint the flower again and give it life if I can—

  I have been painting all day again—Out and up in the canyon this morning—just a hill with bushes on it and a piece of road[227]—

  I'll be out at it again tomorrow morning—It was a fair start—a sort of hill that I wanted to try all last summer and didn't because I was afraid to drive up there alone—

  After lunch a little nap—and I had two letters from you at noon—We just learned that there is a noon mail—I don't know whether it is new or whether we just didn't know about it —I've always had the mail at six at night—

  I painted on my abstraction from the Bear Lake tree[228]—canvas is all covered—it looks as tho it may be a good one—it is small—9 × 24—

  A beaut of a man came and sat with us while we ate supper—German—was in the war —lived in Brazil and Rio de Janeiro for years—He is a sight—and at that a rather inspiring sight tho he seems a bit crazy—And I thought—dear me—if I were built like that I could paint —He made me feel like a mosquito—so little and weak—I should have said before—he is a painter—

  You never saw such hands—I never saw anything more uncanny—

  He was almost as good as Davis—the car thief that they have in jail for twenty years now—

  —Then the moon came clear over the mountain—clear—and the mountain so dark— The water in the little stream seems very loud tonight—

  —I wanted to ride tonight but was tired and thought I had better not—maybe tomorrow—

---

225. O'Keeffe finally responded to Milliken on November 1, 1930, writing that she "would so much rather people would look at [the painting] than read about it." She continued: "The large white flower with the golden heart is something I have to say about white—quite different from what white has been meaning to me. Whether the flower or the color is the focus I do not know. I do know that the flower is painted large to convey to you my experience of the flower—and what is my experience of the flower if it is not color. I know I can not paint a flower. I can not paint the sun on the desert on a bright summer morning but maybe in terms of paint color I can convey to you my experience of the flower or the experience that makes the flower of significance to me at that particular time. Color is one of the great things in the world that makes life worth living to me and as I have come to think of painting it is my effort to create an equivalent with paint color for the world—life as I see it." The Cleveland Museum of Art Archives, as quoted in Cowart, Hamilton, and Greenough, *Georgia O'Keeffe: Art and Letters*, 202.

226. Lynes 561.

227. Possibly Lynes 729.

228. Lynes 745.

—So that is the way the day goes—The Strands and Marins went picnicking up Twining—When I saw them come into supper I was glad I wasn't with them—

—If your insides are bad, why don't you have Margaret grind your food for you— She has a machine—it would be very easy for her—

—Good Night Little One,

—I am tired—Work is too hard work for me—.

—I also made a large drawing of a mountain from up at Bear Lake—I had little drawings for it—

It is 10:20—July 11—30

Time for me to be in bed—

—I wish you were feeling better—it makes things seem a bit out of gear—

—A kiss to you—

Remember—don't let yourself get too down—I would rather go now and do what I can to fix you up rather than have you too completely upset—Don't hesitate to tell me if you want me to come—I know I can do things the others don't do—

Another Good Night kiss—.

Alfred Stieglitz · [Lake George, New York] · July 13, 1930 +

9:30 A.M.—Breakfast over.—Not enough hot water to wash dishes.—Good Morning, you so Faraway Nearest One.—Kiss.—It rained most of the night—And it poured this morning.— Everything is drenched—Up at seven. Went to the post office to get envelopes & stamps & thought there might be some word from you. Sure enough a letter & a postal from Hollywood —Flint.—I hope you haven't hurt yourself. I'd like to telegraph whether you are all right. But would you tell me the truth? You undoubtedly overdid something.—I'll have to wait to hear. —As for being dissatisfied with your painting I can understand how you feel.—It's a great problem you are up against.

And I want to say right here what I have [had] in mind all along. You must not set yourself a date to come back. Your work must come first.—It must.—If you set a date it interferes. So you must stay longer if you feel it will get you anywhere. I am all right. And to feel that I in any way may hinder your growth, your development, your painting just drives me crazy. I understand your conflict.—For there is a conflict.—So you might as well know how I feel about it. And I knew that before you left. Knew it while you were talking Europe—Of course to get down what that country makes you feel is more than a life's work. But anything that one feels so deeply to put into living equivalents is more than a life's work.—Always has been so. Will ever be so.— So don't set yourself a limit—Maybe you feel you must—But I feel you need not to—not quite the way you have set yourself one.—

—As for myself and the seeming contradiction—I must say there is really none. I was examined by both Lee & Jenks because my heart was thumping so hard at nights it kept me awake. It wasn't like two years ago—rushing up & down & skipping, etc.—The beat was normal enough. So I went about everything "normally" & was really what I call well. But I got less sleep than even usually—& the thumping was not pleasant. I knew what Jenks said was right. But I wondered whether Lee might not know something too.—You see I feel that altho' Jenks is still Jenks his marriage—his coming honeymoon trip—etc. all affects his advice. There is an imperceptible difference. It is not only in my imagination.—It's all so subtle.—That's true of all doctors finally, Lee, Roberts—the finest—marriage, Wall Street—etc., etc.—etc.—All called life. As for the Kaolin[229] I was amused too.—Well I'm taking it.—Of course I know that 95% of the "cure" is in myself. Last night my heart was quieter than it has been in months.—Maybe the feeling that something fine—very fine—had gone out into the world from the Hill did something towards bringing this about.—I go right ahead disregarding the heart—not in a foolish way—It's my way finally.—So you have no cause to worry about me in any way.—Knowing you feeling free & happy & at work is as good "medicine" for me as anything.—The music is a great quieter.—

Yes, I can imagine how grand nature is where you are—& what the white light must do.—And that it is very different from anything I have ever experienced. But somehow for the present I still feel it is not for me—much as I'd like to be with you for many reasons.—And for none of those you might imagine.—There's a riddle for a wise woman to solve.—

And now Sweetestheart—I'm going to proof my recent negatives.—I'm curious. I may have something very very beautiful—

A huge kiss—& I do hope you haven't injured yourself in any way.—

Much much love—

Rain has stopped. Sky breaking up in an extraordinary manner.—No day has been without sun.—

Georgia O'Keeffe · Taos, New Mexico · [July 21, 1930]

Dearest:

I am back in Taos—in my big room—it is very nice—ten P.M. I left it very clean so it is very good to return to—

Oh dear what a day—I brought Spud up—and Henwar's mother[230]—and she has almost wrecked us—The two of us almost fell in a heap in the mud when it finally stopped raining tonight and we could leave her at the hotel—I thought the sloppy mud of the street most wonderful when I got out into it and breathed the air without hearing her anymore—We both fairly gasped—

It was raining when I waked up this morning—that discouraged me so I didn't want to get up—As I couldn't go out to work I decided to drive up here this morning—She talked her troubles all the way up here—I argued with her—Spud says he was just having nervous fits on the back seat—She was almost hysterical—

229. Kaolin, a white clay, is used as a digestive aid.
230. O'Keeffe had spent the last few days in Alcalde with Marie Garland and Henwar Rodakiewicz and his mother, Erla Rodakiewicz.

However she seems much better tonight—I took her out to the Pueblo this afternoon at 6:45—rain, mud, and all—It rained all day—

The mud is so slippery the woman next door to me—starting for a walk with her husband—slipped at the edge of the ditch and slid right into it—It was very funny—

I was glad to drive up the canyon road in the mud—The color was lovely—When I finally arrived at the studio after lunch—I read your letters—they are a comfort—ate a melon—made myself a large cup of strong coffee—Stole some of Strand's cream for it—Beck has gone up with Brett—Strand has what he thinks a very satisfactory darkroom over the theatre—seems to be working hard—

I got out all my paintings and looked at them—There are ten—I can't say a great deal for them—The landscape is coming—The three that I did at Marie's[231] move ahead—I painted on one of them all afternoon—It looks pretty good tonight in the darkish room—

But oh dear—oh! dear—they look so thin—and it seems so difficult to paint this light thing I see and not have it thin—

—Anyway—I feel in a great rush to get back there again and at it again[232]—Am going down in the morning—praying for sunshine—

Your letter tonight telling of Ida's book[233] entertains me greatly—I wonder what she has written—

Well—the world is funny—Everything seems funny to me tonight—Wouldn't it be a scream to have Ida write something that would really sell—It is difficult for me to think of anything funnier—

But it is funny too to see all the streets and roads running rivers of mud like thick heavy cream—And it was funny too—to see the way that old lady wore Spud and me to shreds—We plan not to tell Marie—she would love it so—.

Oh what a day!

I wish I could get in bed with you—And I wish my paintings were better—

I would go back across the ditch and tell Strand and Spud—Spud is sleeping in Beck's bed—it is so rainy for him to walk a mile—I would go over and tell them about Ida's book but I'm afraid I might fall into the ditch—

I wish I could sleep by you—

It is one of those nights when I feel everything fell away with the day—So many different things that I feel quite like nothing—

Good Night Dearest,

231. Probably Lynes 725–727.

232. The next day, O'Keeffe again wrote Stieglitz about both her excitement over the landscape and her fears that her paintings were not successful: "When I get out here at work I wish time would stand still—I have never been more excited over the landscape—I sometimes stop to look around—and what I see seems more like music than anything I ever saw—it is really too beautiful—and so beautiful for painting—The days are too short—and I feel so feeble—I am afraid when you see what I have done you will be disgusted after all my raving." She concluded, "Well—it's no use to weep over it—and it does make me enjoy painting" (GOK to AS, July 22, 1930).

233. Ida Ten Eyck O'Keeffe's *Forest Indians* (New York, c. 1934) was a book designed to educate children on the Chippewa Native Americans.

I kiss you a good hard smack—I am not at all sure that red white and blue are the colors I think they are tonight—They may be green, yellow and pink—

Kiss me hard—I need it—

Alfred Stieglitz · Lake George, New York · July 25, 1930

2:15 P.M. We have just come down from Red Top. All full of much very good food. It's eighty-eight degrees in the shade. But so dry it's fine.—Played two rounds of "golf"[234] with Kalonyme this morning. Played well—both did. Then went for mail. Two letters from you. Another from Santa Fe (mailed there—written at Marie's) other from Taos. Mud, etc.—And you feeling very alive—full of good food too—& sleeping without a nightgown—Well,—Well—? You're sweet—Yes, your letters sounded very alive—*all* of you.—

—If you were here now I'd take you upstairs & make you strip—& —& —?—There is no ? about it.—It's just a straight fact.—I'm ready this moment as I write—can opener & all —I feel as if I could squirt great juices into you—down you.—

But you have your muddy roads—You're sweet—

Very, very—

A huge all embracing—Kiss—

Georgia O'Keeffe · [Taos, New Mexico] · [July 29, 1930]

Tuesday—

Well Dearest—

I finally wired you today—I have been worrying about you since Sunday. Had to know how you were right today—I hope you tell me the truth when you say you are well—I don't like it that you have such difficulty sleeping—

I have been painting all day—And I guess it is a hot one—Makes me sick at my stomach—It is the flower I was working on yesterday—large—reddish black—with brilliant blue flowers under it[235]—and it all feels close and hot and bulging out of the canvas—canvas so full—And Oh—it makes me so ill—

Strand likes it much—No one else has seen it—

I started another of the same thing[236]—Have the dark flower painted—will do the blue ones tomorrow—

Oh—I don't know what makes me do such things—Makes me hate myself if I am like that and I suppose I am—

Between the two paintings I went for the mail between three and four—Had your letter —a hot one too—Everything seems hot today—

234. During the 1930s, Stieglitz frequently played miniature golf when he was in Lake George.
235. Lynes 713.
236. Lynes 714.

Strand fell down in Mabel's dining room this noon—I guess he is all right but he seems a bit upset—His hobnail boots slipped on the cement steps—

I have done nothing but work today—

People ask to see my things—I seem to feel I have nothing to show so I don't show anything—

—I am going to read a bit on Mabel's manuscript[237]—I'm not much interested—I haven't even looked at it—

Good Night Dearest—I am beginning to feel right again from the curse—

Everyone says I look so well—Weigh 122½—Beck and I exactly alike—

A kiss—Your hot letter is sweet—

Georgia O'Keeffe · [Espanola, New Mexico] · [August 3, 1930]

Sunday evening—

Good Evening Dearest—

—Well—I wish I could see you—I am sitting in the back yard of the hotel—No one comes out here so we use it entirely—Haven't been on the front porch except the first time we came in—go in and out the back one with our Ford right by it—also by our window—very good—

We had a fine day yesterday—I don't care anything in particular for cave dwellings[238] but they seem to pick pretty fine places for them—always a sheer cliff—a little open space for garden—then the river with its cottonwood trees—

—The drive out and back was fine—the evening particularly lovely—but the morning was quite perfect too—clear—and fine for color—We had a good walk and a good climb too—and the sun was hot—it was fine—We were in bed at twenty to ten—This morning we were off before eight to the east—

—Oh—I almost forgot to tell you that our star was very bright and clear with the moon —and the last sunset glow as we drove up from Santa Fe last night—it was beautiful—I wish you could have seen it as it is here—And I wonder if you remember the plants I had three years ago with huge white flowers on it—Way up on the Puyé cliff—I found it growing as a weed— the sensuous white flowers blooming in the morning till the sun wilts them—also a kind of marigold that we cultivate—

—It seems quite impossible to tell what the country is like—This morning as we drove to the east—it seemed that one was right at the heart of something—

Faraway mountains fine and blue and big looking all around but far enough away not to make one feel shut in—nearer—sort of straight edged and sometimes with many small sharp points—long long ridges—or mountains of pink earth—the river flat—paler—small groups

---

237. Mabel Dodge Luhan, *Lorenzo in Taos* (New York, 1932).

238. O'Keeffe and Beck Strand, who briefly stayed in a hotel in Espanola in early August, had been to the Puye Cliff Dwellings, Santa Clara, New Mexico.

of houses along it—always adobe—small cultivated patches along the river—flowers by the doors—no grass—just hard foot trodden earth—always the dark skin and black eyes of the people—They always wave their hands as greeting—somber and gay at the same time—And sometimes a huge fat mountain—with much dark green on it grows right up out of the barren pinkness—and always here and there soft hills like I tried to paint—only sometimes long stretches of them outlined pale against the burning blue sky—trees a bright yellow green here and there along the river or irrigation ditches—but the principal feeling of it all is grand dry barrenness—And those blue mountains all around—

It all seems like the heart of something—I felt right in the center of something oh—so big—But God only knows what—

It was an awful road—not dangerous—just rough—I drove—so we went slowly—not more than eighteen miles all morning—maybe twenty—

This afternoon we went out by the black mesa again—I walked down to where I could see the river flowing swiftly—muddy—right past the foot of it—

Well I wish I could make you feel just a little of it all—I brought material along—but looking is too good—I made some little no count drawings—that is all—

The day has been burning hot—I have no idea how hot—but hot—We wear as little as possible—and that is very little—

Well—Little One—I am feeling very fine—the food here is very good—A fine breeze blows in from the north tonight—

I must get to bed—We plan to be asleep early—the days go better—

A Good Night kiss—

I wish I could see you tonight—

We will see Strand tomorrow—I think he will bring the mail—

I seem to have written quite a bit—but I'm not tired even tho the days seem a bit active—

Alfred Stieglitz · Lake George, New York · August 6, 1930 +

9 P.M.—Rosenfeld is walking to the Village. I have been looking at the moon playing with a few small silver gray clouds in a very transparent blue sky—& in the West the star slowly descending into night—Cloudless sky—yet farther North in the West—a whole series of most delicate gray cloud shapes—never anything lovelier except perhaps your smile occasionally when you are beginning to feel the endlessness of everything when I'm in you—slowly moving—the beginning of ecstasy—

Here I am—the house & I. And a bit of a cold I have been fighting for some days. I still hope to win out. More stupidity—overheating, golfing & a cold wind springing up—nothing to worry about. Just an annoyance. This afternoon Fred drove me & Lee's superintendent (1040 Park Avenue[239]) & his wife—up to Sabbath Day Point & back. The road is still in a miserable

239. Lee and Lizzie Stieglitz lived at 1040 Park Ave., New York.

shape most of the way & in wet weather dangerous. Fred says it's clay & becomes skiddy.—
The drive took much longer than expected & [when] we got home I found Lizzie worried. I took
the drive as an attention to the people. They are stopping in the Village—at Worden Cottage.
Then too I wanted to see what the road was like—having you in mind—Well, there is mighty
little lake ever to be seen.—At Sabbath Day Point we asked for lemonade at the hotel & were
informed they sold no drinks!!—We saw a buxom female play tennis in a very tight bathing
suit.—This on the same hotel grounds.—

     I had hoped to develop tonight but I'm refraining.—The water too is being turned off
& on.—All too uncertain. Received a short letter from you—still on your trip with Beck.—
I have [been] playing some Bach today.—New records—none too good. English.—I never like
their playing. Colorless.—Like their cooking.—

     Good Night Sweetest One—

     A kiss—

Georgia O'Keeffe · [Alcalde, New Mexico] · [August 8, 1930]

Dearest—

     It is very late—after two—but I must [send] a word—

     Everything goes so fast—Yesterday we went to the Jemez Mountains—the mountains
we see out back of Marie's—It was about 360 miles—very grand country—Seligmann was
up in there somewhere when he was out here—There were nine of us—two cars—Marie
driving one—her new Packard—Henwar his—For the finest part of the mountains I sat in
Henwar's rumble seat—it is a grand place to see from—In the dark coming home I rode with
Marie—Such comfort—it is quite indecent—She is a very careful steady driver—I just give up
to comfort in her car—I have to laugh—It was very late when we got home—nearly two—
I fell right into bed and slept like the dead—was up before eight—the first one usually—Right
after breakfast—I was off with sandwiches for the day—no one up yet—sat by the road out
near the main road—it is much higher than the house and worked on a painting I had started
last time I was down here[240]—I am quite pleased with it—From nine till nearly five—It is
looking toward the mountains we went into yesterday—It was a cool day—I had a very good
day—

     And tonight—last thing—Spud and Henwar and I had a night ride—we ran into a
pouring rain—put up the top—and sat and smelled the rain on the sage—and looked at the
rain and listened to it—the moon made the desert quite light in spite of the rain—I think Spud
wanted to sleep but Henwar and I enjoyed it enormously—

     A day seems to go so fast—and they seem so full—What I was looking at all day today
was just grand—makes me feel I will burst—

     Dearest—I guess you think I am crazy—

     I think of you so often—and wish I could see you going about your day—and hope

---

240. Possibly Lynes 730 or 731.

you are feeling well—How is your indigestion—and your heart—I almost wired you again today—to know how you are right now—

—A Good Night kiss to you—I wish you could see and smell the desert at night when it is wet—it is indescribable—A soft sweet kiss to you—like the moisture on my face out there in the night—

Good Night—

Alfred Stieglitz · Lake George, New York · August 13, 1930

The night is biting clear.—The star—brilliant & large has just set—It's cold. Kalonyme has just gone up—he has a violent headache. Rosenfeld is in his room at work.—It has been a mad sort of day.—Howard & Dorothy[241] arrived at 12:30. Weren't expected till evening.—But the house was ready with food & bed. No words. No excitement. At lunch a discussion was started about industrialism—banking—America—education—etc.—etc.—A terrific discussion all of us men at it—Dorothy listening most of the time.—The discussion lasted till after five!—Kalonyme says the excitement affected his eyes.—There were no tempers lost. All quite amicable but terrific. Wall Street smash started it all.[242] Our leaders. Our institutions. Our masses. Our teachers. Our artists.—And the Hill at peace!—If you can't get hold of the desert & put into form what you feel about it—this is another desert I see—quite as impossible to put into form—too gigantic—too elusive.—The forces of life—the eternal struggle.—Coming & going.—Age upon ages.—And all this discussion really originated in Dorothy's remarking the other night to Elizabeth that in case anything happened to Dorothy & Howard she knew no one whom they would choose to bring up their children comparable to Elizabeth. For everyone seeing her children remarks on their being very different—very wonderful.—Elizabeth wasn't flattered but asked Dorothy a few simple questions.—Because of the happenings on the Hill—because of the happenings in the business crisis—because of much else—because of all "my" life—I naturally was aroused in a very peculiar way because of Dorothy's statement—& inquiry, etc.—I have been seething inside ever since.—I don't want discussions unless they lead to action. Of course America—probably most of the world—is very sick at present. Some may escape the sickness —but not so many as time goes on.—You probably wonder what I'm talking about—Nothing perhaps. Everything perhaps.—

—Kalonyme & I walked to the Village & back. Played only one round of golf. Played very badly.—Both of us. It was a grand day all day.—

The Davidsons leave in the morning.—Tonight the Schubarts are at Red Top.— Sel arrives in Glens Falls tonight. Joe Obermeyer is with her. For a week or so.—Car & all I suppose.—

241. Howard Schubart was Stieglitz's nephew, the son of his sister Selma Stieglitz Schubart. Dorothy was his wife.
242. Despite predictions earlier in August that a revival was on the way, *The New York Times* reported on August 13, 1930, that the recent "bull campaign" on Wall Street had "failed completely." "Leading commission houses," it continued, were not confident of an economic turnaround and cautioned that "there had been too much half-baked optimism, particularly in market circles"; see "Topics in Wall Street," NYT, Aug. 13, 1930, 27.

A queer queer world—queer every day.—Good Night—Sweetestheart—Good Night—A kiss.—

I hope you are painting well.—

Georgia O'Keeffe · Santa Fe, New Mexico · [August 14, 1930]

Thursday Morning—
Good Morning Dearest—

Here I am in Santa Fe again—They couldn't do everything that I needed done on the Ford the other day so I came down this morning to have it finished—It is thirty-two miles from Marie's—I enjoyed the ride—a cool blue morning with a few clouds floating about—and I enjoyed coming alone—no one to remark on the landscape and no one to make me feel I must hurry—The town is very simple to drive in—you could almost drive in it I guess—It is curious the way I discover new things on the road when I am alone—the mountains were fine—they seem like some sort of big black revelation this morning—And your friend feels very good—

I am going to work on the road on the way back this afternoon I think—My hill that I painted over yesterday looked pretty good last night—It is certainly much better than it was.

I saw the evening star last night with the evening glow over the Black Mesa and Jemez Mountains—the mesa dark and sharp against a sort of sharp yellow sky—

They have stairs going to the first roof and a ladder going to the second roof—I ran up there after I was cleaned up for supper—

—I don't know what it is about this country—it just seems to turn all my insides over —Whether I stand up there on the roof—looking at the star and the sharp black line of the mesa against the sunset glow that is almost gone—or drive in the morning light like this morning— And the thing one tries to paint of it is necessarily such a small phase of it—

—I was so glad to hear from your letter yesterday that your cold is better—I hope you were careful so it did not start up again—

—You tell me your daily doings—but you don't tell me much of your daily thinkings— However—maybe I know—

—We had a nice evening last night—Marie, Henwar and I alone—Marie read—we played music—They have some Gregorian chants—it seemed so curious to me to hear that churchly sound in a house—

—I'll be along before long.

I do hope to get a couple more things done—at least—

Will be having the curse soon—that is a nuisance—

A morning kiss to you—

I look forward much to being with you—

Georgia O'Keeffe · [Alcalde, New Mexico] · [August 17, 1930]

Good Morning Dearest:

It is Sunday morning—almost nine—and I am still in bed—have had breakfast—
Marie announced last night that we would all have it in bed—I have the curse—had it
yesterday too—Went out all morning to work—a crazy thing of a church steeple[243]—maybe
nothing—maybe very good I can't tell—but I know I didn't feel like much—Took a nap after
lunch—Then at five went riding with Marie and Ham[244]—her son—He is a strangely beautiful
person—curious—he still looks quite ill—but his face is beautifully cut—light gray eyes—
large—in a very thin dark—beautifully modeled face—So tall you always think his head will
have to bend to go through a door—

We took a drive that I know very well but storm and sunset together over it made
it very grand—gives me such a feeling of the impossibility of doing something with such a
landscape—It might be the end of the earth—or the beginning of it or anything—

The evening was quiet—went to bed early—Henwar and I talked about Beck—
He certainly has it in for her—no use for her at all—Of course he doesn't know her at all—
Says he always feels she is throwing a challenge in his face—and then takes advantage of her
sex—I think he would probably just knock her flat if she gave him half a chance—I wouldn't
want to see it if they had a fight—

If I hadn't felt so good for nothing I would have gone up to Taos last evening—

I have been lying here thinking over my plans—will I do this—or will I do that—
I would like to work longer here but it is so big—and at best I can do so little—It doesn't seem
to matter much whether I do that little or not—I haven't done much but those same hills that I
did last year[245]—It is no use to try today—I'll get too tired too soon—

Well—Little One—I wonder much about you too as I lie here—I seem to have had a
rather bad dream about you—as I was waking up—

It is very still—I'll be getting up and moving out—

I wish you could have had that drive with us yesterday—Everything of out here seemed
to be there—

—A morning kiss to you—When I think of you looking out on the Lake and of what
I will look out on when I get up it does seem so strangely different—I know it is beautiful
there—but what I like best there is the being with you—

What I look out on here seems to just grow into the center of me—if I had you here too
I would probably die—

—It is all so queer—

But I am looking forward so much to seeing you and being with you—

---

243. Lynes 706.
244. Hamilton Garland was Marie Garland's son by Charles Garland, her first husband.
245. Lynes 682, 691, 725, 726.

Alfred Stieglitz · Lake George, New York · August 17, 1930

It's night.—And what a night.—The star shone brilliantly as it set—In spite of a miserable toothache I was out watching it.—It's Sunday night.—It looks like trouble at Peck's tomorrow. —I hate the idea of losing any tooth on my only chewing side—And indications are unfavorable. I hope I'm mistaken.—There seems to be no let-up. Well—that will be lived through too.

—The day was very grand altho' for about ten minutes this noon it rained hard. A shower. The wind veered Northwest & soon the sky was cloudless. The sun was grand. I sat in it a long while—rowed a little too—So you see my sinus was better & the cough some better too. Now comes the darned tooth. I warned Peck when I was there. But he didn't listen—Well I suppose it makes no difference!—

Two letters from you & one from Marin.[246]—All very fine.—I had no letter from Marin until this one.—

And yours—so different from his—and so very you—like all your letters.—I was amused to have you say I never wrote you what I was thinking about. Somehow I thought very much & thought very little at the same time. It has been a most peculiar time for me.[247] A great chance to do much & very little done.—Time just flying when in a way it should have seemed heavy on my hands very often.—Problems.—Problems.—Everywhere.

Flora & Grant Straus came this noon & leave at 10:30 tonight. Just came to say hello. —Lizzie is alone at Red Top.—Kalonyme & Rosenfeld are out walking.—Kalonyme doesn't feel well.—I hope nothing serious.

The house is so silent—I hear a cricket outside.—I hope I'll get some sleep tonight in spite of the tooth. Isn't it just too rotten?—

Good Night—you Sweetestheart—it's a shame to take you away from where you are. Really.—In a way I don't feel it right. Remember you have my sanction to prolong your stay.— A big kiss—

I'm no good—

Georgia O'Keeffe · [Taos, New Mexico] · [August 24, 1930]

Dearest—

I was so busy today I forgot to get paper—Marin was over—liked some of my landscapes—but he said tonight with a laugh—"Oh there are so many things that are good"—

I packed my paintings—about two and a half hours—Beck helped—lunch—Brett

246. In early August 1930 Marin wrote Stieglitz saying that several people had asked him if Stieglitz was coming out to New Mexico. He also related that he found it impossible to capture anything in his art that expressed the spirit of the Santa Domingo dance he had recently seen: to do so would be "like grafting onto perfection. It's like rewriting Bach. To out brilliance the diamond—to out red the ruby" (Marin to AS, Aug. 4–14, 1930).

247. The next day, Stieglitz admitted to Norman: "I'm desperately tired in mind & all primarily because that infernal body of mine insists in giving me no peace.—And I do want to complete some things. And I do want to come to town ready.—The S.W. has no idea of my state.—There was no use in writing" (AS to Norman, Aug. 17, 1930).

and a lot of others together — She came home with me — we talked some — then I packed my trunk — odds and ends are left — and I'll be free for a few days before I take the train — Beck came over with one of the boys and announced coffee — so Brett and I went over —

—A little before six I left them all talking about nothing and went [on] horseback into the hills alone — It is the best way to go in the sunset — the hills such a rich — very dark green — the sage so light — I do like it so much — and I like being alone with it — It was dark when I put the horse in the corral — And I like too the feeling of walking through tall thick green alfalfa with high boots on — had supper alone —

Went to Mabel's for the evening — Her son[248] had come out from Buffalo in an airplane in sixteen hours — Had to land in Santa Fe —

—Then another walk across another alfalfa field in the dark — thick green under your feet — stars over head — and still the tough boots to make you feel safe under foot — and now I get into bed —

A Good Night kiss — it was a full day — The ride tonight made a good end for it. I *want* to be back with you soon.

554   O'KEEFFE LEFT NEW MEXICO on August 29 and arrived back at Lake George a few days later. Once again, she marveled at "how nice" Stieglitz was and told Beck Strand that he even made up for the dullness of the landscape.[249] But she soon realized that his lack of concern about her absence that summer was at least in part due to the daily letters and frequent telephone calls he and Norman were exchanging. By mid-September as the younger woman's due date drew near, Stieglitz became increasingly agitated and ill. His ailments diminished following the birth of Norman's son, Andrew, in late September and evaporated after he briefly went to New York a few weeks later to visit her. When O'Keeffe and Stieglitz returned to the city and reopened An American Place in early November, O'Keeffe's hopes that Norman's two young children would keep her at home were soon dashed. Norman made it clear that she had no intention of abandoning what she saw as her "integral" role at the gallery, the nurturing "family" she had discovered there, or her special relationship with its director.[250] Fully immersing herself in every aspect of Stieglitz's life, Norman began to transcribe some of his stories, read Marin's letters to the photographer, and make a selection of them, which Stieglitz subsequently published.[251] Drawing ever closer to her, Stieglitz also made numerous portraits of Norman throughout the winter and spring of 1930–1931, depicting her as frail, meek, and adoring.[252] They are in stark

248. John Ganson Evans was Mabel Dodge Luhan's son by Karl Evans, her first husband.

249. GOK to Rebecca Strand, Sept. 4, 1930.

250. See Dorothy Norman, *Encounters: A Memoir* (New York, 1987), 96.

251. Many of Stieglitz's stories were later published by Norman in *Twice A Year*: see no. 1 (Fall–Winter 1938), 77–163; nos. 5–6 (1940–1941); nos. 8–9 (1942), 105–136, 156 - 178; nos. 10–11 (1943), 245–265; nos. 14–15 (1946–1947), 188–202. Unpublished stories are now in the Dorothy Norman Papers at the Yale Center for American Literature, Beinecke Rare Book and Manuscript Library, Yale University, and at the Center for Creative Photography, University of Arizona. John Marin, *Letters of John Marin,* ed. and with an intro. by Herbert J. Seligmann (New York, 1931).

252. See Greenough 1363–1371, 1393–1397 (see p. 556).

contrast to the few pictures he made of O'Keeffe at this time, which present her as mature and accomplished but also wary, aloof, and sexless.[253] Lending Norman his Graflex camera, Stieglitz also taught her how to photograph, conferring on her the honor of being his only pupil. And they began to spend many hours together in the darkroom at the Place, where he showed her how to develop and print her pictures. As Norman replaced O'Keeffe as Stieglitz's muse and disciple, he effusively praised her to anyone who would listen, even O'Keeffe. Oblivious to the feelings of others, both Norman and Stieglitz fully believed that their relationship enriched not only their lives but also all those around them. And Norman, who professed to "love" both O'Keeffe and her dedication to her work, even made overtures that spring to form a friendship with the painter and show her how she could adopt some of the younger woman's own "softness."[254]

In the spring of 1931, O'Keeffe was uncertain if she should return to New Mexico that summer, but with Stieglitz's encouragement she left in late April, more than a month earlier than the year before. After stopping in Chicago to visit her friend Ethel Tyrrell and meet with an architect to discuss the use of her paintings in his buildings, she arrived in New Mexico on May 1. Except for brief visits to Taos to see Mabel and Tony Lujan, Frieda Lawrence, and Dorothy Brett, she stayed with Marie Garland and Henwar Rodakiewicz at the H & M Ranch in Alcalde, and used the studio the older woman had recently built.

Stieglitz remained in New York, overseeing the last exhibition of the season at An American Place, a show of Demuth's paintings and watercolors. In an effort to reduce his storage bills, he went through his large collection of work by other artists, consigning some pieces to the new dealer Edith Halpert, keeping some at the Place, returning others to their owners, and even destroying a few.[255] In June, when he went to Lake George and Norman to her summer home in Woods Hole, Massachusetts, both brooded about their relationship in their daily letters and numerous telephone calls. (Stieglitz's letters to Norman from this summer are no longer extant: when her father discovered them and realized the nature of her relationship with the photographer, he made her destroy them.) During these weeks, Stieglitz grew increasingly jealous of the author and critic Gerald Sykes, who visited Norman in June, and she became obsessed with going to the Hill, while both remained "tortured," as Norman wrote, about the "threeness" of their relationship.[256]

Throughout the summer, they also witnessed with great concern the continued fall of the American economy. In mid-May, the Bank of England cut its discount rate to 2½ percent, the lowest it had been since 1909, but "fresh," even "acute weakness" was still seen in the New York Stock Exchange as railroad and industrial stocks were liquidated and the "market was shaken quite severely."[257] By May 17 newspapers reported that "only a handful of the hallowed 'blue chips' which were worshipped during the speculative madness of 1928 and 1929" remained on the New York Stock Exchange.[258] On June 1, the market suffered its sharpest decline since

253. See Greenough 1360–1362 (see p. 557).
254. Norman to GOK, Feb. 13, 1931.
255. See AS to GOK, June 3, 1931.
256. See Norman to AS, July 2 and 3, 1931.
257. "Rate Cut to 2½% by Bank of England" and "Topics in Wall Street," NYT, May 15, 1931, 12 and 35.
258. "Along the Highways of Finance," NYT, May 17, 1931, 45.

Alfred Stieglitz, *Dorothy Norman LXXXII*, 1930–1931. Gelatin silver print, 3¹⁵⁄₁₆ x 2¾ in. (8.4 x 7 cm). Philadelphia Museum of Art (1997.146.159). Copyright © Georgia O'Keeffe Museum/Artists Rights Society (ARS), New York.

October 1930 with sizable losses in industrial, tobacco, and utility stocks. In brokerage circles there was talk of the "possible imminence of a 'selling climax,' or convulsive reaction which might mark the end of the current decline."²⁵⁹

    O'Keeffe's and Stieglitz's letters from the summer of 1931 are, not surprisingly, different from those of other years. Far more controlled and less emotional, Stieglitz's letters are warm but relate his news, not his feelings or ideas, and he speaks far more about O'Keeffe's art than her as a person. For her part, O'Keeffe reveals her genuine affection and loneliness for Stieglitz, but she too does not, as she later said, reveal her "center."

Georgia O'Keeffe · [En route from New York City to Alcalde, New Mexico] · [April 28, 1931]

Dearest—

    I was terribly upset as you left. It seemed as tho I might not be able to bear it—as tho my consciousness were leaving me—I shut my eyes and sat very still—You have been so beautiful in helping me with everything—It makes me wonder if I have done my share—and to that I seem to have no answer—all I seem to know is that I am as I am—

    The river is hazy and lovely—the green very new—almost not there yet—I hope you will have had a good night's sleep by the time you get this and that you are quiet—I feel so very close to you—so much all one thing with you—and I want to say again that I so much look

---

259. "Topics in Wall Street," *NYT*, June 2, 1931, 45.

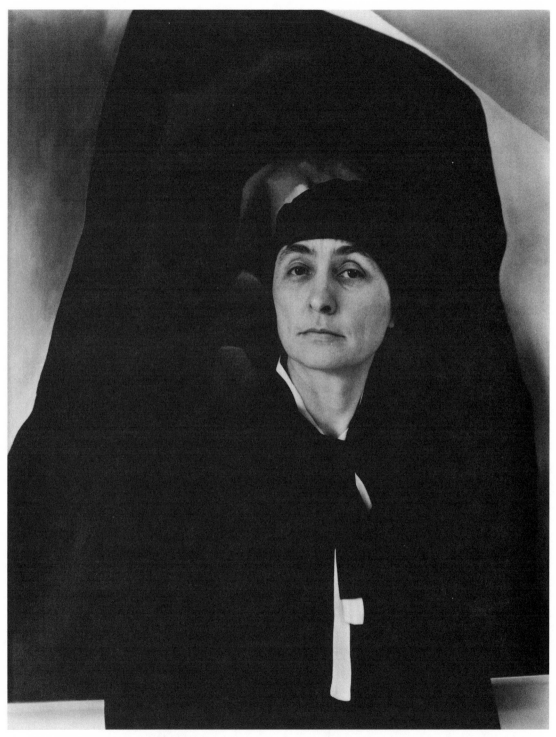

Alfred Stieglitz, *Georgia O'Keeffe*, 1930. Gelatin silver print, 9½ x 7⅜ in. (24.1 x 18.8 cm). Metropolitan Museum of Art, New York (1997.61.43). Copyright © The Metropolitan Museum of Art/Art Resource, NY. Greenough 1319.

forward to the time with you in the country—It will not really be long before we are together again[260]—and in the meantime really try to take care of yourself—

I wish you were riding up the river here with me—it is very lovely—You make me feel like a very much loved girl and I feel I cannot thank you enough for it—

Maybe it is my feeling so much that way that makes me feel this time not so much as tho I am going away from you—Tho I was so completely upset with the last sight of you—

My idea that I will live long is a funny one I suppose—but I know too that I will always carry you with me—I just looked at the lock of hair—it is soft and beautiful and white like you are to me—

A dear—soft—tender kiss to you—

I am going to lie down on the seat—I have a pillow—

Later—Looking at the window again—Spring is such a beautiful time—It is terrible feeling destroyed as I do over going away—I will get myself together soon[261]—I am really terribly fond of you—terribly tied to you—I'll be better soon—

A kiss—

558

Georgia O'Keeffe · [Alcalde, New Mexico] · [May 1, 1931]

Dearest—

Well—here I am in Marie's new studio—and I feel all at home—as tho it is all mine—

It is enough apart from the house so that I feel all by myself—all very good—I wish you could see it—

They met me at Lamy—having driven about ninety miles without any breakfast— It sounds strange in New York but they never give it a second thought—wouldn't even mention it as anything unusual—

The drive out was lovely—the faraway mountains covered with snow—the nearby barrenness—almost the same as in mid-summer—And there is something about all of it that makes me feel so close to the earth—

I had your two first letters in Santa Fe. Marie says to send mail there—they get it every other day if not every day. The letters are so sweet—and mine to you have all been so torn— I was really terribly upset over leaving you—Now that I am here with this feeling of being close to the earth I feel better—

—I'll get settled and be all right. Henwar intended to bring my trunk out on the back of the car this morning but he forgot it till we were nearly here—so after lunch went back for it —seventy miles—And then tonight goes back again to a dinner—some traveling.

---

260. O'Keeffe intended to return to Lake George in July.

261. On April 30, 1931, O'Keeffe told Stieglitz, "This going away from you always just ruins me—seems to break me into millions of pieces and it is so difficult to put them together again."

I was telling Henwar about Flaherty's movie[262] and he says he showed him what he has just before Flaherty went away to Tabu. There were so many similar things in the two[263] that I had wondered about it—

Well—I feel better than I felt on the train—it feels very healthy to be here—

I'll try to see about a car tomorrow—maybe try one they have here—It is very big and not as convenient as my kind I think—

A kiss to you Boy—I think I'll take a walk—the afternoon is a bit cloudy but I think it will not rain. The mountains out back of the house are very grand—and I like being on the ground so much I just feel like jumping up and down on it—

Everyone asks for you—And I am very very fond of you. I wish you were here.

My dearest—dearest—love to you—

My trunk just came—everything all right—.

Alfred Stieglitz · [New York City] · May 6, 1931 +

7:30 P.M. At the Place. What a day.—Ending with the miserable discovery that Zoler has been using stale gum arabicam to mount the Marins. Heaven knows how many in time will have been ruined along the edges.—Of course I should never have trusted him. It's just ghastly. With all the care I have insisted on—the lifeblood I have given to protect the work—Well, I'll get used to this thought too. But I feel I cannot trust anyone anymore to do anything right.—One is a fool for caring.—

—My head is all abuzz. I'm alone.—I got litmus paper to try out the edges of the mounts. Zoler had carefully washed out the stale stuff from his jar when I questioned him.— What laziness—That's all it is. And a subconscious desire to destroy.—Just plain sick.—But as I said I'm solely responsible. The damage has been done.—Heaven knows to how many.—

There were visitors today. Some to see your pictures. Oh! Sweetestheart.

—Mrs. Norman came for an hour to get a story. She hasn't been at the Room since you & she & I lunched together. Looks pale & thin. Page proofs[264] were to turn up today but won't come till Friday.—I hope they'll be all right.—

It's getting dark—& it's so quiet here.—I am not a bit hungry but I guess I'll have to go to the hotel & eat.

Maybe I exaggerate the danger of the acid gum arabicam but it is not that—it's the feeling that anyone like Zoler should profess to have any feeling for me & be so criminally careless knowing better for it was he who told me the gum solution ought to be fresh every time used. Today he doesn't deny he said this but he believes that it will keep three or four or more weeks in an open jar! Great gods & I trusting such a worker with Marins!! Or anything else. And after

---

262. *Tabu: A Story of the South Seas* (1931) was a scripted "documentary" film by F. W. Murnau that Robert Flaherty, creator of *Nanook of the North* (1922), worked on early in its production.

263. Henwar Rodakiewicz had recently completed a film, *The Portrait of a Young Man* (1925–1931).

264. Stieglitz was expecting page proofs for the book *Letters of John Marin*.

knowing his untrustworthiness. Yes, I'll go & eat. And try to be quiet.—It's just a bit much—a sort of last straw.—Of course any bleaching of the watercolors along the edges will be charged to *Watercolor*[265]!!

Well, Good Night—a big kiss—

I oughtn't to write you this. It doesn't do anyone any good. But I am frankly upset.—Hirst helped me greatly.[266] It's something. Much really. Good Night.

A kiss.

Maybe I'll get a letter tomorrow. I understand.—I know you couldn't be in better hands. Kiss—

Alfred Stieglitz · [New York City] · May 8, 1931

Good Morning, Sweetestheart. Good Morning.—A kiss too.—

Here I am.—I have no idea what o'clock. Watch stopped. It must be near ten or so.—The morning is close.—I fooled around 3003[267] awhile. A new chambermaid—old & dried up.—Instructed her to keep hands off toothbrush, glass, etc.—Found them "cleaned" yesterday!—Boiled the outfit at once!!—Also found a pin in bathtub—etc. etc.—All part of life.—I bathed last night.—An event.—Hadn't risked a bath in a week.—Felt good to sit in the water an age.—Counted wash—ready for valet. About thirty handkerchiefs—Now I too use Kleenex.—Thus slowly I become a Modern too.

Jewell phoned yesterday he'd like to see me about the art racket one speaks about.—I have no idea what he's wanting. Coming at eleven today. There is certainly a racket in it as there is a racket generally everywhere in everything today.—Everyday something "new" happens that staggers one even if it doesn't surprise.—So you are most fortunate to be with nearly untouched soil—far away from this mess called city—civilization at its best (or worst or whatever or—or—?)—

Seligmann just called up about matters pertaining to *Marin Letters*. There is no doubt of it that the business people of today—the best of them—are a pretty sloppy lot—all trying to do more than they are able to do properly.—It's a question of proofs & printing—all sorts of details that should be right without any fussiness.—Ever the old story. People like ourselves are just a nuisance in an age of "It'll do"—"It's too good anyway" no matter how bad. "Why care?" "Who cares?" "Why should anyone care?"—"There are more important things."—Etc. etc.—

It is very still here—I wonder have you gotten a car.—And is it satisfactory.—I wonder have you started painting—or are you still in the stages of starting to start—

—I may go to the Tilden-Richards tennis match tonight if there are still tickets to be

560

265. Although watercolor fades in light, Stieglitz wanted to prove that it was an important medium of artistic expression, equal to oil painting, and that it should command similar prices.
266. Virginious Hirst was Stieglitz's ear, nose, and throat doctor.
267. During the winter and spring of 1930 and 1931, O'Keeffe and Stieglitz lived in room 3003 at the Shelton Hotel.

had.[268]—I didn't get any before on account of that nose of mine.—And I'd like to see the match. Had been sort of looking forward to it.—It looks like rain again.—The windows are open in all the rooms & it is comfortable.—

Seligmann on phone again—He's a good workman.—

—A wire from San Francisco California Museum of Art asking for an O'Keeffe flower piece for their show. Would try to sell (!!) Etc. Etc.—Not much. The man was here this spring. He could have arranged if genuine.—All promises—Milliken is the only one so far that could be completely trusted.—Artists are fools generally & let smooth tongued people get away with murder & rape—And then curse everyone that may be innocent.—I have had an experience or two the last few days again. Not worth getting into. And yet incredible. Fortunately I no longer let injustice eat into me.—

You are very sweet, Dearest One.—Yes, you are very much in my mind—In all of me.— A kiss. More later.—

A little later.—A letter from you—postmarked Santa Fe—May 6—11:20 A.M. You with all that space—& I cooped up.—Yes in a way cooped up.—You're sweet.—Also a letter from Brett with a copy of a letter from Frieda.[269] Extraordinary beings.—Some letters both.—Terrific.—

And Frieda due at the ranch soon.—

Not a soul here all morning.—I don't feel as if I were anywhere. But am very quiet. I'll write to Margaret now.

Much much love—& a big kiss.—

Georgia O'Keeffe · [Alcalde, New Mexico] · **May 8, 1931**

Friday afternoon at five—

The wind has blown like mad all day—I was out early—at first thought it too windy —then decided to go anyway—I went out to that funny little church—the one that hung beside the landscape Mrs. Halpert bought[270]—Everything was so hazy—the distant snow-topped mountains like a sort of fairy land—It is absurd the way I love going over these roads—

I painted a tiny little painting[271]—the wind so bad I thought I might not stay out long —However I stayed all morning and went out again after lunch to the painting of my first day —It is one of those things I don't give up readily and don't seem to be able to do anything with.

268. On May 9, 1931, more than fourteen thousand people in Madison Square Garden watched William Tilden II, seven-time winner of the American amateur tennis crown, defeat Vincent Richards, the national professional titleholder, in the first of their series of five matches for the world championship; see "Tilden Turns Back Richards in Four Sets," NYT, May 10, 1931, S1.

269. In her May 3, 1931, letter to Stieglitz, Brett noted she pitied Frieda Lawrence for her "confusion" and enclosed a copy of a letter from Frieda to her in which Frieda wrote: "I gave you so much *fun* and *life* and *care* at the Ranch and all you could do, was to make mischief between Lawrence and me, and you go on saying, I killed him and trifles like that. He loved me so completely and wholly, Lord, I was a fool ever to doubt it, one minute! He didn't want to die and yet he died so splendidly!"

270. The "funny little church" is Lynes 660; Edith Halpert purchased Lynes 725.

271. Lynes 771.

I worked on it for nearly three hours then as the light was too different drove down here to the river—sitting in the car protected from the wind with the sun on my back—

There were two letters from you last night—I hope your cold didn't get bad. There was also the clipping for which thanks also—

I guess you know by now that I am glad I am here and that I like it so much that it seems a bit ridiculous—I just can't bear to stay in the house—that is why I came down here to write you—

The wind just roars through the cottonwood trees—They are big and old and soft gray only beginning to turn green—and tho I say I am by the river I don't see it—and everything looks more like your hair than like a river—I seem to have chosen a particularly dry looking spot—

I got a Ford like my other on what they call a "buy back plan"—If it is in reasonably good condition they guarantee to buy it back in two months—It is a second hand one but it is all right—

My cold is better—it should be entirely gone in a few days—I do so hope yours doesn't develop—It is such a bad time of year to have one—

Marie and Henwar went off to Colorado early this morning to see about a camp Henwar wants to buy up there—It is just a day's drive from here—high up on a pass just a little beyond Colorado Springs—

Paul Jones is here—He is a wiry little man with red hair—a painter—and he does Marie's most elegant cooking—always dinner at night—He is one of those people who can do anything—We get on very well—

Marie will be back Sunday night—

—Well I'll be getting in—have to make my bed and straighten things up a bit—The boy would make it but I said I would rather—then I go out and lock my door and it all seems more mine—

I hope you are all right—I wish I had you here in the sun where it is nice and hot— I would like to ride you around and show you all the things I like so much—I wonder if you would look at it or if you would go to sleep—

I am away a week today—

A kiss you you—

10:30—I played the Victrola—things we play—and it makes me sad—The daytime is very good—out alone with the outdoors—It really gives me a grand feeling—but at night I seem to become a woman again—and wonder—wonder—about you and wish to be near you—

There almost seems to be two of me—Specially when I listen to music that I know so well with you—

I wish I could stand quietly by your bed—cover you and kiss you Good Night—feel the warmth of you—my nose isn't quite good enough to smell much—

Maybe I do stand beside you—I rather think I do—It makes me feel like crying—

I kiss you Good Night—I'll be glad when it is morning—

Georgia O'Keeffe · [Alcalde, New Mexico] · [May 13, 1931]

You Dear Little Bird—

Your Sunday letter is certainly a lonesome little gray affair—

Well—it is three days since then—Maybe you feel better—I am glad you went to the tennis game tho I have a notion that it probably didn't do your sinus any good—

Right at the present moment I am a sight—Have been out with Henwar all day. He doesn't do things by halves and I am so burned from the sun and wind that you get in the open car—it doesn't really feel very good—But we had a grand day—Henwar and the visiting in-law girl[272] on the front seat—Spud Johnson and I in the back—We went up to Taos over a very bad round about road to the east—through strange little Mexican towns—past sand hills—red hills—gray hills—all spotted with piñon bushes looking as tho the pepper shaker had sprinkled them well—far stretches of the desert and hills—and the snow capped mountains that we see from here coming up every little while—Finally over quite a high pass—quite large and beautiful trees and a noisy clear brook—and finally dropped down into the Taos desert with the Taos and Lobo mountains—snow on the top—off to the north—The wild plums are blooming very sweet— all the Taos country looks very beautiful but when we came down the canyon and out on the desert here again—it feels very good—We were out between six and seven hours—It was quite a day—

—I had had a sun bath on the roof this morning—Spud showed me a place where there is a large cushion—quite sheltered from the public—so altogether I am well cooked today—

I just didn't feel like painting this morning—but I will be at it again tomorrow—In my Ford I only get a normal tan—this way you just cook—

—I was so glad to have your three letters when I came back—it made the day quite perfect—tho I wish you a little less sad—

I am away over two weeks—it seems so long—

There is something about this country that makes you feel you don't quite know where you are—A day like today—seeing so many different things—then to sit quiet here in this large room feeling all sheltered from the bright light of the outside—

I must change my dress for supper—There will be no washing—I am too burned— Now don't worry about my sunburn—it goes quickly with me—I only mention it because I was so surprised to get it and it looks so pink and funny—

I kiss you—and hold you close—and wish you had been along—

[May 14, 1931]
Next Morning—

The sunburn is much better—

You are sweet—

---

272. Sylvia was a relation of Marie Garland's.

Alfred Stieglitz · [New York City] · May 16, 1931 +

7 A.M.—Ready for breakfast. A good morning kiss.—

It's a warm hazy sunny morning.—I can breathe. Am much better. Dr. Hirst at 8:45. If only Wall Street wouldn't be so very unfriendly—or maybe I should say if I weren't so ungodly stupid—the world would seem to be not half bad to one like me. As it is, Wall Street or no Wall Street, it is a grand thing to be able to get some air through one's nostrils!!—

You dear Dearest One—How I wish I were of more genuine use—for your sake if no other.—I mean it.—Just caring much, loving—they don't help you or anyone else. Not even myself.—It is quite awful to see one's own idiocies.—It's so good you are far away from all this sepulchral perfection called the Place. For there is a sepulchral perfection there except for the fact the women will mess up the Place with their endless cigarette leavings![273] You should have seen those children's quarters yesterday as I found them. Teachers & mothers—& cigarettes!— If things go on as I see them this country will become one huge cigarette & all sitting around it in adoration. The phallic age replaced by the cigarette one. Coming out of my room yesterday morning to go to breakfast—a father, mother, young looking, & two very young daughters emerged from their quarters—all with cigarettes in their mouth sucking hard.—It turns my stomach still as I see the picture.—And children are punished for sucking their thumbs.—I guess I'm an incorrigible intolerant in certain ways.—Yet I tolerate—but seeing as such & trying to accept it against all I feel is like my trying to accept the scissor grinder sound—walking up & down & training nerves!!—[274]

You're very sweet—And I hope well & full of life & all that's for your good (growth)— I'd better go—A kiss—

6:15 P.M. At Place.—A terrific day.—Eckstein walked in when I stopped. We went to lunch together. Alone. Had about an hour or so. Maybe a little less. Fine. He came back to the Place. Found Seligmann waiting with two Germans—a man & woman.—I was annoyed for a moment. Still as it eventually turned out wouldn't have missed them for anything. Eckstein will be in town for a few days. May see him again. Seemed much pleased about the way I saw his book.[275]—The Germans wanted to see your work. He is a writer. She quite amazing. He too. Are seeing the world.—Dr. Walker walked in.—Shared the view of your pictures. Fell hard for the yellow one with white daisy.[276] The Germans tremendously impressed with the three New Mexico mountain things standing in office.—I took the *White Shell* away and have [sketch of *Poplars Blue & Pink; Green Mountain; Convolution Red*][277]. Look really marvelous. She said

---

273. In May, Stieglitz let the art teachers of the Hessian School of Croyton, New York, install an exhibition in one of the rooms at An American Place.

274. As Stieglitz related to Norman, he was acutely sensitive to certain sounds as a child. In order to become accustomed to the noise of metal being ground, for example, he walked back and forth in front of a scissors grinder weekly for a year, but without success; see "The Scissors Grinder," *Twice A Year,* nos. 10–11 (1942–1943), 256–258.

275. Eckstein, *Noguchi.* On May 14, 1931, Stieglitz wrote O'Keeffe that he had been reading Eckstein's book on the Japanese scientist: "I can't see you reading it through. It's not a book for you—extraordinary as it is."

276. Lynes 642.

277. Probably Lynes 707; probably Lynes 742; Lynes 741; and possibly Lynes 740 or 743.

that back of all the surface of this country she felt something very wonderful happening—
& felt that in your pictures you had that something clearly expressed.—She put it better.—
The *Lake George Door*[278] she said she didn't understand. Naturally she couldn't. I told her why.
The [sketch of an angle] *Abstraction*[279] I don't think they got either. They asked to see photographs of you. I showed some. They said: We never saw such photos. Very simple people. Very
genuine. Solid. Maybe about forty or so. I stood in the office. Seligmann stood—the Germans
finally sat. They asked me about you.—I gave them a short story of you & 291—As I was
speaking Kaye appeared—got a chair & listened very attentively.—It was all very fine—
I wouldn't have missed it for anything. In a way too bad Eckstein didn't stay. He would have
enjoyed it.—

Three photographs came from Boston—Coomaraswamy's wife.[280] Two I like much.
Rosenfeld & Zoler like them all.—Oh yes, McBride also showed up.—We had a short talk.—
Sends love. Thinks I ought to insist that Florine have a show here next season.

Ettie called up.—Wanted to know when Frieda was due!!—Well, Sweetestheart, it has
been a day.—The school section I think had a few visitors—I had no chance to bother.—All the
Demuths are down. Will clear up the place Monday or Tuesday—storage, Of, etc.—Rosenfeld
doesn't know whether he'll go to Taos or not—Finances, etc. very critical.—

I'm tired. I'll walk to the hotel. Zoler is waiting.—Has cleaned up some. I hope to clean
up completely next week.—

Good Night—I hope you are having a grand [time] too—A big kiss.—Your paintings
looked very beautiful.—The Germans didn't care for the Demuths. They are too simple people
for that sort of thing.—

Again Good Night—Another kiss.—

Georgia O'Keeffe · **[Alcalde, New Mexico]** · **[May 17, 1931]** +

Sunday afternoon—1:40—

Good Morning—I was asleep the minute I was in bed it seems—waked in the night
two or three times—and wondered about you—dreamed about you too and you looked so sad
—it made me very sad—and I wondered how you slept—

It was a bright clear morning—I up at seven—painting a little before breakfast—then
off right after breakfast to my pink hill—The same place I came to last Sunday—The heat and
light seemed to hurt my head so after I ate my lunch I started home—but just down the hill I
came to a tall poplar tree by a Mexican house—the tree makes a shade across the road so here
I sit cooling myself and the car—It is a very nice place—Guess it is my curse beginning that
makes my head feel funny—Had ten hours in bed and feel very rested—

I'm just rereading your letter—preferring the school show to a show of "Ambitious

---

278. Lynes 653.

279. Lynes 700 or 701.

280. Doña Luisa Runstein Coomaraswamy was a society photographer who worked under the name Xlata Lotte Llamas.

Young Painters"[281] —I have to laugh—The thought of young painters just turns my stomach —Anyone with a desire to paint ought to be poisoned by the age of twenty—I along with the rest—

Cool enough here now to put on my sweater—what a world—

You say—"don't paint just because I am there"—You are really too sweet—If you hadn't been there God knows what I would be doing—You undoubtedly have something to do with it but I would certainly rather be with the outdoors than anything else out here—and if I don't try to paint it what should I do about it—

I think I would look at things—look for things for painting them—it is the thing I can paint that arrests me—

A cow comes walking down the road—very narrow road—with a soft little calf— all the animals out here seem to have little ones at this time—sheep—goats—horses—cows —chickens—All the animals in Marie's backyard—

Henwar was off early this morning before seven with the dog—the handsomest police dog I ever saw—taking him to Denver to be either doctored or killed—something the matter with his back legs—Too bad—he is such a beautiful animal—

Well—Little Bird—I am quite cool and comfortable in my sweater here in the shade— I had better be traveling home and work some in the house—My head is all right here in the shade—

You know how those heads are—They come and they go—

I am all right—

I kiss you—I'll be going—

Georgia O'Keeffe · [Alcalde, New Mexico] · [May 21, 1931]

This is what my back has been turned to while I make my drawing of those blue mountains with the pink sand wash that I did last year[282]—

—I had a bad headache and ache all over this morning—so I didn't go out to work— Had breakfast—black coffee and orange juice with Henwar—then sat in my door in the sun and sewed till the head was just too bad—Made my room dark and took a powder and lay down—The girl came to call me at twelve for lunch—We ate in the kitchen—it was very good —I ate hoping to feel better—Marie and Sylvia were going for frogs for the fountain—Paul Jones with his aching face and I with my aches finally were persuaded to take the seat of the little Ford—Marie and Sylvia in the rumble—and off we went over the desert and the worst imaginable roads—up the side of the Black Mesa on the other side of the Rio Grande—looking for

281. On May 12, 1931, Stieglitz wrote O'Keeffe that Marin thought the exhibition of the art teachers of the Hessian School was much better than a show of ambitious young painters.

282. This letter includes a sketch of the mountains depicted in Lynes 730 and 731.

frogs—very funny—Of course the frogs were in the water down by the river but we had a great ride—all in a very funny humor—a very fine place—many in fact—that I had never seen except as one sees it from two or three miles distance—

When we came home while Marie planted her greens in the fountain—Sylvia made coffee—I took a bath—Paul lay in the sun suffering with his throat—I felt much improved —my aches gone—We had coffee in the patio—and I thought I would go out on the mesa for the sunset and to work on my drawing again—Henwar came with the mail—two letters and the book—Which reminds me that the spray came a few days ago and did my nose much good—Many thanks—

Your letter today about your Sunday ride and talks with Bragdon was a little sad— makes me want to be with you taking your Sunday ride—all alone—reading a book—I just see you—and it so touches my heart—

After reading your letters in the sunset up on the mesa I went at my drawing—I think it has a bigger freer feeling—

Supper at about 7:20—Henwar announced that in Santa Fe he heard that Walker was in town and that he and the Dasburgs[283] and some others were having supper about fifteen miles down the road tonight—I felt he was the closest thing from you so wanted to see him —Henwar wouldn't go—didn't like the party—so Marie and I started off in her car—The sky still light in the West—a lovely clear new moon with a strange cloud always near it—It is a lovely drive—the outline of the land against the sky always changing—Marie so steady driving—

We found the party at a little roadhouse and I didn't blame Henwar for not liking it— and I was so glad to see him and hear of you—and he seemed equally glad to see me—He has such a nice feeling about you[284]—really so very sweet and nice—said you were wonderful Saturday when he saw you last—

It was so good to see someone who had just seen you—He and Dasburg and I left the others and went outdoors—a bright starlight night with the lovely clear moon—I wish you could have stood there with us just outside the house—a sharp dark severity—really very grand—

The ride with Marie was nice too—Soon after we were home Juan and Eva[285] came in —he had been making a speech at some school graduation—

I soon left and came to my own place—Quite a day in spite of my aches—I think they are about gone—

It was so good to hear from someone who had seen you so recently—You are sweet— everyone seems to know it—

---

283. Andrew and Nancy Lane Dasburg.

284. On May 25, 1931, after seeing Dasburg again, O'Keeffe wrote Stieglitz that he "really makes me sad—he seems such a snarl and he will probably not live long enough to get out of it—it would probably take him about two good lifetimes."

285. Juan, whom O'Keeffe identified only as a "Spanish man," visited Marie Garland and Henwar Rodakiewicz in the summer of 1931 with a Danish woman named Eva.

I send you a kiss through the starlight night—I hope it floats in the open window and touches you quietly for a good dream—

I don't like it when you dream bad things of me—

A gentle little Good Night kiss again—

It is twelve—I must get into bed—

Thursday night

[May 22, 1931]

Friday morning while I wait for breakfast—Good morning!

It is bright and clear—7:40—It really makes me laugh when I realize how glad I was to see someone just from you—It seemed almost like a piece of you come out here—

Here's my egg—

Alfred Stieglitz · [New York City] · May 25, 1931 +

8:50 A.M.—Here I am at the Place early. Was at the dentist's. Wanted him to look at something. Walked there. And walked here. Trying to beat that fool leg of mine. Managing.—And as I came in here I found one letter—yours. Sweet. Very. A kiss. You had the curse.—Had listened to Brahms & Beethoven. You & Henwar—the others not hearing.—I see it all. It's perfect for you. And so for me. The night was restless.—I went to bed at 10:30. Rosenfeld & I had supper. I was stupid. But it was pleasant. Talked about Wagner, Tristan—*Meistersinger.* Then went up— Donald appeared. It was all very quiet. The Davidsons have taken a three room apartment in East 90th Street for twelve hundred dollars a year. Three rooms, kitchenette & bath.

All sorts of "things" run through what I still out of force of habit term my head.— And now I have something to say.—I know you have planned to be at the Lake early in July. —Now I understand how you feel. And heaven knows I feel much as you do.—But I think you owe it to your work first—which is really yourself—to utilize this great opportunity you have where you are. So you must not fix a date. You must be guided by what you are doing.— I mean by all this you are to stay on into July—even into August if essential—Maybe next year you won't get the chance. And remember if I feel the least bit seriously ill or the like I'll let you know.—I write all this now as I feel it's high time to do so.—

I'll probably go to the Lake some time middle of June. I have fixed no date. Rosenfeld is not going to Taos. I asked him whether he'd like to come to the Lake awhile. He said yes if he weren't in the way.—I not only like to have him but his twenty-five dollars a week helps pay part of Margaret's cost—besides paying for the extras to sustain him. I hate to think that way. But there is no choice.—

But please remember Sweetestheart all this must not affect your decision.—In all I do the consideration of *you* comes *first.* It may not always seem to you that way but it is that way all the same. Conditions are difficult. And they'll be more so before they become less so. But I'm not worried. I have "worried" so much I can't any more.—I have spent my capital of worry.—Of course, worry is stupid. But even Farrell, President of the U.S. Steel Trust says the situation is diabolical.[286] So you Dearest One don't worry about me. You know when you appear you'll be only too welcome. I have to laugh when I think of your getting off the train at Albany that morning two years ago & not quite knowing what I was feeling—or you were feeling. And I see you thirteen years ago hopping off the train at the Pennsylvania Station that Sunday June morning & rushing over to me & kissing me—there being nothing else to do.—And Strand's surprised face which you didn't see.—So now you know how I feel. I felt that way when you left. I know you didn't want to leave me. And it was hard to urge you to go.—And still it was the only thing to do—for your health & work's sake—for everything you are—& so I could do nothing differently than I did. And it is in that spirit I say don't set a particular time—I know you'd like to be with me—You know I'd like to have you—But the Hill doesn't run away & the Hill isn't the Southwest—& the summer there is far from stimulating in any way.—I do hope you won't get anything wrong in all this—It's all not easy.—

Your letter is very sweet—I hope the curse isn't torturing you too much.—It must be nearly over now.—

—Tonight Frieda comes to supper.—I wonder what sort of evening it will be.—

I must drop a line to Brett. Haven't written her in ages.—And now I'll get at my job of preparing things for packing, etc. Negatives, material, etc.—

It's cold & dark.—A huge kiss.—And lots of love.—

Had a note from Margaret. Wrote the house will be ready June 1st. She is helping Mrs. Carey clean the Outlook.—

Another kiss.—

Alfred Stieglitz · [New York City] · May 26, 1931

8:45 A.M.—Another day.—Good Morning. A kiss. I'm in 3003.—Breakfast over. Just sitting here a few minutes. Day opens dark gray. Cool. I'm still somewhere—I don't know where.—

—Well, Frieda spent the evening with me. We had supper alone.—What a woman!—I wonder can any other woman quite see her.—She opened up completely.—Never saw a greater inner freedom in anyone.—It is impossible to describe her. Impossible for me.—One might as well try to describe some overwhelming phenomenon of nature to one never having seen something similar or related to it. Seligmann appeared later.—And he fitted in.—She remembered his booklet & also the article he wrote in the *Sun* about *Lady Chatterley's Lover.*[287] —Said Lawrence

286. In a scathing talk that was widely covered in the newspapers, James A. Farrell, president of the United States Steel Corporation, denounced wage reductions and the use of part-time employees by some of the nation's largest iron and steel companies and excoriated executives for "price-shading…taking business for less than its production cost." He blamed this "diabolical business" on the executives, claiming that the solution lay in a more determined price policy, not lower wages; see "Farrell Denounces Cut in Steel Wages and Price Slashing," NYT, May 23, 1931, 1 and 4, and "Along the Highways of Finance," NYT, May 24, 1931, N15.
287. Herbert J. Seligmann, *D. H. Lawrence: An American Interpretation* (New York, 1924). Seligmann wrote a review of Lawrence's *Lady Chatterley's Lover* that was printed in the *New York Sun,* Sept. 1, 1928. The newspaper was so shocked by its content, however, that it remade the literary page to remove this "contaminating essay"; see Harry Thornton Moore, *The Intelligent Heart: The Story of D. H. Lawrence* (New York, 1961), 478.

felt it the best thing written. After that article Seligmann wasn't permitted to write for the *Sun* anymore. He didn't mention that to Frieda. As I said everything was just right — very fine. She related about her first marriage — about Lawrence's death — about their first days — how Lawrence taught her everything — cooking, washing, etc. — His last days. — All in a most living way. All from inside. Nothing calculative. — Spontaneous, intense, full of bursting life, with a terrific life all along the line back of her. — Nothing down — all up! — She said she'd like to see Riverside Drive — The evening was foggy — or rather hazy. So we drove up to 125th Street — & then to her hotel Prince George — 14 East 28th — She related about the famous night scene in Taos.[288] Facts all the same — but the spirit so different. And one knew she was the one telling the truth as far as Lawrence was concerned & about herself she is fearlessly relentlessly frank. — With no bravado about it. — Well, she is a person. You would have enjoyed it all as much as I did & as Seligmann did. He was perfect. He & I went to Childs & I had a chocolate ice-cream! Got to bed at midnight.

Well, Sweetestheart — I kiss you. — I'll tell you more when I see you. — My head is a buzz. — A bit much. I feel as if I had taken a quiet bath in Niagara Falls. —

And now I'll be off for the Place. Going to Weyhe's first. Have found that someone is printing Marin's etchings from the plates Haskell had.[289] — Bad prints! —

6 P.M. 3003 — Another mad day in a way. Still feel pounded & dazed from last night. As I was writing this A.M. in comes the Boni girl.[290] — Also your letter. Very sweet. Very dear. — Curse — Lonely. — Charles's telegram to you. — I wonder will you go camping. I think you will. Particularly after my letter of yesterday telling you I feel you should extend your stay. — Remember, grasp your opportunities. — You're sweet. — Yes, we'll manage together somehow. — Economics! — A kiss — no two — even three. — I told the Boni girl the story of how 291 was begun. She asked. — Anderson called up & announced himself for two P.M. He came. Stayed till 4:30. Saw a lot of your paintings — like particularly the *Yellow Leaves with White Daisy* — & the big *Jack-in-the-Pulpit Abstraction*.[291] — Said the yellow was his yellow. — Asked to see Doves. Liked the *Wind & Clouds* & particularly the *Darkies Swinging in the Park*[292] — A book of his is coming out shortly — called *Perhaps Woman*.[293] — Same Anderson. Talked about Lawrence. Told him some about Frieda. All most entertaining. Frieda is really a heroic sized creature in every way. —

288. Stieglitz may be referring to an incident that took place in 1924 in Taos when Lawrence, jealous that Frieda was dancing with a young man, grabbed Mabel and using her as a "battering ram" darted around the room, bumping and kicking Frieda at every opportunity. Brett later claimed that Lawrence grabbed her and charged into Mabel, who was dancing with the young man; see Lois Palken Rudnick, *Mabel Dodge Luhan: New Woman, New Worlds* (Albuquerque, 1984), 216–217.

289. In 1922 and 1923, in an effort to raise funds for Marin, Stieglitz commissioned Ernest Haskell, an etcher and friend of Marin's, to pull impressions from several plates for which Marin had no prints; see Carl Zigrosser, *The Complete Etchings of John Marin* (Philadelphia, 1969), p. 5 and pls. 49, 57, 58, 59.

290. In May 1931, Miss Ornstein from Boni and Liveright interviewed Stieglitz several times in the hopes of compiling a book of his reminiscences.

291. Lynes 642, 715-720.

292. Morgan 30.5, 30.20. Anderson wrote Stieglitz of the latter painting: "It was just that the one got me as a particular woman gets you though you know there are other beautiful women about.... Perhaps at bottom I'm like Dove, a countryman. The warm earth feeling gets me hardest. It's land love, ground love" (Sherwood Anderson to AS, May 28, 1931).

293. Sherwood Anderson, *Perhaps Women* (New York, 1931).

Zoler here reading. Ditto Strand.

I'm tired. Physically. Otherwise am very alert even tho this scrawl doesn't seem as if I were.—

I must stretch out a bit. Oh yes, I was at Weyhe's before going to the Room this morning.—And also received Phillips' new book in two volumes[294]—Your *Leaves* & *Ranchos Church*[295] reproduced. Look well. Book an improvement over first effort.[296] —

Again a big kiss & a little very alive one—

Georgia O'Keeffe · [Alcalde, New Mexico] · [May 29, 1931]

Dear—dear—You dear Little Bird—

I just have your letter with your long little speech about my staying longer—don't you suppose I know how you feel—You funny one. I still have July first in my head but I don't think much about it—I am thinking of other things—We will see—

Marie and Henwar got off for the camp—truck and all—I got off to my white spot that I found a few days ago—And didn't the heat and the brightness of it almost kill me—You would have laughed to see me crawling around over it with nothing on—Then later in a smock carrying a huge canvas that I held over my head for shade when I got too hot—

I really have a wonderful time—I want a white thing that feels like my red thing[297]— here on the wall

I was exhausted by 3:45—and had nothing but a bum drawing to show for it—Started home—stopping to look at places I specially like—When much to my surprise—in the only shady green place in the twenty-five miles—there is a yell—and there under the trees sit Mabel and Tony—

—I had a drive and took them to supper to a place down the road that they liked so much they are staying the night—It is certainly great riding beside Tony—he singing just a little louder than the hum of the car—that curious Indian rhythm—He seems fine to me as he always does—a rare creature—both looking very well—Mabel her most delightful—

It was very pleasant—lovely moonlight—When I got back here I petted the little blond Dane[298] a little while I read your letters—read her the parts she would like—She has a wisdom tooth hurting—Was in the sitting room playing the Victrola—she hears music too—

Oh dear—I did scramble after that white hill and got very little.

There were two letters from you—The two about Frieda—that must have been a session—Wish I had seen Anderson too. Give him my very warm greetings if you see him again—

Good Night Little One—

294. Duncan Phillips, *The Artist Sees Differently* (New York, 1931).
295. Lynes 465, 662; Phillips, *The Artist*, vol. 2, pls. 179, 177, respectively.
296. Duncan Phillips, *The Enchantment of Art* (Washington, D.C, 1914, 1927).
297. Lynes 790.
298. Eva.

You are sweet—Your letters so dear—so like you—I am glad Rosenfeld goes to Lake George—

A warm sweet kiss to my Boy—I am so fond of you—and I feel so good—

Alfred Stieglitz · [New York City] · June 2, 1931 +

10:30 A.M. Here I'm at the Place.—It's dry & sunny. And I'm just no good.—Wall Street is frightful. I adjust myself constantly—But the shrinkages are ghastly. I have gone through pretty tough times but none like this. To see all one's efforts wiped out gradually—to feel powerless in every respect—yet to laugh & go on & know that those about one need one & that what [one] desires to give them is beyond all possibility—Sweetestheart I have been through it all before—I imagined I had learned a little. I find I had learned less than nothing.

Marin & I had quite a talk last night in a very quiet way—It didn't last long. About affairs—about these times.—No theorizing.—No wishing.—I don't like to mention anything like this to you—You are not helped—nor can you do anything about it.—And don't you worry about it or about me. There is no use.—You keep yourself in shape & keep your wits about you. Grasp the opportunity to the fullest. All else is destructive for yourself & so for me. It's difficult I know but you can do it.—If only everything would go to a complete smash—I know I'd be ready. It's this neither one thing or another that paralyzes.

Bragdon & his pretty friend & I breakfasted together. He is happy in his new job.[299] It's wonderful to see what a change there is in him. A job is a job. You know how I always envied those who had jobs. Of course I had a job in a way too—My own. But that's a different, more difficult kind—And I wanted the easier.—

The Juley boy just brought four prints—two of your *Red Barn*—& two of your [*Autumn?*] *Leaves*[300]—too dark altho' I gave them their own guides. The Reinhardts ordered six of each for themselves. I guess they are trying to give you publicity.[301] I do hope they get some returns for you. The times are impossible but maybe they'll do something—Here comes the letter-carrier with a green envelope.—

I have read—Tony—Mabel—you had my letters about Frieda—your painting. Well it does comfort me to know you having such a great healthy time. Yes, Tony must be a rare one. Mabel is "lucky."—The life down there—the life here—ye gods, one is living—I don't know what this here is.—

A kiss—

----

299. In addition to being an architect, writer, and a follower of Eastern religions, Claude Bragdon was also a set designer. He was currently working with the manager of Madison Square Garden to stage an elaborate spectacle that the manager hoped would attract a sizable audience to the Garden when it was not filled with sporting events; see Claude Bragdon, *The Secret Springs: An Autobiography* (London, 1938), 110–115.

300. Lynes 618; probably Lynes 464.

301. Paul Reinhardt ran the Reinhardt Galleries at 730 Fifth Ave., New York, from 1911 to 1941. His wife, Mary, assisted him from 1924 through 1934. In addition to exhibiting Old Master and contemporary artists, they held several exhibitions of O'Keeffe's work in the early 1930s; see "Paul Reinhardt, Dealer in Art, 56," *NYT*, Jan. 15, 1945, 19.

A phone—the Marin books will be here tomorrow. I hope there won't be too great a heartache.—I have had more than I enjoy for a few days.—

The day is grand—That is a lot—And your letter is grander even than the day—And that is a very great lot—

So I'll get busy in my tinkering way—And that isn't so very grand—it's just nothing—yet it must be done—or at least I think it must.—

A very very sweet kiss—Everywhere—

4:30 P.M. Alone. Quiet as a tomb.—Zoler gone. Seligmann gone. Hartley waited awhile for the John Storrs.[302]—They came. On way to Paris from Chicago.—All gone. The same talk. Dr. Reber said—Dr. Reber invited us—Dr. Reber this, Dr. Reber that.[303] It all turns one's stomach. —And *Creative Art* has come. I hesitate sending you the copy—but you might as well see your frontispiece.[304] Looks well enough.

—What chance has a fool like myself got when I see over & over again how these magazines handle things?—I can't get accustomed to all such sloppiness.—For that is all it is.—Brazen indifference to all that's quality even of a low order.—But I suppose I'm unduly harsh —and ought to keep silent.

—The day is a gorgeous one. Many more packages packed.—There is a general cleaning up.—But it's slow for I have not much vim for the job—or maybe for any job.—

I have no plan for this evening. I'll be alone. Maybe I'll play a few rounds of golf alone. Eat at DeWinter's.—Golf is reduced fifty percent.—It's twenty-five cents a round now. Fifty cents was robbery & I felt like a criminal playing.—

I kiss you Sweetestheart—

I hope all is very well with you—& that painting & all else are running finely.—

Much much love.—

Milton, Jr.'s birthday is tomorrow—I believe it is—I must write a note. Emmy I hear is bound for Europe.

Again a sweet kiss.—

Alfred Stieglitz · [New York City] · June 3, 1931 +

5:45 P.M. Crazy. Crazy. And again crazy.—Such a day.—Josephy phoned—twelve copies of Marin will be up tomorrow afternoon! Balance Friday. Ettie turned up with Demuth. I had just started telling a story to the Boni girl who surprised me in coming at 3:30!—Ettie started talking

---

302. The sculptor John Storrs and his wife, Marguerite De Ville Chabrol Storrs.

303. A "stimulating personality" who visited the United States late in 1930, Dr. Gottlieb Friedrich Reber was a Lausanne collector who believed that the "fundamental creative force" was apparent in his eclectic holdings, which ranged from Egyptian art through Cézanne and Picasso; see Edward Alden Jewell, "Collector Finds Age-Old Creative Energy Here," *NYT*, Nov. 16, 1930, XI2.

304. Stieglitz knew that O'Keeffe would be upset by Mabel Dodge Luhan's article "Georgia O'Keeffe in Taos," *Creative Art* 8 (June 1931), 403–410, because two of her paintings were cropped (Lynes 699, 662) and one *The Lawrence Tree* (Lynes 687), was rotated ninety degrees.

Frieda & Mabel. So the story was interrupted—There was quite a discussion about Mabel's *Lawrence*[305] which I have not read. She thinks it very good. Etc. Etc. All most amusing.— Ettie looks well. Demuth ditto. Both send love. Ettie says she had a fine letter from you.[306] — The telephone has been ringing all afternoon. All sorts of people.—Sykes & Strand are here. They, the Normans, Clurman & I are to go to a Russian movie. First to some Italian restaurant. —Seligmann wanted to come to see me. Zigrosser ditto.—But I chose the youngsters for a change.—I have no idea what the movie is about—oh yes I do—the Five Year Plan.—My head is like a pinwheel in a sixty-mile breeze—Got some things done.—But not as much as I had hoped to. No end of odds & ends.—Have most of the stuff from the hotel over here.

—Rosenfeld called up to find out when I was going to the Lake. I'll know by Friday night when I will have been at Lee's altho' their plans won't entirely guide me. I simply want to be at the house before they come if I can manage. Stupid fixation. Would be just as well to get rid of it. I have so many still to get rid of—I hate them—or really myself because of them.—

Strand is sitting by my side scribbling away at a great rate—to Beck I suppose—He says they are planning to leave for Taos on the 22nd.—

—No letter from you today. Somehow felt there'd be none.—You're very sweet all the same—I send you quite a few kisses—And lots of love—

—It's quiet & I have a chance to do a few more things.—I'm to be called for at 6:45. It's now 6:15.

Good Night—Another kiss—

Georgia O'Keeffe · [Taos, New Mexico] · [June 7, 1931]

Dearest—

Here is your friend in Taos again in my white studio—I really didn't remember how beautiful it is—

I drove up the canyon this morning—slowly—it is so beautiful—Had the first flat tire I have ever had when alone—Two men with a negro chauffeur stopped and helped me when I was about half way through changing the tire—

It is curious the way leaving behind me the work I have been doing there—maybe partially it was the talk with Henwar too[307]—made everything seem different to me this morning—I feel curiously free—as tho I had gotten out from under something—

My curse started a little too—everything seemed fresh and beautiful and simple—

I thought I would sneak into Taos—get a room at a new roadhouse house that I stopped

305. Luhan, *Lorenzo*.

306. On hearing that Ettie Stettheimer might go to New Mexico for the summer, O'Keeffe wrote her on May 19, 1931, afraid that a "tenderly cared for female" like her "would be bored to death" in the small New Mexican village.

307. The day before, O'Keeffe wrote Stieglitz of Rodakiewicz's film: He "has such beautiful material—If he could put it together so that the large unit would be as fine as much of the details—by that I mean single shots—it would be good stuff—You would certainly do wonderful things with it—Of course he is young—but even the young should be able to do it—Too bad he can't be with you some—he has such fine material" (GOK to AS, June 6, 1931).

and looked at and not see anyone for a few days—But I went to see Brett—and just as I got out of my car someone hails me from another car—Mabel—and as I shake hands with her along comes Spud—I really had to laugh—Mabel offering the studio to me with great enthusiasm—I said I'd go over and look at it—

Well—here I am—She and Tony went to Santa Fe for three days to meet Chavez—I said I would stay here till she comes back—Such beautiful quiet—out on the desert tonight—And so grand not to have to talk to anyone after supper—I drove her little Indian—Amelia—out to the pueblo this afternoon—We got another Indian girl and drove along their stream toward the mountain then got out and walked—quite a long walk—always beside—or near the wild little mountain stream that brings water to the pueblo—It was a lovely walk—mostly very large old trees—and always—mixed in with it the silvery sagebrush—here and there—and Amelia showed me the land she owns—I wish you could see the beautiful spots—

—Well—I had a good afternoon with Mabel's cook and her friend—even to the remarks on Frieda and Mabel's treatment of Brett—Mabel wants me to go on their trip around to the Indians to hear the Indian music[308]—I don't know—I'll see—Brett is up at the ranch—

It seems so nice to be here—and so nice that no one else is here—I am certainly fond of my own company—It is all so still and feels so free—My consciousness of all the emotional thing going on as a sort of undercurrent down at Marie's had gotten on my nerves a bit[309]—and I wasn't even aware of it till I got out from under it—

Anyway—I send you much love over the Taos mountains tonight—stretching itself very freely to you—

I wish I could tell you Good Night—feeling all of my body close to you as I kiss you—standing—

My Sunday as been a lovely day—dirty finger nails—some of them broken—red hands very burned and a bit rough—very dirty feet—a few mosquito bites—much dust on me and a hole in my elbow—No beauty I assure you—

Georgia O'Keeffe · [Taos, New Mexico] · [June 10, 1931]

Dearest—Good Morning—

Wednesday—5:30 P.M. And it has been a good day—

I went to bed at eight last night—slept immediately—and got up at 7:30—It was a good night—a good rest—

I went right off after breakfast which didn't take long—I wish you could see the morning as I see it when I go out my door up here on the roof—desert all around to different kinds of mountains on every side—

—I went out to the Ranchos Church and painted like blazes till about 2:15—It rained

308. Mabel Luhan had invited O'Keeffe to accompany her, Tony, and Carlos Antonio de Padua Chávez y Ramirez, the Mexican composer known for incorporating Indian and folk music into his work, on a trip around the Southwest to introduce Chávez to Native American music.

309. Marie Garland and Henwar Rodakiewicz divorced in 1934.

and thundered—and the sun shone again so I have it again with a gray sky[310]—very different from any other—and I think very good—

It comes to me today that purity of spirit and painting have very little in common—maybe nothing at all—

I have been much interested just in painting of late—Something else will come—This is undoubtedly my best day's work so far—I felt so good and the thing is so beautiful—I brought it in at about 2:30 and worked in my room—

The Mexicans that came and looked at it were all surprised—They all told me they thought it the best painting anyone had made of the church—I had to tell them I knew it which surprised some of them—

Well—I really had a good day—

The aspens are green on the mountains—and it has turned cold—There is fresh snow on the tops of the mountains—It is very beautiful—a gray—sharp sort of afternoon—

—I guess it is I getting over the curse—feeling very alive that makes so many things I see so beautiful—The sharp line of a storm—

It is so cold I had to put on stockings—and am on the bed—my legs done up in a blanket—my red shawl around me—

I send you a kiss—

Nothing has happened but that I worked—and rather like my painting—I am getting my paint so it moves pretty fast but don't exactly like what it moves to yet—

It's great to be feeling good again—and it is grand out here—I don't see anyone—

Good Night Little One—

Alfred Stieglitz · [New York City] · June 12, 1931

Good Morning—Sweetest One.—A kiss.

—The sun is out. But it has to battle for its rights. There is still rain in the air.

It's about ten A.M.—A great letter from Dove. He is really doing day laborer's work.[311] Says all he needs is $100.00 a month. Is down. I am advancing him $250—on Phillips' indebtedness to him. He didn't ask for it. But it is a real pleasure to send it. Also sending him a great letter from Anderson which the latter asked me to send if I didn't think it too crazy. It's about some sort of job in Virginia some man there has which Dove might fill.[312] —Holly[313] is seeking a divorce. Asks for $500 a month!! All inevitable.—

---

310. Possibly Lynes 771.

311. In his letter to Stieglitz of June 11, 1931, Dove told him he had done so much work on boat engines at the yacht club where he and Reds lived that he should change his profession to mechanic; see Ann Lee Morgan, *Dear Stieglitz/Dear Dove* (Newark, Del., 1988), 224–255.

312. Sherwood Anderson, who was a great admirer of Dove's work, had written to him, care of Stieglitz, asking if he would be interested in working as a caretaker for Maurice Long in Maryland; see Morgan, *Dear Stieglitz/Dear Dove*, 226.

313. Holly MacDonald Raleigh was married to the illustrator Henry Raleigh, who was also a supporter of Dove's art. Following a tumultuous marriage, they divorced in 1933.

Last night at nine Zoler & I walked to the golf course & played two rounds. His first effort. I played pretty well. Was dripping wet when through. Need exercise badly. I'm wondering will I make the Hill without wreckage. I believe I will—gradually.—I must.—

4 P.M. I was interrupted this morning. All sorts of phones. Odds & ends. Zoler came at 12:30. More bundles. The last I hope. Camera to Of. Josephy with bill for *Marin Letters.* Mr. Glassgold of *Creative Art,* he who is responsible for the slaughter of your pictures, spent over one and a half hours with me.[314] Quite a séance. Thirty-two years old. Thin. Painter who doesn't paint. Teacher at one time. City College—writer, etc.—I think he had an experience. I was kind.— But not mushy.—I wonder how much he got—Rosenfeld here awhile. Seligmann developing.[315] I too a few shots.

Well, the Marin *Letters* came within what I felt would be fair. About $750.00. As there was the typewriter & a few other items the whole outlay on this venture is about $825. I think we'll not have a deficit. That's much.—

Just now a letter from you Dearest One. Taos. At the new roadhouse.—Curse.—Tony came to get you.—All sounds all right. I wonder will you make the trip.—And Charles alone with Mary & an Indian.—Well, life does work out in curious ways.—

I hope you wrote to *Creative Art.* They should rectify their blunders. *The Lawrence Tree*[316] may not be entirely their fault—But all the same they could rectify that blunder too. I wonder too did you meet Frieda. That was to take place before yesterday.—

Tickets for Lake George have been ordered.—Can hardly believe I'm to leave the city & that there is Lake George. All seems foreign. Queer feeling.—But once away I'll undoubtedly be glad. This transitional period always gets terribly on my nerves altho' I'm quiet enough.—Wall Street is not quite as horrible as it was ten days ago—but one can count on nothing. I was in the safe deposit vaults today. Am returning note to Kennerley.[317] —It's a sad picture those "securities" of ours.—Proof of imbecility—on my part—and as for some others—well I dare not think of some of them—

Bragdon gave me tickets for a huge affair he is connected with—Madison Square Garden—one thousand negro singers & bicycle races!![318] —He, Bragdon, doing the lighting & decorations. An attempt to get the people interested in something new!! Tonight Sykes, Mrs. Norman & I probably going. Maybe Seligmann.—

577

314. On June 10, 1931, Stieglitz wrote to Adolph Glassgold, the associate editor of *Creative Art,* expressing his outrage over the periodical's poor reproduction of O'Keeffe's paintings and asking that his name be removed from the magazine's advisory committee.

315. There was a darkroom at An American Place, which Stieglitz, as well as Seligmann, Norman, and a few others, used.

316. Lynes 687.

317. Kennerley had made regular payments on his purchase of six of O'Keeffe's paintings of calla lilies (Lynes 423, 425, 426, 429; appen. 44, 73) until 1931, when he returned them to the artist.

318. Billed as "the *most thrilling and colorful spectacle ever shown in New York,*" the one-thousand-member Negro Choir performed in Madison Square Garden on June 12, 1931, accompanied by bicycle and "motor paved races"; see "Negro Choir," *NYT,* June 11, 1931, 31.

—Your curse must be over—& you are probably in very live trim. I hope feeling on top of the world.—I'm sitting here in Zoler's white outfit. It's too chilly to sit in shirt sleeves & too hot & uncomfortable for my heavy coat.

—The sun has just come out.

I'll see if I can make another photograph.

The Place—empty—looks beautiful—

A big big Big Kiss & much love—

Alfred Stieglitz · [New York City] · June 13, 1931 +

8:20 A.M.—Breakfast over.—Good Morning. You very dear one. A morning kiss.—

It's a gray morning.—A little breeze from the west. Another very restless night.— It was midnight 30 when I got to bed. Seligmann & I had supper at Childs.—Bragdon had given me four tickets for the opening of the big Madison Square Garden show he was interested in helping create. Bicycle races & a chorus of one thousand negro singers!! A real American idea—Incredible—Bicycle races first—then one and a half hours of singing—& more bicycle races. Seligmann & I got there first—Sykes & Mrs. Norman joined us later.—I went chiefly as a compliment to Bragdon who said the chorus would be an overwhelming sight, etc., & that I didn't need to see bicycle races. Well, the chorus was quite a sight—but the singing lasted too long—too much of it. Art too insistent—as usual—Maybe I was in no mood to be much moved. I don't know.—It was seven when I got away from the Place pretty tired after a very hard day in many ways.—But got much really done.—

The bicycle races interested me more than the art—I hadn't seen any in years. I wonder will the combination take. The chorus is seated in the middle of the arena, all dressed in red— touches of blue.—The shiny black hair of the colored folks was quite a spot. The bicycle track is built around the chorus. I think you might have enjoyed it all. I'm not sorry to have seen it. And some bicycling was incredible—one rider who is like Tilden. An Australian.

—I looked for Bragdon at breakfast but I suppose he is resting on his laurels. His job was all right—effective—very. And that's what was wanted.—But as I said the music lasted too long.—

I'll be off now.—Odds & ends ever.—I'm not going to Belmont Park altho' sorely tempted to go to see what should be a memorable race—Jamestown—Twenty Grand—in Belmont Stakes may be the most important three-year-old event of the year.—You saw it several times I believe. At any rate once. Early in the twenties.—

Now I'll really run along.—Another kiss.—

ON JUNE 16, 1931, Stieglitz went to Lake George, where he was joined a few days later by Paul Rosenfeld, who spent several weeks there. Gerald Sykes also arrived for a visit at the end of June. Except for a brief trip to New York on June 29 to see his dermatologist, Dr. Rosen, Stieglitz remained there for the rest of the month.

On June 17, O'Keeffe drove to the Lawrence ranch north of Taos to see Dorothy Brett and Frieda Lawrence, whom she had never met, along with Frieda's lover, the "Captain" Angelo Ravagli. She had such a good visit that she returned the next day with Spud Johnson.

Georgia O'Keeffe · [Taos, New Mexico] · [June 17, 1931]

Wednesday night — 10:45 —
Dearest —

What a day — perfect weather — I was waked soon after dawn — a bird flew into my room — hard against the screen door — fell on the floor and waked me — My watch had stopped — I got up soon — had time to do all sorts of fussing around and got off a little after seven —

I went up to see Frieda — and didn't I have a day — She is certainly some girl — We talked and talked — She liked you very much — But what a woman — I liked her very much — had a great time — The place is quite cleaned up — much order that wasn't there before — And everything seems to be going very smoothly —

Brett likes to talk of tension — I don't feel any — Brett also walks the floor and calls her a bitch and says she is crazy —

The country was so beautiful going up too — so very lovely — the gray sage stretching off and off to far distant mountains is like the sea — it is very wonderful — I never noticed before that the Lawrence Ranch is right up in the Lobo Mountain.

The drive was great — Frieda too and I had a walk of a mile or more along the Lawrence ditch — a quick little stream about twenty inches across that brings their water down — It is through thin but quite untouched woods — lots of small cedars too — no grass — I walked in my bare skin — it was wonderful — so far away there is no chance to meet anyone —

Supper with Brett — Bobby and [Ted][319] came up too — Brett's house is on part of Bobby's home land — It has such a beautiful faraway feeling — Brett's house very neat much to my surprise — I climbed way up on a rocky point for sunset — a very thin new moon — and what a view — desert circling for hundreds of miles it seems — mountains all beyond it — and feeling very close to the top of the Lobo behind me. Very grand — It was a great day — Frieda gave me what's finished of her version of the Lawrence story[320] — I haven't looked at it yet —

We were late coming down — Bobby and [Ted] driving behind me to pick me up if anything went wrong —

I had a letter from you on my way up this morning — also one you forwarded —

Am so tired now I don't remember much about it — I also had a short ride on Lawrence's horse — it was too hot —

---

319. Bobby and Ted Gillett. Lawrence's Kiowa Ranch, where Brett had a small house, was near Del Monte Ranch, owned by Lucy and Arthur Decker Hawk. The Hawks' son, William (Bill), and his wife, Rachel, lived on the ranch with their two children, Walton and Shirley. In the summer of 1913, Brett stayed in one of the cabins on Del Monte Ranch, as did the other Hawk siblings, Betty Hawk Cottam and Bobby Hawk Gillett.

320. Frieda Lawrence, *Not I, But the Wind* (Santa Fe, 1934).

Good Night Dearest—

I'd like to lie next you so quiet—and kiss you Good Night in the dark—and smell you—I am good and tired—

Georgia O'Keeffe · [Kiowa Ranch, New Mexico] · [June 20, 1931]

Dearest—

This visit to Brett's isn't quite like anything else—As I drove down the road that evening coming up here—it occurred to me that Spud might like to come—He had been down at Marie's a day or two before so I stopped to see him—to hear the news and see if he would like to come—He was just finishing cleaning his press for the day—I rolled up his bed and got a splinter in my finger—he finished his cleaning up and we drove off into the sunset—It was a lovely drive—

Brett much pleased to see us—I had my dinner in town—he ate after we got here— It was just after sunset—the lovely new moon—All really very lovely—Everyone dead tired as we had all worked hard all day and a hot day at that—so I took a little walk with Brett—then we all went to bed on the porch—Spud and I on the floor—Brett in a little cot she has—

Well my bones got sharper and sharper—the floor harder and harder—so I saw a most beautiful sunrise creep over this vast expanse of desert and mountains—hundreds and hundreds of miles it must be—We were up early—Spud and I a bit the worse for the hard beds we had—He went off to town at about seven in my Ford—to get at his printing and to get us more food—Brett and I took a ride—then I went out into the bush—took a sunbath and began reading Frieda's manuscript—First early letters to her—then her story—I came down for lunch—steak and onions—grand lunch—Brett and I—Then we both went to sleep—

When we got up—I had acquired a cot by then—I got more sun—It is really just too grand—No one around at all—you can just walk off into the bush—sage and cedar mixed —here and there a tall pine tree—I just walk off with nothing on—it is grand—Later I took a bath in the little brook—very cold—and put on my sweater suit—and all Frieda's outfit came to supper—she and the Captain and two English people who are with her—also Bill Hawk— he is Bobby's brother—and his wife and two children about seven and nine—It was an amusing supper party—Rachel Hawk brought most of the food and we ate on the porch on a carpenter's table with a curtain for a tablecloth—It just wasn't like anything you ever saw—

—Spud was back for the night and he and Brett and I walked almost home with Frieda's party—all walking but the Captain—he on Lawrence's horse—Frieda in quite a dressy white embroidered dress—It was a funny line of folks walking single file—Captain on horseback with gloves on—some with lanterns—some with searchlights—and the sharp clear young moon over it—the woodsy parts dark—the sage in the open always looking frosty—

—Last night I slept better on that cot so I feel first-rate today—For my sunbath this morning I walked a long way through the woods and climbed that pink rock again for the wide wide view—the desert and mountains circle round so very far from up here—

I [am] so taken up with the outdoors when I get out in it I seem to dream the time all away or maybe I just hang it on a tree and forget where—Just walking about—looking is so lovely—

Brett's house is very neat for her—she throws her clothes on the floor anywhere but hasn't accumulated much real dirt yet—Spud is very neat and keeps the kitchen straight— I finished Frieda's [manuscript] this morning and wept over it—I think I'll ask her to send it to you—

—I'll be off again now—This outdoors is perfectly demoralizing to me—I seem to only want to be out in it—

A kiss to you—on the warm wind—across the mountains and the desert—as far as I can see it going to you—

Taos, New Mexico
[June 21, 1931]
Sunday night—Back in Taos—10:30—Bathed—greased and in my bed—

—After writing you Brett and I drove over to Frieda's—Her Captain is quite a boy— Really suffers because he cannot talk English—It is very funny—The ride over is lovely—only a narrow path mostly through woods—We had quite a gay time ending with tea and crackers and Italian sausage and wine—He showed me how to choke a man on his Adam's apple—It was really fun—I like Frieda very much—She makes me feel good—

When we got back to Brett's Spud and I packed up and drove down in the sunset— He driving—I wanted to save my finger—The sky was a bit cloudy but the sunset bright—the light on everything lovely—He came out to supper with me—

And I was much pleased to find mail from you that Marie had sent up—four letters— the last your first one from the Lake—the one written on the train—You do seem a bit lonely —I ought to be there—It makes me get out the calendar and figure—I must either start on the 28th of June or about the 6th of July—and I think it will be the latter—The 28th rushes me a bit—I may stay here till Wednesday afternoon—If the weather is good I may go back to Brett's for another day—would love to paint a red pine tree trunk like you find up in the high mountains—I like so much to just walk around and look up there—it is difficult to sit down and work—Then I want to work down at Marie's again—Tomorrow I go out back of Bobby's again—

The moon over the desert is lovely tonight—I wonder if you are seeing it over the Lake—

I kiss you—and love you so softly—and dearly—You have given me a beautiful world—as only the one who loves can give—I hope I have given you a little too—You have given me much—are always with me—always will be—

I go so hard here I am pretty weary by nighttime when I get to the letter—so if they are scrappy it is because I am only a scrap by night—

I kiss you Little One—Am much with you—even when far away—

So you met Frieda finally. And in the right way.—Yes she is some woman.—A real force. Fearless.—At least fearless as a particular kind of woman.—Bitch! Yes, Brett wrote me that too.[321] If she is, she is an extraordinary type of one.—Me for bitches rather than nondescripts if she represents the bitch type.—What is such a woman to do—What would Brett have her do —be another Brett—or what. At any rate whatever Frieda's nomenclature may be I know she is a very real person—& what a woman as woman.—And it's fine that you met & saw her just as you did.—

I walked to the post office earlier than usual—& on the way down told the golf keeper I'd give him his revenge. As it turned out I beat him two games. Very badly in the second round. He didn't play so well. I played better than Saturday—I drove home—I think I'll walk down again this afternoon. It's a grand day for walking & I'll skip a day printing. And printing is more strenuous than the walk.—Mrs. Ingraham is sending for the wash this afternoon. She phoned several times. Told her we had no vehicle so is sending a niece in a car or something like that.—

So you rode Lawrence's horse. And Lawrence's house is clean.—Naturally.—I'm curious to hear about Frieda's version of Lawrence.—I'm sure it's alive & different.—I'll go out in the sun now—& sit awhile.

A kiss.—

7 P.M.—I walked to the Village a second time. I had some things to do & felt I might as well. —The afternoon is still cool—cold in fact—& the sky has become gray—threatening for awhile—but the west is clearing as the sun is lowering. The wind is east.—Richard was busy all day at Red Top mostly.[322] The house will be opened Wednesday. A week from today Martha arrives. Then goodbye to this heavenly silence.—

For awhile I sat out in the sun & fell asleep.—After the walk. Only slept a few moments.—

I'm eager to hear all about your meeting with Frieda. Details. As a rule I'm not interested.—You were very wise in meeting her without Mabel about. You are very wise.—

It must be near supper time.—Rosenfeld attends to it.—I haven't much appetite. Eat nothing between meals either.—

9:30 P.M.—Mozart's *Symphony.*—Beautiful. We have had very little music. Somehow seem, both of us, to be busy most of the time.—If there were more people I guess there'd be more music.—My appetite was better than I thought it was. Ate quite a meal. Very good fare primarily. Rosenfeld's reading. I have been sorting negatives. Getting ready for tomorrow. I'd like to get a few very fine New York prints. Still waiting for Eastman. Had a nice appreciation from

---

321. On June 2, 1931, Brett wrote Stieglitz saying she was "chilled to the bone" by Frieda Lawrence's behavior since arriving in Taos: "Has Frieda ever loved anyone? Lawrence used to say that he never saw Frieda look affectionate, except when looking at herself in the glass!" Brett insisted that she was "more truly [Lawrence's] widow than Frieda."

322. Richard Menshausen worked for the Stieglitz family from the 1920s through the 1940s.

Goodwin.[323] He had read Marin's *Letters.* Was amazed how Marin had kept free from the complications of modern life—kept detached.—Otherwise haven't heard about the *Letters* from anyone. It's too early. Of course I mentioned Anderson's writing.—

I guess I'll get to bed early. It's a good sleeping night.—All the covers won't be too much.—

Good Night Sweetestheart—Good Night—a kiss—

I hope all is well with you. Everything.—

I have started the Brahms *Concerto*—Kreisler. Rosenfeld asked for it. Sounds great— Kiss.—Kiss. Kiss—

Alfred Stieglitz · Lake George, New York · June 24, 1931

It's nearly 10:45. When this is written I'll go up & take Phanadorm.[324] Rosenfeld is playing De Falla's *Nights in the Garden of Spain,* a rather captivating affair.—A very excellent record as record. Well, it has been a very busy day. And a very beautiful day weather wise. Another mountain day—cool but not cold. Cloudless most of the day. I walked briskly to the post office at about 10:30. Did not play golf but decided to walk home & up the Hill. This taxi business is nonsense. Too expensive besides. Halfway home Ruth Putnam picked me up in her car. She has a secretarial job in the Village. Is a very nice girl. I walked up the hill.—

All afternoon I printed. Five hours work. Not much done. But have a print or two. Am still waiting for Eastman.—Then will get at some large negatives. I wonder.—The day just flew. —I sat for half an hour (five P.M.) in the sun & rested. Some unpleasant financial news. Coupons of some bonds returned with remark "payment deferred."—Unpleasant. But I can't let it disturb me too much. It's all just too ghastly in a way. Well, we'll have to manage somehow. And this all happens in spite of all I have tried to forestall. And started so well & so soundly. There is nothing to say. Money is not for me & it looks not for you either. Too many on the job—& we really not—It all reminds me in a way of my father's lot.—As long as we stay on our feet physically speaking it's all right—

I oughtn't to write you this. But you might as well know.—For awhile yet there is [food] to eat & a roof over the head.—Thanks to some monies *not invested.* Rosenfeld is going to bed & so I suppose I'll have to go up. I'm not a bit sleepy. His sleep is important.—He's really working.—His finances too are in a rotten condition.—

Well, Sweetestheart, Good Night—A Good Night kiss.

More in the morning.—

The night is clear & moonlight—half moon.

I hope everything is fine with you & that the stay with Brett is a real experience. Every day with you is down there—

Good Night again. Another kiss.—

---

323. Walter Goodwin, editor at L. P. Lippincott, not his brother, John.

324. Phanadorm, a barbiturate, was a sleeping pill commonly used at the time.

Georgia O'Keeffe · [Alcalde, New Mexico] · [June 25, 1931]

Dearest—

Your child is very tired again—My days seem to stretch out to eighteen hours days—

I was up a little after six—and it is a little after twelve now and I've been going every minute and I think I have my best painting today. As a matter of fact I know I have—a larger one of those hills like Reinhardts[325] have—This is my second day on it and when I brought it in it looked so good I went right out to find Marie for her to look at it too—It quite pleases me —out there and back is a forty mile drive—It was so hot at about one that I thought of hunting a tree but the nearest one was about five miles away so I didn't—sun really too hot to stand out in it—

I got back at about 5:30—The Strands had been here—I lay on the roof—sun bath —the sun low and not so hot for nearly an hour—Then had your letter—a bath—and stretched a large canvas for tomorrow—and it was dinner time—

Afterward I lay on a bench in the patio—moonlight—Paul Jones brought coffee out there—everyone else sitting about—just a little while—Then got up and went at the bar again[326]—Henwar—Spud and I painted at it all evening—I just now washed my brushes—It is going to be very gay I think—I hope to finish it tomorrow night if Henwar works some on it in the daytime—

And so it goes—and I am tired—Pretty full day—

I am greased all over too—sunburn and hard water make my skin all so dry—

Really—I've done so much today it seems almost impossible—

The breeze tonight is cool and lovely—I am too tired to go up on the roof to look at the moon—I know the sky is full of clouds—

Strands are coming down Saturday—

A sleepy kiss—

Thank you for your letter—urging me again to stay too—There are a few things I must do yet—I understand how you feel—and thank you for it—am glad you are working—

A kiss—A kiss—

—You are very precious—I wonder at myself for being away at all—but I do seem very busy and feel very alive—And I would like to be fluffed besides—

Alfred Stieglitz · Lake George, New York · June 26, 1931

Georgia Sweetestheart,

I have your wonderfully beautiful letter after your stay with Brett. I wired you at once to Alcalde a long day letter which you may or may not get that I'm all right & that I feel you

584

---

325. The larger one is Lynes 790; the Reinhardts owned Lynes 743.

326. O'Keeffe drew a flat pattern of signal flags on the wall behind Henwar's bar at the H & M Ranch, which others helped her paint.

should prolong your stay. You are getting so much that you need that it makes me truly happy to feel that you are getting it. The outdoors—the folks—the life—the opportunity to paint. All singing one grand song. And when I think of this here as a contrast for you it gives me the creeps up my spine. You wrote you might stay through July. You wrote that ten days ago. I feel you should take advantage of the opportunity. When I wrote you I may have sounded lonely but I'm at peace. Georgia dearest, maybe at moments I do feel alone, the Hill & I, but it is a strong aloneness not a weak one. You see I wrote you the doctor was amazed how well I looked. You know I hate to decide for anyone.—But as it was I who felt your way this spring lay south-westward—so it is I now, after the receipt of your letter who say stay the extra month that was in your mind as a possibility.[327]—I have said as much indirectly in other letters. Now you know I am ready for you here—but the Hill will be deadly by comparison to all you are now enjoying. So enjoy while you have the opportunity.—

I'm so glad you like Frieda. You feel about her as I do. Lawrence tho led through hell by her often enough was a lucky man to have such a woman take him. For that's what she did.—

As for the Captain I liked him.—I have to laugh at his riding Lawrence's horse & wearing gloves. A real Italian.—And you have been taught how to kill a man getting hold of his Adam's apple.—My Adam's apple is small. So I'm in danger. Am I?—How much better all your experience than if you had gone with Mabel. Frieda said she'd let me see Lawrence's first letters to her—Maybe she will. She volunteered—

Yes, I like her immensely & I knew you would too.—

I want to get this off by airmail so I'll go to the Village again.

I played two rounds of golf with the professional this morning. He beat me first round —I played badly to begin with—In the second round I played brilliantly—gave him an awful licking. Really played brilliantly.—

I have had an invitation to visit Milton, Jr.,[328] & another to come to Woods Hole. The two could be combined. But I feel my place is here—& that Jr. is better off without me altho' I'd like to photograph.—I'd like to go to Woods Hole but again I feel the Hill is the place where I belong.—

Well, Georgia, Dearest, Whitest Heart—I say once more use your opportunity.

A big sweet kiss.

Lawrence's new book[329] arrived this noon—

Richard just announces to come & look—the weathervane is up! A real event—The arrow point points directly east—The Phanadorm is at work. I feel a bit sleepy. It's sultry. Sun in & out. You are very very sweet.

The rowboat is not yet in the Lake. I must phone Putnam. George is to help. Didn't come when he promised. Or maybe he came & Putnam wasn't there.—I eager to get on the Lake—

A big big kiss.—

---

327. On July 1, 1931, Norman wrote Stieglitz from Woods Hole that she longed "to talk to you for hours," and she calculated that if Gerald Sykes went to Lake George in early July and stayed two weeks, and if O'Keeffe postponed her return until early August, Stieglitz would be alone for two weeks.

328. Stieglitz's son-in-law Milton Stearns lived outside of Boston.

329. D. H. Lawrence, *Apocalypse* (Florence, 1931).

Georgia Sweetestheart. Good Morning.

Here I am again.—I thought it was seven o'clock. I find it is six.—The night for a change was one of those impossible ones—just no sleep. I guess two successive Phanadorm nights are more than I'm entitled to.—I certainly worked hard enough all day yesterday to be entitled to a few hours of real sleep. But sleep wouldn't come. So I tossed about trying to find it.—Somehow I feel rested enough.—The morning is gray & dampish.—The arrow points west. For good weather here at this time of the year the arrow points east during the day & turns west after sunset. Maybe it will turn east a bit later.—But it's weekend—& weekends seem to have a particular cussedness of their own in these parts.—Be it as it may.—

Well weather or no weather I have plenty to do. Yesterday afternoon I sat on the front porch fairly well bared & worked at prints for nearly five hours. There are fifteen ready to mount.—In the evening I worked at a few more. Some are good. Some a question mark. But I'm going ahead all the same. We'll select.—I wonder will you like any. They are particularly "queer" —as I am very queer.—There was a bit of music—Rosenfeld turned on a Bach & then jazz on top of it. We have had no jazz. In reality there has been relatively little music as I believe I've told you.—Then there was silence. I had a few letters to write.—And then I turned on Beethoven *Quartet, 59 No. 2* & sat in the front room working at more prints. We've had no *Quartets* of Beethoven before this year. And what a beautiful one that one is. Such an abundance—

There is the sun.—The western sky is leaden. The hay hasn't been cut so it looks burning copper colored against the dark sky.—Could photograph it but I don't feel like photographing this morning. Not yet.—

I suppose the Strands are installed in Taos long before this. And you have heard directly from Strand about me.—And Beck is reveling in her heaven—And Strand will add to his trophies of photography. What a chance he has. He ought to do some great work this year after the criticism I gave him.[330] My Eastman stuff finally arrived. So there is plain sailing ahead for me.—I made up a new fixing bath last night. So I'm ready to try some large New Yorks. I wonder. Above all it is a question of paper. I know the negatives are all right. Some of them. If I get half a dozen prints—real ones—I'll be satisfied. Soon I'll know.—I may pitch in today. I may not.—Printing large prints is a different matter from small ones. I have to be more careful of paper. A large print spoiled means four small ones—And four small ones means four chances for an AI.—One large one means one chance for an AI or for four chances four times the paper & I haven't much old paper left. Mathematics & Art.—

Lawrence's book *Apocalypse* came yesterday.—

So there is reading enough for me if I want to read.—There is always time for reading— The sun is gone again.—All is grayness once more.—I wired you yesterday to Alcalde & asked for a report when it is delivered. So far no sign of a report—Maybe Marie & Henwar are away —& you still in Taos. And I sent you two airmail letters all about extending your stay through

330. Encouraged by Dorothy Norman, who thought Beck Strand was irresponsible and Paul Strand imitative, Stieglitz had become quite critical of the younger photographer in the past few years, and their friendship was strained.

July. I hope you get the spirit in which the suggestion has been made. Your inspiration lies down there. Why shouldn't you have it? Why not use the opportunity as I'm all right.—I may occasionally sound lonely but you mustn't let that affect you. I'm really in better shape in every way than in ages. Except perhaps the Little Man doesn't show as much interest in life as at one time.—And I'm certainly alive enough for almost anything.—In all events you know how I feel about your staying awhile longer. Now I'll attend to a few matters—

I'm not yet washed, etc—Don't want to disturb Rosenfeld—but I hear him in his bathroom—so I'll take a chance.

Then there is the back bathroom.

A huge kiss to my Sweetestheart—

Your letter of yesterday was very very beautiful.—

Georgia O'Keeffe · [Alcalde, New Mexico] · [June 28, 1931]

Dearest—

I have not written for two nights because I knew the mail would not go—I was so tired—and I thought to write you a longer and better letter all at a time when not so tired and I could really get my breath—

Friday I was off early—at about seven—and was out all day and didn't do a thing—The place I went to ready to work had been the only spot on the thirty miles of road to have a hard rainstorm the day before—and it was all mud so I couldn't do what I intended—the ground being much too wet to sit on—everything much too wet—I looked at it a long time from the car—

It was a day just spent looking—poking along—wading in streams—sunbath—water bath in a little ditch at my white place—At night I worked on the bar—till late—Yesterday Saturday too—I didn't wake up till nine—Paul Jones waked me wide awake with a bucket of soft water he had promised me for my head wash—When he saw me so sleepy he brought me my breakfast on a tray—all so neat and perfect—Henwar and I painted on the bar till four in the afternoon—Then I took my car to be serviced—He came after me—When that was finished I washed my head—

I was dead by suppertime—but then—I am almost every night—Strand was invited for supper—He looked at my paintings and sat on the roof with me while I dried my hair—He seemed to like the paintings—Beck wasn't well.

There was a party after dinner—some thirty people—A bit nondescript—You know I don't like parties—Had a long talk with Ted Stevenson (I think that is his name)—He spoke much of Rosenfeld—seems quite devoted to him—A very nice person—A bit lonely out here as far as his work is concerned I think—I had met and remembered him the first year I was out here—

—Again it was late when I went to bed—and late when I got up—Paul stayed all night—I ate breakfast with everyone—it seemed lazy and groggy—everyone's pulse a bit slow—Paul Strand and I went off to try a new road—each in his own Ford because we expected to get stuck in the mud and one [would] have to pull the other out—Well—it was a new road all right—Very grand to look at—really astonishing—fantastic formations of earth—Then just before we struck the good highway we had to cross a river—It is the Rio Grande—really a great old river—running red from rains on red clay—I was in for turning back—to return the way we went—Strand was all for crossing the river so into it he went—Well—he got stuck in the sand on the far bank—I didn't—He had picked up two Mexicans that wanted a ride—the four of us pulled and pushed and struggled and dug—and finally had to get a team of horses to pull us out—My car wouldn't budge him he was in so deep—It was funny—A very pretty place— The Mexicans were nice—I rather enjoyed it—I was never with anyone stuck in sand before— It hurt Strand mightily to have to pay the Mexicans four dollars for their team—We had a good day—he photographed a little—But all day he was thinking of getting back to Taos before dark—I was quite bored with him—The moon would make going later so easy—

Well he has gone—He must have been there for supper—I really had to laugh at him—

—Now I have had a bath and sit here in my nightgown waiting for supper—I must dress—

—First about your telegram—You must not worry about my returning—I am not rushing—tho the day I had the telegram I had quite decided to go by the fifth or seventh—it may be a little later now—And don't think that if I go I go unwillingly—I will go because I want to—

I kiss you quietly—and very fondly Good Night—

Alfred Stieglitz · Lake George, New York · July 1, 1931 +

4:30 A.M. Early yes.—I took Phanadorm at 11:15. I got the five hours sleep & here I am— Back on the Hill.[331] —Certainly at this time of the year a good swap for town.—Sykes greeted me at the station. He's a very fine person. And young. A great advantage. I feel so far away yet so here—a curious existence.—I stopped at the post office—also at Western Union wired to Zoler to see if vault is locked. I know positively it is. He doesn't know I was in town. Will write him after this.—Came to Hill—Found mail. Nothing from you.—

And Good Morning. Kiss—A very early morning kiss.

After getting my clothes changed I read a long letter from Brett.[332] Lawrence, Frieda, Capitano, Trinidad, etc.—I broke down completely in reading the letter.—And I cried as I haven't cried in a long while. What a woman Brett is after all. And to know how she lives because of Lawrence, that something she has received from him, to find it burning that intensely, that truly in a human being today is rare & very beautiful. And she wrote about Frieda & the others quite rationally. At any rate I was deeply stirred. And I treasure the letter. I must write

331. Stieglitz had gone to New York on June 29 and returned to Lake George the next day.
332. On June 15, 1931, Brett sent Stieglitz a six-page typed letter in which she recounted her recent conversations with Frieda Lawrence about D. H. Lawrence's death, her abiding reverence for the author, and her new understanding that because she would have gone off with Lawrence "without winking an eyelid," she couldn't "very well snub Frieda for her Capitano."

her.[333] It's a letter she begs me not to show to anyone.—But there is nothing in it that I didn't know. It's the spirit, the love that affected me so deeply. As you were affected by what Frieda showed you. I can't ever quite get over the "intricacies" of human relationships when often things that might be simple become so insolubly involved & ugly.—

Well, I got here before Lee's retinue arrived. So I was on the spot—Martha & Fred arrived at six. Red Top is in a mess. Martha threatened to return to town. Same old harangue. Why didn't Margaret [do] this & that? Why?—For the simple reason that orders higher up were different. And I for once let things run. And what a mess things become that way.—

Fred will put the wheels, etc. on & in your Ford & more—he is reliable & I'll watch it. No one will run the car outside of yourself. It's good & sweltering here—I'm glad you're not here at present. It would be a waste of yourself from every angle.—So I'm glad I wired & wrote as I did—Do what you have to do & grasp the opportunity. I have said this over & over again—I repeat it. Heaven knows what's in store later. So set no dates. I'm ready as you know.—All is quiet here & I insist in keeping it so. Whether people understand or not.—I wish you could have walked into 1710[334] as I did—And see the real peace & the [Place] did not smell of the tomb.—

I'm not yet washed or shaved. Rosenfeld is still asleep.—When I hear him stir I can go up. Not a leaf is stirring this morning. At present it is so silent. I like it best so.—

Alfred Stieglitz · Lake George, New York · July 3, 1931

6:40 A.M.

Good Morning—Georgia Sweetestheart.

Finally a letter yesterday. You hadn't written for a few days knowing there'd be no mail —& you were tired from the strenuousness of living & doing.—Of course I was glad to hear.— You are certainly living a full & strenuous [life] & the kind of life you love best. And I'm glad that the opportunity is yours. Here everything continues without any outer excitement. There isn't much to inspire. But it seems to give those who wish to concentrate & work a chance to do so.—The sun continues to burn up vegetation. Not a shower—altho' there was distant thunder beyond the eastern hills all late afternoon yesterday.

Yesterday afternoon was rather interesting. That young musician seemingly somewhat "nutty" at times, the one who wrote about you, "Crazy about O'Keeffes, Room 303." Well he turned up with a friend. For a moment I felt, Oh Lord. The friend was a manly fine-looking person. The young musician teaches at Curtis in Philadelphia—is a nervous—more than nervous —type. When he arrived—they live near Bolton—he remarked to his friend, he said last night, "Why everywhere I see O'Keeffe. Even her abstractions. She paints what is there—what we see

---

333. Stieglitz did not reply to Brett until August 3, 1931, noting that outside of his "regular correspondence with Dorothy Norman, I have been shamefully neglectful of everyone else." He continued: "Your magnificent letter came at a time when I was in a highly wrought up state & when I read it I wept.—Yes, dear Brett, I wept…. Although you asked me to show it to no one I sent it to Dorothy. She can be trusted."

334. An American Place was in room 1710 at 509 Madison Ave., New York.

without knowing." And as they were coming along the road nearing the Lake [he] said to [his] friend, "Look at the sky. Look. I wonder what Stieglitz is doing to the sky?"

I doing to the sky!—It all fitted so absolutely into a particular mood that I seemed spellbound—And was—We walked in your pasture. I hadn't been there. The musician asked to see my tree or your tree. He seemed to remember everything—all most uncanny.—And we sat on the front porch—Rosenfeld, the two visitors & I—Rosenfeld & the musician talked—the youngster quite brilliantly. Scintillating. Is the same person but has matured greatly—The friend was silent—but listened—often smiled. Finally he said something most amusing about death—

I had been listening, spotting prints.—When he mentioned death in such an intelligent way I felt he must come from a minister's family & must be a university man—fitting neither quite. His father is minister. He quit senior class of Colgate in mid-session because he felt the professors "knew all"—& were dead. So he got out. He is an electrician by profession & poet by choice. I then related my feeling about death—its significance in my own life—It was a remarkable few hours. It was a pity Sykes was away having his hair cut. They couldn't stay to supper.—Sykes returned just before they left. You would have enjoyed the session.—It was really fine.—Very unusual.—I never get over my surprise at the human being—so extraordinary—when extraordinary.

590 —In the evening there was much music—a great mixture of Brahms, Bach, Stravinsky—Jazz—*Parsifal, Tristan*—Finally I took Phanadorm—& slept the given four hours & fifty-five minutes. Awake at dawn.—

Later.—Before lunch. Early breakfast. I had it ready for the three of us. Martha & Fred out of the way.—Lee took me to Village—played three rounds of golf—had no business to play third round—Mail very late—waited—A letter from you—Very alive. You—Walker—Frieda to have a party—curse coming—your gathering up your belongings—then coming to the Hill.—

—You're sweet—Kiss.

—The day has grown gray. Need rain badly.—Would spoil holidays. It often does.—

After lunch—I feel lazy. But I'll go over to the Little House & do some developing. Nothing particular. Odds & ends. Experiments—

—I wonder how Frieda's party will have turned out. And whether you staid in Taos a few days—

A kiss Sweetestheart, I'll go over now.—All remains peaceful here—That's fine.— Another kiss—

Georgia O'Keeffe · [Alcalde, New Mexico] · [July 3, 1931]

11:30—I was out all morning—trying to work without any success—clouds—and rain all around—

After lunch—and a bit of stewing Henwar and I drove up to Taos—Saw Beck—looking a bit big eyed—After some time in her house we took her out to Spud's—Between the two I heard all the news—none of any importance—Marie and Paul Jones drove up for supper—and Paul Strand too—

It was a nice evening—quiet but pleasant—really went very well—Came back in the dark—went through heavy rain—The drive up and back was lovely—it is such a beautiful car—the motion of it so fine—And the talk remarkable for Henwar—mostly about the thing between himself and Marie—He isn't a talker—really closemouthed about his own and other people's affairs—and so clean—

Well—there wasn't much left to the imagination when he got through—and such impossible situations there is nothing one can say—nothing one can do for him—

It was curious—driving through the night—slowly—the roads so wet—talking—as I have a notion—he probably never talked to anyone before—All about as I knew it—his telling me rather sweet because he is so male and at the same time so sensitive—I wished that he had been talking with you instead of me—You are so much wiser—

—What he told me I almost knew—that he could talk seemed rather beautiful—because he doesn't talk easily—and even when he is hurt he is sweet about it—

It is late—And when we came in—he got the mailbag and looked in it knowing I wanted my letter—and there was my letter to you from the morning in it—Juan had forgotten to mail—and he also forgotten to get the mail—Henwar said he would go get it tomorrow—Juan doesn't go in on Saturday—

Good Night Dearest—

A kiss—I'm so sleepy—

EVEN THOUGH O'KEEFFE PLANNED to return to Lake George in a few days and Gerald Sykes had arrived only a week earlier, Stieglitz went to Massachusetts in early July. He told O'Keeffe that he wanted to visit his son-in-law Milton Stearns and his grandson Milton, Jr., who lived outside of Boston, and to see his photographs that the Museum of Fine Arts had acquired in 1924. And, he added, he might also go to Woods Hole. But in truth, seeing Norman was his sole objective. In the few weeks that they had been separated, Norman had sent him ever more fervent and provocative letters. In one, after repeatedly referring to Stieglitz as "God," she recounted a dream she had in which a woman implored God to take her: " 'Take you completely?' God asked, 'Yes,' she said. And then suddenly they [were] utterly one." In another, she described her rising excitement before speaking to him on the telephone: "My heart is in my mouth—my throat aches from the pressure of my heart.... Oh how my blood it must be racing." In still others, she implored, "I must see you.... I long to talk to you for hours." When her plans to visit Lake George and spend time alone with Stieglitz were dashed by O'Keeffe's imminent arrival, she proposed they meet in Boston.[335]

Stieglitz left Lake George on July 8 and met Norman in Boston, where the two took the train to Woods Hole. On his way back to Lake George on July 10, he wrote O'Keeffe: "Oh yes,

---

335. Norman to AS, July 2, 7, and 1, 1931.

it was too late to call up Milton in his business. I don't know any other address.—So maybe it's just as well—he probably would have wanted me to go to the seashore, etc. to see Jr.—And I really don't feel like it this time."

Alfred Stieglitz · [Lake George, New York] · July 7, 1931 +

4 P.M.—I had a real sleep—wasn't up till 7:30. Where the day has gone to I don't know. I pitched into breakfast making—sat at the table—had a discussion. It was nine before we arose. A kiss, Sweetestheart—I'm to have no letter from you till Thursday!

A tax collector's notice that if taxes weren't paid on Hill by August 1 the place would be sold at auction!! Herbert has forgotten I suppose. I sent a check at once. The estate can repay me. Lucky there is money in the bank! A fine letter from Dove enclosing another from a man—quite remarkable. Dove may become caretaker in Maryland!! The Anderson suggestion.—

In the meantime Dove has become captain!—Licensed to run his boat with parties. A letter from Seligmann—with copy of what Santayana writes about Marin's *Letters*.[336] You'll see. Most interesting. Other letters. A fine array today.—Also small checks from Mrs. Halpert for Demuth & Marin.[337]—

The day is gray & warm—I want to walk to the Village. Loose bowels a bit. Not bad.

—I may run to Boston for a day or two.—See my prints—see Woods Hole & Milton. Have certain things in mind, I'll tell you about. I haven't decided. [Would] like to fly but it is too costly. Crazy.—I have had this idea all summer but didn't think I'd have the pep to act. You know what a poke in the mud I am—I'm not gone yet. You see I'd like to do this before you get back.—I'll tell you about it.[338]

—Rosenfeld says Lawrence's book is fine. I can't read. Much is turning about in my head.—Sleep does me a lot of good.

Really need to wake up—It's late. The car is waiting. I want to get this off with the mail. All is peaceful still on the Hill. Every day is a day gained.

Sweetestheart—A kiss.

I hope where you were was fine. Brett's I suppose.

336. As Seligmann related in his letter of July 6, 1931, George Santayana wrote him on June 26, 1931, noting that "the dialect" of Marin's letters "at first rather disgusted me—except when I could see the humor of it—but in the end I think that it is justified. It helps to enforce the *Go to Hell* which animates the perfectly spontaneous line. I'll talk as I damn please, and paint as I damn please, and live—as miserable circumstances compel me to live."

337. As the Depression intensified in the early 1930s, Stieglitz allowed Edith Halpert to exhibit and sell works by many of the artists associated with him at her Downtown Gallery.

338. Later that day, Stieglitz told O'Keeffe that he decided "on the spur of the moment" to leave for Boston and Woods Hole early the next morning to see his prints at the Museum of Fine Arts, visit his grandson, and go to Woods Hole. Admitting that it was "quite a trip for such a short stay," he asserted, "it'll do me good. Pull me out of old habits."

Alfred Stieglitz · Woods Hole, Massachusetts · July 9, 1931

Sweetestheart—Good Morning & a kiss.

The house is fast asleep—even children.[339] The foghorn has been tooting all night— still toots—I hear the baby—it's 5:15. It seems very natural to be here—It's very homey— very still—

Mrs. Norman called for me at the Boston station—I was so late we just made the Woods Hole train otherwise would have remained over & I wanted this. She had been at the museum while waiting several hours—The house is small—but nice—Seems just right for them. Quarter acre—We talked & they eat out of doors. It was warm. After supper talked some to Ed & her about themselves—

Very fine—All so natural. She is certainly a rare person—& he a fine fellow. They make a good combination even if not perfect—But it's very wonderful to see how she handles everything. I'm glad I see it here—

—Went to bed at ten.—Didn't sleep—So finally at two took Phanadorm. But here I am downstairs in their living quarters—runs all along the house—& is about sixteen feet wide— All wood. All very simple. Not the way you'd have it.—The bed was good. Room small— four small windows I had open & door open—The fog is heavy—I like the sound of foghorn —it's far away—It's windless—

I'll stay a day & go to Boston & be in Lake George Saturday morning. They wish me to stay longer. But I feel I should be on the Hill—I hear the milkman leaving bottles—Sykes leaves Sunday. I phoned last night to ask if there was mail or telegram from you. There is a letter there. Good—I wonder what's in it.—

I hear the children—their room is on the ground floor—then the Normans' upstairs— I have no idea when they get up. I couldn't stay in bed.—Tried it but just couldn't.

I don't know what the program will be for the day. Last night in the fog—walked a bit. Liked it.—Like it as long as it isn't black—altho' perhaps I'd like it then too.—As long as there is quiet—peace—no discord—And here there seems to be no discord.

—Everywhere flowers—small bits—all like Mrs. Norman. So different from what you'd have & do—& Ida would even do with the material. All more or less conventional but still personal—The children are having a lively time—

In a way it all seems as if I'd been here a long time—& still I feel like some ghost stalking about—

I wonder will I go to Boston today or tomorrow—I'll let her arrange. She'll want to go in with me. And I want it as simple as possible for her.—I'll take the night train from Boston Friday—tomorrow night.

It's so still—& the fog is dense—Nothing is stirring—the children's voices are heard. Sweetestheart—I'll get this in an envelope—A sweet sweet kiss—you Sweetestheart— Georgia dearest—

339. Nancy (b. 1927) and Andrew (b. 1930) Norman.

6 A.M.—The foghorn is blowing.—The house is still. A few birds chirping.—I'm up since 4:55. There goes the horn.—I like the sound.—I hear the children too.—Yet there is a great peace in the house. He is very fine. She really quite beyond belief.—The children very beautiful. Everybody so just right.—I'm glad I came.—A kiss Sweetestheart—Good Morning. At ten she goes to Boston with me to the Museum—I leave for Lake George tonight.—I would [have] loved to stay here a day longer for it's really so restful but I feel I must go. I want to see Sykes & I feel I have been here just the right time.—I took Phanadorm last night so got some sleep.—The day yesterday passed all too quickly.—Walks to the post office—Three letters from you[340]—fine ones—you'll have much to tell me—& I'm eager to hear—everything sounds healthy & growing. Yes, Henwar, I'm glad he spoke to you. That you were ready. And he knew—I knew all along that his opening up to you must come. Yes I would liked to have heard too—not alone but with you—Telling you is one thing—telling me another—even tho the facts remain the same—identical. He needed to tell you.—Relationships. The deepest.—How unfathomable all is—

I snapped a little with Dorothy Norman's camera. The seashore is not the place for her —Some day I'd like her to see the Hill. Ed Norman has given permission. Some day!—Perhaps. —The Hill—with taxes unpaid—All so well kept here without a trace of ostentation—

I phoned last night to Lake George whether there was any word from you.—A letter. Being held. Everything all right there. Sykes on the phone.—

I like that foghorn's sound—but I'm glad I'm not on the water—

A kiss—you Sweetestheart—Georgia—

The morning is a bit chilly. I'm in my cape—I have been reading *Faust*—while waiting till they come to breakfast—I found it lying on the table. A very bad translation.—But ever *Faust*—There are not many books here but all very good ones—I can see you in a house like this & how different it would be. This has the feel of what she is—yours would have the feel of what you are.—Both spirits complete in themselves—both very fine.—But so different.—

I saw *Creative Art* here—Hartley on Florine[341]—Seems all right. But I just can't read such things.—Not now.—I wonder how my photographs will look. As I wrote you I fear my feeling when I see them—I'll see—When I return to the Hill I'll certainly pitch in to printing. —It'll probably not be so hot & I not so tired.—This will have given me what I needed— a foil.—

I sit here unwashed & unkempt—teeth unbrushed—I don't want to disturb anyone —altho' I'm noiseless that I know.—She is a miserable sleeper like I am—& she didn't hear me yesterday morning at three—at four & five—& six going up & downstairs—& everything is heard even more than on the Hill.—I'll go up & see if I can wash a bit—I feel the need badly.

Another kiss—

---

340. O'Keeffe did not write to Stieglitz in Woods Hole. Sykes forwarded these letters from Lake George.
341. Marsden Hartley, "The Paintings of Florine Stettheimer," *Creative Art* 9 (July 1931), 19–24.

Alfred Stieglitz · Boston, Massachusetts · July 10, 1931

6:50 P.M. In four hours I'll be on the train for Lake George. I wanted to stay in Woods Hole another day but something said it's best to go.—Mrs. Norman came to Boston with me. We got here at 12:45. Ate lunch at the Touraine [Hotel] & went to the Museum.—I was amazed at my own prints. I never realized how extraordinarily wonderful they really are.—And I had feared! I must laugh. Well I'm glad I saw them. We looked at other things too. I certainly like the Museum. Its feel is fine. There [is] the personal touch—real caring. The day was one of rain & fog then brilliant sun with amazing banks of clouds.—Really wonderful ones.—I took Mrs. Norman to the station.—She would have liked it had I stayed another day but as I said I felt I'd let a perfect thing be perfect. Because these few hours have been perfect. And very alive.—All so different. I feel quite dazed—But I'll [be] glad to be on the Hill again much as I liked Woods Hole—

I feel pretty tired & drowsy—A kiss Sweetestheart—A kiss.—This is written in the Touraine. I had to change my underwear. I was wringing wet—and I shaved—I'll be glad when I'm on the train.—I'm going out now to get some air—go to the park & look about—kill time —I'm devilishly tired—

Up so early—Wrote you early & mailed the letter—
Another kiss—

Georgia O'Keeffe · [Alcalde, New Mexico] · [July 10, 1931]

Friday Night—
Dearest—

I just sent you a night letter—If you go to Boston and the other places I see no need to rush home—I would just stay here a few days longer—

I just finished packing today—even my suitcase—Everything ready but putting in my last paintings—and that is arranged so that it can be done very quickly as they all fit—Now I feel free for the rest of the time I am here—This afternoon when I had finished packing I went out for a couple of hours and painted on the thing right out in front of the house. I've worked on it much at different times but it was in a bad way—This afternoon it seemed to go particularly well—It looks so much better—I got all excited about it—and wonder why I didn't only paint on that spot all summer—Painting every day as I have since I'm here is certainly the only way to work—Everything seems to have much more go to it—Then when I say that I wonder if it may be only my imagination—

—Strand didn't like the "paint quality" in one of my best paintings—Made me want to knock his hat off or do something to him to muss him up—The painting certainly has no resemblance to a photograph—

Maybe this will all look smeary when I get them in our immaculate place—Here I have been trying to get them to live on a warm earth-colored wall—It is a battle for my color— I think it has been good—

Well—I'm glad to be packed as long as I have it to do—

Don't open my packages when they come—there is nothing in them that would interest you—I am sending a barrel and two packages aside from my box—Nothing but trash[342] I suppose—but it is trash I seem to think I want—

I'll be wondering if you have left the Hill—In a way I hope you have—

If you haven't—we can drive over to Maine when I get home and you can go down to the other places from there—if you want to—

Good Night Little One—Sleep well—I look forward so much to being beside you— Feeling you warm and close—And I want so much to pet you—

O'KEEFFE RETURNED to Lake George on July 16 and soon felt "disgruntled that I thought I had to come East." She wrote her new friend Russell Vernon Hunter, "I do not work.... I walk much and endure the green and that is about all there is to it."[343] Her presence did nothing to diminish the ardor of Norman's and Stieglitz's affair. Immediately after Stieglitz left Woods Hole, Norman feared she might be pregnant. When she realized she was not, she burst into tears, both relieved and grieved that she would not bear Stieglitz's child.[344] By late July and early August, they were exchanging three, four, even five letters a day, often in excess of twenty-five pages each, and their frequent telephone calls, which disturbed both Edward Norman and O'Keeffe, were trying because they could not speak freely.[345] "I want to shriek," Norman wrote after one call, "'Disregard all this—I love you—I love you—that is the important thing.'"[346] As they worked themselves into an emotional frenzy, they decided they had to see each other one more time that summer. On August 26, Stieglitz took an overnight train to Boston, where he met Norman. After checking into a hotel, the two spent the night—in separate rooms, Stieglitz assured O'Keeffe—before taking the train to Woods Hole the next day. After spending one night there, he returned to Lake George.

Alfred Stieglitz · [Albany, New York, en route to Boston, Massachusetts] · August 26, 1931

8:00 P.M.

Sweetestheart—

Here I am alone in the writing room of the Ten-Eyck [hotel] where we ate lunch when you left last summer!—And here I am again.—Two years.—Twice in that time you have been in

---

342. O'Keeffe sent several animal bones to Lake George that she included in paintings made later in the fall (Lynes 772–780, 798, 799), as well as a Native American blanket. Stieglitz also photographed her with the bones and blanket (Greenough 1427–1437).

343. GOK to Russell Vernon Hunter, summer 1931.

344. Norman to AS, Aug. 2, 1931.

345. See Norman to AS, Aug. 4, 1931. A friend of Edward Norman's later remarked that Dorothy "began to treat Edward as beneath her intellectual level. In his presence and mine, she would make long, intimate phone calls from Woods Hole to Stieglitz at Lake George. The implied comparison was devastating to Edward's ego, though she seemed comfortable believing her actions were justified by her high ideals"; see Robert Josephy, *Taking Part: A Twentieth-Century Life* (Iowa City, 1993), 92.

346. Norman to AS, July 14, 1931.

New Mexico.—I induced you to go this spring.—I know how hard it was for you to go.—
And harder really still to have you go. But I know what the life there does for you in every way.
No more radiant woman lives than [when] you are so sure of self. And as you grow surer—
oddly enough I grow less sure of self.—My age has something to do with it. But it's not that
simple.—I had to call you up even tho you said I needn't—I had no choice.—You see as the
train pulled & I was on the road to somewhere—God knows to where—& He probably doesn't
know anymore than I do—for He Himself seems lost these times—I felt a complete letdown
for the first time in several months. What happened to me I don't know. But very much became
suddenly very clear—& that without thinking or feeling.—For I seemed to fear nothing. And I
certainly thought nothing.—

Our fifteen years stood there before me—for it isn't thirteen—but really fifteen, nearly
sixteen. That is a great many years.—And I know what they have been to me & I know what
they have been to you. Both of us consider ourselves failures in respect to the other.—I wonder
could anyone have been less a failure than I during fifteen years with you.—I wonder could
anyone have been less a failure than you during fifteen years with me. In spite of our "failures"
respectively I feel that I still have something to give you if you will let me—& I know you have
very much to give me if I let you—& I know I will let you.—

I feel you are really free!—Whatever you need do—I'll accept. I'll stand by it. And that
without reservations. That came to me clearly before I left Lake George—this morning early
while lying in bed awake—you asleep in your bed.—

I said many things the last few days that sounded feelingless & hard—you said many
things that sounded feelingless & hard. I may have called that forth in you.—When I get back
there'll be none of that from me—I'm sure of that. If I should slip just say: What's that? And let
it go at that.—I do want to work. I do want you to work in peace.—I do need your help. Help
in the broadest sense.—

I must work or go completely crazy. I want to be at my post this season as never before.
—And as far as you & I having separate rooms in the Shelton that is ridiculous unless you
wanted your own quarters. Much I say you don't quite understand. You take it as a criticism
of you when there is no such thought or feeling.—Unfortunately you naturally need many
things which I can't share with you for many causes. And there are a few things I need that are
absolutely meaningless to you.—All that you know.—But in spite of that there is still much we
share if only we'll give ourselves half a chance.—

And we'll give ourselves that I'm sure. You are much wiser than I am—& altho' I'm
pretty much a fool I'm sometimes as wise as you are—or should I say to be gallant—nearly as
wise. So why not use our combined wisdom—you the chief partner having more to give.—

I hope you'll have three real good nights while I'm away—& three full & quiet days
—As for myself I just wonder—and even tho you think I'm foolish in going to Boston & foolish
in phoning to Woods Hole all I can say even if you are right—I had to go to Boston & I had to
phone—something in my system has to get a chance to straighten itself out.—

When I get back I hope you'll see the truth of what I say.—Of course if I were you I'd
act very differently. But if I were you all I have done would never have happened. Much that you

told me the last twenty-four hours was very important for me to hear. Sensing something is one thing—having it told to one is another.—

I'm going to photograph you as soon as I get back.[347] That comes first with me then— You'll see.

With very much love & a real honest kiss—

Your Silly One.—

Alfred Stieglitz · [Boston, Massachusetts] · August 27, 1931

Dearest Heart:

It's been a great day in many respects. A trying one too. I did well to come to Boston.— The night was a long & trying one. Rain.—Slept some. Train one and three-quarters [hours] late! I frantic. But I just caught Dorothy Norman to the minute for the train due one and three-quarters hours before hers pulled in as hers did. I had to run like a sprinter several hundred yards to catch her. I had made no allowance for any such eventuality. You can imagine me. All was well that ends well. After a confab about hotels we came here.[348] She has a room & bath. And I one. Not connecting. It thundered & lightninged—& poured much of the day. So we didn't go out. There was much to say—then lunch & supper. And she isn't at all well. I may go to Woods Hole for a day. Go to a hotel there. I'll see tomorrow. Will wire you if I do, which would mean I'd be in Lake George on Sunday A.M. instead of Saturday.—

I hope all is well at the Lake & you all right & having had a good night's rest. I'm really much quieter & the heart quieter—that terrific nervous strain gone. I see how essential all this was for my health if for no other reason.—Hadn't I come it would have been a big blunder.— I hope you haven't worried any. I didn't wire. I should have I guess—the mess with the trains, the storm, etc. just had me all upset so I never looked [into] wiring. Intended to—But I had written you from train & this ought to reach you tomorrow.

A big big kiss & much love—You're really kind to me—

In haste—

Alfred—

Alfred Stieglitz · [Boston, Massachusetts] · August 28, 1931

Noon. Here I am. I wonder how you are Sweetestheart. Everything seems foreign.—I seem to be nowhere—We talked till fairly late. Very quietly. No excitements.—The night was restless for me—hard rains—lightning & thunder. Still raining now. But it promises to clear up. I wired you I'd be back in Lake George on Sunday morning.—I don't know exactly what time the early train gets in Sunday.—I decided to accompany Dorothy Norman to Woods Hole. I felt it would

347. Greenough 1427–1444.
348. Hotel Statler.

complete something. Ed Norman, Gerald, she & I at supper tonight. I shall room at the Inn. Prefer to.—I stay in Woods Hole until six tomorrow.—That will make the connections in Boston less tiring. I had no idea of going to Woods Hole but got the idea yesterday evening. It wasn't suggested. It has something to do with photography as well as other "reasons."—

I see clearly I want to pitch into work as soon as I get to the Lake. I must do a lot. You'll help me & I'll help you.—I know I'm much quieter & everything is all right.—

It's funny being in this big hotel—a la Commodore. Relatively reasonable. Room & bath $4.50. All very good. Owing to the storming & my trace of sinus—my throat is nearly all right.—I haven't ventured out.—As I'm writing the sun is breaking through. Maybe there'll be sun at Woods Hole. When I was there there was no sun.—It would be fine to have some sun there because of photography as for the pleasure of sun.—

I wonder what you have been doing. Painting?—Walking? Fording? I'm thinking a great deal of you & me. A great deal. I feel we have much to do together. Very much.—There won't be any "rehash" of the past. I'm clear finally as clear as I can be.—I'll be very glad to be back at the Hill. I'm glad it's there. I'm glad you're there. Very glad.—

I must shave now. Mrs. Norman is in her room resting. Her night she says wasn't very good either. She is another poor sleeper.—

Well, Sweetestheart, I'll be back before another letter can reach you. You looked "radiant" when I left—I want to photograph. I'll do it. I hope you have been feeding up.—

A big kiss—

AFTER SPENDING all of September 1931 at Lake George, O'Keeffe and Stieglitz returned to New York in early October to install Marin's exhibition of paintings, watercolors, and etchings at An American Place. Before the October 11 opening, however, O'Keeffe returned to Lake George to prepare for her own December exhibition at the gallery.

On Friday, October 23, O'Keeffe and Margaret Prosser drove to New York and returned to Lake George the next day. Biographies of both O'Keeffe and Stieglitz state that during one of her unannounced visits to the city in the fall of 1931, O'Keeffe found Stieglitz in their rooms at the Shelton Hotel making nude photographs of Norman[349]; some have suggested she found them in bed.[350] There is nothing in their correspondence to confirm this event, but something upsetting to both O'Keeffe and Stieglitz happened during this October visit.

When O'Keeffe went to the city on November 1, she and Stieglitz appear to have reconciled before her return to Lake George on November 4. She again went to New York on November 11 to select frames for her December exhibition and to celebrate her forty-fourth birthday on November 15 with Stieglitz. She returned to Lake George on November 17.

The tone of Stieglitz's letters to O'Keeffe from October and November is much the same as those from earlier in the year: he continued to encourage her to let nothing interfere with the creation of her art and repeatedly reaffirmed the wisdom of her decision to remain in the country

349. See Hunter Drohojowska-Philp, *Full Bloom: The Art and Life of Georgia O'Keeffe* (New York, 2004), 335.

350. Richard Whelan, *Alfred Stieglitz: A Biography* (New York, 1995), 531.

to paint. His letters also indicate that their sex life, despite their recent difficulties, remained an active and important part of their relationship. But hers to him, especially in late October and early November, are different. Shorter and less frequent, they show that she was highly productive, making several new paintings, and was happy with her days alone at the Lake. But they also reveal she was, as she wrote, "stewing much within myself" about their relationship.[351] And both of them appear to have realized that their difficulties stemmed not merely from Stieglitz's infatuation with Norman but also O'Keeffe's independence and their struggles to carve out lives that were viable for both of them.

Alfred Stieglitz · [New York City] · October 10, 1931

The Place—10:30 A.M.—
    Georgia Sweetestheart.
    I have no black ink here only red! I have been reading Mumford[352]—before that glanced through several copies of the London *Sportsman* forwarded from Lake George—The Place is so silent. I'm sitting in my cape—& have the gray sweater on.—And of course you are in my mind all the time. I was glad when Ag[353] phoned. I wasn't nervous but I wanted to know. And now you are speeding up the West Side—towards Lake George! What a beautiful day you have. I'm sure this time you'll have no rain—
    —I feel rather lost.—It's queer how I feel.—I have a very beautiful feeling for you—Georgia Sweetestheart. I wonder whether you realize it.—It's a very deep & quiet one. I'm glad I was in you night before last & yesterday morning & last night—& glad too I controlled myself & that you were in no shape yet to get through!—Georgia Sweetestheart I know Lake George will be beautiful—very beautiful. If I followed my feelings I'd close this up & go to the Lake. Continue to work with you.—And so be with you.—But this must be seen through—the Marins look more & more wonderful & the Place is perfect. I know full well it wouldn't be what it is if *you* & *I* weren't working *together*. Just as I know my prints—my work—wouldn't be in the fine shape it is if it weren't for you.—I may seem grouchy & critical, unfair many times but under the surface Sweetestheart I know what you are to me—& what I am to you—& there is strength in that—growing strength I feel—A kiss—
    —I don't want to get at my prints until I have mounting paper. I think I'll have Zoler stop at Favor Ruhl[354] on Monday, get some paper, have him take it to Of to have cut while he waits. That will save me a day. I want to get those prints mounted. I think I'll go into storage early Monday or Tuesday & see photographs for Julien.[355] I'll look in boxes here today when Zoler comes. I don't want to lift too much.—I might as well get all that off my mind as soon as possible.

351. GOK to AS, Nov. 25, 1931.

352. Lewis Mumford, *The Brown Decades: A Study of the Arts in America, 1865–1895* (New York, c. 1931).

353. Agnes Engelhard, Stieglitz's sister, drove up to Lake George with O'Keeffe.

354. Favor, Ruhl, and Co. was a wholesale dealer in art materials.

355. After working at the Weyhe Gallery in New York, Julien Levy opened his own gallery at 602 Madison Ave. in the fall of 1931. He had contacted Stieglitz to see if the elder photographer would lend his support to the opening exhibition, American Photography Retrospective, on view from November 2 to 20, 1931, and would loan several works from his collection.

—I wouldn't be surprised if no one from the press came today. Saturday is an off day. But it's all right. I don't mind. I rather enjoy the complete solitude—above all the silence.—

I'm going to send you some chocolate & some fruit. I wanted to get the latter for you to take along but didn't think of it till too late last night. And I didn't mention it to you as I didn't want you to delay your getting away.

I'm going to try & take care of myself.—Above all not to worry.—I have still much to learn before I'm ready to die. It's slow business this learning late in life. But I'm really learning.—

I'll go back to Mumford now.—It's easy reading. And my head this morning isn't good for much else.

A big kiss Sweetestheart—Mouth & Fluffy—Take care of yourself—I rather envy you— It's "funny" to feel that I'm not with you in the autumn!—

Georgia O'Keeffe · [Lake George, New York] · October 13, [1931]

Tuesday night—

So the Marin show is really started—critics and all—And you didn't care so much for the Enters performance[356]—

—Well—It has been another beautiful day—

I have been at work—aside from shelves in your Little House—trying to get the oars fixed—fences fixed—and all such nonsense—I have been at a couple of drawings for paintings —nonsense too I suppose—It always takes me a time to get started—I am such a poke—

That is all there is to tell tonight—I might add that the itch has left my head—and that is a comfort—

It has been still and sunny today but cold enough so that it would have seemed very cold if there was a wind like yesterday—

I don't seem to want to play the Victrola at all—I don't know why but I just don't—

It is very nice here—particularly these sunny days—

A Good Night kiss to you Funny One—

Georgia O'Keeffe · [Lake George, New York] · [October 17, 1931] +

It is after eleven and time for me to go to bed—

I have had a good day—Margaret was away all day and I painted in the kitchen— only got up a couple of times all day—and one of those was for lunch—My horse's head— it is a funny painting[357]—

At about twenty to five I went out and looked around—a gray sky—but the atmo-

356. Angna Enters was a mime-dancer who evoked painters and paintings through her performances. Stieglitz saw her perform on October 11, 1931; see John Martin, "The Dance: Visual Art," NYT, Sept. 20, 1931, x10.

357. Lynes 775–777. The next day, O'Keeffe wrote Stieglitz that she was "much pleased" with her horse's head and noted that it was "large and unsaleable—but as things will not sell anyway I might as well suit myself" (GOK to AS, October 18, 1931).

sphere very clear—the pattern of the foliage on the hills very handsome and rich—So beautiful that I drove up the Bolton road to the cemetery—Too beautiful to be looking at it alone—but I would only half see it if I wasn't alone so I guess it is all right—

I got the mail when I came back—Your letter—a bit dreary—and I wonder how you are tonight—Saturday afternoon being over—I realized as I read it that I have only been here a week without you tonight—It seems much longer than that—

Give Demuth my greetings if he is still in town.

I seem to have done so many things this week but I haven't an idea of what they are—It seems ages since I went up the mountain—

Since supper I have been stretching canvases—the skin on my fingers feels all sore—Margaret fixed the oil stove in the cellar and let it smoke so I had to fix that—

I feel I've had a day and am ready for bed—

It was cold driving—much too cold for comfort—

I'm so sleepy my thoughts string out in a funny way—

You sound so forlorn—I wonder if it was just momentary—while you were writing—I'll go down if you want me to—but you don't sound as tho you want that either—

You know I don't have to stay here—even tho I like it—

Margaret told me tonight that she has had a good time this week—She is looking much better—

I ate a pear for lunch—the largest pear I ever ate—it was one you sent me—

My painting is a funny painting—

Good Night.

And I guess this is a funny letter—.

Alfred Stieglitz · [New York City] · October 18, 1931 +

Noon. Two prints are under pressure.—It's slow work. Tables are not large enough. And haven't proper weights handy. And don't want to lift too many boxes.—I'm curious to see the prints completed. Have no particular feeling about them. The yellow reflected light from the buildings makes it all very trying.[358] A gray day would be easier. But I can't wait forever.—Sykes has just phoned. Is coming to lunch.—I have had only one chance to talk to him. Don't intend to talk much.—I want him to tell me about his work, etc.—There is an early print of you peeping out from other prints. Lord it's beautiful. What a pair we were. Really so innocent—very beautiful.—When I think of the things I did of you during this autumn my real feeling for you is in only a couple of the very fine nudes[359]—Maybe there'll be something in the undeveloped last exposures. I haven't worked as yet in the darkroom. The Black Hands[360] are extraordinary but they do not actually express my feeling about you underlying all temporary feelings.—My feel-

358. Stieglitz was trying to photograph the buildings across from An American Place; see Greenough 1374–1381 and 1445–1447.
359. Greenough 1438–1444.
360. Greenough 1427.

ing for you is a much deeper one than you know.—Yes I'm a very funny one.—I'd hate anyone else to be like I am.—

Extras are out. Edison dead.[361] —Queer how unsympathetic I always felt towards him even as a boy.—An extraordinary man of course but something lacking.—But I suppose everyone is lacking in one way or another. Maybe the intuitive feeling that much that was called Edison wasn't Edison at all helped me feel anti as I did.—

I'll look & see if my prints are firmly stuck.—

The wind is kicking up a lot—Otherwise absolutely silent here—

A kiss.—

Georgia O'Keeffe · [Lake George, New York] · [October 20, 1931]

Good morning—

I've had breakfast on the porch—and Richard is here doing a few more things—boat house curtains—gate—cleaning stove pipe—fixing chairs—It is warm and lovely here on the porch in the morning sun—

I didn't write last night—Margaret wasn't well yesterday so I had to cook and last night got in the pantry for some extra scrubbing that it needed—and I went to bed early—

My painting[362] moves along—Margaret likes it—but I don't really think anyone else will—However when I see it on the wall it surprises me—makes me take an extra breath and feel good—

I went on the Lake in the morning—walked a little and in the afternoon lay in the sun a long while—it was such a lovely day—

—I wish you would see the house[363]—it would make you laugh—I am working in the dining room and kitchen—Moved the table from the center of the room—have my bones and other trash all there—

Richard stood in the middle of it and grinned—

The Victrola went wrong again—so I had the man come and fix it again yesterday—I hope it will be all right now—

I'll get off and mail this—

Love—

Georgia

I must be going nutty that I wrote my name up there—Isn't it funny—

603

---

361. Thomas Edison's death on October 18, 1931, was extensively covered in the national newspapers; see "Thomas Edison Dies in Coma at 84," *NYT*, Oct. 18, 1931, 1.

362. Lynes 773.

363. In addition to rearranging the kitchen, O'Keeffe also knocked out a wall in the closet to enlarge her bedroom and painted the floor dark green.

Georgia O'Keeffe · [Lake George, New York] · [October 20, 1931] +

Tuesday night—

Thanks for the Flint article[364]—And three of your letters—Yes—you were much in my mind on Sunday—I spoke of it and Margaret laughed at me—

That painting[365] is up to dry—parts to be repainted—White to be made whiter—

It is the kind of painting that makes me think many funny things about painting—Art —Myself—and maybe America—and then I look at it a bit cross-eyed and say to myself— that maybe it is just nothing after all—So that is that—

We drove a little this afternoon—and then I walked till after dark—the night coming with the moon and sunset together is lovely—It was quite warm today—that is it was not cold—

I haven't done much with the books but stand them up straight—they were falling all about getting all the bindings twisted—

The fire has gone out—it's nearly eleven and a bit chilly so I'd better go up— Good Night Little One—

604
[October 21, 1931]
Next Morning—Good Morning—

I was up a little after six—it is warm and lovely—I've walked a long walk up to Flat Rock—almost to the birches—around through the woods—paths and across spaces—It isn't nine yet—a lovely sunny warm morning—Using myself gives me a kind of feeling of self respect that I don't have when I just sit—

I'll go for the mail—and mail this—

A morning kiss to you—It's a crisp hard smack—then a little soft one—.

Alfred Stieglitz · [New York City] · October 23, 1931

10:17 A.M.—At last I can sit down for a moment to say Hello & Good Morning.—At eight A.M. Zoler & I were at the Lincoln & I got out forty-seven photographs for Julien. Chiefly Steichens. —I hope he'll be satisfied. All night I was fighting an oncoming cold—aspirin—gargling— spraying—treacherous weather—colds all around me—Zoler, Demuth, etc.—I think I have gotten the upper hand of it. I hope so at least.—The photographs will be here this afternoon. Julien can get them from here. There are Days, Steichens, Whites, Eugenes, Keileys, myself, etc.— Steichen will dominate the show. And that tickles me in many ways.

—I have gotten Zoler at my mounting. That is glueing.—He might as well do that.

I have your letter. You drove to Tongue—Your getting up early & watching the rising sun—the mountain—the tree coming to life—everything sounds very solid—& playing Bach

---

364. Ralph Flint, "Recent Work by Marin Seen at 'An American Place,'" *Art News* 30 (Oct. 17, 1931), 3.
365. Lynes 773.

—painting—good—When I think of you here now in this mess—& me with a cold to boot—
I thank my stars you are where you are. You'd be unhappy here.—And I want anything but that.

    More later. There is someone.—

October 24, 1931

    Didn't mail this yesterday. You were here—See what I wrote.—

Alfred Stieglitz · [New York City] · October 24, 1931

Here I am in the Place—Alone—The sun gone.—You have been here.—I wanted to see you.—
You wanted to see me.—You have helped me with my photographs.—We fluffed beautifully.
—You are on the way back to Lake George.—I don't believe you have taken away a fine feeling
about me or your visit.—I feel I have again messed everything. I shouldn't have mentioned my
heart. I shouldn't have had a cold.—There is much I shouldn't have said. It all leads nowhere—
To no greater clarity. No finer feeling. Georgia, Georgia. Yet I'm glad you came.—Very glad.—
I'm sorry you didn't see the Marins in daylight. I'm sorry Margaret didn't see the Place. But
above all I'm sorriest that you should have left feeling as you did. One believes one learns. One
seems not to. It's another illusion. You accept me for what I am you tell me. I accept you for what
you are I tell you.—And yet why these talks that seem to deny this.—

    It's living I suppose—It is said people kill what they love.—Maybe that's true. When
I listen to you when all is said & done I wonder do I see anything straight—do I feel anything
straight—do I feel anything at all.

    All I know as I sit here & look around there is a great feeling of emptiness.—A feeling
that I wish no one would come. It's Saturday & I always dread the Saturday audience. Today
I dread it more than usually.—And you are speeding Lakeward—& I won't be at ease until I
know you on the Hill.—And then—well then—at least I'll know you are your own mistress
and relatively at peace.—Georgia, Sweetestheart, I'm really glad you came.—If I hadn't a cold I
would have made you stay over another day.—For you your not staying is better.—

    I'll mount some prints—again I say you helped me much—Many thanks—I didn't give
you an equivalent for what you gave me.

    When I said nothing has changed just before you left I meant that I had a very beautiful
feeling for you the last ten days—very beautiful—I still have it.—It hasn't changed in spite
of all that was said by both of us.—That was what I meant.—Somehow that feeling lives by
itself—seems apart from all the smallnesses of everyday contacts—

Noon 15.—Tofel just left.—Kalonyme came in right after you had phoned. Was sorry not
to have seen you. I felt sorry too in a way. It might have spared you. He brought McBride's
article.[366]—I am enclosing it. All was very natural. No tension whatever. Wasn't here long. I'm

---

366. [Henry McBride], "John Marin's Annual Show: John Marin's Exhibition at the American Place Evokes Warm Praise,"
New York Sun, Oct. 24, 1931, 12.

so glad you phoned. Didn't dare hope you would. It wasn't because I was nervous about your driving but because I felt terrible that you seemed not to grasp my deep feeling for you—didn't grasp what I was trying to tell you. Georgia.—

Tofel asked to see photographs.—I showed him a few.—He was literally overwhelmed. Said: Grand. It is impossible to think of the medium—it isn't New York—etc., etc.—

2 P.M. After lunch. Went alone. Am alone.—People chatter. Herbert Small took Zoler to lunch. Cardozo announced for noon tomorrow Sunday.—I had hoped in a way to be able to stay in bed till two.—But Cardozo means more. Frances O'Brien sends her love. Enjoyed the Marins. Am not very sociable in my nose-running condition.—Dr. Rugg announces he is coming. Was here twice while I was ill. Is going to the Orient in December.—Wants to see me.—Am not much to see at present.—

I wonder where you are now. Four hours under way. About half way or so.—When you asked shouldn't you come back, Georgia, Sweetestheart, it was very wonderful to know you in the other bed—And yet everything in me that is at all "wise" tells me it would be terrible for you to be in New York now. You couldn't possibly work. It would be bad for your health too.—I'd leave for the Lake at once if someone didn't *have* to be here.—The Place keeps me here. Nothing else.—Many people are coming.—Saturday crowd.—Your Modern Museum friend[367] was here at noon. Sends greetings.—

It's a sticky day. Not enjoyable from a cold point of view—

A letter from Brett. I'll send it to you.[368] —

I'm going to sit in the vault[369] awhile now. Must rest—

A kiss wherever it won't infect you.—And very very much love even if you don't understand.

Georgia O'Keeffe · [Lake George, New York] · [October 24, 1931]

11 P.M. Saturday Night—

I feel I've had a good night's sleep already—I was in bed at seven and slept immediately—I was really tired—then Hall's[370] dogs had a terrible fight and noise down there that waked me up—and I was hot—It is warm like a summer night—raining just a little—And I keep thinking of you—wondering have you gone to bed—and can you breathe—and it almost seems I can hear you breathing here in the other bed—so much so that I almost looked to see—

---

367. Probably Cary Ross, Alfred Barr's assistant at the Museum of Modern Art.

368. Brett wrote Stieglitz a long letter on October 18, 1931, in which she referred to Frieda Lawrence's new "mellow" behavior and Stieglitz's relationship with Dorothy (Dodo) Norman: "So you have Dodo, and she tells me she is deeply involved with a camera. I feel Dodo is the pupil of your heart, that she, more than anybody will learn deeply from you.... I feel the darkroom is going to vibrate with excitement this winter. I simply must come up and see your photographs of this summer, and Dodo's photographs and Georgia's pictures." She concluded: "Yes, you must miss Georgia, but I am glad you have Dodo, but I don't know whether or not to tell you how reflective the windows are in the Room."

369. Stieglitz referred to one of the back rooms at An American Place where he stored paintings and photographs as the "vault."

370. Hall was a neighbor.

I feel like a battlefield terribly torn and dug up—I think there were not thirty words spoken during the drive up—

I would undoubtedly have made it in six hours but I missed Route 4 to Troy and was held up a long time with a bridge into Albany from Rensselaer and traffic in Albany as I went through a congested section—Then we stopped about fifteen minutes for lunch and the seven hours included my stop at the post office and a man stopped me to ask something about you and writing you something about policing this road—And after that Margaret did our Sunday shopping at Cashion's and we rolled in here—including all that—within seven hours—Also my stopping to telephone took time—

I made the fire after telling you we were here—then walked about outside while Margaret got supper—which wasn't long—We ate and both went to bed at seven—Not much time wasted—It was so warm I drove all the way without a sweater or coat—and the air here was soft and warm like a warm summer night—the moon a bit hazy—

Maybe much of the state I am in is due to my curse coming—but I do feel this talking in this way cannot go on—neither of us can afford to be spent that way—At any rate I cannot—

It almost makes me wish not to write—wish to just be still and say nothing to anyone except what is absolutely necessary with the immediate machinery of living—It seems that the words ruin too much—

I hope you do not talk too much—to Paul[371]—it is so bad for your cold to talk—I hate to think of you struggling through two weeks of that—Guess I'll get up and spray my nose and then try to sleep again—

I had thought of Walker and for no reason except that I thought it—thought he was in town—thought of calling him—decided not to—Am glad I missed everyone—it is better so—

Good Night—

I wish you were beside me in the bed—I turned over as tho you were there when the dogs waked me up—

I kiss you very quietly—and very sadly—

Alfred Stieglitz · [New York City] · October 25, 1931 +

I'm glad I phoned. Just had no choice.—And it was good to have such a perfect connection. Zoler is pasting up prints.—I am selecting three paintings to go to a special exhibition in the new Pennsylvania Art Museum—one Marin, one O'Keeffe—one Dove. I'll send a large Marin mountain—the yellow & red Dove—& haven't quite decided which of yours.[372] I'd like to send the large *Jack-in-the-Pulpit*[373] but hate to risk it being scratched. I'll see.—

---

371. Paul Rosenfeld.

372. Stieglitz sent O'Keeffe's painting *Ranchos Church, Taos* (1929; Lynes 662) to Living Artists: Paintings of Our Time, on view at the Pennsylvania Museum of Art (later the Philadelphia Museum of Art) from November 20, 1931, to January 14, 1932, and the Phillips Memorial Gallery sent Dove's *Coal Carrier (Large)* (1930; Morgan 30.6) and Marin's *Near Great Barrington* (1925); see "Henri Marceau, 'Living Artists,'" *Bulletin of the Pennsylvania Museum* 27 (Jan. 1932), 69, 71.

373. Lynes 719.

I can imagine how tired you were last night. And how you slept.—Rosenfeld never found me more stupid. My eyes were watering—nose dripping—cough—& Lord I was tired. Zoler went out for supper.—I went to bed at 10:30. Could breathe some. And that was a lot. —When I awoke I missed you. When I went to bed I missed you.—As I lay in bed I realized how foolish I—how foolish really both of us [were]—knowing full well that under all the recriminations—in spite of all false emphasis of values—no two people could have a deeper feeling for each other than we have. No two really a deeper respect.—Respect in a holy sense. —I'll learn in time how to "behave" as I learned to be alone in the house!—I thought much about Tony & Charles & Eckstein—their significance to you. I fully understood. I saw it all impersonally. That is not always easy.—To see impersonally without the sacrifice of *feeling* that is the real impersonal seeing!—All else is self deception.—

I got up at seven.—Cold somewhat better. Ate at Savarin.—[Julien] is supposed to come sometime this A.M. Cardozo & Herbert come at noon.—

I'll see what Zoler is doing.—I wish I were in Lake George. It must be particularly beautiful. And I'd like to be with you.—Just quiet.—

A big kiss.—

608

Alfred Stieglitz · [New York City] · October 27, 1931

11 A.M. I'm at the Place. Just from Hirst's. I'll stay here till about four. And refuse to talk to anyone. Just control the situation. The doctor said that would be all right—It was a pretty mean night—but I slept some. Larynx mean—sinus some—just outraged at my own stupidities. No one responsible but myself—not a soul!—

Zoler brought me my mail to the hotel before I went to the doctor. An envelope from you—Very very dear one—containing two letters—Beautiful letters—Yes what diabolically destructive things words are—I'll understand if you don't write. The curse made you feel some things differently than you would have felt them at another time. My being ill—harassed in so many ways—made me more sensitive to relatively minor things than should be the case. I feel there can never be *words* between us again.—I know it. We both feel the same thing.—I have a very very deep feeling about all of you—no one can have a deeper.—I even feel I can once more say, "She never told a lie—she never thought one"—Yes Georgia dear one that has come back to me. Came back Sunday night as I lay in bed hardly able to breathe.—It's a very wonderful feeling to have back again.—And I know nothing can ever take it away again—nothing whatever may happen. I know what I'm saying.—

I feel like a criminal because of much I said not only last time but before—criminal in the sense I felt like a criminal when on June 15th 1918 I touched a spot & you threw yourself in a curve as a seal throws itself out of water. Yes I felt like a criminal then—I wonder often wasn't I one then? Didn't I see the wonder & misery both side by side which had come into your life through that touch!—So much chases through my head—trying to get things *straight—straight* in myself. I do know still that we need each other maybe more than ever.—

I know you are fighting the fight of your life to keep intact yourself—I know I am fighting the fight of my life to keep something intact beyond myself—which necessarily includes myself—& includes you—

As I came into the doctor's office I felt that I had not completely gone under—& as I came here—Kopman sad faced—was waiting for me. Couldn't I let him have twenty-five dollars a month for two years. Two other people had promised him such sums. He wants to go to Europe!!—My heavens—will they never understand, those poor devils. Don't they see me at all —I sick really—with all the semblance of wealth—I had to say to him: "Don't you see I'm sick —& I couldn't promise you five dollars a month—Don't you know I'd gladly give if I had it."— And he *knows nothing* has happened for Marin as yet.—

I told him I mustn't talk. He left. Felt sorry.—Levy was here before I got here. He carted off twenty-six photographs. Told Zoler he felt he had made me talk too much yesterday. He all but killed me trying to get me to give him something he had no right to ask for. I wish I had some of the qualities of these young ones—fine as they are in so many ways.

He had threatened not to have the exhibition if I didn't let him have recent work of mine.

Oh well—I guess it's all for the "best"—

The morning is clear & pretty cool. Some lovely fleecy clouds.

—I wonder has the curse come—I do hope you see a bit of light not only for yourself but for *us*.—

I want to do *all* I can here—& to work at my photography—this getting ill is too stupid —it mustn't be—

O'Neill's play seems to have been a great success last night[374]—I won't reserve the tickets for next Monday as I won't be fit to go. Besides I want to go with you when I do go.—There is no hurry.—But if you want to go next Monday with some[one] else just say so—I'll have the tickets held. I'd have no feeling about it.—

A big kiss Georgia dear one—

I hope you're feeling less sad—

What a driver you have become—I found your pocketbook.—I'm enclosing the ticket.—

Again another kiss.—And very much love.—

Alfred Stieglitz · [New York City] · October 27, 1931

4:30 P.M. At hotel. Came home early so as to save me from talking.—I enclosed the telegram I received from you yesterday. Wondered what it meant. Should have guessed! Have you gotten a cold—& from me? Terrible. Like when I brought you one to Maine. Oh Lord.—I sent you the

---

374. Hailed as a "masterpiece," Eugene O'Neill's six-hour trilogy *Mourning Becomes Electra* premiered at the Guild Theatre on October 26, 1931. One critic wrote: O'Neill "has never commanded his theme in all its variety and adumbrations with such superb strength, coolness and coherence"; see "Strange Interludes of Death in Eugene O'Neill's Masterpiece," *NYT*, Oct. 27, 1931, 22.

liquid today by first-class mail special delivery.—I hope you get it early tomorrow & it will help you.—

Well I have had a day.—And I not to talk.—Many visitors. Didn't talk. But Flint showed up & Mather—& lo & behold—Steichen! Had heard I was dying!!—Naturally I was glad to see him. And I did talk. Voice or no voice.—It was really fine.—He thought I was arranging the Levy show!![375] —Amusing. He couldn't make it out. Julien is a wonder. Young. All right.—I won't go into the Steichen hour—I came away. Left him there. He explained why he never came. Reminded me a little of your attitude.—

Well, here I am alone. And it feels good. Beck & Strand came in as I was leaving. Beck suggested coming to the hotel with me but I said it was best for me to be alone. Strand offered to be at Place tomorrow. I said I'd see. I think Hirst helped me today. I was rotten for two days. Feel more like a human again.

So I was (am) supposed to be dying. Maybe I am & don't know it.—Many inquire for you. Very many.—I told Steichen that he & his wife[376] must spend an evening with you & me when you get back.—He asked if I knew what a big influence I have been throughout the country & in what esteem I'm held. I told him that wouldn't give any of us a loaf of bread.—But it was all free from cynicism or any bitterness.—He thinks I look very much like my father. I see some resemblance. But my expression is very different. My mouth & eyes & ears all different.—

Flint was fine. Phillips hasn't paid him either as yet. I hope you & Marin will get your moneys.—Did I tell you Kennerley has hitched up with Rudge the publisher. So I was told. Back to the old love.[377] —

I'm going to lie down a bit.—

I do hope you haven't a cold.—Go to Jenks, he treated me for one & broke it up.— Argyrol & glycerine up the nostrils—don't neglect it—This is very treacherous weather.—

Much love—very much love—& a kiss—

Georgia O'Keeffe · [Lake George, New York] · [October 27, 1931]

11 P.M. In bed—and not sleepy—have been so lazy all day—

You seemed annoyed over the phone when I said you need not worry—I am really all right—The house is very comfortable and Margaret is very kind to me—so kind that it surprises me—

---

375. In a letter to O'Keeffe of October 28, 1931, Stieglitz wrote that Levy "has certainly made a mess of things—being not quite accurate in his statements—trying to make it look as if I were running his first show.—It is getting him into trouble but I told him I'd go ahead—he should stick to *facts* & not be afraid of the mistakes he has made.—So he is going ahead. He is buying three Strand prints for $100 a piece. Gave him that advice. Will come in handy to Strand." Newspaper reviews indicated that the show had been organized with Stieglitz's "cooperation"; see Edward Alden Jewell, "Synthetic View on Photography," *NYT*, Nov. 3, 1931, 35.

376. Steichen was married to Dana Desboro Glover from 1923 until her death in 1957.

377. Before he was president of the Anderson Galleries, Mitchell Kennerley was director of William Edwin Rudge publishers. After Rudge's death on June 12, 1931, he resumed that position.

—Why should you worry—There is nothing to worry about—

I feel a bit paralyzed after the talks with you—as tho something inside me has gone numb—but that will pass too—

I hope to work tomorrow—

I am really all right—

Good Night—

I touch you very gently—

Alfred Stieglitz · [New York City] · November 4, 1931

6 P.M. At the hotel.—I'm glad you are safely installed on the Hill again. And comfortably settled.—And I know I feel very happy that you came down to see me—& I feel you must feel somewhat as I do.—Everything was very fine—including the beautiful fluff—And I was delighted at your moaning & groaning & noisemaking—all very wonderful. I do enjoy it when your enjoyment is so intense.—But as I said everything was fine. And altho' you say you agree with some things I said [and] you disagree with most, I didn't feel any resentments & I hadn't any—so the disagreeing didn't "hurt"—Oh well there is no use going into all that. I feel so much better. And you feel so much better.—That's what I know. That's what's important—I'm sure you'll work with renewed zest & spirit.

—The day was a cut-up one—Marin came early. Had lunch with me. Cary Ross brought his mother.[378] Young Park (or Parker) Frieda's friend from Taos turned up. Chucked his job as dishwasher. Wondered did I know of a job. In speaking with him I suddenly said: "Are you the youngster that carried on so on the ranch."—It was he. So we talked. Quite a youngster. Huxley is in Taos now.—Maybe the Captain is gone. Frieda & Huxley have gone to Mexico. —There were many youngsters around. Male all.—Lee too came to see how my heart was. He was nice. Looked at photographs too.—About thirty to forty people at Place. All virtually in the afternoon.—I didn't get much chance to do anything. Not even write a letter.—

I haven't decided what I'll do with the evening. Didn't have much lunch. Am hungry.—

In a way it's nearly like a dream that you were here—

At the theater last night I felt something wrong with the end. Originally it seems the two darkies strangled the white girl.—

Sweetestheart, Good Night—

I hope you are happy—I'm so glad you came.

A big kiss—

If you were here I'd fluff you tonight—Maybe it's "best" you're not here—

Another kiss—

378. Eliza (Lydia) Mills Ross.

Georgia O'Keeffe · [Lake George, New York] · [November 6, 1931]

Night—And certainly all kinds of day and night gray—then sunny—then rain—very dark—then snow on the mountains to the south—and tonight the same—all black—then rain for awhile and now the stars—

—I painted—a funny painting[379]—And tonight played mostly Wagner—and much of it irritates me so—and much excites me too much—Not for me these days but I tried it anyway—

Read George Moore on "Sex in Art"[380]—and some other things—makes me laugh—I feel like saying it makes me laugh on both sides of my face—That of course means nothing except to me—and what it means to me is as indefinable as a painting—

My painting today is very amusing to me—And may go well if there is any light tomorrow—

So that is my day—I didn't go for the mail till tonight—

—Do you think I am going swimming up here that I wanted my bathing cap—I had to laugh—

I distinctly remember that I did *not* say that I disagreed with most that you said—

Good Night—and a kiss—

I've had a good day—

612

Alfred Stieglitz · [New York City] · November 10, 1931

8:30 A.M.—Am at Dr. Hirst's. Waiting. A little too early—A summer day.—Was at Place—up at 6:45.—Fair night.—Your sweet letter this A.M.—I know how you felt walking wondering would you ever leave the woods again!—A kiss—a good one—

Yesterday afternoon Churchill walked in with Frank Lloyd Wright.—Wright spic & span. Liked the Place. Asked to see the photographs. Sends his greetings to you.—Is certainly a smooth article.—Just returned from Rio de Janeiro, says it's the most beautiful city in the world—unspoiled—untouched by the U.S.A. Curses this country. I asked him if he ever saw Kennerley. He said he didn't & never wanted to because he was the biggest crook in the world—couldn't do a straight thing if he tried to—I guess Kennerley would have about the same thing to say of Wright.—A funny world.—People funny.—He lectures Friday night at the New School[381]—He liked the photographs—but I feel he sees only one thing—like so many "geniuses" do.—And others "see" nothing.—He is certainly a person!—

—Phillips finally sent check for Dove. Will make Dove happy & will refund me five hundred dollars I haven't got to blow in.—

---

379. Probably either Lynes 772, 776, 777, or 778.

380. George Moore, "Sex in Art," in *Modern Painting* (New York, 1893), 226–237.

381. In his lecture of November 13, 1931, Wright declared: "Architecturally speaking, [Radio City] is dead before it is born.... If you stop to think about [skyscrapers] you ask why they are allowed to exist. You must measure all architecture, after all, from its human benefits. Who but the landlord and the bank are benefited by skyscrapers? They are Molochs raised for commercial greatness"; see "Skyscraper Passing Says Frank L. Wright," *NYT*, Nov. 14, 1931, 14.

11 A.M. At the Place. No one in as yet. Am fussing about sorting some more. "Cleaning" up.—*What* will become of all the stuff when we must get out—or when I shuffle off—It gives me the creeps whenever I think of it & I'm forced to think of it very often. Everything looks neat & beautiful—but what does that mean?—The Place is certainly beautiful.

I stopped in at Weyhe's[382]—all sorts of stuff—but no character moving towards any positive beauty—Saw new photographic books. Things that look like something—but are really nothing but empty formulae—bags of tricks.—Awful really. Clever occasionally. But a little cleverness goes a long way.—Obvious cleverness sickens me more & more.—The Marins look more beautiful every day.—

8:15 P.M.—3003.—Terribly tired.—Maybe the warm weather again!—Anita Pollitzer at Place. —Met Dorothy True on street.—Both send their best to you.—Anita lives near Columbia.— Didn't have much chance to talk to her. And I wasn't in much of a mood all day to talk to anyone.—

This evening I went to Hicks & sent you a basket of fruit. You might as well have some decent fruit. And I like to send it to you.—Zoler is here. We ate at "your" restaurant.—

Strand in towards evening.—Had a short talk with him. He looks anything but cheerful. —I started reading *Apocalypse* by Lawrence.

I must stop.—I don't know why I'm so tired.—Feel all right otherwise.

A big kiss—

Georgia O'Keeffe · [Lake George, New York] · [November 10, 1931]

It has been warm like summer today—And the work went better—

I felt pretty good about it till Margaret got after Frankie with a strap and fixed him up well—It seems to make a painting look funny to hear him getting a good thrashing but he certainly needed it—

So that is that—

We went for a walk again right after lunch when it was warmest to the same place we went yesterday but we went into the woods from up back of Cramer's—It was so warm and still and lovely I wanted to undress and let the sun shine on me again—And the painting—it is a new one but I have had it drawn for a long time—I like it—

The one I was disturbed over day before yesterday looks good to me now too and the horse's head with a pink rose[383] over its eye makes me laugh every time I look at it—

I like the way the one went today. It is a jawbone with a black fungus[384]—Sounds diseased but it isn't—

382. A joint exhibition of sculpture by J. B. Flannagan and prints and drawings by Howard Cook was on view at the Weyhe Gallery in New York from November 9 to 28, 1931; see "The Week in New York: Recently Opened Shows," NYT, Nov. 15, 1931, X14.
383. "The one I was disturbed over" is probably either Lynes 772, 776, 777, or 778; "the horse's head with a pink rose" is Lynes 775.
384. Lynes 780.

Margaret admires it much — but she admires them all — I have to laugh.

Good Night — I'll be getting to bed — I'm glad I haven't a small boy to beat up — What a life —

A Good Night kiss to you —

Alfred Stieglitz · [New York City] · November 12, 1931

10:30 A.M. — I have just come from the dentist. — It looks like rain. — I wonder have you decided to come down today.

— I went to bed at ten last night. Remained there till seven this A.M. Tossed about a lot but rested! Came over to the Place before eight — after breakfasting at Savarin's. — Phoned you at 8:30 after the mail had come. Wanted to know how you were & to tell you not to worry about me — that I was all right. The tiredness was natural. No one can help me. — It's due to many causes — the chief one being the everlasting fight I have been putting up against blindness of the powers that be. —

Zigrosser was in yesterday. — The Whitney Museum opens officially on the 18th[385] — I was speaking about the situation — museums — Julien Levy — etc. — Everything half-baked like most of the American bread — Zigrosser thought the more museums the better — & I said the more museums the more necessary that there should be one — even a small one — that had a real standard — That I knew I could show what a museum should be like if I had the chance. Of course the more museums the more chance for "business." — Ye gods — ever the half thing — the pseudo thing. Then he wondered why I didn't make some photographs especially for reproduction!! — As fine a fellow as he is, every word he said seemed to be "wrong" — unseeing. — I just mention him as an example. And he is above the average. — Cary Ross came in too. — I always like to see him. There is something very real there underneath all. — And there were people. — Ross said many people show up at the Matisse show[386] who want to see Mrs. Rockefeller — "starving" artists, etc. — Starving art most of the "starving" artists do. — Certainly a mess everywhere. — Stay in the country as long as you can. New York is impossible. That is to work in. — Of course I want to see you — & you will have to get frames under way. — I'm eager too to see what you have been doing. —

Had a letter from Dove. Has sent me a power of attorney. I asked for one. Has many of

385. An outgrowth of the Whitney Studio Club, the Whitney Museum of American Art opened on 10 West 8th St. in New York on November 17, 1931; see "Whitney Museum to Be Opened Today," *NYT*, Nov. 17, 1931, 27.

386. The Museum of Modern Art opened its third season with the most comprehensive exhibition of Henri Matisse's art ever held in the United States. Organized by Alfred Barr, the museum's founding director, the exhibition was on view from November 3 through December 6, 1931, accompanied by the catalogue *Henri Matisse Retrospective Exhibition*, with an introduction by Alfred Barr (New York, 1931); see Edward Alden Jewell, "A Significant Pioneer," *NYT*, Nov. 8, 1931, XX12. Stieglitz saw the exhibition a few weeks later and wrote O'Keeffe: "He is certainly fiendishly able — '*knows*' about all there is to know about painting. Has charm — knows color — I'm glad I went. It is easy to see why he is such a success. — The Marins look forbidding — severe — austere — drab in a sense — Most interesting to consider two men!" (AS to GOK, Nov. 28, 1931). Stieglitz also told O'Keeffe that Marin said, "Matisse is lousy" (AS to GOK, Nov. 21, 1931).

his things nearly ready.[387] Is at framing—The Phillips money has just come in the nick of time again.—

5 P.M.—A busy day. With what—the Lord knows. A very fine thing happened tho—Weyhe & Churchill brought Holland's foremost architect[388] to see me. He leaves day after tomorrow. Came to see my photographs. Wright seems to mention them in his lectures. They are being talked about. Well this architect is the real article as man. It was a marvelous twenty to twenty-five minutes. He said as soon as [he] opened the door the Place struck him as the real article—a positive relief of simplicity & dignity & feeling of freedom to him as opposed to all he had experienced in America generally. And the photographs impressed him & what I said generally was clear & to the point.—There was no chance to show your things. He glanced at Marin. Said nothing. He came to see the photographs & me.—And was under pressure.—Too bad all these visits are so short. But it was a very fine experience for both him & me. Weyhe couldn't stay.—

As no telegram from you you decided not to come today. Will you come tomorrow? Or Saturday? I wonder. And will you let me know. Or will you just walk in again.—Tonight I shall take some Phanadorm. I must get a real sleep. Haven't taken Phanadorm in at least six weeks. I am due at Hirst's at 8:30 tomorrow—Friday.—

I must get a note off to Dove. And send him his check.—

It looks like rain. Held off all day.

Very much love & a big kiss.—You may not get this letter before I see you.—

Another kiss. I'm eager to see your paintings.—

Alfred Stieglitz · [New York City] · November 17, 1931 +

5:45 P.M. At the Place. Just back from the Whitney Museum.—Well, I was there. And I'm glad I'm here now.—What is one to say.—Bad taste everywhere.—Cheap spirit. No distinction. Cheap goods. Cheap paintings.—Mobs of people.—Mrs. Rockefeller came up to me & said: I'm Mrs. Rockefeller. I'm glad she told me. For a moment I couldn't place her. I told her I had wanted to write her but refrained. She said: Write. So I'll write.—And old Mrs. Walcott was there. Spoke to her.—Artists galore—Kroll (& Mrs.[389]), Demuth, Lawson, oh why enumerate —Your little painting hangs by itself.[390] Looks well. But is really a sketch as you said.—So many bad paintings. Awful. Demuth's *My Egypt*[391] looks well, hangs by itself.—Well I was there. No more of that. An assignation house of art of the third order.—

387. Arthur G. Dove Exhibition—1932, An American Place, New York, Mar. 14–Apr. 9, 1932.

388. Probably the Dutch architect J. J. Oud, who was one of several modern architects featured in Philip Johnson and Henry-Russell Hitchcock's seminal 1932 exhibition at the Museum of Modern Art, The International Style: Architecture Since 1922, Feb. 10–Mar. 23. Their book of the same title was also published in New York that year.

389. Geneviève-Marie-Thérèse Doméc Kroll, wife of the painter Leon.

390. Probably Lynes 612.

391. Charles Demuth, *My Egypt,* 1927, oil on composition board, Whitney Museum of American Art; see Barbara Haskell, *Charles Demuth* (New York, 1987), 129.

I wonder will there be a telegram at the hotel.—It's drizzling.—I'm feeling pretty well. A quiet day.—Everything seems as if in a hidden veil like the city in the fog today.—

I looked at some of your paintings—again.—They wear.—

Beck was in awhile.—Some visitors. I hope you'll get a chance to continue your painting. And that the curse won't upset you too much. It must be a blessing to get back to the Hill—to the peacefulness in contrast to all the unrest here. Terrible unrest. It was lucky you didn't stay over for the opening. It wasn't worth it.—I was there about thirty to forty minutes. Probably not more than thirty.—I don't know.—

I'll go home now & rest before supper.—

I'm sorry Margaret's coming late upset the quiet of the morning. But I'm glad you were here—I wish I hadn't gotten sick—Don't fret about me. I must keep well.

Much much love—& a kiss—

Good Night—

It does seem funny to be writing.—

Alfred Stieglitz · [New York City] · November 18, 1931

4:35 P.M. Hello.—A kiss.—It has been a dull day. Listless. Like the weather. Heavy.—Last night your dear telegram came as we were going to supper.—Yes dear. Very dear.—The night was fair though restless. The heart is pretty well behaved—I haven't taken the Adalin as yet so you see that's proof it's pretty good. I'm going very slowly.—Was up pretty early. At dentist by 8:30.—Then came here. A few people. Very few. Demuth about for quite some time. Mrs. Norman photographed him.[392] He wanted some photographs for publicity. He told her. So she volunteered.—Mrs. Schaefer's daughter was here over two hours beseeching me to let her have an O'Keeffe Show for the Harvard Contemporary Art Society.[393] What two hours!—A nice girl. Has charge of the exhibitions. "You could help so many young people"—I talked for several hours—& when Mrs. Norman came I told her to talk for the young generation to the young woman.—It was an extraordinary séance. You would have enjoyed it. It's the first time I ever heard the case put clearly & fully—the whole business. Now don't laugh—my "feelings" color nothing any more than they color my critical sense about Marin, or you, or Dove, or anyone else. It was important for me what I heard. Important for the future. The young woman was lovely but had no idea but "doing good"—"helping"—to everyone—everyone—but the artist. Gosh! It's maddening.

—I have written to Mrs. Rockefeller. A very informal letter. A nice one—two pages.— I wonder will she come—The more I think of the Whitney business the worse it becomes.—Barr —Flint dropped in & asked for you.—Sends his bestest—I told him you had done some

---

392. *Charles Demuth*, in Dorothy Norman, *Intimate Visions: The Photographs of Dorothy Norman* (San Francisco, 1993), 78–79.

393. Although Stieglitz did not lend any works by O'Keeffe to the Harvard Society for Contemporary Art, he had loaned several of his photographs to the organization in 1930; see Greenough, p. 968.

knockouts!!—Am sending McBride the Marin etching he wanted—It was Glassgold, assistant editor of *Creative Art,* I think you talked to. The one who slaughtered your pictures. Another *Creative Arter* was here yesterday & I asked him.—

—There is a trace of blue in the evening sky. No real rain. Weather warm. Unseasonable. —I hope the Hill has cleared up & that all is fine with you.—

I'm looking forward to your letter—

I want to get at printing. Print those nudes.[394] If all continues well I may begin tomorrow. I have to go slowly. At nine A.M. I have Hirst—another washing out.

The man is ready to wash up the floor. I don't want to sit around while that's going on—

Much much love & a very big kiss—

You're sweet—really—

Georgia O'Keeffe · [Lake George, New York] · [November 23, 1931]

A warm night and another warm morning—like summer—

I have never seen a more beautiful night than last night—a breathless kind of stillness —the mountains a pale gray blue in very white moonlight—the birches shining white—

I walked down to the Lake—almost went out on it—it was so still and warm—but I had no light—Stood a long time looking at the perfect reflection of the mountain—

—All the day yesterday was as perfect—I walked about up in our woods—to all the places I like—in the morning—Then painted—I think it pretty good this morning—worked on it long after dark—and it didn't seem to be much last night—

—I had a dream—waked from it in a perfect rage—broad daylight—just before the sun came—never had such a funny dream experience—

Well it is another day—

Worden was up about the water yesterday and talked a long time—He is quite a boy— Will leave it on awhile yet—

Alfred Stieglitz · [New York City] · November 23, 1931

4:50 P.M. Hello.—Alone. Quite an afternoon.—Bragdon, Demuth, Tofel & his wife, Julien & his wife[395]—& other people. Julien asked me to show his wife some photographs. I did. All looked. She had never seen but two or three. When I showed your hands & skull[396]—very dark print—Bragdon became very excited. Felt he never believed photography could ever attain that plane. Saw a relationship between that photograph & the highest Hindu art—etc., etc.—

---

394. Greenough 1438–1444. A few days later, Stieglitz reported to O'Keeffe that his new photographs of her, especially the nudes, were "quite extraordinary in a way. Hitches up with my old work" (AS to GOK, Nov. 21, 1931).

395. Pearl Tofel, the wife of Jennings Tofel; Joella Levy, the wife of Julien Levy.

396. Greenough 1427.

I listened—Julien quite excited about the whole lot. She said to me you are really a devil when she saw the print Bragdon liked so much. Well it was a memorable few hours. Tofel & his wife had left before the photographs were shown. I had talked about the art situation for an hour or so. All listened intently.—Including Demuth. You would have enjoyed the séance & I thought of you & felt it was better you were working. That painting of yours still haunts me. It's great.—

I'll go to the hotel soon to rest awhile before Kallen comes.[397]

I'm a bit tired. The session took something out of me. But I'm ready. I hope your day was a good one.

A big kiss—

Georgia O'Keeffe · [Lake George, New York] · [November 25, 1931]

9:45—Night—

You are such a silly one—saying your letters give me nothing—What am I to say—there is nothing to say—except that you are silly—

I was so sorry to hear about your tooth this morning—I hope it is better—that you will not have to have it out—

If my letters are queer—Well—maybe I am queer—

My painting tonight makes me laugh again—it is a new one—another horse's head[398] —to me it seems that if I can finish as well as I have started it may be the most beautiful of the fall—but it is another one that makes me laugh—and I really don't know why I laugh because it really isn't funny—only it seems funny to me—Margaret doesn't think it funny at all—So there you are—I have been at it all day—was late starting—almost noon—but worked quite awhile after dark—

Was out with my rope to walk at dusk[399]—it is colder—the mountains dark—

I am stewing much within myself these days but it isn't anything to talk about—just arranging things within myself—There is nothing to say about it because I clear up so gradually even for myself—and what I would say one day I would be very apt to contradict shortly after —so it is best to keep still—

I plan to go down next Tuesday or Wednesday—probably Tuesday—Think I will take the afternoon train from Fort Edward then I will not have to change—Haven't started to pack yet but it will not take me long—

Good Night Little One—I hope your tooth isn't keeping you awake and wearing you out too much—

A quiet little Good Night kiss to you—

---

397. Earlier that same day, Stieglitz told O'Keeffe that Kallen was coming to talk about the influence of photography on painting. However, he felt they should "start with the effect photography had on the world's vision" (AS to GOK, November 23, 1931).
398. Either Lynes 776 or 777.
399. O'Keeffe had been jumping rope for exercise.

10:15 A.M.—I have just read your two letters. Came in from the dentist's—He had some more filling to do.—As for the "bad" tooth it is better. He says to leave it alone for awhile. The trouble may be from the anthrem—As long as I am not over-tortured with pain as I was the day before yesterday I accept as I accept so much these days. Have no choice but to accept.

Your letters are sweet & warm—I knew you'd go on the Lake. I can see you.—See the moon. See the birches. See the shore. See you in the boat. See you walking to the Lake. Walking back. Alone. Feel all you feel. Every bit of it.

Yes—It's a queer world.—Queer & queerer.—And you skip the rope—Walk to the back road.—I see that all too. It's as if I had been there myself. Invisible. You alone.—Not alone. And you have painted maybe the best painting of this fall. Wonderful.

—My letters give you something. I really thought they were too dead to give anyone truly alive anything. And you are truly alive. Very alive.—

—A kiss.—Two kisses.

Well I was at Lee's last night for supper.—The four Davidsons, Lee & Lizzie all dolled up. I naturally not—We went to the concert.[400] A box—second tier.—Very good seats. Rubin (Dr.) in box next to us. Came to speak to me & Lee. I like him.—

The concert was a very fine one. A Mozart symphony he wrote at eighteen—a Bach for violin—a new violinist—Busch—very masculine—very musical—no tricks of the virtuoso —no sentimental saccharine sob taint—A César Franck—Then Beethoven's violin concerto— we have Kreisler's record—& finally *The Flying Dutchman Overture*. The Beethoven was very very beautiful. Busch genuine. But my God Beethoven!!—All of it a rare treat. I think you would have enjoyed it greatly. *The Flying Dutchman* was played with great gusto—but I prefer Munch's rendering as I prefer Munch's rendering of Beethoven.—

The night was very fair. I ate breakfast at the Shelton.—Felt like being nearer the toilet as I was going to the dentist's. Besides the weather was dark & rainy—a few flakes of snow.— I walked to the dentist's & walked from there to the Place.—

Later. A very interesting young painter was here quite awhile. Comes from Texas. Had quite a talk. Mentioned you. Said you were a combination of the primitive & greatest sophistication!! I asked him whether not all women were more or less such a combination.—It was really quite a talk.

—It's snowing now.—Snow that melts as it falls to the pavement.—

You'll be here on Tuesday night you think.—Or not later than Wednesday.

Fine.—Yes, there isn't so much time to prepare[401]—Holidays, etc.—Mrs. Reinhardt wants to see you as soon as you come.—Sibyl Brown called you up on Wednesday.

---

400. Stieglitz attended a "superlative performance" by the Philharmonic Orchestra under the direction of Arturo Toscanini and the debut of the noted violinist Adolph Busch; see "Toscanini Greeted with Great Ovation," *NYT*, Nov. 27, 1931, 30.

401. O'Keeffe's exhibition *Georgia O'Keeffe: Thirty-three New Paintings (New Mexico)* opened on December 27, 1931.

Well, I'd better see if there isn't something for me to do.—There's more than aplenty. *What* is the question.

Much love & a kiss—

Georgia O'Keeffe · [Lake George, New York] · [November 27, 1931]

It is night again—Friday night—

It has been snowing all day—just lightly—but to me very exciting—makes a beautiful light—I working all day on one of the paintings I brought back from town—

At dusk I drove to the garage and got some alcohol in my radiator so it will not freeze —The snow seems to do things to people—they take on a different kind of friendliness—The mechanic that takes the squeaks out of my Ford and greases it had lent me a pair of long-horned Texas steer horns—he didn't want to sell them—I took them back to him today—He is very amusing—always telling me about someone getting killed—

Then I went hunting for the boat man—and when I found him he seemed so nice— he is coming in the morning to see about the boat—

The snow on everything—not very thick but enough to be very pretty—

Then Margaret and I got off and walked—We went almost to the birches—the snow making the roads and paths very easy to follow—very white in the night—It was beautiful—

I am such a fool liking such things—It makes me feel so terribly alive and free—the more I walk—the more I want to walk—and she trots along behind—

The moon came up as we were returning—and over it the longest black cloud I ever saw —from far north to far south along the eastern sky—

It has been an exciting day to me—I feel almost like a simpleton that I can have such an exciting day out of so little—

It makes me not want to go to town—I hate to think of giving up my sateen shirts and corduroys and boots and the old brown coat for town clothes—and the outdoors is really so fine now—and the indoors works so well—

But I suppose I'll be going—

O'KEEFFE RETURNED to New York on November 29, 1931, to install her December exhibition at An American Place. Including paintings of crosses and landscapes from New Mexico and bones she had made at Lake George earlier in the fall, the show sparked much discussion. While some critics, such as Henry McBride, saw the crosses as "elegant shapes charged with solemn mystery," others commented on their connection to surrealism, even cabalism and death.[402] O'Keeffe defended her choice of subject matter by explaining that she was "trying to define my

---

402. Henry McBride, "Skeletons on the Plains," *New York Sun*, Jan. 2, 1932, 8. See Edward Alden Jewell, "Georgia O'Keeffe Shows Work," *NYT*, Dec. 29, 1931, 28.

Alfred Stieglitz, *Lake George from the Hill,* 1932. Gelatin silver print, 7⅜ x 9⅜ in. (18.7 x 23.8 cm). Alfred Stieglitz/Georgia O'Keeffe Archive, Yale Collection of American Literature, Beinecke Rare Book and Manuscript Library. Greenough 1471.

feeling about that country," but she also confided to Russell Vernon Hunter that the critics' comments made her "feel like crawling into a dark—dark hole and staying there a long long time."[403]

Other events that spring and summer also unsettled her. On February 15, 1932, Stieglitz opened an exhibition of 127 of his photographs at An American Place, his first one-person show in eight years. Presenting an overview of his work from the last forty years, the exhibition also included several of his bold, new studies of New York skyscrapers taken from his windows at An American Place and the Shelton Hotel, as well as portraits of O'Keeffe made between 1918 and 1923. Yet the two most recent portraits were of Norman, a public proclamation that the younger woman was his newest muse, confident, and partner. Although O'Keeffe described the exhibition as "beautiful," she also admitted it made her "very sad."[404] Further solidifying her position, Norman spoke to reporters later that spring to announce the formation of the

403. GOK to Russell Vernon Hunter, Dec. 1931–Jan. 1932.
404. GOK to Dorothy Brett, mid-Feb. 1932.

Dorothy Norman Rent Fund to secure the money necessary to renew the lease on An American Place.[405]

As if to suggest the fragility of all relationships, Stieglitz presented a joint exhibition at An American Place that spring of photographs and paintings by Paul and Beck Strand, whose own marriage was also shaky. Despite the younger photographer's steadfast devotion to him for more than fifteen years, Stieglitz had given Strand few exhibitions at any of his galleries and more recently had frequently criticized his work for being too imitative, overly concerned with technique, and devoid of passion and "true seeing." Also, despite the Strands' help in founding and funding An American Place, Norman had made her own dislike of them patently clear.[406] As Paul bitterly recalled many years later, Stieglitz offered the couple the 1932 exhibition yet did nothing to support it—he did not publish a catalogue, nor did he even help hang the show; that job was left to Paul and Beck.[407] When the exhibition closed, Paul gave his key to the gallery to Stieglitz without comment and severed his relationship with his mentor.

As the once close friendships fractured that spring, O'Keeffe asserted even greater independence and struck out on her own. Satisfying a long-standing wish to work on a large scale, she accepted an invitation extended to many American painters and photographers to submit proposals for a mural competition in March 1932. The winning entries, including O'Keeffe's three-panel composition *Manhattan*,[408] were exhibited later that May at the Museum of Modern Art.[409] By June, O'Keeffe was awarded—and accepted—a commission to create a mural for the women's powder room in Rockefeller Center's Radio City Music Hall.[410] With the art dealers Edith Halpert and Mary Reinhardt[411]—not Stieglitz—negotiating the terms of the contract later that summer, she accepted fifteen hundred dollars for her work, substantially less than Stieglitz had commanded for her major paintings and less than male artists, such as Diego Rivera, were to receive for their murals at Rockefeller Center.[412] Stieglitz spent much of the summer trying to persuade O'Keeffe not to proceed with the project, enlisting his friends Louis Kalonyme and others to lobby on his behalf. Acknowledging that "no one in my world wants me to do it," O'Keeffe recognized that her painting was "maybe a bit tender for what it has to stand in that kind of world," but she nevertheless remained resolute.[413]

405. "Stieglitz, at 70, Facing Loss of His Art Gallery," *New York Herald Tribune*, Apr. 29, 1932.

406. See, e.g., AS to Seligmann, Oct. 8, 1928; and AS to Norman, July 23, Aug. 4 and 7, 1929, and July 30, 1932.

407. Paul Strand, as quoted in Drohojowska-Philp, *Full Bloom*, 338.

408. Only one panel is extant, Lynes 801; for reproductions of the other two, see O'Keeffe, *Study for Three-Part Composition, Manhattan*, Peter A. Juley & Son Collection, Smithsonian American Art Museum, negative J0081053.

409. See "Edward Alden Jewell, "The Museum of Modern Art Gives Private Showing Today of Murals by American Painters," *NYT*, May 3, 1932, 19.

410. When Donald Deskey was put in charge of interior decoration at the International Music Hall (Radio City Music Hall) at Rockefeller Center on June 26, 1932, he announced that O'Keeffe was one of several prominent American painters who would create murals for the building; see "Rockefeller City Awards Design Job," *NYT*, June 27, 1932, 32, and Daniel Okrent, *Great Fortune: The Epic of Rockefeller Center* (New York, 2003), 223.

411. Okrent, *Great Fortune*, 225, notes that Halpert helped Deskey negotiate contracts with artists for the Rockefeller Center project. However, O'Keeffe, in a letter to Stieglitz dated July 19, 1932, suggests Reinhardt may also have assisted her. Stieglitz told Norman on December 19, 1932, that Reinhardt "was responsible in getting S.W. into Radio City."

412. In a letter of May 10, 1933, Stieglitz related to O'Keeffe that Rivera was to receive twenty thousand dollars for his mural at Rockefeller Center.

413. GOK to Brett, Sept. 1932, Harry Ransom Humanities Research Center, The University of Texas at Austin.

On May 16, when O'Keeffe, accompanied by her friend Marjorie Content and Stieglitz's niece Georgia Engelhard, went to Lake George to open the house, she was uncertain whether she would go to New Mexico later that summer. She briefly went to New York on May 24 and returned to Lake George the following day, bringing Cary Ross with her, and they in turn were visited by Elizabeth McCausland and Ida and Claudia O'Keeffe. Stieglitz remained in New York, supervising the last show of the season at An American Place, a group exhibition of Demuth, Dove, Hartley, Marin, and O'Keeffe. As he was unsure if the lease on the gallery would be extended, he also spent a considerable amount of time reviewing all his photographs stored there, eliminating those he felt were not "complete."[414]

Still hesitant about the wisdom of her decision, O'Keeffe called Stieglitz on June 1 to say that she would drive to New Mexico with Charles Collier and leave on June 4. On June 2 Stieglitz went to Lake George to say goodbye to her, but while he was there, she once again wavered. He returned to New York on June 3 to allow O'Keeffe to reach a decision on her own.

Alfred Stieglitz · [New York City] · June 1, 1932 +

1 P.M.—You phoned.—An hour ago I held the phone to phone you.—I set it down again as I felt it might "interfere" with the decision you were making. It was a "queer" feeling.—I had not known were you going or were you not. Everyone else laughed & was ever sure you would go. Henwar yesterday said: Of course she's going.—Ross too. Don't imagine that there has been any talk about you. But many asked me were you going. And when I said I didn't know I meant it. —Knowing you as I have known you I felt you had to go—yet I didn't know would you. You have had the desire to drive across the continent—your desires you usually (maybe always) satisfy. There was Charles—the opportunity.—Lake George means little to you.—I know what I am to you. And my hope is that you know what you are to me. I often wonder the latter—The stars are set & don't much vary. We don't vary more than they—I shall take the train for Lake George tomorrow, Thursday, evening. And a little after midnight I'll be in Lake George—I'll return here Friday evening or may leave Lake George with the early morning train on Saturday. I am really at work here getting much in order. I must do it myself. No one can help me. It's my job.—I tore up a lot of meaningless *Equivalents* this morning—prints too dark—Also a few other things. All very quietly.—

—The Dove *Creative Art*[415] is out. I was ready to mail it to you but I'll bring it myself—

Undoubtedly your head & hands are full with preparations for the trip. And remember I don't want to interfere in coming.—I want to see you before you go. That's why I am coming.— Now I'll return to my boxes. Ederheimer was in for a few minutes—he left just as you phoned.

You have a great trip ahead of you. I hope all will go well—the drive—the camping— & all else. Painting this year is really secondary.—

Another kiss & with much love—*au revoir*—

I'll see you tomorrow night. It'll be good to see you & to get a glimpse of the Hill—

414. AS to GOK, May 18, 1932.
415. Paul Rosenfeld, "The World of Arthur G. Dove," *Creative Art* 10 (June 1932), 427–430 and frontispiece.

Georgia O'Keeffe · [Lake George, New York] · [June 1, 1932]

There seems to be no letter to write this morning—

     Charles came last night and I have just about decided to go—

     I will talk with you sometime today—

     It is a lovely morning—

     Charles brought his best girl[416]—she and Georgie are off for a walk—He is still in bed —They drove over from Boston yesterday—We had breakfast in the kitchen—

     I'll talk with you later—

2:30 P.M.—I did not mail the other part of this this morning because I thought I might change my mind—anything that I do seems wrong—It is very difficult to go through the motions of starting—and get myself off when I have really no desire to go—

     I go because I think I'll be able to work—Maybe I am wrong—

     It disturbs me so much that I seem to have nothing to say—

Alfred Stieglitz · [New York City] · June 2, 1932

8 A.M.—It has started to rain.—It's a queer feeling to sit down & write you for you will read this after I have seen you & left again—after the good-bye—I was here till after midnight at work—much accomplished. Zoler helped some. Boxes are piled up & labeled.—It is not exactly the "order" I would like to have—but it is nearer to it than ever before—So that's something. I went to Elizabeth's for supper—got there at 6:40 & left at 7:40, she going out & I glad to get back to work. I didn't want to have her leave for Monsey without having seen her apartment. It's a lovely one. Tiny. Airy. Quiet. The children lovely.—A sense of some balance.—

     —Here is the mail.—Well, last night it was after midnight when we left here. Seligmann was in the darkroom at work. I went to Grand Central to get railroad tickets.—And then walked some. I was dead tired but my head was in a mad state so I walked. Finally near two got to bed. At three I took a hot bath—I thought that might bring some sleep even tho a hot bath usually doesn't.—What a day again. And your voice over the phone.—So many voices these days.—

     This morning a simple letter from Eva about Riki.[417]—Voices too.—Life & Death— more death oftentimes than life—It's queer.—Yet all so damnably simple in spite of its complexity.—

     —I'll read—I have read your two little letters. Yes, I understand.—I know how you feel —It's all difficult—every move becomes more so. Every pleasure more adulterated no matter how keen the pleasure may seem.—Well, you'll be soon on the road. Maybe you'll not read this before you start.—

---

416. Most likely Mary, who would later become his wife.

417. On May 27, 1932, Stieglitz had written O'Keeffe that his friend the painter Riki Hallgarten, whom he "liked immensely," had shot himself in Germany. Eva Herrmann, Hallgarten's companion and the daughter of Stieglitz's friend Frank, wrote Stieglitz from Berlin that Hallgarten had been depressed for three years (Herrmann to AS, May 19, 1932).

As I look at it all dispassionately—there was no escape for you nor for me. You have to do this. That was determined long before you decided. When others said of course she'll go, they seem to have said rightly but yet what made them say so is all wrong. That's the paradox in life. That's what few realize. That's why I dared not come to a conclusion—had no human right to say yea or nay.—

—I want you to enjoy your summer to the fullest.—That's my deepest wish.—Above all others. Of course that includes the hope you remain well.—As for painting don't worry about it. It will perhaps come. Perhaps it won't.—Don't think you owe it to me to come home with anything more than health & a fairly healthy state of mind.—If you paint I know it will be good.—

—I am much in the same state as you are, that's why I know so well how you feel.—The Place here continues to live—I mean the work on the walls.—It's a beautiful room.

Did I tell you that I wrote to Mrs. Fischel a few days ago.—I wonder in what cities you will stop over.—And whom you'll see.—

—On top of a box here there is a print—the photograph I first made of you fifteen years ago—I believe on June 2.[418]—Or it may have been the 3rd. I photographed twice. What I wanted to get is only partly there—Maybe I could coax a better print out of the negative today.—

—Going through all those prints has done something to me which is rather paralyzing—as the age itself seems to lead to paralysis.—And I hate that state—for I feel it is in oneself—& is a form of unnecessary weakness.—

—Georgia dearest do take care of yourself. Don't be rash.—And yet get all out of the opportunity you can.—I know I'm difficult but much is due to the extraordinarily difficult times we are all living in.

Goodbye. I have no idea where my next letter is to reach you—or when—

I have promised not to worry—I'll do my best to keep my word—And I'll take care of myself as best I know how.—And when you return we'll see how we shall arrange to live next winter.[419] —

Goodbye—A very very fond kiss.—

Don't misunderstand what I said about painting. You have no idea what you & your paintings mean to me—and to so many others in a different way than to me.—But I mean you mustn't think I expect.—Or that you must because of me.

Once more Goodbye—

Once more—Be careful of yourself and don't overdo things—

Goodbye—

—Another kiss—

Life is stronger than we are—together or singly.—It's "queer"—

---

418. Greenough 457–460.

419. As Stieglitz's inheritance shrank and O'Keeffe's sales dwindled in the fall of 1931 and throughout 1932, the couple considered renting less expensive rooms than those at the Shelton Hotel.

Georgia O'Keeffe · [Lake George, New York] · [June 2, 1932]

I wonder if you will be coming tonight—

    I hope so—I want to see you—I was up walking about early this morning—everything looking so very lovely—

    I so torn to bits—

    The pasture so lovely—the Lake so still—I walked all around—

    and kiss you gently with the morning.

Alfred Stieglitz · [Albany, New York, en route to New York City] · June 3, 1932

Georgia dear—

    It was all very perfect. I think you feel it was too. Not a harsh word—not a moment's tension!—A great feeling of a closer understanding—Yes it was all very perfect—everything. —And it is wonderful how well kept everything looks—Everything you have done beautifully —as you can do it when you set your mind on anything. I know all the work it represents— work & thought—And the hour near the Lake, the talk—very wonderful—

    It took all my strength not to jump off the moving train as it was leaving—& I was to lose sight of you in a moment or two. I know what you felt—I hope you know what I felt.—

    —You asked if you remained would any time be for you.—Silly. All you want.—

    But you must not let your decision depend on that—Something "deepest" in you must decide—And of course that is not always easy for one to know what is deepest—Yes, what is called love is usually self-love—but I wonder is there not occasionally love as we like to believe it can exist.—

    —It's a queer feeling to be sitting here—the train has started—moving towards New York—You asked me to stay another day. I felt it best for you to be alone & come [to] a decision after the perfection of our complete hours together—complete & rarely beautiful—even tho a bit sad—but we are living in none too happy times.—

    I'd like to peep in now & see what you are doing—I'd like to know what you are thinking—working out in your mind—I'm glad in a way that you are not leaving tomorrow morning—I decided to come away this afternoon & not wait till morning as I could not bear the idea of possibly being on the Hill & see you drive off—Two years ago I came to the Hill & took you to Albany—& saw the train go out from Albany. Even that I could not have stood this year.—We are both queer ones—difficult ones—

    It is pouring pitchforks—the windows are being pelted with rain—I like the sound— The car is empty—people dining I suppose—I'll eat later—I'm not a bit hungry—& have a bit of a headache—eyes probably.—Maybe a little too much controlled excitement!!—

    Georgia—what was it you said at the station as I kissed you goodbye—I heard—

    I'm glad that you are to be in company—I must still assume you are going—even tho you were vacillating today.—I understood.—I repeat I dare not say either Go or Stay. I dare not. —I dare not—Nor dare I wish one or the other.—Can you grasp that in me?—

Good Night for the present—A big kiss—

It was very important for both of us that I came—Another kiss—

I hope you'll have a very Good Night—

Georgia O'Keeffe · Lake George, New York · June 4, 1932

Telegram, 1:28 P.M.

Finally decided definitely not to go.

Love Georgia.

Georgia O'Keeffe · [Lake George, New York] · [June 4, 1932]

I had decided while you were here—And as I went over it I kept feeling the same about it—
so I finally telegraphed you—

That is all there is to say—I am satisfied with my decision—

I walked about over the place this morning—up in the woods—all around—it was a
muggy morning—Must go to Glens Falls for some little things—Am on the way—

A kiss to you—It is all right—I am sorry to have been uncertain so long—

Your letters this morning were sweet—

Thank you—

Alfred Stieglitz · [New York City] · June 4, 1932

8:15 A.M. Here I am at the Place.—Your sweet note asking whether I'm coming—Oh yes, I know
how you felt—how you feel. My own experience gives me that.—Here I am.—I can hardly
believe that I was at the Lake—*that we were really together.* All very wonderful—I am sorely
tempted to phone you to find out how you are. But I'll wait till tonight. I want you to have had
my letters written from the train.—

A good morning kiss. It's hot & sultry. The Place is in order. Looks very neat—& busy
—boxes piled up—labeled—I wonder how your night. How everything.—To my surprise Zoler
met me at the station!! He carried my bag. Walked to the hotel.—Mailed two letters to you at
the post office. Ate some ice-cream. My throat was dry. And I so full—but "quiet."—He says a
man from California was in & was desirous of possibly acquiring an O'Keeffe. Is to come today
or Monday. I wonder. Few people are desirous enough to come again. And Mittler wants to see
me. About the painting I guess. A few others too. Probably nothing of consequence.—It was
nearly one before I went to bed. I was so tired that I was wide awake—I felt I could have walked
forever.—And I was wondering about you & the Hill—all of it—The wonder of life—the
maltreatment people—most people—accord nature wherever they seem to touch it—the hurts
those who love create for each other—Yet the wonder of all—& everything.—

—It's hot. I must get my coat & vest off. I'm glad you put the latter in shape for me. Many thanks. You mustn't believe that I ever take anything for granted even tho I seem not to notice—not to say anything.

A big morning kiss—

I forgot my watch. It must be about 10:30 or thereabouts. I have been replacing prints of you in the large boxes. It's hot work.—But I want some order—certain things together before I get through for the "season." There is quite some work I can do on some prints—here & there spotting—"scraping" too—to release fully what's there. One print which was fine I made much finer in a few minutes—Really is beautiful now—a portrait of you that has the feeling of a shell![420]—It's really a shame we ever had to leave that first studio—It was perfect for me in every way.—

6 P.M.—I have been kept on the jump all day. Many people. Many interested greatly in your work.—I had to harangue quite awhile for a young couple—a fine woman teacher & her husband, a literary man.—Fine. Very fine.—The cripple was [here] & remained several hours *devouring* your things. Also listened. Citkowitz came. Also Marin.—

Above all your telegram came! & I wired you. That tells you.—I couldn't say to you: Go. I couldn't say: Stay. Now I say I feel you have done what I would have done had I been you—which means I feel the "right" thing has happened—I hate to say "right" for it has nothing to do with right or wrong—You will get a chance to work—you & I will be on the Lake often—& together in many ways[421]—I do pray for health for both of us—that I can walk at least up & down the Hill like yesterday morning—If you had decided to go I would have known you had to go & I would have been quiet.—

—I suppose you will have the Shanty put into shape—And I'll have the canvasses shipped to you as you asked me to.—Marin is sitting here.—

Good Night. A kiss. I suppose you feel much relieved that you have finally come to a decision. I know I am for your own sake—which means for my own too—

—You said something about the ocean—going there during the summer sometime. Remember I am in accord with anything you may [feel the need] for doing.—And I can also say I hope to walk up Prospect with you before the season is over!!—

Good Night—

Much much love—And a big kiss.—

628

420. Probably Greenough 521 or 522.

421. In a letter written the next day, Stieglitz confessed, "Yes I'm glad you are staying but in a way it frightens me. Do you know that? It frightens me because I want you to have what I *know* you need most & I wonder am I equal to creating conditions which will bring about what I want for you & what I *know* you need above all things" (AS to GOK, June 5, 1932). A month later, when explaining why he could not visit her in Woods Hole, Stieglitz told Norman he knew O'Keeffe remained in the east because of him (AS to Norman, July 5, 1932).

Alfred Stieglitz · [New York City] · June 7, 1932

9:45 A.M.—Good Morning—Miss O'Keeffe. A kiss Miss O'Keeffe.

—Another day—Fortunately a clear cool one—I have just been at Rosen for a change.
"Trifles."—If an itch continuous be a "trifle."—It is for all others but the one. Continuous—
Of course one becomes accustomed to everything if one lives long enough. If civilization contin-
ues on its present line the itch may become one of its necessities. Maybe its cardinal center.
A scratchy world being taught by its scratchy teacher that one mustn't scratch but to itch with
a smile & thank God the universal for the blessing.—Amen.—

—And Rockefeller, Jr. comes out for reconsideration of Prohibition, reluctantly he
says.[422] —Ye gods. He, Jr. & Sr., were two of the chief guys in furnishing the cash for Hoover's
Noble Experiment.[423] Wilson saw correctly.[424] —And I said it would take fifteen years for the
country to wake up.—It happened to the racetracks. It didn't take a very wise man to see that
Prohibition was a fallacy—an idiot's dream!—Blessed be fallacies & idiots & dreamers—& all
the other wise men & wise women too—

—Lord I was tired last night when I left here. Felt like lying down on the hard floor here
& never getting up again. Walked to Büchler instead, Zoler & I. And then walked to the Shelton
—Getting there I lay on the sofa & fell half asleep. At 10:10 Zoler left—I wanted to bathe &
shampoo—Went to the tub to turn on the water & just couldn't—so tired. Took Phanadorm
—opened all windows—lay under sheet—no woolens of any kind near me—& fell asleep—
slept five hours—& then dozed four more!! A sort of deadened half sleep.—I never want to be
that kind of tired again.

—No letter from you this morning.

Zoler has to go to his family's cemetery today to fix up flowers, etc.—Had to buy a
whole gardener's outfit. His sister's wish!!—I guess madness & imbecility are rapidly overcoming
the world—at least the American section of it.

I never exclude myself from general "charges" of that sort.—

Now I'll get at more boxes & tinker some more in the vault—& continue with the stuff
to go to the Lake. It all clears up but it's mighty slow work—for it is virtually a lone job this
year.—

A kiss—

---

422. On June 6, 1932, John D. Rockefeller, Jr., pronounced Prohibition "a failure." Declaring that its "evils have more than
outweighed its benefits," he urged both the Democratic and Republican parties to work for its repeal; see "Backs Butler Repeal
Plan," *NYT,* June 7, 1932, 1.

423. In a statement issued during the 1928 presidential elections, Herbert Hoover called Prohibition "a great social and economic
experiment, noble in motive and far reaching in purpose." However, the catchphrase "Noble Experiment" stuck in the public's
mind; see Don W. Whisenhunt, *President Herbert Hoover* (New York, 2004), 104.

424. In April 1919, President Woodrow Wilson had argued for a lifting of the wartime ban on the sale of beer and wine, arguing
that demobilization had sufficiently progressed to allow their manufacture and sale without detriment. Bishop James Cannon
and the Anti-Saloon League prevailed, however, and in 1919 Congress enacted the Volstead Act, prohibiting the sale of all liquor,
including wine and beer, over Wilson's veto; see Robert Arthur Hohner, *Prohibition and Politics: The Life of Bishop James Cannon, Jr.* (Columbia, S.C., 1999), 120–125.

11 A.M. Your large mural[425] has just arrived. It's standing on the floor temporarily covering your *Cow Skull*[426] picture. The little sketch they still have hanging in the museum. I had a talk with a Mr. [Blackburn] of that institution. He called me up in regard to letting your mural travel over the country. I had written the museum but there seems to be no coordination between the "departments." He knew nothing of a letter. I told him what I thought of the whole business. He told me your little sketch was hanging in their present show.[427] I told him how absolutely stupid & misleading that was.—Oh heaven protect me from all the imbecilities of the American art world. I told him the good will of a pseudo-surgeon was termed quackery when seen straight! Good will had nothing to do with art—or science—etc.—etc.—

Well your mural here looks very different from over there in Sacred Hall.—It's fine in spite of everything—

I'm at boxes—Shall go back to them—Ettie phoned. She's coming to say Goodbye. And a painter from Philadelphia wants to see me—I don't want to see him but he's coming!—

4:15 P.M. Alone. Ettie came. Duncan came. Ringel, the young German who edited the book *America,*[428] here over three and a half hours—He wanting to write about me. But not knowing how. Feeling it should be done. Duncan talking to him. Dorothy N. in for about half an hour talking to him too. He goes to Cape Cod for part of the summer—Will visit her about a book about me! Of course neither can succeed. An impossible task—much more difficult to write about than Noguchi.[429] The latter was hitched up with a more "positive" thing—It's all so funny because I realize how "well" I have done so much.—

—My watch had stopped.—I inquired the time. It was four. I forgot about lunch. It's too late to eat now. I'll go to supper early.

Ettie was nice. Didn't stay long. Duncan always enjoyable.—If Marin came in I'd play billiards with him tonight. It's cool.—But he won't come in.—The wind is north—It's probably cold at the Lake—

I'll go back to my boxes. Was in the middle of them when Ettie came.—

Goodbye for today.—

I may write later—Another kiss—A big one—

ON JUNE 8, O'Keeffe and Georgia Engelhard drove from Lake George into Canada to the Laurentian Hills, northwest of Montreal. In emulation of her much beloved friend O'Keeffe, Engelhard had started to paint once again, and the two were looking for subjects. After driving toward Québec City, they returned to Lake George on June 10, where O'Keeffe repaired her studio, the Shanty, and, as she told Stieglitz, had "grand thoughts" about the work she would

630

425. Lynes 801.

426. Either Lynes 772, 773, or 799.

427. Lynes 800; Murals by American Painters and Photographers, Museum of Modern Art, May 3–31, 1932.

428. Frederick J. Ringel, *America as Americans See It* (New York, 1932).

429. Eckstein, *Noguchi.*

complete that summer.[430] Stieglitz remained in New York for a few more weeks, attending to last-minute affairs at the gallery, and, as he recounted to O'Keeffe, he also frequently saw Norman.

Georgia O'Keeffe · [Lake George, New York] · [June 10, 1932]

Well—It seems funny to be sitting here—

Georgie and I went to Canada Wednesday morning—got back for lunch today—

We had quite a ride and quite a time—I have the curse—otherwise everything is all right—

We went into the Laurentian Hills—northwest of Montreal—as perfect a kind of landscape as I ever saw—perfectly kept too—very lovely—Then toward Quebec till I got drawings of barns I had in mind—two rather grand crosses[431]—so different from the New Mexico crosses—Sharp and white with obvious hearts on them—

We drove six hundred and ten miles—

I am a bit weary—but I am glad I went.

I find your letters telling about your eye—I hope it is all right—that it doesn't bother you too much—I wonder—will that little lump be gone—

—A branch blew down on the large plum tree—a branch toward the house so we see the trunk much more—It happened since I returned—

We went to the house I thought the Schwabs would be living in on our way down this A.M.—It was empty—but I find here a note saying they may be here today—

I will mail this—then to the Shanty to nail on my wall board—

—Do take care of yourself—

A kiss to you!

Alfred Stieglitz · [New York City] · June 20, 1932

At the Place. 8:45 A.M. Trunk goes today. This P.M.—Ross, Rosenfeld, Zoler & I had supper at Elizabeth Flynn—Ross left—Rosenfeld left soon after. I packed more. And mended the leather grip of the trunk & sewed a pocket in my trousers.

—Had a funny experience at the Place. Ross was in the darkroom getting a drink. He had just come in. I had taken down all the paintings & taken the wire & hooks off of them—& began carrying them into the vault. While there I suddenly thought, here I have been all day alone in the building—excepting the elevator boy—if I had a heart attack what would I do. There was commotion. I went out—three policemen & an ambulance surgeon!! "Where is the person"—I said you must be in the wrong place. They insisted no.—The police got busy on the phone. The white man surgeon said, "I don't understand modern art"—This was in the vault.

---

430. Recounted by Stieglitz in his letter to O'Keeffe of June 18, 1932.

431. Lynes 812, 813.

He had come in. I walked out. He followed. He pointed to your white flower[432] still on the floor & said "I like that. And those mountains (Marin). I don't understand that (Dove). What's this place?" The policemen were frantically phoning. I said to the white man: "For over forty years I have been trying to make Americans think." "Impossible," he said. "Where do you come from" —"Russia," he said. He spoke perfect English. The police said: "It's 57th Street we must go to" —The elevator boy had come in bewildered. Ross had come out wondering. It was one of the funniest things you ever saw. I felt like saying take away the paintings in your ambulance. Or the Place itself—They all disappeared—three cops in blue & the Russian in white—And Ross looked at me. And I told him of my thought just before they came.—

 —One doesn't need to go to a movie—

Now I'll be off to order drugs. Last day before taxes.[433] —Zoler is to get off the packages too. That saves taxes too—No letter from you—

 Good Morning—A kiss—

 I leave at 5:30 P.M. tomorrow. So this is the last letter. I won't wire.

632 ON JUNE 21, Stieglitz arrived in Lake George, where he remained for the next three months. Although he had told O'Keeffe he hoped they would spend much time together that summer, he continued to be obsessed with Norman. Writing the younger woman several times a day, he poured out his faith in her budding talent as a photographer and poet, his passionate love for her, his desolation that they were not together, and his mounting impatience with O'Keeffe. In her ever more numerous letters to him, Norman reciprocated in kind.[434] Because their numerous telephone calls to each other the previous summer had upset O'Keeffe and Edward Norman, they now tried to limit themselves to one call a week, which they carefully planned to ensure that no one else was at home when they spoke—at times Stieglitz even sneaked into the Village to make his calls. Even with this extensive communication, Stieglitz grew increasingly agitated in July and early August as Norman was frequently sick. Following an operation on Norman's adenoids on August 10, his anxiety only intensified.[435]

 Convinced of the sanctity of his love for Norman, Stieglitz did not hide his anguish from O'Keeffe. In letters to Norman he noted that O'Keeffe had told him that he looked like a "'wounded sparrow'" and asked, "'Are you sorry I'm here this year?—I don't seem to exist for you, do I?'" Even when Stieglitz saw O'Keeffe sunbathing nude, he told Norman, he had no desire for her because they had "no spiritual togetherness."[436] Earlier, O'Keeffe had admitted her attraction to the doctor, writer, and teacher Gustav Eckstein, whom she had first met in New

432. Probably Lynes 722.

433. A new excise tax on drugs, tires, and films was scheduled to take effect on June 21, 1932; see "Topics in Wall Street," *NYT*, June 21, 1932, 31.

434. See AS to Norman, and Norman to AS, June–Sept. 1932.

435. As Norman subsequently told Stieglitz, her husband, Edward, said that her doctor did not think her adenoids "were serious enough to cause the general debilitated condition" and instead proposed it might be "a neurotic condition" due to her "too internal, too introspective" life, which her associates, "Stieglitz, especially, innocently encourage"; see Norman to AS, Aug. 17, 1932, and Dorothy Norman, *Encounters: A Memoir* (New York, 1987), 109–110.

436. AS to Norman, June 23, July 10, June 22 and 26, 1932.

Mexico in 1929.[437] Now in early July, as Alfred witnessed his younger brother Lee divorce his wife of more than thirty years, he told Norman he had a dream that O'Keeffe divorced him to marry her "friend" and told him he could not touch her anymore because "that would be adultery—as far as I can see it."[438]

Throughout the summer O'Keeffe tried to keep her focus and managed to make more than a dozen paintings. But the mural she had agreed to paint for the women's powder room at Rockefeller Center's Radio City Music Hall became a strain, as she had no idea when construction on the hall would be completed so that she could start work. She went to the city for a day on July 6 to look at the room and meet with Donald Deskey, the designer in charge of decorations for Radio City Music Hall. She returned to New York for three days on July 18 without first telling Stieglitz why she was going, where she was staying, or even how long she would be gone.

Alfred Stieglitz · Lake George, New York · July 19, 1932

I wonder how long you'll be gone.—And what you are doing. How the city.—I know you are probably rushed. Seeing whom?—Anyone?—I was on the Lake this afternoon. Alone. Seemed funny.—Rowed to the post office.—Had a great headwind coming home. Took me an hour rowing hard—You seem gone a long while.—Nothing here different. All serene. I'm sending this merely to say hello—You may have left the Shelton before it reaches there. Or maybe they won't deliver it to you as they have orders to forward all mail.—

A big kiss.—

Georgia O'Keeffe · [New York City] · [July 19, 1932]

Things were not enough settled to suit me today—so I am staying another day—maybe even till Thursday but I rather think I'll get away tomorrow—Wednesday night—

The town isn't unpleasant—tho I have seen very little of it—Have been busy with sketches all day—tomorrow must settle some things about materials—

Good Night—

A very quiet little kiss to you. Haven't seen anyone but Mary Reinhardt for a few moments—

O'KEEFFE RETURNED to Lake George late in the evening of July 22. A week later, she and Stieglitz had a long talk while they rowed on the lake. Although O'Keeffe was somewhat encouraged by their conversation, Stieglitz was not. The talk was "ghastly," he told Norman, and it convinced him O'Keeffe had "no picture of what I really am—how I function." He concluded

437. See GOK to AS, Aug. 7 and 20, 1929, June 10, 1930, and Aug. 3, 1932; and AS to GOK, Oct. 25, 1931, and Aug. 2, 1932.
438. AS to Norman, July 13, 1932. Lee Stieglitz divorced Lizzie in July 1932 and married Amanda Liebman Hoff later that fall.

there could be nothing more to say, for their relationship was like an ailment that had "gone beyond the doctor's help."[439] O'Keeffe left the next morning for the city and returned to Lake George on August 4.

Alfred Stieglitz · Lake George, New York · August 1, 1932

6:30 A.M.—I am glad we had the talk—Now there is one thing above all things for you to do & that is be as quiet as you can & focus on your job. As I must focus on what I must do here & be ready for the winter. And when I say focus on your job, part of that, & an essential part, is to keep in good physical condition.—Yes I am glad we had the talk. Nothing, as I told you, was not known by me. Yet to hear the spoken word is somewhat different from the intuitive knowing. Why that should be so is a very subtle thing. But even that subtle difference one overcomes.

Please get out of your system the idea that I have any hard feelings about you. For I haven't. I may seem to have. But really I haven't. And haven't had for a long time.—I have to smile a rather sad smile when I think of your sweet saying we have to become acquainted with each other. Georgia dear, don't you know that part of our "trouble" lies in the fact that I know you better than you know yourself & that I know myself too well. And when I say "part" it may be at the root of it all.

—And when you say I did a terrible thing to you, that is a repetition of your saying three years ago that I had robbed you of your faith. No one has ever robbed me of my faith. And sometimes I wonder how it's possible for me to have it still. As for the terrible thing you say I did to you I understand what you mean.—I will have to bear the charge. Whether I'm innocent or not is not for me to say. And as long as you feel the way you do it will remain true for you. Nothing I might say or do would or could undo it, you believing as you do.

—It's a queer feeling I have to know you are not here—are gone. You must take care of yourself. That's my wish.—I want to see you accomplish what you have undertaken without paying the price of a ruined winter. You are demanding much of yourself.—I'll do my best to keep my health. My eyes bother me. I'll begin to poultice them regularly.—There is a difficult time ahead & both of us must be ready for it.—We have still much to do together—No one realizes that better than I do but I want nothing to interfere with your own development spiritually & as artist. I'm afraid I hamper you in many ways.—That is the last thing in the world I wish to do. I know you try the best to help me. I know that.—I try the best to help you.—You must know that. We are not always successful but we must know of each other the good will is there. The flesh is often not as strong as it should be perhaps. My flesh I suppose less so than yours.

—Yes I'm glad we were on the Lake.

I had really hoped for a summer of togetherness. And was glad when you decided not to go to the Southwest—But you see how it works out.—Life the court jester as I have often explained to you.

439. AS to Norman, Aug. 1, 1932.

I know that away from the turmoil of the Hill once on your job you'll feel better. Quieter.

—I'm going to sleep in your bed.—I don't want anyone else in your room until circumstances make other choices impossible.

I wonder will you be at Ross's or at the Shelton—Don't forget the phone number of the former.

I wish I could give you the peace I know you need & wish for. So far I seem to have failed because of not knowing how. I wonder is it given to me to find the way.—I hope so.

The monastery bells are ringing.

I had better go & wash up a bit—

A kiss—A quieting one I hope.—

Later. Ross called up to ask when you were coming—what train. I said you'd phone as soon as you arrived.—

Another kiss. Take care of yourself.

I forgot to give you the chocolate lying on the table here & which I had bought for you & Kalonyme.

Again I say it's queer to feel you gone—I hardly feel part of the house anymore. I'll do my best.—Want to print. I'll develop your negatives tonight.[440] —

—I have nothing much to say to anyone—I'm really glad Rosenfeld is here. He seems closer to me here than anyone else now that you are gone.

Remember your room is ready at any time & so am I. So also the Hill. Remember it is yours—my share—no matter what may come—if the powers that be do not confiscate all—

Georgia O'Keeffe · [New York City] · [August 1, 1932]

I seem to find no writing paper so in between waiting for the telephone I'll use this—

It was sad to see you standing there waving—waving—and feel the train taking me away—I stood looking a long time after I could not see you anymore—

It makes me very sad too when I feel the sort of thing I do to you—

Something seems to be in order for me a bit—but for you I do not know—It seems that I ought to be able to give you a little quiet—a little peace—and I feel as I came away that it is quite the contrary—I am waiting to get you on the telephone—

—As things seem to be moving—I may even decide to go back to the Lake and stay till nearly the first of September—I can't say yet—but a large part of my decision to do so would be influenced by my desire to be with you—You see—I haven't felt that I was with you at all these weeks there—You seemed to be somewhere else always until I was coming away—then you seemed to come to me a little—

---

440. Greenough 1480–1495.

There is really no point to talking about it—It just seems that if I could be with you—quiet—it would be all right—

As it is—the feeling that goes through me when I think of you is a bit as I feel when the sun shines on me—

I hesitate to write—it may all mean nothing to you—but I kiss you very quietly and tenderly—

Ross will be up tomorrow—His telephone is Plaza 3-3000—I am going there—

I feel much better since I am here—the trip down was cool—cold mostly till we were nearly here—the talk quiet—so I feel quite rested compared to yesterday and day before—

I am sorry that there is illness that must disturb you—Again I kiss you—

I wish there were something I could say—but [there] doesn't seem to be—

Except that I some way feel better—closer—if you will let me be and want me—

I kiss you very tenderly—every night and every morning—

Alfred Stieglitz · Lake George, New York · August 2, 1932

636   Georgia dear one—

Yes I was sad as you left. I was sad before. Only you saw my sadness more clearly as you left for in reality you did not want to go.—I was sad because I felt we had been here together for five weeks—& really very little *together* till that last day.—Was it I? Was it you? that prevented. Was it both of us—a little of each—We won't split hairs. We are beyond that stage. You see you have many desires—I have very few—You are young—I am no longer young.—I hate to stop you realizing your desires.—So often I withdraw.[441] Have to. And you misinterpret that as indifference, no longer caring. It's only seeing.—The old must ever see the young go out. The old remains within. But there is still enough "young" in me that needs feeding. What is it in me that needs that feeding.—When you did not go off with E[ckstein] was it because of yourself or me? It makes a great difference which. If you really wished the consummation with him you did a great wrong by him, by yourself & by me. If you come home & find a relationship that makes you feel you were foolish not to have consummated something for yourself then something is wrong somewhere in your makeup as I see life. Of course I understand the complexity of a moment. But a moment does not come out of the clear sky. One is part of the creation of the moment. You know all this maybe better than I do—

So when you went away what made me chiefly sad is that I didn't seem able to give you such excitements as you need for stimulation—the equivalent for many things you crave.

—The world is a hectic condition—I am not hectic in the usual sense—I still have enough left in me to nauseate myself at times. I don't like it. Age perhaps. But I feel I never was hectic in the ordinary sense. I don't always agree with what you do any more than you don't

441. In another letter, written earlier on August 2, 1932, Stieglitz told O'Keeffe: "But you see Georgia dear—you become unreasonably hard—have for years—In turn I seem to withdraw—am forced to—you compel it—As I may do things at times that seem to compel you to withdraw."

agree with what I do.—Should there be the cheapness of compromise—or of distrust—or of resentment.—Of course I know human nature is no formula—is not a switchboard—but it is often more nearly that than is realized.

That Dorothy is ill—& has been ever since her boy was born does disturb me. As I would be disturbed if Marin were ill. As I am disturbed when you are ill. She has work to do.[442] —Work I believe in no matter what anyone else may think to the contrary.—I'm not thinking of you. And I want to see her do it. You are interested in E[ckstein]'s work & in what he is. And I'm glad you are—Of course you consider him of importance—so do I.—I consider Dorothy of equal importance. You consider [her] of no importance. I understand that & accept it as you.—But I can't be affected by it any more than you could be if for some reason I'd feel E[ckstein] of no great consequence as a man or worker. Your work was as important to me the day Anita brought it to me as it ever was since. What the world thinks really matters little. For the world doesn't think—it gradually absorbs & accepts without awareness or consciousness. Again I say you know all this automatically.

As for bringing me peace—Georgia dear that is not the all in all in life—You never brought me peace—no one can bring another peace—But peace & chronic unrest are poles apart.—There is such a thing as moving towards less unrest—call that peace if you will—& there is such a thing as chaos in the guise of convention or any "ism" you may chose. Such at least at present.

—It's a perfect day here. Donald walked with me to the Village. I played golf & beautifully with the professional. Real sleep steadies nerves. I was a deadly shot.

Donald waited.—His kids are fine.—They recited in Sanskrit to me.—Unusual little persons. Sue growing up beautifully. Peggy much improved.—

I wonder what you are doing today. How the city?—How the job? Will you be back to go to St. Huberts. The Engelhard family has driven to the Green Mountains.—Georgia driving your car!—

They have car-itis badly.—I must smile. I have decided to have the barn shingled at my expense.—As a lark—There is the lunch bell—

Much love & a big kiss—

Lunch is over—Rosenfeld & I alone—

Georgia O'Keeffe · [New York City] · [August 2, 1932]

I had your two letters this morning and the cloud this afternoon—The cloud is so beautiful— I looked at it—then covered it so it wouldn't get dirty—

I went to Radio City and after much scrambling about—Ross will tell you of it—

---

442. In addition to the work she did around the gallery, Norman was a budding poet. Stieglitz later helped her publish her poems in a limited edition, *Dualities* (New York, 1933), which included a portrait of Norman by him.

I found the room I am to do—with a solid floor of scaffolding about on a level with my chin
—used for building the curved ceiling—The whole mess was quite a sight—

Since then—more quibbling over canvas etc—till finally when I had my lunch I went
back to the Room and lay on the cot—so tired I was thinking of coming home and going to bed
—It was late when I went to bed last night and I was up before seven so I got tired easily—
While I was trying to decide whether to come home or just stay there—Kalonyme phoned and
came up—He explained to me all the bad things that can come of my doing the thing at Radio
City—

—Well I had thought of it myself—but with the argument I got rested a bit—He
walked over here with me and after getting cool from the walk went on—

I may be up again tomorrow night—It seems that nothing can be done here for a week
—At any rate I will find out something more definite by eleven tomorrow—

—I am going to supper early and to bed early—

Good Night—I kiss you quietly—

Had supper last night with Schwab—

—We will go up to Keene Valley on Saturday if I go back to the Lake tomorrow—

638

Georgia O'Keeffe · [New York City] · [August 3, 1932]

11:15—I just telephoned you about the barn—I was so afraid you would begin on it right away.
—Don't.

I have your two letters—You ask me did I say no to E[ckstein] because of you or
because of myself—It was first because of *us*—because of something we were and had been
together—that meant something in the world to others than ourselves—Secondly—it was
because of you—Myself I considered last—It is all right—I am satisfied with my decisions—
They were the only ones I could make—

That is one reason why a lot of talk you carry on about a lot of other people is so
ridiculous to me—It has all made so many things seem so funny—

I still await telephone calls—

I was frightfully tired last night—Was in bed at eight and not up till after nine—read
for two hours maybe—otherwise—slept—

It rains this morning—

Am going to get out my big painting[443] now and look at it while I wait—

It is pleasant here—

I simply forgot to buy any paper and can't find any here—

A quiet kiss to you—

443. Probably Lynes 801.

Alfred Stieglitz · Lake George, New York · August 3, 1932

6:20 P.M. Just shaved. Feels good. I hate the unclean feeling of my unshaveness & yet I hate to shave!—A bleak miserable day.—Continuous rain. Hard & penetrating. Ross & I walked to the post office & back. Your letter there. I can imagine how your Radio City room looks.—And Kalonyme came to see you.—And he told you about all the bad things that might come because of your Radio City undertaking. I know you thought of all that yourself.

You'll do what your spirit will prompt you to do. And after you have weighed everything for yourself—

I just missed your phone by a couple of minutes. I had to laugh that you thought I might shingle at once. I did get an estimate. It was too rich for my blood just at present. But what a soaking that wood is getting today. I hate to think of it rotting.—

—I wonder will you turn up this weekend to go to St. Huberts.—I am not guessing.—As I wrote you everything is always ready for you to walk in—everything includes myself—! Ross & Rosenfeld just returned from post office to mail their afternoon letters. Fred picked them up on their way back. Everything continues very quiet here.—Sel's closet is up.—I developed this afternoon. You did not move[444]—I don't know how the pictures will turn out. May have something—I don't know.—I think I have something of the dead poplar.[445] Have some ideas.—

—It seems really queer not to have you upstairs—or in the Shanty—or somewhere near.—

I feel stupid & dopey today. Too little sleep I guess. I like your bed really much better than mine. I like the small room too. It is all much more to my own feeling.—

I can't quite see you in New York at this time of year.—Since 1918 you weren't there during the summer months—It was about this time fourteen years ago we came to Lake George.

August 4, 1932

7 A.M. I have just come in. Missed getting a marvelously beautiful photograph. Everything set up. Grasses & raindrops.[446] Large camera. Just as I was about to expose wind sprang up. It had been absolutely windstill all along. I was too late by a minute!!—Sickening. Really.—It would have been maybe the most beautiful thing I ever did.—I had watched the morning for hours. Really before dawn I lay awake. Had slept some. Eyes bother me. Am certainly much of a fool.—

And as I lay there I went over all the ground of years—you & myself. Long before you came. But beginning with the coming of your pictures.—The full significance not only to me personally but abstractly.—Then our first year & from then on—all leading to today.—You. I. —What we have been to each other. What we are to each other. What we have done to each other. What we do to each other. The relationship of all that to others.—I didn't brood—I had no resentments—no hard feelings—I was not sorry for myself—I merely tried to see as clearly as it is possible for me to see. And then I got up and watched the grasses with the raindrops— & the dead poplar illuminated by the early sun & against a very dark sky. And as I tried to

444. Greenough 1480–1495.

445. Greenough 1467–1470.

446. Stieglitz successfully captured this subject the next year; see Greenough 1504–1508.

decide which picture to take first—raindrops or poplar—I decided for the raindrops. It's that time I took to decide which lost me both pictures because the sudden coming of the wind made both impossible.—So here I am writing to you wondering how your evening—how your night—how very much.—And life continues.—The Davidsons, Elizabeth & Donald, leave at 8:55. The Straus gang[447] is to arrive during the day. Elizabeth & Donald don't wish to be here simultaneously with them—Yes, life goes on.—

Your room is certainly like you—and somehow I like it very much—It's compact, has an edge & is practical—Is light—airy.—You can do things for yourself—I haven't that knack for myself—Not in that practical fine sense.

9:20.—Have just come in from front porch—Ross, Rosenfeld & I talking some—The Davidsons gone. Ross asked when you are coming. I said I had no idea.—All is very quiet. Running smoothly. I wonder will the Schaufflers breeze in—When? Mrs. is to sleep in Ag's bed. Ag on porch. Mr. in dining room bed. Even I wonder are you coming.—But dare not speculate as to whether you are or not.—I know you'll do as the spirit moves you.—

The sun is in & out—Looks uncertain.—Negatives are dry. I'll proof them soon.—Am curious.—Technically fine. That's something. Telegram just now from York Harbor—Heavy rains make traveling impossible today. Will come tomorrow!!—And you all may be in St. Huberts.—Well it makes no difference. I'll close this—

Much much love. I do hope you are eating well. And not overdoing.—

A big kiss—

Not so quiet!—Or quiet if you prefer.—

SHORTLY AFTER O'KEEFFE RETURNED from New York City on August 5, she and Engelhard made a second trip to Canada and spent almost three weeks traveling along the St. Lawrence River and into the Gaspé Peninsula. O'Keeffe started several paintings, including *Cross with Red Heart* and *Green Mountains, Canada*.[448] She wrote Stieglitz many lively letters during this trip, but Stieglitz, anxious about Norman's health, seems hardly to have noticed O'Keeffe's absence and wrote her only a few times.

Georgia O'Keeffe · [Berthierville, Québec] · [August 10, 1932]

Dearest—

Everything goes very well with us—We left Plattsburgh before anyone was up—having paid for our room the night before—We went right through Montreal without stopping—a rather shortcut by a different bridge and were up here at the place we wanted to come to around ten—We made ourselves at home in a small, one-room cabin on the river—The St. Lawrence—feels a bit like the ocean—tall trees behind at the road—river in front—car

447. Lee Stieglitz's daughter, Flora, her husband, Hugh Grant Straus, and their children.
448. Lynes 818 and 812.

right beside the door—a small porch—all very good. Then we went out for drawings of our barns—got our canvases stretched—drawings on them—everything ready to paint—Then we drove about thirty miles more up the road to see if it was better—decided it wasn't—had supper up there and drove back into the sunset and wonderful storm clouds—It was very good—We both enjoyed it much—fell right into bed when we got back here and went to sleep immediately—It was a good night—We were up and packed and fed and planted in our field for work at 7:45—Came back here at about two—have been painting indoors for about an hour—Really having an absurdly good time—It is cool and lovely—and the wind blows hard—

I am sending Deskey a night letter today—Wednesday—The idea of being in the city with this cold wind blowing here seems a bit absurd to me—

—The Child[449] remarked this morning as we drove to the place we intended to work— "Why I feel so good I feel like taking my head off and hanging it out the window."

I feel very good too—

Will wire you when I hear from Deskey—

We intend to stay here for at least three days—

A very fresh lively kiss goes to you—

I will be a bit glad if I can't go to town till September—It feels good to get to work again like this—

Georgia O'Keeffe · [Berthierville, Québec] · [August 12, 1932]

Good Morning!

It is a bit gray and sprinkles once in awhile—so we came in from the field at 11:15 as the Kid was working out and I in the car and she kept getting wet—

I am going out again after I mail this—

My wire from Deskey yesterday said "Advise waiting until painting contract is let about September first. You may then execute work in studio or on walls"—So I wired you and settle myself to paint these three weeks—

At the moment it is very good here so I have no definite further plan except that by Monday we will go on to Quebec and beyond it if we don't just decide to stay here altogether—

And we are both much pleased here—At the moment a bit disgusted with the morning rain—but that will pass—It is nice to be out with someone who stays as busy as I do—We really get on very well—

You would have laughed to see us crawling around over the floor stretching canvases last night till nearly midnight—after having driven slowly along the road in the evening light looking at all the places we liked—

I hope everything goes well with you—Tell Agnes her child is fine—

And kiss yourself for me—

---

449. Georgia Engelhard, the daughter of Stieglitz's sister Agnes and her husband, George Herbert, was affectionately called "The Child," "The Kid," "The Kidlet," and, because of her affection for O'Keeffe, "Georgia Minor."

Alfred Stieglitz · [Lake George, New York] · August 14, 1932

As you are so uncertain in your movements & decisions I haven't written to you. But as your letter received this moment says you may stay in Berthierville I'll chase this off to tell you how delighted I am that you are having so *full* a time. And enjoying it hugely. And are at work besides.—I was more than glad that it worked out that you were not to go to the city before September. It did disturb me some to see you cooped up there before you had gotten what I felt enough real air & real sun. Besides which I felt the situation about Radio City so hectic that I knew it would infect you to your disadvantage. But God's ways are queer—& I try to keep my hands off as best I can or know how.—Naturally I'm curious to see what you have been doing.—

All is peaceful on the Hill—I wrote to Ross not to expect you—in case you failed to write yourself or wire. He is due here tomorrow evening per day bus!—Weber turned up last night for a couple of hours after supper!! Came from Montreal with friends on way to New York—I am always glad to see him.—The weather has been gorgeous—cool & clear—marvelous nights.—And days. Have been less active myself. Printed some. Going slowly.—Had been a little too strenuous I guess.—But am all right. Lee was called to New York on Friday.—We take our noon meal at Red Top today—Sunday.—There is no particular news. You know the life here.—It continues.—I found your dear sweet note on the pillow the day you left.

Sweet—

Well continue to have a good time. Everything is all right.

A big kiss—

I'll get this off to the post office. I'll drive down.[450] As Lee is away I get the car for that readily.—

Kiss.—Greetings to the Kid—

Georgia O'Keeffe · [Cap-des-Rosiers, Québec] · [August 17, 1932]

Good Morning—

I think it is Tuesday—no, it is Wednesday—And this is certainly a place—and we have a still better one that we go to today—We got out of the car to take a walk and found a cabin under trees over a grand high rock and the sea with a sandy beach below that is so perfect we still can't believe it true—The sandy beach protected by high rocks at either end and magnificent rocks rising up behind it very high—soft sort of velvety rocks—and out behind a vast cliff that the gulls and wild geese seem to think their own—There is a waterfall rushing down to the sandy beach at one end—a wild fiercely cold one—and at the other end another fall that comes down in fine spray over rich green moss and makes a perfect shower bath—The Kid was so excited she almost lost her mind—and then we even accidentally found the man who owns it

---

450. After O'Keeffe returned from New Mexico in 1929, Stieglitz learned to drive, though he did not drive often or well.

—So we move up there today we think—for a few days—You just couldn't think of anything more perfect—I couldn't imagine such a place existing—the cliff rising up back of it all is as grand as anything I've seen—Well it's pretty good—

Yesterday morning we were up and packed and on the road at five—and it was one of the good days of my life all along the ocean or over mountains through wonderful forest—as beautiful woods as I ever saw—The combination is wonderful—I think you would have liked it —beautiful roads—and all the villages very primitive—just groups of fishermen's houses—All of the way smelling the sea or the woods—It was very good—We found this place[451] for the night quite by accident too—food so good you want to keep on eating indefinitely—Just a family—they haven't even a sign out—You know—one of my lucky moments—five children —all little and so pretty—Georgie and I just look at one another and wonder if we are alive— or dreaming—or what—I think I didn't turn over all night—

It is a bit of a climb up to our cabin over the sea but I can easily take the Ford with all our stuff most of the way—We didn't do it last night because it was too late to get everything settled—

We also found another place that we were on our way back to when we found this— A grand place to paint—

Oh it was a good day yesterday—I think we will have to stay between this place we go to today and the other one a hundred miles down the coast—until near the end of the month—It is wonderful for painting—makes you feel like it anyway—What I will do—I don't know—

I will wire you today—There will not be time for you to write me—I wish you could see it all here—

A kiss to you—

Georgia O'Keeffe · [Cap-des-Rosiers, Québec] · [August 22, 1932]

Good Morning—

You may have known for a long time—that I am no good but you never knew it as well as I know it this morning sitting high up on a slanting white rock watching a roaring sea roll up over the strange circular shapes of rock down below—It is so grand that every once in awhile I have to go into the house and sit down on a chair—

When I first went out this morning—the crows calling on one side on the sand—gulls and wild geese on the other circling about the cliff—The very high cliff partly hidden in fog at the top—sun breaking through in spots out on the water—There was a seal mildly moving down the beach just a little out from where I went in the water yesterday—

The first day we were here it rained a little off and on and we walked and climbed miles—made drawings but nothing came of them—It all just seemed too stupid to try to do

643

---

451. O'Keeffe's stationery indicates that they were staying with H. J. Riffou, who ran a general store in Cap-des-Rosiers.

anything of it when one started—We were so excited that we both hardly slept a wink—Yesterday we stayed more at home—when the tide is low you can walk quite far up the beach and the rocks rising up over you are very grand and very beautiful color from gray to gold—no red—We even took off our clothes and ran up and down the beach—and lay in the sun and climbed about this rock—lay on it for hours watching the water—It is very different on the different sides—Fixed our own supper and were in bed at eight—I don't know when we got up —We seem to get up when it is light—slept hard—We are going on in the morning—This sort of a place is so exciting we would never get anything done unless we came and stayed a long time—The house is a new log house—very small—not very light—but very clean—beds built against the wall—not very wide—Very good place in every way except that it seems to be almost too good—The air is so strangely both warm and cold—With nothing on it is fine in the sun—and it is good too when you have on a sweater & coat buttoned up to the neck—it seems so soft—

Well—I wish you could see it—I think you could not help liking it—It makes me feel very good even if I feel very small at the same time—Even as small as nothing—

A kiss to you from a green and black wave with a shining white top—

644

ON AUGUST 26, O'Keeffe and Georgia Engelhard "breezed in" from Canada, as Stieglitz wrote Norman that day, with "a few beautiful paintings."[452] When asked if he had missed O'Keeffe, Stieglitz replied, "'I missed her as much as she missed me!'"[453] Although O'Keeffe had hoped to start work on her mural at Radio City on September 1, the construction was still far behind schedule. Even though Louis Kalonyme and Cary Ross, who were visiting Lake George, advised her against becoming any more involved with such a "mess," she again went to New York City on September 14 and while there signed a contract with Rockefeller Center to complete her mural by November 1.[454] On her way back to Lake George three days later, she complained to Brett, "I can't paint a room that isn't built and if the time between the building and the opening isn't long enough I can't do it either"; she also admitted that "experimenting so publicly is a bit precarious in every way."[455] To Beck Strand she even more candidly acknowledged, "My Gawd won't I get Hell if I can't make a go of it."[456]

Stieglitz was angered when he discovered that O'Keeffe signed a contract without consulting him and incensed when he learned she was to be paid only fifteen hundred dollars. On September 25, when he went to New York to install the exhibition of Stanton Macdonald-Wright's new paintings at An American Place, he met with Deskey and insisted that O'Keeffe's contract be "redrawn" and that O'Keeffe should be paid five thousand dollars. Deskey later remembered that when he pointed out that the contract had been signed, Stieglitz responded

452. Lynes 805–813.
453. AS to Norman, Aug. 26, 1932.
454. AS to Norman, Sept. 8, 1932. Stieglitz later renegotiated the date to November 15, 1932.
455. GOK to Dorothy Brett, Sept. 14, 1932, Harry Ransom Humanities Research Center, The University of Texas at Austin, as quoted in Cowart, Hamilton, and Greenough, *Georgia O'Keeffe: Art and Letters*, 207.
456. GOK to Rebecca Strand, Oct. 6, 1932.

that O'Keeffe was "a child not responsible for her actions."[457] As a compromise, Stieglitz suggested that O'Keeffe would do the work without cost, except for materials.[458] Staying out of the fray, O'Keeffe remained at Lake George for an additional week before going to New York on October 2.

Georgia O'Keeffe · [En route from Lake George to New York City] · [September 14, 1932]

3:30—We have just left Saratoga—I am so tired—I wanted to write Brett but I seem much too tired—

I ate my sandwich and just sit here—

Maybe part of my broken up feeling is from the curse—I ought to be over feeling badly from it but I don't seem to be—It seems as tho my nerves are all still particularly bare and easily shattered—and all the middle of me much too tired—I will go right to bed in town and be all right in the morning—

—I don't really mind myself being this way as much as I mind what I seem to do to you —and above all I dislike an audience watching it all—It must be unpleasant for them—it is certainly not the sort of thing I would enjoy watching—

Leaving Albany—5 P.M.

I have just sat and tried to be still—and wondered—Everything seems so wrong and I don't see what I can do about it—

I just sit and look out the window in a sort of stupor—

7:25—Yes—I just sat and looked out the window—feeling quite dumb—I am in the day coach on the land side—rather like it as I usually sit on the river side.

I am still so tired and interested most in going to bed—I'll send you my Good Night kiss now—as we are soon in the city—I do not like this going apart—It doesn't seem to go anywhere.

Alfred Stieglitz · [En route from Lake George to New York City] · September 25, 1932

It's 7 P.M.—Just as I was about to write a few lines to you an hour ago who do you think stands before me? Schwab.—We have been talking. He has gone to his car.—It does seem "queer" to be sitting here—a sort of "nowhere"—At four I got out my sandwiches & I ate them & the crackers in one session. I seemed ravenously hungry & they were about the best sandwiches I ever ate. —Really.—Thanks a million times.

457. Letter from Donald Deskey to Laurie Lisle, Nov. 7, 1978, as quoted in Lisle, *Portrait of an Artist: A Biography of Georgia O'Keeffe* (New York, 1980), 205.

458. See AS to GOK, Sept. 26, 1932. Deskey told Lisle that he refused to accept Stieglitz's suggestion that O'Keeffe work for free, although Stieglitz's letter to O'Keeffe of September 26, 1932, contradicts this statement (Lisle, *Portrait of an Artist,* 205).

I wonder did you get home all right. And will you be attending to your rawish throat. I do hope you won't get a cold—Yes I'm glad we had no one around the last few days—you were right!—It would have been impossible with any of the men around except possibly Rosenfeld. But it was better without him too. Schwab says your pictures are liked much. No results as yet.[459]—

I'll be glad when I shall have seen Deskey & finally settled the mural business.—I'll get over with it as soon as possible.

All told I agree with you the summer was a good one—very good in fact.—

Here we are at Harmon.—I wonder will Ross be at the station. In a way I'd rather be alone. Take a hot bath or go to bed. I wonder will you be going to bed very early. I hope so. So that you get a real good rest & break that cold—I'd hate to see you get one. You can't afford it. I'm glad I got some pictures of you this summer.[460] Of course they are not what I had hoped to do. Still a few may seem really good in time.—I'm also very glad you did that spotting—when you are through the prints are so much more *themselves!*—I'll have to mark on the back of prints "Spotted by O'Keeffe"—No joking. I'll stop writing now—too much jostling. You looked so beautiful as you stood at the station—Very lovely! Yes you did.—

Very much love. And a big kiss—

646

Georgia O'Keeffe · [Lake George, New York] · [September 26, 1932]

Good Morning!

It is gray and misty but I feel good—Yesterday was one of my sickish days—I did everything I could to recover and finally the Child and I went walking—at first slowly as I was so miserable—then finally with our usual speed—through the bushes and briars and woods and swamps—Up hill and down with very little attention to paths—just on to the next view or place slightly familiar to cut across—I felt good by the time we got home at six—We went to the Village and got carrots and turnips and onions that we put in the big iron pot whole and cooked with our moose meat—It was very good—a bit like the dish Paul[461] used to make but not rich and greasy the way he made it—

—After supper we got all our paintings down and looked at them and got them ready to pack—And after that got out a lot of reproductions of old drawings that we had collected in the attic in the spring—We had quite a time—and have many more to look at tonight—

It was nearly twelve when we went to bed—

I was glad you telephoned—it was nice to hear your voice—The picture of your little face—sweet—with the very bright eyes as the train pulled out is so clear to me—

Do take care of yourself—I have decided if things are so that I can begin my misery next

459. Teddy Bryner and Arthur Schwab were supporters of Stieglitz and his artists. Over the years they had purchased several Marin watercolors and O'Keeffe paintings and also tried to sell a few.

460. Greenough 1480–1495.

461. Paul Jones.

Monday—I will take the same train that you took down—It will be best with the things I have to carry—

But if you wish to do something else Sunday night—do not stay home because I am arriving—I will find my way in—

A kiss to you—!

In a way I am glad it is a gray day—no temptation to go out—

Do try to keep a bit quiet and take a bit of care of your little self—eyes—etc—

Another little kiss—

Alfred Stieglitz · [New York City] · September 26, 1932

Room 3003—It's 8:10 A.M.—Had breakfast at Childs. Ready for the day. Good morning.— A kiss.—I wonder how you are. Still abed. Oh no—it's 9:10 on the Hill!—After Ross & I had a bite at Childs & I came "home" alone—after awhile I took a real soak in the hot tub. It felt good. Then I went to bed & got a rest. Sleep was fair. I didn't take Phanadorm. It wasn't necessary.—The day is clear & coldish. I'll call up Deskey as soon as possible & try to clean up that business.—I have no idea as to yes or no. Nor have I any wish either way. Really.—If he agrees to a contract according to what I think is fair to both him & you you'll have to see your end of it through.—If he doesn't he prevents you from doing so. That's all there is to it.—So I have no idea what he'll do therefore nor what will happen.—At any rate you are well off now on the Hill.—It's queer the city seems nothing to me at all as I look out. It is as if it were made up of a pasteboard "scenery" in some cheap theatre. The Wonder of the World.—I prefer the "dead" poplar to all this even if you say I am not interested in nature as you are.

—I hope you have broken the beginnings of a cold. And that today you'll be able to get at your *White Flower*.[462] The first one is certainly a wonder.—Real You!—Everything about it quite a "miracle."—You see I not only see the painting—whatever that may mean—but *every-thing* that is "back" of it—that helped it into being.—That's the miracle to me—that that all should exist in the form of *that*. Of course "miracles" are all about us—everything is a miracle if only *seen*.—

—I didn't go to the Place last night. I was in no mood for it. And I didn't want to begin tinkering around.—Ross said Wright had called him up to find out when I'd be in today.—

I'll go to the Place soon. I'll call Deskey from here. Want to attend to several minor matters before going to the Place & still I'm as apt as not to go there first. I want everything well under way by evening.—And no "energy" wasted—

I'm fighting a bit of sinus. If I get a chance may go to Hirst to have a treatment or two. —No use letting the stupid thing run.—I have been thinking about my photographs. I must formulate something. What is to be done with them. It isn't fair to you to put the whole matter up to you. Life has become more & more conflicted—& I believe it won't become less so.—And I do want to conserve your energy for you own life—living—doing & not for taking care of &

---

462. Probably Lynes 816.

placing "things"—Don't misunderstand.—We all are living very contradictory lives that is the root of most of our situations—call them problems in you will.—I hate the idea of property & yet what we produce automatically becomes property—do what we will.—

9 A.M.—I have phoned to Deskey.—I have decided as I have to go to Of's—I'll stop in at Deskey's at 2:30. It won't take long to settle up the whole business.—We'll see. Now I'll be off. More later. A big kiss—

5 P.M. At the Place. Finally a chance to write you. Such a day.—First of all in the Place the "White Room" is *not white*. It's greenish white etc. But it will have to go. The other rooms are not quite right either except the dark gray—At Of's my photographs had not come, there was an hour phoning trying to locate them. Of was closed on Saturday when they tried to deliver so they were sidetracked!! All *my care* was wasted.

    —I was at Deskey's & saw the two men.[463] They accepted all my suggestions. No waste of time.—I may phone you tonight. I'll see about the contract when redrawn.—I want to see the room when it's done with canvas—see how the job is done at the curves, etc.[464]—Am here— Wright just left—no Zoler of course. Ross comes shortly. I'll probably go to the Group opening[465] after all. He too—I wish my photographs were here. It's just fiendish that with all my care I don't seem able to connect!—I should have sent them off either Saturday or before Friday as I originally intended.—

    —I wonder how you are. All this seems idiotic.—The Place is fine in spite of the walls not being right. The floors are glazed—that may affect the color of the wall—probably does.—

    Seligmann had the mimeographs[466] ready. He never fails one.—That's much.—

    I must let down a little. Ate lunch alone at Women's Exchange.—A big kiss. And much love—

Alfred Stieglitz · [New York City] · September 28, 1932

9:15 A.M. Good Morning. I'm at the Place. No mail at all. Can't understand it. I wonder has some fool post office man sent the mail to Lake George. In these days everything is not only possible but likely.—No one seems really to have their wits about them. I as little as the worst.

    Yesterday was a day!—What a waste really.—And how little I know to apply what I learn.

    —And yet the contract is clear. Finally settled to everyone's satisfaction. Now all I hope

---

463. Probably Deskey and S. L. (Roxy) Rothafel, chief of architecture and construction for Radio City Music Hall.

464. Unlike Stuart Davis, whose mural for the men's room at Radio City Music Hall covered a flat surface, O'Keeffe was to paint both curved walls and a domed ceiling in the women's powder room. Stieglitz was concerned that the canvas might not adhere properly on the curved walls.

465. *Success Story*, a new play by John Howard Lawson, performed by the Group Theatre, opened on September 26, 1932, at the Maxine Elliot Theatre.

466. Most of the announcements for shows at An American Place were handwritten by Stieglitz and then mimeographed.

is that you will have quiet during your work time—that nothing will disturb you & above all that you remain well. The rest I know will then be very wonderful. I never question that.—I'll be at the station Sunday night. There can be nothing to keep me.—It is annoying that the mail hasn't come. I'm sure there must be something from you.—But above all it's the frightful strain of uncertainty it emphasizes that one is forced to live under. It was always bad enough but it grows worse & worse.—

Well yesterday Wright was here a good part of the day. Some more pictures came. His strips haven't arrived yet. I hope they'll come today—I want to hang as soon as possible. The invitations go out today.—Ross is as ever a real pleasure. Sensitive & has real feeling & brains.—I'm going to have the wax removed from the floor. People are apt to break their necks slipping—especially women folks.

2:45 P.M. Was interrupted this A.M. Phoned to the post office. A mess there. Finally got my mail. A letter from you!—A fine one.—Lake George sounds so far away. But so does the Place. Wright here.—Black strips on pictures. Will hang tomorrow.—Zoler on deck. Looks less dopey. Have sent him to Deskey with contract signed.—I corrected November 1 to 15.[467] Phoned them. They feel the theatre won't open when announced. I know it won't. Can't.—So there is no use worrying about time in the broad sense. Of course you want to get through as soon as you can. And yet do yourself full justice.

I have Lawrence's *Letters*. A fat volume. Three letters to me included.[468] You mentioned in them.

It's very quiet here. I like it when no one bothers me.—I'll send out the invitations afterwards—It all seems like going through motions without meaning. But the show will be complete in its way. It will attract attention I'm sure. Will it do any more?

5 P.M. Zoler just back—No one disturbed me. I mailed invitations, etc.—Read some Lawrence *Letters* & nearly fell asleep—not because of Lawrence but because of "sleepiness."—I'm glad you are getting these extra days in the country—I'm wondering how *White Flower No. 2*[469] is turning out. Lee dropped in towards noon. Liked the Wrights—The quiet here is incredible when one realizes one is in the heart of New York—

5:30 Seligmann dropped in. In fine shape. Ross in again. Has just left. Is returning for supper. —Everything has the feeling of touch & go today—a sort of "quickness"—concentration. Wright loves the portrait of you with your face (nose) near the left hand edge of paper.[470] The photographs look all right. The mounts are pretty dirty. I wonder what sort of day you have had.—It was drizzly this A.M.—Turned cold suddenly & became clear.—I may call you up after 8:30 to say hello & find out how you are—

467. O'Keeffe's contract with Rockefeller Center is no longer extant.
468. D. H. Lawrence, *The Selected Letters of D. H. Lawrence,* edited with an introduction by Aldous Huxley (London, 1932), 259, 402–403.
469. Lynes 817.
470. Either Greenough 1488 or 1489.

—Good Night—A big kiss—
I hope you have had a fine day. And I hope the nights are good. Very good.
Good Night—
Much love—And love to all—
Remember me to Margaret & Richard. It's "nice" to feel oneself missed a little!—

O'KEEFFE'S VERY PUBLIC EXPERIMENT FAILED. After waiting months for the powder room at Radio City to be completed, Deskey finally told her that she could start work on the mural in mid-October. When she arrived at Radio City, however, she found a "mad house."[471] Even worse, once she started to paint she discovered that the canvas had been applied to wet plaster and was peeling away from the walls. Because she did not think she had enough time to complete the mural once the canvas was properly reapplied, she abandoned the project.[472] Deeply upset and humiliated, she argued with Stieglitz, and before leaving for Lake George at the end of October, she said that they should separate.[473]

For the next several weeks she struggled to regain her confidence but with little success. Although she enjoyed the company of Georgia Engelhard and Margaret Prosser, she was unable to paint. The solitary communion with nature that had once invigorated her spirit and fed her art now gave her more than ample time to brood. She felt "senseless" and "dumb," and, recognizing that "it is the thing I am that makes the work," she also concluded that she was "no good."[474] Although Stieglitz could now see Norman without fear of O'Keeffe's intrusion and told friends that he and the younger woman were "in the deepest living sense…absolutely one," he grew increasingly concerned about O'Keeffe's state.[475] He wrote O'Keeffe every day, relating his activities and the frequent praise others gave her art. He sent her books and records, and he began to call her every night to assess not only her words but also the tone of her voice. To Stieglitz's consternation, O'Keeffe's letters grew more infrequent and scattered, lacking both energy and focus.

O'Keeffe unexpectedly went to New York on November 15 to celebrate her forty-fifth birthday and select frames for her upcoming exhibition at An American Place. Although she still spoke of a separation, Stieglitz dismissed the idea and assured her that she looked much better and that he was "*very glad you came!*"[476] She returned to Lake George the next day.

---

471. GOK to Russell Vernon Hunter, Oct. 1932.

472. When O'Keeffe left the project in late October, she believed she had to have the mural completed by November 15. However, the building did not open until December 27, 1932; see "Radio City Theatre Will Open Tonight," *NYT*, Dec. 27, 1932, 10.

473. See AS to GOK, Oct. 30, 1932.

474. GOK to AS, Nov. 17 and 19, 1932.

475. AS to Norman, Oct. 1, 1932, recounting a conversation he had with Cary Ross.

476. AS to GOK, Nov. 16, 1932.

650

Alfred Stieglitz · [New York City] · October 30, 1932

The Place—It's 5:27—Your train is nearing Saratoga.—I hope you are all right. And the Kidlet awaiting you.—I'm eagerly awaiting half-past eight—I'm glad I went with you to the station—It would have been awful for both of us had I not been able to.—The Place seems particularly empty knowing as I do that you won't be at Childs or at the hotel—And I alone tonight.—No I'm not sentimental—I wonder if my letter told you anything[477]—Oh Georgia why will we torture each other so unnecessarily. I know what I am to you—& I wish I could make you see clearly what you are to me. When you speak of leaving because of me you do not know how ghastly it sounds & how ghastly it is. Each of us is difficult—each in a different way. When you say like yesterday morning that I must hate you at times—I understand & don't understand. I have never had a moment of hatred towards you—Never. Nor anything related to hatred. You see I can't see you hating me at any time—that [is] why I probably can't see why you should feel that I could hate you at any time for even a fraction of a second. If ever I hated anyone it's myself at times.—That's the truth.—I do hope the Hill will bring you a bit of peace—I really envy you for having been able to go.—

　　—Zoler came in at 4:30.—Schwab spent an hour with the Marins[478]—bowled over with the oils!—It has been a very quiet afternoon.—I didn't feel like seeing anyone—& less like talking.—I'll take a bite for supper & return here—call you up & tinker around. I get very little done—I don't want to go to the hotel until it is bedtime. I'll take Adalin. I must sleep. And I'm going to get up early & get things done.—I must go to the dentist—& Rosen & Török.—I have been postponing much.—I who hate procrastination a most guilty one.—Reading Lawrence's *Letters* fits my mood—They make me sadder—

　　Did I tell you Lizzie sent fifty dollars for the Place?—Came this morning—

　　—And now you are in the auto on your way to Lake George—driving at night.— I wonder are you at the wheel. The telephone has been ringing many times today—many "wrong numbers."—I started to say something—& I have forgotten. My head is in a queer state—Ross just came in—Asked whether you had gone. It seems he went to the train leaving at 12:30. Came now to see whether you were leaving with the 6:30 train.—Is gone again.—There were some visitors—Came from the Modern Museum—All spoke of your things—how well they looked[479]—How really fine.—I'm glad you saw them yourself & were satisfied with their presentation.—

　　I think I'll go to supper now.—

　　I may write more later.—Probably will.

　　I can't imagine your not being at supper—I'm not going to the Lexington Avenue Childs. I'll go down Madison Avenue—

---

477. This letter from Stieglitz to O'Keeffe has not survived.

478. On November 7, 1932, Stieglitz opened John Marin: New Oil Paintings and Water Colors and Drawings at An American Place. The exhibition was on view until December 17, 1932.

479. Lynes 654 and 772 were on display at the Museum of Modern Art in their exhibition American Painting and Sculpture, 1862–1942, Oct. 31, 1932–Jan. 31, 1933.

I do hope you are all right—feeling better.—Much better.—

Good Night for the present—

And a real kiss—

7:40 P.M. Back again. Zoler & I went to the Madison Avenue Childs. Ate the twenty-five cent supper & a custard—in all forty cents. Very good. I had no appetite. I just told Zoler he should get two hooks & nails & a hammer.—When we go to the hotel at about ten I want to hang your paintings.—

You must be in Lake George by this time & installed. I wonder how it feels.—Or are you sort of lost as I am sort of lost.—A deadish feeling.—Not pleasant.—I must get to printing & photographing some out of the window.—

—It has grown cold.—I hope you were warm enough in the auto & on the train. I'd hate to see you catch a fresh cold.—Do keep warm enough—take care of the lower regions—bladder—I guess you think I have gone crazy. Maybe I have.—

I have written to Hawley to deliver your letters. I hope you get this.—

9:00 P.M.—Well I'm glad you are installed & found everything comfortable.—I'll take a walk now & then go to the hotel. I'll take a bath and my pill.—After the paintings are hung.—

A kiss—

Good Night!

Alfred Stieglitz · [New York City] · October 30, 1932

Room 3003—10 P.M.—Your paintings are hung. The large one where it was—The small one on the wall where the easel stands.—There is no doubt about it—it is scandalous that you weren't given a fair chance to do that mural—It seems it wasn't to be. Somehow I feel you will get a real chance some day in the not distant future. Maybe that's born of a wish. A wish for you.—It was icy cold when I came in here. And curiously enough when I pushed that button to turn on the light the fuse blew out—The side light burns so there is light. I have sent for the electrician.—

Thanks for my spring suit.—I'll wear it tomorrow.—And thanks too for the belly band[480]—

I really miss you.—And yet I know you are better off than if you were in the place called New York.—

Once more Good Night & another kiss.—

---

480. Stieglitz wore a truss for his hernia.

Georgia O'Keeffe · [Lake George, New York] · [**November 1, 1932**]

The Child met me at Saratoga alone—and we drove over in the dark—

Everything at the house fine as I told you—

I slept well—waked at dawn and got up—heard Margaret go down and Georgie closing her window—it was pouring rain. Has rained all day till nearly five—

We both sewed—Each made ourselves a vest to go with our pants—same material— Talked—and I lay on the bed in the dining room looking out the window—

The rain has stopped—it is still cloudy and windy—

I feel better in my country clothes—my corduroy pants and red shirt and sox—in a few days I guess I'll come to—particularly if the sun would shine and I could get out—

Your letters and one from Ross with a poem—You are a funny one—I seem to have nothing to say that seems worth reading or saying—I just want to be still—

Good Night—

Georgia O'Keeffe · [Lake George, New York] · [**November 3, 1932**]

Thursday—noon—

I didn't write yesterday—There was nothing to say—

I was busy all day tinkering with my materials—Things I must do every once in awhile—

It was gray—rained off and on and finally at about four when it was clearer the Kid and I went for a walk—about six miles up the back road and back the second back road then cut across home through the woods—

I felt better—we ate much and went to bed early—

This morning is clear—She and I paced the porch a long time after breakfast—then both tinkered again—I fixing canvas and such things—so I can paint if I ever want to again— I also settling myself better in my room—She went for a walk—I walked by myself up the back road past the stone schoolhouse till I came to the shadow of the woods—It is cold—ground frozen except where thawing in the sun—

I haven't much ambition to do anything—haven't any in fact—but the house is pleasant —particularly when the sun shines—and maybe when I have things a bit more in order I'll do something about it—I don't know.

I hope all is well with you—I really feel very pleasant in a way—but nothing in my head—and I'd much rather be here than in town—

Be good to yourself—I am glad you like my *White Flowers*[481]—

---

481. Lynes 815–817.

Sunday—It's 8:45 A.M.—I'm about to go to breakfast—Childs. But I want to say good morning before going.—I went to bed at ten—slept till midnight. Got up awhile. Went to bed again. Tossed about. Dreamt a messy dream.—Up again.—To bed again. More dreams—unpleasant. Tossed about but "rested."—Finally got up at eight!—So here I am feeling as if I had been kicked in every part of my body—"rested."—Well, it's another day.—Sort of clearish.

—I do hope you'll get rid of that sinus.—But I'm glad I called up. The connection was very good. So you started to paint & it was no good. I know how difficult it is to get agoing feeling as you do. Really as nearly everyone does these days. But one dare not give in. That would mean complete paralysis.—That's what's threatening the whole country—The world perhaps. —Yesterday was the first day in days that I read no Lawrence or Carswell,[482] etc. So you can imagine how busy I was for Lawrence is really a rare treat to me.

—Well I'd better go. More later—

A morning kiss.—

I suppose you are up & about quite some time still keeping up daylight saving—a fine idea.

Another kisslet!—

8:30 P.M. It's raining. I'm in 3003. Just came from Childs.—Was at Place until 7:30. Ringel, Sykes, a few moments—McCausland & Gutman (*Creative Art*).[483] A few visitors. Nothing of consequence. I tinkered a lot.—Creepy weather. A bit of sinus.—Gutman told me Kuniyoshi is to do "your" room.[484] —Well I guess he can smear off something pretty fast. It will be the opposite in spirit of what you wanted to do.—That's that. I explained to McCausland what happened. Gutman had come with her (are friends) & he heard. Ida brought some pictures. —Four tiny ones & a larger one. Is becoming quite professional. Says Rehn[485] sold one of hers last year. —Didn't ask her particulars. Didn't want to know. Saks (store) she says wants some of her work for window display. Asked my advice. Told her she seemed to know how [to] take care of herself —that I was of no use whatever.—It's all so "funny."—She is certainly learning the trade.

—I am going to take another Adalin tonight—Am a bit on edge. I hate days when I seem to achieve nothing in a way.—At best I achieve little.—Flint says he saw *Americana*[486] a second time & sat nearly downstairs. Says it was awful! Said that last night—So it goes.

—I wonder how your throat & nose are today—If the weather is rotten. I suppose no

---

482. Catherine MacFarlane Carswell, *The Savage Pilgrimage; A Narrative of D. H. Lawrence* (London, 1932).

483. Walter Gutman, an artist and critic who frequently contributed to *Creative Art: A Magazine of Fine and Applied Art,* not O'Keeffe's and Stieglitz's friend the sculptor Ernest Gutman.

484. Yasuo Kuniyoshi created a four-wall mural of exotic flowers for the women's powder room of Radio City Music Hall. Unlike O'Keeffe, who proposed a mural on canvas, Kuniyoshi painted directly onto the plaster; see Christine Roussel, *The Art of Rockefeller Center* (New York, 2006), 72–73.

485. The Rehn Galleries, 683 Fifth Ave., New York, specialized in American art.

486. *Americana*, described as "a little confused in its ideas [but also] extraordinarily beautiful," was a Broadway revue performed at the Shubert Theatre in New York, with sketches by J. P. McEvoy and music by Harold Arlen and others; see "The Play," *NYT*, Oct. 6, 1932, 19.

better.—Someone just phoned & asked me when Dr. Walker's show was to take place.—Well is that out already. I wonder if Walker thinks he is to have a show without those publications.[487] I was clear enough.—Well I'm not going to worry.—

Good Night.—Another kiss.—

Remember me to the Kidlet & Margaret.—

Alfred Stieglitz · [New York City] · November 9, 1932 +

8:15 A.M. Here I am at the Place. A northeast gale is having a grand time. Nearly blew me across the street when I came out of Rosen's.—And it's pouring pitchforks!!—There is your little letter—I'm glad there is that—I feared there mightn't be—& somehow I hoped my fear would be unfounded.—Last night I spent alone. Was glad.—I sat in the armchair & read Lawrence. Then would drop the book into my lap & stare into space awhile & then read some more, etc.—It was election night & I seemed unrelated completely to all that was going on.—I called you up & disturbed you.—It's as if I shouldn't have done that.—For I hate to disturb.—Finally I took an Adalin—I haven't gotten Phanadorm yet—always forget—& went to sleep. The wind had started to kick up—moan & howl—so it took awhile to go off. Well I did sleep some.— Awakening was cold—couldn't get warm. I wondered about you. Whether you kept warm.— And how.—Whether what you felt was in any way related to what I was feeling—Well I went to Rosen. I saw the papers. A landslide. Roosevelt—The country has gone wet.[488]—Anything for a "change."—But the people!—The individuals themselves—how about them?—

There is a letter from Dove.[489] I enclose it. Please let me have it back.—And one from Mellquist.[490] I enclose it too.—I have one from Kopman. Carrying it around unopened for a week. Also a letter from Tofel written three weeks ago. I hadn't opened it[491]—

You say my letter sounded hectic. I wouldn't be surprised if that were true. What a life. —Yesterday printing & running in & out of the darkroom—people—phone—"mind" switching from one thing to another—absolutely unrelated—instantaneously.—Each individual completely oblivious of the fact that after all I too am nothing but an ordinary human.—Of course it's "fun"—beats golf & even motoring—etc.—still it may be a bit hectic at times.—

655

A TERRIBLE RIGHTNESS, 1929–1933

---

487. O'Keeffe had proposed that Stieglitz exhibit the work of the Santa Fe painter and poet Robert Walker at An American Place. Stieglitz was hesitant, however, and agreed to do so only if Walker published a book of poems to accompany the show. On October 30, 1932, Walker wrote Stieglitz that he was not going to publish his poems and therefore did not want to exhibit his paintings at An American Place. Nevertheless, Stieglitz exhibited them in 1936.

488. As part of his campaign for the presidency, Roosevelt had urged the repeal of both the Eighteenth Amendment and the Volstead Act and advocated the return of liquor control to the states.

489. In a letter of November 7[?], 1932, Dove told Stieglitz that he had "probably done the best painting yet," but also lamented that he had "tried to *do* too much" in his work around the house: "You can sew your clothes, weave the wool and make the cloth but when it comes to making the sheep you have to let the ram do it"; Morgan, *Dear Stieglitz/Dear Dove,* 252.

490. On November 7, 1932, Jerome Mellquist wrote Stieglitz, asking if he felt "we are on the verge of a great period in America? That a faith by which men can live again is coming from this place." He added that Stieglitz's work was one of the few "examples we have yet had of this wonder in contemporary America."

491. For the past few years, the painter and writer Jennings Tofel had sent Stieglitz heartfelt letters, detailing his struggles to paint and his impoverished state.

Well I'm glad you are satisfied with the Kidlet's walking powers.—You are certainly a team in many respects—I miss you—yes I do—very much & yet I'm glad you are in a healthier atmosphere than all this is.—I haven't looked at the prints I made yesterday.—So you finally mounted your bits of canvas.—Isn't it a relief?—You certainly are in many respects exactly as I am.—Or should I put it I am like you in many respects. No, I feel if I were not so delinquent you wouldn't be.—Nonsense you'll say.—Well now I'll go & look at the prints.—

A kiss—Whether you want one or not—

11:11 A.M.—Some of the prints look pretty good. I think you'll like some of you.[492] —Very strong. And mighty good looking. That is *you*. I have something I wanted of you.—It's there in the print. But I'll have to get even handsomer prints if I get another chance.—The glossy tree prints[493] are what I want—Well it's another start. Ross just left.—On his way to Baltimore. As he looked at the prints when he saw one he said: God she's a handsome woman. It was one with the cow's skull—you looking out of the Shanty window.[494]

—Still I feel I must do ever better.—That's what gets me crazy here. There are things at Lake George—you (things?!) & the tree I really want to work with—very positively & then this thing here the Place!!—Two selves—really one—Do you understand?

1:30 P.M.—Bruguière left a little while ago.—I showed him some of your things. He liked them tremendously. They looked unusually beautiful. The *Yellow Leaves* (Kennerley)—the *Mountains* (twin of the Whitney one)—*The Skull & Pink Rose*—the *Abstraction* of last year[495] in the white room—Those are the four I showed him.—Can you see them?—An amazing scope & purity (sensitiveness)—

Your show (or maybe shows) will be wonderful. *I want to strike hard*. And will.— I know we—you & Marin (and I—but I'm out of it) are *true* always—& this is the time to establish that if ever there was a time. And it's up to me. True as Lawrence is also true. Maybe even beyond him.—I'm alive once more—Not a bit hectic today. Very clear. And very sure. I slept you know.—And I printed yesterday. And Flint "discovered" the Marin oils, etc., etc.— And election had nothing to do with me—Nor you. Nor Marin. Nor the Place.—Etc. Etc.— I wrote a few lines to Brett. Am dry mounting, Zoler helping.—

I hope you are no longer sad—You mustn't be.—I wonder do you like your white room as much as you did—

It's still pouring—Stray visitors straggle in—Mary Barker of the Group Theatre was here quite awhile. Talked to her a little while. Yesterday the little actress of the Austin car was here. Didn't talk to her as I was printing.—

So Margaret voted.—For whom? Communist?—?—

492. Greenough 1480–1495.
493. Possibly Greenough 1467–1470.
494. Greenough 1430–1433.
495. *Yellow Leaves*, Lynes 642; *Mountains*, Lynes 743; Whitney one, Lynes 790; *Skull & Pink Rose*, Lynes 775; and "*Abstraction* of last year," Lynes 769.

Georgia O'Keeffe · [Lake George, New York] · [November 9, 1932]

4:30—The end of another day—and I really have nothing to write—

The telephone did surprise me last night—I was so sound asleep Margaret had to come right to my door to wake me—I had gone to bed at 8:30—and aside from the few moments at the phone—slept through till dawn—when I got up—

The sun has been out off and on today and I spent nearly three hours out wandering about the woods—

An aimless sort of thing to do I suppose—but there isn't an idea in my head so I get out and use my legs—

Aside from that I've been reading—a little of lots of things—I have half the dining room bed full of books and read on one and then another in a disorderly haphazard sort of way—when I lie there—and it is a good place to lie—Some music too—

—My body is first rate—The rest of me is quite empty—

So that's that—

Georgia O'Keeffe · [Lake George, New York] · [November 10, 1932]

It is a another very wet morning—the rain coming down steadily as tho it will never stop—since way in the night—Clouds over the mountain till the mountain seems almost gone—

Such a wetness.

Your letter yesterday was nice—Mine to you—that you have this morning has nothing in it—nothing at all—That is the way I am—

So I only read—

It would probably be better if I did not write you at all—I am so vacant—

Alfred Stieglitz · [New York City] · November 11, 1932

The Place—8 A.M. It's finally clearing. I have been here since 7:30.—Have been looking at your paintings that came back from Reinhardt's.—Some are very beautiful. I'm glad they are here. I can't do worse by them than they did & perhaps maybe a little better.—But as I said I'm glad they are here. And I'm sure they are glad too.—I can't but feel that fine things are as human as I am.—

—Altho' I was in 3003 all evening last night it was midnight before I went to bed. Zoler was with me awhile.—

—I have just read your letter. It came a few minutes ago.—No, you must write even if you have nothing to write.—And furthermore if you have nothing to paint & feel you'll not get into the mood you might as well come to town. Of course you may feel being alone awhile is what you need or want.—I really don't know how to use words any more. Nearly everything is so twisted & ingrown & everyone so hypersensitive that words seem to hurt—& silence hurts as much or even more—I realize that more & more—

Ettie spoke of Seligmann's poems. Thought them very beautiful. Felt about them as I do. —No one else seems to have felt that way about them. I *know* they are very fine.—I was constantly interrupted while talking to her.—For hours no one would be here then suddenly there'd be quite a swarm (four or five) of "important" people [each of whom] would expect me to talk to them. Goodwin was very fine.—He usually is.—

I guess you'll think me crazy sending you books. But somehow I wanted you to have those volumes whether you'd read them or not.—The quiet here is audible—Yet there is a tomb-like feeling about it all.—That's in me of course. The Marins are so beautiful & so patient.

—I ought to go to the oculist this morning but somehow I haven't the necessary energy to go. The eyes are better—less uncomfortable.—They were certainly a nuisance for about eight weeks.—

Again I say if Lake George gives you nothing you must come back here. I am ready. You must know that. I have a feeling you have much in your head—or wherever you may keep it —which is all wrong about me—and that it affects you in a way which it shouldn't—

I know talking leads nowhere—or if it does it leads to the opposite of [where] it is intended to lead.—Again I say words are the greatest criminals in the world. The original sin is the word.—There is no doubt about that as far as I am concerned. Maybe it is the cardinal sin —& maybe the only sin.—

—If I didn't feel bound to stay here virtually twelve hours a day with the hope that something might happen for Marin I'd surprise you for a day. Just to see how you really are.— That's true.—

A kiss & much love.—

—Yes I'm funny.

Georgia O'Keeffe · [Lake George, New York] · [November 14, 1932]

Monday—A.M.
It is gray and cheerless again this morning—
And I only reading—

Afternoon—The sun came out—Richard was here—I just came from taking him home— Margaret and I walked in [the] very nice woods over near Warrensburg—
I just seem to be tongue-tied—or maybe it is utterly vacant—
Good Night—

Alfred Stieglitz · [New York City] · November 14, 1932

The Place—9:27 A.M.

Good Morning Miss O'Keeffe. A kiss Miss O'Keeffe—

I have just read Vernon Hunter in *Contemporary Arts*.[496] I am sending you two copies. They arrive on your birthday. Odd. I think I asked you yesterday—or maybe day before—had you heard.

—I was at Rosen's. Then went to Hicks & sent you some fruit which I hope you receive with this. It goes Special Handling so ought to be in Lake George tomorrow A.M.—November 15—Your birthday!—Georgia.—I'd like to tell you very much—very much. Really tell you.—But somehow I remain silent as you remain silent. If you don't know I suppose you can't be made to know.

—It was nearly midnight when I left this Place. Ringel was reading in scrapbooks. I read Brett.[497]—It's a beautiful book. Few, very few, will really get it.—If ever a woman loved a man in the deepest sense she loves Lawrence. She has produced a masterpiece of its kind. And she has handled the "unsaid" ending marvelously.[498] Not an inkling. Yet all that's true. I'll send you the manuscript. I want to go through parts of it again & write her. I really wonder will you like it at all.—It has the feeling of soft music to me—soft still firm—& alive. Maybe I read something into the pages which isn't there. I doubt it.—I was charged in doing that with your things.—The two *Blue Lines*[499] for instance. I still feel about that "drawing" as I did from the first.—It exists for me as the sun exists. Walkowitz spoke of it too.—Whatever actually exists in all your things is in that drawing. That's as I see.—

—Ringel & I went to Childs then. We talked.—A drunken man came over to us & said sitting down at our table: "Now don't you let that old philosopher sell you anything you young unsophisticated man," addressing Ringel. There was a most amusing half hour then. The man comes from Washington—

At supper I met Flint who was just finishing. I walked up to 59th Street to get the *Art News*. I enclose clippings.[500] Please send it back. Flint is busy painting. Sends his love—

Went to supper at seven—walked to 59th Street & back here & was here again by 8:30. Outside of reading Brett—talking with Ringel—not so much—& spotting prints—I attended to odds & ends here.—The more there is to do the better I like it as long as there is a sense of life.

—It was two when I got to bed. Really slept several hours without dope. The night was beautiful. It must be very beautiful at the Lake if it is at all like here. Maybe a bit cold. I hope your cough lets up.—It often sticks quite awhile.—

496. Vernon Hunter, "A Note on Georgia O'Keeffe," *Contemporary Arts of the South and Southwest* 1 (Nov.–Dec. 1932), 7.
497. Brett, *Lawrence and Brett*.
498. Brett ended her book not with a discussion of Lawrence's death but with a recollection of her last visit with him on Capri.
499. Lynes 64 (see p. 21).
500. Ralph Flint, "Modern Museum Opens Fine Show of American Art," *Art News* 21 (Nov. 5, 1932), 3–4; Flint, "Marin 1932 Show Has New Trend," *Art News* 21 (Nov. 12, 1932), 10.

Noon 30. The Bentons[501] just left. He excited about the Marins. Really enthusiastic about the "oils." She as ever crazy to have one of your best things.—I told him about your wall. He said he had a hell of a time himself this summer with his murals[502] not putting them on the wall himself—trusting another—

—A few visitors. I fussing with prints. Very slow business. Nothing seems quite right. Gave Benton Marin's *Letters.* I want them out in the world—Possible buyers are as unlikely as the mastodon visiting the Marin show.

5:27 P.M.—I'm alone—unless Zoler counts who is cleaning up. Mumford was here again.— Rosenfeld—About sixty people today. No nibbles.—I wonder will nothing happen like last year.—Mumford very enthusiastic. But that doesn't mean he'll write anything or if he does that it will bear witness to his enthusiasm.

—I have been looking at Brett again. I'm really curious to see how it will strike you. I'll send it Wednesday. I haven't written to her yet. May tonight or tomorrow. Feel a bit tired. Have been going apace. Your things standing here look lovely just now. Happened to look up to see them—Quite a few people look at them.

—I have reread the Vernon Hunter article. It is very good. I only wish he hadn't had to use the word "enlargements."[503] I felt that in the manuscript but didn't wish to interfere. Maybe you did too & said nothing for the same reason I didn't—It's fresh & clearly expressed—

6:30 P.M. I'm still here. Alone now—I shall get the Brett off to you tomorrow which is Tuesday. You'll have it by Wednesday.—

I'm really curious.—I'm afraid it will do one thing above all others—that is make you very sick for the Southwest if you are not that already. If you are it will intensify it terrifically.

In reading Lawrence & Brett I realize more & more how little use I am in a way—what a city person I am.—I also realize more than ever that you are closer to their kind in a way than to my kind.—I often wonder what would have happened had you & Lawrence met—by happened I mean how you would have impressed him & how he would have impressed you.—I'm sure he would have had very little use for me & that I would have liked him very much in spite of it.—

—I have been fixing up some of your prints in the auto.[504] —There is something there—

Good Night—I hope November 15 will be the beginning of a very fine year for you— That is my deepest wish—

Two kisses—A gentle one & one not quite so gentle—

501. Thomas and Rita Piacenza Benton.

502. In 1932, Thomas Hart Benton completed *Arts of Life in America,* a series of large murals in the Whitney Museum of American Art at 10 West 8th St. in New York City. That same year he was also commissioned to paint murals for the Indiana Hall at the Century of Progress exposition at the 1933 Chicago World's Fair.

503. Hunter wrote: "Her flower paintings are not far fetched imaginings but glorified enlargements which would have taken generations of Burbanking to produce in petal and leaf. In pigment they bring a new offering to the altar of aesthetics"; Hunter, "A Note on Georgia O'Keeffe," *Contemporary Arts of the South and Southwest* 1 (Nov.–Dec. 1932), 7.

504. Greenough 1490–1493.

Alfred Stieglitz · [New York City] · [November 16, 1932]

You are at Hirst's.—And soon you'll be here to see how beautiful the Place looks.—It's your work as much as mine & Marin's.—And your work here is as *important* as mine. I know *what we are together.* Please don't think I don't. And you know *what we are together.* The idea of separation is preposterous.—I want you to realize that that is *my* feeling.

Cahill just called up & told me how wonderful your things look at the Museum—that the pastel & the Marin watercolor he hung with the oils! That he hung a Winslow Homer oil & flanked it with your pastel & a Demuth oil[505] making a beautiful wall. And he has the *Cows Skull with White Roses*[506] in the masters' room! All as I hoped it would be & I said nothing!— So Cahill the man I never quite trusted whether rightly or wrongly has done what Barr would never have done nor Abbott[507]—nor anyone else except possibly—probably—you!—It's the spirit of truth & the spirit of beauty—the two are twins—which finally must win out. It takes endless patience to await the moment.—And I'm not always as patient as I know I must be.— That's my chief trouble. And I'm considered endlessly patient. Yet am so impatient at times. I feel the Radio City experience is of value—maybe great value—I want you to enjoy the Hill. I want you to know that whatever you may do I'm with you. Absolutely. I mean this 100 percent— If you want to go to York Beach or elsewhere you must go.—Above all tho get some rest & eat enough & build up.

—Lizzie sent fifty dollars for the Place. Lee had sent fifty dollars.—

—Your *White Flower* is grand. And so is your large *Cross* & the small one[508] very beautiful. If you had only those paintings for the year I'd be more than satisfied with what you have done. I want you to know that—I'll miss you.—I did like our evenings even if they were not exciting.—I'm sorry I seem so unable to make myself clear so frequently—like last night— It's really frightful for I really had felt at peace & felt how wonderful you had been to me all these weeks—and when you said to me: You look beautiful—I felt you were at a relative peace too—I thought I understood—& then!!

Take care of yourself. Give my love to the Hill—to Margaret & Richard & Putnam & the Kidlet. And don't forget to look at the tree for me.—It is ever in my mind—before me— a living symbol—terribly alive—

Walker's letter—Cahill—messages from the vast space of life—voices— I'm glad your little white room is waiting for you—

---

505. American Painting and Sculpture, 1862–1932, Museum of Modern Art, Oct. 31, 1932–Jan. 31, 1933, included two works by O'Keeffe (Lynes 654 and 772), lent by An American Place; Marin, *New Mexico Landscape, Blue Mountain,* lent by An American Place; six works by Winslow Homer, including three oil paintings: *Eight Bells* (1886), lent by the Addison Gallery of American Art, Andover, Mass., *The Gulf Stream* (1899), and *Cannon Rock,* lent by the Metropolitan Museum of Art; and Charles Demuth, *My Egypt* (1925), lent by the Whitney Museum of American Art. See Cahill, *American Painting and Sculpture,* pls. 37, 35, 32, 28. 506. Lynes 772.

507. Holger Cahill served as acting director of the Museum of Modern Art in 1932 while Barr took a one-year leave of absence; Jere Abbott was the associate director of the museum from 1929 to 1932; see Russell Lynes, *Good Old Modern* (New York, 1973), 107.

508. *White Flower,* Lynes 816; *Cross,* Lynes 812; "the small one," Lynes 813.

As for telling me or not telling me in the future—I want you to tell me. It will not make me nervous whatever it may be.—

It is difficult for me not to see you in Radio City for I had really accustomed myself to see you working there.—

That will surprise you.—

Georgia O'Keeffe · [Lake George, New York] · [November 17, 1932]

It is strange to be back here—all as tho I hadn't been away—everything as I left it—even the warm house—

I am glad to be back and I am glad that I was in town—but everything seems a bit like a dream—

My only regret is for the way I feel that I disturb you—and I feel quite helpless about it —maybe I can do better when I get to town—I do not want to disturb you—

Maybe this going down as I have has disturbed you more than not seeing me would have —It may have been a bit crazy but each time I thought I had something to go for—

I know you often say "Don't think!"—Oh—I guess I'm just no good—

I do know that I am very very sorry to have disturbed you in any way—and every way that I did—Not that I think that saying I am sorry helps any—

Writing seems so senseless—but just being seems quite as senseless—

I kiss you Good Night.

When I see myself as I am I know it is the thing I am that makes the work—and it creates lots of trouble it seems—

It is really no use to talk about it—I'll mark myself down as no good—but I'll be busy —So I must go to bed early—

Another Good Night kiss.

[November 18, 1932]

It is morning—Good Morning—! Gray—and warm—

I slept well—have been out on the porch in my wrapper—it is more like warm spring —the feeling in the air—It is so gray and dark I don't see how I can work but I will be at something—

Thank you for the fruit—I had lovely grapefruit for breakfast—

I wonder how you are this morning—I am glad to be back here—

Putnam was up and asked for you—says there has been no sun since we were away—

Afternoon—I've been at the horse's head[509] all day—light bad—

---

509. This painting does not appear to have survived.

Georgia O'Keeffe · [Lake George, New York] · [November 20, 1932]

Good Morning! Sunday morning—Clear and cold—

I finished the Brett manuscript—tomorrow I will mail it to you—

I have nothing to say—Maybe I sidestep by saying it is not my affair—That she will go her way and I see no reason why I should say what I think or what I would do—or what I think I would do—I simply feel like laying it aside and saying it is not my affair[510]—

Think I'll prepare some canvas—

No—the manuscript does not give me the yearning for the West that you thought it would—You see my feeling is different—

You see—I got my feeling alone—it is one of the things that most satisfies my feeling of aloneness—I even get a kind of ecstasy from the vast space—feeling like death—that is close kin to what the male can give me—Still I have always enjoyed it most alone—No one ever seems equal to the country as I feel it[511]—

She is writing about something quite different—

Alfred Stieglitz · [New York City] · November 21, 1932

The Place—10:45 A.M.
Good Morning. A kiss.

—I was here at eight. Went to dentist. Delayed there. Just got back. Must go again next Monday. The disagreeable session comes then—I had hoped it would be today. But the morning is very dark & he needs light. So I'll have a week "looking ahead." But what will be will be. I'm not nervous about it.

—Well, last night I got to the Whitney's[512] sharp nine.—I was the third to arrive.— So had the galleries awhile to myself & looked at the paintings. The room I walked into first had your picture, the Dove, Demuth, Stella, Spencer,[513] in it. Yours looked very distinguished. The finest thing not only in the room but one of the swellest in the whole show. Whether it will be "seen" I don't know.[514] It's so simple & aristocratic.—The Dove looks very well. The Demuth

---

510. In September or October 1932, O'Keeffe had written Brett, "I feel so surely that if [your book] is to be of any value to anyone—it must be your truth as nearly as you are able to put it down.... You must write it truly to the end for yourself— Then if you do not wish to print it to the end stop where you wish." She added, "One's truth must always have a certain amount of fantasy in it." Harry Ransom Humanities Research Center, The University of Texas at Austin.

511. On November 22, 1932, Stieglitz responded to O'Keeffe, writing: "I think I am very clear as to what the Southwest gives you—how you *receive* it.—For that is what you do. Or really 'feel' it.—It's all clearly in your things. Always was. And will be."

512. The Whitney Museum of American Art opened the First Biennial Exhibition of Contemporary American Painting on November 22, 1932; it was on view through January 5, 1933.

513. Lynes 653; Dove, *Red Barge, Reflections,* see Morgan 31.15; Demuth, *Buildings,* see *First Biennial Exhibition of Contemporary American Painting,* Whitney Museum of American Art, exh. cat., pl. 15; Stella, *La Chanson Napolitaine,* pl. 10; Niles Spencer, *Gas House District,* pl. 9.

514. On November 27, 1932, Stieglitz sent O'Keeffe a clipping of an article by Ralph Flint, "Whitney Museum Opens Its First Biennial Show," *Art News* 31 (Nov. 26, 1932), 3–4, in which he wrote that O'Keeffe's *Farmhouse Window and Door* (Lynes 653)

too. But it looks dry. So many of the paintings in the show are stale—things done—not experienced. I looked at the 157 paintings by 157 painters. The crowd gradually gathered. I talked with Mrs. Whitney, & Mrs. Force—Glackens, Speicher, Bouché, Walkowitz, Friedman, Peggy Bacon, Brook, Sheeler, Pollet, Kenneth Hays Miller, Kroll, Pach, and a host of others. Of course with Florine whom I took [home] eventually—but didn't go up with her. It was midnight. Her painting[515] is one of the few real things there. I like it very much. It will amuse you. You didn't miss anything. Not worth sacrificing anything for. Still I'm glad I went.—

I went to sleep quickly. Was up at 6:30.—

—You sounded a bit "down" on the phone last night. And the connection wasn't good. —I hope nothing was wrong.—Flint at supper was amusing. And Duncan is always fine. I wasn't feeling right. Innards kicking up again. "Nerves" or cold or what. Or all three—

—There are a few stray visitors in the rooms walking around. I ought to go to Juley's but will send Zoler with prints & instructions.

—Your letter this morning doesn't sound very bright.—I had hoped you'd perk up!!— And you are reading Freud on Leonardo.[516] And Brett's manuscript. Flint is through with Lawrence *Letters*. Liked them immensely.—

I haven't read anything since Brett—Must go to Török—

—The morning is bleak. More rain? Or possibly a bit of snow?—

Won't I ever get the chance to photograph snow again?—

Georgia O'Keeffe · [Lake George, New York] · [November 27, 1932]

The records came this afternoon—George Pharmer brought them up—I have played first the Beethoven *First*—Then Mozart *Quintet* then the Mozart *Quartette in [G]*—We have the Mozart *Quartette in G*—so I will bring the new one with me when I come down and we can exchange it for something else—Then I played the Beethoven *Second* and after that all the Stravinsky—

And I call that a plenty for one day—I think I enjoyed the Mozart *Quintet* most—

Funny that the day after I played all the Stravinsky here—I had played all the Mozart—

And so it goes—

I had also played the Schubert—

It has been a cold windy day—sun and a little snow with the wind—

I just now went out to look at the thermometer—it is eight above—about nine o'clock I think—I am in bed—

Margaret is absorbed in Mabel's *Lorenzo in Taos*—Having a fine time with it—

"comes near being the most distinguished piece of design in the exhibition, and surely Florine Stettheimer's 'Cathedrals of Fifth Avenue' is the most original canvas on hand."

515. Florine Stettheimer, *Cathedrals of Fifth Avenue*; see Barbara Bloemink, *The Life and Art of Florine Stettheimer* (New Haven, 1995), 181.

516. Sigmund Freud, *Leonardo da Vinci: A Psychosexual Study of Infantile Reminiscence,* trans. A. A. Brill (New York, 1932).

The thermometer went down to five below zero last night[517]—Saturday night—However we are comfortable—It has been a bright clear still cold day—not so cold tonight as last night—The sun goes down behind the mountain at 3:45—a clear warm sunset—warm color—The air has a fine cold smell—

We played the first book of the *Tannhäuser* this afternoon—Margaret came in and listened and seemed to enjoy it much—I enjoyed it too—

There are three books of it—Will finish it tonight—

I am reading *King Richard III*—

Think I will go to town on Wednesday—Will let you know later—will ask about trains tomorrow—

[November 28, 1932]
Monday morning—

I have just ordered my ticket and chair for Wednesday[518]—Will go from Fort Edwards at three—

It is cold and clear again this morning—another zero night—

I played more *Tannhäuser* last night but am not through all of it yet—

I called you last night—wanting to know how you are—also forgot to mail the letter about the records—and felt you would be expecting news this morning—

Good Morning to you—It is so clear and cold here—

O'KEEFFE RETURNED to New York on November 30, ostensibly to prepare for her exhibition at An American Place, on view from January 7 to March 15, 1933. But instead her distress over the failure of her mural and her marriage plunged her into a depression. As her emotional stability weakened, her heart began to beat irregularly, making it difficult for her to walk or even stand, and the headaches that had plagued her adult life returned with a vengeance. Stieglitz's nervous nature, his hypochondria, and his tendency to analyze every comment only exacerbated O'Keeffe's difficulties. Seeking solitude, she moved into her sister Anita Young's apartment in New York City soon after Christmas. Stieglitz's brother Lee initially treated her, but he was soon joined by Edwin Jenks, a New York physician who summered at Diamond Point, near Lake George, and had cared for both Stieglitz and O'Keeffe. At first, Stieglitz visited O'Keeffe every day, but by the middle of January, on the recommendation of her doctors and Young, he saw her only once a week for thirty minutes. On February 1, with no improvement in her condition, O'Keeffe was admitted to Doctors' Hospital on 88th Street and East End Avenue, where Stieglitz, at the discretion of her doctors and nurses, was gradually able to visit her more often.

517. To stay warm at night, O'Keeffe slept in the dining room of the Lake George farmhouse.
518. Just before O'Keeffe left for New York on November 30, 1932, Stieglitz sent her two clippings about Eckstein, announcing his recent return to New York from Spain: "Turns with a Bookworm," *New York Herald Tribune*, Nov. 27, 1932, and "Between the Leaves," *New York Sun*, Nov. 28, 1932.

Throughout the winter and spring of 1933, the rising political volatility and the growing impact of the Depression on O'Keeffe's and Stieglitz's finances aggravated their emotional distress. Like so many others, both Stieglitz and O'Keeffe were alarmed in late January when Hitler was made chancellor of Germany, concerned in March when banks briefly closed, and worried and confused in early April when they had to turn in the small amount of gold they had husbanded as a hedge against inflation. To save money, Stieglitz began making arrangements to dispose of much of his large collection of work by pictorial photographers from the turn of the century. In April, with assistance from Carl Zigrosser, he consented to a long-standing request from William Ivins, curator of prints and drawings at the Metropolitan Museum of Art, and donated 418 photographs and a complete set of *Camera Work* to the museum. He also considered less expensive accommodations at the Shelton Hotel, but, reluctant to leave the place he had shared with O'Keeffe, he instead asked Cary Ross to move into his rooms and split the rent. He further economized by making his breakfast, ironing his own handkerchiefs, and, as he proudly told O'Keeffe, wearing suits from 1916 that did not look too "disreputable."[519]

As the seriousness of O'Keeffe's emotional and physical state grew more apparent, Stieglitz was scared but not chastened. Thereafter, he rarely mentioned Norman in his letters to O'Keeffe, but he did not sever his relationship with the younger woman, nor did she abandon her role at An American Place, where the lease was renegotiated in 1933 and put in her name. Instead, with the March 1933 release of her book of poems, *Dualities,* which Stieglitz helped to edit and publish, she became the latest incarnation of his belief that a woman could be, as he told Norman, a powerful "creative force."[520] To further encourage her, Stieglitz also printed her pamphlets: *It Must Be Said, It Has Been Said, It Might Be Said,* and *It Should Be Remembered.* In 1933 and 1934 Norman was one of the editors of *America and Alfred Stieglitz,* a collection of essays celebrating both his seventieth birthday and his seminal contribution to American art and photography.[521]

From January through mid-March 1933, Stieglitz wrote O'Keeffe several times a day, no doubt hoping to demonstrate that, although absent, she was ever present in his mind. Often no more than a few sentences, these letters provide a diaristic account of his activities and the visitors to the gallery, with their frequent praise of O'Keeffe's art, as well as a recitation of his plans and ruminations. Yet they also show that although he was deeply grieved by her frailty, genuinely missed her, and recognized he upset her, he had little true insight into the causes of her depression and never expressed remorse for his role in precipitating it.[522] Too weak at times even to sit, O'Keeffe did not respond.

---

519. AS to GOK, Feb. 21, 1933.

520. Dorothy Norman, *Dualities* (New York, 1933); AS to Norman, Feb. 22, 1933.

521. *It Must Be Said, It Has Been Said, It Might Be Said,* and *It Should Be Remembered* were a series of small pamphlets compiled and edited by Norman and Stieglitz and published by An American Place between 1932 and 1937. *America and Alfred Stieglitz: A Collective Portrait,* ed. by Waldo Frank, Lewis Mumford, Dorothy Norman, and Paul Rosenfeld (New York, 1934).

522. In a letter to O'Keeffe of November 18, 1932, Stieglitz admitted that he realized he played a role in her depression, but he qualified his responsibility, writing: "For I did feel miserable knowing you so down & much because of 'me'—Yes, 'me' in quotation marks."

Noon 25. I wonder what is happening.—Lee?—You? How you are.—It seems as if you were terribly far away—Cut off since the phone is not next to your bed.—It has been a "queer" morning.—I have been cleaning up some more. Vault. Everything.—Sending out another eighty or so invitations.[523] —John Collier called up.—Tony Lujan & Mirabal are in town to see about Indian affairs.[524] —Want to see you.—I told Collier I wondered.—I know you'd like to see Tony. —And he you.—Will it excite you. Or will it perhaps help you.—Or both?—They are to see President Roosevelt.—Bement was in.—Delighted with the *Green Mountain* & the *Small Cross*—& the *White Barns*[525]—Is very sorry to hear you laid low—And Cortissoz was in. Really looked. Said: Lovely.—Enamored of the *Green Mountain* & *Small Cross*. Also *White Barns* & the bunch of flowers—pastel.[526] —A lady or two strayed in. Otherwise no one. Just light. And a freshness. And cleanness of feeling pervades the Place.—I wonder when will you be able to see it. To see whether I have done pretty well. Whether you would have done it very different.—

Ross & Zoler were at the hotel last night—Nothing exciting. Quite alive.—The Phana-dorm held over some. A man just came in.—The Place looks so perfect that any person seems really out of place.—

I wonder when you'll call up.—

Zoler & I are busy dry mounting a few things. Trying it on Marin's drawings. The crinkling annoyed me & I thought I'd risk a trial. Seems to work.—Also a few of my gravures.—

—I'm going to write to Mrs. Rockefeller. She must see your show. There is no use being too diffident.—It's not with an idea that she should buy but she should see.—If she doesn't come it's her affair.—

5 P.M.—Finally alone. It has been a day of constant coming & going.—I wonder why there has been no phone from you.—There has been no one on the phone since ten A.M.—And then only for a moment or two.—

—Well Cortissoz was here. And Jewell. And a nice young man from the *Chicago News*.[527] Says you talked with him last year. Coming again. Any many people. Cortissoz delighted: *The Green Mountain*—*The Barns*—*Flower* pastel—*The Small Cross*—etc.—Jewell: *Green Mountain*—*White Barns*—old small one.—*The Old Black One*[528]—All enthusiastic.—

523. Stieglitz was sending out invitations to Georgia O'Keeffe: Paintings—New and Some Old, An American Place, New York, Jan. 7–Mar. 15, 1933.

524. In 1933, as secretary of the American Indian Defense Association, John Collier often enlisted Tony and Mabel Luhan to lobby for his causes. Accompanied by Juan Mirabal, Tony Lujan traveled to New York, Washington, D.C., and throughout the Southwest in 1933 to help gain support for the Indian Reorganization Act of 1934. A few months after their visit in January 1933, Collier was appointed Commissioner of Indian Affairs; see Rudnick, *Mabel Dodge Luhan*, 178–179, 261–265.

525. *Green Mountain*, Lynes 818; *Small Cross*, Lynes 813; *White Barns*, Lynes 805, 806, 807, 809, or 811.

526. Lynes 814.

527. Clarence Joseph Bulliett was the art critic for the *Chicago Daily News* in 1933.

528. Possibly Lynes 524 or 811.

Neumann too—He really sees. Feels.—Says: Incarnation of Abstract Beauty.—As beautiful as the creation of a flower.—Is not "painting" in the narrow sense—but said that question of "painting" absurd in front of your pictures. Rosenfeld came again.—Zoler got my lunch at two but it was four before I got a chance to eat it.—At six I'll leave here & go up to you.—I hope I won't be delayed—or rather detained—

8:30 P.M.—Flint, Zoler & I had supper at Childs. Here I am in 3003.—I wasn't satisfied as I left you but I am hoping you will have sleep tonight & will feel stronger in the morning—I feel so helpless as far as helping you. It's a rotten feeling.—Of course I am fighting tooth & nail at the Place. Never more hard—maybe never so hard before.—I hope Tony will be able to come tomorrow.—I may take him up myself—to the door—if he does. But all is uncertain. So don't count on [his] being [able to come] tomorrow. I know he'll want to see you first chance he gets.—
    —I'll send out more invitations now.—
    Good Night—Good Morning—
    And a soft kiss—I do hope you'll sleep—

668   **Alfred Stieglitz · [New York City] · January 14, 1933**

It's just past midnight—I just returned from the opera.—Zoler is unexpectedly here. I'm glad. He remained at the Place. Took out the *Rose*[529]—made new strips—cleaned glass—It lies here on my bed—that is my bed when you are in yours here—The lady[530] comes at 9:45 A.M. with the check.—So all will be ready.—Somehow losing the *Rose* does not give me the pain "losing" many of your pictures gives me—I realize more than ever how "funny" I am about most of your paintings. I have been charged over & over again the last years that I was intolerant towards those who said anything in criticism of any of your work. Do you know that? I the fault-finder.—
    Well it was a day.—At the opera[531] the seats were very good. I sat in mine. But I hardly heard anything or saw anything. I seemed far away from all that was going on in the house. You see I would rather have remained a little longer with you. But I feel I excite you.—That you are quieter when I'm not there.—Maybe I'm wrong.—I do want to see you improve—I wonder will you sleep tonight. Will breathing be easier.—I know you'll have to be patient & I patient too. Very patient.—My arm hurts like the devil. I'll have Zoler rub it with Sloan's & I'll use the electric pad. I may bathe—I don't know.—
    I must read you the Arden letter.—The Jewell review[532] is really fine.—Tomorrow Flint

---

529. Georgia O'Keeffe, *Pink Rose*, oil on canvas, private collection.

530. Probably Madeleine Ruth Cook.

531. Stieglitz saw Elizabeth Rethberg perform Verdi's *Il Trovatore* at the Metropolitan Opera; see "Rethberg Brilliant in 'Il Trovatore,' " *NYT*, Jan. 12, 1933, 20.

532. Elizabeth Arden wrote Stieglitz on January 13, 1929, saying that she hoped "to raise Georgia O'Keeffe's work to the highest place in this kingdom of ours." Edward Alden Jewell, "Georgia O'Keeffe Paintings Offer Five-Year Retrospective at An American Place," *NYT*, Jan. 13, 1933, 13.

comes. And McBride. Sunday Cortissoz & Read. Mumford next week.—It's a grand show. The irony of it all though.—

I wonder at what hour you'll be massaged. You'll like it & it will do you good I'm sure. I'm glad Lee ordered it.

—I'll say Good Night now & get my rub.—

A kiss—And a Good Morning.—

I'll see you in the evening. Maybe you'll call me up. *But don't if it's any effort at all.*— Another kiss.

Alfred Stieglitz · [New York City] · January 17, 1933

The Place—10:10 A.M. Good Morning.—I wonder how you are. And how the night. The heart? Your "strength."—Everything.—A young woman just said "A very beautiful exhibition" & added pointing to the *Black Abstraction*[533]: "A gorgeous thing." And that always gives me a real heartache knowing that in spite of all my care & guardianship it was I who had let the hot water run, etc.[534]—I don't think you know.—But that picture always strikes me as an arraignment of myself by myself. My whole life in a way.—

—I intended going to Török but will wait till tomorrow as I sent Zoler to Of's to have a glass put on your *Horse's Skull with White Rose & Black "Background."*[535]—He is to wait for it.—There was no mail. I got here at nine.—Was up at seven.—Last night after starting to undress I decided to go to Childs. It was nearly midnight.—I ate grilled cakes out of sheer despair & swallowed three cups of hot water lemoned & sugared. Did I sleep?—No worse than usually.—I lay awake a long time thinking of you & me—of us—of all of it—Really of life— of what one is & seems to be—The night seemed endless. You know the feeling. I wish you didn't.—

A friend of Iklé's brought me a tiny volume of Rilke's *Letters to a Young Poet* in German. Costs twenty cents in Germany! Must show it to you.—I have been reading Rilke's *Stories of God*[536]—Iklé sent the volume it seems because of a remark or so I had made to him when he was here. Apropos of his going to Colorado to see his friend—maybe future wife.

Some elderly women have come in.—And the radiators are hammering away merrily for a change.—

—Your large *Cross*[537] looks very wonderful this morning—from here where I'm sitting. The picture glows.—It has never looked so handsome to me before.—The light is just right—no sun but a brilliance.—

---

533. Lynes 574.

534. Records on Lynes 574, now in the collection of the Metropolitan Museum of Art, indicate that O'Keeffe's conservator Caroline Keck told the museum that the painting was varnished while it was still wet, causing the paint to run; Lisa Messinger to the author, Mar. 3, 2009.

535. Lynes 777.

536. Rainer Maria Rilke, *Briefe an einen jungen Dichter* (Leipzig, 1932). Rilke, *Stories of God,* trans. M. D. Herter Norton and Nora Purtscher-Wydenbruch (New York, 1932).

537. Lynes 812.

8:30 P.M. I am *terribly sorry* you seem so despondent. I cannot write tonight.—*I do hope you are quieter.* Or should I remain quiet?

    A kiss—

Alfred Stieglitz · [New York City] · January 17, 1933

3003—11:10 P.M.—It just strikes me all day I thought it was the 16th. It is the 17th. Usually I have been a day ahead—now I find myself a day behind. That's about the state I must be in. Everything runs around in my head as if amuck.—When I'm in the Place somehow with your paintings on the wall there is at least a semblance of order in me. And I am fighting harder than ever—& in a way never was so clear.—But—But—My talk is as if to dead spaces & my voice echoes as if hollow.—

    You must get well—Yes I say *you must.*—

    And you must say: *I will get well*—

    —Mittler is to see me in the morning.[538] What will happen I don't know.—I am alone. And I must decide. I don't know. Haven't the vaguest idea.—

    If I followed my impulse I'd close the Place on April 30—but I dare not follow it.— I have no choice but to go on whatever the space—

    —You are reading Lawrence's *Letters.* I wonder what they mean to you.—At present I can't read anything.—Even Lawrence.—And Lawrence means a lot to me.

    It's a very warm night—I wish the night were over.—I wonder did you quiet down.— I can't understand where my letter to you disappeared to—The one Cary Ross sent you several weeks ago you never got.—I mailed you a letter a short time ago.—I add this. I want to say Good Night.—

    The Room seems emptier tonight than ever.—

    Good Night—A kiss if you want one.—

Alfred Stieglitz · [New York City] · January 19, 1933

The Place—9 A.M. Good Morning. It's a dark gray morning. The Place looks stark, austere— & so quiet. Nothing could be more peaceful than the large room.—I have not been in the other rooms. I have just called up Dun.—He is to pack your *White Rose & Horse's Skull* for Hartford.[539] It is to be called for tomorrow.—It looks very handsome with glass on it. Looked very handsome without.—I put two thousand dollars on it. For what it is that is "low." But I expect

---

538. Mittler was the agent for the building at 509 Madison Ave. He was coming with Edward Norman to negotiate the lease for An American Place.

539. *Horse's Skull with White Rose* (Lynes 777) was shown in An Exhibition of Literature and Poetry in Painting Since 1850, Wadsworth Atheneum, Hartford, Conn., Jan. 24–Feb. 14, 1933.

nothing to happen. Well it will be seen by Father Kelly at least. And that is a huge lot.[540] —What a poverty stricken America in so many respects we live in when all is said & done.

It was nearly one o'clock when I finally fell asleep.—I took Phanadorm at midnight.— The Room seemed emptier than ever. When I knew you away & roaming about—or getting something out of life—busy in your way—the Room seemed empty enough—But now when I know you are bedridden—forced to be inactive in the comparatively free manner you have been accustomed to live—& I am not with you the Room is particularly empty & I feel worthless.[541] —So I'm glad when day comes & the night is over for during the day there is at least the semblance of work—of helping someone to exist—even if not so far down under the outer shell I fully realize that in these days more than ever "helping to exist" is a very barren affair.

—Sleep is a wonderful thing.—I did get some.—

I wonder about you—All the time. I try to be ready for every eventuality—but life beats me to it every time.—I'm no match for it.

—The Of man called for your picture. Quick work.—It's queer how I hate to let anything really good of yours leave my own hands. I'm just as "bad" as I was when Hartley pointed to me while Zoler, he & I sat in gallery seats one night because Hartley "loved to see a certain actor." I had two large portfolios of your watercolors under my arm—He said: "Look at Stieglitz with his game of Heavenly Solitaire."[542] Yes, that's what it was.—He laughed. So did Zoler. I smiled. And nothing has changed. I still feel as I did that night—But the world doesn't feel as it did then. And the watercolors are in the vault here guarded—not under my arms—And there is much else in the vault guarded.—Above all your things.—

Should through some miracle the Place [be] kept intact for another year I hope to bring a lot of stuff from storage down here & finally go through it with some idea. What the idea will be I haven't the slightest notion.—I can't see daylight anywhere.—But I'll know as much as I can when the time comes if it does come.—

—Tonight I'm to dine at 720.[543] —

I have a perfect itch to surprise you this morning & see you. But I dare not. It would do you no good.—I must smile at those flowers Hanna sent you.—I wonder what he had in mind.—

A Good Morning kiss.

I was in the hotel last evening.—All evening.—Am usually there. Ross was at Rosenfeld's.—

540. The Reverend Andrew J. Kelly, founder of the Catholic Library and pastor of St. Anthony Church in Hartford, Conn., was forming a collection of American art, which he gave to St. Joseph College, West Hartford, in 1937; see Vincenza Uccello, *Eugene Higgins, 1874–1958: Artist of Honor*, St. Joseph College Gallery, September 1997, http://www.tfaoi.com/aa/3aa/3aa109.htm.
541. The evening before, Stieglitz wrote O'Keeffe: "You must get on your feet. The Place—the Hill—this—what do you think they signify to me without you? Do you believe that I haven't been aware of all that all these years.—But it isn't only because of me you must get well but because of yourself—of that which you still have to give to the world. For the world needs you more than it needs me—or does it need both of us in the spirit as we live as one in the Place these days.—I mustn't excite you but I must tell you this once & for all" (AS to GOK, Jan. 18, 1933).
542. See AS to GOK, May 3, 1918 (see p. 282).
543. O'Keeffe's sister, Anita Young, lived at 720 Park Ave., New York, with her husband, Robert.

—Everywhere records are being sold at 25–40 percent discount. I am tempted. But refrain.—I do not need them.

You must get well.— *You must.* —

1:15 P.M.—Sime[544] just went out. Zoler with him. A few people here. Sime thought the show the best yet & the *Black Iris*[545] grand.—Noguchi was in. Said no one else can do such pastels. The show your best by far & that your show & the Maillol[546] was the only real thing in town.—

—Anita called up.—Too bad you were upset again. I feared it. I know *exactly* what you feel—& how everything affects you.

You must get well— You will get well—

You must see your show—

Jenks will help you—He understands you & me better psychically than Lee—As for Low I know nothing about him—

—Had a letter from Phillips about Dove.[547] I'll bring it. Dove is in "luck." So it's "lucky" that the picture did not go to Philadelphia.

—I hope you are quiet again—I wonder do my letters upset you—I don't want them to—

3003—9 P.M. Here I am. Quite awhile already. Sort of in a daze. I am not to see you for a week —I can't believe it yet it wasn't unexpected. I'll accept anything as long as you get better. And I'll be patient—so patient. And you will be patient & quiet & give yourself a chance.—You must. —I don't know whether you'll be permitted to read my letters. I'll write all the same.—

I do feel completely lost—Yet I must stick to the post & I will.—If you could but see your rooms.—I'll photograph them[548] so that you'll see a record at least—a poor substitute. —I'm eager to have the talk with Jenks. To hear what he has to say.

—Zoler is here. I'm glad. He was going to go to Jersey. You know me.—Don't worry— I'll do my very best—And I'll take Salsoda finally while you are taking Carlsbad Sprundel!![549] —

—Good Night Georgia—Good Night—

A kiss on the mouth—Very quiet—very gentle.—

I hope you'll have a comfortable night. Anita promised to report daily.—

You must get well. You will.

544. Frank (Sime) Herrmann.

545. Lynes 557.

546. Edward Alden Jewell described Aristide Maillol's exhibition at the Brummer Gallery in New York, January 6–28, 1933, as "one of the most important art events of the season"; see "Art in Review," *NYT,* Jan. 6, 1933, 16.

547. On January 18, 1933, Duncan Phillips wrote Stieglitz: "Mrs. Phillips has just sold to the Whitney Museum a still life.... Her first comments on hearing the news of her success in selling this picture was that she would contribute the $200 to Arthur Dove"; Phillips Collection Archives, as quoted in Sasha M. Newman, *Arthur Dove and Duncan Phillips: Artist and Patron* (Washington, D.C., 1981), 60.

548. Greenough 1499.

549. Carlsbad Sprundel is a mineral water with reputed healing powers used for digestive orders.

7:45 A.M. Another day. Good Morning. A kiss—What a day. Dark. Snowing. Large flakes. Maybe the snowstorm we have been waiting for ever since we moved into 3003.—Waiting for.— And this evening I'm going to be privileged to get a glimpse of you.—I have been waiting all week for *that*.—

    —It was nearly one when I went to bed. I hated the idea. I didn't want to take Phana-dorm again. And I know what that means. So the night was like the night itself—storm-tossed —restless—How I get to see myself—all of myself—how tiny bits of hidden self suddenly present themselves to change the aspect of what one saw before in self—

    And so I discover more & more how little one can really know of others. No matter how close—Of course I knew this all along for many years but never as during the last week. —How impotent one is—or shall I say merely I am. Am & have been.—Vision & blindness— mates—living side by side in oneself.—And how unintelligent one can be—& is.—I again. —All this I knew before. But [did] not see clearly.—And I miss you.—I see our life together— starting way back before 1918 even.—It's all crystal clear—what you are—what I am—what we are together—what the "world"—

    You must get well—You will.

    I wonder what Ed Norman & Mittler have done. They were to meet yesterday. Ross like myself thought all had been settled for a year at least. A few hundred dollars I suppose is the difference between them—But I'm not worrying.—I'll manage somehow—whatever.—

    —I have been thinking more & more of your work—Marin's, mine, Dove's—all seem to disappear as insignificant relatively.—And Marin's is certainly wonderful & mine is not completely negligible—Dove is all right but is not a force like you & Marin & I.—He may become one when he has achieved greater clarity within himself. Yet he is important & counts.—

    I lay in bed. The Christmas balls still hang where you hung them—& the bracelet lies where you put it—the feathers have lain down—I look around the room & see you everywhere—sewing on the sofa.—No I'm not sentimental—A human being!—

    —I'll go now & get some breakfast—

    The flakes are smaller—

    I wonder how your night—And when you receive this I will have seen you with my own eyes.—

    A kiss.—

The Place—8:15 P.M. Ross & I here. Waiting for Smedley. Proofs are to come.[550] Ate at Childs— usual place.—I can hardly believe that I really saw you—sat at your bedside—touched you— heard you—talked to you. A day like today seems unreal. As if it were all pure fantasy.—Well I'm glad you looked less harassed—more yourself. That you are good. Patient. Giving yourself a

---

550. Smedley had photographed some of O'Keeffe's paintings.

full chance.—The half hour passed by much too quickly.—And now I'll have to wait again—I wonder what Jenks will say tomorrow.

—I told you Margy Content was here. She offered a room, etc.—I told you that too.—I'll write to Beck & to Sel.[551] —

—It's so still here.—I got very little done today. I have forgotten what I wanted to do. This morning seems ages away.—

Did I really see you?—Yes I did.—You looked very handsome.—I can never get over life itself—human beings. Kalonyme & I were talking about that. If only there were less gossiping.—But I suppose if that were cut out society as it is termed could close up shop.

—Ross heard this evening that Wright was returning East to make the East his home —His lady[552] told Ross that at Muriel Draper's.—Is that gossip? I'd like him to see your show.—

—I'll send Maurice Sachs a notice. I'll write to Crowninshield.—

Ross says Sachs is a slimy, nasty person.[553] Well that makes no difference—I want him to see your pictures.—

10:11—Smedley gone. Some very good prints. Am glad to have them. But the outlay!!—Well it must be done. I want to get this off—And go to the Shelton—May go to the post office first. I'll see about the time.

Well, Georgia dear, Good Night—

I'm glad I saw you—I do miss you more than you know here & at 3003—& Childs—everywhere. But I must be patient—

I'll try to have my clothes mended—if I get a chance. I don't mind the holes.

Good Night & Good Morning.

A kiss—I hope my visit didn't harm you in any way—& that your night will be good —Another!

Alfred Stieglitz · [New York City] · February 1, 1933

1:00 P.M. I want this to say: *You must not worry about anything & above all not about me. I want you to get well. That's the one thing I want above all things. And you will get well.* I am relying absolutely on you to be good—to give yourself a full chance.—I know the changes must disturb you some[554].—All changes disturb even sensitive well people. I'm glad you decided to act

551. Although Stieglitz's letter to his sister Selma (Sel) Stieglitz Schubart has not survived, he wrote to her daughter-in-law Dorothy Schubart on January 26, 1933, chastizing Dorothy for spreading "absolutely false" rumors of a scandal about him and O'Keeffe and asked if "everything fine [must] be perverted." Oddly, he dictated this letter to Dorothy Norman.

552. Frank Lloyd Wright's third wife was Olga Ivanovna Milanoff.

553. Born in France as Maurice Ettinghausen, Sachs came to New York in the 1920s and became an art dealer. After returning to Paris, he worked for Jean Cocteau and Coco Chanel and was accused of stealing from both of them. In the early years of the German Occupation during World War II Sachs made money by helping Jewish families escape to the unoccupied zone. However, he may have also been an informant for the Gestapo.

554. On February 1, 1933, O'Keeffe decided to check into Doctors' Hospital in New York.

at once. That's you.—I started a letter to you this morning. I'll mail it tonight. I hope this reaches you before nightfall.

So I won't see you tonight but tomorrow. Georgia I know you will be quiet. Won't you. I know how difficult the situation.—But you are equal to it & I am too.

A very gentle kiss—

The hospital *is not out of my way!*—I won't be tired when I come.

Another kiss.

Don't hesitate to use the nurse.—

Welcome & Goodnight.

Alfred Stieglitz · [New York City] · February 2, 1933

The Place—3:15 P.M. At last.—This has been about the maddest day I have experienced in ages. —Here at nine A.M.—And since then every moment it has been like a hurricane. And I the vortex of a whirlwind.—Fortunately I had Phanadormed & slept six solid hours. I went to bed at peace the first time in weeks knowing that you were in a place & room where you could feel free & happy.—So I was really at "peace."—Do you understand?—And when the day opened clear & cheerful I felt at peace again—knowing you taken care of—feeling that you too must feel at relative peace.—And a bit better.—So I came here at nine.—And since then!!—Fortunately you had the nurse call early & I heard that which I needed to hear to give me the strength to face the day.—

Then came the hurricane. People. People. And I was forced to talk about six hours. Women & men. Lee came. Sel phoned, asked for you. Offered me a room to live in.—Clurman & Mellquist.—Elizabeth Arden.—Kootz with quite a wonderful reproduction made by Jaffe in Vienna of my Demuth portrait.[555] They did take out something I had warned Kootz they shouldn't take out.—But he didn't warn them—Then Schwab came & brought T. S. Eliot's (the poet) brother[556] who paints—a sensitive man. Deeply interested in your work—liked particularly the *Abstraction* in gray black & violet—Clurman liked today the pastel of *Roses & Daisy* & the *Barn*[557] next to it—in Marin frame—big expanse of blue sky. Thinks both perfect.

Room 3003—8:45 P.M. Zoler reading paper. Well I saw you. You looked wonderful. I hope I didn't make you too tired. I guess my intensity is too much for you. I'm glad you have such a fine domicile & the river before you!—I am writing to Lee & to Rosenfeld.—I thought tomorrow was Saturday.—I came down in the Second Avenue car. Comes down York Avenue—a block west of East End Avenue.—Was slow but I rested. And there were but two other people in the car. Read some in Maurice Sachs' book.[558] Breezy but no wonder you didn't feel like reading on.

555. Greenough 394.

556. Henry Ware Eliot, Jr.

557. *Abstraction*, Lynes 572; *Roses & Daisy*, Lynes 784; *Barn*, Lynes 807.

558. Maurice Sachs, *The Decade of Illusion: Paris, 1918–1928*, trans. Gwladys Matthews Sachs (New York, 1933).

—Rosenfeld called up Ross & they are together tonight. Here is what Hemingway wrote to Rosenfeld (that is part of letter):

"Dos Passos & I went to see the pictures & I liked them more than I can tell you in a letter. She has an intelligent purity of painting that makes you happy to see. I am very proud we have such a painter. Demuth & Marin I liked too.—What other good, I mean really good, U.S. painters are there alive? I mean I know the dead ones. About four damned good dead ones. I care more about painting than about any single thing probably. It makes me feel better to see good ones. So if you know any good ones I would appreciate your telling me who they are & where you can see the pictures."

Fine.—

After getting to the Shelton I just sat half an hour before going to Childs. It was another terrific day.—But I got little "done." Also had a fine letter from Weber.[559] —Liebovitz turned up —& Walkowitz—Mrs. Halpert came with Elizabeth Arden. The latter is certainly "mad" about your things. Too bad she isn't flush.

—When we visited Walker that night I asked you what the building was in which you now are. It looked so inviting at the time. I forgot whether you knew. Now don't you get excited when you see people. Don't over do anything.—

—I remained ten minutes overtime—I shouldn't have done it. But a few minutes were taken up by Hemingway. I knew you'd like that.—

Well, Good Night, Georgia dear. I want to write to Lee & Rosenfeld & to rest a bit. Good Night.

A kiss.—Two gentle ones. Good Morning!

Alfred Stieglitz · [New York City] · February 12, 1933 +

Sunday—2:30 P.M. Here I am. Back at the Place. The elevator man had sense enough to have the heat on so it's warm.—Ross was here when I came in trimming the folders as they are a bit large for the envelopes.[560]

Well, I have seen you. And I feel like a criminal.—You looked so well & unperturbed when I came & when I left you looked upset. And I had overstayed my time. Did everything wrong.—And you had had a poor night besides. Will I never learn? I hope you are resting now —perhaps sleeping & after a sleep you'll be all right again—I hope so—But I'm glad you are mending—surrounded by flowers—& the water outside with the boats gliding over it—on it. —Water does fascinate me.—

---

559. Max Weber wrote to Stieglitz on January 31, 1933, thanking him for his recent letter with its "kind words which are replete with meaning and warm feeling.... Yes indeed a lifetime did pass since my exhibition at '291' but thank the Gods we are still here to remember the foolish and good things we did and that live after us."

560. Stieglitz was mailing copies of the first number of the occasional publication *It Has Been Said* (February 1933), printed for An American Place and edited by Stieglitz and Dorothy Norman. It included reprints of reviews of O'Keeffe's 1933 exhibition by Henry McBride, Ralph Flint, Elizabeth McCausland, and Lewis Mumford, as well as an extract from Russell Vernon Hunter's 1932 article on O'Keeffe in *Contemporary Arts of the South and Southwest*.

I ate at Childs—59th Street. First warm lunch in many weeks. A plate of soup—a chop & a baked potato.—Curiously enough I ran into Lilias & Seligmann. They were going from lunch to the park to be in the sun.

—I wonder will anyone turn up.—I'll attend to the white shawl first thing in the morning & send it to you when cleaned.

3:40 P.M. McCausland here. Ditto Beck—Several fine people from Massachusetts—Priced—but nothing happened.—A woman. Seems to have been in Intimate Gallery.—

—Last night I was stopped writing through appearance of Marin, Duncan, Kalonyme. —All send their bestest. Duncan was a treat. Kalonyme had a bad headache. Marin always amazes me.

I Phanadormed. I wish you could take something to help you sleep.—I could lie down now and fall asleep. Feel heavy.—

And now I'll have to wait a week to see you again.—Seven days.—I know you misunderstood me this morning. Nothing I wish more than you walking in here unannounced![561] —

4:34 P.M. There are quite some people. The girl who was here so long—was it yesterday or day before—is here again staring & looking.

I am in a daze—

I am going to send you Havelock Ellis' *Fountain of Life*.[562] I don't know whether you ever read in it.—You can read pages here & there. It is full of beauty. I have been ransacking my head to know what you might read without tiring you—or exciting you to the point of tiredness.

—Everyone is gone—I'm alone. Except Ross. He is still folding—

Beck and McCausland remained a long while. Beck ever Beck.—

—I'd like to call you up & find out how you are—I'd know by your voice. But I refrain. I don't want to disturb.—

There is a visitor. Several.

5:15 P.M. Flint was here. In & out. Looking wonderful. Is painting again. Thinks you have a beautiful room where you are—the room itself—the river—the boats—

—Interrupted. A girl from Texas (Houston) with one from California. Both crazy about your work. Priced. The Texan one on acquisition board of museum there. Eventually something may happen—

I have your *Dark Mountain*[563] (New Mexico) standing in the office. Flint was bowled over by it. Really never saw it before!—It's wonderful how people suddenly see a picture.

—Here comes Walkowitz. There are quite a few people.

By hook or crook you'll have to see your things hung here. There are weeks yet even if I

---

561. In the early 1930s, when Norman began to spend a great deal of time at An American Place, O'Keeffe would call before going there.

562. Havelock Ellis, *Fountain of Life: Being the Impressions and Comments of Havelock Ellis* (Boston, 1930).

563. Possibly Lynes 730, 735–737, 739, 793, or 794.

have to keep them up longer than March 15.—I just have the feeling it would be wonderful for you—& for me.

   —But I let the day be sufficient unto the day. Nothing dare be hastened or forced.—

   —Walkowitz is reading the folder. Flint seemed much pleased with it. Was surprised to see his article reprinted. Thought I was going to print the rejected one (*Creative Art*) he had written about me.

   —I am mailing more folders. I hope they'll bring some return eventually.—

   —For the present I'm going to say Good Night.—With a kiss.—And also say a Good Morning. With another kiss.

   —I do hope you will get some real sleep. It is so necessary.—I wonder what sort of an afternoon [you had].

Alfred Stieglitz · [New York City] · February 15, 1933 +

9:30 A.M.
Good Morning, Georgia dear—

   It is wet. Very wet.—Ross has just left with two parcels for you—Ellis book & cleaned shawl. He volunteered. Breakfast went off beautifully—The "work" naturally divided—I actually sat down & had my eggs, juice & water & crackers.—And took it easy.—And dishwashing too was simple. So you had better not call names.—It's as good as Childs & instead of forty cents it costs me about eleven cents now. That is an item nowadays with me—And it's sort of fun. I have even taken a real holiday & not shaved! And a Phanadorm night. So all is well particularly after you bawling me out last night showing me you were getting some strength back. I spent the evening at the tax papers.—I have them nearly done. Found enough memoranda to be able to make a return which has a semblance of accuracy. Of course I invariably cheat ourselves.—A bad habit. Even God doesn't thank one for that. And least of all the U.S. government.—

   —Margules, Zoler, Ross & I were together. Margules left before nine. Zoler before ten. —It was quiet. Very quiet.—No one in an obstreperous mood.

   —And your night?—I wonder.—

   I have put your box of prints & papers back into the vault where they were—up on the shelf.—

1:00 P.M. I have just had your mural[564] out for myself looking at it. It certainly wouldn't go with the show now on. It's very good though.—Much better than the fools realized. Of course I know you painted on it since they saw it.—I have also cleaned up some more. A mess is easily created. "Order" seems impossible to keep.—Schools were here.—A lot of elder women—teachers probably. A creepy lot. To think of them as women is not for me.—Some were intelligent enough—but oh no—too much is shriveling up without.

---

564. Lynes 801.

—Ross said he'd bring me some lunch when he came back.—He did return from his trip uptown.—

Flora Straus' two girls[565] were here with nurse. All three have whooping cough. Sel called up & reiterated her invitation to live up there. Ye gods—I haven't even had time to live with my own thoughts. Or maybe I should say the necessary energy. That's more nearly accurate.— More women.—

—The Maurice Sterne show opened at the Modern yesterday.[566] Ross & Arkin went over. Ross says it was jammed with fashionables. The pictures are tagged with belonging to this collection or that collection. Can't you see it all.

Art as it is arted!—So different from this.—This what happens here—

A kiss—

3003 —8:15 P.M. The wind is howling up here for a change. Zoler & Ross & I here—The afternoon was a torn one. Not pleasant. Not unpleasant. I'm in no very communicative frame of being. Silence suits me most of the times these days. Everything said seems more or less ridiculous.—Looked for some of my own papers & couldn't find them—That always irritates me. There are habits I never seem able to break. And I hate the habits & I hate the inability as it were to break them—This carting around business is rather awful. Still I should be able to master it as I was able in former years.—In the years of *Camera Work*—when my "office" was wherever I was.—

—I wonder did you have a visitor this P.M. Or was Mrs. Schwab a plentiful sufficiency for one day.

There were a few visitors this afternoon. None of interest.—

I feel pretty dead tonight. So I'll say Good Night & also Good Morning—

I'll go to bed early.—A kiss for the night & a kiss for the morning.—

And I apologize for being so stupid.—

Alfred Stieglitz · [New York City] · February 28, 1933 +

The Place—9:15 A.M. It's certainly a windy, cold & sunny morning. Half a gale blowing. March true to form.—I was at Rosen's.—More boracic tonight.—Slow business. A real nuisance.— Rosen showed me the *Times*. An article (short) in Art Column on "The O'Keeffe Family." It seems Catherine has a show at the Delphic Studios. And Ida is announced for a spring show.[567]

---

565. Ann Elizabeth and Virginia Straus were the daughters of Flora and Hugh Grant Straus and the granddaughters of Alfred's brother Lee.

566. Maurice Sterne, Museum of Modern Art, Feb. 14–Mar. 25, 1933.

567. Georgia's younger sisters Catherine O'Keeffe Klenert and Ida Ten Eyck O'Keeffe and her maternal and paternal grandmothers, Isabel Dunham Wyckoff and Mary Catherine O'Keeffe, all had exhibitions of their paintings and watercolors in New York in February and March 1933, prompting *The New York Times*'s critic to note that the season would make "O'Keeffe a family name instead of an individual name in the New York galleries"; see "A Family of Artists," *NYT*, Feb. 28, 1933, 17. Catherine Klenert's exhibition of nineteen paintings of flowers was presented at the Delphic Studios, New York, Feb. 27–Mar. 12, 1933. Stieglitz went

And you of course are mentioned. I'll try to get a *Times* for you. And here I found *Arts &*
Decoration—Kalonyme's article.[568] Very good. And the *Autumn Leaves*[569] large & swell.
Undoubtedly him insisting on size. Maillol & you he features.—I'll mail you a copy. You'll like
what he wrote. It's fine. Honest & has style.—

—The night was fair—It was midnight before I got to bed.—After poulticing I bathed
the lower half of me. Then read some Van Wyck Brooks short essays.[570] Very solid. Very enjoyable. And when Ross returned from the Rosenfeld lecture[571] we talked some.—Not long.—
Affairs. Banks.—The world. Here he comes.

—And you. How are you this morning? And how the night after such a long sleep in the
afternoon?—Maybe the night was good after all.—

11 A.M.—I just finished reading Brooks on William James[572]—read aloud to Ross.—It deals
with values. Mentioned it to Flint yesterday. Thought he'd write an editorial on values. So I am
lending him the book.

There have been two more women visitors. Both gave ten cents each for the leaflet on
you. They were together.—Looked carefully.—Well dressed.—

Now I'm alone.—That hernia certainly raises the devil.—So stupid. Turns my stomach
to be so stupid.—

How burningly clear the sky is.—

1:45 P.M. Milch of Milch Brothers (art business—57th Street) just left.—Has gone in for modernism. Is to have a watercolor show of Homer, Sargent, Eakins, etc. next week.[573] Wanted an
abstract Marin. I let him have one.—I wonder.—It's a fine one. New York—He liked your big
White Flower—the *Roses* pastel—the *White Lily*.[574]—It would be wonderful if through such
people eventually something would be placed. He told me several stories about Phillips. Years
ago. The same Phillips.—But Lord the prices he paid!—

to see the show on March 1, 1933, and sent O'Keeffe the brochure; see AS to GOK, Mar. 1, 1933. Paintings and watercolors by
Ida Ten Eyck O'Keeffe, Isabel Dunham Wyckoff, and Mary Catherine O'Keeffe were shown at the Delphic Studios, Mar 27–
Apr 17[?], 1933. Edward Alden Jewell wrote that despite "a good deal of anticipatory interest" in the work of other members
of the O'Keeffe family "Georgia remains supreme"; see Jewell, "Another O'Keeffe Emerges," NYT, Mar. 29, 1933, 11.

568. Louis Kalonyme, in "The Arts in New York," *Arts and Decoration* 38 (Mar. 1933), 44–45, 59–60, wrote that Aristide
Maillol's sculpture and O'Keeffe's paintings, like Greek sculpture, had a quality of "serenity and purity." O'Keeffe "sees and com-
municates the wonder experienced in physical fulfillment."

569. Lynes 641.

570. Van Wyck Brooks, *Sketches in Criticism* (New York, 1932).

571. Throughout 1933 Rosenfeld delivered a series of lectures at the New School for Social Research on nationalism and internationalism in music, literature, and the visual arts; see "Music Notes," NYT, Feb. 20, 1933, 18.

572. In *Sketches in Criticism*, Van Wyck Brooks blamed William James's philosophy of "self-adaption" for the lack of conviction
among American intellectuals: "They lack conviction because they lack values," he wrote. In addition, he asserted that America
needs to produce "a few good men who are able to look our conventional life in the face and reject it…at the command of a
profound personal vision" (37–45).

573. In addition to providing framing services, Edward and Albert Milch directed the Milch Galleries in New York; this exhibition was entitled Nineteenth and Twentieth Century American Water Colors, Mar. 6–25, 1933.

574. *White Flower*, Lynes 816; two pastels, Lynes 784 and 814, were shown in O'Keeffe's 1933 exhibition at An American Place,
although neither was of a rose; *White Lily*, Lynes 587.

6:30 P.M. It is queer how difficult it is to hear you on the phone. I hardly hear the voice. I don't know whether it is the connection.—So you read Gilman on Sunday.[575] —And felt as I did. Well I didn't want you to miss it.—

I'm going to Childs now & then go to the hotel & take it easy. And poultice.

The evening from the windows here is gorgeous. If my hernia weren't so mean I'd be photographing. Everything but myself is just right for a try!—Sickening—I'm glad you got the candy & I hope you'll like it. It is selected.

Good Night—A kiss.

Good Morning—A kiss.

You must gain that weight.

Alfred Stieglitz · [New York City] · March 9, 1933

The Place—1:50 P.M. Here I am.—It's as if cut off from the world.—Zigrosser in for a few moments. Ross too. Two women for a moment or two. The phone rang twice. Otherwise silence absolute—

—Good morning. A kiss. I didn't Phanadorm so had a mean night. I hope you had a good one. Up at seven. A grand morning. I watched the river & sky—the clouds breaking—Shave—Breakfast—Here by 8:30. Then went to Török. He wasn't to be in till eleven. So marched myself to Ehrich's to see the Enters drawings.[576] —Ehrich's—a terrible place. Drawings hard to see. Put up helter skelter. They are very good. Real Enters. Then I stopped in at Durand Ruel's. Derain & Negro art.[577] —Derain sickening. Negro art looked like fake examples. The gallery as dignified as ever & deserted.—Leon Dabo there. A talk.—Amusing.—Then went to the Delphic to see Catherine's things. What a place. And she stuck off in a corner hung any old way. She has real feeling—but—but—Had a long talk with Mrs. Reed the lady owner. All I say is: Oh Lord.—A "nice" person. Met Goodwin on the avenue. Passed Emmy!—

—Queerer days.—Queerer to come. I'm tired. Have been tinkering here. How out of the world this Place is—& I am.—The women running Ehrich's.—The women at the Delphic. Awful places.—Really awful.—I guess I grow more & more impossible.—

—I wonder how you'd feel in all this mess.—What a godsend a cloister really is—or something akin to it.—But maybe it's no different from what is going on outside of it in the name of Godknowswhat.—

—It's blowing a gale up here. I wonder have you gotten to the street. Taken a walk?—

---

575. In his letter to O'Keeffe of February 26, 1933, Stieglitz included a copy of Lawrence Gilman's article "Ignorance and Bliss," *New York Herald Tribune*, Jan. 26, 1933, 6, in which Gilman lamented the lack of understanding of the "uninstructed music lover."

576. The Theater of Angna Enters, an exhibition of costume drawings, was on view at the Ehrich Galleries, New York, Mar. 6–25, 1933; see "The Dance: Foreign Art," *NYT*, Mar. 5, 1933, X7.

577. An Exhibition of Paintings by Derain and Ancient African Sculpture, Durand-Ruel Galleries, New York, Feb. 20–Mar. 11, 1933.

There is a young man—there is also a young girl—so the Place isn't completely deserted.

I haven't gotten the Dove-Torr notices out yet.[578] Don't quite know what date to open. Everything is so hectic—I don't like to take your things down—that's probably the long & short of it.—

5:50 P.M. I'm sorry you had such a bad headache. Too bad that you must have one occasionally. —Kalonyme came before noon & just left. There has been much talk. Rosenfeld, Arkin's father, etc.—My head is awhirl again. Talk. Talk. Interesting enough still talk—talk.—What does it result in?—At least none of the talk is malicious or gossipy. And that is much.

—Walkowitz & Ross are talking in the large room. There are a few visitors in the small rooms. There were about twenty-five people here this afternoon.—

Tonight I must bathe & surely Phanadorm—I hope Blanche Matthias sees you.—She wondered would she upset you. I said no.—

Zoler hasn't shown up since Saturday. I suppose the money scarcity keeps him at home.

—I wonder will you be able to see your show on Sunday.—I know you won't know till Sunday.—We'll see.

Well I might as well say Good Night—& also Good Morning. A kiss for each.

ON MARCH 10, after more than twenty states had declared bank holidays in an attempt to stop customers from withdrawing their money in a panic, President Franklin D. Roosevelt signed the Emergency Banking Relief Act. Following a four-day national bank holiday, the act allowed insolvent banks to be closed and ones that federal inspectors deemed in good condition to be reopened. Because anxious Americans had reduced the Federal Reserve's gold supply and thereby increased fears of an impending crisis, the act also decreed the end of the gold standard and mandated that all privately owned gold be turned in to the government in exchange for paper money.

On March 12, perhaps as much to please Stieglitz as to satisfy her own curiosity, O'Keeffe went to see her exhibition at An American Place. As she proudly told Beck Strand, she "couldn't stay but a few moments—but I got there."[579] A few weeks later on March 25 O'Keeffe sailed for Bermuda with her friend the photographer Marjorie Content and her teenage daughter, Sue Loeb. They stayed in a small hotel in Cambridge, on the far western end of the island. Although Content and her daughter left on April 11, O'Keeffe stayed on until May.

578. Paintings and watercolors by Arthur Dove and his wife, Helen (Reds) Torr, were on view at An American Place, Mar. 20– Apr. 15, 1933.
579. GOK to Rebecca Strand, Mar. 1933.

Alfred Stieglitz · [New York City] · March 10, 1933

It's 5:15 P.M. What a day. I'll be calling you shortly.—Yes, what a day. The first moment to myself.—Phanadormed last night. Pulled down the shades. So got a real rest.—Was up at 7:30. —After breakfast went to Török. Had to. It was eleven before he saw anyone. Income tax man with him. Two nuns sat in the waiting room with me. When I got here Dove arrived with his load of Doves & Torrs.—Ross came too. We rehearsed. The Doves are very juicy—fine. And Reds is good. I shall give her the dark gray room. Dove liked your *Green & Red Barn*. All the barns. Also the *Green Mountain* & *The Wave*. Also pastel of roses.—Liked the *Yellow Leaves*[580] greatly. He just left with Donald who came about an hour ago.

—Cahill was here. Picked out two of your flowers—*Jack-in-Pulpit* (the one I call the *Ascension*) which was in St. Louis & the large *Red Poppy*.[581] They must go over to the museum tomorrow.[582] I'll take them there myself. Zoler hasn't shown up yet. Bank (Zoler) holiday.—Here comes Margules.—Oh yes Jeanette's[583] mother & brother were here too. Jeanette dances tonight. I'm to go.—

After Phone. Cahill's selection is all right for his purpose. The two paintings looked fine as we had them out. And they will be hung by him to advantage I know. I showed him about ten things —framed.—There was no time for any extra work as the things are wanted tomorrow A.M. He had promised to come last Monday but was ill. The chances are the selection would have been the same.

I wonder why you sounded so "down."—

You ask if I believe Margules about the bank situation. He comes directly from the source. I am going to the Guaranty in the morning. I was in no hurry to be stampeded. I have kept in touch with what is going on.—Don't think I have been asleep. What is happening is what I told the Guaranty people would have to happen if I saw straight.—But I had to play "safe" (!) because of your condition. This I told you.—

I shall bring you a watch on Sunday.—I had hoped to get one to you sooner but it wasn't possible owing to Zoler's taking a banking holiday—or maybe a longer one for all I know.—It doesn't worry me even tho at times it does inconvenience me a bit.—

—There is no news otherwise. About thirty-five people visited the Place. No one of importance.

Good Night—Good Morning.

I wonder what is the matter with you. I know something went wrong.—

A kiss.

580. *Green & Red Barn*, probably Lynes 806; "barns," Lynes 805–811; *Green Mountain*, Lynes 818; *The Wave*, Lynes 644; "pastel of roses," probably Lynes 784 or 814; and *Yellow Leaves*, Lynes 642.

581. *Ascension*, Lynes 716 or 717; *Red Poppy*, Lynes 637 or 638.

582. O'Keeffe's paintings were to be included in Fruit and Flower Paintings, Museum of Modern Art, Mar. 14–31, 1933.

583. Probably Jeanette and Victor Bass.

The Place—10:27 A.M. Well all is ready to receive you.—Too bad it's clouding over. I had hoped the brilliant sunlight would hold until you will have seen your pictures here. Maybe some sun will appear when you come.—At any rate you are to see your show.—I had hoped you would.—All along I have had that in my mind. From the beginning.—It is important for me! —Most of all.

—So here I am—awaiting the moment. I hope you won't be disappointed in the presentation. In the feel of it all—The Place itself.—The starter on duty today just came in. Has a rotten headache. Told him to get some Migranine & take it. Probably has a bilious attack so Migranine won't help much.—A bit of sun is appearing.—Maybe it will last.—

I want the Place to look aglow—cheerful.—The chimes are ringing.—

—The night was fair. I bathed at midnight. Then went to bed. Ross got home at two he says. Heard him but didn't know what time it was. There goes the sun.—The wind is direct —West.—

I wonder are you excited?—

A Good Morning kiss—

There is a bit of sun again.—Tantalizing.—

11:20—I wonder have you started.—Are you on the way.—The sun is coming out. I have been reading *The Times*—sitting in the vault.—It's certainly a disconcerting age to live in & yet an amazing one—Has the Place any significance at all. Rugg just came from Minneapolis—two weeks convention there of educators under the leadership of Dewey.—He said everything was based on "science"—Art seemed non-existent. No one seemed to have anything to say which wasn't simply "Dewey" in one form or another. Finally Rugg was asked by Dewey to say something as they sat together & Rugg was not in accord with what was going on.—So he spoke. He sees the value of creative art as being part of "science"—or paralleling it—And a young teacher at Columbia—a man named Watson spoke for twenty minutes. Said his talk was the finest of all in the two weeks. He wants him to come here. I wish he'd come while your pictures are on the walls. Dove's show, good as it will be, will be more a show of painting than a *message*—or a *clarion call*. I know Kalonyme would not understand what I'm talking about—Walkowitz would. Kalonyme is brilliant—Walkowitz *sees* in a way Kalonyme never can.—Walkowitz seems to stumble over himself when he tries to talk—Kalonyme appears brilliant but is full of fallacies if one *hears* what he is saying.—I am becoming a very good listener at times.—It's a long subject—endless & is usually academic when debated—Rugg is on the track. —It's wonderful here now. So still. And the sun is ablaze.—It's 11:35.—

Noon 5. You were here & are gone.—It all seems so unreal in a way.—I do hope it hasn't taken too much out of you. I know.—I have put your *Rose* where the little *White Apple Blossoms* stood. And the pastel[584] hangs right side up.—So the one man was right & we all wrong. Luckily

---

584. *Rose*, Lynes 784; *White Apple Blossoms*, probably Lynes 711; and "pastel," Lynes 814.

the picture had to be taken down for the screw eye was loose—the picture would have probably fallen before the close of the show.—Gives me the creeps the thought of it.—

—And I came near missing giving you the great watch. I enclose instructions. I hope you or the nurse can manage. The watch cost 89 cents—It is said to be better than the Ingersoll for $1.50.—I hope it will keep some sort of time.—

—I wonder did you like your show.—The Place?—

I have just given the starter Migranine. He can hardly hold his head up.—

—You were really here—but not in this room. You didn't see my corner.—And all the little pictures of yours around me—& your *Dark Green Mountain* next to Marin's *Sea Piece*.[585]

—Above all I hope you'll be all right—that you haven't taken too much out of yourself.—

—I wanted you to come. And you came because you knew that.—Otherwise you wouldn't have come.—I wonder what Jenks said yesterday.—I didn't ask you.—You know I haven't called him up for I feel all is being done that he can do. And you seemed satisfied & seemed to be improving.—The last few days didn't seem so right.—I wonder what happened. What disturbed you. But I don't ask. But I know something did.—

—It's so still here now.—I have plenty I ought to do but somehow I don't.—Yet I make the effort—the will is there.—

—The sun is out—the sky nearly clear.—Thanks for coming—many thanks.— A kiss.

Noon 35. Anita just called me up & told me you had gone to bed. And had taken—or were going to take—some Luminal—She thinks you stood the trip very well. I hope so.—

Another kiss—

I'll call you up at the usual hour—about 5:30.—

I'm cleaning up Zoler's room—just to have something to do.—

1:35. A cloudless sky.—I had a sandwich in the drugstore—I wonder are you asleep or at lunch. —The starter feels better.—Stood in elevator telling me about himself & his family—a story I know but don't mind listening to. Quite a man. Corresponds with Hartley! I'll get busy.— A kiss—

It's so still here—Uncanny in a way—

2:25 P.M. Here I am again. Ross came in to see whether I had had my lunch.—He had been at 85th Street & East End Avenue to see a friend. Says he has such a wonderful penthouse up there. Very beautiful. Is some young man & wife connected with the museum as sort of advisor.—

I wish you could see your pictures in the light now. The whole Place is aglow.—The pastel[586] hung right is very perky.—Funny that I always felt it the other way & today it looks right & much finer right side up.—What queer things one is.—

585. *Dark Green Mountain*, Lynes 818; *Sea Piece*, either Reich 28.64 or 28.65.
586. Lynes 814.

—The idea of putting up Dove & Reds really gives me the creeps even tho they are good. But somehow what is now is the Place for me—you & Marin I feel as part of my own flesh—not so Dove.—Nor anyone else.—And the Place & you are one to me.—And yet I'll have to go through with the "next"—I hate to feel that way. But with Dove having come into something (?) through his mother's death[587] I don't feel so full of the need to get money for him or even fight for his paintings. I do rank him as high as ever as an American artist & his show will be very fine. But somehow your things *satisfy* me—their spirit—& what they actually are.—

The Place glows this afternoon & the office looks beautiful. Ross says he never saw it this way. To the right of me I have your small *Adobe Section,* the sort of L with blue sky & white clouds.—To its right the small *Poppy*—to the left the returned Palmer *Iris.*—Up on top of books on shelf before me—*Shingle, Shell & Green Leaf*—Demuth's favorite—& there is a small photograph of you—done summer before last—very sharp—profile.[588]—

Ross is reading Dorothy Dudley's book.[589]—There have been several visitors—one woman quite excited. With a man.—

I wish it were time to call you. I seem rather impatient today.—I want to know how you really are.

—I'm glad Ross is here. He is very fine. He feels about your paintings as I do. Hates the idea that they are to come down.—Says he feels it all wrong. So do I.

5:45 P.M. Walkowitz here. Otherwise no one. A lively afternoon.—First of all I'm glad to know you [are] relatively all right & that you thought I looked nice.—It's all so queer.—Life ever more so.—A kiss.—Carrie[590] came in. We talked. Then Mrs. Halpert. She certainly sees (feels) pictures. Wondered why *The Door*[591] wasn't up. Said it stood in a class by itself in the Whitney show[592] & said that she had many fights about it. I said I sent it to try out the artists, critics, the visitors & the Whitney Museum. That I knew it to be a very great picture—a masterpiece as a matter of fact. Finally after looking carefully at all your pictures she asked for *The Door.* It was even finer than I had remembered it. Ross was the only one who felt as I did about it at the Whitney. It looked wonderful today.—Stood under the *Green Mountain.*[593]—There were about fifty visitors. The Rilke letter we published is creating a stir.[594]—

—Ross, Walkowitz & I will sup together at Childs or maybe somewhere else. Ross then goes somewhere with Kirstein.—

587. Dove's mother died in January 1933. Although he inherited some property in Geneva, New York, he received no cash and his financial difficulties continued; see Morgan, *Dear Stieglitz/Dear Dove,* 264.

588. *Adobe Section,* Lynes 666; *Poppy,* Lynes 594; *Iris,* Lynes 558; *Shingle, Shell & Green Leaf,* Lynes 540 or 542; "profile," possibly Greenough 1435, 1481, 1309, or 1313.

589. Dorothy Dudley, *Forgotten Frontiers: Dreiser and the Land of the Free: A Novel of Facts* (London, 1932).

590. Carrie Stettheimer was the sister of Florine, a painter, and Ettie, a writer.

591. Lynes 653.

592. First Biennial Exhibition of Contemporary American Painting, Whitney Museum of American Art, Nov. 22, 1932–Jan. 5, 1933.

593. Lynes 818.

594. Cary Ross translated one of Rilke's letters from *Briefe an einen jungen Dichter* and Stieglitz published it: "From Rainer Maria Rilke's Letters to a Young Poet," *It Has Been Said,* no. 2, 1933.

—I'm glad I'll be able to see you Tuesday.

—I'm going to say Good Night now—& also Good Morning—
I hope you'll sleep tonight even tho you won't take medicine.—
I'm glad you were here.—And I'm glad you are glad you came—

Alfred Stieglitz · [New York City] · March 19, 1933

The Place—9:35 A.M.—Rain. Sunday.—Dove at work in Zoler's room. Trying to arrange it so that it is handier for me & that there isn't such a frightful loss of room.—He offered to do it.—The very thought is a relief.—Here since 9:10.—Here comes Ross to help.—The Dove show looks beautiful. It hasn't the *edge* of yours—nor is the presentation as perfect as it would have been had you been here but it does not belie our tradition of aliveness & respect—a certain perfection.

—Yesterday.—I don't think I ever had such a day. Eleven hours on my feet—really "working"—not only directing.—Dove, Ross, Reds & I cooperating without the loss of a moment. Zoler appearing at 3:00 after another week's absence.—Sitting down & looking around. Talking to Reds & Dove.—Ignoring Ross. Ignoring me. I saying "Hello Zoler"—no echo even.—I amused continuing my job—hammering all the nails—engineering—guiding. Seligmann appeared at noon. Very honest. Very fine.—And Rosenfeld appeared later on—The Schwabs flitted in & out—Many people looking for the O'Keeffes.—Your *Red Poppy*[595] seems to be the sensation of the show at the Modern Museum.—

Finally Marin & Duncan arrived. Both surprised at the shows.—Marin saying to Dove he felt a great jump last year & a still greater one this year. That's much for Marin.—And Duncan feels a big jump too. And all surprised at Reds.—The shows pull together. You'll see.—

At seven I was tired. I didn't want to invite the "gang" to supper. I haven't the money.—So there was standing about. Rosenfeld, Ross & I in the hall. The others in the Place. Reds & Dove were going to go but they were talking to Marin & Duncan. Finally it was after half after seven. I went into the Place & said: let's go.—We wound up at Childs.—Zoler took his seat.—It was a funny table. There was no tension but it wasn't "free." These days. Flint showed up. Had eaten. Zoler ate a full meal unperturbed. Rosenfeld sat next to him & felt very uncomfortable. I next to Rosenfeld. Marin to my right—head of the table, etc., etc.—Ross ate for thirty cents. I paid for Marin, Duncan, Zoler, & myself—the others wouldn't let me pay. Duncan wanted to pay. Dove will get some money from the estate so I didn't argue.

I was so damned tired. Broke up after the meal—nearly nine. Went to bed early. Phanadormed. Life!!—You on the phone twice. My mind full of you always.—The nurse saying nothing to you. You saying nothing to her.—Patterns. Ever patterns.—I hope you have slept. In about twenty-five minutes I leave here for the hospital.

—I wonder what is in the shaping.—

---

595. Lynes 594.

Oh yes, yesterday the Davidsons appeared. Wanted the Doves to go to their Hindu in the afternoon!!—But Dove said he doubted being ready.—I must smile. Ever the same story.

—I have your last *Brown Leaf* standing on shelf to my right—covering the small *Red Poppy* & the *New Mexico* bit.[596] The *Leaf* looks much finer in the light here.—Stronger.—Richer—It's very beautiful.

—So you didn't think much of your show. I understand.—It's difficult to think much of anything—no matter what—these times.

Oh yes, Eva was in too yesterday.—Wanted to know if she should call you up. I said: yes. Her communist friends, poets and painters, are imprisoned in Germany & even tortured. The Middle Ages all over again.—Cultured Germany turning to destroy all culture!!—What an age.—

4:45 P.M. Ross is sweeping the floor of the Place. "Zoler's" room is really in shape. You'd be surprised & delighted. And I'm much relieved & beyond irritation. Dove, Reds & Donald (who just came) talking. And I feel delighted you called up for I did feel very unhappy at my bungling way again so as to lead you to feel something *furthest* removed from me.

—You must get certain things about me out of your head for I know them not to be true.[597]

—As for your suggestion about the Marin show—four hundred dollars & under—& my then going to the Lake & coming down during the summer to work at storage things, we'll see.—I want to get everything out of storage as soon as possible to save as much storage as I can. Besides Ross will be able to help me in April. Maybe nowadays—?—In the summer who knows who'll be ready. I can't well do it all alone.—I must decide about certain things. You can't possibly devote your energies to what I must do. I wouldn't permit it.—I won't do anything rash. —I must simplify—money or lack of it demands it finally.—But it isn't merely money. It's the whole situation—the world's—the Place's—etc.

5:15 P.M. The Doves & Donald gone. Ross just going. Walkowitz just came. Likes the show. Feels about it as I do. He said: After O'Keeffe it is difficult. I said: Yes, after O'Keeffe anyone's work would be difficult. And I explained.—And we agreed.—

—But Dove is fine. So is Reds. And I'm glad the spirit is as it is. I must send out some invitations. There is the first silence here in ages as it were.—

—Georgia dear, if there is anything I can do for you & Bermuda just say so.—No, I don't want to come to the boat. I just can't—not because I couldn't leave the Place—but I just can't. You see my real wish is that I could go with you. But I'd be the worst companion you could have. Why?—I must stick to what I call "The Bridge"—You must know that—I wish it weren't essential.

596. *Brown Leaf*, Lynes 787; *Red Poppy*, Lynes 594; New Mexico bit, possibly Lynes 666.

597. A few days earlier O'Keeffe had asked Stieglitz when he planned to go through the paintings, photographs, and other works of art he had in storage. She was, no doubt, worried that he was going to destroy things as he did so often in times of stress; see AS to GOK, Mar. 15, 1933.

—I hope the sun—the warmth—will give you your strength back. Your nerves back. —I'm fighting for you more than ever. Really.—You may not know it but I must tell you.— I want you to know.

—I forgot to ask you about the candy. Is it all gone? You must tell me.—

—I have to get out invitations now & pay some bills—& give my head a chance. Good Night—Good Morning—

Two kisses.—Nice ones. Very.

There is *one* thing you *must* get out of your head & that is that you give me any bother of any kind or are in my way at any time or in any way. Nothing will be thrown away or need be thrown away. It's merely a matter of some sort of order—& that is my job at present. Your job is to get well & to trust me.

Why do I seem to have to upset you?—

Much love & do trust me & don't think of what people say or have said. They don't as a rule say things "right"—I am not talking nor have I talked one tenth as much as you imagine I have. *Listen to me* & try to hear me. It's your welfare above all & everyone I want.—

Again much love & a kiss.—

I am terribly, terribly sorry to have said something you misunderstood for if there is anyone neat & considerate & thoughtful it is you.—I know that as no one else can know it.—

Alfred Stieglitz · [**New York City**] · **March 24, 1933** +

The Place—9:50 A.M.—I—(oh, Good Morning first—& a kiss with the Good Morning) just came in from the Guaranty Trust. Have the money for you to take with you. And deposited Elizabeth Arden[598] & a few other checks for you.—Oh this money business.—What a role it does play. Maybe finally nearly the only role as life is ordered—or disordered—today. Maybe it was always so in one form or another.

The night was restless.—My room seems very empty with the feathers gone—& the bracelet—the only tangible remnant of you the Stettheimer-colored balls!—Of course there is the bag still & the trunk in the other room.—No I'm not sentimental.—The dawn was clear & I was glad you were to have a sunny day—& that tomorrow too will be clear when you sail. Tomorrow!—This will be the last letter sent to the hospital.—It's all beyond me.

—I hope all will begin anew for you when finally you are settled down on the boat. And still more so when you get to Bermuda.—I wish I were going with you. But I'd be the worst companion you could have. The very worst. And it is difficult to fathom why it should be that way.—Get well. Take care of yourself. *You must get well.*—That is regain strength.—You looked very beautiful last night. But you were very tired. Yes, you did want to see Marin & me together. And you I saw as one with us. Three of a kind in a way. Artists I guess. The most foolish

598. Arden had recently purchased Lynes 560.

people in a world like ours. Yes & the wash outside—the rooftops—the river—the gliding boats—the old home—the life that doesn't belong to mad New York—Yes, we three we feel it all as a deeply rooted part of ourselves.—I miss your pictures on the wall. The show is good. But it isn't your show nor Marin's—nor even my stupid photographs.—

—I'll phone you.—

I hope you had a good night.

After phone. Well I'm glad you slept. You sounded rested.—I'll write that letter to go with your will—the old one as Herbert[599] advises you to keep for the present—It is all a complicated business. The old order of things is crumbling fast so that to make wills in times like these is more than difficult—for wills are always made in terms of the past & try to forestall the future. And that future is more uncertain than it has ever been.—Herbert just called up. Your "old" will stands for the present. We'll see how a new one can be worked out if possible later on.— In the meantime dismiss the whole business from your mind & think only of one thing: *to get well*. Then your will automatically becomes negligible for awhile at least.

—I hear Shaw has landed in San Francisco. I had always said he'd come to America. —Well here he is. Seeing America at seventy-seven. That must be an experience. I wonder what he'll *see*.

Georgia O'Keeffe · [Cambridge, Bermuda] · [March 27, 1933]

Well—we are here—Yesterday—Sunday on the boat I was sick all day but I just lay still and ate and drank nothing—and this morning was all right—

I'll not go into the details of getting here—but it is a beautiful group of islands—a feeling like early spring with many mid-summer flowers blooming—The water is a sharp greenish blue like I have only seen in glass—lots of colored people—the whitish houses and sparkling white roofs but the houses not very good as far as shape goes—only the color—

I am really surprised to see how well I seemed to stand getting here—I'll be very quiet for a few days and be all right I think—Am sitting in the sun looking out toward that strange green water—The sun is nice—

I hope you are being good to yourself—I am all right—

With love to the Funny One—

690

599. George Herbert Engelhard, the husband of Alfred's sister Agnes, was an attorney who handled legal issues for O'Keeffe and Stieglitz. This letter also includes a draft of the addendum to her will that O'Keeffe had asked Stieglitz to write. In it she stipulated that in addition to bequests noted in the will, one of her paintings should be given to Anita Young; six each should go to the Art Institute of Chicago and the Metropolitan Museum of Art; four each to the Cleveland Museum of Art, Fogg Art Museum, Museum of Fine Arts, Boston, Toledo Art Museum, Worcester Art Museum, and Brooklyn Museum of Art; and three each to the St. Louis Art Museum and Detroit Institute of Art. Her remaining paintings, watercolors, and drawings were to be "cremated."

Georgia O'Keeffe · [Cambridge, Bermuda] · [April 2, 1933]

Good Morning—Sunday morning—

   The air has a just right sort of feeling as I sit here in the sun looking out on that beautifully streaked strange blue water—

   It seems a bit strange to think of you in that cold gray place—everything here seems to feel like the sky—Yesterday afternoon after lunch we walked—that is—we had a blanket and Marjorie her camera and every short distance Sue and I lay down on the ground—looking at flowers or what not against the sky—great big red or white lilies—strange dark banana flowers—all sorts of things—to the other side of the island—I doubt if it is really more than twelve or fifteen blocks there and back but it is up and down slight hills and there are so many things to look at it seems a long way and I guess we were about three hours loafing along—

   They are nice to be with—and some days they go off on trips and I am alone—that is good too—They are away today—

   I must tell you that I sleep without pills and that this morning I did not wake up till eight o'clock—Slept soundly from about eleven last night—so you know I am doing better—

   We have a little house—two rooms—a fireplace in mine—

   I went to lunch alone today too—great achievement—

   The hotel has lovely gardens around it—I've only gone through that little part yesterday—I'll be creeping about some more—it seems funny to be such a poke but I am improving—I hope you do not worry about me because there is no need—I am all right—

   You know this place where we stay doesn't advertise—The people come by one telling another like we were told—They seem strangely uninteresting to me—it all seems slow like I feel—The man who runs it is young and Irish—red hair—red moustache—looks a little like Waldo Frank except the red hair—makes me laugh—

I've been all day writing a line once in awhile—there is really very little to write—The old girl who rents us the cottage wants to feed me when Marjorie goes—I will see—Anyway—the sun is nice—and everything seems to go very well—

   I hope it goes as well with you—

   I will probably have a letter tomorrow—the boat will be in—

   It seems so funny to be thinking of the mail coming in only once in awhile—

   I do hope you take a little care of yourself—This different climate makes me feel particularly far away—but I think it is good—

   Good Night—just a little kiss to you if you like it—

Sunday night—

9:30 A.M. Another week. Here since 8:30. Expected Herbert to sign will. Phones he'll come tomorrow. Leaves next day for Europe.—Your letter awaited me here. Much delighted.—Felt like real you.—That real you which is soft like the sun. Yet clean-cut. Well, I'm glad you have such a healthy woman near you & one who thinks of cold winds & warns you.—I like anyone thoughtful of you—really thoughtful.—And your Lacto-Dextrin[600] (two) will go off to you today. So you got my letters—one on boat, one on arrival. Yes I am the same. And you are too. Yes.—A kiss.—Get strong gradually.—You will. I'm sure.—

—Last night! Ye gods.—Before going to the Whitney affair was asked to go to hear Chávez & Aaron Copland at League of Composers.[601] They were number one & two on the programme. At French Institute—new hall. All the usual faces.—Fortunately the pieces were short & the agony not long.—The Chávez a mixture of academic & Mexican—I in no mood. The Copland for violin & viola—dry sapless "classic"—I fell asleep I was told.—Good.—

Well, the Whitney affair![602] What am I to say. Either I'm completely dead or I feel one must be ashamed that there is such a thing as painting in America. All the fellowship recipients of the Guggenheim Foundation each had two pictures hung. All from the beginning through this year. Two new Hartleys.[603]—Gave me the creeps—like his hands.[604]—Really awful yet amongst the "best" there. Bouché[605] was the least offensive.—New style. French influence. They too looked like him—color & all. But I won't go into this nightmare of an affair.—I looked at the Benton murals.[606]—They seemed "gigantic" compared to the stuff downstairs. But Benton has no sense of a room—everything jumps at you—tries to smother one.—To read a book in that room would be like having a conversation while the big guns were roaring near one on the battlefield & the louder one talked the less one would hear of what was being said. Mouths would be seen opening & closing—lips moving—one would feel like idiots. But Benton works. He isn't like the proverbial father—.

—Mrs. Force seemed more "the Lady" than ever. Only a bit tougher. Do you know what "the Lady" means?—"Everyone" was there. Flint of course. Billy Ivins—Luther Cary—Glackens & Lawson—Ganso.—Zigrosser.—I mention Ganso as I still feel Weyhe's one great

---

600. Lacto-Dextrin was a digestive aid.

601. The League of Composers, founded in 1923, premiered many pieces by American composers, including Aaron Copland. In April 1933, they performed works by Copland, Carlos Chávez, and Darius Milhaus; see H. H., "Composers Event Proves Popular," *NYT*, Apr. 3, 1933, 13.

602. The Work of Artist Fellows of the John Simon Guggenheim Foundation, Whitney Museum of American Art, New York, Apr. 3–27, 1933; see Edward Alden Jewell, "The Whitney Museum Exhibits the Work of the Artist Fellows of the Guggenheim Foundation," *NYT*, Apr. 9, 1933, X10.

603. Marsden Hartley exhibited *Tollan—Aztec Fantasy* and *Eight Bells Folly—Memorial Picture for Hart Crane;* see *The Work of Artist Fellows of the John Simon Guggenheim Foundation;* exh. cat., Whitney Museum of American Art, New York, Apr. 3–27, 1933, unpaginated.

604. Marsden Hartley, *Morgenrot,* in Townsend Ludington, *Seeking the Spiritual: The Paintings of Marsden Hartley* (Ithaca, N.Y., 1998), 58.

605. Louis Bouché exhibited *Still Life* and *Stamford Gas Works;* see *The Work of Artist Fellows of the John Simon Guggenheim Foundation.*

606. In 1932 Thomas Hart Benton completed *Arts of Life in America,* a suite of four large murals painted for the Whitney Museum of American Art at 10 West 8th St., New York, now in the New Britain Museum of American Art, New Britain, Conn.

crime was to steal Ganso away from cake baking.[607] —Ganso received the Guggenheim this year. Five women were recipients & —three men![608] —Covarrubias was there too. He got the award too. Many inquired of you. All solicitously.—

Room 3003 —10:00 P.M. Raining for a change. Alone. Kalonyme came while I was writing. Then Duncan turned up. And some Dove visitors. One may buy an oil. Dr. Silverberg who bought one about six years ago. Now lives in Washington—The Dove is the only painting he owns. Uses it on his patients—psychoanalysis. He likes it more than ever.—Well, we'll see.—
    Went to the Harriman Gallery at 5:30 to see the Flints.[609] —Look well.—Nice place. Bignon, Maurice Sachs (just back in town) came to talk to me. Ditto Bahr the Chinese man —Marie Sterner, more loud mouthed & stupid than ever—a sort of professional crowd— introduced to Marie Harriman—Flint in clover as always. His things look very well. Hung in small entrance room. Large room Cézannes, Renoirs, Picassos, Matisse, a rotten Derain[610]— a relief room even tho the examples are far from top notchers. But the French can paint.—
    Thunder!—Spring storm blowing up.—
    —It's certainly an austere place ours—What chance has one against all that crowd— Race track toughs are not in it with the art game racketeers.—
    Well I have had enough for awhile.—
    Good Night.
    A big kiss.—
    Do take best care of yourself. I wonder when will you be able to walk to the water & up the incline. Is it much of an "incline"?—

Georgia O'Keeffe · [Cambridge, Bermuda] · **April 10, 1933**

Monday—the 10th—I have your three letters today—There isn't much to write—
    Marjorie and I went to Hamilton this morning on the boat and drove back in a funny buggy—quite a lovely drive—it is about ten or twelve miles—We stopped for lunch on the way —It is the first I have gone anywhere except down to the beach and for short little walks around here—It didn't tire me very much tho I got into my bed for what was left of the afternoon—
    Mostly I go down in my bathing suit and sit on the beach all morning—sometimes again in the afternoon with my clothes on—I can't stand the sun too long—or poke about for a little walk—or sit on the terrace—always lie down after lunch—It has been warmer and not

607. A pupil of Jules Pascin's, Emil Ganso was a largely self-taught artist who supported himself as a baker until 1924, when Erhard Weyhe started to give him a monthly stipend.
608. Lucile Blanch, Georgina Klitgaard, Gwen Lux, Carlotta Petrina, and Mary Tarleton all won Guggenheim Fellowships in 1933, as did Arnold Blanch, Louis Bouché, Miguel Covarrubias, and Emil Ganso; see *The Work of Artist Fellows of the John Simon Guggenheim Foundation.*
609. Ralph Flint's watercolors were on view at the Marie Harriman Gallery until April 18, 1933.
610. Important French Paintings was on view at the Marie Harriman Gallery in New York City in April 1933; see "Exhibition Listing," *Creative Art* 12 (April 1933).

so windy—I really feel much better—Marjorie and Sue go in the morning—I will be all right alone—will stay till sometime in May probably—I am not good for much of anything but sitting and this seems a good place for that—

I will miss them—They have been lovely to be with—but I will be all right alone—I am going to try eating with the old girl who owns the cottage—If it doesn't work I'll go back to the hotel—

I walk better—am really doing very well—

Good Night to you—I must be going to sleep—

It seems strange to be here—but I feel quite at home—

A kiss to you—for quiet for the night—and for the morning too—

Alfred Stieglitz · [New York City] · April 11, 1933

At the Place. It's 3:00 P.M.—A sunny day. Good morning. A kiss.—I didn't get here until ten. Went to Torök before coming here.—A mean night. Overtired & like a fool forgot Phanadorm. Altho' up & about before six—I fussed around. Didn't want to go to the Place before Torök. —When I got here Duncan Phillips & wife[611] were here. Remained over an hour. In love with the Doves. Has no money even tho he could have five he likes for $1100. I am going to send them to Washington so that he can live with them & have them photographed there. I can't afford it here.—He was holding your small *Red Poppy*[612] in his hands when I came in. Had it in the white room.—Says he never saw it. He did. His wife says he did. I remember her liking it at the time & calling his attention to it. She is always quicker than he is. He wants to write about Dove. Likes him better & better.—Wanted me to mark two things ($475 for both) as reserved for him. I said all right. And added you can pay within two years. He said, Oh no, I don't mean buy. I laughed & said that's like saying to some woman you like: You must never marry anyone else & she saying: So we are engaged. And he saying: Oh no I don't know whether I can ever marry you. She laughed. Duncan had come in & introduced him to the Phillipses.

—Seligmann turned up. Very fit. No down pull in him. All ready to go on Friday to Gloucester per new eight-cylinder Ford. He & Lilias expect to live on about $600–$800 for a year. No rent to pay. Seligmann is a real person.—Rosenfeld turned up for a little while. A woman from Chicago came to see your paintings. She teaches children—something rhythmic & was told she'd get fullest pleasure out of O'Keeffe. Phillips was here. Told her to come again. She saw your *White Shell* (large).[613] Thought it wonderful.

—Seligmann saw the Bretts.[614] Was surprised at the strides she has made. They looked particularly well in the light today. All four. If it weren't that I must get at the storage business I'd

611. Marjorie Phillips.

612. Lynes 594.

613. Lynes 707 or 708.

614. Earlier in the year, Brett had sent her paintings to An American Place, hoping Stieglitz would show them.

show her work—& Duncan's.—But I must get at the storage. So the Bretts go to Taos today. Of just called. Brought your two pictures back from the Modern Museum. The two flowers.⁶¹⁵ —

—Some visitors.—Not so dead. Less the sepulcher.—I may keep the Doves up a few days longer than dated.—I met Gallatin as I came from Torök's. Told him he should come & see Dove.—They—what should I call him—ought to buy one for his museum.⁶¹⁶ —

—Yesterday evening I went to Radio City & saw the movie *Cavalcade*⁶¹⁷—quite an extraordinary picture. Saw the building.—Saw Stuart Davis in the gents room.⁶¹⁸—What am I to say.—As men are not privileged to go into the ladies' I didn't see Kuniyoshi's "smears." I'm glad I couldn't go into that room.—Didn't look around for any "art" anywhere.—At Childs met Flint & McBride.—Everyone inquires for you.—

—Tonight I am to hear Shaw at the Met. opera house.⁶¹⁹ You'll see I'm being shown the town. I go for a change.—Nothing else in sight. Whoever isn't prompt for Shaw will not be permitted in. His orders. Fine.—

5:40 P.M. Kalonyme just came. He too is going to Shaw. It has grown dark & rainy looking. Quite a few people. Interest is on the increase.

—Interrupted.—

A rather live woman writes for *Creative Art* now. Really intelligent & sensitive.— Just had a conversation with her.

—Well, I'm off to supper & then to Shaw. Wish you were here to go—

Very much love & a big kiss.—

Alfred Stieglitz · [New York City] · April 17, 1933

The Place—1:00 P.M. Pouring rain. Wet. Wet. Wet. Good morning. Kiss.—Alone.—Well a little before nine I was at the Lincoln.—Gave orders to send all the stuff in my seven vaults to the Place on Thursday. It's Monday today.

—Stopped in at Zigrosser's. Told him what I was doing. Intends calling up Ivins. I am ready to let him (Ivins) have my photography collection & do with it what he chooses. Of course I won't let him have my own things.—So if Ivins comes & wants the things he can have them & I'll feel well rid of them. If not—I'll see—You know what my impulse is. To put the "poor things" out of their misery for they have been tortured long enough.—I then called up Dun.

615. Lynes 716 or 717; Lynes 637 or 638.

616. In 1927 Albert Eugene Gallatin founded the Gallery of Living Art (later renamed the Museum of Living Art) at New York University, which he directed until 1943.

617. Based on a play by Noel Coward, the 1931 movie *Cavalcade* was directed by Frank Lloyd and starred Diana Wynyard and Clive Brook.

618. Stuart Davis, *Men Without Women,* oil on canvas, 1932, men's lounge, Radio City Music Hall, New York; see Lowery Sims, *Stuart Davis: An American Painter* (New York, 1991), 57.

619. On April 11, 1933, George Bernard Shaw delivered a speech entitled "The Future of Political Science in America" at the Metropolitan Opera House; see "Shaw Here Today for Twenty-Six-Hour Visit," *NYT,* Apr. 11, 1933, 21.

He came to the Place. I asked him about one of his men.[620] One out of work. We had a talk. I'd like a man steady for about four weeks. In that time I'll have everything done.—As for the Hartleys I'll call up Mrs. Halpert & have a talk. That when the Hartleys are here. I am satisfied to keep two or three vaults for Marins, etc. but not more.—None of my feelings have changed any the last years. Conditions make it compulsory for me to act. That's all. And the Place gives me the chance I need & it must be utilized. I have no feeling one way or another. It's as if I were depersonalized.—At any rate I have actually finally started.—

    —Your letter came right after Dun had left.—So you too are having rain—& you are having a fire in your queer place. I wonder do you put on wood yourself or must you call someone. Or does someone automatically appear.—And you are reading Beebe.[621] And are enjoying him.—I never read anything of his but know about him & his work.—I can see you having a real good time with him. Your element.

9:30 P.M. I'm here in 3003. And it is raining pitchforks. It had let up for a few hours.—I'm alone. The rain beating against the windowpanes. I was interrupted this afternoon as I was writing. Schwab came in. Also Margules. And Walkowitz—All sat down in the office. And there was talk about the storage stuff. Schwab seems to have been away awhile. Rosenfeld too was present awhile. The talk was serious.—No gossip—thank heavens.—Heidelbach, the architect, turned up later. Is helping get out a book on revolutionary Americans—starting with Jefferson. Wanted to know what I thought about *Cultural Revolutionists of America*—a second volume—It was seven o'clock before I had realized the time slipping away.—

    Flint had been in too. Sold a couple of his things. Enough to pay for some expenses—Low prices he says. I'm glad he is not to go empty-handed.

    —My head is naturally full of the storage business & how I'm going to tackle the problem.—It is certainly an incredible one in an incredible time. But somehow it doesn't bother me. No one can solve it for me.—

    —So the Kid wrote I'm looking well. She must know.—I know I am fairly quiet. I just can't permit myself to be upset by 101 things that formerly set me crazy.—To accept the idiosyncrasies of people without letting the acceptance dull one is a life job I guess.—

    —I think I'll bathe.—

    Good Night—A big kiss—Georgia dear—

    —Last night I dreamt of you very vividly.—

Georgia O'Keeffe · [Cambridge, Bermuda] · [April 19, 1933]

I've been no good—The sun has been shining since Sunday and I liked it so much that I have done little but eat and sleep and get out in it—

    That is all there is to tell—The nights are warmer—that is they are not chilly like they were and the sun on the beach this afternoon made me feel I would melt right down like a

---

620. Stieglitz wanted to have shelves built in the back room of An American Place to store some of his collection of art.
621. Possibly William Beebe, *Nonsuch: Land of Water* (New York, 1932).

candle on a hot day if I didn't get at least get a thin wisp of a bush over my head—really very hot—

I am feeling better—walk better—getting on very well—

Thank you for all the clippings[622]—particularly the Shaw—I was awake early this morning and read it before breakfast—

You ask if I like your letters—you make me laugh—Of course I like your letters—but everything you write about seems strangely far away—

These islands are so queer—it may be that I have fallen off the earth and don't know it—I wouldn't be surprised to wake up any other place and find that I have been dreaming—I think that on islands like these people become even smaller and more gossipy than on real land—They are very funny—

It would be very good for painting but I don't feel that good yet—Good sail boats—too bad Marin isn't here—it is a bit pretty for him but he might like it—

If I would paint I would have to work indoors—the ground is nearly white and the light dazzling—goggles are quite the thing to wear—I was smart enough to bring mine and I wear them.

Good Night—

There are so many bird sounds here in the night.

A kiss to you—I am all right but everything seems very strange to me—

Alfred Stieglitz · [New York City] · April 22, 1933

3003—10:40 P.M. I don't want to let the day pass without a line to you.—Even tho I am more dead than alive. A kiss first. And much love too.—From nine until seven I was at the Place standing—handling pictures—Top speed.—Of's man there four hours—Saturday—A fine worker.—Ross & Walkowitz worked like beavers.—Opening parcels—cleaning up—throwing papers away—mountains of paper.—The Schwabs came & Boyer, of Philadelphia, art dealer, ex-artist, bought a painter from Budapest—a man really sensitive & *knowing art.* Well no one has ever enjoyed the Marins as he did. Was drunk with them. Boyer terrifically moved—silent. Boyer is the man who knows Barnes well. Says Barnes is [re-evaluating] his art ideas.—The man from Budapest & Boyer were there over two hours—also Schwabs excited—much impressed by Budapest artist's vision & what he had to say.—I handled the pictures.—I gave the man Marin's *Letters.* He is coming again with a friend. Wants to see your things too. Was knocked out today.—Thinks Marin the greatest living artist! I take nothing literally. But I know Marin is second to no one.

You ought to see the *Sun*[623] one of yours. Took breath away of everyone.

Got a bite to eat standing up at three.—Margules came. Pitched in. Zoler came. Stood

---

622. Stieglitz sent O'Keeffe "A Test for the Modern Woman," by Mary Ritter Beard, *Current History* (Nov. 1932), 179–183, in which Beard lamented that because American women "have been accustomed to a high degree of personal privilege," they were "unprepared both physically and mentally to cope with financial calamity."

623. Possibly Lynes 608.

around. Kalonyme read Brett[624] & didn't care for it.—Looked at some Marins quietly. Matisse, Picasso, photographs, Hartley, etc., etc. standing about—Rooms gradually assuming some order. People coming in & going out. Mrs. Stix from St. Louis. Also a friend & son. Same Mrs. Stix— I have to be curt with her. Marin showed up. Amused. Delighted at Place—Says it looks cozy.— It looks very dynamic.—A terrific job ahead.—Ringel with a friend—an intelligent friend. A man who seems to have come to 303 & also to the Place. A photographer. Really brainy.—

Finally supper. Marin, Zoler, Walkowitz, Ringel, his friend & I. Kalonyme didn't want to be with Ringel!!—Ringel hadn't been around in a long while. Ross went with Margules to police stations, etc.—

—I am dizzy from too muchness—I'll bathe. Didn't last night—Had breakfast at Childs. Had no eggs here.

When I got to the Place the mail had no letter from you. Disappointed. Wondered— But your letter came with second mail.—Yes I know how you must feel. But I feel too as if I were nowhere—far far away. All this "past" life confronting me—"291"—all it represented—in a certain sense—you & I out of it—

Well I can't begin to tell you what it all means. Even Lafferty turning up.—Rodin, Picabia, Pascin, Picasso, Matisse, Burty, Hartley, Steichen—all the photographers, Duncan, Tofel, Kopman—Marin—& a lot of others—all there in the Place.

—Flint came again—all aflame—Full of ideas!?—

My eyes burn & my head buzzes—Goodnight—

A big kiss—

I'm all right—Now for a bath—& a rest.—

Good Night—Very much love—

April 23, 1933—10:00 A.M.

Sunday Morning. Good Morning.—And a fine big kiss.

—It's a beautiful morning. I'm ready to go to the Place for another onslaught—After a long bath last night I went to bed & slept a few hours.—I lay awake in bed from four till 8:30 —my head full of what to do with all the stuff. It's all very difficult & yet I'm determined to act. Ross & I shall go over now & get all the photographs together so that when Ivins' secretary[625] comes there'll be short shrift one way or another. Some of the Steichens are fine—effective— Steichens!—A surprise to all the men. They understand now why Steichen was a central figure. There are some good Hartleys too. I may keep a few. But I don't know.—I feel the fewer "things" to go to storage the better.—Much is milling in the head I have left—

—I miss you more than I can make you realize.—But I'm hoping that you are getting stronger. All the pictures there called "mine" don't mean anything to me as compared to your well being as far as I am concerned. I am not emotional momentarily about that—I mean it 100 percent.—I want to see you yourself again—*on your feet*.

698

---

624. Brett, *Lawrence and Brett*.

625. When Zigrosser called Ivins to tell him that Stieglitz planned to dispose of his large collection of photographs, he learned that the curator was in Europe. Ivins arranged to send his assistant, Olivia Paine, to An American Place (AS to GOK, Apr. 18, 1933). The Metropolitan Museum picked up the photographs on April 25, 1933.

I'll go now—The Place looks alive—like a junk shop—but an interesting one—A very interesting one—

Another kiss. More later—

3003—10:30 P.M. Another "what a day."—Until 6:30 in the Place—on my feet all day & walked one and a half miles besides after leaving the Place. More packages unpacked—more "order"—Walkowitz & Ross working hard.—Visitors going in & out—Rosenfeld & Porter came to see the Marins.—I am tired.—I hope the Metropolitan Museum turns up tomorrow. Everything together—ready. It would be wonderful if that stuff went out. Ross & Walkowitz bewailed the fact that in reality genuine Internationalism was right there in the Place in concrete form—& of highest educational value. The evolution of photography & the evolution of modern art—I myself am amazed how solidly I have built. But—?—No one is ready. And I have no feeling about it.—Nothing is done impulsively by me. Every move is an inevitable one—

It's too bad you can't see the Place. It never looked so alive. So "useful."—There will be a grand feeling of hallelujah when all the *Camera Works* are gone. Don't think I have forgotten your set.—I haven't.—

You are ever in the Place. And here too.

I'm going to bed. If only to rest even if I don't sleep.—

—And you?—I wonder how you are today.—And how about your weight. You say nothing—I can imagine the gossip in a small place—I do hope you are comfortable—

Well, Georgia dear, Good Night—Again a big kiss—Good Night—

Georgia O'Keeffe · [Cambridge, Bermuda] · **April 26, 1933**

I have your two letters today telling about the arrival of the things from storage—It doesn't seem right that I am not there—I think I would have gone on yesterday's boat but I was just starting the curse—and didn't feel equal to the trip along with it. I will have a week to recover after it and then go—I would not be of any use to you and I know I could not stand the excitement so I suppose there is nothing to say—

I moved over here to the hotel today—think it better—Mrs. Kennerley spent last night with the old girl I have been staying with—It was funny to have her turn up. She says she will report to you.

I do nothing but sit or lie in the sun—Today didn't even go to the beach—just down the lawn a little outside my door—usually I go to the beach—There are lovely cedar trees—and palms—and you will laugh when I tell you that the only flowers blooming nearby are calla lilies—I really had to laugh when I noticed it—

Good Night to you—I must go to bed—I am so sleepy so early it is ridiculous—

A little kiss—

Don't get too tired—All that stuff isn't worth it.

I wish I could see you tonight—smell you.

[April 28, 1933]
Friday afternoon—

The weather has been lovely—There is no news—A funny place—gardens and flowers and trees—and the pale blue green water—I have been pokey—doing nothing but sit and very little walking—Such a funny life—

I have made the acquaintance of the cook—she is quite a girl—"Mr. Gray's right hand man" she says—

While I was lying down after lunch today she came in to visit me—yesterday she stopped and sat with me on the beach—

I keep worrying about you and that stuff—and I feel like such a fool that it should disturb me so when I can do nothing—

Just read *The Bridge of San Luis Rey*[626]—I think you would probably like it—I enjoyed it—

—As I sat here trying to think of something to say—the mail came—letters telling about the photographs going to the museum—and your dream about me—

It is gray this evening—I went down and walked on the beach after the letters—

You see—when I was halfway normal I could walk off a great deal of almost anything —Now I cannot and too much stays with me—

Good Night again—

Alfred Stieglitz · [New York City] · April 30, 1933 +

Room 3003—11:27 A.M. Good morning. A kiss.

It's Sunday morning. I have been real lazy. And intend to remain so for awhile today. Phanadorm at midnight last night.—Clocks set ahead—daylight saving. Slept hard.—The morning is summerlike. Window wide open. No shoes on yet.—Mrs. Kennerley called up at 9:30 & told me about you.—Glowing account. And she spoke about Morley. And asked if I had seen Kennerley.[627]—Asked me to see him. Curiously enough I was on the point of going up to see him when at the Guaranty. It was too early I felt. I have no different feeling about Kennerley than I had that memorable Easter Sunday five years ago.[628] What an eternity since then.—

I didn't write to you yesterday. From early morn till late at night I was going [at] full speed. Where the energy & stamina came from I don't know. I don't think I sat thirty minutes from nine A.M. till after seven. And there was more hauling out of Marins—the Schwabs, Mellquist, the Budapest artist again & Boyer, the Philadelphia dealer—& there were people

700

---

626. Thornton Wilder, *The Bridge of San Luis Rey* (New York, 1928).

627. Mitchell and Helen Rockwell Morley Kennerley divorced in 1929. Morley was their oldest son.

628. Kennerley agreed to buy six of O'Keeffe's calla lily paintings (Lynes 423, 425, 426, 429, appen. 44, 77) on Easter Sunday, April 8, 1928.

asking for O'Keeffes. And I showed O'Keeffes. Also to the Budapest artist. He also looked at a few photographs.—It was all very alive.—Copland appeared. Remained over an hour.—Asked did I know Agnes Meyer & what I thought of her. I took up *291*—"Mental Reactions"[629] & let her speak for herself. And I showed him the de Zayas caricature of Eugene Meyer.[630]—

Everyone loves the Place as it's now. And they all hope I'll keep it that way.—It is alive. And I got the loose prints ready for the museum.—They will call for them. There is a quantity of them. Hundreds. People wandered about & snooped around. I slashed the three Steichen paintings left.[631] They are too bad for words.—Meaningless. I wonder did I ever really think them good—Or did I merely believe in them because they were Steichen—I knew nothing about "art"—or "painting."—I believed in people.—In the being.—And stood by whatever they did. I see it all very clearly. That is myself & my idiosyncrasies.—Well things are moving along.—

Quite a supper table. Flint, Marin, Ross, etc.—Zoler didn't turn up.—Kalonyme present too.—Flint flies to Albuquerque tomorrow. Bound for Taos.—Report has it that Mabel is in a San Francisco hospital. Whether true or not I don't know.—A Dr. Howe of the Rockefeller Institute here last night—formerly at Johns Hopkins, a friend of Ross's.—Blew in.—

—Everything seems to be somewhere & nowhere at the same time. I seem the least movable one in a sense—But I can go the pace of any of them—

—I wonder what you'd say to it all if you saw it completely detached—I wonder.—Would it attract you or repel you or do nothing. I wonder—Flint is more excited than ever by the Marins. Oh yes Walker was in too—Marin saw his evolution. Told me it was very good. Says he has a great deal of knowledge & feeling too—But wonders will he always need the model before him.—I must by hook or crook see what he has done—The *Independent*[632] closes today. I must run over to see the Gutman so that I won't hurt his feelings. Oh these feelings—so easily hurt.—

Flint wants to come to the Place at four for a last look at the Marins—Altho' his job is open to him for next year nothing definite is arranged. Everything is so chaotic.—In a way he'd like to get rid of writing about art.

—Yes I'm glad to have had Mrs. Kennerley's message.—I do hope that when you return you'll continue to do as well—Jenks will be proud of you—

It seems Bob[633] has been in Georgia. I suppose Anita too. His cousin was in & told me so. I had been wondering.—

A big kiss—More later—

I am tempted to take a bus ride but I guess I had better stay here by the open window & take it easy.

629. Agnes Ernst Meyer, "Mental Reactions," *291* 2 (Apr. 1915).

630. Marius de Zayas, *Eugene Meyer, Jr.*, c. 1912, charcoal on paper, Metropolitan Museum of Art, Alfred Stieglitz Collection, 1949.

631. In October 1933, Stieglitz also slashed Steichen's *First Oil*, as well as works by Pamela Colman Smith and "some very rotten Hartleys" (AS to GOK, Oct. 10, 1933).

632. The Seventeenth Annual Exhibition of Society of Independent Artists was on view at the Grand Central Plaza, New York, Apr. 7–30, 1933.

633. Robert Young, husband of O'Keeffe's sister Anita.

Room 3003—11:10 P.M. Somehow the day got away without writing.—I was at the Place before 8:30. When I'm alone I get away earlier.—Cooking my breakfast happens while I shave. And I'm pretty quick with "cooking" & eating. Of course I prefer not to be alone.—At 9:30 I went to Torök's & then over to my barber. Had to wait forty-five minutes. Had a haircut. Feels good. High time. I'll shampoo tonight after writing. Met Dabo on the street. Has a flower show at Knoedler's!!634—Said tell O'Keeffe she opened up a new world to all the world!—I had to smile.—But he at least told the truth.—

You know it was Laurvik who salvaged *Camera Work* in 1908 when I vacated "291" for the first time635 & I threw out all of *Camera Work*. Laurvik got an express wagon & dumped *Camera Work* into Clarence White's & Dabo's studios which adjoined each other. It was in 14th Street. White's skylight leaked—so that the rain & mice played havoc with *Camera Work* in White's studio but the numbers in Dabo's studio were saved. Dabo & White & their friends helped themselves to all the copies they wanted & in due season the copies left over were dumped into the new 291!—In 1917 the second breaking up took place. And now in 1933 another in a way—altho' there have been minor eruptions in years between 1917 & 1933— Oh no—quite a big one in 1923 I believe.636—Yes, a very big one. Or was it 1921? Well, so be it.—The habit.—

A young painter from Maine turned up. Seems to know the Place—also Marin. Goodwin also showed up. Some others too. Goodwin spoke about Mrs. Hare.637 It seems a whole colony is about to go to Santa Fe & Taos. Goodwin says a second Greenwich Village & Woodstock. He seems to distrust such things as much as I frankly am given the creeps hearing about them.—Goodwin certainly a fine fellow.—Kalonyme appeared towards evening.—It was very late when I got away from the Place.—

There was quite a long & terrific thunderstorm overhead. Vivid lightning with simultaneous crashes—& a downpour of rain. It's still raining. It was a sultry semi-foggy day. —Of's man busy all day.—I have stood Marins & O'Keeffes along the walls. When Ross appears I'll hang or Walkowitz. I can't do it alone.—It will be a queerish show.638—Just the large room.—

---

634. Leon Dabo, Flower Paintings of Italy, France and England, Knoedler Gallery, New York, May 1–18, 1933; see "Exhibition Listing," *Art Digest,* May 1, 1933.

635. In February 1908, when the lease on his galleries at 291 Fifth Ave. was about to expire, Stieglitz was told his rent would be doubled and that he must commit to a four-year lease. He refused and vacated the gallery in April 1908. His friend Paul Haviland subsequently leased rooms at 293 Fifth Ave. for Stieglitz to use as a gallery. Although Stieglitz never abandoned the name "291," his gallery remained in this new location until it closed in 1917.

636. After he closed 291 in 1917, Stieglitz stored many books, catalogues, and copies of *Camera Work* and 291, as well as his own photographs, at the Anderson Galleries. In 1922, when Mitchell Kennerley, the owner of the building, needed the room, Zigrosser arranged for many of the books and catalogues to be donated to the library of the Metropolitan Museum.

637. Walter Goodwin, Dorothy Brett's editor at J. P. Lippincott, the publisher of her forthcoming book *Lawrence and Brett: A Friendship,* was also Mrs. Hare's son.

638. In May 1933 Stieglitz mounted a group exhibition of work by Dove, Marin, and O'Keeffe in the two larger galleries of An American Place, with a selection of Walkowitz's work in the smaller one.

I'm out of paper. I'll shampoo.—Good Night. A kiss.—Two.—I do hope you are in fine condition. I wrote to Putnam to turn on the water.—I wonder will this still reach you.—Another kiss.

Georgia O'Keeffe · [Cambridge, Bermuda] · May 6, 1933

Saturday—Good Morning—it is sunny and lovely and still again this morning—

The days have been lovely lately—Yesterday seven of us went on a picnic to as beautiful a place as I ever saw—One of the girls and I had a long wonderful beach to ourselves all morning—We got there first and the others couldn't find us—a beach clean and white and pure looking like hairless skin—sheer high gray coral rocks at the back and at both ends—the water like brilliant pure green and blue glass breaking along the beach—It is all so bright and sparkling one can not look at it long with the naked eye—It was a wonderful day—I had managed the lunch because I had made friends with the cook and no one else had been able to get a good one—It was a great success—I had stopped along the road and bought large bunches of celery and onions right out of the fields—and washed it in the ocean—It was a great day—

I can climb about now and do almost as well as ordinary folks—begin to feel hopeful of doing as well as myself sometime or other—Something ought to come of all this sitting in the sun that I have been doing—

When I got back in the evening your cable was here—it looked very expensive—I had thought of staying longer—the next boat I can go on goes May 23—I will cable you on *Monday May 8* if I am not sailing on Tuesday the 9th.

I do feel much better—

This place is quite strange to me in that it doesn't seem real at all—The ground has a hollow sound—all of it seems to have very little to do with earth and water as I have known it—

A kiss to you—I must get out in the sun—

Alfred Stieglitz · [New York City] · May 8, 1933 +

Noon 27 P.M. Zigrosser just left. Says he came to refresh himself.—Thought the "show" beautiful.—Says the Rivera murals at Radio City very fine.—There is trouble over them because Rivera insists in incorporating Lenin's portrait in them.—I don't know the particulars or at least not accurately.

—I was going through the Hartleys as Zoler came. Some look good. Others awful. I'll keep the good ones.—The others?—I'll see.—

Yesterday afternoon when alone I destroyed a lot of large photogravures of mine.—Not good enough.—I have decided that either a "thing" lived as part of an idea or merely as for itself —let us say for its beauty. The Marins really combine the two.—As I always selected from an idea point of view more than for mere absolute beauty I naturally ever found myself in a "contradictory" position as the search was always really for beauty—for the true.—This isn't very clear but I let it go.—Some day I'll explain.—

—Many de Zayas I tore up.—They were not fine enough as things & had become meaningless as instruments.—I am not destroying anything on the "spur of the moment."—

Later. It's a crazy world.—While sending the photographs to the museum it struck me how surprised all the photographers would be to find themselves in the museum—their great dream —without moving a finger all these years for *photography* or for "the Idea."—And there through me. I had to laugh. A Miss Farnsworth came into my mind. She was very ambitious—Albany —the chief woman photographer in the U.S. in about 1890—I wondered about her & the museum—Wondered had I a Farnsworth[639]—I didn't know.—Well who walks in a little while ago?—Miss Farnsworth! Saw the papers about the museum. Wanted to know was she in the collection, etc., etc.—Ye gods—tombstones will come & ask me.—She talks today like forty years ago.—Colonel Farnsworth's daughter—Albany. Was at Kerhonkson. Knew all about everybody.—A small world. And pretty petty most times.—

Telegram.—Cable. So you stay over. Sail 23rd.—Well I think you are wise.—I believe Margaret is doing some sewing for Sel but is ready to go with you at any time you want her.—

Here comes Ross with my sandwich.—

My envelopes for you I found in my overcoat pocket just now.—So my head isn't entirely gone.—

Another kiss. Thanks for cabling.—

The Place. 6:40 P.M. Just a wish Good Night—And a big kiss—

Tonight is Rosenfeld's last lecture. I'll surprise him by appearing.—I'll take supper somewhere downtown. His lecture begins at 8:20. Kalonyme was here—We talked about the Place & its activities. Everyone feels it has become very alive now that so much of the "past" is also here.

Much much love—

I hope you are a champion bicycle rider!—

Georgia O'Keeffe · [Cambridge, Bermuda] · [May 9, 1933]

My note to you yesterday was only a scrap—Well maybe I am only a scrap—

I thought myself so smart getting about—it is good I really decided yesterday morning not to leave today—I evidently did too much of something because I had to go to bed with my funny heart yesterday afternoon and have been here all day today—Guess I'll have to give up the bicycle—

I feel all right when I keep quiet—it is nothing to worry about—

639. Stieglitz did not donate photographs by Emma Farnsworth to the Metropolitan Museum.

Your letters came at dusk yesterday—a surprise as I thought there was no boat in—the letters about hanging the new show—It was nice to have them—I was so out of sorts over having to go to bed—

My room has a door that most of the guests have to pass on their way to meals—it opens outdoors on the path and they all stop to visit me—It is very amusing—but the colored girls are the funniest—they think I'm so fat that there can't be anything the matter with me—that I just like to stay in bed—I have to laugh—

I'll be up and all right tomorrow I think—

Wednesday—May 10—

Yes I am up today—sitting out under the trees all morning talking with an English woman visiting her son here in the navy. She was so uninteresting that I was quite entertained—I will be all right by tomorrow—

A kiss and a note in the sleeve for the Funny One—

The boat I can go on next goes May 23—arriving in New York on the 25—I think I'll certainly be on it—

Alfred Stieglitz · [New York City] · May 10, 1933

The Place—9:30 A.M. Enclosed will give you pleasure.[640] I knew this was coming. There were rumors about for ten days. I predicted Rivera wouldn't budge. The reporting is brilliant. As Rivera got seven thousand dollars in advance—it seems twenty thousand dollars was the price—& he has been paid in full. He is certainly a *man* above all things.[641]

I'm alone. Of's man is off today. The night was a wild rainy one.—I was glad you weren't on the water. I dreamt you & I were on our way to Lake George & that we were changing in Saratoga.—I suddenly realized that I had left my cape in the train—only had my gray coat on.—Then there was excitement.—A chasing on my part. On & off trains. Moving. Standing still. No cape. And you standing waiting for me & quite faint—pale. I was frantic at myself.—Awful.—I awoke & my heart was having a gay time.—It has been behaving very well.—

I was at Rosen's.—He produces pictures & pictures.

640. As was reported in the clipping Stieglitz sent O'Keeffe, "Rockefeller Center Ousts Rivera Over Painting of Lenin" (*New York Herald Tribune*, May 10, 1933), on May 9, 1933, officials at Rockefeller Center had called Diego Rivera down from his scaffold in the lobby of the RCA Building, where he was working on a mural they had commissioned on modern civilization. After paying Rivera, they canceled the project because the artist refused to remove a portrait of Lenin from it, as John D. Rockefeller, Jr., had requested. In the next few days Stieglitz sent O'Keeffe several other articles about the controversy, including "Rivera Plans Fight to Finish Barred Mural" (*New York Herald Tribune*, May 11, 1933) and "Chicago Drops Rivera Mural; Artist Stunned" (*New York Herald Telegram*, May 11, 1933), which noted that General Motors had cancelled a planned mural by Rivera for its exhibit at the Century of Progress exposition in Chicago, a blow that had reduced Rivera "to a state of incoherence."

641. On May 16, 1933, Rivera wrote Stieglitz that he was "the first to interest yourself in my work here and the first to come to my aid in a combat against the forces that everybody wishes to avoid having against themselves;" see Okrent, *Great Fortune*, 226.

3 P.M. Hallowell just left. Also Margaret—Yes Margaret—She phoned me. Came right down. Looks fine. Is going to the Lake tomorrow. Takes Frankie. Told her she should live in the house. At first wondered but I said all else will be foolish.—So when you come all will be ready & I'll go to the Lake with you for a few days. I would have gone had you come tomorrow.—I am ready.—There is plenty for me to do here yet I am really ready.—

She goes up by bus.—I must try that sometime.—

Hallowell is painting portraits in oil for a living. Is father of a daughter.[642] Those artists have nerve. Ever more it seems.—

—I always forget to get Phanadorm. Must today.—

I wonder are you remaining or are you coming.—

As I wrote you what you decide is best for you is best for me.—That's clear to me. And isn't merely words.—

—More later. I'll see what Of's man is doing—

Another kiss—

O'KEEFFE RETURNED from Bermuda somewhat earlier than expected, arriving back in New York on May 19. Although she was tan and had gained weight, she was still unsteady and did not wish to remain in the city. Instead, Stieglitz took her to Lake George the following day, where she remained for the rest of the summer, under the care of their housekeeper, Margaret Prosser. While Stieglitz was at Lake George, Henri Matisse visited An American Place. Although Stieglitz had exhibited Matisse's work at 291 and had met him in 1909 and 1911, they had not seen each other in the years since. John Dewey later wrote Stieglitz that Matisse was "more interested in your photographs than anything else. He remarked that they did not look like photographs which was the most flattering thing he with his views could say."[643]

Alfred Stieglitz · [En route from Lake George to New York City] · May 23, 1933

4:35 P.M.

Georgia dear—

You on the Hill—I on the train New York bound. And you for a moment believing that I would have had a moment's peace not taking you to the Hill. How little you know me if you could believe anything could have stopped me going with you or staying until I had heard what the doctor would tell you.—I'm glad I didn't have to leave this morning. That we were at the Shanty together & even in the rhubarb field!!—

Saratoga—I had a sandwich. Tell Margaret it was very good. You didn't eat enough for lunch. Don't think I didn't notice the portions you gave Margaret & me & that you had no carrots. I

642. Carolyn Bayard Hallowell.
643. John Dewey to AS, June 4, 1933, courtesy of The Center for Dewey Studies at Southern Illinois University.

didn't want to start an argument! Now you come first. Do you hear.—I'm all right & there is no cause whatever for you to worry.—None.—Not even about money. That sounds queer. Well what isn't queer these days & times.—I want to keep going & I want you to get confidence in yourself back. You will. For I am helping you—& still continue to help you more than ever.—But don't overdo.—I'm glad you are on the Hill. Now don't hesitate to cut the roof off the porch should you want to.[644] Do you hear. I *mean* that.—It will improve the lower room for anyone not only for yourself. I wonder did Dunklee phone you. I asked him to. Thanks for the hat. My other one (lost) looked pretty disreputable.—Stupid about my night clothes but we got to Fort Edward with thirteen minutes to spare!—The road was clear.—Glens Falls was slow.—

6:30 P.M. Sandwiches gone. One cake left.—It is sunny here. I wish I could keep sun for you for a long while—in every way. Soon you'll be eating. Please get it out of your head that I laugh at your increase of flesh. I think it wonderful. Really. Don't you believe anything anymore that I tell you?—For many years I was terribly worried about your weight—I knew it was not right—I enjoy seeing you enjoy your food & that you eat aplenty. I wonder will you remember everything the doctor said.—I'll send you candy tonight—also the tablets.—The candy will not arrive until Thursday.—I think I'll go to Wertheim's tomorrow A.M. & get that off my mind.—A kiss—I'm glad you are finally sleeping where you do.—The only sensible thing to do.

7:30 P.M. I wonder are you at supper. Or is it over.—And what are you doing.—You say I don't notice your clothes. Well I do. The red is very becoming.—You looked very well—I may seem not to see—but I do see mostly—It feels good to have the buttons on my vest. Thanks! Also to have my woolen pajamas clean for a change. Again thanks!—

Room 3003—9:10 P.M. Just got in. Sultry. Had rained. I want to get this off. Ross met me at station with mail. Was unexpected. A letter from Mabel. Will send you a copy.—Don't want to risk losing it. A letter from Waldo (is near Cape Cod)—haven't opened it yet. A long one from McCausland.[645] —And just think!—Yesterday afternoon Matisse was at the Place with Dewey!!—And who do you think did the honors? Walkowitz!! Ross had been there all day & when Walkowitz showed up & asked if Ross didn't want to be relieved awhile, Ross went out for an hour or so.—Well—it [is] queer the fatality of it all. I did want to hear what Matisse would have to say about Marin & you & the Place—& much else—Well it wasn't to be—I'll hear from Walkowitz what happened.—I really wonder what happened. I'll never know except

---

644. In the summer of 1933 O'Keeffe had a portion of the porch roof of the Lake George house cut off to let more light into the first floor; see Greenough 1540–1544.

645. Stieglitz and Elizabeth McCausland had a lively correspondence in May 1933 in which she asked him his opinion of color photography ("As far as I can see color photography as art seems taboo"; AS to McCausland, May 9, 1933) and told him of her training at the New England Printing School ("I love to work with my hands and think printing may be my salvation"; McCausland to AS May 22, 1933). She also sent O'Keeffe her greetings and fondly remembered spending Memorial Day weekend with her the previous year.

possibly from Dewey. I'm writing him now. And writing Matisse c/o his son Pierre. I wouldn't be surprised if Matisse sailed tonight.

Mabel writes Flint is crazy about Taos.—Well I'll send you a copy tomorrow.

Now Good Night. You'll be getting ready for bed shortly. Matisse or no Matisse I'm glad I took you to the Lake & didn't return sooner.—

Mabel writes: I have an article about you in a group called "Makers & Shakers" that is in volume five of her memoirs.[646] But it may appear somewhere this summer she says. The group includes Hutch Hapgood—myself, Margaret Sanger, Emma Goldman & her group & one or two others. She ends it by saying I was the King Lear of the modern art movement in America! And she gives me credit for preparing the ground for the Armory Show & all that happened since then.—She says she wrote it years ago but it stays *true!*

Flint lectured at the Taos Forum.—Said Marin, O'Keeffe, a queer name she forgot & Florine Stettheimer were immortals on the tree of American Art—or rather that Marin & O'Keeffe were the certain immortals & "the other" & Florine were birds in the tree!—So that's the gist of the letter.

Good Night. A kiss. Two.—I hope you sleep really well—

Good Night—

708

Georgia O'Keeffe · Lake George, New York · [May 25, 1933]

Thursday night—

Thanks for the book and the pills and the letters and clippings—

One thing I must say and this is that I did not listen to you and Jenks talking—nor to you and Margaret—I walked into the kitchen when I heard you. I must say for myself that I am not a listener in that way[647]—

It has been lovely here today—I walked up in the woods a little—Margaret with me. She found your hat at the bridge when she went for the mail this afternoon—it was hanging up on a pole or tree where someone had evidently put it when they found it—

I am still mostly sitting—reading and sewing a little—

Too bad about your missing Matisse—

I'm going to have a bath tonight as a great excitement—

There was a very lovely thin new moon at sunset— —so very thin—

Margaret is ironing—I am going to bed—

Good Night—

I hope you have quieted down a bit—

---

646. Mabel Luhan to AS, May 17, 1933. *Movers and Shakers* (New York, 1936) was vol. 3 of Luhan's memoirs. Stieglitz was mentioned several times in the book (pp. 25, 71, 95, and 165), but Luhan did not devote an entire chapter to his activities.

647. Stieglitz responded on May 27, 1933: "You funny one—you misunderstood me. I don't mean that you *listened* in the sense that you read my letter. Must I weigh every word with you.—Can you understand no fun at all. No teasing." He added: "Oh Georgia! Well—well. So I hurt your feelings again when that is the last thing—the very last—I want to do."

Georgia O'Keeffe · [Lake George, New York] · [May 27, 1933]

Saturday night—

    It has been another of those days when I have done nothing—clear and cooler—but sun too hot for me—

    I didn't get up till nearly noon—went for the mail and drove down to the Lake to see if the boat was all right—sat there a little while—This afternoon sat in the hammock—walked up and down from the bridge to the barn a little before supper—

    That is my day—

    I call it nothing—I feel like nothing—

Alfred Stieglitz · [New York City] · May 30, 1933

Decoration Day—The Place—1:00 P.M. Here I am since ten A.M. Not a soul except Ross awhile. He has gone to the Belmont Park races in spite of the drizzly day. Rain on & off.—It was good to hear your voice last night. It sounded strong. And you walked to the back road without ill effects. Great.—There was a stupid girl on the phone.—

    I saw an extraordinary Eisenstein film last night. Seems to be an old one. Not *Potemkin*.—Something like *Ten Days that Changed the World*.—Rivera & his wife[648] walked in & sat right next to me. Curious coincidence. She wanted to know about you.—Hadn't much chance to say anything. You ought to see how thin Rivera is—Must have lost 120 pounds or more. I have been wanting to write to him but somehow didn't.—

    If the day had been fine I might have gone to the races too just to see a horse & to get a day's outing for a change.—I doubt anyone's showing up today. The pictures—yours & Marin's—look particularly beautiful in this gray light.—It's bright & neutral.—They all seem to sing.—I do enjoy them.—A kiss.—I'm glad you are mending so nicely.—I hear Georgia Engelhard leaves for Lake George on Friday.—Now please remember you are not to speed up unconsciously!!—through suggestion.

2:00 P.M. I have been sorting negatives. I found several magnificent unmounted prints of you. Platinums & palladios. Made me positively sick to look at them. They are so beautiful. And I realize how unfair I have been to my own photography & to you too—How relatively irrelevant things seem ever to have been given precedence to the more relevant.—But I suppose that's the mixture in myself. It has been a real shock.—Of course I'm glad there are those few prints. They at least show me that there was something in me which occasionally flowered in a truly worthwhile way. It's fifteen years today that Gaisman took you & Strand & me to Coney Island. It was a raw day for nearly June.—Fifteen years. How innocent we all were—even Gaisman I guess.[649]—

---

648. Sergei Eisenstein's 1928 film *Ten Days That Shook the World*. Rivera was married to Frida Kahlo.
649. On June 4, 1933, Stieglitz recalled O'Keeffe's arrival in New York in 1918: "It's as if it was yesterday & at the same time it's as if it were a dream.—I remember every fraction of a moment.—It was a perfect day like this.—A kiss.—Well I'm glad

I wish I were a better photographer.—The Eisenstein last night—going through a lot of negligible small negatives & the sudden finding of those unmounted prints—together a bit much. Well I'll see this summer.—I must make a decent print or two.—

A kiss!—No two.—

What a hodgepodge one can be when all is said & done—in spite of all one's vision.—The blind spot can certainly be blind!!—I have gotten the set of *Camera Work* ready for Mr. Goldsmith. It's slow progress. Very slow.—

6:40 P.M. Dry mounted some clippings on large cardboards.—And then sat in the armchair & dozed. Drowsy. Weather. Walkowitz sitting at table reading Kootz.[650] It's about time to go to Childs.—Looks as if it might pour any moment.—Rain held off all afternoon.—From dozing I feel more stupefied than I did before. Maybe ate too much lunch. Got it late. Too much food. Tonight I'll go to bed early. Phanadorm. Have a big day ahead of me. I want to go to dentist & to Woolworth's—Bank—etc.—Days are slipping away & I haven't attended to a lot of things which are essential.

Rosenfeld just phoned. Wants to meet us at supper—Lord I'm tired—

I wonder do you rest every two hours as doctor said you should. I wonder are you losing your tan—I wonder much—much—much—

Good Night—A big kiss—

Have you played the Victrola at all. Or would winding be too much strain. Well the Kid can do the winding.—

Again Good Night & one more kiss.—

Georgia O'Keeffe · [Lake George, New York] · [June 3, 1933]

I have not written because there seems really nothing to write—I am feeling better—even much better than a week ago—

Georgie came yesterday—I had discarded most of my clothes before she came—
We spent yesterday afternoon and most of this morning in the sun with nothing on—I cut her hair very short so we feel quite as usual—

I am really quite black—I didn't realize it till I saw myself next [to] her whiteness—
It rained hard this afternoon—the first real rain since I am here—

You asked about the Victrola—No—I haven't even opened it—my nerves seems strangely uninterested—

Sitting on the porch or out in the grass in the sun in my bare skin seems to be the best thing to do these days—It was very good being alone—but it is very good having Georgie too—

The rain was much needed—everything seemed a bit stunted for lack of it—

you came, I hope you are, even though it has meant many a heartache for you—& maybe many for me too. Still they have been worthwhile—mine.—I'm not sentimental."
650. Possibly Samuel Kootz, *Modern American Painters* (New York, 1933).

You speak two or three times about not daring to break down—If you feel like breaking down you had better just shut the door and come up here and sit down instead—

—Don't try to kill yourself the last few days before you get away as you have so often—I'd not be much use in taking care of anything—

Nine packages came yesterday—I have not opened them—am not going to till I have a place to put the books—will have it all fixed Monday—

I am all right—you don't need to worry about me at all—

Georgia O'Keeffe · [**Lake George, New York**] · [**June 12, 1933**]

Monday afternoon—

If I write you I only write about two more days like the one on the gray paper[651]—They are all about alike—Nothing else—

Sun—sitting on the dock—going for the mail—walking a little—

I don't think a great deal of such an existence—That is about all there is to say—

You write about seeing Charles—He wrote and asked me if he could come over—His letter went to Bermuda—then I didn't answer it immediately—He had probably gone to Washington before he had my letter—

So that was that—

I wrote him to come this past weekend if he wanted to.

STIEGLITZ JOINED O'KEEFFE at Lake George on June 16, where the two spent several months together. Unlike earlier summers, Stieglitz invited few visitors to the Hill because, as he wrote, "everybody seems to get on [O'Keeffe's] nerves" and "everything seems to upset her."[652] Instead, he wrote numerous letters. In one, he confided to Dove that "Georgia's condition is pathetic…. I'm certainly far beyond my depths," and he confessed that "at times I feel like a murderer. There is Kitty. Now there is Georgia."[653] Nevertheless he continued to exchange daily letters with Norman. Lamenting the "helpless terror"[654] he felt from the "loneliness…emptiness [and] unkindness" of his new life on the Hill, he wrote longingly of the spiritual, emotional, and physical oneness he and Norman enjoyed.[655] He also focused much of his emotional intensity into his art, creating a series of deeply felt photographs of their farmhouse and the lake, as well as the trees, grasses, and shrubs that defined their vistas.[656] Still unable to paint, O'Keeffe did "nothing all summer," as she told a friend, "but wait for myself to be myself again."[657]

---

651. O'Keeffe's letter of May 27, 1933 (see p. 709), was written on gray paper.

652. AS to Norman, June 18 and 17, 1933.

653. AS to Dove, June 25, 1933; see Morgan, *Dear Stieglitz/Dear Dove,* 277.

654. AS to Norman, June 19, 1933.

655. AS to Norman, June 18, 1933.

656. Greenough 1500–1539.

657. GOK to Russell Vernon Hunter, Oct. 21, 1933.

Stieglitz made a few brief trips to New York during the summer and early fall, but he did not return there until October 1 to install Twenty-Five Years of John Marin, 1908–1932, on view at An American Place from October 12 through December 18, 1933. Throughout the fall he became increasingly involved in the publication of *America and Alfred Stieglitz,* a collection of essays celebrating his seventieth birthday, edited by Waldo Frank, Lewis Mumford, Norman, and others. Preferring the solitude of Lake George, O'Keeffe remained at the Hill with Margaret Prosser. As she was still uncertain where she wanted to live that winter, Stieglitz leased room 2915 at the Shelton Hotel, which Cary Ross again shared with him to reduce expenses. He spent several weekends at Lake George that fall—from October 13 to 15; from October 28 to 30; and from November 14 to 16, when he and O'Keeffe celebrated her forty-sixth birthday. He called her every evening, both to hear her news and to assess the tone of her voice, and he wrote her several times a day, detailing who had come to the gallery and their encouraging words about her art. O'Keeffe responded far less often and less willingly. Asserting that "there was nothing to write," she did not share, as she had once done so readily, the things that moved or excited her nor did she confide in Stieglitz her thoughts or desires.[658]

712 **Alfred Stieglitz · [En route from Lake George to New York City] · September 6, 1933**

Leaving Albany. 7:45 P.M. It is still pouring.—I have been devouring Gertrude Stein—from the first word. And on page 140.[659] A very grand performance. Keen—seen—& grand writing so effortless so alive. I wonder will you enjoy it as I do.—I'll read on shortly—And have eaten my eats.—

I can't begin to tell you how happy in spite of "unhappiness" (!) I am that you seem & are so much better. And that you feel I have been kind—Lord I never wanted to be otherwise to you. And for that matter unkind to anyone. And yet what a brute I have been. I hope you'll continue getting better—& *don't sit on* cold chairs or benches—or get into cold beds without being wrapped up properly—And thanks a million times for putting my things in order—They were rather tattered I confess. But I really don't mind. I guess if I were alone I'd be a pretty ragged affair—as unaware of my clothes as I was of my unspeakably dirty glasses.—

—I hope you will sleep tonight. Will have gotten a real rest & not worry about me. I am tired but all right otherwise.—I'm curious about town. What I'll be moved to do. Or will I seem to drift on—

—It's queer how when people write about me they get the spirit all wrong even in a simple statement. Stein's book has all the semblance of integrity yet where she mentions me the spirit is always left out[660]—Fortunately I don't mind. Her book is grand. She is close to being a genius.

658. GOK to AS, Nov. 6, 1933.

659. Gertrude Stein, *The Autobiography of Alice B. Toklas* (New York, 1933). Stein wrote (p. 140) that Stieglitz had published two of her portraits of Matisse and Picasso in *Camera Work,* special no. (Aug. 1912), 23–25, 29–30, respectively.

660. Stein's references to Stieglitz are brief. In addition to noting his publication of her writings in *Camera Work,* she incorrectly states that he exhibited the Spanish painter and sculptor Manuel Manolo; see Stein, *Autobiography,* 119. Stieglitz did reproduce two of Manolo's drawings in *Camera Work* 39 (July 1912).

In fact I guess she is one—How she writes. How alive everything. Her portrait of Rönnebeck is a wonder.[661]—But all lives. An exciting experience. But I'm not sure you'll like it as I do. I can see McBride wreathed in smiles all the way through & Van Vechten all chuckles[662]—The difference between brother & sister!—She & Leo—Ye gods.—I wonder what would she think of Marin & you & possibly the photographs.—We really have no one like that over here not within miles.

—Later. Read the last paragraph on page 158!! That's Mabel to a hairline. Also page 162 last paragraph—Just to amuse you—See page 163 third paragraph about Demuth.[663]

9:40—I have finished the book. Haven't read a book from cover to cover at one sitting in ages.—I wonder how you are—It seems so funny to think that in one and a half hours I'll be amongst people—millions of them—& skyscrapers—& noise—& smell—& virtually alone—

I dread seeing the walls of the Place—And the floor—Ye gods.—But they will be clean —I hope.—I'll be glad to see your paintings—& Marin's.—I know they will have kept their aliveness for me—

I'm curious too to see how the photographs I have here will look in the office—

—I feel very awake. Not a bit tired. The book has stirred up my blood—& our few little talks have brought me a little peace & much hope—I dread illusions.—

All the windows of the car are closed. It's hot & stuffy. I had my coat & cape on at first. —Weren't too much.—

Alfred Stieglitz · [En route from Lake George to New York City] · October 1, 1933

Albany
Georgia Dear—

I feel as if I were dangling between nowhere & nowhere—Just sheer mad. Talking.— Josephine.[664]—And all the time, you & the Hill—in the back of my head. I can't believe I'll be in New York & you up there walking alone—I not by your side. But I am [by] your side—

661. Stein writes about the sculptor Arnold Rönnebeck's numerous attempts to get her and Toklas to go to Germany in the winter of 1913–1914, even though she repeatedly told him, "I don't like germans"; Stein, *Autobiography*, 125.

662. Stein notes that McBride "did not believe in worldly success. It ruins you, it ruins you, he used to say. But Henry, Gertrude Stein used to answer dolefully, don't you think I will ever have any success, I would like to have a little, you know. Think of my unpublished manuscripts. But Henry McBride was firm, the best that I can wish you, he always said, is to have no success. It is the only good thing. He was firm about that. He was however enormously pleased when Mildred [Aldrich] was successful, and he now says he thinks the time has come when Gertrude Stein could indulge in a little success." She also writes of teasing Carl Van Vechten with intimate details of his failed first marriage with Anna Snyder; Stein, *Autobiography*, 149, 164–168.

663. In *The Autobiography of Alice B. Toklas*, Stein writes that Mabel Dodge (Luhan) confidently described Constance Fletcher "as a very large woman who would wear a purple robe and who was deaf." However, when Stein and Toklas met Fletcher, "she was dressed in green and was not deaf but very short sighted, and she was delightful" (158). Stein also notes that after she had written her "Portrait of Mabel Dodge," Dodge proposed that Stein and Toklas should travel from one country house to the next and make an "exciting and lucrative career" by writing portraits of American millionaires (162). Stein describes a remarkable "landscape" Demuth sent her "in which the roofs and windows are so subtle that they are as mysterious and as alive as the roofs and windows of Hawthorne or Henry James"; Stein, *Autobiography*, 162–163.

664. Possibly Josephine Marks, who was Lee Stieglitz's secretary.

all the time—as you are by mine. And I look through the keyhole to see how you are—Oh and everything. The summer was very hard for us both but I feel very necessary. You are going to get well. The last weeks were very perfect in a way—and important ones—And the drive in the auto yesterday very beautiful & very wonderful. I may seem cruel & hard to you at times—but I'm really not cruel or hard in reality.—

Oh Georgia—I do want to make things start up a bit—I'll fight for you harder than ever. When I say I have no goal, don't misunderstand me.—I'll fight to the last ditch for what I have always fought. What is it? It is nameless.—

I am going to phone tonight—I'm glad Alma[665] is with you—I'll be back to see you if you stay at the Hill.—The trip will take less out of me than not making it.—You must & will get well—You mustn't worry about me—Remember anything you feel you must do I'm back of it.—Absolutely.—Don't try to remember many things I said—for they were not always meant as you heard them. I feel that we are closer together than in a long while—much closer. I want you to know that.—We'll be working *together* I know that.—Much that seemed very "important" to either of us may eventually not seem quite so "important."—I enjoyed our walks—It was wonderful to see you stride out yesterday. But don't overdo—don't force—

I wonder what you'll read when you'll get up & go to bed. What drives & walks you'll take. Remember all that means something very definite to me. So you needn't think your letters must be "interesting."—And I promise you to take as good care of myself as is given to me—

Josephine is reading. She's quite a person. Twenty-two. I was amazed to hear she's that "old."—

—I wonder how my prints will look at the Place—They'll always remind me of you —We do work together in perfect harmony when we get at them—And much more too. I have been very very stupid in many things.—Don't think you are a failure as far as *we* are concerned. Neither of us has been a failure. We weren't always intelligent I guess. But all that is ancient history—There is a fresh start—

And also remember that should you feel you'd like to try some apartment in town eventually I won't stand in the way.—We'll see *how* you are to focus on gaining strength—building up nerves, etc.—Exercise, rest, sleep, plenty of food—*no excitements!*—I wonder will you occasionally play some music—And what?—

6:15 P.M. I have been looking at Cheiro.—Must look up his other books.[666] —I wonder how your afternoon. Did you rest as usual?—

8:30 P.M.—Shelton—Just phoned. You are at a movie in Glens Falls. Great—I hope you'll be all right.—Flint, Margules & Ross met me at station. Am in 2915 but going to Childs to get a "drink"—& something warm.

Lots lots lots of love. And a big kiss—

Yes all will be well—*Must be*—

665. Alma Wertheim.

666. Cheiro (William John Warner), a self-described clairvoyant who taught palmistry, astrology, and numerology; possibly *You and Your Hand: The Last Word on This Fascinating Study* (New York, 1931).

Georgia O'Keeffe · [Lake George, New York] · [October 1, 1933]

10:35—and I am in my bed—

We went to Glens Falls to the movie *Morning Glory*[667]—I think that was the title—and I am still alive and feel very wide awake—not too tired—feeling really very good—lay down before supper.

I am sorry to have missed your call—but Margaret called down the stairs and told me when we came in—

I miss you in so many places and ways—Margaret already has your bed done up for the winter—it seems awful—I may have to have it made so it will not seem so lonely—

With my two naps the afternoon seemed rather short—

Your presence still seems very much about—as tho you have not really gone—something of you seems very much here—

Good Night again—

[October 2, 1933]

10:50 A.M.—Monday morning—I slept very well—and waked up and wondered about you—Every little while I remember that you are in the city and it seems so strange—makes me wish I could see you—exactly what you are doing at the moment—

Alma just got away—we have been talking since soon after seven—at the table then on the porch—the sun warm and lovely—

I am all right—the movie did not tire me too much which pleases me. I feel very good—

And for you—I only hope—and think very fondly of you—

Georgia O'Keeffe · [Lake George, New York] · [October 9, 1933]

After the telephone—You sounded disappointed that I had not written—But I am so dull—so dull—Maybe tomorrow I'll feel better—

It has been gray—

Monday—

[October 10, 1933]

Tuesday Morning—7:30—

I am up and dressed and have finished breakfast and put the car out in the sun—to get the seat warm—

It seems a lovely quiet day—sunny and rather hazy and also rather cold—I slept well and feel much better today—Last night I started to write—was just too tired—

I must tell you that there are two large hoot owls about—They make the strangest noise

---

667. The 1933 movie *Morning Glory* starred Katharine Hepburn, Douglas Fairbanks, Jr., and Adolphe Menjou.

at night—and night before last I saw them—great big things—way up in the top of the old chestnut tree—

The foliage is beginning to be very fine—Rain last night made the ground seem very wet in a nice way when I walked out on it just now—

There were weird dark clouds all yesterday afternoon—very strange ones—and they finally came down—

I hope your lower regions are feeling better—

And naturally I wonder about the Marins—And how your photographs look in town—

A lively wind has come up since I sat here—

A morning kiss to you and a very quiet good night one—

Alfred Stieglitz · [En route from Lake George to New York City] · [October 15, 1933]

Fort Edward—2:45 P.M. You have driven off. I'm standing here on the platform waiting— The "visit" was as perfect as the "weather"—as beautiful—even if a bit "sad."—I feel you are "better"—& will get stronger still—You will for you must.—For your own sake & for mine as I must keep going for your sake & my own—which is typified by the Place. It is the symbol. —Life is certainly incredible. Standing before the old chestnut trees today—they never were more beautiful—to me it was like a ritual—And what you said about the yellow leaf in connection with death—all registered. Everything. And this morning before breakfast was quieting. And you said it should have always been that way. I said nothing for I felt "yes" & couldn't say it for it was self-understood.—You couldn't have said it hadn't you felt my "yes"—

—I hope your driving & my visit will not have taken too much out of you. I'll phone punctually as always—You must have a very good night's rest.—A kiss—a good one.—The train will be here in a few minutes—I'll walk down to where my car will be—Another kiss— Greetings to Margaret & to Richard.—And many many thanks for the perfection—

6:30 I have been reading Wagner[668] by snatches—Really terrific—Also been reading *Times* & *Herald*—mainly about Germany—Heaven only knows—& it doesn't—what we may all be in for. Every hour seems to bring the world closer & closer to an abyss.—

The trip seems long. Car overheated.—Ate sandwich, celery & cake. Feel very full.— I wish it were 8:30. I want to hear how you stood the visit & the drive—I feel as if in a trance—

Get Well—We must work together. That's my goal!—

---

668. Richard Wagner and Mathilde Wesendonck, *Richard Wagner to Mathilde Wesendonck*, trans. William Ashton Ellis (New York, 1905).

8:20 P.M. At phone. Shelton downstairs. Ross met me at station. Walked here. He had Kansas City letter for me. Everything perfect. Receive five hundred as soon as picture[669] is expressed. Balance within a year.—A fine letter from her. I'll send it to you. You must write her at once— Well you see everything has clicked! And I'll feel more satisfied when I get you on the phone—

I'm sure you'll soon feel like painting a little—I'm sure of it—as I'm sure you'll get better & better—stronger—

I'm impatient for the minutes to pass—

Am not tired. Back is better.—Don't worry about me. Get well. There goes the phone—

A big kiss—

I told Ross. He was delighted. He's really very fine.—Young & a little gauche perhaps at times—too conscientious—

Phone started to ring but didn't—It's 8:29—a minute more. Another Kiss—

Read a lot of Wagner—Some day I'll read some of it aloud to you.—

There goes the phone now!—

I hope you got rid of that headache. Good Night—

I wish I were on the Hill—

Georgia O'Keeffe · [Lake George, New York] · [October 15, 1933]

7:30—We have finished supper—

When I had driven some distance away I looked at my watch and I had over ten minutes—time to go back and tell you goodbye again—Your face—and your going seemed so very sad to me—and I feel so helpless—

I drove home slowly—got the newspapers on the way—came in—the house seemed so strange and empty—I drank my orange juice and went back out to the barn and dusted off the car—came in and read the paper some—then went out and walked up and down—I didn't like being in the house and didn't like walking either—so I came in and looked at the paper again and then went out and walked again—then paper again—

I look forward to speaking with you—I have nothing to say but I want to hear you —how you are—My head aches badly—after I speak with you I will go to bed and take something for it—

Good Night—

I am glad you came—it was very nice but I feel so very sad about so many things—

Again Good Night—and such a quiet Good Night kiss—

I wish I could tuck you in—Don't forget to have your buttonholes fixed.

---

669. Rheta Berkley had purchased Lynes 709. As Stieglitz noted in a letter to Berkley of October 16, 1933, O'Keeffe had recently told him that she felt "paralyzed." She "tried to draw but nothing seems to happen." He told Berkley he hoped her purchase of one of O'Keeffe's paintings would "start her again."

717

A TERRIBLE RIGHTNESS, 1929–1933

[October 16, 1933]

Monday morning—I was up and through breakfast by 7:30—

　　　Went to bed and to sleep right after you telephoned—slept till about two—since then have been awake but my headache is gone and I feel all right—It seems fairly warm and sunny—

　　　Richard is here. I am going to have him fix the back porch of the little house.

　　　We were just out talking about it—

　　　It is really very nice out—.

　　　A bright good morning to you—!

　　　I am glad you had the letter from Kansas City when you got back—That is a help—

　　　I'll be starting about my day—

　　　A kiss to you—quietly—

Georgia O'Keeffe · [Lake George, New York] · [October 25, 1933]

Well—you ought to see it here this morning—

　　　It is pretty fine—snow with bright leaves—

　　　I had eaten and been all around up through the pasture by 8:30—hadn't looked at the clock—

　　　It is no use to try to tell of it—You can imagine—

　　　And there is nothing else to tell about.

　　　Richard came down to "fix us up" as he puts it—I'm going to drive him home now tho it is snowing a little and the wind blowing like mad—Sun shining too—I am fine—

　　　A kiss to you—I'll be off—

Alfred Stieglitz · [En route from Lake George to New York City] · October 30, 1933 +

Leaving Fort Edward. 11:20 A.M. I'm glad I got you on the phone. It made me feel very miserable what you said just before I left. And when you said on the phone: That's the way it is—It is not that way for me. Just as I phone every evening—I phone because it gives me something to strengthen me & if it does that for me it must give you something similar even if your "mind" twists it perhaps into something it basically isn't. And as my coming to see you is myself— *I come because I want to.* There is no sacrifice—no ought to—no sense of duty—none of such nonsense—So I'm very glad I came—Very—It was all very perfect except perhaps that I was a bit tired & you too for that matter—I would liked to have taken a drive with you—but didn't suggest it because it was too cold yesterday & both of us too tired.—But I enjoyed the walks yesterday & this morning—I'm even glad I didn't get Ross's letter.—Whatever may be in it can wait—The train shakes so much it's hard to write—Remember in thinking about me even tho I wrote you pretty clearly about my coming—my intentions—you had it all wrong. Of course you had in your mind I wouldn't stay away from the Place both Sunday & Monday.—So you didn't read what I wrote!!—And so it goes.—I was aware absolutely of what I was doing.—A kiss. I wish I were still at the Lake—That's the real truth—What you are you are & what I am I am & if we can't accept each other for what we really are we are hopelessly foolish.—

—I'll call you tonight—

Thanks for the warm bed.—Thanks for the underwear—& all you are solicitious for about me—Don't think I am not fully aware.—I'll send you the Rugg book[670] in a few days—

1:45 P.M. On train from Albany to N. Y. Beautiful weather. Warmer. It's probably so on the Hill. —I still feel bewildered by your feeling.—Still I "understand" it.—In saying you didn't read my letter because you couldn't imagine my remaining away from the Place two days—or at all— you might say I read your letter "wrong" about Margy & her house.[671] —I wondering how you could get to Taos in your physical condition!!—So you see how deeply rooted certain "feelings" about the other are in each of us—And that is what one must pull up by the roots like weeds. I know that about myself & try my best to rid myself of such.—

—I want to see you as well as you can be. That's what I'm after above all things. That's my real goal. But you must help—And I know you are helping—& will help. But you must get certain "ideas" out of your head to achieve our end—your health above all. All else will become relatively easy then. Don't think I'm wasting myself. I'm not—And I am really as careful as I know how to be. I need all my strength to see through what I know there is for me to do. Don't worry about storage. I'll disturb nothing. I know your feeling. And as for the Marin show it will remain up till you will have seen it—

Another kiss—

8:40 P.M. Well I'm glad the cat walked with you in the woods—Also that you and Margaret took Richard home—Why did you think anyone was with me at the phone?

I'll say Good Night. I'll bathe & go to bed early.—A real kiss—

Georgia O'Keeffe · [Lake George, New York] · [October 30, 1933]

I came right home thinking you would telephone—I was quite disturbed—and I was so glad to hear your voice—

But it worries me now that you went away that way because I felt that you had a good quiet day yesterday—and a good night—Then for me to disturb you at the last moment makes me very annoyed with myself—

I wish you would not think any more about it—If I stay alone long enough I will have myself in order and be all right—

670. Probably Harold Rugg, *The Great Technology: Social Change and the Public Mind* (New York, 1933).

671. In her letter to Stieglitz of October 21, 1933, O'Keeffe said that Content had written to her, offering her house in New York City: "She is staying in Taos till nearly Xmas and says her house is empty but for a maid that she thinks quite wonderful—and she tells me that I should go there and stay if I go to town."

Many things that were very important to me are not really so anymore but I haven't them really in place yet—and it makes me say foolish things sometimes—

This afternoon I tinkered and tinkered with something I'm trying to draw—was at it for what was left of the morning too—till four—then went out to get what was left of the sun—Richard came along—going home—So we drove him—There is still a little snow up near Warrensburg—The moon coming up big and white in the daylight.

When we got back I went to walk with the white cat—she followed me all around through the woods and the pasture—so pretty—and she looked so white in the evening light—

And I feel quite rearranged in my head and all right—

There is bright moonlight—a bit hazy—I wish I could kiss you Good Night and make you feel that you need not worry about me—

It is a little after nine—I'm going to bed—

[October 31, 1933]
Tuesday morning—Gray—and quite warm—no sun—everything very still—

I slept pretty well—and feel all right—

Tinkering again—and I seem to get nowhere—

Will go to town—

Good Morning—

Georgia O'Keeffe · [Lake George, New York] · [November 6, 1933]

Good Monday Morning!—It is snowing—

I haven't written for two days—There was nothing to write—

Yesterday Frankie got the wheelbarrow and brought my easel and some other things down from the Shanty for me. He even made efforts to encourage me to paint—getting like others sometimes are—even suggested that I paint the whole front of the barn—

Everything sits here waiting for me and I no good—. Nothing in me—

The snow this morning is pretty—just a little white on everything—You know how it looks—

Richard helped me put the top up on the car—and I plan to go to Glens Falls—

I had thought of it yesterday and [saw] no reason to change my plans just because it is snowing a little—

It is windstill and very pretty out—

My walk around by Hubbel Lane yesterday is the first time I have done it and not been shaky about it—It was good to feel better about such a small adventure—

I may go to New York the end of the week—We'll see how I feel—

Thanks for McBride's page. Jewell evidently thinks differently about Hopper[672]—

672. In "Hopper's One-Man Show," *New York Sun,* Nov. 4, 1933, 11, Henry McBride wrote that Edward Hopper's paintings shown at the Museum of Modern Art were "solid…clear…untroubled," but also "strangely static…petrified and lifeless." On the

The Place—It must be nearly five.—I'm finally alone. Here since nine A.M.—Last night Sel took Ross & me to a movie—a pretty good one:—mixture of the West—Texas—Chicago—pioneer & wealth—early days—decay—Would be much too "exciting" for you.—But I thought of you all the time (something new)—you & your antecedents—where you were rooted—really still are—then myself citified—you the opposite—

I came home pretty tired. Supper rich & good. Even ate crabmeat & didn't realize it until it was down!!—Slept some. Up at seven. Raw cold—threatening snow.—

Found your letter here. Dear.—Alive.—I like the feeling.—I examined my dried negatives. I wonder. Herbert called me up—wouldn't I go to the Philharmonic with them tonight. Ross & the Kid to the horseshow. I said "no"—I'm in no state for concerts.—I'd rather bathe or even walk the street.—There were people here—about fifty.—Rosenfeld & Teddy Bryner—& above all *Duchamp!* As fine as ever. A little older.—Is coming again. He likes the Place.—Brancusi is not coming. There will be fifty-eight Brancusis.[673] —

I wrote to Dorothy Dudley today. She wants a Guggenheim to be able to write a novel.[674] I think I wrote you that.—Had mislaid her letter.—Ever trying to create some "order."—I really give it up. Seems hopeless.

—Tomorrow A.M. I'm due at the dentist's. So you had to go to Dr. Peck. I hope he's right. I hope you didn't have toothache.—My mouth is all sore. Always is after a session at the dentist's.—

My watch stopped. I guessed at the time. Must call up & see.

It's 5:35.—

8:00 P.M. At hotel. Again I left my pen at the Place. Left there at 6:45. Went to Childs. Flint came in. Ross later but he left for the horse show shortly. Brett showed me her paintings today. They disconcerted me some. Too many "outside" influences at work.—Yet she has progressed.—She herself was somewhat startled at what she saw, seeing them in Place. She had another letter from Mabel. Mabel had read part of Frieda's manuscript.[675] —It seems a poem of John Reed's appears in it. Mabel told Frieda that the poem was written for her, Mabel, & she had the original manuscript. And Frieda said: Why my poem is written in his own handwriting! Well Reed certainly must have been a wonder with the ladies. Maybe there are more copies (originals) extant. It also appears (according to Mabel) that the Captain is busy translating the Frieda manuscript into Italian—& there is to be (or already is) a German one.—So the Captain seems to be a useful

other hand, Edward Alden Jewell, "Hopper's Pictures on View Today," *NYT*, Oct. 31, 1933, 19, asserted that the exhibition proved that Hopper was one of "America's most vital, original and accomplished artists." See also Jewell, "This American Painter's Works Admirably Presented," *NYT*, Nov. 5, 1933, 12.

673. Brancusi's sculpture was on view at the Brummer Gallery, Nov. 17, 1933–Jan. 13, 1934; see Edward Alden Jewell, "Brancusi Exhibition," *NYT*, Nov. 18, 1933, 13.

674. Dorothy Dudley did not receive a Guggenheim Foundation grant in 1934. She wrote *Forgotten Frontiers: Dreiser and the Land of the Free: A Novel of Facts* (London, 1932, 1933) and *What Dark Secrets*, with Juanita Sheridan (New York, 1943).

675. Frieda Lawrence, *Not I, but the Wind…*(Santa Fe, 1934).

man in many ways.—Mabel certainly knows how to write letters.—Brett goes to Philadelphia again in the morning. More Stokowski.

9:00 P.M. So it's snowing again at the Lake. It must be very wonderful.—It tried hard here today but without any result.—

You sounded up & about again.—Fine.—Keep it up.

I have been wanting to bathe. Tonight I *must*.—Cute of Frankie to chide you about painting.—

Good Night.—A kiss.

Alfred Stieglitz · [En route from New York City to Lake George, New York] · November 14, 1933

5:20 P.M. On the train for Lake George—the Hill. Seems very natural. Birthday!—Didn't you surprise me last year—coming down & saying: It's my birthday!—And I was glad you came. And that you said what you did.—So why should you be "surprised" (!) that I should come tonight & be with you tomorrow?[676] When I left you last I knew I'd come tonight & hoped you'd be much better—stronger—& that your "birthday" would be a new beginning. That's my great, great hope. It's all too incredible what's happening. Life. Incredible.

Ross got back at noon today. Is in charge. He is a true friend to you & me & to the Place.—I know that. He has his idiosyncrasies as we all seem to have but at heart he is very fine & maybe too honest—for both very fine & too honest may be "faults" at times.—At any rate I feel my leaving the Place for two days is all right. Even if it would have to be closed I'd come. I feel very fit.—I am eager to see for myself how you are.—

—Ross saw the reformatory woman in Baltimore.[677] Another incredible story & happening—all true to the form of "my" life.—

—It's beastly hot in this car.—

Alfred Stieglitz · [En route from Lake George to New York City] · November 16, 1933 +

11:27 A.M. Here I am N.Y. bound on the train after leaving Fort Edward. It's pretty shaky writing—I'm glad I saw you & also that I phoned—I'm glad we had our walks & that one around Hubbel Lane—That seemed so natural—so "normal." Yes I'm satisfied to have come & seen for myself. Keep it up. You will.—The main thing I really have to live for is to see you on

---

676. O'Keeffe responded on November 16, 1933: "It seems funny that you came clear up here for my birthday when year after year it passed without either of us noticing it."

677. Cary Ross was friendly with Scott Fitzgerald and his wife, Zelda, who at that time was in a hospital outside of Baltimore. He had tried to interest the Brummer Gallery and Julien Levy in exhibiting Zelda's drawings and watercolors; see Ross to AS, July 29, 1932, and Sept. 20, 1932. He later exhibited them at his own gallery at 525 East 86th St., New York, in April 1934; see "Art Brevities," *NYT*, Mar. 31, 1934, 9.

your feet again & in contact with the world.—You will have more to give than ever.—And more to receive. I'm sure—

The day is really very perfect this burning clear sky & dry air even if I did freeze a bit owing to my own stupidity & inexcusable laziness—The bed felt good—the food was excellent —Everything really perfect—Don't economize falsely—Get what you need. Take no chances. Don't forget about coal & wood—

I'm going to get Jung's new book[678] & when I have read it I'll let you have it even if you don't "understand" all of it or any of it for that matter.—I have been looking at *The Dial*.[679] It was a pretty decent affair—better than anything we have now.—

Yes I'm very glad I saw you just as I did—It was all very "right"—And I'm glad you read me Henwar's letter[680] & Hunter's too.[681] Two fine fellows.

I see by the paper that Alma's brother[682] is to be head of the Treasury!—Finally a Jew & not Eugene Meyer! I'm very glad Alma & you are friends "again" directly & not via me.—I shall send her Marin's *Letters* at once—Yes you must get well—really well—and you will.—It gives me strength too.—A kiss—

1:17 Waiting Room, Albany. Train late thirty minutes. So here I am patiently waiting. And you at lunch—If I had "spare" cash I'd phone again—I guess I'll walk about a bit to limber up my underpinnings.—It's warm enough in here but I don't like sitting around—How often I wrote to you from here—Way back—& since then—

Yes if I had not run across your way I wonder often would you not have been "better off"—This is not a new thought. Had you not been born I know I would not have been as well off—in the deepest sense—maybe in the only sense—That I know positively.—Now I'll walk up & down a bit.—

Another kiss—

3:15—For some reason we are stopping at Beacon.—Queer feeling. Today is Emmy's & my wedding day—forty years!—And I had just read the name of Vanderbilt's sister—the Vanderbilt who was killed yesterday[683]—Vanderbilt's sister is Muriel with whom Kitty played on board

---

678. Carl Gustav Jung, *Modern Man in Search of a Soul* (London, 1933).

679. *The Dial* was an American magazine published intermittently from 1840 to 1929. During the 1920s, it was an influential source for modernist literature.

680. Henwar Rodakiewicz was in Vera Cruz, Mexico, working as a writer on the film *Los Redes*, released in the United States as *The Wave* (1937); the directors were Emilio Gómez Gabriel and Fred Zinnemann, and the cinematographer, Paul Strand; see Rodakiewicz to GOK, Nov. 5, 1933.

681. Russell Vernon Hunter wrote O'Keeffe long letters on both November 3 and 15, 1933, in which he recounted recent events of his life in Texas and New Mexico and told of the various bullhorns he had collected for her. He also urged her to come to New Mexico even though her doctor might think it "too far and snakey."

682. Alma Wertheim's brother, Henry Morgenthau, Jr., was sworn in as acting secretary of the treasury on November 17, 1933, while Secretary William H. Woodin recuperated from a severe illness; see "Treasury Headed by Morgenthau Jr.," *NYT*, Nov. 16, 1933, 1. He became secretary of the treasury in 1934.

683. William K. Vanderbilt was killed on November 15, 1933, when the car he was driving hit a fruit truck parked by the side of the road near Savannah, Georgia; see "W. K. Vanderbilt is Killed in South," *NYT*, November 16, 1933, 1.

ship going to Europe in 1904.—Mrs. Vanderbilt picking out Kitty as the only child on board she'd like her daughter to play with!!—Ye gods.—And I on my way to a sanatorium in Berlin[684] & Emmy full of clothes to buy in Paris & Kitty booked for a miserable siege in London!! Yes life!—"That's the way it is"—I prefer Eckstein's "That is how it's done."—

6 P.M. At the Place. Citkowitz just left. Got in only five minutes late. Came right here. Jumped right in. Mail. Wrote to Dove.[685] Phillips wants this & that—"Educating" people—Ye gods— always the same story.—And "no money." Rosenfeld phoned. He is coming. Wants a Marin for his lecture tomorrow night on Marin.[686] Ross says many people were here but I seem to have missed nothing.—The Brancusi show will be up for two months.—Opens tomorrow.—I'm sure it will be a genuine event—No humbug—Duchamp left a catalogue here for me.[687] I'll send you one—

The Place looks fine.—I know you'll like it when you are ready to come—But nothing must be forced.

Here comes Rosenfeld—Will spend the evening with Ross & me—

I'll call you at 8:30—

Much much love & a big kiss—

I'm really more [at] the hotel than here.

Another kiss.—

The Marin *Letters* are already packed for Alma!—

Alfred Stieglitz · [New York City] · November 18, 1933

11:30 A.M. A bit out of breath—Over an hour with Cady[688]—Marie's friend.—A clean-cut fellow—twenty-nine.—Knows exactly what he wants. Is looking for a dealer mainly because Dasburg has been swiping his ideas!—They are friends.—He feels it really doesn't matter but he doesn't want to be charged with being an imitator of Dasburg's,—etc., etc.—Marie is in Buzzard's Bay, Mass. That's her address.—Cady returns to the Southwest on Tuesday. Wants to

---

684. As Stieglitz reported in the *American Amateur Photographer*, he "completely collapsed" when he arrived in Europe in 1904 and was told he should undergo a "rest cure" at a private clinic in Berlin; see Richard Whelan, *Alfred Stieglitz: A Biography* (Boston, 1995), 200–201.

685. On November 16, 1933, Stieglitz wrote to Dove, reminding him that Phillips owed him three hundred dollars on *The Red Barge* and that Dove himself should keep after the collector for payment. He added: "I hope you won't let him get away with B. M. (Blue Murder) in all his innocence…. Our last drop of blood doesn't mean a damn to any of them"; Morgan, *Dear Stieglitz/Dear Dove*, 289–290.

686. On November 17, 1933, Stieglitz wrote O'Keeffe that Rosenfeld had a "theory about Marin's palette & says he thinks I hung the show so as to disprove it. First of all I had no idea he had a theory and secondly he doesn't seem to know how I select pictures for a show."

687. On November 17, 1933, Stieglitz told O'Keeffe that Brancusi had written in the catalogue: "Do not look for obscure formulas or mystery. It's pure joy that I give you. Look at them (the sculptures) until you see them.—Those who are closest to God have seen these"; *Brancusi,* exh. cat., Brummer Gallery, New York, Nov. 17, 1933–Jan. 13, 1934. Duchamp was curator of the exhibition.

688. The painter Cady Wells.

get to work. Saw your hands and the wheel. The non-bracelet one.[689] He remarked: "That's a marvel—beautiful. And I have never seen a more beautiful hand." So you see your hands are still perfectly all right—Don't think I haven't been watching them & looking at them.

My head is just awhirl—spinning.—Last night the lecture was good & very short.— Also good. The Schwabs were there—At supper. Dixie Kitchen, Flint, Margules, Ross, Kalonyme & I were together. I went alone to Rosenfeld. Flint still out of a job. The Schwabs & I went to Luchow's for a sandwich! And I dropped in at the Grand Central to mail my letter to you.— Finally have two blankets on my bed. Asked Ross to tell chambermaid—

Noon 30.—Brett just left. Is full of red. Goes to lunches. Says the rich women are all bewailing the "poor artists" but are ever spending piles of money on stupid teas. She hates to go but goes. Says she'll blow up someday.

1:15 P.M. A few people. Very few.—A sort of dead day.—Gray.—Dark.—Doesn't know should it rain or snow or just do nothing but remain dreary. Ross in & out. Says Brancusi show is very fine. Also the watercolor show of Cézanne's at de Hauke's.[690]—Met Eddie Warburg at the Brancusi. Thinks the Brancusi prices too high!—Says so many people are out of work. Ever & ever & ever the same old sentimental story. Yet Eddie Warburg is really far above the average. Told Ross he'd like your *Black Iris*.[691]—I guess he would. Will he guarantee you an annuity for life— a small one even? Ever wanting as private property.—

And Russia finally "recognized" by the U.S.A.[692] We no longer "afraid" of her "lawlessness"—& non-belief in God! And Hartley's friend Bullitt first American ambassador to Russia. It's a great world.—Cady said Henwar's film excited him terribly!![693]—Told him it was you who really started Henwar to take his work seriously not merely to play at it.— McCausland placed a small watercolor of Dove's for twelve dollars.—Sent check. All so pathetic in a way. A woman with a very Hebraic nose is looking at Marins. Brett was to see the Marins yesterday—at Cliffside. Says some of the Marins are very wonderful.—And she sold a sketch in Santa Fe for twenty dollars!—What a world.—I came near wiring you not to drive.

6:10 P.M.—Rugg has just left. Here for hours. Is intensely interested in the book.[694] I think is to write & also be on the committee—actively.—Frank asked him I'm told.—Marin just came in. Many people. Many. Rugg thinks your *Black Iris* the greatest picture in the world. *To me it is second to none.* You know that I don't know any I'd take for it.—

689. Greenough 1519.

690. Cézanne Watercolors, Jacques Seligmann & Co., New York, Nov. 16–Dec. 7, 1933; see Elizabeth Luther Cary, "Cézanne Water-colors Hold Secret of His Art," *NYT,* Dec. 3, 1933, x16. César Mange de Hauke was director of the Seligmann & Co. gallery, later de Hauke & Co.

691. Lynes 557.

692. In November 1933, following William Christian Bullitt's negotiations with Soviet diplomats, the United States formally recognized the Soviet Union. Bullitt had recently worked on Franklin D. Roosevelt's successful election campaign.

693. Henwar Rodakiewicz, *Portrait of a Young Man, 1925–1931,* released in 1932.

694. *America and Alfred Stieglitz.*

Mrs. Neumann was in & with her a very live fine California girl—very sensitive—paints some. Taught arts in the California University.—Husband photographs. Very sensitive & attractive. Crazy about your hands & some of the portraits of you. Also deeply moved by your work & by Marin's.—Well it has been a very live day.—Mozley showed up. Had no time to talk to him.—But in all a mad, mad, mad, very mad day.—I suppose Marin will want to play billiards, I suppose I'll have to. Don't feel like it.

Good Night.—

I do hope all is well with you—that you had a good day—The boat whistles are busy blowing—tooting—must be foggy.—No special news.—A day & what achieved?—O—

A big kiss & much love.

Georgia O'Keeffe · [Lake George, New York] · [November 21, 1933]

Good Morning! And it is cold!

I drove Richard home yesterday—then on up toward the mountains ten miles or so—more and nearly froze by the time I got home—road bare in the middle—snow on either side flying like dust behind cars—but it is beautiful—

It was nine above early this morning. The Schroon River and all the brooks are frozen—

I still plan to go to town on Friday. I am going from Fort Edward on the 3:50 train—then I will not have to change and you can have your supper before you meet me. I will take lunch with me on the train.—You will meet me at eight—. I hate to do it—but some way feel that I must. I plan to stay at Marjorie's—Anyway I will try it. Saturday morning may I go to your room and get my clothes. I have asked Georgie to take things there that she kept for me from the hospital. I will probably have to spend hours there waiting for things to be pressed—I may go and get my head washed while I wait. And Sunday morning I want to go to see the Marins—

I only plan to stay in town a few days—

I get in such an excitement just writing you about it that I have to take something to quiet me—but I want to try. I think it will not be as bad as I imagine—

I thought I would go to see Jenks yesterday but he will not be home till Thursday morning.—Will see him then—before I go.

Now—don't worry about my going down—if for any reason I think I can't make it I'll not go—So don't worry—

Just let me try—

Do take care of yourself—Of course I suppose it isn't as cold for you as it is here—

A kiss to you—

ON NOVEMBER 28, O'Keeffe went to New York City, where she visited several exhibitions, including the Brancusi show at the Brummer Gallery, which, she told Paul Strand later that month, "was lovely—so lovely," and Marin's retrospective at An American Place, which was "very beautiful." She also saw Florine Stettheimer, Duchamp—"and of course talking with him is nice"—and Demuth—"seeing him was one of the nicest things…even if he did seem somewhat shattered." She continued: "The principal things about it all for me were that I could again walk the street a little without fear of losing my mind."[695] She also saw the writer Jean Toomer, whose wife Margery Latimer had recently died in childbirth. Because Toomer was looking for a quiet place to finish his contribution to the forthcoming compilation of essays in honor of Stieglitz, *America and Alfred Stieglitz,* O'Keeffe invited him to Lake George. She returned to Lake George on December 5, 1933, the day before Toomer arrived. Both stayed there together through the end of the month.

Georgia O'Keeffe · [Lake George, New York] · [December 6, 1933]

Do not worry about my cold. I would rather be this way with a cold than the way I was before I went to town—It will pass in a week or so—

 The trip up was pleasant. Even train air seemed so much better than city air that it was a relief to my throat.

 This side of Glens Falls there was snow that Martin said fell in the morning—mountains quite white. It was a great relief—and very pretty tho everything nearby had a dismal sort of feeling with the melting snow around the house. And this morning it is all gray and wet and still.

 I will just have to worry through this cold or sinus or whatever it is and in a week or so will be all right—so don't worry—I don't mind it much. Am sorry Toomer will have to listen to me cough. It is better to be this way up here than in town.

2:15—The sun is out and everything seems still and bright and lovely.

 Jenks is coming to see me and Martin has gone for Toomer—Margaret has walked to town for the mail—she seemed to want to—

 I think there is very little to do for my ailment but for me to wait till I get over it. I don't really mind much except that I don't like to annoy others while I must cough.

 I have hung the Picasso[696] drawing by the door going into my room. It looks very nice with other things in the room as I have it—

 I will give this to Martin to mail—

 A kiss to you. I will lie down till they come—

695. GOK to Paul Strand, Dec. 26, 1933, CCP:PSC.

696. Picasso, *Standing Female Nude,* 1910, charcoal, Metropolitan Museum of Art, Alfred Stieglitz Collection; see Sarah Greenough, *Modern Art and America: Alfred Stieglitz and His New York Galleries* (Washington, D.C., 2001), 37.

Alfred Stieglitz · [New York City] · December 9, 1933 +

The Place—9:45 A.M. Good Morning—A kiss. It's a dark morning. It's making an attempt, futile I fear, to snow.—I remained in bed till after eight.—Didn't feel averse to lying there longer. Dark & I sorish all over. Hadn't taken a sleeping pill but got some rest. Had forgotten.—I felt glad you're on the mend. That meant a lot when I lay awake—Now there is a letter from Toomer.[697] —I'm glad he's there—He says you are very good & mending—And he runs your car. Good. —Yes it's good he's there. Good for himself. For you. And so for me—Even for Margaret too.—

I didn't bathe last night but went to bed a little after ten—Read Jung.[698] —Most enlightening—

It's Saturday.—What will the day bring?—No checks as yet for Marin. Not from the Chicago woman nor the man of the other day. I can't quite understand such people. What are they waiting for?—Or have they changed their minds? If so why don't they let me know?— And so give an edge to all. But I must laugh at myself at all the why-ing. Such a waste.

And you? I wonder did you have a good night?—And are you feeling much better this morning. I'll probably not phone till 8:30 tonight.

I didn't shave.—It feels queer in the city not to be shaved.—Andrew[699] is busy inside—There is certainly always plenty to do.—

10:35 A.M. I have [given] Andrew at Lee's [his] photograph. It will look very beautiful. I guess both Lee & Amanda[700] will be surprised & pleased—

Ross has come in with the latest issue of the *New Republic*. An article by Waldo on Jewry.—It seems to be very fine. I'll send you a copy.—It seems I am mentioned amongst the select.[701] Just a few names.—It always gives me a queer feeling to be mentioned with Einstein & Bergson & a few others of that type. The article is called "Why Should the Jews Survive?"— Waldo is certainly insistent in *placing* us—Yes it does feel queer. I feel so withdrawn into a corner—really ready to hide—Of course I do know that you & Marin & I represent a very exceptional trio.—A very clean-cut one—More later. A kiss.—

8:35 P.M. Well I'm glad you are better.—It's a relief to hear it.—Kalonyme & Marin are here. We ate downstairs.—I'm doubly careful. It was raw out. Margaret says it's eight degrees on the Hill.—I wonder have you gotten coal & wood? Oil?—But it's foolish to ask questions. That's

728

---

697. Toomer wrote Stieglitz on December 8, 1933, that Dr. Jenks had visited O'Keeffe and that she was "in good spirits with eyes twinkling and humor at her cold."

698. Jung's *Modern Man in Search of a Soul*. Stieglitz had previously suggested that O'Keeffe read chapter 10, "The Spiritual Problem of Modern Man," 226–254.

699. Andrew Droth, whom Stieglitz subsequently hired in 1934 to replace Zoler, assisted him at An American Place.

700. Andrew was Lee Stieglitz's butler and chauffeur, and Amanda Liebman Hoff Stieglitz was Lee's second wife. Stieglitz probably gave his brother Greenough 611.

701. Waldo Frank, "Why Should the Jews Survive?" *New Republic,* Dec. 13, 1933, 121–125. Frank asserted that Stieglitz, Albert Einstein, Sigmund Freud, Henri Bergson, and Leon Trotsky "are great, and are leaders, and are Jews. But they are not leaders of Jews. They are leaders of scientists, philosophers, artists, revolutionists. They and other great Jewish men of our times are products of Jewish life; but modern Jewry cannot claim them" (122).

Marjorie Content, *Jean Toomer, 39 West 10th Street, New York City*, 1934.
Gelatin silver print, 3⅞ x 2¹³⁄₁₆ in (9.9 x 7.2 cm). National Gallery of Art,
Washington, R. K. Mellon Family Foundation Fund.

what I hear you say.—Thank Toomer for his letter. I'll write to him.[702]—I feel lazy.—Hope to bathe. I'm too stupid to write. Good Night—Much love—

Another kiss—

Marin & Kalonyme send bestest.

McBride didn't mention Marin[703]!!—

Georgia O'Keeffe · [Lake George, New York] · [December 12, 1933]

It was eight below this morning—And ice more or less across the Lake—It must have been thin as it is about gone except between here and the island—The sun is warm and lovely—everything seems very still and beautiful—The rooms here are so nice with the morning sun—

---

702. Stieglitz wrote Toomer on December 11, 1933: "It is a source of comfort to me to know you on the Hill. Georgia has no idea how much she worries me not only now but has worried me all these years.—It just cannot be helped. I try to be philosophical about it all but there is ever a very big BUT—"

703. Instead of reviewing the recently opened exhibition at An American Place, Twenty-Five Years of John Marin, 1908–1932, McBride used his weekly column in *The New York Sun* (December 9, 1933, 16) to discuss the First Biennial Exhibition of Contemporary American Sculpture, Water Colors, and Prints at the Whitney Museum.

I slept unusually well for me with a wet rag and woolen muffler round my throat—
It seems better this morning—I will keep it done up very warm—

I read a little in the Jung last night—and we played some music—Bach and Spirituals
—Toomer is nice to have about. Thinks his own thoughts—tends to his own affairs—and I to
mine—Sometimes we talk a little—not much—

The front room looks so orderly with the trash off the top shelves—You would be
surprised.—We are burning coal—I forgot to tell you before—And thank you for the cleansing
tissue. You waste so much money on special handling stamps—

I would not say anything if you did not seem to deny yourself little things that I feel you
ought not—I think of it particularly when it is cold like this and I feel you do not eat properly.

I probably cannot get out for a few days but I feel better again this morning and will be
all right in a week or so—I am really getting on all right—You need not worry—I am so glad to
be out of my bed. A throat like this is difficult but it will go too.

A nice cold Good Morning to you.

Georgia O'Keeffe · [Lake George, New York] · [December 13, 1933]

Good Morning Mr. Stieglitz!

It is afternoon—about three—and snowing—but Good Morning just the same.

I am better—I was up before eight—breakfast up for the first time—The thermometer
was eight above this morning instead of eight below like yesterday—

We had frozen pipes—Putnam came—and I have to laugh—drains from both sinks
frozen—He telling me a long tale of what must be done—I persistent about what *can* be done
—sending him down cellar again and again—I couldn't go myself—till he found I was right and
got it fixed—I hate myself when I get persistent like that—but I also dislike it when the water
doesn't run—and it seems that my knowing a bit about the pipes and being absurdly persistent
about what I know and think and want is the only way to keep the plumbing in order—

It is all right now.

Also I have been reading what Toomer has finished of his book.[704] —It seems very good
to me. I was much interested and entertained and sorry that the rest isn't ready to be read.

Between the plumbing and the book—quite a lively day—And in between spells of
looking out the window at the snow coming down—

Last night I read the beginning of the *Golden Flower*[705]—Very hard work for me—
Then as I looked up from that Jung was there on the bookshelves and I read in that a long time
till I get that crazy tired feeling that I get—much too tired.

I had hoped to go outdoors today if only for a few moments—will not because of the
snow—

704. Toomer was working on *Man's Home Companion,* an unpublished drama about modernism and dehumanization, as well as
his essay for *America and Alfred Stieglitz.* O'Keeffe, however, may also have been reading *Caromb,* his 1932 unpublished novel
that discussed the controversy surrounding his interracial marriage to Margery Latimer.

705. Arthur Comte de Gobineau, *The Golden Flower,* trans. Ben Ray Redmans (New York, 1924).

I have the big chair in the front room fixed so I can look out of both windows—my feet up—all wrapped up in that pink blanket—Am going to finish putting the shelves in order when I finish this—

Yesterday I sent you the Meier Graefe article with the very good piece about Marin in it.[706] Thought you might be able to use it and I just happened to find it here—

Wish you could see the snow—and feel how still it is—be here—if only for a few moments.

Be good to yourself—

Georgia O'Keeffe · [Lake George, New York] · [December 15, 1933]

Good Morning!

There really is nothing to write except that I went out for about five minutes this morning—

It snows—queer sleety stuff—

And Toomer is very funny thawing out the car—we all go into hysterics over it—He says he has a hard man's life—that you think you have troubles in New York—but he is here on the spot—that you just don't know—that if you are smart you will stay on that twenty-ninth floor in New York—and so it goes on and on—Really very funny.

The sleet hitting the window hard—

I'm glad your nose is better—

Richard came for a little while this morning—

Alfred Stieglitz · [New York City] · December 17, 1933

2915—11:15 A.M. It's Sunday. Dark.—Foggyish. Warm. It was after one when I got to bed.— Good Morning. Even tho very tired & with the aid of Amytal sleep was spasmodic & not restful. —But remained in bed till nine to give old bones a chance!—

The evening at Stettheimers. Twelve to dinner—the three Stettheimer girls—Ida Rauh —Alma Wertheim, McBride, Paul Rosenfeld, Morss Lovett, myself & several professors whose names I didn't hear. Maybe there were only eleven in all.—I sat between McBride & Florine. Yes there were twelve—Anderson. The dinner was very good. There were cocktails before & Sauterne during. I sipped a cocktail—& drank two glasses of Sauterne. Even sipped a bit of coffee. After dinner Phil Moeller, Duchamp, Kalonyme & Ross appeared. It was a real Stettheimer evening. Groups sitting about. Phil Moeller was trying that game of pushing small balls on a board with spikes & holes—numbered.—Duchamp & I had a talk. He left early. Was tired.—McBride & I talked at table. And Anderson [&] I awhile after dinner.—You know how it is.—Finally

---

706. Probably Julius Meier-Graefe, "A Few Conclusions on American Art," *Vanity Fair,* Nov. 1928, 83, 134, 136, 138, who wrote that Marin steadily progressed to a "freer structural presentation" and now presents "not segments chosen more or less at random, but generalized complexities of light, atmosphere, and vegetation."

at midnight Alma drove [Ross] & me home on her way to her home. And as we came in here Ross said: Isn't it so much nicer here?—Just as you used to say. And I always felt.—It's all such a different world—different way of living. I'm glad I went—I'm glad too it's back of me.—All send their love to you.—But somehow in spite of all, I feel how much better off you are up at the Hill than living that sort of thing more than very occasionally. Of course all the individuals there as individuals are fine enough in themselves. It's the kind of together non-togetherness that means nothing to me whatever.—But I'm a social impossibility.—

It was good to hear your voice even tho it didn't suit me yet. And Jenks has a cold. I was wondering really—day before yesterday—how he avoided one. Really.—I do hope you are gradually improving.—Mellquist & Margules escorted me from the Place here last night—I bathed my hand—& dressed—blue suit—clean shirt—looked presentable & felt comfortable. The hand is a nuisance. Walkowitz said he'd come tomorrow & help me hang the Marins. He is a help. I won't be able to do what I did last time because of the hand but we'll manage. By noon the Marins ought to be at the Place.—I hope that long before midnight they'll be up.[707]—And I'll be much relieved.—In a way I hate to see the present show come down for I know they'll never be such a perfect presentation of Marin again. But I felt that way about your show last year too. And a few shows before—Life—?—I may take the Marins down tonight or may wait until the morning. I have an idea it will happen tonight.

Another kiss—I do hope the nose & throat are clearing up—

More later.

Here are the papers. I'll give them a glance.

Georgia O'Keeffe · Lake George, New York · [December 17, 1933]

Good morning Mr. Stieglitz!

It is Sunday morning—seems warm compared to what we have had but I notice that even tho it is a little after twelve everything outdoors—trees, bushes and grass—is still white with frost.—The Lake is frozen over with here and there rifts in the surface that must be water.—The ice really can not be very thick yet. There has been no wind so it doesn't break up. Yesterday was sunny but thawing at such a pace I didn't go out. It seemed better not to. This morning I had a bath—a great event—then got back into bed hoping not to improve my cold. I think it is all right.

We talked long last night—rather disconnectedly—he telling me about his work in Chicago—Margery—and things he is working on—and we ended the evening between eleven and twelve with his digging out the jazz records—even to *Peter and Johnnie*[708]—

It was very funny—

---

707. Because O'Keeffe had not painted for more than a year and had nothing new to exhibit, Stieglitz gave Marin two back-to-back shows: Twenty-Five Years of John Marin, 1908–1932, Nov. 9–Dec. 10, 1933; and John Marin—New Water Colors, New Oils, New Etchings, Dec. 20, 1933–Feb. 1, 1934.

708. O'Keeffe may be referring to the song *Frankie and Johnny*, a ballad popular in the 1920s about a woman who discovers that her man is cheating on her and shoots him dead.

You know I originally asked him for two weeks—but everything seems to go very well so I asked him yesterday to stay longer if he wants to—He seems very busy upstairs all day and sometimes at night—does our errands for us and gets the mail no matter what the weather—amuses Margaret no end—it is all rather nice—

I wonder if you enjoyed the party—I would have liked to be there for a little while but it wasn't bad here.

I am glad you have the gray mittens—It is very nice to know. I am doing very well thank you. Will not go out till afternoon today if at all on account of my bath. It is gray out—was only twenty-four this morning—

We are going to have roast beef for dinner—It smells good.

Wish you were going to eat with us—

Georgia O'Keeffe · [Lake George, New York] · [December 18, 1933]

It is nearly three—no 3:15—sun shining—I've been sitting in it in the front room since lunch —half asleep.

So far it has been an eventful day for me. After breakfast I went out to walk around with Paul's cane—ice on the snow everywhere so I walked through the grass where the ice broke easily—up past Lee's—across the Morris pastures nearly to the speakeasy and home—Even stopped and fished some watercress out of the Morris Brook. It felt like thawing spring in spite of all the ice.

Toomer was eating his breakfast when I got back—I had my orange juice—a raw egg goes into it now every morning—He went upstairs—I lay down a few minutes then got up and went for the mail—the first time since I am back from town—I felt quite proud—

The magazine you sent—*American Magazine of Art*[709]—came along with your letter— I haven't read the magazine yet. Wanted to put Argerole up my nose before lunch and since lunch I've been lazy—

Anyway I want to tell you I am feeling quite cured—only I will still be very careful. The wind is blowing and the ice breaking on the Lake—it is quite beautiful color—

Last night we talked way into the night—the race problem[710]—We have been ambling along on it since Waldo's article on the Jew[711] that you sent—and last night it spilled all in a heap in quite a wonderful way—It was well past one before I got up to go to bed and if it hadn't been that I thought Margaret would imagine it exceedingly strange, I would have called him down again when I couldn't sleep to go on with things I hadn't said—

709. Inslee A. Hopper, "Vollard and Stieglitz," *American Magazine of Art* 26 (Dec. 1933), 542–545.

710. Although Jean Toomer had attended both all-white and all-black schools and, as O'Keeffe noted earlier (see p. 399), was often mistaken for French, he was of mixed racial and ethnic descent: African American, Dutch, French, German, Jewish, Native American, and Welsh.

711. Frank's provocative article "Why Should the Jews Survive?" sought to "analyze the response of the Jews, particularly in the United States, to Hitler: to expose and study from the response certain traits of modern Jewry" (121).

The way he laid out all his feeling and idea about it was very fine. It certainly wasn't like any talk I ever had with anyone—

This is all so queerly unexpected—having him here—So severe and preoccupied with his own thoughts—And so warm and amusing too.

The cats are lovely too.

Yes I seem really better today.

So a kiss goes to you—I was just too diseased before.

Be good to yourself—.

Alfred Stieglitz · [New York City] · December 18, 1933 +

2915—8:35 P.M. It seems a bit queer not to be calling you up.—I have been dozing—sitting in the armchair. Margules, Marin & Walkowitz were talking. Ross typing Marin's catalogue.[712] Twenty-seven pictures. Well you heard. The Marins were up in three hours!—And the show is very beautiful. The watercolors incredible. The oils "framed" in Marin's own way. Real Marin.—There'll be talk aplenty. I hope McBride will be really fair & give us a real headline for a change. Not merely a sub-headline. But we are non-institutional & non-dealers— non-advertisers!—So maybe he will have to play safe.—

We all had dinner downstairs. Flint saw the show. Still questions the oils.—Rosenfeld very much elated at the whole show.—Well, we'll see what happens. If anything.—

Your voice sounded much better & that was wonderful.—And Rosenfeld showed me a letter Toomer wrote him. Very fine.—About you too. Very fine also.—I agree with what he wrote about Waldo's article.[713] The first to really point out its chief weakness.

And you walked to the stone house.—Margules & Marin are going—Also Walkowitz. My head is tired. My hand did pretty well. It was great the way Andrew, Marin, Walkowitz & I worked together. I did the hammering. Andrew pulled out the nails. Perfectly.—It wasn't a very difficult show to hang.—Still not everyone could have hung it.—

9:11 P.M. Ross has been talking about the Marin show. Feels that watercolors are sheer beauty.—Most of them are truly that.—You'll be surprised when you see them.

—Tomorrow I shall send you the prints for Richard & Margaret.[714] You are to give them to them even if I come up.—I'm going to try some aspirin for my hand.—Ten–twenty grains a day.—Just to see what will happen.—I'll cut out Amytal.—

Well, I'll say Good Night once more—Much love—and a good kiss.—

---

712. *John Marin—New Water Colors, New Oils, New Etchings,* exh. cat., An American Place, New York, Dec. 20, 1933–Feb. 1, 1934.

713. Rosenfeld responded to Toomer's letter on December 21, 1933, noting that "Waldo has always been abnormally concerned with the Jewish problem (in 1921 he told the farmers in Peterboro he was a Catholic) and I think he has a complex on the subject."

714. Greenough 1403 and possibly Greenough 1555.

Georgia O'Keeffe · [Lake George, New York] · [December 19, 1933]

It is after four—a thin—very thin pale moon—and quite dusk already—

    I just finished reading your yesterday's letter—got the mail and Toomer and I drove up over Federal Hill—very icy—we just did make it—he driving—His telling Margaret about it when we returned was very funny—

    —This morning I read in bed till ten—reading *Cane*[715]—he had been talking of the introduction Waldo wrote for it so I read it to be clear about the Waldo talk—

    Then went on to the book—which seems quite an experience to me feeling the South as I do. I wonder how it would seem if I hadn't that association—I think it must seem very warm and beautiful to anyone.

    When I got up I went right out to walk—It was warm and sunny and slippery underfoot. I went up about through the woods then around through Hubbel Lane across Leffingwell's lawns —down on the main road—around to the lake side of the Peabody house where I rested on the porch in the sun—then up the hill—

    After my orange juice and egg lay down and went to sleep till lunch—

    Lunch was amusing—Toomer had told Margaret what a good carver he was so she had chicken because she wanted to see if he really could hit all the joints just right—It was funny —He satisfied her with very neat work—

    And so it goes—

    My black shirt and pink pajamas are hanging on the front porch drying today—They look pretty neat too—

    Yes I am feeling better—Quite all right—almost—

    A kiss to you—

STIEGLITZ WENT to Lake George on December 23 to spend Christmas with O'Keeffe, Toomer, and Prosser. After a "perfect" visit with a "grand" Toomer and with O'Keeffe wearing "the old soft expression" she had when they first met,[716] he returned to New York on December 26. Despite the snow, bitter cold, frozen pipes, and slippery driving conditions, O'Keeffe remained at Lake George. She was still not ready for the pace of the city and recognized that she seemed "to thrive on these winter difficulties and surprises."[717] In addition, Toomer, who had clearly brought her back to life, wanted to stay a bit longer, and she too wanted to spend more time with him.

---

715. Jean Toomer, *Cane*, with an introduction by Waldo Frank (New York, 1923).

716. AS to GOK, Dec. 26, 1933.

717. GOK to AS, Jan. 3, 1934.

11:27 A.M. Well here I am in the train—at Fort Edward about ready to start. Comfortably seated. Writing on a table!! We are starting. Christmas weather! Everything white—& snow falling—& the locomotive as it came down the tracks with its dark gray volumes of smoke & steam reminded me of times when such a sight made me crazy to photograph. And curiously enough it still does! Incurably old as I am.

And what perfect days on the Hill. And you looking very much as you did sixteen & seventeen years ago—the old soft expression—so beautiful.—At last a Christmas at Lake George—never before could there have been such a perfect one—I'm sorry to have missed Richard—but I'm glad we had the drive even tho you felt it was a torture to me. It wasn't. I was very tired & my hand was very miserable & I didn't feel very comfortable still I was glad we went.—Be careful of everything pertaining to yourself—Very careful.—Get those spikes for heels & foot generally. And getting in & out of the car hold onto the door. I speak from experience—It's not over-anything—You are doing so well I don't want any setback that one could prevent.

Yes, everything was perfect—a marvelous spirit—Toomer is a grand person— & Margaret is one too. And you!—Well if you don't know by this time what I think of you or feel for you then all words become ridiculous—You are in a class by yourself—I "envy" the Jenks for the pleasure you will bring into their home with that painting. It's a beautiful gift— but he too is a rare person & deserving of such a rare gift. And she must be fine too. But it's he I have in mind—Don't rush the painting up there. Nor rush the prints to Richard. Wait for safer road.

It's difficult for me to believe that in a few hours the "scene" will have completely changed—& yet I'll be on the Hill as well as at the Place & in 2915.

A kiss.—Two.—Three.—

The train speeds along—snow continues to fall—a real snowstorm—

We are passing thousands of tiny white birches—tens of thousands—no snow on any trees—Oh yes now on pines & evergreens—

Another kiss—I'll eat a sandwich.—

Albany—2:10 P.M. An hour late waiting for train from west. Am in last car—Observation car —All other seats gone—Lucky to get this. Everything jammed. Snowing still. And you all on the Hill through the midday meal. And I wonder did you get your ale. That's very important. It certainly seems to agree with you.

—It's a very queer feeling I have this feeling of being nowhere & whiteness all around —& a conglomeration of people—& I wondering is Walkowitz in charge of the Place—And what?—

I say again the two days & three nights on the Hill were very beautiful, very perfect— The greatest Christmas I could have received was your being virtually your old self—the next would be to know Kitty better & yet I know she is not for the world & the world not for her! —But you have much still to give & much to receive—

Another kiss—

Here we stand—the snow falling quietly—We're in for a real prolonged snowfall I feel—I have never ridden in an observation car in this country. Will it make me a bit dizzy. It's a long train—

You are resting now. I'll eat the balance of my lunch.

Still another gentle kiss—

8 P.M. Here I am in 2915.—It's a very queer feeling. Very queer. Walkowitz reading the paper. We had supper downstairs. It was 5:50 when I got to the Place. He (Walkowitz) got there at 9:15 this A.M. Found Andrew at work. So remained all day. Says about forty visitors came. Mostly students.—I read him Toomer. Says: "If you show that to anyone else no one will be able to write for it is absolutely perfect."[718] And Walkowitz is not easily pleased. I read aloud & it sounded perfect to me too—Walkowitz doesn't know Toomer. Had never heard of him.—A letter from Brett.—I'll send it tomorrow. No I'll enclose it.—It speaks for itself. I wonder is that the hotel owned by McCausland's sister.—No other mail of consequence.—The Place looked fine but I prefer the Hill.

—The City is slippery. I walked from 509 to the hotel. Wanted to get a bit of air. It was windstill & not cold. I can see you on the Hill. I do wonder about the ale. I'll order the coffee tomorrow.

8:23—Rosenfeld just called. Told him how perfect everything was on the Hill. He felt happy about that. Also told him about the Toomer article & what a beautiful thing it was. And that I feared if he & other potential writers read it, it might stop them from writing because of its perfection & inclusiveness. He understood. He is certainly fond of Toomer & a great believer in him. And when I told him you had the expression of fifteen years ago that seemed to take his breath away.—Yes, I said, it's true.—Now it's time to go down & phone. A kiss—

8:38—Well we spoke. And all is ok on the Hill & you are having real snow. And you have your ale—So all is well. It really seems sort of queer to be here—I'll go to bed early. Take a bath. Haven't been out of my underwear since Saturday A.M.—about eighty-four hours.—

I'll say Good Night—& Good Morning & I send much much love & many kisses— & a million & more Thank Yous—

My bestest to Toomer & to Margaret—

I'll look up that frame for Jenks tomorrow.

---

718. In his essay "City Plowman," Toomer drew on his recent experiences at Lake George and wrote about Stieglitz's ability to imbue his art and activities with "an extraordinary sense of significance, a feeling of relatedness." Toomer asserted that in both New York City and Lake George Stieglitz created spaces that expressed his spirit and values; *America and Alfred Stieglitz*, 295–302.

Georgia O'Keeffe · [Lake George, New York] · [December 30, 1933]

Well how are you? I am exhausted—

It was twenty-two below on the front porch again this morning—I've gotten so that when it gets down to ten I think it is warm.

I went out to start the car—It was so cold nothing in it would move—Toomer tried and he could not do anything with it—We had to get Martin and another man and a big heavy truck and with much shoveling and boiling of the engine of the truck—much plowing about and slipping of the wheels they finally dragged my car out of the barn and down the road after about two hours struggling—the wheels at the back refused to move—

There was much running in and out with seemingly nothing happening—They got it out of the barn—then into the deep snow—the ice that is under all the snow is particularly thick out in front of the barn—It was snowing—with a little wind—and I can tell you it was bitter —but they got at these winter difficulties with great gusto and amusement—

They say that almost everyone's car is frozen—I'm going to leave it down in Martin's Garage where he has a fire till the weather modifies a little now—

The cold and snow are wonderful but your bare hand just sticks seemingly frozen immediately to metal when you touch it—

I walked around the circle in the back yard twelve or fourteen times and had to keep rubbing my face [so it wouldn't] get so numb—

Last night at about 11:30 the Village snowplow made us a visit—came up from the main road and circled about the back yard—That is a great help—It is a strange looking monster —sort of a cross between a boat and the devil—riding about in the most beautiful moonlight—

Now we are plowed out and the car is frozen in—

Well—such weather can't last—and I don't mind it anyway—

Toomer is going West tomorrow—he thinks he must so that is that—We will miss him—He has certainly been lots of fun—and I guess very good for me—

Everything here is all right now that my Ford is in a warm place—

A kiss to you—

Alfred Stieglitz · [New York City] · December 31, 1933 +

Room 2915—11:20 P.M. I have been looking thro' the Sunday papers.—Have been sitting in an armchair.—Should I bathe or shouldn't I?—Not a bit sleepy.—Wondering are you fast asleep.—The wind is starting up—As I look out of the window the streets are wet—thawing still.—I guess I'll not bathe but go to bed—see the old year out in bed & see the new year in there too.—How glad I am that you are on the road to real health again. How I remember last year—you at Anita's.—Well I won't look back—I start the year with going to the Place— a day like other days.—Whether anyone comes or not is immaterial. There is plenty for me to do.—More than plenty.—As last Sunday we were far away from what is usually termed

Christmas—so today—tonight—we both—tho not physically as close as last Sunday—are far removed from what is called New Year.—

Good Night once more—another Good Night kiss—I'll lotion my head—it needs it badly—& I'll go to bed—

Good Night—another kiss—& very much love.

It's 11:33—

Midnight. It's New Year—1934—The City is agog with whistles & bells—sirens—I have been in bed—I jumped up to say Hello—If I didn't feel you were asleep I'd phone now. But I hope you are fast asleep & comfortably resting—

Oh Georgia.—And I am seventy finally.—I never expected to see that age.—Yes seventy. —And you on the road to full recovery.—That's my gift from you.—

Again much, much love—I'll hop into bed again.—Another kiss—the first in 1934!—

There is shouting—still bells & whistles—all sorts of noises—1934—January 1st— Do be careful.—

Biographical Dictionary

The individuals listed below are frequently referred to in the letters by first name only. They are identified more fully in the dictionary that follows.

Agnes/Ag: see Engelhard, Agnes Stieglitz

Alexis: see O'Keeffe, Alexis Wyckoff

Alma: see Wertheim, Alma Morgenthau

Anita: from 1915 to 1932, see Pollitzer, Anita

Anita: for 1933, see Young, Anita Natalie

Arthur: Macmahon, Arthur Whittier

Beck: see Strand, Rebecca Salsbury

Betty: see O'Keeffe, Elizabeth Jones

Billie Mac: see McMeans, Annette Harris

Brack: see Harris, Thomas Brackenridge

Captain: see Ravagli, Angelo

Catherine: see Klenert, Catherine Blanche O'Keeffe

Charles: see Collier, Charles W.

Claudia/Claudie: see O'Keeffe, Claudia Ruth

Dr. Mac: see McMeans, Robert Lee

Donald: see Davidson, Donald Douglas

Dorothy: from 1915 to 1925, see True, Dorothy

Dorothy: from 1926 to 1933, see Norman, Dorothy Stecker

Edward/Ed: see Norman, Edward

Elizabeth: see Davidson, Elizabeth Stieglitz

Emmy: see Stieglitz, Emmeline Obermeyer

Ethel: see Tyrrell, Ethel Louise

Ettie: see Stettheimer, Henriette Walter

Eva: see Herrmann, Eva

Florine: see Stettheimer, Florine

Frances: see O'Brien, Frances

Frankie: see Prosser, Frank

Fred: from 1916 to 1918, see Heyser, Fred Theodore

Fred: from 1929 to 1933, see Fred (Lake George handyman)

Frieda: see Lawrence, Frieda

Georgie/Babse/The Kid/The Kidlet: see Engelhard, Georgia

Henwar: see Rodakiewicz, Henwar

Herbert: see Engelhard, George Herbert

Hodge: see Kirnon, Hodge

Ida: see O'Keeffe, Ida Ten Eyck

Julien: see Levy, Julien

Kitty: see Stearns, Katherine Stieglitz

Leah: see Harris, Leah

Lee: see Stieglitz, Leopold

Lewis: see Callaghan, Lewis

Lilias: see Seligmann, Lilias

Lizzie: see Stieglitz, Elizabeth Stieffel

Mabel: see Luhan, Mabel Dodge

Margaret: see Prosser, Margaret

Marie: from 1915 to 1928, see Boursault, Marie Rapp

Marie: from 1929 to 1933, see Garland, Marie

Marjorie/Margy: see Content, Marjorie

Miriam: see Hapgood, Miriam

Paul: see Strand, Paul

Peggy: see Davidson, Elizabeth Margery

Pete: see Dozier, José Pitman Guadalupe

Ray: see Klenert, Raymond

Reds: see Torr, Helen

Richard: see Menschausen, Richard

Sel: see Schubart, Selma Stieglitz

Sibyl: see Browne, Sibyl

Spud: see Johnson, William

Sue: see Davidson, Sue

Ted: see Reid, James Warren

Tony: see Lujan, Antonio

Waldo: see Frank, Waldo

Willard: see Austin, Don Willard

Well-known composers, musicians, politicians, scientists, and vocalists are not included, nor are persons mentioned only in the footnotes. Celebrated artists and authors are included only if they had a direct connection with O'Keeffe or Stieglitz. Nicknames and pseudonyms, as well as surnames acquired through marriage, are given in parentheses. All individuals are American unless otherwise noted.

Abbott, Jere (1897–1982): associate director of the Museum of Modern Art, 1929–1932; director of the Smith College Museum of Art until 1946.

Ackerman, Charles Clarence (1867–1964?): O'Keeffe's landlord in Canyon, Texas, 1916–1917.

Ackerman, Ralph E. (1902–1972): son of O'Keeffe's landlord in Canyon, Texas.

Ackerman, Susie (1870–?): O'Keeffe's landlord in Canyon, Texas, 1916–1917.

Adams, Ansel (1902–1984): landscape photographer who met O'Keeffe in Taos in 1929 and became close friends with her and Stieglitz; Stieglitz exhibited his photographs in 1936; helped found the photography department at the Museum of Modern Art and championed environmental causes.

Aisen, Maurice (1885–1942): Rumanian-born chemist; supporter of modern art; contributor to *Camera Work*.

Alexander, Elizabeth W. (1866–1947): wife of the painter John W. Alexander; founder of the Arden Galleries, New York, in 1917 with Mrs. James C. Rogerson.

Allatini, Rose (Eunice Buckley) (1890–1980): Viennese-born author and wife of Cyril Kay Scott.

Allen, Lloyd Green (Lanky) (1864–1949): professor of mathematics and head of the department at West Texas State Normal College, 1910–1932; dean of the college, 1919–1927.

Anderson, Sherwood (1876–1941): author of *Winesburg, Ohio* (1919) and other works; a friend of O'Keeffe, Stieglitz, Dove, and other members of the Stieglitz circle in the 1920s and 1930s.

Arden, Elizabeth (born: Florence Nightingale Graham) (1884–1966): Canadian-born businesswoman who built a cosmetics empire; art collector who acquired O'Keeffe's paintings.

Arensberg, Louise (1879–1953): wife of Walter Arensberg and hostess of their lively salon in New York during World War I.

Arensberg, Walter Conrad (1878–1954): critic, poet, and art collector who fostered the careers of Marcel Duchamp and other avant-garde artists in New York during World War I.

Arkin, Arthur E. L. (1872–1937): Russian-born father of David Arkin.

Arkin, Beatrice Wortis (1909–1991): wife of David Arkin; teacher.

Arkin, David I. (1906–1980): Russian-born poet, painter, songwriter, and teacher.

Austin, Don Willard (1878–1953): friend of O'Keeffe's in Amarillo and San Antonio in 1917–1918; insurance salesman.

Austin, Mary (1868–1934): writer, poet, feminist, and champion of Native American and Hispanic American rights.

Baasch, Kurt W. (1891–1964): Venezuelan-born, German-educated photographer who was a member of the Camera Club of New York; a friend of Paul Strand's.

Bacon, Margaret Frances (Peggy) (1895–1987): painter, printmaker, and illustrator.

Baer, Maximilian Adelbert (Max; Madcap Maxie) (1909–1959): Hall of Fame boxer in the 1930s and onetime Heavyweight Champion of the World.

Bahr, Abel William (1878–1959): collector and scholar of Chinese art; friend of Charles Freer.

Barker, Mary Taylor (1908–?): actress, writer, and director.

Barnes, Albert C. (1872–1951): inventor and collector of modern European and American art; founder of the Barnes Foundation, a private museum he established in 1922 in Merion, Pennsylvania.

Barnes, Djuna (1892–1982): modernist poet, author, and playwright; member of the Provincetown Players and the Greenwich Village bohemian community during World War I.

Barr, Alfred Hamilton (1902–1981): Princeton- and Harvard-trained art historian; first director of the Museum of Modern Art from 1929 to 1943.

Barton, Ralph (1891–1931): caricaturist; third husband of Carlotta Monterey O'Neill.

Bass, Jeanette (?–?): child dancer who visited and corresponded with Stieglitz in the late 1920s.

Bass, Victor (?–?): brother of Jeanette Bass.

Bauschmied, Elsa (1889?–1912): Alfred Stieglitz's daughter; born to a German woman in Munich; died giving birth to Stieglitz's granddaughter, Elsa Lidauer.

Bayley, R. Child (1869–1934): British electrical engineer, journalist, and photographer; editor of *Photography* and *The Amateur Photographer and Photography*.

Beckett, Marion (1886–1949): modernist painter whose work Stieglitz exhibited in 1915.

Belasco, David (1853–1931): theatrical manager and producer known for his spectacular stage settings and lighting.

Bell, Clive (1881–1964): British art critic who defended abstract art; author of *Art* (1914), which was widely read by the Stieglitz artists.

Bell, Martha T. (Domestic Science) (1880–1950?): teacher of domestic science at West Texas State Normal College, 1916–1918.

Bellows, George (1882–1925): realist painter known for his paintings of New York City and teacher at the Art Students League of New York.

Bement, Alon (1876–1954): painter and professor at Teachers College, Columbia University; O'Keeffe studied with him in 1912 at the University of Virginia and assisted him there in the summers of 1913–1916.

Bement, Katherine Emmet (1878–1960): wife of Alon Bement; actress.

Benn, Ben (born: Benjamin Rosenberg) (1884–1983): Russian-born modernist painter known for his bold use of color.

Benton, Rita Piacenza (1896–1975): Italian-born wife of Thomas Hart Benton.

Benton, Thomas Hart (1889–1975): modernist painter who embraced Regionalism and became known for his murals.

Berg, Benjamin Nathan, M.D. (1897–1988): instructor of experimental pathology at Columbia College of Physicians and Surgeons; O'Keeffe's doctor in the 1920s.

Berk, A. B., M.D. (1867–1927): Hungarian-born dermatologist and head of dermatology at Mt. Sinai Hospital.

Berkman, Alexander (1870–1936): Russian-born anarchist; editor of *Mother Earth* (1907–1915) and *The Blast* (1916–1917); companion of Emma Goldman, with whom he was deported to Russia in 1917.

Birnbaum, Martin (1878–1970): Hungarian-born lawyer; manager of the Berlin Photographic Company, 1910–1916, which sold reproductions of works of art; partner of Scott and Fowles, New York, 1916–1926, which exhibited old master paintings and modern art.

Blackburn, Alan R. Jr. (1907?–1999?): executive secretary and exhibition coordinator, Museum of Modern Art.

Blaine, William Henry (Physical Education) (1884–1964?): teacher of physical education at West Texas State Normal College, 1912–1920.

Bliss, Lizzie P. (1864–1931): collector, patron of the arts, and a founder of the Museum of Modern Art.

Bluemner, Oscar F. (1867–1938): German-born modernist painter whose work Stieglitz exhibited in 1915 and 1928; known for his use of brilliant, prismatic color planes.

Bodansky, Artur (1877–1939): Austrian-born conductor of the Metropolitan Opera from 1915 to 1939; specialized in German work.

Bolton, Buck W. (1896–1955): junior at West Texas State Normal College, 1916–1917.

Bouché, Louis (1896–1969): painter and director of the Belmaison Gallery, part of Wanamaker's Gallery of Decorative Arts, New York.

Bouguereau, William-Adolphe (1825–1905): French academic painter.

Bourgeois, Stephen (1881–1964): French-born founder and director of the Bourgeois Gallery, New York, 1914, which exhibited modern European and American art.

Boursault, Albert K. (1863–1913): advertising agent and member of the Photo-Secession.

Boursault, Mrs. Albert (?-?): mother of George Boursault.

Boursault, George (1890–1987): son of Albert Boursault and husband of Marie Rapp.

Boursault, Marie Rapp (1894–1988): music student; Stieglitz's secretary at 291 from 1911 to 1917.

Boyce, Neith (1872–1951): wife of Hutchins Hapgood; journalist, author, and member of the Greenwich Village bohemian community; founder of the Provincetown Players.

Boyer, Charles Philip (?–?): Russian-born director of the Mellon Galleries, Philadelphia, which showed modern art.

Boyesen, Bayard (1882–1964?): son of Hjalmar Hjorth Boyesen; poet, anarchist, lecturer at Columbia, and a principal at the Ferrer Center and Modern School, New York, a gathering place for cultural and political radicals.

Boyesen, Hjalmar Hjorth (1848–1895): Norwegian-born author and professor of Germanic languages at Columbia University.

Bragdon, Claude Fayette (1866–1946): architect, writer, set designer, and follower of Eastern religions; lived at the Shelton Hotel and was a close friend of O'Keeffe's and Stieglitz's in the 1920s and 1930s.

Brancusi, Constantin (1876–1957): Rumanian-born modernist sculptor whose work Stieglitz exhibited in 1914 and reproduced in *Camera Work*; celebrated for his highly simplified forms.

Breckenridge, Hugh Henry (1870–1937): painter and teacher at the Pennsylvania Academy of the Fine Arts.

Brett, The Honorable Dorothy (1883–1977): British-born painter and devotee of D. H. Lawrence, whom she followed to Taos, New Mexico; close friend of O'Keeffe's and Stieglitz's in the late 1920s and 1930s.

Brigman, Anne Wardrope (Annie) (1869–1950): pictorial photographer known for her nude depictions of women; member of the Photo-Secession whose photographs Stieglitz exhibited in 1905 and 1906 and reproduced in *Camera Work*.

Brill, Abraham Arden, M.D. (1874–1948): Austrian-born psychoanalyst; studied with C. G. Jung and translated works by Freud into English.

Brixey, Richard De Wolfe (1881–1943): president of the Kerite Insulated Wire and Cable Company; a collector of O'Keeffe's paintings.

Brook, Alexander (1898–1980): realist painter of still lifes, landscapes, and portraits.

Brooks, Van Wyck (1886–1963): literary critic, historian, biographer, and author of *The*

Wine of the Puritans: A Study of Present Day America (1908) and *The Ordeal of Mark Twain* (1920).

Brown, Mary Morgan (Expression) (1873–1938): head of the speech department at West Texas State Normal College, 1916–1918.

Browne, Hetty Sibyl Turnipseed (1875–1966): director of an experimental primary school, Winthrop College, Rock Hill, South Carolina, in the 1910s; director of the River Road School, San Antonio.

Browne, Sibyl (1892–1979): daughter of Hetty Browne; artist and author; student of Diego Rivera; instructor at Teachers College, Columbia University.

Bruce, Patrick Henry (1881–1936): modernist painter influenced by cubism and purism who resided in Paris from 1904 to 1933.

Bruguière, Francis Joseph (1879–1945): photographer known for his portraits and abstractions, which Stieglitz reproduced in *Camera Work*.

Bruno, Guido (1884–1942): Greenwich Village publisher of *Bruno's Weekly* (1915–1916) and *Bruno Chap Books* (1915–1916); champion of Imagist poets and opponent of censorship.

Bryner, Edna (Teddy) (1866–1967): novelist with an interest in Eastern religions; with her husband, Arthur Schwab, a collector and supporter of Stieglitz and his artists.

Buffet-Picabia, Gabrielle (1881–1985): first wife of Francis Picabia; musicologist; author whose writings Stieglitz published in *Camera Work*.

Bull, Mary Elizabeth (?–?): daughter of Nina Bull, who lived with her mother in the rooms that once housed 291, 1917–1918.

Bull, Nina (1880?–1968?): occupant who moved into the rooms that once housed 291 with the intention of establishing an art-lending library, 1917–1918.

Bulliet, Clarence Joseph (1883–1952): art critic for the *Chicago Daily News*.

Bullitt, William Christian, Jr. (1891–1967): diplomat, journalist, and novelist; first American ambassador to the Soviet Union.

Bunting, Charles Henry (1875–1961): professor of pathology at the University of Wisconsin Medical School.

Burke, Mary William Ethelbert Appleton (Billie) (1884–1970): actress.

Burty, Frank (Burty-Haviland) (1886–1971): French modernist painter whose work Stieglitz exhibited in 1914.

Busch, Adolph (1891–1952): German violinist and composer.

Bynner, Harold Witter (1881–1968): poet, writer, and follower of Taoism; hosted many visiting actors, artists, and writers in his Santa Fe home.

Caffin, Caroline Scurfield (1864–?): British-born wife of Charles Caffin.

Caffin, Charles Henry (1854–1918): British-born New York art critic for *Harper's Weekly*, the *New York Sun*, and *New York American*; author of several books, including *Photography as a Fine Art* (1901); frequent contributor to *Camera Work*.

Cahill, Holger (born: Sveinn Kristján Bjarnason) (1887–1960): Icelandic-born curator at the Newark Museum; acting head of the Museum of Modern Art in 1932; director of the Federal Arts Project, part of the Works Project Administration, 1935–1943.

Callaghan, Lewis (1906–1983): photographer and New Mexico resident who met O'Keeffe in 1929.

Cane, Melville (1879–1980): attorney, reporter for the *New York Evening Post,* and poet.

Cardozo, Benjamin N. (1870–1938): New York attorney and member of the New York Supreme Court; appointed to the United States Supreme Court in 1932.

Carles, Arthur Beecher (1882–1952): modernist painter whose work Stieglitz exhibited in 1910 and 1912; influenced by Matisse.

Carswell, Catherine MacFarlane (1879–1946): Scottish author and journalist; biographer of D. H. Lawrence, among others.

Cary, Elizabeth Luther (1867–1936): art critic for *The New York Times.*

Cézanne, Paul (1839–1906): French postimpressionist painter whose highly influential work Stieglitz exhibited in 1910 and 1911 and reproduced in *Camera Work.*

Chase, William Merritt (1849–1916): impressionist painter and influential teacher at the Pennsylvania Academy of the Fine Arts and the Art Students League, New York, where O'Keeffe studied with him in 1907–1908.

Chávez y Ramirez, Carlos Antonio de Padua (1899–1978): Mexican composer, conductor, and journalist; founder of the Mexican Symphonic Orchestra.

Cheiro (born: William John Warner) (1866–1936): Irish astrologer, occult figure, and clairvoyant who taught palmistry and numerology; author of several books.

Churchill, Henry Stern (1893–1962): architect, city planner, and author.

Citkowitz, Israel (1908–1974): composer and piano teacher.

Clurman, Harold (1901–1980): theater director; founder of the Group Theatre; drama critic for *The New Republic.*

Coady, Robert J. (1882–1921): founder and codirector of the Washington Square Gallery, New York, 1914; later renamed the Coady Gallery, 1917–1919, which exhibited modern European art and African sculpture; editor of *The Soil* (1916–1917).

Coburn, Alvin Langdon (1882–1966): pictorial photographer known for his portraits and cityscapes, which Stieglitz exhibited in 1907 and 1909 and reproduced in *Camera Work*; associated with Ezra Pound and British Vorticists during World War I.

Cohan, Georgette (later: Souther; Rowse) (1900–1988): daughter of the Broadway producer George M. Cohan.

Collier, Charles W. (1909–1987): son of John Collier; O'Keeffe's friend and traveling companion in the late 1920s and early 1930s.

Collier, John (1884–1968): social reformer, and advocate for Native American rights; Commissioner of Indian Affairs, 1933–1945; instrumental in the passage of the Indian Reorganization Act of 1934.

Concha, John (?–?): Native American who traveled with O'Keeffe to Santa Fe and Las Vegas, New Mexico, in 1929.

Content, Marjorie (Margy) (1895–1984): photographer who traveled with O'Keeffe to Bermuda in 1933; married Jean Toomer in 1934.

Cook, Madeleine Ruth (Madge) (1906–1946): daughter of Alfred and Ruth Meyer Cook, niece of Eugene Meyer and Aline Liebman; poet.

Coomaraswamy, Ananda Kentish (Kūmaraswāmī) (1877–1947): Sri Lankan–born historian, philosopher, and curator of Indian, Persian, and Mohammedan art at the Museum of Fine Arts, Boston; responsible for the acquisition of Stieglitz's photographs by the museum in 1924.

Coomaraswamy, Doña Luisa Runstein (Xlata Lotte Llamas) (1903–1969): Argentine-born society photographer; third wife of Ananda Coomaraswamy.

Coombs, Elizabeth Maury (1874–1957): short story author who contributed to *The Century Magazine* and *Lippincott's Monthly Magazine*.

Cooper, Ruth Margaret (?–?): teacher in the Training School of West Texas State Normal College, 1916–1919.

Cortissoz, Royal (1869–1948): art historian; critic for the *New York Herald Tribune* from 1891 to 1948.

Cosgrave, John O'Hara (1866–1947): Australian-born editor and publisher of *Everybody's* (1900–1911) and the Sunday supplement of *New York World* (1912–1927).

Cottam, Elizabeth Hawk (Betty) (1902–?): with siblings William Hawk and Bertha Hawk Gillett, owned Del Monte Ranch outside of Taos; O'Keeffe's friend in the early 1930s.

Cousins, Robert Barstow (1861–1932): founding president of West Texas State Normal College, 1909–1918.

Covarrubias, José Miguel (1904–1957): Mexican-born caricaturist whose work was frequently published in *The New Yorker* and *Vanity Fair* in the 1920s and 1930s.

Covert, John (1882–1960): modernist painter and one of founders of the Society of Independent Artists.

Cox, Kenyon (1856–1919): academic painter and teacher at the Art Students League of New York.

Craig, Edward Gordon (1872–1966): British actor, director, and set designer whose work Stieglitz exhibited in 1910–1911 and reproduced in *Camera Work*.

Cramer, Konrad (1888–1963): German-born modernist painter and photographer.

Crane, Hart (1899–1932): modernist poet influenced by T. S. Eliot; author of *The Bridge* (1930); a friend of O'Keeffe's and Stieglitz's in the 1920s.

Crowninshield, Frank (1872–1947): French-born art and theater critic who wrote for *Vanity Fair*.

Dabo, Leon (1865–1960): tonalist landscape painter.

Daniel, Charles (1878–1971): art dealer and director of the Daniel Gallery, New York, 1913–1932, which exhibited modern American art.

Daniel, Margery Durant Campbell (later: Green) (?–1969): fiancée of Mitchell Kennerley in 1928.

Dannenberg, George (1882–1978): painter; student with O'Keeffe at the Art Students League in New York from 1907 to 1908 and her correspondent from 1908 to 1912.

Dasburg, Andrew (1887–1979): modernist painter influenced by cubism; moved to Santa Fe in 1921 and to Taos in 1932.

Dasburg, Nancy Lane Kauffmann (?–?): second wife of Andrew Dasburg (m. 1928; d. 1932); actress.

Davey, Randall (1887–1964): painter; student of Robert Henri's; resident of Taos.

Davidson, Donald Douglas (1878–1948): Scottish-born husband of Alfred's niece Elizabeth; gardener at Lake George; close friend of O'Keeffe, Stieglitz, and many of the artists associated with them from the late 1910s to the 1940s; involved with Vedantism and Eastern religions.

Davidson, Elizabeth Margery (Peggy) (later: McManus; Bodkin) (1919–1995): Alfred's grandniece, daughter of Elizabeth Davidson and her husband, Donald; frequent visitor to Lake George.

Davidson, Elizabeth Stieglitz (1897–1956): Alfred Stieglitz's niece, daughter of Leopold and Elizabeth Stieglitz, wife of Donald Davidson, and close friend of Stieglitz, O'Keeffe, and many of the artists associated with them from the late 1910s to the 1940s; involved with Vedantism and Eastern religions; director of the Ramakrishna Vivekananda Center, New York.

Davidson, Florence L. (1886–1962): wife of Jo Davidson.

Davidson, Gilbert Cummings (1900–1974): son of Donald Davidson and his first wife, Lucille Valentini; mechanical engineer.

Davidson, Jo (1883–1952): modernist sculptor known for his realist portraits.

Davidson, Sue (later: Lowe) (b. 1922): Alfred's grandniece, daughter of Elizabeth and Donald Davidson; frequent visitor to Lake George; Stieglitz's biographer.

Davies, Arthur Bowen (1863–1928): artist known for his ethereal figure paintings; one of the organizers of the 1913 International Exhibition of Modern Art at the New York Armory.

Davis, J. Lyman (Sixteen Silk Shirts) (1897–1988?): senior at West Texas State Normal College, 1916–1917.

Davis, Stuart (1892–1964): modernist artist who painted a mural at Radio City Music Hall.

Day, Frank (?–?): student at West Texas State Normal College, 1916–1917.

Dearth, Henry Golden (1864–1918): tonalist painter.

De Falla y Matheu, Manuel (1876–1946): Spanish composer.

de Hauke, César Mange (1900–?): French-born art dealer; director of Jacques Seligmann & Co. Gallery, New York; later de Hauke & Co.

Demuth, Charles (1888–1935): modernist painter known for his cityscapes, abstract portraits, and watercolors; Stieglitz exhibited his work in 1922, 1925, and 1926, and yearly from 1929 to 1932 and 1936 to 1938; close friend of O'Keeffe's, to whom he bequeathed many paintings.

Deskey, Donald (1894–1989): designer responsible for the interiors of Radio City Music Hall.

Dewald, Jacob (1888–1940): German-born investment banker, collector, and supporter of Stieglitz and his galleries.

Dewey, John (1859–1952): philosopher and educational reformer.

De Zayas, Marius (1880–1961): Mexican-born artist; cofounder of 291; cofounder of the Modern Gallery, 1915–1918, and the de Zayas Gallery, 1919–1921, which exhibited modern European and American art; Stieglitz exhibited his art in 1909, 1910, 1913, and 1914 and reproduced it in *Camera Work*.

Dodge, Mabel: see Luhan, Mabel Ganson Evans Dodge Sterne.

Dove, Arthur (1880–1946): modernist painter celebrated for his early abstractions, landscapes, and collages; Stieglitz exhibited his art in 1910, 1912, and yearly from 1925 to 1927 and 1929 to 1946; close friend of O'Keeffe's and Stieglitz's.

Dove, Helen Torr: see Torr, Helen (Reds).

Dow, Arthur Wesley (1857–1922): painter, printmaker, and influential teacher at Teachers College, Columbia University, where O'Keeffe studied with him in 1916.

Dozier, José Pitman Guadalupe (Pete) (1898–1982): gardener and horse wrangler for Mabel Dodge Luhan; later a guide at Ghost Ranch.

Draper, Muriel (1886–1952): socialite whose weekly salon attracted a wide range of artists, writers, and photographers.

Dreier, Katherine S. (1877–1952): painter and collector who in 1920 founded the Société Anonyme, Inc., with Marcel Duchamp and Man Ray to champion modern art in the United States.

Droth, Andrew (1886?–?): assistant at An American Place from 1934 to 1950.

Du Bois, Guy Pène (1884–1958): painter.

Duchamp, Marcel (R. Mutt) (1887–1968): French modernist painter and sculptor most closely associated with Dada and surrealism; highly influential in twentieth-century avant-garde artistic practice.

Dudley, Dorothy (later: Harvey) (1884–1962): poet and author.

Dufour, Elise R. (?–1929): dancer and teacher of dance.

Dun: New York packer and shipper who worked for Stieglitz in the 1930s.

Duncan, Charles (1887?–1952): artist and sign painter whose work Stieglitz exhibited in 1916.

Dunklee, George (1879–1936): Lake George handyman who ran a taxi service.

Duveen, Joseph (1869–1939): British art dealer who sold many paintings to Americans; friend of the art historian Bernard Berenson.

Eastman, George (1854–1932): inventor of the first practical roll film, 1884, and the Kodak camera, 1888; founder of Eastman Kodak Company, 1892; manufacturer of cameras, films, and printing papers.

Eckstein, Gustav (1890–1981): author and professor at the University of Cincinnati whose work on physiology, psychiatry, and animal behavior with Ivan Pavlov was celebrated in the 1930s and 1940s; O'Keeffe's close friend in the late 1920s and early 1930s.

Eddy, Arthur Jerome (1859–1920): Chicago attorney; early collector of modernist art; author of *Cubists and Post-Impressionism* (1914).

Ederheimer, Richard R. (1878–1959): painter, print dealer, and collector.

Eggers, George William (1883–1958): painter and director of The Art Institute of Chicago, 1916–1921, and the Worcester Art Museum in Worcester, Massachusetts.

Eisenstein, Sergei Mikhailovich (1898–1948): Soviet film theorist; director of *The Battleship Potemkin* (1925) and *Ten Days That Shook the World* (1928).

Eliot, Henry Ware, Jr. (1879–1947): painter and brother of the poet T. S. Eliot.

Ellis, Havelock (1859–1939): British scientist who studied and wrote extensively on sex, including the six-volume *Studies in the Psychology of Sex* (1897–1910, 1928).

Engelhard, Agnes Stieglitz (1869–1952): Alfred's sister, wife of George Herbert Engelhard, and mother of Georgia.

Engelhard, George Herbert (1870–1945): husband of Alfred's sister Agnes and father of Georgia; attorney.

Engelhard, Georgia (Babse; The Child; The Kid; The Kidlet; Georgia Minor; Georgie) (later: Cromwell) (1906–1986): Alfred's niece; daughter of his sister, Agnes Stieglitz Engelhard and her husband, George; Stieglitz exhibited her drawings in 1912, 1914, and 1916; painter, photographer, and mountaineer; close friend of O'Keeffe's and Stieglitz's.

Enters, Anita (Angna) (1897–1989): dancer, mime, painter, writer, and wife of Louis Kalonyme.

Eugene, Frank (1865–1936): pictorial photographer, member of the Photo-Secession whose work Stieglitz exhibited in 1907 and reproduced in *Camera Work;* professor of photography.

Evans, John Ganson (1902–1978): Mabel Dodge Luhan's son by her first husband, Karl Evans; author and government employee.

Farnsworth, Emma Justine (1860–1952): pictorial photographer.

Farrell, James A. (1863–1943): president of the United States Steel Corporation, 1911–1932.

Field, Hamilton Easter (1876–1922): painter; critic for the *Brooklyn Daily Eagle;* collector of American modernist art.

Fischel, Marguerite Kaufmann (1889–1950): composer who studied with Ernest Bloch; cerebral palsy specialist; collector of O'Keeffe's art.

Fisher, Harrison (1877–1934): commercial artist whose work was published in *Cosmopolitan* and *The Saturday Evening Post.*

Fisher, William Murrell (1889–1969): British-born poet and critic; employee at the Metropolitan Museum of Art.

Fitzgerald, Desmond (1846–1926): Boston critic and collector of French impressionism who built a gallery in Brookline, Massachusetts.

Flaherty, Robert Joseph (1884–1951): filmmaker who directed and produced the first successful documentary film, *Nanook of the North* (1922).

Fleischmann, Leon Samuel (1889–1946): husband of Helen Kastor (m. 1915) and Marjorie Content (m. 1929); poet, reporter, and counselor in the French Ministry of Foreign Affairs.

Flint, Ralph (1885–1968): painter; critic for *The New York Times* and *The Christian Science Monitor;* editor of *Art News.*

Force, Juliana Rieser (1876–1948): Gertrude Whitney's secretary; director of the Whitney Studio Club and the Whitney Museum of American Art, New York, 1918–1948.

Fowler, Ruby (later: Reid) (1896–1995): O'Keeffe's friend in Canyon, Texas, 1917–1918; Ted Reid's girlfriend and subsequently his wife.

Fox, William Henry (1859–1952): director of the Brooklyn Museum of Art, 1912–1934.

Frank, Waldo (1889–1967): social historian and political activist; associate editor of *The Seven Arts* (1916–1917); author of *The Re-Discovery of America: An Introduction to a Philosophy of American Life* (1929); coeditor of *America and Alfred Stieglitz* (1934).

Fred: Lake George handyman.

Freer, Charles (1854–1919): railroad car manufacturer, art collector, and founder of the Freer Gallery of Art, Washington, D.C.

Freytag-Loringhoven, Elsa von, Baroness (1874–1927): German-born poet, sculptress, and member of the New York Dada circle of artists.

Friedman, Arnold (1879–1946): postal clerk who became a painter.

Gág, Wanda (1893–1946): illustrator, printmaker, and author of the children's book *Millions of Cats* (1928).

Gaisman, Henry J. (1869–1974): inventor of the safety razor, the "autographic" camera back, and many other patents.

Gale, Zona (1874–1938): native of Portage, Wisconsin; journalist and author of *Miss Zulu Bett* (1920).

Gallatin, Albert Eugene (1881–1952): collector of modern art; opened The Gallery of Living Art at New York University in 1927, renamed the Museum of Living Art in 1936.

Ganso, Emil (1895–1941): baker who became a painter.

Garland, Hamilton (Ham) (1900–1983): Marie Garland's son by her first husband, Charles.

Garland, Marie Tudor (1870–1949): author and heiress who gave up a $10 million estate from first husband, Charles Garland, to marry Francis Cushing Greene; later married Swinburne Hale, Henwar Rodakiewicz (m. 1927; d. 1934), and J. Allen Fiske; owned H & M Ranch, Alcalde, New Mexico, where O'Keeffe stayed in the summers of 1929–1931.

Geller, Henry William (Agriculture) (?–1918): Rumanian-born agriculture professor at West Texas State Normal College, 1914–1918.

Gerard, James Watson (1867–1951): lawyer, diplomat, and American ambassador to Germany, 1913–1917.

Gillett, Bertha Hawk (Bobby) (1905–1994?): wife of Ted Gillett; with siblings Elizabeth Hawk Cottam and William Hawk, owned Del Monte Ranch outside of Taos; O'Keeffe's friend in the early 1930s.

Gillett, Ted (?–?): husband of Bertha Hawk Gillet; O'Keeffe's friend in the early 1930s.

Gilman, Lawrence (1878–1939): author, music critic, and contributor to the *New York Herald Tribune*.

Gist, Robert D., M.D. (1882–1955): physician in practice with Dr. Robert McMeans, Amarillo, Texas, who treated O'Keeffe in 1918.

Glackens, William James (1870–1938): painter associated with the Ashcan School and member of The Eight.

Glassgold, C. Adolph (1899–1985): editor of *Creative Art*; employee of the Whitney Museum of American Art; coordinator of the Works Project Administration's Index of American Design.

Gleizes, Albert (1881–1953): French modernist painter celebrated for his cubist portraits, landscapes, and still lifes.

Gleizes, Juilette Roche (1884–1982): wife of Albert Gleizes; painter.

Goepfert: see March, Louise Goepfert.

Goldman, Emma (1869–1940): Russian-born New York anarchist and political activist who opposed World War I and was deported to Russia.

Goldsmith, Alfred F. (1881–1947): New York bookseller; owner of At the Sign of the Sparrow bookstore.

Goodwin, John (1913–?): son of Walter and Elizabeth Goodwin (later: Hare); visitor to Taos in 1929.

Goodwin, Walter L., Jr. (1902–1978): son of Walter and Elizabeth Goodwin (later: Hare); editor at L. P. Lippincott and founder of Rydal Press, Santa Fe.

Grafly, Charles (1862–1929): academic sculptor and teacher at the Pennsylvania Academy of the Fine Arts, Philadelphia.

Green, Louise (1891–1986?): housekeeper who worked for the Stieglitz family in Lake George.

Greene, Belle da Costa (1883–1950): librarian to J. P. Morgan and first director of the Pierpont Morgan Library.

Griffin, William V. (?–?): art collector who supported Marsden Hartley for four years in the mid-1920s.

Gris, Juan (born: José Victoriano González-Pérez) (1887–1927): Spanish painter and sculptor celebrated for his cubist portraits and still lives.

Gutman, Ernest (1903–1980): abstract sculptor who was friends with Stieglitz in the 1930s.

Gutman, Walter (1903–1986): New York stock analyst, artist, and critic.

Hagen, Walter Charles (1892–1969): golfer.

Hallgarten, Riki (?–1932): German painter.

Hallowell, Carolyn Bayard (1931–2003): daughter of Robert Hallowell; psychiatric social worker.

Hallowell, Robert (1886–1939): artist and publisher.

Halpert, Edith Gregor (born: Fivoosiovitch) (1900–1970): Russian-born wife of Samuel Halpert; art dealer and founder of the Downtown Gallery, New York, 1926–1970, which showed work by American modernists.

Hanna, Leonard C., Jr. (1889–1957): Cleveland iron ore miner, philanthropist, and collector.

Hapgood, Charles H. (1904–1982): son of Neith Boyce and Hutchins Hapgood, who traveled with O'Keeffe in 1929; history professor, author, and advocate of polar shift.

Hapgood, Hutchins (1869–1944): husband of Neith Boyce; member of the Greenwich Village bohemian community; anarchist and journalist for the *New York Globe;* author of *The Spirit of the Ghetto* (1902) and *A Victorian in the Modern World* (1933).

Hapgood, Miriam (later: DeWitt) (1906–1990): daughter of Hutchins Hapgood and Neith Boyce; traveled with O'Keeffe in 1929; painter, environmentalist, and author.

Hapgood, Neith Boyce: see Boyce, Neith.

Hare, Elizabeth Sage Goodwin (1878–1948): socialite mother of O'Keeffe's and Stieglitz's friends Walter L. Goodwin, Jr., and John Goodwin; friend and supporter of D. H. Lawrence.

Harriman, Marie Norton Whitney (1903–1970): wife of Cornelius Vanderbilt Whitney; later married the statesman W. Averell Harriman; ran the Marie Harriman Gallery, New York, 1930–1942.

Harris, Frank (1856–1931): British-born author, journalist, editor, and publisher.

Harris, Leah (later: Bentley) (1888–1966): county nutritionist in West Texas and O'Keeffe's close friend in Texas from 1916 to 1918.

Harris, Mose C. (Moses) (1843–1922): father of O'Keeffe's friends Leah and Brock Harris and Annette Harris McMeans; printer, journalist, and founder of the *San Antonio Evening News;* editor of *The Texas Republic.*

Harris, Thomas Brackenridge (Brack) (1884–?): Leah Harris's brother and O'Keeffe's friend in 1918.

Harrison, Lowell Birge (1854–1929): tonalist painter.

Harter, Richard H. (1897–?): student at West Texas State Normal College, 1916–1917.

Hartley, Marsden (1877–1943): modernist painter, poet, and essayist most celebrated for his abstract portraits and expressionist landscapes; Stieglitz exhibited his work repeatedly from 1909 through 1937; thereafter Hartley's work was handled by other New York dealers.

Harvey, Frederick Henry (Fred) (1835–1901): British-born entrepreneur who developed a chain of restaurants and hotels along western U.S. railroad lines.

Haskell, Ernest (1876–1925): painter and printmaker.

Havemeyer, Louisine (1855–1929): collector of impressionist art; friend of Mary Cassatt's; philanthropist and suffragette.

Haviland, Paul Burty (1880–1950): French photographer whose family owned the Haviland china company; writer; associate editor of *Camera Work;* cofounder of 291 and the Modern Gallery, 1915–1918; Stieglitz reproduced his photographs in *Camera Work.*

Hawk, Rachel (1898–1992): wife of William Hawk; O'Keeffe's friend in the early 1930s.

Hawk, Shirley (b. 1925): daughter of William and Rachel Hawk.

Hawk, Walton (b. 1923): son of William and Rachel Hawk.

Hawk, William (Bill) (1891–1975): with siblings Elizabeth Hawk Cottam and Bertha Hawk Gillet, owned Del Monte Ranch outside of Taos; O'Keeffe's friend in the early 1930s.

Henderson, Hunt (1877?–1972?): New Orleans collector of O'Keeffe's paintings.

Henning, Harris B. (1904–1940): Leah Harris's nephew, son of her sister Dean Harris Henning.

Henri, Robert (1865–1929): painter associated with the Ashcan School; member of The Eight; influential teacher at the Art Students League of New York.

Herbin, Auguste (1882–1960): French cubist and abstract painter.

Herrmann, Eva (1901–1978): daughter of Stieglitz's college classmate Frank Simon Herrmann; painter.

Herrmann, Frank Simon (Sime) (1866–1942): Stieglitz's classmate at City College of New York and traveling companion in Europe in the 1880s; painter.

Herschmann, Arthur J. (1874–1950): baritone and mechanical engineer.

Herzig, Katherine (?–?): Hedwig Stieglitz's nurse in the early 1920s.

Heyser, Fred Theodore (1894?–1963?): senior at West Texas State Normal College, 1916–1917.

Hibbets, Anna I. (1876–1966): Irish-born graduate of West Texas State Normal College; teacher in Normal College training school, 1912–1920; professor of primary education at West Texas State, 1922–1944.

Hill, Joseph Abner (History) (1877–1973): professor of history at West Texas State Normal College, 1910–1918; president of the college, 1918–1948.

Hillery, Mrs. (?–?): art teacher at West Texas State Normal College before O'Keeffe arrived in 1916.

Hillquit, Morris (1869–1933): labor lawyer; leader of the socialist party; congressional candidate in 1908; New York mayoral candidate in 1917.

Hirst, Virginius B., M.D. (1891–1952): Stieglitz's ear, nose, and throat doctor.

Howe, William A. (1862–1940): New York State medical inspector; advocate of public health instruction.

Hughes, Charles Evans, Sr. (1862–1948): Republican governor of New York, 1907–1910; Republican presidential candidate in 1916; secretary of state, 1921–1925; chief justice of the United States, 1930–1941.

Hume, Martha Beatrice (Mattie) (1898–?): junior at West Texas State Normal College, 1916–1917.

Hunter, Russell Vernon (1900–1955): painter, teacher, and arts administrator in Santa Fe; a friend of O'Keeffe's in the 1930s.

Huxley, Aldous (1894–1963): British author, best known for *Brave New World* (1932); friend of D.H. and Frieda Lawrence.

Iklé, Charles F. (1874–1963): German-born collector of work by the Stieglitz artists.

Ilse (?–?): cook who worked for the Stieglitz family at Lake George in the summer of 1926.

Ingraham, Mrs. (?–?): laundress at Lake George.

Ivins, William Mills, Jr. (Billy) (1881–1961): curator in the department of prints at the Metropolitan Museum of Art, 1916–1946.

James, William (1842–1910): philosopher, psychologist, and author of numerous books on free will and pragmatism.

Jeffers, Robinson (1887–1962): poet known for his works about the California coast.

Jeffers, Una Call Kuster (1884–1950): wife of Robinson Jeffers.

Jenks, Edwin B., M.D. (1880–1945): New York physician who had a home in Diamond Point, New York, and treated O'Keeffe and Stieglitz.

Jenks, Ruth Guernsey (1880–1952): wife of physician Edwin Jenks.

Jewell, Edward Alden (1888–1947): art critic for the *New York Tribune* and *The New York Times*.

Johnson, William Willard (Spud) (1897–1968): author, poet, and editor of *Laughing Horse* (1922–1939); friend of O'Keeffe's in 1929 and the early 1930s.

Jones, D. Paul (?–1962): painter and cook for Marie Garland in 1931.

Josephy, Robert (1903–1993): book designer who worked on *Letters of John Marin* (1931).

Kahlo, Frida (born: Magdalena Carmen Frida Kahlo y Calderón) (1907–1954): wife of Diego Rivera; Mexican modernist painter celebrated for her self-portraits and vibrant color.

Kahn, Otto Hermann (1867–1934): investment banker and arts patron.

Kallen, Horace (1882–1974): German-born philosopher and educator; founder of the New School for Social Research; advocate of cultural plurism.

Kalonyme, Louis B. (born: Kantor) (1900–1961): husband of Angna Enters; art and drama critic; friend of Eugene O'Neill's.

Kandinsky, Wassily (1866–1944): Russian-born abstract artist whose art and writings Stieglitz published in *Camera Work;* his book *The Spiritual in Art* (1914) influenced many Stieglitz artists.

Kastor, Helen (later: Fleischmann; Joyce) (1894–1963): wife of the poet Leon Fleischmann (m. 1915) and of Giorgio Joyce (m. 1930), James Joyce's son.

Katherine: cook and housekeeper for the Stieglitz family in Lake George in the 1920s.

Keiley, Joseph Turner (1869–1914): pictorial photographer known for his portraits; member of the Photo-Secession; critic and close associate of Stieglitz; Stieglitz exhibited his photographs in 1905, 1906, and 1907 and reproduced them and his writings in *Camera Work.*

Kelly, Reverend Andrew J. (?–1948): founder of the Catholic Library; pastor of St. Anthony Church in Hartford, Connecticut; collector of American art; donor to St. Joseph's College Gallery, West Hartford, Connecticut.

Kennerley, Helen Rockwell Morley (1883–1963): first wife of Mitchell Kennerley; mother of Morley.

Kennerley, Mitchell: (1878–1950): British-born business manager of *The Smart Set;* publisher of *The Forum;* president of the Anderson Galleries, New York, 1916–1929.

Kennerley, Morley (1902–1985): son of Mitchell and Helen Kennerley; publisher.

Kerfoot, John Barrett (1865–1927): member of the Camera Club of New York; literary critic for *Life;* frequent contributor to *Camera Work.*

Kirnon, Hodge (1891–1962): Montserrat-born elevator operator at 291, 1912–1917; member of the Harlem Renaissance; publisher of *The Promoter;* lecturer; contributor to *New York Amsterdam Star News.*

Kirstein, Lincoln Edward (1907–1996): writer, critic, and cofounder of the School of American Ballet.

Klenert, Catherine (later: Krueger) (b. 1923): Georgia's niece; daughter of Raymond and Catherine Klenert.

Klenert, Catherine Blanche O'Keeffe: (1895–1987): Georgia's sister; wife of Raymond Klenert and mother of Catherine; painter.

Klenert, Mary Ellen (1870–1961): Ray Klenert's mother.

Klenert, Raymond (Ray) (1895–1985): husband of Georgia's sister Catherine; president of the First National Bank of Portage, Wisconsin.

Kline, Jessie M. (1895–1986): instructor in the music department at West Texas State Normal College, 1913–1918.

Kootz, Samuel (1898–1982): art dealer, art historian, and author of *Modern American Painters* (1930).

Kopman, Benjamin (1887–1965): Russian-born painter and printmaker.

Kreisler, Fritz (1875–1962): Austrian violinist and composer.

Kreymborg, Alfred (1883–1966): poet and novelist; editor of *The Glebe* (1913–1914),

The Others: A Magazine of New Verse (1915–1917), and *The Broom: An International Magazine of the Arts* (1921–1924).

Kroll, Geneviève-Marie-Thérèse Doméc (1898–1987): wife of the painter Leon Kroll.

Kroll, Leon (1888–1974): realist painter and muralist.

Kühn, Heinrich (1866–1944): German scientist and pictorial photographer known for his portraits and landscapes; Stieglitz exhibited his work in 1906 and reproduced it in *Camera Work*.

Kuhn, Walt (1877–1949): painter known for his figure studies; one of the organizers of the 1913 International Exhibition of Modern Art at the New York Armory.

Kuniyoshi, Yasuo (1893–1953): Japanese-born painter and printmaker who painted a mural for the women's lounge at Radio City Music Hall.

Kurt, Melanie (1880–1941): Austrian-born opera singer who performed at the Metropolitan Opera from 1914 to 1917.

Lachaise, Gaston (1882–1935): French-born sculptor celebrated for his female nudes; Stieglitz exhibited his work in 1927.

Lachaise, Isabel Dutaud Nagle (1872–1957): wife of Gaston Lachaise and his frequent model.

Lafferty, Réné (1888–?): painter whose work Stieglitz exhibited in 1916.

Latimer, Margery (1899–1932): native of Portage, Wisconsin; first wife of Jean Toomer (m. 1931); writer, feminist, and author of *Nellie Bloom and Other Stories* (1929).

Laurvik, John Nilsen (1877–1953): Norwegian-born art critic and photographer; Stieglitz exhibited his photographs in 1909 and published his writings in *Camera Work*.

Lawrence, David Herbert Richards (1885–1930): British author, poet, playwright, and critic whose passionate and sexually explicit writings, such as *Lady Chatterley's Lover* (1928), were admired by the Stieglitz circle.

Lawrence, Frieda (born: Emma Maria Frieda Johanna Baroness Frelin von Richthofen) (1879–1956): French-born second wife of D. H. Lawrence; author of *Not I, but the Wind* (1934); married Angelo Ravagli in 1950.

Lawson, Ernest (1873–1939): Canadian-born landscape painter associated with The Eight.

Leffingwell, Lucy Hewett (1881–1959): wife of Russell Leffingwell; neighbor of the Stieglitz family at Lake George.

Leffingwell, Russell Cornell (1878–1960): chairman of J. P. Morgan; assistant secretary of the treasury, 1917–1920; neighbor of the Stieglitz family at Lake George.

Lentz (1861–1917): Colorado engineer whom O'Keeffe met in 1917.

Lester, Lewis T. (1858–1934): father of Rector Llamo Lester; rancher; founder of the Stockman's National Bank, Canyon, Texas; member of the local board of trustees of West Texas State Normal College.

Lester, Rector Llano (1887–1975): son of Lewis T. Lester; Yale-educated Randall County attorney and judge; O'Keeffe's friend in 1917.

Lever, Hayley (1876–1958): Australian-born painter, etcher, and teacher.

Levy, Julien (1906–1981): director of the Julien Levy Gallery, New York, 1931–1949; champion of surrealism and modern photography.

Lewis, Allen (1873–1957): painter and printmaker whose work Stieglitz exhibited in 1909 and reproduced in *Camera Work*.

Lewisohn, Sam (1884–1951): New York financier; collector and donor to the Metropolitan Museum of Art and the Brooklyn Museum of Art.

Lie, Jonas (1880–1940): Norwegian-born tonalist painter.

Liebman, Aline Meyer (1879–1966): sister of Eugene Meyer, cousin of Emmeline Stieglitz, and wife of Charles J. Liebman; supporter of Stieglitz and his artists; painter.

Liebman, Charles J. (1887–1957): husband of Aline and cousin of Emmeline Stieglitz; early supporter of Stieglitz and his artists; businessman.

Liebovitz, David (1892–1968): author.

Litchfield, Donald (1891–1966): British-born painter and critic at the *New York American*; fiancé of the photographer Consuelo Kanaga.

Locke, Alain LeRoy (1885–1954): writer and philosopher; editor of *Survey Graphic;* author of several studies on the Harlem Renaissance.

Loeb, Jacques, M.D. (1859–1924): German-born scientist; head of physiology at the Rockefeller Institute for Medical Research, New York.

Loeb, Solomon (1828–1903): German-born banker and founder of Kuhn, Loeb and Company.

Loeb, Susan (later: Sandburg) (b. 1916): daughter of Marjorie Content and her first husband, Harold A. Loeb; traveled to Bermuda with O'Keeffe in 1933; dancer and office manager.

Lovett, Robert Morss (1870–1956): professor of English at the University of Chicago; editor

of *The Dial, The New Republic,* and *Poetry*; political activist.

Loy, Mina (born: Mina Gertrude Löwry) (1882–1966): British-born poet and painter; member of the New York Dada circle; briefly married to Arthur Craven.

Luhan, Mabel Ganson Evans Dodge Sterne (1879–1962): wife of Karl Evans (m. 1900), Edwin Dodge (m. 1904), Maurice Sterne (m. 1916), and Tony Lujan (m. 1923); art patron whose homes in Florence, New York City, and Taos became centers for painters, photographers, poets, and authors; O'Keeffe's hostess in 1929 and 1930.

Lujan, Albert (?–?): brother of Antonio Lujan.

Lujan, Antonio (Tony Luhan) (1880–1963): Taos Pueblo Native American who married Mabel Dodge Sterne in 1923 and formed a close friendship with O'Keeffe beginning in 1929.

Lumpkin, Katherine (1897–1988?): Y.W.C.A. secretary in Charlottesville, Virginia; friend of Claudia and Georgia O'Keeffe in 1916.

Macbeth, Robert Walker (1884–1940): son of William Macbeth and director of the Macbeth Gallery, New York, 1918–1940.

Macbeth, William (1851–1917): Irish-born founder of the Macbeth Gallery, New York, 1892, which exhibited American art.

Macdonald-Wright, Stanton (1890–1973): modernist painter who, with Morgan Russell, founded Synchronism, based on the belief that painting could evoke musical sensations; Stieglitz exhibited his work in 1917 and 1932.

Macknight, Dodge (1860–1950): painter who was a friend of Vincent Van Gogh's.

Macmahon, Arthur Whittier (1890–1980): political science professor at Columbia University from

1913 to 1958; O'Keeffe's beau in 1915 and 1916.

MacMonnies, Frederick William (1863–1937): sculptor.

Mahan, W. B (?–?): professor of English at West Texas State Normal College, 1917–1922.

Maillol, Aristide (1861–1944): French sculptor and painter.

Man Ray (Emmanuel Rudinsky) (1890–1976): modernist painter and photographer most closely associated with Dada and Surrealism.

Manet, Édouard (1832–1883): French painter whose influential art examined modern life; Stieglitz exhibited his work in 1910.

Manship, Paul (1885–1966): modernist sculptor known for his figurative works.

March, Louise Goepfert (1900–1987): Swiss-born art historian; manager of the Opportunity Gallery, New York; follower of G. I. Gurdjieff's.

Marcos, John (?–?): Native American who traveled with O'Keeffe in 1929.

Marcosson, Isaac Frederick (1877–1961): financial editor of *The Saturday Evening Post*; author of *The War After the War* (1916) and *The Business of War* (1917).

Margules, De Hirsh (1899–1965): Rumanian-born modernist painter and poet.

Marin, John (1870–1953): modernist painter celebrated for his watercolors of landscapes and cityscapes; close friend of O'Keeffe and Stieglitz, who steadfastly supported his work and reproduced it in *291* and *Camera Work* and exhibited it almost yearly from 1909 to 1917, and again from 1925 to 1946; beginning in 1929, Stieglitz started most fall seasons at An American Place with shows of Marin's work.

Marin, John, Jr. (1914–1988): son of the painter John Marin and his wife, Marie.

Marin, Marie Jane Hughes (?–1945): wife of the painter John Marin.

Martha: Lee and Lizzie Stieglitz's cook in the early 1930s.

Martha: cook and housekeeper for the Stieglitz family in Lake George in the 1920s.

Martin: Lake George mechanic and garage owner in the early 1930s.

Mather, Frank Jewett, Jr. (1868–1953): art historian, professor at Princeton University, and critic; author of *The American Spirit in Art* (1927) and *Modern Painting* (1927).

Matisse, Henri (1869–1954): French modernist painter and sculptor celebrated for his striking color and innovative form; Stieglitz exhibited his work in 1908, 1910, and 1912 and reproduced it in *Camera Work*.

Matisse, Pierre (1900–1989): son of the painter Henri and director of the Pierre Matisse Gallery, New York, from 1931 to 1989.

Matthias, Blanche Coates (1887–1983): poet; art critic for the *Chicago Evening Post* and *Chicago Herald and Examiner*; friend of O'Keeffe's.

Maury, Elizabeth (1861–?): mother of Louis and Judith; friend of O'Keeffe's in San Antonio in 1918.

Maury, Judith (?–?): friend of O'Keeffe's from Virginia who was in San Antonio in 1918.

Maury, Louis (1887–1964): son of Elizabeth and friend of O'Keeffe's in San Antonio in 1918.

McBride, Henry (1867–1962): art critic for the *New York Sun, The Dial,* and *Creative Arts*.

McCausland, Elizabeth (1899–1965): art critic for the *Springfield Sunday Union and Republican*.

McGregor, J. F. (?–1917): Alaskan miner; secretary-treasurer of the Panhandle State Fair and Amarillo County treasurer in 1914; O'Keeffe's friend from 1912 to 1917.

McMeans, Annette Harris (Billie Mac; Annellie) (1877–1957): Leah Harris's sister and wife of Robert McMeans.

McMeans, Robert Lee, M.D. (Dr. Mac) (1866–1936): husband of Annette and brother-in law of Leah Harris; Johns Hopkins–trained Amarillo physician who treated O'Keeffe in 1918.

Meier-Graefe, Julius (1867–1935): German art critic and novelist.

Mellon, Andrew W. (1855–1937): banker, industrialist, art collector, and founder of the National Gallery of Art; secretary of the treasury from 1921 to 1932.

Mellquist, Jerome (1906–1963): art historian, critic, editor, and author of *The Emergence of American Art* (1942).

Menshausen, Richard (1879–?): handyman who worked for the Stieglitz family from the 1920s through the 1940s.

Metzinger, Jean (1883–1956): French cubist painter.

Meyer, Agnes Ernst (1887–1970): wife of Eugene Meyer, Jr.; art critic for the *New York Sun;* cofounder of 291 and the Modern Gallery, 1915–1918, which exhibited modern European and American art; early collector of work by the Stieglitz artists.

Milch, Albert (1881–1951): Austrian-born co-owner of the Milch Art Gallery, New York, which exhibited works by American artists.

Milch, Edward (1865–1954): Austrian-born co-owner of the Milch Art Gallery, New York, which exhibited works by American artists.

Miller, Kenneth Hayes (1876–1952): painter and teacher at the Art Students League, New York.

Milliken, William Mathewson (1889–1978): director of the Cleveland Museum of Art from 1930 to 1958.

Minuit, Peter: see Paul Rosenfeld.

Mirabal, Juan (?–?): Native American who traveled with O'Keeffe in 1929 and worked with Tony Lujan on the Indian Reorganization Act of 1934.

Mitchell, R. Milton, Jr. (1880–1939): treasurer of the Anderson Galleries, New York.

Mittler (?–?): agent for 509 Madison Ave., New York, which housed An American Place.

Moeller, Phillip (1880–1958): producer and director who cofounded the Washington Square Players and worked for the Theatre Guild.

Montross, Newman Emerson (1849–1932): founder of the Montross Gallery, New York, 1885–1932, which showed American impressionism and modern European and American work.

Moore, George (1852–1933): Irish painter, poet, and critic; author of *Modern Painting* (1893) and *The Brook Kerith* (1916).

Morelock, Horace Wilson (1873–1966): professor and head of the English department at West Texas State Normal College, 1910–1923; president of Sul Ross Teachers College, 1923–1945.

Morgan, John Pierpont (1837–1913): financier, banker, and art collector.

Morgenthau, Henry, Jr. (1891–1967): Alma Wertheim's brother; secretary of the treasury during the Franklin D. Roosevelt administration.

Mörling, Alie (?–?): art student and roommate of Elizabeth Stieglitz Davidson.

Morse, Mrs.: housekeeper for Charles and Florence Schauffler in York Beach, Maine, in the 1920s.

Mozley: landlord and agent for An American Place, 509 Madison Avenue, New York.

Muck, Karl (1859–1940): German-born conductor of the Boston Symphony Orchestra who was accused of treason and interned during World War I.

Mumford, Lewis (1895–1990): historian noted for his studies of cities and urban architecture; author of *Sticks and Stones* (1924) and *The Brown Decades: A Study of the Arts in America, 1865–1895* (1931); coeditor of *America and Alfred Stieglitz* (1934).

Mutt, R.: see Duchamp, Marcel.

Nadelman, Elie (1882–1946): Polish-born modernist sculptor known for his figurative works; Stieglitz exhibited his sculpture in 1915–1916.

Naumburg, Margaret (Margy) (1890–1983): first wife of Waldo Frank; educator and founder of the Walden Schools.

Neumann, Elsa Schmidt (1894–1970): wife of J. B. Neumann; mosaic artist.

Neumann, Jsrael Ber (1887–1961): Austrian-born art dealer; founder and director of J. B. Neumann's Print Room, New York, 1924, and later the New Art Circle gallery; supporter of modern artists.

Noguchi, Hideyo Seisaku (1876–1928): Japanese-born microbiologist who discovered the causative agent of syphilis.

Noguchi, Isamu (1904–1988): sculptor and landscape architect.

Norman, Andrew E. (1930–2004): son of Dorothy and Edward Norman; journalist and reporter for the *Current* and the *Newark Star Ledger*.

Norman, Dorothy Stecker (1905–1997): writer, poet, photographer, social activist, and supporter of An American Place; editor of *Twice A Year;* coeditor of *America and Alfred Stieglitz* (1934); author of *Alfred Stieglitz: An American Seer* (1973); Stieglitz's lover from 1931 until his death in 1946.

Norman, Edward (1900–1955): husband of Dorothy Norman and son of the vice president of Sears, Roebuck; philanthropist.

Norman, Nancy N. (later: Lassalle) (b. 1927): daughter of Dorothy and Edward Norman; director of the School of American Ballet at Lincoln Center.

Obermeyer, Bertha (1863–?): wife of Theodore Obermeyer.

Obermeyer, Ernest (1862–1937): brother of Stieglitz's first wife, Emmeline; husband of Henrietta; director of Obermeyer and Liebmann Breweries.

Obermeyer, Henrietta (1870–1936): wife of Ernest Obermeyer.

Obermeyer, Joseph (1865–1943): brother of Stieglitz's first wife, Emmeline; Stieglitz's friend in Berlin in the 1880s; partner with him in the Photochrome Engraving Company, New York, 1891–1895; director of Obermeyer and Liebmann Breweries; later beau of Stieglitz's sister Selma.

Obermeyer, Theodore (1861–1926): brother of Stieglitz's first wife, Emmeline.

O'Brien, Frances (1904–1990): portrait painter who briefly studied with O'Keeffe in 1926.

Of, George Ferdinand, Jr. (1876–1954): painter and frame maker who framed works for the Stieglitz artists from the early 1900s through the 1940s.

O'Keeffe, Alexis Wyckoff (1892–1930): Georgia's brother; civil engineer and importer.

O'Keeffe, Barbara June (later: Sebring) (b. 1928): Georgia's niece; daughter of Alexis and Elizabeth O'Keeffe; teacher, graphic designer, and painter; one of the founders of the Georgia O'Keeffe Foundation.

O'Keeffe, Claudia Ruth (Claudie) (1899–1984): Georgia's sister; teacher and founder of a Montessori school in Beverly Hills, California.

O'Keeffe, Elizabeth Jones (Betty) (later: Duttenhofer) (1902–1967): wife of Georgia's brother Alexis and mother of Barbara June and John.

O'Keeffe, Francis Calixtus (1853–1918): Georgia's father; farmer; grocery and feed store owner; purveyor of concrete blocks; owner of a creamery; building inspector.

O'Keeffe, Francis Calixtus, Jr. (1885–1959): Georgia's brother; architect.

O'Keeffe, Ida Ten Eyck (1889–1961): Georgia's sister; nurse and painter.

O'Keeffe, Ida Ten Eyck Totto (1864–1916): Georgia's mother.

O'Keeffe, John Robert (1930–1951): Georgia's nephew; son of Alexis and Elizabeth O'Keeffe.

Oppenheim, James (1888–1932): poet, novelist, and coeditor of *The Seven Arts*.

Orage, Alfred Richard (1873–1934): British intellectual, follower of theosophy, and translator of the writings of G. I. Gurdjieff.

Oud, Jacobus Johannes Pieter (1890–1963): Dutch architect associated with De Stijl.

Pach, Walter (1883–1958): artist, critic, and champion of modern art; one of the organizers of the 1913 International Exhibition of Modern Art at the New York Armory.

Palmer, Winthrop Bushnell (1899–1988): wife of Carleton H. Palmer, president of E. R. Squibb & Sons; collector of O'Keeffe's paintings.

Parrish, Maxfield (1870–1966): painter and illustrator.

Pascin, Jules (1885–1930): Bulgarian-born modernist painter who lived in America from 1914 to 1920.

Peck, Gordon C., M.D. (1893?–1949): dentist who lived in Glens Falls, New York.

Pemberton, Murdock (1888–1982): art critic for *The New Yorker* from 1925 to 1932 and during the 1950s and 1960s.

Pharmer, George (1895–1969): Lake George resident.

Phillips, Duncan (1886–1966): collector of modern art; founder of the Phillips Memorial Art Gallery in Washington, D.C., 1920 (later: The Phillips Collection); important supporter of the Stieglitz artists.

Phillips, Marjorie Acker (1894–1985): wife of Duncan Phillips; collector of modern art; painter.

Picabia, Francis (1879–1953): French-Spanish-Cuban modernist artist associated with Dadaism and surrealism; Stieglitz exhibited his work in 1913, 1915, and 1928 and reproduced it in *Camera Work* and *291;* cofounder of the Modern Gallery, 1915–1918, which exhibited modern European and American art.

Picasso, Pablo (1881–1973): Spanish modernist painter and sculptor celebrated for founding cubism; Stieglitz exhibited his highly influential work in 1911 and 1914–1915 and reproduced it in *Camera Work.*

Pollet, Joseph (1897–1979): German-born realist painter.

Pollitzer, Aline (1896–1991): cousin of O'Keeffe's friend Anita Pollitzer; child welfare advocate.

Pollitzer, Anita (1894–1975): art student with O'Keeffe at Teachers College, Columbia University; active member of the National Woman's Party.

Pollitzer, Sigmund, M.D. (1859–1937): uncle of O'Keeffe's friend Anita Pollitzer; dermatologist and head of the American Dermatological Association.

Porter, Fairfield (1907–1975): modernist painter.

Prosser, Margaret (1899?–1970): Canadian-born housekeeper for the Stieglitz family at Lake George from 1927 to 1946.

Prosser, Frank (Buckie, Frankie) (b. 1923): son of Margaret and Frank Prosser.

Putnam, Lewis L. (1878–?): caretaker for the Stieglitz family at Lake George.

Putnam, Ruth Lillian (1912–?): daughter of Lewis Putnam; secretary.

Quinn, John (1870–1924): attorney and art patron; one of the organizers of the 1913 International Exhibition of Modern Art at the New York Armory; an early collector of modernist paintings.

Raleigh, Holly MacDonald (1907–?): wife of the illustrator Henry Raleigh, who was a supporter of Dove's work.

Rapp, Marie: see Boursault, Marie Rapp.

Rauh, Ida (1877–1970): wife of Max Eastman; feminist, socialist, poet, sculptor, and actress; founding member of the Provincetown Players.

Ravagli, Angelo (Captain) (1891–1976): Italian officer who was Frieda Lawrence's companion after the death of D. H. Lawrence and the manager of her ranch in Taos; they married in 1950.

Read, Helen Appleton (1887–1974): art critic for the *Brooklyn Daily Eagle;* associate editor of *Vogue.*

Reber, Gottlieb Friedrich, M.D. (1880–1959): Swiss art collector who acquired many works by Picasso.

Reed, Alma Marie Sullivan (1889–1966): journalist; founder of the Delphic Studio, New York, which exhibited work by Mexican artists.

Reed, John Silas (Jack) (1887–1920): journalist and poet; founding member of the Communist Labor Party; author of *Ten Days That Shook the World* (1919), a firsthand account of the Bolshevik Revolution.

Reeves, Herman (1892–?): brother of Thomas Reeves and O'Keeffe's friend in Canyon, Texas, 1916–1918.

Reeves, Luella (1890–1975): wife of Thomas Reeves and O'Keeffe's friend in Canyon, Texas, 1916–1918.

Reeves, Thomas Vinseno (1883–1979): Randall Country district clerk in 1916–1917; husband of Luella Reeves and O'Keeffe's friend in Canyon, Texas, in 1916–1918.

Rehn, Frank K. M. (1886–1956): employee at the Milch Galleries; owner and founder of the Rehn Galleries, New York, 1918–1981, which exhibited America art.

Reid, James Warren (Ted) (1895–1983): senior at West Texas State Normal College, 1916–1917; O'Keeffe's beau in 1917 and 1918; teacher, school superintendent, and coordinator of veterans' affairs.

Reid, John W. (1866–1947): professor of chemistry and physics and head of the chemistry department at West Texas State Normal College from 1910 to 1922; Texas state senator from 1925 to 1929.

Reid, Ruby: see Fowler, Ruby.

Reinhardt, Mary Woodward (later: Lasker) (1900–1994): art dealer and with her husband, Paul Reinhardt, director of the Reinhardt Gallery, New York; advocate for medical research and founder of the Lasker Foundation.

Reinhardt, Paul (1889–1945): art dealer and, with his wife, Mary, director of the Reinhardt Gallery, New York.

Renoir, Pierre-Auguste (1841–1919): French impressionist painter whose work Stieglitz exhibited in 1910.

Rhoades, Elizabeth (1857–?): mother of Katherine N. Rhoades.

Rhoades, Katharine Nash (1885–1965): painter whose work Stieglitz exhibited in 1915 and reproduced in *291*; employee at the Freer Gallery of Art in the 1920s.

Richards, Vincent (1903–1959): champion tennis player.

Ringel, Frederick Julius (1904–1976): author and a contributor to *America and Alfred Stieglitz* (1934).

Ritchie, George (1900–?): nephew of Jennie Ritchie; student at West Texas State Normal College.

Ritchie, Jennie C. (1870–1944): instructor and professor of English at West Texas State Normal College from 1910 to 1941.

Rivera, Diego (1886–1957): husband of Frida Kahlo; Mexican modernist painter celebrated for his politically charged murals.

Rivera, Frida: see Kahlo, Frida.

Rockefeller, Abby Aldrich (1874–1948): wife of John D. Rockefeller II; collector of modern American and European art; founder of the Museum of Modern Art.

Rockefeller, John Davidson, Jr. (1874–1960): heir of Standard Oil industrialist John D. Rockefeller; philanthropist; developer of Rockefeller Center.

Rodakiewicz, Erla (1872–?): Polish-born mother of Henwar Rodakiewicz.

Rodakiewicz, Henwar (1903–1976): fourth husband of Marie Garland; later married Margaret Plummer Bok; writer, director, and filmmaker.

Rodin, Auguste (1840–1917): French sculptor and draftsman celebrated for his expressive figurative works; Stieglitz exhibited his art in 1908 and 1910 and reproduced it in *Camera Work*.

Rolanda, Rosa (1897–1962): wife of *New Yorker* artist Miguel Covarrubias; modern dancer, painter, and photographer.

Rönnebeck, Arnold (1885–1957): German-born modernist sculptor, painter, and printmaker.

Rosen, Isadore, M.D. (1881–1974): chief of dermatology at Mt. Sinai Hospital; Stieglitz's dermatologist for many years.

Rosenfeld, Paul (Paul Minuit) (1890–1946): journalist and music critic; editor of *The Seven Arts,* author of *Port of New York: Essays on Fourteen American Moderns* (1924), and coeditor of *America and Alfred Stieglitz* (1934); loyal champion of the Stieglitz artists.

Ross, Cary (1903–1950?): Yale-educated poet; assistant to Alfred Barr at the Museum of Modern Art; director of small gallery in his home in New York City.

Ross, Eliza Mills McClung (Lydia) (1883–1965?): mother of Cary Ross.

Rothafel, Samuel Lionel (Roxy) (1882–1936): manager of the Strand, Rialto, Rivoli, and Roxy theaters; opening manager for Radio City Music Hall.

Rousseau, Henri (1844–1910): French primitive painter whose work Stieglitz exhibited in 1910.

Rubin, Samuel (1901–1978): Russian-born founder of the Fabergé perfume company; philanthopist; a founder of the American Symphony Orchestra.

Rudge, William Edwin (1876–1931): printer, typographer, and publisher.

Rugg, Harold Ordway (1886–1960): professor of education at Teachers College, Columbia University; coeditor of *America and Alfred Stieglitz* (1934).

Russell, Arthur William Bertrand (1872–1953): British philosopher, author, historian, and advocate of social reform.

Ryder, Albert Pinkham (1847–1917): painter whose visionary work influenced many American modernist painters.

Sachs, Maurice (Ettinghausen) (1906–1945): French writer and art dealer.

Sam: Leah Harris's friend in San Antonio in 1918.

Sanborn, Frank B. (1831–1917): abolitionist; friend and biographer of John Brown, Ralph Waldo Emerson, and Henry David Thoreau.

Sanborn, Louisa A. (1834–?): wife of Frank Sanborn.

Sanger, Margaret Higgins (1879–1966): birth-control advocate; founder of the American Birth Control League (later Planned Parenthood).

Santayana, George (1863–1952): Spanish-born philosopher and author.

Sarter, Emilie (1893–1976): art critic; manager of concerts, lectures, and art exhibits.

Sayer, Evelyn (1892–1963?): author of a review on O'Keeffe's 1916 exhibition at 291.

Schamberg, Morton (1881–1918): modernist sculptor, painter, and photographer.

Schauffler, Bennet F. (1893–1979): son of Florence and Charles Schauffler; husband of Marjorie; attorney and director of the National Labor Relations Board.

Schauffler, Charles E. (1865–1936): husband of Florence Schauffler; father of Allan, Henry, Bennet, Leslie, Goodrich, and Charles; civil engineer.

Schauffler, Florence M. (1867–1964): wife of Charles Schauffler; mother of Allan, Henry, Bennet, Leslie, Goodrich, and Charles; hosted

O'Keeffe and Stieglitz on their visits to York Beach, Maine, in the 1920s.

Schauffler, Katharine K. (1898–1983): wife of Leslie Schauffler.

Schauffler, Leslie R. (1895–1970): son of Charles and Florence Schauffler and husband of Katharine.

Schauffler, Marjorie (Margie) (1897–1983): wife of Bennet Schauffler and mother of Richard.

Schauffler, Richard (Dick) (1921–1990): son of Bennet and Marjorie Schauffler.

Schmeling, Maximillian Adolph Otto Siegfried (Max) (1905–2005): German boxer; Heavyweight Champion of the World, 1930 and 1932; later fought Joe Louis.

Schroder, Miss (?–?): part of the "291 marriage"; married the poet Turner.

Schubart, Dorothy Obermeyer (1893–1985): wife of Stieglitz's nephew William Howard; painter.

Schubart, Louis H. (1862?–1927): college friend of Stieglitz's; husband of his sister Selma; father of William.

Schubart, Selma Stieglitz (1871–1957): Alfred's sister; daughter of Edward and Hedwig Stieglitz; wife of Louis Schubart; mother of William.

Schubart, William Howard (1892–1953): son of Alfred's sister Selma and Louis H. Schubart; banker; partner of Lazard Frères and Company; adviser to O'Keeffe.

Schwab, Arthur (1882–1966): director of Hammersley Manufacturing; with his wife, Edna Bryner, a collector and supporter of Stieglitz and his artists.

Schwab, Edna: see Bryner, Edna (Teddy).

Scott: agriculture teacher from Georgia who was a friend of O'Keeffe's in 1915–1916.

Scott, Cyril Kay (born: Frederick Creighton Wellman) (Cyril Meir Scott) (1879–1960): British composer, anthropologist, journalist, economist, and author.

Seligmann, Herbert J. (1891–1984): writer for the *New Republic* and the *New York Evening Post;* close friend of Stieglitz's in the 1920s.

Seligmann, Lilias Hazewell MacLane (1893–1964): wife of Herbert Seligmann; dancer.

Sessions, Roger Huntington (1896–1985): composer, critic, and music teacher.

Severini, Gino (1883–1966): Italian futurist painter whose work Stieglitz showed in 1917.

Sheeler, Charles (1883–1965): modernist painter and photographer celebrated for his cityscapes and views of American industry.

Shirley, Douglas Alfred (1882–1949): professor of physics at West Texas State Normal College, 1913–1949; dean of the college, 1923–1949; O'Keeffe's landlord, 1917–1918.

Shirley, Louise (1915–2006): daughter of Willena and Douglas Shirley; teacher.

Shirley, Willena (1886–1975): wife of Douglas Shirley; O'Keeffe's landlord in Canyon, Texas.

Signac, Paul (1863–1935): French postimpressionist painter.

Silverberg, William V. (1897–1967): psychoanalyst and founder of the American Academy of Psychoanalysis.

Simonson, Lee (1888–1967): architect, painter, and set designer for the Provincetown Players.

Sisley, Alfred (1839–1899): French impressionist painter of English descent.

Sloan, John French (1871–1951): painter; member of The Eight; a leading figure in the Ashcan School of painters; known for his urban genre paintings.

Sloan, Tod (1874–1933): jockey who popularized the Monkey Crouch, a forward-seat style of riding; known for his flamboyant lifestyle.

Small, Hannah (1903–1992): Alfred's cousin; great-granddaughter of Edward Stieglitz's sister Zerlina.

Small, Herbert (1881–1931): Alfred's cousin; son of Hedwig Stieglitz's younger sister Ida.

Smedley, William (1899?–1968?): commercial photographer who photographed works of art for Stieglitz.

Smith, Pamela Colman (1878–1951): British-born artist, illustrator, and writer whose drawings Stieglitz showed at 291 in 1907, 1908, and 1909.

Smith, Polly Gertrude (Gertie) (?–?): student at West Texas State Normal College, 1916–1917.

Speicher, Eugene (1888–1962): portrait and landscape painter; student with O'Keeffe at the Art Students League in 1907 and 1908.

Spencer, Niles (1893–1952): precisionist painter.

Sportsman, Beverly B. (1896–1962?): a senior at West Texas State Normal College, 1916–1917.

Stafford, Benjamin Alvis (Fatty Latin; Latin) (1892–1930): Latin professor at West Texas State Normal College, 1910–1925; O'Keeffe briefly boarded with him and his family in 1916.

Stearns, Katherine Stieglitz (Kitty) (1898–1971): Alfred and Emmeline's daughter; wife of Milton Sprague Stearns; after the birth of her son, Milton Sprague Stearns, Jr., she was institutionalized for the rest of her life.

Stearns, Milton Sprague (1893–1957): Katherine Stieglitz's husband.

Stearns, Milton Sprague, Jr. (b. 1923): son of Katherine and Milton Stearns; manufacturer and financial consultant.

Steichen, Clara Smith (1875–1952): first wife of Edward Steichen, mother of Kate and Mary.

Steichen, Edward (1879–1973): pictorial photographer and painter known for his portraits, landscapes, and cityscapes; organized many exhibitions of European modernist art at 291; Stieglitz exhibited his photographs at 291 yearly from 1906 through 1910 and reproduced them in *Camera Work;* Stieglitz disapproved of Steichen's work for *Vanity Fair* in the 1920s and 1930s; they later reconciled.

Steichen, Kate Rodina (1908–1988): daughter of Edward and Clara Steichen; administrative assistant at Doubleday Publishing Company.

Steichen, Mary, M.D. (later: Calderone) (1904–1998): daughter of Edward and Clara; physician and public health advocate.

Stein, Gertrude (1874–1946): sister of Leo Stein; collector, champion of modern artists, and author whose writings Stieglitz published in *Camera Work.*

Stein, Leo (1872–1947): brother of Gertrude Stein; art collector and critic.

Stella, Joseph (1877–1946): Italian-born modernist painter; associated with futurism and precisionism.

Sterne, Maurice (1877–1957): husband of Mabel Dodge (m. 1916); modernist painter and sculptor.

Sterner, Marie (Lintott) (1880–1953): art dealer who worked at Knoedler & Co. and then opened the Marie Sterner Gallery, which exhibited modern art.

Stettheimer, Carrie Walter (1878–1944): one of three Stettheimer sisters; hostess who organized their celebrated soirées; creator of dollhouse replica of their home.

Stettheimer, Florine (Florrie) (1874–1944): one of three Stettheimer sisters; painter celebrated for her portraits of New York's literati.

Stettheimer, Henriette Walter (Ettie; Henri Waste) (1875–1955): one of three Stettheimer sisters; writer celebrated for her witty conversation.

Stevens, Frances Simpson (1894–1976): painter associated with the Italian Futurists.

Stevenson, Philip Theodore (1896–1965): author and playwright.

Stieglitz, Amanda Liebman Hoff (1873–1938): Leopold Stieglitz's second wife.

Stieglitz, Edward (1833–1909): German-born husband of Hedwig; father of Alfred, Flora, Julius, Leopold, Agnes, and Selma; successful importer of wool; amateur painter.

Stieglitz, Elizabeth: see Davidson, Elizabeth.

Stieglitz, Elizabeth Stieffel (Lizzie) (1865–1955): Leopold Stieglitz's first wife; mother of Elizabeth Stieglitz Davidson and Flora B. Straus.

Stieglitz, Emmeline Obermeyer (Emmy) (1873–1953): Alfred's first wife; mother of Katherine; sister of Ernest, Joseph, and Theodore Obermeyer.

Stieglitz, Hedwig (1844–1922): German-born wife of Edward; mother of Alfred, Flora, Julius, Leopold, Agnes, and Selma.

Stieglitz, Julius Oscar (1867–1937): Alfred's brother; renowned chemist; head of the chemistry department at the University of Chicago.

Stieglitz, Katherine (Kitty): see Stearns, Katherine.

Stieglitz, Leopold (Lee), M.D. (1867–1956): Alfred's brother; married to Elizabeth and Amanda; father of Elizabeth Stieglitz Davidson and Flora B. Straus; physician to many leading New York families.

Stix, Erma Kingsbacker (1884–?): St. Louis collector of O'Keeffe's paintings.

Storrs, John (1885–1956): modernist sculptor.

Storrs, Marguerite De Ville Chabrol (1881–1959): French wife of the painter John Storrs; writer.

Stovel, Rex (?–?): Canadian-born playright, actor, and butler whose writings Stieglitz published in *Camera Work*.

Strand, Paul (1890–1976): modernist photographer and filmmaker known for his portraits, cityscapes, and landscapes; Stieglitz exhibited his work in 1916, 1925, 1929, and 1932 and reproduced it in *Camera Work;* disciple, supporter, and close friend of Stieglitz and O'Keeffe from the early 1910s to 1932, when Strand severed their relationship.

Strand, Rebecca Salsbury (Beck) (later: James) (1891–1968): daughter of the self-proclaimed creator of Barnum and Bailey's "Buffalo Bill's Wild West Show"; wife of Paul Strand; close friend of O'Keeffe's and Stieglitz's from the early 1920s through the early 1930s; secretary and painter.

Stránský, Joseph (1872–1936): Czech-born conductor of the New York City Philharmonic, 1911–1923.

Straus, Ann Elizabeth (later: Gertler) (b. 1922): daughter of Flora and Hugh Grant Straus; granddaughter of Alfred's brother's Leopold.

Straus, Flora Stieglitz (1895–1994): Alfred's niece; daughter of Leopold and Elizabeth Stieglitz.

Straus, Hugh Grant (1890–1961): Flora Stieglitz Grant's husband; Leopold Stieglitz's son-in-law.

Straus, Hugh Grant Jr. (1915–1990): son of Flora and Hugh Grant Straus, grandson of Alfred's brother Leopold.

Straus, Virginia Babette (1925–2001): daughter of Flora and Hugh Grant Straus; granddaughter of Alfred's brother Leopold.

Swim, Bobby (?–?): jockey who won the 1876 Kentucky Derby on Aristides, owned by William Astor, Jr.

Sykes, Gerald (1903–1984): author, philosopher, and critic; friend of Dorothy Norman's.

Taylor, Will Douglas (1898–1997?): student at West Texas State Normal College, 1916–1918.

Terrill, Frances Dobbins (1880–1963): wife of Reuben Terrill; O'Keeffe's friend from 1916 to 1918.

Terrill, Reuben Aubrey (1875–1940): editor of the *Randall County News;* member of the local board of trustees of West Texas State Normal College; head of the industrial arts department at West Texas State Normal College; O'Keeffe's friend from 1916 to 1918.

Tilden, William (1893–1953): tennis champion.

Tofel, Jennings (1891–1959): Polish-born painter.

Tofel, Pearl (1905–?): wife of Jennings Tofel.

Toomer, Jean (1894–1967): husband of Margery Latimer (m. 1931); husband of Marjorie Content (m. 1934); author of *Cane* (1923); contributor to *America and Alfred Stieglitz* (1934); close friend of O'Keeffe's in 1933.

Török, Ervin, M.D. (1877–1947): Hungarian-born New York ophthalmologist; Stieglitz's doctor for many years.

Torr, Helen (Reds) (1886–1967): second wife of Arthur Dove (m. 1932); painter whose work Stieglitz exhibited in 1933.

Totto, Alletta (Ollie) (1856–1958): Georgia's maternal aunt.

Totto, Charles Wyckoff (1912–1974): Georgia's cousin; son of Leonore and Alletta Totto's brother Charles; attorney.

Totto, Leonore (Lola) (1867–1938): Georgia's maternal aunt.

Trask, Katrina (1853–1922): wife of Spencer Trask; poet and philanthropist; founder of the artists' retreats Amitola on Lake George and Yaddo in Saratoga, New York.

Trask, Spencer (1844–1909): husband of Katrina Trask; New York financier and philanthropist; founder of the artists' retreats Amitola on Lake George and Yaddo in Saratoga, New York.

Traubel, Horace (1858–1919): poet and biographer of Walt Whitman.

True, Dorothy (later: Palmer; Crockett) (1893–1970?): O'Keeffe's friend at the Art Students League in New York from 1907 to 1908 and at Columbia Teachers College from 1914 to 1915; painter.

Turner (?–?): young poet who frequently visited 291 in 1916 and 1917; part of the "291 marriage"; married Miss Schroder.

Tyrrell, Ethel Louise (1893–1985?): daughter of Henry Tyrrell; art educator, furniture designer, and potter.

Tyrrell, Henry (?–?): art critic for the *Christian Science Monitor* and the *New York World.*

Vanderbilt, Muriel (1902–1982): socialite and childhood playmate of Katherine Stieglitz.

Vanderbilt, William K. (1907–1933): scion of the Vanderbilt family and brother of Muriel.

Van Gogh, Vincent (1853–1890): French postimpressionist painter whose work Stieglitz reproduced in *Camera Work*.

Van Vechten, Carl (1880–1964): writer, photographer, and patron of the Harlem Renaissance; literary executor of Gertrude Stein.

Varney, Jane Wyckoff Totto (Jennie; Auntie) (1833–1918): Georgia's maternal great aunt; wife of Erza; took care of Georgia and her siblings.

Varnum, Fred (1854?–1924): caretaker for the Stieglitz family in Lake George for more than thirty years.

Walcott, Mary Vaux (1860–1940): wife of Charles D. Walcott, secretary of the Smithsonian Museum; painter.

Walker, Robert (1894–1940): New Mexican painter and poet whose work Stieglitz exhibited in 1936.

Walkowitz, Abraham (1878–1965): modernist painter whose work Stieglitz exhibited in 1913, 1913–1914, and 1916–1917, and reproduced in *Camera Work*.

Warburg, Edward Mortimer Morris (Eddie) (1908–1992): philanthropist; founder of the Harvard Society for Contemporary Art, the American Ballet, and the Museum of Modern Art, where he was a trustee.

Watkins, Kindred Marion (Watson; Murray) (1887–1952): friend of O'Keeffe's in 1917–1918; worked at Connell Motor Company in Amarillo.

Watson, Gordon (?–?): professor of education at Teachers College, Columbia University.

Weber, Max (1881–1961): Polish-born modernist painter whose work Stieglitz exhibited in 1910 and 1911.

Weichsel, John (1870–1946): physician, critic, and founder of the People's Art Guild, 1915–1918, an artists' cooperative.

Weir, Julian Alden (1852–1919): impressionist painter.

Wells, Cady (1904–1954): Taos painter.

Wertheim, Alma Morgenthau (later: Weiner) (1887–1953): with her first husband, Maurice, supporter of Stieglitz and his artists.

Wertheim, Anne Rebe (later: Langman; Simon; Werner) (1914–1996): daughter of Alma and Maurice; magazine writer and environmentalist.

Wertheim, Maurice (1886–1950): with first wife, Alma, supporter of Stieglitz and his artists; New York investment banker; owner of *The Nation*.

Weyhe, Erhard (1883–1972): German-born book dealer; founder of the Weyhe Gallery, New York.

White, Clarence H. (1871–1925): pictorial photographer known for his portraits and figurative works; member of the Photo-Secession whose work Stieglitz exhibited in 1906 and reproduced in *Camera Work*; founder and director of the Clarence H. White School of Modern Photography, 1914–1925.

Whitney, Gertrude Vanderbilt (1875–1942): sculptor, art patron, and collector; founder of the Whitney Museum of American Art in 1931.

Williams, Edith Clifford (1885–1971): painter who exhibited in the Society of Independent Artists Exhibitions, 1917–1919.

Wilson, Francis Vaux (1874–1938): painter and illustrator.

Worden, Edwin J. (?–?): member of the Caldwell, New York, board of supervisors; owner of the Hotel Lake George.

Wrather, James Rufus, M.D. (1866–1956): physician in practice with Dr. Robert McMeans, Amarillo, Texas, who treated O'Keeffe in 1918.

Wright, Frank Lloyd (1867–1959): architect and writer; leader of the Prairie style of architecture; teacher and founder of Taliesin East, in Green Spring, Wisconsin, and Taliesin West, in Scottsdale, Arizona.

Wright, Olga Ivanovna Milanoff (Olgivanna; Olga) (1897–1985): third wife of Frank Lloyd Wright.

Wright, Stanton Macdonald: see Macdonald-Wright, Stanton.

Wright, Willard Huntington (S. S. Van Dine) (1888–1929): artist and critic; author of *Modern Painting* (1915) and *The Future of Painting* (1923); also a mystery writer.

Young, Anita Natalie (1891–1985): Georgia's sister and wife of Robert Young.

Young, Ella (1867–1956): Irish poet, political activist, and mystic; visited Mabel Dodge Luhan in 1929.

Young, Robert R. (Bob) (1898–1958): husband of Georgia's sister Anita; financier; chairman of the board of the Allegheny Corporation and the New York Central Railroad.

Zigrosser, Carl (1891–1975): founder and director of the E. Weyhe Gallery, New York, from 1919 to 1940; later curator of prints, drawings, and rare books at the Philadelphia Museum of Art.

Zoeller, Louis, M.D. (1876–1945): veterinarian and resident of Waring, Texas; O'Keeffe's neighbor in 1918.

Zoler, Emil (1878–1959): artist, anarchist, and member of the Wobblies; helped Stieglitz at his galleries from 1909 through the mid-1930s.

Zorach, William (1887–1966): modernist sculptor, painter, and printmaker.

Acknowledgments

IN 1981 GEORGIA O'KEEFFE asked me to select and edit letters that she and Alfred Stieglitz had exchanged over the course of their thirty-one-year relationship, with the purpose of publishing this important and revealing correspondence. Thirty years later, with this volume, the first of two, I am honored to have begun to fulfill that request.

When I began work on this book, I had no idea of the scope of their letters or the complex issues they raised—the tangled web of their chronology; their innumerable references to tantalizing but frequently obscure details; and their occasional illegibility. Nor did I initially comprehend the ways their correspondence demanded an intimate familiarity with not only their art but also the minutia of their daily activities and their relationships with a constantly changing cast of family, friends, and acquaintances. Yet as soon as I delved into the project and heard the compelling voices of the authors, I understood that their letters would allow O'Keeffe and Stieglitz to tell the story of their lives and love in their own rich, resonant words.

I owe my largest debt of gratitude to Miss O'Keeffe herself, not only for the opportunity to work on this engrossing project but also for the confidence she showed in me at a very early stage in my life. I am also indebted to the people she hired, probably in the 1940s and 1950s, who made a preliminary organization of their correspondence and, under her supervision, transcribed many of her letters to Stieglitz. I do not know their names, unfortunately, and so am unable to thank them in person, but the lessons they silently gave me in decoding O'Keeffe's writing have proved invaluable.

I am also indebted to many scholars of O'Keeffe and Stieglitz who have been unstinting in their assistance and encouragement at all stages of this endeavor. Sue Davidson Lowe, Stieglitz's grandniece and biographer, shared with me the privileged perspective she gained from the time she spent with both Stieglitz and O'Keeffe as a child and young adult, as well as her extensive knowledge of the large Stieglitz family. She and Barbara Buhler Lynes, author of the indispensible *Georgia O'Keeffe: A Catalogue Raisonné,* have answered innumerable questions of both great import and, no doubt, seemingly mind-numbing trivia with insight, grace, and patience. Also to be thanked in this regard are Sarah Whitaker Peters, Hunter Drohojowska-Philp, Judith Mara Gutman, Laurie Lisle, and Richard Whelan for the critical work they have done to illuminate the accomplishments of these two artists and for their assistance with this book. Wanda Corn also offered significant input as I worked to shape the selection of letters and their presentation; I thank her for her time, expertise, and support.

I also wish to acknowledge the important role that my friend and colleague Mary Yakush, former senior editor at the National Gallery of Art, played in this publication. Ever since we worked together on *Georgia O'Keeffe: Art and Letters*, the 1987 catalogue published by the Gallery, she has encouraged me with her own interest in this project. In 2000 she spent several months reading and transcribing letters, and in 2004–2005 and again in 2007 she worked extensively with me to devise a structure and texts that would enable both authors' voices to remain paramount while still providing readers with necessary contextual information. I thank her for her assistance and wise counsel.

My colleagues at the National Gallery also deserve special recognition. I especially wish to thank Earl A. Powell, director; Franklin Kelly and Alan Shestack, present and former deputy directors; and Elizabeth Cropper, dean of the Center for Advanced Study in the Visual Arts, for their steadfast support and for awarding me the Ailsa Mellon Bruce Curatorial Sabbatical Fellowship in 2004–2005 and Robert Smith Fellowships in 2005, 2006, and 2007. These awards enabled me to take precious time away from my work at the National Gallery to complete necessary research. Judy Metro also deserves special thanks for her unfailingly astute advice and for reading the manuscript at a critical stage of its completion. Curators, conservators, and members of the Gallery's library have also greatly assisted my work. I would especially like to thank Charles Brock, Ted Dalziel, Mariam Dirda, Ruth Fine, Constance McCabe, Tom McGill, Greg Most, Kimberly Schenck, Wil Scott, and Neal Turtell. Present and former members of the department of photographs, including Emma Acker, Molly Bloom, Sarah Gordon, Sarah Kennel, Mark Levitch, Kathleen McGovern, Sara Cooling Trucksess, Diane Waggoner, and Matthew Witkovsky, are also to be thanked for listening for so many years to the stories of my work on this project with good humor and for performing their own jobs so superbly, which enabled me to devote more time to this book.

I was also fortunate to have the help of many talented people who transcribed letters and completed research. I thank Sarah Benditt, Alice Carver-Kubik, Adam Greenhalgh, Marcie

Hocking, Arpad Kovacs, Liliana Milkova, Andrea Nelson, Erin O'Toole, John Palmer, Gabriella Sarraf, John Scribner, Annie Stuart, Terri Weissman, and my daughter Sophia Cikovsky for their assistance. Janet Blyberg and Joel Lefever also deserve special thanks.

Throughout the years, numerous other individuals have helped me bring this book to fruition. I particularly wish to thank Agapita Lopez, former director of the Georgia O'Keeffe Foundation, for sharing with me her knowledge of O'Keeffe's life and her great skill in deciphering the painter's handwriting; Catherine Krueger and Raymond Krueger, chair of the board of directors of the Georgia O'Keeffe Foundation, for information about Catherine Klenert and the O'Keeffe family; June O'Keeffe Sebring, also on the board of the Georgia O'Keeffe Foundation, for additional insights into the O'Keeffe family; and Sidnye Johnson of the Cornette Library, West Texas A&M University, for invaluable details about O'Keeffe's colleagues at West Texas State Normal College. I also thank Bill Green and Warren Stricker of the Panhandle Plains Historical Museum; Rob Groman, Kevin Hill, and Gayle Brown of the Amarillo Public Library; Sandra Hanna of the Amarillo District Court House; Joann Holt at the Amarillo Bar Association for helping to make O'Keeffe's years in Canyon, Texas, come alive; and Anne Stewart for sharing her knowledge of Leah Harris and O'Keeffe's time in Waring, Texas. I also wish to acknowledge the kind assistance of William Agee, Doris Bry, Eleanor Caponigro, Mariana Cook, Michelle Delaney, Peggy Edwards, Eugene Gaddis, Jim Goldberg, Laura Harris, Daniel Hartwig, Michelle Harvey, Anne Havinga, Tom Hinson, David Hogue, Beth Jaffe-Davis, Hans Kraus, Nancy Norman Lassalle and Abigail Norman, Joseph Lichtenberg, Peter MacGill, Anthony Montoya, Francis Naumann, Sasha Nicholas, Lesley Poling-Kempes, Jill Quasha, Katy Rawdon, Lois Rudnick, Janet Russek, Betsy Schulberg, Will South, Roger Taylor, Sharyn Udall, and Michael Weil, Jr. And I would be greatly remiss if I did not note the invaluable assistance provided to me by Lawrence Barth and the support of Kevin and Karen Kennedy.

During the past thirty years, I have spent untold hours at the Beinecke Rare Book and Manuscript Library at Yale University. Yet despite my familiarity with both the place and the people, I still consider it a rare privilege every time I visit that remarkable institution. I wish to gratefully acknowledge the former director, Frank Turner, as well as his predecessors, for their support of this project. I am especially indebted to Nancy Kuhl and Patricia Willis, present and former curators of the Yale Collection of American Literature, for their invaluable help and advice. From the security people to archivists to those in charge of access services, the staff has been exceptionally professional, while simultaneously extending me numerous kindnesses that have made my stays more enjoyable and my work more productive. I wish to extend my deepest thanks to all of them, especially Stephen Jones, Sandra Markham, Karen Nagle, and Timothy Young. Librarians at other institutions have also been generous with their time and expertise, among them Amy Rule and Leslie Calmes of the Center for Creative Photography and Eumie Imm-Stroukoff of the Georgia O'Keeffe Museum Research Center. I also thank the staffs of the Cleveland Museum of Art library; the Harry Ransom Humanities Research Center, The University of Texas at Austin; and the Manuscript and Archive Division of the New York Public Library.

The staff of Yale University Press also deserves special recognition. For more than six years, Patricia Fidler has watched this book evolve and has astutely guided it to publication. I thank her for her steadfast enthusiasm, support, and counsel, and for assembling an excellent team, including Sarah Henry, John Palmer, Katherine Boller, Kristin Swan, Michelle Komie, and David Luljak, who have brought the book to fruition with intelligence and grace. I am particularly grateful to Karen Gangel, who has worked so thoroughly and meticulously with me to edit the manuscript and who has approached each issue with good cheer and enthusiasm, and to Heidi Downey, for her gifted oversight of this complicated project. As a special tribute, I wish to thank my friend and colleague Margaret Bauer for her stunning design, especially her inspired jacket, which so eloquently expresses the spirit of the letters.

Finally, I thank my husband, Nicolai Cikovsky, and my daughters, Sophia and Emily, for patiently enduring my absorption in this project and, as always, for their love and support.

Concordance of Artworks by Stieglitz and O'Keeffe

The "G." numbers below refer to works listed in Sarah Greenough, *Alfred Stieglitz: The Key Set* (Washington, 2002). The "L." numbers refer to works listed in Barbara Buhler Lynes, *Georgia O'Keeffe: Catalogue Raisonné* (New Haven, 1999).

Greenough Concordance

G. 92–96, e.g., *The Terminal*: 93n199

G. 208–211, *Gossip—Katwyk*: 358n94

G. 225–226, *The Landing of the Boats*: 358n94

G. 227, *The Fisherman's Return*: 358n94

G. 228, *The Beach, Katwyk*: 358n94

G. 229, *The Incoming Boat*: 358n94

G. 230, *Unloading*: 358n94

G. 231–232, *At Anchor*: 358n94

G. 266, *The Street—Design for a Poster*: 227n457

G. 227–280, *The Hand of Man*: 87n188

G. 284, *Snapshot—In the New York Central Yards*: 87n188, 93n199, 161n339

G. 285, *The Railroad Yard, Winter*: 87n188, 93n199, 161n339

G. 286, *In the New York Central Yards*: 87n188, 93n199, 161n339

G. 320, *Hedwig Stieglitz*: 44n98

G. 321, *Hedwig Stieglitz and Agnes Engelhard*: 44n98

G. 322, *Self-Portrait*: 44n98

G. 323, *Emmeline Stieglitz*: 44n98

G. 328, *Kitty Stieglitz*: 44n98

G. 379, *Lake George, Oaklawn*: 43n96

G. 388, *Brancusi Exhibition at 291*: 221n450

G. 393, *291—Picasso-Braque Exhibition*: 221n450

G. 394, *Charles Demuth*: 675n555

G. 413, *Ma*: 37n82

G. 414, *Kitty Stieglitz*: 37n82

G. 415, *Kitty Stieglitz*: 37n82, 44n98

G. 416, *Unknown Woman*: 37n82

G. 421, *From the Back-Window—291—Snow-Covered Tree, Back-Yard*: 221n450

G. 429, *From the Back-Window—291—Wall Closing In*: 39n89, 372n127

G. 431, *William Zorach*: 372n127

G. 436, *Lake George*: 37n83

G. 437–438, *Abraham Walkowitz*: 37n82

G. 439–441, *Shadows in Lake*: 37n82

G. 442–452, *Ellen Koeniger, Lake George*: 37n82

G. 453, *Leo Stein*: 168n358, 179n378

G. 457–459, *Georgia O'Keeffe at 291*: 149, 150n317, 161n330, 253n502, 625n418

G. 460, *Georgia O'Keeffe at 291*: 150n317, 161n330, 226n, 253n502, 625n418

G. 487–507, *Georgia O'Keeffe*: 299n568

G. 508–511, *Georgia O'Keeffe—Torso*: 299n568

G. 512–513, *Georgia O'Keeffe—Hands*: 299n568

G. 1508, *Little House, Lake George*: 639n446, 711n656

G. 1509–1510, *Little House, Lake George*: 711n656

G. 1511, *Back of Little House*: 711n656

G. 1512, *Equivalent 27A*: 711n656

G. 1513, *Equivalent 27B*: 711n656

G. 1514, *Equivalent 27C*: 711n656

G. 1515, *Georgia O'Keeffe—Hand and Wheel*: 711n656

G. 1516–1518 *Georgia O'Keeffe*: 711n656

G. 1519, *Georgia O'Keeffe—Hand and Wheel*: 711n656, 725n689

G. 1520–1534, *Georgia O'Keeffe*: 711n656

G. 1535, *Georgia O'Keeffe —Hands*: 711n656

G. 1536–1539, *Georgia O'Keeffe*: 711n656

G. 1540, *House, Leaves and Tree*: 707n644

G. 1541–1543, *House and Grape Leaves*: 707n644

G. 1544, *House, Lake George*: 707n644

G. 1555, *Margaret Prosser*: 734n714

G. appen. 3, *Fred Varnum*: 44n98

G. appen. 4–8, *Hedwig Stieglitz*: 44n98

G. appen. 9–8, *Lake George*: 44n98

G. appen. 11–12, *George and Agnes Engelhard*: 44n98

G. appen. 13–17, *Georgia Engelhard*: 44n98

G. appen. 18–20, *Abraham Walkowitz*: 44n98

Lynes Concordance

L. 44, *Untitled (Portrait of Dorothy True)*: 141n304

L. 45, *No. 2—Special*: 2n5, 57n129

L. 46, *No. 5—Special*: 2n5, 57n129

L. 47, *No. 7—Special*: 2n5, 57n129

L. 48, *No. 3—Special*: 2n5, 57n129

L. 49, *No. 4—Special*: 2n5, 57n129

L. 50, *Early Abstraction*: 2n5, 15n31, 17n37, 46n103, 47n105, 57n129

L. 52, *No. 12—Special*: 2n5, 17n38, 57n129, 126n271, 129n278, 231n462

L. 53, *No. 20—Special*: 29n60, 34n77, 35n78

L. 54, *No. 9—Special*: 2n5

L. 55, *Untitled*: 2n5, 57n129

L. 56, *Second, Out of My Head*: 2n5, 57n129

L. 57, *No. 32—Special*: 57n129, 268n528

L. 58, *Special No. 33*: 57n129

L. 61, *No. 14—Special*: 20n43, 29n59, 34n76

L. 62, *First Drawing of the Blue Lines*: 20n43, 79n170, 129n278

L. 63, *Black Lines*: 20n43, 129n278

L. 64, *Blue Lines*: 20n43, 20n44, 29n58, 77n164, 79n169, 81n172, 84n179, 89n195, 125n268, 144n309, 231n462, 446n81, 453n90, 457n95, 659n499

L. 66, *Abstraction*: 15n32, 94n201, 94n204, 159n336, 260n515, 304n569

L. 81, *Untitled (Red, Blue, Yellow)*: 18n39, 23n49

L. 82, *Untitled (Red, Blue and Green)*: 18n39, 23n49

L. 83, *Abstraction, Pale Sun*: 18n39, 23n49

L. 84, *Blue, Green and Red*: 18n39, 23n49, 166

L. 85, *Red and Green No. I*: 18n39, 23n49

L. 86, *Red and Green No. III*: 18n39, 23n49

L. 87, *Red and Green No. IV*: 18n39, 23n49

L. 88, *Red and Blue No. I*: 18n39, 23n49

L. 89, *Red and Blue No. II*: 18n39, 23n49

L. 90, *Anything*: 18n39, 23n49, 199n411

L. 91, *Blue No. I*: 18n39, 23n49, 31n65f

L. 92, *Blue No. II*: 18n39, 23n49, 31n65

L. 93, *Blue No. III*: 18n39, 23n49, 31n65

L. 94, *Blue No. IV*: 18n39, 23n49, 31n65

L. 95, *Untitled (House and Landscape)*: 18n39, 23n49

L. 96, *Untitled (Houses and Landscape)*: 18n39, 23n49

L. 97–98, *Untitled (Abstraction)*: 18n39, 18n40

L. 99, *Abstraction*: 18n39, 18n40, 110n238, 125n268, 144n309, 155n331, 197n408

L. 100, *Untitled (Boy)*: 18n39, 22n45

L. 101, *Untitled (Girl)*: 18n39, 22n45

L. 102–103, *Untitled (Landscape)*: 18n39

L. 104, *Evening*: 18n39, 23n49

L. 105, *Green Hill*: 18n39, 23n49

L. 106, *Pink and Blue Mountain*: 18n39, 23n49

L. 107, *Landscape, Layered Mountain*: 18n39, 23n49

L. 108, *Blue Hill No. I*: 18n39, 23n49

L. 109, *Blue Hill No. II*: 18n39, 23n49

L. 110, *Blue Hill No. III*: 18n39, 23n49

L. 111, *Untitled (Tent Door at Night)*: 18n39, 23n49

L. 112, *Untitled (Tent Door at Night)*: 18n39, 23n49, 31n69

L. 113, *Tent Door at Night*: 18n39, 23n49, 31n69

L. 114, *Untitled (Abstraction)*: 18n39, 31n69

L. 116, *I—Special*: 56n128

L. 117, *No. 12 Special*: 56n128

L. 118, *No. 8—Special*: 31n70, 41n91, 56n128

L. 119, *Blue I*: 31n70, 41n91, 66n, 119n258, 150n317, 151n321, 166n354

L. 120, *Blue II*: 31n70, 41n91, 66n, 71n152

L. 121, *Untitled (Abstraction)*: 31n70, 41n91, 71n151

L. 128, *Train at Night in the Desert*: 84n178, 138n298, 231n462, 232n463

780

782

Index

Page numbers in *italic* type indicate illustrations.

784

786

digestive aids, 420n24, 544n229, 672n549. *See also* Salsanos

Dixie Kitchen restaurant, New York City, 725

Doctors' Hospital, New York City, 665, 674n554

Dodge, Mabel. *See* Luhan, Mabel Dodge

Dorothy Norman (AS, G. 1363–1371 and 1393–1397), 554n252

Dorothy True (AS, G. 604), 376n135

Dos Passos, John, 676

Dove, Arthur: *Chinese Music,* 375n134; *Coal Carrier,* 607n372; critical reception of, 623; *Darkies Swinging in the Park,* 570, 570n292; exhibitions of, 359, 360, 368, 372, 375, 377, 456, 615, 615n387, 623, 682, 682n578, 683, 686–88, 693, 695, 702n638; finances of, 407, 496, 576, 576n311, 576n312, 592, 612, 615, 672n547, 686, 686n587, 724n685; *Moon and Sea,* 375n134; *Nigger Goes a-Fishing,* 375n134; O'Keeffe and, 1, 79, 233; *The Red Barge,* 724n685; *Red Barge, Reflections,* 663; Stieglitz and, 189, 226, 226n454, 232–33, 316, 406, 407, 576, 592, 614–15, 655, 655n489, 686, 711, 724; supporters of, 407, 576, 576n312, 576n313, 615, 672, 672n547, 694; *Wind & Clouds,* 570; work of, 77, 79, 418, 632, 655n489, 673, 684, 725

Dow, Arthur Wesley, x, 1, 141, 141n304, 212

Downtown Gallery, 592

Dozier, José Pitman Guadalupe (Pete), 424, 424n39, 473, 476, 481, 484

Draper, Muriel, 674

Dreier, Katherine S., 368, 371–73, 371n124, 373n129

Dreiser, Theodore, "Life, Art and America," 112, 112n242

Droth, Andrew, 728, 728n699, 734, 737

drugs. *See* medicines and remedies

Duchamp, Marcel, 89, 124–25, 130, 332–33, 721, 724, 724n687, 727, 731; *The Baroness Shaves Her Pubic Hair* (with May Ray), 294n563; *The Bride Stripped Bare by Her Bachelors, Even (The Large Glass),* 125, 125n266, 333; *The Fountain,* 130, 130n281, 130n283, 135

Dudley, Dorothy, 721; *Forgotten Frontiers,* 686, 686n589, 721; *What Dark Secrets,* 721n674

Dufour, Elise, 325, 325n37

Dumas, Alexander, "A Marriage of Convenience," 282, 282n553

Dun (art packer and shipper), 670, 695–96

Duncan, Charles, 2n5, 12, 51, 52n117, 68, 68n144, 74–75, 77, 85, 89, 630, 664, 677, 687, 693, 694–95, 699

Duncan, Isadora, 135, 198

Dunklee, George, 467, 707

Durand-Ruel Galleries, 681, 681n577

Dürer, Albrecht, 402

Duveen, Joseph, 419, 419n20

Dying Poplar and Live Branch—Lake George (AS, G. 1469), 639n445, 656n493

Eakins, 680

Early Abstraction (GOK, L. 50), 2n5, 15n31, 17n37, 46n103, 47n105, 57n129

East River from the 30th Story of the Shelton Hotel (GOK, L. 620), 381n150, 422n34, 424n41

Eastman, Max, 141n305

Eckstein, Gustav, 406, 494, 494n, 509, 524, 527, 529, 529n195, 529n196, 529n197, 564, 565, 608, 632–33, 636–38, 665n518, 724; *Noguchi,* 564n275, 630

economy, 88–90, 105, 105n229, 196, 407, 527, 530, 530n201, 531, 536, 550, 550n242, 555–56, 564, 568–69, 572, 577, 666, 682

eczema, 47n104. *See also* skin disease

Eddy, Arthur Jerome, *Cubists and Post-Impressionism,* 82, 82n175

Ederheimer, Richard R., 623

Edgemere, New York, 53–54

Edison, Thomas, 603, 603n361

Eduardo (adoptee of Mabel Dodge Luhan), 424n40

education. *See* teaching and education

Eggers, George, 536

Egyptian art, 319, 320, 325, 573n303

Ehrich Galleries, 681, 681n576

Eighteenth Amendment, 655n488

Einstein, Albert, 728, 728n701

Eisenstein, Sergei, *Ten Days That Shook the World,* 709, 709n648

El Greco: *Fray Hortensio Félix Paravicino,* 320, 320n21; *Saint Martin and the Beggar,* 390, 390n178

El Navajo Hotel, Gallup, New Mexico, 446n83

Eliot, Henry Ware, Jr., 675, 675n556

Eliot, T. S., 675

Elizabeth and Donald Davidson (AS, G. 697), 346n79, 356n92

Elizabeth Flynn restaurant, 631

Ellen Koeniger, Lake George (AS, G. 442–452,) 37n82

Ellis, Havelock, ix; *Fountain of Life,* 677n561, 678

Emergency Banking Relief Act, 682

Emmeline Stieglitz (AS, G. 323), 44n98

Engelhard, Agnes Stieglitz (sister), 76n, 196, 244, 341, 341n66, 342–43, 343n67, 350, 370, 430, 452, 600, 600n353, 637, 641

800

804

806

and I want to draw a
little spot — like a
of some kind — or
the plains — The
sky — makes
deep That I'd break
of it I would
filled my